Introduction to Women's, Gender & Sexuality Studies

Introduction to Women's, Gender & Sexuality Studies

Interdisciplinary and Intersectional Approaches

SECOND EDITION

Edited by

L. Ayu Saraswati
University of Hawai'i

Barbara L. Shaw
Allegheny College

Heather Rellihan
Anne Arundel Community College

New York   Oxford
OXFORD UNIVERSITY PRESS

Oxford University Press is a department of the University of Oxford. It furthers the University's objective of excellence in research, scholarship, and education by publishing worldwide. Oxford is a registered trade mark of Oxford University Press in the UK and certain other countries.

Published in the United States of America by Oxford University Press
198 Madison Avenue, New York, NY 10016, United States of America.

For titles covered by Section 112 of the US Higher Education Opportunity Act, please visit www.oup.com/us/he for the latest information about pricing and alternate formats.

Library of Congress Cataloging-in-Publication Data

CIP data is on file at the Library of Congress
9780190084806

Printing number: 9 8 7 6 5 4 3 2 1
Printed by LSC Communications, Inc., United States of America

Contents

Preface   xi
Acknowledgments   xviii

SECTION ONE   **MAPPING THE FIELD: AN INTRODUCTION TO WOMEN'S, GENDER, AND SEXUALITY STUDIES**   1

1. bell hooks, "Feminist Politics: Where We Stand"   23

2. Allan Johnson, "Patriarchy, The System: An It, Not a He, a Them, or an Us"   26

3. Anne Fausto-Sterling, "The Five Sexes, Revisited"   35

4. Ijeoma A., "Because You're a Girl"   40

5. C. J. Pascoe, "Making Masculinity: Adolescence, Identity, and High School"   46

6. *Eli Clare, "The Mountain"   55

7. *Robin DiAngelo, "Nothing to Add: A Challenge to White Silence in Racial Discussions"   62

8. Audre Lorde, "There Is No Hierarchy of Oppressions"   75

9. Ashley Currier and Thérèse Migraine-George, "Queer/African Identities: Questions, Limits, Challenges"   76

10. M. Soledad Caballero, "Before Intersectionality"   80

11. *Kimberly Williams Brown and Red Washburn, "Trans-forming Bodies and Bodies of Knowledge: A Case Study of Utopia, Intersectionality, Transdisciplinarity, and Collaborative Pedagogy" (new)   81

SECTION TWO   **HISTORICAL PERSPECTIVES IN WOMEN'S, GENDER, AND SEXUALITY STUDIES**   87

Nineteenth Century

12. Angelina Emily Grimké, "An Appeal to the Christian Women of the South"   112

13. *Seneca Falls Convention, "Declaration of Sentiments and Resolutions"   114

14. Sojourner Truth, "1851 Speech"   117

15. Ida B. Wells, "A Red Record"   117

Twentieth Century

16. *The New York Times*, "141 Men and Girls Die in Waist Factory Fire"   121

17. Daughters of Bilitis, "Statement of Purpose"   123

18. Leslie Feinberg, interview with Sylvia Rivera, "I'm Glad I Was in the Stonewall Riot"   124

19. Pat Mainardi, "The Politics of Housework"   126

20. Anne Koedt, "The Myth of the Vaginal Orgasm"   130

21. Radicalesbians, "The Woman-Identified Woman"   135

22. Chicago Gay Liberation Front, "A Leaflet for the American Medical Association"   139

23. The Combahee River Collective, "A Black Feminist Statement"   141

24. Jo Carrillo, "And When You Leave, Take Your Pictures With You"   147

25. bell hooks, "Men: Comrades in Struggle"   148

26. Gloria Anzaldúa, "La Conciencia de la Mestiza/Towards a New Consciousness"   156

27. *National Organization for Men Against Sexism, "Tenets"   161

28. Angela Davis, "Masked Racism: Reflections on the Prison Industrial Complex"   163

Twenty-First Century

29. *Jackson Katz, "Memo to Media: Manhood, Not Guns or Mental Illness, Should Be Central in Newtown Shooting"   167

30. Tina Vasquez, "It's Time to End the Long History of Feminism Failing Transgender Women"   171

31. *Ashwini Tambe, "Reckoning with the Silences of #MeToo"   174

32. *Women's March, "Guiding Vision and Definition of Principles"   178

SECTION THREE   **SOCIOPOLITICAL ISSUES IN WOMEN'S, GENDER, AND SEXUALITY STUDIES**   183

Rethinking the Family

33. Rebecca Barrett-Fox, "Constraints and Freedom in Conservative Christian Women's Lives"   216

34. Jessica E. Birch, "Love, Labor, and Lorde: The Tools My Grandmother Gave Me"   220

35. Monisha Das Gupta, "'Broken Hearts, Broken Families': The Political Use of Families in the Fight Against Deportation"   224

36. *Sarah Mirk, "Popaganda: Queering Family Values"   229

Gender and Sexuality in the Labor Market

37. Marlene Kim, "Policies to End the Gender Wage Gap in the United States"   239

38. Dean Spade, "Compliance Is Gendered: Struggling for Gendered Self-Determination in a Hostile Economy"   245

39. *Catherine Rottenberg, "The Rise of Neoliberal Feminism"   257

40. *Fernando Tormos-Aponte, "The Politics of Survival"   270

Reproductive Politics

41. Kathy E. Ferguson, "Birth Control"   275

42. *Loretta Ross, "The Color of *Choice*: White Supremacy and Reproductive Justice"   279

43. *Yifat Susskind, "Population Control Is Not the Answer to Our Climate Crisis"   291

Gendered Violence

44. *V. Efua Prince, "June" (new)   293

45. Beth Richie, "A Black Feminist Reflection on the Antiviolence Movement"   299

46. *Courtney Bailey, "A Queer #MeToo Story: Sexual Violence, Consent, and Interdependence" (new) 302

47. Joey L. Mogul, Andrea J. Richie, and Kay Whitlock, "False Promises: Criminal Legal Responses to Violence Against LGBT People" 307

48. Isis Nusair, "Making Feminist Sense of Torture at Abu-Ghraib" 317

Popular Culture and Media Representations

49. *Jaelani Turner-Williams, "A Quick History of TV's Elusive Quest for Black Lesbians" 321

50. Judith Kegan Gardiner, "Women's Friendships, Popular Culture, and Gender Theories" (updated) 324

51. Meda Chesney-Lind, "Mean Girls, Bad Girls, or Just Girls: Corporate Media Hype and the Policing of Girlhood" 329

52. *Elly Belle, "Knee-Jerk Biphobia: What Responses to Miley Cyrus's Breakup Say About Queer Erasure" 333

SECTION FOUR **EPISTEMOLOGIES OF BODIES: WAYS OF KNOWING AND EXPERIENCING THE WORLD** 337

53. Janet Mock, from *Redefining Realness* 357

54. *Ari Agha, "Singing in the Cracks" (new) 363

55. *Cheryl Chase, "Hermaphrodites with Attitude: Mapping the Emergence of Intersex Political Activism" 368

56. *C. Winter Han, "Being an Oriental, I Could Never Be Completely a Man: Gay Asian Men and the Intersection of Race, Gender, Sexuality, and Class" 375

57. Dominique C. Hill, "(My) Lesbianism Is Not a Fixed Point" 384

58. *Christina Crosby, "Masculine, Feminine, or Fourth of July" 387

59. Aleichia Williams, "Too Latina to Be Black, Too Black to Be Latina" 392

60. *Kristina Gupta, "Feminist Approaches to Asexuality" (new) 393

61. Gloria Steinem, "If Men Could Menstruate" 398

62. No'u Revilla, "How to Use a Condom" 400

63. *Lailatul Fitriyah, "Can We Stop Talking About the 'Hijab'?: Islamic Feminism, Intersectionality, and the Indonesian Muslim Female Migrant Workers" (new) 401

64. L. Ayu Saraswati, "Cosmopolitan Whiteness: The Effects and Affects of Skin-Whitening Advertisements in Transnational Indonesia"   406

65. Chimamanda Ngozi Adichie, from *Americanah*   416

66. Kimberly Dark, "Big Yoga Student"   421

67. *Jessica Vasquez-Tokos and Kathryn Norton-Smith, "Resisting Racism: Latinos' Changing Responses to Controlling Images over the Life Course"   423

68. *Joanna Gordon, "Sketches" (new)   427

69. *Christina Lux, "10,000 Blows" (new)   428

SECTION FIVE

SCIENCE, TECHNOLOGY, AND THE DIGITAL WORLD

   429

70. Emily Martin, "The Egg and the Sperm: How Science Has Constructed a Romance Based on Stereotypical Male–Female Roles"   447

71. *Glenda M. Flores, "Latina/x *Doctoras* [Doctors]: Negotiating Knowledge Production in Science" (new)   455

72. *Liam Oliver Lair, "Navigating Transness in the United States: Understanding the Legacies of Eugenics" (new)   459

73. *Clare C. Jen, "Oppositional Scientific Praxis: The 'Do' and 'Doing' of #CRISPRbabies and DIY Hormone Biohacking" (new)   465

74. Wendy Seymour, "Putting Myself in the Picture: Researching Disability and Technology"   470

75. *Vandana Shiva "The Hijacking of the Global Food Supply"   476

76. *Naciza Masikini and Bipasha Baruah, "Gender Equity in the 'Sharing' Economy: Possibilities and Limitations" (new)   483

77. *Rachel Charlene Lewis, "Technology Isn't Neutral: Ari Fitz on How Instagram Fails Queer Black Creators"   488

78. *Sima Shakhsari "The Parahumanity of the YouTube Shooter: Nasim Aghdam and the Paradox of Freedom"   491

79. Aliette de Bodard, "Immersion"   495

SECTION SIX   **ACTIVIST FRONTIERS: AGENCY
                    AND RESISTANCE**   505

80. Lila Abu-Lughod, "Do Muslim Women Really Need Saving?
    Anthropological Reflections on Cultural Relativism and
    Its Others"   530

81. Beenash Jafri, "Not Your Indian Eco-Princess: Indigenous
    Women's Resistance to Environmental Degradation"   541

82. Elizabeth R. Cole and Zakiya T. Luna, "Making Coalitions
    Work: Solidarity Across Difference Within US Feminism"   546

83. *Evette Dionne, "Turning Fury into Fuel: Three Women
    Authors on Publishing's New Investment in Anger"   554

84. DaMaris B. Hill, "Concrete"   559

85. *Wangari Maathai, "An Unbreakable Link: Peace,
    Environment, and Democracy"   563

86. *Christina E. Bejarano, "The Latina Advantage in US Politics:
    Recent Example with Representative Ocasio-Cortez" (new)   567

87. Michael Winter, "I Was There"   572

88. Sarah E. Fryett, "Laudable Laughter: Feminism and Female
    Comedians"   574

89. Guerrilla Girls, "When Racism & Sexism Are No Longer
    Fashionable"   579

90. *Alison Bechdel, "The Bechdel Test"   580

91. Kathleen Hanna/Bikini Kill, "Riot Grrrl Manifesto"   582

92. *Heather Rellihan, "An Interview with Tarana Burke" (new)   583

Readings with asterisks (*) indicate that they are new to this edition.

Readings with (new) indicate that they have never been published before.

Index   589

Preface

Women's studies departments and programs are undergoing rapid transformation at all levels of higher education, transitioning from women's studies and feminist studies to women's and gender studies, and most recently to women's, gender, and sexuality studies. With this transformation came the need for a comprehensive and accessible introductory textbook that addresses the current state of the field. *Introduction to Women's, Gender & Sexuality Studies: Interdisciplinary and Intersectional Approaches* was the first text to reflect these exciting changes; this second edition updates section introductions and some readings to reflect some of the most pressing contemporary issues in our rapidly changing world.

Introduction to Women's, Gender & Sexuality Studies continues to be designed to appeal to a full range of programs and departments. Our core mission as teachers and scholars in creating this text is to be accessible and represent the rigor in the field. We present complex interdisciplinary feminist and queer concepts and theories that are approachable for first- and second-year students entering a women's, gender, and sexuality studies classroom, and supply pedagogical scaffolding to engage a new generation of learners. Innovative in the field, the second edition of *Introduction to Women's, Gender & Sexuality Studies* continues to be a comprehensive mix of anthology and textbook that provides thorough overviews that begin each section; robust and engaging pedagogy that encourages students to think critically and self-reflexively as well as take action; and supplemental online resources for instructors (see Online Resources in this section for further information).

Introduction to Women's, Gender & Sexuality Studies offers students a strong foundation that teaches them to think in and across disciplines. We include key primary historical sources that represent broad social movements that helped shape the field; an introduction to contemporary issues that elucidates the connections and tensions between individuals and social institutions; and recent work in science, technology, and digital cultures to emphasize the importance of interdisciplinary approaches to women's, gender, and sexuality studies. In the sections that follow, we integrate new work from established scholars and emerging voices alongside key foundational creative and critical readings to introduce learners to multiple perspectives. Finally, we provide a range of genres (including poetry, short stories, interviews, op-eds, and feminist magazine articles) to complement the scholarly selections and acknowledge the roots of creative and personal expression in the field.

Introduction to Women's, Gender & Sexuality Studies emphasizes interdisciplinarity and intersectionality. This edited collection represents women's, men's, intersex, nonbinary and/or genderqueer, transgender, asexual, lesbian, gay, bisexual, and pansexual identities and experiences through scholarship in traditional disciplines and those that emerge from interdisciplinary fields. We proceed from the recognition that all identities are multifaceted social categories that require deep and contextual examinations in order to understand power dynamics that create sociocultural inequalities, hierarchies, oppressions, and privileges that shape our lives. Intersectionality is critical because it recognizes that universal and stabilized understandings of "women," "gender," and "queer" marginalize or exclude the voices, experiences, interests, and struggles of those who live their lives within material contexts of race, class, nationalities, abilities, religions, and age.

For example, we include readings that allow learners to comprehend "gay men" or "Asian women" through the prism of skin color, religion, and/or body image. Other articles emphasizing the history of race, class, and ability call into question how "reproductive rights" have been exclusively positioned as empowering white, middle-class women in order to underscore how people in Indigenous, Black, gay, lesbian, and/or disabled communities struggle for the right to have children. Intersectionality requires framing any experience/issue from standpoints based on complex identity formations and within relations of power. *Introduction to Women's, Gender & Sexuality Studies* takes this theoretical cornerstone as its conceptual framework and brings it to life with accessible and rigorous perspectives.

Please note that some of the readings may evoke certain (uncomfortable) feelings in the readers. Yet, as Saraswati argues in her book *Seeing Beauty Sensing Race in Transnational Indonesia*, "sensing is ... an epistemic apparatus" (3). Hence, it is important to be mindful of whatever feelings that may arise because they will, if addressed critically and mindfully, provide us with a mode of knowing and understanding the issue and the world better, which is the foundation for transformation.

A NOTE ABOUT TERMINOLOGY

This reader purposefully uses a variety of racial/ethnic terminologies (e.g., Native American/American Indian/Indigenous; Black/African American; Latino/Latina/ Latinx and Chicano/a; and Asian/Asian diaspora/Pacific Islander) depending on the context, and as a way to honor certain individuals' and groups' preferences. For example, whereas "African American" may be used to refer to people of African descent who are living in the United States, "Black" may be deployed as a political and cultural term in reference to "Black Lives Matter." It is important that students are exposed to these various terms and understand the different ways in which they are used to allow them to grapple with the complexity of race and ethnicity rather than providing privileged terms that affix and stabilize their meaning in a fluid world.

ORGANIZATION

Introduction to Women's, Gender & Sexuality Studies is divided into six sections. Each section begins with an introductory essay that frames the fields of study, contextualizing the selected readings and concluding with discussion questions that reinforce comprehension of key concepts while prompting critical thinking and self-reflection.

- Section One, "Mapping the Field: An Introduction to Women's, Gender, and Sexuality Studies," engages concepts that serve as cornerstones of the field: social constructions that move beyond the dualities of sex and gender; the complexity of patriarchy as well as the categories of "women," "gender," and "queer" through intersectional approaches; the interlocking systems of oppression and privilege; how interdisciplinary approaches are critical to addressing complex contemporary sociopolitical issues; and the centrality of praxis and self-reflexivity in writing, oral communication, and activism.
- Section Two, "Historical Perspectives in Women's, Gender, and Sexuality Studies," traces the development of identity politics and social movements in the field. Beginning with nineteenth and early twentieth-century organizing around abolition, suffrage, lynching, and working conditions and moving through to the present day, this section follows the evolving questions over how to define "women's issues" or "queer issues" and how intersectional identities complicate notions of what counts as women's and queer activism. This section allows students to engage with primary sources that both contextualize and complicate the critical and creative texts in other sections.
- Section Three, "Sociopolitical Issues in Women's, Gender, and Sexuality Studies," sets up some of the key contemporary issues in the field and challenges students to understand the power relations embedded in everyday experiences of family, work, reproduction, violence, and popular culture and media representations from multiple perspectives.
- Section Four, "Epistemologies of Bodies: Ways of Knowing and Experiencing the World," examines the production of knowledge surrounding bodies and the cultural politics and social stratifications of embodiment, representation, and identity construction. The essays in this section critically analyze how labels (such as feminine, masculine, fat, queer, trans, disabled, racialized, reproductive, and sexual) are attached to and provide meanings for how bodies *can* and *should* be experienced.
- Section Five, "Science, Technology, and the Digital World," includes essays that map out the changes afforded by sciences and technologies, and the

challenges of living as gendered, sexualized, racialized, and classed people in a digital age.

- Section Six, "Activist Frontiers: Agency and Resistance," emphasizes the roots of the field: activism. The readings in this section provide models of feminist and queer activism and avenues for understanding the interplay of agency and social change.

KEY FEATURES

Dynamic Approach *Introduction to Women's, Gender & Sexuality Studies* combines the best features of both traditional textbooks and anthologies. The standard single-voice textbook approach is useful because it succinctly summarizes key events or issues, provides context, and presents information in accessible language. However, part of the ethos of women's, gender, and sexuality studies as a field is to engage multiple and contested ideas, accomplished most effectively through an anthology of diverse readings. *Introduction to Women's, Gender & Sexuality Studies* provides the best of both worlds by featuring in-depth introductory narratives for each section *and* a range of readings from canonical to emerging voices.

The section introductions provide the social and historical context for the selected readings that follow. Depending on the section, this may include an overview of important developments in the field, a historiography of pivotal issues, biographical information about influential thinkers, definitions of key vocabulary terms, and other background information necessary for understanding how the readings that follow are in conversation with one another. The selected pieces include both primary and secondary sources. The primary texts encourage critical thinking skills by providing the opportunity to engage with archival materials and subjective narratives; secondary texts ask learners to interpret, evaluate, and synthesize while modeling scholarly writing. Many selections are included in their entirety; we also feature robust excerpts from longer sources. This allows for a balance between depth and breadth.

Interdisciplinary and Intersectional *Introduction to Women's, Gender & Sexuality Studies* encourages interdisciplinary analysis of United States–based and transnational cultural identities through critical and creative works. Each section includes multiple perspectives and genres, encouraging students to develop broad-based and multifaceted understandings of the complex issues surrounding "women," "gender," and "sexuality." A unique section emphasizing science, technology, and digital cultures adds to our understanding of women's, gender, and sexuality studies as an interdisciplinary field.

New Works While the majority of selections included in this anthology are foundational texts—either frequently published or cited materials—*Introduction to Women's, Gender & Sexuality Studies* also includes new scholarship (critical essays as well as creative work) to expand current debates with new voices.

Rather than relying only on where the field has been, *Introduction to Women's, Gender & Sexuality Studies* points to future directions that actualize the emerging field of women's, gender, and sexuality studies.

PEDAGOGY

Introduction to Women's, Gender & Sexuality Studies includes pedagogical tools designed to facilitate learning and develop critical and creative thinking skills. Each section introduction includes one of each of the following boxed features:

- **Intersectional Analysis** Students will be presented with a case study that is related to the theme of each section. This case study is followed by a series of questions that specifically prompt students to critically think about the issue from an intersectional perspective. By doing this exercise, students will have an opportunity to apply the concept of intersectionality to a thoughtfully chosen topic, giving them a better understanding of both "intersectionality" as a mode of analysis and the rich content of the section's topic. These case studies will illustrate to students how intersectional analysis is about complex relations of power and why it is necessary for better understanding the world around them.
- **Engaged Learning** This pedagogical tool features an engaging activity that allows students to further explore the topic of each section. It encourages students to make connections between the concepts presented in each section and their everyday lives. This exercise guides students through a "hands-on" activity with focused questions designed to further their understanding of the materials through application, analysis, and self-reflection.
- **Activism and Civic Engagement** Students will be presented with a brief description of either an activist, activist group, or activist method followed by reflection, or a suggestion for a civic engagement activity designed to encourage students to take an active role in making changes in their communities and to illustrate the connection between the theories they learn in class and activism.
- **Transnational Connections** By analyzing a case study or doing an activity, students will learn the transnational aspect of the topic discussed in each section. These case studies and activities will emphasize the interconnectedness of our world and how decisions we make in our lives not only affect people in other parts of the world and vice versa, but also are shaped by transnational sociopolitical, economic, and affective conditions.

Additional pedagogical resources to enhance student learning and engagement include:

- **Learning Objectives** In light of the current focus on learning outcomes and assessment, each section introduction begins with specific learning objectives to guide students toward an understanding of key topics and overarching themes.

- **Marginal Glosses** This feature in the section introductions provides quick definitions for key terms and concepts as soon as students first encounter them in the text. These key terms are collected again in an alphabetized list at the end of each section introduction (to allow for quick review).
- **Headnotes** Introducing each reading selection, these narratives provide brief biographies of the authors, information about the historical context, and/or information about the original publishing context.
- **Critical Thinking Questions** Listed at the end of each section, these questions provide an opportunity to assess understanding and encourage self-reflection in developing arguments and perspectives.
- **Online Resources** In addition to the printed text, a website will be maintained that provides supplementary learning materials. Links will be provided for further readings including both primary and secondary sources that may be used for understanding the context surrounding any given topic, inspire debate around a particular issue, or allow for the application of a theoretical premise to a real-life example. The site will also contain suggested activities that can be developed either in the traditional face-to-face classroom or in an online learning environment. The site will collate and organize links to multimedia content that could be incorporated into a lecture, used as a prompt for classroom discussion or online discussion forums, or provided to students as supplementary classroom preparation. The site will also include selected texts originally included in the first edition but not in the second edition.

NEW THIS EDITION

- **Unpublished Works** reflect new contributions to the field. These readings are indicated by (new) in the Table of Contents.

  Kimberly Williams and Red Washburn, "Trans-forming Bodies and Bodies of Knowledge: A Case Study of Utopia, Intersectionality, Transdisciplinarity, and Collaborative Pedagogy"

  V. Efua Prince, "June"

  Courtney Bailey, "A Queer #MeToo Story: Sexual Violence, Consent, and Interdependence"

  Ari Agha, "Singing in the Cracks"

  Kristina Gupta, "Feminist Approaches to Asexuality"

  Lailatul Fitriyah, "Can We Stop Talking About the 'Hijab'?: Islamic Feminism, Intersectionality, and the Indonesian Muslim Female Migrant Workers"

  Joanna Gordon, "Sketches"

  Christina Lux, "10,000 Blows"

  Glenda M. Flores, "Latina/x *Doctoras* [Doctors]: Brown Women Negotiating Knowledge Production in Science"

Liam Lair, "Navigating Transness in the United States: Understanding the Legacies of Eugenics"

Clare C. Jen, "Oppositional Scientific Praxis: The 'Do' and 'Doing' of #CRIS-PRbabies and DIY Hormone Biohacking"

Naciza Masikini and Bipasha Baruah, "Gender Equity in the 'Sharing' Economy: Possibilities and Limitations"

Christina E. Bejarano, "The Latina Advantage in US Politics: Recent Example with Representative Ocasio-Cortez"

Heather Rellihan, "An Interview with Tarana Burke"

- **New Readings** The second edition includes 38 new readings (not included in the first edition) from a diverse range of contemporary voices. These readings are indicated by a * in the Table of Contents.
- **Environmental Issues** Key works have been included that address this topic because thinking critically about environmental issues and climate change is increasingly imperative in today's world and women's, gender, and sexuality studies offers tools to understand how it impacts people's daily lives.
- **Moments and Movements in History** Several readings have been included to provide context and intersectional framing for recent historical developments like the Women's March and the MeToo movement.
- **Updated Essays** Previous contributors were invited to update their essays or include newer works to address the evolving fields of science and digital technology.

Acknowledgments

The editors would like to thank Claire Moses for her insightful feedback as we developed the reader during the early stages. We would also like to thank Lynn Bolles, who has been an important guide for each of us in our understandings of interdisciplinarity and intersectionality. Our fantastic OUP editors Sherith Pankratz and Meg Botteon have truly been amazing to work with. We are so lucky to have their guidance and help. Our project manager Patricia Berube and copyeditor Wendy Walker have gone above and beyond in making sure that our book is the best that it can be. Grace Li has also been tremendously helpful throughout the process. We thank our OUP family immensely.

The feedback from kind and generous anonymous reviewers has helped the formation of this reader:

Patricia Ackerman, The City College of New York
Amanda Koontz Anthony, University of Central Florida
Lisa Arellano, Colby College
Barbara A. Barnes, University of California
Tammy Birk, Otterbein University
Penny-Bee Kapilialoha Bovard, University of Hawai'i at Mānoa
Brandy Boyd, Maryville University
Emily Burrill, University of North Carolina at Chapel Hill
Nicole Carter, Wright State University
Lynn Comella, University of Nevada
Sarah E. Dougher, Portland State University
Nehal Elmeligy, University of Cincinnati
Matthew B. Ezzell, James Madison University
Jerilyn Fisher, Hostos Community College
Melissa M. Forbis, Stony Brook University
Ann Fuehrer, Miami University
Amy C. Gregg, University of Hawai'i at Hilo
Julianne Guillard, University of Richmond
Yalda Nafiseh Hamidi, Stony Brook University
Laura Harrison, Minnesota State University

Margaret Ann Harrison, City College of San Francisco
Alison Hatch, University of Colorado-Boulder
L. Justine Hernandez, St. Edwards University
Jill Hersh, Montclair State University
Julietta Hua, San Francisco State University
Elizabeth A. Hubble, University of Montana
Loraine Hutchins, Montgomery College, Takoma Park
Tara Jabbaar-Gyambrah, Niagara University
Alison Kibler, Franklin and Marshall College
Lisa King, Edgewood College
Christy Kollath-Cattano, College of Charleston
Angela LaGrotteria, Lorain County Community College
Rachel A. Lewis, George Mason University
Miranda Miller, Gillette College
Kristan Poirot, Texas A&M University
Leandra Preston-Sidler, University of Central Florida
Dynette I. Reynolds, Weber State University
Danielle Roth-Johnson, University of Nevada, Las Vegas
Ariella Rotramel, Connecticut College
Sami Schalk, University of Wisconsin-Madison
Ann Schofield, University of Kansas
Beth Sertell, Ohio University
Harleen Singh, Brandeis University
Racheal Stimpson, Alamance Community College
Rebecca Tolley-Stokes, East Tennessee State University
Avery Tompkins, Transylvania University
Jessica Turcat, Oklahoma State University
Kathleen Turkel, University of Delaware
Cameron A. Tyrrell, University of Kentucky
Dahlia Valle, Kingsborough Community College
Sujey Vega, Arizona State University
Cheryl Waite, Community College of Aurora
Jennifer A. Wagner-Lawlor, Pennsylvania State University
Mary Ruth Warner, University of Delaware
Lauren Weis, American University
Heying Jenny Zhan, Georgia State University

SECTION ONE

Mapping the Field: An Introduction to Women's, Gender, and Sexuality Studies

TABLE OF CONTENTS

1. bell hooks, "Feminist Politics: Where We Stand" 23
2. Allan Johnson, "Patriarchy, The System: An It, Not a He, a Them, or an Us" 26
3. Anne Fausto-Sterling, "The Five Sexes, Revisited" 35
4. Ijeoma A., "Because You're a Girl" 40
5. C. J. Pascoe, "Making Masculinity: Adolescence, Identity, and High School" 46
6. *Eli Clare, "The Mountain" 55
7. *Robin DiAngelo, "Nothing to Add: A Challenge to White Silence in Racial Discussions" 62
8. Audre Lorde, "There Is No Hierarchy of Oppressions" 75
9. Ashley Currier and Thérèse Migraine-George, "Queer/African Identities: Questions, Limits, Challenges" 76
10. M. Soledad Caballero, "Before Intersectionality" 80
11. *Kimberly Williams Brown and Red Washburn, "Trans-forming Bodies and Bodies of Knowledge: A Case Study of Utopia, Intersectionality, Transdisciplinarity, and Collaborative Pedagogy" (new) 81

1

Women's, gender, and sexuality studies is an interdisciplinary field of study and emerges as part of a long history of feminist, queer, antiracist, anticapitalist, and anticolonial movements. As an academic field it is concerned with issues of gender, sexuality, race, ethnicity, class, nationality, abilities, age, body size, and religion. It also provides lenses or ways of seeing how sociocultural dynamics of power craft our understanding of gender, transgender, and queer and its effect on our daily life. Scholars, artists, and activists in women's, gender, and sexuality studies (1) question what we know and how we know it, (2) craft theories and practices that work to end oppression, inequality, and inequities and pursue social justice and transformational change, (3) empower individuals and groups marginalized by sociopolitical systems, and (4) generally agree that there is no single or "correct" feminist or queer way of being, doing, and living. In the remainder of this introduction, you will learn key concepts (such as feminism, queer, gender, transgender, oppression, privilege, intersectionality, and interdisciplinarity) that provide the foundation for understanding women's, gender, and sexuality studies.

WHAT DOES FEMINISM AND QUEER HAVE TO DO WITH IT?

In our changing and precarious global political landscape that includes health and environmental crises alongside Black Lives Matter and antiracist movements, historical and contemporary critiques, insights, and re-imaginings that emerge from women's, gender, and sexuality studies are vital for helping make sense of a changing world and contributing to actions toward social transformation. As students will explore throughout this book, women, people of color, and LGBTQPAI+ communities have made some political, social, and economic progress over the decades. Feminist and queer thought and activism have provided foundations for these changes and will continue to provide frameworks for how to pursue justice and freedom. Yet, in popular discourse, feminism can be met with suspicion and sometimes hostility. In the English language, using the "f-word" is considered obscene; it shows anger, contempt, and disrespect to whoever (or whatever) is on the receiving end. Feminism seems to have similar cultural meanings. By now many of us have heard the stereotypes of feminists: angry, unshaven, dykes, bitchy, man-hating, and aggressive. bell hooks in her piece "Feminist Politics" (included in this section) makes the simple statement that feminism is "a movement to end sexism, sexist exploitation, and oppression" and uses this definition because it "implies that all sexist thinking and action is the problem," regardless of who is doing it (p. 23). When asked, most individuals may readily agree that people should not be exploited or oppressed. How is it then that when feminists come together to fight against individual, institutional, and systematic sexism for protections, rights, social justice, and freedom, feminism becomes suspect? How or why might this sentiment have taken hold? bell hooks suggests that all of us learn antifeminism through U.S. patriarchal mass media because it seeks to undermine gender justice, which for her moves beyond equality and "the freedom to have abortions, to be lesbians, to challenge rape and domestic violence" (p. 23).

Feminism has a long and contentious history in which its strongest advocates did not always agree with one another on the goals of the movement or the strategies for social change. As you will learn in more detail in Section Two, women (and some men) were inspired by women's personal narratives and public speeches as well as abolition movements in the mid-nineteenth century to begin advocating for women's equality with men while others sought liberation from subjugation. Demanding everything from the right to vote to sexual autonomy, early feminists challenged the cultural belief that white, middle-class, and wealthy men innately deserved respect and dignity that was materially accompanied by access to education, work, and citizenship, while white, middle-class, and wealthy women were expected to be pious, pure, submissive, and domestic, thus best suited to be mothers and wives (Welter 1966, 152). Women's, gender, and sexuality studies also traces its roots to movements such as the turn-of-the-twentieth-century antilynching movement led in part by African American journalist, newspaper owner, and grassroots activist Ida B. Wells; the labor movement organized by working-class, Jewish immigrant women in the early twentieth century; and mid-twentieth-century women's groups such as Radicalesbian, WITCH (Women's International Conspiracy from Hell), and the Red Stockings who made it clear that eradicating patriarchal culture and crafting a women-centered one was the only means to liberation. The crucial questions that beget grassroots movements for change form the backbone of feminist and queer inquiry in women's, gender, and sexuality studies. As Marilyn Boxer notes in *When Women Ask the Questions*, "From the beginning, the goal of women's studies was not merely to study women's position in the world but to change it" (Boxer 1988, 13). Given the expansiveness of feminist politics today, it is critical to understand how the last century and a half of movements for civil rights and social justice fundamentally shaped the field and that **patriarchy** remains a central feature that reinforces racism, classism, homophobia, transphobia, nationalism, ageism, and ableism in our daily lives.

Some people often assume that patriarchy is the idea that all men dominate and control all women. As Allan Johnson explains in "Patriarchy, the System: An It, Not a He, a Them, or an Us" (included in this section), this oversimplified approach emphasizes individual actions and reactions rather than seeing patriarchy as a system in which we all—men, women, nonbinary, genderqueer, and transgender people—participate. Patriarchy is cultural—knit into the fabric of U.S. society—and upheld by individuals *and* **social institutions**

Patriarchy: Cultural system in which men hold power and are the central figures in the family, community, government, and larger society.

Social institutions: Rule-governed social arrangements that have survived across time and appear natural and normal but in fact represent one way of being in the world (e.g., the nuclear family, a well-armed military, and a capitalist economy).

Queer: Once a pejorative term, it has been reclaimed to describe sexual identities and political issues in lesbian, gay, bisexual, pansexual, polyamorous, transgender, questioning, asexual, and intersexed communities; used to push back against oversimplified and assumed definitions of lesbian and gay identity.

LGBTQPAI+: An acronym used to identify and politically unite lesbian, gay, bisexual, transgender, questioning and queer, pansexual and polyamory, asexual and ally, and intersexed communities. The plus indicates that the acronym is fluid; as more queer identities are named, they can be added. The plus can also signify that people identify with more than one of these categories.

Transgender: Term used to represent a diverse group of people whose gender identity and/or gender expression differs from the gender assigned at birth. Trans may include but is not limited to transwomen, transmen, nonbinary, gender nonconforming, genderfluid, genderqueer, genderless, agender, third gender, and two-spirited.

Genderqueer: Individuals who self-identify outside of the woman/man gender binary.

through the law, media, family, education, and religion. Johnson provides an example that makes this very clear: if we think about patriarchy as the actions of individuals, "we might ask why a particular man raped, harassed, or beat a woman. We wouldn't ask however what kind of society would promote persistent patterns of such behavior" (p. 27). If one in four women experience rape on college campuses, social change will depend on getting to the roots that produce, maintain, and reproduce violence; this means looking closely at cultural myths about sexualities, genders, races, and socioeconomic status and how these narratives become embedded in social institutions that protect violence through silence. As Johnson argues, if society is oppressive, then people who grow up and live in it will accept, identify with, and participate in it as "normal." Feminist and queer inquiry intervenes in systems of subjugation and injustice, and, while there is significant overlap between feminist and queer studies, they are not synonymous.

In her essay "Queer," Jennifer Purvis posits that women's, gender, and sexuality studies "is always already queer," which she defines as "twisting" and "making strange" (Purvis 2012, 190). In this context, feminism is intended to be inclusive of **queer**. Once a derogatory term hurled at lesbians and gay men, "queer" has been reclaimed by **LGBTQPAI+** communities as a term of self-identification as lesbian, gay, bisexual, transgender, questioning, pansexual, polyamorous, asexual, and intersexual. "Queer" is an umbrella term used to bring together people (1) who have been marginalized in U.S. society because of their sexualities and gender identities and expressions and (2) whose descriptions and feelings do not fit easily within and may resist categories of lesbian, gay, bisexual, or **transgender**. In the latter case, it becomes an inclusive term for those who self-identify as **genderqueer**. Queer can also be its own sexual identity (in some acronyms it can be the "Q"), and it can signify someone's politics. For scholars, practitioners, artists, and activists who fight for the political and legal protections, rights, and freedoms of all queer people, the phrase "queer nation" can represent the need for a continued national political voice. It is also important to note that when "queer" is deployed in the struggle for social justice, it assumes solidarity, which does not always exist between the various groups of people under its purview. For example, the queer community won a significant victory when the Supreme Court ruled in July 2015 that states must allow same-sex marriage. It is also true that this milestone is limited to those who want to participate in marriage—a historically **heteronormative** institution. As such, gay marriage unites and divides the queer community.

Purvis's statement that women's, gender, and sexuality studies "is always already queer" is a bold one, particularly for some feminists. It *still* matters that lesbians, bisexual/pansexual, transgender, and asexual people who identify as women and femme do not have the same unearned privileges, opportunities, and rights as gay, bisexual, pansexual, asexual, and polyamorous men because of sexism *and* have a history of exclusion in feminism. This was true in the late 1960s when the cofounder of the National Organization for Women, Betty Friedan, named lesbians as the "lavender menace" and is happening today as some trans women fight for acceptance and inclusion in the women's movement, colleges, and other groups and social institutions (both of these examples will be examined closely in Section Two). When feminism excludes queer and transgender people, it replicates the power relations of patriarchy, racism, classism, ableism, and nationalism. Therefore, if feminism is to be queer it will mean that scholars, practitioners, artists, and activists will need to continue challenging the social norms that define the social categories of "women" and "men"—indeed, the binary of gender itself. And if queer communities are feminist, it will require consistent and public challenges to sexism, patriarchy, racism, classism, and ableism. This matters so that all minoritized people's voices and experiences are valued and included in movements, laws, social institutions, creative communities, and scholarship.

Heteronormative: A worldview or ideology that assumes and promotes heterosexuality as a preferred sexual orientation and expression.

LEARNING AND UNLEARNING GENDER AND SEXUALITY

Learning gender begins before any of us can even process it. In the United States, the relatively recent social media phenomenon of the "gender-reveal party" is a case in point. Also, when the baby is born, many doctors still announce, "It's a healthy baby girl!" or "It's a healthy baby boy!" This simple act of looking at the baby's genitals and announcing their sex begins the process of assigning children a **gender status**. If it is a girl, friends may purchase gifts of pink or pastel clothing, exclaim how beautiful she is going to be when she grows up, and comment that she is such a good, quiet baby. If it is boy, he may receive blue or brightly colored clothing and told that he is smart or active or will be the next star athlete or scientist. Knowing the sex of the baby sets the stage for how the child will be socialized into their **gender identity** and treated as a person.

Gender status: The gender assigned to children and used to socialize them into boy/man and girl/woman; may also be referred to as gender assignment.

As this scenario demonstrates, there is an easy and unconscious slippage between sex and gender. We readily accept that female and male represent the biological differences between men and women and that two sexes exist. In "The Five Sexes, Revisited" (included in this section), Anne Fausto-Sterling, a biologist and gender studies scholar, provides evidence that there is wide variation of sexes in the natural world—including among humans. While the language she uses in this piece reflects its publication date, this foundational piece made clear that a binary system of sex and gender is a powerful **social construction** and has been institutionalized as a scientific fact through medicine, education, family, and religion. If, as Fausto-Sterling estimates, 1.7 percent of all births are people with varying degrees of intersexed development and sex exists on a spectrum, then it is important to consider the implications for gender (Fausto-Sterling 2000, 51). As Sharyn Graham Davies suggests in her research, Western cultures have much that they can learn from more global—and more open-minded—cultures, like the Bugis in South Sulawesi, Indonesia, who recognize five genders.

Gender identity: An individual's gendered sense of self.

Social constructionism: Theory that our knowledge of gender, race, class, sexuality, ethnicity, body size, ability, religion, and nationality is tied to social processes that have their basis in relations of power and is therefore constantly being created and recreated by human beings within specific cultural contexts.

While gender may *appear* to be a natural and simple outgrowth of sex, it is a social process "constantly created and re-created out of human interaction, out of social life, and is the texture and order of that social life" (Lorber 1994, 99–100). We enact and express gender every day, and it is one of the central ways we organize our lives. From deciding what to wear to how we sit, talk, and generally take up public space to what kinds of labor we perform, gender arrangements shape our lives. They are not built on individual efforts, hard work, or abilities but on hierarchies of power that socialize men/boys to be dominant and women/girls to be subordinate. This structure finds its legitimization through the social constructions of family, religion, law, media, education, work, and language. In her very personal piece "Because You're a Girl," Ijeoma A. recounts her experiences of being raised in a family that embraced traditional customs characteristic of villages in eastern Nigeria. She spent her childhood in Lagos living under her family's Four Commandments that taught her how to become a good woman prepared for marriage: (1) her "office" is the kitchen, (2) she is responsible for all the chores in the home, (3) she is accountable for the children and their actions, and (4) of course, she must pledge complete and total allegiance to the man in charge first, before herself (p. 41). Angered by the patriarchal constrictions, Ijeoma finds pathways through education to rethink what it means to "be a girl" and how to navigate living in-between U.S. American and Nigerian cultures.

Binary gender formations makes sense because they are systematized, reflected, and reinforced in our everyday lives: toy stores are clearly divided; it is still significant to name female astronauts, engineers, and scientists and male nurses, schoolteachers, and social workers. The use of language in the previous sentence represents the power of gendered assumptions. "Gender is such a familiar part of daily life, it usually takes a deliberate disruption of our expectations of how women and men are supposed to act to pay attention to how it is produced" (Lorber 1994, 100). While individuals and communities of people actively disrupt social patterns, gender also continues to exist as a system based on hierarchies of power that is recognizable. For example, how are men perceived if they want to stay home and raise a family or if young women decide to remain single throughout their lifespan? Are they the same if reversed? If the answer is no, systems of gender and power continue to shape our lives. Can transgender people move freely through larger political, economic, and social worlds without being misgendered, diagnosed, and/or discriminated against? If the answer is no, gender continues to matter.

In "Making Masculinity" (included in this section), C. J. Pascoe begins by narrating a scene that may sound familiar: at an annual high school assembly, the most popular boy will be crowned "Mr. Cougar" to the loud cheers of his classmates. In this particular case, when the two highest vote-getting candidates run onto the floor, they are dressed like "nerds" and proceed to perform a skit in which they save their girlfriends from "gangstas" (young Black men who volunteered to be run off the stage) and are transformed into handsome, rugged, all-American guys. This scene illustrates that "[t]his masculinizing process happens through a transformation of bodies, the assertion of racial privilege, and a shoring up of heterosexuality and is a stark reminder of how limiting masculinity is

ACTIVISM AND CIVIC ENGAGEMENT

Log on to Twitter, Instagram, or Snapchat and access #growinguptrans. If the hashtag is not active, search social media for a similar community talking about what it means to grow up trans, nonbinary, or genderqueer. If you cannot find this hashtag or one similar, start one as a class. Participants use #growinguptrans to raise awareness; it represents resilience and creates a self-determined community of how people walk through the world. Posts can range from detailing street harassment (when, where, and what took place), to what it means to be silenced, to supporting people. Read the entries and make two lists. In the first, detail how people experience daily life; in the second, write down how they use the hashtag to practice self-care and empower themselves. Reflect on your own experiences of what it was like to grow up in your town/city and think about the similarities to and differences from #growinguptrans. Think carefully about family life, your experiences in school, what you learned through the media, how religion shaped your worldview, and how romance and attraction mattered as you grew up.

QUESTIONS

1. Examine your two lists carefully. Do you see any patterns that indicate what trans, nonbinary, and genderqueer people generally face in their daily life? What dominates each list? Why do you think these two things are at the top of the list? What role does sexism, patriarchy, racism, and classism play in people's lives?

2. Do the issues cut across cultural differences, or do you see additional patterns based on race, class, sexuality, ability, and religious beliefs?

4. Name one small change all of us could make that might alter how we discuss transgender, nonbinary, and genderqueer issues. Share it with your class.

5. As a class, translate your suggestion into a community action. Whether real or hypothetical, what would you include and why?

for boys and men" (p. 47). If adolescent boys are perceived as tough, in control, focused on sports and girls, white, and not to care about others, they will be rewarded for their gender performances (see Gardiner 2002; Halberstam 1998; hooks 1981; Messner 1997; Segal, 1990; Wiegman 2002). If a young man steps outside these narrow bounds, his peers will police and control his behavior by publicly ridiculing him as a "fag," which, as Pascoe learned during her field research, remains an insult for adolescents. She argues in this piece "how heteronormative and homophobic discourses, practices, and interactions (among students, teachers, and administrators) . . . produce masculine identities" (p. 48).

If gender is a form of social control and a social construction that can be changed, in "The Mountain" (in this section) Eli Clare asks us to think about this in relation to disabilities, particularly physical disabilities. In explaining how dominant narratives of disability circulate around us—often as mediated stories of inspiration, medicalized as "disordered," and sometimes as a reason for bullying, discrimination, and violence—Clare draws on the mountain as a metaphor to argue that a "supercrip" narrative (disabled people completing grand challenges) exists so that ableism can persist uninterrupted and the violence of the "supercrip" is made invisible. This is particularly significant since people, for example, in wheelchairs or with cerebral palsy, blindness, deafness, and/or

Down syndrome have material conditions that circumscribe their lives and can result in "lack of access, lack of employment, lack of education, lack of personal attendant services" (p. 56). Clare suggests that it is our bodies that become the places people can call home and where they can find refuge: "I will never find home on the mountain. This I know. Rather home starts here in my body, in all that lies imbedded beneath my skin" and that the body can become home "only if it is understood that the stolen body can be reclaimed" (p. 60, 61). Reclamation here becomes a process for understanding and resisting how a harmful, normalizing culture names and steals what it means to be disabled. Since disability and gender narratives are socially constructed and performed by us every day, we collectively can and do change the ways stereotypes circulate to uphold inequities. Students enter women's, gender, and sexuality studies courses telling personal narratives of how they refuse bullying by finding community, practice self-care, refuse controlling gender expressions, join boys' soccer teams as the only girl, and resist and persist through stereotypes. Feminist and queer inquiry also remains interested in clarifying the underlying material and social circumstances that constrain and can control people's everyday lives. Until relations of power are addressed consistently across social institutions (from families, religion, and the law to media and language), fundamental and sustained sociopolitical change will remain elusive.

BEYOND THE GENDER BINARY

In 1990, gender studies scholar Judith Butler argued in *Gender Trouble* that our understandings of gender are too closely mapped to how we understand the body (for more on the body see Section Four). Rather than think of the body as constituting sex and gender, she and others suggest that it is more productive to understand gender performances as a fluid, social process based on repetition and reinforcement (see Halberstam 1998; Muñoz 2009). Gender flexibility disrupts the static assumption that to be born male equals being a man/masculine/attracted to women and that to be born female means being a woman/feminine/attracted to men. It also challenges the concept that "masculine" and "feminine" have universal meanings. This shift away from the certainty of the social construction of gender is both embraced and challenged by feminists and queer scholars. It is liberating for those who understand gender binaries as too limiting yet of great concern for those who see structural inequalities still tied to the bodies of women, lesbians, gay men, bisexuals, pansexuals, transgender, intersex, and asexual people. It is also important to note that Butler articulates how gender fluidity and flexibility may come at a personal cost ranging from possible teasing and being outcast, to bullying and being disowned, to discrimination and physical violence; this again suggests to us that the personal is indeed political and it will take all of us working together to make social change.

In *Transgender History*, Susan Stryker uses the term transgender "to refer to people who move away from the gender they were assigned at birth, people who cross over (*trans-*) the boundaries constructed by their culture to define and contain that gender" (Stryker 2008, 1). The term describes the full spectrum of someone's gender identity and expression, not their sexuality, and may include people who seek medical interventions to transition from one gender to another. The term **cisgender** is used to describe an individual whose gender assignment, gender identity, and gender expression align with the gender assigned at birth. Its use as an adjective before "woman" or "man" is necessary "to resist the way that 'woman' or 'man' can mean 'nontransgendered woman' or 'nontransgendered man' by default, unless the person's transgender status is explicitly named" (Stryker 2008, 22). And while these terms and their attending politics have received media attention, activists such as Sylvia Rivera and Marsha P. Johnson were pioneers of liberation movements in the mid-1960s, demanding rights, protections, and justice through political, legal, and sociocultural change; they will be honored for their work in New York City with a new monument. Books, journals, courses, academic programs, blogs, and activist platforms are dedicated to the history and complexity of reimagining what transgender means and the struggle for freedom. Learning the importance of pronouns to avoid misgendering people as well as the general meaning of terms that describe people's everyday lives is a starting place to create community and to take part in feminist and queer solidarity activism and knowledge building.

> **Cisgender:** A term that describes when an individual's gender assigned at birth aligns with their gender identity and gender expression.

The following glossary from the Southern Policy Law Center's "Teaching Tolerance" project provides an overview of key terms:

Affirmed gender (*noun*)	The gender by which one wishes to be known. This term is often used to replace terms like "new gender" or "chosen gender," which imply that a person's gender was chosen rather than simply innate.
Agender (*adj.*)	Describes a person who does not identify with any gender identity.
Ally (*noun*)	A person who does not identify as LGBTQ, but stands with and advocates for LGBTQ people.
Androgynous (*adj.*), Androgyne (*noun*)	Used to describe someone who identifies or presents as neither distinguishably masculine or feminine.
Aromantic (*adj.*)	A romantic orientation generally characterized by not feeling romantic attraction or a desire for romance.
Asexual (*adj.*)	Used to describe people who do not experience sexual attraction or do not have a desire for sex. Many experience romantic or emotional attractions across the entire spectrum of sexual orientations. Asexuality differs from celibacy, which refers to abstaining from sex. Also *ace*, or *ace community*.
Assigned sex (*noun*)	The sex that is assigned to an infant at birth based on the child's visible sex organs, including genitalia and other physical characteristics. Often corresponds with a child's *assigned gender* and *assumed gender*.
Binary system (*noun*)	Something that contains two opposing parts; binary systems are often assumed despite the existence of a spectrum of possibilities. Gender (man/woman) and sex (male/female) are examples of binary systems often perpetuated by our culture.

Continued

Biological sex (*noun*)	A medical classification that refers to anatomical, physiological, genetic or physical attributes that determine if a person is assigned male, female or intersex identity at birth. Biological sex is often confused or interchanged with the term "gender," which encompasses personal identity and social factors, and is not necessarily determined by biological sex. See *gender*.
Bisexual, Bi (*adj.*)	A person emotionally, romantically or sexually attracted to more than one sex, gender or gender identity though not necessarily simultaneously, in the same way or to the same degree.
Cisgender (*adj.*)	Describes a person whose gender identity (*defined below*) aligns with the sex assigned to them at birth.
Cissexism (*noun*)	A system of discrimination and exclusion that oppresses people whose gender and/or gender expression falls outside of normative social constructs. This system is founded on the belief that there are, and should be, only two genders—usually tied to assigned sex.
Coming out (*verb*)	A lifelong process of self-acceptance and revealing one's queer identity to others. This may involve something as private as telling a single confidant or something as public as posting to social media.
Demisexual (*adj.*)	Used to describe someone who feels sexual attraction only to people with whom they have an emotional bond—often considered to be on the asexual spectrum.
Gay (*adj.*)	Used to describe people (often, but not exclusively, men) whose enduring physical, romantic and/or emotional attractions are to people of the same sex or gender identity.
Gender (*noun*)	A set of social, physical, psychological and emotional traits, often influenced by societal expectations, that classify an individual as feminine, masculine, androgynous or other. Words and qualities ascribed to these traits vary across cultures.
Gender dysphoria (*noun*)	Clinically significant distress caused when a person's assigned birth gender is not the same as the one with which they identify.
Gender expression (*noun*)	External appearance of one's gender identity, usually expressed through behavior, clothing, haircut or voice, and which may or may not conform to socially defined behaviors and characteristics typically associated with being masculine or feminine.
Gender-fluid (*adj.*)	A person who does not identify with a single fixed gender and whose identification and presentation may shift, whether within or outside of the male/female binary.
Gender identity (*noun*)	One's innermost feeling of maleness, femaleness, a blend of both or neither. One's gender identity can be the same or different from their sex assigned at birth.
Gender neutral (*adj.*)	Not gendered, usually operating outside the male/female binary. Can refer to language (e.g., pronouns), spaces (e.g., bathrooms) or identities.
Gender nonconforming (*adj.*)	A broad term referring to people who do not behave in a way that conforms to the traditional expectations of their gender or whose gender expression does not fit neatly into a category. Also, *gender expansive*.
Genderqueer (*adj.*)	Describes a person who rejects static categories of gender (i.e. the gender binary of male/female) and whose gender expression or identity falls outside of the dominant social norms of their assigned sex. They may identify as having aspects of both male and female identities, or neither.
Gender roles (*noun*)	The social behaviors and expression that a culture expects from people based on their assigned sex (e.g., girls wear pink; boys don't cry; women care for home and child; men are more violent), despite a spectrum of various other possibilities.

Heteronormativity (*noun*)	Coined by social critic Michael Warner, the term refers to a societal assumption of certain norms: 1) that there are two distinct sexes; 2) that male and female functions and characteristics are distinctly different; and 3) that traits such as attraction and sexual behavior correspond to anatomy. Those who do not fit these norms—be it through same-sex attraction, a nonbinary gender identity, or nontraditional gender expression—are therefore seen as *abnormal*, and often marginalized or pressured to conform to norms as a result.
Heterosexism (*noun*)	The assumption that sexuality between people of different sexes is normal, standard, superior or universal while other sexual orientations are substandard, inferior, abnormal, marginal or invalid.
Heterosexual (*adj.*)	Used to describe people whose enduring physical, romantic and/or emotional attraction is to people of the opposite sex. Also *straight*.
Heterosexual/cisgender privilege (*noun*)	Refers to societal advantages that heterosexual people and cisgender people have solely because of their dominant identities. This can include things as simple as safely holding hands with a romantic partner in public or having safe access to public bathrooms. This can also include systemic privileges such as the right to legally donate blood, to adopt children without facing possible rejection because of your sexual orientation, or to play organized sports with others of the same gender identity.
Homophobia* (*noun*)	A fear or hostility toward lesbian, gay and/or bisexual people, often expressed as discrimination, harassment and violence.
Intersex (*adj.*)	An umbrella term describing people born with reproductive or sexual anatomy and/or a chromosome pattern that can't be classified as typically male or female.
Latinx (*adj.*)	A gender-expansive term for people of Latin American descent used to be more inclusive of all genders than the binary terms *Latino* or *Latina*.
Lesbian (*adj.*)	Used to describe a woman whose enduring physical, romantic and/or emotional attraction is to other women.
LGBTQ (*noun*)	An acronym for "lesbian, gay, bisexual, transgender and queer." Less often, the Q stands for "questioning." Acronyms like LGBTQIA also include the intersex and asexual communities, while acronyms like LGBTQ attempt to envelop an entire community of people who hold identities that are not cisgender or heterosexual.
Misgender (*verb*)	To refer to someone in a way that does not correctly reflect the gender with which they identify, such as refusing to use a person's pronouns or name.
Nonbinary (*adj.*)	An umbrella term that refers to individuals who identify as neither man or woman, or as a combination of man or woman. Instead, nonbinary people exhibit a boundless range of identities that can exist beyond a spectrum between male and female.
Outing (*verb*)	The inappropriate act of publicly declaring (sometimes based on rumor and/or speculation) or revealing another person's sexual orientation or gender identity without that person's consent.
Pansexual (*adj.*)	Used to describe people who have the potential for emotional, romantic or sexual attraction to people of any gender identity, though not necessarily simultaneously, in the same way or to the same degree. The term *panromantic* may refer to a person who feels these emotional and romantic attractions, but identifies as asexual.
Preferred pronouns (*adj.*)	The pronoun or set of pronouns that an individual personally uses and would like others to use when talking to or about that individual. Can include variations of he/him/his, she/her/hers, they/their/theirs, among others. This term is being used less and less in LGBTQ circles, as it suggests one's gender identity is a "preference" rather than innate. *Recommended replacement: "Your pronouns, my pronouns, their pronouns, etc."*

Continued

Queer (*adj.*)	Once a pejorative term, a term reclaimed and used by some within academic circles and the LGBTQ community to describe sexual orientations and gender identities that are not exclusively heterosexual or cisgender.
Questioning (*adj.*)	A term used to describe people who are in the process of exploring their sexual orientation or gender identity.
Same-gender loving (*adj.*)	A term coined in the early 1990s by activist Cleo Manago, this term was and is used by some members of the Black community who feel that terms like gay, lesbian and bisexual (and sometimes the communities therein) are Eurocentric and fail to affirm Black culture, history and identity.
Sexual orientation (*noun*)	An inherent or immutable emotional, romantic or sexual attraction to other people; oftentimes used to signify the gender identity (or identities) to which a person is most attracted.
Third gender (*noun*)	A gender identity that is neither male nor female, existing outside the idea that gender represents a linear spectrum between the two. Sometimes a catchall term or category in societies, states or countries that legally recognize genders other than male and female.
Transgender (*adj.*)	An umbrella term for people whose gender identity differs from the sex they were assigned at birth. Not all trans people undergo transition. Being transgender does not imply any specific sexual orientation. Therefore, transgender people may identify as straight, gay, lesbian, bisexual or something else. Also, *trans*.
Transitioning (*verb*)	A process during which some people strive to more closely align their gender identity with their gender expression. This includes *socially transitioning*, during which a person may change their pronouns, the name they ask to be called or the way they dress to be socially recognized as another gender. This includes *legal transitioning*, which may involve an official name change and modified IDs and birth certificates. And this includes *physically transitioning*, during which a person may undergo medical interventions to more closely align their body to their gender identity. Transgender and nonbinary people transition in various ways to various degrees; self-identification alone is enough to validate gender identity.
Transphobia* (*noun*)	The fear and hatred of, or discomfort with, transgender people. This may manifest into transphobic actions, such as violence, harassment, misrepresentation or exclusion.
Transsexual (*adj.*)	A less frequently used term (considered by some to be outdated or offensive) which refers to people who use medical interventions such as hormone therapy, gender-affirming surgery (GAS) or sex reassignment surgery (SRS) as part of the process of expressing their gender. Some people who identify as transsexual do not identify as transgender and vice versa. *Only use this term if someone who specifically identifies as such asks you to.*
Two Spirit (*adj.*)	An umbrella term in Native culture to describe people who have both a male and female spirit within them. This encompasses many tribe-specific names, roles and traditions, such as the *winkte* of the Lakota and *nadleeh* of the Navajo people. This term often describes Native people who performed roles and gender expression associated with both men and women. This term should be used only in the context of Native culture.

University of California, Davis's LGBTQIA Resource Center offers this note on words like this: We've been intentionally moving away from using words like "transphobic," "homophobic," and "biphobic" because (1) they inaccurately describe systems of oppression as irrational fears and (2) for some people, phobias are a very distressing part of their lived experience and co-opting this language is disrespectful to their experiences and perpetuates ableism.

Reprinted with permission of Teaching Tolerance, a project of the Southern Poverty Law Center. www.tolerance.org.

Knowing that sex and gender exist beyond binaries and that disabilities are understood through harmful normalizing assumptions helps us to unlearn limiting and harmful stereotypes. This is not just a matter of philosophical or political debate but has material consequences for the freedom, safety, well-being, equity, and social justice people seek.

OPPRESSION, PRIVILEGE, AND INTERSECTIONALITY

Oppression is the primary force that keeps marginalized people from achieving full equality, social justice, and freedom. It is best understood as a system of barriers that operate socially and institutionally to disempower groups of people based on their gender, race, class, ethnicity, sexuality, ability, religion, body size, and/or nationality and can be internalized. "Oppression" can also refer to how individual people can suppress and control one another psychologically. In Marilyn Frye's classic essay "Oppression," she argues that in patriarchal cultures *all* women are oppressed and men are not because "networks of forces and barriers . . . expose one to penalty, loss, or contempt whether one works outside the home or not, is on welfare or not, bears children or not, marries or not, stays married or not, is heterosexual, lesbian, both or neither" (Frye 1983, 3–4). Frye makes clear that women universally are affected by the **double binds** that oppression creates.

While it is true that women face similar oppressions—such as the stigma tied to menstruation or being told never to walk alone at night or wear revealing clothing to "prevent" rape (rather than insisting that boys/men not rape)—**women of color** (and people of color) may experience oppression differently than white women (and white men) and in multiple ways. In Deborah King's "Multiple Jeopardy and Multiple Consciousness: The Context of a Black Feminist Ideology," she points out that Black women recognize that "the interactive oppressions that circumscribe our lives provide a distinctive context for black womanhood" (King 1988, 42). While white people may experience oppression based on class, sexuality, body size, age, religion, and abilities, whiteness is not marked as a racial category in the United States. Therefore, white people experience unearned cultural privileges *because* they are not Black, Latinx, Native American, and/or Asian American. More broadly speaking, **privilege** is deeply connected to oppression and defined as a set of unearned advantages enjoyed by those who are empowered by U.S. social hierarchies (e.g., male, Christian, heterosexual, able-bodied, and/or young adults). It can be differentiated from sexism, racism, homophobia, classism, ableism, ageism, and prejudice because people with privilege may be unconscious of it and not acting overtly to subordinate others. Peggy McIntosh's essay "White Privilege: Unpacking the Invisible Knapsack" examines this social process and provides a compelling list of individual examples that detail the white privilege she personally experiences and the male privilege she does not. Robin DiAngelo's reading in this section,

Oppression: A social system of barriers that operate institutionally and interpersonally to disempower people because of their gender, race, class, sexuality, ethnicity, religion, body size, ability, and/or nationality.

Double bind: When a person faces two problematic choices as the only ones socially available (e.g., a woman can be labeled as a "slut" if sexually active and a "tease" or "prude" if not).

Women of color: A sociopolitical term used in the United States to describe African American/Black, Asian American, Latina/x, and Native American/Indigenous women.

Privilege: Cultural benefits and power granted to people through social and institutional inequalities.

INTERSECTIONAL ANALYSIS

Gina Metallic, coming out as two-spirit native womyn. Growing up in a small Indigenous community in Canada that she describes as both homophobic and transphobic because of colonization and Christianity, Metallic now identifies as a cisgender, feminist, two-spirit Mi'kmaq womyn deeply connected to her family and community. She told her story to the *Montreal Gazette* in August 2015 so that others might know that it is possible to be both queer and native and that there is support.

source: Justin Tang/The Gazette

A Case Study: Gina Metallic grew up in Listuguj, a small Mi'Kmaq community on the Gaspé Peninsula in Quebec, Canada. In her own words in the online version of the *Montreal Gazette*, she identifies as "a granddaughter, daughter, sister, aunt and a soon-to-be-wife. I also identify as a cisgender two-spirit Mi'kmaq womyn—a biological female inhabited at once by spirits of both male and female gender. I'm also a feminist who chooses to identify as 'womyn' rather than 'woman.'" In 1990 at the Third Annual First Nations Conference in Winnipeg, Canada, the term "two-spirited" was defined as "an Aboriginal who identifies with both male and female gender roles." When asked what identifying as two-spirited means to her, she discusses it historically and in her own life. According to her community elders and family members, two-spirited people hold respected positions in Indigenous communities: marriage counselors, medicine people, and visionaries. When Europeans arrived in the Americas, they enforced Christianity, and two-spirited people were either exiled or killed. Today, Metallic openly embraces her identity and has found support through the maternal side of her family but still experiences rejection from her father's side, which she attributes to the lasting effects of colonialism. Through ongoing work with a traditional healer, Metallic better understands her own history and has found a community of two-spirited womyn. In coming out, she writes, "I have realized that 'gay pride' and 'native pride' can co-exist. Being two-spirit empowers me to take agency over my body, sexuality, my gender and my culture."

QUESTIONS

1. Do some further investigations into what "two-spirited" means, take notes, and in a paragraph describe it in your own words, making clear how it is similar to and different from identifying as gender fluid.

2. Why is it important to know the Indigenous history of two-spirited people?

3. Is it possible for someone who does not identify as Indigenous to be two-spirited? Why or why not?

4. How does Gina Metallic's story of identifying as Indigenous, cisgender, womyn, feminist, and two-spirited add to your understanding of queer? How does it help you think through how people live in the world as they embody and inhabit many communities? Why is personal narrative a crucial tool for understanding how people identify?

"Nothing to Add: A Challenge to White Silence in Racial Discussions," draws on and pushes McIntosh's ideas to argue that whiteness itself is a framework for understanding why discussions about race and racism are met with silence. She argues that "if silence is not strategically enacted from an antiracist framework, it functions to maintain white power and privilege and must be challenged."

In other words, explaining race and confronting racism cannot be done on the backs of people of color so that they are the bridge to social change. DiAngelo's work investigates how white people might practice speaking up—even if it is for the first time—so that social transformation is possible. Whether it is within families, through education, in the media, and/or through other social institutions, acknowledging individual privileges does not go far enough in changing the material and social conditions of racism.

Intersectionality references the two-fold idea that people's identities are complex, often not fitting easily into named social categories of gender, race, class, and sexuality, *and* that sexism, racism, classism, homophobia, ableism, religious persecution, and nationalism are interlocking systems of power that shape our lives and social institutions (Collins and Bilge 2016). People are members of various identity groups *simultaneously*, and their position in each of these groups may bring them more or less power based on U.S. social hierarchies. While we can trace Black women's activism through collective archives to the early days of the republic in the United States, the collective work of The Combahee River Collective (included in Section Two) lay the theoretical groundwork for a contemporary understanding of intersectionality. Emphasizing the centrality of race/gender/class/sexuality as interlocking structures of power, many contemporary feminists honor the work of those who came before them in such foundational texts as Angela Davis's *Women, Race, & Class* (1981); bell hooks's *Ain't I a Woman?* (1981); Hazel Carby's "White Woman Listen!" (1982); Cherríe Moraga and Gloria Anzaldúa's edited volume *This Bridge Called My Back* (1983); Barbara Smith's edited collection *Home Girls* (1983); Alice Walker's *In Search of Our Mother's Gardens* (1983); Audre Lorde's *Sister Outsider* (1984); Barbara Christian's *Black Feminist Criticism* (1985); and Patricia Hill Collins' *Black Feminist Thought* (1990). Scholarly and creative writers responded to white, middle-class feminist assumptions that all women experience oppressions similarly. Women marginalized by sociopolitical systems in the United States—Black women, women of color, lesbians of color, working poor women, and **third world women**—argued that feminism and queer communities must grapple with how normalized cultural differences shape people's everyday lives if they are to work together in solidarity for social change.

In a 1988 article, Kimberlé Crenshaw coined the term "intersectionality" as a way for scholars and practitioners to describe these intricacies as well as make clear the impossible "choice" women, lesbians of color, and poor women face in being asked to fight for their rights as women *or* as Black, Chicana/Latina/x, Asian American, Native American, third world *or* queer *or* poor (Allen 1986; Anzaldúa 1990; Asian Women United of California 1989; García 1989; Mohanty, Russo, and Torres 1991; Moraga 1983). Turning particularly to how the law demands that Black women must "choose" their legal pathway based on race or gender to pursue workplace discrimination cases, Crenshaw theorized the need to see how interlocking oppressions created hierarchies of power. Audre Lorde poignantly and personally elucidates this point in her essay "There Is No Hierarchy of Oppressions" (included in this section) with this statement: "I simply do not believe that one aspect of myself can possibly

Intersectionality: Theoretical term used to discuss the interlocking systems of oppression of gender, race, class, sexuality, age, ability, religion, and nationality that shape people's experience and access to power.

Third world women: Women who inhabit or whose (familial) origins reflect Asian, African, and Latin American geographies; used as a political term to reflect the colonial power relations between the first world (the West or Global North) and the third world (or Global South).

profit from the oppression of any other part of my identity" (p. 75). She goes on to point out that, in the lesbian community, she is both Black and a lesbian, and in the Black community, she is both Black and a lesbian. How then can she fight against racism and not homophobia and sexism? This question and the insights based on the lived experiences of U.S. women of color now form the intersectional approaches that are foundational in understanding women's, gender, and sexuality studies.

Engaged Learning

In Peggy McIntosh's "White Privilege: Unpacking the Invisible Knapsack" (available online) she notes that many of the privileges she experiences as a white woman and a professor are based on not being racially profiled by the police. Imagine how significant this is when we consider the brutality that people of color disproportionately experience in the United States. If you are not familiar with the recent history of the police murdering black men, do a quick internet search for George Floyd, Michael Brown, Eric Garner, Philando Castile, Allen Locke, Freddi Gray, Paul Castaway, and Samuel DuBose (among too many other names). Do the same search through the archives of *Al Jazeera* and/or the online magazine *The Root* or *Colorlines*. Two of the men named here identified as Indigenous. According to the Lakota People's Law Project, Native Americans are most likely to be killed by law enforcement (Agorist 2015). Expand the search to see what other names of people emerge and what communities they represent.

In one month alone (July 2015), five Black women died in police custody. Did your search tell you about the lives of Breonna Taylor Sandra Bland, Alexia Christian, Meagan Hockaday, Kayla Moore, Shelly Frey, Tanisha Anderson, Alberta Spruil, Miriam Carey, and Michelle Cusseaux, and other people whose names we do not know? What about the nearly thirty trans women of color killed in 2019, including Dana Martin, Ellie Marie Washtock, Jazzaline Ware, Ashanti Carmon, Claire Legato, Muhlaysia Booker, Michelle "Tamika" Washington, Paris Cameron,

Chynal Lindsay, Denali Berris Stuckey, Tracy Single, Bubba Walker, Kiki Fantroy, Pebbles LeDime "Dime" Doe, Bailey Reeves, Bee Love Slater, Jamagio Jamar Berryman, Itali Marlowe, Brianna BB Hill, Nikki Kuhnhausen, and Yahira Nesdby? For more information on the underreported violence against African American women and women of color follow #SayHerName and consult the work of the African American Policy Forum. To learn more about violence against trans women of color, follow #StopTransMurders, #ProtectTransWomen, and #SayHerName and consult the TransWomen of Color Collective, Sylvia Rivera Law Project (SRLP), the Trevor Project, the Human Rights Campaign (HRC), and Somos Familia Valle, to name a few.

QUESTIONS

1. Choose two news stories about either police brutality or the far-reaching violence against women of color and look carefully at what words and images frame the story. Whose voices are the experts in telling the story? Can you detect anything that may be left out of it?

2. What does this exercise reveal about objectivity in reporting and the silences regarding violence?

3. When framed through an intersectional lens, how does this exercise ask us to think through violence beyond individual incidences?

4. Find stories of resilience and representations of race that depict joy, reparations, thriving, and the beauty in life. Where did you find them and what did you learn from them?

Intersectionality also matters in a global context. Ashley Currier and Thérèse Migraine-George's article "Queer/African Identities: Questions, Limits, Challenges" (included in this section), examines antigay violence that specific African states perpetuate against the people in their respective countries. In asking us to think carefully about what constitutes a nation and its people and how this intersects with queer identity, they argue that violent backlashes most certainly negatively affect gay, lesbian, bisexual, and transgender people *and* violence and discrimination does not "predetermine the content and contours of queer African identities" (p. 77). While the U.S. popular media only presents specific African nations as showing open hostility toward queer communities, the authors interview activists in Liberia, Malawi, and South Africa and draw on queer African literature and films to provide more "complicated dimensions of generating, representing, and nurturing queer identities" (p. 77). Rather than showing African queer communities only as victims of the stigma and violence in their homelands (which by itself only serves to reinforce oversimplified and sensational media constructions), Currier's and Migraine-George's research honors the complexity of queer life—the resilience of LGBTQPAI+ people, the continued stigma attached to bisexuality, and the joy and beauty of being queer in Africa—by amplifying the voices of activists who are working to make a difference.

Pride in Global Spaces. LGBTQPAI+ pride rallies take place all over the world and help us to understand that the movement to end discrimination and marginalization of queer-identified people is transnational. Participants here hold posters in support of the LGBTQPAI+ community in Manila during the twenty-first Pride Parade on June 27, 2015. The press reported that thousands marched through main streets to celebrate the queer community.
Source: J Gerard Seguia/Pacific Press/Alamy Live News

In her poem "Before Intersectionality" (included in this section), M. Soledad Caballero reminds us that while "intersectionality" is a relatively new term in academia, immigrant women, men, trans, nonbinary, and genderqueer people from Spanish-speaking countries have always lived at the crossroads of gender, race, class, sexuality, and nationality, yet can be rendered invisible by the culturally-produced Black/white racial binary in the United States. Her poem names the violence Latinx immigrants face; gives voice to the pain, isolation, and invisibility of young people living in between English- and Spanish-speaking cultures; and reaches out to anyone who may feel like they do not belong. It also speaks to the dimensions of what needs to be considered in order for us to care about, empathize with, and work toward social change across cultural borders.

To fully understand intersectionality, it is important to acknowledge that whiteness *is* a racial category—but one that has unearned privileges (including the privilege of remaining silent) and therefore can remain unmarked. Just as

TRANSNATIONAL CONNECTIONS

Zanele Muholi, photographer and self-identified visual activist, was born in 1972 in South Africa. She has dedicated her life's work to telling the stories of lesbians and transgender and intersexed people in South Africa through images. In her 2014 series *Faces and Phases, 2006–2014*, Muholi creates portraits of more than two hundred individuals in the lesbian community, which as an archive makes a political statement on how South African lesbians exist and thrive in the midst of stigma and violence. The "Isibonelo/Evidence" exhibition at the Elizabeth A. Sackler Center for Feminist Art at the Brooklyn Museum (2015) featured eighty-seven of Muholi's works from *Faces and Phases*, *Weddings*, and the video *Being Scene* that incorporates firsthand accounts of what it is like to live in places where LGBTQPAI+ rights are constitutionally protected but often not defended. Her thought-provoking and sensitive photography also makes a point of focusing on love, intimacy, and daily life in close-knit lesbian and transgender communities. In Muholi's own words, she does this work because "it heals me to know that I am paving the way for others who, in wanting to come out, are able to look at the photographs, read the biographies, and understand that they are not alone" (qtd. in Schwiegershausen 2015). Do an internet search on "Zanele Muholi" and choose a comprehensive website that provides her biography and images of her work. At the time of publication, we can recommend https://www.artsy.net/artist/zanele-muholi.

QUESTIONS

1. Muholi uses the term "visual activist" (instead of "visual artist") to describe her work. What does this mean to you as you read her biography and look at her photography?

2. The people in Muholi's photographs look back at the people who are looking at them. This is a central feature of portraiture. Why is it important that many of her photographs of the South African LGBTQPAI+ community are done in this style?

3. Both Muholi and Currier and Migraine-George discuss love and empowerment in African queer communities. How does this focus help you rethink what it means to be queer and transgender in Africa? Why is this important?

4. Zanele Muholi's work is affirming and empowering of queer and transgender people. How might you use this approach to think through LGBTQPAI+ issues in your home town/city?

oppression must be understood in relation to privilege, social constructions of Blackness and Brownness are deeply connected to whiteness, and we cannot understand the empowerment of one without the disempowerment of the other. Second, while no one person is *responsible* for this way of thinking, guilt as a response to sexism, racism, classism, homophobia, and transphobia does very little to contribute to efforts toward social change as it recenters whiteness. Audre Lorde writes powerfully in *Sister Outsider*, "Guilt is not a response to anger; it is a response to one's own actions or lack of action. If it leads to change, then it can be useful, since it is then no longer guilt but the beginning of knowledge" (Lorde 130). It is only through **self-reflexivity**, careful listening, and understanding identity, cultural power, and social structures through intersectional and transnational lenses that we can understand, protest, address, and begin to transform systematic inequalities more fully and accurately.

INTERDISCIPLINARITY

Given the expansive landscape of the field, students and anyone picking up this text may be wondering, "What does *not* count as women's, gender, and sexuality studies?" Indeed, the field encompasses the study of all people and the social dynamics that shape their lives. To tell the stories of people's complex lives, especially of individuals and groups that are marginalized and made to seem invisible and/or hypervisible in the dominant culture, researchers must be self-reflexive about the kinds of questions they ask as well as how they go about collecting information. The same can be said for educators and how they go about sharing knowledge, engaging with one another, and working closely with students. As the final reading in this section, Kimberly Williams Brown and Red Washburn model collaborative, self-reflexive approaches to creating more equitable classrooms. Instructors and students might ask ourselves, as we enter women's, gender, and sexuality studies classes, how we collectively might translate what Brown and Washburn are doing into practice with one another—in the classroom and beyond. Their essay shows us the possibilities of doing feminist-queer solidarity work. It suggests that this is how we can reimagine a future based on connection and reaching across disciplinary and cultural boundaries in the name of transdisciplinarity and in search of utopias.

In addition to entering interdisciplinary work self-reflexively, women's, gender, and sexuality studies values **praxis** and draws on a range of primary and secondary sources to make knowledge claims and frame political issues. Primary sources may include personal narratives, historical archives (official collections and those that are more intimate, such as diaries), quantitative research, ethnographies, art, literature, television and film, newspapers and online sources, scientific experiments, and critical legal analysis. Secondary sources, or those written by other scholars in the field, provide historical and cultural context for framing arguments. Both are necessary for analyzing subject matter.

Self-reflexivity: The deliberate examination of how and why people come to their beliefs, ideas, and knowledge in the context of broader (gender, race, class, sexuality, abilities, age, religion, and nationalities) power relations; a necessary step in pursuing feminist and queer scholarship, activism, and institutional practices.

Praxis: The integration of learning theoretical concepts with social justice actions so that one's own behaviors in the world reflect the liberatory philosophies of feminism and queer approaches.

Naming women's, gender, and sexuality studies as an interdisciplinary field of study and praxis means that there is no one framework, no one method, and no one theory that explains feminist and queer cultures, issues, and politics. Rather, it requires multiple modes of knowing and doing to produce the most accurate and politically engaged work possible. The reading selections included in this book draw from across traditional disciplines (such as English, political science, and sociology) as well as the humanistic interdisciplinary fields that also emerged from twentieth-century social movements (such as Africana studies, ethnic studies, Latino/a/x studies, Asian American studies, Native American studies, Puerto Rican studies, transgender studies, and disability studies) to show the exciting and engaging possibilities for doing interdisciplinary work.

Critical Thinking Questions

1. Understanding oppression means that those caught in a network of social, political, economic, and cultural forces can face double binds. In this introductory section, an example of a double bind is when young women who choose to be sexually active are labeled whores and young women who choose not to be sexually active are called teases or prudes. What other double binds do you see and/or experience across gender identities/expressions and sexualities? Think critically about your answers through an intersectional approach.

2. How does Robin DiAngelo's work on white silence and fragility contribute to understanding the social construction of race and racism? How might we acknowledge individual unearned privilege and begin working collectively toward dismantling oppression? What are some of the first steps to take given the perspectives conveyed through the readings in this first section?

3. Reflect on your experiences learning about sexuality—whether it was through a sex education class, from your parents, with your friends, YouTube, or from reading on your own. What did you learn? How was it gendered? Was it intersectional? What do you think it should include for the next generation?

4. Given what you have learned about intersectionality, including disability, what do you think it means for you as a student to be self-reflexive when talking about feminist and queer issues, cultural identities, and power?

GLOSSARY

Cisgender 9	Genderqueer 4	Intersectionality 15
Double bind 13	Gender status 5	LGBTQPAI+ 4
Gender identity 5	Heteronormative 4	Oppression 13

Patriarchy 3

Praxis 19

Privilege 13

Queer 4

Self-reflexivity 19

Social construction 5

Social institutions 3

Third world women 15

Transgender 4

Women of color 13

WORKS CITED

Agorist, Matt. "Police Are Killing Native Americans at Higher Rate Than Any Race, and Nobody Is Talking About It." *The Free Thought Project.com*, August 2, 2015, thefreethoughtproject.com/police-killing-native-americans-higher-rate-race-talking/.

Allen, Paula Gunn. *The Sacred Hoop: Recovering the Feminine in American Indian Traditions*. Beacon Press, 1986.

Boxer, Marilyn. *When Women Ask the Questions: Creating Women's Studies in America*. Johns Hopkins UP, 1998.

Butler, Judith. *Gender Trouble: Feminism and the Subversion of Identity*. Routledge, 1990.

Carby, Hazel. "White Woman Listen! Black Feminism and the Boundaries of Sisterhood." In *The Empire Strikes Back: Race and Racism in 70s Britain*, edited by the Centre for Contemporary Cultural Studies. Routledge, 1982.

Christian, Barbara. *Black Feminist Criticism: Perspectives on Black Women Writers*. Teachers College Press, 1985.

Collins, Patricia Hill. *Black Feminist Thought: Knowledge, Consciousness, and the Politics of Empowerment*. Routledge, 1990.

Collins, Patricia Hill, and Sirma Bilge. *Intersectionality*. Polity, 2016.

Crenshaw, Kimberlé. "Mapping the Margins: Intersectionality, Identity Politics, and Violence Against Women of Color." *Stanford Law Review*, vol. 43, no. 124, 1993, pp. 1241–99.

Davies, Sharyn Graham. "What We Can Learn From An Indonesian Ethnicity That Recognizes Five Genders." *The Conversation*, June 16, 2016.

Davis, Angela. *Women, Race, & Class*. Vintage Books, 1981.

Fausto-Sterling, Anne. *Sexing the Body: Gender Politics and the Construction of Sexuality*. Basic Books, 2000.

Frye, Marilyn. *The Politics of Reality: Essays in Feminist Theory*. Crossing Press, 1983.

García, Alma. "The Development of Chicana Feminist Discourse, 1970–1980." *Gender & Society*, vol. 3, no. 2, 1989, pp. 217–38.

Gardiner, Judith Kegan. *Masculinity Studies and Feminist Theory*. Columbia UP, 2002.

Halberstam, Judith. *Female Masculinity*. Duke UP, 1998.

hooks, bell. *Ain't I a Woman? Black Women and Feminism*. South End Press, 1981.

hooks, bell. *Black Looks: Race and Representation*. South End Press, 1992.

hooks, bell. *Feminism Is for Everybody: Passionate Politics*. Pluto Press, 2000.

hooks, bell. *Feminist Theory: From Margin to Center*. South End Press, 1984.

hooks, bell. *We Real Cool: Black Men and Masculinity*. Routledge, 2003.

King, Deborah. "Multiple Jeopardy, Multiple Consciousness: The Context of a Black Feminist Ideology." *Signs: Journal of Women in Culture and Society*, vol. 14, no. 1, 1988, pp. 42–72.

Lorber, Judith. "'Night to His Day': The Social Construction of Gender." In *Paradoxes of Gender*. Yale UP, 1994.

Lorde, Audre. *Sister Outsider*. Crossing Press, 1984.

Messner, Michael. *Politics of Masculinities: Men in Movements*. Sage Publications, 1997.

Metallic, Gina. "My Coming Out: Finding My True Identity Meant Re-Connecting with My Culture." *Montreal Gazette*, August 5, 2015, montrealgazette.com/life/my-coming-out-finding-my-true-identity-meant-reconnecting-with-my-culture.

Mohanty, Chandra Talpade, Ann Russo, and Lourdes Torres, editors. *Third World Women and the Politics of Feminism*. Indiana UP, 1991.

Moraga, Cherríe. *Loving in the War Years: Lo Que Nunca Pasó Por Sus Labios*. South End Press, 1983.

Moraga, Cherríe, and Gloria Anzaldúa, eds. *This Bridge Called My Back: Writings by Radical Women of Color*. Kitchen Table, Women of Color Press, 1983.

Muholi, Zanele. *Faces and Phases, 2006–2014*. Steidl Verlag, 2014.

Muñoz, José Esteban. *Cruising Utopia: The Then and There of Queer Futurity*. New York UP, 2009.

Purvis, Jennifer. "Queer." In *Rethinking Women's and Gender Studies*, edited by C. Orr, A. Braithwaite, and D. Lichtenstein. Routledge, 2012.

Schwiegershausen, Erica. "See Zanele Muholi's Powerful Portraits of the LGBTI Experience in South Africa." *The Cut*, New York Media, January 7, 2015, nymag.

com/thecut/2015/01/powerful-portraits-of-queer-life-in-south-africa.html.

Segal, Lynne. *Slow Motion: Changing Masculinities, Changing Men*. Virago, 1990.

Smith, Barbara, ed. *Home Girls: A Black Feminist Anthology*. Kitchen Table, Women of Color Press, 1983.

Southern Poverty Law Center. "The Acronym and Beyond: A Glossary of Terms." *Teaching Tolerance*. https://www.tolerance.org/magazine/publications/best-practices-for-serving-lgbtq-students/lgbtq-terms-definitions-the-acronym-and-beyond.

Stryker, Susan. *Transgender History*. Seal Press, 2008.

Walker, Alice. *In Search of Our Mother's Gardens*. Harcourt Brace Jovanovich, 1983.

Welter, Barbara. "The Cult of True Womanhood: 1820–1860." *American Quarterly*, vol. 18, no. 2, 1966, pp. 151–74.

Wiegman, Robyn. "Unmaking: Men and Masculinity in Feminist Theory." In *Masculinity Studies and Feminist Theory*, edited by Judith Gardiner. Columbia UP, 2002.

FEMINIST POLITICS:
Where We Stand (2000)

Born Gloria Jean Watkins, award-winning feminist scholar and cultural critic bell hooks is the author of over three dozen books and has contributed original work to seven collections and numerous periodicals. Her writing explores the intersections of race, class, gender, sexuality, spirituality, teaching, and the media and spans several genres, including nonfiction, poetry, memoir, and children's literature. She has been an acclaimed and outspoken social justice activist throughout her career and the bell hooks Institute in Berea, Kentucky, is dedicated to documenting her life and work. The Institute's mission is to end exploitation and oppression through critical thinking, teaching, and dialogue. "Feminist Politics: Where We Stand" is a chapter in her text *Feminism Is for Everybody*, an accessible and lively introduction to feminism designed for students and the general public.

Simply put, feminism is a movement to end sexism, sexist exploitation, and oppression. This was a definition of feminism I offered in *Feminist Theory: From Margin to Center* more than 10 years ago. It was my hope at the time that it would become a common definition everyone would use. I liked this definition because it did not imply that men were the enemy. By naming sexism as the problem it went directly to the heart of the matter. Practically, it is a definition which implies that all sexist thinking and action is the problem, whether those who perpetuate it are female or male, child or adult. It is also broad enough to include an understanding of systemic institutionalized sexism. As a definition it is open-ended. To understand feminism it implies one has to necessarily understand sexism.

As all advocates of feminist politics know, most people do not understand sexism, or if they do, they think it is not a problem. Masses of people think that feminism is always and only about women seeking to be equal to men. And a huge majority of these folks think feminism is anti-male. Their misunderstanding of feminist politics reflects the reality that most folks learn about feminism from patriarchal mass media. The feminism they hear about the most is portrayed by women who are primarily committed to gender equality—equal pay for equal work, and sometimes women and men sharing household chores and parenting. They see that these women are usually white and materially privileged. They know from mass media that women's liberation focuses on the freedom to have abortions, to be lesbians, to challenge rape and domestic violence. Among these issues, masses of people agree with the idea of gender equity in the workplace—equal pay for equal work.

Since our society continues to be primarily a "Christian" culture, masses of people continue to believe that god has ordained that women be

hooks, bell. "Feminist Politics: Where We Stand." Feminism is for Everybody. Boston: South End Press, 2000. Pluto Press, pp. 1–6 subordinate to men in the domestic household. Even though masses of women have entered the workforce, even though many families are headed by women who are the sole breadwinners, the vision of domestic life which continues to dominate the nation's imagination is one in which the logic of male domination is intact, whether men are present in the home or not. The wrongminded notion of feminist movement which implied it was anti-male carried with it the wrongminded assumption that all: female space would necessarily be an environment where patriarchy and sexist thinking would be absent. Many women, even those involved in feminist politics, chose to believe this as well.

There was indeed a great deal of anti-male sentiment among early feminist activists who were responding to male domination with anger. It was that anger at injustice that was the impetus for creating a women's liberation movement. Early on most feminist activists (a majority of whom were white) had their consciousness raised about the nature of male domination when they were working in anti-classist and anti-racist settings with men who were telling the world about the importance of freedom while subordinating the women in their ranks. Whether it was white women working on behalf of socialism, black women working on behalf of civil rights and black liberation, or Native American women working for indigenous rights, it was clear that men wanted to lead, and they wanted women to follow. Participating in these radical freedom struggles awakened the spirit of rebellion and resistance in progressive females and led them towards contemporary women's liberation.

As contemporary feminism progressed, as women realized that males were not the only group in our society who supported sexist thinking and behavior— that females could be sexist as well—anti-male sentiment no longer shaped the movement's consciousness. The focus shifted to an all-out effort to create gender justice. But women could not band together to further feminism without confronting our sexist thinking. Sisterhood could not be powerful as long as women were competitively at war with one another. Utopian visions of sisterhood based solely

on the awareness of the reality that all women were in some way victimized by male domination were disrupted by discussions of class and race. Discussions of class differences occurred early on in contemporary feminism, preceding discussions of race. Diana Press published revolutionary insights about class divisions between women as early as the mid-'70s in their collection of essays *Class and Feminism.* These discussions did not trivialize the feminist insistence that "sisterhood is powerful"; they simply emphasized that we could only become sisters in struggle by confronting the ways women—through sex, class, and race—dominated and exploited other women, and created a political platform that would address these differences.

Even though individual black women were active in contemporary feminist movement from its inception, they were not the individuals who became the "stars" of the movement, who attracted the attention of mass media. Often individual black women active in feminist movement were revolutionary feminists (like many white lesbians). They were already at odds with reformist feminists who resolutely wanted to project a vision of the movement as being solely about women gaining equality with men in the existing system. Even before race became a talked-about issue in feminist circles it was clear to black women (and to their revolutionary allies in struggle) that they were never going to have equality within the existing white supremacist capitalist patriarchy.

From its earliest inception feminist movement was polarized. Reformist thinkers chose to emphasize gender equality. Revolutionary thinkers did not want simply to alter the existing system so that women would have more rights. We wanted to transform that system, to bring an end to patriarchy and sexism. Since patriarchal mass media was not interested in the more revolutionary vision, it never received attention in mainstream press. The vision of "women's liberation" which captured and still holds the public imagination was the one representing women as wanting what men had. And this was the vision that was easier to realize. Changes in our nation's economy, economic depression, the loss of jobs, etc., made the climate ripe for our nation's citizens to accept the notion of gender equality in the workforce.

Given the reality of racism, it made sense that white men were more willing to consider women's rights when the granting of those rights could serve the interests of maintaining white supremacy. We can never forget that white women began to assert their need for freedom after civil rights just at the point when racial discrimination was ending and black people, especially black males, might have attained equality in the workforce with white men. Reformist feminist thinking focusing primarily on equality with men in the workforce overshadowed the original radical foundations of contemporary feminism which called for reform as well as overall restructuring of society so that our nation would be fundamentally anti-sexist.

Most women, especially privileged white women, ceased even to consider revolutionary feminist visions, once they began to gain economic power within the existing social structure. Ironically, revolutionary feminist thinking was most accepted and embraced in academic circles. In those circles the production of revolutionary feminist theory progressed, but more often than not that theory was not made available to the public. It became and remains a privileged discourse available to those among us who are highly literate, well-educated, and usually materially privileged. Works like *Feminist Theory: From Margin to Center* that offer a liberatory vision of feminist transformation never receive mainstream attention. Masses of people have not heard of this book. They have not rejected its message; they do not know what the message is.

While it was in the interest of mainstream white supremacist capitalist patriarchy to suppress visionary feminist thinking which was not anti-male or concerned with getting women the right to be like men, reformist feminists were also eager to silence these forces. Reformist feminism became their route to class mobility. They could break free of male domination in the workforce and be more self-determining in their lifestyles. While sexism did not end, they could maximize their freedom within the existing system. And they could count on there being a lower class of exploited subordinated women to do the dirty work they were refusing to do. By accepting and indeed colluding with the subordination of working-class and poor women, they not only ally themselves with the existing patriarchy and its concomitant sexism; they give themselves the right to lead a double life, one where they are the equals of men in the workforce and at home when they want to be. If they choose lesbianism they have the privilege of being equals with men in the workforce while using class power to create domestic lifestyles where they can choose to have little or no contact with men.

Lifestyle feminism ushered in the notion that there could be as many versions of feminism as there were women. Suddenly the politics was being slowly removed from feminism. And the assumption prevailed that no matter what a woman's politics, be she conservative or liberal, she too could fit feminism into her existing lifestyle. Obviously this way of thinking has made feminism more acceptable because its underlying assumption is that women can be feminists without fundamentally challenging and changing themselves or the culture. For example, let's take the issue of abortion. If feminism is a movement to end sexist oppression, and depriving females of reproductive rights is a form of sexist oppression, then one cannot be anti-choice and be feminist. A woman can insist she would never choose to have an abortion while affirming her support of the right of women to choose and still be an advocate of feminist politics. She cannot be anti-abortion and an advocate of feminism. Concurrently there can be no such thing as "power feminism" if the vision of power evoked is power gained through the exploitation and oppression of others.

Feminist politics is losing momentum because the feminist movement has lost clear definitions. We have those definitions. Let's reclaim them. Let's share them. Let's start over. Let's have T-shirts and bumper stickers and postcards and hip-hop music, television and radio commercials, ads everywhere and billboards, and all manner of printed material that tells the world about feminism. We can share the simple yet powerful message that feminism is a movement to end sexist oppression. Let's start there. Let the movement begin again.

2. • *Allan Johnson*

PATRIARCHY, THE SYSTEM:
An It, Not a He, a Them, or an Us (2014)

Allan Johnson is a cultural critic, novelist, sociologist, public speaker, and blogger interested in social justice through unraveling privileges tied to gender, race, and class. He is the author of eight books and several essays that span nonfiction, memoir, and fiction. Following the publication of *The Gender Knot*, from which this article is excerpted, he transitioned from academe to public speaking working as a diversity trainer in corporations, including IBM, GE, and BankBoston.

"When you say patriarchy," a man complained from the rear of the audience, "I know what you *really* mean—me!" A lot of people hear "men" whenever someone says "patriarchy," so that criticism of male privilege and the oppression of women is taken to mean that all men—each and every one of them—are oppressive people.

Some of the time, men feel defensive because they identify with patriarchy and its values and do not want to face the consequences these produce or the prospect of giving up male privilege. But defensiveness can also reflect a common confusion about the difference between patriarchy as a kind of society and the people who participate in it. If we are ever going to work toward real change, it is a confusion we will have to clear up.

To do this, we have to begin by realizing that we are stuck in a model of social life that views everything as beginning and ending with individuals, Looking at things in this way, the tendency is to think that if bad things happen in the world and if the bad thing is something big, it is only because there are bad people who have entered into some kind of conspiracy. Racism exists, then, because white people are racist bigots who hate members of racial and ethnic minorities and want to do them harm. The oppression of women happens because men want and like to dominate women and act out hostility toward them. There is poverty and class oppression because people in the upper classes are greedy, heartless, and cruel.

The flip side of this individualistic model of guilt and blame is that race, gender, and class oppression are actually not oppression at all but merely the sum of individual failings on the part of people of color, women, and people living in poverty, who lack the right stuff to compete successfully with whites, men, and others who know how to make something of themselves.

What this kind of thinking ignores is that we are all participating in something larger than ourselves or any collection of us. On some level, most people are familiar with the idea that social life involves us in something larger than ourselves, but few seem to know what to do with that idea. Blaming everything on "the system" strikes a deep chord in many people,[1] but it also touches on a basic misunderstanding of social life, because blaming the system (presumably society) for our problems doesn't take the next step to understanding what that might mean. What exactly is a system and how could it run our lives? Do we have anything to do with shaping *it*, and if so, how? How do we participate in patriarchy, and how does that link us to the consequences? How is what we think of as normal life related to male privilege, women's oppression, and the hierarchical, control-obsessed world in which everyone's lives are embedded?

Without asking such questions, not only can we not understand gender fully, but we also avoid taking responsibility either for ourselves or for patriarchy. Instead, "the system" serves as a vague, unarticulated catch-all, a dumping ground for social problems, a scapegoat that can never be held to account and that, for all the power we think it has, cannot talk back or actually *do* anything.

[. . .]

If we see patriarchy as nothing more than men's and women's individual personalities, motivations, and behavior, then it won't occur to us to ask about larger contexts—such as institutions like the family, religion, and the economy—and how people's lives are shaped in relation to them. From an individualistic perspective, for example, we might ask why a particular man raped, harassed, or beat a particular woman. We would not ask, however, what kind of society would promote persistent *patterns* of such behavior in everyday life, from wife-beating jokes to the routine inclusion of sexual coercion and violence in mainstream movies. We would be quick to explain rape and battery as the acts of sick or angry men, but without taking seriously the question of what kind of society would produce so much male anger and pathology or direct it toward sexual violence rather than something else. We would be unlikely to ask how gender violence might serve other more normalized ends such as masculine control and domination and the proving of manhood. . . .

In short, the tendency in this patriarchal society is to ignore and take for granted what we can least afford to overlook in trying to understand and change the world. Rather than ask how social systems produce social problems such as men's violence against women, we obsess over legal debates and titillating but irrelevant case histories soon to become made-for-television movies. If the goal is to change the world, this will not help. We need to see and deal with the social roots that generate and nurture the *social* problems that are reflected in and manifested through the behavior of individuals. We cannot do this without realizing that we all participate in something larger than ourselves, something we did not create but that we now have the power to affect through the choices we make about *how* to participate.

Some readers have objected to describing women as "participating" in patriarchy. The objection is based on the idea that participation, by definition, is something voluntary, freely chosen, entered into as equals, and that it therefore makes no sense that women might participate in their own oppression. But that is not my meaning here, and it is not a necessary interpretation of the word. To participate is to have a *part* in what goes on, to do something (or not) and to have that choice affect the consequences, regardless of whether it is conscious or unconscious, coerced or not. Of course, the *terms* of women's participation differ dramatically from those that shape men's, but it is participation, nonetheless.

This is similar to the participation of workers in the system of capitalism. They do not participate as equals to the capitalists who employ them or on terms they would choose if they could. Nevertheless, without workers, capitalism cannot function as a system that oppresses them.

The importance of participation can be seen in the many ways that women and working-class people respond to oppression—all the forms that fighting back or giving in can take. To argue that women or workers do not participate is to render them powerless and irrelevant to patriarchy's and capitalism's past, present, and future, for it is only as participants that people can affect anything. Otherwise, women and workers would be like pieces of wood floating down a river, which, as history makes clear, has never been the case.

[...]

Even more so, we cannot understand the world and our lives in it without looking at the dynamic relationship between individual people and social systems. Nor can we understand the countless details—from sexual violence to patterns of conversation to unequal distributions of power—that make up the reality of male privilege and the oppression of women.

As Figure 2 shows, this relationship has two parts. The arrow on the right side represents the idea that as we participate in social systems, we are shaped as individuals. Through the process of socialization, we learn how to participate in social life—from families, schools, religion, and the mass media, through the examples set by parents, peers, coaches, teachers, and public figures—a continuing stream of ideas and images of people and the world and who we are in relation to them.

Through all of this, we develop a sense of personal identity—including gender—and how this positions us in relation to other people, especially in terms of inequalities of power. As I grew up watching movies and television, for example, the message was clear that men are the most important people because they are the ones who do the most important things, as defined by patriarchal culture. They are the strong ones who build; the heroes and superheroes who fight the good fight; the geniuses, writers, and artists; the bold leaders; and even the evil—but always interesting—villains.

[...]

Invariably, some of what we learn through socialization turns out not to be true and then we may have to deal with that. I say "may" because powerful forces encourage us to keep ourselves in a state of denial, to rationalize what we have been taught. It is a way to keep it safe from scrutiny, if only to protect our sense of who we are and ensure our being accepted by other people, including family and friends. In the end, the default is to adopt the dominant version of reality and act as though it's the only one there is.

In addition to socialization, participation in social systems shapes our behavior through paths of least resistance, a concept that refers to a feature of social systems that guides the conscious and unconscious choices we make from one moment to the next. When a young male college student at a party, for example, observes another man taking sexual advantage of a young woman who is clearly so drunk that she has little idea of what is happening, there are many things he could do. The options vary, however, in how much social resistance they are likely to provoke. They range from asking to join in or standing by to watch as if it were some kind of entertainment to walking away and pretending he doesn't know what is happening or stepping in to intervene before it goes any further. And, of course, as a human being he could do plenty of other things—sing, dance, go to sleep, scratch his nose, and so on. Most of these possibilities won't even occur to him, which is one of the ways that social systems limit our options. But of those that do occur to him, usually one will risk provoking less social resistance than all the rest. The path of least resistance in such a situation is to go along and not make any trouble, to not get in the way of

SOCIAL SYSTEMS

We make social systems happen.

INDIVIDUALS

As we participate in systems, our lives are shaped by *socialization* and *paths of least resistance.*

Figure 2 Individuals and systems

another man making use of a woman, to not risk being accused of siding with a woman against a man and thereby appearing to be less of a man himself, and unless he is willing to deal with the greater resistance that would follow, that is the choice he is most likely to make.

[. . .]

This brings us to the arrow on the left side of the figure, which represents the fact that human beings are the ones who make social systems happen. A classroom, for example, does not happen as a social system unless and until students and teachers come together and, through their choices from moment to moment, *make* it happen in one way or another. Because people make systems happen, then people can also make systems happen differently. And when systems happen differently, the consequences are different as well. In other words, when people step off paths of least resistance, they have the potential not simply to change other people but to alter the way the system itself happens.

Given that systems shape people's behavior, this kind of change can be powerful. When a man objects to a sexist joke, for example, it can shake other men's perception of what is socially acceptable and what is not so that the next time they are in this kind of situation, their perception of the social environment itself—not just of other people as individuals, whom they may or may not know personally—may shift in a new direction that makes old paths (such as telling sexist jokes) more difficult to choose because of the increased risk of social resistance.

The dynamic relationship between people and social systems represents a basic sociological view of the world at every level of human experience, from the global capitalist economy to casual friendships to the patriarchal system in which women and men participate. Thus, patriarchy is more than a collection of women and men and cannot be understood by understanding *them*. *We* are not patriarchy, no more than people who believe in Allah *are* Islam or Canadians *are* Canada. Patriarchy is a kind of society

organized around certain kinds of social relationships and ideas that shape paths of least resistance. As individuals, we participate in it as we live our lives. Paradoxically, our participation both shapes our lives and gives us the opportunity to be part of changing or perpetuating it. But *we are not it*, which means patriarchy can exist without men having oppressive personalities or actively conspiring with one another to defend male privilege.

THE SYSTEM

In general, a system is any collection of interrelated parts or elements that we can think of as a whole. A car engine, for example, is a collection of parts that fit together in certain ways to produce a whole that is culturally identified as serving a particular purpose. A language is a collection of parts—letters of the alphabet, words, punctuation marks, and rules of grammar and syntax—that fit together in certain ways to form something we identify as a whole. In the same way, a family or a society qualify as systems that differ in what they include and how those elements are organized.

[. . .]

In spite of all the good reasons not to use individual models to explain social life, doing so constitutes a path of least resistance because personal experience and motivation are what we know best. As a result, we tend to see something like patriarchy as the result of poor socialization through which men learn to act dominant and masculine and women learn to act subordinate and feminine. While there is certainly some truth to this, it fails to explain patterns of privilege and oppression. It is no better than trying to explain war as simply the result of training men to be warlike, without looking at economic systems that equip armies at huge profits and political systems that organize and hurl armies at each other. . . . Socialization is merely a process, a mechanism for training people to participate in social systems. Although it tells us how people learn to participate, it does not illuminate the systems themselves. Accordingly, it can tell us something about the *how* of a system like patriarchy but very little of the *what* and the *why*.

[. . .]

Patriarchy is a way of organizing social life through which such wounding, failure, and mistreatment are bound to occur. If fathers neglect their sons, it is because fathers move in a world that makes pursuit of goals other than deeply committed fatherhood a path of least resistance.[2] If heterosexual intimacy is prone to fail, it is because patriarchy is organized in ways that set women and men fundamentally at odds with one another in spite of all the good reasons they otherwise have to get along together and thrive. And men's use of coercion and violence against women is a pervasive pattern only because force and violence are supported in patriarchal society, because women are designated as desirable and legitimate objects of male control, and because in a society organized around control, force and violence *work.*

We cannot find a way out of patriarchy or imagine something different without a clear sense of what patriarchy is and what it's got to do with us. Thus far, the alternative has been to reduce our understanding of gender to an intellectual gumbo of personal problems, tendencies, and motivations. Presumably, these will be solved through education, better communication skills, consciousness raising, heroic journeys and other forms of individual transformation, and the mere passage of time. Since this is not how social systems actually change, the result is widespread frustration and cycles of blame and denial, which is precisely where most people in this society seem to have been for many years.

We need to see more clearly what patriarchy is about as a system. This includes cultural ideas about men and women, the web of relationships that structure social life, and the unequal distribution of power, rewards, and resources that underlies privilege and oppression. We need to see new ways to participate by forging alternative paths of least resistance, for the system does not simply run us like hapless puppets. It may be larger than us, it may not be us, but it does not happen except *through* us.

And that is where we have the power to do something about it and about ourselves in relation to it.

PATRIARCHY

The key to understanding any system is to identify its various aspects and how they are arranged to form a whole. To understand a language, for example, we have to learn its alphabet, vocabulary, and rules for combining words into meaningful phrases and sentences. A system like patriarchy is more complicated because there are many different aspects, and it can be difficult to see how they are connected.

Patriarchy's defining elements are its male-dominated, male-identified, male-centered, and control-obsessed character, but this is just the beginning. At its core, patriarchy is based on a set of symbols and ideas that make up a culture embodied by everything from the content of everyday conversation to the practice of war. Patriarchal culture includes ideas about the nature of things, including women, men, and humanity, with manhood and masculinity most closely associated with being human and womanhood and femininity relegated to the marginal position of other. It is about how social life is and what it is supposed to be, about what is expected of people and about how they feel. It is about standards of feminine beauty and masculine toughness, images of feminine vulnerability and masculine protectiveness, of older men coupled with younger women, of elderly women alone. It is about defining women and men as opposites, about the "naturalness" of male aggression, competition, and dominance on the one hand and of female caring, cooperation, and subordination on the other. It is about the valuing of masculinity and manhood and the devaluing of femininity and womanhood. It is about the primary importance of a husband's career and the secondary status of a wife's, about child care as a priority in women's lives and its secondary importance in men's. It is about the social acceptability of anger, rage, and toughness in men but not in women, and of caring, tenderness, and vulnerability in women but not in men.

Above all, patriarchal culture is about the core value of control and domination in almost every area of human existence. From the expression of emotion to economics to the natural environment, gaining and exercising control is a continuing goal. Because of this, the concept of power takes on a narrow definition in terms of "power over"—the ability to control others, events, resources, or oneself in spite of resistance—rather than alternatives such as the ability to cooperate, to give freely of oneself, or to feel and act in harmony with nature.[3] To have power over and to be prepared to use it are culturally defined as good and desirable (and characteristically masculine), and to lack such power or to be reluctant to use it is seen as weak if not contemptible (and characteristically feminine).

[. . .]

The main use of any culture is to provide symbols and ideas out of which to construct a sense of what is real. Thus, language mirrors social reality in sometimes startling ways. In contemporary usage, for example, the words "crone," "bitch," and "virgin" describe women as threatening or heterosexually inexperienced and thus incomplete. In their original meanings, however, these words evoked far different images.[4] The crone was the old woman whose life experience gave her insight, wisdom, respect, and the power to enrich people's lives. The bitch was Artemis-Diana, goddess of the hunt, most often associated with the dogs who accompanied her. And the virgin was merely a woman who was unattached, unclaimed, and unowned by any man and therefore independent and autonomous. Notice how each word has been transformed from a positive cultural image of female power, independence, and dignity to an insult or a shadow of its former self, leaving few words to identify women in ways both positive and powerful.

Going deeper into patriarchal culture, we find a complex web of ideas that define reality and what is considered good and desirable. To see the world through patriarchal eyes is to believe that women and men are profoundly different in their basic natures, that hierarchy is the only alternative to chaos,

and that men were made in the image of a masculine God with whom they enjoy a special relationship. It is to take as obvious the ideas that there are two and only two distinct sexes and genders; that patriarchal heterosexuality is natural and same-sex attraction is not; that because men neither bear nor breastfeed children, they cannot feel a compelling bodily connection to them; that on some level every woman, whether heterosexual, lesbian, or bisexual, wants a "real man" who knows how to take charge of things, including her; and that females cannot be trusted, especially when they're menstruating or accusing men of abuse.

In spite of all the media hype to the contrary, to embrace patriarchy still is to believe that mothers should stay home and that fathers should work outside the home, regardless of men's and women's actual abilities or needs.[5] It is to buy into the notion that women are weak and men are strong and that women and children need men to support and protect them, despite the fact that in many ways men are not the physically stronger sex, that women perform a huge share of hard physical labor in many societies (often larger than men's), that women's physical endurance tends to be greater than men's over the long haul, and that women tend to be more capable of enduring pain and emotional stress.[6]

[. . .]

To live in a patriarchal culture is to learn what is expected of men and women—to learn the rules that regulate punishment and reward based on how individuals behave and appear. These rules range from laws that require men to fight in wars not of their own choosing to the expectation that mothers will provide child care. Or that when a woman shows sexual interest in a man or merely smiles or acts friendly, she gives up her right to say no and to control her own body from that point on. And to live under patriarchy is to take into ourselves ways of feeling—the hostile contempt for women that forms the core of misogyny and presumptions of male superiority, the ridicule that men direct at other men who show signs of vulnerability or weakness, or the fear and insecurity that every woman must deal with when she exercises the right to move freely in the world, especially at night and by herself in public places.

[. . .]

The prominent place of misogyny in patriarchal culture, for example, doesn't mean that every man and woman consciously hates all things that are culturally associated with being female. But it does mean that to the extent that we do not feel such hatred, it is *in spite of* prevailing paths of least resistance. Complete freedom from such feelings and judgments is all but impossible. It is certainly possible for heterosexual men to love women without mentally fragmenting them into breasts, buttocks, genitals, and other variously desirable parts. It is possible for women to feel good about their bodies, to not judge themselves as being too big, to not abuse themselves to one degree or another in pursuit of impossible male-identified standards of beauty and sexual attractiveness.

All of this is possible, but to live in patriarchy is to breathe in misogynist images of women as objectified sexual property valued primarily for their usefulness to men. This finds its way into everyone who grows up breathing and swimming in it, and once inside us it remains, however unaware of it we may be. When we hear or express sexist jokes and other forms of misogyny, we may not recognize it, and even if we do, we may say nothing rather than risk other people thinking we're too sensitive or, especially in the case of men, not one of the guys. In either case, we are involved, if only by our silence.

The symbols and ideas that make up patriarchal culture are important to understand because they have such powerful effects on the structure of social life. By "structure," I mean the ways privilege and oppression are organized through social relationships and unequal distributions of power, rewards, opportunities, and resources. This appears in countless patterns of everyday life in family and work, religion and politics, community and education. It is found in family divisions of labor that exempt fathers from most domestic work even when both parents

work outside the home, and in the concentration of women in lower-level pink-collar jobs and male predominance almost everywhere else. It is in the unequal distribution of income and all that goes with it, from access to health care to the availability of leisure time. It is in patterns of male violence and harassment that can turn a simple walk in the park or a typical day at work or a lovers' quarrel into a life-threatening nightmare. More than anything, the structure of patriarchy is found in the unequal distribution of power that makes male privilege possible, in patterns of male dominance in every facet of human life, from everyday conversation to global politics. By its nature, patriarchy puts issues of power, dominance, and control at the center of human existence, not only in relationships between men and women but among men as they compete and struggle to gain status, maintain control, and protect themselves from what other men might do to them.

[. . .]

THE SYSTEM IN US IN THE SYSTEM

One way to see how people connect with systems is to think of us as occupying social positions that locate us in relation to people in other positions. We connect, for example, to families through positions such as mother, daughter, and cousin; to economic systems through positions such as vice president, secretary, or unemployed; to political systems through positions such as citizen, registered voter, and mayor; and to religious systems through positions such as believer and clergy.

How we perceive the people who occupy such positions and what we expect of them depend on cultural ideas—such as the belief that mothers are naturally better than fathers at child care. Such ideas are powerful because we use them to construct a sense of who we and other people are. When a woman marries a man, for example, how people (including her) perceive and think about her will change as cultural ideas about what it means to be a wife come into play—ideas about how wives feel about their husbands, what is most important to wives, what is expected of them, and what they may expect of others.

From this perspective, *who* we and other people think we are has a lot to do with *where* we are in relation to social systems and all the positions we occupy in them. We would not exist as social beings without our participation in one social system or another. It is hard to imagine just who we would be and what our existence would consist of if we took away all of our connections to the symbols, ideas, and relationships that make up social systems. Take away language and all that it allows us to imagine and think, starting with our names. Take away all the positions that we occupy and the roles that go with them–from daughter and son to occupation and nationality— and with these all the complex ways our lives are connected to other people. Not much would be left over that we would recognize as ourselves.[7]

We can think of a society as a network of interconnected systems within systems, each made up of social positions and their relations to one another. To say, then, that I am white, male, college educated, non-disabled, and a nonfiction author, novelist, sociologist, U.S. citizen, heterosexual, husband, father, grandfather, brother, and son identifies me in relation to positions which are themselves related to positions in various systems, from the entire world to the family of my birth.

In another sense, the day-to-day reality of a society exists only through what people actually do as they participate in it. Patriarchal culture, for example, places a high value on control and manhood. By themselves, these are just abstractions. But when men and women actually talk and men interrupt women more than women interrupt men, or men ignore topics introduced by women in favor of their own or in other ways control conversation,[8] or when men use their authority to harass women in the workplace, then the reality of patriarchy as a kind of society and people's sense of themselves as gendered beings within it actually happen in a concrete way.

In this sense, like all social systems, patriarchy exists only through people's lives. Through this dynamic relationship, patriarchy's various aspects are there for us to see over and over again. This has two

important implications for how we understand the system. First, to some extent people will experience patriarchy as external to them. This does not mean the system is a distinct and separate thing, like a house in which we live. Instead, by participating in patriarchy we are *of* patriarchy and it is *of* us. Both exist *through* the other, and neither exists without the other.

Second, patriarchy is not static. It is an ongoing *process* that is continually shaped and reshaped. Since the thing we are participating in is patriarchal, we tend to behave in ways that create a patriarchal world from one moment to the next. But we have some freedom to break the rules and construct everyday life in different ways, which means the paths we choose to follow can do as much to change patriarchy as they can to perpetuate it.

We are involved in patriarchy and its consequences because we occupy social positions in it, which is all it takes. Because patriarchy is, by definition, a system of inequality organized around culturally created gender categories, we cannot avoid being involved in it. *All* men and *all* women are therefore involved in this oppressive system, and none of us can control *whether* we participate, only *how*. As Harry Brod argues, this is especially important in relation to men and male privilege:

> We need to be clear that there is no such thing as giving up one's privilege to be "outside" the system. One is always *in* the system. The only question is whether one is part of the system in a way which challenges or strengthens the status quo. Privilege is not something I *take* and which I therefore have the option of *not* taking. It is something that society *gives* me, and unless I change the institutions which give it to me, they will continue to give it, and I will continue to *have* it, however noble and egalitarian my intentions.[9]

Because privilege is conferred by social systems, people do not have to *feel* privileged to *be* privileged. When I do presentations, for example, I usually come away feeling good about how it went and, therefore, about myself and my work. If anyone were to ask me to explain why things went so well, I would probably mention my ability, my years of ex-perience in public speaking, the quality of my ideas, and the interest and contributions of the audience. The last thing that would occur to me, however, would be that my success was aided by my gender, that if I had performed in exactly the same way but was perceived to be a woman, research shows quite clearly that I would have been taken less seriously, evaluated less positively along many dimensions, and have less of my success attributed to my own efforts and ability.

The difference between the two outcomes is a measure of male privilege, and there is little I can do to get rid of it, because its authority rests not in me but in society itself, especially in cultural images of gender. The audience does not know it is conferring male privilege on me, and I may not be aware that I'm receiving it. But the privilege is there nonetheless. That all of this may feel natural and non-privileged only deepens the system's hold on all who participate in it.

[. . .]

NOTES

1. Sam Keen, *Fire in the Belly: On Being a Man* (New York: Bantam Books, 1991), 207.

2. For a history of American fatherhood, see Robert L. Griswold, *Fatherhood in America: A History* (New York: Basic Books, 1993).

3. For a thorough discussion of this distinction, see Marilyn French, *Beyond Power: On Men, Women, and Morals* (New York: Summit Books, 1985).

4. For discussions of language and gender, see Jane Caputi, *Gossips, Gorgons, and Crones* (Santa Fe, NM: Bear, 1993); Mary Daly, *Gyn/Ecology: The Metaethics of Radical Feminism* (Boston: Beacon Press, 1978); Margaret Gibbon, *Feminist Perspectives on Language* (New York: Longman, 1999); Dale Spender, *Man Made Language* (London: Pandora, 1980); Robin Lakoff, *Language and Woman's Place*, rev. ed. (New York: Harper and Row, 2004); Barbara G. Walker, *The Women's Encyclopedia of Myths and Secrets* (San Francisco: Harper and Row, 1983); and Barbara G. Walker, *The Woman's Dictionary of Symbols and Sacred Objects* (San Francisco: Harper and Row, 1988). For a very different slant on gender and language, see Mary Daly (in cahoots with Jane Caputi), *Webster's First New Intergalactic Wickedary of the English Language* (Boston: Beacon Press, 1987).

5. See Arlie Hochschild, *The Second Shift: Working Parents and the Revolution at Home*, rev. ed. (New York: Viking/Penguin, 2012).

6. See, for example, Rosalyn Baxandall, Linda Gordon, and Susan Reverby, eds., *America's Working Women: A Documentary History—1600 to the Present*, rev. ed. (New York: Norton, 1995); Ashley Montagu, *The Natural Superiority of Women* (New York: Collier, 1974); Robin Morgan, ed., *Sisterhood Is Global* (New York: Feminist Press, 1996); and Marilyn Waring, *If Women Counted: A New Feminist Economics* (San Francisco: HarperCollins, 1990).

7. Some would no doubt argue, with good reason, that our social selves mask more essential selves, but that's another argument for another place.

8. There is a substantial research literature documenting such genderized patterns of conversation. See, for example, Laurie P. Arliss, *Women and Men Communicating: Challenges and Changes*, 2nd ed. (Prospect Heights, IL: Waveland Press, 2000); N. Henley, M. Hamilton, and B. Thorne, "Womanspeak and Manspeak: Sex Differences and Sexism in Communication," in *Beyond Sex Roles*, edited by A. G. Sargent (New York; West, 1985), 168–85; P. Kollock, P. Blumstein, and P. Schwartz, "Sex and Power in Interaction, *American Sociological Review* 50, no. 1 (1985): 34–46; L. Smith-Lovin and C. Brody, "Interruptions in Group Discussions: The Effect of Gender and Group Composition," *American Sociological Review* 51, no. 3 (1989): 424–35; and Mary M. Talbot, *Language and Gender. An Introduction*, 2nd ed. (Cambridge, UK: Polity Press, 2010).

9. Harry Brod, "Work Clothes and Leisure Suits: The Class Basis and Bias of the Men's Movement," in *Men's Lives*, edited by Michael S. Kimmel and Michael A. Messner (New York: Macmillan, 1989), 280.

3. • *Anne Fausto-Sterling*

THE FIVE SEXES, REVISITED (2000)

Anne Fausto-Sterling is the Nancy Duke Lewis Professor Emerita of Biology and Gender Studies at Brown University, the founder and director of the Science & Technology Studies Program at Brown, and fellow of the American Association for the Advancement of Science. Author of three books and more than sixty scholarly articles, her work strives to dismantle conversations that depend on either/or ways of seeing the world (e.g., nature/nurture and male/female) to develop theories that demonstrate interconnectedness. In "The Five Sexes, Revisited," While the language in the piece reflects its publication date, Fausto-Sterling's groundbreaking work continues to challenge readers to interrogate how dualities found in cultural and gender differences become bodily differences despite scientific evidence that there are more than two sexes.

As Cheryl Chase stepped to the front of the packed meeting room in the Sheraton Boston Hotel, nervous coughs made the tension audible. Chase, an activist for intersexual rights, had been invited to address the May 2000 meeting of the Lawson Wilkins Pediatric Endocrine Society (LWPES), the largest organization in the United States for specialists in children's hormones. Her talk would be the grand finale to a four-hour symposium on the treatment of genital ambiguity in newborns, infants born with a mixture of both male and female anatomy, or genitals that appear to differ from their chromosomal sex. The topic was hardly a novel one to the assembled physicians.

Yet Chase's appearance before the group was remarkable. Three and a half years earlier, the American Academy of Pediatrics had refused her request for a chance to present the patients' viewpoint on the treatment of genital ambiguity, dismissing Chase and her supporters as "zealots." About two dozen intersex people had responded by throwing up a picket line. The Intersex Society of North America (ISNA) even issued a press release: "Hermaphrodites Target Kiddie Docs."

It had done my 1960s street-activist heart good. In the short run, I said to Chase at the time, the picketing would make people angry. But eventually, I assured her, the doors then closed would open. Now, as Chase began to address the physicians at their own convention, that prediction was coming true. Her talk, titled "Sexual Ambiguity: The Patient-Centered Approach," was a measured critique of the near-universal practice of performing immediate, "corrective" surgery on thousands of infants born each year with ambiguous genitalia. Chase herself lives with the consequences of such surgery. Yet her audience, the very endocrinologists and surgeons Chase was accusing of reacting with "surgery and shame," received her with respect. Even more remarkably, many of the speakers who preceded her at the session had already spoken of the need to scrap current practices in favor of treatments more centered on psychological counseling.

What led to such a dramatic reversal of fortune? Certainly, Chase's talk at the LWPES symposium was a vindication of her persistence in seeking attention for her cause. But her invitation to speak was also a watershed in the evolving discussion about how to treat children with ambiguous genitalia. And that discussion, in turn, is the tip of a biocultural iceberg—the gender iceberg—that continues to rock both medicine and our culture at large.

Chase made her first national appearance in 1993, in these very pages, announcing the formation of ISNA in a letter responding to an essay I had written for *The Sciences*, titled "The Five Sexes" [March/April 1993]. In that article I argued that the two-sex system embedded in our society is not adequate to encompass the full spectrum of human sexuality. In its place, I suggested a five-sex system. In addition to males and females, I included "herms" (named after true hermaphrodites, people born with both a testis and an ovary); "merms" (male pseudo-hermaphrodites, who are born with testes and some aspect of female genitalia); and "ferms" (female pseudohermaphrodites, who have ovaries combined with some aspect of male genitalia).

I had intended to be provocative, but I had also written with tongue firmly in cheek. So I was surprised by the extent of the controversy the article unleashed. Right-wing Christians were outraged, and connected my idea of five sexes with the United Nations–sponsored Fourth World Conference on Women, held in Beijing in September 1995. At the same time, the article delighted others who felt constrained by the current sex and gender system.

Clearly, I had struck a nerve. The fact that so many people could get riled up by my proposal to revamp our sex and gender system suggested that change—as well as resistance to it—might be in the offing. Indeed, a lot has changed since 1993, and I like to think that my article was an important stimulus. As if from nowhere, intersexuals are materializing before our very eyes. Like Chase, many have become political organizers, who lobby physicians

and politicians to change current treatment practices. But more generally, though perhaps no less provocatively, the boundaries separating masculine and feminine seem harder than ever to define.

Some find the changes under way deeply disturbing. Others find them liberating.

Who is an intersexual—and how many intersexuals are there? The concept of intersexuality is rooted in the very ideas of male and female. In the idealized, Platonic, biological world, human beings are divided into two kinds: a perfectly dimorphic species. Males have an X and a Y chromosome, testes, a penis and all of the appropriate internal plumbing for delivering urine and semen to the outside world. They also have well-known secondary sexual characteristics, including a muscular build and facial hair. Women have two X chromosomes, ovaries, all of the internal plumbing to transport urine and ova to the outside world, a system to support pregnancy and fetal development, as well as a variety of recognizable secondary sexual characteristics.

That idealized story papers over many obvious caveats: some women have facial hair, some men have none; some women speak with deep voices, some men veritably squeak. Less well known is the fact that, on close inspection, absolute dimorphism disintegrates even at the level of basic biology. Chromosomes, hormones, the internal sex structures, the gonads and the external genitalia all vary more than most people realize. Those born outside of the Platonic dimorphic mold are called intersexuals.

In "The Five Sexes" I reported an estimate by a psychologist expert in the treatment of intersexuals, suggesting that some 4 percent of all live births are intersexual. Then, together with a group of Brown University undergraduates, I set out to conduct the first systematic assessment of the available data on intersexual birthrates. We scoured the medical literature for estimates of the frequency of various categories of intersexuality, from additional chromosomes to mixed gonads, hormones and genitalia. For some conditions we could find only anecdotal evidence; for most, however, numbers exist. On the basis of that evidence, we calculated that for every 1,000 children born, seventeen are intersexual in some form. That number—1.7 percent—is a ball-park estimate, not a precise count, though we believe it is more accurate than the 4 percent I reported.

Our figure represents all chromosomal, anatomical and hormonal exceptions to the dimorphic ideal; the number of intersexuals who might, potentially, be subject to surgery as infants is smaller—probably between one in 1,000 and one in 2,000 live births. Furthermore, because some populations possess the relevant genes at high frequency, the intersexual birthrate is not uniform throughout the world.

Consider, for instance, the gene for congenital adrenal hyperplasia (CAH). When the CAH gene is inherited from both parents, it leads to a baby with masculinized external genitalia who possesses two X chromosomes and the internal reproductive organs of a potentially fertile woman. The frequency of the gene varies widely around the world: in New Zealand it occurs in only forty-three children per million; among the Yupik Eskimo of southwestern Alaska, its frequency is 3,500 per million.

Intersexuality has always been to some extent a matter of definition. And in the past century physicians have been the ones who defined children as intersexual—and provided the remedies. When only the chromosomes are unusual, but the external genitalia and gonads clearly indicate either a male or a female, physicians do not advocate intervention. Indeed, it is not clear what kind of intervention could be advocated in such cases. But the story is quite different when infants are born with mixed genitalia, or with external genitals that seem at odds with the baby's gonads.

Most clinics now specializing in the treatment of intersex babies rely on case-management principles developed in the 1950s by the psychologist John Money and the psychiatrists Joan G. Hampson and John L. Hampson, all of Johns Hopkins University in Baltimore, Maryland. Money believed that gender identity is completely malleable for about eighteen months after birth. Thus, he argued, when a treatment team is presented with an infant who has ambiguous genitalia, the team could make a gender assignment solely on the basis of what made the best surgical sense. The physicians could then simply encourage the parents to raise the child according to the surgically assigned gender. Following that course, most physicians maintained, would eliminate psychological distress for both the patient and the parents. Indeed, treatment teams were never to use such words as "intersex" or "hermaphrodite"; instead, they were to tell parents that nature intended the baby to be the boy or the girl that the physicians had determined it was. Through surgery, the physicians were merely completing nature's intention.

Although Money and the Hampsons published detailed case studies of intersex children who they said had adjusted well to their gender assignments, Money thought one case in particular proved his theory. It was a dramatic example, inasmuch as it did not involve intersexuality at all: one of a pair of identical twin boys lost his penis as a result of a circumcision accident. Money recommended that "John" (as he came to be known in a later case study) be surgically turned into "Joan" and raised as a girl. In time, Joan grew to love wearing dresses and having her hair done. Money proudly proclaimed the sex reassignment a success.

But as recently chronicled by John Colapinto, in his book *As Nature Made Him*, Joan—now known to be an adult male named David Reimer—eventually rejected his female assignment. Even without a functioning penis and testes (which had been removed as part of the reassignment) John/Joan sought masculinizing medication, and married a woman with children (whom he adopted).

Since the full conclusion to the John/Joan story came to light, other individuals who were reassigned as males or females shortly after birth but who later rejected their early assignments have come forward. So, too, have cases in which the reassignment has worked—at least into the subject's mid-twenties. But even then the aftermath of the surgery can be problematic. Genital surgery often leaves scars that reduce sexual sensitivity. Chase herself had a complete clitoridectomy, a procedure that is less frequently performed on intersexuals today. But the newer surgeries, which reduce the size of the clitoral shaft, still greatly reduce sensitivity.

The revelation of cases of failed reassignments and the emergence of intersex activism have led an increasing number of pediatric endocrinologists, urologists and psychologists to reexamine the wisdom of early genital surgery. For example, in a talk that preceded Chase's at the LWPES meeting, the medical ethicist Laurence B. McCullough of the Center for Medical Ethics and Health Policy at Baylor College of Medicine in Houston, Texas, introduced an ethical framework for the treatment of children with ambiguous genitalia. Because sex phenotype (the manifestation of genetically and embryologically determined sexual characteristics) and gender presentation (the sex role projected by the individual in society) are highly variable, McCullough argues, the various forms of intersexuality should be defined as normal. All of them fall within the statistically expected variability of sex and gender. Furthermore, though certain disease states may accompany some forms of intersexuality, and may require medical intervention, intersexual conditions are not themselves diseases.

McCullough also contends that in the process of assigning gender, physicians should minimize what he calls irreversible assignments: taking steps such as the surgical removal or modification of gonads or genitalia that the patient may one day want to have reversed. Finally, McCullough urges physicians to abandon their practice of treating the birth of a child with genital ambiguity as a medical or social emergency. Instead, they should take the time to perform a thorough medical workup and should disclose everything to the parents, including the uncertainties about the final outcome. The treatment mantra, in other words, should be therapy, not surgery.

I believe a new treatment protocol for intersex infants, similar to the one outlined by McCullough, is close at hand. Treatment should combine some basic medical and ethical principles with a practical but less drastic approach to the birth of a mixed-sex child. As a first step, surgery on infants should be performed only to save the child's life or to substantially improve the child's physical well-being. Physicians may assign a sex—male or female—to an intersex infant on the basis of the probability that the child's particular condition will lead to the formation of a particular gender identity. At the same time, though, practitioners ought to be humble enough to recognize that as the child grows, he or she may reject the assignment—and they should be wise enough to listen to what the child has to say. Most important, parents should have access to the full range of information and options available to them.

Sex assignments made shortly after birth are only the beginning of a long journey. Consider, for instance, the life of Max Beck: Born intersexual, Max was surgically assigned as a female and consistently raised as such. Had her medical team followed her into her early twenties, they would have deemed her assignment a success because she was married to a man. (It should be noted that success in gender assignment has traditionally been defined as living in that gender as a heterosexual.) Within a few years, however, Beck had come out as a butch lesbian; now in her mid-thirties, Beck has become a man and married his lesbian partner, who (through the miracles of modern reproductive technology) recently gave birth to a girl.

Transsexuals, people who have an emotional gender at odds with their physical sex, once described themselves in terms of dimorphic absolutes—males trapped in female bodies, or vice versa. As such, they sought psychological relief through surgery. Although many still do, some so-called transgendered people today are content to inhabit a more ambiguous zone. A male-to-female transsexual, for instance, may come out as a lesbian. Jane, born a physiological male, is now in her late thirties and living with her wife, whom she married when her name was still John. Jane takes hormones to feminize herself, but they have not yet interfered with her ability to engage in intercourse as a man. In her mind Jane has a lesbian relationship with her wife, though she views their intimate moments as a cross between lesbian and heterosexual sex.

It might seem natural to regard intersexuals and transgendered people as living midway between the poles of male and female. But male and female, masculine and feminine, cannot be parsed as some kind of continuum. Rather, sex and gender are best conceptualized as points in a multidimensional space. For some time, experts on gender development have distinguished between sex at the genetic level and at the cellular level (sex-specific gene expression, X and Y chromosomes); at the hormonal level (in the fetus, during childhood and after puberty); and at the anatomical level (genitals and secondary sexual characteristics). Gender identity presumably emerges from all of those corporeal aspects via some poorly understood interaction with environment and experience. What has become increasingly clear is that one can find levels of masculinity and femininity in almost every possible permutation. A chromosomal, hormonal and genital male (or female) may emerge with a female (or male) gender identity. Or a chromosomal female with male fetal hormones and masculinized genitalia—but with female pubertal hormones—may develop a female gender identity.

The medical and scientific communities have yet to adopt a language that is capable of describing such diversity. In her book *Hermaphrodites and the Medical Invention of Sex*, the historian and medical ethicist Alice Domurat Dreger of Michigan State University in East Lansing documents the emergence of current medical systems for classifying gender ambiguity. The current usage remains rooted in the Victorian approach to sex. The logical structure of the commonly used terms "true hermaphrodite," "male pseudohermaphrodite" and "female pseudohermaphrodite" indicates that only the so-called true hermaphrodite is a genuine mix of male and female. The others, no matter how confusing their body parts, are really hidden males or females. Because true hermaphrodites are rare—possibly only one in 100,000—such a classification system supports the idea that human beings are an absolutely dimorphic species.

At the dawn of the twenty-first century, when the variability of gender seems so visible, such a position is hard to maintain. And here, too, the old medical consensus has begun to crumble. Last fall the pediatric urologist Ian A. Aaronson of the Medical University of South Carolina in Charleston organized the North American Task Force on Intersexuality (NATFI) to review the clinical responses to genital ambiguity in infants. Key medical associations, such as the American Academy of Pediatrics, have endorsed NATFI. Specialists in surgery, endocrinology, psychology, ethics, psychiatry, genetics and public health, as well as intersex patient-advocate groups, have joined its ranks.

One of the goals of NATFI is to establish a new sex nomenclature. One proposal under consideration replaces the current system with emotionally neutral terminology that emphasizes developmental processes rather than preconceived gender categories. For example, Type I intersexes develop out of anomalous virilizing influences; Type II result from some interruption of virilization; and in Type III intersexes the gonads themselves may not have developed in the expected fashion.

What is clear is that since 1993, modern society has moved beyond five sexes to a recognition that gender variation is normal and, for some people, an arena for playful exploration. Discussing my "five sexes" proposal in her book *Lessons from the Intersexed*, the psychologist Suzanne J. Kessler of the State University of New York at Purchase drives this point home with great effect:

> The limitation with Fausto-Sterling's proposal is that . . . [it] still gives genitals . . . primary signifying status and ignores the fact that in the everyday world gender attributions are made without access to genital inspection. . . . What has primacy in everyday life is the gender that is performed, regardless of the flesh's configuration under the clothes.

I now agree with Kessler's assessment. It would be better for intersexuals and their supporters to turn everyone's focus away from genitals. Instead, as she suggests, one should acknowledge that people come in an even wider assortment of sexual identities and characteristics than mere genitals can distinguish. Some women may have "large clitorises or fused labia," whereas some men may have "small penises or misshapen scrota," as Kessler puts it, "phenotypes with no particular clinical or identity meaning."

As clearheaded as Kessler's program is—and despite the progress made in the 1990s—our society is still far from that ideal. The intersexual or transgendered person who projects a social gender—what Kessler calls "cultural genitals"—that conflicts with his or her physical genitals still may die for the transgression. Hence legal protection for people whose cultural and physical genitals do not match is needed during the current transition to a more gender-diverse world. One easy step would be to eliminate the category of "gender" from official documents, such as driver's licenses and passports. Surely attributes both more visible (such as height, build and eye color) and less visible (fingerprints and genetic profiles) would be more expedient.

A more far-ranging agenda is presented in the International Bill of Gender Rights, adopted in 1995 at the fourth annual International Conference on Transgender Law and Employment Policy in Houston, Texas. It lists ten "gender rights," including the right to define one's own gender, the right to change one's physical gender if one so chooses

and the right to marry whomever one wishes. The legal bases for such rights are being hammered out in the courts as I write and, most recently, through the establishment, in the state of Vermont, of legal same-sex domestic partnerships.

No one could have foreseen such changes in 1993. And the idea that I played some role, however small, in reducing the pressure—from the medical community as well as from society at large—to flatten the diversity of human sexes into two diametrically opposed camps gives me pleasure.

Sometimes people suggest to me, with not a little horror, that I am arguing for a pastel world in which androgyny reigns and men and women are boringly the same. In my vision, however, strong colors coexist with pastels. There are and will continue to be highly masculine people out there; it's just that some of them are women. And some of the most feminine people I know happen to be men.

4. • *Ijeoma A.*

BECAUSE YOU'RE A GIRL (2002)

Ijeoma A. was born and raised in West Africa. Her first trip to the United States was to attend college in Ohio. Her essay included here grew out a column she contributed to a popular student publication in which she shared what it was like growing up in West Africa as well as her experiences as a migrant negotiating US culture.

It was a Sunday night in Lagos during the African Cup series. In these parts, we lived by soccer. Often, you'd hear the tale of the lover who threatened his sweetheart because she walked past the television, obstructing his vision for a precious second while the Nigerian Eagles were playing. Indeed, soccer was serious business.

This year, Nigeria had made it to the finals, and tonight's game was going to be watched by everybody who was anybody that knew somebody. I couldn't miss this game for the world. We had an earlier-than-recommended dinner, and before long, all of us—two brothers, five cousins and myself—littered ourselves around the miniature TV screen

A., Ijeoma. "Because You're a Girl." *Colonize This!: Young Women of Color on Today's Feminism*. Ed. D. Hernández and Bushra Rehman. Emeryville, CA: Seal Press, 2002, Page 215–228 to witness this lifetime event. It was then that the unmistakable voice of my mother burst through the bustle, with a distinctly familiar hint of irritation: "Ijeoma, when exactly did you intend to clean up?"

"Only me?" I responded. "Could one of the boys help this time? I don't want to miss the game. Please!"

"Ije! You're a girl and we're raising you to become a woman some day. Now, stop being stubborn and go clean that kitchen up!"

My heart ached. Ten people were a lot to clean up after, especially on a finals night. As I dug through a bottomless sink of dirty dishes, the boys and my parents were in the living room, screaming, yelling and cheering. I felt so small. I was alone, with filthy mountains of blackened pots and kettles surrounding me in that small, somber kitchen. Once in a while, one of the boys would stop by and ask me where he might place an empty glass he had just used so that I wouldn't forget to wash it. I would use such opportunities to ask "Who's winning?!" Then I was alone again, sulking at soccer ball-shaped saucers that constantly reminded me I would be spending the core of the Eagles' game cleaning up in the kitchen; because I was a girl.

Although I was raised in Nigeria's capital city of Lagos, most of my guardians (my parents, uncles, aunts and older cousins) were raised in the rural villages of Eastern Nigeria. As a result, my upbringing was not as diluted of traditional customs as is typical in the big and populated cities of Nigeria. My parents, uncles and aunts had Four Commandments incorporating what a woman's responsibilities were to her family:

1. Her office is the kitchen.
2. She is responsible for all the chores in the home.
3. She is accountable for the children and their actions.
4. And, of course, she must pledge complete and total allegiance to the man in charge first, before herself.

I know my guardians believed that they were looking out for my best interests by molding me in accordance with these ideas. Frankly, I can

understand why. In our society, it is considered every woman's destiny to be married one day and have children. Deviations from that fate usually ended up in an unhappy ever after of spite and loneliness. Being a woman in her late twenties with no suitors to pop the Question seemed the greatest shame a woman could endure. Thus, by raising me in accordance with these Four Commandments, my guardians hoped to ensure that I would not have to endure the mockery or the pain of being an old unmarried woman. However, despite their good intentions, I was never able to appreciate this way of life wholeheartedly.

Everything in my childhood substantiated the need for women to submit. The stability of our society depended heavily on it. Fairytales were laden with morals of submission, as well as forewarnings against the girl who talked back, or the wife who tried to be the second captain on a ship that demanded just one. Before long, like other girls I was convinced that something bad would happen to me if I rocked the boat. I decided that I would dutifully execute anything my family demanded, since I didn't want the same fate as the girls in those tales who dared to go against our customs. My family's approval was all that I lived for, and I wanted my parents to be proud of me. But, whenever I was alone, I'd often catch myself wishing that I were born a boy.

As I observed my family's dynamics, it became evident that my brothers and cousins didn't have the same "duties to the family" as I did. Every morning, I had to get up early to dust and sweep. I would get in trouble if breakfast weren't ready by the time the boys got hungry. It was also my responsibility to ensure that my younger brother bathed and dressed himself appropriately for the day. Of course, I had to do the dishes when everyone was done and then get myself ready in time for school or church, depending on what day it was.

I really wanted to be a good daughter, but at night I would dream that I could wake up a little later the next morning, and like a boy find my breakfast already waiting for me. I would take off my slippers and tease my toes with the fresh feel of a dustless floor that had already been swept and mopped . . . just like the boys did each morning. At times I would gather the courage to inquire about the discrepancies in the division of labor, but would be silenced with an abrupt: "It's a woman's job to do those things." Whenever I persisted, I became the subject of corrosive criticism that was sometimes accompanied by some form of punishment. Thus, I learned to conform and embrace the life that had been carved out for me.

On the surface I was the good girl that my family wanted me to be. I grew content with my predicament as I got older and even impressed my parents with my devotion to serve. Deep down, however, I despised my submission. I hated taking orders and cleaning after people. I usually had to consciously press my lips firmly together, so I wouldn't say "inappropriate" things whenever I was assigned a chore, or if one of the boys complained about his meal. One night, I was doing the dishes while the rest of the family enjoyed a sitcom in the living room. A cousin then came into the kitchen, slightly irritated that there were no clean glasses available for him to take a drink. He then instructed me to hurry up with the dishes when I suddenly snapped at him, "Well maybe if you learned to wash your own dirty dishes I wouldn't ever have to listen to you whine like that over a glass!" Neither of us could believe what I had just said. As expected, I was reported, and then punished for my impudence.

On another occasion, I had just baked some chicken to accompany the Sunday lunch my mother had prepared. According to our customs, the heart was a part of the chicken that could only be eaten by the oldest man at the table. As I placed the poultry pieces neatly in a serving dish, something made me swiftly snatch the heart from the dish and toss it into my mouth. It tasted really, really good, but suddenly I became afraid. How would I account for the missing heart? What was going to happen to me? I promptly decided that I would blame the merchant who sold us the chicken. At the table, I swore that he must have taken the heart out before selling the bird to us, because I didn't recall seeing it with the rest of the chicken. Fortunately, everyone believed me.

In my day-to-day experiences school became my refuge, an oasis in the midst of all the mindless house cleaning and cooking. In the classroom I didn't feel so passive. Despite my gender, my teachers often sought my insight in resolving problems that they used to test the students. I was encouraged to develop my own ideas, since productive class discussions depended highly on the individuality and diversity of the students. Something about school made me feel "great" about myself. I would suddenly become more talkative and would volunteer my opinions in various situations without the fear of reproach. It seemed my teachers were not as focused on gender as my family, and I often wondered about that irregularity. They were more interested in a student's ability to absorb their teachings and then use them in productive ways, irrespective of gender. They made me believe that being a girl wasn't really a factor in my ability to answer a test question, and I found this new way of thinking rather refreshing. In the classroom, gender didn't rank the boys higher than the girls. Instead, it was your academic excellence that earned you your respect and the teacher's favor. If you had an interest in student leadership, or if you wanted membership in exclusive school organizations, your grades were inspected, and it was those grades that earned you your rank.

For me, this was ample incentive to excel. Although I had little power over my predicament at home, I had a magnitude of control over my school performance, and fortunately my efforts didn't go unnoticed. Before too long, I was appointed Class Captain in primary-3 (equivalent to the third grade in American schools). As a Class Captain, I was in charge of the classroom's cleanliness, but in very different capacity than at home. In the classroom, I supervised the cleaning, and I assigned the different chores to my fellow classmates. In school, I had the ability to enforce the change that I was powerless at creating in my own home. I made sure that the boys worked just as hard as the girls, and I ensured that their hands got just as dirty from sweeping and scrubbing the floors. Thereafter, I would take my shoes off and indulge my feet in that nice feeling you get from walking on a really clean floor.

As Class Captain, it was also my responsibility to enforce the School Rules on my peers. Since I was in charge, I would momentarily forget about my family's ideals of Woman's submission to Man. Whenever I spoke, my words had to be obeyed since I embodied the school authorities in the classroom. As a result of my position, I was always the first in line for school assemblies and field trips, the first to be seated at important school functions, and even the first to receive my report card at the end of each trimester. At home my place had always been after the boys. But in the classroom, I was Number One; ahead of the other girls, and of course before the boys. I valued my relationship with the other girls, however, given my background, male respect had a closer resemblance to the "forbidden fruit" and so I tended to focus more of my efforts on obtaining it. This taste of power made me feel that I could potentially transcend my fate of becoming a family Cook and Maid in my future husband's house. I suddenly felt like I could achieve more with my life: do great things, make a lasting difference.

As I became an adolescent, the demands on my time seemed to increase exponentially, especially in conjunction with my academic obligations. Since I received little help, I often found myself grumbling about all the "because-you're-a-girl" rhetoric. Whenever I lamented openly, my mother and aunts would try to comfort me: "You're a big girl now and you may marry soon. These are the things your husband and his family will expect of you, and we're only preparing you to handle them." I really hated to hear that. If my forty-eight-hour days were indicative of my life with a husband, then I didn't ever want to get married. Of course, the family hated to hear that. Still, as a minor I had to fulfill the demands of my family.

By my senior year of high school, my resources were stretched as thin as they could get. I pressured myself to do well in school because I was very addicted to the prominence my previous grades had earned me in the student government. My father also pressured me to score only the highest grades. He had gotten so accustomed to my excellent performance in earlier years that he was unwilling to

accept anything less during my senior year. Nonetheless, I was still expected to fulfill all my "duties to the family." No one seemed to understand that in order to keep stellar grades, it would be helpful to have fewer chores at home. "If you don't do them, who will?" was their response. I believe my situation was exacerbated simply because I was the "only" girl in a large family of men. Perhaps if I had a sister or two, one of them could have covered for me while I studied for exams. Maybe then, my sessions slaving in the kitchen while the boys watched the TV would not have been so lonely and harrowing.

During this year my father revealed his plans to educate me abroad. To gain admission to an American college, I had to satisfy several other academic requirements in addition to my schoolwork. No one seemed to empathize with me, and so I began to see my father's intention to send me to the United States as my ticket out of these stressful conditions and an escape from my future as a "good wife." This thought motivated me to excel academically despite the odds and to earn admission and a scholarship to attend Oberlin College in Ohio.

✱ ✱ ✱

After arriving in America, I was not quite sure how to proceed with my life. For the past seventeen years I had become accustomed to someone else telling me how and when to live. Now, I was suddenly answerable to only myself—a role I had never learned to play. I found myself waiting for someone to tell me my chores. After living in a cage all my life, I guess I found this new environment a little too big to live in. Despite the liberating utopia that America represented, it took me a long time to let go of my previous life. How could the world suddenly expect me to take initiative when it had always trained me to receive my opinions from others? Sometimes I felt the sudden urge to do something really outrageous, like sleeping in for a couple of extra hours in the morning. "Would someone come to scold me and yank me out from under my blanket?" I would wait and see. If nothing happened, I would get up and leave my bed unmade indefinitely. Then I would wait again. Would my roommate report me?

Perhaps my parents would be notified of my misbehavior and then force me to return to Nigeria. I would then become afraid and return to my room to make the bed.

I was taken aback as I learned that my roommate was messier than I was; she claimed she had always been that way. How could her parents tolerate that? Didn't they worry that she would never find a good husband? As I opened up to her, I was stunned by everything she shared about herself. She had never had to clean her brother's room. "He does that his damned self," she said, a bit surprised that I had thought that she had ever waited on him. Also, she had never cooked in her life. She probably couldn't even tell you how to boil water, yet she wasn't ashamed.

Slowly I fell in love with America. Sometimes I would hang out with the boys, just so I could say "No" to them. Whenever I felt really bold, I'd say, "Do it your damned self," just like my roommate. Once, I cooked an African meal for some of my American friends. I didn't make anything complicated, simply because I didn't want to generate too many dirty dishes. I wasn't sure I could handle the same loads as I used to in Nigeria. To my surprise, however, one of the boys offered to do the dishes when we were done eating. I paused and then said, with my accent, "Yeah, do it your damned self!" He thought that was funny and so we laughed about it.

Gradually I found myself saying and doing things I wouldn't have dared to in the past, in West Africa. I finally felt light and free. I was able to focus on my studies without needing to rush home and cook lunch. I now had "leisure" time to sit around and chat with people from all over the world. I could sleep in longer, and I could experience "idle" moments when I simply did nothing. I could make boys clean after themselves, and I could do it with authority. And sometimes, just to be cheeky, I would even make them clean up after me. I really loved this new life that I was allowed to live.

Whenever I returned home for the holidays, I always underwent psychological conflicts within myself. My family had missed my cooking. They missed me too, however they had also missed my services. After two semesters of being my own master, I had to readjust to being the passive daughter they had been used to in previous years. Once, I told a cousin to do something "his damned self." I was very frustrated. It wasn't easy reassuming my domestic role, especially after a whole year of retirement. He was livid. Before long, the rest of the family clamored around me, inquiring about what possessed me to say something like that. I remained quiet and listened to them answer the question for themselves: "She's gone to America, and now she has forgotten about her heritage." "Why did they send her there? Now look at what she is becoming." "She thinks she is American." My father returned home from work and, of course, I was spoken to sternly. I was never to repeat that behavior again.

But had America really changed me? I vehemently oppose that theory. It is true that as I progressed through college, my relationship with my family clearly experienced a metamorphosis. Although I was still respectful of my elders, I gradually became less restrained in expressing my true sentiments in various situations. I no longer followed orders passively as I had in the past, and little by little, I acquired the audacity to question them. Of course, I didn't always have my way, but at least I made it known that I was not always happy with the kind of life that they felt was right for me. This perceived impudence was not always welcomed, and I was repeatedly accused of disregarding my homeland's traditions and thinking that I was now an American.

But my theory is that America introduced me to Me. Growing up, I had numbed myself to the dissatisfactions I felt in a society that favored boys. My only option was to conform, so I brainwashed myself into thinking that I was happy. That was the only way I knew to keep a level head. I lived an emotionally uncomfortable life plagued with internal conflicts. It was always my reflex to suppress my true opinions on the gender inequalities for the fear of reproach from a conservative society that I loved more than myself. Each time I felt violated because one of the boys was being treated like a first-class citizen at my expense, a voice inside me affirmed that I was being treated unjustly, but I would dismiss it as the voice of a wayward extremist. America helped me realize that all that time, I had been dismissing myself, choosing instead to embrace the beliefs of a society that taught me that I was inferior to my male counterparts. American society was conducive to nurturing that part of me that didn't believe that I was weaker by virtue of my gender. America didn't change me, but rather it simply allowed me to discover myself.

As I continued to enjoy this growing sense of empowerment, I became acquainted with American feminism. Quite frankly, I didn't know what to make of it. It surprised me that any American woman could be discontent with the gender conditions of the same country I credited for liberating me. America felt like the Promised Land, and I wondered what else an American feminist could want. In my patriarchal background, women were considered the property of the male breadwinner. My aunt's husband, for instance, would use her as a punching bag without compunction after say, a stressful day at work. As a young woman I choked on these realities; my hands were tied when it came to protesting how my uncle handled my aunt, whom he considered his "property." At least in the United States my aunt could have been shielded from battery since her husband might have feared the threat of arrest. Thus, from my first perspective, America was surely the feminist's paradise.

It was interesting to learn later that many years ago, America's situation was quite similar to the current one in my natal country. I find this encouraging since it indicates that my people may one day embrace some of the values I now enjoy in America. Therefore, I do support the feminist and womanist movements in the United States, simply because these were forces that drove the change in America. I may eventually participate in the U.S. feminist struggles; perhaps I will gain some insight into what it would take to effect change in my country. For now, however, I am still living my American

dream. I am so addicted to the freedoms I have enjoyed here, and I hope I can keep them, irrespective of the country in which I finally decide to settle down.

Today I am an independent woman working in the United States. I am very happy with my life, and I feel more fulfilled than I ever have. Occasionally, however, I find myself missing home. There are many aspects of the Nigerian society, besides the gender inequalities, that I failed to appreciate until I came to America. I miss the Nigerian sense of community; the security of knowing that I can depend on my next-door neighbor to worry if she doesn't see me for several days. Here in the United States, my neighbor of two years still isn't sure whether or not I have children. Come to think of it, we don't even know each other's names. I also miss Nigerian food, the obstinate devotion to family, and the festive celebrations. I miss home. However, irrespective of how nostalgic I get, I know deep inside that America is the best option for me right now. I have deviated so much from my childhood's domestic and subservient lifestyle that I don't think it will ever be possible for me to adopt it again. The only way I could return to that life would be to erase the past six years I spent in America. Without those years I would never have tasted the sweet wine of independence that has gotten me drunk and addicted today.

I think that my family is gradually coming to terms with the person that I have become. I wouldn't say that my relatives are thrilled, but they recognize the futility of compelling me to marry a man from my community who is attached to its "good wife" values. They know that I will probably tell him to do his cooking and laundry his damned self, just like I have already told some members of my family to date. However, I wouldn't necessarily conclude that an American would make the perfect companion for me either, since he may not embody the Nigerian values that I love and miss.

It is difficult to predict what the future holds for me, since I am very much in the middle of the two worlds that have molded me into who I am today.

I have decided that I will go anywhere destiny takes me, provided that I have primary control over my life and that my opinions count, despite my gender. Anything less would not be a life for me. I have worked and struggled very hard to become the intelligent, independent and strong woman that I am today. I absolutely cannot ignore all that I have endured and achieved by settling for a passive life as Adam's Rib. Some may choose to call me a rebel, but I am simply a woman searching for a happier life. One in which I am allowed to love myself, and not sacrifice that love in favor of a society's values.

5. • C. J. Pascoe

MAKING MASCULINITY:
Adolescence, Identity, and High School (2007)

C. J. Pascoe, a professor of sociology at the University of Oregon, researches the constructions of gender, sexuality, and inequalities in youth culture and is the award-winning author of *Dude You're a Fag: Masculinity and Sexuality in High School* (excerpted here). Her research has been featured in *The New York Times*, *The Wall Street Journal*, *The Toronto Globe and Mail*, *American Sexuality Magazine*, and *Inside Higher Ed*. Pascoe's most recent book, coauthored with Tristan Bridges, is *Exploring Masculinities: Identity, Inequality, Continuity, and Change* (2015). She is a public advocate for antibullying and harassment policies, and her most recent projects investigate youth culture, sexuality, homophobia, and new media.

REVENGE OF THE NERDS

Cheering students filled River High's gymnasium. Packed tightly in the bleachers, they sang, hollered, and danced to loud hip-hop music. Over their heads hung banners celebrating fifty years of River High's sports victories. The yearly assembly in which the student body voted for the most popular senior boy in the school to be crowned Mr. Cougar was under way, featuring six candidates performing a series of skits to earn student votes.

Two candidates, Brent and Greg, both handsome, blond, "all-American" water polo players, entered the stage dressed like "nerds" to perform their skit, "Revenge

of the Nerds." They wore matching outfits: yellow button-down shirts; tight brown pants about five inches too short, with the waistbands pulled up clownishly high by black suspenders; black shoes with white knee socks; and thick black-rimmed glasses held together with white tape. As music played, the boys started dancing, flailing around comically in bad renditions of outdated dance moves like the Running Man and the Roger Rabbit. The crowd roared in laughter when Brent and Greg rubbed their rear ends together in time to the music. Two girls with long straight hair and matching miniskirts and black tank tops, presumably the nerds' girlfriends, ran out to dance with Brent and Greg.

Reprinted with permission of University of California Press from C.J. Pascoe, *Dude, You're a Fag: Masculinity and Sexuality in High School*, University of California Press, 2007; permission conveyed through Copyright Clearance Center, Inc.

Suddenly a group of white male "gangstas" sporting bandannas, baggy pants, sports jerseys, and oversized gold jewelry walked, or, more correctly, gangsta-limped, onto the stage. They proceeded to shove Brent and Greg, who looked at them fearfully and fled the stage without their girlfriends. The gangstas encircled the two girls, then "kidnapped" them by forcing them off the stage. After peering timidly around the corner of the stage, Brent and Greg reentered. The crowd roared as Brent opened his mouth and, in a high-pitched feminine voice, cried, "We have to get our women!"

Soon a girl dressed in a sweat suit and wearing a whistle around her neck carried barbells and weight benches onto the stage. Greg and Brent emerged from behind a screen, having replaced their nerd gear with matching black and white sweat pants and T-shirts. The female coach tossed the barbells around with ease, lifting one with a single hand. The audience hooted in laughter as the nerds struggled to lift even the smallest weight. Brent and Greg continued to work out until they could finally lift the weights. They ran up to the crowd to flex their newfound muscles as the audience cheered. To underscore how strong they had become, Brent and Greg ripped off their pants. The crowd was in hysterics as the boys revealed, not muscled legs, but matching red miniskirts. At first Greg and Brent looked embarrassed; then they triumphantly dropped the skirts, revealing matching shorts, and the audience cheered.

Brent and Greg ran off stage as stagehands unfurled a large cloth sign reading "Gangstas' Hideout." Some of the gangstas who had kidnapped the girlfriends sat around a table playing poker, while other gangstas gambled with dice. The nerds, who had changed into black suits accented with ties and fedoras, strode confidently into the hideout. They threw the card table in the air, causing the gangstas to jump back as the cards and chips scattered. Looking frightened at the nerds' newfound strength, the gangstas scrambled out of their hideout. After the gangstas had fled, the two miniskirted girlfriends ran up to Brent and Greg, hugging them gratefully. Several African American boys, also dressed in suits and fedoras, ran onto the stage, dancing while the former nerds stood behind them with their arms folded. After the dance, the victorious nerds walked off stage hand in hand with their rescued girlfriends.

I open with this scene to highlight the themes of masculinity I saw during a year and a half of fieldwork at River High School. The Mr. Cougar competition clearly illuminates the intersecting dynamics of sexuality, gender, social class, race, bodies, and institutional practices that constitute adolescent masculinity in this setting. Craig and Brent are transformed from unmasculine nerds who cannot protect their girlfriends into heterosexual, muscular men. This masculinizing process happens through a transformation of bodies, the assertion of racial privilege, and a shoring up of heterosexuality.

The story line of the skit—Brent and Craig's quest to confirm their heterosexuality by rescuing their girlfriends—posits heterosexuality as central to masculinity. Brent and Craig's inability to protect "their women" marks their physical inadequacy. Their appearance—tight, ill-fitting, outdated clothes—codes them as unmasculine. Their weakness and their high-pitched voices cast them as feminine. Their homoerotic dance moves position them as homosexual. By working out, the boys shed their weak, effeminate, and possibly homosexual identities. Just in case they didn't get their message across by bench-pressing heavy weights, the boys shed their last remnants of femininity by ripping off their matching miniskirts. They become so physically imposing that they don't even have to fight the gangstas, who flee in terror at the mere hint of the nerds' strength.

This skit lays bare the ways racialized notions of masculinity may be enacted through sexualized tropes. The gangstas symbolize failed and at the same time wildly successful men in their heterosexual claim on the nerds' women. Their "do-rags," baggy pants, shirts bearing sports team insignias, and limping walks are designed to invoke a hardened inner-city gangsta style, one portrayed on television and in movies, as a specifically black cultural style. In representing black men, the gangstas symbolize hypersexuality and invoke a thinly veiled imagery of the black rapist (Davis 1981), who threatens white men's control over white women. But in the end, the gangstas are vanquished by the white, middle-class legitimacy of the nerds, turned masculine with their newfound strength. The skit also portrays black men as slightly feminized in that they act as cheerleaders and relieve the white heroes of the unmasculine practice of dancing.

Markers of femininity such as high voices and skirts symbolize emasculation when associated with male bodies. The girlfriends also signal a relationship between femininity and helplessness, since they are unable to save themselves from the gangstas. However, the female coach symbolizes strength, a sign of masculinity the nerds initially lack. The students in the audience cheer her as she engages in a masculinized practice, lifting weights with ease, and they laugh at the boys who can't do this. Male femininity, in this instance, is coded as humorous, while female masculinity is cheered.

[. . .]

My findings illustrate that masculinity is not a homogenous category that any boy possesses by virtue of being male. Rather, masculinity—as constituted and understood in the social world I studied—is a configuration of practices and discourses that different youths (boys and girls) may embody in different ways and to different degrees. Masculinity, in this sense, is associated with, but not reduced or solely equivalent to, the male body. I argue that adolescent masculinity is understood in this setting as a form of dominance usually expressed through sexualized discourses.[1]

Through extensive fieldwork and interviewing I discovered that, for boys, achieving a masculine identity entails the repeated repudiation of the specter of failed masculinity. Boys lay claim to masculine identities by lobbing homophobic epithets at one another. They also assert masculine selves by engaging in heterosexist discussions of girls' bodies and their own sexual experiences. Both of these phenomena intersect with racialized identities in that they are organized somewhat differently by and for African American boys and white boys. From what I saw during my research, African American boys were more likely to be punished by school authorities for engaging in these masculinizing practices. Though homophobic taunts and assertion of heterosexuality shore up a masculine identity for boys,

the relationship between sexuality and masculinity looks different when masculinity occurs outside male bodies. For girls, challenging heterosexual identities often solidifies a more masculine identity. These gendering processes are encoded at multiple levels: institutional, interactional, and individual.

[. . .]

WHAT DO WE MEAN BY MASCULINITY?

Sociologists have approached masculinity as a multiplicity of gender practices (regardless of their content) enacted by men whose bodies are assumed to be biologically male. Early in the twentieth century, when fears of feminization pervaded just about every sphere of social life, psychologists became increasingly concerned with differentiating men from women (Kimmel 1996). As a result, part of the definition of a psychologically "normal" adult came to involve proper adjustment to one's "gender role" (Pleck 1987). Talcott Parsons (1954), the first sociologist to really address masculinity as such, argued that men's "instrumental" role and women's "expressive" role were central to the functioning of a well-ordered society. Deviations from women's role as maternal caretakers or men's role as breadwinners would result in "role strain" and "role competition," weakening families and ultimately society.

With the advent of the women's movement, feminist gender theorists examined how power is embedded in these seemingly neutral (not to mention natural) "gender roles" (Hartmann 1976; Jaggar 1983; Rosaldo and Lamphere 1974; Rubin 1984). Psychoanalytic feminist theorists explicitly addressed masculinity as an identity formation constituted by inequality. Both Dorothy Dinnerstein (1976) and Nancy Chodorow (1978) argued that masculinity, as we recognize it, is the result of a family system in which women mother. Identification with a mother as the primary caregiver proves much more problematic in the formation of a gender identity for a boy than for a girl child, producing a self we understand as masculine characterized by defensive ego boundaries and repudiation of femininity. Feminist psychoanalytic theorists equate contemporary masculinity with a quest for autonomy and separation, an approach that influences my own analysis of masculinity.

Recognizing the changes wrought for women by feminist movements, sociologists of masculinity realized that feminism had radical implications for men (Carrigan, Connell, and Lee 1987). Frustrated with the paucity of non-normative approaches to masculinity, and what they saw (a bit defensively) as feminist characterizations of masculinity as "unrelieved villainy and all men as agents of the patriarchy in more or less the same degree" (64), these sociologists attempted to carve out new models of gendered analysis in which individual men or men collectively were not all framed as equal agents of patriarchal oppression.

The emergent sociology of masculinity became a "critical study of men, their behaviors, practices, values and perspectives" (Whitehead and Barrett 2001, 14). These new sociologists of masculinity positioned themselves in opposition to earlier Parsonian theories of masculinity, proffering, not a single masculine "role," but rather the idea that masculinity is understandable only in a model of "multiple masculinities" (Connell 1995). Instead of focusing on masculinity as the male role, this model asserts that there are a variety of masculinities, which make sense only in hierarchical and contested relations with one another. R. W. Connell argues that men enact and embody different configurations of masculinity depending on their positions within a social hierarchy of power. *Hegemonic masculinity*, the type of gender practice that, in a given space and time, supports gender inequality, is at the top of this hierarchy. *Complicit masculinity* describes men who benefit from hegemonic masculinity but do not enact it; *subordinated masculinity* describes men who are oppressed by definitions of hegemonic masculinity, primarily gay men; *marginalized masculinity* describes men who may be positioned powerfully in terms of gender but not in terms of class or race.

Connell, importantly, emphasizes that the content of these configurations of gender practice is not always and everywhere the same. Very few men, if any, are actually hegemonically masculine, but all men do benefit, to different extents, from this sort of definition of masculinity, a form of benefit Connell (1995) calls the "patriarchal dividend" (41).

This model of multiple masculinities has been enormously influential, inspiring countless studies that detail the ways different configurations of masculinity are promoted, challenged, or reinforced in given social situations. This research on how men do masculinity has provided insight into practices of masculinity in a wide range of social institutions, such as families (Coltrane 2001), schools (Francis and Skelton 2001; Gilbert 1998; Mac an Ghaill 1996; Parker 1996), the workplace (Connell 1998; Cooper 2000), the media (Craig 1992; Davies 1995), and sports (Curry 2004; Edley and Wetherell 1997; Majors 2001; Messner 2002). This focus on masculinity as what men do has spawned an industry of cataloguing "types" of masculinity: gay, black, Chicano, working class, middle class, Asian, gay black, gay Chicano, white working class, militarized, transnational business, New Man, negotiated, versatile, healthy, toxic, counter, and cool masculinities, among others (Messner 2004b).

While Connell intends this model of masculinities to be understood as fluid and conflictual, the multiple masculinities model is more often used to construct static and reified typologies such as the ones listed by Michael Messner. These descriptions of masculinity are intended to highlight patterns of practice in which structure meets with identity and action, but they have the effect of slotting men into masculinity categories: a hegemonic man, a complicit man, a resistant man (or the multitude of ever-increasing types of masculinities catalogued above). While these masculinities may be posited as ideal types, they are sometimes difficult to use analytically without lapsing into a simplistic categorical analysis. Because of the emphasis on masculinities in the plural, a set of types some men can seemingly step in and out of at will, this model runs the risk of collapsing into an analysis of styles of masculinity, thereby deflecting attention from structural inequalities between men and women. In other words, we must always pay attention to power relations when we think in pluralities and diversities; otherwise we are simply left with a list of differences (Zinn and Dill 1996). Additionally, the category of "hegemonic masculinity" is so rife with contradictions it is small wonder that no man actually embodies it (Donaldson 1993). According to this model both a rich, slim, soft-spoken businessman and a poor, muscular, violent gang member might be described as hegemonically masculine. At the same time neither of them would really be hegemonically masculine, since the businessman would not be physically powerful and the poor gang member would lack claims on institutional gendered power. Because of some of these deployment problems, those studying masculinities have for some time called for a more sophisticated analysis of masculinity (Messner 1993; Morgan 1992).

To refine approaches to masculinity, researchers need to think more clearly about the implications of defining masculinity as what men or boys do. This definition conflates masculinity with the actions of those who have male bodies. Defining masculinity as "what men do" reifies biologized categories of male and female that are problematic and not necessarily discrete categories to begin with (Fausto-Sterling 1995). In the end, masculinity is framed as a social category based on an assumed biological difference that in itself is constituted by the very social category it purports to underlie. This is not to say that sociologists of masculinity are biological determinists, but by assuming that the male body is the location of masculinity their theories reify the assumed biological basis of gender. Recognizing that masculinizing discourses and practices extend beyond male bodies, this book traces the various ways masculinity is produced and manifested in relation to a multiplicity of bodies, spaces, and objects. That is, this book looks at masculinity as a variety of practices and discourses that can be mobilized by and applied to both boys and girls.

BRINGING IN SEXUALITY

Heeding the admonition of Carrigan, Connell, and Lee (1987) that "analysis of masculinity needs to be related as well to other currents in feminism" (64), I turn to interdisciplinary theorizing about the role of sexuality in the construction of gender identities. Building on studies of sexuality that demonstrate that sexuality is an organizing principle of social life, this book highlights intersections of masculinizing and sexualizing practices and discourses at River High.

Thinking about sexuality as an organizing principle of social life means that it is not just the property of individuals. Sexuality, in this sense, doesn't just indicate a person's sexual identity, whether he or she is gay or straight. Rather, sexuality is itself a form of power that exists regardless of an individual's sexual identity. Thinking about sexuality this way can be initially quite jarring. After all, usually we discuss sexuality as a personal identity or a set of private practices. However, researchers and theorists have increasingly argued that sexuality is a quite public part of social life (Foucault 1990). Though sexuality was initially studied as a set of private acts, and eventually identities, by physicians and other medical professionals intent on discerning normal from abnormal sexuality, social theorists are now documenting the ways institutions, identities, and discourses interact with, are regulated by, and produce sexual meanings.

In this sense, *sexuality* refers to sex acts and sexual identities, but it also encompasses a range of meanings associated with these acts and identities. The meanings that vary by social class, location, and gender identity (Mahay, Laumann, and Michaels 2005) may be more important than the acts themselves (Weeks 1996). A good example of this is heterosexuality. While heterosexual desires or identities might feel private and personal, contemporary meanings of heterosexuality also confer upon heterosexual individuals all sorts of citizenship rights, so that heterosexuality is not just a private matter but one that links a person to certain state benefits.

Similarly contemporary meanings of sexuality, particularly heterosexuality, for instance, eroticize male dominance and female submission (Jeffreys 1996, 75). In this way what seems like a private desire is part of the mechanisms through which the microprocesses of daily life actually foster inequality.

Interdisciplinary theorizing about sexuality has primarily taken the form of "queer theory." Like sociology, queer theory destabilizes the assumed naturalness of the social order (Lemert 1996). Queer theory moves the deconstructive project of sociology into new areas by examining much of what sociology sometimes takes for granted: "deviant" sexualities, sexual identities, sexual practices, sexual discourses, and sexual norms (Seidman 1996). In making the taken-for-granted explicit, queer theorists examine sexual power as it is embedded in different areas of social life and interrogate areas of the social world not usually seen as sexuality—such as the ways heterosexuality confers upon an individual a variety of citizenship rights (A. Stein and Plummer 1994). The logic of sexuality not only regulates intimate relations but also infuses social relations and social structures (S. Epstein 1994; Warner 1993).

. . . Queer theory draws on a postmodern approach to studying society that moves beyond traditional categories such as male/female, masculine/feminine, and straight/gay to focus instead on the instability of these categories. That is, we might think of "heterosexual" and "homosexual" as stable, opposing, and discrete identities, but really they are fraught with internal contradictions (Halley 1993). To this end, queer theory emphasizes multiple identities and multiplicity in general. Instead of creating knowledge about categories of sexual identity, queer theorists look to see how those categories themselves are created, sustained, and undone.

One of the ways a queer theory approach can bring studies of masculinity in line with other feminist theorizing is to uncouple the male body from definitions of masculinity. The masculinities literature, while attending to very real inequalities between gay and straight men, tends to look at sexuality as inherent in static identities attached to male bodies, not as a major organizing principle of social life (S. Epstein 1994; Warner 1993). As part of its deconstructive project, queer theory often points to disjunctures between pairings thought of as natural and inevitable. In doing so queer theorists may implicitly question some of the assumptions of the multiple masculinities model—specifically the assumption that masculinity is defined by the bodily practices of boys and men—by placing sexuality at the center of analysis. Eve Sedgwick (1995), one of the few theorists to address the problematic assumption of the centrality of the male body to academic discussions of masculinity, argues that sometimes masculinity has nothing to do with men and that men don't necessarily have anything to do with masculinity. As a result "it is important to drive a wedge in, early and often and if possible conclusively, between the two topics, masculinity and men, whose relation to one another it is so difficult not to presume" (12).

Assuming that masculinity is only about men weakens inquiries into masculinity. Therefore it is important to look at masculinizing processes outside the male body, not to catalogue a new type of masculinity, but to identify practices, rituals, and discourses that constitute masculinity. Doing so indicates the centrality of sexualized meanings to masculinity in relation to both male and female bodies.

Dislodging masculinity from a biological location is a productive way to highlight the social constructedness of masculinity and may even expose a latent sexism within the sociological literature in its assumption that masculinity, as a powerful social identity, is only the domain of men. Judith Kegan Gardiner (2003) points out in her review of gender and masculinity textbooks "the very different investments that men, including masculinity scholars, appear to have in preserving masculinity as some intelligible and coherent grounding of identity in comparison to the skepticism and distance shown by feminists towards femininity" (153). Indeed, gender scholars who study women have not been nearly as interested in femininity as scholars of men have been in masculinity.

It is not that bodies are unimportant. They are. Bodies are the vehicles through which we express gendered selves; they are also the matter through which social norms are made concrete. What is problematic is the unreflexive assumption of an embodied location for gender that echoes throughout the masculinities literature. Looking at masculinity as discourses and practices that can be mobilized by female bodies undermines the conflation of masculinity with an embodied state of maleness (Califia 1994; Halberstam 1998; Paechter 2006). Instead, this approach looks at masculinity as a recognizable configuration of gender practices and discourses.

Placing sexuality at the center of analysis highlights the "routinely unquestioned heteronormative expectations and proscriptions that exist as background context in contemporary U.S. culture," assumptions that "emerge when traditional normative gender boundaries are crossed" (Neilsen, Walden, and Kunkel 2000, 292). Examining these heteronormative structures and how masculine girls and feminine boys challenge them gets at contemporary constructions of masculinity in adolescence. Studying gender transgressions in adolescence provides empirical evidence to bolster and extend some of the claims of queer theory, an approach that often relies on literary or artistic examples for its data (Gamson and Moon 2004, 49).

RETHINKING MASCULINITY, SEXUALITY, AND BODIES

Attending to sexuality and its centrality to gendered identities opens insight into masculinity both as a process (Bederman 1995) and as a field through which power is articulated (Scott 1999) rather than as a never-ending list of configurations of practice enacted by specific bodies. My research indicates that masculinity is an identity that respondents think of as related to the male body but as not necessarily specific to the male body. Interviews with and observations of students at River High indicate that they recognize masculinity as an identity

expressed through sexual discourses and practices that indicate dominance and control.[2]

As scholars of gender have demonstrated, gender is accomplished through day-to-day interactions (G. Fine 1989; Hochschild 1989; Thorne 2002; West and Zimmerman 1991). In this sense gender is the "activity of managing situated conduct in light of normative conceptions of attitudes and activities appropriate for one's sex category" (West and Zimmerman 1991, 127). People are supposed to act in ways that line up with their presumed sex. That is, we expect people we think are females to act like women and males to act like men. People hold other people accountable for "doing gender" correctly.

The queer theorist Judith Butler (1999) builds on this interactionist approach to gender, arguing that gender is something people accomplish through "a set of repeated acts within a highly rigid regulatory frame that congeal over time to produce the appearance of substance, of a natural sort of being" (43). That is, gender is not just natural, or something one is, but rather something we all produce through our actions. By repeatedly acting "feminine" or "masculine" we actually create those categories. Becoming gendered, becoming masculine or feminine, is a process.

Butler argues that gendered beings are created through processes of repeated invocation and repudiation. People constantly reference or invoke a gendered norm, thus making the norm seem like a timeless truth. Similarly, people continually repudiate a "constitutive outside" (Butler 1993, 3) in which is contained all that is cast out of a socially recognizable gender category. The "constitutive outside" is inhabited by what she calls "abject identities," unrecognizably and unacceptably gendered selves. The interactional accomplishment of gender in a Butlerian model consists, in part, of the continual iteration and repudiation of an abject identity. The abject identity must be constantly named to remind individuals of its power. Similarly, it must be constantly repudiated by individuals or groups so that they can continually affirm their identities as normal and as culturally intelligible. Gender, in this sense, is "constituted through the force of exclusion and abjection, one which produces a constitutive outside to the subject, an abjected outside, which is, after all, 'inside' the subject as its own founding repudiation" (Butler 1993, 3). This repudiation creates and reaffirms a "threatening specter" (3) of failed gender, the existence of which must be continually repudiated through interactional processes.

Informed by this interactionist approach to gender, in which gender is not just a quality of an individual but the result of interactional processes, this study examines masculinity as sexualized processes of confirmation and repudiation through which individuals demonstrate mastery over others. Building on the insights of the multiple masculinities literature, I emphasize that this definition of masculinity is not universal but local, age limited, and institutional and that other definitions of masculinity may be found in different locales and different times. Examining masculinity using Butler's theory of interactional accomplishment of gender indicates that the "fag" position is an "abject" position and, as such, is a "threatening specter" constituting contemporary American adolescent masculinity at River High. Similarly, drawing on Butler's concept of the constitution of gender through "repeated acts within a highly rigid regulatory frame" elucidates how seemingly "normal" daily interactions of male adolescence are actually ritualized interactions constituting masculinity. These repeated acts involve demonstrating sexual mastery and the denial of girls' subjectivity. The school itself sets the groundwork for boys' interactional rituals of repudiation and confirmation, like those illustrated in the opening vignette.

Butler also suggests ways to challenge an unequal gender order. Individuals who deliberately engage in gender practices that render them culturally unintelligible, such as practices that are at odds with their apparent sex category, challenge the naturalness and inevitability of a rigid gender order. Some girls at River High engage in precisely this sort of resistance by engaging in masculinizing processes. While challenging an unequal gender order at the level of interactions does not necessarily address larger structural inequalities, it is an important component of social change. That said, doing gender differently by engaging in gender practices not "appropriate" for one's sex category, such as drag, also runs the risk of reifying binary categories of gender. Resistance, in this model, is fraught with danger, since it is both an investment in gender norms and a subversion of them. Sometimes it challenges the gender order and sometimes it seems to bolster it.

[. . .]

NOTES

1. This is not to say that women don't possess this sort of subjectivity, but these qualities are what students at River High associate with masculinity.
2. While trying to retain the insight that there are multiple masculinities that vary by time and place, I self-consciously use the singular *masculinity* in this text because students at River talk about masculinity as a singular identity that involves practices and discourses of sexualized power and mastery.

REFERENCES

Bederman, Gail. 1995. *Manliness and Civilization: A Cultural History of Gender and Race in the United States, 1880–1917.* Chicago: University of Chicago Press.

Butler, Judith. 1993. *Bodies That Matter: On the Discursive Limits of "Sex."* New York: Routledge.

Butler, Judith. 1999. *Gender Trouble: Feminism and the Subversion of Identity.* New York: Routledge.

Califia, Pat. 1994. "Butch Desire." In *Dagger: On Butch Women,* edited by L. Burana and L. Roxie Due, 220–24. San Francisco: Cleis Press.

Carrigan, T., B. Connell, and J. Lee. 1987. "Towards a New Sociology of Masculinity." In *The Making of Masculinities: The New Men's Studies,* edited by H. Brod, 63–102. Boston: Allen and Unwin.

Chodorow, Nancy. 1978. *The Reproduction of Mothering: Psychoanalysis and the Sociology of Gender*. Berkeley: University of California Press.

Coltrane, Scott. 2001. "Selling the Indispensable Father." Paper presented at the conference "Pushing the Boundaries: New Conceptualizations of Childhood and Motherhood," Temple University, Philadelphia.

Connell, R. W. 1995. *Masculinities*. Berkeley: University of California Press.

Connell, R. W. 1998. "Masculinities and Globalization." *Men and Masculinities* 1, no. 1:3–23.

Cooper, Marianne. 2000. "Being the 'Go-to Guy': Fatherhood, Masculinity and the Organization of Work in Silicon Valley." *Qualitative Sociology* 23, no. 4:379–405.

Craig, Steve. 1992. *Men, Masculinity, and the Media*. Research on Men and Masculinities Series 1. Newbury Park, CA: Sage Publications.

Curry, Timothy Jon. 2004. "Fraternal Bonding in the Locker Room: A Profeminist Analysis of Talk about Competition and Women." In *Men's Lives*, edited by Michael Messner and Michael Kimmel, 204–17. Boston: Pearson.

Davies, Jude. 1995. "'I'm the Bad Guy?' *Falling Down* and White Masculinity in Hollywood." *Journal of Gender Studies* 4, no. 2:145–52.

Davis, Angela. 1981. *Women, Race and Class*. New York: Vintage Books, 1981.

Dinnerstein, Dorothy. 1976. *The Mermaid and the Minotaur: Sexual Arrangements and Human Malaise*. New York: Harper Perennial.

Donaldson, Mike. 1993. "What Is Hegemonic Masculinity?" *Theory and Society* 22, no. 5:643–57.

Edley, Nigel, and Margaret Wetherell. 1997. "Jockeying for Position: The Construction of Masculine Identities." *Discourse and Society* 8, no. 2:203–17.

Epstein, Steven. 1994. "A Queer Encounter." *Sociological Theory* 12:188–202.

Fausto-Sterling, Ann. 1995. "How to Build a Man." In *Constructing Masculinity*, edited by Maurice Berger, Brian Wallis, and Simon Watson, 127–34. New York: Routledge.

Fine, Gary Alan. 1989. "The Dirty Play of Little Boys." In *Men's Lives*, edited by Michael Kimmel and Michael Messner, 171–79. New York: Macmillan.

Foucault, Michel. 1990. *The History of Sexuality*. Vol. 1. Translated by Robert Hurley. New York: Vintage Books.

Francis, Becky, and Christine Skelton. 2001. "Men Teachers and the Construction of Heterosexual Masculinity in the Classroom." *Sex Education* 1, no. 1:9–21.

Gamson, Joshua, and Dawne Moon. 2004. "The Sociology of Sexualities: Queer and Beyond." *Annual Review of Sociology* 30:47–64.

Gardiner, Judith Kegan. 2003. "Gender and Masculinity Texts: Consensus and Concerns for Feminist Classrooms." *NWSA Journal* 15, no. 1:147–57.

Gilbert, Rob. 1998. *Masculinity Goes to School*. New York: Routledge.

Halberstam, Judith. 1998. *Female Masculinity*. Durham: Duke University Press.

Halley, Janet E. 1993. "The Construction of Heterosexuality." In *Fear of a Queer Planet: Queer Politics and Social Theory*, edited by Michael Warner, 82–102. Minneapolis: University of Minnesota Press.

Hartmann, Heidi. 1976. "Capitalism, Patriarchy and Job Segregation by Sex." *Signs* 1:137–70.

Hochschild, Arlie Russell. 1989. *The Second Shift*. New York: Avon.

Jaggar, Alison. 1983. *Feminist Politics and Human Nature*. Totowa, NJ: Rowman and Allanheld.

Jeffreys, Sheila. 1996. "Heterosexuality and the Desire for Gender." In *Theorising Heterosexuality*, edited by Diane Richardson, 75–90. Buckingham: Open University Press.

Kimmel, Michael S. 1996. *Manhood in America: A Cultural History*. New York: Free Press.

Lemert, Charles. 1996. "Series Editor's Preface." In *Queer Theory/Sociology*, edited by Steven Seidman, vii–xi. Cambridge: Blackwell.

Mac an Ghaill, Martain. 1996. "What about the Boys? Schooling, Class and Crisis Masculinity." *Sociological Review* 44, no. 3:381–97.

Mahay, Jenna, Edward O. Laumann, and Stuart Michaels. 2005. "Race, Gender and Class in Sexual Scripts." In *Speaking of Sexuality: Interdisciplinary Readings*, edited by J. Kenneth Davidson Sr. and Nelwyn B. Moore, 144–58. Los Angeles: Roxbury.

Majors, Richard. 2001. "Cool Pose: Black Masculinity and Sports." In *The Masculinities Reader*, edited by Stephen Whitehead and Frank Barrett, 208–17. Cambridge: Polity Press.

Messner, Michael. 1993. "'Changing Men' and Feminist Politics in the United States." *Theory and Society* 22, no. 5:723–27.

Messner, Michael. 2002. *Taking the Field: Women, Men and Sports*. Minneapolis: University of Minnesota Press.

Messner, Michael. 2004b. "On Patriarchs and Losers: Rethinking Men's Interests." Paper presented at the Berkeley Journal of Sociology Conference: Rethinking Gender, University of California, Berkeley, March.

Morgan, David. 1992. *Discovering Men*. New York: Routledge.

Neilsen, Joyce McCarl, Glenda Walden, and Charlotte A. Kunkel. 2000. "Gendered Heteronormativity: Empirical

Illustrations in Everyday Life." *Sociological Quarterly* 41, no. 2:283–96.

Paechter, Carrie. 2006. "Masculine Femininities/Feminine Masculinities: Power, Identities and Gender." *Gender and Education* 18, no. 3:253–63.

Parker, Andrew. 1996. "The Construction of Masculinity within Boys' Physical Education." *Gender and Education* 8, no. 2:141–57.

Parsons, Talcott. 1954. *Essays in Sociological Theory*. New York: Free Press.

Pleck, Joseph H. 1987. "The Theory of Male Sex-Role Identity: Its Rise and Fall, 1936 to the Present." In *The Making of Masculinities: The New Men's Studies*, edited by Harry Brod, 21–38. Boston: Allen and Unwin.

Rosaldo, Michelle, and Louise Lamphere. 1974. "Introduction." In *Woman, Culture and Society*, edited by Michelle Rosaldo and Louise Lamphere. Stanford: Stanford University Press.

Rubin, Gayle. 1984. "Thinking Sex: Notes for a Radical Theory of the Politics of Sexuality." In *Pleasure and Danger: Exploring Female Sexuality*, edited by Carol Vance, 267–319. London: Pandora.

Scott, Joan Wallach. 1999. *Gender and the Politics of History*. New York: Columbia University Press.

Sedgwick, Eve Kosofsky. 1995. "'Gosh, Boy George, You Must Be Awfully Secure in Your Masculinity!'" In *Constructing Masculinity*, edited by Maurice Berger, Brian Wallis, and Simon Watson, 11–20. New York: Routledge.

Seidman, Steven. 1996. "Introduction." In *Queer Theory/Sociology*, edited by Steven Seidman, 1–29. Oxford: Blackwell.

Stein, Arlene, and Ken Plummer. 1994. "'I Can't Even Think Straight': Theory and the Missing Sexual Revolution in Sociology." *Sociological Theory* 12, no. 2:178–87.

Thorne, Barrie. 2002. "Gender and Interaction: Widening the Conceptual Scope." In *Gender in Interaction: Perspectives on Femininity and Masculinity in Ethnography and Discourse*, edited by Bettina Baron and Helga Kotthoff, 3–18. Philadelphia: John Benjamins.

Warner, Michael. 1993. "Introduction." In *Fear of a Queer Planet: Queer Politics and Social Theory*, edited by Michael Warner, vii–xxxi. Minneapolis: University of Minnesota Press.

Weeks, Jeffrey. 1996. "The Construction of Homosexuality." In *Queer Theory/Sociology*, edited by Steven Seidman, 41–63. Cambridge: Blackwell.

West, Candace, and Don Zimmerman. 1991. "Doing Gender." In *The Social Construction of Gender*, edited by Judith Lorber, 102–21. Newbury Park, CA: Sage Publications.

Whitehead, Stephen, and Frank Barrett. 2001. "The Sociology of Masculinity." In *The Masculinities Reader*, edited by Stephen Whitehead and Frank Barrett, 1–26. Malden, MA: Blackwell.

Zinn, Maxine Baca, and Bonnie Thornton Dill. 1996. "Theorizing Difference from Multiracial Feminism." *Feminist Studies* 22, no. 2:321–31.

6. • *Eli Clare*

THE MOUNTAIN (2009)

Eli Clare is a writer, speaker, activist, teacher, and poet who weaves scholarship and storytelling to contribute to disability studies through an intersectional lens. Author of three books, including *Exile and Pride* (2009, excerpted here), *The Marrow's Telling* (2007), and *Brilliant Imperfection: Grappling with Cure* (2017), Clare has worked in a variety of communities, organizations, and institutions offering multimedia talks, lectures, classroom presentations, and retreats, and actively keeps a blog on his personal webpage (eliclare.com).

I. A METAPHOR

The mountain as metaphor looms large in the lives of marginalized people, people whose bones get crushed in the grind of capitalism, patriarchy, white supremacy. How many of us have struggled up the mountain, measured ourselves against it, failed up there, lived in its shadow? We've hit our heads on glass ceilings, tried to climb the class ladder, lost fights against assimilation, scrambled toward that phantom called normality.

We hear from the summit that the world is grand from up there, that we live down here at the bottom because we are lazy, stupid, weak, and ugly. We decide to climb that mountain, or make a pact that our children will climb it. The climbing turns out to be unimaginably difficult. We are afraid; every time we look ahead we can find nothing remotely familiar or comfortable. We lose the trail. Our wheelchairs get stuck. We speak the wrong languages with the wrong accents, wear the wrong clothes, carry our bodies the wrong ways, ask the wrong questions, love the wrong people. And it's goddamn lonely up there on the mountain. We decide to stop climbing and build a new house right where we are. Or we decide to climb back down to the people we love, where the food, the clothes, the dirt, the sidewalk, the steaming asphalt under our feet, our crutches, all feel right. Or we find the path again, decide to continue climbing only to have the very people who told us how wonderful life is at the summit booby-trap the trail. They burn the bridge over the impassable canyon. They redraw our topo maps so that we end up walking in circles. They send their goons—those working-class and poor people they employ as their official brutes—to push us over the edge. Maybe we get to the summit, but probably not. And the price we pay is huge.

Up there on the mountain, we confront the external forces, the power brokers who benefit so much from the status quo and their privileged position at the very summit. But just as vividly, we come face-to-face with our own bodies, all that we cherish and despise, all that lies imbedded there. This I know because I have caught myself lurching up the mountain.

II. A SUPERCRIP STORY

I am a gimp, a crip, disabled with cerebral palsy. The story of me lurching up the mountain begins not on the mountain, but with one of the dominant images of disabled people, the supercrip. A boy without hands bats .486 on his Little League team. A blind man hikes the Appalachian Trail from end to end. An adolescent girl with Down syndrome learns to drive and has a boyfriend. A guy with one leg runs across Canada. The nondisabled world is saturated with these stories: stories about gimps who engage in activities as grand as walking 2,500 miles or as mundane as learning to drive. They focus on disabled people "overcoming" our disabilities. They reinforce the superiority of the nondisabled body and mind. They turn individual disabled people, who are simply leading their lives, into symbols of inspiration.

Supercrip stories never focus on the conditions that make it so difficult for people with Down syndrome to have romantic partners, for blind people to have adventures, for disabled kids to play sports. I don't mean medical conditions. I mean material, social, legal conditions. I mean lack of access, lack of employment, lack of education, lack of personal attendant services. I mean stereotypes and attitudes. I mean oppression. The dominant story about disability should be about ableism, not the inspirational supercrip crap, the believe-it-or-not disability story.

I've been a supercrip in the mind's eye of nondisabled people more than once. Running cross-country and track in high school, I came in dead last in more races than I care to count. My tense, wiry body, right foot wandering out to the side as I grew tired, pushed against the miles, the stopwatch, the final back stretch, the last muddy hill. Sometimes I was lapped by the front-runners in races as short as the mile. Sometimes I trailed everyone on a cross-country course by two, three, four minutes. I ran because I loved to run, and yet after every race, strangers came to thank me, cry over me, tell me what an inspiration I was. To them, I was not just another hopelessly slow, tenacious high school athlete, but supercrip, tragic brave girl with CP, courageous cripple. It sucked. The slogan on one of my favorite T-shirts, black cotton inked with big fluorescent pink letters, one word per line, reads PISS ON PITY.

[. . .]

My lurching up the mountain is another kind of supercrip story, a story about internalizing supercripdom, about becoming supercrip in my own mind's eye, a story about climbing Mount Adams last summer with my friend Adrianne. We had been planning this trip for years. Adrianne spent her childhood roaming New Hampshire's White Mountains and wanted to take me to her favorite haunts. Six times in six years, we set the trip up, and every time something fell through at the last minute. Finally, last summer everything stayed in place.

I love the mountains almost as much as I love the ocean, not a soft, romantic kind of love, but a deep down rumble in my bones. When Adrianne pulled out her trail guides and topo maps and asked me to choose one of the mountains we'd climb, I looked for a big mountain, for a long, hard hike, for a trail that would take us well above tree line. I picked Mount Adams. I think I asked Adrianne, "Can I handle this trail?" meaning, "Will I have to clamber across deep gulches on narrow log bridges without hand railings to get to the top of this mountain?" Without a moment's hesitation, she said, "No problem."

I have walked from Los Angeles to Washington, DC, on a peace walk; backpacked solo in the southern Appalachians, along Lake Superior, on the beaches at Point Reyes; slogged my way over Cottonwood Pass and down South Manitou's dunes. Learning to walk took me longer than most kids—certainly most nondisabled kids. I was two and a half before I figured out how to stand on my own two feet, drop my heels to the ground, balance my weight on the whole long flat of each foot. I wore orthopedic shoes—clunky, unbending monsters—for several years, but never had to suffer through physical therapy or surgery. Today, I can and often do walk unending miles for the pure joy of walking. In the disability community I am called a walkie, someone who doesn't use a wheelchair, who walks

rather than rolls. Adrianne and I have been hiking buddies for years. I never questioned her judgment. Of course, I could handle Mount Adams.

The night before our hike, it rained. In the morning we thought we might have to postpone. The weather reports from the summit still looked uncertain, but by 10 A.M. the clouds started to lift, later than we had planned to begin but still okay. The first mile of trail snaked through steep jumbles of rock, leaving me breathing hard, sweat drenching my cotton T-shirt, dripping into my eyes. I love this pull and stretch, quads and calves, lungs and heart, straining.

[. . .]

The trail divides and divides again, steeper and rockier now, moving not around but over piles of craggy granite, mossy and a bit slick from the night's rain. I start having to watch where I put my feet. Balance has always been somewhat of a problem for me, my right foot less steady than my left. On uncertain ground, each step becomes a studied move, especially when my weight is balanced on my right foot. I take the trail slowly, bringing both feet together, solid on one stone, before leaning into my next step. This assures my balance, but I lose all the momentum gained from swinging into a step, touching ground, pushing off again in the same moment. There is no rhythm to my stop-and-go clamber. I know that going down will be worse, gravity underscoring my lack of balance. I watch Adrianne ahead of me hop from one rock to the next up this tumble trail of granite. I know that she's breathing hard, that this is no easy climb, but also that each step isn't a strategic game for her. I start getting scared as the trail steepens, then steepens again, the rocks not letting up. I can't think of how I will ever come down this mountain. Fear sets up a rumble right alongside the love in my bones. I keep climbing. Adrianne starts waiting for me every 50 yards or so. I finally tell her I'm scared.

She's never hiked this trail before so can't tell me if this is as steep as it gets. We study the topo map, do a time check. We have many hours of daylight ahead of us, but we're both thinking about how much time it might take me to climb down, using my hands and butt when I can't trust my feet. I want to continue up to tree line, the pines shorter and shorter, grown twisted and withered, giving way to scrub brush, then to lichen-covered granite, up to the sun-drenched cap where the mountains all tumble out toward the hazy blue horizon. I want to so badly but fear rumbles next to love next to real lived physical limitations, and so we decide to turn around. I cry, maybe for the first time, over something I want to do, had many reasons to believe I could, but really can't. I cry hard, then get up and follow Adrianne back down the mountain. It's hard and slow, and I use my hands and butt often and wish I could use gravity as Adrianne does to bounce from one flat spot to another, down this jumbled pile of rocks.

[. . .]

I thought a lot coming down Mount Adams. Thought about bitterness. For as long as I can remember, I have avoided certain questions. Would I have been a good runner if I didn't have CP? Could I have been a surgeon or pianist, a dancer or gymnast? Tempting questions that have no answers. I refuse to enter the territory marked *bitterness*. I wondered about a friend who calls herself one of the last of the polio tribe, born just before the polio vaccine's discovery. Does she ever ask what her life might look like had she been born five years later? On a topo map, bitterness would be outlined in red.

I thought about the model of disability that separates impairment from disability. Disability theorist Michael Oliver defines impairment as "lacking part of or all of a limb, or having a defective limb, organism or mechanism of the body."[1] I lack a fair amount of fine motor control. My hands shake. I can't play a piano, place my hands gently on a keyboard, or type even fifteen words a minute.

Whole paragraphs never cascade from my fingertips. My longhand is a slow scrawl. I have trouble picking up small objects, putting them down. Dicing onions with a sharp knife puts my hands at risk. A food processor is not a yuppie kitchen luxury in my house, but an adaptive device. My gross motor skills are better but not great. I can

walk mile after mile, run and jump and skip and hop, but don't expect me to walk a balance beam. A tightrope would be murder; boulder hopping and rock climbing, not much better. I am not asking for pity. I am telling you about impairment.

Oliver defines disability as "the disadvantage or restriction of activity caused by a contemporary social organisation which takes no or little account of people who have physical [and/or cognitive/intellectual] impairments and thus excludes them from the mainstream of society."[2] I write slowly enough that cashiers get impatient as I sign my name to checks, stop talking to me, turn to my companions, hand them my receipts. I have failed timed tests, important tests, because teachers wouldn't allow me extra time to finish the sheer physical act of writing, wouldn't allow me to use a typewriter. I have been turned away from jobs because my potential employer believed my slow, slurred speech meant I was stupid. Everywhere I go people stare at me, in restaurants as I eat, in grocery stores as I fish coins out of my pocket to pay the cashier, in parks as I play with my dog. I am not asking for pity. I am telling you about disability.

In large part, disability oppression is about access. Simply being on Mount Adams, halfway up Air Line Trail, represents a whole lot of access. When access is measured by curb cuts, ramps, and whether they are kept clear of snow and ice in the winter; by the width of doors and height of counters; by the presence or absence of Braille, closed captions, ASL, and TDDs; my not being able to climb all the way to the very top of Mount Adams stops being about disability. I decided that turning around before reaching the summit was more about impairment than disability.

But even as I formed the thought, I could feel my resistance to it. To neatly divide disability from impairment doesn't feel right. My experience of living with CP has been so shaped by ableism—or to use Oliver's language, my experience of impairment has been so shaped by disability—that I have trouble separating the two. I understand the difference between failing a test because some stupid school rule won't give me more time and foiling to summit

Mount Adams because it's too steep and slippery for my feet. The first failure centers on a socially constructed limitation, the second on a physical one.

At the same time, both center on my body. The faster I try to write, the more my pen slides out of control, muscles spasm, then contract trying to stop the tremors, my shoulder and upper arm growing painfully tight. Even though this socially constructed limitation has a simple solution—access to a typewriter, computer, tape recorder, or person to take dictation—I experience the problem on a very physical level. In the case of the bodily limitation, my experience is similarly physical. My feet simply don't know the necessary balance. I lurch along from one rock to the next, catching myself repeatedly as I start to fall, quads quickly sore from exertion, tension, lack of momentum. These physical experiences, one caused by a social construction, the other by a bodily limitation, translate directly into frustration, making me want to crumple the test I can't finish, hurl the rocks I can't climb. This frustration knows no neat theoretical divide between disability and impairment. Neither does disappointment nor embarrassment. On good days, I can separate the anger I turn inward at my body from the anger that needs to be turned outward, directed at the daily ableist shit, but there is nothing simple or neat about kindling the latter while transforming the former. I decided that Oliver's model of disability makes theoretical and political sense but misses important emotional realities.

I thought of my nondisabled friends who don't care for camping, hiking, or backpacking. They would never spend a vacation sweat-drenched and breathing hard halfway up a mountain. I started to list their names, told Adrianne what I was doing. She reminded me of other friends who enjoy easy day hikes on smooth, well-maintained trails. Many of them would never even attempt the tumbled trail of rock I climbed for an hour and a half before turning around. We added their names to my list. It turned into a long roster. I decided that if part of what happened to me up there was about impairment, another part was about desire, my desire to climb mountains.

I thought about supercrips. Some of us—the boy who bats .486, the man who through-hikes the A.T.—accomplish something truly extraordinary and become supercrips. Others of us—the teenager with Down syndrome who has a boyfriend, the kid with CP who runs track and cross-country—lead entirely ordinary lives and still become supercrips. Nothing about having a boyfriend or running cross-country is particularly noteworthy. Bat .486 or have a boyfriend, it doesn't matter; either way we are astonishing. In the creation of supercrip stories, nondisabled people don't celebrate any particular achievement, however extraordinary or mundane. Rather, these stories rely upon the perception that disability and achievement contradict each other and that any disabled person who overcomes this contradiction is heroic.

To believe that achievement contradicts disability is to pair helplessness with disability, a pairing for which crips pay an awful price. The nondisabled world locks us away in nursing homes. It deprives us the resources to live independently.[3] It physically and sexually abuses us in astoundingly high numbers.[4] It refuses to give us jobs because even when a workplace is accessible, the speech impediment, the limp, the ventilator, the seeing-eye dog are read as signs of inability.[5] The price is incredibly high.

[. . .]

And here, supercrip turns complicated. On the other side of supercripdom lie pity, tragedy, and the nursing home. Disabled people know this, and in our process of knowing, some of us internalize the crap. We make supercrip our own, particularly the type that pushes into the extraordinary, cracks into our physical limitations. We use supercripdom as a shield, a protection, as if this individual internalization could defend us against disability oppression.

I climbed Mount Adams for an hour and a half scared, not sure I'd ever be able to climb down, knowing that on the next rock my balance could give out, and yet I climbed. Climbed surely because I wanted the summit, because of the love rumbling in my bones. But climbed also because I wanted to say, "Yes, I have CP, but see. See, watch me. I can climb mountains too." I wanted to prove myself once again. I wanted to overcome my CP.

Overcoming has a powerful grip. Back home, my friends told me, "But you can walk any of us under the table." My sister, a serious mountain climber who spends many a weekend high up in the North Cascades, told me, "I bet with the right gear and enough practice you *could* climb Mount Adams." A woman who doesn't know me told Adrianne, "Tell your friend not to give up. She can do anything she wants. She just has to want it hard enough." I told myself as Adrianne and I started talking about another trip to the Whites, "If I used a walking stick, and we picked a dry day and a different trail, maybe I could make it up to the top of Adams." I never once heard, "You made the right choice when you turned around." The mountain just won't let go.

III. HOME

I will never find home on the mountain. This I know. Rather home starts here in my body, in all that lies imbedded beneath my skin. My disabled body: born prematurely in the backwoods of Oregon, I was first diagnosed as "mentally retarded," and then later as having CP. I grew up to the words *cripple*, *retard*, *monkey*, *defect*, took all the staring into me and learned to shut it out.

My body violated: early on my father started raping me, physically abusing me in ways that can only be described as torture, and sharing my body with other people, mostly men, who did the same. I abandoned that body, decided to be a hermit, to be done with humans, to live among the trees, with the salmon, to ride the south wind bareback.

My white body: the only person of color in my hometown was an African American boy, adopted by a white family. I grew up to persistent rumors of a lynching tree way back in the hills, of the sheriff running people out of the county. For a long time after moving to the city, college scholarship in hand, all I could do was gawk at the multitude of humans: homeless people, their shopping carts and bedrolls, Black people, Chinese people, Chicanos,

drag queens and punks, vets down on Portland's Burnside Avenue, white men in their wool suits, limos shined to sparkle. I watched them all, sucking in the thick weave of Spanish, Cantonese, street talk, formal English. This is how I became aware of my whiteness.

My queer body: I spent my childhood, a tomboy not sure of my girlness, queer without a name for my queerness. I cut firewood on clearcuts, swam in the river, ran the beaches at Battle Rock and Cape Blanco. When I found dykes, fell in love for the first time, came into a political queer community, I felt as if I had found home again.

The body as home, but only if it is understood that bodies are never singular, but rather haunted, strengthened, underscored by countless other bodies. My alcoholic, Libertarian father and his father, the gravedigger, from whom my father learned his violence. I still dream about them sometimes, ugly dreams that leave me panting with fear in the middle of the night. One day I will be done with them. The white, working-class loggers, fishermen, and ranchers I grew up among: Les Smith, John Black, Walt Maya. Their ways of dressing, moving, talking helped shape my sense of self. Today when I hear queer activists say the word *redneck* like a cuss word, I think of those men, backs of their necks turning red in the summertime from long days of work outside, felling trees, pulling fishnets, baling hay. I think of my butchness, grounded there, overlaid by a queer, urban sensibility. A body of white, rural, working-class values. I still feel an allegiance to this body, even as I reject the virulent racism, the unexamined destruction of forest and riven. How could I possibly call my body home without the bodies of trees that repeatedly provided me refuge? Without queer bodies? Without crip bodies? Without transgender and transsexual bodies? Without the history of disabled people who worked as freaks in the freak show, displaying their bodies: Charles Stratton posed as General Tom Thumb, Hiram and Barney Davis billed as the "Wild Men from Borneo"? The answer is simple. I couldn't.

The body as home, but only if it is understood that place and community and culture burrow

deep into our bones. My earliest and most enduring sense of place is in the backwoods of Oregon,
where I grew up but no longer live, in a logging
and fishing town of a thousand that hangs on to
the most western edge of the continental United
States. To the west stretches the Pacific Ocean;
to the east the Siskiyou Mountains rise, not tall
enough to be mountains but too steep to be hills.
Portland is a seven-hour drive north; San Francisco, a twelve-hour drive south. Douglas fir and
chinook salmon, south wind whipping the ocean
into a fury of waves and surf, mark home for me.
Marked by the aching knowledge of environmental destruction, the sad truth of that town
founded on the genocide of Native peoples, the
Kwatami and Coquelle, Talkema and Latgawa. In
writing about the backwoods and the rural, white,
working-class culture found there, I am not being
nostalgic, reaching backward toward a re-creation
of the past. Rather I am reaching toward my bones.
When I write about losing that place, about living
in exile, I am putting words to a loss which also
grasps at my bones.

The body as home, but only if it is understood
that language too lives under the skin. I think of
the words *crip, queer, freak, redneck.* None of these
are easy words. They mark the jagged edge between
self-hatred and pride, the chasm between how the
dominant culture views marginalized peoples and
how we view ourselves, the razor between finding
home, finding our bodies, and living in exile, living
on the metaphoric mountain. Whatever our relationships with these words—whether we embrace
them or hate them, feel them draw blood as they
hit our skin or find them entirely fitting, refuse
to say them or simply feel uncomfortable in their
presence—we deal with their power every day. I
hear these words all the time. They are whispered
in the mirror as I dress to go out, as I straighten my
tie and shrug into my suit jacket; on the streets as
folks gawk at my trembling hands, stare trying to
figure out whether I'm a woman or man; in half the
rhetoric I hear from environmentalists and queer
activists, rhetoric where rural working-class people
get cast as clods and bigots. At the same time, I use

some, but not all, of these words to call out my
pride, to strengthen my resistance, to place myself
within community. *Crip, queer, freak, redneck* bur-
rowed into my body.

The body as home, but only if it is understood
that bodies can be stolen, fed lies and poison, torn
away from us. They rise up around me—bodies
stolen by hunger, war, breast cancer, AIDS, rape;
the daily grind of factory sweatshop, cannery saw-
mill; the lynching rope; the freezing streets; the
nursing home and prison. African American drag
performer Leonard/Lynn Vines, walking through
his Baltimore neighborhood, called a "drag queen
faggot bitch" and shot six times. Matt Shepard—
gay, white, young—tied to a fence post in Wyoming
and beaten to death. Some bodies are taken for
good; other bodies live on, numb, abandoned, full
of self-hate. Both have been stolen. Disabled people
cast as supercrips and tragedies; lesbian, gay, bi, and
trans peoples told over and over again that we are
twisted and unnatural; poor people made responsible for their own poverty. Stereotypes and lies
lodge in our bodies as surely as bullets. They live
and fester there, stealing the body.

The body as home, but only if it is understood
that the stolen body can be reclaimed. The bodies
irrevocably taken from us: we can memorialize them
in quilts, granite walls, candlelight vigils; remember and mourn them; use their deaths to strengthen
our will. And as for the lies and false images, we
need to name them, transform them, create something entirely new in their place, something that
comes close and finally true to the bone, entering
our bodies as liberation, joy, fury, hope, a will to
refigure the world. The body as home.

[. . .]

The mountain will never be home, and still I
have to remember it grips me. Supercrip lives inside
my body, ready and willing to push the physical limitations, to try the "extraordinary," because
down at the base of the mountain waits a nursing
home. I hang on to a vision. Someday after the revolution, disabled people will live ordinary lives, neither heroic nor tragic. *Crip, queer, freak, redneck* will

be mere words describing human difference. Super-crip will be dead; the nursing home, burnt down; the metaphoric mountain, collapsed in volcanic splendor. Post-revolution I expect there will still be

literal mountains I want to climb and can't, but I'll be able to say without doubt, without hesitation, "Let's turn around here. This one is too steep, too slippery for my feet."

NOTES

1. Quoted in David Hevey, *The Creatures Time Forgot: Photography and Disability Imagery* (London: Routledge, 1992), 9.
2. Ibid., 9.
3. Marta Russell, *Beyond Ramps* (Monroe, ME: Common Courage Press, 1998), 96–108.
4. Dick Sobsey, *Violence and Abuse in the Lives of People with Disabilities* (Baltimore: Paul H. Brookes Publishing, 1994), 68.
5. Joseph Shapiro, *No Pity: People with Disabilities Forging a New Civil Rights Movement* (New York: Times Books, 1994), 27–28.

7. • *Robin DiAngelo*

NOTHING TO ADD:
A Challenge to White Silence in Racial Discussions (2012)

Robin DiAngelo is an affiliate associate professor of education at the University of Washington with research interests in critical whiteness studies and critical discourse analysis. She is an award-winning educator and writer with numerous publications such as *White Fragility: Why It Is So Hard for White People to Talk About Racism* (2018), which debuted on the *New York Times* Bestseller List. She travels extensively giving keynote presentations on critical racial and social justice education to colleges, universities, foundations, civic organizations, and nonprofits. The reading here was published by the *Journal of Understanding and Dismantling Privilege* in 2012.

As unconscious, habits of white privilege do not merely go unnoticed. They actively thwart the process of conscious reflection on them, which allows them to seem nonexistent even as they continue to function

(Sullivan, 2006, pp. 5–6).

As a white person involved in national antiracist education in the United States for the last 15 years, I have had the unique opportunity to observe, across time and place, consistent patterns of white engagement in discussions about race. Although like most white people, I have been socialized to avoid explicit racial discussions, years of intentional commitment and practice have enabled me to continually challenge

Reprinted with permission of Robin DiAngelo.

this socialization. On a daily basis, I lead or participate in racial discussions, working with both primarily white groups and cross-racial groups—sometimes alone and sometimes with a co-facilitator of color.[1] My position leading these discussions allows me a kind of concentrated exposure to the discourses and practices taken up in racial dialogues that function to support white domination and privilege ("whiteness"). Although these discourses and practices have been well documented by others (see Bonilla-Silva, 2006; Picca & Feagin, 2007; Pollock, 2005; Trepagnier, 2007), I focus on the group dynamics involved in the production of whiteness in "real time"; the unspoken, unmarked norms and behavioral patterns that bolster the advantageous social position of whites at the expense of people of color.[2]

In cross-racial discussions it is easy to be distracted by white participants who dominate; indeed, facilitators spend a lot of energy strategizing about how to rein these participants in. For example, in the educational film, *The Color of Fear* (1994), in which a racially diverse group of men discuss racism, the white man who continually dominates the discussion and invalidates the men of color receives the greatest amount of attention in every discussion of the film I have attended. Yet there is another white man in the film who is at the other end of the participation spectrum, one who rarely speaks and has to be asked directly to join in. This participant receives little if any attention following the film, but his role in the discussion is no less racially salient. In this paper, I want to direct our attention to the often neglected end of the participation continuum—white silence—and provide an analysis of and challenge to that silence. Using whiteness theory as the frame, I will explicate the various ways that white silence functions in discussions of race to maintain white privilege, and challenge common white rationales for this silence. These rationales include: "It's just my personality—I rarely talk in groups"; "Everyone has already said what I was thinking"; "I don't know much about race, so I will just listen"; "I don't feel safe / don't want to be attacked, so I am staying quiet"; "I am trying to be careful not to dominate the discussion"; "I don't want to be misunderstood

/ say the wrong thing / offend anybody"; and "I don't have anything to add."[3] In so doing, I hope to provide an accessible challenge to silence for white participants in these discussions, regardless of the context in which it may occur—in the classroom, workplace, workshops, or professional development seminars. My goal is to unsettle the complacency that often surrounds this silence and motivate silent whites to break their silence.

THEORETICAL FRAMEWORK

Although mainstream definitions of racism are typically some variation of individual "race prejudice," which anyone across any race can have, whiteness scholars define racism as encompassing economic, political, social, and cultural structures, actions, and beliefs that systematize and perpetuate an unequal distribution of privileges, resources, and power among white people and people of color (Hilliard, 1992). This unequal distribution benefits whites and disadvantages people of color overall and at the group level (although individual whites may be "against" racism, they still benefit from a system that privileges their group). Racism is not fluid within the United States in that it does not flow back and forth, one day benefiting whites and another day (or even era) benefiting people of color. The direction of power between whites and people of color is historic, traditional, normalized, and deeply embedded in the fabric of U.S. society (Mills, 1999; Feagin, 2001). Whiteness refers to the dimensions of racism that serve to elevate white people over people of color (DiAngelo, 2006a); whiteness is the relationship of dominance between whites and people of color. This domination is enacted moment by moment on individual, interpersonal, cultural, and institutional levels (Frankenberg, 2001).

Frankenberg (1997) defines whiteness as multidimensional: "Whiteness is a location of structural advantage, of race privilege. Second, it is a 'standpoint,' a place from which white people look at ourselves, at others, and at society. Third, 'whiteness' refers to a set of cultural practices that are usually unmarked and unnamed" (p.1). Race is conceptualized as a constellation of processes and practices rather than as an isolated entity. These processes and practices include basic rights, values, beliefs, perspectives, and experiences purported to be commonly shared by all but that are actually only afforded in any consistent way to white people. Thus, to name whiteness is to refer to a set of relations that are historically, socially, politically, and culturally produced, and that are intrinsically linked to dynamic relations of white racial domination (Dyer, 1997; Lipsitz, 1999; Frankenberg, 2001; Roediger, 2007).

Whiteness is both "empty," in that it is normalized and thus typically unmarked, and content laden or "full," in that it generates norms and reference points, ways of conceptualizing the world, and ways of thinking about oneself and others, regardless of where one is positioned relationally within it (Dyer, 1997; Frankenberg, 2001). This definition counters the dominant representation of racism in mainstream education as isolated in discrete incidents that some individuals may or may not "do," and goes beyond naming specific privileges. Whiteness is dynamic, relational, and operating at all times and on myriad levels. Whites are theorized as actively shaped, affected, defined, and elevated through their racialization, and their individual and collective consciousness formed within it (Thandeka, 2000; Van Ausdale & Feagin, 2002; Morrison, 1992; Tatum, 1997).

Within the current racial construct, white racial comfort and sense of racial equilibrium are rooted in norms and traditions that uphold relations of inequality; one of these norms is to avoid talking openly about race, especially in mixed-race groups. When white normative taboos against talking directly about race are broken, especially within the context of deliberately challenging the norms that hold racial inequality in place, it is uncomfortable and destabilizing for many whites, and they will seek to regain their comfort and sense of racial stability (DiAngelo, in press). Therefore, whatever moves whites make in a racial discussion that are intended to regain or maintain racial comfort or the racial equilibrium that has been interrupted by the

discussion itself necessarily work to maintain traditional racial relations. In this context, when whites employ silence to maintain some degree of comfort, that silence functions (albeit seldom explicitly) as a means to regain white dominance.

ANTIRACIST EDUCATION

Antiracist educators, like whiteness theorists, conceptualize racism as a multilayered, multidimensional, ongoing, adaptive process that functions to maintain, reinforce, reproduce, normalize, and render invisible white power and privilege. Antiracist education deliberately goes beyond the "celebrating differences" approach common to most diversity training and centers the analysis on the social, cultural, and institutional power that so profoundly shapes the meaning and outcome of racial difference. Antiracism education recognizes racism as embedded in all aspects of society and the socialization process; no one who is born into and raised in Western culture can escape being socialized to participate in these relations (Van Ausdale & Feagin, 2002). Antiracist education seeks to interrupt these relations of inequality by educating people to identify, name, and challenge the norms, patterns, traditions, structures, and institutions that keep racism and white supremacy in place. A key aspect of this education process is to "raise the consciousness" of white people about what racism is and how it works. To accomplish this, the dominant conceptualization of racism as isolated to individual acts that only some (bad) individuals do, rather than as a system we are all enmeshed in, must be countered.

Race is a dynamic and ongoing production; there is no race-neutral space. As Dyer (1997) states, race is "never not a factor, never not in play" (p.1). Focusing on specific incidences of racism rather than on racism as an all-encompassing system makes a personal, interpersonal, cultural, historical, and structural analysis difficult (Macedo & Bartolome, 1999). Using a relational and systematic definition of whiteness and racism allows whites to explore their own relationship to racism and move beyond isolated incidences and/or intentions.

In the following section, I focus on one key way that whiteness is reproduced within the context of antiracist education: white silence. I discuss common white rationales for white silence in discussions of race, and challenge these rationales from an antiracist framework. I acknowledge that silence can, of course, be a constructive mode of white engagement in racial discussions, by differentiating between the temporary and contextual silence that results from active listening and silence as the primary or only mode of engagement.

OVERALL EFFECTS OF WHITE SILENCE

In racial dialogue, white silence functions overall to shelter white participants by keeping their racial perspectives hidden and thus protected from exploration or challenge. Not contributing one's perspectives serves to ensure that those perspectives cannot be expanded. While one can, of course, gain deeper understanding through listening, there are several problems with this being one's primary mode of engagement. Listening alone leaves everyone else to carry the weight of the discussion. And, of course, if everyone chose this mode no discussion (and hence no learning) would occur at all. On the other hand, one may have something to say that is insightful and contributes to everyone's learning, but if a lack of confidence can't be overcome, everyone loses.

The role of silent whites is critical to protecting whiteness, for white dominance depends, in part, on the silence of other whites (Mura, 1999; Picca & Feagin, 2007). In the context of particularly difficult discussions, white silence serves to embolden explicitly resistant participants because it establishes that no challenge will be forthcoming, and can even imply agreement. Even if whites who are silent find the behavior of their peers problematic, their silence allows explicitly resistant participants to continually dictate the agenda of the discussion and rally resources around themselves as facilitators (and others)

work to move them forward. At the minimum, the resistant participants receive no social penalty from other whites, and the silence effectively maintains white solidarity. Although silent whites might recognize and be troubled by the behavior of some of their white cohorts, they ultimately maintain their white privilege by not contesting this behavior. An internal awareness of whiteness is a necessary start, but if it isn't accompanied by a change in behavior, alliance with whiteness remains intact.

Silence has different effects depending on what move it follows. For example, if white silence follows a story shared by a person of color about the impact of racism on their lives, that silence serves to invalidate the story. People of color who take the social risk of revealing the impact of racism only to be met by white silence are left with their vulnerability unreciprocated. Whites could offer validation, for example, by sharing how the story impacted them, what insight they gained from hearing it, or what questions it raised for them. Conversely, when white silence follows a particularly problematic move made by a white participant, that silence supports the move by offering no interruption; in essence, white silence operates as a normative mechanism for these tactics. When white silence follows a white, antiracist stand (such as challenging one's fellow whites to racialize their perspectives), it serves to isolate the person who took that stand. This isolation is a powerful social penalty and an enticement to return to the comfort of white solidarity. In this context, white silence denies the support that is critical to other whites working to develop antiracist practice.

WHEN IS WHITE SILENCE A CONSTRUCTIVE MOVE IN RACIAL DIALOGUE?

White silence, when used strategically from an antiracist framework, can be a constructive move in racial discussions. Indeed, too much white participation simply reinscribes the white dominance and centrality embedded in the larger society. I am arguing that white silence based on the rationale

I will discuss in this article is not a constructive move. I am also arguing against white silence as one's default mode of engagement. What differentiates constructive use of white silence from a reinforcement of white racism is that the person is using his or her best judgment, based in an antiracist framework and at each phase of the discussion, of how to engage with the goal of deepening racial self-knowledge, building antiracist community, and interrupting traditional racist power relations. No one way for whites to engage is likely to be effective in all contexts, but antiracist white engagement asks that one continually grapple with the question of how best to interrupt white power and privilege. The following are generally good times for whites to just listen when in inter-racial groups:

- When people of color are discussing the sensitive issue of internalized racial oppression.
- When one tends to take up a lot of airspace and, in recognition of the history of white dominance, is trying to pull back and have a less dominant voice.
- When other whites have already spoken first and most to an issue in the discussion.
- When intentionally trying not to speak first and most in the discussion.
- When a person of color has spoken and one feels drawn to re-explain, clarify, or "add to" his or her point (and thereby "say it better" and have the last word on the matter).
- When a facilitator asks for whites to just listen, hold back, or not go first.

The above list addresses silence in the context of racially mixed groups. In all-white settings, the dynamics are different because whites are not navigating their relationships to people of color in the group. In the context of all-white groups, white silence functions to pass up the opportunity to explore one's racial perspectives, feelings, blind spots, and assumptions without fear of causing microaggressions[4] to people of color. To not take advantage of a structured discussion in an all-white group prevents community building and antiracist alignment

among whites, and fails to support those whites who are actively taking risks and being vulnerable in the pursuit of antiracist growth. In this context, the main reason for white silence should be for periods of personal reflection, to provide time and space for other more reticent whites who need a slower pacing to speak up, and because the person is someone who tends to speak often. These forms of silence can more authentically be seen as active listening.

RATIONALES FOR WHITE SILENCE AND AN ANTIRACIST CHALLENGE

"IT'S JUST MY PERSONALITY; I RARELY TALK IN GROUPS."

Our personalities are not separate from the society in which we were raised.

All whites are socialized in a white-dominant society. Seeing one's patterns of engagement as merely a function of a unique personality rather than as sociopolitical and coproduced in relation with social others is a privilege only afforded to white people (McIntosh, 1988). By focusing on ourselves as individuals, whites are able to conceptualize the patterns in our behavior that have a racist impact as "just our personality" and not connected to intergroup dynamics. For example, I might be an extrovert and talk over people when I am engaged in a discussion. I can say, "That is just my personality, I do that to everyone. That is how we talked at the dinner table in my family. And because I do it to everyone, it can't be racism." However, when I talk over a person of color, the impact of that behavior is different because we bring the racial history of our groups with us (DiAngelo, 2006c). While white people tend to see themselves as individuals, people of color tend to see us as white individuals, thus the meaning of cutting off or talking over a person of color is very different. Conversely, remaining silent in an inter-racial dialogue also has a cross-racial impact. Antiracist action requires us to challenge our patterns and respond differently than we normally would (Thompson, 2001). The freedom to remain oblivious to that fact, with no sense that this obliviousness has any consequences of importance, is a form of white privilege. In effect, we are saying, "I will not adapt to you or this context, I will continue to act the way I always act and you will have to adapt to me." Participants of color seldom see themselves as having the option to disengage or withdraw from the discussion based solely on their personal preferences for engagement (DiAngelo, 2010). They understand that dominant culture does not position them as individuals and has a different set of stereotypical expectations for them. If they hold back, they reinforce these expectations, a concern that puts constant pressure on them. Two people of color in a recent cross-racial discussion express these expectations:

RICH (POC): Well, in terms of putting ourselves out there, I think I put myself out there too. But if I was to come into this group and not put myself out there, everybody would look at me kind of strange, because I'm a person of color. So, oh, my god, this person of color is not putting himself out there. What's up with that? This is a dialogue about race; you're supposed to put yourself out there. So, I mean, Tiffany has put herself out there, but I don't know how much Tiffany should be commended—well, I guess she should be commended in the sense that she is like probably the only white person that put herself out there. But I think everybody should be putting themselves out there.

LAURA (POC): I feel frustrated by the fact that white people can just choose to disengage, where I'm supposed to say something, and like if I don't say something, then I'm the quiet Asian one or something like that. And so, I feel like I need to put myself out there even more just to contradict that. And that gets really tiring to me . . . to constantly feel like I have to display something, when—even if I don't feel like saying anything; I might want to step back, but I'm conscious all the time of what that looks like to people.

As these two participants make clear, the pressure of being seen as people of color compels them to speak up, even when they don't want to. Not speaking up because one doesn't want to—without penalty—is a privilege they are not afforded; if they remain silent they don't challenge the racism that constricts their lives. Their comments also illustrate the difference in the way white people and people of color often conceptualize themselves. Whites tend to see themselves as unique individuals and not members of a racial group whose actions represent that group. People of color, who don't have that luxury, want whites to meet them half way—to understand white patterns at the group level and push through the temporary discomfort of not engaging in their "preferred" mode in order to challenge those patterns. Challenging whiteness requires, as Rich expresses above, "putting ourselves out there" and engaging differently in order to break problematic racial dynamics.

"EVERYONE HAS ALREADY SAID WHAT I WAS THINKING" OR "I DON'T HAVE MUCH TO ADD."

Perhaps others have expressed our sentiments, but no one will express them the way that we will. It's essential to the discussion to hear everyone's voice, and even vocalizing one or two sentences makes a difference. Further, it is important to support those who have voiced our perspective—to validate it and give people of color a read of the room; they cannot assume everyone has already said what we are thinking. In fact, given the history of harm between white people and people of color, people of color may assume whites haven't spoken because they are not aligned with what has been said and don't want to reveal that misalignment. It is important for us to contribute our thoughts in order to demonstrate to people of color that what they have shared has made a difference in terms of helping increase our understanding. If we are moved or gained insight from what someone shared, we should say so, even if others have also said it.

Sometimes the reticence to speak is based on a perception that those who have expressed similar thoughts are far more articulate, and that we won't be as eloquent. In my experience, openness, humility, and vulnerability are the most important aspects of participation, not perfection. Positioning ourselves as having less of value to contribute than others in the group may be rooted in dominant culture's expectation that knowledge should be a form of "correct" information. Yet sharing what we are thinking, whether "right" or "wrong," articulate or clumsy, is important in terms of building trust, conveying empathy, or validating a story or perspective.

"I AM TRYING TO BE CAREFUL NOT TO DOMINATE THE DISCUSSION."

While it is important not to dominate discussions in general and, as a white person, not to dominate an inter-racial discussion in particular, the problem with this strategy is that it is inflexible. Antiracist practice asks us to think strategically—to be racially attentive to who is talking, when, how much, and for how long. As a white person in the discussion, we need to ask ourselves when it is a constructive time to speak up and when is it most constructive to just listen. The more practiced we become in racial discussions, the more easily we will be able to make sound strategic judgments about where and when to enter. When we remain silent we leave the weight of the dialogue on either people of color or other, more dominant whites. If these dominant whites are expressing hostility, we aren't challenging them; if they are taking risks, we aren't supporting them. When one is trying not to dominate the discussion and so never joins in, one errs on the opposite side of domination—ineffective passivity.

"I FEEL INTIMIDATED BY PEOPLE IN THIS GROUP WHO HAVE POWER OVER ME."

Complex sociopolitical power relations circulate in all groups, and there are other identities besides race at play in any discussion. While one is in a power position as a white person, there are other identities that may obscure that sense of that power because they position us in a subordinated (or "target") position—i.e., gender or class. Because we "swim against the current" in our target identities, they are generally more salient to us. However, not being

salient does not mean inoperative; indeed, much of the power we derive from our dominant identities is in its unremarkable, taken-for-granted status. In a setting in which I feel intimidated because my target identities are more salient to me, this feeling of intimidation may indeed be coming from a place of internalized inferiority. But, in practice, my silence colludes with racism and ultimately benefits me by protecting my white privilege and maintaining racial solidarity with other white people. This solidarity connects and realigns me with white people across other lines of difference that separate us, such as gender or class. When I work to keep my race privilege salient and speak up in this context, I not only break white solidarity, I simultaneously interrupt (and thus work to heal the "lie" of) my internalized inferiority where I am also in a target position.

In situations in which we may share key identities such as race and gender with someone but fear there may be repercussions because he or she holds more power in the specific context than we do—e.g., I am a staff worker and my supervisor is in the room, or the professor who is grading me is in the group—a different kind of courage is needed. This is the courage to put our integrity to do the right thing above the possibility of repercussions. Ultimately, we have to make a decision. Do I protect myself and maintain white solidarity and power, or do I authentically engage in antiracist practice?

"I DON'T KNOW MUCH ABOUT RACE, SO I WILL JUST LISTEN."

Dyer (1997) states: "There is a specificity to white representations, but it does not reside in a set of stereotypes so much as in narrative structural positions, rhetorical tropes and habits of perception" (p. 12). One of these narrative structural positions is that of racial innocence. This position functions as a kind of blindness; an inability to think about whiteness as an identity or as a "state" of being that would or could have an impact on one's life, and thus be a source of meaning. Because whites are socially positioned as individuals, or "just people" (the writer, the man, the friend) while people of color are always positioned as members of a racial group (the Latino writer, the Asian man, the black friend) we have the privilege of seeing ourselves as outside of race and thus unfamiliar with it (DiAngelo, 2006c). The white claim that one does not know much about race is particularly problematic because, while it positions whiteness as "innocence," it simultaneously reinforces the projection of race onto people of color—they have race, not us, and thus are the holders of racial knowledge. In so doing, we position ourselves as standing outside of hierarchical social relations—as if the oppression of people of color occurs in a vacuum. White obliviousness is not benign; it has material consequences because it allows us to ignore the impact of racism on people of color while enjoying its benefits at their expense.

Many whites have not thought about race in the way that antiracist education conceptualizes it, but once we are introduced, it's important to share our thoughts. If I have never thought about these issues before, what am I thinking about them now as a result of the discussion? What specifically is new to me? What questions do I have? What insights am I having? What emotions am I feeling? Why might I have never thought about these things before, and what role might this play in keeping racism in place? In other words, how might racism depend on white people not thinking about these issues? Being new to the concepts is not an end point or a pass to only listen and not speak; it is a key entry point into the discussion and into furthering self-knowledge.

While as white people we may not have thought explicitly about race from an antiracist perspective, we do have knowledge of how we are socialized into denial of ourselves as racialized. We can speak to why we believe we don't know anything about race—for example, if we don't know much about it, who do we believe does and why do they have this knowledge when we do not? Further, why have we not sought out this knowledge prior to this conversation? Many white people who grew up in segregated neighborhoods and attended segregated schools with primarily white teachers often believe that they were completely unaware of race until later

in childhood. I have found a series of reflection questions helpful at unpacking this belief: At what age was I aware that people of color existed, and black people in particular? (Most whites acknowledge that they knew by age five, if not earlier.) What was I told about them? Where did they live? Why did they live there and not in my neighborhood? What was it like where they lived? Was it considered nice and was I encouraged to go to the places where they lived? Was I taught that I had lost anything by their absence? If I was not taught I had lost anything by not knowing people of color, what has that meant for my relationships with them? While these questions were not likely explicitly addressed in childhood, somehow we had to make sense of our racially segregated worlds. Explorations such as these have the potential to reveal our racial paradigms, an essential precursor to antiracist action; they are a great place to start engaging in the discussion without depending on people of color to teach us.

"I ALREADY KNOW ALL THIS."

While the previous rationale positions the listener as racially innocent and thus only able to absorb the discussion, this rationale positions the listener as so sophisticated as to be beyond the discussion. This claim gives the message to the people of color in the group that there is nothing to be gained from what they might share—their stories, experiences, perspectives, or feelings. This claim is particularly problematic because it conveys superiority; reinscribing the historical invalidation of people of color as not having any knowledge of value to white people, elevating oneself above other whites in the group and the potential to work together with them against racism, and accomplishing all of this by presenting oneself as so advanced as to be beyond the discussion.

The antiracist framework undergirding these discussions holds that racism is a deeply embedded, complex system that will not end in our lifetimes, and certainly not end through our complacency. If one sincerely believes one's understanding of racism is more advanced than the discussion allows for (which can happen when the majority of the white participants are very new to the concepts and the facilitators assess that they must move at a slower pace), then the antiracist way to engage is to make strategic points that will help guide the other white people. Whites who have more knowledge than the majority of the group are in an excellent position to "mentor from the sidelines." They can share their process and how they came to their current understanding, validate the struggle while reinforcing its worthiness, take the discussion deeper, and back up the facilitators and participants of color.

We may have an intellectual grasp of the dynamics, but awareness of racial inequity alone is not enough to trump our participation. White people, while served well by the dynamics of whiteness, are simultaneously in a prime position to interrupt it, yet to do so we must take unambiguous action. Claiming that we already know is meaningless without demonstration of that knowledge, and remaining silent is not a demonstration of antiracist action or understanding. People of color involved in antiracist endeavors generally assume that all whites have a racist perspective unless demonstrated otherwise (Sue, 2003; hooks, 1995). To not explicitly take up an antiracist stance in such a context can only reinforce the perception that we are actively choosing to align with whiteness. Being "advanced" is not a reason for us to disengage; the disengagement itself makes the claim unconvincing.

"I NEED TIME TO PROCESS."

In my experience, participants who use this rationale seldom return after processing and share the results, suggesting that this may be a deflection against "putting ourselves out there," rather than an expression of a sincere difference in how people process information. We may indeed need time to process, but taking the time we need is still a privilege not everyone can afford. At the minimum, we can try articulating what we are hearing that we need to process, and then let the group know that these are new ideas, that we are feeling overwhelmed, and we want to let things settle in. At the minimum, we

can let the group know why we need the time to process and what we will be processing, rather than remain silent and leave others to wonder. When we have had time to process, we can share the results with the group.

It's also helpful to distinguish between the need to process and the need to sound controlled, correct, and coherent. If composure is what we are waiting for, we are working at cross-purposes to the discussion. Emotions, confusion, inner conflict, and inarticulation are all usually welcome in racial discussions. Vulnerability and openness build trust, and while thoughtfulness and respect are critical, control and composure are not necessary and can be counterproductive.

"I DON'T WANT TO BE MISUNDERSTOOD."

To not speak up in case we are misunderstood is to protect our perspective from deepening or expanding. It is not possible, given the embeddedness of racism in the culture, for white people not to have problematic racial assumptions and blind spots. Of course, it is uncomfortable and even embarrassing to see that we lack certain forms of knowledge, but we can't gain the knowledge we lack if we don't take risks. It is imperative that we enter the discussion with a willingness (even enthusiasm) to have our assumptions uncovered so we can increase our knowledge and cross-racial skills, for how will we realize that we have misconceptions and only a partial view if we don't share our views and open them up to exploration?

When whites do feel misunderstood in a racial discussion, it is usually because we were given feedback on an assumption we made or a blind spot we have in our racial awareness. Sadly, pointing out gaps in a white person's understanding is often experienced as being attacked or judged. When we insist that the issue is that we were misunderstood, rather than engage with the possibility that we are the ones who don't understand the feedback we have received, we close ourselves off to further learning. By insisting that the problem is that we have been misunderstood, we place the responsibility for the "misunderstanding" onto those who we believe have misunderstood us—usually the participants of color. There is no opening in this position for the possibility that the lack of understanding could be ours. If we are unable or unwilling to consider this possibility, or the corollary possibility that people of color might have information that we do not, we cannot gain new insight into how racism functions. If the only way one will engage in cross-racial discussion is to never be challenged, there is minimal point to the discussion.

"I DON'T FEEL SAFE."

Sub-discourses: "I don't want to be attacked." "I don't want to be judged."

The safety discourse, while one of the most familiar and understandable, is also one of the most problematic. On the surface it conveys a kind of vulnerability and desire for protection. Unfortunately, it rests on a lack of understanding of historical and ongoing institutional, cultural, and interpersonal power relations between white people and people of color. While the feelings may be real for white people struggling with a sense of safety, some reflection may help clarify the difference between actual safety and what is more realistically a concern about comfort. To help differentiate safety from comfort, one might ask what safety means from a position of social, cultural, historical, and institutional power? If one does not fear that one is in actual physical harm, then some reflection on what one fears is actually at risk can offer much insight. Often, it is our self-image: Because we have been taught that only bad people participate in racism, we often fear that if it is somehow revealed that we participate in racism, we will lose face and be judged. Indeed, many white people feel very uncomfortable in racial discussions, but this discomfort is actually a positive sign, for it indicates that the status quo (unnamed and unexamined racism) is being challenged. It is therefore critical that we feel uncomfortable and not confuse discomfort with danger. As for being judged, there is no human objectivity—all people judge and we cannot protect ourselves from judgments in

any context. But feeling judged, while dismaying, should not be confused with safety.

Further, the language of safety is not without significance in this context. By employing terms that connote physical threat, we tap into the classic discourse of people of color (particularly African Americans) as dangerous and violent. This discourse twists the actual direction of danger that exists between whites and people of color. The history of extensive and brutal violence perpetrated by whites; slavery, genocide, lynching, whipping, forced sterilization, and medical experimentation, to mention a few, is trivialized when we claim we don't feel safe or are under attack when in the rare situation of merely talking about race with people of color. By implying potential victimization, we obscure the power and privilege we wield and have wielded for centuries. The safety discourse also illustrates how fragile and ill equipped most white people are to confront racial tensions, and our subsequent projection of this tension onto people of color (DiAngelo, 2006b; Morrison, 1992). People of color seldom have the luxury of withdrawing because they don't feel safe. It doesn't benefit people of color to remain silent, as it does us. To not put themselves "out there" makes them complicit in their own oppression, as Rich and Laura express above. If people of color are not self-advocating and pushing back against whiteness, they can't depend on white people to do it for them, as has been amply demonstrated time and again in racial discussions—often via white silence. While the pushing back we might get from people of color can be very uncomfortable, that discomfort is a key way to unsettle our world views and create the stretching and growing that is necessary for authentic change.

"I DON'T WANT TO OFFEND ANYBODY."

Similar to "I don't want to be misunderstood," this rationale allows one to protect oneself against alternative perspectives, responses, constructive conflict, or taking the risks that could potentially expand one's awareness. This rationale is unfair to people of color because, if we fear offending, it can only be assumed that is because we are having offensive thoughts or are hostile toward what is being said. If this is the case, to not put our disagreement into the room is to deny the group knowledge of where we are coming from and the ability for others to make any adjustments they might need in response to our hostility. If we are not hostile to what is being said but just worried that we may inadvertently offend someone, how will we learn that what we think or say is offensive if we don't share it and open ourselves up to feedback? In effect, by not taking this intentional opportunity to discover which ideas we hold are offensive, we protect these ideas and enable them to surface at a later date and offend someone else. In the unique and often rare learning environment of racial discussions, to remain silent so as not to offend is to offend twice—once through our silence and again in our unwillingness to discover and change racially problematic dimensions in our thinking. If unsure, we can simply offer our thoughts with openness and humility rather than as declarations of certainty or truth: "Please let me know if something is off in my thinking, but here is how I am responding to this . . . ," Can you help me understand why . . . ?" "I have often heard . . . what are your thoughts on that?"

"Anything I say won't be listened to because I am white."

At the point that this discourse emerges, we have usually been challenged in the way we conceptualize race—either directly or via the content of the dialogue, and we are unable to rise to that challenge. Clearly we have not understood the objectives of the discussion or the theoretical framework that it rests on: There is a relationship of unequal power between white people and people of color that all of us have been taught to collude in, but that only white people benefit from. One way that antiracist education tries to interrupt this relationship is by acknowledging the power differential and affirming the perspectives of those whose voices dominant society seldom hears or validates (Schiele, 2000). In turn, challenging white perspectives is necessary because the way that dominant culture understands race actually functions to hold racism in place. The issue is not that we won't be listened to because we are white; the issue is that—counter to what we are accustomed to—our perspectives will be challenged at times and are not going to be affirmed just because we are white.

A NOTE ON THE SILENCE OF PEOPLE OF COLOR IN RACIAL DISCUSSIONS

Although this analysis is limited to a white person addressing white silence in racial discussions, I would be remiss if I did not at least raise the issue of the silence of people of color and offer some preliminary thoughts. First, as should be clear via my argument thus far, the silence of whites has a very different foundation and impact than the silence of people of color, based on the unequal positioning of the two groups in society; these silences are not equivalent. For Laura and Rich, quoted above, silence is generally not an option. However, there are several key reasons why people of color, including Laura and Rich, may at times choose silence in a racial discussion, including: (1) in response to resistance or hostility expressed (consciously or not) by white participants (this unconscious expression of hostility could include silence based on many of the reasons discussed above); (2) a lack of trust based on well-founded experience that one will be penalized for challenging white perspectives; (3) a sense of hopelessness in the face of white denial; (4) taking risks and being vulnerable about one's racial experiences and perspectives and being met with silence, argumentation, or rationalization, all of which function as forms of invalidation; (5) being outnumbered in ratio to white people and assessing that there are no allies present for support were one to challenge white privilege; or (6) being acutely aware of the power differentials and choosing to protect oneself in the face of inevitable hurt.

It is important to keep in mind that so much of how white racism operates is invisible to and/or denied by white people; a room that seems perfectly comfortable to white people may not feel that way to people of color. In fact, given white racism as the status quo, the more comfortable a space is for white people, the more likely it is to be harmful to people of color. Further (and especially for well-intended whites) because we are deeply invested materially, psychically, socially, and politically as the producers and beneficiaries of white privilege, the very behaviors we think are benign or even supportive (as I have argued above) may be the very behaviors that are so toxic to people of color. Adding to these roots of our denial, our very identities as good people rests on our not seeing our racism. As Sullivan (2006) states, "As unconscious habit, white privilege operates as nonexistent and actively works to disrupt attempts to reveal its existence" (pp. 1–2). In other words, whites work hard not to see white privilege, which is a key way we keep it protected and intact. In this context, it should be clear why people of color might choose silence.

IN CONCLUSION

It may be clear at this point that much of the rationale for white silence is based on a racial paradigm that posits racism as isolated to individual acts of meanness (McIntosh, 1988) that only some people do. This dominant paradigm of racism as discreet, individual, intentional, and malicious acts makes it unlikely that whites will see our silence as a function of, and support to, racism and white privilege.

To challenge one's most comfortable patterns of engagement in a racial dialogue, while it may be counterintuitive, is necessarily to interrupt one's racial socialization. From an antiracist perspective, we can assume that our racial socialization has not prepared us to be competent in cross-racial relationship building. Although consistent silence in racial discussions often feels benign to those who practice it, in this paper I have argued that no form of white engagement that is not informed by an antiracist perspective is benign. Going against one's "grain" for engagement, while difficult, is necessary and will result in the least harmful and most authentic and rewarding engagement. A white student expresses this powerfully in a class-assigned journal entry. In response to a person of color in the class sharing the impact of a recent racist incident, she writes:

As Jane finished speaking, and I raised my hand, I became completely overwhelmed by the enormity of what she had said. I was terrified that anything that I said would seem trivial or, even more frightening, would make things worse. I felt paralyzed by the moment, feeling in my stomach how utterly raw and open Jane seemed—but my need to speak, to address what she had said, despite the probability that I would mess it up, was greater than my guilt or my shame or my desire to remain quiet. I realized that the notion that I can make it worse—that I do have that power—requires that I speak. I realized that, in our silence, we are complicit. In my silence for the past four weeks of this course—and for a lifetime before it—I have been complicit. I no longer feel comfortable letting my silence speak for me—it is inarticulate and offensive. I would rather blunder along than stay silent. I hope the people around me, who witness my blundering, can see beyond the errors . . . because remaining silent—maintaining my complicity—is no longer conscionable (Student Journal, July 5, 2009).

NOTES

1. Of course whites frequently engage in discussions of race, in both implicit and explicit ways, e.g., discourses on "good neighborhoods and schools" and racialized comments and jokes. I am not referring to this form of discussion on race. I am referring to intentional facilitated explorations of our racial socialization, feelings, and perspectives for the purpose of deepening cross-racial awareness, either in all-white or inter-racial groups.

2. Of course whites frequently engage in discussions of race, in both implicit and explicit ways, e.g., discourses on "good neighborhoods and schools" and racialized comments and jokes. I am not referring to this form of discussion on race. I am referring to intentional facilitated explorations of our racial socialization, feelings, and perspectives for the purpose of deepening cross-racial awareness, either in all-white or inter-racial groups.

3. A special thank you to Anika Nailah and John Kent for invaluable feedback on earlier drafts.
4. Microaggressions are the myriad slights that people of color endure on a daily basis, most often from well-intended whites. Consistently being met by white silence

in an inter-racial discussion, even when well intended, often functions as a microaggression towards people of color. See Sue et al. (2007). Racial microaggressions in everyday life. *American Psychologist, 62*(4), 271–286.

REFERENCES

Applebaum, B. (1997). Good liberal intentions are not enough! Racism, intentions and moral responsibility. *Journal of Moral Education*, 26(4), 409–421.

Bonilla-Silva, E. (2006). *Racism without racists: Color-blind racism and the persistence of racial inequality in the United States* (2nd ed.). New York: Rowman & Littlefield.

DiAngelo, R. (2006a). The production of whiteness in education: Asian international students in a college classroom. *Teachers College Record*, 108(10), 1960–1982.

DiAngelo, R. (2006b). "I'm leaving!": White fragility in racial dialogue. In B. McMahon & D. Armstrong (Eds.), *Inclusion in urban educational environments: Addressing issues of diversity, equity, and social justice (pp. 213–240)*. Centre for Leadership and Diversity. Ontario Institute for Studies in Education of the University of Toronto.

DiAngelo, R. (2006c). My race didn't trump my class: Using oppression to face privilege. *Multicultural Perspectives*, 8(1), 51–56.

DiAngelo, R. (2010). Why can't we all just be individuals?: The discourse of individualism in anti-racist education. *InterActions: UCLA Journal of Education and Information Studies*, 6(1), 1548–3320.

Dyer, R. (1997). *White*. New York: Routledge.

Feagin, J. (2001). *Racist America*. New York: Routledge.

Frankenberg, R. (1997). Introduction: Local Whitenesses, localizing Whiteness. In R. Frankenberg (Ed.), *Displacing Whiteness: Essays in social and cultural criticism* (pp. 1–33). Durham, NC: Duke University Press.

Frankenberg, R. (2001). Mirage of an unmarked Whiteness. In B. Rasmussen, E. Klinerberg, I. Nexica, & M. Wray (Eds.), *The making and unmaking of Whiteness* (pp. 72–96). Durham, NC: Duke University Press.

Hilliard, A. (1992). *Racism: Its origins and how it works. Paper presented at the meeting of the Mid-West Association for the Education of Young Children*, Madison, WI.

hooks, b. (1995). *Killing rage*. New York: Henry Holt.

Lipsitz, G. (1999). *The possessive investment in whiteness: How white people profit from identity politics*. Philadelphia, PA: Temple University Press.

Macedo, D., & Bartolome, L. (1999). *Dancing with bigotry: Beyond the politics of tolerance*. New York: St. Martin's Press.

McIntosh, P. (1988). White privilege and male privilege: A personal account of coming to see correspondence through work in women's studies. In M. Anderson & P. Hill Collins (Eds.), *Race, class, and gender: An anthology* (pp. 94–105). Belmont, CA: Wadsworth.

Mills, C. (1999). *The racial contract*. Ithaca, NY: Cornell University Press.

Morrison, T. (1992). *Playing in the dark: Whiteness in the literary imagination*. Cambridge, MA: Harvard University Press.

Mura, D. (1999). Explaining racism to my daughter. In T. B. Jelloun, C. Volk, & P. Williams (Eds.), *Racism explained to my daughter* (pp. 93–137). New York: The New Press.

Picca, L., & Feagin, J. (2007). *Two-faced racism: Whites in the backstage and frontstage*. New York: Routledge.

Pollock, M. (2005). *Colormute: Race talk dilemmas in an American school*. Princeton, NJ: Princeton University Press.

Roediger, D. (2007). *The wages of whiteness: Race and the making of the American working class* (2nd ed.). New York: Verso.

Schiele, J. H. (2000). *Human service and the Afro-centric paradigm*. Binghamton, NY: Haworth.

Sue, D. W. (2003). *Overcoming our racism: The journey to liberation*. San Francisco: Jossey-Bass.

Sullivan, S. (2006). *Revealing whiteness: The unconscious habits of racial privilege*. Bloomington, IN: Indiana University Press.

Tatum, B. (1997). *"Why are all the black kids sitting together in the cafeteria?": And other conversations about race*. New York: Basic Books.

Thandeka (2000). *Learning to be White*. New York: Continuum Publishing Group.

Thompson, B. (2001). *A promise and a way of life: White antiracist activism*. Minneapolis, MN: University of Minnesota Press.

Trepagnier, B. (2007). *Silent racism: How well-meaning white people perpetuate the racial divide*. Boulder, CO: Paradigm Publishers.

Van Ausdale, D., & Feagin, J. (2002). *The first R: How children learn racism*. New York: Rowman & Littlefield.

8. • *Audre Lorde*

THERE IS NO HIERARCHY OF OPPRESSIONS (1983)

Audre Lorde, born in New York in 1934 to Caribbean immigrant parents Frederic Byron and Linda Belmar Lorde, self-identified as a "black feminist lesbian mother poet." She dedicated her life and creative work to the struggle for liberation of all oppressed people, elucidating how racism, sexism, and homophobia work together to create injustices. Among her eighteen publications is the highly acclaimed collection of poetry *The Black Unicorn* (1978), which deals with lesbian relationships and love in accessible and affective ways. Her essays in *The Cancer Journals* (1980), *I Am Your Sister: Black Women Organizing Across Sexualities* (1985), *Sister Outsider: Essays and Speeches* (1984), and *Zami: A New Spelling of My Name* (1982) are required reading for anyone interested in feminist, queer, antiracist social justice work. It was a great loss to so many communities when she died in 1992 of cancer.

I was born Black, and a woman. I am trying to become the strongest person I can become to live the life I have been given and to help effect change toward a liveable future for this earth and for my children. As a Black, lesbian, feminist, socialist, poet, mother of two including one boy and a member of an interracial couple, I usually find myself part of some group in which the majority defines me as deviant, difficult, inferior or just plain "wrong."

From my membership in all of these groups I have learned that oppression and the intolerance of difference come in all shapes and sexes and colors and sexualities; and that among those of us who share the goals of liberation and a workable future for our children, there can be no hierarchies of oppression. I have learned that sexism and heterosexism both arise from the same source as racism.

"Oh," says a voice from the Black community, "but being Black is NORMAL!" Well, I and many Black people of my age can remember grimly the days when it didn't used to be!

I simply do not believe that one aspect of myself can possibly profit from the oppression of any other part of my identity. I know that my people cannot possibly profit from the oppression of any other group which seeks the right to peaceful existence. Rather, we diminish ourselves by denying to others what we have shed blood to obtain for our children. And those children need to learn that they do not have to become like each other in order to work together for a future they will all share.

Within the lesbian community I am Black, and within the Black community I am a lesbian. Any attack against Black people is a lesbian and gay issue, because I and thousands of other Black women are part of the lesbian community. Any attack against lesbians and gays is a Black issue, because thousands of lesbians and gay men are Black. There is no hierarchy of oppression.

I cannot afford the luxury of fighting one form of oppression only. I cannot afford to believe that freedom from intolerance is the right of only one particular group. And I cannot afford to choose between the fronts upon which I must battle these forces of discrimination . . . wherever they appear to destroy me. And when they appear to destroy me, it will not be long before they appear to destroy you.

Lorde, Audre. "There is no hierarchy of oppressions." Bulletin: *Homophobia and Education.* Council on Interracial Books for Children, 1983.

9. • *Ashley Currier and Thérèse Migraine-George*

QUEER/AFRICAN IDENTITIES:
Questions, Limits, Challenges (2017)

Ashley Currier is professor and head of women's, gender, and sexuality studies at the University of Cincinnati, and she researches lesbian, gay, bisexual, transgender, and queer (LGBTQ) organizing in southern and West Africa. Her books include *Out in Africa: LGBT Organizing in Namibia and South Africa* (2012) and *Politicizing Sex in Contemporary Africa: Homophobia in Malawi* (2019). Her research has appeared in leading feminist and queer studies journals, including *Feminist Formations*, *Gender & Society*, *GLQ*, *Journal of Lesbian Studies*, *Sexualities*, *Signs: Journal of Women in Culture and Society*, and *Women's Studies Quarterly*.

Thérèse Migraine-George is a professor and head of the department of Romance and Arabic languages and literatures at the University of Cincinnati. She is the author of *African Women and Representation: From Performance to Politics* (2008), *From Francophonie to World Literature in French: Ethics, Poetics, and Politics* (2013), two novels, a book of essays, and numerous articles and book chapters focusing on African and Francophone literatures and cultures, women writers, and queer studies.

"Queer Africanness" has been associated with hardship and violent realities over the past twenty years. The now-infamous homophobic statement made by Zimbabwean President Robert Mugabe in 1995 that homosexuals are "worse than pigs and dogs" generated visibility for queer African movements, communities, and identities and a political backlash against African gender and sexual dissidents that continues today (Aarmo 262). By "gender and sexual dissidence," we mean both lived gender and sexual variance and gender and sexual minorities' organized resistance. The backlash instigated by Mugabe's comments constrains how African gender and sexual dissidents express "queer" identities. For instance, Sarah, a lesbian who volunteers at a Liberian HIV/AIDS activist organization that works with lesbian, gay, bisexual, and transgender (LGBT) persons, explains in an interview that passersby who observe people entering the organization's office in Monrovia would assume that visitors were lesbian or gay. In light of the organization's reputation as the "office of lesbians" and gay men, lesbian, bisexual, and transgender (LBT) women are reluctant to participate in activities the organization sponsors. Sarah explains that some LBT women "don't want to be seen" associating with the organization. When Sarah tried to recruit LBT women to join an LGBT rights campaign, they asked her, "Are we coming to be put on television? Are we going to be put [in the] newspaper?" (Currier, Interview). These women feared being outed as gender and/or sexual minorities and becoming victims of anti-LGBT prejudice.

Although the continuing antigay backlash affects how, when, and why queer Africans articulate gender and sexual minority identities and claims, it does not completely predetermine the content and contours of queer African identities. In this essay, we consider the complicated dimensions of generating, representing, and nurturing queer identities in African countries hostile to gender and sexual diversity. We marshal insights derived from original fieldwork conducted with LGBT activists in Liberia, Malawi, and South Africa and analyses of literary and cultural depictions of African queerness.

SCRUTINIZED IDENTITIES

Queer African communities respond not only to local opponents but also to a legacy of scientific racism, sexism, and homophobia. In the nineteenth century, scientific racism and ethnocentrism pervaded investigations of African sexualities. Exemplified by European fascination with the bodies of African women like Saartjie "Sara" Baartman, scientific and colonial racism distorted Euro-American perceptions of African sexual practices and bodies, as research by Clifton Crais and Pamela Scully and Siobhan Somerville shows. Such views promoted racist, heteronormative views of African women as temptresses who lured white men into adulterous relationships and African men as sexual predators who raped white women. Scholars, including Signe Arnfred and Sylvia Tamale, work to dispel racist and ethnocentric misconceptions of African sexualities, just as African LGBT activists confront the lingering effects of colonial constructions of race, gender, and sexuality. Such effects include the notions that "homosexuality is un-African" and that Western governments use LGBT rights to undermine African sovereignty (Msibi 68).

Over the past ten years, African antigay opponents have attempted to constrain how queer African communities portray themselves and to limit the political claims they can make. In 2006, a white South African lesbian couple, Engelina de Nysschen and Hannelie Botha, stood trial for abusing and murdering their son (Ndaba). At the time, South Africa was one of the few countries in the world with legislation prohibiting discrimination on the basis of sexual orientation, and the Constitutional Court had recently issued a ruling asking lawmakers to legalize same-sex marriage. Members of the African Christian Democratic Party (ACDP) viewed the trial as a chance to argue that lesbians were violent and should not have access to the same rights and protections as heterosexual South Africans. Reverend Kenneth Meshoe, the ACDP leader, used the case to denounce same-sex marriage and to call on lawmakers not to legalize same-sex marriage. Meshoe stated, "Parliament must do more to protect children who are exposed to such sinful relationships" (Xaba 4). The fact that the lesbian women were white bolstered claims underlying Meshoe's opposition that same-sex sexualities were un-African, white phenomena. It was precisely this type of misrepresentation against which South African LGBT activists had been working. Although Meshoe's call to deny queer South Africans access to marriage equality went unheeded, it was one of many homophobic assertions intended to limit the social and political space queer Africans could safely claim. Ultimately, the court sentenced De Nysschen to 25 years and Botha to 20 years in prison (Ndaba).

BISEXUALS' SECONDARY MARGINALIZATION

In light of antiqueer sentiments, one might expect that queer African communities are safe spaces for all gender and sexual dissidents. Yet not all queer constituents—specifically, bisexual persons—receive a warm embrace in queer African community spaces. For some black South African lesbians, bisexuality was a term laden with perilous connotations. Black lesbian activists with the Forum for the Empowerment for Women (FEW) sponsored "antiviolence training" workshops intended to educate black lesbians about "corrective rape," a term black South African lesbian activists devised to describe the punitive intentions of antilesbian sexual violence (Currier 64, 2). At one such workshop in 2006, FEW addressed antilesbian violence and intimate partner violence in lesbian relationships. The workshop leader provocatively asked if anyone in the audience believed that there was an instance in which a woman deserved to be beaten. One lesbian woman bluntly stated that she "hated bisexuals" and that bisexual women needed punishment because, after sleeping with men, they sleep with women, exposing lesbians to HIV/AIDS. The workshop leader disapproved and advised women that if they were in a relationship with someone who held similar views, their partners would eventually become physically abusive, implying a close connection between beliefs about gender and sexual norms and violent action. Within this workshop setting, no woman who identified as bisexual likely felt comfortable disclosing her sexual identity. Such marginalization, which Cathy J. Cohen names "secondary marginalization," involves marginalized members within disenfranchised groups experiencing "the denial of access not only to dominant resources and structures, but also to many of the indigenous resources and institutions needed for their survival" (70, 75). Such ostracism can alienate and make less privileged queers feel unsafe and unwelcome in LGBT communities.

Bisexuality also acquired a negative valence for some LGBT and HIV/AIDS activists in Liberia and Malawi. In interviews, some activists derided married, bisexually active men for putting their wives at risk for contracting HIV and sexually transmitted infections (STIs) and for not being liberated enough, even in a homophobic society, to acknowledge what activists assumed to be an overriding sexual desire for men. These views resonate with the stereotype of some US men of color who have sex with men as being "on the down low," a category that portrays these men as endangering heterosexual women of color (Snorton 122). Arthur, a gay man and HIV/AIDS activist in Liberia, pitied married, bisexually active men whom he assumed were too insecure to live exclusively as gay men and embrace their sexual attractions to men as a step toward gay authenticity.

There are some people even living complicated lives because you want to cover up so you get married to a woman, but you're not satisfied [sexually]. You call your friend: "Can I bring my friend to your house?" Why can't people be who they're supposed to be? (Currier, Interview)

Activists' disapproval of married men's bisexual activity was premised on a sense of sexual agency and liberation. The logic went like this: if men could be secure in their sexual desires for men in societies like Liberia and Malawi where antihomosexual sentiments suffused political debate, they could commit to one partner. For such activists, gay authenticity—the alignment of sexual desires, behaviors, and identity in a linear fashion—would serve as the social substrate on which LGBT activist organizations could advance their political projects.

ACTIVISM, AGENCY, AND QUEER IDENTITIES

Although insistence on gender and sexual "authenticity" could result in unreasonable demands on African LGBT persons, narratives of authenticity produced an unexpected variant of the sexual liberation logic in some movements, which involved expressing sexual agency. For instance, some Malawian gay men involved with LGBT organizing spontaneously disclosed in interviews that an older boy or man had raped them when they were younger. Both men were in their twenties and worked as HIV/AIDS peer educators at a Malawian LGBT movement organization. Although, when recounting these sexual encounters, these men did not label them as "rape," they clearly conveyed that they did not want to have sex (Currier and Manuel 295). Both men's HIV/AIDS educational training and experiences working as peer educators counseling men who have sex with men transformed their sense of sexual agency. Just as they advised men to turn down sex with men they did not desire, these two men became aware that they could reject sex with men who propositioned them, a possibility that did not occur to their younger selves. By articulating the principles of sexual consent that were important to them, these peer educators confirmed how LGBT activism resulted in the reorganization of their sexual agency and identities.

Such renewed sexual agency has also translated into wider representations of same-sex desire in African literatures and cultures, which had afforded little space to such representations. African "homosexualities" have usually not been depicted as an expression of identity politics, which in Western countries were borne out of gay and lesbian liberation movements, but rather have been submerged in subtext. While transgressing sociocultural norms, the female homoeroticism illustrated in the works of postcolonial Francophone African novelists, such as Calixthe Beyala and Ken Bugul, registers the prohibition associated with such desires in patriarchal African cultures (Etoke 176–177, 186). Considered to be the first feature film about homosexuality in sub-Saharan Africa, Mohamed Camara's 1997 film *Dakan* broke new ground by portraying the irrepressible attraction and love between two Guinean male high school students. Although the film celebrates their relationship as an authentic alternative to heteronormativity, it closes on the protagonists' forced departure for an unknown place and future (Migraine-George 46). Recent documentaries, such as *Born This Way* and *Call Me Kuchu*, similarly focus on the ostracism experienced by queer Africans in Cameroon and Uganda.

However, literary and cultural representations of African same-sex sexualities treat queer relationships as legitimate modes of pleasure and commitment. The Nigerian writer Chimamanda Ngozi Adichie, now a high-profile figure in US media (she was notably quoted by pop star Beyoncé in one of her songs), broached the topic of same-sex desire in a collection of short stories, *The Thing around Your Neck* (2009). In an op-ed, "Why Can't He Just Be Like Everyone Else?" Adichie publicly opposes the antigay law passed

in January 2014 by the Nigerian government, declaring: "If anything, it is the passage of the law itself that is 'unafrican.' It goes against the values of tolerance and 'live and let live' that are part of many African cultures." Another example is the photographer and activist Zanele Muholi, whose internationally exhibited work focuses on black South African lesbians. While documenting homophobic violence, Muholi's photographs illustrate a multifaceted sensuality. A BBC journalist described one of her pictures of two women kissing as one of "art history's greatest kisses," alongside famous artworks by European artists, such as Auguste Rodin and Gustav Klimt. Such representations capture the complexity of the public and private lives of queer Africans.

While examining queer African identities, one needs to account for how colonial homophobia, scientific racism, local forms of stigmatization, and perceived Western meddling in African sovereign affairs fuel anti-LGBT discrimination in Africa (Ekine and Abbas). Despite the looming threat of antiqueer violence and discrimination, queer persons, whether in Africa or elsewhere, manifest resilience and creativity in determining their lives and futures. Online social media enable them to network within a global queer community in which people increasingly view identities as fluid and borderless. Activists and gender and sexual dissidents throughout Africa and cultural depictions of queer Africans defy easy categorization, insisting that observers consider cultural, economic, social, and political similarities and distinctions when discussing queerness on the African continent.

ACKNOWLEDGMENTS

Funding from the National Science Foundation (SES-0601767) supported Ashley Currier's fieldwork in South Africa, and funding from the American Sociological Association Fund for the Advancement for the Discipline supported her research in Liberia.

WORKS CITED

Aarmo, Margrete. "How Homosexuality Became 'Un-African': The Case of Zimbabwe." *Female Desires: Same-Sex Relations and Transgender Practices across Cultures.* Edited by Evelyn Blackwood and Saskia E. Wieringa. Columbia UP, 1999, pp. 255–80.

Adichie, Chimamanda Ngozi. *The Thing around Your Neck.* Alfred A. Knopf, 2009.

_____. "Why Can't He Just Be Like Everyone Else?" *The Scoop*, 18 Feb. 2014, www.thescoopng.com/chimamanda-adichie-why-cant-he-just-be-like-everyoneelse/.

Arnfred, Signe, editor. *Re-Thinking Sexualities in Africa.* Nordic Africa Institute, 2004.

Camara, Mohamed, director. *Dakan.* Les Films du 20ème et La Sept Cinéma/California Newsreel, 1997.

Cohen, Cathy J. *The Boundaries of Blackness: AIDS and the Breakdown of Black Politics.* U of Chicago P, 1999.

Crais, Clifton C., and Pamela Scully. *Sara Baartman and the Hottentot Venus: A Ghost Story and a Biography.* Princeton UP, 2009.

Currier, Ashley. Interview by Thérèse Migraine-George. Monrovia, Liberia, 10 July 2013.

Currier, Ashley. *Out in Africa: LGBT Organizing in Namibia and South Africa.* U of Minnesota P, 2012.

Currier, Ashley, and Rashida A. Manuel. "When Rape Goes Unnamed: Gay Malawian Men's Responses to Unwanted and Nonconsensual Sex." *Australian Feminist Studies*, vol. 81, 2014, pp. 289–305. *MasterFILE Complete*, doi:10.1080/08164649.2014.959242.

Ekine, Sokari, and Hakima Abbas, editors. *Queer African Reader.* Pambazuka Press, 2013.

Etoke, Nathalie. "Mariama Barry, Ken Bugul, Calixthe Beyala, and the Politics of Female Homoeroticism in Sub-Saharan Francophone African Literature." *Research in African Literatures*, vol. 40, no. 2, 2009, pp. 173–89.

Call Me Kuchu. Directed by Katherine Fairfax Wright and Malika Zouhali-Worrall. Docurama, 2013.

Farago, Jason. "Art History's Greatest Kisses." *Culture*, BBC, 13 Feb. 2015, www.bbc.com/culture/story/20150213-art-historys-greatest-kisses.

Kadlec, Shaun, and Deb Tullmann, dirs. *Born This Way.* Good Docs, 2014.

Migraine-George, Thérèse. "Beyond the 'Internalist' vs. 'Externalist' Debate: African Homosexuals' Local-Global Identities in Two Films, *Woubi Chéri* and *Dakan.*" *Journal of African Cultural Studies*, vol. 16, no. 1, 2003, pp. 45–56.

Murray, Stephen, and Will Roscoe. *Boy-Wives and Female Husbands: Studies in African Homosexualities.* St. Martin's Press, 1998.

Msibi, Thabo. "The Lies We Have Been Told: On (Homo) Sexuality in Africa." *Africa Today*, vol. 58, no. 1, 2011, pp. 55–77. *Project MUSE*, doi:10.2979/africatoday. 58.1.55.

Ndaba, Baldwin. "Mom, Lesbian Lover Imprisoned for Boy's Death." *The Star*, 28 November 2006, www.iol.co.za/news/south-africa/mom-lesbian-lover-imprisoned-for-boy-s-death-1.305130#.VbY2FXhjqS0.

Snorton, C. Riley. *Nobody Is Supposed to Know: Black Sexuality on the Down Low.* U of Minnesota P, 2014.

Somerville, Siobhan B. *Queering the Color Line: Race and the Invention of Homosexuality in American Culture.* Duke UP, 2000.

Tamale, Sylvia, editor. *African Sexualities: A Reader.* Pambazuka Press, 2011.

Xaba, Phindile. "Same-sex Sin Blamed for Child's Murder." *Sowetan*, 24 March 2006, p. 4.

10. • *M. Soledad Caballero*

BEFORE INTERSECTIONALITY (2017)

M. Soledad Caballero is a full professor of English at Allegheny College. Her scholarly work focuses on British Romanticism, travel writing, post-colonial literatures, women's gender, and sexuality studies, and interdisciplinarity. She was a 2017 CantoMundo fellow, has been nominated for two Pushcart Prizes, and has been named a finalist for the *Missouri Review*'s Jeffry E. Smith poetry prize, the *Mississippi Review*'s annual editor's prize, and the Lucille Medwick Memorial Award. Her poem "Myths

We Tell" won the 2019 Joy Harjo poetry prize for *Cutthroat: A Journal of the Arts*. Her poems have appeared in the *Missouri Review*, the *Mississippi Review*, the *Iron Horse Literary Review*, *Memorius*, the *Crab Orchard Review*, *Anomaly*, and other venues. Her book *Birds of Prey* won the 2019 Benjamin Saltman Poetry Award and will be published by Red Hen Press.

After school, you hid in the bathroom
examining the day's insults
stuck to your face. You punched
lockers. You slammed bedroom
doors. I tried books. I tried invisibility. We
lived our sadness through each other. We
lived our silence too. We straddled
emptiness. Spanish in whispers,
our parents' accents, their immigrant fears.
South Carolina 1986. There were
only two colors, only two histories
to choose. We were neither.

11. • *Kimberly Williams Brown and Red Washburn*

TRANS-FORMING BODIES AND BODIES OF KNOWLEDGE:
A Case Study of Utopia, Intersectionality, Transdisciplinarity, and Collaborative Pedagogy (new)

Kimberly Williams Brown, an assistant professor in education and Africana studies at Vassar College, holds a Ph.D. from Syracuse University in Cultural Foundations of Education. Her academic areas of focus are immigration/migration studies, women's and gender studies, and intergroup dialogue. Her work centers Afro-Caribbean women teachers and undocumented Black immigrants. Her other intellectual interests include critical feminist pedagogy particularly in decolonial feminist theories; Black feminist theories; transnational feminist theories; Indigenous feminisms and Caribbean feminist theories; and critical race theory and methodologies.

Red Washburn is an associate professor of English and director of women's and gender studies at Kingsborough and also teaches women's and gender studies at Brooklyn College and the Graduate Center. Their articles appear in *Journal for the*

Study of Radicalism, Women's Studies: An Interdisciplinary Journal, Journal of Lesbian Studies, and *Theory and Praxis: Women's and Gender Studies at Community Colleges*; Washburn also published *Crestview Tree Woman*, a poetry collection, and edited issues of *Sinister Wisdom*. They are a coordinator for the Lesbian Herstory Archives, the Rainbow Book Fair, and the Center for LGBTQ Studies.

INTRODUCTION

In "Body of Knowledge: Black Queer Feminist Pedagogy, Praxis, and Embodied Text," Lewis states, "I teach what I am, I am what I teach, an intersectionality, an interdisciplinarity, a complex epistemology, and pedagogical location. I live and perform my multiple social identities, both visible and invisible, and teach both through institutional knowledge and my own 'embodied text.' As I teach through these embodiments, it has become apparent that the methods through which we teach women's studies must be intersectional and interdisciplinary, while recognizing the body as a site of learning and knowledge" (Lewis 49). This passage highlights the ways in which bodies and bodies of knowledge intersect in personal and professional ways. The subjects we are and the subject we teach overlap. We are trans and Black with many other identities that are at different points salient and subordinate, and we do transdisciplinary, intersectional work that centers and deconstructs power hierarchies. In the summer of 2018, we accepted a co-teaching opportunity at Vassar College in the Exploring Transfer Program, a program focused on intersectionality, transdisciplinarity, and collaborative pedagogy. The program partners a community college professor (Red) with a Vassar College professor (Kim) to work with community college students across the nation who live on campus for six weeks and take co-taught courses. The primary goal is that community college students will see Vassar College, and colleges like it, as a place to which they can transfer. Through our work in this program, we thought about a number of questions: 1) what it means to be trans and Black among other identities doing transdisciplinary work, thinking about boundaries and boundary objects, as well as intersectional and marginalized bodies (i.e., bodies outside the gender binary, bodies of women, and bodies of color, that cannot be translated; and 2) what it means to do collaborative work—co-teach, co-present, co-write—as a knowledge project in transformative justice. In this piece we want to foreground how our identities and lived experiences are text as much as they are teaching strategy and embodied practice.

TRANSDISCIPLINARY STUDIES AND UTOPIAS

Transdisciplinarity is grounded in the modes of inquiry rooted in academic programs that emerged in conjunction with social movements. Transdisciplinary studies have roots in, yet also critique, traditional disciplines and their canons in English, history, philosophy, art, sociology, biology, etc. in order to center marginalized women and trans people in texts, through histories, and lived experiences. Transdisciplinarity examines race, class, gender, ethnicity, sexuality, disability, religion, and age, etc. as intersecting and interlocking identities that impact how texts are written and how disciplines come to be. It also acknowledges these social identities across the spectrum of difference as inextricably linked to systems of power: racism, sexism, cissexism, ethnocentrism, ableism, and Islamophobia. In addition, it is comprised of multiple voices that share in knowledge production, meaning, and dissemination as a democratic practice of diversity, inclusion, belongingness, and freedom.

Transdisciplinary studies help us imagine and create utopias. Utopias are ongoing scholarly and activist projects that use tools of remembering and reimagining to bring about social change. Utopias defy temporality or time-specific associations. They are not linear and are not bound by a place or a destination. Utopias are co-created in community and have the goal of liberation at their fore. The thought that one can reshape canonical disciplines that are often culturally homogenous and represent one set of ideas is powerful and utopic because the very act provides space to create better heterogeneous and intellectual worlds.

Lastly, one way in which we have experienced utopia through our use of transdisciplinary studies is through the student-centered and dialogue-focused classroom environment where respect for consensus and dissent are balanced and epistemic authority is shared between students and professors. Furthermore, it recognizes a critical intimacy between students and professors that centers trust, kindness, empathy, vulnerability, and other non-cognitive skills that are just as essential as learning outcomes devoted to information literacy, style, and citation. It humanizes all of us in critical ways that breed ideal intellectual spaces.

BODIES AND THE POLITICS OF SELF-REFLEXIVITY

RED

I am a white, queer, and trans professor with Irish-Catholic working-class roots in upstate New York. The politics of my everyday life have invited me into a critique of our world. I grew up as a girl, learned from a young age to be obedient, submissive, and feminine. I did not conform to any of those norms. I challenged Catholic structures, patriarchal orders, and gender norms. I was a tomboy who expressed myself through writing, guitar, basketball, softball, and cats, and I fought with the men in my family who were abusive to girls and women. I saw poverty all around me in Newburgh, NY, and even now, with the cultural capital I have gained as a professor, I still feel out of place in upper-middle-class and affluent environments, especially wine-and-cheese gatherings. I was taught to be straight and chaste, that there was a boy's room and a girl's room, and yet had a handful of girl crushes and emulated the masculine boys and men in my circles long before

I came out as queer and trans. I witnessed racism during my childhood, even in a largely Black, Latinx, and white trash community, and I have been trying to unlearn it since college, though it is a life-long process as a white person with unearned privilege. I think about my identities, the body I live in, and how I walk in space in the world every day.

My personal experiences have been greatly informed by the identities and bodies I have held over the course of my life. They translate to my professional expectations, intentions, practices, and responses, as well. Many times before I walk into class to teach, I have experienced harm on the street, in the bathroom, in my place of work, in my neighborhood, on the train, and any place that requires identification (e.g. the store, the post office, the gym, and bars). I am harassed, misgendered, and I have been assaulted many times because of my gender and sexuality, especially by cis, white, straight frat guys and airport security. Still, I know my whiteness has allowed me to live through the worst situations I have experienced, especially perpetrated by cops. I use queer, postcolonial, and feminist theory to teach about my experiences with homophobia, transphobia, and classism as well as unpack my white and national privilege and I create curricula and events around these issues as the Director of Women's and Gender Studies at Kingsborough Community College. My work is in critical theory, women's and trans autobiography and poetry, and feminist, queer, and postcolonial social movements in the U.S. and Ireland. I want to change curricula as much as I want to change the world, and I believe critical consciousness is essential to social action.

KIM

I am a Black Caribbean woman who grew up middle class and has lived in the U.S. for 20 years. When I left Jamaica for college in the United States in 1999, I was not aware of the politics of being Black that had shaped U.S. society. Yes, I was aware of slavery and its effects but not aware of the palpable, subtle and structural ways in which racism worked in the U.S. I knew I was Black, but I did not quite understand how my Blackness would organize my life, my ability to move freely and my ability to access resources. My scholarship and my teaching in the Educational Studies Department at Vassar College are intersectional, decolonial, and steeped in feminist praxis because of my personal experiences of becoming critical of my socialization. My intellectual journey through these transdisciplinary spaces allowed me to make sense of my immigrant status, my Blackness, my gender and my class locations. It is no coincidence that I teach what I am, to return to Lewis' statement that "I teach what I am, I am what I teach, an intersectionality, an interdisciplinarity, a complex epistemology, and pedagogical location" (Lewis 49), because to understand how I was and am located socially, I have to continue to learn about histories of oppression, power, and liberation.

I focus mostly on Caribbean women's migrant labor because this group of women is often understudied and misunderstood. I also use intergroup dialogue methodology and praxis to work across difference and work through power hierarchies. My feminist politics were piqued as a little girl growing up in a conservative Christian church wondering why boys and girls had different rules that dictated dress and demeanor. Later, those politics were sharpened through my realization of the materiality of power and power hierarchies. It is from this place that I teach and write. I am what I teach and what I teach is what I am because these are the intersectional places from which I access the world and make meaning, create space, and work towards liberation.

PEDAGOGIES OF POSSIBILITY AND SOCIAL DIFFERENCE

Through our work co-teaching at Vassar College in the Exploring Transfer Program, we began to think about utopias as part of the academic burgeoning of utopia studies, particularly in how utopias intersect with transdisciplinary scholarship, and in conversation with our lived experiences as professors in trans and Black bodies. In particular, we were interested in the trends in queer sexuality and

futurity/"cruising utopia" (Muñoz), postmodernism and Afrofuturism/"outlaw genres," and disability studies/"crip futures." We co-taught "Feminist Utopias and Afrofuturism" and situated our understanding of the aforementioned utopias within a critical race and feminist theory framework of Afrofuturism. We each came to teaching this course with different academic expertise and different lived experiences: Red's expertise is not in Afrofuturism and they are white and trans and Kim is cis and Black. Using these differences as strengths, we created a learning experience of promise and hope by practicing the values of transdisciplinarity, intersectionality, collaboration, and affect. This collaboration was informed by our work in women's, gender, and sexuality studies, English, history, sociology, and education. It was also informed by our social location and personal histories as well as our pedagogical practices, and self-reflexivity. Our race, gender, class, ethnicity, and sexuality construct our identities, and shape our lives and work. The class was therefore informed by our intellectual merger of scholarship, creativity, and activist pedagogical work, as well as the ways our bodies were read, misread, appreciated, and included as texts for students and to enhance learning.

We incorporated our bodies and our lived experiences into the class in many ways. For example, in our teaching we are critical of the ways our professional "successes" are unconsciously informed by privilege and oppression in our society. We also used the lived experiences of the students in the class as sites for discussion. Students at Vassar are disproportionately white and upper middle class. Yet, many of the students in the Exploring Transfer Program are working-class students of color, some of whom are queer, trans, and immigrant. Just as we used our own bodies and experiences as texts for the class, we drew upon the lived experiences of the students as sites for discussion. For example, we discussed our shared yet different experiences with imposter syndrome: that we did not feel like we belonged at Vassar as students and professors who lived on the margins of a socially constructed idea of "normal" or "average." Through affirming and reimagining belongingness and by using empathy and vulnerability, we created possibilities in the classroom for new ways of being and connecting across power and difference.

We discussed systems of power and our lived experiences with oppression. We read a number of theoretical texts in feminist studies, critical race studies, queer studies, and disability studies that helped us think about how our bodies are texts across different disciplines. Some of the authors we discussed included Sara Ahmed, Chandra Talpade Mohanty, Kimberlé Williams Crenshaw, and Jose Muñoz. We discussed the intersections of identities and bodies in interlocking and complicated ways. Using the concept of utopia as a theoretical frame, we discussed what a utopia would look like for our class and for our world with rampant injustice. We opened up our minds and pushed our bodies physically and metaphorically by learning outside the classroom during Freedom Friday field trips and reflecting on how our bodies translate outside in the world on colonized land (the students researched colonialism and Indigenous life at many of the locations), expanding the spaces from which knowledge can emerge. We embraced organic intellectualism to discover ways of being and knowing in and outside the classroom, in personal and professional contexts. We discussed self-disclosure as connection that transcends space and place by going to art museums, and discussing the power inherent in curating, and capturing life and culture through the mode of museology. Our classrooms were on the grass, in parking lots, at the lake, and up a steep mountain. In these places we engaged the "web of oppression" activity, which is a web created out of yarn and index cards that highlight statistics on structural inequality and which provided an alternative text (different from reading articles and books) and mode of representing multiple oppressions at their intersections.

These classrooms allowed and encouraged students to share their personal experiences with colonialism and gentrification as well as the generational trauma associated with home and exile. Making ourselves vulnerable as professors, and naming our privilege, helped cultivate a different kind of learning. For example, Red shared with the class their experience of being transmasculine, nonbinary, and queer, which for them means not belonging in spaces such as bathrooms, doctors' offices, families, administrative forms, pools, gyms, etc.. Red also pointed out that as a white person with U.S. citizenship standing on Indigenous land, they took up space and reproduced power. Two trans students, Hanniel and Padraig (pseudonyms), confided in Red that they were the first professor who got them, their identities, and pronouns, and that through the course they were able to study who they are and write about it to create possibilities for them as intellectuals and agents. By embodying and examining the politics of bodies and space, we reclaimed them and created spaces for solidarity.

Similarly, Kim realized early in the class that as a Black Caribbean woman, her body, how she showed up in class, and her belief systems meant a lot to predominantly racially marginal students. It seemed the students of color were especially interested not just in her intellectual engagement with them but also in her personal engagement with them. For example, one student, Ebony (pseudonym), asked her personal questions about how she worked through difficulties in her family life, why she was motivated to get a Ph.D., and how to work through confusing experiences with sexuality. Many teachers would argue that is beyond the scope of their teaching and arguably it is. However, for Ebony, it was Kim's ability to be honest with her that opened her up to the possibility of learning content that for her was too foreign, and too invasive because we asked students to share deeply about themselves. As feminist educators, we often ask students to share about themselves and marvel at their inability to do so when we do not share about ourselves. Prior to Kim sharing her experiences with Ebony, she was one of the more difficult students in the class who had trouble connecting to and understanding how insidious power relationships can be. After sharing, Ebony was more open and collaborated with her peers in ways that were meaningful to her and for us.

Our ability to collaborate, as professors, across our multiply intersecting identities and power hierarchies of race, gender, class, sexuality, and ethnicity was a gift. We shared mutual gratitude and critique, a critical friendship, from which students also benefited because they saw professors struggling together through many of the conceptual understandings of intersectionality. For instance, we can recall two classes where we both checked ourselves in front of students for our respective white and straight privileges, and tried to find ways to call in and unpack them publicly with acknowledgment and accountability, as we continued to honor each other, our histories, and our knowledges. Those moments built trust between us and, more importantly, with our students.

In addition, we greatly benefited from the structure of co-written lesson plans that allowed us insight into each other's pedagogical styles, intellectual capacity, and creative abilities. The students also witnessed us struggling with different lived experiences and we challenged dominant ways of knowing in what we taught and how we taught it, but we also had moments of frustration and contradiction in how our bodies traveled and how we performed across space and place. It shifted knowledge communities in a way that opened us up, humanized us, drew us all closer, and deepened intimacy for us all beyond a mind and body duality.

CONCLUSION

We believe that intersectional, transdisciplinary, and collaborative work are key components of utopia. How we create and rethink a better world, a better future, both in and outside of the classroom across difference and power can look different for different people. Our bodies are implicated in the process that is utopic which is not shortsighted and cannot be prescriptive. Every day in the class we taught together, we showed appreciation for each other through verbal affirmations in class. These appreciations allowed us to see others' humanity by being generous and considerate of the ways in which we had contributed to the process of building community, and—we hoped—a utopic space and ideology. However, this is not to say that we created perfect spaces that were conflict free. In fact, while we incorporated gratitude into every class to create a sense of intellectual and emotional balance, we worked through conflict and used our appreciations as a process-driven enterprise to create social change. Appreciations allowed us to feel as safe and heard as possible and yet question how power played out in our time together.

We also often think about the other ways we fell short of creating utopic ideology and space, by not having as many resources as necessary for students to deal with their trauma, and how we might work towards repairing that through other modes of mentoring and resource-sharing without an over-reliance on institutional support. This project and the aforementioned examples illustrate the beauty of transdisciplinary, intersectional, and affective academic work as a utopic project in intellectual and emotional possibility across communities of difference. We believe that through transdisciplinary and intersectional work we can embrace our frustrations and contradictions in spaces to create possibility, empathy, and solidarity as we struggle together to get free.

WORKS CITED

Ahmed, Sara. "Feminist Killjoys." *The Promise of Happiness* (2010): 50–87.

Crenshaw, Kimberlé. "Mapping the Margins: Intersectionality, Identity Politics, and Violence against Women of Color." *Stanford Law Review.* 43 (1990): 1241.

Lewis, Mel Michelle. "Body of Knowledge: Black Queer Feminist Pedagogy, Praxis, and Embodied Text." *The Journal of Lesbian Studies* 15.1 (2011): 49–57.

Mohanty, Chandra. "Under Western Eyes: Feminist Scholarship and Colonial Discourses." *Feminist Review.* 30.1 (1988): 61–88.

Muñoz, José Esteban, et al. *Cruising Utopia: The Then and There of Queer Futurity.* NYU Press, 2019.

SECTION TWO

Historical Perspectives in Women's, Gender, and Sexuality Studies

TABLE OF CONTENTS

NINETEENTH CENTURY

12. Angelina Emily Grimké, "An Appeal to the Christian Women of the South" 112
13. *Seneca Falls Convention, "Declaration of Sentiments and Resolutions" 114
14. Sojourner Truth, "1851 Speech" 117
15. Ida B. Wells, "A Red Record" 117

TWENTIETH CENTURY

16. *The New York Times*, "141 Men and Girls Die in Waist Factory Fire" 121
17. Daughters of Bilitis, "Statement of Purpose" 123
18. Leslie Feinberg, interview with Sylvia Rivera, "I'm Glad I Was in the Stonewall Riot" 124
19. Pat Mainardi, "The Politics of Housework" 126
20. Anne Koedt, "The Myth of the Vaginal Orgasm" 130
21. Radicalesbians, "The Woman-Identified Woman" 135
22. Chicago Gay Liberation Front, "A Leaflet for the American Medical Association" 139
23. The Combahee River Collective, "A Black Feminist Statement" 141
24. Jo Carrillo, "And When You Leave, Take Your Pictures With You" 147
25. bell hooks, "Men: Comrades in Struggle" 148

26. Gloria Anzaldúa, "La Conciencia de la Mestiza/Towards a New Consciousness" 156
27. *National Organization for Men Against Sexism, "Tenets" 161
28. Angela Davis, "Masked Racism: Reflections on the Prison Industrial Complex" 163

TWENTY-FIRST CENTURY

29. *Jackson Katz, "Memo to Media: Manhood, Not Guns or Mental Illness, Should Be Central in Newtown Shooting" 167
30. Tina Vasquez, "It's Time to End the Long History of Feminism Failing Transgender Women" 171
31. *Ashwini Tambe, "Reckoning with the Silences of #MeToo" 174
32. *Women's March, "Guiding Vision and Definition of Principles" 178

History and activism are inextricably intertwined: if want equality today, we have to understand the past. Chandra Talpade Mohanty notes that "[f]eminist analysis has always recognized the centrality of rewriting and remembering history . . . not merely as a corrective to the gaps, erasures, and misunderstandings of hegemonic masculinist history, but because the very practice of remembering and rewriting leads to the formation of politicized consciousness and self-identity" (Mohanty 1991, 34). For most of American history, narratives that chronicled politics, work, medicine, religion, and other aspects of life focused largely, if not exclusively, on privileged men. However, our knowledge of women's lives developed rapidly after the 1970s as an increasing number of historians started writing about women. The very decision to *focus* on women, to see women as *historical actors*, was itself a revolutionary political act. Historians worked to recover the stories of women who had made significant contributions to their society but who were then overlooked, and therefore devalued, by the mostly male historians who recorded the stories of their times. The same process has been true for LG-BTQPAI+ history and the histories of other marginalized groups; the stories of the subordinate group were often absent or misperceived in histories written by the dominant group. Telling the stories of subordinate groups gives us a richer—and more accurate—understanding of American history.

Feminist and queer activism need not focus exclusively, or even primarily, on gender or sexual identity. Focusing on gender discrimination only, for example, is a luxury usually only afforded to women who are privileged by other categories of identity. For example, as we discussed in Section One, for women of color the fight against race-based discrimination has often been just as pressing as the fight against sexism. Furthermore, as historian Elsa Barkley Brown explains, the differences between women are *relational*—one is always affecting the other. So it's not only that race- and class-based differences alter the experience of being a woman; it's that "middle-class women live the lives they do precisely *because* working-class women live the lives they do. White women and women of color not only live different lives but white women live the lives they do in large part *because* women of color live the ones they do" (Barkley Brown 1992, 298 [emphasis ours]). To explore these issues of relational differences, this section focuses on three interconnected subjects within U.S. history: (1) examples of women and LGBTQPAI+ people organizing for progressive change in their communities; (2) activism to advance the interests of women and LGBTQPAI+ communities and seek justice and equity around race, class, gender, sexual orientation, and other identities; and (3) activism to expose, challenge, and destabilize social hierarchies where one identity group is given more access to social, political, and/or economic power.

The scope of this section is necessarily modest. Restricting ourselves to the past two hundred years, and focusing on the United States, the narrative is grounded in an intersectional approach that highlights the relational aspects of privilege and oppression. This does not mean that feminist and queer activism are limited to the United States or that there aren't earlier examples. Furthermore, while the sections move in chronological order, this is not to suggest a linear narrative but rather to group events in ways that allow for intersectional analysis within a historical context. Meant to supplement and contextualize the primary documents that follow, this introduction is *a* history of organizing in the United States, but it is not *the* history. Indeed, one way in which the following narrative diverges from more traditional feminist histories is in its move away from the "wave" metaphor that has commonly been used to structure and canonize the history of feminism into three distinct periods: the First Wave, the Second Wave, and the Third Wave. This wave model has been criticized for focusing mostly on the activism of more privileged women. Even as the following history challenges the wave model, it *will* privilege certain stories over others. While feminist and queer historians challenge dominant narratives, they are not immune from the bias of their own experience. Therefore, it is common for feminist and queer historians to point out the limitations in another historian's work, perhaps noting, for example, the ways in which the historian's class privilege causes them to reproduce a class-biased narrative even while they are trying to dismantle a male-biased narrative. Feminist and queer scholarship is dynamic and ever-changing, and the ethic of the field of women's, gender, and sexuality studies encourages these types of critiques, understanding that everyone's knowledge is "situated" (Haraway 1988). Part of becoming an active learner with strong critical thinking skills is imagining what stories are left out and why. We encourage you to do that with this history, as with all histories.

LEARNING OBJECTIVES

By the end of this section, you will have a better understanding of:

1. The connections between the abolitionist movement, anti-lynching campaigns, and the suffrage movement.

2. How women's labor organizing helped regulate the workplace and fight inequalities of class and gender.

3. How housewives organized in women's auxiliaries and as consumers, and how the limitations of the post-World War II constructions of women's roles affected some housewives.

4. How differences of race and class affected women's demands around reproductive control.

5. How the medical community's constructions of sexuality affected women, lesbians, and gay men and how the articulation of lesbian and gay rights changed over time.

6. The role of intersectional analysis in the evolution of feminist and queer activism.

Engaged Learning

In a group, compare and contrast different histories to understand how subjectivity, bias, and power affect one's version of events.

QUESTIONS

1. Write a one-page history of your course since the beginning of the semester.
2. Read your classmates' histories and read your professor's history.
3. Analyze the collection of histories by asking: What did each person include in their version of events? What did they leave out? What accounts for the differences between various histories of the same events? Are there places where two or more histories are saying conflicting things? If so, how do you decide which version to use?

4. Think about the narrative you wrote. Are there ways in which your subjectivity affected what you wrote? For example, did you talk about the lectures because you really like the professor? Did you talk more about what happened in the classroom because you didn't complete all of the reading assignments? Why do you think you didn't mention some of the things that your classmates talked about?
5. Consider your fellow classmates and the professor. Which of these class historians has the most power? If the president of your college came to your class and asked for the "official history" of the course, whose narrative do you think they would take? Why? What would be forgotten if that was the only story recorded?

THE ABOLITIONIST MOVEMENT, ANTI-LYNCHING CAMPAIGNS, AND THE SUFFRAGE MOVEMENT, 1830–1920

Frederick Douglass, a man born into slavery who became a leader in both the abolitionist movement and the suffrage movement, said, "When the true history of the anti-slavery cause shall be written, women will occupy a large space in its pages, for the cause of the slave has been peculiarly women's cause" (qtd. in Davis 1981, 30). One reason white women—poor young women working in factories as well as wealthier social reformers—were so active in the abolitionist movement was because many drew connections between women's oppression and slavery. For example, Sarah and Angelina Grimké, white sisters from a wealthy family who had grown up on a plantation in South Carolina where they witnessed first-hand the horrors of slavery, moved to Philadelphia after converting to Quakerism and began speaking out publicly against slavery. Even among the progressive Quakers, many found the idea of women lecturing about political issues "unnatural" and therefore objectionable, but, despite strong opposition, Sarah and Angelina continued to voice their opinions lecturing for the American Anti-Slavery Society and writing on the subjects of gender and race.

We might ask whether it was fair for white women to compare themselves to slaves. After all, women like the Grimké sisters were able to advocate for abolition because they had education and leisure time, both of which were a result of the wealth from their family's slave-holding plantation. This strategy

Abolitionists gather to oppose Fugitive Slave Act. Angelina Grimké stands in the background with other abolitionists, including Frederick Douglass (seated, left of center), at the Fugitive Slave Law Convention in Cazenovia, New York, on August 22, 1850. The convention, attended by over two thousand people, including many formerly enslaved people like Emily and Mary Edmonson (standing row, left of center and right of center, dressed in plaid), was called to protest the proposal of the Fugitive Slave Act of 1850.
Source: © The Art Archive/Alamy Stock Photo

was effective, though, in getting white women to see their affinity with Black women, as demonstrated by Angelina's "An Appeal to the Christian Women of the South" (included in this section) in which she challenges the religious arguments used to support slavery and tells Southern women that ending slavery is part of their Christian duty.

Women's experiences in the abolitionist movement helped develop their political consciousness and provided crucial activist training. Lucretia Mott, an abolitionist who helped with the Underground Railroad, was one of the organizers of the first U.S. conference on women's rights, the 1848 Seneca Falls Convention, envisioned by Mott and other organizers as "the inauguration of a rebellion such as the world had never before seen" (Stanton et al. 1881, 68). Indeed, the attendees made many radical statements, articulated in the document that emerged out of the convention, the "Declaration of Sentiments" (included in this section). This document shows the influence of the abolitionist movement, as many of the ideas highlighted in the "Declaration of Sentiments" echoed those made years earlier in Quaker meetings and antislavery organizations (Hewitt 2010, 18).

Unfortunately, male journalists at the time represented the convention as "excessively silly" (Hulin and Avery 1848). Referring to the convention as "the most shocking and unnatural incident in the history of womanity," the *Oneida Whig* asked, "If our ladies will insist on voting and legislating, where, gentlemen, will be our dinners and our elbows? where our domestic firesides and the holes in our stockings?" With similar disdain, *The Mechanic's Advocate* reported: "The women who attend these meetings, no doubt at the expense of their more appropriate duties . . . affirm, as among their rights, that of unrestricted franchise, and assert that it is wrong to deprive them of the privilege to become legislators, lawyers, doctors, divines, etc. etc. . . . Now it requires no argument to prove that this is all wrong. Every true-hearted female will instantly feel that it is unwomanly."

The newspaper comments foreshadowed many of the arguments against women's suffrage: women were weak, in need of men's protection, and best suited to taking care of the house and children. Sojourner Truth, a gifted orator, challenged these arguments in her 1851 speech (included in this section) by calling attention to the intersections of gender and race. Truth had been born into slavery and had done hard manual labor and therefore observed, "I have plowed and reaped and husked and chopped and mowed, and can any man do more than that?" (p. 117). Exposing the conflict between gendered ideology and the treatment of poor and enslaved women, Truth asks: If women are inherently weak, why was she able to do the same work as a man?

The relationship between the abolitionist movement and those working for women's rights was severely damaged after the Civil War when the Fourteenth and Fifteenth Amendments to the Constitution were passed to raise the status of formerly enslaved Black men, giving them the right to vote. Outraged that Black men would vote while women remained disenfranchised, some activists believed that Black leaders should withhold their support for the amendments in solidarity with women. This issue was so divisive that in 1869 activists for women's rights divided into two organizations, the National Woman Suffrage Association (NWSA), who opposed the Fifteenth Amendment because it didn't include women, and the American Woman Suffrage Association (AWSA), who supported the amendment. The organizations didn't reunite until 1890. Although many in the NWSA had been abolitionists, after the Civil War they ignored issues important to Black women like lynching and interracial rape, seeing them as "'race questions,' irrelevant to the . . . goal of 'political equality of women'" (Newman 1999, 6). Therefore, while the suffragist slogan "Votes for Women" suggests advocacy for *all* women, some activists privileged white women's lives at the expense of Black women.

Despite the lack of support from some suffrage circles, Black women like Ida B. Wells launched campaigns to address racial discrimination in the post-slavery era. Her 1895 pamphlet "A Red Record" (included in this section) exposed the horror of lynching. Lynching was a form of domestic terrorism used to maintain white supremacy, but "before lynching could be consolidated as a popularly accepted institution . . . its savagery and its horrors had to be convincingly justified" (Davis 1981, 185). The myth of the Black male rapist who preyed on white women became this justification, as evidenced in the following statement by South Carolina Senator Ben Tillman: "When stern and sad-faced white men put to death a creature in human form who has deflowered a white woman, they have avenged the greatest wrong, the blackest crime" (qtd. in Davis 1981, 187). Wells exposed the image of the Black male rapist as a racist myth, thereby helping to turn the public against lynching.

Some activists argued that the Fourteenth and Fifteenth Amendments *did* give women the right to vote because the Fourteenth Amendment made *all* persons born or naturalized in the United States citizens and the Fifteenth Amendment gave *all citizens* the right to vote. In 1872, Susan B. Anthony attempted to vote using this justification, but she was arrested. While her attempt to vote was unsuccessful, her trial helped undermine a key argument

Ida B. Wells, journalist and activist. Wells, here about thirty-one years of age, documented and exposed the motivations underlying lynching. Her work was central to the antilynching movement.

Source: Pictorial Press Ltd/Alamy Stock Photo

against women's suffrage: that women didn't have the intellectual capacity to understand politics. Pointing out the hypocrisy of a democracy that denies half of its citizens the right to vote, Anthony's testimony (included in our supplementary online material at www.oup.com/he/saraswati2e) demonstrates her knowledge of the Constitution and U.S. history.

Suffragists focused on two primary strategies in the late nineteenth century. First, they focused on getting women the right to vote at the state level; second, they introduced a constitutional amendment that stated: "The right of citizens of the United States to vote shall not be denied or abridged by the United States or any State on account of sex." The Nineteenth Amendment was first introduced in Congress in 1878 but was not ratified until 1920—forty-two years later. It took many new and daring strategies to change public opinion. To this end, under the leadership of Alice Paul and Lucy Burns, suffragists picketed outside the White House. In 1917, after months of picketing, 218 suffragists were arrested. In prison, some of them went on a hunger strike, risking their lives for the cause. Although the passing of the Nineteenth Amendment was a major victory, it was not a complete victory because, in practice, suffrage was only afforded to certain women (Hewitt 2010, 31): African American women were barred from voting by local discriminatory measures, most of which weren't removed until the 1965 Voting Rights Act. The Chinese Exclusion Act restricted citizenship, and thus voting, for Chinese women and men until 1943. Many Native Americans were not considered citizens until 1924, and even then some states didn't allow Native Americans to vote.

ACTIVISM AND CIVIC ENGAGEMENT

Voting is a not just a right but a responsibility. Your vote is one of the most powerful tools for making social change. To be an effective voter, you must educate yourself about the issues. Sharing your knowledge can be an effective way to influence others.

QUESTIONS

1. Divide into groups. Each group should research one local, state, or federal office (e.g., school board member, attorney general, senator). Determine who holds the position or, if there is an upcoming election, who is competing for the position. Research the individual(s), looking at things like their policy statements, biography, voting history, and any news coverage.

2. Based on your findings, discuss with your group members whether you think the individual(s) are strong or weak on social justice issues. Be sure to explain what information you used to form your opinion.

3. Discuss how important social justice issues should be in determining whether you should vote for a candidate. Would you support the individual(s) you researched?

4. Share your information with the class and take notes on the information the other groups offer so that you have them as a reference for upcoming elections.

LABOR ORGANIZING AND THE EQUAL RIGHTS AMENDMENT, 1870–1930

Labor organizing was a major area of women's activism in the late nineteenth and early twentieth centuries. For example, beginning in 1903, the Women's Trade Union League (WTUL) brought together women across racial, ethnic, class, and religious differences and successfully mobilized factory workers, suffragists, college students, and their affluent allies (Boris and Orleck 2011, 34). With leadership from immigrant women, especially Jewish women who immigrated from eastern Europe, bringing with them socialist ideals, these activists helped bring about new laws regulating the extremes of capitalism that emerged with the Industrial Revolution: ending child labor, creating a minimum wage, restricting the length of work days, and creating basic safety standards. Theresa Serber Malkiel's 1910 *Diary of a Shirtwaist Striker* (included in our supplementary online material at www.oup.com/he/saraswati2e) gives us insight into the lives of women labor activists who fought both class and gender discrimination.

On March 25, 1911, a devastating fire at the Triangle Shirtwaist Factory demonstrated the need for basic safety protections. The New York City factory employed many immigrant girls and women who worked long hours for low pay. An article in *The New York Times* (included in this section) reported that

Factory fire kills 146 in New York City on March 25, 1911. The Triangle Shirtwaist Fire is an infamous moment in the history of worker rights. One hundred forty-six victims, most of them young immigrant women, died because of the lack of sufficient fire exits and other basic safety standards. Here victims are seen in coffins on the sidewalk where many jumped nine stories to their death to avoid the flames.

Source: Everett Collection Historical/Alamy Stock Photo

more than 140 workers were killed in the fire. Most, if not all, of these deaths could have been prevented with basic safety precautions. The factory owners were not convicted of manslaughter, a charge many thought they deserved, but the fire was a turning point in labor regulation. Prior to this, the government had resisted workers' calls to regulate private business. However, after the fire, public outrage and women's organizing spurred government officials to act, creating some of the basic safety regulations that we take for granted today.

Despite the many victories for women labor activists, ethnic, racial, and class differences created and reinforced divisive hierarchies within wage-earning women, detracting from their organizing power. For example, women who worked in department stores considered themselves above "factory girls" even though their wages were often lower (Kessler-Harris 1981, 135–37). Similarly, factory workers saw themselves as superior to domestic workers, despite the fact that domestic workers often earned higher wages (135–36). A worker in 1915 explained: "Intelligent people set no stigma on factory workers who are well bred and ladylike. These girls are received in good circles anywhere. . . . But no one has ever invited someone's maid or cook to their home for afternoon tea or any other social affair" (qtd. in Kessler-Harris 1981, 136). Black women created divisions within the bottom tier of the labor market, where they preferred laundry and domestic work over agricultural field work, which had associations with slavery (137). Employers exploited these hierarchies to control wages. If the workplace was more "genteel"—as defined by the race and ethnicity of its workers—women would choose to work there even if the wages were lower than other employment. Thus racial and ethnic discrimination hurt even the white, native-born women who were at the top of the social hierarchy because it depressed wages for all women.

Women workers also had to contend with male workers who saw women's increasing role in the labor market as competition for scarce resources. As men began to unionize in larger numbers, they were effective in using gender ideology to discourage women's advancement in the workforce (Kessler-Harris 1981, 142). Organizing around demands like an eight-hour day and equal pay, the Boston Working Women's League was created in 1869 by Jennie Collins, Aurora Phelps, and Elizabeth Daniels and serves as an example of how women fought against gender and class discrimination (Vapnek 2010, 311, 320). Collins also used her writing to advocate for change. In 1871, she wrote *Nature's Aristocracy: A Plea for the Oppressed*, becoming one of the first working-class women to publish her own book. In it she criticizes class inequality and explains the relational aspect between wealthy women's privilege and poor women's oppression, noting that while some wealthy women give to charity, they are simultaneously producing the *need* for charity by exploiting those whom they employ with low wages.

The class struggle between working-class women and wealthier women can be seen in the conflict over the Equal Rights Amendment (ERA), a proposed constitutional amendment (first introduced into Congress in 1923) that aimed to ensure that men and women were treated equally under the law. The amendment read: "Equality of rights under the law shall not be denied or abridged by the United States or by any state on account of sex." The language of the amendment immediately worried women labor activists in groups like the WTUL and the National Consumers League (NCL) that had been lobbying for protective laws for women: limiting the amount of hours women worked, increasing women's wages, and protecting women from unsafe working conditions (Orleck 2015, 32). Because the ERA was intended to remove any legal differentiation based on sex, women labor activists feared that, if it passed, the laws protecting women workers would be lost. ERA supporters, however, believed that any legal differentiation between the sexes—even in terms of laws benefiting women—undermined feminist progress; the idea that women needed special protective laws, they argued, positioned women as inferior to men (Orleck 2015). Attempts at compromise between the two groups failed. Congress didn't pass the ERA until 1972. The next phase required ratification by thirty-eight states, but the amendment failed to reach that mark before time expired in 1982. Decades later, though, the fight to ratify the ERA has been revived. In 2017 Nevada ratified the amendment, followed by Illinois in 2018 and Virginia in 2020, gaining the amendment the additional states needed to meet the thirty-eight-state requirement. Despite these significant developments, the future of the ERA is unclear; it remains to be determined whether the original deadline can be extended, or what other legal wrangling might be necessary or possible for the ERA to be added to the Constitution.

Both sides of the early ERA debate wanted to improve women's lives, but their different positions exposed a major issue for feminist activism that still resonates today: is it possible to create a women's coalition if various groups of women will have different, and sometimes opposing, interests around a particular issue?

INTERSECTIONAL ANALYSIS

A Case Study: In 2013, the chief operating officer of Facebook, Sheryl Sandberg, published *Lean In: Women, Work, and the Will to Lead*, in which she discusses gender equality in the workforce and what women can do to increase their success. Sandberg's approach has been criticized by feminist scholars like Susan Faludi and bell hooks, who argue that Sandberg's approach is a cooptation of feminism that undermines gender equality and female solidarity. Watch Sandberg's TED Talk, "Why We Have Too Few Women Leaders" (http://www.ted.com/ talks/sheryl_sandberg_why_we_have_too_few_women_leaders?language=en), where she summarizes some of the main points from her book.

QUESTIONS

1. What are Sandberg's main strategies for producing more women leaders?
2. Using intersectional analysis, which women do you think Sandberg is talking about?
3. How does she propose to address structural sexism?
4. Why do you think feminist critics say Sandberg is coopting feminism?

HOUSEWIVES REVOLT! 1930–1970

While wage-earning women used unions to organize and effect change, women who weren't in the labor market also played important roles through women's auxiliaries. These support organizations were affiliated with a union and made up of workers' wives and family members. The story of the working-class, Mexican American women in the Mine-Mill Ladies Auxiliary 209 is a great example. In 1950 in New Mexico, Mexican American mineworkers went on strike to protest wage policies and hiring practices that paid Mexican American workers less than white workers at the Empire Zinc mine (Orleck 2015, 62). After the Empire Zinc owners won a court order to prevent the men from picketing outside the mine, Virginia Chacón, the wife of the mine's local union president, suggested that the wives and children of the miners picket in the men's place (62). The women, part of Mine-Mill Ladies Auxiliary 209, continued the picketing. They were harassed and ultimately jailed for their actions (62). Those arrested were told they would be released from jail if they would not return to the picket line, but they refused (Cargill 1983, 208–209). Even once the men returned to the picket line, many women continued to strike, and their efforts remained important to the overall union strategy (209).

Although women's participation in the strike won the respect of male Mexican American activists, it did not result in substantive changes to women's subordinate status in the union or in their families (Cargill 1983, 243–46). Despite the fact that the male miners were able to recognize inequalities based on race, ethnicity, and class, they had not developed the same level of consciousness around gender. The women's most important demand—indoor plumbing in the company-owned housing—was not made a priority during the strike and few women maintained influence in the union organizations after the strike (244–46).

Housewives also entered into collective action as buyers. In the 1930s, 1940s, and 1950s, poor and working-class women across the country "staged anti-eviction protests, consumer boycotts, rent strikes and protests for better education and affordable public housing . . . Echoing the language of trade unionism, [housewives] asserted that housing and food, like wages and hours, could be regulated by organizing and applying economic pressure" (Orleck 2015, 44). Building on their experiences as labor activists, organizers of the housewives' movement like Clara Lemlich Shavelson, Rose Schneiderman, and Pauline Newman recognized that while working-class women held little power in the workforce, they could use their power as *consumers* to effectively pressure businesses to lower prices and government to increase regulation and address price gouging (45–48).

The 1935 meat boycott in Hamtramck, Michigan, is a good example. In light of the pervasive unemployment around the country, a large increase in the cost of meat drove women to organize. On July 27, 1935, the Hamtramck Women's Committee picketed the local shopping district, demanding a 20 percent cut in the price of meat and blocking the entrance to food stores

(White 2014, 114). When shoppers exited the stores, the picketers searched their bags, taking and destroying any meat they found (114). The first day alone, the picketers were credited with a loss of $65,000 in sales (114–15). These women activists were successful not only in cutting the prices of meat and other food staples but in creating a new consumer consciousness that lives on today (Orleck 2015, 48).

Perhaps the best-known story of housewife revolt was spurred by Betty Friedan's 1963 book *The Feminine Mystique*, which chronicles the stories of middle-class, white women who found the role of housewife unfulfilling. Friedan describes the problem: "As she made the beds, shopped for groceries, matched slipcover material, ate peanut butter sandwiches with her children, chauffeured Cub Scouts and Brownies, lay beside her husband at night—she was afraid to ask even of herself the silent question—'Is this all?'" (15). Friedan explains that while these women felt empty, dissatisfied, and depressed, they didn't have the words to describe their situation. It was "the problem that has no name." Women were too ashamed to tell their friends and family about it. After all, they said, what could they complain about? According to the images of the "happy housewife" presented on TV and in women's magazines, they had a perfect life. If they weren't happy, the women reasoned, there must be something wrong with *them*. The power of *The Feminine Mystique* was that in making these stories public, women began to realize that it was not an *individual* problem. The problem was in the culture's expectations: the post–World War II construction of femininity created unrealistic and unfulfilling roles for women.

It's important to understand Friedan's critique within the historical context of the 1950s. For the women Friedan described, their identity was defined as *relational*: they were someone's wife and someone's mother. The idea that they "could be a person in [their] own right, in addition to being a wife and mother, seemed completely new to many women" (Coontz 2011, xxi). Books and magazines regularly encouraged women to be better wives by being more sel*fless*. If she worked outside the home, she was told to make sure it didn't "take priority in her life" or "become more important to her than his" work (qtd. in Coontz 2011, 16). Women were also encouraged to submit to their husbands, to become "the perfect follower," making her husband "feel that he is the boss at home," and never to "appear to know more than [her husband] does" (qtd. in Coontz 2011, 15, 16).

The Feminine Mystique is an important marker in the history of feminist organizing—both for what it said and what it didn't say. Despite its usefulness in providing a language to discuss female subordination, Friedan makes concerning generalizations about women. While her account did reflect the lives of many middle-class, white women, it did not represent *all* women. Indeed, the book makes the stories of women of color and other less privileged women all but invisible. For example, because racial discrimination usually prevented Black men from making enough money to support their families, it was common for Black women to work outside the home. These women would not have identified with the stories told in Friedan's book. Historian Stephanie Coontz notes the way in which the exclusion of Black women's stories limited the book: "In ignoring the experience of African-American women in *The Feminine Mystique*, Friedan missed an opportunity to prove that women could indeed combine family commitments with involvement beyond the home" (Coontz 2011, 126). Because *The Feminine Mystique* became such a well-known example of feminism in the 1960s, and because it privileged the stories of white, middle-class women while claiming to speak for all women, this book is often pointed to as an example of the ways in which the feminist movement reproduced hierarchies of race and class while challenging them in terms of gender.

THE PERSONAL IS POLITICAL: HOUSEWORK AND REPRODUCTIVE CHOICE, 1960–1980

In the 1960s and 1970s, the feminist slogan "the personal is political" challenged the idea that social and family concerns were "private" matters and therefore outside of the realm of politics. For example, in her 1970 article "The Politics of Housework" (included in this section), Pat Mainardi argues that the unequal distribution of housework is based on the subordination of women. Because men are seen as superior, they are excused from housework; because men don't do housework, it is not valued. Housework is unpaid and it depletes women's leisure time, time that women could use to improve their status through increased education and more political activism.

The recognition that individual problems in the home, in marriages, and in the family were connected to larger structures of inequality encouraged women to mobilize on a number of fronts. For example, many feminist activists argued for the widespread availability of birth control and access to abortion (this is discussed more in Section Three).

However, often poor women and women of color viewed the issues of birth control and abortion differently than white, middle- and upper-class women. While "the personal is political" mantra encouraged privileged feminists to recognize that male controls over female reproduction were tools of patriarchy, there wasn't the same recognition that the regulation of minority women's reproduction advanced racial oppression. For example, in the 1960s and 1970s, when the civil rights movement was challenging white supremacy, coerced sterilization of women of color became commonplace. Presented as antipoverty initiatives, women of color were routinely sterilized by state authorities without informed consent or through coercion. African American girls like Minnie Lee (age fourteen) and Mary Alice Relf (age twelve) were sterilized without their parents' informed consent "on the grounds that they were 'at risk' of early sexual activity" (Gordon 2014, 114). In other cases women were told they would lose their welfare benefits if they didn't agree to be sterilized (114). One woman, Mexican American Helena Orozco, testified that her doctor said that if she "did not consent to the tubal ligation that the doctor repairing [her] hernia would use an inferior type of stitching material" (qtd. in Gordon 2014, 115). The effects of sterilization programs on women of color are shocking: in Puerto Rico, a third of women of childbearing age were sterilized by 1968 (Roberts 1997, 94). Similarly, between 1970 and 1976, the Indian Health Services clinics had sterilized between 25 and 42 percent of Native American women of childbearing age (Orleck 2015, 99).

Women-of-color activists organized to end these practices. Dr. Helen Rodriguez-Trias, who founded the Coalition to End Sterilization Abuse (CESA) and cofounded the Committee for Abortion Rights and Against Sterilization Abuse (CARASA), successfully lobbied New York City to provide information about sterilization in a woman's native language and to require a waiting period between childbirth and sterilization (Orleck 2015, 98). Women of All Red Nations (WARN), a Native American women's organization that organized around this issue, noted ending the forced sterilization of Native women as one of their major goals (143). However, while women of color were organizing to prevent forced sterilization, white, middle-class feminists advocated for unfettered access to *all* methods of birth control including sterilization, seeing this as tied to women's liberation. Therefore, groups like the National Abortion Rights Action League (NARAL) and Planned Parenthood opposed sterilization restrictions (Roberts 1997, 96). Dorothy Roberts argues, "Focusing on the obstacle the regulations would pose to middle-class white women, they ignored the ravages on minority women's bodies the new law would help to prevent" (96).

ACTIVISM AROUND SEX AND SEXUALITY, 1950–1980

Anatomy textbooks from the early nineteenth century defined the clitoris as "passive and unimportant to female sexual expression," but at least the clitoris was discussed: by the twentieth century the clitoris wasn't even labeled in most anatomy textbooks (Gerhard 2000, 452). Therefore, it shouldn't be surprising that when Freud published *Three Essays on the Theory of Sexuality* in 1905, he defined the clitoral orgasm as "immature," while he positioned the vaginal orgasm as the "normal" response to sexual intercourse. Women who didn't experience vaginal orgasm through intercourse were pathologized as "frigid." This figuring of women's sexuality both assumed and legitimated heterosexuality as the only healthy orientation.

Writing in the 1950s and 1960s, sex researchers like Alfred Kinsey, William Masters, and Virginia Johnson presented a very different view of women's sexuality. They rejected the claim that a clitoral orgasm was somehow deficient or inferior; indeed, they presented it as central to female sexual pleasure (Gerhard 2000, 462). Anne Koedt's 1970 article "The Myth of the Vaginal Orgasm" (included in this section) helped to redefine women's sexuality with a focus on the clitoris. As one scholar observes, "When Koedt attacked [the vaginal orgasm] as a myth, or more pointedly, as a fraudulent misinformation campaign that created a host of psychological problems for women, she appeared to challenge the very foundation of heterosexuality as it was understood in psychoanalytic, medical, and popular discourse" (Gerhard 2000, 449).

Compulsory heterosexuality: A term coined by Adrienne Rich meaning that patriarchal institutions and social norms create and enforce the expectation that all people are heterosexual.

In her 1980 essay "Compulsory Heterosexuality and Lesbian Existence," Adrienne Rich examines the ways in which heterosexual norms have been constructed in the interest of patriarchy. She says that **compulsory heterosexuality** naturalizes opposite-sex attraction as normal and universal and pressures people to conform. Like Koedt, Rich sees the construction of sexuality as about power. She argues that compulsory heterosexuality perpetuates male privilege and marks lesbians as deviant. As with the anatomy textbooks discussed previously, an examination of the treatment of homosexuality in the field of medicine helps demonstrates how our understanding of sexuality is connected to larger social issues.

Beginning in the late nineteenth century, most in the medical community saw homosexuality as a "sickness," a perversion of "normal" sexuality that required treatment (Frank 2014, 9). This representation of homosexuality supported and legitimated large-scale discrimination, which was heightened by the Cold War fervor in the 1950s. The argument went something like this: because homosexuals were "sick," most homosexuals were "in the closet." This meant they could be blackmailed—and if they could be blackmailed, they could be motivated to take actions against the United States. Therefore, gays were seen as an inherent threat to the safety and security of the nation. While the blackmail argument was conveniently overblown to support discriminatory measures, being outed did have consequences. As gay activist Harry Hay explains, "The moment a person was listed as a homosexual [following arrest], his name appeared on the front page of the newspaper. The moment that happened you lost your job, you lost your insurance, you lost your credit" (qtd. in Frank 2014, 10).

The legitimation that the medical community gave to gay discrimination helps explain the strategies of early LGBT activists. Often referred to as part of the homophile movement, activists organizations like the Mattachine Society, founded in 1950, and the Daughters of Bilitis, founded in 1955, laid the foundation for the challenges to social and legal discrimination that would come later. However, from today's vantage point they don't seem radical because they largely focused on assimilationist strategies, emphasizing the commonalities between homosexuals and heterosexuals and encouraging gays and lesbians to conform to heterosexual norms and behaviors. For example, the "Statement of Purpose" for the Daughters of Bilitis (included in this section) encourages the lesbian to "make her adjustment to society" as opposed to demanding that society change its treatment of lesbians (p. 123). While these organizations have been criticized for their strategies of accommodation, the incredible persecution of gays and lesbians during the Cold War era may have made this feel like the only realistic alternative (Adam 1995, 70).

In the 1960s, in conjunction with other social movements, gay and lesbian activists began to question the accommodation strategies of the homophile movement and began to take a more militant approach (Adam 1995, 75).

The Stonewall riots of 1969 are perhaps the most noted marker of this transition from assimilation to liberation. On the night of June 27–28, 1969, police raided a New York City bar that LGBT folks patronized called the Stonewall Inn. This was nothing new; police often raided gay bars. However, as Sylvia Rivera describes in her interview with Leslie Feinberg, "I'm Glad I Was in the Stonewall Riot" (included in this section), this time the patrons rebelled. Unbiased contemporaneous first-person accounts of Stonewall are limited. Reports from mainstream publications of the time are imbued with homophobia and transphobia. Indeed, gay rights activist Dick Leitsch's 1969 account, published in the newsletter of the New York Mattachine Society, provides a rare glimpse of the Stonewall uprising written from the activists' point of view at the time. Leitsch describes how "an almost solid mass of people—most of them gay" chanted "'Gay Power,' 'We Want Freedom Now,' and 'Equality for Homosexuals'" as they blocked traffic on "Christopher Street, from Greenwich to Seventh Avenue." While the overall significance of Stonewall is debated by scholars— did it really represent *the* turning point for gay rights?—what we know is that "Stonewall and its aftermath gave something to the gay community, particularly its younger generation, that it had never had: it transformed a shared narrative of oppression into a new narrative of rebellion" (Frank 2014, 38).

After Stonewall we start to see a shift in the tenor of queer activism. For example, the Gay Liberation Front (GLF), founded in 1969, was markedly different from the earlier homophile organizations in that it attacked "the consumer culture, militarism, racism, sexism, and homophobia" and emphasized

A group gathers outside the boarded-up Stonewall Inn in New York City after June 1969 uprising. Stonewall patrons rebelled against police harassment, igniting a mass protest that became an important turning point in the gay rights movement.
Source: Photo by Fred W. McDarrah/Getty Images

"coming out" as necessary to gay liberation (Rimmerman 2015, 23). After the GLF broke up, the Gay Activists Alliance (GAA) became more visible (24). The GAA focused on the single issue of gay rights and was less radical than the GLF; however, the GAA adopted a focus on political elections that proved to be a very effective strategy, and it was successful at establishing institutional structures (24–26).

One of the most visible early successes of post-Stonewall activism was the removal of homosexuality from the American Psychiatric Association's *Diagnostic and Statistical Manual of Mental Disorders* in 1973. The Chicago Gay Liberation Front handed out leaflets (included in this section) to doctors at the American Medical Association's 1970 convention. They demanded an end to the pathologizing of homosexuality as a "sickness," arguing that the problem didn't lie in the individual psychology and behavior of gays and lesbians but rather in the social system that discriminates against them.

By the 1970s, feminist and queer activists shared many connections. By exposing the socially constructed nature of gender, feminists had implicitly challenged all "natural" identities; by challenging the connection between sex and procreation, emphasizing and encouraging a valuing of sex for pleasure, some antigay arguments were weakened. However, there were those within the women's movement who feared that incorporating the issues of the queer community would hurt them politically. Indeed, in 1969 National Organization for Women (NOW) leader Betty Friedan referred to the lesbians within the women's movement as a "lavender menace." In protest to her comment but also in recognition of the larger issues around the silencing of lesbians in the women's movement, a group of lesbian feminists called the Radicalesbians distributed a manifesto called "The Woman-Identified Woman" (included in this section), which argued that lesbians should be central to the women's movement. By 1971, Friedan changed her opinion on lesbians and NOW adopted a resolution supporting gay rights (Gordon 2014, 91). Despite the progress around sexual orientation, writers like Tina Vasquez, in her article "It's Time to End the Long History of Feminism Failing Transgender Women" (included in this section), suggest that trans women continued to be marginalized within feminist activism.

IDENTITY POLITICS AND PRIVILEGE: CROSSING BORDERS, UNDERSTANDING ALLIANCES, AND QUEER IDENTITIES, 1970–PRESENT

In the 1980s, the question of identity politics and privilege came to the forefront of many feminist debates. Many less privileged women (working-class women, women of color, and lesbians) argued that they were marginalized within the women's movement of the 1960s and 1970s. These critiques noted that publicly recognized feminist leaders were white, middle-class, straight women and that the platforms of many feminist organizations focused on issues that reflected the lived experiences of white, middle-class, straight women. For example, as bell hooks points out, "[w]omen in lower-class and poor groups, particularly those who are non-white, would not have defined women's liberation as woman gaining equality with men . . . Knowing that men in their groups do not have social, political, and economic power, they would not deem it liberatory to share their social status" (hooks 2000, 19). Less privileged women may not have been intentionally excluded, but, in large and small ways, they were made to feel like second-class citizens within the movement. This debate caused many more privileged women to reflect on the ways in which they were simultaneously *perpetuating* hierarchies of race, class, and sexual orientation even while they were *challenging* hierarchy in terms of gender. Many of the white, middle-class, straight women had previously seen themselves as oppressed, and having to accept that they were also the oppressor was often difficult to acknowledge.

As discussed in Section One, in the 1980s and 1990s many scholars explored the role of simultaneous oppression and intersectional identities. For example, Benita Roth notes that Black feminists challenged their marginalization in both the women's movement and the civil rights movement simultaneously, challenging "white feminist movements for ignoring economic and survival issues common to the Black community, and for failing to examine personal racism" and challenging "the Black Civil Rights movement as it shifted into a Black liberation/nationalist movement that seemed to be recreating its gender politics along white middle class patriarchal lines" (Roth 2003, 49). Born of this marginalization, Black feminist activism incorporated an intersectional perspective that looked at race, class, and gender simultaneously, positioning these social hierarchies as mutually reinforcing. Angela Davis's "Masked Racism: Reflections on the Prison Industrial Complex" (included in this section) exemplifies the legacy of this type of scholarship. Here she looks at how the **prison industrial complex** relies on concepts of criminality that both emerge from and reinforce the subordination of the poor and people of color.

While Black feminists had been vocal about the intersections of race, class, and gender, they were sometimes silent on issues of heterosexual privilege. To address this, the Combahee River Collective, a Black lesbian feminist organization in the 1970s, issued "A Black Feminist Statement" (included in this section). In it they emphasize that racial, sexual, heterosexual, and class oppressions are all interconnected, and they argue for an alternative "to universalistic visions of sisterhood that erased differences between women" (Roth 2003, 52). Part of the legacy of this era of Black feminism is an understanding that systems of oppression work together: the idea that some people should be accorded more rights and privileges because of socially constructed ideas around difference is the underlying premise in *all* social hierarchies. Therefore, if one's work implicitly or explicitly supports this premise in regard to race, class, or sexual orientation, the argument for gender equality is weakened. Consequently, all efforts to promote gender equality must simultaneously address other social hierarchies.

Prison industrial complex: The industry and its supporters who promote institutional punishment as the solution for social problems in order to further political and financial self-interest.

Third world feminism:
Feminist activism that
emerges from the lived
experiences of women
from the geographical
third world and from
women of color living in
powerful countries like
the United States.

Using Benedict Anderson's idea of "imagined communities," Chandra Talpade Mohanty defines **third world feminism** as an alliance of women "with
divergent histories and social locations, woven together by the *political* threads
of opposition to forms of domination that are not only pervasive but also systemic" (4). Therefore, she positions this alliance based not on essentialist identities, not on biology or culture, but on consciousness: "the *way* we think
about race, class, and gender—the political links we choose to make among
and between struggles" (Mohanty 1991, 4). For Mohanty, it is the "common
context of struggle" that creates a "potential commonality" for "the peoples of
Africa, Asia, Latin America, and the Middle East, as well as 'minority' populations (people of color) in the United States and Europe" (7, 2).

Many third world feminists critiqued what they saw as mainstream U.S.
(white) feminism's "narrow conception of feminist terrain as an almost singularly antisexist struggle" (Johnson-Odim 1991, 315). While third world
feminists support the fight for gender equality, they also face discrimination
based on factors like race, class, and nation. Therefore, for feminism to improve the lives of third world women, activists must address other social hierarchies as well as *the position of the societies* in which Third World women
find themselves" (Johnson-Odim 1991, 320 [emphasis ours]). This means that
privileged women in the United States and Europe must interrogate their
complicity in the imperialist relationships that bring their own countries
wealth at the expense of others. As Jo Carrillo's poem "And When You Leave,
Take Your Pictures With You" (included in this section) represents, many
third world women see feminism's superficial inclusion of women of color as
more for show than for substance.

In the introduction to their influential 1981 book *This Bridge Called My
Back: Writings by Radical Women of Color*, Cherríe Moraga and Gloria Anzaldúa
say their motivation "began as a reaction to the racism of white feminists," but
soon "became a positive affirmation of the commitment of women of color to
our own feminism" (Moraga and Anzaldúa 1981, xxiii). The lived experiences
of women of color have given rise to transformative concepts like Anzaldúa's
mestiza **consciousness.** In "La Conciencia de la Mestiza/Towards a New
Consciousness" (included in this section), Anzaldúa champions the liberatory
potential of "borderlands" as a space that can embrace ambiguity and contradictions and can challenge binaries.

Mestiza consciousness:
A term coined by Gloria
Anzaldúa that emerges
out of her lived experi-
ence as a Chicana and
means a sense of self that
embraces borders and
ambiguity and challenges
dualistic thinking.

Historian Susan Stryker notes the connections between Anzaldúa's articulation of hybrid and intersectional identities and queer theory (Stryker 2008,
124). Reclaiming the previously pejorative word "queer," activists now use
the term to refer to empowering concepts of identity that resist traditional
categorizations. As discussed in Section One, queer identity refers to fluidity
in terms of gender and sexuality but can also be used to mean any identity that
is nonnormative or outside of traditional boundaries.

The debates about privilege, intersectionality, and alliances during this
time period also examined the role of men in feminist activism. In bell hooks's
"Men: Comrades in Struggle" (included in this section) she observes that

TRANSNATIONAL CONNECTIONS

The question of how to define women's issues has been at the heart of debates around feminist activism. Choose three countries and do an internet search for women's organizations based in that country. Decide on the criteria you will use to define "women's organizations" and select at least one women's organization from each country. Read about the work of each organization and look for their mission statement or a list of their goals.

QUESTIONS

1. Compare and contrast the women's organizations from different countries. How does each organization define its focus?

2. How is the organization funded? Who is the audience for the organization's website? How might the funding source affect the framing of women's issues?

3. What narratives about women travel across these countries? Are there certain themes that structure a transnational discourse around women's issues? What tensions might there be in a definition of women's issues from a transnational perspective?

viewing men as the enemy emerges from a gender-only focus. If one's vantage point is informed by understandings of intersectionality, men become part of the struggle. And indeed, men benefit from feminism. For example, challenging rigidly defined definitions of masculinity has created new definitions of fatherhood, encouraging men to spend more time with their children. We see significant examples of men engaging in feminist activism during this time period, both as allies to women and to improve the lives of boys and men. For example, the National Organization for Men Against Sexism (NOMAS) formed in the 1970s when a group of men in a women's studies course at the University of Tennessee held a conference on men and masculinities and began to articulate the ideological underpinnings that would later structure their organization ("A Brief History of NOMAS"). In 1982 the group began to formalize into a national organization, adopting the current name in 1990 and then in 1992 incorporating a stronger focus on intersectionality because of the recognition that "[a]ll oppressions are linked, and a consciousness of any oppression leads to an awareness of them all" ("A Brief History of NOMAS," "Tenets" p. 161). NOMAS advocates for positive changes in men's lives, stating that "[t]raditional masculinity includes many positive characteristics in which we take pride and find strength, but it also contains qualities that have limited and harmed us" ("Statement of Principles"). As demonstrated in their "Tenets" (included in this section), NOMAS positions this work to enhance men's lives as necessarily pro-feminist, gay/LGBT-affirming, and anti-racist.

Emerging out of the understanding that men had a responsibility and a self-interest in thinking critically about gender and power, scholars like R. W. Connell contributed to more nuanced understandings of the social construction

Hegemonic masculinity: A term used by R. W. Connell that reflects hierarchies between different types of masculinity in addition to the hierarchy of masculinity over femininity.

of masculinity. For example, Connell uses the concept of "hegemonic masculinity" to explore different kinds of masculinities, and the hierarchies between and among them. Connell argues, "To recognize diversity in masculinities is not enough. We must also recognize the *relations* between the different kinds of masculinity: relations of alliance, dominance and subordination. These relationships are constructed through practices that exclude and include, that intimidate, exploit, and so on. There is a gender politics within masculinity" (37). Thus Connell encourages us to analyze masculinity as "a place in gender *relations*, the *practices* through which men and women engage that place in gender, and the *effects* of these practices in bodily experience, personality and culture" (Connell 2005, 71 [emphasis ours]). Scholars like Connell who study the social construction of masculinity as a relational concept connected to power argue that more sophisticated understandings of masculinity can provide insight into social problems like violence. For example, in his article "Memo to Media: Manhood, Not Guns or Mental Illness, Should Be Central in Newtown Shooting" (included in this section), Jackson Katz positions "violence as a gendered phenomenon" and argues that to understand school shootings like the one at Sandy Hook Elementary School in 2012, where a gunman shot and killed twenty young children and six adults, we have to acknowledge that men are the ones committing most of these types of rampage killings (p. 168). To appropriately address the ongoing problem of gun violence in the United States, Katz says that we have to make gender a central focus of the conversation and "have a thoughtful conversation about manhood" (p. 168).

Many of the questions that have been central to this section—questions about social justice organizing, privilege, and identity politics—are reflected in two recent historical events: the MeToo movement and the Women's March each provide case studies on both the necessity of, and the difficulties inherent in, engaging in truly intersectional activist work. In January 2017, immediately following and reacting to the inauguration of the forty-fifth president of the United States, Donald Trump, activists came together in a global show of resistance. An estimated three to five million people joined in marches across the United States—likely making it the largest single-day protest in U.S. history—and there were approximately 260 marches in other countries around the world (Chenoweth and Pressman 2017). Organizers then built on the momentum of these grassroots nonviolent direct action events to "harness the political power of diverse women and their communities to create transformative social change": since 2017, the Women's March has continued to organize an annual march in Washington, DC, and support sister marches in other locations around the country and the world, but their mission also includes "providing intersectional education on a diverse range of issues and creating entry points for new grassroots activists & organizers to engage in their local communities through trainings, outreach programs and events" ("Mission and Principles"). Their comprehensive platform is based on the belief that "Women's Rights are Human Rights and Human Rights are Women's Rights" and that "[o]ur liberation is bound in each other's" (p. 179, 178). Their intentional focus on intersectionality is evidenced in the naming of key areas of focus for their work: "Ending Violence, Reproductive Rights, LGBTQIA Rights, Worker's Rights, Civil Rights, Disability Rights, Immigrant Rights, Environmental Justice" ("Mission and Principles"). They also emphasize their intersectional approach in how they tell the story of their work. In their "Guiding Vision and Definition of Principles" (included in this section) they position the work of the Women's March as building on the legacies of other social movements, including "the suffragists and abolitionists, the Civil Rights Movement, the feminist movement, the American Indian Movement, Occupy Wall Street, Marriage Equality, Black Lives Matter, and more" (p. 179).

The MeToo movement began in 2006 with the work of Tarana Burke (see an interview with Tarana Burke and more discussion of hashtag activism in Section Six) but reached a global audience in 2017 through a viral hashtag. In response to the allegations of sexual violence against Hollywood mogul Harvey Weinstein, actress Alyssa Milano tweeted a suggestion from a friend, "If all the women who have been sexually harassed or assaulted wrote 'Me too.' as a status, we might give people a sense of the magnitude of the problem." Milano asked that people who had experienced sexual violence reply to her tweet with "me too." The hashtag has since been used millions of times, creating an international conversation and helping to "de-stigmatize the act of surviving by highlighting the breadth and impact of sexual violence worldwide" (Anderson and Toor 2018; "History & Vision").

In her article "Reckoning with the Silences of #MeToo" (included in this section), Ashwini Tambe chronicles the emergence of the hashtag #MeToo, reflecting on the power of social media as a vehicle for a widespread and deeply moving national and international conversation that led to real consequences that included the toppling of abusive men in power, a shift in the public response to survivors and their stories, and a deepening public awareness of the pervasiveness of sexual violence. Tambe's contribution to our understanding of the MeToo movement lies in her answers to two key questions: "Why Now?" and "What's Left Out?" (p. 175, 176). Through these questions she analyzes the specific social and historical context out of which the MeToo movement surfaced and explores how the emotional and psychological pain revealed in these testimonials travels in complicated ways connected to larger narratives around race and class and in ways that sometimes lack the nuanced dialogues that are useful in fully understanding the many faces of coercion.

The successes and challenges of both the Women's March and the MeToo movement illustrate the importance of intersectional activist movements and remind us of the important questions that frame this section: How do we define feminist and queer activism? Who gets to speak and what stories do we tell about these movements for social change? Who benefits from the stories we tell? Why are some people's concerns or contributions less visible than others? These questions are important because how we remember the past, and how we understand the limitations of our histories, will influence our strategies around current issues.

Critical Thinking Questions

1. How have differences in race, class, and sexual orientation created conflict within women's activism?

2. What strategies have been used to advocate for women and queer communities?

3. When the Equal Rights Amendment was first proposed, women labor activists were against it because they supported protective legislation for women, legislation that relied on a legal differentiation between the sexes. Today we still have protections for women written into our laws. For example, only men can be drafted for war. Do you think protective legislation undermines arguments for gender equality?

4. Compare the "Statement of Purpose" of the Daughters of Bilitis with the Chicago Gay Liberation Front's "A Leaflet for the American Medical Association." What are the assumptions that inform each document? How do they differ?

5. How does Gloria Anzaldúa's concept of the *mestiza* challenge social hierarchies?

GLOSSARY

Compulsory heterosexuality 102

Hegemonic masculinity 108

Mestiza consciousness 106

Prison industrial complex 105

Third world feminism 106

WORKS CITED

"A Brief History of NOMAS." *NOMAS*, March 5, 2015, nomas.org/history/.

Adam, Barry. *The Rise of a Gay and Lesbian Movement.* Twayne Publishers, 1995.

@Alyssa_Milano. "If You've Been Sexually Harassed or Assaulted Write 'Me Too' as a Reply to This Tweet." *Twitter*, October 15, 2017, 4:21 p.m., twitter.com/Alyssa_Milano/status/919659438700670976.

Anderson, Benedict. *Imagined Communities: Reflections on the Origin and Spread of Nationalism.* Rev. ed. Verso, 2006.

Anderson, Monica, and Skye Toor. "How Social Media Users Have Discussed Sexual Harassment Since #MeToo Went Viral." Pew Research Center, October 11, 2018, www.pewresearch.org/fact-tank/2018/10/11/how-social-media-users-have-discussed-sexual-harassment-since-metoo-went-viral/.

Barkley Brown, Elsa. "'What Has Happened Here': The Politics of Difference in Women's History and Feminist Politics." *Feminist Studies*, vol. 18, no. 2, 1992, pp. 295–312.

"Bolting Among the Ladies." *Oneida Whig*, August 1, 1848. https://www.loc.gov/exhibits/treasures/images/vc006199.jpg.

Boris, Eileen, and Annelise Oleck. "Feminism and the Labor Movement: A Century of Collaboration and Conflict." *New Labor Forum*, vol. 20, no. 1, 2011, pp. 33–41.

Cargill, Jack. "Empire and Opposition: The 'Salt of the Earth' Strike." In *Labor in New Mexico: Unions, Strikes, and Social History Since 1881*, edited by Robert Kern. University of New Mexico Press, 1983.

Chenoweth, Erica and Jeremy Pressman. "This Is What We Learned by Counting the Women's Marches." February 7, 2017. https://www.washingtonpost.com/news/monkey-cage/wp/2017/02/07/this-is-what-we-learned-by-counting-the-womens-marches/.

Collins, Jenni, and Judith Ranta. *Nature's Aristocracy or, Battle Wounds in the Time of Peace: A Plea for the Oppressed*, edited by Russell H. Conwell. Lee and Shepard Publishers, 1871.

Connell, R. W. *Masculinities*. 2nd ed. University of California Press, 2005.

Coontz, Stephanie. *A Strange Stirring: The Feminine Mystique and American Women at the Dawn of the 1960s*. Basic Books, 2011.

Davis, Angela Y. *Women, Race and Class*. Vintage Books, 1981.

Frank, Walter. *Law and the Gay Rights Story: The Long Search for Equal Justice in a Divided Democracy*. Rutgers UP, 2014.

Friedan, Betty. *The Feminine Mystique*. W. W. Norton, 1963.

Gerhard, Jane. "Revisiting 'The Myth of the Vaginal Orgasm': The Female Orgasm in American Sexual Thought and Second Wave Feminism." *Feminist Studies*, vol. 26, no. 2, 2000, pp. 449–76.

Gordon, Linda. "The Women's Liberation Movement." In *Feminism Unfinished: A Short, Surprising History of American Women's Movements*. Liveright Publishing, 2014, pp. 69–145.

Haraway, Donna. "Situated Knowledges: The Science Question in Feminism and the Privilege of Partial Perspective." *Feminist Studies*, vol. 14, no. 3, 1988, pp. 575–99.

Hewitt, Nancy A. "From Seneca Falls to Suffrage? Reimagining a 'Master' Narrative in U.S. Women's History." In *No Permanent Waves: Recasting Histories of U.S. Feminism*, edited by Nancy Hewitt. Rutgers, 2010, pp. 15–38.

"History & Vision." *Me Too Movement*, metoomvmt.org/about/.

hooks, bell. *Feminist Theory: From Margin to Center*. South End Press, 2000.

Hulin, G. H., and J. A. Avery, editors. *The Recorder {Syracuse}*, August 3, 1848. https://www.loc.gov/exhibits/treasures/images/vc006198.jpg.

Johnson-Odim, Cheryl. "Common Themes, Different Contexts: Third World Women and Feminism." *Third World Women and the Politics of Feminism*, edited by Chandra Talpade Mohanty et al. Indiana UP, 1991, pp. 314–27.

Kessler-Harris, Alice. *Women Have Always Worked: A Historical Overview*. Feminist Press, 1981.

Leitsch, Dick "Police Raid on N.Y. Club Sets off First Gay Riot" (1969). http://www.advocate.com/society/activism/2012/06/29/our-archives-1969-advocate-article-stonewall-riots.

"Mission and Principles—Women's March 2020." womensmarch.com/mission-and-principles.

Mohanty, Chandra Talpade. "Cartographies of Struggle: Third World Women and the Politics of Feminism." In *Third World Women and the Politics of Feminism*, edited by Chandra Talpade Mohanty et al. Indiana UP, 1991, pp. 1–47.

Moraga, Cherríe, and Gloria Anzaldúa. "Introduction." In *This Bridge Called My Back: Writings by Radical Women of Color*, edited by Cherríe Moraga and Gloria Anzaldúa. Kitchen Table: Women of Color Press, 1983, pp. xxii–xxvi.

Newman, Louise Michele. *White Women's Rights: The Radical Origins of Feminism in the United States*. Oxford UP, 1999.

Orleck, Annelise. *Rethinking American Women's Activism*. Routledge, 2015.

Rich, Adrienne. "Compulsory Heterosexuality and Lesbian Existence." *Women: Sex and Sexuality, Signs: Journal of Women in Culture and Society*, special issue, vol. 5, no. 4, 1980, pp. 631–60.

Rimmerman, Craig. *The Lesbian and Gay Movement: Assimilation or Liberation*. 2nd ed. Westview Press, 2015.

Roberts, Dorothy. *Killing the Black Body: Race, Reproduction, and the Meaning of Liberty*. Vintage Books, 1997.

Roth, Benita. "Second Wave Black Feminism in the African Diaspora: News from New Scholarship." *African Feminisms III, Agenda: Empowering Women for Gender Equity*, special edition, no. 58, 2003, pp. 46–58. doi:10.1080/10130950.2003.9674493.

Stanton, Elizabeth Cady, et al. *History of Woman Suffrage (1848–1861)*. Vol. 1, 1881.

Stryker, Susan. *Transgender History*. Seal Press, 2008.

Tanner, John. "Women out of Their Latitude." *The Mechanic's Advocate*, August 12, 1848. https://www.loc.gov/exhibits/treasures/images/vc006200.jpg.

Vapnek, Lara. "Staking Claims to Independence: Jennie Collins, Aurora Phelps, and the Boston Working Women's League, 1865–1877." In *No Permanent Waves: Recasting Histories of U. S. Feminism*, edited by Nancy Hewitt. Rutgers UP, 2010, pp. 305–28.

White, Ann Folino. *Plowed Under: Food Policy Protests and Performance in New Deal America*. Indiana UP, 2014.

12. • *Angelina Emily Grimké*

AN APPEAL TO THE CHRISTIAN WOMEN OF THE SOUTH (1836)

Angelina Emily Grimké and her sister Sarah were influential abolitionists and women's rights activists. Born in 1805 to a slave-holding family in South Carolina, Grimké had first-hand experience with the institution of slavery. Leaving her parents' home and rejecting their lifestyle, Grimké became a Quaker and moved to Philadelphia. In 1835 she sent a letter to abolitionist William Lloyd Garrison condemning slavery. He published the letter in his antislavery newspaper, *The Liberator*, and afterward Grimké began giving speeches against slavery. Because she spoke to audiences of both men and women, she faced strong criticism for stepping outside the bounds of appropriate female behavior. While her initial focus was on abolition, Grimké came to see that, in order to be a strong abolitionist, she had to advocate for women's rights as well. In "An Appeal to the Christian Women of the South," Grimké uses religious rhetoric and biblical references to argue that slavery is a sin and that it is women's Christian duty to end the practice.

Respected Friends,

It is because I feel a deep and tender interest in your present and eternal welfare that I am willing thus publicly to address you. Some of you have loved me as a relative, and some have felt bound to me in Christian sympathy, and Gospel fellowship; and even when compelled by a strong sense of duty, to break those outward bonds of union which bound us together as members of the same community, and members of the same religious denomination, you were generous enough to give me credit, for sincerity as a Christian, though you believed I had been most strangely deceived. I thanked you then for your kindness, and I ask you *now*, for the sake of former confidence, and former friendship, to read the following pages in the spirit of calm investigation and fervent prayer. It is because you have known me, that I write thus unto you.

[. . .]

"The *supporters* of the slave system," says Jonathan Dymond in his admirable work on the Principles of Morality, "will *hereafter* be regarded with the *same* public feeling, as he who was an advocate for the slave trade *now is*." It will be, and that very soon, clearly perceived and fully acknowledged by all the virtuous and the candid, that in *principle* it is as sinful to hold a human being in bondage who has been born in Carolina, as one who has been born in Africa. All that sophistry of argument which has been employed to prove, that although it is sinful to send to Africa to procure men and women as slaves, who have never been in slavery, that still, it is not sinful to keep those in bondage who have come down by inheritance, will be utterly overthrown. We must come back to the good old doctrine of our forefathers who declared to the world, "this self-evident truth that *all* men are created equal, and that they have certain *inalienable* rights among which are life, *liberty*, and the pursuit

New York, American Anti-Slavery Society, 1836

of happiness." It is even a greater absurdity to suppose a man can be legally born a slave under *our free Republican* Government, than under the petty despotisms of barbarian Africa. If then, we have no right to enslave an African, surely we can have none to enslave an American; if it is a self-evident truth that *all* men, everywhere and of every color are born equal, and have an *inalienable right to liberty*, then it is equally true that *no* man can be born a slave, and no man can ever *rightfully* be reduced to *involuntary* bondage and held as a slave, however fair may be the claim of his master or mistress through wills and title-deeds. . . .

[. . .]

But perhaps you will be ready to query, why appeal to *women* on this subject? *We* do not make the laws which perpetuate slavery. *No* legislative power is vested in *us; we* can do nothing to overthrow the system, even if we wished to do so. To this I reply, I know you do not make the laws, but I also know that *you are the wives and mothers, the sisters and daughters of those who do;* and if you really suppose *you* can do nothing to overthrow slavery, you are greatly mistaken. You can do much in every way: four things I will name. 1st. You can read on this subject. 2d. You can pray over this subject. 3d. You can speak on this subject. 4th. You can *act* on this subject. I have not placed reading before praying because I regard it more important, but because, in order to pray aright, we must understand what we are praying for; it is only then we can "pray with the understanding and the spirit also."

[. . .]

The *women of the South can overthrow* this horrible system of oppression and cruelty, licentiousness and wrong. Such appeals to your legislatures would be irresistible, for there is something in the heart of man which *will bend under moral suasion*. There is a swift witness for truth in his bosom, *which will respond to truth* when it is uttered with calmness and dignity. If you could obtain but six signatures to such a petition in only one state, I would say, send up that petition, and be not in the least discouraged by the scoffs and jeers of the heartless, or the resolution of the house to lay it on the table. It will be a great thing if the subject can be introduced into your legislatures in any way, even by *women*, and *they* will be the most likely to introduce it there in the best possible manner, as a matter of *morals* and *religion*, not of expediency or politics. You may petition, too, the different ecclesiastical bodies of the slave states. Slavery must be attacked with the whole power of truth and the sword of the spirit. You must take it up on *Christian* ground, and fight against it with Christian weapons, whilst your feet are shod with the preparation of the gospel of peace. And *you are now* loudly called upon by the cries of the widow and the orphan, to arise and gird yourselves for this great moral conflict, with the whole armour of righteousness upon the right hand and on the left.

[. . .]

Sisters in Christ, I have done. As a Southerner, I have felt it was my duty to address you. I have endeavoured to set before you the exceeding sinfulness of slavery, and to point you to the example of those noble women who have been raised up in the church to effect great revolutions, and to suffer for the truth's sake. I have appealed to your sympathies as women, to your sense of duty as *Christian women*. I have attempted to vindicate the Abolitionists, to prove the entire safety of immediate Emancipation, and to plead the cause of the poor and oppressed. I have done—I have sowed the seeds of truth, but I well know, that even if an Apollos were to follow in my steps to water them, *"God only* can give the increase." To Him then who is able to prosper the work of his servant's hand, I commend this Appeal in fervent prayer, that as he "hath *chosen the weak things of the world*, to confound the things which are mighty," so He may cause His blessing, to descend and carry conviction to the hearts of many Lydias through these speaking pages. Farewell—Count me not your "enemy because I have told you the truth," but believe me in unfeigned affection,

Your sympathizing Friend,
Angelina E. Grimké.

DECLARATION OF SENTIMENTS AND RESOLUTIONS (1848)

The Seneca Falls Convention took place on July 19–20, 1848, bringing together around three hundred men and women in Seneca Falls, New York, for the first women's rights convention in US history. Prior to the convention, a document called the "Declaration of Sentiments" was drafted by Elizabeth Cady Stanton with help from other organizers. The document, which was modeled after the Declaration of Independence, was a statement of principles and a list of injustices that resulted in women's oppression. The convention voted on a series of "Resolutions" that they believed would help remedy the injustices outlined in the "Declaration of Sentiments," among which was a statement that women should have the right to vote. While the other resolutions, including those demanding equality in law and opportunity, were unanimously approved, the suffrage resolution barely passed and only after a fervent plea for support from Frederick Douglass. Asking for women's right to vote was seen as too extreme by many of the convention attendees.

DECLARATION OF SENTIMENTS

When, in the course of human events, it becomes necessary for one portion of the family of man to assume among the people of the earth a position different from that which they have hitherto occupied, but one to which the laws of nature and of nature's God entitle them, a decent respect to the opinions of mankind requires that they should declare the causes that impel them to such a course.

We hold these truths to be self-evident: that all men and women are created equal; that they are endowed by their Creator with certain inalienable rights; that among these are life, liberty, and the pursuit of happiness; that to secure these rights governments are instituted, deriving their just powers from the consent of the governed. Whenever any form of government becomes destructive of these ends, it is the right of those who suffer from it to refuse allegiance to it, and to insist upon the institution of a new government, laying its foundation on such principles, and organizing its powers in such form, as to them shall seem most likely to effect their safety and happiness. Prudence, indeed, will dictate that governments long established should not be changed for light and transient causes; and accordingly all experience hath shown that mankind are more disposed to suffer, while evils are sufferable, than to right themselves by abolishing the forms to which they are accustomed. But when a long train of abuses and usurpations, pursuing invariably the same object, evinces a design to reduce them under absolute despotism, it is their duty to throw off such government, and to provide new guards for their future security. Such has been the patient sufferance of the women under this government, and such is now the necessity which constrains them to demand the equal station to which they are entitled.

From Stanton, Elizabeth Cady, Susan B. Anthony, and M.J. Cage. *A History of Woman Suffrage*, vol. 1 (Rochester, N.Y.: Fowler and Wells, 1889)

The history of mankind is a history of repeated injuries and usurpations on the part of man toward woman, having in direct object the establishment of an absolute tyranny over her. To prove this, let facts be submitted to a candid world.

He has never permitted her to exercise her inalienable right to the elective franchise.

He has compelled her to submit to laws, in the formation of which she had no voice.

He has withheld from her rights which are given to the most ignorant and degraded men—both natives and foreigners.

Having deprived her of this first right of a citizen, the elective franchise, thereby leaving her without representation in the halls of legislation, he has oppressed her on all sides.

He has made her, if married, in the eye of the law, civilly dead.

He has taken from her all right in property, even to the wages she earns.

He has made her, morally, an irresponsible being, as she can commit many crimes with impunity, provided they be done in the presence of her husband. In the covenant of marriage, she is compelled to promise obedience to her husband, he becoming, to all intents and purposes, her master—the law giving him power to deprive her of her liberty, and to administer chastisement.

He has so framed the laws of divorce, as to what shall be the proper causes, and in case of separation, to whom the guardianship of the children shall be given, as to be wholly regardless of the happiness of women—the law, in all cases, going upon a false supposition of the supremacy of man, and giving all power into his hands.

After depriving her of all rights as a married woman, if single, and the owner of property, he has taxed her to support a government which recognizes her only when her property can be made profitable to it.

He has monopolized nearly all the profitable employments, and from those she is permitted to follow, she receives but a scanty remuneration. He closes against her all the avenues to wealth and distinction which he considers most honorable to himself. As a teacher of theology, medicine, or law, she is not known.

He has denied her the facilities for obtaining a thorough education, all colleges being closed against her.

He allows her in Church, as well as State, but a subordinate position, claiming Apostolic authority for her exclusion from the ministry, and, with some exceptions, from any public participation in the affairs of the Church.

He has created a false public sentiment by giving to the world a different code of morals for men and women, by which moral delinquencies which exclude women from society, are not only tolerated, but deemed of little account in man.

He has usurped the prerogative of Jehovah himself, claiming it as his right to assign for her a sphere of action, when that belongs to her conscience and to her God.

He has endeavored, in every way that he could, to destroy her confidence in her own powers, to lessen her self-respect, and to make her willing to lead a dependent and abject life.

Now, in view of this entire disfranchisement of one-half the people of this country, their social and religious degradation—in view of the unjust laws above mentioned, and because women do feel themselves aggrieved, oppressed, and fraudulently deprived of their most sacred rights, we insist that they have immediate admission to all the rights and privileges which belong to them as citizens of the United States.

[. . .]

RESOLUTIONS

Whereas, the great precept of nature is conceded to be, "that man shall pursue his own true and substantial happiness." Blackstone in his Commentaries remarks, that this law of Nature being coeval with mankind, and dictated by God himself, is of course superior in obligation to any other. It is binding over all the globe, in all countries and at all times; no human laws are of any validity if contrary to this, and such of them as are valid, derive their force, and all their validity, and all their authority, mediately and immediately, from this original; therefore;

Resolved, That such laws as conflict, in any way, with the true and substantial happiness of woman, are contrary to the great precept of nature, and of no validity; for this is "superior in obligation to any other."

Resolved, That all laws which prevent woman from occupying such a station in society as her conscience shall dictate, or which place her in a position inferior to that of man, are contrary to the great precept of nature, and therefore of no force or authority.

Resolved, That woman is man's equal—was intended to be so by the Creator, and the highest good of the race demands that she should be recognized as such.

Resolved, That the women of this country ought to be enlightened in regard to the laws under which they live, that they may no longer publish their degradation, by declaring themselves satisfied with their present position, nor their ignorance, by asserting that they have all the rights they want.

Resolved, That inasmuch as man, while claiming for himself intellectual superiority, does accord to woman moral superiority, it is pre-eminently his duty to encourage her to speak, and teach, as she has an opportunity, in all religious assemblies.

Resolved, That the same amount of virtue, delicacy, and refinement of behavior, that is required of woman in the social state, should also be required of man, and the same transgressions should be visited with equal severity on both man and woman.

Resolved, That the objection of indelicacy and impropriety, which is so often brought against woman when she addresses a public audience, comes with a very ill-grace from those who encourage, by their attendance, her appearance on the stage, in the concert, or in feats of the circus.

Resolved, That woman has too long rested satisfied in the circumscribed limits which corrupt customs and a perverted application of the Scriptures have marked out for her, and that it is time she should move in the enlarged sphere which her great Creator has assigned her.

Resolved, That it is the duty of women of this country to secure to themselves their sacred right to the elective franchise.

Resolved, That the equality of human rights results necessarily from the fact of the identity of the race in capabilities and responsibilities.

Resolved, therefore, That, being invested by the Creator with the same capabilities, and the same consciousness of responsibility for their exercise, it is demonstrably the right and duty of woman, equally with man, to promote every righteous cause, by every righteous means; and especially in regard to the great subjects of morals and religion, it is self-evidently her right to participate with her brother in teaching them, both in private and in public, by writing and by speaking, by any instrumentalities proper to be used, and in any assemblies proper to be held; and this being a self-evident truth, growing out of the divinely implanted principles of human nature, any custom or authority adverse to it, whether modern or wearing the hoary sanction of antiquity, is to be regarded as a self-evident falsehood, and at war with the interests of mankind.

Resolved, That the speedy success of our cause depends upon the zealous and untiring efforts of both men and women, for the overthrow of the monopoly of the pulpit, and for the securing to women an equal participation with men in the various trades, professions, and commerce.

14. • *Sojourner Truth*

1851 SPEECH

Sojourner Truth was an African American abolitionist and women's rights activist born into slavery circa 1797 under the name Isabella Baumfree. She escaped from slavery in 1826 and renamed herself Sojourner Truth in 1843. Truth was illiterate but dictated her memoir, *The Narrative of Sojourner Truth: A Northern Slave*, which was published in 1850. After the Civil War, Truth advocated for land grants for former slaves and desegregation. She continued her activist work until her death in 1883. Truth's 1851 speech was presented at the Ohio Women's Rights Convention.

May I say a few words? Receiving an affirmative answer, she proceeded; I want to say a few words about this matter. I am a woman's rights. I have as much muscle as any man, and can do as much work as any man. I have plowed and reaped and husked and chopped and mowed, and can any man do more than that? I have heard much about the sexes being equal; I can carry as much as any man, and can eat as much too, if I can get it. I am as strong as any man that is now. As for intellect, all I can say is, if woman have a pint and man a quart—why can't she have her little pint full? You need not be afraid to give us our rights for fear we will take too much, for we can't take more than our pint'll hold. The poor men seem to be all in confusion, and don't know what to do. Why children, if you have woman's rights give it to her and you will feel better.

You will have your own rights, and they won't be so much trouble. I can't read, but I can hear. I have heard the Bible and have learned that Eve caused man to sin. Well if woman upset the world, do give her a chance to set it right side up again. The lady has spoken about Jesus, how he never spurned woman from him, and she was right. When Lazarus died, Mary and Martha came to him with faith and love and besought him to raise their brother. And Jesus wept—and Lazarus came forth. And how came Jesus into the world? Through God who created him and woman who bore him. Man, where is your part? But the women are coming up, blessed be God, and a few of the men are coming up with them. But man is in a right place, the poor slave is on him, woman is coming on him, and he is surely between a hawk and a buzzard.

Sojourner Truth Speech, Anti-Slavery Bugle (Salem, Ohio), June 21, 1851

15. • *Ida B. Wells*

A RED RECORD (1895)

Ida B. Wells (later Wells-Barnett) was born into slavery in 1862 but received a strong education and became a successful member of the new black middle class, working first as a schoolteacher and later becoming a journalist. Wells was active in both the

From Wells-Barnett, Ida B. "The Case Started." *The Red Record: Tabulated Statistics and Alleged Causes of Lynching in the United States*. Chicago: Donahue & Hanneberry Printers, Binders, and Engravers, 1895 civil rights movement and the suffrage movement. She became known for her writing on race and became an editor of the antisegregationist Memphis newspaper *Free Speech and Headlight*. After three black businessmen who were friends of Wells were lynched by a white mob, she began a campaign to expose the injustice and horror of lynching. The following excerpt from her pamphlet "A Red Record" demonstrates how Wells challenged the underlying arguments that legitimated lynching.

Beginning with the emancipation of the Negro, the inevitable result of unbridled power exercised for two and a half centuries, by the white man over the Negro, began to show itself in acts of conscienceless outlawry. During the slave regime, the Southern white man owned the Negro body and soul. It was to his interest to dwarf the soul and preserve the body. Vested with unlimited power over his slave, to subject him to any and all kinds of physical punishment, the white man was still restrained from such punishment as tended to injure the slave by abating his physical powers and thereby reducing his financial worth. While slaves were scourged mercilessly, and in countless cases inhumanly treated in other respects, still the white owner rarely permitted his anger to go so far as to take a life, which would entail upon him a loss of several hundred dollars. The slave was rarely killed, he was too valuable; it was easier and quite as effective, for discipline or revenge, to sell him "Down South."

But Emancipation came and the vested interests of the white man in the Negro's body were lost. The white man had no right to scourge the emancipated Negro, still less has he a right to kill him. But the Southern white people had been educated so long in that school of practice, in which might makes right, that they disdained to draw strict lines of action in dealing with the Negro. In slave times the Negro was kept subservient and submissive by the frequency and severity of the scourging, but, with freedom, a new system of intimidation came into vogue; the Negro was not only whipped and scourged; he was killed.

Not all nor nearly all of the murders done by white men, during the past thirty years in the South, have come to light, but the statistics as gathered and preserved by white men, and which have not been questioned, show that during these years more than ten thousand Negroes have been killed in cold blood, without the formality of judicial trial and legal execution. And yet, as evidence of the absolute impunity with which the white man dares to kill a Negro, the same record shows that during all these years, and for all these murders only three white men have been tried, convicted, and executed. As no white man has been lynched for the murder of colored people, these three executions are the only instances of the death penalty being visited upon white men for murdering Negroes.

Naturally enough the commission of these crimes began to tell upon the public conscience, and the Southern white man, as a tribute to the nineteenth-century civilization, was in a manner compelled to give excuses for his barbarism. His excuses have adapted themselves to the emergency, and are aptly outlined by that greatest of all Negroes, Frederick Douglass, in an article of recent date, in which he shows that there have been three distinct eras of Southern barbarism, to account for which three distinct excuses have been made.

The first excuse given to the civilized world for the murder of unoffending Negroes was the necessity of the white man to repress and stamp out alleged "race riots." For years immediately succeeding the war there was an appalling slaughter of colored people, and the wires usually conveyed to Northern people and the world the intelligence, first, that an insurrection was being planned by Negroes, which, a few hours later, would prove to have been vigorously resisted by white men, and controlled with a resulting loss of several killed and wounded. It was always a remarkable feature in these insurrections and riots that only Negroes were killed during the rioting, and that all the white men escaped unharmed.

From 1865 to 1872, hundreds of colored men and women were mercilessly murdered and the almost invariable reason assigned was that they met their death by being alleged participants in an insurrection or riot. But this story at last wore itself out. No insurrection ever materialized; no Negro rioter was ever apprehended and proven guilty, and no dynamite ever recorded the black man's protest against oppression and wrong. It was too much to ask thoughtful people to believe this transparent story, and the Southern white people at last made up their minds that some other excuse must be had.

Then came the second excuse, which had its birth during the turbulent times of reconstruction. By an amendment to the Constitution the Negro was given the right of franchise, and, theoretically at least, his ballot became his invaluable emblem of citizenship. In a government "of the people, for the people, and by the people," the Negro's vote became an important factor in all matters of state and national politics. But this did not last long. The Southern white man would not consider that the Negro had any right which a white man was bound to respect, and the idea of a republican form of government in the Southern states grew into general contempt. It was maintained that "This is a white man's government," and regardless of numbers the white man should rule. "No Negro domination" became the new legend on the sanguinary banner of the sunny South, and under it rode the Ku Klux Klan, the Regulators, and the lawless mobs, which for any cause chose to murder one man or a dozen as suited their purpose best. It was a long, gory campaign; the blood chills and the heart almost loses faith in Christianity when one thinks of Yazoo, Hamburg, Edgefield, Copiah, and the countless massacres of defenseless Negroes, whose only crime was the attempt to exercise their right to vote.

But it was a bootless strife for colored people. The government which had made the Negro a citizen found itself unable to protect him. It gave him the right to vote, but denied him the protection which should have maintained that right. Scourged from his home; hunted through the swamps; hung by midnight raiders, and openly murdered in the light of day, the Negro clung to his right of franchise with a heroism which would have wrung admiration from the hearts of savages. He believed that in that small white ballot there was a subtle something which stood for manhood as well as citizenship, and thousands of brave black men went to their graves, exemplifying the one by dying for the other.

The white man's victory soon became complete by fraud, violence, intimidation and murder. The franchise vouchsafed to the Negro grew to be a "barren ideality," and regardless of numbers, the colored people found themselves voiceless in the councils of those whose duty it was to rule. With no longer the fear of "Negro Domination" before their eyes, the white man's second excuse became valueless. With the Southern governments all subverted and the Negro actually eliminated from all participation in state and national elections, there could be no longer an excuse for killing Negroes to prevent "Negro Domination."

Brutality still continued; Negroes were whipped, scourged, exiled, shot and hung whenever and wherever it pleased the white man so to treat them, and as the civilized world with increasing persistency held the white people of the South to account for its outlawry, the murderers invented the third excuse—that Negroes had to be killed to avenge their assaults upon women. There could be framed no possible excuse more harmful to the Negro and more unanswerable if true in its sufficiency for the white man.

Humanity abhors the assailant of womanhood, and this charge upon the Negro at once placed him beyond the pale of human sympathy. With such unanimity, earnestness and apparent candor was this charge made and reiterated that the world has accepted the story that the Negro is a monster which the Southern white man has painted him. And today, the Christian world feels, that while lynching is a crime, and lawlessness and anarchy the certain precursors of a nation's fall, it can not by word or deed, extend sympathy or help to a race of outlaws, who might mistake their plea for justice and deem it an excuse for their continued wrongs.

[. . .]

If the Southern people in defense of their lawlessness, would tell the truth and admit that colored men and women are lynched for almost any offense, from murder to a misdemeanor, there would not now be the necessity for this defense. But when they intentionally, maliciously and constantly belie the record and bolster up these falsehoods by the words of legislators, preachers, governors and bishops, then the Negro must give to the world his side of the awful story.

A word as to the charge itself. In considering the third reason assigned by the Southern white people for the butchery of blacks, the question must be asked, what the white man means when he charges the black man with rape. Does he mean the crime which the statutes of the civilized states describe as such? Not by any means. With the Southern white man, any mésalliance existing between a white woman and a colored man is a sufficient foundation for the charge of rape. The Southern white man says that it is impossible for a voluntary alliance to exist between a white woman and a colored man, and therefore, the fact of an alliance is a proof of force. In numerous instances where colored men have been lynched on the charge of rape, it was positively known at the time of lynching, and indisputably proven after the victim's death, that the relationship sustained between the man and woman was voluntary and clandestine, and that in no court of law

could even the charge of assault have been successfully maintained.

[. . .]

In his remarkable apology for lynching, Bishop Haygood, of Georgia, says: "No race, not the most savage, tolerates the rape of woman, but it may be said without reflection upon any other people that the Southern people are now and always have been most sensitive concerning the honor of their women—their mothers, wives, sisters and daughters." It is not the purpose of this defense to say one word against the white women of the South. Such need not be said, but it is their misfortune that the chivalrous white men of that section, in order to escape the deserved execration of the civilized world, should shield themselves by their cowardly and infamously false excuse, and call into question that very honor about which their distinguished priestly apologist claims they are most sensitive. To justify their own barbarism they assume a chivalry which they do not possess. True chivalry respects all womanhood, and no one who reads the record, as it is written in the faces of the million mulattoes in the South, will for a minute conceive that the Southern white man had a very chivalrous regard for the honor due the women of his own race or respect for the womanhood which circumstances placed in his power. That chivalry which is "most sensitive concerning the honor of women" can hope for but little respect from the civilized world, when it confines itself entirely to the women who happen to be white. Virtue knows no color line, and the chivalry which depends upon complexion of skin and texture of hair can command no honest respect.

[. . .]

141 MEN AND GIRLS DIE IN WAIST FACTORY FIRE (1911)

Despite the gains achieved through the New York Shirtwaist Strike of 1909, working conditions in the garment industry remained dangerous. The Triangle Shirtwaist Factory was one of the largest garment companies in Manhattan and employed mostly immigrant women as factory workers. This account of the fire in *The New York Times* describes the deaths of 141 workers (later found to be 146) and the horror of onlookers. This tragedy demonstrated the inadequacies of existing worker protections and became a rallying cry for improved government regulation and increased unionization.

Three stories of a ten-floor building at the corner of Greene Street and Washington Place were burned yesterday, and while the fire was going on 141 young men and women—at least 125 of them mere girls—were burned to death or killed by jumping to the pavement below.

The building was fireproof. It shows now hardly any signs of the disaster that overtook it. The walls are as good as ever; so are the floors; nothing is the worse for the fire except the furniture and 141 of the 600 men and girls that were employed in its upper three stories.

Most of the victims were suffocated or burned to death within the building, but some who fought their way to the windows and leaped met death as surely, but perhaps more quickly, on the pavements below.

[. . .]

The victims who are now lying at the Morgue waiting for some one to identify them by a tooth or the remains of a burned shoe were mostly girls from 16 to 23 years of age. They were employed at making shirtwaists by the Triangle Waist Company, the principal owners of which are Isaac Harris and Max Blanck. Most of them could barely speak English. Many of them came from Brooklyn. Almost all were the main support of their hardworking families.

There is just one fire escape in the building. That one is an interior fire escape. In Greene Street, where the terrified unfortunates crowded before they began to make their mad leaps to death, the whole big front of the building is guiltless of one. Nor is there a fire escape in the back.

[. . .]

LEAPED OUT OF THE FLAMES

At 4:40 o'clock, nearly five hours after the employees in the rest of the building had gone home, the fire broke out. The one little fire escape in the interior was never resorted to by any of the doomed victims. Some of them escaped by running down the stairs, but in a moment or two this avenue was cut off by flame. The girls rushed to the windows and looked down at Greene Street, 100 feet below them. Then one poor, little creature jumped. There was a plate glass protection over part of the sidewalk, but

"141 Men and Girls Die in Waist Factory Fire." *New York Times* March 26, 1911.

she crashed through it, wrecking it and breaking her body into a thousand pieces.

Then they all began to drop. The crowd yelled "Don't jump!" but it was jump or be burned—the proof of which is found in the fact that fifty burned bodies were taken from the ninth floor alone.

They jumped, they crashed through broken glass, they crushed themselves to death on the sidewalk. Of those who stayed behind it is better to say nothing—except what a veteran policeman said as he gazed at a headless and charred trunk on the Greene Street sidewalk hours after the worst cases had been taken out:

> "I saw the Slocum disaster, but it was nothing to this."
>
> "Is it a man or a woman?" asked the reporter.
>
> "It's human, that's all you can tell," answered the policeman.

It was just a mass of ashes, with blood congealed on what had probably been the neck.

Messrs. Harris and Blanck were in the building, but they escaped. They carried with them Mr. Blanck's children and a governess, and they fled over the roofs. Their employees did not know the way, because they had been in the habit of using the two freight elevators, and one of these elevators was not in service when the fire broke out.

[. . .]

"It's the worst thing I ever saw," said one old policeman.

Chief Croker said it was an outrage. He spoke bitterly of the way in which the Manufacturers' Association had called a meeting in Wall Street to take measures against his proposal for enforcing better methods of protection for employees in cases of fire.

NO CHANCE TO SAVE VICTIMS

[. . .]

It may convey some idea too, to say that thirty bodies clogged the elevator shaft. These dead were all girls. They had made their rush there blindly when they discovered that there was no chance to get out by the fire escape. Then they found that the elevator was as hopeless as anything else, and they fell there in their tracks and died.

The Triangle Waist Company employed about 600 women and less than 100 men. One of the saddest features of the thing is the fact that they had almost finished for the day. In five minutes more, if the fire had started then, probably not a life would have been lost.

Last night District Attorney Whitman started an investigation—not of this disaster alone but of the whole condition which makes it possible for a firetrap of such a kind to exist. Mr. Whitman's intention is to find out if the present laws cover such cases, and if they do not to frame laws that will.

GIRLS JUMP TO SURE DEATH. FIRE NETS PROVE USELESS— FIREMEN HELPLESS TO SAVE LIFE

[. . .]

How the fire started no one knows. On the three upper floors of the building were 600 employees of the waist company, 500 of whom were girls. The victims—mostly Italians, Russians, Hungarians, and Germans—were girls and men who had been employed by the firm of Harris & Blanck, owners of the Triangle Waist Company, after the strike in which the Jewish girls, formerly employed, had become unionized and had demanded better working conditions. The building had experienced four recent fires and had been reported by the Fire Department to the Building Department as unsafe on account of the insufficiency of its exits.

The building itself was of the most modern construction and classed as fireproof. What burned so quickly and disastrously for the victims were shirtwaists, hanging on lines above tiers of workers, sewing machines placed so closely together that there was hardly aisle room for the girls between them, and shirtwaist trimmings and cuttings which littered the floors above the eighth and ninth stories.

Girls had begun leaping from the eighth story windows before firemen arrived. The firemen had trouble bringing their apparatus into position because of the bodies which strewed the pavement and sidewalks. While more bodies crashed down among them, they worked with desperation to run their ladders into position and to spread fire nets.

[. . .]

Five girls who stood together at a window close to the Greene Street corner held their places while a fire ladder was worked toward them, but which stopped at its full length two stories lower down. They leaped together, clinging to each other, with fire streaming back from their hair and dresses. They struck a glass sidewalk cover and crashed through it to the basement. There was no time to aid them. With water pouring in upon them from a dozen hose nozzles the bodies lay for two hours where they struck, as did the many others who leaped to their deaths.

One girl, who waved a handkerchief at the crowd, leaped from a window adjoining the New York University Building on the westward. Her dress caught on a wire, and the crowd watched her hang there till her dress burned free and she came toppling down.

[. . .]

17. • *Daughters of Bilitis*

STATEMENT OF PURPOSE (1955)

The Daughters of Bilitis (DOB) was the first lesbian civil rights organization in the United States. It formed in San Francisco in 1955 and later opened up chapters across the country. While initially functioning as more of a social club where lesbians could meet and interact safely, DOB quickly grew into an activist organization. In 1956 DOB began publishing *The Ladder*, the first nationally distributed lesbian publication, which became an important source of information for lesbians across the country and created a sense of community. The goals of DOB seem modest by today's standards and, along with others that were part of the homophile movement, they are often criticized for their assimilationist rhetoric. However, the pioneering work of the DOB laid the groundwork for more radical activism.

A women's organization for the purpose of promoting the integration of the homosexual into society by:

1. Education of the variant, with particular emphasis on the psychological, physiological and sociological aspects, to enable her to understand herself and make her adjustment to society in all its social, civic and economic implications— this to be accomplished by establishing and maintaining as complete a library as possible of both fiction and non-fiction literature on the sex deviant theme; by sponsoring public discussions on pertinent subjects to be conducted by leading members of the legal, psychiatric, religious and other professions; by advocating a mode of behavior and dress acceptable to society.

Daughters of Bilitis. "Statement of Purpose" *The Ladder*. 1955.

2. Education of the public at large through acceptance first of the individual, leading to an eventual breakdown of erroneous taboos and prejudices; through public discussion meetings aforementioned; through dissemination of educational literature on the homosexual theme.

3. Participation in research projects by duly authorized and responsible psychologists, sociologists and other such experts directed towards further knowledge of the homosexual.

4. Investigation of the penal code as it pertains to the homosexual, proposal of changes to provide an equitable handling of cases involving this minority group, and promotion of these changes through due process of law in the state legislatures.

18. • Leslie Feinberg, interview with Sylvia Rivera

I'M GLAD I WAS IN THE STONEWALL RIOT (1998)

Sylvia Rivera was a long-time activist for the LGBTQPAI+ community, particularly for genderqueer and other groups who felt marginalized within the gay rights movement. She was an influential member of several activist organizations including the Gay Liberation Front (GLF), Gay Activists Alliance (GAA), and the Street Transvestite Action Revolutionaries (STAR). While other readings in this section provide contemporaneous historical accounts, most of the reports of the Stonewall riot written at the time reflect a heavily biased, heteronormative, cisgender perspective. Therefore, to include a first-person, queer history of the uprising, we have chosen a retrospective piece, written three decades after the riots, and positioned it chronologically in terms of the time period it discusses rather than the year it was published. Here, in an interview with Leslie Feinberg that was included in Feinberg's book, *Trans Liberation: Beyond Pink or Blue*, Rivera tells her story of the Stonewall riot and discusses her other activist work.

I left home at age 10 in 1961. I hustled on 42nd Street. The early 60s was not a good time for drag queens, effeminate boys or boys that wore makeup like we did.

Back then we were beat up by the police, by everybody. I didn't really come out as a drag queen until the late 60s.

When drag queens were arrested, what degradation there was. I remember the first time I got arrested, I wasn't even in full drag. I was walking down the street and the cops just snatched me.

We always felt that the police were the real enemy. We expected nothing better than to be treated like we were animals—and we were.

We were stuck in a bullpen like a bunch of freaks. We were disrespected. A lot of us were beaten up and raped.

When I ended up going to jail, to do 90 days, they tried to rape me. I very nicely bit the shit out of a man.

I've been through it all.

In 1969, the night of the Stonewall riot, was a very hot, muggy night. We were in the Stonewall [bar] and the lights came on. We all stopped dancing. The police came in.

They had gotten their payoff earlier in the week. But Inspector Pine came in—him and his morals squad—to spend more of the government's money.

We were led out of the bar and they cattled us all up against the police vans. The cops pushed us up against the grates and the fences. People started throwing pennies, nickels, and quarters at the cops.

And then the bottles started. And then we finally had the morals squad barricaded in the Stonewall building, because they were actually afraid of us at that time. They didn't know we were going to react that way.

We were not taking any more of this shit. We had done so much for other movements. It was time.

It was street gay people from the Village out front—homeless people who lived in the park in Sheridan Square outside the bar—and then drag queens behind them and everybody behind us. The Stonewall Inn telephone lines were cut and they were left in the dark.

One *Village Voice* reporter was in the bar at that time. And according to the archives of the *Village Voice*, he was handed a gun from Inspector Pine and told, "We got to fight our way out of there."

This was after one Molotov cocktail was thrown and we were ramming the door of the Stonewall bar with an uprooted parking meter. So they were ready to come out shooting that night.

Finally the Tactical Police Force showed up after 45 minutes. A lot of people forget that for 45 minutes we had them trapped in there.

All of us were working for so many movements at that time. Everyone was involved with the women's movement, the peace movement, the civil-rights movement. We were all radicals. I believe that's what brought it around.

You get tired of being just pushed around.

STAR came about after a sit-in at Weinstein Hall at New York University in 1970. Later we had a chapter in New York, one in Chicago, one in California and England.

STAR was for the street gay people, the street homeless people and anybody that needed help at that time. Marsha and I had always sneaked people into our hotel rooms. Marsha and I decided to get a building. We were trying to get away from the Mafia's control at the bars.

We got a building at 213 East 2nd Street. Marsha and I just decided it was time to help each other and help our other kids. We fed people and clothed people. We kept the building going. We went out and hustled the streets. We paid the rent.

We didn't want the kids out in the streets hustling. They would go out and rip off food. There was always food in the house and everyone had fun. It lasted for two or three years.

We would sit there and ask, "Why do we suffer?" As we got more involved into the movements, we said, "Why do we always got to take the brunt of this shit?"

Later on, when the Young Lords [revolutionary Puerto Rican youth group] came about in New York City, I was already in GLF [Gay Liberation Front]. There was a mass demonstration that started in East Harlem in the fall of 1970. The protest was against police repression and we decided to join the demonstration with our STAR banner.

That was one of first times the STAR banner was shown in public, where STAR was present as a group.

I ended up meeting some of the Young Lords that day. I became one of them. Any time they needed any help, I was always there for the Young Lords. It was just the respect they gave us as human beings. They gave us a lot of respect.

It was a fabulous feeling for me to be myself— being part of the Young Lords as a drag queen—and my organization [STAR] being part of the Young Lords.

I met [Black Panther Party leader] Huey Newton at the Peoples' Revolutionary Convention in Philadelphia in 1971. Huey decided we were part of the revolution—that we were revolutionary people.

I was a radical, a revolutionist. I am still a revolutionist. I was proud to make the road and help change laws and what-not. I was very proud of doing that and proud of what I'm still doing, no matter what it takes.

Today, we have to fight back against the government. We have to fight them back. They're cutting back Medicaid, cutting back on medicine for people with AIDS. They want to take away from women on welfare and put them into that little work program. They're going to cut SSI.

Now they're taking away food stamps. These people who want the cuts—these people are making millions and millions and millions of dollars as CEOs.

Why is the government going to take it away from us? What they're doing is cutting us back. Why can't we have a break?

I'm glad I was in the Stonewall riot. I remember when someone threw a Molotov cocktail, I thought: "My god, the revolution is here. The revolution is finally here!"

I always believed that we would have a fight back. I just knew that we would fight back. I just didn't know it would be that night.

I am proud of myself as being there that night. If I had lost that moment, I would have been kind of hurt because that's when I saw the world change for me and my people.

Of course, we still got a long way ahead of us.

19. • *Pat Mainardi*

THE POLITICS OF HOUSEWORK (1970)

Pat Mainardi belonged to a radical feminist group called the Redstockings, which was formed in New York in 1969. One of the activist strategies of the group was consciousness-raising, a practice that used group discussion to make links between individual experiences and larger structures of exploitation and discrimination. Mainardi's article illustrates the feminist slogan "the personal is political" by demonstrating how housework, something that seemed trivial and apolitical, was really connected to the undervaluing of women's work and therefore to women's oppression more generally.

. . . Liberated women—very different from Women's Liberation! The first signals all kinds of goodies, to warm the hearts (not to mention other parts) of the most radical men. The other signals—HOUSEWORK. The first brings sex without marriage, sex before marriage, cozy housekeeping arrangements ("I'm living with this chick") and the self-content of knowing that you're not the kind of man who wants a doormat instead of a woman. That will come later. After all, who wants that old commodity anymore, the Standard American Housewife, all husband, home and kids. The New

Mainardi, Pat. "The Politics of Housework" This text is from: *Notes from the Second Year: Women's Liberation: Major Writings of the Radical Feminists* (1970)

Commodity, the Liberated Woman, has sex a lot and has a Career, preferably something that can be fitted in with the household chores—like dancing, pottery, or painting.

On the other hand is Women's Liberation—and housework. What? You say this is all trivial? Wonderful! That's what I thought. It seemed perfectly reasonable. We both had careers, both had to work a couple of days a week to earn enough to live on, so why shouldn't we share the housework? So I suggested it to my mate and he agreed—most men are too hip to turn you down flat. You're right, he said. It's only fair.

Then an interesting thing happened. I can only explain it by stating that we women have been brainwashed more than even we can imagine. Probably too many years of seeing television women in ecstasy over their shiny waxed floors or breaking down over their dirty shirt collars. Men have no such conditioning. They recognize the essential fact of housework right from the very beginning. Which is that it stinks.

Here's my list of dirty chores: buying groceries, carting them home and putting them away; cooking meals and washing dishes and pots; doing the laundry; digging out the place when things get out of control; washing floors. The list could go on but the sheer necessities are bad enough. All of us live to do these things, or get someone else to do them for us. The longer my husband contemplated these chores, the more repulsed he became, and so proceeded the change from the normally sweet considerate Dr. Jekyll into the crafty Mr. Hyde who would stop at nothing to avoid the horrors of housework. As he felt himself backed into a corner laden with dirty dishes, brooms, mops and reeking garbage, his front teeth grew longer and pointier, his fingernails haggled and his eyes grew wild. Housework trivial? Not on your life! Just try to share the burden.

So ensued a dialogue that's been going on for several years. Here are some of the high points:

- "I don't mind sharing the housework, but I don't do it very well. We should each do the things we're best at." MEANING: Unfortunately I'm no good

at things like washing dishes or cooking. What I do best is a little light carpentry, changing light bulbs, moving furniture (how often do *you* move furniture?). ALSO MEANING: Historically the lower classes (black men and us) have had hundreds of years' experience doing menial jobs. It would be a waste of manpower to train someone else to do them now. ALSO MEANING: I don't like the dull stupid boring jobs, so you should do them.

- "I don't mind sharing the work, but you'll have to show me how to do it." MEANING: I ask a lot of questions and you'll have to show me everything every time I do it because I don't remember so good. Also don't try to sit down and read while I'M doing my jobs because I'm going to annoy hell out of you until it's easier to do them yourself.

- "We used to be so happy!" (Said whenever it was his turn to do something.) MEANING: I used to be so happy. MEANING: Life without housework is bliss. No quarrel here. Perfect Agreement.

- "We have different standards, and why should I have to work to your standards? That's unfair." MEANING: If I begin to get bugged by the dirt and crap I will say, "This place sure is a sty" or "How can anyone live like this?" and wait for your reaction. I know that all women have a sore called "Guilt over a messy house" or "Household work is ultimately my responsibility." I know that men have caused that sore—if anyone visits and the place *is* a sty, they're not going to leave and say, "He sure is a lousy housekeeper." You'll take the rap in any case. I can outwait you. ALSO MEANING: I can provoke innumerable scenes over the housework issue. Eventually doing all the housework yourself will be less painful to you than trying to get me to do half. Or I'll suggest we get a maid. She will do my share of the work. You will do yours. It's women's work.

- "I've got nothing against sharing the housework, but you can't make me do it on your schedule." MEANING: Passive resistance. I'll do it when I damned well please, if at all. If my job is doing dishes, it's easier to do them once a week. If taking out laundry, once a month. If washing the floors, once a year. If you don't like it, do it yourself oftener, and then I won't do it at all.

- "I hate it more than you. You don't mind it so much." MEANING: Housework is garbage work. It's the worst crap I've ever done. It's degrading and humiliating for someone of *my* intelligence to do it. But for someone of *your* intelligence . . .

- "Housework is too trivial to even talk about." MEANING: It's even more trivial to do. Housework is beneath my status. My purpose in life is to deal with matters of significance. Yours is to deal with matters of insignificance. You should do the housework.

- "This problem of housework is not a man–woman problem. In any relationship between two people one is going to have a stronger personality and dominate." MEANING: That stronger personality had better be *me*.

- "In animal societies, wolves, for example, the top animal is usually a male even where he is not chosen for brute strength but on the basis of cunning and intelligence. Isn't that interesting?" MEANING: I have historical, psychological, anthropological and biological justification for keeping you down. How can you ask the top wolf to be equal?

- "Women's Liberation isn't really a political movement." MEANING: The Revolution is coming too close to home. ALSO MEANING: I am only interested in how I am oppressed, not how I oppress others. Therefore the war, the draft and the university are political. Women's Liberation is not.

- "Man's accomplishments have always depended on getting help from other people, mostly women. What great man would have accomplished what he did if he had to do his own housework?" MEANING: Oppression is built into the system and I, as the white American male, receive the benefits of this system. I don't want to give them up.

* * *

Participatory democracy begins at home. If you are planning to implement your politics, there are certain things to remember:

1. He *is* feeling it more than you. He's losing some leisure and you're gaining it. The measure of your oppression is his resistance.

2. A great many American men are not accustomed to doing monotonous repetitive work which never issues in any lasting, let alone important, achievement. This is why they would rather repair a cabinet than wash dishes. If human endeavors are like a pyramid with man's highest achievements at the top, then keeping oneself alive is at the bottom. Men have always had servants (us) to take care of this bottom strata of life while they have confined their efforts to the rarefied upper regions. It is thus ironic when they ask of women—where are your great painters, statesmen, etc.? Mme. Matisse ran a millinery shop so he could paint. Mrs. Martin Luther King kept his house and raised his babies.

3. It is a traumatizing experience for someone who has always thought of himself as being against any oppression or exploitation of one human being by another to realize that in his daily life he has been accepting and implementing (and benefiting from) this exploitation; that his rationalization is little different from that of the racist who says "Black people don't feel pain" (women don't mind doing the shitwork); and that the oldest form of oppression in history has been the oppression of 50% of the population by the other 50%.

4. Arm yourself with some knowledge of the psychology of oppressed peoples everywhere, and a few facts about the animal kingdom. I admit playing top wolf or who runs the gorillas is silly but as a last resort men bring it up all the time. Talk about bees. If you feel really hostile bring up the sex life of spiders. They have sex. She bites off his head.

The psychology of oppressed peoples is not silly. Jews, immigrants, black men and all women have employed the same psychological mechanisms to survive: admiring the oppressor, glorifying the oppressor, wanting to be like the oppressor, wanting the oppressor to like them, mostly because the oppressor held all the power.

5. In a sense, all men everywhere are slightly schizoid—divorced from the reality of maintaining life. This makes it easier for them to play games with it. It is almost a cliché that women feel greater grief at sending a son off to a war or losing him to that war because they bore him, suckled him, and raised him. The men who foment those wars did none of those things and have a more superficial estimate of the worth of human life. One hour a day is a low estimate of the amount of time one has to spend "keeping" oneself. By foisting this off on others, man has seven hours a week—one working day more to play with his mind and not his human needs. Over the course of generations it is easy to see whence evolved the horrifying abstractions of modern life.

6. With the death of each form of oppression, life changes and new forms evolve. English aristocrats at the turn of the century were horrified at the idea of enfranchising working men—were sure that it signaled the death of civilization and a return to barbarism. Some workingmen were even deceived by this line. Similarly with the minimum wage, abolition of slavery, and female suffrage. Life changes but it goes on. Don't fall for any line about the death of everything if men take a turn at the dishes. They will imply that you are holding back the Revolution (their Revolution). But you are advancing it (your Revolution).

7. Keep checking up. Periodically consider who's actually *doing* the jobs. These things have a way of backsliding so that a year later once again the woman is doing everything. After a year make a list of jobs the man has rarely if ever done. You will find cleaning pots, toilets, refrigerators and ovens high on the list. Use time sheets if necessary. He will accuse you of being petty. He is above that sort of thing (housework). Bear in mind what the worst jobs are, namely the ones that have to be done every day or several times a day. Also the ones that are dirty—it's more pleasant to pick up books, newspapers, etc., than to wash dishes. Alternate the bad jobs. It's the daily grind that gets you down. Also make sure that you don't have the responsibility for the housework with occasional help from him. "I'll cook dinner for you tonight" implies it's really your job and isn't he a nice guy to do some of it for you.

8. Most men had a rich and rewarding bachelor life during which they did not starve or become encrusted with crud or buried under the litter. There is a taboo that says women mustn't strain themselves in the presence of men—we haul around 50 lbs of groceries if we have to but aren't allowed to open a jar if there is someone around to do it for us. The reverse side of the coin is that men aren't supposed to be able to take care of themselves without a woman. Both are excuses for making women do the housework.

9. Beware of the double whammy. He won't do the little things he always did because you're now a "Liberated Woman," right? Of course he won't do anything else either . . .

I was just finishing this when my husband came in and asked what I was doing. Writing a paper on housework. Housework? he said. *Housework?* Oh my god, how trivial can you get. A paper on housework.

20. • *Anne Koedt*

THE MYTH OF THE VAGINAL ORGASM (1970)

Anne Koedt was a founding member of the New York Radical Feminists. "The Myth of the Vaginal Orgasm" was included in the feminist publication *Notes from the Second Year.* It quickly became a seminal text in feminist scholarship by arguing that contemporary understandings of female pleasure were inaccurate because they were produced in a male-dominated society. Koedt argues that women achieve orgasms through their clitoris and that the focus on vaginal orgasms is a mischaracterization of female pleasure that has caused many women to be sexually deprived while blaming themselves.

Whenever female orgasm and frigidity is discussed, a false distinction is made between the vaginal and the clitoral orgasm. Frigidity has generally been defined by men as the failure of women to have vaginal orgasms. Actually the vagina is not a highly sensitive area and is not constructed to achieve orgasm. It is the clitoris which is the center of sexual sensitivity and which is the female equivalent of the penis.

I think this explains a great many things: First of all, the fact that the so-called frigidity rate among women is phenomenally high. Rather than tracing female frigidity to the false assumptions about female anatomy, our "experts" have declared frigidity a psychological problem of women. Those women who complained about it were recommended psychiatrists, so that they might discover their "problem"—diagnosed generally as a failure to adjust to their role as women.

The facts of female anatomy and sexual response tell a different story. There is only one area for sexual climax, although there are many areas for sexual arousal; that area is the clitoris. All orgasms are extensions of sensation from this area. Since the clitoris is not necessarily stimulated sufficiently in the conventional sexual positions, we are left "frigid."

Aside from physical stimulation, which is the common cause of orgasm for most people, there is also stimulation through primarily mental processes. Some women, for example, may achieve orgasm through sexual fantasies, or through fetishes. However, while the stimulation may be psychological, the orgasm manifests itself physically. Thus, while the cause is psychological, the *effect* is still physical, and the orgasm necessarily takes place in the sexual organ equipped for sexual climax—the clitoris. The orgasm experience may also differ in degree of intensity—some more localized, and some more diffuse and sensitive. But they are all clitoral orgasms.

All this leads to some interesting questions about conventional sex and our role in it. Men have orgasms essentially by friction with the vagina, not

Koedt, Anne. "The Myth of the Vaginal Orgasm." *Notes from the Second Year: Women's Liberation: Major Writings of the Radical Feminists* (1970)

the clitoral area, which is external and not able to cause friction the way penetration does. Women have thus been defined sexually in terms of what pleases men; our own biology has not been properly analyzed. Instead, we are fed the myth of the liberated woman and her vaginal orgasm—an orgasm which in fact does not exist.

What we must do is redefine our sexuality. We must discard the "normal" concepts of sex and create new guidelines which take into account mutual sexual enjoyment. While the idea of mutual enjoyment is liberally applauded in marriage manuals, it is not followed to its logical conclusion. We must begin to demand that if certain sexual positions now defined as "standard" are not mutually conducive to orgasm, they no longer be defined as standard. New techniques must be used or devised which transform this particular aspect of our current sexual exploitation.

FREUD—A FATHER OF THE VAGINAL ORGASM

Freud contended that the clitoral orgasm was adolescent, and that upon puberty, when women began having intercourse with men, women should transfer the center of orgasm to the vagina. The vagina, it was assumed, was able to produce a parallel, but more mature, orgasm than the clitoris. Much work was done to elaborate on this theory, but little was done to challenge the basic assumptions.

To fully appreciate this incredible invention, perhaps Freud's general attitude about women should first be recalled. Mary Ellman, in *Thinking About Women*, summed it up this way:

> Everything in Freud's patronizing and fearful attitude toward women follows from their lack of a penis, but it is only in his essay *The Psychology of Women* that Freud makes explicit . . . the deprecations of women which are implicit in his work. He then prescribes for them the abandonment of the life of the mind, which will interfere with their sexual function. When the psychoanalyzed patient is male, the analyst sets himself the task of developing the man's capacities; but with women patients, the job is to resign them to the limits of their sexuality. As Mr. Rieff puts it: For Freud, "Analysis cannot encourage in women new energies for success and achievement, but only teach them the lesson of rational resignation."

It was Freud's feelings about women's secondary and inferior relationship to men that formed the basis for his theories on female sexuality.

Once having laid down the law about the nature of our sexuality, Freud not so strangely discovered a tremendous problem of frigidity in women. His recommended cure for a woman who was frigid was psychiatric care. She was suffering from failure to mentally adjust to her "natural" role as a woman. Frank S. Caprio, a contemporary follower of these ideas, states:

> . . . whenever a woman is incapable of achieving an orgasm via coitus, provided her husband is an adequate partner, and prefers clitoral stimulation to any other form of sexual activity, she can be regarded as suffering from frigidity and requires psychiatric assistance. (*The Sexually Adequate Female*, p. 64.)

The explanation given was that women were envious of men—"renunciation of womanhood." Thus it was diagnosed as an anti-male phenomenon.

It is important to emphasize that Freud did not base his theory upon a study of woman's anatomy, but rather upon his assumptions of woman as an inferior appendage to man, and her consequent social and psychological role. In their attempts to deal with the ensuing problem of mass frigidity, Freudians created elaborate mental gymnastics. Marie Bonaparte, in *Female Sexuality*, goes so far as to suggest surgery to help women back on their rightful path. Having discovered a strange connection between the non-frigid woman and the location of the clitoris near the vagina,

> it then occurred to me that where, in certain women, this gap was excessive, and clitoridal fixation obdurate, a clitoridal-vaginal reconciliation might be effected by surgical means, which would then benefit the normal erotic function. Professor Halban, of Vienna, as much a biologist as surgeon, became

interested in the problem and worked out a simple operative technique. In this, the suspensory ligament of the clitoris was severed and the clitoris secured to the underlying structures, thus fixing it in a lower position, with eventual reduction of the labia minora. (p. 148.)

But the severest damage was not in the area of surgery, where Freudians ran around absurdly trying to change female anatomy to fit their basic assumptions. The worst damage was done to the mental health of women, who either suffered silently with self-blame, or flocked to the psychiatrists looking desperately for the hidden and terrible repression that kept from them their vaginal destiny.

LACK OF EVIDENCE?

One may perhaps at first claim that these are unknown and unexplored areas, but upon closer examination this is certainly not true today, nor was it true even in the past. For example, men have known that women suffered from frigidity often during intercourse. So the problem was there. Also, there is much specific evidence. Men knew that the clitoris was and is the essential organ for masturbation, whether in children or adult women. So obviously women made it clear where they thought their sexuality was located. Men also seem suspiciously aware of the clitoral powers during "foreplay," when they want to arouse women and produce the necessary lubrication for penetration. Foreplay is a concept created for male purposes, but works to the disadvantage of many women, since as soon as the woman is aroused the man changes to vaginal stimulation, leaving her both aroused and unsatisfied.

It has also been known that women need no anesthesia inside the vagina during surgery, thus pointing to the fact that the vagina is in fact not a highly sensitive area.

Today, with extensive knowledge of anatomy, with Kinsey, and Masters and Johnson, to mention just a few sources, there is no ignorance on the subject. There are, however, social reasons why this knowledge has not been popularized. We are living in a male society which has not sought change in women's role.

ANATOMICAL EVIDENCE

Rather than starting with what women *ought* to feel, it would seem logical to start out with the anatomical facts regarding the clitoris and vagina.

The Clitoris is a small equivalent of the penis, except for the fact that the urethra does not go through it as in the man's penis. Its erection is similar to the male erection, and the head of the clitoris has the same type of structure and function as the head of the penis. G. Lombard Kelly, in *Sexual Feeling in Married Men and Women*, says:

> The head of the clitoris is also composed of erectile tissue, and it possesses a very sensitive epithelium or surface covering, supplied with special nerve endings called genital corpuscles, which are peculiarly adapted for sensory stimulation that under proper mental conditions terminates in the sexual orgasm. No other part of the female generative tract has such corpuscles. (Pocketbooks; p. 35.)

The clitoris has no other function than that of sexual pleasure.

The Vagina—Its functions are related to the reproductive function. Principally, 1) menstruation, 2) receive penis, 3) hold semen, and 4) birth passage. The interior of the vagina, which according to the defenders of the vaginally caused orgasm is the center and producer of the orgasm, is:

> like nearly all other internal body structures, poorly supplied with end organs of touch. The internal entodermal origin of the lining of the vagina makes it similar in this respect to the rectum and other parts of the digestive tract. (Kinsey, *Sexual Behavior in the Human Female*, p. 580.)

The degree of insensitivity inside the vagina is so high that "Among the women who were tested in our gynecologic sample, less than 14% were at all conscious that they had been touched." (Kinsey, p. 580.)

Even the importance of the vagina as an *erotic* center (as opposed to an orgasmic center) has been found to be minor.

Other Areas—Labia minora and the vestibule of the vagina. These two sensitive areas may trigger off a clitoral orgasm. Because they can be effectively stimulated during "normal" coitus, though infrequent, this kind of stimulation is incorrectly thought to be vaginal orgasm. However, it is important to distinguish between areas which can stimulate the clitoris, incapable of producing the orgasm themselves, and the clitoris:

> Regardless of what means of excitation is used to bring the individual to the state of sexual climax, the sensation is perceived by the genital corpuscles and is localized where they are situated: in the head of the clitoris or penis. (Kelly, p. 49.)

Psychologically Stimulated Orgasm—Aside from the above mentioned direct and indirect stimulations of the clitoris, there is a third way an orgasm may be triggered. This is through mental (cortical) stimulation, where the imagination stimulates the brain, which in turn stimulates the genital corpuscles of the glans to set off an orgasm.

WOMEN WHO SAY THEY HAVE VAGINAL ORGASMS

Confusion—Because of the lack of knowledge of their own anatomy, some women accept the idea that an orgasm felt during "normal" intercourse was vaginally caused. This confusion is caused by a combination of two factors. One, failing to locate the center of the orgasm, and two, by a desire to fit her experience to the male-defined idea of sexual normalcy. Considering that women know little about their anatomy, it is easy to be confused.

Deception—The vast majority of women who pretend vaginal orgasm to their men are faking it to, as Ti-Grace Atkinson says, "get the job." In a new bestselling Danish book, *I Accuse* (my own translation), Mette Ejlersen specifically deals with this common problem, which she calls the "sex comedy."

This comedy has many causes. First of all, the man brings a great deal of pressure to bear on the woman, because he considers his ability as a lover at stake. So as not to offend his ego, the woman will comply with the prescribed role and go through simulated ecstasy. In some of the other Danish women mentioned, women who were left frigid were turned off to sex, and pretended vaginal orgasm to hurry up the sex act. Others admitted that they had faked vaginal orgasm to catch a man. In one case, the woman pretended vaginal orgasm to get him to leave his first wife, who admitted being vaginally frigid. Later she was forced to continue the deception, since obviously she couldn't tell him to stimulate her clitorally.

Many more women were simply afraid to establish their right to equal enjoyment, seeing the sexual act as being primarily for the man's benefit, and any pleasure that the woman got as an added extra.

Other women, with just enough ego to reject the man's idea that they needed psychiatric care, refused to admit their frigidity. They wouldn't accept self-blame, but they didn't know how to solve the problem, not knowing the physiological facts about themselves. So they were left in a peculiar limbo.

Again, perhaps one of the most infuriating and damaging results of this whole charade has been that women who were perfectly healthy sexually were taught that they were not. So in addition to being sexually deprived, these women were told to blame themselves when they deserved no blame. Looking for a cure to a problem that has none can lead a woman on an endless path of self-hatred and insecurity. For she is told by her analyst that not even in her one role allowed in a male society—the role of a woman—is she successful. She is put on the defensive, with phony data as evidence that she better try to be even more feminine, think more feminine, and reject her envy of men. That is, shuffle even harder, baby.

WHY MEN MAINTAIN THE MYTH

1. *Sexual Penetration is Preferred*—The best stimulant for the penis is the woman's vagina. It supplies the necessary friction and lubrication. From

a strictly technical point of view this position offers the best physical conditions, even though the man may try other positions for variation.

2. *The Invisible Woman*—One of the elements of male chauvinism is the refusal or inability to see women as total, separate human beings. Rather, men have chosen to define women only in terms of how they benefited men's lives. Sexually, a woman was not seen as an individual wanting to share equally in the sexual act, any more than she was seen as a person with independent desires when she did anything else in society. Thus, it was easy to make up what was convenient about women; for on top of that, society has been a function of male interests, and women were not organized to form even a vocal opposition to the male experts.

3. *The Penis as Epitome of Masculinity*—Men define their lives greatly in terms of masculinity. It is a *universal*, as opposed to racial, ego boosting, which is localized by the geography of racial mixtures.

The essence of male chauvinism is not the practical, economic services women supply. It is the psychological superiority. This kind of negative definition of self, rather than positive definition based upon one's own achievements and development, has of course chained the victim and the oppressor both. But by far the most brutalized of the two is the victim.

An analogy is racism, where the white racist compensates his feelings of unworthiness by creating an image of the black man (it is primarily a male struggle) as biologically inferior to him. Because of his power in a white male power structure, the white man can socially enforce this mythical division.

To the extent that men try to rationalize and justify male superiority through physical differentiation, masculinity may be symbolized by being the *most* muscular, the most hairy, the deepest voice, and the biggest penis. Women, on the other hand, are approved of (i.e., called feminine) if they are weak, petite, shave their legs, have high soft voices, and no penis.

Since the clitoris is almost identical to the penis, one finds a great deal of evidence of men in various societies trying to either ignore the clitoris and emphasize the vagina (as did Freud), or, as in some places in the Mideast, actually performing clitoridectomy. Freud saw this ancient and still practiced custom as a way of further "feminizing" the female by removing this cardinal vestige of her masculinity. It should be noted also that a big clitoris is considered ugly and masculine. Some cultures engage in the practice of pouring a chemical on the clitoris to make it shrivel up into proper size.

It seems clear to me that men in fact fear the clitoris as a threat to their masculinity.

4. *Sexually Expendable Male*—Men fear that they will become sexually expendable if the clitoris is substituted for the vagina as the center of pleasure for women. Actually this has a great deal of validity if one considers *only* the anatomy. The position of the penis inside the vagina, while perfect for reproduction, does not necessarily stimulate an orgasm in women because the clitoris is located externally and higher up. Women must rely upon indirect stimulation in the "normal" position.

Lesbian sexuality could make an excellent case, based upon anatomical data, for the extinction of the male organ. Albert Ellis says something to the effect that a man without a penis can make a woman an excellent lover.

Considering that the vagina is very desirable from a man's point of view, purely on physical grounds, one begins to see the dilemma for men. And it forces us as well to discard many "physical" arguments explaining why women go to bed with men. What is left, it seems to me, are primarily psychological reasons why women select men at the exclusion of women as sexual partners.

5. *Control of Women*—One reason given to explain the Mideastern practice of clitoridectomy is that it will keep the women from straying. By removing the sexual organ capable of orgasm, it must be assumed that her sexual drive will diminish. Considering how men look upon their women as

property, particularly in very backward nations, we should begin to consider a great deal more why it is not in the men's interest to have women totally free sexually. The double standard, as practiced for example in Latin America, is set up to keep the woman as total property of the husband, while he is free to have affairs as he wishes.

6. *Lesbianism and Bisexuality*—Aside from the strictly anatomical reasons why women might equally seek other women as lovers, there is a fear on men's part that women will seek the company of other women on a full, human basis. The establishment of clitoral orgasm as fact would threaten the heterosexual *institution*. For it would indicate that sexual pleasure was obtainable from either men *or* women, thus making heterosexuality not an absolute, but an option. It would thus open up the whole question of *human* sexual relationships beyond the confines of the present male-female role system.

BOOKS MENTIONED IN THIS ESSAY

Sexual Behavior in the Human Female, Alfred C. Kinsey, Pocketbooks

Female Sexuality, Marie Bonaparte, Grove Press

Sex Without Guilt, Albert Ellis, Grove Press

Sexual Feeling in Married Men and Women, G. Lombard Kelly, Pocketbooks

I Accuse (Jeg Anklager), Mette Ejlersen, Chr. Erichsens Forlag (Danish)

The Sexually Adequate Female, Frank S. Caprio, Fawcett Gold Medal Books

Thinking About Women, Mary Ellman, Harcourt, Brace & World

Human Sexual Response, Masters and Johnson, Little, Brown

Also see:

The ABZ of Love, Inge and Sten Hegeler, Alexicon Corp.

---

21. • *Radicalesbians*

THE WOMAN-IDENTIFIED WOMAN (1970)

"The Woman-Identified Woman" was distributed at the Second Congress to Unite Women on May 1, 1970, a conference sponsored by the National Organization for Women (NOW). The manifesto came about specifically as a response to the comment made by NOW president Betty Friedan that lesbians were a "lavender menace" that detracted from the credibility of the women's movement but also more generally to the feeling on the part of many lesbians that their issues weren't being taken seriously within feminist circles. To call attention to this silencing and to respond to Friedan's comments, a group of women wearing T-shirts that said "lavender menace," who came to be known as the Radicalesbians, took over the conference, voicing anger over their exclusion and challenging the idea that lesbianism was a threat to the women's movement. "The Woman-Identified Woman" articulates a lesbian-feminist politics that positioned lesbianism as a form of resistance to patriarchy.

"The Woman-Identified Women" (1970). From *Documents from the Women's Liberation Movement*, Special Collections Library, Duke University.

What is a lesbian? A lesbian is the rage of all women condensed to the point of explosion. She is the woman who, often beginning at an extremely early age, acts in accordance with her inner compulsion to be a more complete and freer human being than her society—perhaps then, but certainly later—cares to allow her. These needs and actions, over a period of years, bring her into painful conflict with people, situations, the accepted ways of thinking, feeling and behaving, until she is in a state of continual war with everything around her, and usually with herself. She may not be fully conscious of the political implications of what for her began as personal necessity, but on some level she has not been able to accept the limitations and oppression laid on her by the most basic role of her society—the female role. The turmoil she experiences tends to induce guilt proportional to the degree to which she feels she is not meeting social expectations, and/or eventually drives her to question and analyze what the rest of her society more or less accepts. She is forced to evolve her own life pattern, often living much of her life alone, learning usually much earlier than her "straight" (heterosexual) sisters about the essential aloneness of life (which the myth of marriage obscures) and about the reality of illusions. To the extent that she cannot expel the heavy socialization that goes with being female, she can never truly find peace with herself. For she is caught somewhere between accepting society's view of her—in which case she cannot accept herself—and coming to understand what this sexist society has done to her and why it is functional and necessary for it to do so. Those of us who work that through find ourselves on the other side of a tortuous journey through a night that may have been decades long. The perspective gained from that journey, the liberation of self, the inner peace, the real love of self and of all women, is something to be shared with all women—because we are all women.

It should first be understood that lesbianism, like male homosexuality, is a category of behavior possible only in a sexist society characterized by rigid sex roles and dominated by male supremacy. Those sex roles dehumanize women by defining us as a supportive/serving caste in relation to the master caste of men, and emotionally cripple men by demanding that they be alienated from their own bodies and emotions in order to perform their economic/political/military functions effectively. Homosexuality is a by-product of a particular way of setting up roles (or approved patterns of behavior) on the basis of sex; as such it is an inauthentic (not consonant with "reality") category. In a society in which men do not oppress women, and sexual expression is allowed to follow feelings, the categories of homosexuality and heterosexuality would disappear.

But lesbianism is also different from male homosexuality, and serves a different function in the society. "Dyke" is a different kind of put-down from "faggot," although both imply you are not playing your socially assigned sex role—are not therefore a "real woman" or a "real man." The grudging admiration felt for the tomboy and the queasiness felt around a sissy boy point to the same thing: the contempt in which women—or those who play a female role—are held. And the investment in keeping women in that contemptuous role is very great. Lesbian is the word, the label, the condition that holds women in line. When a woman hears this word tossed her way, she knows she is stepping out of line. She knows that she has crossed the terrible boundary of her sex role. She recoils, she protests, she reshapes her actions to gain approval. Lesbian is a label invented by the man to throw at any woman who dares to be his equal, who dares to challenge his prerogatives (including that of all woman as part of the exchange medium among men), who dares to assert the primacy of her own needs. To have the label applied to people active in women's liberation is just the most recent instance of a long history; older women will recall that not so long ago, any woman who was successful, independent, not orienting her whole life about a man, would hear this word. For in this sexist society, for a woman to be independent means she can't be a woman—she must be a dyke. That in itself should tell us where women are at. It says as clearly as can be said: woman and person are contradictory terms. For a lesbian is not considered a "real woman." And yet, in popular thinking, there is really only one essential difference between a lesbian and other women: that of sexual orientation—which is to say, when you strip off all the packaging, you must finally realize that the essence of being a "woman" is to get fucked by men.

"Lesbian" is one of the sexual categories by which men have divided up humanity. While all women are dehumanized as sex objects, as the objects of men, they are given certain compensations: identification with his power, his ego, his status, his protection (from other males), feeling like a "real woman," finding social acceptance by adhering to her role, etc. Should a woman confront herself by confronting another woman, there are fewer rationalizations, fewer buffers by which to avoid the stark horror of her dehumanized condition. Herein we find the overriding fear of many women toward exploring intimate relationships with other women: the fear of her being used as a sexual object by a woman, which not only will bring no male-connected compensations, but also will reveal the void which is woman's real situation. This dehumanization is expressed when a straight woman learns that a sister is a lesbian; she begins to relate to her lesbian sister as her potential sex object, laying a surrogate male role on the lesbian. This reveals her heterosexual conditioning to make herself into an object when sex is potentially involved in a relationship, and it denies the lesbian her full humanity. For women, especially those in the movement, to perceive their lesbian sisters through this male grid of role definitions is to accept this male cultural conditioning and to oppress their sisters much as they themselves have been oppressed by men. Are we going to continue the male classification system of defining all females in sexual relation to some other category of people? Affixing the label lesbian not only to a woman who aspires to be a person, but also to any situation of real love, real solidarity, real primacy among women is a primary form of divisiveness among women: it is the condition which keeps women within the confines of the feminine role, and

it is the debunking/scare term that keeps women from forming any primary attachments, groups, or associations among ourselves.

Women in the movement have in most cases gone to great lengths to avoid discussion and confrontation with the issue of lesbianism. It puts people uptight. They are hostile, evasive, or try to incorporate it into some "broader issue." They would rather not talk about it. If they have to, they try to dismiss it as a "lavender herring." But it is no side issue. It is absolutely essential to the success and fulfillment of the women's liberation movement that this issue be dealt with. As long as the label "dyke" can be used to frighten women into a less militant stand, keep her separate from her sisters, keep her from giving primacy to anything other than men and family— then to that extent she is controlled by the male culture. Until women see in each other the possibility of primal commitment which includes sexual love, they will be denying themselves the love and value they readily accord to men, thus affirming their second-class status. As long as male acceptability is primary—both to individual women and to the movement as a whole—the term lesbian will be used effectively against women. Insofar as women want only more privileges within the system, they do not want to antagonize male power. They instead seek acceptability for women's liberation, and the most crucial aspect of the acceptability is to deny lesbianism—i.e., deny any fundamental challenge to the basis of the female role.

It should also be said that some younger, more radical women have honestly begun to discuss lesbianism, but so far it has been primarily as a sexual "alternative" to men. This, however, is still giving primacy to men, both because the idea of relating more completely to women occurs as a negative reaction to men, and because the lesbian relationship is being characterized simply by sex, which is divisive and sexist. On one level, which is both personal and political, women may withdraw emotional and sexual energies from men, and work out various alternatives for those energies in their own lives. On a different political/psychological level, it must be understood that what is crucial is that women begin disengaging from male-defined response patterns. In the privacy of our own psyches, we must cut those cords to the core. For irrespective of where our love and sexual energies flow, if we are male-identified in our heads, we cannot realize our autonomy as human beings.

But why is it that women have related to and through men? By virtue of having been brought up in a male society, we have internalized the male culture's definition of ourselves. That definition views us as relative beings who exist not for ourselves, but for the servicing, maintenance and comfort of men. That definition consigns us to sexual and family functions, and excludes us from defining and shaping the terms of our lives. In exchange for our psychic servicing and for performing society's non-profit-making functions, the man confers on us just one thing: the slave status which makes us legitimate in the eyes of the society in which we live. This is called "femininity" or "being a real woman" in our cultural lingo. We are authentic, legitimate, real to the extent that we are the property of some man whose name we bear. To be a woman who belongs to no man is to be invisible, pathetic, unauthentic, unreal. He confirms his image of us—of what we have to be in order to be—as he defines it, in relation to him—but cannot confirm our personhood, our own selves as absolutes. As long as we are dependent on the male culture for this definition, for this approval, we cannot be free.

The consequence of internalizing this role is an enormous reservoir of self-hate. This is not to say the self-hate is recognized or accepted as such; indeed most women would deny it. It may be experienced as discomfort with her role, as feeling empty, as numbness, as restlessness, a paralyzing anxiety at the center. Alternatively, it may be expressed in shrill defensiveness of the glory and destiny of her role. But it does exist, often beneath the edge of her consciousness, poisoning her existence, keeping her alienated from herself, her own needs, and rendering her a stranger to other women. Women hate both themselves and other women. They try

to escape by identifying with the oppressor, living through him, gaining status and identity from his ego, his power, his accomplishments. And by not identifying with other "empty vessels" like themselves, women resist relating on all levels to other women who will reflect their own oppression, their own secondary status, their own self-hate. For to confront another woman is finally to confront one's self—the self we have gone to such lengths to avoid. And in that mirror we know we cannot really respect and love that which we have been made to be.

As the source of self-hate and the lack of real self are rooted in our male-given identity, we must create a new sense of self. As long as we cling to the idea of "being a woman," we will sense some conflict with that incipient self, that sense of I, that sense of a whole person. It is very difficult to realize and accept that being "feminine" and being a whole person are irreconcilable. Only women can give each other a new sense of self. That identity we have to develop with reference to ourselves, and not in relation to men. This consciousness is the revolutionary force from which all else will follow, for ours is an organic revolution. For this we must be available and supportive to one another, give our commitment and our love, give the emotional support necessary to sustain this movement. Our energies must flow toward our sisters not backwards towards our oppressors. As long as women's liberation tries to free women without facing the basic heterosexual structure that binds us in one-to-one relationship with a man, how to get better sex, how to turn his head around—into trying to make the "new man" out of him, in the delusion that this will allow us to be the "new woman." This obviously splits our energies and commitments, leaving us unable to be committed to the construction of the new patterns which will liberate us.

It is the primacy of women relating to women, of women creating a new consciousness of and with each other which is at the heart of women's liberation, and the basis for the cultural revolution. Together we must find, reinforce and validate our authentic selves. As we do this, we confirm in each other that struggling incipient sense of pride and strength, the divisive barriers begin to melt, we feel this growing solidarity with our sisters. We see ourselves as prime, find our centers inside of ourselves. We find receding the sense of alienation, of being cut off, of being behind a locked window, of being unable to get out what we know is inside. We feel a realness, feel at last we are coinciding with ourselves. With that real self, with that consciousness, we begin a revolution to end the imposition of all coercive identifications, and to achieve maximum autonomy in human expression.

22. • *Chicago Gay Liberation Front*

A LEAFLET FOR THE AMERICAN MEDICAL ASSOCIATION (1970)

After the 1969 Stonewall riots, queer activist groups formed under the name the Gay Liberation Front (GLF). Emboldened with a new revolutionary fervor, these activists challenged the prevailing social norms around homosexuality, including the belief that homosexuals were "sick." Up until the mid-twentieth century, the consensus within the medical and psychiatric communities was that homosexuality was an illness that should be treated. However, influenced by Alfred Kinsey and other pioneering researchers in the 1950s and 1960s, an increasing number of doctors began to question this view. Gay activists like those in the GLF argued that the pathologization of homosexuality encouraged antigay attitudes and that to the extent that homosexuals experienced psychological problems, the cause was the discrimination they faced, not something intrinsic to their sexual orientation. Activists in the Chicago GLF distributed "A Leaflet for the American Medical Association" to doctors attending the association's 1970 convention. Three years later the American Psychiatric Association removed homosexuality from its list of psychiatric disorders.

The establishment school of psychiatry is based on the premise that people who are hurting should solve their problems by "adjusting" to the situation. For the homosexual, this means becoming adept at straight-fronting, learning how to survive in a hostile world, how to settle for housing in the gay ghetto, how to be satisfied with a profession in which homosexuals are tolerated, and how to live with low self-esteem.

The adjustment school places the burden on each individual homosexual to learn to bear his torment. But the "problem" of homosexuality is never solved under this scheme; the anti-homosexualist attitude of society, which is the cause of the homosexual's trouble, goes unchallenged. And there's always another paying patient on the psychiatrist's couch.

Dr. Socarides claims, "A human being is sick when he fails to function in his appropriate gender

---

Chicago Gay Liberation Front. *A Leaflet for the American Medical Association.* 1970.

identity, which is appropriate to his anatomy." Who determined "appropriateness"? The psychiatrist as moralist? Certainly there is no scientific basis for defining "appropriate" sexual behavior. In a study of homosexuality in other species and other cultures, Ford and Beach in *Patterns of Sexual Behavior* conclude, "Human homosexuality is not a product of hormonal imbalance or 'perverted heredity.' It is the product of the fundamental mammalian heritage of general sexual responsiveness as modified under the impact of experience."

Other than invoking moral standards, Dr. Socarides claims that homosexuality is an emotional illness because of the guilt and anxieties in homosexual life. Would he also consider Judaism an emotional illness because of the paranoia which Jews experienced in Nazi Germany?

We homosexuals of gay liberation believe that the adjustment school of therapy is not a valid approach to society.

We refuse to adjust to our oppression, and believe that the key to our mental health, and to the mental health of all oppressed peoples in a racist, sexist, capitalist society, is a radical change in the structure and accompanying attitudes of the entire social system.

Mental health for women does not mean therapy for women—it means the elimination of male supremacy. Not therapy for blacks, but an end to racism. The poor don't need psychiatrists (what a joke at 25 bucks a throw!)—they need democratic distribution of wealth. OFF THE COUCHES, INTO THE STREETS!

We see political organizing and collective action as the strategy for effecting this social change. We declare that we are healthy homosexuals in a sexist society, and that homosexuality is at least on a par

with heterosexuality as a way for people to relate to each other (know any men that don't dominate women?).

Since the prevalent notion in society is that homosexuality is wrong, all those who recognize that this attitude is damaging to people, and that it must be corrected, have to raise their voices in opposition to anti-homosexualism. Not to do so is to permit the myth of homosexual pathology to continue and to comply in the homosexual's continued suffering from senseless stigmatization.

A psychiatrist who allows a homosexual patient—who has been subject to a barrage of anti-homosexual sentiments his whole life—to continue in the belief that heterosexuality is superior to homosexuality, is the greatest obstacle to his patient's health and well-being.

We furthermore urge psychiatrists to refer their homosexual patients to gay liberation (and other patients who are victims of oppression to relevant liberation movements). Once relieved of patients whose guilt is not deserved but imposed, psychiatrists will be able to devote all their effort to the rich—who do earn their guilt but not their wealth, and can best afford to pay psychiatrists' fees.

We are convinced that a picket and a dance will do more for the vast majority of homosexuals than two years on the couch. We call on the medical profession to repudiate the adjustment approach as a solution to homosexual oppression and instead to further homosexual liberation by working in a variety of political ways (re-educating the public, supporting pickets, attending rallies, promoting social events, etc.) to change the situation of homosexuals in this society.

Join us in the struggle for a world in which all human beings are free to love without fear or shame.

23. • *The Combahee River Collective*

A BLACK FEMINIST STATEMENT (1977)

The Combahee River Collective was an activist group who wanted to draw attention to the intersecting oppressions of race, class, gender, and sexual orientation. After attending a meeting of the National Black Feminist Organization in 1973, members of the Collective saw the need for a new organization, one with a more radical vision and that would better address issues that were important to black lesbians. They named their new group the Combahee River Collective to honor Harriet Tubman, who led the 1863 Union raid that freed 750 slaves along the Combahee River in South Carolina during the American Civil War. In the mid-1970s, the Collective used meetings and retreats to articulate a politics of black feminism out of which emerged "A Black Feminist Statement." This document is regarded as a seminal text in the critique of white feminists' gender-only focus and helped trigger an increased emphasis on intersectionality within the field of women's, gender, and sexuality studies.

We are a collective of Black feminists who have been meeting together since 1974. During that time we have been involved in the process of defining and clarifying our politics, while at the same time doing political work within our own group and in coalition with other progressive organizations and movements. The most general statement of our politics at the present time would be that we are actively committed to struggling against racial, sexual, heterosexual, and class oppression, and see as our particular task the development of integrated analysis and practice based upon the fact that the major systems of oppression are interlocking. The synthesis of these oppressions creates the conditions of our lives. As Black women we see Black feminism as the logical political movement to combat the manifold and simultaneous oppressions that all women of color face.

We will discuss four major topics in the paper that follows: (1) the genesis of contemporary Black feminism; (2) what we believe, i.e., the specific province of our politics; (3) the problems in organizing Black feminists, including a brief herstory of our collective; and (4) Black feminist issues and practice.

1. THE GENESIS OF CONTEMPORARY BLACK FEMINISM

Before looking at the recent development of Black feminism we would like to affirm that we find our origins in the historical reality of Afro-American women's continuous life-and-death struggle for survival and liberation. Black women's extremely negative relationship to the American political system (a system of white male rule) has always been determined by our membership in two oppressed racial and sexual castes. As Angela Davis points out in "Reflections on the Black Woman's Role in the Community of Slaves," Black women have always embodied, if only in their physical manifestation, an adversary stance to white male rule and have actively

Reprinted with permission of Zillah R. Eisenstein from *Capitalist Patriarchy and the Case for Socialist Feminism*. Ed. Zillah R. Eisenstein. New York: Monthly Review Press, 1979; permission conveyed through Copyright Clearance Center, Inc.

resisted its inroads upon them and their communities in both dramatic and subtle ways. There have always been Black women activists—some known, like Sojourner Truth, Harriet Tubman, Frances E. W. Harper, Ida B. Wells Barnett, and Mary Church Terrell, and thousands upon thousands unknown—who had a shared awareness of how their sexual identity combined with their racial identity to make their whole life situation and the focus of their political struggles unique. Contemporary Black feminism is the outgrowth of countless generations of personal sacrifice, militancy, and work by our mothers and sisters.

A Black feminist presence has evolved most obviously in connection with the second wave of the American women's movement beginning in the late 1960s. Black, other Third World, and working women have been involved in the feminist movement from its start, but both outside reactionary forces and racism and elitism within the movement itself have served to obscure our participation. In 1973, Black feminists, primarily located in New York, felt the necessity of forming a separate Black feminist group. This became the National Black Feminist Organization (NBFO).

Black feminist politics also have an obvious connection to movements for Black liberation, particularly those of the 1960s and 1970s. Many of us were active in those movements (Civil Rights, Black nationalism, the Black Panthers), and all of our lives were greatly affected and changed by their ideologies, their goals, and the tactics used to achieve their goals. It was our experience and disillusionment within these liberation movements, as well as experience on the periphery of the white male left, that led to the need to develop a politics that was antiracist, unlike those of white women, and antisexist, unlike those of Black and white men.

There is also undeniably a personal genesis for Black Feminism, that is, the political realization that comes from the seemingly personal experiences of individual Black women's lives. Black feminists and many more Black women who do not define themselves as feminists have all experienced sexual oppression as a constant factor in our day-to-day existence. As children we realized that we were different from boys and that we were treated differently. For example, we were told in the same breath to be quiet both for the sake of being "ladylike" and to make us less objectionable in the eyes of white people. As we grew older we became aware of the threat of physical and sexual abuse by men. However, we had no way of conceptualizing what was so apparent to us, what we *knew* was really happening.

Black feminists often talk about their feelings of craziness before becoming conscious of the concepts of sexual politics, patriarchal rule, and most importantly, feminism, the political analysis and practice that we women use to struggle against our oppression. The fact that racial politics and indeed racism are pervasive factors in our lives did not allow us, and still does not allow most Black women, to look more deeply into our own experiences and, from that sharing and growing consciousness, to build a politics that will change our lives and inevitably end our oppression. Our development must also be tied to the contemporary economic and political position of Black people. The post-World War II generation of Black youth was the first to be able to minimally partake of certain educational and employment options, previously closed completely to Black people. Although our economic position is still at the very bottom of the American capitalistic economy, a handful of us have been able to gain certain tools as a result of tokenism in education and employment which potentially enable us to more effectively fight our oppression.

A combined antiracist and antisexist position drew us together initially, and as we developed politically we addressed ourselves to heterosexism and economic oppression under capitalism.

2. WHAT WE BELIEVE

Above all else, our politics initially sprang from the shared belief that Black women are inherently valuable, that our liberation is a necessity not as an adjunct to somebody else's but because of our need as human persons for autonomy. This may seem so obvious as to sound simplistic, but it is apparent that no other ostensibly progressive movement has ever considered our specific oppression as a priority or worked seriously for the ending of that oppression. Merely naming the pejorative stereotypes attributed to Black women (e.g. mammy, matriarch, Sapphire, whore, bulldagger), let alone cataloguing the cruel, often murderous, treatment we receive, indicates how little value has been placed upon our lives during four centuries of bondage in the Western hemisphere. We realize that the only people who care enough about us to work consistently for our liberation are us. Our politics evolve from a healthy love for ourselves, our sisters and our community which allows us to continue our struggle and work.

This focusing upon our own oppression is embodied in the concept of identity politics. We believe that the most profound and potentially most radical politics come directly out of our own identity, as opposed to working to end somebody else's oppression. In the case of Black women this is a particularly repugnant, dangerous, threatening, and therefore revolutionary concept because it is obvious from looking at all the political movements that have preceded us that anyone is more worthy of liberation than ourselves. We reject pedestals, queenhood, and walking ten paces behind. To be recognized as human, levelly human, is enough.

We believe that sexual politics under patriarchy is as pervasive in Black women's lives as are the politics of class and race. We also often find it difficult to separate race from class from sex oppression because in our lives they are most often experienced simultaneously. We know that there is such a thing as racial-sexual oppression which is neither solely racial nor solely sexual, e.g., the history of rape of Black women by white men as a weapon of political repression.

Although we are feminists and lesbians, we feel solidarity with progressive Black men and do not advocate the fractionalization that white women who are separatists demand. Our situation as Black people necessitates that we have solidarity around the fact of race, which white women of course do not need to have with white men, unless it is their negative solidarity as racial oppressors. We struggle together with Black men against racism, while we also struggle with Black men about sexism.

We realize that the liberation of all oppressed peoples necessitates the destruction of the political-economic systems of capitalism and imperialism as well as patriarchy. We are socialists because we believe that work must be organized for the collective benefit of those who do the work and create the products, and not for the profit of the bosses. Material resources must be equally distributed among those who create these resources. We are not convinced, however, that a socialist revolution that is not also a feminist and antiracist revolution will guarantee our liberation. We have arrived at the necessity for developing an understanding of class relationships that takes into account the specific class position of Black women who are generally marginal in the labor force, while at this particular time some of us are temporarily viewed as doubly desirable tokens at white-collar and professional levels. We need to articulate the real class situation of persons who are not merely raceless, sexless workers, but for whom racial and sexual oppression are significant determinants in their working/economic lives. Although we are in essential agreement with Marx's theory as it applied to the very specific economic relationships he analyzed, we know that his analysis must be extended further in order for us to understand our specific economic situation as Black women.

A political contribution which we feel we have already made is the expansion of the feminist principle that the personal is political. In our consciousness-raising sessions, for example, we have in many ways gone beyond white women's revelations because we are dealing with the implications of race and class as well as sex. Even our Black women's style of talking/testifying in Black language about what we have experienced has a resonance that is both cultural and political. We have spent a great deal of energy delving into the cultural and experiential nature of our oppression out of necessity because none of these matters has ever been looked at before. No one before has ever examined the multilayered texture of Black women's lives. An example of this kind of revelation/conceptualization occurred at a meeting as we discussed the ways in which our early intellectual interests had been attacked by our peers, particularly Black males. We discovered that all of us, because we were "smart" had also been considered "ugly," i.e., "smart-ugly." "Smart-ugly" crystallized the way in which most of us had been forced to develop our intellects at great cost to our "social" lives. The sanctions in the Black and white communities against Black women thinkers is comparatively much higher than for white women, particularly ones from the educated middle and upper classes.

As we have already stated, we reject the stance of lesbian separatism because it is not a viable political analysis or strategy for us. It leaves out far too much and far too many people, particularly Black men, women, and children. We have a great deal of criticism and loathing for what men have been socialized to be in this society: what they support, how they act, and how they oppress. But we do not have the misguided notion that it is their maleness, per se—i.e., their biological maleness—that makes them what they are. As Black women we find any type of biological determinism a particularly dangerous and reactionary basis upon which to build a politic. We must also question whether lesbian separatism is an adequate and progressive political analysis and strategy, even for those who practice it, since it so completely denies any but the sexual sources of women's oppression, negating the facts of class and race.

3. PROBLEMS IN ORGANIZING BLACK FEMINISTS

During our years together as a Black feminist collective we have experienced success and defeat, joy and pain, victory and failure. We have found that it is very difficult to organize around Black feminist issues, difficult even to announce in certain contexts that we *are* Black feminists. We have tried to think about the reasons for our difficulties, particularly since the white women's movement continues to be strong and to grow in many directions. In this section we will discuss some of the general reasons for the organizing problems we face and also talk specifically about the stages in organizing our own collective.

The major source of difficulty in our political work is that we are not just trying to fight oppression on one front or even two, but instead to address a whole range of oppressions. We do not have racial,

sexual, heterosexual, or class privilege to rely upon, nor do we have even the minimal access to resources and power that groups who possess any one of these types of privilege have.

The psychological toll of being a Black woman and the difficulties this presents in reaching political consciousness and doing political work can never be underestimated. There is a very low value placed upon Black women's psyches in this society, which is both racist and sexist. As an early group member once said, "We are all damaged people merely by virtue of being Black women." We are dispossessed psychologically and on every other level, and yet we feel the necessity to struggle to change the condition of all Black women. In "A Black Feminist's Search for Sisterhood," Michele Wallace arrives at this conclusion:

> We exist as women who are Black who are feminists, each stranded for the moment, working independently because there is not yet an environment in this society remotely congenial to our struggle—because, being on the bottom, we would have to do what no one else has done: we would have to fight the world.[1]

Wallace is pessimistic but realistic in her assessment of Black feminists' position, particularly in her allusion to the nearly classic isolation most of us face. We might use our position at the bottom, however, to make a clear leap into revolutionary action. If Black women were free, it would mean that everyone else would have to be free since our freedom would necessitate the destruction of all the systems of oppression.

Feminism is, nevertheless, very threatening to the majority of Black people because it calls into question some of the most basic assumptions about our existence, i.e., that sex should be a determinant of power relationships. Here is the way male and female roles were defined in a Black nationalist pamphlet from the early 1970s:

> We understand that it is and has been traditional that the man is the head of the house. He is the leader of the house/nation because his knowledge of the world is broader, his awareness is greater, his understanding is fuller and his application of this information is wiser . . . After all, it is only reasonable that the man

be the head of the house because he is able to defend and protect the development of his home . . . Women cannot do the same things as men—they are made by nature to function differently. Equality of men and women is something that cannot happen even in the abstract world. Men are not equal to other men, i.e. ability, experience or even understanding. The value of men and women can be seen as in the value of gold and silver—they are not equal but both have great value. We must realize that men and women are a complement to each other because there is no house/family without a man and his wife. Both are essential to the development of any life.[2]

The material conditions of most Black women would hardly lead them to upset both economic and sexual arrangements that seem to represent some stability in their lives. Many Black women have a good understanding of both sexism and racism, but because of the everyday constrictions of their lives, cannot risk struggling against them both.

The reaction of Black men to feminism has been notoriously negative. They are, of course, even more threatened than Black women by the possibility that Black feminists might organize around our own needs. They realize that they might not only lose valuable and hardworking allies in their struggles but that they might also be forced to change their habitually sexist ways of interacting with and oppressing Black women. Accusations that Black feminism divides the Black struggle are powerful deterrents to the growth of an autonomous Black women's movement.

Still, hundreds of women have been active at different times during the three-year existence of our group. And every Black woman who came, came out of a strongly-felt need for some level of possibility that did not previously exist in her life.

When we first started meeting early in 1974 after the NBFO first eastern regional conference, we did not have a strategy for organizing, or even a focus. We just wanted to see what we had. After a period of months of not meeting, we began to meet again late in the year and started doing an intense variety of consciousness-raising. The overwhelming feeling that we had is that after years and years we had finally found each other. Although we were not doing political work as a group, individuals continued their involvement in Lesbian politics, sterilization abuse and abortion rights work, Third World Women's International Women's Day activities, and support activity for the trials of Dr. Kenneth Edelin, Joan Little, and Inéz García. During our first summer when membership had dropped off considerably, those of us remaining devoted serious discussion to the possibility of opening a refuge for battered women in a Black community. (There was no refuge in Boston at that time.) We also decided around that time to become an independent collective since we had serious disagreements with NBFO's bourgeois-feminist stance and their lack of a clear political focus.

We also were contacted at that time by socialist feminists, with whom we had worked on abortion rights activities, who wanted to encourage us to attend the National Socialist Feminist Conference in Yellow Springs. One of our members did attend and despite the narrowness of the ideology that was promoted at that particular conference, we became more aware of the need for us to understand our own economic situation and to make our own economic analysis.

In the fall, when some members returned, we experienced several months of comparative inactivity and internal disagreements which were first conceptualized as a Lesbian–straight split but which were also the result of class and political differences. During the summer those of us who were still meeting had determined the need to do political work and to move beyond consciousness-raising and serving exclusively as an emotional support group. At the beginning of 1976, when some of the women who had not wanted to do political work and who also had voiced disagreements stopped attending of their own accord, we again looked for a focus. We decided at that time, with the addition of new members, to become a study group. We had always shared our reading with each other, and some of us had written papers on Black feminism for group discussion a few months before this decision was made. We began functioning as a study group and also began discussing the possibility of starting a

Black feminist publication. We had a retreat in the late spring which provided a time for both political discussion and working out interpersonal issues. Currently we are planning to gather together a collection of Black feminist writing. We feel that it is absolutely essential to demonstrate the reality of our politics to other Black women and believe that we can do this through writing and distributing our work. The fact that individual Black feminists are living in isolation all over the country, that our own numbers are small, and that we have some skills in writing, printing, and publishing makes us want to carry out these kinds of projects as a means of organizing Black feminists as we continue to do political work in coalition with other groups.

4. BLACK FEMINIST ISSUES AND PROJECTS

During our time together we have identified and worked on many issues of particular relevance to Black women. The inclusiveness of our politics makes us concerned with any situation that impinges upon the lives of women, Third World and working people. We are of course particularly committed to working on those struggles in which race, sex, and class are simultaneous factors in oppression. We might, for example, become involved in workplace organizing at a factory that employs Third World women or picket a hospital that is cutting back on already inadequate heath care to a Third World community, or set up a rape crisis center in a Black neighborhood. Organizing around welfare and daycare concerns might also be a focus. The work to be done and the countless issues that this work represents merely reflect the pervasiveness of our oppression.

Issues and projects that collective members have actually worked on are sterilization abuse, abortion rights, battered women, rape and health care. We have also done many workshops and educationals on Black feminism on college campuses, at women's conferences, and most recently for high school women.

One issue that is of major concern to us and that we have begun to publicly address is racism in the white women's movement. As Black feminists we are made constantly and painfully aware of how little effort white women have made to understand and combat their racism, which requires among other things that they have a more than superficial comprehension of race, color, and Black history and culture. Eliminating racism in the white women's movement is by definition work for white women to do, but we will continue to speak to and demand accountability on this issue.

In the practice of our politics we do not believe that the end always justifies the means. Many reactionary and destructive acts have been done in the name of achieving "correct" political goals. As feminists we do not want to mess over people in the name of politics. We believe in collective process and a nonhierarchical distribution of power within our own group and in our vision of a revolutionary society. We are committed to a continual examination of our politics as they develop through criticism and self-criticism as an essential aspect of our practice. In her introduction to *Sisterhood is Powerful* Robin Morgan writes:

> I haven't the faintest notion what possible revolutionary role white heterosexual men could fulfill, since they are the very embodiment of reactionary-vested-interest-power.

As Black feminists and Lesbians we know that we have a very definite revolutionary task to perform and we are ready for the lifetime of work and struggle before us.

NOTES

1. Wallace, Michele. "A Black Feminist's Search for Sisterhood," *The Village Voice*, 28 July 1975, pp. 6–7.

2. Mumininas of Committee for Unified Newark, *Mwanamke Mwananchi (The Nationalist Woman)*, Newark, N.J., ©1971, pp. 4–5.

24. • *Jo Carrillo*

AND WHEN YOU LEAVE, TAKE YOUR PICTURES WITH YOU (1981)

Jo Carrillo is a professor at University of California Hastings College of the Law. Her poem, "And When You Leave, Take Your Pictures With You," was published in an influential anthology of feminist writings called *This Bridge Called My Back: Writings by Radical Women of Color*. The poem criticizes the romanticized image of a global sisterhood and the appropriation of third world women and their struggle by white, privileged feminists.

Our white sisters
radical friends
love to own pictures of us
sitting at a factory machine
wielding a machete
in our bright bandanas
holding brown yellow black red children
reading books from literacy campaigns
holding machine guns bayonets bombs knives
Our white sisters
radical friends
should think
again.

Our white sisters
radical friends
love to own pictures of us
walking to the fields in hot sun
with straw hat on head if brown
bandana if black
in bright embroidered shirts
holding brown yellow black red children

reading books from literacy campaigns
smiling.
Our white sisters radical friends
should think again.
No one smiles
at the beginning of a day spent
digging for souvenir chunks of uranium
of cleaning up after
our white sisters
radical friends

And when our white sisters
radical friends see us
in the flesh
not as a picture they own,
they are not quite as sure
if
they like us as much.
We're not as happy as we look
on
their
wall.

Carrillo, Jo. "And When You Leave, Take Your Pictures With You." *This Bridge Called My Back: Writings by Radical Women of Color*. Eds. Cherríe Moraga and Gloria Anzaldúa. New York: Kitchen Table: Women of Color Press, 1981. 63–4.

25. • *bell hooks*

MEN: COMRADES IN STRUGGLE (1984)

bell hooks is the pen name of Gloria Jean Watkins, an influential feminist scholar whose work uses intersectional analysis to interrogate social inequality. hooks is a prolific writer with more than thirty books, including *Ain't I a Woman: Black Women and Feminism, Teaching to Transgress: Education as the Practice of Freedom*, and *Feminism Is for Everybody: Passionate Politics*. She founded the bell hooks Institute in Berea, Kentucky, in 2014. In "Men: Comrades in Struggle," hooks illustrates the importance of intersectionality, arguing that the binary view of women as oppressed and men as oppressor overlooks the ways in which race and class also confer or restrict privilege. She contends that anti-male feminist rhetoric and separatist ideology alienates women of color as well as poor and working-class women because these women feel connected to men in their communities through the recognition of a common struggle.

Feminism defined as a movement to end sexist oppression enables women and men, girls and boys, to participate equally in revolutionary struggle. So far, contemporary feminist movement has been primarily generated by the efforts of women—men have rarely participated. This lack of participation is not solely a consequence of anti-feminism. By making women's liberation synonymous with women gaining social equality with men, liberal feminists effectively created a situation in which they, not men, designated feminist movement "women's work." Even as they were attacking sex-role divisions of labor, the institutionalized sexism which assigns unpaid, devalued, "dirty" work to women, they were assigning to women yet another sex-role task: making feminist revolution. Women's liberationists called upon all women to join feminist movement, but they did not continually stress that men should assume responsibility for actively struggling to end sexist oppression. Men, they argued, were all-powerful, misogynist, oppressor—the enemy. Women were the oppressed—the victims. Such rhetoric reinforced sexist ideology by positing in an inverted form the notion of a basic conflict between the sexes, the implication being that the empowerment of women would necessarily be at the expense of men.

As with other issues, the insistence on a "woman only" feminist movement and a virulent anti-male stance reflected the race and class background of participants. Bourgeois white women, especially radical feminists, were envious of and angry at privileged white men for denying them an equal share in class privilege. In part, feminism provided them with a public forum for the expression of their anger as well as a political platform they could use to call attention to issues of social equality, demand change, and promote specific reforms. They were not eager to call attention to the fact that men do not share a common social status, that patriarchy does not negate the existence of class and race privilege or exploitation, that all men do not benefit equally from sexism. They did not want to acknowledge that bourgeois white women,

hooks, bell. "Men: Comrades in Struggle." *Feminist Theory: From Margin to Center*. 2nd. Ed. Cambridge, MA, South End Press: 2000. 68–83.

though often victimized by sexism, have more power and privilege, are less likely to be exploited or oppressed, than poor, uneducated, non-white males. At the time, many white women's liberationists did not care about the fate of oppressed groups of men. In keeping with the exercise of race and/or class privilege, they deemed the life experiences of these men unworthy of their attention, dismissed them, and simultaneously deflected attention away from their support of continued exploitation and oppression. Assertions like "all men are the enemy" and "all men hate women" lumped all groups of men in one category, thereby suggesting that they share equally in all forms of male privilege. One of the first written statements that endeavored to make an anti-male stance a central feminist position was the "Redstockings Manifesto." Clause III of the manifesto reads:

> We identify the agents of our oppression as men. Male supremacy is the oldest, most basic form of domination. All other forms of exploitation and oppression (racism, capitalism, imperialism, etc.) are extensions of male supremacy: men dominate women, a few men dominate the rest. All power situations throughout history have been male-dominated and male-oriented. Men have controlled all political, economic, and cultural institutions and backed up this control with physical force. They have used their power to keep women in an inferior position. All men receive economic, sexual, and psychological benefits from male supremacy. All men have oppressed women.

Anti-male sentiments have alienated many poor and working-class women, particularly non-white women, from feminist movement. Their life experiences have shown them that they have more in common with men of their race and/or class group than with bourgeois white women. They know the sufferings and hardships women face in their communities; they also know the sufferings and hardships men face, and they have compassion for them. They have had the experience of struggling with them for a better life. This has been especially true for black women. Throughout our history in the United States, black women have shared equal responsibility in all struggles to resist racist oppression. Despite

sexism, black women have continually contributed equally to anti-racist struggle, and frequently, before contemporary black liberation effort, black men recognized this contribution. There is a special tie binding people together who struggle collectively for liberation. Black women and men have been united by such ties. They have known the experience of political solidarity. It is the experience of shared resistance struggle that led black women to reject the anti-male stance of some feminist activists. This does not mean that black women were not willing to acknowledge the reality of black male sexism. It does mean that many of us do not believe we will combat sexism or woman-hating by attacking black men or responding to them in kind.

Bourgeois white women cannot conceptualize the bonds that develop between women and men in liberation struggle and have not had as many positive experiences working with men politically. Patriarchal white male rule has usually devalued female political input. Despite the prevalence of sexism in black communities, the role black women play in social institutions, whether primary or secondary, is recognized by everyone as significant and valuable. In an interview with Claudia Tate, black woman writer Maya Angelou explains her sense of the different role black and white women play in their communities:

> Black women and white women are in strange positions in our separate communities. In the social gatherings of black people, black women have always been predominant. That is to say, in the church it's always Sister Hudson, Sister Thomas, and Sister Wetheringay who keep the church alive. In lay gatherings it's always Lottie who cooks, and Mary who's going to Bonita's where there is a good party going on. Also, black women are the nurturers of children in our community. White women are in a different position in their social institutions. White men, who are in effect their fathers, husbands, brothers, their sons, nephews, and uncles, say to white women or imply in any case: "I don't really need you to run my institutions. I need you in certain places and in those places you must be kept—in the bedroom, in the kitchen, in the nursery, and on the pedestal." Black women have never been told this.

Without the material input of black women as participants and leaders, many male-dominated institutions in black communities would cease to exist; this is not the case in all white communities.

Many black women refused participation in feminist movement because they felt an anti-male stance was not a sound basis for action. They were convinced that virulent expressions of these sentiments intensify sexism by adding to the antagonism which already exists between women and men. For years black women (and some black men) had been struggling to overcome the tensions and antagonisms between black females and males that is generated by internalized racism (i.e., when the white patriarchy suggests one group has caused the oppression of the other). Black women were saying to black men, "We are not one another's enemy," "We must resist the socialization that teaches us to hate ourselves and one another." This affirmation of bonding between black women and men was part of anti-racist struggle. It could have been a part of feminist struggle had white women's liberationists stressed the need for women and men to resist the sexist socialization that teaches us to hate and fear one another. They chose instead to emphasize hate, especially male woman-hating, suggesting that it could not be changed. Therefore no viable political solidarity could exist between women and men. Women of color from various ethnic backgrounds, as well as women who were active in the gay movement, not only experienced the development of solidarity between women and men in resistance struggle, but recognized its value. They were not willing to devalue this bonding by allying themselves with anti-male, bourgeois white women. Encouraging political bonding between women and men to radically resist sexist oppression would have called attention to the transformative potential of feminism. The anti-male stance was a reactionary perspective that made feminism appear to be a movement that would enable white women to usurp white male power, replacing white male supremacist rule with white female supremacist rule.

Within feminist organizations, the issue of female separatism was initially separated from the anti-male stance; it was only as the movement progressed that the two perspectives merged. Many all-female, sex-segregated groups were formed because women recognized that separatist organizing could hasten female consciousness-raising, lay the groundwork for the development of solidarity among women, and generally advance the movement. It was believed that mixed groups would get bogged down by male power trips. Separatist groups were seen as a necessary strategy, not as a way to attack men. Ultimately, the purpose of such groups was integration with equality.

The positive implications of separatist organizing were diminished when radical feminists, like Ti-Grace Atkinson, proposed sexual separatism as an ultimate goal of feminist movement. Reactionary separatism is rooted in the conviction that male supremacy is an absolute aspect of our culture, that women have only two alternatives: accepting it or withdrawing from it to create subcultures. This position eliminates any need for revolutionary struggle, and it is in no way a threat to the status quo. . . .

[. . .]

During the course of contemporary feminist movement, reactionary separatism has led many women to abandon feminist struggle, yet it remains an accepted pattern for feminist organizing, e.g., autonomous women's groups within the peace movement. As a policy, it has helped to marginalize feminist struggle, to make it seem more a personal solution to individual problems, especially problems with men, than a political movement that aims to transform society as a whole. To return to an emphasis on feminism as revolutionary struggle, women can no longer allow feminism to be another arena for the continued expression of antagonism between the sexes. The time has come for women active in feminist movement to develop new strategies for including men in the struggle against sexism.

All men support and perpetuate sexism and sexist oppression in one form or another. It is crucial that feminist activists not get bogged down in intensifying our awareness of this fact to the extent that we do not stress the more unemphasized point, which is that men can lead life-affirming, meaningful lives without exploiting and oppressing women. Like women, men have been socialized to passively accept sexist ideology. While they need not blame themselves for accepting sexism, they must assume responsibility for eliminating it. It angers women activists who push separatism as a goal of feminist movement to hear emphasis placed on men being victimized by sexism; they cling to the "all men are the enemy" version of reality. Men are not exploited or oppressed by sexism, but there are ways in which they suffer as a result of it. This suffering should not be ignored. While it in no way diminishes the seriousness of male abuse and oppression of women, or negates male responsibility for exploitative actions, the pain men experience can serve as a catalyst calling attention to the need for change. Recognition of the painful consequences of sexism in their lives led some men to establish consciousness-raising groups to examine this. Paul Hornacek explains the purpose of these gatherings in his essay "Anti-Sexist Consciousness-Raising Groups for Men":

> Men have reported a variety of different reasons for deciding to seek a C-R group, all of which have an underlying link to the feminist movement. Most are experiencing emotional pain as a result of their male sex role and are dissatisfied with it. Some have had confrontations with radical feminists in public or private encounters and have been repeatedly criticized for being sexist. Some come as a result of their commitment to social change and their recognition that sexism and patriarchy are elements of an intolerable social system that needs to be altered.

Men in the consciousness-raising groups Hornacek describes acknowledge that they benefit from patriarchy and yet are also hurt by it. Men's groups, like women's support groups, run the risk of overemphasizing personal change at the expense of political analysis and struggle.

Separatist ideology encourages women to ignore the negative impact of sexism on male personhood. It stresses polarization between the sexes. According to Joy Justice, separatists believe that there are "two basic perspectives" on the issue of naming the victims of sexism: "There is the perspective that men oppress women. And there is the perspective that people are people, and we are all hurt by rigid sex roles." Many separatists feel that the latter perspective is a sign of co-optation, representing women's refusal to confront the fact that men are the enemy—they insist on the primacy of the first perspective. Both perspectives accurately describe our predicament. Men do oppress women. People are hurt by rigid sex-role patterns. These two realities co-exist. Male oppression of women cannot be excused by the recognition that there are ways men are hurt by rigid sex roles. Feminist activists should acknowledge that hurt—it exists. It does not erase or lessen male responsibility for supporting and perpetuating their power under patriarchy to exploit and oppress women in a manner far more grievous than the psychological stress or emotional pain caused by male conformity to rigid sex-role patterns.

Women active in feminist movement have not wanted to focus in any way on male pain so as not to deflect attention away from the focus on male privilege. Separatist feminist rhetoric suggested that all men share equally in male privilege, that all men reap positive benefits from sexism. Yet the poor or working-class man who has been socialized via sexist ideology to believe that there are privileges and powers he should possess solely because he is male often finds that few, if any, of these benefits are automatically bestowed on him in life. More than any other male group in the United States, he is constantly concerned about the contradiction between the notion of masculinity he was taught and his inability to live up to that notion. He is usually "hurt," emotionally scarred because he does not have the privilege or power society has taught him "real men" should possess. Alienated, frustrated, pissed off, he may attack, abuse, and oppress an individual woman or women, but he is not reaping positive benefits from his support and perpetuation of sexist ideology. When he beats or rapes women, he is not exercising privilege or reaping positive rewards; he may feel satisfied in exercising the only form of domination allowed him. The ruling-class male power structure that promotes his sexist abuse of women reaps the real material benefits and privileges from his actions. As long as he is attacking women and not sexism or capitalism, he helps to maintain a system that allows him few, if any, benefits or privileges. He is an oppressor. He is an enemy to women. He is also an enemy to himself. He is also oppressed. His abuse of women is not justifiable. Even though he has been socialized to act as he does, there are existing social movements that would enable him to struggle for self-recovery and liberation. By ignoring these movements, he chooses to remain both oppressor and oppressed. If feminist movement ignores his predicament, dismisses his hurt, or writes him off as just another male enemy, then we are passively condoning his actions.

The process by which men act as oppressors and are oppressed is particularly visible in black communities, where men are working-class and poor. In her essay "Notes for Yet Another Paper on Black Feminism, or, Will the Real Enemy Please Stand Up?" black feminist activist Barbara Smith suggests that black women are unwilling to confront the problem of sexist oppression in black communities:

> By naming sexist oppression as a problem it would appear that we would have to identify as threatening a group we have heretofore assumed to be our allies—Black men. This seems to be one of the major stumbling blocks to beginning to analyze the sexual relationships/sexual politics of our lives. The phrase "men are not the enemy" dismisses feminism and the reality of patriarchy in one breath and also overlooks some major realities. If we cannot entertain the idea that some men are the enemy, especially white men and in a different sense Black men, too, then we will never be able to figure out all the reasons why, for example, we are beaten up every day, why we are sterilized against our wills, why we are being raped by our neighbors, why we are pregnant at age twelve, and why we are at home on welfare with more children than we can support or care for. Acknowledging the sexism of Black men does not mean that we become "man-haters" or necessarily eliminate them from our lives. What it does mean is that we must struggle for a different basis of interaction with them.

Women in black communities have been reluctant to publicly discuss sexist oppression, but they have always known it exists. We too have been socialized to accept sexist ideology, and many black women feel that black male abuse of women is a reflection of frustrated masculinity—such thoughts lead them to see that abuse is understandable, even justified. The vast majority of black women think that just publicly stating that these men are the enemy or identifying them as oppressors would do little to change the situation; they fear it could simply lead to greater victimization. Naming oppressive realities, in and of itself, has not brought about the kinds of changes for oppressed groups that it can for more privileged groups, who command a different quality of attention. The public naming of sexism has generally not resulted in the institutionalized violence that characterized, for example, the response to black civil rights struggles. (Private naming, however, is often met with violent oppression.) Black women have not joined feminist movement not because they cannot face the reality of sexist oppression; they face it daily. They do not join feminist movement because they do not see in feminist theory and practice, especially those writings made available to masses of people, potential solutions.

So far, feminist rhetoric identifying men as the enemy has had few positive implications. Had feminist activists called attention to the relationship between ruling-class men and the vast majority of men, who are socialized to perpetuate and maintain sexism and sexist oppression even as they reap no life-affirming benefits, these men might have been motivated to examine the impact of sexism in their lives. Often feminist activists talk about male abuse of women as if it is an exercise of privilege rather than an expression of moral bankruptcy, insanity, and dehumanization. For example, in Barbara Smith's essay, she identifies white males as "the primary oppressor group in American society" and discusses the nature of their domination of others. At the end of the passage in which this statement is made she comments: "It is not just rich and powerful capitalists who inhibit and destroy life. Rapists, murderers, lynchers, and ordinary bigots do, too, and exercise very real and violent power because of this white male privilege." Implicit in this statement is the assumption that the act of committing violent crimes against women is either a gesture or an affirmation of privilege. Sexist ideology brainwashes men to believe that their violent abuse of women is beneficial when it is not. Yet feminist activists affirm this logic when we should be constantly naming these acts as expressions of perverted power relations, general lack of control over one's actions, emotional powerlessness, extreme irrationality, and, in many cases, outright insanity. Passive male absorption of sexist ideology enables them to interpret this disturbed behavior positively. As long as men are brainwashed to equate violent abuse of women with privilege, they will have no understanding of the damage done to themselves or the damage they do to others, and no motivation to change.

Individuals committed to feminist revolution must address ways that men can unlearn sexism. Women were never encouraged in contemporary feminist movement to point out to men their responsibility. Some feminist rhetoric "put down" women who related to men at all. Most women's liberationists were saying, "Women have nurtured, helped, and supported others for too long—now we must fend for ourselves." Having helped and supported men for centuries by acting in complicity with sexism, women were suddenly encouraged to withdraw their support when it came to the issue of "liberation." The insistence on a concentrated focus on individualism, on the primacy of self, deemed "liberatory" by women's liberationists, was not a visionary, radical concept of freedom. It did provide individual solutions for women, however. It was the same idea of independence perpetuated by the imperialist patriarchal state which equates independence with narcissism, and lack of concern with triumph over others. In this way, women active in feminist movement were simply inverting the dominant ideology of the culture—they were not attacking it. They were not presenting practical alternatives to the status quo. In fact, even the statement "men are the enemy" was basically an inversion of the male supremacist doctrine that "women

are the enemy"—the old Adam and Eve version of reality.

In retrospect, it is evident that the emphasis on "man as enemy" deflected attention away from focus on improving relationships between women and men, ways for men and women to work together to unlearn sexism. Bourgeois women active in feminist movement exploited the notion of a natural polarization between the sexes to draw attention to equal-rights effort. They had an enormous investment in depicting the male as enemy and the female as victim. They were the group of women who could dismiss their ties with men once they had an equal share in class privilege. They were ultimately more concerned with obtaining an equal share in class privilege than with the struggle to eliminate sexism and sexist oppression. Their insistence on separating from men heightened the sense that they, as women without men, needed equality of opportunity. Most women do not have the freedom to separate from men because of economic interdependence. The separatist notion that women could resist sexism by withdrawing from contact with men reflected a bourgeois class perspective. In Cathy McCandless's essay "Some Thoughts about Racism, Classism, and Separatism," she makes the point that separatism is in many ways a false issue because "in this capitalist economy, none of us are truly separate." However, she adds:

> Socially, it's another matter entirely. The richer you are, the less you generally have to acknowledge those you depend upon. Money can buy you a great deal of distance. Given enough of it, it is even possible never to lay eyes upon a man. It's a wonderful luxury, having control over who you lay eyes on, but let's face it: most women's daily survival still involves face-to-face contact with men whether they like it or not. It seems to me that for this reason alone, criticizing women who associate with men not only tends to be counterproductive; it borders on blaming the victim. Particularly if the women taking it upon themselves to set the standards are white and upper- or middle-class (as has often been the case in my experience) and those to whom they apply these rules are not.

Devaluing the real necessities of life that compel many women to remain in contact with men, as well as not respecting the desire of women to keep contact with men, created an unnecessary conflict of interest for those women who might have been very interested in feminism but felt they could not live up to the politically correct standards.

Feminist writing did not say enough about ways women could directly engage in feminist struggle in subtle, day-to-day contacts with men, although they have addressed crises. Feminism is politically relevant to the masses of women who daily interact with men both publicly and privately if it addresses ways that interaction, which usually has negative components because sexism is so all-pervasive, can be changed. Women who have daily contact with men need useful strategies that will enable them to integrate feminist movement into their daily life. By inadequately addressing or failing to address the difficult issues, contemporary feminist movement located itself on the periphery of society rather than at the center. Many women and men think feminism is happening, or happened, "out there." Television tells them the "liberated" woman is an exception, that she is primarily a careerist. Commercials like the one that shows a white career woman shifting from work attire to flimsy clothing exposing flesh, singing all the while "I can bring home the bacon, fry it up in the pan, and never let you forget you're a man," reaffirm that her careerism will not prevent her from assuming the stereotyped sex-object role assigned women in male supremacist society.

Often men who claim to support women's liberation do so because they believe they will benefit by no longer having to assume specific, rigid sex roles they find negative or restrictive. The role they are most willing and eager to change is that of economic provider. Commercials like the one described above assure men that women can be breadwinners or even "the" breadwinner, but still allow men to dominate them. . . .

[. . .]

Men who have dared to be honest about sexism and sexist oppression, who have chosen to assume responsibility for opposing and resisting it, often find themselves isolated. Their politics are disdained by anti-feminist men and women, and are often ignored by women active in feminist movement. Writing about his efforts to publicly support feminism in a local newspaper in Santa Cruz, Morris Conerly explains:

> Talking with a group of men, the subject of Women's Liberation inevitably comes up. A few laughs, snickers, angry mutterings, and denunciations follow. There is a group consensus that men are in an embattled position and must close ranks against the assaults of misguided females. Without fail, someone will solicit me for my view, which is that I am 100% for Women's Liberation. That throws them for a loop and they start staring at me as if my eyebrows were crawling with lice.
>
> They're thinking, "What kind of man is he?" I am a black man who understands that women are not my enemy. If I were a white man with a position of power, one could understand the reason for defending the status quo. Even then, the defense of a morally bankrupt doctrine that exploits and oppresses others would be inexcusable.

Conerly stresses that it was not easy for him to publicly support feminist movement, that it took time:

> Why did it take me some time? Because I was scared of the negative reaction I knew would come my way by supporting Women's Liberation. In my mind I could hear it from the brothers and sisters. "What kind of man are you?" "Who's wearing the pants?" "Why are you in that white shit?" And on and on. Sure enough the attacks came as I had foreseen but by that time my belief was firm enough to withstand public scorn.
>
> With growth there is pain . . . and that truism certainly applied in my case.

Men who actively struggle against sexism have a place in feminist movement. They are our comrades. Feminists have recognized and supported the work of men who take responsibility for sexist oppression—men's work with batterers, for example. Those women's liberationists who see no value in this participation must rethink and re-examine the process by which revolutionary struggle is advanced. Individual men tend to become involved in feminist movement because of the pain generated in relationships with women. Usually a woman friend or companion has called attention to their support of male supremacy. Jon Snodgrass introduces the book he edited, *For Men Against Sexism: A Book of Readings*, by telling readers:

> While there were aspects of women's liberation which appealed to men, on the whole my reaction was typical of men. I was threatened by the movement and responded with anger and ridicule. I believed that men and women were oppressed by capitalism, but not that women were oppressed by men. I argued that "men are oppressed too" and that it's workers who need liberation! I was unable to recognize a hierarchy of inequality between men and women (in the working class) nor to attribute it to male domination. My blindness to patriarchy, I now think, was a function of my male privilege. As a member of the male gender caste, I either ignored or suppressed women's liberation.

> My full introduction to the women's movement came through a personal relationship. . . . As our relationship developed, I began to receive repeated criticism for being sexist. At first I responded, as part of the male backlash, with anger and denial. In time, however, I began to recognize the validity of the accusation, and eventually even to acknowledge the sexism in my denial of the accusations.

Snodgrass participated in the men's consciousness-raising groups and edited the book of readings in 1977. Towards the end of the 1970s, interest in male anti-sexist groups declined. Even though more men than ever before support the idea of social equality for women, like women they do not see this support as synonymous with efforts to end sexist oppression, with feminist movement that would radically transform society. Men who advocate feminism as a movement to end sexist oppression must become more vocal and public in their opposition to sexism and sexist oppression. Until men share equal responsibility for struggling to end sexism, feminist movement will reflect the very sexist contradictions we wish to eradicate.

Separatist ideology encourages us to believe that women alone can make feminist revolution—we cannot. Since men are the primary agents maintaining and supporting sexism and sexist oppression, they can only be successfully eradicated if men are compelled to assume responsibility for transforming their consciousness and the consciousness of society as a whole. After hundreds of years of anti-racist struggle, more than ever before non-white people are currently calling attention to the primary role white people must play in anti-racist struggle. The same is true of the struggle to eradicate sexism—men have a primary role to play. This does not mean that they are better equipped to lead feminist movement; it does mean that they should share equally in resistance struggle. In particular, men have a tremendous contribution to make to feminist struggle in the area of exposing, confronting, opposing, and transforming the sexism of their male peers. When men show a willingness to assume equal responsibility in feminist struggle, performing whatever tasks are necessary, women should affirm their revolutionary work by acknowledging them as comrades in struggle.

26. • *Gloria Anzaldúa*

LA CONCIENCIA DE LA MESTIZA/ TOWARDS A NEW CONSCIOUSNESS (1987)

Gloria Anzaldúa was a queer Chicana writer and scholar whose use of the terms *"mestizaje"* and "the new *mestiza"* represented significant contributions to the fields of queer, feminist, Chicana, and postcolonial scholarship. *Mestizaje* is a rejection of traditional dualistic and hierarchical identity constructions, and the embracing of this concept is what gives the new *mestiza* an ability to use her multiple identities as a source of strength and vision. Anzaldúa's writing is grounded in her lived experience as a Chicana who grew up on the Texas–Mexico border, and she used the ambiguity of borderlands to rethink traditional concepts of race, gender, sexuality, and nation. Moving between English and Spanish, her writing style reflected her theoretical work. "La Conciencia de la Mestiza/Towards a New Consciousness" is a section from *Borderlands/La Frontera: The New Mestiza*, one of Anzaldúa's best-known works.

Por la mujer de mi raza
hablará el espíritu.[1]

José Vasconcelos, Mexican philosopher, envisaged *una raza mestiza, una mezcla de razas afines, una raza de color—la primera raza síntesis del globo.* He called it a cosmic race, *la raza cósmica,* a fifth race embracing the four major races of the world.[2] Opposite to the theory of the pure Aryan, and to the policy of racial purity that white America practices, his theory is one of inclusivity. At the confluence of two or more genetic streams, with chromosomes constantly "crossing over," this mixture of races, rather than resulting in an inferior being, provides hybrid progeny, a mutable, more malleable species with a rich gene pool. From this racial, ideological, cultural and biological cross-pollination, an "alien" consciousness is presently in the making—a new *mestiza* consciousness, *una conciencia de mujer.* It is a consciousness of the Borderlands.

UNA LUCHA DE FRONTERAS/ A STRUGGLE OF BORDERS

Because I, a *mestiza,*
continually walk out of one culture
and into another,
because I am in all cultures at the same time,
alma entre dos mundos, tres, cuatro,
me zumba la cabeza con lo contradictorio.
Estoy norteada por todas las voces que me hablan
simultáneamente.

The ambivalence from the clash of voices results in mental and emotional states of perplexity. Internal strife results in insecurity and indecisiveness. The *mestiza*'s dual or multiple personality is plagued by psychic restlessness.

In a constant state of mental nepantilism, an Aztec word meaning torn between ways, *la mestiza* is a product of the transfer of the cultural and spiritual

Anzaldúa, Gloria. "La Conciencia de la Mestiza/ Towards a New Consciousness" *Borderlands/La Frontera: The New Mestiza.* 2nd. Ed. San Francisco, Aunt Lute Books, 1999. 99–113.

values of one group to another. Being tricultural, monolingual, bilingual, or multilingual, speaking a patois, and in a state of perpetual transition, the *mestiza* faces the dilemma of the mixed breed: which collectivity does the daughter of a darkskinned mother listen to?

El choque de un alma atrapado entre el mundo del espíritu y el mundo de la técnica a veces la deja entullada. Cradled in one culture, sandwiched between two cultures, straddling all three cultures and their value systems, *la mestiza* undergoes a struggle of flesh, a struggle of borders, an inner war. Like all people, we perceive the version of reality that our culture communicates. Like others having or living in more than one culture, we get multiple, often opposing messages. The coming together of two self-consistent but habitually incompatible frames of reference[3] causes *un choque*, a cultural collision.

Within us and within *la cultura chicana*, commonly held beliefs of the white culture attack commonly held beliefs of the Mexican culture, and both attack commonly held beliefs of the indigenous culture. Subconsciously, we see an attack on ourselves and our beliefs as a threat and we attempt to block with a counterstance.

But it is not enough to stand on the opposite river bank, shouting questions, challenging patriarchal, white conventions. A counterstance locks one into a duel of oppressor and oppressed; locked in mortal combat, like the cop and the criminal, both are reduced to a common denominator of violence. The counterstance refutes the dominant culture's views and beliefs, and, for this, it is proudly defiant. All reaction is limited by, and dependent on, what it is reacting against. Because the counterstance stems from a problem with authority—outer as well as inner—it's a step towards liberation from cultural domination. But it is not a way of life. At some point, on our way to a new consciousness, we will have to leave the opposite bank, the split between the two mortal combatants somehow healed so that we are on both shores at once and, at once, see through serpent and eagle eyes. Or perhaps we will decide to disengage from the dominant culture, write it off altogether as a lost cause, and cross the

border into a wholly new and separate territory. Or we might go another route. The possibilities are numerous once we decide to act and not react.

A TOLERANCE FOR AMBIGUITY

These numerous possibilities leave *la mestiza* floundering in uncharted seas. In perceiving conflicting information and points of view, she is subjected to a swamping of her psychological borders. She has discovered that she can't hold concepts or ideas in rigid boundaries. The borders and walls that are supposed to keep the undesirable ideas out are entrenched habits and patterns of behavior; these habits and patterns are the enemy within. Rigidity means death. Only by remaining flexible is she able to stretch the psyche horizontally and vertically. *La mestiza* constantly has to shift out of habitual formations; from convergent thinking, analytical reasoning that tends to use rationality to move toward a single goal (a Western mode), to divergent thinking,[4] characterized by movement away from set patterns and goals and toward a more whole perspective, one that includes rather than excludes.

The new *mestiza* copes by developing a tolerance for contradictions, a tolerance for ambiguity. She learns to be an Indian in Mexican culture, to be Mexican from an Anglo point of view. She learns to juggle cultures. She has a plural personality, she operates in a pluralistic mode—nothing is thrust out, the good the bad and the ugly, nothing rejected, nothing abandoned. Not only does she sustain contradictions, she turns the ambivalence into something else.

She can be jarred out of ambivalence by an intense, and often painful, emotional event which inverts or resolves the ambivalence. I'm not sure exactly how. The work takes place underground—subconsciously. It is work that the soul performs. That focal point or fulcrum, that juncture where the *mestiza* stands, is where phenomena tend to collide. It is where the possibility of uniting all that is separate occurs. This assembly is not one where severed or separated pieces merely come together. Nor is it a balancing of opposing powers. In attempting to work out a synthesis, the self has added a third element which is greater than the sum of its severed parts. That third element is a new consciousness—a *mestiza* consciousness—and though it is a source of intense pain, its energy comes from continual creative motion that keeps breaking down the unitary aspect of each new paradigm.

En unas pocas centurias, the future will belong to the *mestiza*. Because the future depends on the breaking down of paradigms, it depends on the straddling of two or more cultures. By creating a new mythos—that is, a change in the way we perceive reality, the way we see ourselves, and the ways we behave—*la mestiza* creates a new consciousness.

The work of *mestiza* consciousness is to break down the subject–object duality that keeps her a prisoner and to show in the flesh and through the images in her work how duality is transcended. The answer to the problem between the white race and the colored, between males and females, lies in healing the split that originates in the very foundation of our lives, our culture, our languages, our thoughts. A massive uprooting of dualistic thinking in the individual and collective consciousness is the beginning of a long struggle, but one that could, in our best hopes, bring us to the end of rape, of violence, of war.

LA ENCRUCIJADA/THE CROSSROADS

A chicken is being sacrificed
    at a crossroads, a simple mound of earth
a mud shrine for *Eshu*,
    Yoruba god of indeterminacy,
who blesses her choice of path.
    She begins her journey.

Su cuerpo es una bocacalle. La mestiza has gone from being the sacrificial goat to becoming the officiating priestess at the crossroads.

As a *mestiza* I have no country, my homeland cast me out; yet all countries are mine because I am every woman's sister or potential lover. (As a lesbian I have no race, my own people disclaim me; but I am all races because there is the queer of me in all races.) I am cultureless because, as a feminist, I challenge the collective cultural/religious male-derived beliefs of Indo-Hispanics and Anglos; yet I am cultured because I am participating in the creation of yet another culture, a new story to explain the world and our participation in it, a new value system with images and symbols that connect us to each other and to the planet. *Soy un amasamiento*, I am an act of kneading, of uniting and joining that not only has produced both a creature of darkness and a creature of light, but also a creature that questions the definitions of light and dark and gives them new meanings.

We are the people who leap in the dark, we are the people on the knees of the gods. In our very flesh, (r)evolution works out the clash of cultures. It makes us crazy constantly, but if the center holds, we've made some kind of evolutionary step forward. *Nuestra alma el trabajo*, the opus, the great alchemical work; spiritual *mestizaje*, a "morphogenesis,"[5] an inevitable unfolding. We have become the quickening serpent movement.

Indigenous like corn, like corn, the *mestiza* is a product of crossbreeding, designed for preservation under a variety of conditions. Like an ear of corn—a female seed-bearing organ—the *mestiza* is tenacious, tightly wrapped in the husks of her culture. Like kernels she clings to the cob; with thick stalks and strong brace roots, she holds tight to the earth—she will survive the crossroads.

Lavando y remojando el maíz en agua de cal, despojando el pellejo. Moliendo, mixteando, amasando, haciendo tortillas de masa.[6] She steeps the corn in lime, it swells, softens. With stone roller on *metate*, she grinds the corn, then grinds again. She kneads and moulds the dough, pats the round balls into *tortillas*.

We are the porous rock in the stone *metate*
squatting on the ground.
We are the rolling pin, *el maíz y agua*,
la masa harina. Somos el amasijo.
Somos lo molido en el metate.
We are the *comal* sizzling hot,

the hot *tortilla*, the hungry mouth.
We are the coarse rock.
We are the grinding motion,
the mixed potion, *somos el molcajete*.
We are the pestle, the *comino, ajo, pimienta*,
We are the *chile colorado*,
the green shoot that cracks the rock.
We will abide.

EL CAMINO DE LA MESTIZA/
THE MESTIZA WAY

Caught between the sudden contraction, the breath sucked in and the endless space, the brown woman stands still, looks at the sky. She decides to go down, digging her way along the roots of trees. Sifting through the bones, she shakes them to see if there is any marrow in them. Then, touching the dirt to her forehead, to her tongue, she takes a few bones, leaves the rest in their burial place.

She goes through her backpack, keeps her journal and address book, throws away the muni-bart metro-maps. The coins are heavy and they go next, then the greenbacks flutter through the air. She keeps her knife, can opener and eyebrow pencil. She puts bones, pieces of bark, *hierbas*, eagle feather, snakeskin, tape recorder, the rattle and drum in her pack and she sets out to become the complete *tolteca*.

Her first step is to take inventory. *Despojando, desgranando, quitando paja.* Just what did she inherit from her ancestors? This weight on her back—which is the baggage from the Indian mother, which the baggage from the Spanish father, which the baggage from the Anglo?

Pero es difícil differentiating between *lo heredado, lo adquirido, lo impuesto.* She puts history through a sieve, winnows out the lies, looks at the forces that we as a race, as women, have been a part of. *Luego bota lo que no vale, los desmientos, los desencuentos, el embrutecimiento. Aguarda el juicio, hondo y enraízado, de la gente antigua.* This step is a conscious rupture with all oppressive traditions of all cultures and religions. She communicates that rupture,

documents the struggle. She reinterprets history and, using new symbols, she shapes new myths. She adopts new perspectives toward the dark-skinned, women and queers. She strengthens her tolerance (and intolerance) for ambiguity. She is willing to share, to make herself vulnerable to foreign ways of seeing and thinking. She surrenders all notions of safety, of the familiar. Deconstruct, construct. She becomes a *nahual*, able to transform herself into a tree, a coyote, into another person. She learns to transform the small "I" into the total Self. *Se hace moldeadora de su alma. Según la concepción que tiene de sí misma, así será.*

QUE NO SE NOS OLVIDEN
LOS HOMBRES

> *"Tú no sirves pa' nada—*
> you're good for nothing.
> *Eres pura vieja."*

"You're nothing but a woman" means you are defective. Its opposite is to be *un macho.* The modern meaning of the word "machismo," as well as the concept, is actually an Anglo invention. For men like my father, being "macho" meant being strong enough to protect and support my mother and us, yet being able to show love. Today's macho has doubts about his ability to feed and protect his family. His "machismo" is an adaptation to oppression and poverty and low self-esteem. It is the result of hierarchical male dominance. The Anglo, feeling inadequate and inferior and powerless, displaces or transfers these feelings to the Chicano by shaming him. In the Gringo world, the Chicano suffers from excessive humility and self-effacement, shame of self and self-deprecation. Around Latinos he suffers from a sense of language inadequacy and its accompanying discomfort; with Native Americans he suffers from a racial amnesia which ignores our common blood, and from guilt because the Spanish part of him took their land and oppressed them. He has an excessive compensatory hubris when around Mexicans from the other side. It overlays a deep sense of racial shame.

The loss of a sense of dignity and respect in the macho breeds a false machismo which leads him to put down women and even to brutalize them. Coexisting with his sexist behavior is a love for the mother which takes precedence over that of all others. Devoted son, macho pig. To wash down the shame of his acts, of his very being, and to handle the brute in the mirror, he takes to the bottle, the snort, the needle, and the fist.

Though we "understand" the root causes of male hatred and fear, and the subsequent wounding of women, we do not excuse, we do not condone, and we will no longer put up with it. From the men of our race, we demand the admission/acknowledgment/ disclosure/testimony that they wound us, violate us, are afraid of us and of our power. We need them to say they will begin to eliminate their hurtful put-down ways. But more than the words, we demand acts. We say to them: We will develop equal power with you and those who have shamed us.

It is imperative that *mestizas* support each other in changing the sexist elements in the Mexican-Indian culture. As long as woman is put down, the Indian and the Black in all of us is put down. The struggle of the *mestiza* is above all a feminist one. As long as *los hombres* think they have to *chingar mujeres* and each other to be men, as long as men are taught that they are superior and therefore culturally favored over *la mujer*, as long as to be a *vieja* is a thing of derision, there can be no real healing of our psyches. We're halfway there—we have such love of the Mother, the good mother. The first step is to unlearn the *puta/virgen* dichotomy and to see *Coatlalopeuh-Coatlicue* in the Mother, *Guadalupe*.

Tenderness, a sign of vulnerability, is so feared that it is showered on women with verbal abuse and blows. Men, even more than women, are fettered to gender roles. Women at least have had the guts to break out

of bondage. Only gay men have had the courage to expose themselves to the woman inside them and to challenge the current masculinity. I've encountered a few scattered and isolated gentle straight men, the beginnings of a new breed, but they are confused, and entangled with sexist behaviors that they have not been able to eradicate. We need a new masculinity and the new man needs a movement.

Lumping the males who deviate from the general norm with man, the oppressor, is a gross injustice. *Asombra pensar que nos hemos quedado en ese pozo oscuro donde el mundo encierra a las lesbianas. Asombra pensar que hemos, como femenistas y lesbianas, cerrado nuestros corazónes a los hombres, a nuestros hermanos los jotos, desheredados y marginales como nosotros.* Being the supreme crossers of cultures, homosexuals have strong bonds with the queer white, Black, Asian, Native American, Latino, and with the queer in Italy, Australia and the rest of the planet. We come from all colors, all classes, all races, all time periods. Our role is to link people with each other—the Blacks with Jews with Indians with Asians with whites with extraterrestrials. It is to transfer ideas and information from one culture to another. Colored homosexuals have more knowledge of other cultures; have always been at the forefront (although sometimes in the closet) of all liberation struggles in this country; have suffered more injustices and have survived them despite all odds. Chicanos need to acknowledge the political and artistic contributions of their queer. People, listen to what your *jotería* is saying.

The *mestizo* and the queer exist at this time and point on the evolutionary continuum for a purpose. We are a blending that proves that all blood is intricately woven together, and that we are spawned out of similar souls.

[. . .]

NOTES

1. This is my own "take off" on José Vasconcelos' idea. José Vasconcelos, *La Raza Cósmica: Misión de la Raza Ibero-Americana* (México: Aguilar S.A. de Ediciones, 1961).

2. Vasconcelos.

3. Arthur Koestler termed this "bisociation." Albert Rothenberg, *The Creative Process in Art, Science, and*

Other Fields (Chicago, IL: University of Chicago Press, 1979), 12.

4. In part, I derive my definitions for "convergent" and "divergent" thinking from Rothenberg, 12–13.

5. To borrow chemist Ilya Prigogine's theory of "dissipative structures." Prigogine discovered that substances interact not in predictable ways as it was taught in science, but in different and fluctuating ways to produce new and more complex structures, a kind of birth he

called "morphogenesis," which created unpredictable innovations. Harold Gilliam, "Searching for a New World View." *This World* (January, 1981), 23.

6. *Tortillas de masa harina:* corn tortillas are of two types, the smooth uniform ones made in a tortilla press and usually bought at a tortilla factory or supermarket, and *gorditas*, made by mixing *masa* with lard or shortening or butter (my mother sometimes puts in bits of bacon or *chicharrones*).

27. • *National Organization for Men Against Sexism*

TENETS (1980s)

The National Organization for Men Against Sexism (NOMAS) is an activist organization focused on intersectional advocacy for men. Maintaining that gender equality is a men's issue, the organization supports feminism and argues that both men and women benefit from reducing sexism and challenging traditional and limiting gender norms. Recognizing the ways in which sexism intersects with other types of oppression, the organization articulates an intersectional commitment to fighting social inequalities related to sexual orientation, gender, and race. NOMAS's "Tenets" lay the foundation for its activism, articulating the ways in which pro-feminist, gay/LGBT-affirmative, and antiracist work helps improve men's lives. An evolving document, the "Tenets" have been revised many times since they were originally written in the 1980s. The version included here reflects the most recent revisions, but we date it in the 1980s to reflect the start of this document and the long history of the organization's work.

PRO-FEMINIST

Whatever psychological burden men have to overcome, women are still the most universal and direct victims of our patriarchy. Our organization must take a highly visible and energetic position in support of women's struggle for equality. Our movement was born directly out of and continually nourished by feminism. Our support for women's

rights and specific women's issues must be vigorous and unmistakable. The simple truth is that oppression of gays, homophobia, women's oppression, and men's numerous sex role burdens and wounds are all part of the institution of patriarchy. Each injustice associated with sex contributes to all of the others. All oppressions are linked, and a consciousness of any oppression leads to an awareness of them all. The uniqueness and great potential strength of our

https://nomas.org/tenets/

movement is that we span all these categories of oppressions. Most people in this country have never heard gay men speak up for women's rights. Most people have not heard heterosexual men speak out forcefully for the civil rights of Gay men and Lesbians. Most people have not heard women speak knowledgeably and sympathetically about men's sex role burdens. In NOMAS, all of these things take place at every conference or meeting. There is something very special and wonderful in the breadth of our vision as a social movement, which speaks more persuasively than any of us could do alone. The totality of our opposition to the consequences of patriarchy is no weak point at all, but our greatest strength. We are not standing up as men to create a movement that cares only about men's sex role issues, or only about gay rights, or only about supporting women's fight against sexism. What is most special about our movement is that we have seen the connections between all these injustices, and are committed to ending all of them.

GAY/LGBT AFFIRMATIVE

This is the greatest challenge to our integrity, and one of our greatest opportunities to make a real difference in people's lives; to create positive social change. The homophobia of the majority of American men can hardly be underestimated. We speak out for Gay Rights, even in light of frightening and alienating the majority of men before they can hear anything else we have to say, not only because gays are among the most oppressed minorities in the world today, or because gay men and women have been a vital part of our movement, but, because the oppression (heterosexism) of gays is tightly linked to sexism—which is unquestionably the most potent single factor which makes most heterosexual men afraid to deviate from the traditional male sex role. We advocate for Gay Rights to heal the incalculable damage that homophobia, and the fear and confusion that it engenders, has done to both homosexual and heterosexual men. From this position, it

is natural to cite and dispel the popular myths about homosexuality, to mention the incredible fear and suffering and anxiety that oppression inflicts on gay Americans, and to staunchly advocate an end to all discrimination based on sexual orientation.

ANTI-RACIST

The enduring injustice of racism, which, like sexism, has long divided humankind into unequal and isolated groups, is of particular concern to us. Racism touches all of us and remains a primary source of inequality and oppression in our society. NOMAS is committed to examine and challenge racism in ourselves, our organizations, and our communities.

ENHANCING MEN'S LIVES

It is important to be clear about the ways that most men's lives can become happier and more fulfilling by un-learning large parts of the male role. Realistically, this is the main positive personal gain we have to offer the average, thoughtful but uninvolved man who might be interested in joining our movement. The satisfaction of being part of a struggle against social injustice will also be important, but these are the ways in which a man's own personal life can most clearly be improved, even in the short run. These benefits are all very real. Some of the main issues in this general category are:

- More (and better) time spent with one's children. The traditional male is a financial provider and authority, but has little time for daily, affectionate parenting, and little emotional preparation for dealing with the needs of children.
- Genuine male friendships. By overcoming competitiveness, homophobia, inexpressiveness, and several other aspects of the traditional male role, men can begin to experience intimacy, trust, and real support in their relationships with other men. Instead of chums, men can have real male friends.

- Putting work in perspective. Instead of building their entire identities around career status and being a Provider, men can develop other sources of satisfaction and self-esteem, such as the quality of their personal relationships with others.
- Emotional expressiveness. By overcoming the traditional male denial of most emotions and feelings, men can have more meaningful relationships, richer and fuller emotional lives and even be physically healthier.
- Compulsive competition. By rethinking the obsession with Winning that so many men are socialized into, we can free ourselves to relate to people in many other, more satisfying and more productive ways.
- Sensitivity and interpersonal skills. Men can learn to be good listeners, to be gentle, to be sensitive to other people's needs and feelings, and able to nurture.
- Sexual pleasure. No area of human experience is more thoroughly influenced by male role posturing and pressures than the ability to give and receive sexual pleasure. People are each different, but the male role demands just one traditional masculine sexual style. On top of his other problems, macho man doesn't have much fun.
- Unlearning aggressiveness. Physical and verbal aggressiveness, an important aspect of traditional masculinity, has taken a terrible toll on women and children, and on men themselves. This society is challenged with the misery caused by male violence, and aggression brings no happiness to the men who are trapped in it.
- Fear of femininity. The ridiculous stigma of doing, saying, or enjoying anything considered feminine is learned very early and continues to haunt and limit traditional men all their lives. It's a simple but profound relief to realize that we can say, wear, eat, enjoy, play, and do whatever we want without warring about what category it falls into.

This is not an exhaustive list. These issues should not be the only concern of the anti-sexist men's movement, but they deserve a major place.

---

28. • *Angela Davis*

MASKED RACISM: REFLECTIONS ON THE PRISON INDUSTRIAL COMPLEX (1998)

Angela Davis is distinguished professor emerita in the history of consciousness and feminist studies departments at the University of California, Santa Cruz. A scholar, activist, and author, her work demonstrates a commitment to fighting oppression based on race, class, and gender. She has published numerous books, including *Women, Race, and Class* and *Are Prisons Obsolete?* and she is a founding member of Critical Resistance, a grassroots organization calling attention to racism in the criminal justice system and working to end the prison industrial complex. In "Masked

Davis, Angela. "Masked Racism: Reflections on the Prison Industrial Complex." *Colorlines*. Race Forward, 10 Sept. 1998. Web. 1 Feb. 2016.

Racism: Reflections on the Prison Industrial Complex," Davis analyzes the growing prison population, the privatization of the corrections system, and the use of racist narratives to justify the exploitation of prison populations for corporate profit.

Imprisonment has become the response of first resort to far too many of the social problems that burden people who are ensconced in poverty. These problems often are veiled by being conveniently grouped together under the category "crime" and by the automatic attribution of criminal behavior to people of color. Homelessness, unemployment, drug addiction, mental illness, and illiteracy are only a few of the problems that disappear from public view when the human beings contending with them are relegated to cages.

Prisons thus perform a feat of magic. Or rather the people who continually vote in new prison bonds and tacitly assent to a proliferating network of prisons and jails have been tricked into believing in the magic of imprisonment. But prisons do not disappear problems, they disappear human beings. And the practice of disappearing vast numbers of people from poor, immigrant, and racially marginalized communities has literally become big business.

The seeming effortlessness of magic always conceals an enormous amount of behind-the-scenes work. When prisons disappear human beings in order to convey the illusion of solving social problems, penal infrastructures must be created to accommodate a rapidly swelling population of caged people. Goods and services must be provided to keep imprisoned populations alive. Sometimes these populations must be kept busy and at other times—particularly in repressive super maximum prisons and in INS detention centers—they must be deprived of virtually all meaningful activity. Vast numbers of handcuffed and shackled people are moved across state borders as they are transferred from one state or federal prison to another.

All this work, which used to be the primary province of government, is now also performed by private corporations, whose links to government in the field of what is euphemistically called "corrections" resonate dangerously with the military industrial complex. The dividends that accrue from investment in the punishment industry, like those that accrue from investment in weapons production, only amount to social destruction. Taking into account the structural similarities and profitability of business–government linkages in the realms of military production and public punishment, the expanding penal system can now be characterized as a "prison industrial complex."

THE COLOR OF IMPRISONMENT

Almost two million people are currently locked up in the immense network of U.S. prisons and jails. More than 70 percent of the imprisoned population are people of color. It is rarely acknowledged that the fastest growing group of prisoners are black women and that Native American prisoners are the largest group per capita. Approximately five million people—including those on probation and parole—are directly under the surveillance of the criminal justice system.

Three decades ago, the imprisoned population was approximately one-eighth its current size. While women still constitute a relatively small percentage of people behind bars, today the number of incarcerated women in California alone is almost twice what the nationwide women's prison population was in 1970. According to Elliott Currie, "[t]he prison has become a looming presence in our society to an extent unparalleled in our history—or that of any other industrial democracy. Short of major wars, mass incarceration has been the most thoroughly implemented government social program of our time."

To deliver up bodies destined for profitable punishment, the political economy of prisons relies on racialized assumptions of criminality—such as images of black welfare mothers reproducing criminal children—and on racist practices in arrest, conviction, and sentencing patterns. Colored bodies constitute the main human raw material in this vast experiment to disappear the major social problems of our time. Once the aura of magic is stripped away from the imprisonment solution, what is revealed is racism, class bias, and the parasitic seduction of capitalist profit. The prison industrial system materially and morally impoverishes its inhabitants and devours the social wealth needed to address the very problems that have led to spiraling numbers of prisoners.

As prisons take up more and more space on the social landscape, other government programs that have previously sought to respond to social needs—such as Temporary Assistance to Needy Families—are being squeezed out of existence. The deterioration of public education, including prioritizing discipline and security over learning in public schools located in poor communities, is directly related to the prison "solution."

PROFITING FROM PRISONERS

As prisons proliferate in U.S. society, private capital has become enmeshed in the punishment industry. And precisely because of their profit potential, prisons are becoming increasingly important to the U.S. economy. If the notion of punishment as a source of potentially stupendous profits is disturbing by itself, then the strategic dependence on racist structures and ideologies to render mass punishment palatable and profitable is even more troubling.

Prison privatization is the most obvious instance of capital's current movement toward the prison industry. While government-run prisons are often in gross violation of international human rights standards, private prisons are even less accountable. In March of this year, the Corrections Corporation of America (CCA), the largest U.S. private prison company, claimed 54,944 beds in 68 facilities under contract or development in the U.S., Puerto Rico, the United Kingdom, and Australia. Following the global trend of subjecting more women to public

punishment, CCA recently opened a women's prison outside Melbourne. The company recently identified California as its "new frontier."

Wackenhut Corrections Corporation (WCC), the second largest U.S. prison company, claimed contracts and awards to manage 46 facilities in North America, U.K., and Australia. It boasts a total of 30,424 beds as well as contracts for prisoner health care services, transportation, and security.

Currently, the stocks of both CCA and WCC are doing extremely well. Between 1996 and 1997, CCA's revenues increased by 58 percent, from $293 million to $462 million. Its net profit grew from $30.9 million to $53.9 million. WCC raised its revenues from $138 million in 1996 to $210 million in 1997. Unlike public correctional facilities, the vast profits of these private facilities rely on the employment of non-union labor.

THE PRISON INDUSTRIAL COMPLEX

But private prison companies are only the most visible component of the increasing corporatization of punishment. Government contracts to build prisons have bolstered the construction industry. The architectural community has identified prison design as a major new niche. Technology developed for the military by companies like Westinghouse is being marketed for use in law enforcement and punishment.

Moreover, corporations that appear to be far removed from the business of punishment are intimately involved in the expansion of the prison industrial complex. Prison construction bonds are one of the many sources of profitable investment for leading financiers such as Merrill Lynch. MCI charges prisoners and their families outrageous prices for the precious telephone calls which are often the only contact prisoners have with the free world.

Many corporations whose products we consume on a daily basis have learned that prison labor power can be as profitable as third world labor power exploited by U.S.-based global corporations. Both relegate formerly unionized workers to joblessness and many even wind up in prison. Some of the companies that use prison labor are IBM, Motorola, Compaq, Texas Instruments, Honeywell, Microsoft, and Boeing. But it is not only the hi-tech industries that reap the profits of prison labor. Nordstrom department stores sell jeans that are marketed as "Prison Blues," as well as t-shirts and jackets made in Oregon prisons. The advertising slogan for these clothes is "made on the inside to be worn on the outside." Maryland prisoners inspect glass bottles and jars used by Revlon and Pierre Cardin, and schools throughout the world buy graduation caps and gowns made by South Carolina prisoners.

"For private business," write Eve Goldberg and Linda Evans (a political prisoner inside the Federal Correctional Institution at Dublin, California), "prison labor is like a pot of gold. No strikes. No union organizing. No health benefits, unemployment insurance, or workers' compensation to pay. No language barriers, as in foreign countries. New leviathan prisons are being built on thousands of eerie acres of factories inside the walls. Prisoners do data entry for Chevron, make telephone reservations for TWA, raise hogs, shovel manure, make circuit boards, limousines, waterbeds, and lingerie for Victoria's Secret—all at a fraction of the cost of 'free labor.'"

was added to the California State University system and none to the University of California system. In 1996-97, higher education received only 8.7 percent of the State's General Fund while corrections received 9.6 percent. Now that affirmative action has been declared illegal in California, it is obvious that education is increasingly reserved for certain people, while prisons are reserved for others. Five times as many black men are presently in prison as in four-year colleges and universities. This new segregation has dangerous implications for the entire country.

By segregating people labeled as criminals, prison simultaneously fortifies and conceals the structural racism of the U.S. economy. Claims of low unemployment rates—even in black communities—make sense only if one assumes that the vast numbers of people in prison have really disappeared and thus have no legitimate claims to jobs. The numbers of black and Latino men currently incarcerated amount to two percent of the male labor force. According to criminologist David Downes, "[t]reating incarceration as a type of hidden unemployment may raise the jobless rate for men by about one-third, to 8 percent. The effect on the black labor force is greater still, raising the [black] male unemployment rate from 11 percent to 19 percent."

DEVOURING THE SOCIAL WEALTH

Although prison labor—which ultimately is compensated at a rate far below the minimum wage—is hugely profitable for the private companies that use it, the penal system as a whole does not produce wealth. It devours the social wealth that could be used to subsidize housing for the homeless, to ameliorate public education for poor and racially marginalized communities, to open free drug rehabilitation programs for people who wish to kick their habits, to create a national health care system, to expand programs to combat HIV, to eradicate domestic abuse—and, in the process, to create well-paying jobs for the unemployed.

Since 1984 more than twenty new prisons have opened in California, while only one new campus

HIDDEN AGENDA

Mass incarceration is not a solution to unemployment, nor is it a solution to the vast array of social problems that are hidden away in a rapidly growing network of prisons and jails. However, the great majority of people have been tricked into believing in the efficacy of imprisonment, even though the historical record clearly demonstrates that prisons do not work. Racism has undermined our ability to create a popular critical discourse to contest the ideological trickery that posits imprisonment as key to public safety. The focus of state policy is rapidly shifting from social welfare to social control.

Black, Latino, Native American, and many Asian youth are portrayed as the purveyors of violence, traffickers of drugs, and as envious of commodities that they have no right to possess. Young black and Latina women are represented as sexually promiscuous and as indiscriminately propagating babies and poverty. Criminality and deviance are racialized. Surveillance is thus focused on communities of color, immigrants, the unemployed, the undereducated, the homeless, and in general on those who have a diminishing claim to social resources. Their claim to social resources continues to diminish in large part because law enforcement and penal measures increasingly devour these resources. The prison industrial complex has thus created a vicious cycle of punishment which only further impoverishes those whose impoverishment is supposedly "solved" by imprisonment.

Therefore, as the emphasis of government policy shifts from social welfare to crime control, racism sinks more deeply into the economic and ideological structures of U.S. society. Meanwhile, conservative crusaders against affirmative action and bilingual education proclaim the end of racism, while their opponents suggest that racism's remnants can be dispelled through dialogue and conversation. But conversations about "race relations" will hardly dismantle a prison industrial complex that thrives on and nourishes the racism hidden within the deep structures of our society.

The emergence of a U.S. prison industrial complex within a context of cascading conservatism marks a new historical moment, whose dangers are unprecedented. But so are its opportunities. Considering the impressive number of grassroots projects that continue to resist the expansion of the punishment industry, it ought to be possible to bring these efforts together to create radical and nationally visible movements that can legitimize anti-capitalist critiques of the prison industrial complex. It ought to be possible to build movements in defense of prisoners' human rights and movements that persuasively argue that what we need is not new prisons, but new health care, housing, education, drug programs, jobs, and education. To safeguard a democratic future, it is possible and necessary to weave together the many and increasing strands of resistance to the prison industrial complex into a powerful movement for social transformation.

---

29. • *Jackson Katz*

MEMO TO MEDIA: MANHOOD, NOT GUNS OR MENTAL ILLNESS, SHOULD BE CENTRAL IN NEWTOWN SHOOTING (2013)

Jackson Katz is an antiviolence activist whose work focuses on the social construction of American masculinity. He is an award-winning filmmaker well known for his films *Tough Guise* and *Tough Guise 2*, which examine what he sees as a crisis in masculinity. He argues that cultural norms encourage a style of manhood steeped

Reprinted with permission of Jackson Katz.

in misogyny, homophobia, and violence. Katz works with boys and men in schools, sports organizations, and the military to change the definition of manhood as a way to address the social problems of bullying, sexual assault, and domestic violence. In "Memo to Media: Manhood, Not Guns or Mental Illness, Should Be Central in Newtown Shooting," originally published on HuffPost, Katz explains that because males commit the majority of school shootings, and indeed most of the violence in our society, effectively addressing tragedies like the massacre at Sandy Hook Elementary School in 2012 necessitates a discussion of manhood and the construction of masculinity.

Many of us whose work touches on the subject of masculinity and violence have long been frustrated by the failure of mainstream media—and much of progressive media and the blogosphere as well—to confront the gender issues at the heart of so many violent rampages like the one on December 14 in Connecticut.

My colleagues and I who do this type of work experience an unsettling dichotomy. In one part of our lives, we routinely have intense, in-depth discussions about men's emotional and relational struggles, and how the bravado about "rugged individualism" in American culture masks the deep yearning for connection that so many men feel, and how the absence or loss of that can quickly turn to pain, despair, and anger. In these discussions, we talk about violence as a gendered phenomenon: how, for example, men who batter their wives or girlfriends typically do so not because they have trigger tempers, but rather as a means to gain or maintain power and control over her, in a (misguided) attempt to get their needs met.

We talk amongst ourselves about how so many boys and men in our society are conditioned to see violence as a solution to their problems, a resolution of their anxieties, or a means of exacting revenge against those they perceive as taking something from them. We share with each other news stories, websites and YouTube videos that demonstrate the connection between deeply ingrained cultural ideas about manhood and individual acts of violence that operationalize those ideas.

And then in the wake of repeated tragedies like Newtown, we turn on the TV and watch the same

predictable conversations about guns and mental illness, with only an occasional mention that the overwhelming majority of these types of crimes are committed by men—usually white men. Even when some brave soul dares to mention this crucial fact, it rarely prompts further discussion, as if no one wants to be called a "male-basher" for uttering the simple truth that men commit the vast majority of violence, and thus efforts to "prevent violence"—if they're going to be more than minimally effective—need to explore why.

Maybe the Newtown massacre will mark a turning point. Maybe the mass murder of young children will force the ideological gatekeepers in mainstream media to actually pry open the cupboards of conventional thinking for just long enough to have a thoughtful conversation about manhood in the context of our ongoing national tragedy of gun violence.

But initial signs are not particularly promising. In the days since the shooting, some op-eds and blog posts have spoken to the gendered dynamics at the heart of this and other rampage killings. But most mainstream analysis has steered clear of this critical piece of the puzzle.

What follows is a brief list of suggestions for how journalists, cable hosts, bloggers and others who will be writing and talking about this unbelievable tragedy can frame the discussion in the coming days and weeks.

1) Make gender—specifically the idea that men are gendered beings—a central part of the national conversation about rampage killings. Typical

news accounts and commentaries about school shootings and rampage killings rarely mention gender. If a woman were the shooter, you can bet there would be all sorts of commentary about shifting cultural notions of femininity and how they might have contributed to her act, such as discussions in recent years about girl gang violence. That same conversation about gender should take place when a man is the perpetrator. Men are every bit as gendered as women.

The key difference is that because men represent the dominant gender, their gender is rendered invisible in the discourse about violence. So much of the commentary about school shootings, including the one at Sandy Hook Elementary, focuses on "people" who have problems, "individuals" who suffer from depression, and "shooters" whose motives remain obtuse. When opinion leaders start talking about the *men* who commit these rampages, and ask questions like: "why is it almost always men who do these horrible things?" and then follow that up, we will have a much better chance of finding workable solutions to the outrageous level of violence in our society.

2) Use the "M-word." Talk about masculinity. This does not mean you need to talk about biological maleness or search for answers in new research on brain chemistry. Such inquiries have their place. But the focus needs to be sociological: individual men are products of social systems. How many more school shootings do we need before we start talking about this as a social problem, and not merely a random collection of isolated incidents? Why are nearly all of the perpetrators of these types of crimes men, and most of them white men? (A recent piece by William Hamby is a step in the right direction.)

What are the cultural narratives from which school shooters draw lessons or inspiration? This does not mean simplistic condemnations of video games or violent media—although all cultural influences are fair game for analysis. It means looking carefully at how our culture defines manhood, how boys are socialized,

and how pressure to stay in the "man box" not only constrains boys' and men's emotional and relational development, but also their range of choices when faced with life crises. Psychological factors in men's development and psyches surely need to be examined, but the best analyses see individual men's actions in a social and historical context.

3) Identify the gender subtext of the ongoing political battle over "guns rights" versus "gun control," and bring it to the surface. The current script that plays out in media after these types of horrendous killings is unproductive and full of empty clichés. Advocates of stricter gun laws call on political leaders to take action, while defenders of "gun rights" hunker down and deflect criticism, hoping to ride out yet another public relations nightmare for the firearms industry. But few commentators who opine about the gun debates seem to recognize the deeply gendered aspects of this ongoing controversy. Guns play an important emotional role in many men's lives, both as a vehicle for their relationships with their fathers and in the way they bolster some men's sense of security and power.

It is also time to broaden the gun policy debate to a more in-depth discussion about the declining economic and cultural power of white men, and to deconstruct the gendered rhetoric of "defending liberty" and "fighting tyranny" that animates much right-wing opposition to even moderate gun control measures. If one effect of this tragedy is that journalists and others in media are able to create space for a discussion about guns that focuses on the role of guns in men's psyches and identities, and how this plays out in their political belief systems, we might have a chance to move beyond the current impasse.

4) Consult with, interview and feature in your stories the perspectives of the numerous men (and women) across the country who have worked with abusive men. Many of these people are counselors, therapists, and educators who can provide all sorts of insights about how—and

why—men use violence. Since men who commit murder outside the home more than occasionally have a history of domestic violence, it is important to hear from the many women and men in the domestic violence field who can speak to these types of connections—and in many cases have first-hand experience that deepen their understanding.

5) Bring experts on the air, and quote them in your stories, who can speak knowledgeably about the link between masculinity and violence. After the Jovan Belcher murder-suicide, CNN featured the work of the author Kevin Powell, who has written a lot about men's violence and the many intersections between gender and race. That was a good start. In the modern era of school shootings and rampage killings, a number of scholars have produced works that offer ways to think about the gendered subtext of these disturbing phenomena.

Examples include Rachel Kalish and Michael Kimmel's piece "Suicide by Mass Murder: Masculinity, Aggrieved Entitlement and Rampage School Shootings," Douglas Kellner's "Rage and Rampage: School Shootings and Crises of Masculinity," and a short piece that I co-wrote with Sut Jhally after Columbine, "The national conversation in the wake of Littleton is missing the mark."

There have also been many important books published over the past 15 years or so that provide great insight into issues of late 20th and 21st century American manhood, and thus provide valuable context for discussions about men's violence. They include *Real Boys*, by William Pollack; *Raising Cane*, by Michael Thompson and Dan Kindlon; *New Black Man*, by Mark Anthony Neal; *Why Does He Do That?* by Lundy Bancroft; *Dude You're a Fag*, by C.J. Pascoe; *Guyland*, by Michael Kimmel; *I Don't Want to Talk About It*, by Terrence Real; *Violence*, by James Gilligan; *Guys and Guns Amok*, by Douglas Kellner; *On Killing*, by David Grossman; and two documentary films: *Hip Hop: Beyond Beats and Rhymes*, by Byron Hurt; and *Tough Guise*, which I created and Sut Jhally directed.

6) Resist the temptation to blame this shooting or others on "mental illness," as if this answers the why and requires no further explanation. Even if some of these violent men are or were "mentally ill," the specific ways in which mental illness manifests itself are often profoundly gendered. Consult with experts who understand the gendered features of mental illness. For example, conduct interviews with mental health experts who can talk about why men, many of whom are clinically depressed, comprise the vast majority of perpetrators of murder-suicides. Why is depression in women much less likely to contribute to their committing murder than it is for men? (It is important to note that only a very small percentage of men with clinical depression commit murder, although a very high percentage of people with clinical depression who commit murder are men.)

7) Don't buy the manipulative argument that it's somehow "anti-male" to focus on questions about manhood in the wake of these ongoing tragedies. Men commit the vast majority of violence and almost all rampage killings. It's long past time that we summoned the courage as a society to look this fact squarely in the eye and then do something about it. Women in media can initiate this discussion, but men bear the ultimate responsibility for addressing the masculinity crisis at the heart of these tragedies. With little children being murdered en masse at school, for God's sake, it's time for more of them to step up, even in the face of inevitable push back from the defenders of a sick and dysfunctional status quo.

30. · *Tina Vasquez*

IT'S TIME TO END THE LONG HISTORY OF FEMINISM FAILING TRANSGENDER WOMEN (2014)

Tina Vasquez is a writer whose work focuses on issues related to gender, sexuality, and race. She was formerly the associate editor of *Black Girl Dangerous* and has written for blogs and websites like Jezebel, Bitch Media, and Everyday Feminism. Her article "It's Time to End the Long History of Feminism Failing Transgender Women," originally published online at Bitch Media and later included in the 20th anniversary edition of *Bitch* magazine, won a 2015 Impact Award from The Media Consortium. The article analyzes the use of feminist discourse to discriminate against the trans community.

[. . .]

In her 2013 article "Unpacking Transphobia in Feminism" on the website The TransAdvocate, writer Emma Allen explained that radical feminists such as [Cathy] Brennan assert that trans women are a problem because they perpetuate the idea that "gender roles are biologically determined rather than socially constructed" is the antithesis of feminism. "Radical feminists claim that gender oppression can only be abolished by getting rid of the whole concept of gender and they view transgender people as a threat to that ideal," Allen wrote.

Janice Raymond's 1979 book *The Transsexual Empire: The Making of the She-Male* shaped the notion that transgender rights have no place in feminism. Max Wolf Valerio reflected on the book in his 2006 memoir *The Testosterone Files: My Hormonal and Social Transformation from Female to Male*, writing that "Raymond postulated that all transsexuals were dupes of the patriarchy, 'mutilating' their bodies in order to live out stereotyped sex roles instead of changing those roles through a rigorously applied program of radical feminism." Other feminist writing of the 1970s also hit on the anti-transgender ideas. Mary Daly's 1978 book *Gyn/Ecology* compared the drag queen "phenomenon" to blackface and included assertions such as: "The surgeons and hormone therapists of the transsexual kingdom . . . can be said to produce feminine persons. They cannot produce women."

Drawing from that history, Brennan, fellow attorney Elizabeth Hungerford, and other modern-day feminists continue to actively question the inclusion of trans people in women's spaces. These feminists refer to themselves as "radical feminists" or "gender critical feminists." In 2008, trans women and trans advocates started referring to this group as "trans-exclusionary radical feminists" or TERFs, a term Brennan considers a slur. Cristan Williams, managing editor of The TransAdvocate and founder of Houston's Transgender Center and the Transgender Archive, asserts that TERFs should be recognized as a hate group by the Southern Poverty Law Center.

(To that end, a petition calling for the Southern Poverty Law Center to track the activities of the Gender Identity Watch website as a hate group was recently circulated and garnered nearly 7,000 signatures.)

This debate is not just feminist-theory inside baseball. Though outspoken, politically active trans-exclusionary radical feminists are relatively few in number, their influence on legislation and mainstream perceptions of transgender people is powerful and real.

For example, transgender people were able to readily obtain government-funded healthcare prior to 1980. That year, Janice Raymond wrote a report for the Reagan administration called "Technology on the Social and Ethical Aspects of Transsexual Surgery" which informed the official federal position on medical care for transgender people. The paper's conclusion reads, "The elimination of transsexualism is not best achieved by legislation prohibiting transsexual treatment and surgery, but rather by legislation that limits it and by other legislation that lessens the support given to sex-role stereotyping." In her book *Transgender History*, Susan Stryker says that the government curtailed transgender access to government social services under Reagan, "In part in response to anti-transgender feminist arguments that dovetailed with conservative politics."

[. . .]

The belief that transgender women are "not really women" sadly finds traction among many people—not just conservative politicians, but some mainstream feminists. However, few people use the tactics of the most outspoken trans-exclusionary activists to promote their ideas.

"TERFs do a good job of colonizing feminist discourse by framing their hate as a 'feminist critique of gender,' thereby representing the hate that follows as the feminist position. It's not," says TransAdvocate editor Williams.

The problem is that when trans-exclusionary feminists speak, a lot of people listen. Take the Michigan Womyn's Festival for example which takes place each August and attracts performers like Le Tigre and the Indigo Girls. Since its inception in 1976, the

feminist music festival has asked that only "womyn-born-womyn" attend. In 2006, the festival's founder, Lisa Vogel, defended her stance, writing, "As feminists, we call upon the transwomen's community to help us maintain womyn-only space, including spaces created by and for womyn-born womyn."

In response to a 2013 petition opposing the festival's ongoing exclusion of trans women, Vogel continued to defend the festival's stance, writing, "The Festival, for a single precious week, is intended for womyn who at birth were deemed female, who were raised as girls, and who identify as womyn. I believe that womyn-born womyn is a lived experience that constitutes its own distinct gender identity."

This idea that "women-born-women" need space away from transgender women impacts not just music festivals, but legislation. As policies promoting the creation of gender-neutral bathrooms continue to gain traction around the country, Brennan and other trans-exclusionary feminists have devoted time to arguing that trans women are somehow dangerous to cisgender women in public restrooms. In 2011, Brennan and Elizabeth Hungerford teamed up to write a letter to the United Nations urging opposition to laws prohibiting discrimination based on gender identity and gender expression. In her interview with Bustle, Brennan explained her thinking:

> Our whole lives we are raised very much aware of our vulnerability as women, so I don't understand why when a man says he's a woman, all of a sudden the penis is no longer (an issue) . . . Men rape women and girls in bathrooms all the time, so it's not like women's concerns about that aren't reasonable. And these laws are broadly enough written to justify the entry of anyone into a (women-only) space.

To imply that trans women pose a threat to cisgender women in restrooms is misinformation that preys on unfounded fears. I searched for news stories in which transgender women have assaulted cisgender women in bathrooms, coming across nothing but news stories detailing the attacks on transgender women themselves.

Indeed, if anyone is in harm's way in public restrooms, it's trans people, who can face abuse or assault no matter which restroom they choose. A 2011 survey of 6,000 transgender Americans found that more than half of the people surveyed reported experiencing harassment in public accommodations, including bathrooms, restaurants, and hotels. This is why there has been a push to make public restrooms a little safer for those who are trans, including legislation in Philadelphia that requires all new or renovated city-owned buildings to include gender-neutral bathrooms. There's also California's School Success and Opportunity Act, which mandates that transgender students must be included in school activities on the basis of their identified gender rather than their assigned sex. This extends to using bathrooms and locker rooms consistent with their gender. The Transgender Law Center heralded the law, which passed in August 2013, as a change that will save lives.

In contrast to that positive, progressive narrative around gender-neutral bathrooms, there was one story about the "dangers" of trans girls in girl's restrooms that popped up in the fall. In October, the right-wing organization Pacific Justice Institute altered press that a transgender teenager was harassing students in the girls' restroom at Florence High School in Colorado. The *Daily Mail*, Fox Nation, and at least one local TV station picked up the story, with Fox posting a short piece including the misgendering line, "When parents complained, school officials said the boy's rights as a transgender trumped their daughters' privacy rights." While some outlets referred to the minor as Jane Doe, Gender Identity Watch posted the name of the teen in question, describing her as a "male student" who "claims to be transgender."

It turns out, the story was false. The TransAdvocate's Cristan Williams quickly called the school's superintendent to inquire about the story and was told that the story was based on the complaint of one parent who was opposed to allowing the transgender student to use the girl's restroom; there were no actual reported incidents of harassment.

After this incident, the teen's mom said her daughter was struggling with harassment because of the story and was in such bad shape, the family had her on suicide watch.

It's clear from this example that trans-exclusionary feminists don't just spend their days making waves on social media—some get mainstream attention and hold successful, powerful positions. Cathy Brennan has used her skills as a lawyer to threaten legal action against a magazine that published an article critical of her. She also served as a liaison to the American Bar Association's Commission on Sexual Orientation and Gender Identity from 2008-2009. She appeared on Roseanne Barr's weekly radio program specifically to discuss her radical feminism and beliefs on female biology and gender identity. Trans-exclusionary feminists Janice Raymond and Mary Daly worked as well-respected, tenured professors. Like-minded feminist thought leader Sheila Jeffreys is still an established professor in Australia. Her forthcoming book *Gender Hurts*, from major publisher Routledge, will argue that "the ideology and practice of transgenderism" is harmful.

This approach to feminism is beyond troubling—it's downright dangerous, considering that the transgender community is one of the nation's most vulnerable. According to a 2011 study from the Anti-Violence Project, 40 percent of anti-LGBT murder victims were transgender women. A report from the National Transgender Discrimination Survey conducted by the National Gay & Lesbian Task Force and the National Center for Transgender Equality, found that transgender people faced double the rate of unemployment of the general population, with 63 percent of the transgender people surveyed reporting they experienced a serious act of discrimination that majorly affected their ability to sustain themselves. These numbers are even worse for trans people of color, especially trans women of color, the deaths of whom have been deemed a "state of emergency."

For these reasons, the concern these feminists elicit among trans women is serious. Trans blogger and womanist Monica Roberts has been blogging as TransGriot for years, discussing the intersections between race and the violence experienced by trans women of color and writing about the importance of knowing black trans history. Roberts routinely writes about how closely white privilege is tied to radical feminists' ability to incite scorn toward a vulnerable minority and not only get away with it, but remain gainfully employed in the process.

[. . .]

It has been said that feminism has failed the transgender community. It's hard to disagree. Trans women have been weathering a storm of hate and abuse in the name of feminism for decades now and for the most part, cisgender feminists have failed to speak out about it or push against it.

[. . .]

. . . It seems the tide is turning. People in queer communities are demanding that the silencing of trans women be addressed. Cisgender feminists are speaking out about Brennan's activism. Radical feminists like Julie Bindel are distancing themselves from trans-exclusionary groups. Healthcare is becoming more accessible for trans people, including the removal of health exclusions. Workplace discrimination bills are being expanded to encompass gender identity and as discussed previously, gender-neutral bathrooms are becoming law. "Transphobic" is now in the *Oxford English Dictionary* and even Facebook now has the option to set your gender to "custom."

Though change has been far too slow and painful, trans pioneer Autumn Sandeen, who was the first to be officially recognized by the Pentagon as a transgender service member, expresses hope that transphobia is becoming less acceptable.

"Every major gay-rights organization includes trans people in their mission statements. Trans people are more public than ever before and the media is moving beyond telling transition stories. Even though we've experienced so much hate from certain feminists, the real support is coming from feminist and queer circles," Sandeen said. "Transphobia is no longer acceptable in the name of feminism, so while people like Brennan are free to express their anti-trans sentiments and meet with like-minded feminists while excluding trans women, there is now a cost for expressing those viewpoints."

[. . .]

Trans women have been saddled with the responsibility of taking on trans-exclusionary feminists for far too long—but it's not their issue to deal with alone. Cisgender feminists, such as myself, have to make it clear that our feminism loves and supports trans women and that we will fight against transphobia. As Williams said, it's time to expose trans-exclusionary feminists for who they really are.

[. . .]

31. • *Ashwini Tambe*

RECKONING WITH THE SILENCES OF #METOO (2018)

Ashwini Tambe is professor of women's studies at the University of Maryland, College Park. She is also the editorial director of *Feminist Studies*, a leading journal in women's studies. Her 2009 book *Codes of Misconduct: Regulating Prostitution in Late*

Tambe, Ashwini. "Reckoning with the Silences of #MeToo." *Feminist Studies*. Vol. 44, No. 1 (2018), pp. 197–203

Colonial Bombay examines the regulation and criminalization of sex work through the lens of state coercion and empire. Her 2019 book *Defining Girlhood in India: A Transnational History of Sexual Maturity Laws* continues her transnational feminist approach to understanding the relationship between the state and female sexuality. "Reckoning with the Silences of #MeToo," first published in *Feminist Studies*, explores the narratives around sexual violence, power, and coercion that circulated through the hashtag #MeToo.

The past six months have been an important time for US feminism. For women's studies professors, it's been heartening to find the world outside our classrooms taking up conversations about sex and power that we've been having for decades. In this piece, I will reflect on three questions: What is going on? Why is it happening now? And what forms of feminism have been overlooked in the coverage of the #MeToo movement? I spend the longest time on the third question, because I'm concerned about how #MeToo has advanced a version of public feminism that is, in some ways, out of step with currents in academic feminism.

WHAT'S GOING ON?

Although feminists have long championed public speak-outs for survivors of sexual violence—whether in Take Back the Night open mics since the 1980s or the workshops also called "MeToo" that Tarana Burke started in Alabama in 2007—the viral force of the hashtag #MeToo in mid-October 2017 took most people by surprise. Within the first twenty-four hours, it had been retweeted half a million times. According to Facebook, nearly 50 percent of US users are friends with someone who posted a message about experiences of assault or harassment. #MeToo was by no means just a US phenomenon: Facebook and Twitter feeds in various parts of the world, notably Sweden, India, and Japan, were rocked for days by this hashtag. Then came the slew of powerful cis-men, largely in the US media and entertainment industries, who were forced to swiftly resign after allegations of sexual

misconduct. This toppling continues and has expanded beyond the media to other industries where reputations matter: politics, music, architecture, and, somewhat belatedly, higher education. In an important way, the ground beneath us has shifted. #MeToo has tilted public sympathy in favor of survivors by changing the default response to belief, rather than suspicion; the hashtag has revealed how widespread sexual coercion is.

WHY NOW?

We need to theorize, on a cultural scale, why this movement against sexual harassment and violence in the United States has happened now rather than, say, three years ago, when Bill Cosby was accused by multiple women, or after Roger Ailes, CEO of Fox News, was deposed. #MeToo's impact may seem sudden, but it is a part of a groundswell in women's activism since the November 2016 elections. The Women's March was the largest globally coordinated public gathering in history. The 3-million-strong Facebook group Pantsuit Nation saw hundreds of thousands of posts about experiences of misogyny. Unprecedented numbers of women are running for US political office this year. The signature affective note running through this political moment is a fierce rage about the election of Donald Trump.

Trump's impunity, I suggest, serves as a trigger provoking the fury at the heart of #MeToo. There are many reasons to find fault with Trump, but it is distinctly galling that he faced no consequences after acknowledging being a sexual predator. For victims of sexual trauma, it is already painful to watch perpetrators roam free because of how high the burdens of proof are in legal cases. When a person such as Trump is grandly affirmed by an election, it retraumatizes victims. Right after the election, therapists and counseling centers were flooded with patients seeking help with processing past events. The ballast provided by women's feverish organizing and the instant power of social media has facilitated a collective emboldening. Trump has made the comeuppance of all powerful men feel more urgent.

But from the inception of #MeToo, I have also watched its racial and class politics with some wariness: whose pain was being centered, I wondered? A colleague recently asked aloud: is #MeToo a white women's movement? Another wondered, is this a moral panic? These questions underline the importance of feminist insights that are overlooked in dominant coverage of the movement.

WHAT'S LEFT OUT?

Critical race feminism offers important insights when exploring the question of whether this is a white women's movement. The answer is complicated—both yes and no. Obviously, sexual violence and harassment are not white women's problems alone. They have been a pervasive workplace experience for women of color—whether we are talking about enslaved women or the vast majority of women in low-wage service professions. The viral reach of the hashtag around the globe—driving changes in laws in places such as Sweden and shaking up the elite professoriate in the Indian academy—makes clear that sexual violence is not only a US white women's issue.[1] But if we look at US media coverage of the movement and the most striking spokespersons as well as casualties in recent scandals, it is certainly white women's pain that is centered in popular media coverage. There are a few exceptions, such as the *New York Times* December 2017 feature on Ford's Chicago auto assembly plant and Oprah Winfrey's Golden Globes speech about Recy Taylor, but by and large, it is young white women's complaints, such as those by victims of Roy Moore or Larry Nassar, that

have the most visibility.[2] This is a familiar problem in a racist society. It has been commented on for a long time—including in Kimberlé Crenshaw's classic article about how to understand intersectionality in domestic violence cases.[3] Black women are regularly also pressured by black men not to speak publicly about harassment. Apart from the logic of protecting a community's image—the logic that dramatically shaped the Clarence Thomas hearings and the vilification of Anita Hill—it is worth keeping in mind that the primary instrument of redress in #MeToo is public shaming and criminalization of the perpetrator. This is already too familiar a problem for black men. We know the history of how black men have been lynched based on unfounded allegations that they sexually violated white women. We know how many black men are unjustly incarcerated. The dynamics of #MeToo, in which due process has been reversed—with accusers' words taken more seriously than those of the accused—is a familiar problem in black communities. Maybe some black women want no part of this dynamic.

#MeToo's affective focus on pain is also out of step with currents in contemporary academic feminism that center pleasure, play, and healing. Many lessons from feminist debates over sex and sexuality in the past few decades have not been absorbed, as #MeToo displays.

The rapid series of scandals have produced a conflation in the public imagination of different types of problem behaviors. It is pretty clear that what Larry Nassar and Roy Moore did, trapping unsuspecting younger women and girls, is predatory. But predatory sex is not the same thing as transactional sex. Charlie Rose and Harvey Weinstein's wrongs are more complicated because they involve trading promotions or film roles in exchange for sexual favors. These kinds of transactions happen frequently.

In many contexts—both within and outside marriage—sex is exchanged for security, affection, and money. So, a crucial point to keep in mind is that not all transactional sex is coerced. As sex positive feminists would argue, we need to guard against casting all transactions as coercion. The question is, how to discern coercion within contexts of transaction.

Not all seemingly consensual transactions are free of coercion, of course. A common mistake of philosophical liberalism (and some sex positive feminism) is to presume that any exchange arises out of, and generates, symmetry between two actors. But transacting in sex, or getting something in exchange for sex, does not mean that coercion is absent. In fact, coercion can also work in seemingly consensual ways.

We need, in this moment, a broader lens to understand coercion beyond the liberal understanding of verbal consent. Many of the scandals in the news involve women who went along with sex without saying no—but who would have preferred not to. Men such as Charlie Rose should have asked themselves: under what conditions could women have said no to their advances? Was it difficult for women to refuse? Was the men's institutional position, or age, or wealth, tilting their decision? Coercion, in other words, should be defined by more than just whether someone says yes or no. It hinges on whether one has power over that other person such that they might interpret a request as force—or even as a threat. If s/he faces negative consequences for saying no to a sexual advance, then that sexual advance is coercive.

This broad definition of coercion extends beyond contexts of sexual harassment to other abuses of power. In fact, if we take sex out of the picture for a moment, it becomes much easier for most people to recognize such coercion: most people relate to the problem of being forced to do something that they really don't want to do.

So why is it hard to take sex out of the picture? Perhaps it is not a surprise that a movement against sexual coercion, rather than, say, domestic violence, has received this level of news attention; sexual harassment stories gain traction because the details make for sensational copy. Many powerful people ask for inappropriate personal favors—such as John Conyers asking his subordinates to babysit for him—but the infractions that really seem to exercise our attention are related to sex. This predilection is not simply an outgrowth of a repressed interest in sex; it is because readers conflate sex and selfhood—many people see any experience of sexual coercion as eroding a woman's core sense of self.

We need not view sex this way, of course: equating sex with selfhood is a historically specific mandate connected to norms of middle-class respectability. Many sex workers express different understandings of their sexual activity—they don't treat their sexual encounters as signaling their virtue (or lack of it). Asexual people also protest that we give sex undue centrality in the way we define ourselves.

So, if we are to ask, what makes coercion in workplaces so common, we will need to do more than just fire those who are accused of forcing sex. We will need to look at the factors that generate cis-male dominance in the workplace: historical wage discrimination, childcare policies, and the way skills are defined and valued in masculinist ways. When men are systematically privileged by workplace policies and practices, they regularly ascend to powerful positions. This is why when we see the words "coach" or "boss" or "director" or "executive," we imagine male figures first. Our goal shouldn't only be to unseat coaches, bosses, directors, and executives who have abused their power. We need to re-script misogynistic practices that make it difficult for women to inhabit these roles in the first place. And we need to create alternatives to a politics of retribution that only focuses on punishment rather than transforming workplace hierarchies.

NOTES

1. Rick Noack, "Sweden Proposes Tough Sexual Assault Law," *Washington Post*, December 20, 2017, https://www.washingtonpost.com/news/worldviews/wp/2017/12/20/amid-metoo-movement-and-fear-of-immigrants-sweden-proposes-tough-sexual-assault-law/?utm_term=. edfo257oc5b4; Elizabeth Cassin and Ritu Prasad, "Student's 'Sexual Predator' List Names Professors," *BBC*, November 6, 2017, http://www.bbc.com/news/blogs-trending-41862615.

2. Susan Chira and Catrin Einhorn, "How Tough Is It to Change a Culture of Harassment? Ask Women at Ford," *New York Times*, December 19, 2017, https://www.nytimes.com/interactive/2017/12/19/us/ford-chicago-sexual-harassment.html; Madison Park, "Recy Taylor Is 'A Name I Know . . . You Should Know, Too,' Oprah says," *CNN*, January 10, 2018, https://www.cnn. com/2018/01/08/us/recy-taylor-oprah-winfrey-golden-globes-speech/index.html.

3. Kimberlé Williams Crenshaw, "Mapping the Margins: Intersectionality, Identity Politics, and Violence Against Women of Color," *Stanford Law Review* 43, no. 6 (July 1991): 1241–99.

32. • *Women's March*

GUIDING VISION AND DEFINITION OF PRINCIPLES (2019)

The Women's March is a women-led, intersectional, social justice movement committed to education and grassroots activism. In January 2017 people came together around the world as an act of resistance after the inauguration of Donald Trump as the forty-fifth president of the United States. Emerging out of this historic event, the Women's March continues to organize nonviolent direct action events like the annual Women's March in Washington, DC, and has assembled an inclusive leadership structure to develop initiatives and work in coalition with other activist groups to further the goals stipulated in the organization's "Unity Principles." In "Guiding Vision and Definition of Principles," the Women's March explains the importance of intersectionality as a foundation for activism and articulates the principles that guide the work of the organization.

OVERVIEW & PURPOSE

The Women's March on Washington is a women-led movement bringing together people of all genders, ages, races, cultures, political affiliations, disabilities and backgrounds in our nation's capital on January 19, 2019, to affirm our shared humanity and pronounce our bold message of resistance and self-determination.

Recognizing that women have intersecting identities and are therefore impacted by a multitude of social justice and human rights issues, we have outlined a representative vision for a government that is based on the principles of liberty and justice for all. *As Dr. King said, "We cannot walk alone. And as we walk, we must make the pledge that we shall always march ahead. We cannot turn back."*

Our liberation is bound in each other's. The Women's March on Washington includes leaders of organizations and communities that have been building the foundation for social progress for generations. We welcome vibrant collaboration and honor the legacy of the movements before us—the suffragists and abolitionists, the Civil Rights Movement, the feminist movement, the American Indian Movement, Occupy Wall Street, Marriage Equality, Black Lives Matter, and more—by employing a decentralized, leader-full structure and focusing on an ambitious, fundamental and comprehensive agenda.

#WHY WE MARCH

We are empowered by the legions of revolutionary leaders who paved the way for us to march, and acknowledge those around the globe who fight for our freedoms. We honor these women and so many more. They are #WHYWEMARCH.

Bella Abzug • Corazon Aquino • Ella Baker • Grace Lee Boggs • Berta Cáceres • Rachel Carson • Shirley Chisholm • Angela Davis • Miss Major Griffin Gracy • LaDonna Harris • Dorothy I. Height • bell hooks • Judith Heumann • Dolores Huerta • Marsha P. Johnson • Barbara Jordan • Yuri Kochiyama • Winona LaDuke • Audre Lorde • Wilma Mankiller • Diane Nash • Sylvia Rivera • Barbara Smith • Gloria Steinem • Hannah G. Solomon • Harriet Tubman • Edith Windsor • Malala Yousafzai

VALUES & PRINCIPLES

- We believe that Women's Rights are Human Rights and Human Rights are Women's Rights. This is the basic and original tenet for which we unite to March on Washington.
- We believe Gender Justice is Racial Justice is Economic Justice. We must create a society in which all women—including Black women, Indigenous women, poor women, immigrant women, disabled women, Jewish women, Muslim women, Latinx women, Asian and Pacific Islander women, lesbian, bi, queer and trans women—are free and able to care for and nurture themselves and their families, however they are formed, in safe and healthy environments free from structural impediments.

- Women have the right to live full and healthy lives, free of all forms of violence against our bodies. One in three women have been victims of some form of physical violence by an intimate partner within their lifetime; and one in five women have been raped. Further, each year, thousands of women and girls, particularly Black, Indigenous and transgender women and girls, are kidnapped, trafficked, or murdered. We honor the lives of those women who were taken before their time and we affirm that we work for a day when all forms of violence against women are eliminated. We believe that gun violence is a women's issue and that guns are not how we keep our communities free from violence.
- We believe in accountability and justice for police brutality and ending racial profiling and targeting of communities of color and Indigenous peoples. Women of color and Indigenous women are killed in police custody at greater rates, and are more likely to be sexually assaulted by police, and women with disabilities are disproportionately likely to experience use of force at the hands of police, and sexual assault in general. We also call for an immediate end to arming police with the military grade weapons and military tactics that are wreaking havoc on communities of color and sovereign tribal lands. No woman or mother should have to fear that she or her loved ones will be harmed at the hands of those sworn to protect.
- We believe it is our moral imperative to dismantle the gender and racial inequities within the criminal justice system. The rate of imprisonment has grown faster for women than men, increasing by 700% since 1980, and the majority of women in prison have a child under the age of 18. Incarcerated women also face a high rate of violence and sexual assault. We are committed to ensuring access to gender-responsive programming and dedicated healthcare including substance abuse treatment, mental and maternal health services for women in prison. We believe in the promise of restorative justice and alternatives to incarceration. We are also committed to disrupting the school-to-prison pipeline that prioritizes

incarceration over education by systematically funneling our children—particularly children of color, queer and trans youth, foster care children, and girls—into the justice system.

- We believe in Reproductive Freedom. We do not accept any federal, state or local rollbacks, cuts or restrictions on our ability to access quality reproductive healthcare services, birth control, HIV/AIDS care and prevention, or medically accurate sexuality education. This means open access to safe, legal, affordable abortion and birth control for all people, regardless of income, location or education. We understand that we can only have reproductive justice when reproductive health care is accessible to all people regardless of income, location or education.

- We believe in Gender Justice. We must have the power to control our bodies and be free from gender norms, expectations and stereotypes. We must free ourselves and our society from the institution of awarding power, agency and resources disproportionately to masculinity to the exclusion of others.

- We firmly declare that LGBTQIA Rights are Human Rights and that it is our obligation to uplift, expand and protect the rights of our gay, lesbian, bi, queer, trans, two-spirit or gender nonconforming brothers, sisters and siblings. This includes access to non-judgmental, comprehensive healthcare with no exceptions or limitations; access to name and gender changes on identity documents; full anti-discrimination protections; access to education, employment, housing and benefits; and an end to police and state violence.

- We believe in an economy powered by transparency, accountability, security and equity. We believe that creating workforce opportunities that reduce discrimination against women and mothers allow economies to thrive. Nations and industries that support and invest in caregiving and basic workplace protections—including benefits like paid family leave, access to affordable childcare, sick days, healthcare, fair pay, vacation time, and healthy work environments—have shown growth and increased capacity.

- We believe in equal pay for equal work and the right of all women to be paid equitably. We must end the pay and hiring discrimination that women, particularly mothers, women of color, Indigenous women, lesbian, queer and trans women still face each day in our nation, as well as discrimination against workers with disabilities, who can currently legally be paid less than federal minimum wage. Many mothers have always worked and in our modern labor force; and women are now 50% of all family breadwinners. We stand for the 82% of women who become moms, particularly moms of color, being paid, judged, and treated fairly. Equal pay for equal work will lift families out of poverty and boost our nation's economy.

- We recognize that women of color and Indigenous women carry the heaviest burden in the global and domestic economic landscape, particularly in the care economy. We further affirm that all care work—caring for the elderly, caring for the chronically ill, caring for children and supporting independence for people with disabilities—is work, and that the burden of care falls disproportionately on the shoulders of women, particularly women of color. We stand for the rights, dignity, and fair treatment of all unpaid and paid caregivers. We must repair and replace the systemic disparities that permeate caregiving at every level of society.

- We believe that all workers—including domestic and farm workers—must have the right to organize and fight for a living minimum wage, and that unions and other labor associations are critical to a healthy and thriving economy for all. Undocumented and migrant workers must be included in our labor protections, and we stand in full solidarity with the sex workers' rights movement. We recognize that exploitation for sex and labor in all forms is a violation of human rights.

- We believe Civil Rights are our birthright. Our Constitutional government establishes a framework to provide and expand rights and freedoms—not restrict them. To this end, we must protect and restore all the Constitutionally-mandated rights to all our citizens, including voting rights, freedom to worship without fear of intimidation or harassment, freedom of speech, and protections for all citizens regardless of race, gender, age or disability. We honor and respect tribal laws and jurisdictions.

- We support Indigenous women's right to access, own, develop and control land and its resources. We affirm that now is the time for the U.S. implementation of the UN Declaration on the Rights of Indigenous Peoples and to honor existing treaty rights and fulfill promises made.

- We believe that all women's issues are issues faced by women with disabilities and Deaf women. As mothers, sisters, daughters, and contributing members of this great nation, we seek to break barriers to access, inclusion, independence, and the full enjoyment of citizenship at home and around the world. We strive to be fully included in and contribute to all aspects of American life, economy, and culture.

- We believe it is time for an all-inclusive Equal Rights Amendment to the U.S. Constitution. Most Americans believe the Constitution guarantees equal rights, but it does not. The 14th Amendment has been undermined by courts and cannot produce real equity on the basis of race and/or sex. And in a true democracy, each citizen's vote should count equally. All Americans deserve equality guarantees in the Constitution that cannot be taken away or disregarded, recognizing the reality that inequalities intersect, interconnect and overlap.

- Rooted in the promise of America's call for huddled masses yearning to breathe free, we believe in immigrant and refugee rights regardless of status or country of origin. It is our moral duty to keep families together and empower all aspiring Americans to fully participate in, and contribute to, our economy and society. We reject mass deportation, family detention, violations of due process and violence against queer and trans migrants. Immigration reform must establish a roadmap to citizenship, and provide equal opportunities and workplace protections for all. We recognize that the call to action to love our neighbor is not limited to the United States, because there is a global migration crisis. We believe migration is a human right and that no human being is illegal.

- We believe that every person, every community and Indigenous peoples in our nation have the right to clean water, clean air, and access to and enjoyment of public lands. We believe that our environment and our climate must be protected, and that our land and natural resources cannot be exploited for corporate gain or greed—especially at the risk of public safety and health.

- We recognize that to achieve any of the goals outlined within this statement, we must work together to end war and live in peace with our sisters and brothers around the world. Ending war means a cessation to the direct and indirect aggression caused by the war economy and the concentration of power in the hands of a wealthy elite who use political, social, and economic systems to safeguard and expand their power.

ABOUT THIS DOCUMENT

The guiding vision and definition of principles were prepared in 2017 by a broad and diverse group of leaders. The Women's March on Washington is grateful to all contributors, listed and unlisted, for their dedication in shaping this agenda.

J. Bob Alotta, Executive Director, Astraea Lesbian Foundation for Justice
Monifa Bandele, Vice President, MomsRising
Zahra Billoo, Council on American Islamic Relations— San Francisco Bay Area
Gaylynn Burroughs, Director of Policy & Research, Feminist Majority Foundation
Melanie L. Campbell, Convener, Black Women's Roundtable, President & CEO, NCBCP
Sung Yeon Choimorrow, Executive Director, National Asian Pacific American Women's Forum
Alida Garcia, Immigrant Rights & Diversity Advocate
Alicia Garza, National Domestic Workers Alliance
Indigenous Women Rise Collective
Carol Jenkins, Board of Directors, ERA Coalition
Dr. Avis Jones-DeWeever, President, Incite Unlimited, LLC
Carol Joyner, Director, Labor Project for Working Families, Family Values @ Work

Janet Mock, Activist and author of *Redefining Realness* and *Surpassing Certainty*

Jessica Neuwirth, President, ERA Coalition

Terry O'Neill, President, National Organization for Women (NOW)

Carmen Perez, Executive Director, The Gathering for Justice

Jody Rabhan, Director of Washington Operations, National Council of Jewish Women

Kelley Robinson, Deputy National Organizing Director, Planned Parenthood Federation of America

Kristin Rowe-Finkbeiner, Executive Director and Co-Founder, MomsRising

Linda Sarsour, Founder, MPower Change

Heidi L. Sieck, Co-Founder/CEO, #VOTEPROCHOICE

Emily Tisch Sussman, Campaign Director, Center for American Progress

Jennifer Tucker, Senior Policy Advisor, Black Women's Roundtable

Winnie Wong, Activist, Organizer and Co-Founder, People for Bernie

SECTION THREE

Sociopolitical Issues in Women's, Gender, and Sexuality Studies

TABLE OF CONTENTS

RETHINKING THE FAMILY

33. Rebecca Barrett-Fox, "Constraints and Freedom in Conservative Christian Women's Lives" 216

34. Jessica E. Birch, "Love, Labor, and Lorde: The Tools My Grandmother Gave Me" 220

35. Monisha Das Gupta, "'Broken Hearts, Broken Families': The Political Use of Families in the Fight Against Deportation" 224

36. *Sarah Mirk, "Popaganda: Queering Family Values" 229

GENDER AND SEXUALITY IN THE LABOR MARKET

37. Marlene Kim, "Policies to End the Gender Wage Gap in the United States" 239

38. Dean Spade, "Compliance Is Gendered: Struggling for Gendered Self-Determination in a Hostile Economy" 245

39. *Catherine Rottenberg, "The Rise of Neoliberal Feminism" 257

40. *Fernando Tormos-Aponte, "The Politics of Survival" 270

REPRODUCTIVE POLITICS

41. Kathy E. Ferguson, "Birth Control" 275

42. *Loretta Ross, "The Color of *Choice*: White Supremacy and Reproductive Justice" 279

43. *Yifat Susskind, "Population Control Is Not the Answer to Our Climate Crisis" 291

GENDERED VIOLENCE

44. *V. Efua Prince, "June" (new) 293
45. Beth Richie, "A Black Feminist Reflection on the Antiviolence Movement" 299
46. *Courtney Bailey, "A Queer #MeToo Story: Sexual Violence, Consent, and Interdependence" (new) 302
47. Joey L. Mogul, Andrea J. Richie, and Kay Whitlock, "False Promises: Criminal Legal Responses to Violence Against LGBT People" 307
48. Isis Nusair, "Making Feminist Sense of Torture at Abu-Ghraib" 317

POPULAR CULTURE AND MEDIA REPRESENTATIONS

49. *Jaelani Turner-Williams, "A Quick History of TV's Elusive Quest for Black Lesbians" 321
50. Judith Kegan Gardiner, "Women's Friendships, Popular Culture, and Gender Theories" (updated) 324
51. Meda Chesney-Lind, "Mean Girls, Bad Girls, or Just Girls: Corporate Media Hype and the Policing of Girlhood" 329
52. *Elly Belle, "Knee-Jerk Biphobia: What Responses to Miley Cyrus's Breakup Say About Queer Erasure" 333

Feminist and queer scholars, activists, and practitioners do not all agree on how to address and analyze topics examined in women's, gender, and sexuality studies. This dynamic nature of interdisciplinarity gives the field its breadth, depth, and vibrancy. In this section, readings about gender, sexuality, and the family; labor market and neoliberal feminism; reproductive politics; gendered violence; and popular culture and media representations ask students to consider multiple points of view. Social, political, economic, and deeply human issues are full of tensions, and as Audre Lorde so eloquently evokes in *Sister Outsider*, our intellectual, political, and creative work is required in order to find multiple paths toward social change and justice.

RETHINKING THE FAMILY

Families or kinship systems are central organizing structures of people globally. As sites of both reproduction and production, they take care of our basic human needs as well as provide love, care, protection, discipline, and sometimes neglect and abuse; teach us about who we are as gendered and sexualized beings as well as shape our belief systems and worldviews; and prepare us for the public worlds of school, work, and sometimes to have our own families. Early feminist scholars Louise Tilly and Joan Scott argue in *Women, Work & Family* that the gendered labor within families is deeply tied to economic structures. While it matters that (some, not all) women bear children, the cultural meanings ascribed

Nuclear family: Social construction that creates the family as a married man and woman living together with at least one child.

to motherhood, fatherhood, the role of children, and what "counts" as work are social constructions that are not universally practiced across genders, sexualities, race, class, abilities, and nationalities. These roles and philosophies are woven into socioeconomic systems and dominant political ideologies so much so that we collectively may not spend time thinking about their meanings. This section briefly analyzes the social institutions of marriage and family as they shifted from home-based agriculture to industrialization and again under postindustrial neoliberalism.

Prevailing ideas about marriage and families are deeply tied to relations of power. In the United States, it may appear as though the **nuclear family** is "normal" and has been central to development of the society, yet this view is oversimplified and historically inaccurate when we begin to think intersectionally. From historians' marking of their arrival in Jamestown, Virginia, in 1607 to the end of the colonial period in 1763, the labor of white, Christian **settler-colonials** in the New World was gendered and the work was valued for its contributions to the family and community. In this context, family is defined more as an extended kinship network since it required having as many children as possible to produce needed goods for exchange, sale, and use.

Dominant constructions of marriage and family were (and are) deeply tied to property ownership—which has a long history of racial and gendered exclusion (see Taylor 2019)—as well as religious beliefs that shape what moral behavior means. In the early republic and as industrialization took hold, the ideal marriage of white, wealthy men and women meant that the household was a combination of opposite but complementary gender roles. Men dominated the public sphere while women's domain was in the home. Men were understood to be strong and rational and to provide for the family, while "[t]he attributes of True Womanhood, by which a woman judged herself and was judged by her husband, her neighbors, and society were piety, purity, submissiveness, and domesticity" (Welter 1966, 152). Women's responsibilities were to love, honor, and obey their husbands and rear the children. Christianity and nineteenth-century law anchored men's superiority by naming women as property—first of their fathers and later their husbands. While this may seem like a far cry from how marriage is practiced today, Rebecca Barrett-Fox makes clear in "Constraints and Freedoms in Conservative Christian Women's Lives" (included in this section) that "gender fundamentalism" is alive and well in

LEARNING OBJECTIVES

By the end of this section, you will have a better understanding of:

1. How historical constructions of family and work are connected and significant to understanding contemporary formations of gender and sexuality.

2. How social constructions of gender, race, class, sexuality, age, disabilities, and nationality stratify the labor market and how neoliberal feminism prevents us from understanding the material and social conditions created by political economies.

3. How intersectional approaches to reproductive politics produce contested meanings about reproductive choice, justice, and freedom.

4. How gender-based violence is tied to structures of race, class, sexuality, age, disabilities, nationality, and transnational politics.

5. How popular culture and media representations play an integral role in understanding gender, race, class, sexuality, religion, age, ability, and nationality.

Settler-colonials: White Europeans who immigrated to the Americas; the term is used to emphasize how indigenous peoples inhabited the land now called the United States.

the Fundamentalist Church of Jesus Christ of Latter-Day Saints (FLDS), Quiverfull, and other conservative religious groups. Men continue to exercise power and control over women in the name of religious practices; in the case of the FLDS, this includes polygamy.

The modern idea of gendered division of labor was further solidified during American industrialism and Henry Ford's introduction of the Five Dollar Day in 1914. When the Ford Motor Company proposed its higher standard of living, the intention was to stabilize, standardize, and control its male workforce while creating an economically comfortable American middle class. By offering men a livable wage, it meant that more married working-class and immigrant women could stay home in greater numbers. The legacy of this paradigm is that men emerged as the culturally appropriate "breadwinner" for the family, and it provided the foundation for what would become the gender wage gap (discussed in detail in the "Gender and Sexuality in the Labor Market" section). Moreover, wage work associated with the domestic sphere—jobs that include cleaning, working with children, and caregiving—retain less cultural value and today disproportionately affect low-income women of color and immigrant women. In her essay "Love, Labor, and Lorde: The Tools My Grandmother Gave Me" (included in this section), Jessica Birch considers a feminist response to the devaluing of domestic and care work.

Despite the concerted efforts of religion, government, and industry to secure the nuclear, patriarchal family as the dominant ideological and organizing structure in the United States, family structures and relationships have varied greatly historically and today. As historian Stephanie Coontz argues, the nuclear family in the United States is a heteronormative cultural construction representing a nostalgic past that never really existed the way we might imagine. In "It's All in the Family," Patricia Hill Collins names family as "an imagined traditional family ideal . . . and a privileged exemplar of intersectionality" (Collins 1998, 62–63). This section explores the multiple ways the state exerts control over kinship ties and specifically the ways in which family was and is torn apart through colonization, enslavement, mass incarceration, and immigration; historically denied to lesbian and gay people because of heteronormative definitions of marriage; and is reconfigured in contemporary U.S. households, including with chosen family.

Prior to contact with settler-colonials, family structures in Native American populations were more accurately described as small communities within specific tribes. They drew on the strength of extended kinship ties, where elders taught the young. The earth, the sky, objects, animals, and activities (such as hunting, fishing, and weaving) crafted meaning in people's lives and were not to be conquered and controlled. As poet and novelist Paula Gunn Allen (1939–2008), a Laguna Pueblo descendent, explains in "Where I Come From Is Like This," in such an environment gender was fluid: "women" and "men" did not hold the same meanings as they do in white settler traditions. Because settler-colonials perceived indigenous communities as "uncivilized" and a threat to the expanding United States, many Native American children were removed from their communities by the Bureau of Indian Affairs and Christian missionaries and placed in boarding schools and adoptive families to enforce assimilation. This included socializing children to adhere to rigid white U.S. constructions of gender (see Briggs 2012; Smith 2015). At the time of this writing, similar processes can be seen at work when children are separated from their families and caregivers at the U.S. southern border and incarcerated because of Trump administration policies, and sometimes are placed in foster care systems or adopted.

Beginning with the colonial era in the New World, African, African Caribbean, and African American enslaved populations were forced by plantation owners to become Christian and live in rudimentary family dwellings. Yet slaveholding white men and women did not recognize the marriage of Black men and women and sold children into enslavement across the South. Scholars know through collected oral histories and literature that extended kinship networks provided people with strength, resilience, and resistance to brutal conditions, and created underground pathways toward freedom. Because enslavement left a legacy of poverty, after Emancipation (1863) many Black women needed to work to sustain themselves and/or their families and kinship networks. Being the "true woman" was not available to women of color or immigrant women, including those considered free Black women and/or those who could trace their ancestry through substantial economic means. "True womanhood" was a social production of white femininity. Rather, Black women and men found ways to determine for themselves what family and community meant (and continues to mean) despite structures of racial violence (Collins 1998).

American immigration laws over the past two centuries have separated families. Historically, one of the most restrictive policies focused on Chinese immigration. The Page Act (1875) denied entrance to anyone considered "undesirable." It was specifically used to bar all Asian women (regardless of their country of origin) from entering the United States even if their fathers, husbands, sons, and extended family members had been working for the railroads and other industries in the western United States for over twenty years. Established in 1882 and propelled by fear and **xenophobia**, the Chinese Exclusion Act prohibited men and women from entering the country and gave the U.S. government power to repatriate workers and their families. This act was law until Congress drafted a measure to rescind it in 1943. As students of history, today's travel bans and border closings represent contemporary U.S. exceptionalism, racism, and exclusionary thinking.

In today's global economy, it is necessary to think about family, labor, and immigration under the regimes of **neoliberalism**. As corporations receive tax breaks, CEOs post record salaries, social programs become privatized or eliminated, workers fear losing their jobs and must work twice as hard for less wages and fewer benefits, a toxic environment is created for documented and undocumented immigrants alike. Economic precarity fuels xenophobia. While very few U.S. American citizens actually will do the work associated with some

Xenophobia: Irrational and intense dislike of people from other countries.

Neoliberalism: Set of economic policies that shape social formations and people's lived experiences by favoring a free-market economy, deregulation of industry, and the privatization of government social programs that erodes the middle class and emphasizes individual responsibility.

INTERSECTIONAL ANALYSIS

In 2013, the Supreme Court heard arguments in *Adoptive Family v. Baby Girl* in which a white family in South Carolina sued for permanent custody of "Baby Veronica" after the birth father, Dusten Brown, and the Cherokee Nation alleged that she was unlawfully taken from them in Oklahoma. The birth mother, Christina Maldonado, and Brown never married; soon after the birth of Veronica and unbeknownst to Brown, Maldonado relinquished the child to Nightlife Christian Adoption Agency. Subsequently, a couple in South Carolina—a state whose laws are unfavorable to birth fathers— adopted the baby. Brown is Cherokee, and according to the Indian Child Welfare Act (ICWA) of 1978, all efforts must be made to keep American Indian children with American Indian families. Therefore, Brown's attorney successfully argued that the ICWA applied to the case and Brown should gain custody of Baby Veronica. However, the adoptive couple's counsel, Paul Clement, was able to produce arguments so that the Supreme Court of the United States (SCOTUS) was willing to hear the case. In a 5–4 decision, SCOTUS handed down the verdict that the noncustodial parent (Brown) could not invoke the ICWA to win custody of his child when the custodial parent, who was not Cherokee, voluntarily and legally initiated the adoption process.

QUESTIONS

1. The birth mother told the Nightlife Christian Adoption Agency that there might be difficulties because Brown is Cherokee and could invoke ICWA for custodial rights. Look online to learn more about the case. How did the adoption agency circumvent the law?

2. Given the history of removing American Indian children from their homes to socialize them to be Christian—what scholar Andrea Smith (2015) names as a mode of genocide in *Conquest*—why is it important that Brown and his attorneys invoked ICWA to argue for the birth father's rights in this case?

3. The Baby Veronica case was sensationalized in U.S. media, and many supporters launched "Save Baby Veronica" websites. Look specifically at http://www.saveveronica.org/. Take notes on the language and images that are used throughout the site. What patterns do you perceive, and what are the messages that are telegraphed?

4. What relations of power are at work in this specific case? Do you think it was an injustice to the father? Did the adoptive parents receive justice?

5. Is this historical case relevant to contemporary feminism? How so or why not?

immigrant labor (e.g., seasonally picking fruits and vegetables), the phrase "they are taking our jobs" circulates easily through U.S. media and at kitchen tables and informs electoral politics. Economic policies not only shape family structures; they also craft competition among middle- and low-income people by establishing social hierarchies of who is "deserving" of employment and wealth and who must provide the labor for others to acquire profit, governing power, and influence over social policies—all of which undercut the middle and working classes. Thus neoliberal policies have both created the material and social conditions for low-paying, backbreaking work *and* the pervasive "us versus them" rhetoric that feeds sexism, xenophobia, racism, and classism.

In her essay "'Broken Hearts, Broken Families': The Political Use of Families in the Fight Against Deportation" (included in this section), Monisha

Das Gupta explains that following September 11, 2001, Congress crafted laws that target and incarcerate immigrants suspected of drug smuggling and use, weapon possession, and/or terrorism and expedited their deportation. At the time of writing, the U.S. executive branch of government doubled down on these efforts by expanding "detention centers" and travel bans in an attempt to halt immigration from particular regions of the world. These practices punish human beings fleeing from economic and political turmoil and those searching for new opportunities. With more tightly patrolled borders, immigrants from Latin America, the Caribbean, Asia, and Africa experience the effects most directly. Das Gupta examines the cultural and legal representational strategies of the New York–based group Freedom for Families, which works to keep immigrant families together in the United States by featuring fathers as caregivers and integral members of normative family structures.

It is important to note that while documented and undocumented immigrant households fight to stay together, lesbian, gay, and transgender couples successfully have argued for their right to marry and be recognized as a family under state and federal law. In addition to being recognized by the state and the general public as loving households, advocates insist that the financial and health benefits tied to marriage must be extended to gay and lesbian couples. For example, the rate of taxation is lowered for a couple who files jointly; families receive the Child Tax Credit based on how many children are in a state-recognized household; and married couples pay less for health insurance, can make health care decisions in the event the other is incapacitated, and can be named as the beneficiaries of retirement and other funds. While the Defense of Marriage Act (1996) circumvented gay marriage recognizing same-sex partnerships, legal marriage for gays and lesbians received its first victory in Massachusetts in 2004. However, other states did not have to acknowledge its legality, and advocates pushed for a comprehensive federal law. On June 26, 2015, in a 5–4 ruling in *Obergefell vs. Hodges*, the Supreme Court proclaimed same-sex marriage a right under the U.S. Constitution.

The fight for marriage equality divides the LGBTQPAI+ community. Some question if it really gets us any closer to equality since marriage favors state-sanctioned lesbian and gay couples over people (regardless of their sexuality) who choose to be single or live in domestic partnerships (see Duggan 2004; Muñoz 2009; Spade 2015). In "Queering Family Values" (included in this section), a podcast transcribed in 2017 and reposted in 2019 on the BitchMedia website, queer feminist activists Margaret Jacobsen and Yasmin Nair discuss what it means from their points of view when we politicize what family means. While Jacobsen speaks personally and asks readers to focus on how family and the home might primarily be seen as a place of kindness, compassion, and safety rather than one that defines and regulates gender and gender roles, Nair reframes family as people and animals we choose to bring close to us, build intimacies with, and become "familiars," while critiquing the family unit as an apparatus of the state that limits our freedoms. This wide-ranging interview

Latinas protest deportation. As political rhetoric and immigration policies tighten U.S. and European borders, women take to the streets in protest to keep families together. In the United States, "illegal" immigration is not just about people crossing to find safety, security, and economic opportunity; it is also widely supported by corporations and big agricultural conglomerates that demand cheap labor.
Source: Bob Kreisel/Alamy Stock Photo

asks students to question and think through what constitutes a family, why that is, and how it might be reimagined.

While marriage and restrictive definitions of "family" allow the state and religious institutions to shape "normal" and "desirable" nuclear families, statistics from the U.S. Census Bureau reflect changing household arrangements. From 1967 to 2019, there has been a steady decline in the nuclear family, from 70 percent to approximately 50 percent of U.S. households (U.S. Census Current Population Survey). Economic struggles brought on by neoliberal policies, combined with women pursuing higher education and entering the workforce in increased numbers, divorce rates, and more people opting for flexible and cooperative living arrangements, including crafting families that are chosen, mean that as a social institution our everyday experiences of family have changed.

Love has no bounds. Feminist and queer scholars, activists, and practitioners celebrate and advocate for families and communities across gender, sexuality, racial, class, and national divides. While gay marriage allows people to marry whom they choose, it does not guarantee a world free of housing discrimination, employment discrimination, microaggressions, and violence. How might emphasizing love rather than social divisions help us make these changes?
Source: Ad Council

GENDER AND SEXUALITY IN THE LABOR MARKET

In a patriarchal capitalist society, women's and LGBTQAI+ peoples' independence is tied to their ability to earn money. When we look at women's employment rates over the past fifty years, it is not surprising that we see significant change. Today, the U.S. Department of Labor Women's Bureau website reports that in 2016 46.8 percent of women participate in the labor force, with a projection of 47.2 percent by 2024. The data also suggests that nearly 70 percent remain in the labor force until they are at least fifty-four years old. Not only have more women entered the paid workforce, they are also moving into positions where they have real decision-making power. While some women advance, it is clear that progress is not evenly distributed. Most of these gains have been experienced by middle- and upper-class women, while women in low-wage jobs, who are more likely to be women of color, have experienced little improvement in their overall employment outlook (Boushey 2014, 50). Nearly two-thirds of minimum-wage workers are women (45). These jobs pay low wages, have low job security, rarely offer paid sick leave, and often come with schedules that change from week to week, making it difficult to plan childcare, pursue more education, or hold a second job. Moreover, gains have not been evenly distributed across the range of professions, with traditionally male-dominated fields like science, technology, engineering, and math showing little substantial improvement for women beyond slightly increased representation (51).

Second shift: A term coined by sociologist Arlie Hochschild (1989) referring to the household and caregiving labor performed by women in addition to their wage work.

Because women's labor force participation has increased but social institutions have not adapted, many women in the paid labor force experience the **second shift**. The hours of household, childcare, and eldercare work that women complete in addition to their paid employment are often overlooked because the labor is supposed to be done out of love. Yet housework and caretaking are both vital to a capitalist economy, and when women take on a disproportionate amount of this unpaid labor, they have less leisure time, less time to devote to their education or career advancement, and less time to participate in civic and recreational activities.

Until June 15, 2020 with the Supreme Court's ruling in *Bostock v. Clayton County, GA*, there had been little progress around LGBTQPAI+ rights. With this ruling, LGBTQAI+ workers' rights are protected under the 1964 Civil Rights Act and can no longer be legally denied employment or fired based on their sexual orientation, gender identity, and/or gender expression. Culturally, workplace discrimination will remain an issue if workers cannot afford legal representation or feel comfortable coming forward with allegations. Perhaps with this new ruling there will be new information collected regarding LGBTQPAI+ unemployment making it even more visible as a social problem; right now, this data is limited though it suggests that lesbian, gay, bisexual, and transgender workers experience a higher unemployment rate than the heterosexual and cisgender population. Gay and bisexual men historically have received lower wages—between 10 percent and 32 percent lower—than their heterosexual counterparts (*A Broken Bargain* 2013, 7, 34; Bagri 2017). In a recent paper, two economists found evidence that this gay male earnings penalty no longer exists and that federal data suggests that gay men earn more than heterosexual men (Carpenter and Eppnick 2017). More studies with refined methods will need to analyze this data not only to confirm this finding but also to take into account how gender, race, disability, and socioeconomic status affect wage earning within LGBTQPAI+ communities. In the United States, transgender workers have an unemployment rate twice the national average. For transgender people of color, the situation is even bleaker: their unemployment numbers are as much as *four times* the national average (7). Employment discrimination, higher rates of unemployment, hostile work environments, and wage penalties all contribute to the fact that queer communities are more likely to experience poverty (8).

THE GENDER PAY GAP

Gender pay gap: The average difference between men's and women's earnings.

The pay differential between men's and women's average earnings is referred to as the **gender pay gap** and it is significant that what we most often measure does not account for trans, nonbinary, and genderqueer experiences. These lost wages affect women's economic power, but it's not only women who are affected. Because women make up a large share of breadwinners and co-breadwinners, these lost wages affect *families* and *households*.

When we compare the median incomes for full-time, year-round, male and female workers in the United States, women earn only about 79 percent of what men earn (Hill 2015, 5). However, while 79 percent is the median difference, this number varies depending on several factors, including region, race, disability, and national origin. For example, women in the District of Columbia make about 90 percent of what their male counterparts earn, whereas in Louisiana, that number drops to 65 percent (7). In every racial and ethnic group, women earn less than men, but there is significant variation. For example, African American women earn about 90 percent of what African American men earn, while white women earn 78 percent of what white men earn (10). When we use white men's salary as the benchmark, we find that Latinas make only 54 percent of their salary, American Indian and Alaska Native women make 59 percent, Native Hawaiian and Pacific Islander women make 62 percent, and African American women make 63 percent. Asian American women experience the smallest gap compared to white men, earning 90 percent of their earnings (11).

Because the pay gap is caused in part by how women act in the labor market, a superficial analysis of the problem, indeed a neoliberal one, might lead us to blame women for their lower pay. However, research tells us that it is more accurate to see choices in labor force participation as "constrained" because there are structural variables that limit or influence the options afforded to women, queer people, people of color, and immigrants.

Women are socialized by their families, religion, and/or the media and may feel social pressure to *choose* gendered professions, causing **occupational segregation**, and there are two types: horizontal and vertical segregation. Horizontal segregation occurs when men and women staff certain career fields disproportionately. For example, K-12 teachers are overwhelmingly female while construction workers are overwhelmingly male. Horizontal segregation matters because the jobs staffed by women tend to pay less. This raises the question: Do we as a society value certain jobs less? In attempting to answer that question, it is interesting to note that the pay gap exists even when men hold traditionally "female" jobs or women hold traditionally "male" jobs. In 2013, full-time female registered nurses earned only 88 percent of the median weekly earnings of their male counterparts (Hill 2015, 16). In 2018, this translated to male nurses earning over $6,000/year more than female nurses (Lagasse 2018). The gap was wider in the traditionally male field of computer programming, where females earned only 81 percent compared to their male peers (Hill 2015, 16).

Horizontal segregation is particularly damaging for women employed in occupations with lower educational requirements. While men without college degrees tend to work in industries that are heavily unionized, we find women without college degrees disproportionately in industries that are *not*

Occupational segregation: The division of men and women in the workforce.

unionized. Unionized workers receive higher wages and better benefits, and there is a lower pay gap between male and female employees. An analysis of 2012 data found that full-time, unionized female workers earned 90 percent of what their male coworkers did (Boushey 2014, 52; Corbett and Hill 2012, 32). The unionization of domestic care workers in places like California and Hawai'i demonstrates that union organizing can bring about important gains for women in female-segregated jobs.

Vertical segregation refers to gender stratification *within* an occupation or career field. For example, women now make up about one-third of doctors and lawyers in the United States, which represents a significant change from the 1970s when these jobs were overwhelmingly male. However, women are poorly represented at the top of these professions. Women make up about 50 percent of law school graduates and about 45 percent of law firm associates, for example, but only 28 percent of nonequity partners and only 18 percent of equity partners (Rikleen 2015, 2). When we look more closely at *which* women hold top positions, we find that women of color are significantly less likely than their white counterparts to make it into leadership positions. We also see token status when we look at LGBTQPAI+ lawyers, where only 2 percent of female and 1 percent of male equity partners identify as LGBTQPAI+ (6). Horizontal and vertical segregation matter because these divisions solidify gender, racial, sexual, ability, and class hierarchies.

Women who have children may face added barriers. First, they may opt for an occupation that allows them more flexibility to enter and exit the labor market during prime reproductive years. Often these jobs do not require advanced education and are low paying. Second, since women are still expected to be the primary caretakers, they are much more likely to leave the workforce for longer periods of time or work part-time if they can afford to do so. The **mother pay penalty** refers to the wages women lose once they become mothers. Conversely, men experience wage increases in their jobs and advancement in their career, referred to as the **fatherhood bonus**, if they have children. According to sociologist Michelle Budig in "The Fatherhood Bonus and the Motherhood Penalty," the pay gap related to parenthood seems to be increasing while the gender pay gap seems to be eroding very slowly over time. Women's sacrifice becomes particularly problematic in the case of divorce. A married stay-at-home mother who returns to the workforce will lose future earnings because of her leave of absence, but if she stays married, those lost wages will be shared with her spouse. In the case of divorce, the woman bears the brunt of those lost wages. This does not mean that women should not be stay-at-home parents, work part-time, or stay in a marriage for economic reasons. It does suggest that when our culture pressures women to make those sacrifices, we end up with gender-based economic inequality.

Another cause of the pay gap is that women are less likely to negotiate their salaries, ask for a raise, or ask for a promotion. In *Women Don't Ask: Negotiation and the Gender Divide*, Babcock and Laschever provide a useful example of how much is at stake in not understanding the art of negotiation.

Mother pay penalty: Lost wages that mothers experience in comparison to non-mothers.

Fatherhood bonus: Increased wages and career advancement that fathers experience when being a part of a family structure because they are perceived as needing to provide for people and fulfilling their responsibilities as citizens within patriarchy and capitalism.

A twenty-two-year-old man and an equally qualified twenty-two-year-old woman are each offered a job for $25,000 a year. If the man negotiates his salary to $30,000 but the woman accepts the original offer, and each receives a 3 percent cost of living increase every year for thirty-eight years, at the end of his career the man's salary will be $92,243 while the woman's salary will be $76,870 (Babcock and Laschever 2003, 5).

Workers from marginalized groups are more vulnerable to the glass ceiling, sexual harassment, and wage theft in the labor market. The **glass ceiling** refers to the phenomenon whereby women, LGBTQPAI+, and people of color move into professional positions but then for reasons that are invisible but deeply structural, they have difficulty advancing. The reason it is referred to as a *glass* ceiling is because subtle things, like prejudice in hiring and promotion, microaggressions in the workplace, and lack of mentoring arguably does more to hold workers back than earlier practices of denying them employment. Hostile work environments also affect people's ability to do their best work and advance. Unwelcome sexual advances, requests for sexual favors, and offensive comments cause emotional distress and physical health problems and can push people out of jobs even though it is the workplace climate that should be changing. Women across racial, ethnic, and class differences have been the most commonly acknowledged victims of sexual harassment, but, according to the website for Catalyst, an organization dedicated to changing workplace culture, "nearly one in ten LGBTQPAI+ employees left a job because the environment was unwelcoming." Wage theft refers to employer violations of minimum wage and overtime laws, forced unpaid "off-the-clock" work, erasing work hours on time cards, stealing tips, and issuing incorrect paychecks. A 2010 report on workers in Chicago, Los Angeles, and New York City found that women and immigrant workers were most likely to experience minimum wage violations and that African Americans had three times as many violations as whites (Bernhardt et al. 2010, 43). In 2018, the magazine *Sojourners* reported that women of color and immigrant home health care workers "are only paid for half the hours they work" even though the state they work in has a $15/hour minimum wage. Since these professions often involve 24/7 care, many hours simply are not accounted for. In cases where employees are undocumented, abuse is rampant because wages are unregulated and there is good reason to fear reporting it.

Popular initiatives to address gender-based inequalities in the labor market tend to fall under three general strategies that aim to reform the existing system: (1) make all salary information public; if workers see the discrepancies, they have better footing to demand equal pay for equal work; (2) give women and LGBTQPAI+ people equal access and equal opportunities in the paid workforce; and (3) value and reward care work. In "Policies to End the Gender Wage Gap in the United States" (included in this section), Marlene Kim discusses six specific initiatives: using existing laws to prosecute discrimination, adopting family-friendly policies like paid parental leave and publicly funded childcare, establishing comparable-worth standards to ensure

Glass ceiling: Invisible barriers structurally tied to gender, race, class, sexuality, age, ability, and nationality that prevent job and career advancement for women, queer-identified people, and people of color.

that jobs that require similar skills and responsibilities are rewarded equitably, increasing unionization, prohibiting pay secrecy, and focusing on change at the state level.

To ensure progress is equitable, we must look at how race, ethnicity, class, sexualities, citizenship status, disability, and age affect the gendered experience of work. For example, the United States is the only industrialized country in the world that does not provide paid leave for new mothers. The U.S. Family and Medical Leave Act (FMLA) allows for twelve weeks of *un*paid leave. For working poor, low-income, and even many middle-class women, taking unpaid leave is not an option. At best, FMLA is a safety net for some people, but overall the policy is designed to benefit industries and institutions, not employees.

For LGBTQPAI+ workers, federal nondiscrimination legislation now exists and workplace culture needs to shift to ensure that workers cannot be treated unfairly based on sexual orientation, gender identity, or gender expression and that workplace benefits can be extended to domestic partners. However, as Dean Spade contends in "Compliance Is Gendered: Struggling for a Gendered Self-Determination in a Hostile Economy" (included in this section), "[a]ccess to participation in the U.S. economy has always been conditioned on the ability of each individual to comply with norms of gendered behavior and expression, and the U.S. economy has always been shaped by explicit incentives that coerce people into normative gender and sexual structures, identities, and behaviors" (p. 247). Nonbinary, agender, genderqueer, and transgender people face barriers that the law cannot address because transphobia is deeply enmeshed in how people think. Feminist and queer movements interested in social change must focus on finding just, intersectional approaches to alleviate the violence of poverty and the U.S. economic system itself, not reforming a broken system that was never meant to protect trans and genderqueer people, and especially trans and genderqueer people of color.

As feminist and queer scholars, activists, and practitioners work toward fundamental social change, there has also been a rise in neoliberal feminism. According to Catherine Rottenberg in "The Rise of Neoliberal Feminism" (included in this section), there has been a discursive shift in which women are told and tell one another to take personal and full responsibility for their positions in the labor force, work done at home, and their own well-being. Disregarding structural inequities built by centuries of oppression and imperialism, this version of "feminism" suggests that to be a contributing subject to society, a woman (regardless of race, gender identity and expression, ability, and socioeconomic as well as citizenship status) simply needs to put forth her best individual effort to be rewarded. Feminist liberation movements that have organized around understanding how systems of power work are hollowed out by neoliberal feminism. This is best represented by books written by women in power, such as *Lean In* by Sheryl Sandberg in which she argues that good education, hard work, and a willingness to put forward whatever it takes will ensure individual success and women's leadership in a capitalist labor market—thus disregarding how systems of structural inequity and power operate. In her piece, Rottenberg asks students to take seriously the question "why is there any need for a *feminism* informed by the norms of neoliberalism?" (p. 257). Each woman's success is not a political success if it only serves to secure individual wealth and divisive national practices that are embedded in the U.S. labor market.

In an age of austerity and uncertainty for the U.S. mainland, Puerto Rico experiences it exponentially and this, too, is a feminist issue. Whether it is in the wake of a natural disaster or the ongoing neocolonial reach and neglect of the U.S. government, Puerto Rico unemployment rate in January 2020 was 8.9 percent compared to the mainland U.S. rate of 3.6 percent in the same month. In June 2020 during the global pandemic, this rate shot up to 23 percent in Puerto Rico while the mainland U.S. rate was 11.1 percent. In Fernando Tormos-Aponte's "The Politics of Survival" (included in this section), it becomes clear that when the political Left (ranging from students to environmentalists to feminists) works in solidarity rather than against one another, they experience victories against neoliberal regimes. The examples that Tormos-Aponte gives are resisting tuition hikes and stopping oil pipelines from cutting across the island and disrupting the biodiversity. Moving from solidarity toward mutual aid under what Naomi Klein names as "disaster capitalism" is another way in which communities can come together to work against the consolidation of government and economic power. At the time of writing this introduction, the world is gripped by the COVID-19 pandemic—everyday life looks like ghost towns as we collectively "flatten the curve" to avert overwhelming health care systems. Governments around the world have been slow to act to protect people's health (including the health of doctors and nurses) at the same rate they may be protecting their nation's economies. According to Mariame Kaba and Dean Spade in a podcast/interview, "Solidarity Not Charity: Mutual Aid and How to Organize in the Age of Corona Virus" on the *Democracy Now!* website (March 20, 2020), community projects offer logistical support for getting rent money and food directly to people who need it to survive. Feminist and queer activists-scholars-teachers have known for decades that smaller acts of sharing and working together matter and that members of local communities, whether in Puerto Rico or elsewhere, have the agency and power to make a difference that affects the many rather than the few and that sustained change will need new economic, political, and social structures.

SEX WORK AS LABOR

Sex work and **sex trafficking** are not synonymous. Sex work represents a paid industry that can include pornography, street prostitution, indoor prostitution (such as escort services, massage parlors, and brothels), phone sex, exotic dancing, and online nude modeling. Most collected data focuses on prostitution: Stephanie Chen of CNN reports that 1 million to 2 million women in the United States and 40 million to 42 million women globally participate

Sex work: Paid work within the sex industry.

Sex trafficking: Forced work against people's wills within the sex industry and often as the result of being made vulnerable due to poverty, refugee status, and as women/girls and LGBTQPAI+ youth/adults.

in prostitution. These figures do not account for the number of LGBTQPAI+ people in sex work industries. Sex trafficking refers to those victims who are forced into the industry against their will and mostly without pay. Feminist, queer, and human rights scholars and organizations use the term "sex work" to emphasize that, regardless of its legal status, women, men, and LGBTQPAI+ individuals make constrained economic choices to enter sex labor. Since it is an intricate (and largely an underground) commercial economy, workers do not benefit from international, federal, and state regulations. Therefore, sex workers' rights are framed as human rights. They need protection from pimps and syndicates stealing their money; protection from violence, discrimination, and social marginalization; and access to health services and housing. It is particularly unjust that sex workers are frequently criminalized while the men involved (whether a consumer or those who control labor) are not prosecuted. Feminist and queer scholars, activists, and practitioners disagree on whether to decriminalize, legalize, and/or unionize sex work, though all agree that the power embedded in the social construction of gender, race, class, age, sexuality, and nationality produces economic conditions that require sex workers to persist within violent patriarchal and capitalist paradigms.

TRANSNATIONAL CONNECTIONS

It is relatively easy to find international organizations that work to eliminate sex trafficking (see humantrafficking.org). With transnational feminism's recent interest in naming sex work as a form of labor that is tied to political, economic, and social global systems of gender, migration, race, class, neocolonialism, and neoliberalism, spend time locating feminist and/or queer organizations that advocate sex workers' rights. We suggest starting with International Union of Sex Workers and Amnesty International, though see if you can find organizations in specific countries that advocate for inclusion in women's, civil, human, and labor rights.

QUESTIONS

1. Why do you think it is easier to find organizations that seek to end sex trafficking compared to ones that advocate for safe conditions for sex work, and how might this be tied to assumptions about gender, race, class, and nationalities as well as neoliberalism?

2. If sex work (not trafficking) is to be seen as a form of labor, what kinds of rights and protections would workers need?

3. In global locations where sex work is illegal and not regulated—for example, in parts of Africa, South Asia, and the United States—rates of sexually transmitted infections, including HIV/AIDS, are high and disproportionately affect the working poor and homeless. How might health outcomes be tied to cultural issues, including the stigmatizing of sex work? What might be one intervention for lowering disease and the stigma?

4. Sex work is also tied to sex tourism in places such as the Dominican Republic. With 41 percent of the population living below the national poverty line and the general economic prospects above that of some other Caribbean nations, why might state and local governments on this small island be uninterested in regulating sex work and protecting the workers?

REPRODUCTIVE POLITICS

Reproductive issues have played a role in U.S. politics since the turn of the twentieth century. The origin of the movement is historically attributed to Margaret Sanger (1879–1966). A nurse by profession, she was a public advocate for contraception after watching her mother suffer because she bore eleven children and had seven miscarriages. As a nurse, Sanger witnessed women dying from unregulated abortions. She devoted her life to making birth control legal by challenging the state and federal **Comstock Laws** and providing it to all women, especially struggling, poor mothers. "She knew that women could not achieve full equality unless they had control over their reproductive lives" (May 2010, 14).

However, this popular narrative hides contested histories of the movement. First, as historians Linda Gordon in *The Moral Property of Women: A History of Birth Control Politics in America* and Kathy Ferguson in her article "Birth Control" (included in this section) conclude, its radical roots in anarchism and socialism are largely unknown and ignored, and it fails to acknowledge that Sanger's advocacy among low-income immigrant women, Black women, and disabled women was linked to the **eugenics movement** (see Davis 1983; Roberts 1998; Washington 2008).

The legacies of these divisions in reproductive politics can be seen today. Generally, reproductive rights advocates agree that people across the spectra of race, ethnicity, class, and abilities benefit from comprehensive sex education;

Comstock Laws: Federal act passed in 1873 criminalizing the use of the U.S. Postal Service to exchange materials and information the government deemed obscene, such as pornography, contraceptives, and information on abortion.

Eugenics movement: In the late nineteenth and early twentieth century, the belief that a superior human race could be produced by controlling the reproduction of those deemed incapable or inferior by those who considered themselves superior in terms of race, looks, and abilities found popular support as well as generous funding from organizations such as the Carnegie Institution and Rockefeller Foundation.

Margaret Sanger, birth control advocate and supporter of eugenics. Sanger is widely known as the founder of the modern birth control movement, advocating for working-poor mothers struggling under deplorable living conditions in the early twentieth century. Archival evidence, such as this photograph taken on March 23, 1925, at the annual Neo-Malthusian and Birth Control Conference and her writing for the *Birth Control Review*, tie her to eugenics organizations.
Source: Bettmann/Getty Images

affordable birth control (and its availability through health insurance); a robust, federally funded Planned Parenthood; available and affordable abortion options; and reproductive technologies (such as sperm and egg donation, IVF, and surrogacy). What matters greatly are the conditions under which birth control is enforced and procedures (such as abortion, sterilization, and surrogacy) are performed. The next section looks closely at contemporary feminist and queer perspectives on what reproductive "choice" and "justice" mean.

REPRODUCTIVE CHOICE

The slogan "My Body, My Choice" was a rallying cry for many women across the United States throughout the 1960s and 1970s and continues to be an integral part of today's political landscape. Pro-choice positions emphasize that *all* women inherently have the right to control their fertility and if/when they will carry a pregnancy to term. While it may seem for some like common sense to argue for access to safe and effective birth control, the protection of legal abortion procedures, and women's rights to their bodies, for others it remains highly contested. Conservative religious institutions (as Rebecca Barrett-Fox inscribes in "Constraints and Freedom in Conservative Christian Women's Lives") teach that sex is between a husband and wife, and while it can and should be pleasurable, birth control is unnecessary. Moreover, pro-life advocates have restricted access to care in a handful of states by arguing that abortion providers (who often work out of free-standing clinics or doctor's offices) must provide facilities and standards equivalent to those of full hospitals as well as admitting privileges in hospitals. In June 2020, the Supreme Court in *June Medical Services v. Russo* struck down in a 5-4 vote a Louisiana law that mandated doctors to have admitting privileges for the same reasons it did so in Texas four years earlier, noting that it put a burden on women seeking an abortion. Ultimately, pro-life activists, policymakers, and lawmakers would like to see *Roe v. Wade* overturned by the Supreme Court and birth control fully privatized. In July 2020, they were handed a partial victory when the Supreme Court ruled in *Little Sisters of the Poor v. Pennsylvania* that employers with religious or moral objections to birth control could opt out of the Affordable Care Act provisions that it be covered. However, legal experts suggest that this will be challenged in the months and years ahead.

In the 1960s, federal approval of the birth control pill coincided with feminists' call for a sexual revolution. As historian Elaine Tyler May makes clear in *America and the Pill: A History of Promise, Peril, and Liberation*, there was momentum for women "to pursue sex, education, work and marriage when and how they liked it . . . [and while] the pill encouraged this trend, it did not create it" (May 2010, 71). Women themselves did. The pill's form assisted. It was discreet; she did not need to rely on her partner to agree to it; it required no interruption immediately before sex (unlike the diaphragm, cervical cap, sponge, and spermicide); and at the time it was considered safer than the intrauterine devise or IUD. The pill represented freedom and independence for those who had access to it.

In the United States, birth control and the legalization of abortion in *Roe v. Wade* (1973) were and still are largely framed politically as "health initiatives"—not women's rights—and purposefully so because it is an effective political strategy for ensuring both are available. It is important to note that for women to secure certain forms of birth control (such as an IUD), they must see a doctor. This simple step makes women's reproductive "choice" a constrained one. "A variety of scholars and activists have critiqued the choice paradigm because it rests on essentially individualistic, consumerist notions of 'free choice' that do not take into consideration all the social, economic, and political conditions that frame the so-called choices women are supposed to make" (Smith 2005, 127).

REPRODUCTIVE JUSTICE

When it comes to issues of reproduction, one person's freedom or choice can be another's oppression. This is especially clear in thinking about the difference between reproductive choice and reproductive justice. Marginalized communities, including low-income women, immigrant women, and women of color in the United States, including Puerto Rico, have a long history of not having a "choice" when it comes to reproduction.

The historical legacy of enslavement, colonization, and immigration policies has been coercive abuse. Black feminist scholars, such as Angela Davis in *Women, Race, & Class* and Dorothy Roberts in *Killing the Black Body: Race, Reproduction and the Meaning of Liberty*, have written extensively on how Black women were forced—and frequently raped—to produce children. In the 1980s, low-income women of color seeking state assistance ("welfare") were forced to use the implantable contraceptives Norplant and Depo Provera in exchange for money and food. What the women did not know at the time, and as Roberts reveals in *Killing the Black Body*, was that they were the test subjects for these new birth control methods. Scholars have documented how indigenous women were sterilized without their consent through National Indian Health Services (Gurr 2014; Smith 2015). Spanish-speaking Puerto Rican women in New York and Latinx individuals in Los Angeles report signing consent forms but not being able to understand what they signed because it was never translated. Between 1929 and 1976, North Carolina forcibly sterilized more than seven thousand men, women, and children, many of whom were poor, Black, and/or mentally challenged. According to Eric Mennel of National Public Radio in "Payments Start for N.C. Eugenics Victims," the state set aside $10 million in reparations in 2013 to be dispersed through the Office of Justice for Sterilization Victims, though many will not qualify given bureaucratic stipulations or may never see the money because they are quite elderly and the process of reparations is slow.

In "Birth Control" (included in this section), Kathy Ferguson suggests studying the radical philosophies of nineteenth- and twentieth-century anarchists and socialists will help us find pathways toward reproductive justice and freedom. They understood that birth control was one tenet of a larger struggle for freedom and that all members of society would not be free, including those who engage in sex outside of heterosexual, procreative marriage, if one member experienced control exercised by the state, churches, and families. By adjusting the frame, Ferguson asks us to understand that history does not march steadily toward progress. If we continue to react to contemporary politics by rolling our eyes and silently wondering "isn't this the twenty-first century?", the ideological forces that insist sex is heteronormative, tied to marriage, and procreative will also continue to erode women's access to birth control, abortion, and other reproductive care.

Reproductive justice expands what is meant by reproductive politics. While interested in birth control and abortion, this intersectional approach centers the lives of indigenous women, women of color, and trans/non-binary people to insist that systems of power must be examined and reconfigured so that reproduction can be self-determined by those made vulnerable within health, economic, and sociopolitical systems. According to SisterSong: Women of Color Reproductive Justice Collective, reproductive justice is defined as "the human right to maintain bodily autonomy, have children, not have children, and parent the children we have in safe and sustainable communities." Loretta Ross, a co-founder and national coordinator of SisterSong, has written extensively on the history of abortion in the Black community, edited *Undivided Rights* (2004), co-wrote with Rickie Solinger *Reproductive Justice: An Introduction* (2017), and served as lead editor of *Radical Reproductive Justice* (2017). The next reading in this section, "The Color of Choice, " is an early articulation of reproduction justice in which Ross names clearly how white supremacy, "an interlocking system of racism, patriarchy, homophobia, ultranationalism, xenophobia, anti-Semitism, and religious fundamentalism that creates a complex matrix of oppressions faced by people of color" (p. 280), is the root of why women of color resist "the reproductive politics of both the Right and the Left" (p. 280). This piece and *The Color of Violence: The Incite! Anthology* (originally published in 2006), in which it is found, have become foundational to understanding the shift from individual reproductive rights to a social justice framework of reproductive justice.

When we act in the name of reproductive freedom globally, US-based scholars, activists, and practitioners must be knowledgeable about the specific histories of population control that have been created and recreated for decades. With the climate crisis looming in our everyday lives, Yifat Susskind warns us in "Population Control Is Not the Answer to Our Climate Crisis" (included in this section) that "arguments for population control are reemerging in mainstream and even liberal discussions around limiting women's fertility in the name of environmental sustainability" (p. 291). A superficial reading of this dynamic might suggest that people are deeply concerned about the future we leave for the people on the planet. However, history teaches us that it is low-income women in the Global South who become targets for population control policies (Hartmann 2016). Susskind reminds readers how the contraception trials and sterilization abuses of the 1970s were invigorated by the same kind of rhetoric emerging today. What remains consistent is the need to recognize that the root of the problem is based in how capitalism produces "resource scarcity . . . [and] unequal distribution of basic necessities" (p. 292). Focusing on the birth rate diverts our attention from how corporations and the wealthy accelerate the climate crisis. If we pay attention to the activists calling for global economic justice, Susskind argues that we have a better chance of addressing one of the most pressing issues of our era. To advocate for reproductive freedom means activists, scholars, and practitioners understand how an intersectional and transnational approach must inform our theories and actions directing attention toward economic, political, and social structures that shape our interconnected lives.

ACTIVISM AND CIVIC ENGAGEMENT

Reproductive justice is a critical sociopolitical issue in women's, gender, and sexuality studies, yet individual reproductive rights and access to abortion and birth control dominate mainstream media and electoral politics. The following exercises help us to understand why abortion/birth control access "is necessary, but not enough" (SisterSong).

QUESTIONS

1. Visit SisterSong's website. Why is it important to have a reproductive justice organization crafted by and for indigenous women, women of color, and trans/non-binary people?

2. What does it mean to "mobilize . . . around our lived experiences," and why is this integral to understanding intersectional approaches to reproductive issues?

3. SisterSong contends that reproductive justice is a human right and draws on the internationally accepted United Nations Declaration of Human Rights to claim that reproductive decisions must be protected. Why do they ground their work in human rights instead of making it a health issue?

4. Why is it important that "comprehensive sexual education, alternate birth options, funded prenatal care and family leave, domestic violence programming, liveable wages, freedom from police violence and incarceration, and safe homes/communities" be included in the definition of reproductive justice? How might we reimagine the curriculum in sex education to include issues of reproductive justice?

5. Look closely at the Q/TPOC Birthwerq Project or another collective/organization that centers queer/trans people of color and reproductive justice. At the time of publication, the Q/TPOC Birthwerq Project had a Twitter and Facebook social media presence. What might it mean that "trans visibility is not enough"? How is being policed or incarcerated a reproductive justice issue? Is there a group in your community that serves a similar mission to the Birthwerq Project? If not, can you find one in your state? If so, what does it emphasize? If not, how might you and your class advocate for more racial, class, genderqueer, transgender, and disability awareness within your community?

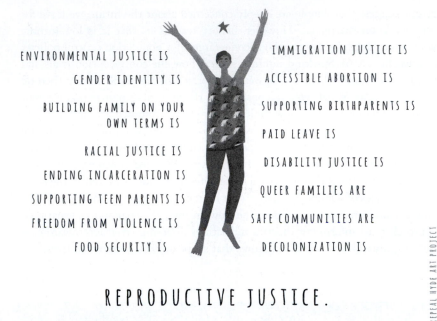

ENVIRONMENTAL JUSTICE IS

GENDER IDENTITY IS

BUILDING FAMILY ON YOUR
OWN TERMS IS

RACIAL JUSTICE IS

ENDING INCARCERATION IS

SUPPORTING TEEN PARENTS IS

FREEDOM FROM VIOLENCE IS

FOOD SECURITY IS

IMMIGRATION JUSTICE IS

ACCESSIBLE ABORTION IS

SUPPORTING BIRTHPARENTS IS

PAID LEAVE IS

DISABILITY JUSTICE IS

QUEER FAMILIES ARE

SAFE COMMUNITIES ARE

DECOLONIZATION IS

REPRODUCTIVE JUSTICE.

REPEAL HYDE ART PROJECT

Reproductive justice, an intersectional movement for social change. Reproductive justice movements are deeply interested in women's access to birth control, abortion clinics, repealing the Hyde Amendment, supporting *Roe v. Wade*, and advocating for the right to have children. Started by women of color, it also makes clear how the well-being of all marginalized people is deeply connected to justice within all social systems—whether it is living in communities with lead-free water or the abolition of the prison system.
Source: Megan Smith

GENDERED VIOLENCE

The statistics are startling. According to the National Organization for Women's website, three women are killed per day in the United States, a third of them murdered by an intimate partner; one in five women on U.S. college campuses will experience rape and sexual assault; and 4.8 million women in the United States experience physical assaults and rape within a domestic partnership. The United Nations, through its UN Women website, reports that 70 percent of women have experienced violence from an intimate partner, 120 million girls experience forced or coerced intercourse or other forced sex acts, and 88 percent of women have experienced verbal sexual harassment; 133 million girls and women in twenty-nine countries experience some form of female genital mutilation; and women and girls account for 70 percent of all sex trafficking victims. While the United Nations World's Women 2015 Report celebrates women's abilities to live longer, healthier lives and that more girls are receiving formal education, violence against women and girls darkens these advances.

Interpersonal sexual violence: Intimate partner violence or domestic violence, rape, and emotional or psychological violence within privatized relationships.

Gendered violence is ubiquitous and these stark numbers do not sufficiently address the **interpersonal sexual violence** that women of color and

LGBTQPAI+ communities experience. Moreover, this privatized violence does not address the **state violence** that women, men, queer, and trans people experience. These acts of bodily and psychological harm are largely unseen by the broader public for two reasons. First, the very institutions meant to protect LGBTQPAI+ and racial/ethnic communities, such as the U.S. Justice Department, the police, and the State Department, can perpetuate it. Specific examples include police brutality and murder, racial profiling and mass incarceration, xenophobia linked to anti-Arab and anti-Muslim violence, and hate crimes and homelessness in LGBTQPAI+ communities. Second, misogyny colludes with culturally accepted practices that harm and kill women, such as sex trafficking, female genital mutilation, and femicide. Although instances of systemic violence may appear to be isolated events, when investigated carefully, it becomes clear how historical processes and the social meanings ascribed to gender, race, class, sexuality, disability, religion, and nationality create an atmosphere where the unthinkable becomes a daily reality.

State violence: Harm that government, social institutions, industry, and individual members of society perpetuate based on stereotypical and interlocking ideas about gender, race, class, sexuality, religion, and nationality; also referred to as structural violence.

Antiviolence scholars, activists, and practitioners argue that private incidents of intimate partner violence and rape must be understood as public acts that require political attention; physical violence, abuse, and coercive sex are acts of power tied to toxic enactments of gender; and shelter systems and the law must be seen as safety nets and not solutions to addressing, preventing, and eliminating sexual violence. By proclaiming that violence can and does happen to anyone, feminists have consistently (and to some degree successfully) pushed US state and federal legislatures to craft laws that punish perpetrators found guilty of rape, sexual assault, and domestic violence. Yet, according to the statistics on the Rape, Abuse and Incest Network (RAINN) website, 68 percent of sexual assaults are not reported to the police, and 98 percent of rapists will not spend a day in jail or prison. SafeHorizon, the largest nonprofit victim services agency in the United States, notes that "most domestic violence incidents are *never* reported."

Collectively, we live in a rape culture. This explains why women, LGBTQPAI+ people, disabled people, and other minoritized groups do not use the structures for reporting sexual violence available to them through schools, the military, workplaces, or the police and why so few cases are successfully prosecuted through court systems. One in five women experiences sexual assault on college campuses and only two percent of victims report it to police and four percent to campus authorities. From a young age, girls are taught that they must keep themselves safe—through modest dress, monitoring when and with whom they consume alcohol, being careful on social media, and never walking alone at night. Rape culture curtails women's freedom; patriarchy, racism, classism, homophobia, transphobia, and xenophobia insist that women are responsible and therefore to blame if men (or anyone else) assault them.

Scholars, activists, and practitioners acknowledge that we do not know enough about sexual violence perpetrated against women of color, men, and LGBTQPAI+ communities for at least four reasons: (1) we do not invest as

Engaged Learning

Bystander intervention is a method used to disrupt public harassment and violence. It relies on evidence-based research in the social sciences (such as psychology and sociology) to train individuals to step out of their comfort zone and intervene when people, especially women, people of color, and LGBTQPAI+ people, may not be able to stop the violence themselves. According to the authors' research in "Friends of Survivors: The Community Impact of Unwanted Sexual Experiences," they discovered that most college campus victim/survivors of sexual violence confide in their friends (more so than parents/caregivers and university officials) and this can lead to community trauma. Bystander training can be one mechanism for stepping in before violence takes place. Hollaback! and Green Dot partner on their website (https://www.ihollaback.org/bystander-resources/) to train bystanders to (1) create a distraction, (2) delegate someone to get help, (3) document the incident, and (4) direct attention to the victim and ask if they are okay (ensuring one's own safety), and delay or slow things down to make sure the person is okay and the perpetrator is no longer on the scene. Full training is available on the website, and we recommend working with the Title IX coordinator on your campus if one is available. Complete the training and as a class develop an action plan to advocate that students across campus stand up to racial, anti-LGBTQPAI+, and sexual violence as a community.

Bystander intervention: A strategy for preventing violence, including gender-based violence, by training individuals to disrupt social norms that perpetuate victim blaming and the privatization of violence.

many resources into collecting this data historically and today, nationally and internationally; (2) given the harsh realities of racism, xenophobia, homophobia, and transphobia, some victims/survivors choose to protect members of their communities at their own personal cost; (3) members of the LGBTQPAI+ community may not be out and therefore do not feel like they can disclose violence in their relationships; and (4) others do not feel safe reporting to campus personnel and/or the police because their needs may be ignored and because of possible police brutality. For example, Angela Davis writes in "Rape, Racism and Myth of the Black Rapist" (1983) that "rape laws as a rule were framed originally for the protection of men of the upper classes, whose daughter and wives might be assaulted. What happens to working-class women has usually been of little concern to the courts" (172). She goes on to detail the ways in which white supremacy created cultural narratives that Black men rape white women in order to "justify" lynching and now incarcerating Black men; when Black women were/are raped by white men, they have nowhere to turn and their experiences are silenced. V. Efua Prince lays bare this process in her award-winning essay "June" (included in this section). Moving seamlessly between the violence of enslavement and the contemporary violence perpetrated against Black women, Prince's stark work weaves how sexual violence in the African American community must also be understood within historical narratives of trauma in the diaspora. Reflecting on the contemporary feminist movement, Beth Richie critiques the absence of racial and class analysis in antiviolence scholarship and movements, despite Davis's early interventions, in "A Black Feminist Reflection on the Antiviolence Movement" (included in this section). She argues that "a reassessment of the responses that have been central to antiviolence work—in particular, the reliance on law enforcement as the principal provider of women's safety" is central to creating change and bringing justice into the lives of Black women and women of color (p. 301).

For the first time in its history, the Centers for Disease Control and Prevention produced a press release in 2013 detailing the data it collected on interpersonal and sexual violence based on sexual orientation. According to its website, the agency found that "lesbians and gay men reported IPV and SV over their lifetimes at levels equal to or higher than those of heterosexuals . . . and bisexual women (61.1 percent) report a higher prevalence of rape, physical violence, and/or stalking by an intimate partner compared to both lesbian and heterosexual women." The report suggests that the LGBTQPAI+ community "suffer[s] a heavy toll of sexual violence and stalking" and that sexism and homophobia are deeply connected such that bisexual women experience a disproportionate amount of harm. In "A Queer #MeToo Story" (the next reading included in this section), Courtney Bailey expands our understanding of #MeToo by critiquing its heteronormative assumptions and contextualizing her experiences within a long-term relationship, at times in graphic detail, to articulate a vision of sexual agency and bodily integrity. In making a shift from consent and bodily autonomy—both of which rely on a singular self—to agency and bodily integrity, Bailey argues that agency relies on a radical interdependence. In her own words, "if we take agency as our starting point rather than consent, sexual mutuality and reciprocity do not arise from one person respecting or merging with another person. Instead, they arise from the very grounds that makes personhood possible" (p. 306). What remains true is that if intimate partner violence and sexual violence continue to be perceived only as heterosexual crimes linked to straight masculinity, violence in LGBTQPAI+ communities will remain invisible.

According to Joey L. Mogul, Andrea J. Richie, and Kay Whitlock, the authors of "False Promises: Criminal Legal Responses to Violence Against LGBT People" (included in this section), there has been a notable spike in stranger and intimate violence in LGBTQPAI+ communities. In 2008, the National Coalition of Anti-Violence Programs "reported over 2,000 instances of homophobic and transphobic violence . . . representing a 26 percent increase over 2006 figures" (p. 308). More recently, the online magazine, *The Advocate*, reported that twenty-one trans women of color were murdered in 2015 and 2019 and acknowledged that the number was undoubtedly higher since these statistics represent what was reported to the police. While many incidents are supposed to be investigated as **hate crimes**, Mogul, Ritchie, and Whitlock argue that "the same criminalizing archetypes that permeate treatment of queers in other contexts also profoundly inform police approaches to LGBT victims of crime" (Mogul et. al 2011, 102). In the United States, justice is tied to the thoroughness of police work. If LGBTQPAI+ community members experience gender, racial, and sexual discrimination, bias, and violence in that very process, people will distrust authorities and will stop reporting crimes. As the

Hate crime: Violence motivated by race, color, religion, ethnicity, national origin, sexual orientation, gender, gender identity or expression, or disability.

authors contend, so long as we focus on violence as individual acts and not "dismantling the systemic forces that promote, condone, and facilitate homophobic and transphobic violence" (p. 311), we will continue to see continued violence and systemic protection of perpetrators.

Following the terrorist attacks of September 11, 2001, and President George W. Bush's decision to wage war in the Middle East under false claims that Iraq was producing weapons of mass destruction, the Southern Poverty Law Center reported a dramatic increase in anti-Arab and anti-Muslim hate groups in the United States. **Islamophobia** is fueled by government promises to fight "terrorism" in the name of US national security and the repeated media construction of Muslims as "anti-American jihadists." As Isis Nusair argues in "Making Feminist Sense of Torture at Abu-Ghraib" (included in this section), when facile ideologies embedded in **orientalism** misrepresent one of the oldest and the most widely practiced religions in the world, it does the cultural work needed to condone war, justify torture, and violate human and women's rights.

It can be overwhelming to take all this in at once, but it is necessary to understand how interpersonal and structural violence are linked before we can even begin addressing gender, sexual, and racial violence with the goal of

Islamophobia: Prejudice produced by fear of Islam or Muslims.

Orientalism: Delimiting Western representations of Asian and Middle Eastern cultures so as to produce and reproduce stereotypes and tropes embedded in colonialism and imperialism.

The complexity of "Muslim women." In today's world, some media outlets and politicians drawing ties between Muslim communities and terrorism have incited violence and amplified cultural divides. Muslim women are at home in countries across Asia, Africa, the Middle East, Europe, and the Americas and cannot be reduced to oversimplified and deliberately crafted stereotypes. Here, women march in the Annual Muslim Day Parade in New York City (2013) demanding better from the dominant culture.
Source: Ethel Wolovitz/Alamy Stock Photo

prevention and elimination. Violence is all around us, perhaps so much so that collectively we become desensitized, tune it out, or grow numb to it. However, one of the first steps in combating this scourge is to become aware of its depth and dimensions and discuss violence openly.

POPULAR CULTURE AND MEDIA REPRESENTATIONS

In 1975, feminist film theorist Laura Mulvey argued that the structures of Hollywood films represented women through the **male gaze** for all audience members. The male gaze crafted women on screen as passive, helpless, and in need of rescue; sexualized but not sexual; and available for men's pleasure. Since 1975, feminist and queer scholars have debated how much agency marginalized communities have in popular culture and the ways in which representations of women and LGBTQPAI+ people either reinforce harmful stereotypes or allow the boundaries of gender, race, social class, sexuality, abilities, religion, and nationalities to be challenged.

Male gaze: How the production of visual arts is crafted by and through patriarchal interpretations of the world, and therefore film, television, and art represent women as objects rather than subjects.

Pop culture is among the most readily accessible and easily digestible cultural texts. As an "agent of socialization" and a pedagogical tool, it teaches us how to see, live, and be in this world (D'Enbeau 2009, 17; Kellner 2015, 7; Lindner 2004, 409). How feminism and queer identity is represented *in* pop culture matters because many people may first learn about gender, race, sexuality, feminism, and LGBTQPAI+ communities through pop culture (Hollows and Moseley 2006, 1). In Sut Jhally's film *Stuart Hall: Representations and the Media*, cultural theorist and sociologist Stuart Hall argues that representation is constitutive of reality, and it is through representations that we make sense of the world. Skewed media representations undoubtedly contribute to a distorted perception of reality. Psychological research has shown, for example, that when people are exposed to sexually explicit advertisements, they tend to show "greater gender role stereotyping, rape myth acceptance, and acceptance of sexual aggression against women" (Lindner 2004, 410).

Would a solution to this problem then be to have more "accurate" representations of people the world? The answer to this question may not be that simple. Wanting to see an "authentic" representation of a social group is in itself troubling because it is often based on the assumption that there is an essence to what is being represented. For example, it assumes that the creative minds of any given media product have access to knowing what a wealthy heterosexual Muslim woman's life *really* looks like. With different histories and fluid experiences even within the same group of people, any attempt to construct *a* representation of anything or anyone will be fraught with some form of misrepresentation. It is thus important to be critical of how a cultural text is produced, circulated, and consumed; to be aware of the relations of power within these media agents and agencies; and to understand how certain politics and ideologies limit and shape the production of texts (Kellner 2015, 11). The first step to analyzing any media representation requires us to ask, "[w]ho does visibility benefit, and on what terms is it offered? For whose purposes, and under whose control do media artifacts circulate?" (Mann 2014, 293).

Sociologist Patricia Hill Collins argues in *Black Feminist Thought* that the dominant media representations of Black Americans function as "controlling images." These representations usually deploy the stereotypical figures of the mammy, matriarch, welfare mother, and jezebel. Working-class Black men are often represented as "athletes" or "criminals" (being "inherently violent and/or hyper-heterosexual") and middle-class Black men as "sissies and sidekicks" (being "friendly and deferential; . . . loyal both to dominant societal values such as law and order as well as to individuals who seemingly uphold them; . . . a safe, nonthreatening Black identity") (Collins, "Booty Call," 2012, 320, 323–324). Hence, representations of Black people in US media do not necessarily challenge racial hierarchy; they may even do the cultural work of further cementing inequalities. Specifically focusing on Black lesbians on television, Jaelani Turner-Williams, in her essay "A Quick History of TV's Elusive Quest for Complex Black Lesbians" (included in this section), demonstrates how "thoughtfully crafted Black lesbians are still an anomaly on TV" (p. 322).

Pop culture has also failed to provide us with critical representations not only in terms of race, gender, and sexuality, but also in terms of class. In her essay "Women's Friendships, Popular Culture, and Gender Theories," Judith Kegan Gardiner argues that in American films, friendships have indeed functioned to "reinforce class and gender binaries and . . . reassure individuals that they are performing their social roles appropriately" (p. 324).

It is challenging to find representations that empower women and LGBTQPAI+ communities. In contemporary media, **postfeminism** appears to do this work. However, when we apply a critical lens to its mode of representation, we can see that it functions as another way of limiting how we interpret gender, race, class, sexuality, abilities, age, and nationalities and the *only* way in which we have access to feminism in mass-circulated media (Tasker and Negra 2007, 2). Postfeminism is both a popular and academic term. It circulates in much the same way that postracial does by suggesting that we have moved beyond the need for feminism because gender equality and justice have been realized. One of the primary reasons it has popular traction is because Hollywood films and television shows (such as *Sex in the City* and *Scandal*) feature independent and empowered women who appear to no longer need broader sociopolitical changes to achieve their personal goals. It is important to note that women in these shows often are simultaneously sexualized and interpreted as in control of their sexuality. What such critique ignores is that individual characters, even those who claim to be successful and empowered, are nonetheless living within patriarchal, racist, classist, homophobic, transphobic, and xenophobic social structures and that their self-proclaimed liberation does not represent *all* women's liberation.

As a scholarly term, postfeminism first was conceptualized within feminist media studies and has two identifiable strategies (Hollows and Moseley 2006, 7). First, it refers to a form of subjectivity (or being) that values "agency, freedom, sexual pleasure, fashion, consumer culture, hybridism, humor, and the

Postfeminism: The ways in which everyday people assume that gender equality and justice has been achieved and, within feminist media studies, the ways in which media outlets appropriate feminism to sell ideas, images, and products to consumers.

renewed focus on the female body" (Adriaens and Van Bauwel 2014, 191). Second, it flags an economically independent subject that "promote[s] an aesthetic of wealth, to display privileged whiteness, heterosexuality, normative Western beauty ideals and individualism" (Wilkes 2015, 18). In this way, it suggests that feminism is an individualistic pursuit that can be reflected in what we buy (which ultimately reflects how others see and produce goods for us) rather than bell hooks's definition in Section One that emphasized feminism as a movement for social change.

Postfeminist television shows and movies often represent feminism *as* history (something that happened in the past [i.e., in the 1960s and 1970s]) rather than embedded *in* an ongoing history. In the 1980s, there was an increase in the number of women and girls seen on television, but any sense of their political and social progress was not represented. This phenomenon cannot be separated from how major television networks contributed to a return to conservative values in US society and a "backlash against feminism" (see Faludi 1991; Kellner 2015).

For example, television featured more young female characters (Ivins-Hulley 2014, 1198). However, as Kristen Myers found in her study of forty-five episodes of four TV series targeted at preteen girls (*Hannah Montana*, *Suite Life on Deck*, *Wizards of Waverly Place*, and *iCarly*), these shows circulate "antifeminist" messages. They "celebrated beauty and heterosexual coupling, demonized strong and unattractive women, and valorized antisocial girls" (Myers 2013, 198–199, 203). These programs featured "strong girl characters" that seemed to defy traditional notions of femininity, but when analyzed carefully, they were simply "heterosexy bullies, not feminists" (Myers 2013, 201). Indeed, in recent media, girls have been represented as bullies, more violent than ever before (and "meaner" than boys). Yet, as Meda Chesney-Lind shows in "Mean Girls, Bad Girls, or Just Girls: Corporate Media Hype and the Policing of Girlhood" (included in this section), this story is far more complicated. She deflates this media hype by providing context and statistics that show why girls only *seem* to be more violent or meaner than boys.

Girls, women, and LGBTQPAI+ people are not passive consumers of pop culture in their everyday lives. With the relatively recent boom of social media, people's engagement with pop culture has been reconfigured. New digital media provide alternative spaces for marginalized voices and force us to rethink old notions of "expertise, authority, and communication skills" (Mann 2014, 295). The participation of Black women media makers in social media such as Twitter and Tumblr "far outweighs their participation in other media channels" (Mann 2014, 294). Feminist zines and fan fiction challenge problematic gender ideologies and find new outlets online (Spiers 2015, 9). As Susan Driver shows in her book *Queer Girls and Popular Culture: Reading, Resisting, and Creating Media*, pop culture becomes a "process through which queer girls creatively imagine possibilities, forge connections, make meanings, and articulate relations" (Driver 2007, 14). New media provide an outlet to experiment with nonheteronormative identities.

Although changes have occurred in media as they broadcast shows that focus on same-sex couples or transgender people, heterosexuality still remains the hegemonic norm. Often, when LGBTQPAI+ identities are represented in media, they perpetuate rather than challenge existing stereotypes. In the case of bisexual and pansexual identities of celebrities such as Miley Cyrus that Elly Belle observes in "Knee-Jerk Biphobia: What Responses to Miley Cyrus's Breakup Say About Queer Erasure" (included in this section), "representations of queerness are stifled by a popular culture that, despite some promising changes, remains heteronormative" (p. 334).

Could fetishizing bisexual celebrities for heterosexual males' fantasies or transgender celebrities for voyeuristic media consumption by the general public be another form of the male gaze that Mulvey theorized over forty years ago? Perhaps it more accurately reflects straight and queer men and women's participation in crafting meanings ascribed to gender and sexuality in popular culture? Might we need a more structural analysis of how media institutions use sex—and a very particular version of sex—to sell their products? Regardless of how we answer these questions, it is clear we need more than just representations of difference; it matters greatly *how* gender, race, social class, age, abilities, and nationalities are constructed. The next time you hear someone say with ease that "sex sells"—whether it is in reference to products in advertisements or how a film is promoted to draw in an audience—you may want to ask which kind of sex they are referring to, because it appears as though only the bodies of young, white, slim women who wear sexy outfits and pose in submissive and seductive positions for heterosexual men sell. If we expand the notion of "sex" to include bodies of people of color and/or with disability and in different sizes, older women, or same-sex couples, then perhaps sex does not sell. By asking these kinds of critical questions, we can engage with popular culture and media representations in productive ways so that we might one day see a full range of empowered feminist and queer identities reflected back to us.

This section has asked students to think about a range of issues central to feminist and queer studies, from the social constructions of family and work to intersectional representations of straight and queer communities in popular culture. In each section, you have seen how some people's freedom might be others' oppressions and how this is yoked to our understandings of gender, race, social class, sexuality, religion, age, abilities, and nationality; you have also learned that feminist and queer scholars, activists, and practitioners do not always agree on how to address inequalities. Rather, as bell hooks argues in *Feminism Is for Everybody*, they offer ideas for social change based on philosophies of reform or revolution. As you reflect on the sociopolitical issues in this section, let's ask: Can equality and social justice be approached—perhaps even achieved—by working within the existing system? Will it require rethinking and new political initiatives that reconfigure gender, race, social class, sexuality, abilities, age, religion, and nationality so that social institutions are rebuilt on new foundations?

Critical Thinking Questions

1. How is the history of the social construction of families integral to our understanding of occupational segregation, the gender pay gap, sexual harassment, and discrimination in the contemporary labor market? How do intersectional approaches shed light on your answers to this question?

2. Why is it important to frame sex work as labor and not just as an extension of patriarchy and global capitalism?

3. In your own words, what are the philosophical and political differences between reproductive choice and reproductive justice? What role does intersectionality play?

4. Do some investigations into how scholars and the media discuss violence against trans communities, and especially trans communities of color. What are the stories that are told? How does the television series *Pose* rewrite this representation?

5. Can you think of media texts (television shows, films, podcasts etc.) that construct an empowered feminist or queer gaze (beyond *Pose*)? If so, what are they, where are they found, and how do they resist controlling images? If not, why do you think this is the case and why does it matter in thinking about social transformation and justice?

GLOSSARY

Bystander intervention 206
Comstock Laws 199
Eugenics movement 199
Fatherhood bonus 194
Gender pay gap 192
Glass ceiling 195
Hate crime 207

Interpersonal sexual
violence 204
Islamophobia 208
Male gaze 209
Mother pay penalty 194
Neoliberalism 187
Nuclear family 185
Occupational segregation 193

Orientalism 208
Postfeminism 210
Second shift 192
Settler-colonials 185
Sex trafficking 197
Sex work 197
State violence 205
Xenophobia 187

WORKS CITED

Adriaens, Fien, and Sofie Van Bauwel. "*Sex and the City*: A Postfeminist Point of View? Or How Popular Culture Functions as a Channel for Feminist Discourse." *Journal of Popular Culture*, vol. 47, no. 1, 2014, pp. 174–95.

Allen, Paula Gunn. *The Sacred Hoop: Recovering the Feminine in American Indian Traditions*. Reissued ed. Beacon Press, 1992.

Babcock, Linda, and Sara Laschever. *Women Don't Ask: Negotiation and the Gender Divide*. Princeton UP, 2003.

Bagri, Neha Thirani. "New Research Confirms the "Sexuality Pay Gap" Is Real." *Quartz* January, 12, 2017.

Bernhardt, Annette, et al. "Broken Laws, Unprotected Workers: Violations of Employment and Labor Laws in America's Cities." *Unprotected Workers Organization*, 2010, www.unprotectedworkers.org/index.php/broken_laws/index.

Boushey, Heather. "A Woman's Place Is in the Middle Class." In *The Shriver Report: A Woman's Nation Pushes Back from the Brink*, edited by Olivia Morgan et al., 2014, pp. 45–73.

Briggs, Laura. *Somebody's Children: The Politics of Transracial and Transnational Adoption*. Duke UP, 2012.

A Broken Bargain: Discrimination, Fewer Benefits and More Taxes for LGBT Workers. Movement Advancement Project/Center for American Progress/Human Rights Campaign, June 2013, www.lgbtmap.org/file/a-broken-bargain-full-report.pdf.

Budig, Michelle. "The Fatherhood Bonus and the Motherhood Penalty: Parenthood and the Gender Gap in Pay." *Third Way Fresh Thinking*, September 2, 2014, content.thirdway.org/publications/853/NEXT_-_Fatherhood_Motherhood.pdf.

Carpenter, Christopher S. and Samuel T. Eppnick. "Does It Get Better?: Recent Estimates of Sexual Orientation Earnings in the United States. *Southern Economic Journal* 84:2 (2017): 426-441.

"CDC Releases Data on Interpersonal and Sexual Violence by Sexual Orientation." *CDC Newsroom*, January 25, 2013, www.cdc.gov/media/releases/2013/p0125_NISVS.html.

Chen, Stephanie. "'John Schools' Try to Change Attitudes about Paid Sex." *CNN*, August 28, 2009, www.cnn.com/2009/CRIME/08/27/tennessee.john.school/index.html?eref=rss_us.

Collins, Patricia Hill. *Black Feminist Thought: Knowledge, Consciousness, and the Politics of Empowerment.* 10th anniversary ed. Routledge, 2000.

Collins, Patricia Hill. "Booty Call: Sex, Violence, and Images of Black Masculinity." In *Media and Cultural Studies Keyworks*, edited by Meenakshi Gigi Durham and Douglas M. Kellner, 2nd ed. Wiley-Blackwell, 2012, pp. 318–37.

Collins, Patricia Hill. "It's All in the Family: Intersections of Gender, Race, and Nation." *Hypatia*, vol. 13, no. 3, 1998, pp. 62–82.

Corbett, Christianne, and Catherine Hill. *Graduating to a Pay Gap: The Earnings of Men and Women One Year After College Graduation.* American Association of University Women, 2012, www.aauw.org/files/2013/02/graduating-to-a-pay-gap-the-earnings-of-women-and-men-one-year-after-college-graduation.pdf.

Davis, Angela. *Women, Race and Class.* Vintage Books, 1983.

D'Enbeau, Suzy. "Feminine and Feminist Transformation in Popular Culture: An Application of Mary Daly's Radical Philosophies to *Bust* Magazine." *Feminist Media Studies*, vol. 9, no. 1, 2009, pp. 17–36.

"Domestic Violence: Statistics and Facts." *SafeHorizon*, 2015, www.safehorizon.org/page/domestic-violence-statistics—facts-52.html.

Driver, Susan. *Queer Girls and Popular Culture: Reading, Resisting, and Creating Media.* Peter Lang, 2007.

Duggan, Lisa. *Twilight of Equality: Neoliberalism, Cultural Politics, and the Attack on Democracy.* Beacon Press, 2004.

"Facts and Figures: Ending Violence Against Women." *UN Women*, October 2015, www.unwomen.org/en/what-we-do/ending-violence-against-women/facts-and-figures.

Faludi, Susan. *Backlash: The Undeclared War Against American Women.* Crown Publishing, 1991.

Gordon, Linda. *The Moral Property of Women: A History of Birth Control Politics in America.* University of Illinois Press, 2007.

Gurr, Barbara. *Reproductive Justice: The Politics of Health Care for Native American Women.* Rutgers UP, 2014.

Hartmann, Betsy. *Reproductive Rights and Wrongs: the Global Politics of Population Control.* 3rd ed. Haymarket Books, 2016.

Hill, Catherine. *The Simple Truth About the Gender Pay Gap.* American Association of University Women, Fall 2015, www.aauw.org/research/the-simple-truth-about-the-gender-pay-gap/.

Hochschild, Arlie. *The Second Shift.* Avon Books, 1989.

Hollows, Joanne, and Rachel Moseley. *Feminism in Popular Culture.* Berg, 2006.

hooks, bell. *Feminism Is for Everybody.* Pluto Press, 2000.

Incite! Women of Color Against Violence. *The Color of Violence: The Incite! Anthology.* Reprint. Duke, 2016.

Ivins-Hulley, Laura. "Narrowcasting Feminism: MTV's *Daria*." *Journal of Popular Culture*, vol. 47, no. 6, 2014, pp. 1198–212.

Jhally, Sut, director. *Stuart Hall: Representation and the Media.* Media Education Foundation, 1997.

Kellner, Douglas. "Cultural Studies, Multiculturalism, and Media Culture." In *Gender, Race, and Class in Media*, edited by Gail Dines and Jean M. Humez. 4th ed. Sage Publications, 2015, pp. 7–19.

Killaway, Mitch, and Sunnivie Brydum. "These Are the U.S. Transwomen Killed in 2015." *Advocate*, December 11, 2015, www.advocate.com/transgender/2015/12/11/these-are-trans-women-killed-in-2015.

Lagasse, Jeff. "Male Nurses Still Make $6,000-plus More Than Women, New Survey Shows." HealthcareITNews, June 2018, https://www.healthcareitnews.com/news/male-nurses-still-make-6000-plus-more-women-new-survey-shows.

Lindner, Katharina. "Images of Women in General Interest and Fashion Magazine Advertisements from 1955 to 2002." *Sex Roles*, vol. 51, no. 7/8, 2004, pp. 409–21.

Mann, Larisa. "What Can Feminism Learn from New Media?" *Communication and Critical/Cultural Studies*, vol. 11, no. 3, 2014, pp. 293–97.

May, Elaine Tyler. *America and the Pill*. Basic Books, 2010.

McMurray, Anaya. "Hotep and Hip-Hop: Can Black Muslim Women Be Down with Hip-Hop?" *Meridians*, vol. 8, no. 1, 2008, pp. 74–92.

Mennel, Eric. "Payments Start for N.C. Eugenics Victims, But Many Won't Qualify." *Shots: Health News*, National Public Radio, November 5, 2014.

Miller-Young, Mirelle. *A Taste for Brown Sugar: Black Women in Pornography*. Duke UP, 2014.

Muñoz, José Esteban. *Cruising Utopia: The Then and There of Queer Futurity*. New York UP, 2009.

Myers, Kristen. "Anti-Feminist Messages in American Television Programming for Young Girls." *Journal of Gender Studies*, vol. 22, no. 2, 2013, pp. 192–205.

Quick Take: Lesbian, Gay, Bisexual, and Transgender Workplace Issues. Catalyst, 2015, http://www.catalyst.org/knowledge/lesbian-gay-bisexual-transgender-workplace-issues.

Rikleen, Lauren Stiller. "Women Lawyers Continue to Lag Behind Male Colleagues: Report of the Ninth Annual NAWL Survey on Retention and Promotion of Women in Law Firms." *National Association of Women Lawyers*, 2015, heinonline.org/HOL/LandingPage?handle=hein.journals/wolj100&div=32&id=&page=.

Roberts, Dorothy. *Killing the Black Body: Race, Reproduction and the Meaning of Liberty*. Vintage Books, 1998.

Ross, Loretta, Lynn Roberts, Erika Derkas, Whiteney Peoples, and Pamela Bridgewater-Toure. *Radical Reproductive Justice: Foundations, Theory, Practice, and Critique*. Feminist Press, 2017.

Ross, Loretta, and Rickie Solinger. *Reproductive Justice: An Introduction*. University of California Press, 2017.

Ruiz, Vicki, and Ellen Carol DuBois, editors. *Unequal Sister: An Inclusive Reader in U. S. Women's History*. 4th ed. Routledge, 2007.

Smith, Andrea. "Beyond Pro-Life versus Pro-Choice: Women of Color and Reproductive Justice." *NWSA Journal*, vol. 17, no. 1, 2005, pp. 119–40.

Smith, Andrea. *Conquest: Sexual Violence and American Indian Genocide*. Duke UP, 2015.

"Solidarity Not Charity: Mutual Aid and How to Organize in the Age of Coronavirus." *Democracy Now!*, March 20, 2020, https://www.democracynow.org/2020/3/20/coronavirus_community_response_mutual_aid.

Spade, Dean. *Normal Life: Administrative Violence, Critical Trans Politics and the Limit of the Law*. Duke UP, 2015.

Spiers, Emily. "'Killing Ourselves Is Not Subversive': Riot Grrrl From Zine to Screen and the Commodification of Female Transgression." *Women: A Cultural Review*, vol. 26, no. 1/2, 2015, pp. 1–21.

"Statistics." *RAINN: Rape, Abuse, and Incest National Network*, 2009, rainn.org/statistics.

Tasker, Yvonne, and Diane Negra. "Introduction: Feminist Politics and Postfeminist Culture." In *Interrogating Post-Feminism*, edited by Yvonne Tasker and Diane Negra, Duke UP, 2007, pp. 1–26.

Taylor, Keeanga-Yamahtta. *Race for Profit: How Banks and the Real Estate Industry Undermined Black Homeownership*. University of North Carolina Press, 2019.

Tilly, Louise A., and Joan W. Scott. *Women, Work and Family*. Routledge, 1989.

U.S. Census Bureau. U.S. Current Population Survey. July 2020. https://www.census.gov/programs-surveys/cps.html

U.S. Department of Labor. *Data and Statistics*. January 2015, www.dol.gov/wb/stats/stats_data.htm.

"Violence Against Women in the United States: Statistics." *National Organization for Women*, 2015, now.org/resource/violence-against-women-in-the-united-states-statistic/.

Washington, Harriet. *Medical Apartheid: The Dark History of Medical Experimentation on Black Americans from Colonial Times to the Present*. Reprint ed. Anchor Books, 2008.

Welter, Barbara. "The Cult of True Womanhood: 1820–1860." *American Quarterly*, vol. 18, no. 2, 1966, pp. 151–74.

Wilkes, Karen. "Colluding with Neo-Liberalism: Post-Feminist Subjectivities, Whiteness and Expressions of Entitlement." *Feminist Review*, vol. 110, 2015, pp. 18–33.

33. • *Rebecca Barrett-Fox*

CONSTRAINTS AND FREEDOM IN CONSERVATIVE CHRISTIAN WOMEN'S LIVES (2017)

Rebecca Barrett-Fox is the visiting coordinator of online learning at Hesston College, where she promotes feminist, compassionate, just pedagogy. She is also a scholar of gender and sexuality, race and ethnicity, and religion, especially as they intersect with hate groups and rightwing and conservative social and political movements. She is the author of God Hates: Westboro Baptist Church, American Nationalism, and the Religious Right (University Press of Kansas 2016) as well as numerous peer-reviewed articles. .

Hannah (who shared her story over a course of interviews but requested that her real name and identifying information not be shared) hoists her toddler daughter into the swing on the playground as her older daughter climbs the slide. Her friend Rachel should arrive soon with her own preschoolers, and Hannah is anxious. Rachel is pregnant again, as Hannah should be now, too—except that her third pregnancy ended a month ago in the stillbirth of a yearned-for baby boy. She attends a two hundred–person independent fundamentalist church—a congregation that interprets the Bible literally and espouses conservative political and social views and has no official ties to any other church. She loves her church and values the intergenerational mentoring of other women. They model for her Proverbs 31 womanhood, a template of femininity drawn from a Biblical passage describing the ideal wife and mother as both beautiful and hardworking. Broadly rejecting what they see as government interference, they homeschool their own many children. Despite their busy lives, after her stillbirth, members of the church provided several weeks' worth of meals and babysitting for the girls so that Hannah and her husband could focus on the funeral. Now, Hannah is not sure she can bear to see Rachel. She is blessed to

have Quiverfull friends—families who believe that any form of birth control is a sin. As Psalm 127:4–5 in the King James Version (KJV) of the Bible states, "As arrows are in the hand of a mighty man; so are children of the youth. Happy is the man that hath his quiver full of them." However, she sometimes feels that the other wives in her church have made childbearing a competition—one in which a stillbirth is a sign of failure. She worries that her feelings may be rooted in jealousy and resolves to devote more prayer to the issue.

For conservative and fundamentalist Christians like Hannah, gender identities and roles are informed by orthodoxy ("right belief"), which tells participants what they should *believe* about gender, sex, and sexuality, and orthopraxis ("right practice"), which tells them what they should *do*. Hannah's beliefs about fertility shape her hopes about childbearing; her beliefs about gender shape her ideas about mothering. Though many women find such constraints oppressive, others find them empowering—a paradox that has often puzzled observers. In *You Can Be the Wife of a Happy Husband*, self-help author and motivational speaker Darien B. Cooper explains the liberating effects of constraints that she experienced in her own life-long marriage to her husband, saying,

"Submission never means that our personalities, abilities, talents, or individuality should be buried. Rather, they are to be directed so they can be maximized and reflect the goodness and glory of God" (Cooper 2010, 23). Though there are many varieties of conservative Christianity, each stresses submission of the individual's life to the will of God, a will that is committed to gender *complementarianism*—the idea that God created everyone with a sex that aligns with a masculine or feminine gender and that God values and loves men and women equally but has created them for different roles (Council on Biblical Manhood and Womanhood). Strife, unhappiness, and inequality are not the result of gender distinctions but of people's fight against them. Christian gender manuals, such as *The Total Woman*, *The Power of a Praying Wife*, *Raising a Modern-Day Knight*, and *Wild at Heart: Discovering the Secrets of a Man's Soul*, stress that marital harmony comes from embracing the limitations that conservative belief places on our lives and then excelling within those limits. While the details of orthopraxis vary among conservative Christian groups, three domains of women's lives, explored in this essay, are the targets of religious control: sexuality, bodies, and marriage and reproduction.

SEXUALITY

As the sexual revolution began to reshape mainstream American culture, many conservative Christians, such as Tim and Beverly LaHaye in *The Act of Marriage* (1976), argued for sexual passion in marriage. In their handbook, the LaHayes explained how new couples could achieve sexual pleasure—including orgasms for the bride, an explicit recognition that women deserve sexual pleasure. More recently, some conservative churches have tried pro-sex programming. Sermon series about sex's importance, along with ad campaigns promoting these series, are especially popular in nondenominational megachurches known for recruiting new members. Books such as *Holy Sex!* and *Intended for Pleasure* suggest that sex is created by God for human pleasure,

not just procreation, and that heterosexual married partners have a mutual obligation to have great sex. Pastor Ed Young and his wife Lisa encourage a seven-day "sexperiment" (also the title of their 2012 book) in which congregants commit to having sex every day for a week. Pastor Mark Driscoll, coauthor with his wife Grace Driscoll of *Real Marriage* (2013), has gone further, listing all the kinds of sex that the figures in the Bible's Song of Solomon had that Christians, too, should be having: fellatio, cunnilingus, "sacred stripping" (erotic dance for one's partner alone), and outdoor sex.

Yet these explicit commands for Christians to have sex are still presented within the narrow confines of married monogamous heterosexuality. Hebrews 13:4 of the KJV admonishes that "marriage be held in honor by all, and the bed undefiled" and warns that that "fornicators and adulterers God will judge." This verse is often used to explain that *only* heterosexual, cisgender marital sex is honorable; even if LGBTQ+ people are legally married, sex is sinful. Additionally, among more conservative groups, divorce is sinful (though being the victim of a divorce is not), and any remarriage, even between opposite-sex partners, may be considered adultery.

Within conservative Christian culture, as in secular culture, women are seen as less interested in sex's physical aspects and more interested in emotional connection, whereas men are depicted as primarily interested in physical sensation. Explains Juli Slattery on the website for Focus on the Family, a conservative Christian media organization:

> A woman's sexual desire is far more connected to emotions than her husband's sex drive is. A man can experience sexual arousal apart from any emotional attachment. He can look at a naked woman and feel intense physical desire for her, while *at the same time* he may be completely devoted to and in love with his wife. For most women, this just doesn't compute. (para. 5)

Christian gender manuals consistently frame sex as *resulting from* emotional connection for women and *causing* emotional connection for men—giving women, who control access to sex, an inherent power advantage. In this view, men do not seek emotional connection to women, though women *need* emotional connection for sex. In contrast, because men are attracted to women's physical bodies, men are inherently tempted by women. Indeed, writers often coach men on how to express, within a range of acceptable "masculine" styles, those emotions that will connect them to women—and lead to holy sex. In contrast, because women are not attuned to men's physical desire, both married and unmarried women must be frequently reminded that their bodies tempt men; their appearances must be policed to protect men they encounter. The American Decency Association, a conservative Christian organization that opposes "indecent" media, ranging from pornography to lingerie catalogues, reminds women of their duty in one of their radio spots:

> Ladies, God calls you to walk in this world as a candle among straw or gunpowder. A fire can injure and destroy many lives. Are you aware of how powerful your dress affects men? Does your style of dress help or hinder men? Bring glory to God as you honor God by your modesty. (Johnson 2015)

First, women must recognize normative standards of sexual attractiveness, such as exposed knees and cleavage, then must refuse to adopt them for men's sake. In this way, every woman must morally guard men's spirituality and sexuality with her own body.

BODIES

Gender embodiment varies across conservative Christian subcultures, but modesty, however, defined, is valued highly, as is gender difference. In many groups, modesty and gender distinctiveness mean unisex dress is prohibited. Amish, conservative Mennonites, FLDS, and River Brethren, some Pentecostals and Baptists, and others require women to wear dresses that cover the majority of the leg and hide the outline of breasts. FLDS dress codes, for example, never allow women to show

ankles, and both Amish and conservative Mennonites wear "cape dresses," which include an apronlike top to de-emphasize breasts. Among the most conservative groups, cosmetics are forbidden, as is hair cutting because 1 Corinthians 11:15 of the KJV declares that "if a woman have long hair, it is a glory to her: for her hair is given her for a covering." Some groups mandate long or uncut hair, sometimes in combination with head coverings such as the *kapp* (Amish), *Mitz* (Hutterite), or scarf or bonnet to indicate submission to the God-ordained hierarchy described in 1 Corinthians 11:3: "that the head of every man is Christ; and the head of the woman is the man; and the head of Christ is God." For groups that adopt head coverings, it is evidence of a woman's agreement with male leadership in the family and church and her willingness to be under the authority of men.

Among evangelical churches that are theologically and politically conservative while still engaging mainstream culture more than sects such as the Amish, women have to negotiate more ambiguous standards. Southern Baptists, Covenant Evangelicals, members of the Church of Christ, women in nondenominational churches, and many others must be simultaneously modest and attractive to their husbands without tempting other men. They must also put enough effort into their appearance that their husbands and others know that they care about being attractive to and therefore respectful of their husbands without prompting lust in other men or allowing such effort to interfere with other wifely duties. They face a double bind: if they fail to comply with these codes, they are either slovenly or vain, either disrespectful of their husbands' needs to have an attractive wife or disrespectful of other husbands (and their wives) by tempting men.

MARRIAGE AND REPRODUCTION

Because marriage is so highly valued (and perhaps because premarital sex is prohibited), conservative Christians tend to marry and have children (and more of them) at a younger age than their peers. While most Protestants have long accepted birth control methods and most Catholics who reject artificial birth control still use natural family planning (tracking fertility and abstaining from sex during ovulation), the most conservative groups do not. Families involved in the Quiverfull Movement, which reaches across denominations, reject all efforts to control family size or the spacing between births, including periodic abstinence within marriage. In this view, children are *always* a blessing from God, and therefore contraceptives or abstaining during times of female fertility is a rejection of God's blessing and, by extension, God's plan and God's authority. Pregnancy avoidance is thus a rejection of the hierarchy of authority over women's lives: God, then husband.

Men, like women, must accept their place in this hierarchy: the head of the family—a term often reviled outside of conservative Christian subculture but one that proponents insist makes sense. Male "headship" means taking responsibility for the family, eschewing laziness and controlling behaviors and, for Quiverfull families, openness to large families. They can only do this, though, when women give them respect—something that may be difficult for women (Smith 2014, 95). In this model, men need respect and women need love, and only when they give each other what they require will marriage be happy (Eggerichs 2004, 5).

FREEDOM IN CONSTRAINT

Not every woman yields all domains of her life easily or fully to the doctrines and practices of her conservative Christian religion. Even when such groups thrive, women are not simply doing what they are told. They innovate, pushing beliefs to allow new practices. Religion has been a place where women lead before they can do so in other domains, such as politics or the workplace. The Salvation Army, a group organized around the masculine metaphor of the military, allowed nineteenth-century women

to travel to cities, an opportunity they would have likely not had otherwise, to evangelize. Pentecostalism's somatic focus allows women's bodies to be inhabited by the Holy Spirit, giving them spiritual authority at least sometimes. Amish sects carefully proscribe women's dress, including the type and color of cloth, the style of dress, and the process for creating clothing, but within those confines, women express themselves with pride. Women who live in religious enclaves find support and community in them absent in the secular world, even if they must sometimes negotiate the rules of those communities carefully and creatively, as the story of Hannah, profiled at the beginning of this essay, suggests.

Hannah suffered eight miscarriages before undergoing a partial hysterectomy. Even as she mourned the loss of her fertility, she felt relieved not to have to suffer further pregnancy losses. During her fertility struggles, she had internalized implication that her "closed womb" was due to weak faith or unconfessed sin, but when biological children were no longer the measure of God's love for her, Hannah was able to approach her husband about alternatives to achieving her dream of motherhood. They soon adopted two children from Belarus, and they hope to adopt through domestic foster care. In this way, Hannah's body continues to rear, if not bear, children, cementing her place under her husband's headship and thus indicating her willingness to submit to God's gendered will for her life. Keeping her focus on maintaining that hierarchal relationship, rather than obsessing about fertility, has, Hannah shares, made her more available to God's directions for her life and brought two wonderful children into it. Like many women who willingly remain in their conservative tradition, she has found that the narrow confines of her faith have allowed her a deeper experience of it. Only by listening to women's own stories and their interpretations of their experiences can scholars hope to understand what, on the surface, seems like a paradox between women's subjugation and their liberation.

WORKS CITED

Cooper, Darien B. *You Can Be the Wife of a Happy Husband: Discovering the Keys to Marital Success*. Rev. ed. Destiny Image, 2010.

Driscoll, Mark and Grace. *Real Marriage: The Truth About Sex, Friendship, and Life Together*. Thomas Nelson, 2013.

Eggerichs, Emerson. *Love and Respect: The Love She Most Desires, the Respect He Desperately Needs*. Thomas Nelson, 2004.

Focus on the Family, www.focusonthefamily.com/marriage/sex-and-intimacy/understanding-your-husbands-sexual-needs/sex-is-a-physical-need.

Johnson, Bill. "Decency Minute." *American Family Minute*, September 3, 2015, www.americandecency.org/decency_minute/AFR/decencyminute1.08.26.15.mp4.

LaHaye, Tim, and Beverly LaHaye. *The Act of Marriage: The Beauty of Sexual Love*. Zondervan, 1998.

Slattery, Juli. "Sex Is a Physical Need." In *No More Headaches*, Tyndale House, 2009.

Smith, Leslie Durrough. *Righteous Rhetoric: Sex, Speech, and the Politics of Concerned Women for America*. Oxford UP, 2014.

Young, Ed, and Lisa Young. *Sexperiment: 7 Days to Lasting Intimacy with Your Spouse*. FaithWords, 2012.

---

34. • *Jessica E. Birch*

LOVE, LABOR, AND LORDE:
The Tools My Grandmother Gave Me (2017)

Jessica E. Birch, an assistant teaching professor in ethnic studies and women's, gender, and sexuality studies at Bowling Green State University, focuses her teaching and research on how cultural narratives justify and perpetuate social inequality, using feminist theory, critical race theory, critical pedagogy, multiethnic literature analysis, and cultural studies. She is the area chair for Race & Ethnicity and Popular Culture & Pedagogy for the Midwest Popular Culture Association and has done a series of workshops on pedagogical inclusivity at the National Women's Studies Association Conference. Recent publications include contributions in *Gothic and Racism* (Universitas Press, 2015), *Race and the Vampire Narrative* (Sense Publishers, 2015), *The Supernatural Revamped: From Timeworn Legends to 21st Century Chic* (Fairleigh Dickinson University Press, 2016), *The Wiley-Blackwell Encyclopedia of Gender and Sexuality Studies* (Wiley-Blackwell, 2016), and *Women's Rights in Popular Culture* (Greenwood Press, 2017).

At the National Women's Studies Association Annual Conference, a button proclaims, "This is a recipe for success, not cookies." Feminist theorists describe that idea as the public/private distinction. Men's lives are public, because men participate politically and economically. Women's lives are private, focusing on care work—childrearing, cleaning, and cooking. This is the story society discursively tells about women (because, for society, women are all the same). On one side lies success: financial gain, career advancement, and societal impact; on the other, mixing bowls derail women from success.

Care work is unpopular in the contemporary neoliberal United States. Neoliberalism is an ideology—a set of narratives that shape society—that operates "to reestablish the conditions for capital accumulation and to restore the power of economic elites" (Harvey 2005, 19). One of the ways it does this is by demanding individualism, telling us that society is composed of a set of individuals, each of whom has an obligation only to herself, rather than community members who have obligations to care for each other.

Personal responsibility is the driving theme of neoliberalism. American society prizes independence and self-sufficiency, so we assume the powerful have earned their rewards. Each person sinks or swims on her own merits—and the only actions that matter are the ones in the job market.

This is why I bake cookies for my students.

❋ ❋ ❋

My grandmother's funeral: someone is talking about my grandmother's biscuits. After the sermon, delivered by a man with hair like Don King's, a sweaty forehead, and the rolling cadence that differentiates preachers from ministers, come the eulogies. A man from the church group replaces biscuit woman. Leaning heavily on the podium, he fixes the congregation with a watery, sharp eye.

"I'm talking about some **FRIED CHICKEN.**" I've never heard anyone address poultry with such vehemence. Wiping his forehead with a purple-striped handkerchief that matches his tie, he sighs heavily. "Anna made some damned fine fried chicken. Her fried chicken was so good, it made hot sauce cry! You hear me?"

Behind me to the left, a reflexive "Amen, brother" bursts out.

❋ ❋ ❋

On the campaign trail in 1992, Hillary Rodham Clinton says, "I could have stayed home and baked cookies and had teas, but what I decided to do was fulfill my profession" (Swinth 2012, 1).

Clinton has a profession. My grandmother had a job. My grandmother did not have teas. She did not stay home. She scrubbed white women's toilets, took care of white women's children, and washed white women's clothes. After working a full day, her hat still pinned perfectly, her dress still starched, her white gloves still perfectly clean, Anna Roberson came home to the house paid for by the blistered, calloused hands the gloves hid. There she scrubbed her own toilet, took care of her own children, and washed her own clothes in the bathtub.

We who are "poor, who are lesbians, who are Black, who are older," we are the women who know, as Audre Lorde says, "that survival is not an academic skill" (Lorde 2007, 112). Survival in a world that tries to smother us before we can breathe, much less speak, is an act of resistance, an act that matters. My grandmother did more than survive. She had plans.

Later in life, she married the man I knew as my grandfather, a man who had a good job working for the city. Sometimes, then, she stayed home. She worked on her plans. When he entered high school—she herself had never gone to high school—she bought my father a violin. As a black boy in Pittsburgh in the 1950s, he took violin lessons, playing in the orchestra of the newly desegregated high school. He learned how to box, because he had to, and he was good at it, because he had to be to survive. And every Sunday, every holiday, my grandmother laid out a spread of food like the Baby Jesus Himself was coming down for dinner.

❋ ❋ ❋

I am nine. My aunts and uncles and cousins are all there when my grandmother drags me by the wrist into her bathroom. She is slender, skin dark and smooth like rye bread, tiny birdlike hands, and smoothly coiffed hair. Next to her, I look like a loaf of bread left out in the rain: pale, puffy, and unwanted.

The scale says I am 120 pounds. I step off the scale. She steps on: 92 pounds. She waits until we are again sitting on the beds with the red satin spreads—there is no space for couches—to say, "You're fat. Sloppy. Look at your thighs."

I look. When the tears well up in my eyes, I pick up my book, pretending to read.

❋ ❋ ❋

In 1972, Shirley Chisholm was the first black person and the first woman to run for the US presidency. She ran under the slogan "unbought and unbossed" (Davies 2009, 392), as Carole Boyce Davies explains, contrasting Chisholm with Condoleezza Rice's loyalty to the George W. Bush administration. When a "black and/or female subject" gains power, and with that power begins "working publicly against the larger interests of the group to which s/he belongs," that is "condification" (395). That's what Davies calls it when women work against the interests of other women. Condification is another word for women who internalize oppression so hard they lose everything, including their knowledge of who they are, where they've been, and how they got there.

When women with professions pay minimal wages to Anna Robersons to clean their homes, to cook their meals, to care for their children, they are engaging in condification. The narrative of family as a free choice disregards the material circumstances of women's lives and their interconnectedness. As Elsa Barkley Brown points out, these women "live the lives they do . . . because working class women live the lives they do . . . [and] white women live the lives they do . . . because women of color live the ones they do" (Brown 1992, 287). Some women support the status quo because it gives them a free pass into the privilege club. As members, they promote individualism to justify their insistence that they belong in the club.

Condification creates women who, "day by day," accept "tyrannies" that they "attempt to make [their] own," and perhaps one day, as Audre Lorde suggests, they may "sicken and die of them, still in silence" (2007, 41)—but I hope they do not. I am not a religious woman, but I pray that they may someday realize that their silence is imposed upon them by those who feed their fear like my grandmother fed her family. May they remember the defiant taste of their deeply buried words. May they remember themselves. May they remember that they are us.

✳ ✳ ✳

I am eleven. I ask my grandmother how to make apple pie. She stares at me for a long moment. I think she's going to tell me I'm fat. Instead, she says, "Watch."

She peels three McIntoshes, her small hands curving the paring knife around them, each peel coming off in one long spiral. Then she hands me an apple and waits. The family's running joke is that if my grandmother met God, she'd have a list of instructions ready. Now, my grandmother the talker says nothing.

My peels are choppy little hunks, wasting apple flesh. I cringe, trying to make them match hers, but then I'm slow. I know too well that when the Lord gave out patience, my grandmother didn't wait in line to get hers. At the twelfth apple, she shifts her weight, and I lay down the knife. She picks it up, slices one of the apples into quarters, puts it down.

When I put the second pie in the oven and look at my grandmother, she gives me a small nod. One movement of her head, down and then up.

For the rest of the visit, she does not tell me I'm fat.

✳ ✳ ✳

When my grandmother dies, we learn that she was born December 14, 1906, not December 24, 1916. Every year, we carefully wrapped a birthday present in birthday paper and a Christmas present in Christmas paper. She saved the paper from both. Gave it back to us as we left so we could reuse it. What kind of person lies to her family about her age and her birthday? The kind of person my grandmother was, I guess.

I wonder if I know what kind of person my grandmother was at all.

✳ ✳ ✳

The first year of my Ph.D. program, in a feminist theory course, one of my classmates says, "If you're not going to stay home to take care of your children, you don't deserve to have them."

No one disagrees with her, including our professor. I am the only person in this room who was in daycare as a child.

I know now that feminism, unlike survival, is often academic, because "the convenient omission of household works' problems from the programs of 'middle class' feminists past and present has often turned out to be a veiled justification . . . of their own exploitative treatment of their maids" (Davis 1983, 96). The "contemporary American culture" that Betty Friedan describes in *The Feminine Mystique* (1997) applies only to a specific set of women—women who, like Clinton, had a choice.

If the Devil had opened her screen door, Anna Roberson would have looked him in the eye and told him, in the voice she used for white people, debt collectors, disrespectful children, and catcalling men, that he was not welcome in her home. There were—and are—thousands of Anna Robersons. Many of them do not get college degrees, or even high school diplomas. Most of them are strong, physically and emotionally. Some, like my grandmother, are what my father calls "a hard woman": a woman who takes no disrespect and gives no compliments.

These women are not Friedan's housewives, whose days involved "smiling as they ran the new electric waxer over the spotless kitchen floor . . . [and] kept their new washing machines and dryers running all day" (Friedan 1997, 61). Women of color and working-class women "have rarely been offered the time and energy to become experts at domesticity" (Davis 1983, 232), because becoming an expert at domesticity has generally required the support of a (white) man with a (middle- to upper-class) stable income.

The work of women who had no choices except whether to survive provided choices to my classmates' mothers. I got my determination from women like my grandmother, who stepped up to vote knowing that they might be beaten and would be jailed. We are not the same, my classmates and I—and I do not want to be like them. Audre Lorde writes, "[The] master's tools will never dismantle the master's house. They may allow us temporarily to beat him at his own game, but they will never enable us to bring about genuine change" (Lorde

2007, 112). Succeeding by standing on the necks of others is the master's game, not mine.

My face is hot, but the voice that comes out of my mouth is my grandmother's, her ice-cold, diamond-sharp voice, girded by the hardness of Pittsburgh steel forged in the mills we can smell from her house when the wind is strong: "I don't believe I heard you correctly."

✳ ✳ ✳

As I begin teaching my first class, I must decide what to do when students fail assignments. My preliminary syllabus says that major assignments can be revised for partial credit. Colleagues tell me, "Some of them just don't want to work—save your time and energy. Failing is failing."

I think of my grandmother, who gave me the freedom to find my way in the kitchen, knowing that if I failed, I'd waste what precious little food we had. I remember those who came before me, who fought the first, most dangerous steps of the same battle I fight: my grandmother, Angela Davis, Shirley Chisholm, Mary McLeod Bethune, Audre Lorde, Fannie Lou Hamer, Rose Parks, Ella Baker, and all those whose names history has forgotten but whose actions live on. They did not save their time and energy. Unlike food, time and energy are free. They are mine to give, and I have a debt that will always be owed.

I revise my syllabus: *All assignments may be revised and resubmitted for full credit. Learning is a process, and we will figure it out together. No failure is final.*

✳ ✳ ✳

After the funeral, we go to my grandmother's house, except that it's not my grandmother's house anymore. The church brings food: green beans, macaroni and cheese, collard greens, ham. Fried chicken. Everyone tells stories as they fill their plates. I sit on the red satin bedspread. The chicken is dry, and the hot sauce I pour on it doesn't even whimper, much less sob.

✳ ✳ ✳

In my Introduction to Gender Studies course, my student bites into a butterscotch-oatmeal cookie, saying, "I thought feminists would laugh at me if I said I baked with my son on weekends. But my grandmother taught me how. Who taught you?"

I see my grandmother's hands, putting Sunday dinner on the table set with the blue-and-white china she'd acquired, piece by piece. And I realize something: I know what kind of person my grandmother was. She was unbought and unbossed, her whole life. She helped make a world in which I don't always have to be a hard woman, taught me how to survive when I do have to be. She was a woman whose pride in care work was a form of love.

To my student, I say, "My grandmother taught me."

WORKS CITED

Brown, Elsa Barkley. "'What Has Happened Here': The Politics of Difference in Women's History and Feminist Politics." *Feminist Studies*, vol. 18, no. 2, 1992, pp. 295–312.

Collins, Patricia Hill. *Black Feminist Thought: Knowledge, Consciousness, and the Politics of Empowerment*. 2nd ed. Routledge, 2000.

Davies, Carol Boyce. "'Con-di-fi-cation': Black Women, Leadership, and Political Power." In *Still Brave: The Evolution of Black Women's Studies*, edited by Stanlie M. James et al. Feminist Press at CUNY, 2009.

Davis, Angela. *Women, Race, and Class*. Random House, 1983.

Friedan, Betty. *The Feminine Mystique*. W. W. Norton, 1997.

Harvey, David. *A Brief History of Neoliberalism*. Kindle ed. Oxford UP, 2005.

Lorde, Audre. *Sister Outsider: Essays and Speeches*. Reprint ed. Crossing Press, 2007.

Swinth, Kirsten. "Hillary Clinton, Cookies, and the Rise of Working Families." *CNN*, March 16, 2012, www.cnn.com/2012/03/16/opinion/swinth-hillary-clinton/.

35. • *Monisha Das Gupta*

"BROKEN HEARTS, BROKEN FAMILIES":
The Political Use of Families in the Fight Against Deportation (2017)

Monisha Das Gupta holds a joint appointment as associate professor in the departments of ethnic studies and women's studies at the University of Hawai'i at Mānoa. She is currently completing *Settling Migration: Migrant Organizing in an Era of Deportation and Dispossession*, which is under contract with Duke University Press. Her first book, *Unruly Immigrants*, dealt with feminist, queer and labor organizing in South Asian communities on the East Coast and won awards in sociology and Asian American studies. Her recent contributions on immigrant and gender justice appear in the *Amerasia Journal* and a co-authored chapter in *Our Voices, Our History: Asian*

American and Pacific Islander Women (NYU Press, 2020). She is active in the migrant rights movements in Honolulu and Los Angeles that address local police and immigration enforcement and also works closely with UNITE HERE Local 5, which organizes hotel workers in Honolulu.

In the course of my involvement in the immigrant rights movement since it was reenergized in 2006, when documented and undocumented migrants poured out on the streets of cities across the United States to protest anti-immigrant federal legislation, I joined an anti-deportation rally in Manhattan at the invitation of Families for Families in the summer of 2009. I was in New York for a few weeks to learn about migrant organizing, and was curious about Families for Freedom (FFF), which had been formed in 2002 in the wake of escalating deportations post-9/11. From its inception, it has been made up entirely of deportees and their loved ones. Those not directly affected by deportation are allies but not members. The organization represents migrants from the Caribbean, Latin America, Asia, and Africa. The members have a range of immigration status—some are undocumented, others legal permanent residents (LPRs), and still others asylum seekers. Many of them live in mixed-status families with members who are US citizens.

The rally that day in front of the Federal Plaza, which houses the immigration court, was for an FFF organizer, the then fifty-two-year-old Brooklyn resident Roxroy Salmon, a Jamaican national and an LPR. He was appearing before an immigration judge for a hearing on his deportation case. Many of us who had gathered that morning held signs that read "Broken Hearts, Broken Families. Stop Deportation Now," "Help Keep Children Safe. Stop Deportation," and "A Family United Is a Happy Family." During the several hours we waited for Roxroy, we sang and chanted about the attentiveness with which Roxroy cared for his mother and his children, three of whom lived with him; we communicated to all those who passed us on that busy street that we were standing up against a state practice that separated children from their parents. Hours later, Roxroy, who had

been building the campaign against his deportation for two years, emerged to tell us that the judge had ordered his deportation for two minor drug convictions over twenty years ago.

As I examined FFF's representational strategies, I wondered what would make criminalized men of color, like Roxroy, sympathetic figures. Reading member testimonies on its older website,[1] I found that the emphasis on Roxroy's caregiving in his family was not exceptional. It was a theme that ran through the narratives of and about other men who had been deported or were in deportation proceedings. Was the portrayal of these men as loving and caring fathers a move on their part to represent themselves in the public eye as migrants deserving of reprieve? As a feminist, I wanted to find out how the organization mobilized families, the public appeal to which made me wary because "the family" and family values have been appropriated by the Right to push a conservative white heteropatriarchal agenda to promote sexual, economic, and political control over women, measures that are particularly punitive for poor women.

What set FFF apart from many others, which appealed to normative ideas of the family in fighting deportation, was its unwavering commitment to publicly advocating the rights of criminalized members, most of whom, mirroring the prison population, were men of color. Its entry point—the role of deportation in tearing apart families—helps us piece together how deportation, working hand in hand with mass incarceration, reorganizes kinship arrangements as well as the division of labor within families. The testimonies that were carried on its older website and my interviews with organizers reveal the ways in which the state intrudes in the lives of migrants of color to put not only their economic viability at risk but also their ability to do carework in the private sphere. This type of state violence, feminist theorists of color have reminded us, has historically shaped communities of color, which are not allowed to shield their private lives from state intervention (Cohen 2004).

Migrants, who often share the same inner-city neighborhoods with African Americans and Chicanos, are subject to heavy policing and racial profiling, which have led to the mass incarceration of the minoritized citizenry in the United States. But for noncitizens the consequences of encounters with the criminal legal system are somewhat different from those suffered by citizens. Under current law, they are barred for their lifetime from returning to the United States regardless of the lives they built and of their intimate ties to US-born spouses, children, and siblings.

The legal grounds for the permanent removal of lawfully present immigrants and undocumented migrants with criminal convictions had been consolidated in 1996. With the passage of the Illegal Immigration Reform and Immigrant Responsibility Act (IIRIRA) in 1996, immigration judges lost the discretion they had exercised from 1976 onward to waive the removal of long-term LPRs with criminal records by taking into account the hardship to US-born or LPR family members (Hing 2006, 58–64). The IIRIRA expanded the definition of aggravated felony to misdemeanors and low-level offenses for noncitizens. Those with such convictions are subject to mandatory detention and removal. The changes to the law have been applied zealously in the twenty-first century. In this period, several federal programs authorized local police to find out whether arrested noncitizens had immigration (civil) violations. This federal–local law enforcement cooperation enhanced the ability of immigration authorities to identify deportable migrants. In 2014, the Immigration and Customs Enforcement removed 315,943 people and reported that 85 percent of the 102,224 individuals removed from the interior (i.e., not at the border) had criminal convictions (US Department of Homeland Security 2014). These numbers show that the criminal legal system has become a key partner in the business of deporting migrants who lived in the United States.

The removal of "criminal aliens" as an immigration priority has broad public support fed by racialized discourses about criminality and the need for law and order. The division this discourse creates between "good" migrants, who deserve legalization, and "bad" criminal migrants, who need to be expelled permanently, is so powerful that it has also entrenched itself in immigrant activism. A FFF organizer at the time, Manisha Vaze, pointed out the pervasiveness of this divisive argument in the movement when she observed, "I hear it all over— we want to keep the hardworking undocumented family-oriented immigrants in this country. But those criminals should be deported. And there is no real analysis of what it means to be a criminal for immigration purposes" (Vaze 2009). The importance of FFF's work lies in offering an analysis of how criminalization works in the lives of migrants of color and in situating the deportation crisis in the daily struggles of these migrants.

The FFF members, many of whom had criminal convictions, faced a difficult task, akin to that shouldered by those who advocate prisoners' rights, because the public perceives them as lawbreakers and deadbeat dads who are unable to financially and emotionally support their families. These racialized expectations about normative fatherhood were codified into law in 1996 as part of restructuring welfare and reducing public assistance for single mothers, whose benefits were tied to stringent child support collection and paternity establishment requirements (Curran and Abrams 2000). The FFF men's accounts as well as those of their partners and children directly counter the stereotypical casting of men who have criminal convictions as uncaring and irresponsible (see Pallares 2014 on the emergence of the family as a political subjectivity and site of racial resistance in the immigrant rights movement). They present in loving detail the work they did in caring not only for their biological children but also stepchildren from their partners' previous marriages as well as elderly parents. They eloquently express the ways in which their indefinite separation from their children or their constant fear of deportation interfered with their ability to be good fathers.

Howard, a FFF member deported to Jamaica for not complying with a prior deportation order, described his feelings on being separated from his US citizen wife, who sponsored him for residency, and three children: "Even though I'm not locked up, it feels like prison. I worry about time I used to spend with kids. We spent precious time together. I don't want my kids to grow up without a father" ("Barbara and Howard" 2015). From his wife's testimony, we learn that Howard used to "pick up the children from school; take them to the library, park and McDonald's." After Howard's deportation, his wife, who worked at a drugstore, had difficulty picking up one of their children from school on time because of her work schedule and was told that the school would notify the Office of Children and Family Services for neglect if she were repeatedly late. Like Howard's wife, who remarked, "Life has turned upside down since our husbands were taken away," Carol, whose Guyanese husband was arrested for marijuana possession, expressed her frustration with her new role as a single mother as a result of her husband's nine-month-long incarceration at an immigration detention center. In her testimony, she confessed, "Raising a daughter without any help is a struggle. . . . Natasha got sick last week. . . . No matter how much it hurt, I had to send her to school and go to work as a home health aide" ("Carol and Linden" 2015). Carol's narrative points to an irony that is typical of a society where commodified and paid carework is done by women of color for other, better-off families while struggling to take care of their own. In this racialized and gendered division of labor, families that lose a caregiver to deportation do not have the resources to replace the emotional and physical labor. Jani, an African American woman, in asking for sanctuary for her Haitian husband, Jean, who had a criminal record, recounted the crucial role he played in her life by taking care of their children so that she could attend college and earn her bachelor's degree.

Joe, an asylum seeker from China, in his testimony to the congregants of St. Paul of the Apostle Church, expressed his and his wife's constant anxiety of being separated from their small children. He said, "As parents facing deportation, we feel helpless to protect our own children. . . . We love our children's smiles. We want to see them grow. We want to be in their daily life. . . . I have been working in a restaurant for ten years. . . . Today I am twenty-eight. I am a young father. I want to be a good father. . . . My daughter here—she is the oldest child. She is two now. I take her to the playground, even if I am tired. She has a lot of energy. She deserves the best." Both Howard and Joe articulate what they consider to be the qualities of good fatherhood; both emphasize time spent with their children and focus on everyday tasks of taking care of them and the daily, mundane pleasures of fatherhood. Similarly, when testifying with her nine-year-old son, Joshua, to the United Nations Special Rapporteur, Kathy McArdle, who continues to sit on FFF's board, shared an ordinary but tender domestic moment while recounting the horrors of Calvin's arrest at their home early one morning by eight armed immigration agents. Recalling the interactions Calvin had with their son, she said, "Their greatest joy was probably the tickle fights they used to have, and just quiet moments together that can never be duplicated by phone calls." In the magazine *Colorlines*, an older Joshua is quoted as remembering his father's cooking: "I miss his cooking. I really liked his rice that he used to make. It had coconut milk in it" (Wessler 2009). Calvin, an LPR, had lived in the United States for thirty-three years at the time of his arrest and deportation in 2004.

Janis Rosheuvel, former executive director of FFF, attributes the focus on men's caregiving in their households to the lived experience of these families. Fathers struggling to find work often become the primary caretakers, cooking their children dinner, taking them to the park, and helping them with their homework. FFF, she noted, represents men and women who jointly care for their children and elderly to survive in decaying urban areas while working low-paying jobs without adequate benefits (Rosheuvel 2010). These inner-city men of color have few prospects of gainful employment, especially if they have a criminal record or are undocumented. Roxroy, for example, could not financially support his family. Instead, he took on the role of the person who took care of his children; his mother, who suffered from

Alzheimer's disease; and his infant grandchild. This work ensured that his eighteen-year-old daughter could attend a local university. His life story, Rosheuvel points out, is not an exception when it comes to members of the organization.

The testimonies from FFF members challenge us to apply the feminist insights about kinship arrangements in communities of color where men's place in their families cannot be read straightforwardly through the hegemonic scripts about masculinity that is contingent on breadwinning. The emotional content of the testimonies of FFF members sheds light on the reorganization of kinship and the everyday caregiving tasks in migrant and mixed-status families through immigration enforcement. Deportation not only serves to deprive migrants of their livelihood, discipline them for their activism, and target their biological reproduction (Buff 2008; Chavez 2008) but also impacts their ability to care for their family members and households.

In the application of deportation policy, we can discern a set of codes that appeal to morality to devalue the relationships of criminalized migrants to their loved ones. The folding together of law enforcement, national security, and immigration enforcement constantly reminds FFF that their members and their loved ones are under attack because they fall outside of nationally and racially marked familial arrangements considered normative. In this context, Rosheuvel's insistence that "Our *family* is valuable; our family deserves justice; our family should have access to relief and justice like any other family" rests on the recognition that deportees' kinship ties are devalued because they do not conform to dominant ideologies that govern the family as an institution (Rosheuvel 2010). The revaluation renders visible the emotional and material labor of migrant men in their

households. The stories of domesticity, intimacy, and tenderness under social and economic circumstances that strain heteronormative versions of these affective states counteract the dehumanizing portrayals of these men as dangerous criminals, terrorists, and men who flout the "rule of law," a concept that reifies the state's sovereignty exercised through its right to deport. Deportation practices that mandate lifetime separation of family members themselves create new configurations of nonnormative kinship, desire, and intimacy. These split families may signal a restructuring of heterosexuality by unmooring it from heteronormativity, as feminist scholar Jasbir Puar suggests (2007, 146). The long-distance arrangements raise afresh questions about what it means to negotiate heterosexuality as well as affective and caregiving structures in an era of deportation.

Simply put, FFF's narratives of good fathering are not just a strategic choice to cast these men as respectable, domesticated, and deserving of public sympathy. They confront us with the ways in which deportation becomes an instrument through which the state continues to define "the family." However, in the immigrant rights movement, discussions about the relationship between immigration regulation and the regulation of gender and sexuality are rare outside of feminist and queer spaces. As an immigrant feminist who is involved in the movement, the process of interrogating my skepticism about FFF's mobilization of "families" and attending to FFF's analysis of the intersection between the criminal legal system and immigration enforcement underlines the importance of recognizing that the organization of gender and sexuality lies at the heart of immigration policy and, thus, addressing state control over our intimate lives needs to be central to visions of justice for migrants and their loved ones.

NOTE

1. The older version of the FFF webpage is archived at wayback.archive.org/ and can be accessed by searching for www.familiesforfreedom.org/index.htm. Some of the personal narratives quoted here can be accessed by clicking on the Truth Commission link. The testimonies of Jean and Jani, Joe and Mei, and Josh and Kathy used here are no longer online, but the stories about Joe and Mei and Josh and Kathy can be accessed at familiesforfreedom.org/families/kathy-josh-calvin and familiesforfreedom.org/families/chen-family.

WORKS CITED

"Barbara and Howard." *Families for Freedom*, familiesforfreedom.org/families/barbara-howard. Accessed September 11, 2015.

Buff, Rachel Ida. "The Deportation Terror." *American Quarterly*, vol. 60, no. 3, 2008, pp. 523–51.

"Carol and Linden." *Families for Freedom*, familiesforfreedom.org/families/carol-linden. Accessed September 11, 2015.

Chavez, Leo R. *The Latino Threat: Constructing Immigrants, Citizens, and the Nation*. Stanford UP, 2008.

Cohen, Cathy. "Deviance as Resistance: A New Research Agenda for the Study of Black Politics." *Du Bois Review*, vol. 1, no. 1, 2004, pp. 27–45.

Curran, Laura, and Laura Abrams. "Making Men into Dads: Fatherhood, the State and Welfare Reform." *Gender & Society*, vol. 14, no. 5, 2000, pp. 662–78.

Hing, Bill Ong. *Deporting Our Souls: Values, Morality, and Immigration Policy*. Cambridge UP, 2006.

Pallares, Amalia. *Family Activism: Immigrant Struggles and the Politics of Noncitizenship*. Rutgers UP, 2014.

Puar, Jasbir. *Terrorist Assemblage: Homonationalism in Queer Times*. Duke UP, 2007.

Rosheuvel, Janis. Personal interview. 2010.

US Department of Homeland Security, Immigration and Customs Enforcement. *FY 2014 ICE Immigration Removals*. 2014, www.ice.gov/removal-statistics.

Vaze, Manisha. Personal interview. 10 July 2009.

Wessler, Seth. "Double Punishment." *Colorlines*, October 9, 2009, www.colorlines.com/articles/double-punishment.

ADDITIONAL RESOURCES

Detention Watch Network. www.detentionwatchnetwork.org/.

Families for Freedom. familiesforfreedom.org/.

---

36. • *Sarah Mirk*

POPAGANDA:
Queering Family Values (2019)

Sarah Mirk, an adjunct professor in contemporary art practices at Portland State University, is a visual journalist and author who has worked for alternative weekly media outlets, *The Stranger*, *The Portland Mercury*, and *Bitch Media*. The selection included here was one of many feminist podcasts in her Popaganda series that reached over 10,000 listeners. She is the author of several books, is currently at work on an illustrated oral history of Guantanamo Bay, is a contributing editor at *The Nib*, and currently is at work producing a zine a day for a year.

"Family values" has been co-opted by right-wing folks. But what the hell! Feminists have strong values, and we have strong families, too. On today's episode, we're queering family values. For a lot of queer folks, the traditional concept of family is wrought with complicated feelings—a lot of blood families refuse to accept or celebrate queerness, so LGBTQ people have in many ways redefined "family" for themselves. I talk with two queer feminist activists about what the word "family" means to them and which "family values" they try to live by and teach.

Writer and photographer Margaret Jacobsen and writer Yasmin Nair are two awesome feminist thinkers who have different ideas on what it means to have a family, what it means to get married, and how our ideas of family shape our ideas of the world.

This podcast was be transcribed by Cheryl Green of StoryMinders. We're proud to make Popaganda accessible to people who are Deaf or hard of hearing.

FULL TRANSCRIPT

SARAH MIRK: This is Popaganda, the feminist response to pop culture podcast. I'm Sarah Mirk.

[theme music]

Do you feel like the values that you try to imbue your family with have changed at all since Trump was elected?

MARGARET JACOBSEN: I don't know if they've changed as much as I feel like perhaps I've just seen the importance of us continuing to build our family and creating, especially in our home, just a safe space to exist as a non-monogamous, queer family.

SARAH: That's Margaret Jacobsen, a writer, photographer, and member of an extraordinarily beautiful family [chuckles]. This spring at Bitch, we're exploring the theme of "family values." That's a term that has been co-opted by right-wing folks in the United States. In our media and in our politics, claims of "family values" are used to defend everything from repealing abortion access to transphobic bathroom bills to policing women's sexuality.

You know, people use family values in a really narrow way. It means like this kind of retro shit.

[recorded clip with dramatic music, 1950s-era sound]

NARRATOR: This boy and girl coming home from school look quite content with life. And why not? They're looking forward to an important date: Dinner at home with the family. Mother, too, changes from her daytime clothes. The women of this family seem to feel that they owe it to the men of the family to look relaxed, rested, and attractive at dinnertime.

SARAH: Politicians use the framing of "family values" as essentially the political equivalent of this mom from *The Simpsons*.

[recorded clip]

WOMAN: [high-pitched, bubbly, wavering, yelping voice] Oh! Won't somebody please think of the children?!?!

SARAH: But what the hell [laughs]! Feminists have strong values, and we have strong families, too. Why do Republicans get a monopoly on defining what family values means?

On today's episode, we're queering family values. For a lot of queer folks, the traditional concept of family is wrought with complicated feelings. A lot of blood families refuse to accept or celebrate queerness. So LGBTQ people have in many ways redefined "family" for themselves.

On this episode, I talk with two queer feminist activists about what the word "family" means to them and what "family values" they try to live by and teach. Margaret Jacobsen and Yasmin Nair are two amazing feminist writers and thinkers who have different ideas on what it means to have a family, what it means to get married, and how our ideas of family shape our ideas of the world. Listen in.

[song from Steven Universe, voice with piano accompaniment, lyrics below]

♪ Why don't you talk to each other?
Why don't you talk to each other?
Just give it a try.

Why don't you talk about what happened?
I know you're trying to avoid it,
But I don't know why.
You might not believe it.
You might not believe it,
But you've got a lot in common.
You really do.
You both love me, and I love both of you. ♪

SARAH: Just kickin' it off with a little relationship advice from Steven Universe [laughs].

All right, Margaret Jacobsen.

MARGARET: Hi, I'm Margaret Jacobsen. I'm a photographer and writer that lives in Portland.

SARAH: That's like . . . selling it short a bit. Margaret is an awesome activist who organizes lots of events centering on race, gender, and identity, including a regular self-care day for Black women—Margaret is Black—and the Women's March in Portland in January. Proudly non-monogamous and also non-binary, Margaret's social media feed feels like a vision into a better, more gorgeous world filled with kids and friends and loving partners who make time for each other and also make lots of good food together.

I asked Margaret about being non-binary and using the pronoun "they."

MARGARET: I identify as non-binary, just meaning I don't really see myself on the gender binary. And gender for me, I think I used to identify as genderqueer or gender fluid, but since gender isn't something I personally believe in, then non-binary fits my identity a lot better.

SARAH: So to start it off, I asked Margaret, "Who's in your family?"

MARGARET: So I guess I would start with my ex-husband. We live seven minutes from each other. We do a lot of stuff together. We're just no longer married. And then I am engaged to my partner, Noah, and we live together. And then there is my partner that lives outside of the house, Pace. Yeah, so I would say there's—how many is that?—like six of us [chuckles].

SARAH: That's six including Margaret's two kids, Riley and Beck, who are seven and eight and also extremely adorable.

So Margaret has a strong family and also really strong values. But still, the phrase "family values" instantly induces some cringing.

MARGARET: I think I'm one of those people that also gets [laughing] really anxious when people say that! And a lot of that is because of how I grew up, which was very religious, very Christian, and family values were definitely: Like a mom and a dad that were married with kids [chuckles], and it's just wholesome. Whatever wholesome means. Boring, I guess.

SARAH: [laughs] Is that what wholesome means?

MARGARET: I don't know!!! 'Cause I feel like I just don't know what people mean when they're saying that something is wholesome. I don't get it. I don't get what's not wholesome. But I think for me and for my partners, our family values are really centered around compassion and kindness and kind of trying to have an infinite amount of love and capacity. We have an open-door policy in our home, and we're always trying to host people and have dinners and just having the house always be full of people that are kind of our chosen family.

Growing up, I think that my parents tried really hard to have family time and family trips, and I felt like they were trying really hard to fit into an idea of what family is and doing it in a traditional way. And traditional, I guess, simply meaning what society perceives as the normal; it's what the majority is. And I think as a kid all I really wanted was to be surrounded by a lot of people and to just share space and food and time with people who I knew loved me and that I loved. And my daughter has always been kind of inviting everybody into her life. If she meets you, and she likes you, she's like, "Great. You're welcome here," you know? And we all try to have that mentality. So I think that that's what our family values are rooted in, is always having open arms. No one gets turned away, and there's no expectations to show up perfectly. It's like show up as you are, and that's enough. That's all we want.

SARAH: How do you feel like your family is similar to the family you grew up in, and how is it different? Is there anything you've taken from your parents in a good way or anything you've intentionally very much left behind?

MARGARET: I think that the cooking is something that I took because it was a thing that we would do with my mom. It felt like a really sacred time, and I know for her, she would tell us stories about cooking with her own father. And we do that around here a lot. There's a lot of cooking, and not just in my house, but in my ex-husband's house.

SARAH: You all cook dinner together, or what does it look like?

MARGARET: Sometimes we cook dinner together. Sometimes he'll make food and bring it over here. Or we'll just make food, and he'll come over. Same with my partner, Pace. We try really hard to do a family dinner where everyone's there, where it's all the partners [chuckles], including my ex-husband and his partner and then the kids. And my parents were really good about having meals together every night, and we have to work really hard to do that just because I'm really busy. And I don't see the importance of family meals, but my kids really, really love them. I will sometimes be like, "We can do it next week or something. I'm writing and studying whatever." And they get really excited about it. It reminds me of like I was always really excited as a kid too, to just sit down with my family and us all be together. Because during the day, we weren't always together. We were all over the place. But other than that, I don't know.

My parents really prided themselves on taking us to church together, and they didn't like to play board games, and maybe we would watch movies together. So I think with my kids, I try to make everything a family thing. Like we all go outside and play together. We play a lot of board games, and we play Magic, and we watch a lot of TV together. And we cuddle every weekend morning. It used to be every morning, but not so much now that they're in school. So it's just doing lots of little things and doing it together and making it they get really

excited. And they ask for it all the time, where it's like, "Can we do this as a family? Can we do this?" It's like, I'm going to the grocery store, like, "Can we go as a family?" So yeah. I think that's what I do a little bit differently than my family did.

SARAH: How did your family get to be so adorable [laughs]?

MARGARET: Oh [laughs]!

SARAH: That's a real question. I think a lot of people have very tense relationships with their partners, and especially with their ex-partners, and with their kids. In so many families there's so much tension all around. Hearing you talk about your family just sounds like in some ways, it's a bundle of love. I'm sure you have problems, too.

MARGARET: [laughs]

SARAH: How do you manage conflict, and how does it wind up being so sweet?

MARGARET: I think that I would say therapy [laughs]! We do a lot of therapy. I'm just a really big supporter of therapy. Quickly, I was adopted when I was a baby, and I've kind of just always been a very empathetic, sensitive person, and I've always wanted just a family of my own. My kids are like my first blood relatives, which is crazy and blows my mind. And then my ex-husband was my first serious partner and is my best friend. So when we were talking about separating, it was a really long conversation about how do we preserve what we have, because it's special? It's not a thing that we're just gonna throw away because we shouldn't be together anymore. It's something that definitely should continue. We did couple's therapy, which was great. It helped us learn how to communicate better. And then we've just implicated all of those things that we learned there. Now we do family therapy with our kids, and that's really awesome. We make sure that the four of us spend time together too.

SARAH: You mean your kids and your ex-partner?

MARGARET: Yeah. So the kids and my ex-husband. But then also it was very natural for us when I started to be with my partner. The kids are very, they're just really excited to have more adults love them. So that's been really—I don't know—it's just been really nice. We're all really good communicators, and we all really work hard on our communicating. And that was something I didn't know how to do as a kid. I didn't know how to advocate for myself or speak up for myself, and my kids do a really wonderful job of being like, "I don't feel like this is for me," or, "I wanna do something different," or, "This would make me feel better." So we encourage a lot of that. So I would say that that helps us [chuckles] because we can be really honest about our expectations. I would also say that non-monogamy has helped us [chuckles] with our communication and appreciating each other and trusting each other because you do have to work with so many people. So it makes sense that those skills and tools would also apply to when you have children and ex-partners. It's not just limited to partners that you're romantic with.

Yeah, we have a lot of love and a lot of gratitude. I would say that my daughter especially is really good about bringing people together and loving people and appreciating them. When you're around her, you're like, "Oh my gosh! I wanna be just like you when I grow up!"

SARAH: So in this similar way to how non-monogamy has shaped your family dynamics, how do you feel like queerness has shaped your family? Do you ever think about how your family would be different if you were binary and straight?

MARGARET: I mean, I lived like that for a really long time. I mean, I think I always was like, "I'm queer," but we didn't talk about it. Then they saw me just being married to their dad. And so I think that we were already very much like, "You can be whoever you wanna be, and we're good with it." But they definitely saw a very hetero example. Then now, I think I like the way that my kids view people and being attracted to people and when they talk about it. It is so like, what they're attracted to, who they really enjoy is so diverse. The other day, my son was like, "I don't think I'm gay," [laughs] but kind

of sad. But also still being able to be like, "But this man is really cute, and this person's handsome," and not feeling shame or anything around it or embarrassed. A lot of our friends are non-binary. So that's been really fun to have those conversations with my daughter where she's like, "OK. I don't have to just be a girl forever. I can be so many other things." I'm like, "Yeah! Yeah!" I don't know if we would've had those conversations necessarily; I can't tell. But I do think that I'm psyched that they're growing up in a house with a queer parent.

Kids have this way of looking at things where you explain it to them, they think about it, and then they're like, "Great" [chuckles]. Now can we go do this thing?" They might have more questions, but they're not questions in the way where they're like, "That's wrong, and this is the right way." It's more questions like, "Oh, how did you know? Why do you feel that way?"

SARAH: That they're like, "Uh, can we stop talking about gender and sexuality so we can go watch TV?"

MARGARET: Yeah, sometimes they're like, "We know!!!!" [laughs] 'Cause I'm like, let me turn this into a lesson, and they're like, "We already know, Mom!" I'm like, "You're right."

SARAH: [chuckles] So that's all super positive. I'm wondering about how violence and fear affects your family in any way. I would think especially now with Trump in office, we're hearing a lot of homophobia. We're hearing a lot of worries about people not being able to be with people they love and families getting broken up. Is that something that affects your family in a significant way?

MARGARET: I would say before that, we were already in a place of—So my kids are mixed. I'm Black, and their dad is white. For the last two years, we had been having a lot of conversations about violence from policemen on Black men and women. And then particularly, when Tamir Rice was killed, that was a really big deal for us. That's when we told the kids, "You don't get to play with toy guns. Anything that looks like it could be used as a weapon you don't get to play with." So I think for my kids, they were already living with a certain reality. And then they understand that there's also, yes, homophobia. I think, to me and them, there's the thing of like if a queer person is white, they're still white. And then we're still Black. So even if we were straight, our skin color would still set us apart.

SARAH: Where do you guys find role models for your kids and for relationships, especially in pop culture? Our pop culture is pretty straight, pretty white. Are there TV shows or movies or books that your kids love that you feel like represent your family or people that you want them to be like?

MARGARET: Huh. We've been trying to get them more books with other kids of color in them [laughs], which is not . . . At first I was like, "Where are these books? There are none." And then once you start finding them, you're like, "Wow. There's so many. Why aren't these in libraries? Why aren't these at the school?" And then, there isn't very much on TV or in books about non-binary people, non-binary couples. There isn't very much about polyamory, I guess, either. And if it is, I feel like we just can't relate to it. We can't relate to middle-class white people in a triad where it's a man and two women, and they're still cis people.

But for my kids, I run a Black self-care day. So they participate in that. I do a Black women's tea, Black women femme tea, and Riley, my daughter, participates in that as well. And I run a discussion group where it's a mixture of people of color and white people, and we come and we talk about race and whatnot. And they're a part of that. So we try to make sure that they're also, aside from what they're reading or watching, they're also around other people who are similar. That's why we live in this huge house that's always full of people. We usually do Friday night dinners for Shabbat. My partner is Jewish. And that's always other polyamorous people or non-monogamous people and queer people and non-binary people. And there, they also see this example of what the world is like. And that is their world. These Friday night dinners, that's what their reality is.

SARAH: I feel like you've made such a beautiful universe for your kids.

MARGARET: [laughs] Trying.

SARAH: I know a lot of queer people have complicated feelings about marriage, and you're getting married to your partner, Noah. Can you talk about the decision to get married and why that feels special to you and how it's complicated?

MARGARET: Yeah. That's so funny 'cause this is the second time I'm getting married. I loved being married the first time, but I know that we also got married under the guise of we were both so religious. And it feels differently this time. It feels like I get to make the choice. There's very few things that I believe in doing as a ritual [chuckling]. I'm just not that kind of person. But this seems like one that I could invest in. And the fact that I'm going to bring all of these people that I love and share in this, I guess, union with another human—which is crazy—I'm really excited about. The first time I got married, we eloped. It was awesome, and it was really intimate. This time, I feel like I'm making a really big choice, and I'm making this choice in front of all of these people, this commitment, and they're there. I always thought like if I get divorced, I'll never get married again, and I'll just have a long-time partner or something. When I met my partner, within a few months, I was like, "I'm gonna marry you. You're a person that I would like to build a life with for hopefully the rest of my life and watch that evolve and have you as my anchor."

SARAH: Why does it feel important to you to get married? What's the difference there?

MARGARET: I don't know. I've been thinking about that a lot. I know that it feels really important, and I know I'm really happy with my choice in proposing to him. I think there's also—I had this conversation with Noah, actually the other day, where I was like—I actually don't want to ever not be partnered with you. And I feel like making this choice to do that is me also committing to putting in this effort that I don't know if I would've done outside of that. Which sounds really shitty, but I think it's important to me to make this commitment to this person that I think is the I don't wanna say my soul mate; I don't like that word.

SARAH: [laughs] What's wrong with soul mate?

MARGARET: I just don't know why. I'm really weird about words like soul mate and lover. Ack! Oh my god.

SARAH: Is it because you don't believe in souls, or is it just too cheesy?

MARGARET: [laughs] I just don't like the word! I think souls are so real [laughs]! This is my person, and I have a lot of conversations with other non-monogamous people and other non-hierarchical people about this. I do think that I've found my person and that I want to be married to them.

SARAH: There's a lot of critique of marriage of saying it's a patriarchal, heteronormative institution.

MARGARET: Yeah.

SARAH: You can't take it and make it your own. How are you trying to take it and make it your own, or is it a moot point 'cause you're just like, "Fuck it"?

MARGARET: I do believe in things where it must be dismantled in order to change but also believe that some things have to be changed by doing them. I don't think that I am anyone that does uphold a lot of like, I don't uphold patriarchy. Or at least I don't try to. I think it's impossible for me to fit into what is "norm." So for me, getting married, I don't think that is me being normal or upholding anything. I think it's me making my choice because I was given a choice. And there's also the part of me that people who are Black and white weren't always able to get married. That's still such a recent thing. That's something I also wanna take advantage of. That's not a thing I take for granted at all. Being able to be with my white partners, that's not a thing I take lightly.

So that also, to me, is this form of resisting what is normal. I think maybe if I was a white person who was cis, then maybe I don't need to get married. But I'm not that, you know? Our whole wedding is

two days of just celebration and just ridiculous. I'm getting married in a suit and then changing into a gown and then also wearing a jumpsuit, and we're having a crawfish boil. It's all these things that are just us and celebrating who we are.

SARAH: I'm glad celebrating who you are involves a jumpsuit [chuckles].

MARGARET: [laughs] I actually don't know! I don't know who I was before jumpsuits. I don't know how I was existing.

[music with lyrics]

> ♪ Hug me closer, mother, closer
> Put your arms around me tight
> For I'm holding tight, dear mother
> And I feel so strange tonight ♪

SARAH: You can follow Margaret and their whole beautiful family on Instagram and all the other places @margejacobsen.

Next up, Yasmin Nair.

YASMIN: As you may know, I do a lot of critiques of a lot of people and things, right? And I take care to be careful in my critiques. I do the same thing in my personal life, which is if I'm critical of someone, I'm not just gonna throw mud at them. I'm gonna be like, "This is why this is fucked up!" [chuckles] So.

SARAH: [chuckles] That's her! Keep listening.

[song from above continued]

> ♪ As I lay upon my bed
> How I'm trying to be patient
> And to think of what you said
> Just before the lamps were lighted
> Just before the children came
> While the room was very quiet
> I heard someone call my name ♪

SARAH: Just a quick plug here. Popaganda is produced by the team here at Bitch Media. If you didn't know, Bitch is an independent, non-profit feminist media organization. We're entirely funded by our Beehive members, subscribers, and like-minded sponsors. So if you liked today's episode of Popaganda, please become a member online at BitchMedia.org today. Let us know if you liked the show in your order comments.

OK. On with the show.

SARAH: Yasmin Nair is a prolific writer whose work focuses on sexuality, queer theory, and critiques of capitalism. She's been particularly critical of the mainstream gay rights movement and the push for same-sex marriage. She's the cofounder of a group called Against Equality. Yasmin, who is originally from Calcutta, India, and now lives in Chicago, is just a fascinating person to talk to, one of those people who makes even a simple question really interesting and complicated.

Like, I asked the basic question of who she thinks of as her family, and she contested the basic idea of family.

YASMIN: Right. So in terms of I prefer to not think of it as a family unit, but I do think of myself as occupying and being part of a very strong, and in some cases, very old network of friends and familiars, including cats and friends with cats and cats with friends. But no, I think of it as a network of friendships, actually, sort of a complicated series of networks that function a bit like, I guess, the rings around Saturn [chuckles]. That's how I think of my people, my tribes.

SARAH: So what do you think of reclaiming the word "family"? Why do you see yourself in a tribe or in a network of friendships or in a pile of cats [chuckles], but not in a family?

YASMIN: Right. And for a lot of queers, I think reclaiming family's important. A lot of people will call out to alternative families or families of choice, for instance; that's how they refer to them. For me, I'm also a Marxist feminist. So for me, it's also about being critical about the notion of a family as something that's very much implicated in a particular state apparatus, and to put it brutally, is mostly about collecting taxes. We tend to think of the family as a kind of naturally occurring, intimate configuration, and it's actually something that's very much socially, politically, and certainly economically constructed. In order to enable the state, really, to benefit the most. And it also enables a certain kind of patriarchy, as we all know. The idea of the family always involves who is the head of the family? Who are the subordinates in the family? Who's the breadwinner and so on? And it's not that that cannot be "subverted," but it's just that I see it pointless to sort of even try and subvert a structure that has been with us for millennia and has been so troubling for women, children, queer people, anyone who's outside that rigidly defined idea of family.

SARAH: Yeah, when you think about it, friendships are a really powerful force. Friendships, I feel like, are often discounted and devalued, especially in comparison to blood relatives.

YASMIN: I have noticed especially in the United States, when I moved here, I did notice that a lot of people use the phrase "we're just friends." And I always thought, what do you mean JUST friends? Friends are the best!! That's the most intense relationship. Your husband should be your friend.

SARAH: This is maybe too big of a question, but how do you feel like queerness impacts your idea of family and the way you see those lifelong relationships?

YASMIN: Yes, it was very much a part of also defining friends and friendships in my life. My friends and I, when I was at Purdue in the '90s, we formed a very close-knit band of groups. And we were very particular about defining ourselves as queer. This was also 1992, around the time when queer theory was becoming a thing in the university. I think queerness was very integral to that because what queerness, at least for us, as we were thinking through and theorizing it, not just in the texts we were writing but in our lives, was about first of all not heeling to the usual conventional boundaries of what was acceptable. So for instance, queerness meant that you could be friends with somebody and perhaps have a sort of almost sibling relation—and I had this—almost sibling kind of relationship with somebody, which might then shift into a cozy or a sexual relationship and then go back to being friends without sex and then at the same time be involved in helping each other figure out how to get this person they were interested in, you might be interested in, interested back in you and so on.

So what I think queerness really allowed us to do was to really think that relationships are very complicated, and it's OK to be complicated. Whereas I think if we had been—And that was very much deliberate on our parts. We would say, I think in our relationships, we were constantly asking each other how do we remain connected to each other with a kind of integrity that is actually fundamentally queer without screwing each other over, without of course hurting each other, but also being aware that queerness means that we get to test these boundaries of who you can be and who you can't be.

SARAH: So this is a show about family values. So what do you see as the core values that define your friendships? What are your friendship values, I guess?

YASMIN: Well, one value would be that you stay friends with someone even when they're going through a terribly hard time, or even when [chuckles] they're being complete assholes. And I think that's also the test of a friendship. So there are people, for instance, in the outer ambit who might—Am I allowed to use the word "asshole" on this? Do I have to change it?

SARAH: [laughs] No, we call people assholes all the time.

YASMIN: So I think one, and I've been very different kinds of people over the years, people have stuck with me, the same as I hope is true of my relationships with them. So I think one feature of how one defines a friendship and how one sustains is to see people through very hard times, even when they're being very hard on you. So that's really important because what matters is that relationship that you had with them for a long time, the relationship that actually makes the two of you who you are and that evolves. I think also really for me, what makes friendship, in a way, more dynamic than family

where a lot of people simply feel that they have to stick with someone because blood, because related.

SARAH: Let's talk about your thoughts on marriage. So you've published a lot of writing about queer critiques of marriage, and in part, it's because it involves relationships with a capitalist state that you say is exploitive at its core. So how has your thinking on marriage evolved? How do you think of marriage these days, now that it's legal for all LGBT people in the United States, thanks to the Supreme Court's decision about three years ago on the Defense of Marriage Act?

YASMIN: I think the problem with marriage has always been that it is a sign of the neoliberal times overtaking us. So when gay marriage did not become legal because people thought, oh, these sweet, sad gay couples just need to be happy and have children and all of that. Gay marriage became legal because it helped make the neoliberal state stronger. So what do I mean by that? Neoliberalism is fundamentally about the privatization of resources. There are longer arguments to be made about what it is and so on. But in essence, it is about privatizing resources like education, healthcare, housing, even water, for instance, that should actually be given over to the public. But these things have, increasingly over the last 40-odd years, become severely privatized.

So what gay marriage did was to actually mark a change even to gay community where in the '90s, for instance, during the AIDS crisis, gay people were marching; queers were marching for universal healthcare as a response to the AIDS crisis, as a response to the fact that people were literally dying because hospitals would not take care of them. Forget about healthcare. What happened in the '90s is you saw the gay community's pivoting around after it became a "manageable crisis," for mostly wealthy and mostly white gay men. And then you saw movement towards marriage. And then argument then became, well, if we can get married, we can get our partners on our healthcare, right? So what gay marriage represents is the ultimate privatization of something as essential as healthcare and along with it, things like citizenship. So you had the argument, which they won, that gay people should be able to get their marriage partners into the country for citizenship. So it's no surprise, for instance, that in Britain where they have, they've had for many years, a National Health Service, in Britain now, as that weakens, there's a rise in support for gay marriage, which is all, again, about the privatization of healthcare. So all of that is no surprise.

So that's my fundamental critique of gay marriage. It's not so much that it represents a cultural or social assimilation but that it is a movement that has helped become a vital cog for neoliberalism and the privatization of resources.

SARAH: I think a lot of feminist people feel that way, really conflicted about the institution of marriage and building their basic family unit around marriage. In the United States at least, marriage is such obviously a messy institution that mashes together tax law, healthcare policies, romantic love, economic history, monogamy. Is there anywhere that you see relationships that are defined in a way that resonates with you more? Like examples of where you say, "Ah, yeah. That works."

YASMIN: Well, in Scandinavia, for instance, in places like Sweden and Norway, it doesn't really matter whether you're married or not. The same is true of Canada. So for me, it's not so much about relationships; it's about what do people expect, and what do they get from the state? So in Canada, for instance, when gay marriage became legal, a lot of Canadian gays just shrugged their shoulders and went on their way. You see, they didn't have to get married. It didn't make a difference to them. People didn't have to get married because of healthcare issues. The same is true in places like Sweden and Norway where men and women get leave for childcare, for pregnancy and so on. The system works for everyone. So you don't have to affirm yourself as some sad gay person or some marvelously fruitful married couple. You don't have to move through this affective register to prove your worth as a human being, to get something as basic as healthcare, or for that matter, education.

SARAH: These issues around marriage and who has the right to be married, so much of it comes down to rights in our society and how certain rights—especially around taxes and healthcare in the United States—are only given to people who are married. But other hand, a lot of queer people have pushed back on that said that marriage is something that's really important and worth fighting for and worth defending the right to get married. Weddings can be beautiful expressions of love and especially our statement of happiness and joy and celebration of relationships that are so often demeaned. So I know a lot of queer feminists have problems with marriage, sure, but still want to get married themselves. How do you talk to the friends in your life who wanna get married about that choice and those tricky feelings?

YASMIN: I have been the official wedding photographer [laughs] for friends' unions. So I don't have any problem with that at all. My attitude about marriage is simply, again, this is about individuals. Fine. If you and another person feel that marriage means something to you, and I love you enough, I'll be there. And that's different. My response to all of them is it's one thing to say that personally, on an individual level for me, this is what marriage means. That's fine. What I don't like is when you fight for the system to become such that only married people like you can access the benefits. So that's different.

In Sweden people do get married. Not as often as here, perhaps, but they do get married in very different ways. But for one thing, I'm not sure any other country has quite the marriage industrial complex that we have here. It's really quite ridiculous. But it's one thing to have an emotional and affective tie to marriage. That's fine. I really don't care about that. But for me what matters, again, is what are you and what are we fighting for in terms of the benefits, the basic, fundamental rights that people should have regardless of whether or not they're married. So I really don't have a problem with people wanting to be married. Friends of mine are married, and that's fine with me. There's a difference between an individual, personal choice and how you fight for that personal choice to become the system-wide choice that everybody then has to sign onto.

[music]

SARAH: There's no right way to have a family. That's what's cool about the idea of reframing "family values," that there can be a diversity of values, and families can look all sorts of ways. Too often, families that don't fit a narrow, old-school idea of respectability are seen as bad. In so many ways, our society sends the message that in order to have a "good" family, you need to have two monogamous, wealthy, married parents, two kids would be ideal, everybody gets along harmoniously. But life is messier than that, and that's good! Whether your family is made of friends or made of many lovers or made of a husband and kids, you can form your own values and live by them. Having a strong family that looks just the way you want it to is actually a powerful act of resistance.

[music]

Hey, thanks for listening to the show today.

Our episode was produced by Alex Ward of Sounds Like Pictures. If you're looking for a transcript of this show, you're in luck. Cheryl Green of StoryMinders transcribes all Popaganda episodes. The transcript is available on our website, BitchMedia. org. We're proud to make the podcast accessible to people who are D/deaf or Hard-of-Hearing.

Our jingle is by Mucks and Owen Wuerker. Additional music was provided by Blue.Sessions. You can look up their creative and minimalist sounds by going to Google and typing in Sessions.Blue.

Please feel 100% encouraged to send me ideas, feedback, and criticisms on the show. I'm sarah@b-word.org. I'd love to hear from you.

Popaganda is produced by the team here at Bitch Media. We're an independent, non-profit feminist media organization that's entirely funded by our Beehive members, subscribers, and like-minded sponsors. So if you learned something new on today's episode of Popaganda, please become a member online at BitchMedia.org today. Let us know that you liked the show in your order comments. We read through them all, and they make us feel so special. OK, thanks for listening. Bye!

[theme music]

---

37. • *Marlene Kim*

POLICIES TO END THE GENDER WAGE GAP IN THE UNITED STATES (2013)

Marlene Kim, a professor of economics at the University of Massachusetts, Boston, specializes in discrimination of the working poor and wrote *Race and Economic Opportunity in the Twenty-first Century* (Routledge 2007) as well as numerous articles. She is the recipient of the first Rhonda Williams Prize from the International Association of Feminist Economics (2002). The following article originally was published in the *Review of Radical Political Economics* (2013).

Women continue to earn less than men in the United States. Among full-time workers, on average women earned 82 percent of men's wages in 2011. Gender wage gaps are pervasive among all races and ethnicities: Asian women earned 23 percent, white women 18 percent, and black and Hispanic women 9 percent less than men of the same race (U.S. Bureau of Labor Statistics 2012). Thus, although women's wages have increased over the past thirty years, they remain stubbornly below men's.

Much of the explanation for these wage differentials is that women work in different jobs than men, and these are lower paid. Although women have made some progress over the past thirty years in some professional occupations, such as law and medicine, women work in the lower-paying specialties of these fields, and they remain in the same low-paid jobs in which they had always worked, such as office support and service occupations (England 2010). Little progress has been made in traditionally male blue-collar jobs such as construction (England 2010). Research continues to show that entry into high-paid top executive jobs remains difficult for women (Smith 2012). Thus, over-representation in lower-paid jobs and underrepresentation in higher-paid ones continue to reduce women's pay.

There is a lively debate about the cause of these occupational differences. Neoclassical economists believe that women are less productive and that they choose lower-paying jobs in order to care for their families. Women work fewer years than men, and if they work at all, women with young children are more likely to work part-time compared to men with young families (O'Neill 2004). Anticipating their family needs, women choose occupations that allow them flexibility in the hours they work, such as nursing and teaching, and they avoid jobs that require highly specific skills and knowledge that become quickly outdated, such as in physics, knowing that they may take time off to raise families (O'Neill 2004; O'Neill and O'Neill 2005).

Critics of these neoclassical explanations control for factors that can explain productivity differences, including education level, hours worked, working part-time, having young children at home, and being married. These studies generally find that even with these controls, women earn less than men (Blau and Kahn 2007). To counter the argument that women are less career-focused or motivated, scholars find that even after adding controls for job aspirations and occupational preferences, women earn less than men (Blau and Ferber 1991). Finally, to dispute the argument that women major in less remunerative areas, such as the liberal arts rather than engineering or sciences, Weinberger and Joy (1997) add controls for college major, the university attended, and grade point average. They find that even when attending the same college and having the same college major and GPA, women earn less than men.

Audit and correspondence studies in hiring indicate that men are favored over women, even with the same qualifications. David Neumark (1996) found that when résumés for similarly-qualified women and men were left in restaurants, men received higher call-back rates in higher-paid restaurants, while women were favored in the lower-paid ones. Other studies find that women's qualifications are often overlooked, while men's qualifications are often used to justify their higher pay (Bergmann 1996). Mothers are perceived as less competent and less committed to working and consequently are recommended for lower salaries. They are also less likely to be recommended to be hired or to be promoted into management (Corell et al. 2007).

Thus, given that gender disparities in wages may result from bias, policies are needed to remedy these. Such policies can be divided into two strategies: increasing access to higher-paying jobs, and increasing pay in the jobs in which women already work.

1. ENFORCING EXISTING EQUAL OPPORTUNITY STATUTES

If women are less likely to be hired into higher-paying jobs because of discrimination, enforcing existing statutes would help alleviate this. In a cross-country analysis, Doris Weichselbaumer and Rudolf Winter-Ebmer (2007) find that laws mandating equal treatment in workplaces reduce the gender wage gap.

Indeed, Title VII of the 1964 Civil Rights Act in the United States, which mandates non-discrimination regarding gender in the workplace, has been very successful in mitigating discrimination when this law is enforced (Leonard 1989).

In addition, enforcing affirmative action mandates can also increase women's employment and pay (Leonard 1989). Affirmative action requires that companies that receive government contracts examine the gender and racial composition of their workplaces in broad occupational categories and compare this with the composition of workers available to work. When workplaces are deficient in their representation of women or minorities, employers must use voluntary goals and timetables and take affirmative steps so that the gender and racial composition in their workplace reflects the composition of the workers available. Affirmative steps include publicizing the availability of jobs, recruiting underrepresented workers, and training and mentoring them. In egregious cases of discrimination, courts can mandate hiring quotas so that employers are forced to hire underrepresented workers.

Affirmative action has been successful in increasing the proportion of women in jobs, but it has been dismantled by the courts (Leonard 1989). Despite critics' allegations, it does not lead to weaker candidates being hired or a loss in productivity in the firm (Holzer and Neumark 1999; Leonard 1989).

2. FAMILY-FRIENDLY POLICIES

Family-friendly policies allow women to work so that they do not have to choose between their careers and their families. Many countries that have family-friendly policies have higher labor participation rates among women than in the United States, since women in these countries can have both a job and a family. Parental leave, especially paid leave, as well as part-time work and child care policies, increase the proportion of mothers who work (Hofferth 1996; Joech 1997; Gornick et al. 1998), and moderate-length paid parental leave and publicly-funded child care can increase earnings for mothers

(Budig et al. 2012).[1] Thus, adopting paid family leave and child care policies that are available in many industrialized countries can reduce the gender wage gap.

One must ensure that family-friendly policies do not reinforce the gendered division of labor, however (Bergmann 1997; Singley and Hynes 2005). Allowing part-time work only in low-paid female jobs, paid parental leave for women but not men (e.g. women receive disability payments for childbirth in some U.S. states), and higher pay for men ensures that women rather than men will care for families. Thus, part-time work should be available in high-paying fields, both parents should be required to take alternating periods of "use or lose" paid parental leave, and families should not forfeit the higher pay of fathers who take such leave (Singley and Hynes 2005).

3. COMPARABLE WORTH

Besides increasing access to higher-paying jobs, another strategy to improve women's earnings is to increase pay in the jobs in which women work. Comparable worth, also known as pay equity, is one such strategy. To comprehend it, one must understand that employers' compensation systems meet three different goals: to adequately recruit and retain workers, they pay market wages (hence they perform or purchase salary surveys); to pay more for occupations that are evaluated as having greater worth (often measured as having greater duties and responsibilities), they conduct job evaluations; and to motivate hard work, they pay more for more productive workers even within occupations (hence they use performance appraisals). (See Milkovich et al. 2010.)

Comparable worth addresses the second of these goals. It advocates that when employers conduct job evaluations, they should not underpay jobs simply because women are employed. Occupations evaluated as having the same value to the employer should be paid the same, whether women or men perform the work.

This is not the case in the United States. The greater the proportion of women in an occupation, the lower the pay, and even employers' own job evaluations often indicate that women's occupations should receive higher pay (England 1992). In addition, there is much historical evidence that employers commonly paid less to occupations filled by women. For example, in 1945, Westinghouse and General Electric paid 70.5 cents per hour for women's jobs having 50–62 job evaluation points, but 84.5 cents per hour for men's occupations with the same number of points (Newman 1976). Kim (1999) similarly shows that when the State of California established its pay system in the 1930s, it paid occupations primarily held by women less than those primarily held by men, where otherwise the duties and responsibilities were the same. Because the employer maintains the existing salary relationships among occupations, this underpayment to female-dominated occupations continues into the present, even when market wages are accounted for.

Thus scholars believe that employers should reevaluate their job evaluation systems to ensure that women's occupations are no longer underpaid. Indeed, research indicates that when comparable worth is implemented at the state level (for public sector workers), the wage gap is reduced (Hartmann and Aaronson 1994) once these inequities are remedied.

4. UNIONIZATION

Unionized workers earn ten to thirty percent more than non-union workers (Freeman and Medoff 1986), and the union wage premium is higher among women than among men in public sector jobs (Freeman and Leonard 1987). The result is that unionization decreases the gender wage gap (Cho and Cho 2011). Thus, unionizing workers in typically female jobs and industries can reduce the gender wage gap.

Women are less likely to belong to unions, however, even though they are more likely to favor them, because historically organizing drives occurred in manufacturing and blue-collar jobs, where men typically worked (Freeman and Medoff 1986).

Given the decline of these jobs and the rise of the service sector, including health care, education, and other sectors in which women work, unionizing women is critical to revitalizing union density in the nation. However, this will require changes in the law so that organizing drives can occur without union-busting tactics of employers (Freeman and Medoff 1986).

5. PAY SECRECY

An interesting strategy to close the gender pay gap is to prohibit pay secrecy. Pay secrecy includes rules, policies, and practices that forbid workers from sharing information on their earnings. Even though the National Labor Relations Act (NLRA) of 1935 mandates that employees have the right to share information on wages, most employers either formally or informally forbid this (Institute for Women's Policy Research 2010). Feminists are concerned that women may be underpaid because they do not know that they are paid less than men, as in the case of Lilly Ledbetter. Ledbetter worked as a manager for Goodyear Tire for twenty years before receiving an anonymous note that the male managers in her position were paid more than she.

Six states (California, Vermont, Michigan, Colorado, Illinois, and Maine) forbid employers from retaliating against employees for sharing information about their earnings (Kim 2012). These laws are important because the NLRA does not cover supervisors; hence Lilly Ledbetter could have been fired had she inquired about the pay of male managers. In addition, because the remedies under the NLRA are mild, limited to back wages minus any earnings in other jobs, employers commonly ignore this law (Freeman and Medoff 1986).

Research indicates that in states that outlaw pay secrecy, wages are higher for women, even when accounting for standard human capital controls as well as state effects. In other words, wages for women increased in the same state after such laws were passed compared to similar women in the state before these laws were in effect (Kim 2012). Thus expanding pay secrecy laws to other states would benefit women, increasing their pay and lowering the gender wage gap.

6. POLICIES TO END THE GENDER WAGE GAP

Because the wage gap results from multiple causes, no single policy can end it, and multiple remedies are required. Title VII and affirmative action address the problem of women being employed in low-paying jobs and being overlooked for higher-paid ones. Family-friendly policies would ensure that women can work and retain their jobs. Comparable worth, unionization, and pay secrecy laws can allow women to increase their pay in the jobs in which they already work. Research indicates that all of these policies improve women's wages and lower the gender wage gap.

But national legislation has been introduced many times in these areas. The Paycheck Fairness Act has been introduced by Congress 20 times, most recently in 2012. This legislation proposed to increase the remedies and penalties under Title VII and also outlaw pay secrecy. Comparable worth and family-friendly laws have also been introduced but never passed by Congress. Labor law reform that would make it easier to elect unions and that would increase the penalties to employers and remedies to employees under the NLRA also have failed in Congress.

Given this political reality, advocates should follow the very successful political strategy of the radical right. The right failed to pass federal legislation outlawing abortions, so it took its campaign to the states. Over the years, it has limited abortions with state laws mandating parental consent, waiting periods, and other conditions so that in many states abortions are effectively unavailable. A similar campaign is now being waged over unions, with Michigan recently becoming a Right to Work state.

Let us follow this example. Individual states have passed stronger laws on non-discrimination, pay secrecy, comparable worth, and paid family leave. States should continue to take this lead. Advocates can assess and target the states most likely to pass such legislation, and researchers can study and disseminate the effects of these policies on the gender wage gap, leading to more support for these policies. In addition, states can be pro-active in identifying and remedying unequal pay for women. The Attorney General's Office in Vermont, for example, explicitly asks during every intake of any complaint (including minimum wage or maximum hour violations) whether women are underpaid at work, and if women answer affirmatively, they initiate and investigate a pay discrimination complaint. In this way, they proactively uncover and resolve problems that women encounter in their workplaces. States can use this as a model to uncover, investigate, and remedy underpayment to women. Instead of attempting to pass the same legislation that continues to fail on a national level, women can reap the rewards of higher pay through targeted state and local initiatives and legislation that can remedy the problem of unequal pay that women face.

[. . .]

NOTE

Acknowledgments: Arsenia Reilly provided excellent research assistance. Joya Misra provided useful feedback. The errors in this paper remain the author's.

1. Extensively long paid leaves for mothers may relegate them to low-paid jobs after they return from their long absence (Budig et al. 2012).

REFERENCES

Bergmann, B. R. 1997. Work-family policies and equality between women and men. In *Gender and family issues in the workplace*, ed. F. D. Blau and R. G. Ehrenberg. New York: Russell Sage.

Bergmann, B. R. 1996. *In defense of affirmative action*. New York: Basic Books.

Blau, F. D., and M. A. Ferber. 1991. Career plans and expectations of young women and men: The earnings gap and labor force participation. *Journal of Human Resources* 26: 581–607.

Blau, F. D., and L. M. Kahn. 2007. The gender pay gap: Have women gone as far as they can? *Academy of Management Perspectives* 21: 7–23.

Budig, M. J., J. Misra, and I. Boeckmann. 2012. The motherhood penalty in cross-national perspective: The importance of work-family policies and cultural attitudes. *Social Politics* 19: 163–193.

Cho, D., and J. Cho. 2011. How do labor unions influence the gender earnings gap? A comparative study of the US and Korea. *Feminist Economics* 17: 133–157.

Correll, S. J., S. Benard, and I. Paik. 2007. Getting a job: Is there a motherhood penalty? *American Journal of Sociology* 112: 1297–1339.

England, P. 2010. The gender revolution: Uneven and stalled. *Gender and Society* 24(2): 149–166.

England, P. 1992. *Comparable worth: Theories and practice*. New York: Aldine de Gruyer.

Freeman, R., and J. S. Leonard. 1985. Union maids: Unions and the female workforce. NBER Working Paper 1652.

Freeman, R., and J. Medoff. 1986. *What do unions do?* New York: Basic Books.

Gornick, J. C., M. K. Meyers, and K. E. Ross. 1998. Public policies and the employment of mothers: A cross-national survey. *Social Science Quarterly* 79: 35–54.

Hartmann, H. I., and S. Aaronson. 1994. Pay equity and women's wage increases: Success in the states, a model for the nation. *Duke Journal of Gender Law and Policy* 1: 69–87.

Hofferth, S. L. 1996. Effects of public and private policies on working after childbirth. *Work and Occupations* 23: 378–404.

Holzer, H., and D. Neumark. 1999. Assessing affirmative action. NBER Working Paper 7323.

Joech, J. M. 1997. Paid leave and timing of women's employment before and after birth. *Journal of Marriage and the Family* 59: 1008–21.

Institute for Women's Policy Research. 2010. Pay secrecy and paycheck fairness.

Kim, M. 1999. Inertia and discrimination in the California State civil service. *Industrial Relations* 38: 46–68.

Kim, M. 2012. Pay secrecy and the gender wage gap. Mimeo.

Leonard, J. 1989. Women and affirmative action. *Journal of Economic Perspectives* 3: 6175.

Milkovich, G., G. Newman, and B. Gerhart. 2010. *Compensation*. New York: McGraw-Hill.

Newman, W. 1976. Presentation III. In *Women and the workplace: The implications of occupational segregation*, ed. B. B. Reagan and M. Blaxall, 265–272. Chicago: University of Chicago Press.

Neumark, D. 1996. Sex discrimination in restaurant hiring: An audit study. *Quarterly Journal of Economics* 111: 915–941.

O'Neill, J. E. 1994. The gender gap in wages, circa 2000. *American Economic Review* 93: 309–314.

O'Neill, J. E. and D. M. O'Neill. 2005. What do wage differentials tell us about labor market discrimination? NBER Working Paper 11240.

Singley, S. G., and K. Hynes. 2005. Transitions to parenthood: Work-family policies, gender, and the couple context. *Gender and Society* 19: 376–397.

Smith, R. 2012. Money, benefits and power: A test of the glass ceiling and glass escalator hypotheses. *The Annals of the American Academic of Political and Social Science* 639: 149–172.

U.S. Bureau of Labor Statistics. 2012. Highlights of women's earnings in 2011. Report 1038. www.bls.gov/cps/cpswom2011.pdf.

Weichselbaumer, D., and R. Winter-Ebmer. 2007. International gender wage gaps. *Economic Policy* 237–287.

Weinberger, C., and L. Joy. 2007. Relative earnings of black college graduates. In *Race and economic opportunity in the twenty-first century*, ed. M. Kim, 50–72. London: Routledge.

38. • *Dean Spade*

COMPLIANCE IS GENDERED:
Struggling for Gendered Self-Determination in a Hostile Economy (2006)

> Dean Spade, a professor at the Seattle University School of Law, founded the Sylvia Rivera Law Project, a nonprofit collective that provides free legal services to transgender, intersex, and nonconforming people who are low income and/or people of color. Spade is currently the co-editor of the online journal *Enough* and originally published *Normal Life: Administrative Violence, Critical Trans Politics, and the Limits of the Law* with South End Press; it was reissued with Duke University Press in 2015. The public can access multimedia talks, additional writing, and teaching information at http://www.deanspade.net. The following article originally appeared in *Transgender Rights*, edited by P. Currah, R. Juang, and S. Price Minter (Minnesota 2006).

[. . .]

Since the emergence of poor-relief programs in sixteenth-century Europe, governments have developed varying strategies of social welfare to quell resistance among those who inhabit the necessary lowest level of the capitalist economy: the pool of unemployed whose presence keeps wages low and profit margins high.[1] Throughout their history, relief systems have been characterized by their insistence on work requirements for recipients, their vilification of recipients of relief, and their ability to paint the necessary failures of the economic systems they prop up as moral failures of the individuals who are most negatively affected by those systems.[2]

Feminist theorists have provided vital insight into how public relief systems have also operated through moralistic understandings of sexuality and family structure to force recipients into compliance with sexist and heterosexist notions of womanhood and motherhood. The creation of coercive policies requiring this compliance have usually been mobilized by appeals to white supremacist notions of white motherhood and racial purity, as well as depictions of Black women as oversexualized, lazy, and morally loose. Feminist theorists have provided a picture of how the day-to-day surveillance of low-income people and the rigid and punitive rule systems used in social services create a highly regulated context for the gender expression, sexuality, and family structure of low-income women who often rely on these systems to get out of economically dependent relationships with men. This fits into a broader analysis of how gendered models of citizenship, and gender and race hierarchies in the economy, operate to dominate the lives of low-income people most forcefully and directly affect the ability of all people to determine and express our gender, sexuality, and reproduction.

Unfortunately, this analysis has not yet been applied to examine how gender regulation of the poor applies to those who face some of the most dire consequences of a coercive binary gendered economy, those who transgress the basic principles of binary gender. Much feminist analysis of binary gender transgression has focused on the pathologizing medical discourses that have defined popular understandings of gender role distress to reinscribe meaning into rigid notions of "male" and "female."[3] However, as transgender liberation movements proliferate, and feminist analysis of gender transgression becomes more nuanced and sophisticated, it is essential that we bring along the feminist analysis of gender regulation in work and public assistance systems in order to account for the extreme economic consequences that gender-transgressive people face because of our gender identities and expressions.

Similarly, many lesbian, gay, and bi activists and theorists have tended to miss the vital connection between economic and anticapitalist analysis and the regulation of sexual and gender expression and behavior. The most well-publicized and well-funded LGB organizations have notoriously marginalized low-income people and people of color, and framed political agendas that have reflected concern for economic opportunity and family recognition for well-resourced and disproportionately white LGB populations. Feminist, anticapitalist, and antiracist analysis has been notably absent from mainstream discourses about LGBT rights, and low-income people, people of color, and gender-transgressive people have been notoriously under-represented from leadership and decision-making power in these movements.[4]

This is particularly distressing given the economic realities that people who transgress gender norms face. Economic and educational opportunity remain inaccessible to gender transgressive people because of severe and persistent discrimination, much of which remains legal,[5] but for low-income people caught up in the especially gender-regulating public relief systems and criminal justice systems that dominate the lives of the poor, the gender regulation of the economy is felt even more sharply.

Many trans people start out their lives with the obstacle of abuse or harassment at home, or being kicked out of their homes because of their gender identities or expressions. Some turn to foster care, but often end up homeless when they experience harassment and violence at the hands of staff and other residents in foster care facilities (most of which are sex segregated and place trans youth according to birth sex designation).[6] The adult homeless shelter system, similarly, is inaccessible because of the fact that most facilities are sex segregated and will either turn down a trans person outright or refuse to house them according to their lived gender identity.[7] Similarly, harassment and violence against trans and gender nonconforming students is rampant in schools, and many drop out before finishing or are kicked out. Many trans people also do not pursue higher education because of fears about having to apply to schools and having their paperwork reveal their old name and birth sex because they have not been able to change these on their documents. Furthermore, trans people face severe discrimination in the job market and are routinely fired for transitioning on the job or when their gender identities or expressions come to their supervisors' attention.[8]

Trans people also have a difficult time accessing the entitlements that exist, though in a reduced and diminished format, to support poor people. Discrimination on the basis of gender identity occurs in welfare offices, on workfare job sites, in Medicaid offices, in Administrative Law Hearings for welfare, Medicaid, and Social Security Disability benefits. These benefit programs have been decimated in the last ten years and are generally operated with a punitive approach that includes frequent illegal termination of benefits and the failure to provide people their entitlements. For most people seeking to access these programs consistently during a time of need, the availability of an attorney or advocate to help navigate the hearings process has been essential to maintaining benefits. Unfortunately, most poverty attorneys and advocacy organizations are still severely lacking in basic information about serving trans clients and may reject cases on the basis of a person's gender identity or create such an unwelcoming environment that a trans client will not return for services. Based on community awareness of this problem, many trans people will not even seek these services, expecting that they will be subjected to humiliating and unhelpful treatment. The resulting lack of access to even the remaining shreds of the welfare system leaves a disproportionate number of trans people in severe poverty and dependent on criminalized work such as prostitution or the drug economy to survive. This, in turn, results in large numbers of trans people being entangled in the juvenile and adult criminal justice systems where they are subjected to extreme harassment and violence.

Given these conditions, the need for an understanding of the operations of gender regulation on gender-transgressive people in the context of poverty is urgent. . . . I want to begin to suggest how we could reexamine what we know from feminist and LGB analysis of gender, sexual, and reproductive regulation, to see how this applies to the lives of low-income transgender, transsexual, intersex, and other gender-transgressive people. I come to these questions as a poverty lawyer working for these populations, and I want to use feminist, queer, and anticapitalist analysis of the operation of poverty alleviation programs and other methods of controlling and exploiting poor people to contextualize case studies from the day-to-day lives of my clients. I want to begin a conversation about what it means that almost all of the institutions and programs that exist to control and exploit poor people and people of color in the United States are sex segregated, especially in a context where membership in a sexual category is still determined with regard to access to medical technologies that are prohibitively expensive to all but the most well-resourced gender-transgressive people. . . .

Now is the time to recognize that no project of gender and sexual self-determination will be meaningful if it fails to engage resistance to an inherently violent and hierarchical capitalist economic system that grounds its control over workers and the poor in oppressive understandings of race, sex, gender, ability, and nationality.[9] To address homophobic and transphobic domination in pursuit of a better world, we need to start from an understanding of the experiences of those who face the intersection of multiple oppressions, centralize the analysis that this intersectionality fosters, and think concretely about what strategies a movement dedicated to these principles would engage.

CAPITALISM, ACCESS TO INCOME, AND THE USE OF SOCIAL WELFARE POLICIES TO REGULATE GENDER AND SEXUALITY AND PROMOTE WHITE SUPREMACY

Access to participation in the U.S. economy has always been conditioned on the ability of each individual to comply with norms of gendered behavior and expression, and the U.S. economy has always been shaped by explicit incentives that coerce people into normative gender and sexual structures, identities, and behaviors. At the same time the U.S. economy has, since its inception, been structured to recognize and maintain access to wealth for white people and to exploit the labor, land, and resources of native people, immigrants, and people of color. Property ownership itself has been a raced and gendered right throughout U.S. history, and an individual's race, gender, and sexuality have operated as forms of property themselves.[10] Similarly, interventions that would appear to seek to remedy the exploitative and damaging outcomes of our economic system have often been structured to control gendered behavior and expression and incentivize misogynist and heterosexist family norms. These interventions have typically been mobilized by white supremacy and the desire to benefit white workers and families to the disadvantage of people of color and immigrants. For example, the first wage and hour laws in the United States were passed under a notion of protectionism for women, the logic being that since women really did not belong in the workplace anyway, if they had to work outside the home, it was the states' role to intervene in their labor contracts to protect them from exploitation.[11] Similarly, since the inception of poor relief in the United States, programs have been structured to support gendered divisions of labor and promote heterosexual family structure and have been mobilized by discourses of racial purity.[12] . . .

[. . .]

Anyone who has lived through the last ten years of "welfare reform" rhetoric in the United States will notice that racist and sexist rhetoric and policy in the realm of welfare is still strongly with us. Such rhetoric is still being used to formulate welfare policies that control the gender and sexual behavior and expression of women and firmly tie economic survival and advantage to racial status. The most recent well-publicized massive overhaul of the welfare system, the "welfare reform" of the mid-1990s, was motivated, structured, and sold to the American public through racist and sexist understandings of poverty, work, and family structure. Its results have lived up to its intentions, with poor women of color suffering horribly under the new system.[13] Holloway Sparks writes about how the changes in welfare policy in the mid-1990s were based on a concept of contractual citizenship in which low-income people needed to be obligated to work and meet certain moral standards in order to earn their rights to public benefits.[14] Public benefits recipients were cast in the media as pathological, amoral people caught in a "cycle of dependency." Welfare mothers were depicted as people who couldn't stop having more and more children and committing welfare fraud.[15] The media uproar focused on racist and sexist images of black "welfare queens" and irresponsible teenage mothers. The mobilization of these images was an essential part of the creation of the Personal Responsibility and Work Opportunity Reconciliation Act of 1996 (PRWORA).[16]

The purpose and result of vilifying welfare recipients and focusing on sexual morality and gender role transgression is the creation of coercive policies designed to force poor people to obey rigid gender and family norms. Marriage incentives and requirements that mothers disclose the paternity of their children are only the most explicit examples of how the moral performance on which benefit receipt is conditional is fundamentally a requirement that poor women rigidly obey conservative notions of gender role and

family structure. As countless critics have pointed out, these requirements create horrendous obstacles to women struggling with domestic violence who cannot safely disclose paternity or comply with other aspects of the "maintenance and sustenance of two-parent families" dictated by welfare policy.[17] Additionally, for lesbian mothers the rigidity with which family structure is viewed and regulated by welfare policies and rules makes benefits inaccessible or dependent on remaining closeted.[18]

[. . .]

The example of the PRWORA passage, as well as more recent activity around reauthorizing PRWORA, which has included increasing discussion of "healthy marriage promotion,"[19] demonstrates that social welfare programs are explicitly designed to promote oppressive and racialized understandings of gender, sexuality, and family structure. The depiction of the lives of poor women that motivated the PRWORA, and behind which both Democrats and Republicans rallied, made it clear that poor women were responsible for their poverty and that the only remedy was to coerce them into marriage and work. These morality-based understandings of poverty play out in the day-to-day operation of social services programs that emphasize surveillance and gender regulation of poor people.

FAILING TO COMPLY

The climate of vilification of the poor and pathologization of the conditions and consequences of poverty produce and operate through day-to-day punitive and coercive structures within poverty service provision. These programs often focus on notions of "compliance" and "noncompliance" among participants. Feminist theorists have provided helpful analysis in this area, examining the ways that access to homeless and domestic violence shelters is mediated through punitive processes where those looking for assistance are treated as morally and intellectually deficient and subjected to humiliating violations of privacy as an integral part of the disincentification of receiving services.[20] Navigating benefits systems, shelter systems, essential medical services, and entanglement with the criminal justice system that is now a central aspect of low-income existence in order to survive is increasingly tied to the ability of each person to meet highly gendered and raced behavioral and expression requirements.[21] While feminist analysis has exposed the hidden agendas of poverty policies to shape women's work and family structure and inhibit the ability of women to be economically independent and escape violent relationships, this analysis has not extended to examine the effects of this system on poor people who also transgress the coercive binary gender system that maintains sexism.

The following two stories from my work with low-income gender-transgressive people illustrate the particular ways in which the incorporation of rigid binary gender expectations into social service provision and the criminal justice system operate in the lives of gender-transgressive people.

JIM'S STORY

Jim is an intersex person.[22] He was raised as a girl, but during adolescence began to identify as male. To his family, he remained female identified, but in the world he identified as male. The stress of living a double life was immense, but he knew it was the only way to maintain a relationship with his family, with whom he was very close. When Jim was nineteen, he was involved in a robbery for which he received a sentence of five years' probation. During the second year of that probation period, Jim was arrested for drug possession and was sentenced to eighteen months of residential drug treatment. Jim was sent to a male residential facility. In a purportedly therapeutic environment, Jim discussed his intersex status with his therapist. His confidentiality was broken, and soon the entire staff and residential population were aware that Jim was intersex. Jim was facing such severe rape threat with no support or protection from staff that he ultimately ran away from the facility. I met Jim after he had turned himself in, wanting to deal with his criminal justice status so that he could safely apply to college and get on with his life. Jim was in a Brooklyn men's jail, again facing severe rape threat because the jail refused to continue his testosterone treatments, which caused him to menstruate, and when he was strip-searched while menstruating other inmates and staff learned of his status. Jim and I worked together to try to convince the judge in his case that Jim could safely access drug treatment services only in an outpatient setting because of the rape threat he continually faced in residential settings. Even when we had convinced the judge of this, though, we faced the fact that most programs were gender segregated and would not be a safe place for Jim to be known as intersex. When I contacted facilities to find a place for Jim, staff at all levels would ask me questions like "Does he pee sitting or standing?" and "Does he have a penis?" indicating to me that Jim would be treated as a novelty and his intersex status would be a source of gossip. Even the few lesbian and gay drug treatment programs I identified seemed inappropriate because Jim did not identify as gay and was, in fact, quite unfamiliar with gay and lesbian communities and somewhat uncomfortable in queer spaces. Eventually, the judge agreed to let Jim try outpatient treatment, but on a "zero tolerance" policy, where a single relapse would result in jail time. Jim was under enormous stress, engaged in treatment where he was always afraid he might be outed and where his participation in the daily hours of group therapy required hiding his identity. He relapsed and was sentenced to two years in state prison. When I went before the judge to request that Jim be placed in women's prison because of his well-founded fear of sexual assault in men's facilities, the judge's response was "He can't have it both ways." Once again, Jim's intersex status, and his inability to successfully navigate the gender requirements of the extremely violent system in which he was entangled because of involvement in nonviolent poverty-related crimes, was considered part of his criminality and a blameworthy status.

BIANCA'S STORY

Bianca is a transgender woman. In 1999 she was attending high school in the Bronx. After struggling with an internal understanding of herself as a woman for several years, Bianca eventually mustered the courage to come out to her peers and teachers at school. She and another transgender student who were close friends decided to come out together, and arrived at school one day dressed to reflect their female gender identities. They were stopped at the front office and not allowed to enter school. Eventually, they were told to leave and not come back. When their parents called the school to follow up and find out what to do next, their calls were never returned. They were given no referrals to other schools, and no official suspension or expulsion documents. Because of their families' poverty and language barriers, they were never able to successfully get documentation or services from the schools. I met Bianca three years later. She had been trying to find an attorney to take the case and had never found one, and when I met her and began investigating the possibility of bringing a lawsuit, I discovered that the statute of limitations had run out, and she no longer had a claim. When I met Bianca, she was homeless and unemployed and was trying to escape from an abusive relationship. She was afraid to go to the police both because of the retaliation of her boyfriend and because she rightly feared that the police would react badly to her because of her transgender status. Her IDs all said her male name and gender, and there would be no way for her to seek police protection without being identified as transgender. As we searched for places for Bianca to live, we ran up against the fact that all the homeless shelters would only place her according to birth gender, so she would be a woman in an all-men's facility, which she rightly feared would be unsafe and uncomfortable. Women's shelters for domestic violence survivors were unwilling to take her because they did not recognize her as a woman. When Bianca went to apply for welfare she was given an assignment to attend a job center to be placed in a workfare program. When she tried to access the job center, she was severely harassed outside, and when she entered she was outed and humiliated by staff when she attempted to use the women's restroom. Ultimately, she felt too unsafe to return, and her benefits were

terminated. Bianca's total lack of income also meant that she had no access to the hormone treatments that she used to maintain a feminine appearance, which was both emotionally necessary for her and kept her safe from some of the harassment and violence she faced when she was identifiable as a trans woman on the street. Bianca felt that her only option for finding income sufficient to pay for the hormones she bought on the street (it would have been more expensive from a doctor, since Medicaid would not cover it even if she could successfully apply for Medicaid) was to engage in illegal sex work. This put her in further danger of police violence, arrest, and private violence. Additionally, because she was accessing injectable hormones through street economies, she was at greater risk of HIV infection and other communicable diseases.

These two cases are typical of my clients in that almost everyone who comes to the Sylvia Rivera Law Project for services is facing serious consequences of failing to fit within a rigid binary gender structure in multiple systems and institutions: welfare, adult or juvenile justice, public education, voluntary or mandated drug treatment, homeless services, and mental and physical health care. Compliance is a central issue that my clients face in these systems. They are unable to comply or "rehabilitate" because to do either means to match stereotypes associated with their birth genders. Some are kicked off welfare because they fail to wear birth-gender appropriate clothing to "job training" programs that require them to.[23] Others are labeled "sex offenders" in juvenile justice simply because of their transgender identities despite the fact that their criminal offenses were not sex-related, and forced to wear sex offender jumpsuits while locked up and attend sex offender therapy groups. If they cannot or will not remedy their gender transgressions, they cannot complete the rehabilitation process required for release. Some clients lose housing at youth or adult shelters because staff argue that their failures to dress according to birth gender means they are not seriously job hunting, a requirement of the program to maintain housing. The ways that these systems, apply rigid gendered expectations to poor people, which are notably not applied to nonpoor people, are manifold, because these systems operate through detailed surveillance coupled with extensive discretion on the part of individual caseworkers and administrators. I find my clients serving the role of example, particularly in adult and juvenile justice contexts, by being humiliated, harassed, or assaulted because of their gender transgressions in a way that communicates clearly to others entangled in those systems exactly what is expected of them. For many transgender, transsexual, or intersex people, this violence results in long-term severe injuries and in death.[24]

The other vitally important component to the inability of gender-transgressive poor people to access benefits and services is the fact that gender segregation remains a central organizing strategy of systems of social control. Employed people with stable housing are subjected to far fewer gender-segregated facilities on a daily basis than poor or homeless people. While we all must contend with bathrooms or locker rooms that are gender segregated, those of us with homes and jobs may even be able to avoid those a good deal of the time, as opposed to homeless people who must always use public facilities that are likely to be segregated and highly policed. Additionally, all the essential services and coercive control institutions (jails, homeless shelters, group homes, drug treatment facilities, foster care facilities, domestic violence shelters, juvenile justice facilities, housing for the mentally ill) that increasingly dominate the lives of poor people and disproportionately of people of color use gender segregation as a part of the gendered social control they maintain.[25] For the most part, these institutions recognize only birth gender, or rely on identity documents such as birth certificates to determine gender. In every state in the United States that allows people to change their gender markers on their birth certificates, evidence of sex reassignment surgery is required.[26]

As I have written elsewhere,[27] the reliance on medical evidence in all legal contexts in which transgender and other gender-transgressive people struggle for recognition or rights is highly problematic. Whether seeking to prove our marriages valid so that we can keep our parental rights or access our spouse's estate,[28] or attempting to change our names and gender on our identity documents so that we can apply for educational or employment opportunities,[29] or when attempting to access sex-segregated facilities of various kinds,[30] medical evidence remains the defining factor in determining our rights. This is problematic because access to gender-related medical intervention is usually conditioned on successful performance of rigidly defined and harshly enforced understandings of binary gender,[31] because many gender-transgressive people may not wish to undergo medical intervention, and because medical care of all kinds, but particularly gender-related medical care, remains extremely inaccessible to most low-income gender-transgressive people.[32]

[. . .]

ASKING FOR MORE

The most well-funded organizations in the lesbian and gay movement do not provide direct legal services to low-income people, but instead focus their resources on high-profile impact litigation cases and policy efforts. Most of these efforts have traditionally focused on concerns central to the lives of nonpoor lesbian and gay people and have ignored the most pressing issues in the lives of poor people, people of color, and transgender people. The "gay agenda" has been about passing our apartments to each other when we die, not about increasing affordable housing or opposing illegal eviction. It has been about getting our partnerships recognized so our partners can share our private health benefits, not about defending Medicaid rights or demanding universal health care. It has been about getting our young sons into Boy Scouts, not about advocating for the countless/uncounted queer and trans youth struggling against a growing industry of youth incarceration. It has been about working to put more punishment power in the hands of an overtly racist criminal system with passage of hate crimes laws, not about opposing the mass incarceration of a generation of men of color, or fighting the abuse of queer and trans people in adult and juvenile justice settings.

The debates about gender identity inclusion in the federal Employment Non-Discrimination Act (ENDA)[33] or the exclusion of gender identity protection from New York States Sexual Orientation Non-Discrimination Act (SONDA)[34] are only the most blatant examples of the mainstream lesbian and gay movement's lack of commitment to gender-transgressive populations, but the failure of "LGBT" dollars, services, and resources to reach the lives of low-income people is even more widespread. What it means in the lives of low-income gender-transgressive people is that not only do they lack essential legal protections, they cannot find effective advocacy to access the fair treatment, services, or benefits they are entitled to. Unfortunately, the trend in gender rights litigation toward the recognition of gender identity change only in the context of medicalization maintains this imbalance. The history of gender rights litigation seems to be progressing with increasing recognition of membership in the "new" gender category, but only for those transgender people who have undergone medical intervention. The vast majority of gender-transgressive people who will either not want or not be able to afford such intervention remain unprotected. . . .

On a broader level, though, the distribution of resources (services, policy and legislative advocacy, direct representation) is something that our movements can be more responsible about than they have been. Transgender and gender-transgressive movements are at a moment of building and expansion, and in some senses institutionalization. We are increasingly forming organizations, we are seeking funding, and we are forming a growing national and international conversation seeking an end to the inequality and oppression we have struggled against. It is in this moment that it is most urgent for us to examine where our resources have been going, and what unintentional consequences may result from

following the model of the lesbian and gay rights movement. Inevitably, given the context of capitalism in which transliberation activism occurs, and the economic/educational privilege that usually accompanies the ability to secure paid "movement leader" jobs in nonprofits and to raise money to start and maintain movement organizations, the voices of low-income people and people of color will remain underincluded without a serious commitment to intervention.[35] . . .

[. . .]

The notion that we should put our movement resources into a struggle for gender identity nondiscrimination in employment, but not concern ourselves with the fact that there is no one to represent struggling gender-transgressive people being harassed on workfare jobsites or raped in prisons or falsely arrested for prostitution, indicates a problem in terms of the depth and breadth of liberation we are seeking. LGBT movement activists have the power to determine whether the liberation we pursue will follow a tolerance model, making room for those who can access private employment and housing to not experience discrimination there because of their gender identities (and possibly conditioned on medical intervention), or we can quest for a broader liberation that demands gender self-determination for all people regardless of their positions in capitalist economies. To make the latter real, we need to strategize beyond a notion that if we win rights for the most sympathetic and normal of our lot first, the others will be protected in time. Instead, we should be concerned that the breadth of our vision will determine the victories we obtain. If we want to end oppression on the basis of gender identity and expression for all people, we need to examine how the rigid regulation of binary gender is a core element of participation in our capitalist economy, how the hyperregulation of poor peoples' gender and sexuality has propped up that system, and how this has resulted in disproportionate poverty and incarceration for poor, gender-transgressive people. Starting from that analysis, we can undertake strategies to combat these problems and make sure that our activism does not further entrench this regulation by relying on pathologization and medicalization to articulate gender rights.

[. . .]

Many people generously provided editorial advice for this chapter. Thanks to Craig Willse, Paisley Currah, Danny McGee, Franklin Romeo, Jenny Robertson, Bridge Joyce, and Richard M. Juang for their help. The asterisks that appear with page numbers in these notes refer to screen page numbers from a database.

NOTES

1. Frances Fox Piven and Richard Clower, *Regulating the Poor* (New York: Vintage, 1993).
2. Ibid.
3. Janice Raymond, *The Transsexual Empire* (New York: Teachers College Press, 1994); Dwight B. Billings and Thomas Urban, "The Socio-Medical Construction of Transsexualism: An Interpretation and Critique," *Social Problems* 29 (1982): 266, 276. Billings and Urban are engaged in an anticapitalist critique of the gender-regulating process of sex reassignment therapy and the adoption of norm-supporting narratives by patients seeking medical interventions. However, rather than focusing on the problems of a coercive system that demands the performance of rigid gender norms by people seeking body alteration, they vilify transgender people for performing these narratives. The resulting analysis paints trans subjects as clueless gender upholders, who are buying our way out of our gender distress and ruining any radical potential for disrupting gender norms. For more on the strategic uses of medical narratives by trans subjects, and the attribution of oppressive medical understandings of gender to trans people, see Dean Spade, "Mutilating Gender," *makezine* (spring 2002), http://makezine.org/mutilate.html.
4. Theorists and activists who produce intersectional and multi-issue queer and trans analysis and activism continually critique these failures. See, for example, Eli Clare, *Exile and Pride* (Cambridge, MA: South End, 1999); Amber Hollibaugh, "Queers without Money," *Village Voice*, June 2001; Cathy Cohen, "Punks, Bulldaggers, and Welfare Queens: The Radical Potential of Queer Politics?" *GLQ* 3 (1997): 437; Craig Willse and Dean Spade, "Confronting the Limits of Gay Hate Crimes Activism: A Radical Critique," *Chicano-Latino Law Review* 21 (2000): 38–49; Sylvia Rivera, "Queens in Exile, the Forgotten Ones," in *Genderqueer: Voices from Beyond the Binary*, ed. Joan Nestle et al. (New York: Alyson, 2002), 67-85; Richard E. Blum, Barbara Ann Perina, and Joseph Nicholas DeFilippis, "Why Welfare Is a Queer Issue," *NYU Review of Law and Social Change* 26 (2001): 207.
5. According to the National Gay and Lesbian Task Force, 76 percent of the U.S. population lives in jurisdictions that are not covered by antidiscrimination laws that include prohibitions on gender identity discrimination. See L. Mottet, "Populations of Jurisdictions with Explicitly Transgender Anti-Discrimination Laws" (Washington, DC: National Gay and Lesbian Task Force, 2003), http://ngltf.org/downloads/TransIncPops.pdf. Even those who are covered may find these laws ineffectual when they try to enforce their rights before biased judges. See *Goins v. West Group*, 635 N.W.2d 717 (Minn. 2001) (finding that an employer's refusal to allow a transgender employee access to the women's bathroom was not gender identity discrimination); *Hispanic AIDS Forum v. Bruno*, 792 N.Y.S. 2d 43 (2005). Further, even for those who live in jurisdictions where gender identity discrimination is prohibited, seeking redress may be difficult because of a lack of attorneys willing to take cases with transgender plaintiffs and because of the failure of city governments to enforce these provisions. See *Local Laws of the City of New York* 3, 2002, http://www.council.nyc.ny.us/pdf_files/bills/law02003.pdf; Duncan Osborne, "Trans Advocates Allege Foot-Dragging," Gay City News, June 17, 2004; Cyd Zeigler Jr., "Trans Protection Compromised?" *New York Blade*, May 28, 2004.
6. *Doe v. Bell*, 2003 WL 355603 at *1–2 (N.Y. Sup. Ct. 2003) (finding that group home's policy forbidding transgender youth from dressing in skirts and dresses was illegal).
7. L. Mottet and J. Ohle, *Transitioning Our Shelters: A Guide to Making Homeless Shelters Safe for Transgender People* (Washington, DC: National Gay and Lesbian Task Force, 2003). In 2006 transgender advocates succeeded in winning a written policy in the Department of Homeless Service of New York City addressing the rights of

transgender people seeking shelter in the city's facilities. The policy explicitly states that transgender people may not be placed in shelters that do not comport with their self-identified gender and may not be forced to wear clothing associated with their birth gender. Years of advocacy were required to put this policy, which is not yet being enforced as of this writing, in place. A handful of cities in North America, including Boston, San Francisco, and Toronto, have policies addressing the discrimination and exclusion transgender people face in shelter systems. For more information on these policies, see www.srlp.org.

8. *Oiler v. Winn-Dixie Louisiana, Inc.*, 2002 WL 31098541 at *1 (September 16, 2002) (where a grocery store loader and truck driver was fired for cross-dressing off the job).

9. I use the term *gender self-determination* throughout this chapter, and more broadly in my political work, as a tool to express opposition to the coercive mechanisms of the binary gender system (everything from assignment of birth gender to gender segregation of bathrooms to targeting of trans people by police). I use this term strategically while also recognizing that any notion of self-determination is bound up in understandings of individuality that support capitalist concepts like individual freedom to sell labor" that obscure the mechanisms of oppression we are seeking to overcome. While I want to think past and reconceptualize articulations of individuality and replace them with understandings of community-centered change, mobilizing around ending coercive gender within a political framework where we still experience ourselves through heavily entrenched concepts of individuality and freedom requires strategic employment of ideas like self-determination.

10. See Cheryl I. Harris, "Whiteness as Property," in *Critical Race Theory Reader*, ed. Kimberlé Crenshaw, Neil Gotanda, Garry Peller, and Kendall Thomas (New York: New Press, 1996), 276–91. Harris traces the racial origins of property ownership, both in terms of how race has defined, property status with one's ability to own property or to be property of another determined by race—and in terms of how racial identity itself has been attributed a property status through libel and slander laws. She argues that racial identity still has property value recognized and protected by American law. Gender and sexual orientation have also, at times, had property status protected in various ways in the law. In the case of gender, clearly the right to own property has at times been a gender-based right, and, additionally, we see value being assigned to sexuality in tort claims of Loss of Consortium, typically

brought by spouses claiming that they have been damaged by the loss of sexual service from their spouses because of whatever tort was committed. Additionally, defamation cases regarding false accusations of homosexuality similarly indicate a legal protection of heterosexual identity. See E. Yatar, "Defamation, Privacy, and the Changing Social Status of Homosexuality: Re-Thinking Supreme Court Gay Rights Jurisprudence," *Law and Sexuality* 12 (2003): 119–56.

11. The court decisions establishing protection for women laborers are based on this protectionist logic: "It is manifest that this established principle is peculiarly applicable in relation to the employment of women in whose protection the state has a special interest. That phase of the subject received elaborate consideration in *Muller v. Oregon* (1908) 208 U.S. 412, 28 S.Ct. 324, 326, 52 L.Ed. 551, 13 Ann.Cas. 957, where the constitutional authority of the state to limit the working hours of women was sustained. We emphasized the consideration that 'woman's physical structure and the performance of maternal functions place her at a disadvantage in the struggle for subsistence' and that her physical well-being 'becomes an object of public interest and care in order to preserve the strength and vigor of the race.' We emphasized the need of protecting women against oppression despite her possession of contractual rights. We said that 'though limitations upon personal and contractual rights may be removed by legislation, there is that in her disposition and habits of life which will operate against a full assertion of those rights. She will still be where some legislation to protect her seems necessary to secure a real equality of right.' Hence she was properly placed in a class by herself, and legislation designed for her protection may be sustained, even when like legislation is not necessary for men, and could not be sustained'" (*West Coast Hotel v. Parrish*, 57 S.Ct. 578, at 583 [upholding Washington State's minimum wage law for women]).

12. Gwendolyn Mink, "The Lady and the Tramp: Gender, Race, and the Origins of the American Welfare State," in *Women, the State, and Welfare*, ed. Linda Gordon (Madison: University of Wisconsin Press, 1990), 92–122.

13. See J. Heinz and N. Folbre, *The Ultimate Field Guide to the U.S. Economy: A Compact and Irreverent Guide to Economic Life in America* (New York: New Press, 2000).

14. Holloway Sparks, "Queens, Teens, and Model Mothers: Race, Gender, and the Discourse of Welfare Reform," in *Race and the Politics of Welfare Reform*, ed. Sanford F. Schram, Joe Soss, and Richard C. Fording (Ann Arbor: University of Michigan Press, 2003), 188–89.

15. See Susan James and Beth Harris, "Gimme Shelter: Battering and Poverty," in *For Crying Out Loud: Women's*

Poverty in the United States, ed. Diane Dujon and Ann Withorn (Boston: South End, 1996), 57–66.

16. Sparks, "Queens, Teens, and Model Mothers," 171. Then senator John Ashcroft utilized the contractual view of citizenship described by Sparks during one of the final debates on welfare reform in the 104th Congress: "I think it is time for us to limit the amount of time that people can be on welfare. It is time for us to provide disincentives to bear children out of wedlock. It is time for us to provide powerful incentives for people to go to work. It is time for us to say that, if you are on welfare, you should be off drugs. It is time for us to say that, if you are on welfare, your children should be in school . . . You have to be responsible for what you are doing. We are not going to continue to support you in a way in which you abdicate, you simply run from, you hide from, your responsibility as a citizen" (quoted in Sparks, "Queens, Teens, and Model Mothers," 190).

17. Sparks, "Queens, Teens, and Model Mothers," 189.

18. See Blum, Perina, and DeFilippis, "Why Welfare Is a Queer Issue," 207.

19. Current Republican proposals for the reauthorization include an increase in work requirements to forty hours a week and $200 million in federal grants plus $100 million in state matching grants for marriage promotion programs. See Jonathan Riskind, "House Set to Revisit Welfare Reform This Week: Legislators to Vote on Bill Very Similar to One Passed in May," *Columbus Dispatch*, February 12, 2003. See also Sharon Tubbs and Thomas C. Tobin, "When Government Wants Marriage Reform," *St. Petersburg Times*, February 8, 2003; Sharon Lerner, "Marriage on the Mind: The Bush Administration's Misguided Poverty Cure," *The Nation*, July 5, 2004.

20. See Roofless Women's Action Research Mobilization, "A Hole in My Soul: Experiences of Homeless Women," ed. Marie Kennedy, in Dujon and Withorn, *For Crying Out Loud*, 41–56.

21. I recently participated in a bar association panel about queer and trans youth in juvenile justice and foster care at which a youth service provider smilingly described continued efforts to not let the transgender youth leave the residence she supervised looking like "hos." Her determination that an aspect of receiving housing at her facility should include compliance with particular expressions of femininity, and her use of a racialized term to indicate the prohibited expression, exemplifies the type of race/gender expression management that typically becomes the concern of poverty service providers measuring compliance.

22. Intersex people are people who have physical conditions that make their bodies difficult to classify under current medical understandings of what constitutes a "male"

or "female" body. Intersex activists are working to stop the infant and childhood surgeries that intersex people are frequently subjected to as doctors attempt to bring their bodies into line with medical expectations of what a male or female body should look like. For more information on intersex conditions and intersex activism, see the Web site of the Intersex Society of North America, www.isna.org.

23. Blum, Perina, and DeFilippis, "Why Welfare Is a Queer Issue," 213.

24. See Remembering Our Dead, http://www.rememberingourdead.org.

25. A common response to questions about the wisdom of sex segregation in jails, prisons, shelters, and other contexts is a concern for women's safety and a suggestion that sex segregation exists to prevent violence against women. While women's safety should be of paramount concern to service providers and corrections staff, there is not sufficient evidence that sex segregation policies are motivated by concern for women's safety or that women are safe in these institutions. In fact, systemic sexual assault and violence against women are more often than not a fundamental part of the coercive control exercised over poor women in these institutions. Examining the violence against women and gender-transgressive people in these settings should be a project that advocates for women's safety are deeply engaged in with advocates for gender self-determination, as these two populations are frequently targets for related violence. The first step may be to acknowledge that control of low-income people, not safety, is the aim of these institutions. See R. Ralph, "Nowhere to Hide: Retaliation against Women in Michigan State Prisons," *Human Rights Watch* 10 (1998), http://hrw.org/reports98/women/.

26. See *Ala. Code* § 22–9A-19 (2002) (order of court of competent jurisdiction and surgery required); *Artz. Rev. Stat.* § 36–326 (2001) (change may be made based on sworn statement from licensed physician attesting to either surgical operation or chromosomal count, although registrar may require further evidence); *Ark. Code Ann.* § 20–18–307 (2002) (order of court of competent jurisdiction and surgery required); *Cal. Health & Safety Code* § 103425, 103430 (2002 Supp.) (court order and surgery apparently required); *Colo. Rev. Stat. Ann.* § 25–2–115 (2002) (same); *D.C. Code Ann.* § 7–217 (2002) (same); *Ga. Code Ann.* § 31–10–23 (2002) (same); *Haw. Rev. Stat.* § 338–17.7 (2002) (physician affidavit and surgery required; registrar can require additional information); 410 Ill. Comp. Stat. 535/17 (2002) (same); *Iowa Code* § 144.23 (2002) (physician affidavit and surgery "or other treatment"); *La. Rev. Stat. Ann.*

§ 40: 62 (2002) (order of court of competent jurisdiction and surgery required); *Mass. Ann. Laws chap.* 46, § 13 (2002) (same); *Mich. Comp. Laws* § 333.2831 (2002) (affidavit of physician certifying sex reassignment surgery); *Miss. Code Ann.* § 41-57-21 (2001) (registrar may correct certificate that contains incorrect sex on affidavit of two persons having personal knowledge of facts; not clear whether restricted to initial error in certificate or includes gender change); *Mo. Rev. Stat* § 193.215 (2001) (order of court of competent jurisdiction and surgery required); *Neb. Rev. Stat.* § 71–604.1 (2002) (affidavit of physician as to sex reassignment surgery and order of court of competent jurisdiction changing name required); N.J. Stat. Ann. 26:8–40.12 (2002) (certificate from physician attesting to surgery and order of court of competent jurisdiction changing name); *N.M. Stat. Ann.* § 24–14–25 (2002) (same); N.C. Gen. Stat. 130A-118 (2001) (affidavit of physician attesting to sex reassignment surgery); *Or. Rev. Stat.* § 432.235 (2001) (order of court of competent jurisdiction and surgery required); *Utah Code Ann.* § 26–2–11 (2002) (order of Utah District Court or court of competent jurisdiction of another state required; no specific requirement of surgery); *Va. Code Ann.* § 32.1-269 (2002) (order of court of competent jurisdiction indicating sex has been changed by "medical procedure"); *Wis. Stat.* § 69.15 (2001) (order of court or administrative order) cited in Matter of Heilig, 2003 WL 282856 at *15 n.8 (Md. 2003). See also. Lambda Legal Defense and Education Fund, Resources: Transgender Issues, http://www.lambdalegal.org/cgi-bin/iowa/documents/record?record=1162 (November 12, 2002) (accessed March 30, 2003).

27. Dean Spade, "Resisting Medicine, Re/modeling Gender," *Berkeley Women's Law Journal* 18 (2003): 16–26.

28. *In re Estate of Gardiner*, 42 P.3d 120 (Kan. 2002); *Kantaras v. Kantaras*, Case No. 98–5375CA (Circuit Court of the Sixth Judicial Circuit, Pasco County, Florida, February 19, 2003).

29. See, for example, *In re Rivera*, 165 Misc.2d 307, 627 N.Y.S,2d 241 (Civ. Ct. Bx. Co. 1995); *Application of Anonymous*, 155 Misc.2d 241, 587 N.Y.S.2d 548 (N.Y.City Civ.Ct, August 27, 1992); *Matter of Anonymous*, 153 Misc.2d 893, 582 N.Y.S.2d 941 (N.Y.City Civ.Ct., March 27, 1992); but see, *In re Guido*, 2003 WL 22471153, 2003 NY. Slip Op. 23821 (NY. Civ.Ct, October 24, 2003).

30. See Jody Marksamer and Dylan Vade, "Gender Neutral Bathroom Survey," http://www.transgenderlaw-center.org/documents/safe_WC_survey_results.html (2001) (accessed March 30, 2003). See Dean Spade, "2 Legit 2 Quit, Piss & Vinegar," http://www.makezine.org/2legit.html (accessed March 14, 2003).

31. See Spade, "Resisting Medicine," 16–26, for a broader discussion of the gender regulation accomplished by medical approaches to gender role distress.

32. Most states in the United States still explicitly exclude "sex reassignment related care" from Medicaid coverage, and most medical insurance companies still exclude this care from coverage. See *Smith v. Rasmussen*, 249 F.3d 755 (8th Cir. 2001) (reversing district court's ruling and holding that Iowa's rule denying coverage for SRS was not arbitrary or inconsistent with the Medicaid Act); *Rush v. Parham*, 625 F.2d 1150 (5th Cir. 1980) (reversing district court's ruling that Georgia's Medicaid program could not categorically deny coverage for SRS); 18 NYCRR § 505.2(1). See N.Y. St. Reg. (March 25, 1998) at 5; Ill. Admin. Code tit. 89 at 140.6(1); 55 Pa. Code at 1163.59(a)(1); Alaska Admin. Code tit 7, at 43.385(a)(1); Medicare Program: National Coverage Decisions, 54 Fed. Reg. 34555, 34572 (August 21, 1989); 32 C.F.R. at 199.4(e)(7) (excluding sex reassignment surgeries from the Civilian Health and Medical Program of the Uniformed Services); but see *J.D. v. Lackner*, 80 Cal. App. 3d 90 (Cal. Ct. App. 1978).

33. See L. Mottet, *Partial Equality* (Washington, DC: National Gay and Lesbian Task Force, 2003), http://www.ngltf.org/library/partialeq.htm.

34. H. Humm, "Unity Eludes SONDA Advocates, Gender Identity Divides Duane, Pride Agenda," *Gay City News*, December 13, 2002, http://www.gaycitynews.com/gcn29/unity.html; K. Krawchuk, "SONDA Bill Heads to Senate," *Capital News* 9 (Albany, NY), 2002, http://www.capitalnews9.com/content/headlines/?SecID=33&ArID=7580.

35. Significant inequalities in access to education persist. In 1997 less than 75 percent of African Americans and less than 55 percent of Latinos had completed four years of high school, and less than 14 percent of either group had completed four years of college. Cuts in financial aid for college students have reinforced a decline in the percentage of low-income high school graduates going to college (Heinz and Folbre, *Ultimate Field Guide to the U.S. Economy*, 74). Further, the end of affirmative action policies in higher education and new rules making people with drug convictions ineligible for federal financial aid have reduced access to higher education for poor communities and communities that are overexposed to police enforcement.

39. • *Catherine Rottenberg*

THE RISE OF NEOLIBERAL FEMINISM (2014)

Catherine Rottenberg is an associate professor of American and Canadian Studies at the University of Nottingham (UK). She has particular research interests in comparative African American and Jewish American literary studies and postfeminism neoliberal, and popular feminism. Rottenberg has published numerous articles and chapters in edited collections. The article selected for this anthology originally appeared in *The Journal of Cultural Studies* (2014).

A new trend is on the rise: increasingly, high-powered women are publicly and unabashedly espousing feminism. One has only to think of Anne-Marie Slaughter's "Why Women Still Can't Have It All," a piece that appeared in *The Atlantic* in July 2012 and quickly became the most widely read article in the magazine's history.[1] Then, in March 2013, Sheryl Sandberg's *Lean In* hit the shelves and instantly became a *New York Times'* best-seller.[2] These self-declared feminist manifestos, the first written by a former State Department Director of Policy Planning and Princeton professor and the other by the Chief Operating Officer at Facebook, are being read in such large numbers—and generating so much discussion and media attention—that commentators have begun comparing Sandberg to Betty Friedan and Slaughter, by association, to Gloria Steinem.[3] They have announced that the Sandberg–Slaughter disagreement about the best way to facilitate women's ability to balance work and family is "the most notable feminist row since Ms. Friedan refused to shake Gloria Steinem's hand decades ago."[4] In an era often described as post-feminist (McRobbie 2009), it appears that feminism is currently being revived in the US public domain.

In the wake of *Lean In*'s publication and the ensuing media blitz, there has also been a flurry of criticism in various popular venues, ranging from the

New York Times to *Al-Jazeera*.[5] Critics, particularly radical and socialist feminists, have acknowledged that voices like Sandberg's have helped to reinvigorate a public discussion about continued gender inequality in the USA, but they have also underscored that this emergent feminism is predicated on the erasure of the issues that concern the overwhelming majority of women in the USA and across the globe.[6] In addition, there have been debates about the increasing compatibility of mainstream feminism with the market values of neoliberalism (e.g. Eisenstein 2009, Fraser 2013). What does it mean, many longtime feminists are asking, that a movement once dedicated, however problematically, to women's liberation is now being framed in extremely individualistic terms, consequently ceasing to raise the spectre of social or collective justice? Building on this question, my concern revolves around a related but slightly different conundrum: namely, why is there any need for a feminism informed by the norms of neoliberalism?

I suggest that Sandberg's feminist manifesto can be seen as symptomatic of a larger cultural phenomenon in which neoliberal feminism is fast displacing liberal feminism. By examining in some detail the language and shifting discursive registers in the extraordinarily successful *Lean In* we can, I propose, gain insight into an on-going cultural process in which mainstream liberal feminism is being disarticulated and transmuted into a particular mode of neoliberal governmentality (Larner 2000, Brown 2005). Unlike classic liberal feminism whose *raison d'être* was to pose an immanent critique of liberalism, revealing the gendered exclusions within liberal democracy's proclamation of universal equality, particularly with respect to the law, institutional access, and the full incorporation of women into the public sphere, this new feminism seems perfectly in sync with the evolving neoliberal order. Neoliberal feminism, in other words, offers no critique—immanent or otherwise—of neoliberalism. More specifically, *Lean In* reveals the ways in which the husk of liberalism is being mobilized to spawn a neoliberal feminism, as well as a new feminist (and not simply a female) subject. Individuated in the extreme, this subject is feminist in the sense that she is distinctly aware of current inequalities between men and women. This same subject is, however, simultaneously neoliberal, not only because she disavows the social, cultural and economic forces producing this inequality, but also because she accepts full responsibility for her own well-being and self-care, which is increasingly predicated on crafting a felicitous work–family balance based on a cost-benefit calculus. The neoliberal feminist subject is thus mobilized to convert continued gender inequality from a structural problem into an individual affair.

In what follows, I briefly define neoliberal governmentality and its specific mode of governance, while arguing that a new form of feminism is coalescing. I then proceed by demonstrating how *Lean In* utilizes terms borrowed from liberal feminism, but effectively calls into being a new neoliberal feminist subject, one that is distinct from her liberal feminist counterpart. Focusing on three of Sandberg's central phrases—(1) internalizing the revolution; (2) lean in; and (3) the leadership ambition gap—I show how they are all informed by a market rationality. Finally, I pose the question of why neoliberalism has spawned a feminist rather than simply a female subject at all. While this emerging form of feminism can certainly be understood as yet another domain

neoliberalism has colonized by producing its own variant, I suggest that it simultaneously serves a particular cultural purpose: it hollows out the potential of mainstream liberal feminism to underscore the constitutive contradictions of liberal democracy, and in this way further entrenches neoliberal rationality and an imperialist logic. Each woman's success becomes a feminist success, which is then attributed to the USA's enlightened political order, as well as to its moral and political superiority.

NEOLIBERAL RATIONALITY

In her germinal article, "Neoliberalism and the End of Liberal Democracy," Wendy Brown argues that it is critical to understand the current US political landscape as one in which neoliberal rationality has become the dominant mode of governance. This mode of governance is neither limited to the economic sphere nor to state policies but rather "produces subjects, forms of citizenship and behavior, and a new organization of the social" (Brown 2005, p. 37). Consequently, neoliberalism is never simply about a set of economic policies or an economic system that facilitates intensified privatization, deregulation, and corporate profits, but rather is itself a modality of governmentality in the Foucauldian sense of regulating the "conduct of conduct" (Foucault et al. 1991, Lemke 2002, Brown 2005). Neoliberalism, in other words, is a dominant political rationality that moves to and from the management of the state to the inner workings of the subject, normatively constructing and interpellating individuals as entrepreneurial actors. New political subjectivities and social identities subsequently emerge. One of the hallmarks of our neoliberal age, Brown proposes, is precisely the casting of every human endeavor and activity in entrepreneurial terms (p. 40).

Drawing on Brown as well as the work of Nikolas Rose (1993) and other contemporary theorists of governmentality (e.g. Barry et al. 1996), Wendy Larner (2000) has similarly argued that neoliberalism is both a political discourse about the nature of rule and a set of practices that facilitate the governing of individuals. This form of governance transforms the logic by which institutions such as schools, workplaces, health and welfare agencies operate, while creating a new form of selfhood, which "encourages people to see themselves as individualized and active subjects responsible for enhancing their own well-being" (Larner 2000, p. 13). Collective forms of action or well-being are eroded, and a new regime of morality comes into being, one that links moral probity even more intimately to self-reliance and efficiency, as well as to the individual's capacity to exercise his or her own autonomous choices. Most disturbing for Larner, however, is the way neoliberal governmentality undoes notions of social justice, while usurping the concept of citizenship by producing economic identities as the basis for political life.

More recently, the prominent feminist theorist Nancy Fraser (2013) has decried the growing complicity of certain dominant stands of feminism with neoliberal capitalism. In her provocative article, "Feminism, Capitalism, and the Cunning of History," Fraser claims that second-wave feminism's ultimate privileging of recognition (i.e. identity claims) over redistribution (i.e. economic justice) is responsible for the convergence of contemporary feminism with neoliberal capitalism. The foregoing of economic analyses, particularly by poststructuralist feminists, in other words, has led, disastrously, to strengthening the spirit of the neoliberal stage of capitalism. The current merging of feminism with neoliberalism is consequently understood as the legacy of second-wave feminism's myopic refusal to sustain a materialist critique.[7] While I do not agree with Fraser's ascription of culpability, I do believe that her article is a key intervention in the discussion, since it underscores the emergence of a contemporary mode of feminism profoundly informed by a market rationality.

However, the question of why neoliberalism has any need of feminism at all still remains. The emergence of neoliberal feminism during this particular historical juncture serves specific objectives, as I will argue, but to place the blame on the shoulders of second-wave feminism is, as Ozlem Aslan and Zeynep Gambetti have convincingly argued, to "misrepresent the 'cunning of history,'" while

subscribing to a causal view of the past that "constructs unitary subjects" (p. 145). My claim, therefore, is that the contemporary convergence between neoliberalism and feminism involves the production of a new kind of feminism that is eviscerating classic, mainstream liberal feminism.[8] This neoliberal feminism, in turn, is helping to produce a particular kind of feminist subject. Using key liberal terms, such as equality, opportunity, and free choice, while displacing and replacing their content, this recuperated feminism forges a feminist subject who is not only individualized but entrepreneurial in the sense that she is oriented towards optimizing her resources through incessant calculation, personal initiative and innovation. Indeed, creative individual solutions are presented as feminist and progressive, while calibrating a felicitous work–family balance becomes her main task. Inequality between men and women is thus paradoxically acknowledged only to be disavowed, and the question of social justice is recast in personal, individualized terms.

THE LIBERAL HUSK OF *LEAN IN*

Lean In is a site in which we can very clearly discern the processes by and through which liberal feminism is disarticulated, and the neoliberal feminist subject is born. The book is a mixture of personal anecdotes, motivational language, and journalism—all of which is larded with "hard facts" and statistics. It is a quick read, and Sandberg is careful to introduce pithy and catchy phrases as a way of attracting as wide an audience as possible. Moreover, she self-consciously details how she would like her text to be read: *Lean In* should not be understood as a memoir, self-help book or a career management guide, but rather draws on these genres in order to engender a "feminist manifesto," one dedicated to convincing women to pursue their goals vigorously (Sandberg 2013, pp. 9–10). The book is motivated by a desire to revive a feminist discussion and make good on the promise of "true equality"—one of the central cornerstones of liberal democracy. Liberal feminism accordingly appears to serve as the text's scaffolding.

In the very first pages of *Lean In*, Sandberg majestically announces that women in the USA and the developed world are better off today than they have ever been in the entire history of humankind: "We stand on the shoulders of the women who came before us, women who had to fight for the rights we now take for granted" (p. 4). She also insists that women in the West should be grateful because they are centuries ahead of the unacceptable treatment of women in places like Afghanistan and Sudan. It is only by sheer luck that some women are born into families in the USA rather than "one of the many places in the world where women are denied basic rights" (Sandberg 2013, p. 38).

The discussion is thus immediately framed within a progressive trajectory and a well-worn binary that positions the liberated West in opposition to the subjugated rest. The USA and western democracies are presented as the pinnacles of civilization, which have been moving towards the key goal of true equality between men and women. "Gender equality," in turn, becomes the benchmark for civilization, as Sara Farris has recently underscored, while liberal principles are set up as the unassailable standards of the good (Farris 2012). At first glance, this framing seems to deflect the question of continued inequality at home by projecting true oppression elsewhere, and it is no coincidence that Sandberg mentions by name countries that have been represented endlessly in Western media as torn apart by Islamic extremism. This, as Ann Norton has persuasively argued, is part of an Islamophobic discourse that endlessly depicts the Muslim world as particularly hostile to women, which then serves to shore up US national sentiment and nation building (p. 67).

But *Lean In* does not ultimately use this anti-Islam trope to turn the "gaze of feminists and other potential critics away from the continuing oppression of women in the West" (Norton 2013, p. 67). Instead, Sandberg turns a critical eye on the USA itself, declaring that despite tremendous progress there is still work to be done, particularly when it comes to women occupying positions of power and leadership. In government, in industry, and in corporations, she tells us, women are still lagging behind

in terms of representation at the top. Gender inequality is thus associated with a dearth of women in the higher echelons of powerful institutions. On the one hand, then, Sandberg conceives of liberalism and the liberal feminist struggle as responsible for producing the contemporary cultural landscape, which is one of historic opportunities for women in the West in general and in the USA more specifically. On the other hand, she proceeds to map out what needs to be done in order to move beyond the current impasse and finally fulfill the promises of the women's movement as well as of liberal democracy itself.

It is also in these first few pages that Sandberg sets up her own progressive liberal credentials by summoning the notion of equality and underscoring just how central a principle it is. Lamenting the fact that the feminist revolution of the 1970s has stalled, she proclaims that "the promise of equality is not the same as true equality" (p. 7). This and other statements, interspersed in the text, make it clear that Sandberg is attempting to situate herself within a longer liberal feminist tradition; her objective, she repeatedly states, is to move towards a more equal world. In addition, throughout the book she alludes to other key liberal political principles, such as fair treatment and equal opportunity. And while the text's language is not always coherent or consistent, the emphasis is certainly on creating conditions that would allow women to make freer choices about work and family. Sandberg even gestures towards the structural inequalities that still exist in the USA. She tells her reader that she is aware that institutional barriers remain and admits that there is a need to eliminate them. But these remarks are limited and made in passing, while the vast majority of the book focuses on what are considered the more substantial barriers to women's success: the internal ones.

Before turning to an examination of the book's key terms, it is important to note that the "lean in" language and framework are reminiscent, in many ways, of other now classic feminist texts geared to "popular culture and media exposure" (Stansell 2010, p. 206), such as *The Feminine Mystique* and *The Beauty Myth*. All of these books—Sandberg's included—attempt to identify the source of a recurrent (liberal) paradox: Given that women's opportunities and progress are no longer obstructed by discriminatory laws and exclusionary institutions, what are the causes of (white middle-class) women's continued inequality in the USA? If Betty Friedan's objective was to uncover the powerful cultural norms and pressures of femininity, namely, the feminine mystique, which kept white middle-class women in the domestic sphere in the post-Second World War era, Naomi Woolf's aim was to expose the way in which contemporary ideals of female beauty—endlessly produced in the mass media—helped to create an atmosphere of self-loathing and psychological warfare among a new generation of middle-class women who had grown up in the wake of the women's movement and who were entering the public sphere in record numbers. Sandberg, too, is addressing a similar question (and a similarly privileged white [upper] middle-class audience), and like Friedan, she is ultimately interested in encouraging women to pursue professional careers.[9] Yet, in contrast to both Friedan and Wolf, *Lean In*'s focus is decidedly not on confronting or changing social pressures, but rather on what "women can change themselves," their "internal obstacles" (Sandberg 2013, p. 10). The shift in emphasis: from an attempt to alter social pressures towards interiorized affective spaces that require constant self-monitoring is precisely the node through which liberal feminism is rendered hollow and transmuted into a mode of neoliberal governmentality.

The demand for self-realization and self-transformation is, of course, nothing new in the USA. It was as Christine Stansell (2010) has so meticulously documented, a central part of the women's movement in the 1970s and has a much longer history in US culture: from the American Dream discourse and the Horatio Alger myth, through New Age cults and contemporary meditation and yoga trends. Indeed, Sandberg draws on a wide variety of recognizably American discourses, such as American exceptionalism, as well as the highly profitable how-to-succeed literary genre, some of which she explicitly acknowledges and some of which serve as the implicit palimpsest for her brand of feminism. Anne Applebaum (2013) describes *Lean In* as the "first truly successful,

best-selling 'how to succeed in business' motivational book to be explicitly designed and marketed to women." Yet, despite the hype surrounding its publication, there is nothing particularly new about Sandberg's book, Applebaum claims, except the fact of its female authorship and its target audience.

While Applebaum's critique is timely in that it highlights the specifically entrepreneurial aspect of *Lean In*, this kind of criticism ultimately fails to underscore what is indeed new in feminist manifestos like Sandberg's. If we understand *Lean In* as a significant intervention in the feminist discussion, which I believe we must, then the book can be read as marking (and marketing) a change in current articulations of mainstream liberal feminism and as participating in the production of a new feminist subject. This subject willingly and forcibly acknowledges continued gender inequality but, as I show, her feminism is so individuated that it has been completely unmoored from any notion of social inequality and consequently cannot offer any sustained analytic of the structures of male dominance, power, or privilege. In this emergent feminism, then, there is a liberal wrapping, while the content—namely, its mode of operation—is neoliberal through and through.

TIPPING THE SCALES: METAMORPHOSING LIBERALISM INTO NEOLIBERALISM

True to its title, *Lean In* is primarily concerned with encouraging women to "lean in" to their careers. The book lays out various strategies for facilitating women's ability to foster their professional ambition. In the process, Sandberg coins three phrases, which play a central role in *Lean In* and which have, since the book's publication, begun to circulate in the public domain and the mass media: internalizing the revolution, lean in, and the leadership ambition gap. Before turning to explore how they operate together to produce a specific kind of feminist consciousness, I briefly lay out the book's rationale for introducing these particular terms.

According to Sandberg's logic, the first and fundamental step in reorienting women towards a successful career is "internalizing the revolution." This presumably involves accepting (by making personal) the need to keep moving towards true equality between men and women (signifying, in this context, equal representation in powerful institutions). By coming to terms with and working through their internal obstacles, women will then be able to muster the self-confidence necessary to push themselves forward towards their professional goals. The text suggests that it is incumbent on women to create effective ways of overcoming their fears—of being too outspoken, aggressive, or more powerful than men. Getting rid of these internal impediments is crucial for expediting women's ability to lean into their careers, which becomes the second crucial stage in reorienting their priorities. Women, in Sandberg's words, too often "hold ourselves back in ways both big and small, by lacking self-confidence, by not raising our hands, and by pulling back when we should be leaning in" (p. 8). Only when women finally internalize the revolution, triumph over their internal obstacles and actively lean in to their careers will they be poised to accomplish one of *Lean In*'s key feminist objectives: closing the "leadership ambition gap." Eliminating this gap constitutes the final stage in the reorientation process. Indeed, the surest way to reach the still elusive goal of gender equality is by encouraging more women to move up the professional ladder and into leadership positions. Sandberg maintains that as more and more "women begin entering into high-level positions, giving strong and powerful voice to their needs and concerns, conditions for all women will improve" (p. 7).

This amorphous "ambition gap" very quickly comes to stand in for inequality, radically reducing inequality to the absence of women in positions at the top. Consequently, other classic liberal feminist goals, such as fair treatment, equal institutional access, and women's full integration into the public sphere, are expediently elided, while climbing the power hierarchy ultimately becomes the feminist objective. Through the book's shifting discursive registers, *Lean In*—using a liberal frame while performatively undoing that very same frame—thus demonstrates very clearly how neoliberal feminism takes shape under the legitimating cloth of liberal feminist discourse.

Premising her manifesto on the conviction that gender inequality still exists in the USA, Sandberg patriotically invokes the liberal notions of equality, equal opportunity, and free choice in order to reinvigorate a public feminist discussion. Yet, when examined more closely, the three central phrases she invents overrun and then evacuate her liberal framework, effectively replacing it with a different rationality. "Internalizing the revolution," "lean in" and closing the "ambition gap" operate together in the text in order to call into being a subject who is compelled and encouraged to conform to the norms of the market while assuming responsibility for her own well-being. Moreover, "true equality" is predicated upon individuals moving up the professional ladder, one woman at a time.

The notions of internalizing the revolution and lean in, first and foremost, conjure up a discrete and isolated feminist consciousness. The call to internalize revolution is particularly disconcerting as it assumes that the revolution has in some sense already taken place, and therefore all women need to do is to rouse themselves by absorbing and acting on this reality. Moreover, it not only neutralizes the radical idea of collective uprising by atomizing the revolutionary agents and transferring the site of activity from the public arena to each individual's psyche, but also conceptualizes change as an internal, solipsistic and affective matter. There is no orientation beyond the self, which makes this form of feminism distinct. Revolution, in other words, is transformed from mass mobilization into an interiorized and individual activity, thereby stripping it of any potential political valence in the Arendtian sense of "acting in concert" (Gordon 2002). This turn inward helps to produce an individuated feminist agent who, alone, is accountable for garnering her own "revolutionary" energy. That energy, of course, is not being steered towards the toppling of any political order or even about coming to an awareness of systemic male domination, as was the goal of even liberal feminism in the 1970s, but rather such energy is transmogrified into ambition and metamorphosized into the nurturing of each individual woman's desire to reach the top of the power pyramid. The exhortation to lean in to their careers thus effectively reorients women away from conceptions of solidarity and towards their own particular development, which, to stay on "track" as it were, requires constant self-monitoring.

Angela McRobbie (2013) has argued in a slightly different context that the lean in groups that Sandberg has managed to create—by sheer force of will—are ghostly resurrections of the consciousness-raising groups of the 1970s. Rather than serving as a vehicle for raising women's awareness of sexual politics or the ramifications of male dominance and sexism in women's everyday lives, these lean in groups are geared to encourage women to help "play the corporate game more deftly" (McRobbie 2013, p. 24). The very conception of encouraging women in these groups to "lean in" to their individual careers is antithetical to working together towards any common goal. What is reinforced and (re)produced in these groups, then, is precisely the entrepreneurial subject who is encouraged to take her own personal initiative in order to improve her career prospects, particularly in the corporate world.

The last chapter of *Lean In* is entitled "Working Together Toward Equality." The trajectory of this final chapter parallels the process of liberal feminism's disarticulation in the book more generally: initially summoning the hallowed and today uncontroversial liberal political principle of formal equality, Sandberg very quickly moves on to personal anecdotes as well as expressions of concern about the increasing numbers of high potential women who are "off-ramping" the career track, particularly when they have children, concluding with her by now familiar solution to the stalled revolution: more women in positions of power. There is no dwelling on the signification of "true equality" beyond the "trickle down" statement that it will be achieved only when more women "rise to the top of every government and every industry" (Sandberg 2013, p. 159). Indeed, with lightning speed, the text moves from its mention of equality to honing in on encouraging women to "seek challenges and lean in" (Sandberg 2013). The chapter then ends with a passionate exhortation to individual women to strive to reach the highest echelons of their respective organizations. This is a strange concept of working together indeed—even from a liberal feminist perspective—since each woman is urged to set her own goals within her own career path and then reach for them with gusto. Working together this is not—working separately for a similar but separate goal, perhaps.

In these final pages Sandberg ironically converts the notion of "working together" into its polar opposite. Moreover, she confidently assumes that having more women in the leadership position will automatically ensure fairer treatment for all women, because shared experience leads to empathy (p. 171). This is exactly the kind of top-down approach for which many feminists have already harshly criticized Sandberg.[10] Not only is the address directed to a tiny number of women, but her whole agenda operates to inculcate the norms of the market, which divide rather than unify even these extremely privileged women. While this is a key point, my focus here, however, is less on the kinds of exclusions upon which this kind of feminism is predicated—which, again, many critics have rightly been quick to underscore—and more on the hows and whys of its emergence, even though these aspects are, of course, inextricably implicated in one another.

No longer concerned with classic liberal feminist notions, such as "equal moral personhood" or each person "being an end in and of herself," which have a long history in the West and in the USA (Stansell 2010, Abbey 2011), this new feminism inaugurates a subject who is being called upon to "provide for [her] own needs and service [her] own ambitions" (Brown 2006, p. 694). She may conceive of herself as an end, but everyone else becomes mere means. This feminist subject's "moral" probity, moreover, is measured by how well and efficiently she provides for her own self-care, which entails calculation, initiative and innovation. Neoliberal feminism is predominantly concerned with instating a feminist subject who epitomizes "self-responsibility," and who no longer demands anything from the state or the government, or even from men as a group; there is no longer any attempt to confront the tension between liberal individualism, equality, and those social pressures that potentially obstruct the realization of "true" equality. Moreover, as David Eng has cogently pointed out in a different context, this subject is also a post-race one who helps to ensure, yet again, "the forgetting of race" (Eng 2010, p. 4). The creation of the neoliberal feminist subject thus bolsters the assumption that the struggle for racial equality—just like the feminist revolution—has, in some sense, already occurred, been successful and is, consequently, a thing of the past. At most, there is a gesturing towards the importance of professional women speaking up in their respective workplaces so as to make targeted or surgical improvements. There is no mention of collective solutions to historic injustices: indeed, the neoliberal feminist subject is divested of any orientation toward the common good.

HAPPILY EVER AFTER: AFFECT AND THE NEW FEMINIST IDEAL

If, up until now, I have underscored the concern with inspiring women to "dream big" professionally, here it is crucial to underscore that *Lean In*'s emphasis on career development is not intended, by any means, to come at the expense of family life. On the contrary, Sandberg's call on women to lean in to their careers is presented in the text as a reaction to and an attempt to counter a rising and disturbing trend, where "highly trained women are scaling back and dropping out of the workforce in high numbers" when they have children (p. 14). The book, time and again, intimates that once individual women value their own professional development more highly and "lean in" to their careers, they will be better poised to carve out a more effective and felicitous work–family balance. Consequently, the feminist ideal being presented here is emphatically not the one-dimensional or one-track professional woman

who sacrifices family for career, but rather a high-powered woman who manages to balance a spectacularly successful career with a satisfying home life. In this way, neoliberal feminism not only interpellates a subject responsible for her own self-care but this subject is also normalized by this address, called upon to desire both professional success and personal fulfillment, which almost always translates into motherhood. What is reinforced is the message that "progressive" and successful women's well-being can only (or, reading more generously, is most likely) be found by following a particular path: only certain choices can bring women in closer proximity to well-being and true feminist consciousness.

Furthermore, the notion of pursuing happiness is identified with an economic model of sorts in which each woman is asked to calculate the right balance between work and family. The promise of emancipation and happiness this feminism holds out hinges not only on one's active desire to cultivate a profession and on having a spouse and children, but also on one's ability to calibrate a perfect equilibrium between the private and the public spheres. Happiness, therefore, plays a crucial role in this new feminism: it becomes the objective of a particular calculus, functions as a normalizing matrix, and serves to deflect attention away from the process by which neoliberal feminism is rapidly displacing mainstream liberal feminism.

As I have argued elsewhere, advocating a happy work–family balance is one of the ways in which the emergent feminism disavows the gendered contradictions constitutive of the public–private divide within the liberal imagination, while simultaneously providing fertile ground for the expansion of neoliberal rationality.[11] The widespread mobilization and acceptance of terms, such as a happy work–family balance, operate, in other words, to shore up the gendered presuppositions that make the liberal production of space possible—namely, the public–private distinction—while allowing for the continued evisceration of the foundations upon which that spatiality has been built. The task of pursuing happiness consequently not only orients us away from countering the rise of neoliberal feminism, but also from attempting to imagine spatiality and social relations in new ways.

To make good on the new millennium's feminist promise, then, it seems that "progressive" ambitious women are compelled and encouraged to pursue happiness through constructing a self-tailored work–family balance. The turn to a notion of a happy balance, moreover, helps to further convert mainstream liberal feminism from a discourse—even if tangentially—concerned with social pressures to one that produces a subject who is constantly turned inwards, monitoring herself. After all, the goal of crafting and maintaining a felicitous equilibrium—which might entail, for instance, making up lost time with children after investing too many hours at work, or finding creative solutions to unexpected conflicts, such as planning an important conference call after the children's bedtime—is elusive, since well-being is famously difficult to gauge, but, as a consequence of affect's very elusiveness, requires constant calculation and optimizing of personal resources. Thus, the quest for not just a sane equilibrium but a satisfying equilibrium further inscribes an entrepreneurial subject and a market rationality—since in order to be successful and content, even for a period of time, efficiency, innovation and a cost–benefit calculus are paramount.

This new feminist norm appears to have already taken hold in the US cultural imagination. In a July 12, 2013, article in the *New York Times*, for example, Kate Taylor describes a rising phenomenon among middle-class undergraduate women in elite universities. Holding up women like Sandberg, Slaughter and Marissa Mayer as their role models,[12] Taylor describes how potentially high-achieving young women are no longer interested in investing in relationships during their college years—years when they feel they need to be concerned with building their professional résumés. The reasons these university students give for their decision to find "hookup buddies" rather than boyfriends is the "low risk and low investment of hooking up." Their orientation is one thoroughly informed by a cost–benefit metrics. Importantly, however, these women do not reject the family part of the equation. Rather, the women

interviewed by Taylor declared that they would likely defer marriage until their late 20s or early 30s when they felt they had already established themselves professionally. This careful calculation in the present, in other words, will make it possible to craft that elusive work–family balance later on.

Sandberg's "how-to-reinvigorate-feminism" program is not only a *New York Times* best-seller, but her TED talks have attracted millions of viewers. Her message, though—as I have indicated—is not unique. Indeed, the buzz surrounding Sandberg's book occurred in the wake of the media hype surrounding Anne-Marie Slaughter's "Why Women Still Can't Have it All," an essay that immediately went viral and, within a week of its publication, had been accessed by over one million people. These women have clearly tapped into a cultural sore spot, and they are quickly becoming the most visible representatives of mainstream feminism in the USA in the early twenty-first century.

[. . .]

While Sandberg urges women to reaffirm their commitment to work, Slaughter urges women to reaffirm their commitment to family. Yet, the end goal is the same for both women: namely, providing women more latitude so that they can carve out their own felicitous work–family balance. "Why Women Still Can't Have it All" focuses on legitimating women's "natural" commitment towards their children, and, in the article, Slaughter urges high-powered women to speak out about the value of family, exhorting them to demand changes in the norms of their respective workplaces. Yet Slaughter, again like Sandberg, is adamant about encouraging women not to abandon their career aspirations, even when they have children, and her overall objective is precisely to facilitate each woman's ability to continue cultivating their professional ambitions while fulfilling their desire for a satisfying family life. Slaughter does gesture more towards the need for institutional change than Sandberg, yet change is ultimately understood as the consequence of high-powered women taking personal initiative and demanding things like flex time. Moreover, Slaughter calls upon the same elite cadre of highly successful women—thus initiating the identical top-down, elitist and exclusionary approach. The very turn to a language of affect, namely, the importance of the pursuit of personal happiness (through balance), unravels any notion of social inequality by placing the responsibility of well-being, as well as the burden of unhappiness, once again, on the shoulders of individual women.

Even in the heyday of the feminist movement in the early 1970s, the call for self-transformation or self-empowerment was accompanied by some form of critique of systemic male domination and/or structural discrimination. Today, by contrast, the emergent feminism is contracting, shining its spotlight, as well as the onus of responsibility on each female subject while turning that subject even more intensively inward. As a result, neoliberal feminism is—not surprisingly—purging itself of all elements that would orient it outwards, towards the public good. Yet, simply claiming that this discourse is not really feminist or constitutes some sort of backlash against "true" feminism is too easy and, I believe, misguided, both because such a claim assumes that there is one true definition of feminism (and that "we" have or know it), and because it misses the opportunity to understand the kind of cultural work the emergence of neoliberal feminism—which tracts like *Lean In* and "Why Women Still Can't Have It All" reflect and (re)produce—is currently "doing."

✳ ✳ ✳

By way of conclusion, I would like to offer a set of speculations about why we are witnessing the emergence of a neoliberal feminism. To begin with, it is important to ask the question of why neoliberalism acknowledges and revives a discourse about continued gender inequality at all. This in and of itself seems somewhat paradoxical, given neoliberalism's disregard and steady erosion of liberal political principles, such as liberty, formal equality, solidarity and the rule of law. Why, in other words, is there any need for the production of a neoliberal feminism, which draws attention to a specific kind of inequality? Given that neoliberal rationality individuates subjects, eliding structural inequalities

while instating market rationality, why is there any need for a feminist variant when a female (as opposed to a feminist) neoliberal subject might do the job just as well or better?

The rise of neoliberal feminism, I posit, can be traced to multiple sources. One has to do with the ability of neoliberal rationality, as the dominant or hegemonic mode of governance, to colonize more and more domains (Harvey 2005).[13] In the USA, all strands of feminism, even liberal feminism, have always operated, at least in theory, as a critique of the dominant political order. This critique has ranged from an immanent one—embodied in liberal feminism—which endeavored to show up the contradictions between liberal democracy's theoretical commitment to equality and its actual practice of gendered exclusions and discrimination, to a revolutionary one, which insisted on an overhaul of the patriarchal or masculinist foundations of modern society. From this perspective, the production of neoliberal feminism makes cultural sense, since it becomes one more domain that neoliberal governmentality colonizes and remakes in its own image. This is a process, in Stuart Hall's words, that performs the massive work of "transcoding while remaining in sight of the lexicon on which it draws" (2011, p. 711). As more and more white middle-class women enter and remain in the public sphere even after they have children—by choice and increasingly by necessity—this emergent feminist discourse helps to neutralize the potential critique from other strands of feminism. No longer concerned with issues, such as the gendered wage gap, sexual harassment, rape or domestic violence, ambitious individual middle-class women themselves become both the problem and the solution in the neoliberal feminist age. And by tapping into what Sara Ahmed has termed the current "happiness industry" (Ahmed 2010), neoliberal feminism attempts to ensure that the new feminist subject is oriented and orients herself towards the goal of finding her own personal and felicitous work–family balance.

In addition, the public acknowledgement of continued gender inequalities in the USA may actually serve to bolster a waning sense of liberal democracy's perfectibility and even continued feasibility. At a time when the political principles of liberal democracy are being eroded by the norms and practices of the market, the production of neoliberal *feminism* may help to sustain the weakening belief that the USA still aspires to fulfill liberal democracy's promise of "true equality" (while simultaneously diffusing the threat from other forms of emancipatory movements, like anti-racist and/or radical feminism). Whereas in recent years the so-called plight of women in Muslim countries served to deflect attention away from continued gender inequality in the USA, today a specific kind of internal critical gaze may have become increasingly necessary in order to do some of the same cultural work. The publication of these self-proclaimed feminist tracts not only creates the powerful impression that the USA is willing and able to sustain self-critique, but also—and importantly—that it is still committed to and governed by liberal rather than neoliberal or market principles.

This ostensible self-critique, in other words, serves to bolster the US's sense of openness, as well as moral and political superiority while (re)inscribing an imperialist logic. On the one hand, the "progressive" critical eye is turned back on the USA itself, which, I posit, marks a new development in the neoliberal landscape. Moving beyond the strategic use of homonationalism or "queer liberalism," where there is an instrumentalization of gay and lesbian rights so that western democracies and the USA can assert a kind of global progressive superiority (Puar 2007, Eng 2010), neoliberal feminism may be the latest discursive modality to (re)produce the USA as the bastion of progressive liberal democracy. Rather than deflecting internal criticism by shining the spotlight of oppressive practices onto other countries while overtly showcasing its progressive superiority, this discursive formation actually generates its own internal critique of the USA. Yet it simultaneously inscribes and circumscribes the permissible parameters of that very same internal critique. In this way, the USA can continue touting its much more enlightened because self-critical and always-improving gender relations, while continuing to mobilize "gender equality" as the benchmark for civilization. This, too, helps to neutralize criticism

from other strands of feminism, as well as from other countries about continued gender inequality inside the USA, helps to forget, yet again, racial inequality by focusing on a post-racial and individualized ("progressive") feminist subject, and serves to justify continued imperialist intervention in countries that do not respect the liberal principle of gender equality. On the other hand, the turn "inward"—both to the USA and into interiorized affective spaces—helps to further entrench neoliberalism by "responsibilizing" women and by producing individuated feminist subjects who have transmuted liberation into self-care and melded neoliberal rationality with an emancipatory project.

It seems clear that there is fertile ground for the emergent neoliberal feminism. The fact that Sandberg and Slaughter have so quickly become highly visible representatives of mainstream feminism seems to point to a much broader truth about contemporary US society. Rather than end on a defeatist note, however, I suggest that we need to return to the insights of Stuart Hall (2011) and Wendy Larner (2000), who have been careful to underscore that neoliberalism is not a seamless monolithic apparatus. Despite the power and influence of neoliberal rationality, it is also constantly generating internal contradictions and incoherencies. Consequently, if there are still to be alternative visions to the "neoliberalization of everything," then it may be more urgent than ever to change our own critical orientation. Rather than simply rejecting or denouncing these neoliberal feminist manifestos, perhaps we may do better by identifying and working within the potential fault lines of their logic and conceits. To begin with, then, we could highlight the gaping irreconcilability of the notion of "true gender equality" with the turn towards happiness and intricate processes of individuation. After all, the turn to positive affect and to intensified individuation in neoliberal feminism is exactly the turn away from the questions of social justice, and the common good that were, at the very least, a source of tension within classic liberal feminism. Indeed, glaring inconsistencies emerge as these manifestos move from a discourse of equal rights and social justice to a discourse of positive affect. In "Why Women Still Can't Have It All," for example, Slaughter acknowledges that the crisis she explores is one that is most relevant for "high potential" upwardly mobile women, and yet she calls for a national happiness project. If the feminism that Slaughter advocates does not address and cannot take into account the reality of the vast majority of US women, then a national project it clearly is not. Thus, while underscoring these contradictions and incoherencies, we would also do well to point out that the personal well-being of women like Sandberg and Slaughter, who likely constitute less than 0.1% of the general population, is increasingly coming at the expense of the 99.9%, namely, the overwhelming majority of poor, working class, and middle-class women in the USA.

NOTES

Acknowledgments: I would like to extend a profound thank you to the anonymous readers as well as to David Eng, Sara Farris, Neve Gordon, Moon-Kie Jung, Angela McRobbie, Jacinda Swanson, Joan Scott, Niza Yanay, Danielle Allen and Lila Corwin Berman for their insights and very helpful comments.

1. Wikipedia entry on Anne-Marie Slaughter. Available at: http://en.wikipedia.org/wiki/Anne-Marie_Slaughter [Accessed July 30, 2013]
2. See, for example, Suddath (2013).
3. Professor Slaughter was the first woman to hold the position of Director of Policy Planning in the State Department.
4. Kantor (2013).
5. See, Kantor (2013), Huffer (2013), and Eisenstein (2013).
6. See, for example, Rottenberg (2013) and Eisenstein (2013).
7. In many ways Fraser's current argument can be seen to recapitulate her earlier indictment of the decoupling of "cultural politics from social politics" (1997, p. 2). In *Justice Interruptus*, she describes the increasing tendency of social movements and feminists to privilege recognition over redistribution. Her later work, however, not only takes on the perspective of hindsight, arguing that this privileging only intensified over the years, but more specifically targets second-wave feminism for having failed to sustain a critique of capitalism. Furthermore, she suggests that second-wave feminism, by forfeiting the demand for economic redistribution, ended up serving as a key enabler for "the new spirit of neoliberalism" (2012, p. 220). In this later work, Fraser also adopts a three- rather than two-dimensional account of injustice: in addition to her well-known insistence that a truly emancipatory feminism must integrate demands for redistribution and recognition, in *Fortunes of Feminism* she adds the demand for political representation (2012, p. 225).
8. My claim is thus more in line with Angela McRobbie (2013) who has recently suggested that we are witnessing the folding of US liberal feminism into current neoliberal modes of governmentality. However, unlike McRobbie—whose concern is primarily with what she terms the new norm of "maternal-familialism" that aims to reify the nuclear family structure as an enterprise, thus legitimizing the extinction of public services—my focus is on the way neoliberal feminism is not only eviscerating liberal feminism but helping to produce a particular kind of feminist—as opposed to a female—subject.
9. It is perhaps important to remember that *The Feminine Mystique*, published in 1963, is not only considered part of the liberal feminist tradition but is often credited with sparking the beginning of second-wave feminism. *The Beauty Myth*, by contrast, was first published in 1990, at a time when the term postfeminism was gaining currency. Wolf's text is often considered part of so-called third-wave feminism as well as a critique of liberal feminist assumptions. What is interesting, however, is that despite the many differences between these feminist manifestos, they all return to a similar liberal paradox.
10. See, for example, Rottenberg and Huffer.
11. I have also argued that this new feminist ideal—what I term the Balanced Woman—helps to keep women with one foot firmly planted in the private sphere. But this is only one of the many effects of the emergence of the new norm of "progressive" womanhood (2014).
12. Marissa Mayer is President and CEO of Yahoo!. She was also ranked number 14 on the list of America's most powerful businesswomen of 2012 by *Fortune* Magazine.

13. David Harvey has argued that neoliberalism has not only become hegemonic as a mode of discourse, but it has become common sense: "It has pervasive effects on ways of thought to the point where it has incorporated into the common-sense way many of us interpret, live in, and understand the world" (2005, p. 3).

REFERENCES

Abbey, R. (2011) *The Return of Feminist Liberalism*, Durham, England, Acumen.

Ahmed, S. (2010) *The Promise of Happiness*, Durham, NC, Duke University Press.

Applebaum, A. (2013) *How to Succeed in Business* [Homepage of NEW YORK REVIEW], [online] Available at: http://www.nybooks.com/articles/archives/2013/jun/06/sheryl-sandberg-how-succeed-business/?pagination=false (accessed 6 June 2013).

Aslan, Ö. & Gambetti, Z. (2011) "Provincializing Fraser's history: feminism and neoliberalism revisited," *History of the Present*, vol. 1, no. 1, pp. 130–147.

Barry, A., Osborne, T. & Rose, N. S. (1996) *Foucault and Political Reason: Liberalism, Neo-liberalism, and Rationalities of Government*, Chicago, University of Chicago Press.

Brown, W. (2005) "Neo-liberalism and the end of liberal democracy," *Theory & Event*, vol. 7, no. 1, pp. 37–59.

Brown, W. (2006) "American nightmare: neoliberalism, neoconservatism, and dedemocratization," *Political Theory*, vol. 34, no. 6, pp. 690–714.

Eisenstein, H. (2009) *Feminism Seduced: How Global Elites Use Women's Labor and Ideas to Exploit the World*, Boulder, CO, Paradigm.

Eisenstein, Z. (2013) "'Leaning in' in Iraq," Available at: http://www.aljazeera.com/indepth/opinion/2013/03/20133231141149557391.html

Eng, D. L. (2010) *The Feeling of Kinship: Queer Liberalism and the Racialization of Intimacy*, Durham, NC, Duke University Press.

Farris, S. R. (2012) "Femonationalism and the 'regular army' of labor called migrant women," *History of the Present*, vol. 2, no. 2, pp. 184–199.

Foucault, M., et al. (1991) *The Foucault Effect: Studies in Governmentality*, Chicago, University of Chicago Press.

Fraser, N. (1997) *Justice Interruptus: Critical Reflections on the "Postsocialist" Condition*, New York, Routledge.

Fraser, N. (2013) *Fortunes of Feminism: From State-managed Capitalism to Neoliberal Crisis*, London, Verso Books.

Gordon, N. (2002) "On visibility and power: an Arendtian corrective of Foucault," *Human Studies*, vol. 25, no. 2, pp. 125–145.

Hall, S. (2011) "The neo-liberal revolution," *Cultural Studies*, vol. 25, no. 6, pp. 705–728.

Harvey, D. (2005) *A Brief History of Neoliberalism*, Oxford, Oxford University Press.

Huffer, L. (2013) "It's the Economy Sister," Available at: http://www.aljazeera.com/indepth/opinion/2013/03/201331885644977848.html

Kantor, J. (2013) "A Titan's How-To on Breaking the Glass Ceiling," *New York Times*, 21 February, Available at https://www.nytimes.com/2013/02/22/us/sheryl-sandberg-lean-in-author-hopes-to-spur-movement.html?pagewanted=all&_r=0

Larner, W. (2000) "Neo-liberalism: policy, ideology, governmentality," *Studies in Political Economy*, vol. 63, pp. 5–25.

Lemke, T. (2002) "Foucault, governmentality, and critique," *Rethinking Marxism*, vol. 14, no. 3, pp. 49–64.

McRobbie, A. (2009) *The Aftermath of Feminism: Gender, Culture and Social Change*, London, Sage Publications Limited.

McRobbie, A. (2013) "Feminism, the family and the new 'mediated' maternalism," *New Formations*, vol. 80–81, 119–137.

Norton, A. (2013) *On the Muslim Question*, Princeton, Princeton University Press.

Puar, J. K. (2007) *Terrorist Assemblages: Homonationalism in Queer Times*, Durham, NC, Duke University Press.

Rose, N. (1993) "Government, authority and expertise in advanced liberalism," *Economy and Society*, vol. 22, no. 3, pp. 283–299.

Rottenberg, C. (2013) "Hijacking Feminism," Available at: http://www.aljazeera.com/indepth/opinion/2013/03/201332510121757700.html

Rottenberg, C. (2014) "Happiness and the liberal imagination: how superwoman became balanced," *Feminist Studies*, vol. 40, no. 1, 144–168.

Sandberg, S. (2013) *Lean In: Women, Work, and the Will to Lead*, New York, Alfred A. Knopf.

Stansell, C. (2010) *The Feminist Promise: 1792 to the Present*, New York, Modern Library.

Suddath, C. (2013) *Sheryl Sandberg's "Lean In" Brand Goes Global*. http://www.businessweek.com/articles/2013-03-22/sheryl-sandbergs-lean-in-brand-goes-global (accessed 22 March 2013).

40. • *Fernando Tormos-Aponte*

THE POLITICS OF SURVIVAL (2018)

> Fernando Tormos-Aponte, a postdoctoral research associate at the University of Maryland, Baltimore County, a visiting scholar at Johns Hopkins University, and a research fellow at the Southern Methodist University Latino Center for Leadership Development, has research interests in social movements, identity politics, social policy, and transnational politics. His work has appeared in numerous journals and in the edited collection *The Legacy of Second-Wave Feminism in American Politics*. The piece here appeared in *Jacobin* in 2018.

Puerto Rico's left is rebuilding in the wake of two disasters: Hurricane María and a neoliberal onslaught.

Puerto Rico's left-wing forces have long tried to unify, a goal that has proven difficult to reach and even harder to sustain. At its strongest, the Left has faced intense repression from both the United States and the island's colonial government. Yet, activists and left-wing intellectuals agree that deeper differences account for the collective inability to build unity.

Historically, left-wing forces in Puerto Rico have split over the national question. Pro-independence groups, arguably the largest sector, have prioritized decolonization while socialists, feminists, and environmentalists have proposed a broader anti-oppression praxis centered on social and economic issues. Other groups, such as the Movimiento Socialista de Trabajadores, do not see these struggles as mutually exclusive, calling for the formation of a socialist republic in Puerto Rico.

Today a new wave of leftist organizing is emerging, one free from traditional Marxist or nationalist dogmas. This new Puerto Rican left is organizing for economic justice and against colonialism while putting a greater emphasis on gender, sexuality, and race. It aims to foster young leadership, articulate new solidarities, and revive the practice of community organizing. It is learning from the errors of the past while picking up the sediments of previous struggles.

But, if the Left wants to remain relevant, it must collaborate with the youth, community, feminist, farmer, and environmental-justice groups that are bringing new energy to the island.

THE STRUGGLE AGAINST NEOLIBERALISM

In 2010, Luis Fortuño's conservative administration attacked the Puerto Rican public sector. The economy was in crisis, and Fortuño and his advisory council were confident that the problem had a familiar solution—economic austerity. His government went after unions, social policies, and most violently, higher education.

In response, a popular front came together in order to defeat a common enemy: Fortuño and the private interests he so faithfully represented. The island had seldom been so polarized, with neoliberal forces preparing to strike a fatal blow and opposition groups looking for ways to resist. The Puerto Rican left aimed to build an emancipatory struggle connected to the global wave of resistance

Fernando Tormos-Aponte, "The Politics of Survival," *Jacobin*, April 2, 2018. Reprinted with permission of Jacobin Magazine.

that included Occupiers, Indignados, Pingüinos, and Arab Spring activists.

Labor leaders, scholar-activists, pro-independence leaders, feminists, the Christian left, environmentalists, lawyers, and other sectors seized the opportunity, forming a coalition of thirty-five organizations called Todo Puerto Rico por Puerto Rico. They aimed to ride the momentum built by University of Puerto Rico (UPR) students while preparing for the widely anticipated neoliberal attack on public higher education. Veteran organizers saw the student movement as a model to imitate as they expanded, sustained, and escalated the Todo Puerto Rico por Puerto Rico coalition.

The students used democratic decision-making and deliberative practices to plan direct actions, set the terms of negotiations with university administrators and government officials, and ratify the agreements made at the table. They also devoted significant efforts to recruiting new organizers for youth groups, including the Unión de Juventudes Socialistas, J-23, Juventud Hostosiana, Juventud del Partido Independentista Puertorriqueño, Organización Socialista Internacional, Federación Universitaria Pro Independencia, and MASFALDA. These practices of democratic and inclusive debate—coupled with a strong organizational structure—allowed the students to occupy the UPR's main campus for sixty-two days.

Thanks to this wave of activism, the Puerto Rican left scored important victories during the Fortuño administration (2009–2013). Not only did students stop a system-wide tuition hike and save tuition waivers for athletes, student workers, and honor students, but environmentalists also blocked the construction of a natural-gas pipeline and the development of the North Ecological Corridor, which would have sacrificed the area's unique biodiversity in order to build luxury resorts. Civil-rights lawyers united to defeat a referendum in which the Fortuño administration tried to curtail the right to bail.

These sectors eventually came together at a massive People's Assembly, where they organized an island-wide work stoppage and mobilized tens of thousands at marches. The movement began

to resemble the campaigns that eventually drove the US military out of Vieques Island in 2003. It seemed like the stage was set for a broader emancipatory struggle, one that could transition from resistance to revolution.

Unfortunately, the forces committed to continuing the colonial and neoliberal order in Puerto Rico proved to be stronger than those that fought to subvert it.

THE BALANCE OF FORCES

The Puerto Rican left has resisted a number of neoliberal attacks in the past, but the fiscal and humanitarian crisis brought on by Hurricane María is testing this ability. In the wake of the storm, both veteran and new activists have had to migrate or accept jobs with entities complicit in neoliberal policy making. But left-wing activism is still taking place and, in some instances, deepening its practices.

Socialist, environmentalist, and youth-activist groups had set up a network of mutual-assistance centers, which grew in the aftermath of the storm. When these solidary brigades reached areas in the mountainous regions two weeks after María's landfall, they discovered that residents didn't need their help. They had already prepared, sourcing water from wells and storing enough food to last for weeks.

The organizers quickly recognized that the people's needs entailed more than just basic goods. This lesson forced the Puerto Rican left to acknowledge that its relevance would depend on listening to and learning from these communities.

Since the storm, the farmers' and food-sovereignty movements have drawn support from Vía Campesina and the climate-justice movement to provide rapid response to frontline communities affected by the disaster. Mutual-aid groups from the Puerto Rican diaspora and the Climate Justice Alliance have joined local activists to get supplies to local farmers, rebuild ecosystems, and coordinate relief efforts with local and US labor unions.

They are resisting the nonprofit, corporate, and government-led network that has raised millions of dollars in donations since the disaster, calling attention to the fact that funds raised in the name of relief have yet to reach the Puerto Rican population and denouncing government efforts to implement false solutions, such as privatizing public utilities and education. They are working to politicize the recovery process, which has already produced widespread frustration, manifesting as roadblocks, picket lines, and occupations of government buildings.

On the other hand, right-wing forces have strong allies not only among the Republican-led government in Washington but also within the island's major political parties: the New Progressive Party (NPP) and the Popular Democratic Party (PDP).

The NPP's base includes religious fundamentalists, and its ample campaign funding comes from local capitalists. Sheltered by the darkness that swept the island after the hurricane, the NPP exploited the crisis to sidestep legislative hearings, silence the opposition, introduce a religious-freedom bill, grant no-bid contracts to dubious providers, and push conservative criminal-justice reforms.

In January, Governor Ricardo Rosselló confirmed his intentions to continue the legacy of his father, former governor Pedro Rosselló, by selling the island's besieged power authority. A week later, he announced the privatization of the primary and secondary public school system. Last week he announced a sweeping labor reform and the closure of a number of government agencies.

His father had tried to win public support for similar schemes by claiming that the revenue gained from privatizing public goods would fund social spending, including public employee pensions and universal health care. Instead, his administration took on expensive mega-projects, which handed lucrative contracts over to campaign donors but failed to raise the money necessary to sustain welfare programs.

The government's efforts to privatize Puerto Rico's Public Power Authority (PREPA) and public education prove that the Puerto Rican right feels strong. The NPP has long wanted to enact these policies, but previous administrations deemed public sector unions—and the Left more generally—too strong to undertake such an attack.

The crisis that followed Hurricane María opened the door for the Rosselló administration to consolidate its plans. Line workers are exhausted, toiling around the clock to restore power while facing attacks from citizens who blame them for the government's inability to restore power. Meanwhile, many teachers are working in schools without electricity.

The privatization announcement was carefully timed. Vulture funds have been looking over the governor's shoulder, pressuring him to include PREPA's privatization in the fiscal recovery proposal. Though it's ironic that someone who ran as an erudite technocrat with a sophisticated plan for every possibility failed to prepare for a natural disaster. Selling off the few remaining public assets was always part of his vision—even if he never revealed it on the campaign trail.

A week after the announcement, UTIER, the PREPA workers' union, issued a call for solidarity across all sectors of the Puerto Rican left to renew their resistance to privatization. Many have answered.

The new generation of leftist organizers has shed much of the old left's baggage. While they disagree about tactics, these debates have not been as divisive as they once were. Younger activists did not have to take sides on the extremely divisive issue of armed struggle, as those groups have mostly disbanded. Now debate centers on electoral participation, on mutual-assistance projects, and on diversification.

THE ELECTORAL QUESTION

Pedro Albizu Campos once referred to ballot boxes as coffins designed for the burial of the Puerto Rican nation. Under his leadership, the nationalist party militarized, rejecting the electoral process. The Puerto Rico Independence Party (PIP) stepped in to provide an electoral alternative for left-wing voters. Though these two sectors have come together to resist militarism, right-wing influences on public education, the displacement of marginalized communities, repression, and environmentally hazardous projects, the disagreement over electoral participation has persisted.

In 2016, the Obama administration created an unelected Fiscal Control Board with the power to impose fiscal policies in order to recover Puerto Rico's ballooning debt. That year's elections revealed a growing discontent with the island's three main parties and with the electoral process more generally. Between 2012 and 2016, Puerto Rico experienced a remarkable 22 percent drop in electoral turnout (from 77 to 55 percent). While these numbers are still higher than turnout in the United States, Puerto Rico has historically experienced voter turnout nearing 80 percent.

The Left has not figured out how to address voters' obvious frustration. Leftists who reject the electoral process argue that participating in elections legitimizes the colonial order, while others argue that boycotting will limit the Left's ability to curtail government corruption and hold elected officials accountable. This group is further divided between those who support the PDP in order to defeat right-wing candidates and those that who support the more left-wing parties, the PIP and the Working People's Party (PPT). The first tactic handed the PDP slim victories against two recent NPP re-election bids: both Rosselló and Fortuño lost by a margin of less than .6 percent. Without the Left's support, Puerto Rico would have had uninterrupted NPP rule since 2000.

In recent elections, neither the PIP nor the PPT has passed the 3 percent threshold necessary to remain in the ballot for future elections. The pro-independence party has failed to do so since 2004, but have been able to win at-large seats in the House and Senate. The PPT, which participated in elections for the first time in 2012, has never had legislative representation. Given this landscape, the Left's ability to claim electoral victory seems significantly limited.

Various voices within the Left have suggested forming a party combining the PIP and the PPT, but party leaders don't agree—at least not yet. Some argue that the Left must address its internal differences and define the purpose of these alliances before uniting. These critics only feel compelled to join a coalition focused on building radical democracy, as opposed to one that prioritizes the question of status.

POWER TO THE PEOPLE

Despite these electoral failures, left-wing forces have shown their strength in the streets and in communities.

Umbrella organizations like Jornada Se Acabaron las Promesas and the Concertadón Puertorriqueña en Contra de la Junta have joined culture workers like Papel Machete and AgitArte to mount a sustained campaign against the Fiscal Control Board.

Feminists from growing organizations like the Colectiva Feminista en Construcción have built popular resistance to patriarchy, neoliberalism, and authoritarianism. They disrupted two of the island's main highways on two separate occasions, mobilized hundreds for a feminist assembly, formed a mutual-assistance center, and forced the resignation and prosecution of Guaynabo mayor Hector O'Neill for sexual assault against a municipal employee.

An amalgam of leftist organizations called for an island-wide work stoppage and thousands flooded Puerto Rico's financial district in Hato Rey during the May 1 demonstrations.

The farmers' movement has grown dramatically in the past decade, with a growing number of independent and sustainable farming projects underway. Activist leaders have joined other activists at the United Nations climate-change negotiations and have strengthened their ties with the anti-capitalist farmer's movement Vía Campesina.

The environmental-justice movement has successfully mobilized against pipeline projects and used the media attention following Hurricane María to call for a just energy transition.

The network of mutual-assistance centers throughout the island has breathed new life into the Left. They are working to meet the needs of isolated communities that the state, local, and federal governments have ignored, moving the people from resilience to resistance.

While some have warned that the Left should also pressure the state to meet its responsibilities to the population, these activists have criticized the false dichotomy of bottom-up and top-down approaches to organizing. The vitality of the Puerto Rican left, they argue, must come from a synthesis of these approaches.

EMANCIPATORY DIVERSITY

Puerto Rican feminists argue that the Left's vitality will also depend on its ability to build more inclusive leadership groups. While left-wing groups have long fought to diversify government, schools, and other societal institutions, some have resisted internal diversification.

Historically, the Puerto Rican left has been at its strongest when it has identity, ideological, and tactical diversity. The upsurge that it experienced in the 1960s came when leaders focused on organizing marginalized groups and workers, fostering unity in diversity, strengthening youth and student groups, opening dialogue across different sectors of the Left, and developing international relationships of solidarity. These approaches encouraged collaboration despite disagreements about tactics, electoral participation, and organizing priorities. It also allowed the Left to deploy new tactical repertoires, mounting massive campaigns, organizing strikes, and supporting cultural work.

Some have dismissed these calls to diversify, expressing a desire to avoid what they consider a postmodern or neoliberal concern for identity. But others see diversity as a form of strength. Adopting this second approach entails building opportunities for dialogue despite differences, amplifying marginalized group's voices and perspectives, and prioritizing the issues of oppressed groups while fighting against shared grievances. Most importantly, it involves building leadership from the bottom up and trusting those without prestigious educations who possess the knowledge that comes from the pedagogy of the oppressed.

New groups have taken important steps in this direction. Members of the Juventud Hostosiana, which took a prominent role in the most recent student strike, have embraced diversity and declared themselves intersectional feminists, anti-colonialists, and ecologists.

The leaders of the feminist organization Colectiva Feminista en Construcción also played active roles in the student movement. The Colectiva, now a powerful force within the Puerto Rican left and in Puerto Rican politics more generally, has adopted an intersectional feminist organizing praxis and pushed the Left to fulfill its commitment to ending oppression by aiming to defeat capitalism and patriarchy simultaneously.

THE PATH FORWARD

Moving forward, the American and international left must refrain from using Puerto Ricans as a pawn in their battles against the Trump administration and afford them a substantive role in these efforts. Rather than framing the urgency of supporting Puerto Ricans in terms of their US citizenship, advocates must ground solidarity in the values of radical democracy and emancipation.

This orientation runs counter to how mainstream American politicians treat Puerto Ricans. The Democrats have launched voter-registration campaigns in hopes of using recent migrants as cannon fodder for the war against the Republicans—a cause that few Puerto Ricans seem eager to join. Liberals hope to enlist the Puerto Rican diaspora in the 2018 midterm elections, forgetting that Puerto Ricans, and Latinxs more generally, have often failed to reap the promised benefits of Democratic electoral victories.

In the days that followed Hurricane María, Puerto Ricans took matters into their own hands. Groups of retired line workers and electricians restored power in isolated sectors. Communities came together to rebuild their own bridges, literally and metaphorically. Collectively, they dispelled the myths that portray them as lazy and dependent on the government.

Hurricane María did not only bring devastation to the island. It also opened opportunities for both the Left and the Right. In the next months, the Left can defeat the neoliberal attacks on its public services and institutions, but only if it continues to embrace the energy of the alliances of unions, environmentalists, farmers, students, and scholar-activists that have formed on the ground, in the Puerto Rican diaspora, and internationally.

41. • *Kathy E. Ferguson*

BIRTH CONTROL (2017)

Kathy E. Ferguson, a professor of political science and women's studies at the University of Hawai'i, is currently writing a book on the activism of anarchist women advocating for reproductive and sexual freedom, labor rights, and an end to war. She has received several teaching, research, and service awards from the University of Hawai'i and from the field of political science, most recently for scholarship that directly benefits local communities. An earlier version of this essay first appeared in the blog *The Contemporary Condition* on July 14, 2015.

The second decade of the twenty-first century is witnessing significant political attacks on women's ability to use birth control—the Supreme Court case *Burwell v. Hobby Lobby* (2014), the presidential campaigns of Mitt Romney, Ted Cruz, and Rick Santorum, and a plethora of state-level initiatives from conservative and religious sources: such assaults often elicit disbelief from progressive women. We thought those battles were over. We thought we had won. A Planned Parenthood ad reminds us that it's not the 1950s anymore: "It is unbelievable that in 2014 we are still fighting about women's access to basic health care like birth control." Progressive women often ask, sarcastically, if this is 1915, not 2015, as if the passage of a hundred years were a guarantor of progress.

However, a stronger grasp of the history of the birth control movement suggests otherwise: the anarchists and socialists who fought those battles in the early twentieth century would not, I think, be surprised that the issue is still with us. I imagine that Emma Goldman, Alexander Berkman, Marie Equi, Ida Rauh, Crystal Eastman, Eugene Debs, Walter Adolphe Roberts, and many, many others working for access to contraception would know better, because they understood birth control as a central tenet of a larger struggle. Rather than looking at opposition to birth control as a lingering remnant of an otherwise settled past, the earlier radicals

encourage us to see birth control as inextricably woven into other ongoing struggles for freedom and community. Rather than assuming progress and being repeatedly surprised at its absence, we could learn from earlier struggles to locate our understanding of birth control in a more radical frame.[1]

The anarchists and socialists who fought for birth control in the late nineteenth and early twentieth centuries did not think they were winning a definitive war but that they were engaging in a prolonged and messy set of battles in which victories came at significant costs. They understood that if women did not control their own reproduction, someone else would control it, since states, capitalists, churches, and families have serious investments in controlling women's bodies. It wasn't just attitudes that needed to be changed but also institutions. They fought for birth control, not as a private decision between a woman and her doctor but as a potentially revolutionary practice that radically challenged prevailing power arrangements, including that of men over women, capitalists over workers, militaries over soldiers, and churches over parishioners.

The Supreme Court decision in *Burwell v. Hobby Lobby* offers an unwelcome opportunity to think about birth control through an appreciation of its radical past. Many good questions have been asked regarding the *Hobby Lobby* ruling—why do for-profit corporations have religious rights? Why is men's sexuality unproblematic, so that insurance coverage for Viagra and vasectomies is uncontested, while women's sexuality is subject to scrutiny? Why are straightforward medical distinctions between preventing conception and aborting a fetus ignored or confused? Why do many conservatives decry recreational sex on the part of women but seem unconcerned that men might have sex for fun?

While recognizing the legitimacy of these queries, I want to raise a different question: Why are we surprised? Why is our indignation tinged with disbelief: "How could this happen in this day and age?" Critics routinely call the decision "hopelessly backward" and accuse critics of wanting to "turn back the clock," as though there were a single historical timeline that carries us forward unless someone pushes us back. This is an utterly inadequate view of history. Instead, we need to locate both our victories and our defeats within multidirectional and open-ended historical processes, not steps in a single unfolding drama. We won't understand the tenacity of efforts to control women's sexuality until we give up the comforting assumption that history is a story of progress, and look more closely at the stakes and the terms of political struggle.

RECLAIMING OUR RADICAL PAST

Linda Gordon rightly points out, in her landmark study *Woman's Body, Woman's Right* (1976) that the radical roots of the struggle for birth control are largely unknown today. The situation faced by women in the United States in the early twentieth century with regard to controlling their reproduction was dire. The main problem was not a lack of known birth control technology, since, as Gordon documents, ancient, effective forms of birth control were selectively available, but in the United States it had been largely forced underground. In 1873 the passage of the Comstock Law, which criminalized sending "obscene" material through the mail, gathered birth control, sexuality, and radical ideas in general into its elastic net of prohibitions. During this time, various barrier and suppository methods,

called pessaries, were known and available to wealthy women through their doctors but largely unknown or unavailable to the poor. Diaphragms and condoms had to be smuggled into the United States from Europe. Politics, rather than technology, made birth control unavailable to most American women, and to change that situation political struggle was required.

From a contemporary point of view, it is startling to realize that many anarchists and socialists placed women's access to birth control at the heart of social revolution. We are accustomed to seeing the medicalized perspective—the claim that reproductive choices are questions of women's health and should be left to women and their doctors—as the feminist position, the position we must defend. Yet, there is another set of feminist voices, radical voices, voices that aimed to free women as well as liberate workers, end war, and transform society. Jamaican writer Walter Adolphe Roberts championed birth control both to enhance women's freedom and to advance the cause of social revolution (Roberts 1917, 7). Emma Goldman and Alexander Berkman located women's control over their reproduction as a central aspect of workers' struggles and antiwar activism. Emma Goldman's journal *Mother Earth* devoted its April 1916 issue to birth control. Alexander Berkman's journal *The Blast* concentrated on birth control in its February 12, 1916, issue and mentioned it in several others. While they supported Margaret Sanger in her early activism, they objected to Sanger's later strategy, which legitimized the birth control movement by aligning it with (mostly male) doctors. The radicals felt this approach removed birth control from the larger political context while giving power over women (including midwives) to doctors rather than to women themselves. Understanding these arguments can help feminists today learn from our own movement's past and perhaps shape current reproductive struggles as steps toward more radical political change.

Anarchists and socialists who embraced birth control framed it as a revolutionary demand to include sexual and reproductive freedom as necessary aspects of social justice and individual autonomy. Controlling one's own reproduction was part of transforming society. These progressive women and men integrated the liberation of women's sexuality into their vocal anticapitalist, antiwar mass movements. Just as capitalism sought to control the laboring bodies of workers and militaries sought to control the fighting bodies of soldiers, so did patriarchal families, churches, professions, and governments seek to control the reproductive bodies of women. Restrictions on birth control, they concluded, served the interests of states by producing an endless supply of cannon fodder for imperial wars, the interests of capital by generating a reserve army of labor to keep wages down, and the interests of organized religion by maintaining women's subservience and vulnerability within families and communities. A free society would be a society in which workers control their own labor, soldiers control their own fighting, and women control their own wombs. The radicals watched with dismay as their vision of a transformed society was displaced by the rise of a coalition between feminists, doctors, and the state to privatize contraception as an issue "between a woman and her doctor." Understanding the potentially radical implications of women's reproductive freedom, they also saw that some kinds of birth control reform could reinforce patriarchy rather than challenge it.

Attention to these struggles can reframe contemporary debates over birth control. The *Hobby Lobby* decision and other contraceptive losses for women are not temporary backsliding or inexplicable throwbacks to an earlier era but instead indicate ongoing and predictable unrest over proper standards of sexuality and of women's place. It would not surprise earlier anarchist and socialist feminists that the current Gilded Age, driven by neoliberal values and global corporate priorities, includes a resurgent war on women's reproductive autonomy. These radicals would, however, likely recoil from the pallid notion that birth control is a "women's issue" rather than a central aspect of a larger system of exploitation and control. A fuller grasp of our radical past can help us think of history as a dynamic network of shifting relations, operating at different paces in response to various challenges. The birth control movement then becomes a site of struggle, not an unfolding of a telos of development. We can look for the forgotten victories and lost possibilities of human freedom recorded there and bring those minoritarian views back into contemporary discussions.

HOW CAN BIRTH CONTROL BE MORE RADICAL?

How might a greater appreciation of birth control's radical past change feminism's present and future? Perhaps it could give us an alternative to being on the defensive: rather than asking for healthcare, we might demand freedom. Rather than seeing doctors as our main partners, we might see unions, antiwar groups, civil rights organizations, environmental groups, alternative spiritual movements, and other radical communities as coalition partners. There is a vibrant history of such coalitions: the early years of the journal *The Birth Control Review* brought together labor leaders like Eugene Debs, antiwar activists such as John Haynes Holmes, and civil rights activists including W. E. B. Du Bois to endorse women's access to birth control as a central aspect of freedom for all oppressed people. Today, we could make common cause with others who are similarly disadvantaged by, for example, judicial rulings granting corporations personhood, defining money as speech, and attributing religious identity to for-profit businesses. We might become bolder, not more cautious, in our thinking and acting.

For example, feminists often stress the difference between preventing and terminating pregnancy in order to use opposition to abortion to promote acceptance of birth control. Abortion and contraception are two separate issues, we say. Hobby Lobby's court arguments are invalid because they confuse technologies that prevent fertilization with technologies that remove fertilized eggs, we point out. We invite people who oppose abortion to agree with us about birth control because, if all women had access to birth control, there would be fewer abortions. These are very old arguments: birth control activist Mary Ware Dennett made the exact same claims in her 1926 book advocating the removal of contraception from the category of obscenity (Dennett

1926, 12). Perhaps we need to stop concentrating on these arguments. Even though these claims are accurate, they don't appear to be working. I suspect they give up too much. While clearly abortion and contraception are different, it is their common value to women who want to control their fertility that makes both birth control and abortion into targets of conservative wrath.

Also, feminists often stress the priority of the relationship "between a woman and her doctor" to discredit other possible relations, say, between a woman and her employer, a woman and her husband, a woman and her Supreme Court justices. Perhaps we need to stop doing that too. Medicalization of contraception has come to be the progressive position, the position we have to defend. But that only happened because more radical, more feminist perspectives were sidelined. Maybe it's time to stress women's freedom—and access to affordable and high-quality healthcare would surely be an aspect of that freedom—rather than women's health as our primary goal. When Sandra Fluke bravely testified before Congress in 2012 about the importance of oral contraception for treating health issues other than pregnancy, she was vilified as a slut and a prostitute anyway (Moorhead 2012). So perhaps it's time to demand access to the birth control techniques that we want rather than parsing our desires to downplay sexual freedom. Calling on the courts to consider the "plight" of women who use contraception for non-sexual purposes implicitly suggests that those uses are somehow more legitimate, that women who have a "plight" are more worthy of consideration than women who have a cause. If contraceptives were sold over-the-counter at affordable prices or distributed for free at accessible clinics, then women's reasons for wanting them would be irrelevant and the opportunities to judge women's sexuality might diminish.

Further, feminists sometimes speak of opposition to birth control as psychological, a question of men's fears of women's sexual autonomy. Joan Walsh (2014) of Salon.com writes of a deep fear of women's freedom on the Right; Dan Savage (2015) writes on *Slog*, "it's sex for pleasure that they hate." I don't disagree with either of these claims, but I want to push them further—opposition to women's reproductive freedom is not primarily a bad attitude or emotional hang-up. The interests of material structures and institutions that distribute resources, organize labor, conduct war, and administer spirituality are fully in play. Birth control keeps coming back as an issue not just because men don't get it but because capitalism, the state, empire, war, and patriarchal religions are still in power, and those institutions have an enormous stake in controlling women's sexuality. Controlling access to physical pleasure, managing demographic change, disciplining labor, and ensuring inheritance, among other outcomes, are at issue.

Finally, feminists need to give up the comforting idea that history is on our side, that progress toward fuller rights and greater equality is written into the order of things, once we dispense with those irrational, wrong-thinking obstructionists. History, I think, isn't on anyone's side; more importantly, there are many histories, many trajectories, and many different futures past. When feminists assure us, as Joan Walsh recently did, that "the right's crippling panic over women's autonomy will eventually doom it to irrelevance" (2014), or, as Amanda Marcote commented, "the anti-sex argument is a losing argument" (2014), we should question the implicit progress narrative folded into such guarantees. We are neither doomed nor blessed—rather, we have multiple opportunities to struggle for a better world and we should think carefully about their possibilities.

NOTE

1. My thanks to Nicole Sunday Grove, Jairus Grove, and Lori Marso for their help on this essay. An earlier version appeared in *The Contemporary Condition*, July 14, 2014.

WORKS CITED

Bauman, Nick. "The Republican War on Contraception." *Mother Jones*, February 9, 2012, www.motherjones.com/politics/2012/02/republican-war-birth-control-contraception.

Dennett, Mary Ware. *Birth Control Laws: Shall We Keep Them, Change Them or Abolish Them*. Grafton Press/Frederick H. Hitchcock, 1926.

Gordon, Linda. *Woman's Body, Woman's Right: The History of Birth Control in America*. Penguin Books, 1976.

Marcote, Amanda. "The Religious Right's No. 1 Obsession: Policing Women's Sex Lives by Any Means Necessary." *Salon*, July 3, 2014, www.salon.com/2014/07/03/the_religious_rights_1_obsession_policing_womens_sex_lives_by_any_means_necessary_partner/.

Moorhead, Molly. "In Context: Sandra Fluke on Contraceptives and Women's Health." *Tampa Bay Times*, March 6, 2012, www.politifact.com/truth-o-meter/article/2012/mar/06/context-sandra-fluke-contraceptives-and-womens-hea/.

Roberts, Walter Adolphe. "Birth Control and the Revolution." *The Birth Control Review*, June 1917, p. 7.

Savage, Dan. "Republicans in Colorado Vote for More Abortions," *Slog*, Stranger, May 1, 2015, www.thestranger.com/blogs/slog/2015/05/01/22147727/republicans-in-colorado-vote-for-more-abortions.

Walsh, Joan. "GOP's Culture War Disaster: How This Week Highlights a Massive Blindspot." *Salon*, July 3, 2014, www.salon.com/2014/07/03/gops_culture_war_disaster_how_this_week_highlighted_a_massive_blind_spot/.

42. • *Loretta Ross*[1]

THE COLOR OF *CHOICE*:
White Supremacy and Reproductive Justice (2006)

Loretta Ross has been a visiting professor of practice in the school of social transformation at Arizona State University and in women's studies at Hampshire College, served as the co-founder and national coordinator of SisterSong, and was National Co-Director of the 2004 March for Women's Lives in Washington DC. She has appeared in several media outlets, won numerous awards for her leadership in reproductive justice, and is a nationally recognized trainer/organizer in building human rights movements that center intersectional approaches to reproductive justice. She has written extensively on African American women and reproductive justice activism. Ross's recent publications include *Reproductive Justice: An Introduction*, co-written with Rickie Solinger (California, 2017), and a co-edited collection *Radical Reproductive Justice* (Feminist Press, 2017).

> [T]he regulation of reproduction and the exploitation
> of women's bodies and labor is both a tool and a result
> of systems of oppression based on race, class, gender,
> sexuality, ability, age and immigration status.[2]

It is impossible to understand the resistance of women of color to the reproductive politics of both the Right and the Left without first comprehending how the system of white supremacy constructs different destinies for each ethnic population of the United States through targeted, yet diffuse, policies of population control. Even a cursory examination of the reproductive politics dominating today's headlines—such as debates on abortion and welfare—reveals that some women are encouraged to have more children while others are discouraged. Why are some women glorified as mothers while others have their motherhood rights contested? Why are there obstacles for women who seek abortions while our society neglects mothers and children already here? As we move toward "designer babies" made possible by advances in assisted reproductive technologies, does anyone truly believe that all women will have an equal right to benefit from these "new reproductive choices," that children of all races will be promoted, or that vulnerable women will not be exploited?

Women of color reproductive justice activists oppose all political rationales, social theories, and genetic justifications for reproductive oppression against communities of color, whether through blatant policies of sterilization abuse or through the coercive use of dangerous contraceptives. Instead, women of color activists demand "reproductive justice," which requires the protection of women's human rights to achieve the physical, mental, spiritual, political, economic and social well-being of women and girls.[3] Reproductive justice goes far beyond the demand to eliminate racial disparities in reproductive health services, and beyond the right-to-privacy–based claims to legal abortion made by the pro-choice movement and dictated and limited by the US Supreme Court. A reproductive justice analysis addresses the fact that progressive issues are divided, isolating advocacy for abortion from other social justice issues relevant to the lives of every woman. In the words of SisterSong president Toni Bond, "We have to reconnect women's health and bodies with the rest of their lives."[4] In short, reproductive justice can be described as reproductive rights embedded in a human rights and social justice framework used to counter all forms of population control that deny women's human rights.

WHITE SUPREMACY AND POPULATION CONTROL ON THE RIGHT, AND LEFT

> Population control is necessary to maintain the
> normal operation of US commercial interests around
> the world. Without our trying to help these coun-
> tries with their economic and social development, the
> world would rebel against the strong US commercial
> presence.[5]

Although the United States does not currently have an explicit population control policy, population control ideologies march from the margins to the mainstream of reproductive politics and inform policies promoted by the Right and the Left. Fears of being numerically and politically overwhelmed by people of color bleach meaning from any alternative interpretations of the constellation of population control policies that restrict immigration by people of color, encourage sterilization and contraceptive abuse of people of color, and incarcerate upwards of 2 million people, the vast majority of whom are people of color.

The expanded definition of white supremacy as I use it in this essay is an interlocking system of racism, patriarchy, homophobia, ultranationalism, xenophobia, anti-Semitism, and religious fundamentalism that creates a complex matrix of oppressions faced by people of color in the United States. As a tenacious ideology in practice, it is evidenced on both the Right and the Left—in the Far Right, the Religious Right, paleoconservatives, neoconservatives, neoliberals, and liberals. Abby Ferber, a researcher on the intersection of race, gender, and white supremacy, writes that "defining white supremacy as extremist in its racism often has the result of absolving the mainstream population of its racism, portraying white supremacists as the racist fringe in contrast to some non-racist majority."[6]

White supremacy not only defines the character of debates on reproductive politics but it also explains and predicts the borders of the debate. In other words, what Americans think as a society about women of color and population control is determined and informed by their relationship to white supremacy as an ideology, and these beliefs affect the country's reproductive politics. Both conservatives and liberals enforce a reproductive hierarchy of privatization and punishment that targets the fertility, motherhood, and liberty of women of color.

Population control policies are externally imposed by governments, corporations, or private agencies to control—by increasing or limiting—population growth and behavior, usually by controlling women's reproduction and fertility. All national population policies, even those developed for purportedly benign reasons, put women's empowerment at risk. Forms of population control include immigration restrictions, selective population movement or dispersal, incarceration, and various forms of discrimination, as well as more blatant manifestations, such as cases in which pregnant illegal immigrants and incarcerated women are forced to have abortions. According to a 1996 study by Human Rights Watch, abuses of incarcerated women not only include denial of adequate health care, but pressure to seek an abortion, particularly if the woman is impregnated by a prison guard.[7]

Meanwhile, impediments are placed in the way of women who voluntarily choose to terminate their pregnancies. The only logic that explains this apparent moral inconsistency is one that examines precisely who is subjected to which treatment and who is affected by which reproductive policy at which time in history. Women of color have little trouble distinguishing between those who are encouraged to have more children and those who are not, and understanding which social, political, and economic forces influence these determinations.

Population control policies are by no means exclusively a twentieth-century phenomenon. During the Roman Empire, the state was concerned with a falling birthrate among married upper-class couples. As has been the case for elite classes throughout history, procreation was seen as a duty to society. Emperor Augustus consequently enacted laws containing positive and negative incentives to reproduction, promoting at least three children per couple and discouraging childlessness.[8] Augustus probably knew that the falling birthrate was not a result of abstention among Roman men and women, but rather of contraceptive and abortifacient use by Roman women to control their fertility. Through legislation, he asserted the state's interest in compelling citizens to have more children for the good of society.[9] Because no ancient Roman texts offer the perspectives of women on this issue, it is difficult to ascertain what women thought of this territorial assertion of male privilege over their private lives. However, the Roman birthrate continued to decline despite the emperor's orders, suggesting that Roman women probably did what most women have done throughout the ages: make the decisions that make sense for them and refuse to allow men to control their fertility. As historian Rickie Solinger points out, "The history of reproductive politics will always be in part a record of women controlling their reproductive capacity, no matter what the law says, and by those acts reshaping the law."[10]

Despite the Roman failure to impose the state's will on individual human reproductive behavior, many governments today have refused to recognize the virtual impossibility of regulating human reproductive behavior through national population policies. China and Romania have instituted population control measures with catastrophic results. Even governments seeking to achieve their population objectives through more benign policies, such as offering financial incentives for women to have children, can only report negligible results. Despite government and moralistic pronouncements, women perceive their reproductive decisions as private, like their periods and other health concerns. Even when the law, the church, or their partners oppose their decisions, they tend to make the decision about whether or not to use birth control or abortion, or to parent, for themselves.

This lived reality has not stopped lawmakers from trying to assert control over women's reproduction. Who gets targeted for positive, pronatalist policies encouraging childbirth versus negative, antinatalist policies that discourage childbirth is determined by powerful elites, informed by prejudices based on race, class, sexual identity, and immigration status. Policies that restrict abortion access, distort sex and sexuality education, impose parental notification requirements for minors, allow husbands to veto options for abortion, and limit use of emergency and regular contraception all conspire to limit access to fertility control to white women, especially young white women. Meanwhile, women of color face intimidating obstacles to making reproductive choices, including forced contraception, sterilization abuse, and, in the case of poor women and women of color on social assistance, welfare family caps. These population control policies have both domestic and international dimensions, which are rarely linked in the minds of those who believe that the struggle is principally about abortion.

Internationally, the fertility rate of women of color is the primary preoccupation of those determined to impose population controls on developing countries. According to the United Nations, in 2000, more than one hundred countries worldwide had large "youth bulges"—people aged fifteen to twenty-nine accounted for more than 40% of all adults. All of these extremely youthful countries are in the developing world, where fertility rates are highest, and most are in sub-Saharan Africa and the Middle East. Many of the young people who make up these "youth bulges" face dismal prospects because of deliberate underdevelopment. Over the past decade, youth unemployment rates have risen to more than double the overall global unemployment rate. In the absence of a secure livelihood, many experts believe that discontented youth may resort to violence or turn to insurgent organizations as sources of social mobility and self-esteem. Recent studies show that countries with large youth bulges were roughly two and a half times more likely to experience an outbreak of civil conflict than countries below this benchmark.[11]

To respond to these alarming trends, many on the Right and the Left want to restrict the growth of developing world populations, and in this context, "family planning" becomes a tool to fight terrorism and civil unrest. Some on the Left want to increase access to family planning, economic development, and education as a way to curb population growth, even if achieved through the coercive use of contraceptives and sterilization. Some on the Right prefer military interventions and economic domination to achieve population control.

The Bush administration's family planning and HIV/AIDS policies are also having the impact of serving as tools of population control in the Global South. The US government's "ABC program" (A is for abstinence, B is for being faithful, and C for condom use) is purportedly designed to reduce the spread of HIV/AIDS. Critics of the policy point out that the ABC approach offers no option for girls or women coerced into sex, for married women who are trying to get pregnant yet have unfaithful husbands, or for victims of rape and incest who have no control over when and under what conditions they will be forced to engage in sexual activity. As a result, instead of decreasing the spread of HIV/AIDS, some suspect the ABC policy of actually increasing the ravages of the disease. In combination with the US government's failure to provide funding for and access to vital medications for individuals infected with HIV, the effects are deadly.

Meanwhile, right-wing policies that appear to be pronatalist—such as the Global Gag Rule which prohibits clinics in developing countries that receive USAID funds from discussing abortion—are, in fact, achieving the opposite result. Catering to its radical antiabortion base, the Bush administration has withdrawn funds from programs for family planning for women around the world, withholding $136 million in funding for the United Nations Population Fund (UNFPA) since 2002. This money could have prevented at least 1.5 million induced abortions, 9,400 maternal deaths, and 154,000 infant and child deaths.[12] In September 2005, the US State Department announced that it was denying funding to UNFPA for the fourth year.

One might ask why staunch conservatives are opposed to family planning in developing countries when family planning so clearly limits population growth and reduces the need for abortions. One of the leading causes of death for women in developing countries is maternal mortality—death from childbirth. The UN estimated a worldwide total of 529,000 maternal deaths in the year 2000, with less than 1% of deaths occurring in developed nations.[13] Women of color cannot help but observe that family planning is not nearly as efficient in reducing populations of color as factors such as maternal mortality, infant mortality, and AIDS. We are also not oblivious to the wealth of natural resources like oil, gold, and diamonds in the lands where these populations are shrinking—after all, a depopulated land cannot protect itself.

Overt and covert population control policies are also at play on the domestic front. In October 2005, former secretary of education William Bennett declared on his radio talk show that if "you wanted to reduce crime . . . if that were your sole purpose, you could abort every Black baby in this country, and your crime rate would go down." While Bennett conceded that aborting all African American babies "would be an impossible, ridiculous, and morally reprehensible thing to do," he still maintained that "the crime rate would go down."

Bennett is merely echoing widespread perceptions by many radical and moderate conservatives in the United States who directly link social ills with the fertility of women of color. The Heritage Foundation, a right-wing think tank influential in the national debates on reproductive politics, offers the following analysis: "Far more important than residual material hardship is behavioral poverty: a breakdown in the values and conduct that lead to the formation of healthy families, stable personalities, and self-sufficiency. This includes eroded work ethic and dependency, lack of educational aspiration and achievement, inability or unwillingness to control one's children, *increased single parenthood and*

illegitimacy [emphasis added], criminal activity, and drug and alcohol abuse."[14]

This mainstream white supremacist worldview is based on the notion that people are poor because of behaviors, not because they are born into poverty. In reality, according to Zillah Eisenstein, "poverty is tied to family structures in crisis. Poverty is tied to the unavailability of contraceptives and reproductive rights. Poverty is tied to teenage pregnancy. Poverty is tied to women's wages that are always statistically lower than men's. Poverty is tied to the lack of day care for women who must work. Poverty is tied to insufficient health care for women. Poverty is tied to the lack of access to job training and education."[15]

It would be logical to assume that people who claim to value all human life from the moment of conception would fiercely support programs that help disadvantaged children and parents. Sadly, this is not the case. Surveys show that, on average, people who are strongly opposed to abortion are also more likely to define themselves as political conservatives who do not support domestic programs for poor families, single mothers, people of color, and immigrants.[16] They are also opposed to overseas development assistance in general, and to specific programs for improving women's and children's health, reducing domestic violence, helping women become more economically self-sufficient, and lowering infant mortality.[17]

Perspectives from the Left are hardly more reassuring to women of color. Is Bennett, a member of the Heritage Foundation, any worse than an environmentalist who claims that the world is overpopulated and drastic measures must be taken to address this catastrophe? Betsy Hartmann writes about the "greening of hate," or blaming environmental degradation, urban sprawl, and diminishing natural resources on poor populations of color. This is a widely accepted set of racist myths promoted by many in the environmental movement, which is moving rather alarmingly to the right as it absorbs ideas and personnel from the white supremacist movement, including organizations such as the Aryan Women's League.[18]

The reality is that 20% of the world's population controls 80% of the global wealth. In other words, it is not the population growth of the developing world that is depleting the world's resources, but the overconsumption of these resources by the richest countries in the world. The real fear of many in the population control movement is that the developing world will become true competitors for the earth's resources and demand local control over their natural wealth of oil and minerals. Rather than perceiving overconsumption by Americans, agricultural mismanagement, and the military-industrial complex as the main sources of environmental degradation, many US environmentalists maintain that the fertility of poor women is the root of environmental evil, and cast women of color, immigrant women, and women of the Global South as the perpetrators, rather than the victims, of environmental degradation.[19] This myth promotes alarmist fears about overpopulation, and leads to genocidal conclusions such as those reached by writers for *Earth First! Journal* who said, "The AIDS virus may be Gaia's tailor-made answer to human overpopulation," and that famine should take its natural course to stem overpopulation.[20]

Population control groups on the Left will often claim that they are concerned with eliminating gender and economic inequalities, racism, and colonialism, but since these organizations address these issues through a problematic paradigm, inevitably their efforts are directed toward reducing population growth of all peoples in theory and of people of color in reality.[21] In fact, these efforts are embedded within the context of a dominant neoliberal agenda which trumps women's health and empowerment. And some pro-choice feminists have supported the neoliberal projects of "privatization, commodification, and deregulation of public health services that . . . have led to diminished access and increasing mortality and morbidity of women who constitute the most vulnerable groups in both developing and developed countries."[22]

Similarly, the pro-choice movement, largely directed by middle-class white women, is oblivious to the role of white supremacy in restricting reproductive options for all women, and, as a result, often inadvertently colludes with it. For instance, a study published in 2001 in the *Quarterly Journal of Economics* by John J. Donohue III, a professor of law at Stanford University, and Steven D. Levitt, a professor of economics at the University of Chicago, claimed that the 1973 legalization of abortion prevented the birth of unwanted children who were likely to have become criminals. Of course, the authors state that these children would have been born to poor women of color. They also disingenuously and incorrectly assert that "women who have abortions are those most at risk to give birth to children who would engage in criminal activity,"[23] and conclude that the drop in crime rates approximately eighteen years after the *Roe v. Wade* decision was a consequence of legal abortion. Despite the quickly revealed flaws in their research, some pro-choice advocates continue to tout their findings as justification for keeping abortion legal, adopting a position similar to Mr. Bennett's.[24]

Indeed, the pro-choice movement's failure to understand the intersection between race, class, and gender led leaders of the movement to try their own "Southern Strategy" in the 1980s. Central to this strategy was an appeal to conservative voters who did not share concerns about women's rights, but who were hostile to the federal government and its public encroachment on individual choice and privacy. Some voters with conservative sympathies were pruned from the antiabortion movement for a while, uneasily joining the ranks of the pro-choice movement in an admittedly unstable alliance based on "states' rights" segregationist tendencies.[25] Not surprisingly, on questions of abortion policy—whether the government should spend tax money on abortions for poor women or whether teenagers should have to obtain parental consent for abortions—the alliance fell apart. And this appeal to conservative, libertarian Southern voters drove an even deeper wedge in the pro-choice movement, divorcing it from its original base of progressive white women and alienating women of color.

Meanwhile, the Right pursued its population control policies targeting communities of color both overtly and indirectly. Family planning initiatives in the Deep South in the 1950s encouraged women of color (predominantly African American women) to use contraceptives and sterilizations to reduce the growth of our populations, while obstacles were simultaneously placed in the paths of white women seeking access to these same services. A Louisiana judge, Leander Perez, was quoted as saying, "The best way to hate a nigger is to hate him before he is born."[26] This astonishingly frank outburst represented the sentiments of many racists during this period, although the more temperate ones disavowed gutter epithets.

For example, conservative politicians like Strom Thurmond supported family planning in the 1960s when it was used as a racialized form of population control, aimed at limiting Black voter strength in African American communities.[27] When it was presented as a race-directed strategy to reduce their Black populations, North Carolina and South Carolina became the first states to include family planning in their state budgets in the 1950s. One center in Louisiana reported that in its first year of operation, 96% of its clients were Black. The proportion of white clients never rose above 15%.[28] Generally speaking, family planning associated with women of color was most frequently supported; but support quickly evaporated when it was associated with white women.

Increased federal spending on contraception coincided with the urban unrest and rise of a militant Civil Rights movement in the late 1960s. In 1969, President Nixon asked Congress to establish a five-year plan for providing family planning services to "all those who want them but cannot afford them."[29] However, the rationale behind the proposed policy was to prevent population increases among Blacks—this would make governance of the world in general, and inner cities in particular, difficult. Reflecting concerns strikingly similar to those driving US population policies overseas, Nixon pointed to statistics that showed a "bulge" in the number of Black Americans between the ages of five and nine. This group of youngsters who would soon enter their teens—"an age group with problems that can create social turbulence"—was 25% larger than ten years before.[30] This scarcely disguised race- and class-based appeal for population control persuaded many Republicans to support family planning.

Today the US government's less obvious—but no less effective—approach of promoting policies overseas that contribute to high maternal mortality rates and devastation as a result of HIV/AIDS was also recently revealed to have a counterpart on the domestic front. Images of chaos and death as Hurricane Katrina's floodwaters engulfed Black neighborhoods shocked many Americans. But according to Jean Hardisty, a researcher on white supremacy in America, these pictures of poor New Orleans residents, many of them Black women and their children, revealed some essential truths:

> Much of the white public will never understand that those images were more than the result of neglected enforcement of civil rights laws, or the "failure" of the poor to rise above race and class. They were images of structural racism. In one of the poorest cities in the country (with 28% of New Orleanians living in poverty—over two times the national poverty rate), the poor were white as well as African American. But, the vast majority (84%) of the poor were Black. This is not an accident. It is the result of white supremacy that is so imbedded in US society that it has become part of the social structure. Structural racism is not only a failure to serve people equally across race, culture and ethnic origin within private and government entities (as well as "third sector" institutions, such as the print, radio and TV media and Hollywood). It is also the predictable consequence of legislation at the federal, state, and local level.[31]

This racial illiteracy on the part of white people is part of the hegemonic power of whiteness. Through a historical mythology, white supremacy has a vested interest in denying what is most obvious: the privileged position of whiteness. For most people who are described as white, since race is believed to be "something" that shapes the lives of people of color, they often fail to recognize the ways in which their own lives and our public policies are shaped by race. Structural or institutionalized racism is not merely a matter of individual attitudes, but the result of centuries of subordination and objectification that reinforce population control policies.

Politicians have continuously used policies of population control to conquer this land, produce an enslaved workforce, enshrine racial inequities, and preserve traditional power relations. For just as long, women of color have challenged race-based reproductive politics, including the forced removal of our children; the racialization and destruction of the welfare system; the callousness of the foster care system that breaks up our families; and the use of the state to criminalize our pregnancies and our children. These become an interlocked set of public policies which Dorothy Roberts calls "reproductive punishment." She observes that the "system's racial disparity also reinforces negative stereotypes about . . . people's incapacity to govern themselves and need for state supervision."[32]

Reproductive politics are about who decides "whether, when, and which woman can reproduce legitimately and *also* the struggles over which women have the right to be mothers of the children they bear."[33] Entire communities can be monitored and regulated by controlling how, when, and how many children a woman can have and keep. This is particularly true for women on Native American reservations, incarcerated women, immigrant women, and poor women across the board, whose reproductive behavior is policed by an adroit series of popular racist myths, fierce state regulation, and eugenicist control. The use of the "choice" framework in the arena of abortion, as Rhonda Copelon points outs, underwrites "the conservative idea that the personal is separate from the political, and that the larger social structure has no impact on [or responsibility for] private, individual choice."[34]

For the past thirty years, women of color have urged the mainstream movement to seriously and consistently support government funding for abortions for poor women. The 1977 Hyde Amendment prohibited the use of taxpayer funds to pay for abortions for women whose health care is dependent on the federal government, and it affects women on Medicaid, women in the military and the Peace Corps, and indigenous women who primarily rely on the Indian Health Service for their medical care. Yet despite its obvious targeting of poor women of color, pro-choice groups have not made repealing the Hyde Amendment a priority because polling data has indicated that the majority of Americans do not want taxpayer money used to pay for abortions.

When the Freedom of Choice Act was proposed by pro-choice groups in 1993, it retained the provisions of the Hyde Amendment. According to Andrea Smith, one NARAL Pro-Choice America (formerly known as the National Abortion Rights Action League) petition in favor of the act stated that "the Freedom of Choice Act (FOCA) will secure the original vision of *Roe v. Wade*, giving *all* women reproductive freedom and securing that right for future generations" [emphasis added].[35] As Smith wryly points out, apparently poor women and indigenous women did not qualify as "women" in the eyes of the writers of this petition.

In a 1973 editorial, the National Council of Negro Women pointed out the link between civil rights activism and reproductive oppression that mitigated the concept of choice for oppressed communities:

> The key words are "if she chooses." Bitter experience has taught the Black woman that the administration of justice in this country is not colorblind. Black women on welfare have been forced to accept sterilization in exchange for a continuation of relief benefits and others have been sterilized without their knowledge or consent. A young pregnant woman recently arrested for civil rights activities in North Carolina was convicted and told that her punishment would be to have a forced abortion. We must be ever vigilant that what appears on the surface to be a step forward, does not in fact become yet another fetter or method of enslavement.[36]

Yet currently the hard-core Right has begun to demand the political disenfranchisement of people receiving public assistance. For example, in 2005 a law was proposed in Georgia that would have required voters to have driver's licenses or other forms of state identification to vote; right-wing proponents complained that the bill didn't go far enough, and that the vote should be taken away from welfare recipients.[37] And while linking political enfranchisement to population control is blatantly coercive and antidemocratic, it has not been unusual in United States. In 1960, when the city of New Orleans was ordered to desegregate its schools, local officials responded by criminalizing the second pregnancies of women on public assistance; after they were threatened with imprisonment and welfare fraud, many of these African American women and children disappeared from the welfare rolls.[38] The Right is often blatant in its determination to restrict the fertility of women of color, and thus control our communities. They endlessly proffer an array of schemes and justifications for intruding on the personal decisions of women of color and for withholding the social supports necessary to make healthy reproductive decisions.

On the other hand, in its singular focus on maintaining the legal right to abortion, the pro-choice movement often ignores the intersectional matrix of race, gender, sovereignty, class and immigration status that complicates debates on reproductive politics in the United States for women of color. The movement is not the personal property of middle-class white women, but without a frank acknowledgement of white supremacist practices in the past and the present, women of color will not be convinced that mainstream pro-choice activists and organizations are committed to empowering women of color to make decisions about our fertility, or to reorienting the movement to include the experiences of *all* women.

MOBILIZING FOR REPRODUCTIVE JUSTICE

Prior to the 1980s, women of color reproductive health activists organized primarily against sterilization abuse and teen pregnancy, yet many were involved in early activities to legalize abortion because of the disparate impact illegal abortion had in African American, Puerto Rican, and Mexican communities. Most women of color refrained from joining mainstream pro-choice organizations, preferring instead to organize autonomous women of color organizations that were more directly responsive to the needs of their communities. The rapid growth of women of color reproductive health organizations in the 1980s and 1990s helped build the organizational strength (in relative terms) to generate an analysis and a new movement in the twenty-first century.

This was a period of explosive autonomous organizing.[39] Women of color searched for a conceptual framework that would convey our twinned values—the right to have and not to have a child—as well as the myriad ways our rights to be mothers and parent our children are constantly threatened. We believed these values and concerns separated us from the liberal pro-choice movement in the United States, which was preoccupied with privacy rights and maintaining the legality of abortion. We were also skeptical about leaders in the pro-choice movement who seemed more interested in population restrictions than women's empowerment. Some promoted dangerous contraceptives and coercive sterilizations, and were mostly silent about economic inequalities and power imbalances between the developed and the developing worlds. Progressive women of color felt closest to the radical wing of the women's movement that articulated demands for abortion access and shared our class analysis, and even closer to radical feminists who demanded an end to sterilization and contraceptive abuse. Yet we lacked a framework that aligned reproductive rights with social justice in an intersectional way, bridging the multiple domestic and global movements to which we belonged.

We found an answer in the global women's health movement through the voices of women from the Global South. By forming small but significant delegations, women of color from the United States participated in all of the international conferences and significant events of the global feminist movement. A significant milestone was the International Conference on Population and Development in 1994 in Cairo, Egypt. In Cairo, women of color witnessed how women in other countries were successfully using a human rights framework in their advocacy for reproductive health and sexual rights.

Shortly after the Cairo conference, drawing on the perspectives of women of color engaged in both domestic and international activism, women of color in the United States coined the term "reproductive justice." In particular, we made the link between poverty and the denial of women's human rights, and critiqued how shared opposition to fundamentalists and misogynists strengthened a problematic alliance between feminists and the population control establishment.

The first step toward implementing a reproductive justice framework in our work was taken two months after the September Cairo conference. A group of African American women (some of whom became cofounders of the SisterSong Women of Color Reproductive Health Collective) spontaneously organized an informal Black Women's Caucus at a national pro-choice conference sponsored in 1994 by the Illinois Pro-Choice Alliance in Chicago. We were attempting to "Bring Cairo Home" by adapting agreements from the Cairo program of action to a US-specific context. In the immediate future, we were very concerned that the Clinton administration's health care reform proposals were ominously silent about abortion rights, which appeared to renege on the promises the Administration made at Cairo. Even without a structured organization, we mobilized for a national signature ad in the *Washington Post* to express our concerns, raising twenty-seven thousand dollars and collecting six hundred signatures from African American women to place the ad in the *Post*. After debating and rejecting the choice framework in our deliberations, we called ourselves Women of African Descent for Reproductive Justice. We defined reproductive justice, at that time, as "reproductive health integrated into social justice," bespeaking our perception that reproductive health is a social justice issue for women of color because health care reform without a reproductive health component would do more harm than good for women of color. Three years later, using human rights as a unifying framework

and reproductive justice as a central organizing concept, the SisterSong Women of Color Reproductive Health Collective was formed in 1997 by autonomous women of color organizations.

SisterSong maintains that reproductive justice—the complete physical, mental, spiritual, political, economic, and social well-being of women and girls—will be achieved when women and girls have the economic, social, and political power and resources to make healthy decisions about our bodies, sexuality, and reproduction for ourselves, our families, and our communities in all areas of our lives. For this to become a reality, we need to make change on the individual, community, institutional, and societal levels to end all forms of oppression, including forces that deprive us of self-determination and control over our bodies, and limit our reproductive choices to achieve undivided justice.[40]

An instructive example of how the reproductive justice framework employed by SisterSong has influenced the mainstream movement is the organizing story behind the March for Women's Lives in Washington, D.C., on April 25, 2004. The march, which mobilized 1.15 million participants, was the largest demonstration in US history. Originally organized to protest antiwoman policies (such as the badly named Partial Birth Abortion Ban Act) and to call attention to the delicate pro-choice majority on the Supreme Court, it also exposed fissures in the pro-choice movement that have not been fully analyzed.

Mobilizing for the march uncovered cleavages on the Left. The event's original title, the "March for Freedom of Choice," reflected a traditional focus on a privacy-based abortion rights framework established by the Supreme Court. At the same time, the dominant issue on the American Left was the illegal war against Iraq, not abortion politics. Tens of millions of people had marched around the globe to protest Bush's invasion in February 2003. As the initial organizing for the march progressed in 2003, it became clear that targeted supporters would not turn out in sufficient numbers if the march focused solely on the right to legal abortion and the need to protect the Supreme Court. Abortion isolated from other social justice issues would not work.

Ultimately, in order to broaden the appeal of the march and mobilize the entire spectrum of social justice activists in the United States, organizers sought a strategic framework that could connect various sectors of US social justice movements. They approached SisterSong in the fall of 2003, asking for endorsement of and participation in the march. SisterSong pushed back, expressing problems with the march title and the then all-white decision-makers on the steering committee. SisterSong demanded that women of color organizations be added to the highest decision-making body, and counteroffered with its own "reproductive justice" framework. (The original March organizers were the Feminist Majority Foundation, the National Organization for Women, Planned Parenthood Federation of America, and NARAL Pro-Choice America. Eventually, the National Latina Institute for Reproductive Health, the Black Women's Health Imperative and the American Civil Liberties Union were added to the march steering committee.) Reproductive justice was a viable way to mobilize broader support for the march. It also had the potential to revitalize an admittedly disheartened pro-choice movement. The central question was: were pro-choice leaders ready and willing to finally respect the leadership and vision of women of color?

Through the leadership of Alice Cohan, the march director, the March for Freedom of Choice was renamed in the fall of 2003, and women of color organizations were added to the steering committee. Using the intersectional, multi-issue approach fundamental to the reproductive justice framework, march organizers reached out to women of color, civil rights organizations, labor, youth, antiwar groups, anti-globalization activists, environmentalists, immigrants' rights organizations, and many, many others.

The success of the march was a testament to the power of reproductive justice as a framework to mobilize and unite diverse sectors of the social justice movement to support women's human rights in the United States and abroad. Just as importantly, it also showed how women of color have to take on the Right and the Left when asserting control over our bodies, our communities, and our destinies.

> I am not wrong: Wrong is not my name
> My name is my own my own my own
> and I can't tell you who in the hell set things up like this
> but I can tell you that from now on my resistance
> my simple and daily and nightly self-determination
> may very well cost you your life.
>
> —June Jordan

NOTES

1. I write this essay from the perspective of an African American woman, sterilized by the Dalkon Shield intrauterine device in the 1970s, when I was 23 years old. I have since been active in the movement for reproductive justice, trying to ensure that what I experienced will never happen to another woman, even though I am a grandmother now. Rather than perceiving my lived experience as a deficit as a writer (or myself as a victim), I prefer to see it as an asset in understanding how the politics of race intertwine with the politics of class and gender in the United States. My body has served as a site of many of the battles over reproductive politics in this country. My passion now is borne of the conviction that population control is not a hysterical conspiracy offered by people of color but a real determinant of many conditions in our lives.

2. Asian Communities for Reproductive Justice, "Reproductive Justice: A New Vision for Advancing Our Movement for Reproductive Health, Reproductive Rights and Reproductive Justice," http://www.reproductivejustice. org/download/ACRJ_A_New_Vision.pdf (accessed October 15, 2005).

3. Ibid.

4. Founded in 1997, the SisterSong Women of Color Reproductive Health Collective is the only national coalition of women of color organizations and individuals in the United States that unites our collective voices to ensure "Reproductive Justice" through securing human rights for communities of color. Reproductive Justice is a fresh and exciting human rights-based analysis offered by women of color that is increasingly being used by many organizations to link reproductive health and population concerns

to environmental, economic, racial, and other social justice issues. With our national office in Atlanta, Georgia, the SisterSong Collective is now comprised of seventy-six local, regional, and national grassroots organizations representing six populations in the United States: Native American/indigenous, Black/African American/Caribbean, Latina, Middle Eastern/North African, and Asian/Pacific Islander, as well as individual women of color affiliated with mainstream organizations, and white and male allies. The Collective is governed by the Management Circle, a board of directors composed of twenty-one organizational and individual members. Membership in the Collective is open: everyone can be a member of SisterSong. The mission of SisterSong is to amplify and strengthen the collective voices of indigenous women and women of color to ensure reproductive justice through securing human rights. Our core strategic goals are to: 1) Create opportunities for women of color to build a national movement for reproductive justice in the United States; 2) strengthen women of color organizations by providing training, information, and analyses on reproductive health and organizational development issues; and 3) build alliances among women of color and between women of color and the mainstream movement through shared advocacy work. SisterSong publishes a national newspaper by and for women of color on reproductive justice issues called *Collective Voices* and can be reached at www.sistersong.net.

5. Quoted in Andrea Smith, *Conquest: Sexual Violence and American Indian Genocide* (Cambridge, MA: South End Press, 2005), 80.

6. Abby L. Ferber, *White Man Falling: Race, Gender and White Supremacy* (New York: Rowman & Littlefield, 1998), 9.

7. Human Rights Watch, "All Too Familiar: Sexual Abuse of Women in US State Prisons," Summary and Recommendations, December 1996, http://hrw.org/reports/1996/us1.htm (accessed March 18, 2006).

8. Rosalind Pollack Petchesky, *Abortion and Woman's Choice: The State, Sexuality and Reproductive Freedom* (Boston: Northeastern University Press, 1990), 70.

9. John T. Noonan, *Contraception: A History of Its Treatment by the Catholic Theologians and Canonists* (Cambridge, MA: Harvard University Press, 1966), 21–2.

10. Rickie Solinger, *Pregnancy and Power: A Short History of Reproductive Politics in America* (New York: New York University Press, 2005), 3.

11. World Watch Institute, "State of the World 2005 Trends and Facts—Population and Security," http://www.worldwatch.org/features/security/tf/2 (accessed July 30, 2005).

12. Leila Hessini, "Globalizing Radical Agendas," *Collective Voices* 1, Issue 1, www.sistersong.net (accessed August 8, 2005).

13. World Health Organization, "World Health Report 2005," http://www.who.int/whr/2005/whr2005_en.pdf (accessed September 9, 2005).

14. Heritage Foundation, "Where We Stand: Our Principles on Building on Welfare Reform," http://www.heritage.org/research/features/mandate/2005/copic.cfm?copic=17 (accessed November 15, 2005).

15. Zillah Eisenstein, "Katrina and Her Gendering of Race and Class," Women's Human Rights Net, www.whrnet.org/docs/issue-katrina.hcml (accessed September 30, 2005).

16. Ruth Dixon-Mueller and Paul K. B. Dagg, *Abortion and Common Sense* (Philadelphia: XLibris Corporation, 2002), 225–6.

17. Ibid., 226.

18. James Ridgeway, *Blood in the Face: The Ku Klux Klan, Aryan Nations, Nazi Skinheads, and the Rise of New White Culture* (New York: Thunder's Mouth Press, 1990), 174.

19. Betsy Hartmann, "The Greening of Hate at Home and Abroad," *ZNet*, December 10, 2003.

20. Izaak Walton, League of America, http://www.overpopulation.org (accessed August 8, 2005).

21. Smith, *Conquest*, 78.

22. Rhonda Copelon and Rosalind Petchesky, "Reproductive and Sexual Rights as Human Rights," in *From Basic Needs to Basic Rights*, ed. Margaret Shuler (Washington, DC: Women, Law and Development International, 1995), 355.

23. John J. Donohue III and Steven D. Levitt, "The Impact of Legalized Abortion on Crime," *The Quarterly Journal of Economics* 116, Issue 2 (May 2001), 379.

24. Alexander Sanger, *Beyond Choice: Reproductive Freedom in the 21st Century* (New York: Public Affairs Books, 2004), 67.

25. William Saletan, *Bearing Right: How the Conservatives Won the Abortion War* (Berkeley, CA: University of California Press, 2003), 2.

26. Martha C. Ward, *Poor Women, Powerful Men: America's Great Experiment in Family Planning* (Boulder: Westview Press, 1986), 31.

27. Thomas B. Littlewood, *The Politics of Population Control* (Notre Dame, IN: University of Notre Dame Press, 1977), 51, 139.

28. Ward, *Poor Women*, 59.

29. Littlewood, *Politics of Population Control*, 54.

30. Ibid., 56.

31. Jean Hardisty, "Hurricane Katrina and Structural Racism: A Letter to White People," October 2005, http://www.jeanhardisty.com/blog_katrina.html (accessed October I, 2005).

32. Dorothy Roberts, *Shattered Bonds: The Color of Child Welfare* (New York: Basic Books, 2002), 237.

33. Solinger, *Pregnancy and Power*, 38.

34. Quoted in Rickie Solinger, "Poisonous Choice," in *"Bad" Mothers: The Politics of Blame in Twentieth-Century America*, eds. Molly Ladd-Taylor and Lauri Umansky (New York: New York University Press, 1998), 385.

35. Smith, *Conquest*, 96.

36. National Council of Negro Women, editorial, *Black Woman's Voice* 2, no. 2 (January/February 1973).

37. Dan T. Carter, "George Wallace and the Rightward Turn in Today's Politics," *Public Eye* magazine, Winter 2005, http://www.publiceye.org/magazine/v19n3/carter_wallace.html (accessed July 20, 2006).

38. Solinger, *Pregnancy and Power*, 137.

39. Jael Silliman et al., *Undivided Rights: Women of Color Organize for Reproductive Justice* (Cambridge, MA: South End Press, 2004), 42–3.

40. Asian Communities for Reproductive Justice, "Reproductive Justice."

43. • *Yifat Susskind*

POPULATION CONTROL IS NOT THE ANSWER TO OUR CLIMATE CRISIS (2019)

Yifat Susskind is the director of MADRES and partners with women's human rights activists from Latin America, the Middle East, Asia, and Africa to create community-based programs that respond to war and climate disasters. She has written extensively in international studies and her work has appeared in *The New York Times*, *The Washington Post*, *Foreign Policy in Focus*, *The Guardian*, and *The Huffington Post*. The following essay was originally published in *Ms. Magazine*.

"If we can get rid of enough people," the El Paso terrorist wrote in his grotesque manifesto, "then our way of life can be more sustainable." His bigoted rampage left little doubt who he meant by "we" and "our way of life." The eco-fascism of the far-right couches its racist intent as concern for the environment, demonizes women of color for "overpopulation" and stokes fears of an end to white racial "purity" and power. It uses the current specter of looming ecological collapse to reawaken a genocidal impulse as old as the United States, wiping out those deemed unfit to survive.

Only a few people defend the most horrific expression of these beliefs. But today, arguments for population control are reemerging in mainstream and even liberal discussions around limiting women's fertility in the name of environmental sustainability.

This isn't the first time women's bodies have been treated as a means to a demographic end. Recall such ugly initiatives, all mainstream in their day, to forcibly sterilize Black, Latina, and Indigenous women, to treat Puerto Rican women like lab rats in contraceptive trials to keep the island's population down and to fund sterilization camps in India.

Invariably, even the most nefarious population control projects claim to serve some unassailable social good, like poverty reduction or peace. After

Ms. September 24, 2019. https://msmagazine.com/2019/09/24/population-control-isnt-the-answer-to-our-climate-crisis/

Hurricane Katrina, a Louisiana representative proposed paying people who receive state assistance $1,000 in exchange for being sterilized. He explained the benefits of reducing the number of poor people, citing the likelihood of more frequent hurricanes and the need to conserve resources.

The reproductive justice movement then emerged to redefine these policies as human rights abuses. But today, the monster of population control has been reanimated, and these gains are again under threat.

Most people now know better than to use the discredited term "population control." Neither will you hear mainstream voices talking about "black overpopulation." Listen, instead, for rights-based and social justice language that positions contraception and family planning as core strategies to reduce carbon emissions.

For instance, a USAID blog entry for World Population Day links family planning to protecting "people, planet, prosperity, peace and partnership," before going on to say that "by slowing rapid population growth, family planning can help to decrease the sheer number of poor people."

Today's mainstream population control advocates offer full-throated support for reproductive rights. They point to a happy coincidence that women's freedom to limit childbearing is also a key solution to climate change. Win-win propositions are inherently appealing, but we should be skeptical of solutions that ask little of those who have caused the problem.

Women around the world will tell you that access to healthcare, family planning, contraception and abortion remain critical unmet needs. True reproductive justice, as conceived by women who have long been targeted for population control, includes the option to choose how many children to have and raise them in a safe, healthy environment. But those seeking to instrumentalize these basic rights as climate solutions segue too seamlessly and singularly to the emissions-cutting benefits of women bearing fewer children—not just any women, but the same poor Black and brown women who have always been blamed for "having too many babies."

Whatever their political underpinnings, population-based approaches to climate change are steeped in three falsehoods.

One is that the world's population is exploding. The rate of growth has actually been slowing since the 1960s; from 1990 to 2019, the global fertility rate fell from 3.2 births per woman to 2.5.

Another is that the main threat we face is resource scarcity, when in fact the problem isn't sheer numbers—it's unequal distribution of basic necessities. The planet cannot provide for 7.5 billion people exploiting resources at the rate of the richest, but it could support many more if the wealthiest used a fairer share and policies enabled poorer communities to end over-reliance on fragile ecosystems.

Finally, there is the myth that larger populations accelerate climate change, when a country's carbon emissions cannot be extrapolated only from its population size. The U.S. is less than 5 percent of the world population but responsible for 15 percent of emissions. Meanwhile, countries in sub-Saharan Africa, commonly cited as prime candidates for population control policies, are among the lowest carbon polluters.

That's obvious when you remember that climate chaos is a direct consequence of industrial policy—but recognizing that truth brings you to a very different set of strategies than encouraging poor women to have fewer babies. The scapegoating of women ultimately draws attention away from the real culprits behind our climate catastrophe: fossil fuel and energy companies, and their scandalous success in supplanting government regulation with subsidies and tax loopholes. It diverts attention from the need to change an economic system that demands limitless resource exploitation and profit-seeking.

Policymakers must seize the change to beat back the idea that population control is a solution to climate breakdown. Most importantly, they can learn from women on the frontlines of climate change worldwide, whose innovative solutions and calls for global economic justice are the real answer to climate breakdown.

44. • *V. Efua Prince*

JUNE (new)

V. Efua Prince is a professor of African American Studies at Wayne State University whose research centers on the complexities of home. Her writing often takes an interdisciplinary form as history, poetry, drama, and performance, in order to transform the history of black women into political art. She is the author of *Burnin' Down the House: Home in African American Literature* (2005), *Daughter's Exchange* (2018), and numerous other creative works. First published in *The Masters Review*, Prince's award-winning essay, "June," represents the interconnectedness of rape with global and historical factors.

1

I dreamed I was carrying a dead man on my back. The stench of his decomposing flesh poisoned each breath. His weight bent my shoulders like a sack filled with cotton. He had been dead long enough for his flesh to yield its contents so I was soiled beneath the mass. But I held his arms and kept a labored pace. When I woke, I buried him without ceremony. I did not mark the date.

2

What's left? Memory. But where is it lodged? In the brain as images? In the flesh as disease or scar tissue? In the air like a virus? In the soil like seed? In the marrow of bone.

3

It was my baby, all grown up looking like herself but also a lot like me when I was her age. It was she that brought it all back.

No, she didn't do it.

All she did was stretch out and fill in. Legs long as a drag queen's with a switch full of conjure—drawing on her roots in New Orleans. New Orleans is just too much. Music at all hours of the day and night. That's why they always dancing in the streets. They eat anything that walk, swim, or crawl. They prone to painting their houses in audacious hues. Even the plants wear too many colors. Air so thick down there that nothing bothers to mind.

Then too, her breasts grew way past any size I'm familiar with. Folks always looking at her saying, "Jill Scott." She open her mouth and they expect blue notes to slide out. She be looking at them through luxurious eyes. Ethiopians walking up to her speaking

Amharic and when she shakes her head at them they say, "Where you from?" She says, "Virginia." They say, "Oh. Where your people from?" "New Orleans," she says. "And Maryland." They look confused.

Those aren't places to be from.

4

I felt guilty. So when he called me and talked incessantly about whatever he was talking about I felt compelled to keep the line open. Although sometimes I put the phone down and did other things. No matter, when I got back to the phone, he'd still be talking. We had dated for nearly five years. Then I broke up with him and left whatever love I had for him on a shelf. He would call long distance and hold me on the phone crying, yelling, accusing, pleading,

One morning he showed up at my house. I went to school in Virginia. I lived off-campus and nearly 200 miles away from him but there he was. I let him in. My day hadn't started yet so I went to the bathroom and showered. I put on my underclothes, wrapped myself in a towel and returned to my room where he was waiting. It's been too long now and I don't recall exactly how he approached me but he started tussling with me. He tied my wrists with one of his wife-beaters. Because I lived alone on the first floor of a house, I kept knives and scissors around in the event that a stranger would come into my abode entertaining the thought that I was a victim. So when he pushed me onto my bed with my hands bound, I retrieved the blade I kept tucked between my box spring and bed frame and cut myself loose. He became enraged. "You cut my shirt!" Then he picked me up and threw me onto the front porch, locking me out of my house. There I was—humiliated. In my bra and panties locked out of my own house in front of my neighbors and whomever happened by. I didn't dare make too much noise. I curled up as small as I could and I waited for release.

5

"It's always been a mystery to me how men can feel themselves honoured by the humiliation of their fellow beings"—Mahatma Gandhi

6

". . . a group of touts attacked a woman at one of the major bus stations in the capital, Harare, [Zimbabwe] and stripped her naked for the 'crime' of wearing a mini-skirt. She managed to escape after paying a commuter omnibus crew $2 to hide her from the mob."—Sally Nyakanyanga, 2015

7

Where you from?
Virginia.

8

In 1619 twenty Africans were off loaded at Old Point Comfort in the area which was to become Fort Monroe in Hampton, Virginia, about 40 miles from the British settlement at Jamestown.

9

Sometimes I imagine a woman being coerced into sex with two or three men in public. She is initially reluctant but eventually gives herself over to the pleasure. For years I would pray and ask God to heal my mind. I don't bother God with this anymore. Now I think this is memory. I think it has something to do with things that happened when I was a very young child.

10

Virginia. New Orleans. Maryland.
Those aren't places to be from.

11

The boundaries of territory in its earliest formation were vaguely identified, particularly its western limits, and thus Virginia was conceived as extending from "sea to sea."

12

When Europe began carving up the world to serve their royal houses, it justified its aggression using the machinations of binary thinking. Binary thinking conceives of experience in terms of oppositions—such as right or wrong, us or them, up or down—which one imagines as inherent rather than constructed. This vision of the world as essentially oppositional is reflected in European religion that pictures divinity in terms of good and evil, light and darkness, heaven and hell. Europeans used this conceptual frame to impose order on their experiences. Human experience is chaotic enough with the confounding intrusions of every day mysteries such as lightning strikes, predators, the bubonic plague, famine, war, and about a million other things lurking in the shadows to suddenly kill you. But for Europeans living during the 16th–19th centuries the realm of possibility was undergoing dramatic expansion.

When the world seemed flat, with the sun revolving around the Earth, folks could imagine themselves at the center of all things. Then Nicolaus Copernicus insisted that accurate perception required complex calculations, which were beyond the average person's frame of reference. Copernicus had science; those operating without the benefit of telescopes and equations needed *something* that could make sense of it all. Imagine the bewilderment propagated within poor societies by adventurers funded by venture capitalists seeking an untold cache of spices, sugar, and gold that they hoped to extract from exotic and distant lands. Even for those who stayed put, these new notions changed what people hoped for, how they saw themselves, and where they thought they were. But because their frame of reference tended to conceptualize in terms of the binary, these ocean journeys yielded for Europeans a "New World" rather than an expanded worldview.

In fact, the conceptual framework fostered by binary thinking encourages a kind of cognitive dissonance. Human beings make analogical comparisons in order to encode something not yet experienced. We come to understand the new thing by mapping it onto something familiar. In this way conceptual maps are merely a long series of associations between dissimilar things. The comparison, then, between what the Europeans knew and what they were freshly encountering is quite natural. However, the trouble comes with the insistence that these encounters be mapped in terms of binary oppositions. Binary thinking represented the lands on the other side of the Atlantic as a *world* somehow distinct, somewhere separate and apart from the world Europeans had already known. Rather than a "New World" and an "Old World," there is, for all practical purposes, just one world.

13

Virginia is a metaphor for the New World.

14

"On the thirty-third day after leaving Cadiz I came into the Indian Sea, where I discovered many islands inhabited by numerous people. I took possession of all of them for our most fortunate King by making public proclamation and unfurling his standard, no one making any resistance."—Christopher Columbus, 1493

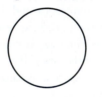

15

When we think of rape we are encouraged to envision it as a problem between individuals. The reality, however, is much more pernicious. Rape is an ideology.

16

Knock Knock
Who's there?
Me

Me who?
Let me in my house motherfucker

17

According to Michael Doran in his *Atlas of County Boundary Changes in Virginia 1634–1895*, "Either as an Anglicized modification of a local chieftain's name (Win-gi-na) or in unabashed flattery of the distaff English sovereign, [Sir Walter] Raleigh's lands became known as Virginia."

18

Virginia. Virgin land. No one lives there. A wilderness peopled not but by savages.

19

Knock Knock
Who's there?
No one
No one who?
Noonenoonenoonenoone

20

More than 350 years ago, Captain John Smith might have walked the ground beneath the porch I crouched on. The great Captain might have paused on this patch of earth to finger the charter for the Virginia Company given him by the sovereign King James. He might have offered a trifle in exchange for a smile from an Indian child right on this ground. Capt. Smith might have had corn grown on this very patch of earth. He might have rested on a log right here on his way to visit Chief Powhatan. He might have squatted here too, to take aim at an Indian warrior shooting buckshot in defense of his land. He might have taken aim to piss. This might very well have been the actual spot where John Smith himself carved a hole in the dirt wherein he relieved his bowels.

I should erect a monument.

21

There are no heroes.
Villains neither.

22

People do not talk about the horrendous conditions in Europe as an explanation for European colonialism and imperialism. Instead, school children are shown pictures of pilgrims seeking religious freedoms. One of the best known of these early settlers is John Winthrop whose vision of founding a "city upon the hill" is indicative of a kind of binary thinking. The pilgrim story of a people fleeing religious persecution, intent on building a model society, casts the travelers in the light of a hero. Winthrop draws this image from Matthew 5: 14–16 in the New Testament of the Bible which states, "You are the light of the world. A town built on a hill cannot be hidden." By representing their actions in the language of this sacred text, Winthrop

associates their actions with that of Jesus Christ—the ultimate Western hero.

23

While the pilgrims finally settle the Massachusetts Bay Colony, Winthrop set out in 1620 with a charter for Virginia.

24

"Rape is not the problem. Rape is a symptom of the problem. And the answer is not to attempt to stop men from raping women, but to categorically change women's values and status in their communities"—Abigail Disney, 2012

25

The Chinese still grieve over Japanese aggressions during the early parts of World War II, which resulted in what is known as the Rape of Nanjing. Estimates range widely but official records state that 200,000 Chinese were massacred and some 20,000–30,000 were raped during the Japanese campaign beginning in December 1937. In *Nanjing Requiem* Chinese American novelist Ha Jin writes about the heroic efforts of an American missionary, Minnie Vautrin, to spare young women from the horrors of the Japanese occupation. Western readers love heroes. Creating heroes provides a way to elevate an individual out of her social, cultural, and historical circumstances. It alleviates responsibility for collective action, so long as we can look to heroic action for change. But rape is not really about individuals, especially during times of war. After killing those whom one intends to kill, then what is a more effective strategy for dominating a resistant people than rape? Raping a woman in front of her family and friends is extremely effective at unraveling the fabric of the community. The sense of shame born by the women and the sense of failure born by the men undermine the foundational security needed to stabilize a community. Rape is psychologically devastating, not to mention the myriad concerns to one's health and well-being. And what of the children born of rape? Who will love them and more importantly *how* will they love them? What kind of love results in the aftermath of rape?

26

Funny thing: I don't remember how I got off the porch.

27

How one loves in the aftermath of rape is a question that African Americans are still resolving. In the wake of slavery, society has demonstrated the extended capacity to envision the rape of black women at the hands of white men, partly because it reinforces the illusion of white, male power as well as the desirability of black women. More recently, African American women authors like Alice Walker and Ntozake Shange popularized (a terrible characterization but I think accurate) the image of black women victimized at the hands of black men. However, if we begin to explore the dynamics of rape and the culture it breeds then we might see more clearly the men who are not just perpetrators but those who are victims as well. For instance, while rape is largely perpetuated against women the notion that it is exclusively violent men

acting against women is preposterous. Do we have any idea how many men were raped under slavery?

It's been years since the United Nations Security Council declared rape a war crime, unanimously adopting Resolution 1820, which called for the immediate and complete halt to acts of sexual violence in 2008. Yet on July 6, 2014, *The Guardian* published "Turning a blind eye to rape crimes in the Democratic Republic of the Congo," accusing the prime minister, Augustin Matata Ponyo, of refusing to acknowledge that state security services outside of the conflict region, including the capital of Kinshasa, are using rape as torture. Rape is such an effective means of subduing a people precisely because of the inclination to turn a blind eye on an act so heinous that it threatens to corrode the very foundation of civilization. Rape has the potential to leave its victims incapacitated and unable to raise a family—there is no more devastating impact of war.

Outside the boundaries of war, rape is more circumspect. The subject of rape as a military tactic remains taboo and the United States has been adopting measures to curb sexual assaults within the ranks of its own military. On another front, in April 2014 the White House appointed a task force to curb sexual assaults on college campuses. Rape is all over the news these days. According to a survey reported by the Associated Press 9 July 2014, 2 in 5 (that's 40%) colleges/universities have not investigated a single rape in the previous five years. Nevertheless, the White House estimates that one in five women (that's 20%) graduate as victims of sexual assault. And if one in five women, how many young men? And how many are graduating as rapists? Rape should not be built in to the cost of education.

28

Funny Thing: In 1421, when Admiral Zhing's Ming fleet reached the Western Hemisphere from China he did not find Virginia. He wasn't looking for a New World—and so he did not find one. He encountered land—fecund—but not vacant. Desirable—but not prone.

45. • *Beth Richie*

A BLACK FEMINIST REFLECTION ON THE ANTIVIOLENCE MOVEMENT (2000)

Beth Richie, professor of African American studies and criminology, law, and justice at the University of Illinois at Chicago, is the author of *Arrested Justice: Black Women, Violence, and America's Prison Nation* (NYU Press, 2012) and *Compelled to Crime: The Gender Entrapment of Black Battered Women* (Routledge, 1995). The short list of her awards includes the Audre Lorde Legacy Award from the Union Institute, the Advocacy Award from the US Department of Health and Human Services, and the Visionary Award from the Violence Intervention Project. Richie serves on the board of numerous organizations and is a founding member of Incite! Women of Color Against Violence. The following article originally appeared in *Signs* (2000).

For the feminist-based antiviolence movement in the United States, the new millennium marks the beginning of an interesting third decade that poses particular challenges and concerns for Black feminist activists and our work to end violence against women. The mainstream social movement, organized over twenty years ago in response to an emerging consciousness that regarded gender violence as the most extreme point along the continuum of women's oppression, can claim numerous victories, such as legal reforms that protect the rights of battered women and sexual assault survivors, the criminalization of sexual harassment, and legislative moves to call attention to the needs of children who witness domestic violence. In addition, an elaborate apparatus of social services has been developed to provide emergency shelter, crisis intervention counseling, medical and legal advocacy, and ongoing assistance with housing, employment, and custody issues that women who experience violence need. African-American and other women of color have been at the forefront of the most radical dimensions of this work.

Services and support at the individual level have been matched with an array of academic and public policy initiatives designed to address violence against women. There are several journals dedicated to presenting new research and intervention discussions related to gender violence, and at least four university-based research centers focus on violence against women. Each year witnesses a growing number of national conferences on issues related to gender violence, which attract a range of audiences, some with more activist goals and others with more professional and bureaucratic interests. The National Institute for Justice, the Centers for Disease Control, the Departments of Housing and Urban Development and Health and Human Services, and—paradoxically—even the Department of Defense have established federal initiatives that attempt to reduce or respond to violence against women in this country. The feminist campaign at the grassroots level has influenced government and public policy to a considerable extent, which has resulted in a significant influx of public funding for victim

Beth Richie, "A Black Feminist Reflection on the Antiviolence Movement" *Signs* 25:4 (Summer 2000): 1133–1137. The University of Chicago Press services, law enforcement training, and prevention services. This growth, due in no small part to the grassroots activism of survivors and other women, has deeply influenced the mainstream consciousness. Evidence of this influence appears in several recent public awareness campaigns and opinion polls that suggest that tolerance for gender-based violence has decreased significantly in the past ten years. Feminist activism has paid off; we have witnessed a considerable shift in public consciousness with regard to the problem of violence against women.

Arguably, a critical dimension of the public awareness campaign that has led to this expansion in resources for, and the credibility of, the antiviolence movement in this country is the assertion that violence against women is a common experience, that any woman or child can be the victim of gender violence. In fact, many of us who do training, public speaking, teaching, and writing on violence against women traditionally begin our presentations by saying, "It can happen to anyone." This notion has become a powerful emblem of our rhetoric and, some would argue, the basis of our mainstream success. Indeed, many people in this country finally understand that they and their children, mothers, sisters, coworkers, and neighbors can be victimized by gender violence—that it really *can* happen to anyone.

The ideas that any woman can be a battered woman and that rape is every woman's problem were part of a strategic attempt by early activists to avoid individualizing the problem of domestic and sexual violence, to focus on the social dimensions of the problem of gender violence, and to resist the stigmatization of race and class commonly associated with mainstream responses to social problems. This approach was based not only on the empirical data available at the time but also on the lived experiences of most women who—at many points in our lives—change our behavior to minimize our risk of assault. This generalized construction helped to foster an analysis of women's vulnerability as both profound and persistent, rather than as particular to any racial/ethnic community, socioeconomic position, religious group, or station in life. As a result, from college campuses

to private corporations, from public housing complexes to elite suburban communities, and in all manner of religious institutions progress has been made in increasing awareness that violence against women is an important social problem that requires a broad-based social response.

And yet, as a Black feminist activist committed to ending violence against women, something seems terribly wrong with this construction at this point in time, something that leaves many African-American women and other women of color still unsafe and renders our communities for the most part disconnected from the mainstream antiviolence movement. I would even argue that the notion that every woman is at risk—one of the hallmarks of our movement's rhetorical paradigm—is in fact a dangerous one in that it has structured a national advocacy response based on a false sense of unity around the experience of gender oppression. For, as the epistemological foundation of the antiviolence movement was institutionalized, the assumption of "everywoman" fell into the vacuum created by a white feminist analysis that did not very successfully incorporate an analysis of race and class.

In the end, the assumed race and class neutrality of gender violence led to the erasure of low-income women and women of color from the dominant view. I contend that this erasure, in turn, seriously compromised the transgressive and transformative potential of the antiviolence movement's potentially radical critique of various forms of social domination. It divorced racism from sexism, for example, and invited a discourse regarding gender violence without attention to the class dimensions of patriarchy and white domination in this country.

Put another way, when the national dialogue on violence against women became legitimized and institutionalized, the notion that "It could happen to anyone" meant that "It could happen to those in power." Subsequently, the ones who mattered most in society got the most visibility and the most public sympathy; those with power are the ones whose needs are taken most seriously. When mainstream attention to the needs of victims and survivors was gradually integrated into the public realm of social service and legal protection and became visible in research studies, "everywoman" became a white middle-class woman who could turn to a private therapist, a doctor, a police officer, or a law to protect her from abuse. She consumed the greater proportion of attention in the literature, intervention strategies were based on her needs, she was featured in public awareness campaigns, and she was represented by national leaders on the issue of violence against women.

So what began as an attempt to avoid stereotyping and stigma has resulted in exactly that which was seen early in the antiviolence movement as a threat to the essential values of inclusion, equality, and antioppression work. The consequence of this paradigmatic problem is that victimization of women of color in low-income communities is invisible to the mainstream public, at best. Worse yet, when poor African-American, Latina, Native American women and other women of color are victimized, the problem is cast as something other than a case of gender violence.

Similarly, scholarship and activism around racial/ethnic and class oppression often ignores gender as an essential variable. This argument is supported by the growing body of research on women who use drugs, women in prison, women who live in dangerous low-income neighborhoods, lesbians of color, or young women who are involved with street gangs. Where women and girls are included in these studies or activist campaigns, they are seen as "special cases" within those populations rather than as women per se. Gender is not considered a central, defining part of their identity, and their experiences are subsumed by other master categories, typically race and class. They are essentially de-gendered, which renders them without access to claims of gender oppression and outside the category of individuals at risk of gender violence.

It is here, at a critical crossroads, that I ponder my work in the antiviolence movement as a Black feminist activist and academic. From here I offer critical observations and make recommendations for the future. First, it seems that to continue to ignore the race and class dimensions of gender oppression will seriously jeopardize the viability and legitimacy of the antiviolence movement in this country, a dangerous development for women of color in low-income communities, who are most likely to be in both dangerous intimate relationships and dangerous social positions. The overreliance on simplistic analyses (as in the case of "everywoman") has significant consequences for the potential for radical social change. I suggest that we revisit our analytic frame and develop a much more complex and contextualized analysis of gender violence, one rooted in an understanding of the historical and contemporary social processes that have differentially affected women of color.

I argue for a reassessment of the responses that have been central to antiviolence work—in particular, the reliance on law enforcement as the principal provider of women's safety. For over a decade, women of color in the antiviolence movement have warned against investing too heavily in arrest, detention, and prosecution as responses to violence against women. Our warnings have been ignored, and the consequences have been serious: serious for the credibility of the antiviolence movement, serious for feminist organizing by women of color, and, most important, serious for women experiencing gender violence who fall outside of the mainstream.

The concern with overreliance on law enforcement parallels a broader apprehension about the expansion of state power in the lives of poor women of color in this country. Just as the antiviolence movement is relying on legal and legislative strategies to criminalize gender violence, women in communities of color are experiencing the negative effects of conservative legislation regarding public assistance, affirmative action, and immigration. And, while the antiviolence movement is working to improve arrest policies, everyday safety in communities of color is being threatened by more aggressive policing, which has resulted in increased use of force, mass incarceration, and brutality. The conflict between the anti-violence movement's strategy and the experiences of low-income communities of color has seriously undermined our work as feminists of color fighting violence against women.

Obviously, leadership emerges as central to this dilemma. While there is a renewed call for unity and diversity from some corners of our movement, others (women of color who have dedicated years to this work) are appalled at the persistent whiteness of the nationally recognized leadership. As the bureaucratic and institutional apparatus of the antiviolence movement grows—bringing more funding, more recognition, and also more collaborations with partners who do not share our radical goals—there is little evidence of increasing racial/ethnic and class diversity. Despite some notable exceptions, the lack of women of color in leadership roles in antiviolence programs is startling and contrasts sharply with the rhetoric of inclusion, diversity, and commitment to antioppression work. While there may be structural excuses for this, the fact that so few national organizations (even feminist ones) have successfully promoted the leadership of women of color is almost a mockery of the values on which the movement was built. Given the similar invisibility of women of color as leaders in struggles for racial justice (again, with some exceptions), the situation can seem dire as we face the new millennium.

Yet, for better or worse, the solutions are not enigmatic; they exist within our core values and the principles on which the antiviolence movement was organized. Feminist women of color need to step forward as never before, reclaiming our place as leaders both in the antiviolence movement and in struggles for gender equality in our communities. The antiviolence movement needs only to acknowledge the contradictions between its rhetoric and practice and to deal honestly with the hypocrisy in its work. As members of a social justice movement committed to ending oppression, we must reconsider the complexity of rendering justice by paying attention to specific vulnerabilities of race and class. As we claim victories on some very important fronts, our understanding of gender oppression must be broadened to include state-sanctioned abuse and mistreatment of women. If we are prepared to go there, we can begin the millennium ready to face the really hard, radical work of ending violence against women—for each and any woman.

---

46. • *Courtney Bailey*

A QUEER #METOO STORY:
Sexual Violence, Consent, and Interdependence (new)

Courtney Bailey, an associate professor of communication arts at Allegheny College, specializes in critical cultural studies and feminist, queer, and critical race theory. She has a particular interest in visual culture and visual representations of the body in popular culture. Her research has appeared in *Disability Studies Quarterly, Queer Studies in Media & Popular Culture, QED: A Journal of GLBTQ Worldmaking, Communication and Critical Cultural Studies*, and the *Journal of Popular Culture*. Focusing on her own experiences with disability and sexual/gendered violence, this essay was written for this collection and explores the potential of writing from personal experience while still grounding that experience in larger theoretical insights.

INTRODUCTION

I think of myself as one of the lucky ones, a woman who somehow moves through the world of heteropatriarchy without encountering the worst kinds of sexual violence. Sure, I have some experiences that I problematically file under "bad sex," but I tell myself they cannot match the horrific stories emerging from the era of Trumpism and #MeToo. In many rape accounts, forced penetration (usually penile-vaginal) emerges as the primary site of trauma. This makes sense given that penetration itself carries so much cultural baggage: according to dominant U.S. culture, it is an indispensable component of procreation, the consummation of heteroromanticism, and the sign that sex "really" happened.

My queer story of sexual violence exists on the fringes, recognizable only if seen around the corner of the "textbook" case in which a man violates a woman via penile penetration. I suggest instead that sexual violence *feminizes* victims and *masculinizes* perpetrators, no matter how they individually identify. Dominant culture *produces* the categories of women and men through acts of gendered sexual violence. This binary constructs masculinity and femininity as mutually exclusive opposites, insists they are the only two options, and renders femininity inferior and masculinity superior (Stryker 2006, 253). Because anti-rape social movements understandably focus on violence against women perpetrated by men, they usually center heterosexuality and/or heterosex. This essay centers queer sexual experiences instead, arguing for an understanding of the stakes of sexual violence that shifts from consent and bodily autonomy to sexual agency and bodily integrity.

The following story contains sexually explicit and violent scenes. I respect strategies used to minimize voyeurism and re-traumatization, such as eliding the details of a sexual assault. But such strategies only erase the very things I need to say. I err on the side of specificity because the white heteropatriarchal devil really is in the details.

THE STORY OF KIM

I meet Kim through an online dating site, and we embark on a loving nine-year relationship also fraught with mistreatment and abuse. When we first decide to have sex, I tell her that penetration physically hurts me so it's off limits. She nods and honors my wishes . . . until the night she jams her finger up my ass with no warning. Surprised and shocked, I feel thrown off balance. I feel guilty because my dislike of penetration keeps denying *her* a pleasurable sensation, purportedly the pinnacle of sexual and emotional intimacy. I want desperately to prove that I'm not selfish, frigid, and aloof; I want to show her how much I love her, so I stay silent. My silence arises, at least in part, from the demands of hegemonic femininity, including passivity, selflessness, and deference to others (Bordo 2004 11–12). Kim takes my silence as permission to penetrate me anally whenever she decides it's in my (her) best interest, which is not often but often enough.

She also threatens me with rape on more than one occasion, usually right before I leave for work. "One of these days, I'm going to tie you to the bed and rape you all day long, over and over again," she says in a flirty tone as if she's giving me a sexy compliment. I laugh these statements off until my feminist conscience rears its head and I tell her to knock it off. "But it's just a joke!" she exclaims, as if a woman raping another woman is *prima facie* ridiculous. Once we divorce and I begin to understand our relationship as abusive, her rape jokes appear more like rape fantasies of control, possession, and dominance.

I wonder if my boundaries come across like a challenge to her, an eerie echo of the infamous "no means yes, and yes means anal" slogan popularized by Yale fraternity members in 2010 (Orbey 2018). This slogan relies on the peculiar cultural charge that adheres to anal penetration, simultaneously forbidden and the ultimate sign of heterosexual male conquest. Heteropatriarchy frames women's pain around penetration as expected and normal, desired and desirable, proof of her chastity, and a guarantee of greater male pleasure at her expense—hence the value accorded to "tightness" (Loofbourow 2018). Anal sex heightens this dynamic because of its taboo status. By doing something that will presumably hurt her and that society frowns up, he asserts his will in the face of reluctance and resistance. In the cultural imaginary, anal heterosex becomes a realm where real men prove themselves and real women exist for male sexual gratification and bravado.

What happens when this dynamic plays out between two queer-identified women? Kim exerted a masculinist form of power over me, but our status as queer women complicates it. Historically excluded from and marginalized by masculinist power, queer women can only access it in partial, limited, and unstable ways. In the absence of a penis and clearly demarcated gender roles, we can only approximate heterosex by engaging in a shadowy, perverse version of it. My experience of anal penetration at Kim's hands is either proof of sexual/gendered pathology or "not that bad."

WHEN CONSENT IS NOT ENOUGH

Mainstream anti-rape activism usually presumes that consent is the cure for sexual violence and that to enact consent, we need more/better communication (Harding 2015, 44–46; Friedman 2017, 188–89). Activists assume that well-intentioned people know how to read interpersonal cues and simply need to pay more attention to them. But *how* do people know? As a scholar of communication, I believe communication constructs our reality; that is, it shapes our understanding of ourselves, others, and the world. Far from a panacea, communication is part of the problem because it produces and circulates dominant norms. For instance, Hollywood often propagates a "no eventually means yes" model of heterosex, in which *both women and men have always already consented.* These scenes depict the man as an aggressive pursuer who won't take no for an answer (McIntosh 2018, "Abduction;" McIntosh 2018, "Stalking"). When the woman explicitly resists, he persists until she reveals, often enthusiastically, that she really wanted it

all along. If this sort of portrayal pervades the cultural air we breathe, then we learn that women's verbal and non-verbal cues of resistance do not, in fact, mean "stop." They mean "keep going."

My experiences of sexual abuse, therefore, are not just a matter of interpersonal miscommunication. U.S. rape culture frames my silence and non-verbal cues as an invitation for Kim to keep going, to overpower me, until I give in and start enjoying myself because maybe I want it to happen. Women don't want to be subjected to rape and perhaps qualifying as a "real" (white, cis, straight, middle-class) woman under the dominant rules requires being "rapeable." Perhaps being acknowledged as rapeable brings with it protection—the masculinist, paternalistic and controlling kind.

Yet what do we do when white heteropatriarchy deems white women perfect victims, black and brown women never victims, black and brown men always perpetrators, and white men heroic saviors? What do we do when these systems deny lesbians sexual agency by portraying them either as nonsexual in the absence of straight men or hyper-sexual in the presence of straight men? What do we do when these systems need a clear distinction between men and women and so punish trans, non-binary, and genderqueer folks? Consent may not be a strong enough term to bear the weight of what it needs to accomplish under these conditions, especially when considered outside the white, heteronormative charmed circle (Rubin 1984, 153).

SHOULD I CALL IT RAPE?

As the astute reader might note, I have not explicitly called my experience of anal penetration "rape." If communication constructs our world, then it's not just a matter of semantics; it's a matter of reality, politics, and belief. Calling what happened to me "rape," for one thing, invokes a legalistic framework of crime and punishment, which locates the remedy for sexual violence in the criminal justice system. Turning to this framework allows anti-rape activists to agitate for important reforms like affirmative consent laws (Friedman and Valenti 2008, 5). Yet even when the legal system decides to prosecute rapists, a rare occasion indeed, it can re-traumatize victims/survivors by enacting a kind of "second rape." It thus *produces* sexual violence as an integral part of its punitive functions. By conceptualizing rapists as irredeemable monsters, a legalistic framework settles for blaming evil individuals rather than interrogating the systems that make rape possible in the first place.

Like all spheres of life, sex exists within systems of domination and oppression, lending it a potentially traumatic quality even outside technical or legal definitions. White supremacy, for instance, hypersexualizes women of color, thereby excusing—and erasing—sexual violence against them (Hill Collins 2005, 121). Heteropatriarchy eroticizes male domination and female subordination under the rubric of romantic love (Griffin 2008, 501). Treating rape as a singular, aberrant incident, therefore, obscures the ubiquity of rape culture and its normalization of sexual violence (Dworkin 1987, 66).

The injurious potential of sex exists alongside pleasure, intimacy, and love, but that does not necessarily mitigate it. Laura Kipnis argues that dominant notions of romantic love imagine intimacy as the merging of true selves, which she describes in the following terms:

> Lovers fashion themselves after doctors wielding long probes to penetrate the tender regions. Try to think of yourself as just one big orifice: now stop clenching and relax . . . Needless to say, all this opening up will leave you feeling somewhat vulnerable, lying there psychically spread-eagled . . . But remember, it's for your own good—even if it subjects you to whatever pain [or] chafing the partner may happen to inflict on you. (2003, 76)

This passage suggests that sexual violations are normative, that is, culturally expected and encouraged. Kim's actions, then, are hardly aberrations or deviations from romantic love; on the contrary, romantic love justifies and expects those actions in the name of wholeness and completeness, of two interior selves becoming one. Kim's penetration of me is for my own good, showing me what it's truly like to open up to someone else.

Alongside my concerns about legalistic and romantic frameworks, I also worry about reinforcing the pernicious myths that link queer people to sexual perversion. The last thing I want to do is give homo/transphobia more ammunition, especially in an era when lawmakers are rationalizing the persecution of LGBTQPAI+ communities in the name of "religious liberty." The last thing I want to do is give sexism more ammunition, especially in an era where lawmakers are undermining reproductive justice and a self-avowed sexual abuser sits in the White House. The last thing I want to do is provide fodder for the male gaze, which has historically co-opted lesbian sexuality for straight male titillation (Ristock 2002, 16). Refusing the term "rape," then, might be a protective move that attempts to shield queer and lesbian communities from further voyeurism, trivialization, and violence (Girschick 2002, 11).

But still I wonder, is refusing to use it running away from something far too daunting to confront? For all its limitations, the word "rape" carries a certain kind of weight; it has a certain kind of specificity and rhetorical force. Calling it rape does not feel liberatory or redemptive, but by not calling it that, am I trying to distance myself from it and, in the process, underselling it? As Ristock and Girschick note in their studies of woman-to-woman sexual violence, the pacifism, gentleness, and care for others associated with hegemonic femininity can make it difficult to believe that women are even capable of intimate violence, especially when rape typically connotes brutal male force and aggression (Ristock 2002, 48; Girschick 2002, 93). Maybe I feel like a finger up the ass cannot compete with a dick up, well, anything. If lesbians cannot have "real" sex, then we cannot have real rape, and Kim's insistence that it's just a joke lingers. In this context, calling it rape refuses simplistic conflations of queerness with liberation and gives shape to harms otherwise erased or marginalized. Perhaps calling it rape opens up as many possibilities as it shuts down, including rethinking rape (and sex) itself.

CONCLUSION: SEXUAL AGENCY, BODILY INTEGRITY, AND INTERDEPENDENCE

Although often treated as interchangeable, the terms "consent" and "agency" do not index the same thing. Consent remains anchored to the notion of the autonomous individual with free will, historically the exclusive property of hegemonic masculinity. Rather than locating the self in free will and self-sufficiency, agency places the self within larger sociopolitical systems and it recognizes that these contexts both enable and constrain creative riffs on dominant norms. Agency relies upon a radical notion of interdependence in which we only make sense in relation to one another (e.g., men only exist because women do, and vice versa). If we take agency as our starting point rather than consent, sexual mutuality and reciprocity do not arise from one person respecting or merging with another person. Instead, they arise from the very grounds that make personhood possible.

Along with sexual agency, I invoke bodily integrity to signify what's at stake in sexual violence. Bodily integrity does not refer to a body that is impermeable, but one that is inviolable. All bodies are permeable and interdependent. Inviolability recognizes and respects such interdependence, refusing both complete separation and complete merging. In my own case, I suffer not because my partner fails to respect my free will and bodily autonomy (which dominant culture denies me anyway), but because she breaks the promise of mutuality and reciprocity necessary for sexual agency and bodily integrity.

It's tempting to assume that love represents a viable alternative to rape culture. But our love never quite escapes the dominant terms of (hetero)romance because it is constituted, in part, by those very terms. The romantic belief in an internal, true self contributes to the Western fantasy of the atomized individual, one who enjoys autonomy, independence, willpower, and control. The harm of sexual violence arises from one individual's decision to breach another's sense of self. This view cannot capture the damage sexual violence does to *relationships* among and within people. If we are defined through our relationships, then sexual violence shatters the grounds of selfhood, only to remake it—and our relationships—in the image of dominant structures.

In sum, *the harm of sexual violence arises not from a violation of independence, but from a violation of interdependence.* The alternative of sexual agency and bodily integrity I propose here does not presume to eliminate such harm completely; after all, we're still operating within dominant culture, and my alternative is a riff, not a totally different song. Like consent, it's aspirational, a goal to put our energies toward. It may be harder to enact than consent, given that it challenges deeply cherished values in U.S. culture, including the belief that my desires are my own, I should control my own body, and love conquers all. If we truly seek a just and compassionate world, we need to interrogate these beliefs, even when they might serve our own interests.

The textbook case certainly enjoys the most attention in public discourse and the #MeToo movement's status as a hashtag makes it open to a range of different, even contradictory stories. Mine will never be perceived as media-worthy as the ones around Bill Cosby, Harvey Weinstein, and Brett Kavanaugh, but it exists nonetheless, ready and waiting to be shared. Sharing it is not only key to my survival, but an extension of my politics. Like bearing witness, sharing this essay represents an enactment of interdependence. From one feminist to another, I could not—and would not—be here without you.

WORKS CITED

Bordo, Susan. *Unbearable Weight: Feminism, Western Culture, and the Body.* University of California Press, 2004.

Dworkin, Andrea. *Intercourse.* New York: The Free Press, 1987.

Friedman, Jacyln. *Unscrewed: Women, Sex, Power, and How to Stop Letting the System Screw Us All.* New York: Seal Press, 2017.

Friedman, Jaclyn, and Jessica Valenti, editors. *Yes Means Yes: Visions of Female Sexual Power and a World Without Rape*. New York: Perseus Books Group, 2008.

Girschick, Lori B. *Woman-to-Woman Violence: Does She Call It Rape?* Boston, MA: Northeastern UP, 2002.

Griffin, Susan. "Rape: The All-American Crime." *Women: Images and Realities*, 4th ed. Edited by Amy Kesselman, Lily D. McNair, and Nancy Schniedewind. New York: McGraw Hill, 2008, pp. 499–506.

Harding, Kate. *Asking for It: The Alarming Rise of Rape Culture—and What We Can Do About It*. Boston: De Capo Press, 2015.

Hill Collins, Patricia. *Black Sexual Politics*. New York: Routledge, 2005.

Kipnis, Laura. *Against Love: A Polemic*. New York: Pantheon Books, 2003.

Loofbourow, Lili. "The Female Price of Male Pleasure." *The Week*, January 25, 2018, theweek.com/articles/749978/female-price-male-pleasure. Accessed October 10, 2018.

McIntosh, Jonathan. "Abduction as Romance." *YouTube*, uploaded by Pop Culture Detective, June 20, 2018, www.youtube.com/watch?v=t8xL7w1POZ0.

McIntosh, Jonathan. "Stalking for Love." *YouTube*, uploaded by Pop Culture Detective, February 28, 2018, www.youtube.com/watch?v=rZ1MPc5HG_I&t=4s.

Orbey, Eren. "The Long Decline of DKE, Brett Kavanagh's Fraternity at Yale." *The New Yorker*, September 25, 2018, https://www.newyorker.com/culture/culture-desk/the-long-decline-of-dke-brett-kavanaughs-fraternity-at-yale. Accessed July 29, 2019.

Ristock, Janice. *No More Secrets: Violence in Lesbian Relationships*. New York: Routledge, 2002.

Rubin, Gayle. "Thinking Sex: Notes for a Radical Theory of the Politics of Sex." *Pleasure and Danger*, edited by Carole Vance. New York: Routledge, 1984, pp. 143–178.

Stryker, Susan. "My Words to Victor Frankenstein Above the Village of Chamounix." *The Transgender Studies Reader*, edited by Susan Stryker and Stephen Whittle. New York: Routledge, 2006, pp. 244–256.

47. • *Joey L. Mogul, Andrea J. Richie, and Kay Whitlock*

FALSE PROMISES:
Criminal Legal Responses to Violence Against LGBT People (2011)

The following piece, excerpted from *Queer (In)Justice: Criminalization of LGBT People in the U.S.* (Beacon, 2011), was collective written by the three authors. Joey Mogul is a partner at the People's Law Office, where he fights for justice for people who have suffered from police and other state torture, abuse, and misconduct. He also directs a clinic at DePaul University's College of Law. Andrea Richie is a leading black lesbian police misconduct attorney who has written extensively on the profiling and policing of women of color and litigated *Tikkun v. City of New York*, a ground-breaking case that challenged unlawful searches of trans people in police custody. In 2014 she was awarded a Senior Soros Justice Fellowship to continue her work. Kay Whitlock is an activist and writer committed to dismantling structural violence. She co-authored *Considering Hate* (with Michael Bronski; Beacon, 2015) and is the co-founder and co-editor (with Nancy Heitzeg) of the Criminal Injustice Series on the blog *Critical Mass Progress*.

In March 2002 April Mora, a lesbian teen of African American and Native American descent, was walking to a store in Denver, Colorado, to get a soft drink. A car pulled up behind her and the driver called out, referring disparagingly to Mora as a "dyke." Two other men jumped from the car, attacked her, and pinned her to the ground. When Mora screamed, one man with a knife cut her tongue, causing blood to gather in her throat. He held a knife to her neck while the other used a razor blade to carve the word "dyke" on her left forearm and "R.I.P." into the flesh of her stomach. Choking, she fought to get free. The man with the razor cut her face. Before leaving her on the street, both men kicked her in the ribs, telling her she was lucky they hadn't raped her, and that next time, they would.

Dazed, injured, and bloodied, Mora walked back home and called her girlfriend, Dominicque Quintana, at school. When Quintana arrived, they called an ambulance and the police. The scene that unfolded when the police arrived both compounded and complicated the homophobic ferocity of the original attack. According to Quintana's mother, who lived with the two young women, the police immediately wanted to know if Mora and her girlfriend had been fighting, and if they were on drugs. They did not search for the men who attacked Mora, instead insisting that she take a polygraph to prove she was telling the truth.

After the young women were finally allowed to leave for the hospital, officers remaining on the scene focused their investigation on a "self-infliction of injury" theory. Quintana's mother later recounted that "the police went into my house and looked for a razor and the tee shirt April had been wearing. The police trashed April and Dominicque's bedroom in the basement and went through the freezer, too." Though the health care providers who treated Mora offered to confirm in writing that the injuries she suffered could not have been self-inflicted, the police nevertheless insisted on focusing on Mora rather than on investigating her account of events, thereby foreclosing any opportunity to locate her attackers.[1]

Violence against LGBT people at the hands of strangers on the streets and family members in our homes continues to be reported at alarming rates across the country. According to the National Coalition of Anti-Violence Programs (NCAVP), a national network of thirty-five local organizations providing services to and advocating on behalf of LGBT people, in 2008 there were over two thousand instances of homophobic and transphobic violence reported to just thirteen local organizations across the country, representing a 26 percent increase over 2006 figures.[2] Homophobic and transphobic violence spans a spectrum from brutal physical attacks such as that experienced by Mora, to pervasive verbal abuse and harassment. While commonplace, physical assaults make up the minority of reported incidents. Nevertheless, the viciousness and impunity of the violence in many instances shocks the conscience, prompts outrage, and spurs demands for action.

[. . .]

Unfortunately, but perhaps not surprisingly given the central role played by the criminal legal system in policing sexual and gender nonconformity, April Mora's experience with seeking protection and accountability from the police is also not unique. LGBT people across the country consistently report that police often focus on them, rather than their assailants, when they are victims of violence, by questioning their account or blaming them for bringing violence upon themselves. With appalling frequency, LGBT victims of violence are subjected to further homophobic or transphobic verbal or physical abuse at the hands of law enforcement authorities that are charged with protecting them. Often, police refuse to take reports, neglect to classify violence as motivated by anti-LGBT sentiment or as domestic violence, or fail to respond altogether.[3] For many LGBT people, and particularly LGBT people of color, immigrants, youth, and criminalized queers, reliance on the police and criminal legal system for safety is simply not an option because of the risk of adverse consequences.

[. . .]

VIOLENCE AGAINST LGBT PEOPLE

The virulently homophobic and transphobic assault April Mora experienced constitutes what is generally understood to be a *hate crime*, a term used to describe violence motivated, in whole or in part, by actual or perceived race, color, religion, ethnicity, national origin, sexual orientation, gender, gender identity or expression, or disability. According to the FBI, the majority of identity-related violence is motivated by race, followed by violence based on religion, homophobia, and national origin.[4] Indeed, the grisly 1998 murder of James Byrd, Jr., who was beaten and then dragged behind a truck to his death by three white supremacists in Jasper, Texas, remains foremost among iconic representations of present-day manifestations of hate crimes in the United States.

Recognizing that many forms of violence are motivated by a range of intentions and hostilities, the terms *racist*, *sexist*, *anti-Semitic*, *anti-Muslim*, and *homophobic and transphobic violence* are used here in an effort to more accurately describe the phenomena under discussion: the terms *bias* or *hate crime* suggest that such violence is motivated entirely by prejudice (presumably irrational) and not informed by historical patterns of dominance and subordination that produce tangible political, social, and economic benefits for majority groups. Regardless of the terminology used or its targets, there is no question that such violence is abhorrent, structural, and pervasive.

Where violence against LGBT people is concerned, the problem is difficult to quantify for a variety of reasons. Like many forms of gender and sexuality-based violence, it is underreported across the board, and particularly to law enforcement officials.[5] Numerous factors may contribute to LGBT individuals' reluctance to report violence they experience, including fear of retribution by their attackers, and of disclosure of sexual orientation, gender identity, or immigration status, perceptions that police will not take the report seriously, or will blame them for the violence, and participation in informal or criminalized economic activity, including

sex work.[6] According to the NCAVP, "Because anti-LGBT violence has historically been poorly addressed by law enforcement (and because law enforcement officials remain one of the prime categories of offenders documented by NCAVP each year), it is very often underreported to police even in jurisdictions where relationships between law enforcement and the LGBT population have improved." As a result, LGBT antiviolence activists and service providers generally agree that much—perhaps even most—harassment and violence against queers is never reported.[7]

Moreover, official figures do not even accurately depict the number of incidents that *do* come to the attention of law enforcement, due to police officers' failure to adequately and appropriately respond to, classify, document, and report such instances.[8] While the FBI issues an annual report that includes data on incidents reported to law enforcement where a motive based on sexual orientation and, more recently, gender identity or expression has been ascribed, it relies on inconsistent, voluntary reporting by a small and unrepresentative number of local law enforcement agencies. In 2007, for example, only 2,025 out of nearly 17,000 law enforcement agencies reported hate crime data to the federal Uniform Crime Reporting Program.[9] The most reliable source of national data on anti-LGBT violence is compiled annually by the NCAVP. Although limited by resources and the fluctuating capacity of its member organizations to consistently collect and report data, the NCAVP's reports document incidents of homophobic and transphobic violence reported directly to its member organizations, including incidents in which victims have declined to report to the police, or where law enforcement refused classification as a hate crime.

The NCAVP's 2008 report paints a sobering picture. In addition to an increase of 26 percent over 2006 figures in incidents of vandalism, verbal abuse, and physical abuse, the incidence of sexual assaults reported to be motivated by homophobia and transphobia rose sharply for the third consecutive year. While murders represent only a small fraction of violence experienced by LGBT people, their numbers increased by 28 percent from 2007 to 2008, and, according to the NCAVP, constituted "the highest number of deaths since 1999."[10]

Since racially motivated violence makes up the majority of reported hate crimes, it is not surprising that LGBT people of color are overrepresented among those targeted for homophobic and transphobic violence.[11] Transgender people also experience high levels of violence: 12 percent of the total number of reported incidents of violence targeted transgender people, and transgender and gender-nonconforming people report some of the most pervasive and egregious forms of harassment and abuse.[12] Even among LGB people who do not identify as transgender, gender nonconformity has been found to be a predictor of both "every day discrimination" and violence.[13] Finally, despite the prevailing perception that gay men are "the natural and most frequent targets of homophobic hate crime," some estimate that one in five lesbians have been assaulted in an antilesbian incident in their lifetimes.[14]

No matter which numbers or populations we look at, homophobic and transphobic violence against LGBT people in the United States clearly demands a response. The question is whether responses rooted in a criminal legal system invested in policing and punishing sexual and gender deviance, rather than in community-based accountability and systemic change, are effective in actually preventing and protecting queers from violence.

THE "HATE CRIME" FRAMEWORK

The predominant response to violence against LGBT people over the past decade has focused on enactment of legislation against hate crimes. In almost all cases, the underlying violation—criminal mischief, harassment, malicious intimidation or threat, vandalism, arson, assault, battery, rape, or murder—is already subject to criminal penalties.[15] The addition of provisions specific to motivations for already-criminalized activity is intended to ensure harsher punishment of such

offenses and promote law enforcement measures intended—at least in theory—to deter and prevent such violence.

[. . .]

In 1981, the Anti-Defamation League (ADL)[16] developed a "model" template for hate crime laws, promoted as an effective response to the problem of harassment, intimidation, and violence based on a victim's actual or perceived race, religion, or national origin. Sexual orientation and gender were later added to the ADL model. The core feature of the ADL approach is "a 'penalty-enhancement' concept: criminal activity motivated by hate is subject to a stiffer sentence" on the grounds that the harm extends beyond the individual, affecting the entire community.[17]

The model is based on the theoretical swift and harsh "retribution" for violence directed at any member of a particular group, without reference to historical context, the complexities of intersecting power relations, or consequences to members of other oppressed groups. The powerful appeal of such an approach rests in its implied promise that, by framing communities historically targeted for ongoing harassment and violence as "crime victims," law enforcement will "be on our side."

[. . .]

In 1982, the National Gay Task Force initiated the first national antiviolence organizing project to document and increase public awareness of violence against lesbian and gay people, and mobilize "community indignation about hate crimes [in order to] finally end the long-ignored epidemic of anti-LGBT violence." The primary policy tool for bringing about an end to this violence would be "the passage of state and federal laws that recognize LGBT vulnerability to crimes motivated by anti-LGBT hate and prejudice."[18] Other national, state, and local groups representing LGBT communities also quickly embraced the hate crime framework. State hate crime legislation rapidly proliferated, particularly as advocates worked to expand the original list of protected categories to include actual or perceived ethnicity, sexual orientation, mental or physical disability, gender, and gender identity or expression. By late 2009, forty-five states had legislation addressing bias-motivated harassment and violence. Laws vary with regard to protected categories, though most include race, religion, ethnicity, and national origin. Twelve states and the District of Columbia include both gender identity and sexual orientation, while eighteen states only include sexual orientation.[19]

[. . .]

New federal hate crime laws passed as well, beginning with the 1990 Hate Crimes Statistics Act. Sentencing enhancements were tucked into the much broader 1994 Violent Crime Control and Law Enforcement Act.[20] In 2009, the Local Law Enforcement Enhancement Act (LLEEA), also known as the Matthew Shepard and James Byrd, Jr. Hate Crimes Prevention Act, authorized the Department of Justice to assist or, where local authorities are unwilling or unable, take the lead in state and local investigations and prosecutions.

A push for the creation of specialized law enforcement units to investigate and prosecute hate crimes accompanied the rapid spread and expansion of these laws, a call taken up by many LGBT organizations. Such units now exist in a growing number of locales. In many more community liaisons are charged with educating law enforcement officers about affected communities and facilitating appropriate responses to hate crimes.[21]

[. . .]

Closer examination of the hate crime framework reveals substantive flaws in this approach. A central shortcoming is its exclusive focus on individual acts of violence rather than on dismantling the systemic forces that promote, condone, and facilitate homophobic and transphobic violence. Hate or bias-related violence is portrayed as individualized, ignorant, and aberrant—a criminal departure by individuals and extremist groups from the norms of society, necessitating intensified policing to produce safety. The fact is many of the individuals who engage

in such violence are encouraged to do so by mainstream society through promotion of laws, practices, generally accepted prejudices, and religious views. In other words, behavior that is racist, homophobic, transphobic, anti-Semitic, anti-Muslim, and anti-immigrant, and violence against disabled people, does not occur in a political vacuum. And it is not always possible to police the factors that encourage and facilitate it.

For instance, violence against LGBT people generally increases in the midst of highly visible, homophobic, right-wing political attacks. Michigan saw the largest increase (207 percent) in anti-LGBT incidents reported to NCAVP in 2007, as the state's attorney general was concluding a three-year campaign against domestic partnership benefits.[22] In 2008, during the volatile backlash that accompanied the statewide Yes on Proposition 8 campaign to reverse a California Supreme Court decision permitting same-sex couples to marry, Community United Against Violence (CUAV) reported a large increase in reported anti-LGBT violence.[23] Other tensions also produce notable increases in violence against LGBT people who are immigrants or people of color. For example, attacks against South Asian and Middle Eastern LGBT people surged in the aftermath of the anti-Arab and anti-Muslim rhetoric following 9/11.[24]

Because they fail to address larger social forces influencing individual acts of violence, and instead focus on harsher punishment of individuals rather than prevention, there is no proactive "protection" in hate crime laws, despite the claims of supporters.[25] While the presumed deterrent value of enhanced penalties is advanced as a central argument for the laws, the hate crime statutes currently in place in thirty states and the District of Columbia do not appear to deter much, if any, harassment and violence. More than two decades after the first LGBT embrace of hate crime laws, as NCAVP figures illustrate, violence directed against queers remains a serious problem.

[. . .]

LGBT people of color do not escape the problematic effects of the hate crime framework. Police profile LGBT people of color, particularly youth, as potential perpetrators of hate crimes in predominantly white, gay urban enclaves. Given prevailing perceptions of LGBT people as predominantly, if not exclusively, white, people of color are perceived by police and residents to be criminally "out of place" in these neighborhoods. Archetypes framing people of color as inherently dangerous and more violently homophobic than whites further contribute to law enforcement targeting, aggressively harassing, stopping, and questioning LGBT people of color about the "legitimacy" of their presence in LGBT-identified areas. . . .

[. . .]

LAW ENFORCEMENT RESPONSES TO ANTI-LGBT VIOLENCE

The hate crime framework is further compromised by placing primary responsibility for preventing violence in the hands of a criminal legal system that is itself responsible for much of the LGBT violence. As journalist Richard Kim has noted, "It seems improbable that the passage of hate crimes laws would suddenly transform the state into a guardian of gay and lesbian people."[26] Recent NCAVP data underscores the point: the 2008 report concludes that "law enforcement officers remain one of the prime categories of offenders documented by NCAVP each year."[27] Over the past three decades LGBT people have increasingly turned to police and prosecutors for protection, only to be met with responses that further devalue queer lives, sometimes placing victims in greater jeopardy. Nevertheless, resources allocated by hate crime legislation for responding to and reducing violence continue to be directed almost exclusively to the expansion of policing, prosecution, and punishment.

But instances in which law enforcement–based approaches have failed to address or further contributed to the problem abound. For example, the Anti-Violence Project (AVP) of the Los Angeles Gay and Lesbian Center reported a case in which several youth in a car saw a Latina transgender woman, stopped, and proceeded to beat and stab her. Los

Angeles Police Department officers responding to the scene demanded the victim's driver's license, which identified her as female, refused to accept it, and insisted that paramedics on the scene examine her genitals. The paramedics did not comply with the demand. Witnesses to the attack alleged the officers inquired in an intimidating fashion about their immigration status.[28] As in April Mora's case, criminalizing archetypes framing transgender and gender-nonconforming people as inherently deceptive and unworthy of protection drove police response, which in turn led the victim and witnesses to refuse to speak further to the police, even though they had information that could have helped identify the assailants.

Unfortunately, such responses do not appear to be the product of an aberrant few insensitive, untrained officers. Researchers studying police response to violence against LGBT people in Minnesota over a ten-year period described numerous instances of 911 operators failing to send assistance, police mocking and laughing at victims, and officers blaming victims for the violence they experienced. Overall, police engaged in verbal harassment of victims of homophobic and transphobic violence in 32 percent of all incidents in which police responded, although this percentage decreased over time.[29]

[. . .]

The Minnesota researchers found that "there continues to be a significant percentage of incidents where officers refuse to file a report indicating that a crime has occurred. Over the course of the nine years, on average, officers refused in 31 percent of the cases to file a general incident report."[30] More recent figures compiled by the NCAVP indicate a 27 percent rate of refusal to classify violence against LGBT people as motivated by sexual orientation or gender identity.[31]

The Minnesota study also found that, despite deliberate efforts on the part of local LGBT anti-violence activists to build strong relationships with local police departments through education, outreach, sharing information about specific incidents, and advocating on behalf of victims of crime, negative interactions with police continued. More than half of the incidences of violence reported by LGBT people over this period were met with "negative" responses by law enforcement, compared to 20 percent positive responses. Although negative responses decreased by 50 percent over a nine-year period, they still made up the bulk of police-related incidents reported. The authors concluded, "While Minnesota has a reputation as one of the best states in the nation that offers protection against bias-motivated violence and intimidation, we still found low levels of reporting, refusal by police to indicate bias when requested by the victim, and police misconduct against those in the GLBT community."[32]

For almost thirty years, hate crime laws have existed as a kind of untouchable "third rail" of mainstream LGBT politics. In some respects debates around hate crime laws seem to powerfully distill all of the insult, harm, and fear born by queers for centuries. Many LGBT people—especially those who have little ongoing contact or engagement with policing and prison systems and their broader social and economic impacts—respond as if any challenge to these laws is an active betrayal of wounded gay people, an almost intentional reinfliction of murderous violence.

But it is also becoming apparent to at least some supporters of such legislation that, while data collection, civil remedies, and other provisions might be useful and important in particular contexts, penalty enhancements are largely ineffective. Three prominent transgender advocates hinted as much when they wrote, in 2006, "Including transgender people in hate crime laws does not create a change by enhancing penalties but by educating legislators, the media, the police, and the courts about the violence faced by trans people and by asking the public at large to side with the victims rather than the perpetrators of hate."[33] The NCAVP has distanced itself from penalty enhancements over a period of several years, and in 2008, NCAVP affirmed its opposition to enhanced penalties for those convicted of hate crimes.[34] In 2009, the Sylvia Rivera Law Project (SRLP), joined by FIERCE, INCITE! Women of Color Against Violence, Queers for Economic Justice (QEJ), Right Rides, the Transgender Intersex

Justice Project (TGIJP), and the Transformative Justice Law Project (TJLP), declared their opposition to the Matthew Shepard and James Byrd, Jr. Hate Crimes Prevention Act. Placing their stand within a larger context of opposition to mass incarceration, militarization, and colonialism, they said, "The evidence . . . shows that hate crimes laws and other 'get tough on crime' measures do not deter or prevent violence. Increased incarceration does not deter others from committing violent acts motivated by hate, does not rehabilitate those who have committed past acts of hate, and does not make anyone safer."[35]

DOMESTIC VIOLENCE IN QUEER RELATIONSHIPS

Over the past two decades, in addition to demanding protection from homophobic and transphobic violence at the hands of strangers, LGBT individuals and communities have increasingly sought protection for violence in intimate relationships. Although historically even more invisible than its heterosexual counterpart, the existence of violence in the context of queer relationships is being brought to light by antiviolence advocates working to counter reluctance both within and outside queer communities to recognize it. In so doing they have come up against resistance on the part of LGBT people concerned about feeding negative perceptions of queers as well as resistance on the part of policymakers loath to appear to be condoning homosexuality by providing protections to victims of violence in homosexual relationships.[36] Despite these challenges, by 2008, thirty-seven states provided for civil orders of protection against an intimate partner of the same sex under varying circumstances, although the availability of this remedy in reality varies from judge to judge and jurisdiction to jurisdiction.[37]

Fifteen organizations in fourteen jurisdictions across the country provide services to LGBT survivors of domestic violence (DV) and jointly report on the populations they serve in an annual report published by the NCAVP. They define domestic violence as "a pattern of behavior where one partner coerces, dominates, and isolates the other to maintain power and control over their partner."[38] While this is a welcome expansion beyond a domestic violence frame that encompasses only physical abuse in heterosexual relationships, it does not include violence queers experience in other intimate relationships, including at the hands of family members such as parents, siblings, and extended family members, as well as caregivers. A significant proportion of homophobic and transphobic violence takes place within or near our homes, and often represents some of the most brutal violence experienced by LGBT people.[39] The widely used term *same-sex domestic violence*, which appears to reflect an effort to shoehorn queer lives into mainstream domestic violence discourse, similarly excludes these experiences of violence, as well as those of transgender people involved in heterosexual relationships. Recognizing that LGBT people, and particularly queer youth and elders, are vulnerable to violence in a multitude of intimate contexts beyond monogamous relationships that mirror heterosexual marriage, many LGBT anti-violence activists use the broader term *LGBT domestic violence* to reflect this reality and distinguish these experiences from violence experienced at the hands of strangers or public authorities.

A recent study found, based on a review of the literature, that police are less likely to intervene in domestic violence cases that involve gay or lesbian couples. The study's authors suggest that failure to do so may be based on homophobia, and on notions that "women cannot be abusers and men cannot be abused." They also note that such beliefs are likely held not only by law enforcement officers, but also by others who will determine survivors' success in obtaining safety through in the criminal legal system, including witnesses, health care workers, attorneys, judges, and jurors. As a result, the researchers conclude, lesbian and gay people who experience domestic violence "may not receive equal protection under the law."[40]

[. . .]

In far too many cases, police heap harassment and abuse on top of that already experienced at the hands of an intimate. NCAVP data indicates that, of the 18 percent of cases of LGBT DV reported to affiliates across the country in which the police intervened, police misconduct, including verbal abuse, use of slurs, and physical abuse, was reported in 6 percent. Arrest of survivors in addition to or instead of abusers took place in an additional 6 percent. And, overall reports of police misconduct in DV cases increased by 93 percent in 2008. In Los Angeles, which consistently reports the largest number of LGBT DV cases per year, a misarrest was reported in over 97 percent of cases in 2007: "Frequently both parties are arrested or law enforcement officers threaten to arrest both."[41] . . .

[. . .]

In some cases, police failure to respond, combined with an absence of alternative community-based responses, can prove deadly. On March 28, 1998, Marc Kajs was shot by his former partner at the restaurant where he worked in Houston, Texas. A lawsuit brought by Kajs' mother alleged that, although he contacted police to report abuse by the former partner on at least six separate occasions, each time officers failed to file written reports or offer him assistance. On the last occasion Kajs sought help from the police, he ran into a police station at two thirty in the morning while being chased by his former partner, who threatened him in front of a police officer. Kajs told the officer he was frightened, that the man had threatened his life and that of his friends and family members, and asked for protection. The officer gave him an incident number and sent him back out on the street with his abuser, telling him to return the following Monday. Kajs was dead before Monday came around.[42]

In many more cases, as with hate crimes, queers feel unable to seek protection from the criminal legal system, fearing ineffective or homophobic responses, disclosure of their sexual orientation or gender identity, or arrest, deportation, loss of custody of children, or other adverse outcomes.[43] NCAVP suggests that this is particularly true for LGBT people of color and LGBT immigrants. It is also the case for a substantial number of transgender people. According to NCAVP, "Since police officers were perpetrators in almost half (48 percent) of the incidents of anti-transgender violence [in 2000], transgender people are not likely to seek police protection from an abusive partner." The number of incidents reported to NCAVP member organizations in which police were called decreased by 41 percent in 2008.[44]

[. . .]

Not surprisingly, the situation doesn't much improve once queer survivors of DV reach the courts. As the National Resource Center on Domestic Violence notes, "In the overtly hierarchical structure of the legal system . . . survivors of violence in same-gender/gender variant relationships are not routinely afforded the same protections as those employed to protect privileged heterosexual victims of domestic violence."[45] Not only do queer survivors face generic and pervasive homophobic treatment, but in some jurisdictions courts continue to refuse to enforce existing protections for people who experience LGBT DV on the grounds that they believe doing so would put gay relationships on equal legal footing with heterosexual marriage.[46] Further aggravating the situation, the STOP DV program of the Los Angeles AVP reports a lack of awareness among legal professionals regarding domestic partnership law and custody and visitation issues in LGBT relationships, which may lead to hesitation to offer assistance because the issues appear too complicated.[47]

[. . .]

For transgender women, the problem is endemic. Archetypes of transgender people as deceptive, mentally unstable, and sexually degraded permeate responses to DV committed against them as much as they do other law enforcement activities. A San Antonio woman, who called the police for help when her boyfriend broke a window and some of her personal possessions, was arrested on the mere word of her abuser that she was "bipolar." A young African American transgender woman living in Los Angeles who repeatedly called police for assistance when her boyfriend was abusive was told each time that there was nothing the officers could do, despite the presence of visible bruises on her body. However, one morning two undercover officers knocked on her door and told her she was under arrest pursuant to an old warrant on a solicitation charge. In 2002, in Washington, DC, a transgender woman choked by her male partner managed to call police only to be arrested, handcuffed, pushed down the stairs, and referred to by male pronouns throughout her subsequent detention. Although charges against her were eventually dismissed, the message was clear: gender "deception" can be met with violence, with no recourse to the law.[48]

[. . .]

The challenge is to develop bolder justice visions and new frameworks for naming, analyzing, and confronting the myriad forms of individual and systemic violence that not only hurt individuals, but also destabilize entire communities—to shift our focus to our communities, to help them grow stronger, more just, more stable, and more compassionate. LGBT people need to deeply question whether institutions rooted in the control and punishment of people of color, poor people, immigrants, *and* queers can ever be deployed in the service of LGBT interests without abandoning entire segments of queer communities to continuing state violence. But how do we start to break out of the old frames, confront the inhumanity of criminal archetypes, and begin to open up what Angela Y. Davis calls "new terrains of justice"?[49]

NOTES

1. "CAVP Condemns Assault on Lesbian Youth," Colorado Anti-Violence Project, www.coavp.org/content/view/35/44/ (accessed September 13, 2009); and Amnesty International, *Stonewalled: Police Abuse and Misconduct Against Lesbian, Gay, Bisexual and Transgender People in the U.S.* (New York: Amnesty International USA, 2005), 76.

2. National Coalition of Anti-Violence Projects, *Hate Violence Against Lesbian, Gay, Bisexual, and Transgender People in the United States 2008*, 2009 Release Edition, www.ncavp.org/publications/NationalPubs.aspx (accessed September 5, 2009).

3. Kristina B. Wolff and Carrie L. Cokeley, "To Protect and Serve? An Exploration of Police Conduct in Relation to the Gay, Lesbian, Bisexual and Transgender Community," *Sex Cult* II (2007): 1–23; and Amnesty, *Stonewalled*, 67, 78.

4. Federal Bureau of Investigation, *Uniform Crime Report: Hate Crime Statistics 2008*, www.fbi.gov/ucr/hc2008/documents/abouthc.pdf (accessed February 11, 2010).

5. See U.S. Department of Justice, Bureau of Justice Statistics, *Criminal Victimization, 2004*, Office of Justice Programs, NCJ 210674 (Washington, DC, September 2005); U.S. Department of Justice, Bureau of Justice Statistics, *Rape and Sexual Assault: Reporting to Police and Medical Attention, 1992–2000*, Office of Justice Programs, NCJ 194530 (Washington, DC, August 2002); and Wolff and Cokeley, "To Protect and Serve?"

6. Wolff and Cokeley, "To Protect and Serve?"; Amnesty, *Stonewalled*, 67–68; and Suzanna M. Rose, "Community Interventions Concerning Homophobic Violence and Partner Violence Against Lesbians," *Journal of Lesbian Studies* 7, no. 4 (2003): 125–39.

7. NCAVP, *Hate Violence in 2008*, 16–17.

8. See, e.g., Wolff and Cokeley, "To Protect and Serve?" See also Amnesty, *Stonewalled*, 75–77.

9. U.S. Department of Justice, *Hate Crimes Statistics, 2007*, Uniform Crime Reporting Program, Federal Bureau of Investigation (Washington, DC, October 2008), www.fbi.gov/ucr/htm (accessed October 12, 2009).

10. NCAVP, *Hate Violence in 2008*, 5.

11. Ibid., 7; and FBI, *Uniform Crime Report.*

12. Amnesty, *Stonewalled*, 70.

13. Allegra R. Gordon and Ilan H. Meyer, "Gender Nonconformity as a Target of Prejudice, Discrimination, and Violence Against LGB Individuals," *Journal of LGBT Health Research* 3, no. 3 (2007): 55–71.

14. Rose, "Community Interventions," 131.

15. James B. Jacobs and Kimberly Potter, *Hate Crimes: Criminal Law & Identity Politics* (New York: Oxford University Press, 1998), 29–44.

16. The ADL states that its mission is fighting "anti-Semitism and all forms of bigotry in the United States and abroad." The organization has been critiqued for its embrace of centrist/extremist theory, which fashions bigotry and violence as the product of extremism on the part of individuals while ignoring systemic forms of violence against marginalized groups by the state. See "Focus on Individual Aberration," www.publiceye.org/liberty/Repression-and-ideology-06.html (accessed February 2, 2010). ADL has also been critiqued for its uncritical support of the policies and practices of the State of Israel, and its efforts to suppress dissenting voices. See, e.g., Edward W. Said and Christopher Hitchens, eds., *Blaming the Victims: Spurious Scholarship and the Palestinian Question* (New York: Verso, 1988), 10, 12. See also, e.g., Eric Alterman, "The Defamation League," *Nation*, February 16, 2009.

17. Anti-Defamation League, *ADL Model Legislation* (2003), www.adl.org/99hatecrime/penalty.asp (accessed September 15, 2009); Anti-Defamation League, *Hate Crimes Laws Introduction* (2003), www.adl.org/99hatecrime/intro.asp (accessed September 15, 2009); and Levin, "Slavery to Hate Crime," 237.

18. National Gay and Lesbian Task Force Action Fund, *Hate Crimes Protections Historical Overview*, www.thetaskforce.org/issues/hate_crimes_main_page/ overview (accessed September 10, 2009).

19. National Gay and Lesbian Task Force Action Fund, *Map of Hate Crime Laws in the U.S.* (updated July 14, 2009), www.thetaskforce.org/reports_and_research/hate_crimes_laws (accessed September 8, 2009). Two states include sexual orientation in data collection laws/provisions only.

20. See Levin, "Slavery to Hate Crimes," 235–41. See also Jacobs and Potter, *Hate Crimes*, 29–44.

21. See, e.g., Amnesty, *Stonewalled*, 98–99.

22. National Coalition of Anti-Violence Programs, *Anti-Lesbian, Gay, Bisexual and Transgender Violence in 2007* (2008), www.ncavp.org/publications/NationalPubs.aspx (accessed September 5, 2009).

23. NCAVP, *Hate Violence in 2008.*

24. See National Coalition of Anti-Violence Programs, *Anti-Lesbian, Gay, Bisexual and Transgender Violence in 2002* (2003), 5, www.ncavp.org/publications/NationalPubs.aspx (accessed February 5, 2010). See also American Friends Service Committee, *Is Opposing the War an LGBT Issue?*, produced in partnership with the National Youth Action Coalition (2003), www.afsc.org/lgbt/ht/display/ContentDetails/i/i8752 (accessed February 4, 2010).

25. Richard Kim, "The Truth About Hate Crimes Laws," *Nation*, July 12, 1999, www.thenation.com/article/truth-about-hate-crimes-laws (accessed October 15, 2009).

26. Kim, "Truth About Hate Crimes."

27. NCAVP, *Hate Violence in 2008*, 16.

28. Amnesty, *Stonewalled*, 69.

29. Wolff and Cokeley, "To Protect and Serve?" 12, 18.

30. Wolff and Cokeley, "To Protect and Serve?" 13.

31. NCAVP, *Hate Violence in 2008, 13.*

32. Wolff and Cokeley, "To Protect and Serve?" 12, 19.

33. Paisley Currah, Richard Juang, and Shannon Minter, eds., *Transgender Rights* (Minneapolis: University of Minnesota Press, 2006), xxiii. See also Lee, "Prickly Coalitions," 110–11.

34. NCAVP, *Hate Violence in 2008*, 86.

35. See SLRP's Web site: http://srlp.org/fedhatecrimelaw (accessed February 2010).

36. National Coalition of Anti-Violence Programs, *Lesbian, Gay, Bisexual and Transgender Domestic Violence in the United States in 2007* (2008), 3, www.avp.org (accessed February 14, 2010); National Resource Center on Domestic Violence, *LGBT Communities and Domestic Violence: Information and Resources* (Pennsylvania, 2007), www.nrcdv.org (accessed February 14, 2010); and Amnesty, *Stonewalled*, 80.

37. Sheila M. Seelau and Eric P. Seelau, "Gender-Role Stereotypes and Perceptions of Heterosexual, Gay and Lesbian Domestic Violence," *Journal of Family Violence* 20, no. 6 (2005): 363–71, 363; and NCAVP, *Domestic Violence in 2007*.

38. National Coalition of Anti-Violence Programs, *Lesbian, Gay, Bisexual and Transgender Domestic Violence in the United States in 2008* (2009), 6, 11. NCAVP is moving toward the use of the term *intimate partner violence* to describe this phenomenon.

39. Ibid., 6, 11, 12. The NCAVP recognizes the existence of violence in these contexts, but nevertheless focuses its reporting on *intimate partner violence* and *domestic violence*, using these terms synonymously. Nearly one-third of all incidents reported to the NCAVP took place in or near a private residence.

40. Seelau and Seelau, "Gender-Role Stereotypes," 364–70.

41. NCAVP, *Domestic Violence in 2007*, 24, 19; and NCAVP, *Domestic Violence in 2008*, 2.

42. Harvey Rice, "Judge Again Dismisses Law Suit over Gay Domestic Violence Case," *Houston Chronicle*, February 4, 2004; Harvey Rice, "Expert Questions Police Report on Gay Man's Death," *Houston Chronicle*, December 19, 2003; Rosanna Ruiz, "Court Reinstates Mom's Suit over Death of Gay Son," *Houston Chronicle*, December 15, 2001; Wendy Grossman, "Bullets After Brunch," *Houston Press*, May 4, 2000; and Amnesty, *Stonewalled*, 82.

43. NCAVP, *Domestic Violence in 2007*, 19, 24; NRCDV, *LGBT Communities and Domestic Violence*; Danica R. Borenstein et al., "Understanding the Experiences of Lesbian, Bisexual and Trans Survivors of Domestic Violence: A Qualitative Study," *Journal of Homosexuality* 51, no. 1 (2006): 159–81, 162, 172; and Rose, "Community Interventions," 131.

44. NCAVP, *Domestic Violence in 2008*, 3; NCAVP, *Domestic Violence in 2007*, 16; and National Coalition of Anti-Violence Programs, *Lesbian, Gay, Bisexual and Transgender Domestic Violence in the United States in 2000*, www.avp.org (accessed February 14, 2010).

45. NRCDV, *LGBT Communities and Domestic Violence*.

46. NCAVP, *Domestic Violence in 2007*, 35; and NRCDV, *LGBT Communities and Domestic Violence*.

47. NCAVP, *Domestic Violence in 2007*, 25.

48. NRCDV, *LGBT Communities and Domestic Violence*.

49. Angela Y. Davis, *Are Prisons Obsolete?* (New York: Seven Stories, 2003), 21.

48. • *Isis Nusair*

MAKING FEMINIST SENSE OF TORTURE AT ABU-GHRAIB (2017)

Isis Nusair is an associate professor of international studies and women's and gender studies at Denison University. She is the translator of Ramy Al-Asheq's *Ever Since I Did Not Die* (2020), and the co-writer/director with Laila Farah of the performance *Weaving the Maps: Tales of Survival and Resistance*. She is the co-editor with Rhoda Kanaaneh of *Displaced at Home: Ethnicity and Gender Among Palestinians in Israel* (2010). She is completing a book on the effect of war and displacement on Iraqi women refugees in

Jordan and the United States and is conducting research with Syrian refugees in Germany. The following piece was written for this collection; a longer, more theoretical examination of the subject can be found in *Feminism and War: Confronting U.S. Imperialism*, edited by R. Riley, C. Mohanty, and M. Bruce Pratt (Zed Books, 2008).

I analyze in this essay how the essentializing and dichotomizing discourses of Orientalism justified, facilitated, and shaped gendered, racialized, and sexualized torture at the Abu-Ghraib prison outside Baghdad. The torture at Abu-Ghraib remains a sign of what constitutes Orientalist militarized hyper-masculine domination and power over Iraq and by extension the Middle East and North Africa.

The *Taguba Report* on the treatment of Abu-Ghraib prisoners in Iraq states that the intentional abuse of detainees by American military police personnel at Abu-Ghraib post 2003 included the following acts: punching, slapping, and kicking detainees; jumping on their naked feet; videotaping and photographing naked male and female detainees; forcibly arranging detainees in various sexually explicit positions for photographing; forcing detainees to remove their clothing and keeping them naked for several days at a time; forcing naked male detainees to wear women's underwear; forcing groups of male detainees to masturbate themselves while being photographed and videotaped; arranging male detainees in a pile and then jumping on them; positioning a naked detainee on a MRE box, with a sandbag on his head, and attaching wires to his fingers, toes, and penis to simulate electric torture; writing "I am a Rapest" (sic) on the leg of a detainee alleged to have forcibly raped a fifteen-year old fellow detainee and then photographing him naked; placing a dog chain or strap around a naked detainee's neck and having a female soldier pose for a picture; a male MP guard having sex with a female detainee; and using military working dogs (without muzzles) to intimidate and frighten detainees, resulting in at least one case of a dog biting and severely injuring a detainee.

Orientalism, as a body of thought and system of representation, helps us frame these US military actions in Iraq. Orientalism splits the world into the Occident versus the Orient, positing essential differences between the two that are hard to overcome

(Said 1979). This binary opposition is not only a means to set boundaries but a representation that is interlocked with the will to rule over others. This was illustrated in the aftermath of the September 11, 2001, attacks when President George W. Bush's discourses on terrorism divided the world into "good versus evil" and "us against them." This representation reinforced an absolute view of the world without offering a way of understanding the economic and political contexts that contributed to them. Furthermore, on September 16, 2001, Bush made the association between the war on terrorism and the war against Islam and described it as a "crusade," giving the conflict a clear religious dimension (Hatem 2003/2004, 84). The Bush doctrine, as it came to be called, argued that if you "harbor them, feed them, house them, you are just as guilty and you will be held accountable." This dispensed with legal niceties and embraced the lawless motif of the Old West: "get them dead or alive" and "smoke them in their caves/holes" (Hatem 2003/2004, 84). In a press conference on September 17, 2001, Bush explained that the United States faced a new enemy, one that has no borders and an extensive network. Yet his representation did not go beyond describing it as a barbarian whose objectives were incomprehensible.

Within Orientalism, the taming and civilizing mission of the "barbaric" Orient requires the dissemination of rational procedures of Western institutions of law and order and reorganization of Oriental cultures along the principles of the modern, progressive, and civilized West (Yegenoglu 1998). In order to be able to construct the West and the Orient as different, the machinery of colonial discourse uses terms such as "primitive," "backward," and "traditional." This pushes the cultural other back in time, implying and inscribing an "articulation and ordering of cultural difference" that is gendered and racialized (Yegenoglu 1998, 96). This representation facilitated the conceptual gendered division between the nation (masculine) and the enemy other (feminine) and the successful reproduction of US intervention as a superior moral mission (Shepherd 2006).

Manifest Orientalism refers to various stated views about Oriental society, languages, literatures, and history while latent Orientalism refers to an almost unconscious and untouchable act. Latent Orientalism achieves power through its everydayness and naturalness, its taken-for-granted authority (Said 1979). It also encourages a peculiarly male and sexist conception of the world (Yegenoglu 1998). The connection between latent and manifest Orientalism is illustrated in the military psychology assessment report (*AR 15-6 Investigation*) indicating that "soldiers were immersed in Islamic culture, a culture with different worship and belief systems that they were encountering for the first time." It explains how the "association by soldiers of Muslims with terrorism could exaggerate difference and lead to fear and to a devaluation of people." Difference between US soldiers and Iraqi prisoners reached such a level that, according to a military dog-handler, even dogs "came not to like Iraqi detainees. They [the dogs] did not like the Iraqi culture, smell, sound, skin-tone, hair-color or anything about them."

Orientalism constructs the Middle East as the place of sensuality, irrationality, corrupt despotism, mystical religiosity, and sexually unstable Arabs. It also makes Western inquiry into the nature of the "Islamic mind" and "Arab character" perfectly legitimate as a means to control that "other" (Yegenoglu 1998). In a *New Yorker* May 14, 2004, article titled "How a Secret Pentagon Program Came to Abu-Ghraib," Seymour Hersh states that the notion that Arabs are particularly vulnerable to sexual humiliation became a talking point among prowar Washington conservatives in the months before the 2003 invasion of Iraq. "The Patai book [*The Arab Mind*], an academic told me, was 'the bible of the neocons on Arab behavior . . .' [where] two themes emerged—'one, that Arabs only understand force and, two that the biggest weakness of Arabs is shame and humiliation'" (Hersh 2004).

Even though Islam's "oppression" of women formed some element of the European narrative of Islam from early on, the issue of women only emerged as the centerpiece of the Western narrative of Islam in the nineteenth century as Europeans established themselves as colonial powers in Muslim countries (Ahmed 1992). Fusion between women and culture and the idea that other men, men in colonized societies or societies beyond the borders of the civilized West, oppressed women was to be used, in the rhetoric of colonialism, "to render morally justifiable its project of undermining or eradicating the cultures of colonized people" (Ahmed 1992, 151). Accordingly, Islam was "innately and immutably oppressive to women, that the veil and segregation epitomized that oppression, and that these customs were the fundamental reasons for the general and comprehensive backwardness of Islamic societies" (Ahmed 1992, 152). Only "if these practices 'intrinsic' to Islam (and therefore Islam itself) were cast off could Muslim societies begin to move forward on the path of civilization" (Ahmed 1992, 152).

By posing and presupposing that the veil is hiding something, the subject turns the veil into a mask that needs to be penetrated, a mask behind which the other is suspected of hiding some dangerous secret threatening his unity and stability. The grand narrative of the colonial gaze is made up of tales of unveiling, fantasies of penetrating, domesticating, reforming, and thus controlling her (Yegenoglu 1998). The aggressive, hostile, and violent act of unveiling, stripping, penetrating, and tearing apart Iraqi bodies at Abu-Ghraib where the body is left nude, exposed, and laid bare is a guarantee for the colonial power that the body and consequently the mind become knowable, observable, visible, and thereby manipulative. This gendered, racialized, and sexualized violence maintains discipline and secures the boundaries between the private and public and between community, nation, and state. Within this context, they are all bodies to be disciplined. This is evident in Sherene Razack's (2004) analysis that what took place at Abu-Ghraib is part of a larger "national project of dominating racially inferior peoples" and that the violence in these photos is a sexualized colonial violence that "the soldiers understand to be one between conquerors and racially, morally and culturally inferior" others.

What took place at Abu-Ghraib is part of a constructed heterosexual, racialized, and gendered script that is firmly grounded in the colonial desires and practices of the larger social order (Richter-Montpetit 2007). This construction of difference is laden with negative cultural, gendered, racial, and social connotations. It is associated with constructions of power and hierarchy in that the detainees, seen as "other," are sexually tortured and humiliated in ways that are most often associated with the violence inflicted on women's bodies. Sexual domination and national conquest are part of a militarist hypersexuality that endorses elements of masculinity, such as rigid gender roles, vengeful and militarized reactions, and obsession with order, power, and control (Burnham 2004; Eisenstein 2004; Enloe 2000).

Photos of torture and abuse at Abu-Ghraib are evident of the violent act of unveiling, stripping, and penetration, the ultimate act of cultural and sexual domination over an emasculate Iraqi order. Male Iraqi prisoners were represented in the Abu-Ghraib photos as the opposite of what a US militarist and hypersexual soldier should be. The Iraqi prisoners were represented as helpless, obedient, and docile (read feminine) others. They were sexually dominated, degraded, and forced to simulate homosexual acts. Within this homophobic, militarized, racist, and sexist representation, the US military defined their position as well as the nature of their domination over Iraqi others. Taking over 1,800 pictures of torture of Iraqi prisoners at Abu-Ghraib marks not only the difference between "us" and "them" in terms of sexuality, religion, belief system, and culture but makes these pictures available for the whole world to see. The act of taking a picture automatically implies distancing the self from its objectified other, and the process of reproducing these orchestrated images marked and recorded these representations of absolute and essential *difference from* and *domination over* those others.

Torture at Abu-Ghraib was first exposed not by a digital photograph but by a letter that was smuggled out of the prison. A woman prisoner inside the jail managed to smuggle out a note in December 2003. The contents of the letter were so shocking that Amal Kadham Swadi and other Iraqi women lawyers who had been trying to gain access to the US jail found them hard to believe. The note claimed that US guards had been raping women detainees and that several of the women were now pregnant. The note added that women had been forced to strip naked in front of men, and it urged the Iraqi resistance to bomb the jail to spare the women further shame. Swadi, one of seven female lawyers who represented women detainees in Abu-Ghraib, began to piece together a held without charge in various detention centers in Iraq (Harding 2004).

The statement from the *Taguba Report* that "a male MP [Military Police] guard having sex with a female detainee," seems to be as far as US officials are willing to admit that actual rape of Iraqi women took place at Abu-Ghraib. Within the logic of Orientalist domination, male Iraqi prisoners are still men, although weak and emasculate others. Acknowledging the actual rape of Iraqi women would shatter the civilizing and rescuing rhetoric of the US military mission. Although the moral superiority and saving mission was severely damaged by the release of the photos of abuse and torture at Abu-Ghraib, the Bush administration blamed the torture in the pictures on a few "bad apples." This focus on the action of the few stands in stark opposition to Human Rights Watch's analysis (Brody 2004) that what created the climate for Abu-Ghraib was part of a larger continuum of torture and mistreatment of detainees during the US wars in Afghanistan and Iraq and in Guantanamo Bay (a US military prison in Cuba where detainees were held after 2002). Within the sexist and hierarchical logic of militarized hypermasculinity, penetration of and dominance over Iraqi male prisoners could still be justified as something to be resolved between men. After all, and despite women comprising about 15 percent of the US military, waging war is still constructed within the domain of the masculine. Acknowledging the rape of Iraqi female prisoner exposes the undifferentiated power of penetration and control over not only the bodies of Iraqis but the land and its resources. This exposure, in turn, strips naked and tears apart the moral foundation of the US masculinized and militarized "liberation" mission in Iraq.

WORKS CITED

Ahmed, Leila. *Women and Gender in Islam*. Yale UP, 1992.

AR 15-6 Investigation—Allegation of Detainee Abuse at Abu-Ghraib: Psychological Assessment. American Civil Liberties Union, www.aclu.org/files/projects/foiasearch/pdf/DODDOA000309.pdf. Accessed January 10, 2005.

Brody, Reed. "The Road to Abu-Ghraib." *Human Rights Watch*, June 2004, www.hrw.org/reports/2004/usa0604/.

Burnham, Linda. "Sexual Domination in Uniform: An American Value." *CounterPunch*, May 18, 2004, www.counterpunch.org/2004/05/22/an-american-value/.

Eisenstein, Zillah. "Sexual Humiliation, Gender Confusion and the Horrors at Abu Ghraib." *ZNet*, June 22, 2004, zcomm.org/znetarticle/sexual-humiliation-gender-confusion-and-the-horrors-at-abu-ghraib-by-zillah-eisenstein/.

Enloe, Cynthia. *Maneuvers: The International Politics of Militarizing Women's Lives*. University of California Press, 2000.

Harding, Luke. "The Other Prisoners." *The Guardian*, May 19, 2004, www.theguardian.com/world/2004/may/20/iraq.gender.

Hatem, Mervat. "Discourses on the 'War on Terrorism' in the US and its View of the Arab, Muslim, and Gendered 'Other.'" *Arab Studies Journal*, vol. 11, no. 2/12.1, 2003/2004, pp. 77–97.

Hersh, Seymour M. "The Gray Zone: How a Secret Pentagon Program Came to Abu-Ghraib." *The New Yorker*, May 24, 2004, www.newyorker.com/magazine/2004/05/24/the-gray-zone.

Patai, Raphael. *The Arab Mind*. Hatherleigh Press, 2002.

Razack, Sherene. "When Is Prisoner Abuse Racial Violence?" *Selves and Others*, May 24, 2004.

Richter-Montpetit, Melanie. "Empire, Desire and Violence: A Queer Transnational Feminist Reading of the Prisoner 'Abuse' in Abu-Ghraib and the Question of 'Gender Equality.'" *International Feminist Journal of Politics*, vol. 9, no. 1, 2007, pp. 38–59. *Academic Search Premier*, doi:10.1080/14616740601066366.

Said, Edward. *Orientalism*. Vintage Books, 1979.

Shepherd, Laura. "Veiled References: Constructions of Gender in the Bush Administration Discourse on the Attacks on Afghanistan Post-9/11." *International Feminist Journal of Politics*, vol. 8, no. 1, 2006, pp. 19–41.

Yegenoglu, Meyda. *Colonial Fantasies: Toward a Feminist Reading of Orientalism*. Cambridge UP, 1998.

---

49. • *Jaelani Turner-Williams*

A QUICK HISTORY OF TV'S ELUSIVE QUEST FOR BLACK LESBIANS (2019)

Jaelani Turner-Williams is a writer and freelance journalist based in Columbus, OH. Her writings focus mostly on music and can be found in *Remezcla*, *Okayplayer*, *Vinyl Me, Please*, and *Bitch*.

There's recently been a much-needed shift in television's approach to portraying Black lesbian relationships: Characters are being given more complexity onscreen, as they are offered the chance to explore their queerness in ways typically reserved for white queer women.

Ellen DeGeneres, who made headlines when she came out on "The Puppy Episode" of her '90s comedy series *Ellen*, is considered the start of representation for white lesbianism on television (though she wasn't the first lesbian on screen, she was the game-changer due to her reach and popularity).

Though "The Puppy Episode" earned awards and acclaim, ABC's advertisers were less than thrilled. The network cancelled *Ellen* after airing one additional season. Later, *Buffy*'s Willow Rosenburg (Alyson Hannigan) explored relationships with women that began as subtle physical connections and became much more overt as the series went on. Rosenberg shared her first onscreen kiss with another woman during the Season 5 episode "The Body." Lesbianism on television also took a dramatic turn on The-N teen series *South of Nowhere*, with protagonist Spencer Carlin (Gabrielle Christian) questioning her sexuality after befriending her openly lesbian classmate Ashley Davies (Mandy Musgrave). Shows ranging from *The L Word*, which wrapped in 2009, to Netflix's *Everything Sucks* (2018) feature well-rounded white lesbians who are given depth.

However, thoughtfully crafted Black lesbians are still an anomaly on TV. Overall, there are still pervasive stereotypes about Black women that bleed into pop culture: they're desexualized or sex-crazed, aggressive or passive, anti-male or existing solely for the male gaze. Their identities are often unclear, with few Black lesbians proclaiming themselves as such. Altogether, these limited character formulas leave little to no room for Black lesbians to be fleshed out, and an even smaller possibility for their characters to be at the center of a multidimensional storyline. And when these stories are told, there tends to be a male protagonist whose storyline overshadows theirs. For example, Spike Lee's 2004 film *She Hate Me* centers on Jack Armstrong (Anthony Mackie), a sperm donor who's in high demand among some lesbians in New York City, including his ex-girlfriend Fatima Goodrich (Kerry Washington) and her girlfriend Alex Guerrero (Dania Ramirez). It's still rare for the narrative to prioritize the Black lesbians themselves in a real, human way.

Historically, Black lesbians have been mostly depicted in indie films, including *The Watermelon Woman* (1996), *Mississippi Damned* (2009), and *Pariah* (2011), which often limited their reach. While both *The Women of Brewster Place* and *The Color Purple* (1985) shined a brief light on Black lesbianism, there hadn't yet been a film or series that migrated beyond a surface-level trajectory and really delved into Black lesbian experiences. If Black lesbians weren't struggling with their identity, they were being confronted or even isolated by their families. Take bible-thumping mother Audrey's (Kim Wayans) dysfunctional and abusive relationship with her butch daughter Alike (Adepero Oduye) in the 2011 indie film *Pariah* or Theresa (Paula Kelly) and Lorraine (Lonette McKee) being treated as outcasts in the 1989 TV adaptation of Gloria Naylor's 1982 book *The Women of Brewster Place*. Though Brewster Place is a tenement that's primarily run by Black women, Lorraine still struggles with internalized homophobia: She refers to a nearby nightclub as the home of "fags" and avoids being seen in public with Theresa. Lorraine's fears are warranted as she'd been pushed out of a teaching position in Detroit because of her sexuality, and an intrusive neighbor, Miss Sophie (Olivia Cole), intentionally outs her and Theresa to get them shunned by the neighborhood.

Prior to the 2000s, Black lesbians were rarely physical in film. If there was a glimmer of intimacy, it resulted in one partner being hushed, notably in 1996's *Set It Off* when bank robber Cleo Sims (Queen Latifah) dates a woman named Ursula (Samantha MacLachlan). Despite Sims's loud, gun-toting bravado, Ursula is virtually mute and detached throughout the film, until later when she cries after seeing Sims gunned down on television. *The Color Purple*, an adaptation of Alice Walker's 1982 novel, suggests a lesbian relationship between nightclub singer Shug Avery (Margaret Avery) and docile, battered protagonist, Celie Harris Johnson (Whoopi Goldberg). (The book is much more explicit and definitive about their relationship.) Though Celie and Shug share a kiss, their sex scene in the book was expunged from the film to prevent homophobic backlash. This minimizing of physical intimacy has started to shift: Though Netflix's adaptation of *She's Gotta Have It* has been called out for queerbaiting, Opal Gilstrap (Ilfenesh Hedera) and Nola Darling's (Dewanda Wise) relationship is worth watching. Season 3 opens with an unflinching sex scene between Darling and Gilstrap, and rather than catering to the male gaze, the two are fully intertwined—clasped fingers and all—in a way that truly prioritizes their pleasure rather than that of male viewers.

Black lesbians aren't perfect, and that should be reflected onscreen. Take *Dear White People* for example: After "running out of lesbians in one semester," Kelsey Phillips (Nia Jerver), a junior at Winchester University, decides to stop dating. Then, she's corralled by bi-curious friend Brooke Morgan (Courtney Sauls) to begin dating. As Morgan shamelessly flirts with Phillips following a meaningless stint of random hookups with men, she voices her interest in giving women a try. Phillips forewarns Morgan that "the lady pond is already cloudy enough without a straight-but-curious girl dipping a toe." Somehow, this encourages Morgan to up the ante on her seemingly futile attempts until Phillips clarifies her lesbianism and explains why she's nervous about pursuing anything with Morgan: "I don't want to be just some part of an experiment, so if you're on some sort of sexual journey, please don't make me a stop along the way." Phillips says after romantically decorating her dorm room for a tryst with Morgan. Emptily assuring Phillips that the two are connected, the next morning, Morgan awkwardly dodges Phillips's invite for another date, instead texting a male suitor while she's still in Phillips's bed. With Morgan continuously giving Phillips the cold shoulder, it becomes clear that Morgan was using her to fill an experimental void, and had no plans of taking their relationship further.

As the third season of *Dear White People* focuses keenly on LGBTQ students, Phillips and Morgan's affair is solely based on Morgan's unfulfilling relationships with men rather a true connection that takes Phillips's feelings into consideration. The move was opportunistic, a dynamic that's also captured in *Pariah*. While the teenage Alike wants to date Bina (Aasha Davis) after the two have a sleepover, Bina rebukes her motives, saying that they were just having fun. Similarly, the relationship between Morgan and Phillips plays into the stereotype that WLW relationships are simply disposable girl crushes. While *Dear White People* and *Pariah* can be critiqued for leaning into this trope, it's noteworthy in the sense that *Dear White People* is giving Black queer women the space to make mistakes and to question their sexualities, something typically reserved for white characters and actresses. A large part of this is demand for more human characters.

TV writers have begun listening and adhering to an overwhelming insistence from lesbian audiences that lesbians be progressive characters who are treated with the same care afforded to straight characters. Actress and screenwriter Lena Waithe has played a large role in this, beginning with the *Master of None* episode "Thanksgiving," which garnered Emmy-winning acclaim. The episode follows Denise (Waithe) as she attempts to come out to her family over the span of nearly 20 years.

Now, Waithe is bringing former YouTube series *Twenties* to the small screen in a feat that further illustrates her dedication to showcasing Black lesbian stories. The forthcoming BET series will revolve around Hattie, a queer Black woman who comes to terms with her sexuality with the help of her straight friends Marie and Nia. As Waithe's passion project comes to life, it provides additional space for Black lesbian visibility in television, breaking down barriers for women who deserve to see themselves fairly personified. In 2019, Queer Black women viewers expect the characters that represent them to have range, and the complexity of their relationships to be visible, rather than miniscule or unseen entirely. Millennial and Gen-Z audiences are more open to queer representation, and there's an urgency for media to reflect the times. Moving ahead, television can continue the pace of diversifying the writers' room, especially with queer Black women, to fulfill these narratives.

50. • *Judith Kegan Gardiner*

WOMEN'S FRIENDSHIPS, POPULAR CULTURE, AND GENDER THEORIES (UPDATED)

Judith Kegan Gardiner is Professor of English and of Gender and Women's Studies, *Emerita*, at the University of Illinois at Chicago. Her publications include two monographs, three edited collections of critical essays, and over 100 essays and chapters. Recent publications discuss feminist theories, masculinity studies, contemporary women writers, popular culture, and pedagogy. She is a member of the editorial collective of the interdisciplinary journal *Feminist Studies* and the editor of the collection of essays, *Approaches to Teaching Alison Bechdel's* Fun Home (Modern Language Association, 2018). The book was nominated for the 2019 Teaching Literature Award. The following essay is an updated and expanded version of her previously published article, "Friendship, Gender Theories, and Social Change" (2017).

An online cartoon pictures three young white women facing each other across a table. They say, "Oh my God, I love you guys." The caption reads: "Girl Friendship: lasts 2–3 years." The accompanying illustration shows two young white men sitting side by side with video game controllers in their hands. One says, "asshole," and the other says, "bitch," presumably to each other. The caption reads: "Guy Friendship: lasts forever." Despite its inaccuracy, the cartoon reinforces long-standing stereotypes that men and women, and their same-sex friendships, are not only different but opposite. In Geoffrey Greif's terms, men's friendships are "shoulder to shoulder," while women's are "face to face" (Greif 2009, 134).

Much current ethnography and sociology continues to endorse these gendered oppositions, polarizing men's and women's friendships according to twentieth-century theories of gender influenced by Freudian psychology. However, recent popular culture as well as scholarly research shows convergences between men's and women's friendships

in real life, particularly for young adults. Looking especially at American women's friendships in the contexts of gender theories, social change, and representations in movies and television, I describe some paradoxical developments. Current gender and women's studies textbooks develop intersectional analyses that define categories of gender (masculine/feminine) as mutually created by and creating the social categories of race, ethnicity, social class, sexuality and sexual orientation, as well as age, nationality, and ability status. Contemporary film and television illustrate how some of these categories create contradictions that are represented in current American popular culture. On the one hand, Americans experience friendship as a realm of freedom from the restrictions of families and workplaces. On the other, I claim that friendships reinforce class and gender binaries and so reassure individuals that they are performing their social roles appropriately. Thus while friendships seem—and are—freer from constraint than most other social connections, they still flourish chiefly through what social scientists call *homophily*—that is, between people freely choosing to associate with those of similar race, ethnicity, religion, social class, gender, and sexual orientation. Despite this familiar picture, significant changes are indeed taking place concerning who forms friendships with whom, what such friendships mean, and how they are depicted in popular culture.

For example, the film *Crazy Rich Asians* (2018) delivers a spectacular global Cinderella story in which brilliant and beautiful Asian American economics professor Rachel Chu (Constance Wu) travels to Singapore for a wedding, where she learns that her boyfriend Nick (Henry Golding) is extremely wealthy. Contending with Nick's cold and snobbish mother, Rachel finds support from her eccentric girlfriend, played by rapper Awkwafina. The women friends model a thoroughly positive relationship in contrast to the other bitchy women surrounding Nick. Meanwhile, the groom and Nick enjoy a guys' getaway hidden from obnoxious male partygoers. The one out gay man in the film acts like a girlfriend in helping Rachel dress appropriately. The unconventional twist in the plot, showing recent flexible attitudes to sexual morality, is that Rachel is not only poorer than Nick but unknowingly the daughter of a woman who ran off to America, pregnant with her lover's, not her husband's, child. Although the prospective mother-in-law at first objects to this scandal, she finally warms to Rachel's steely composure proved in a mahjong game and accepts her as a future daughter-in-law.

The "chick flick" *Bridesmaids* (2011) also shapes its plot around difficulties preceding a friend's wedding, but rather than focusing on family conflict or heterosexual relationships, the movie focuses on rivalries between the main character, the bride, and a richer woman connected with the groom. The central character, Annie (Kristen Wiig), and the rich woman vie for "best friend" status with the bride, establishing the emotional core of the film and validating the poorer woman's friendship.

These films portray their characters as subject to the emotionally intense female friendships predicted by cultural feminist theorists like Nancy Chodorow and Adrienne Rich. However, whereas former gender theories contrasted men's and women's friendships in accordance with supposedly opposing psychologies, here the women are also competitive and the men can be nurturing. Raewyn Connell reminds us that because "dichotomous gender symbolism" is still so strong globally, it is "not surprising that when researchers look at sex and gender, what they see is difference," even when the differences are minor, decreasing, and variable in their social contexts (Connell 2009, 44). Thus in recent popular films, friends act as positive support, often in contrast to fractious family relationships. Ethnicity, at least in the genre of romantic comedy, remains governed by the broad inclusiveness of American liberalism. What the movies demonstrate to their viewers, however, is the implicit classism that unites friends within the same social classes while rewarding their good-hearted protagonists with material success, rich partners, and social mobility upward.

Friendship remains more important in contemporary lives than current gender theories attest. It continues to be little theorized even though friendships in fact provide significant emotional support, especially for young adults undergoing the stresses of insecure economies, more mobile relationships, and confusion around gender and sexuality. Although people of all ages enjoy and benefit from friendships, friendship is increasingly associated with youth, leisure, same-sex bonding, and experiences of consumption within shared markets of sports, travel, and shopping. While friendships bless people with the pleasures of similarity and comradeship, I argue that a major function of the institution of friendship is that it reassures individuals that they are performing gender appropriately and so reinforces society's established gender norms and other social boundaries. On the other hand, contemporary friendships are indeed changing shape. Peter Nardi claims that for gay men, friendships "mean more and last longer" than romantic relationships (Nardi 1999, 3). More LGBT people are openly enjoying each other's company and also forming gay/heterosexual friendships. Ideals for friendship are converging for both genders, and cross-gender friendships are increasing (Felmlee, Sweet, and Sinclair 2012).

The 2019 film *Booksmart* illustrates popular culture's growing flexibility about gender and sexual identities. It revises the traditionally male buddy film to feature two young women. Smart, hardworking students Amy (Kaitln Dever) and Molly (Beanie Feldstein) decide to have one wild party night before they graduate. Both seek their crushes, lesbian Amy on a girl and straight Molly on a boy. The two friends seem equally smart and middle class, and the fact that Amy is a lesbian does not disturb the friendship. Both young women get promising erotic interests in new partners by the end of the film, although Amy is heading off not to college, but to bring menstrual products to third world women. Meanwhile, the friends overcome rivalries over dominance with one another in their rite of passage using their private code word "Malala." In this way, the two privileged white teenagers show their multicultural awareness as they invoke the name of Malala Yousafzai, a young Pakistani activist and Nobel Prize winner who suffered a disfiguring assassination attempt because of her campaign for women's rights to education.

The convergence in male and female psychologies, personalities, and life experiences that some feminist theorists seek has only partly occurred (Lorber 1995). Young women swear and drink more like their male peers, and young men may be more comfortable with physical intimacy and self-disclosure between friends than previously. Today's social forces simultaneously expand liberatory possibilities for American friendships and also conservatively reinforce established hierarchies of power and privilege.

Twentieth-century cultural feminist theorists, who see men and women as deeply different, described male psychology as autonomous, competitive, and defensive, in contrast to interdependent women's psychologies. Adrienne Rich (1980) claimed that all women exist on a "lesbian continuum," whatever their sexual preferences, so that women naturally bond with other women, while men are loyal to other men and masculine institutions. Nancy Chodorow (1978) argued that mother-dominated childrearing in households of stay-at-home mothers and employed fathers produced these asymmetries. Dual parenting, in which both parents shared daily care for their children, she proposed, would produce more autonomous women and more empathic men. U.S. family structures have changed dramatically since the post–World War II gender norms these theorists described. Male and female personalities have converged in some respects. Later marriage and childbearing, a divorce rate of almost 50 percent, and longer life expectancies, especially for women, have led to over 27 percent of Americans living in single-person households (American Psychological Association 2015). Many women are raising children without a father present. As more Americans stay single longer, these demographic changes may result from and encourage sexual experimentation outside of marriage; open lifestyles for people who identify as lesbian, gay, transgender, or nonbinary; and desires for community and friendship outside traditional nuclear families—all changes supported by liberal feminists who view men and women as fundamentally similar. Most research on American friendships is based on information from college students, so the scholarship of friendship is skewed toward middle-class, well-educated, and predominantly white youth. For many, college relationships continue into years of relative freedom from family obligations but also into occupations destabilized by a precarious economy.

Racial, ethnic, and class differences also affect friendship choices. For example, working-class African American men form closer, more mutually supportive ties than their upwardly mobile peers (Franklin 1992). For gender theorist Michael Kimmel, homophobia still crucially inhibits men's friendships: "The single cardinal rule of manhood . . . is to offer constant proof that you are not gay"

(Kimmel 2008, 50). In contrast, Eric Anderson (2009) contends that men's friendships now are less homophobic. As more people openly identify as gay or lesbian, gay/straight friendships have also increased along with greater acceptance of nonbinary gender expression. "Doing gender" also means "doing friendship," and friendship becomes a way of doing gender (West and Zimmerman 1987).

Changes in technology and workplaces are also reshaping friendships. Fewer Americans work in factories with large numbers of fellow workers, while more people face screens on which they can develop online friendships, find groups with similar tastes, discover fellow sufferers from afflictions, or join supporters of the same sports teams (Gardiner 2016). Online, dominant tendencies to associate only with one's own demographic may be countered by cross-gendered avatars or reinforced by niche-targeted websites. Alison Winch claims that for the social network Facebook, friendships are "its content, its market, and its worth" (Winch 2013, 191).

Cross-culturally, friendships are bound by fewer constraints than marriage and kinship. In some situations, as queer and postcolonial feminists note, friendships overlap with sexual relations, from American "friends with benefits" to Caribbean "Mati work," in which married working-class Afro-Caribbean women are sexually intimate with women friends (Wekker 1999). Friendships may also overlap with ethnic kinship structures, as with Mexican "comadres" (López 2012). And Americans often agree with political theorist Robert Putnam, who says, "everyone needs a best friend; I am blessed to be married to mine" (Putnam 2000, 213).

Some aspects of feminist theory are now widely accepted, even when not identified as such, like criticism of advertising's sexualization of women's bodies—and, increasingly, of men's. Winch decries the "thinspiration," which says that losing weight "empowers" "girlfriend culture" (Winch 2013, 50). Using a materialist feminist analysis, she asserts that women's friendships in the United States and the United Kingdom now incorporate attitudes shaped by contemporary capitalism: that is, women bond in consumer activities like shopping and compete to become more desirable objects for men. Men, in turn, bond through sports, cars, and video games, all mediated by the capitalist marketplace. Popular advice books claim that friendships boost people's health and well-being but also describe conflict and betrayal in women's friendships and competition in men's, while both genders seek loyalty and intimacy (Bertsche 2011). Girls' friendships provide spaces to try out feelings and shape identities. Boys' friendships reveal stress through joking and sports, while younger boys are more intimate than homophobic teens (Way 2011).

In past decades, U.S. popular culture has included fresh attention to mixed-sex groups of young adult friends, as in the television programs *Seinfeld* (1989–1998) and *Friends* (1994–2004), both of which can still be seen streaming. These programs expose the unstable, often comically immature relationships of both male and female characters. Even if each episode features the trivia of independent living, the supportive, mixed-sex friendship groups remain intact. More recent television series feature female-centric sitcoms like *Girls* (2012–17) and *Broad City* (2009–11, 2017–19). More racially and sexually diverse are the incarcerated women in the award-winning television series *Orange Is the New Black* (2013–19). The central character, Piper (Taylor Schilling), is a middle-class white bisexual among a wide array of jailed women, including a transsexual inmate and disabled women, who are continually forming and changing friendships and hostile rivalries as the plot lines reveal American problems with drugs, crime, racism, and immigration.

We can conclude, then, from these disparate cultural representations and from current scholarly research on gender that today's friendships are not as polarized between men and women as the cartoon beginning this essay pronounced. At the same time, such popular representations continue both to inhibit social change and to hide those changes that have in fact occurred. Friendships among both men and women may be diminishing somewhat in number and duration as people move more often, change employers, grow dispirited when unemployed or cheerfully overextended while juggling childcare and work (Putnam 2000). Liberal feminists may welcome the convergence in gendered lifestyles; cultural feminists may mourn the loss of female-specific activities; materialist feminists point out the economic contexts shaping such changes. Intersectional and queer theorists chafe at the simplistic categories "men" and "women" and join postcolonial scholars and theorists of color in demanding more nuanced analyses for specific social categories and contexts.

American friendships cushion the constraints of more structured institutions like the workplace and the family. They support American ideologies of individual freedom, autonomy, and freedom of association and play a large part in people's happiness. They consolidate social hierarchies of power and privilege, yet are now becoming less polarized and more encouraging of flexible attitudes toward gender and sexuality and of ethnicities and social classes.

WORKS CITED

American Psychological Association. http://www.apa.org/marriage, 2015. Web.

Anderson, Eric. *Inclusive Masculinity: The Changing Nature of Masculinities*. Routledge/Taylor & Francis, 2009. Print.

Bertsche, Rachel. *MWF Seeking BFF: My Yearlong Search for a New Best Friend*. Ballantine, 2011. Print.

Chodorow, Nancy. *The Reproduction of Mothering: Psychoanalysis and the Sociology of Gender*. University of California Press, 1978. Print.

Connell, Raewyn. *Gender in World Perspective*. 2nd ed. Polity, 2009. Print.

Felmlee, Diane, Elizabeth Sweet, and H. Colleen Sinclair. "Gender Rules: Same- and Cross-Gender Friendship Norms." *Sex Roles* vol. 66, 2012, pp. 518–29. Print.

Franklin, Clyde. "'Hey Home—Yo, Bro': Friendship Among Black Men." In *Men's Friendships*, edited by Peter M. Nardi. Sage, 1992, pp. 201–14. Print.

Gardiner, Judith Kegan. "Women's Friendships, Feminist Friendships." *Feminist Studies* vol. 42, no. 2, 2016, 484–501. Print.

Greif, Geoffrey L. *Buddy System: Understanding Male Friendships*. Oxford UP, 2009. Print.

Kimmel, Michael. *Guyland: The Perilous World Where Boys Become Men*. Harper, 2008. Print.

López, Adriana, ed. *Count on Me: Tales of Sisterhoods and Fierce Friendships*. Atria, 2012. Print.

Lorber, Judith. *Breaking the Bowls: Degendering and Feminist Change*. Norton, 1995. Print.

Nardi, Peter M. *Gay Men's Friendships: Invincible Communities*. Chicago & London: Chicago, 1999. Print.

Putnam, Robert D. *Bowling Alone: The Collapse and Revival of American Community*. Simon and Schuster, 2000. Print.

Rich, Adrienne. "Compulsory Heterosexuality and Lesbian Existence." *Signs* vol. 5, no. 4, 1980, pp. 631–60. Print.

Way, Niobe. *Deep Secrets: Boys' Friendships and the Crisis of Connection*. Harvard, 2011. Print.

Wekker, Gloria. "What's Identity Got to Do with It?: Rethinking Identity in Light of Mati Work in Suriname." In *Female Desires: Same-Sex and Transgender Practices across Cultures*, edited by Evelyn Blackwood and Saskia E. Wieringa. Columbia UP, 1999, pp. 119–38. Print.

Winch, Alison. *Girlfriends and Postfeminist Sisterhood*. Palgrave Macmillan, 2013. Print.

West, Candace, and Don H. Zimmerman, "Doing Gender." *Gender and Society* vol. 1, no. 2, 1987, pp. 125–51. Print.

51. • *Meda Chesney-Lind*

MEAN GIRLS, BAD GIRLS, OR JUST GIRLS:
Corporate Media Hype and the Policing of Girlhood (2017)

Meda Chesney-Lind, a Professor of women's studies, *Emerita*, at the University of Hawai'i, is nationally recognized for her work on women and crime; her testimony before Congress resulted in national support of gender-responsive programming for girls in the juvenile justice system. Her book on girls' use of violence, *Fighting for Girls* (co-edited with Nikki Jones in 2010), won an award from the National Council on Crime and Delinquency. In 2013, the Western Society of Criminology named an award after her honoring "significant contributions to the fields of gender, crime and justice" and made her the inaugural recipient. She was elected President of the American Society of Criminology in 2017; she is currently serving as past President of the Society. The following article was written specifically for the first edition.

It seems as though the bad news about American girls just keeps coming, at least if you watch television or read the papers. Girls are going "wild," girls are "mean" (and certainly meaner than boys), and girls are even getting as violent as boys. Current media coverage of modern girlhood, at least in the United States, is virtually all grim, and it is also clear as to the source of the problem—girls are getting more like boys and that is bad news for girls.

As an example, on June 19, 2001, an ABC report on trends in gang membership maintained that girls are "catching up with boys in this one area," "joining gangs for the same reasons as boys," and doing the same activities as boys: selling drugs and committing murder (Gibbs 2001). Likewise, on July 28, 2009, New Jersey Attorney General Anne Milgram announced that law enforcement officials dismantled an all-female–led, gang-involved narcotics ring. Dubbing the investigation "Operation Bloodette," Milgram went on to state that she wished "this was not one [glass] ceiling women were

breaking" and that "women are taking over dominant roles in traditionally male-dominated gangs" (Read 2009). Finally, in March 2006, ABC's *Good Morning America* contributed to these stories with its series titled "Why Girls Are Getting More Violent: Violence Is on the Rise Among High School Girls." One segment was labeled "Girls Are Beating and Bullying."

This last headline introduces a theme closely related to the news media's obsession with girls' violence—a focus on "mean" girls. The manipulative and damaging characteristics of girls' social worlds have been the subject of high-profile best-selling books like *Odd Girl Out* (Simmons 2002) and *Queen Bees and Wannabes* (Wiseman 2002). These, in turn, spawned hit movies, like *Mean Girls*, and also innumerable articles. *The New York Times Magazine* ran a cover story titled "Girls Just Want to Be Mean," where the author noted "it is not just boys who can bully" (Talbot 2002, 24), and other media outlets quickly jumped on the bandwagon, running stories titled "Girl Bullies Don't Leave Black Eyes, Just Agony" (Elizabeth 2002), "She Devils" (Metcalf 2002), and "Just Between Us Girls: Not Enough Sugar, Too Much Spite" (Bennett 2002).

Books like *Odd Girl Out* and *Queen Bees and Wannabes* all rely on recent psychological research on aggression, particularly what is called "relational," "covert," or "indirect" aggression (Underwood et al. 2001, 248). The concept of relational or covert aggression relates to a repertoire of passive and/or indirect behaviors (e.g., rolling eyes, spreading rumors, ostracizing, and ignoring), used with the "intent to hurt or harm others" (Crick and Grotpeter 1995), and thus the concept expands the range of behaviors that are considered aggressive in nature.

By identifying a "relational," "covert," or "indirect" aggression, rather than a physical type of aggression, researchers argued that they shattered the myth of the nonaggressive girl (Bjorkqvist and Niemela 1992). These researchers note that when these indirect aggressions are considered, girls are as aggressive as boys. In fact, they claimed that they were not only shattering myths but that they were unraveling years of gender bias in which male researchers tended to only look at male problems. Bjorkqvist and Niemela argued that researchers, "the majority being males, . . . may, for personal reasons, find male aggression easier to understand and a more appealing object of study" (1992, 5).

While this characterization of the "discovery" has been widely accepted, there are reasons to be a bit more skeptical that this concept benefits girls. First, does this aggression really challenge stereotypes and myths about girls? Thinking about the behaviors included in relational aggression, this research is arguing that girls and women are manipulative, sneaky, mean-spirited, and backstabbing—hardly new ideas, which may, in fact, be one reason that the public and the media embraced them so quickly.

More importantly, the literature on relational aggression does not consistently support the notion that girls specialize in these forms of aggression while boys are more physically aggressive (Chesney-Lind, Morash, and Irwin 2007). For example, University of Georgia researchers randomly selected 745 sixth-graders from nine middle schools across six school districts in northeast Georgia. The student participants took computer surveys each spring semester for seven years, from sixth to twelfth grade (Orpinas et al. 2014).

Key findings included the following. First, covert and relational aggression is extremely common; 96 percent of the students who participated in the study reported at least one act of relational aggression (meaning basically everyone is mean sometimes), and 92.3 percent of boys and 94.3 percent of girls said they'd been the victim of such an attack at one point during the study period. Second, they found that boys admitted to significantly more acts of relational aggression than girls did, and girls were more likely to be victims. Finally, and of the greatest significance, of the meanest kids (the ones who fell into the "high" relational aggression group), 66.7 percent were boys and 33.3 percent were girls (Orpinas et al. 2014).

So while the media focuses on the "meanness" of girls, the reality is that boys might be meaner than girls. But what of the media hype regarding those "bad" girls who are using violence, including those in gangs? Are girls really seeking violent equality with their male counterparts, as the media insist? There is also an important racial element to this discussion. Stock media imagery of girls, particularly girls in gangs, tends to suggest that these girls are just as menacing as their male counterparts. *Newsweek* did this by using a stereotypical headline, "Girls Will Be Girls," while showing a picture of a black girl holding a gun and wearing a mask, with the subtitle "Some girls carry guns. Others hide razor blades in their mouths" (Leslie et al. 1993). In essence, black and Latina violence is positioned in ways that invite a contrast to the assumed "nonviolence" of white girls.

Media accounts of this "problem" also are caused by girls trying to act like boys. There's nothing new about this argument, by the way. In the 1920s, opponents of women's suffrage fretted about increases in "intensely immoral" behavior among the "modern age of girls" and, in the 1930s, commentators contended that "women becoming more criminally minded" as a result of "the fight for Emancipation" (Pollock 2014, 84). By the 1970s, the argument was that the second wave of feminism had "caused" a surge in women's serious crimes (Chesney-Lind 1986).

The current media backlash to efforts to improve both girls and women's lives, though, has settled on girls' commission of violent crimes, particularly but not always in gangs. Is this true that girls are more violent today than in decades past?

Certain data, which the media tend to rely on heavily, suggests that girls are getting in trouble more often than in the past and also that they are engaged in more serious delinquent behavior. In 1983, arrests of girls accounted for roughly one in five arrests (21.4 percent), but by 2013, girls accounted for nearly one in three juvenile arrests (28.8 percent) (Federal Bureau of Investigation 2014). And while both male and female arrests have been declining in recent years, arrests of juvenile boys decreased far more steeply, decreasing 26.5 percent during the first decade of the twenty-first century compared to a decrease in girls' arrests of only 15.4 percent. The much-vaunted "crime drop," at least among youth, was really a crime drop in just boys' official delinquency.

Data on juvenile courts suggests that the number of girls' cases referred to the court has also increased. The National Center for Juvenile Justice noted that most of the surge in male and female delinquency cases occurred between 1985 and 1997. During that time period, the reported increase in cases involving girls grew 97 percent versus a 52 percent increase for boys (Puzzanchera and Hockenberry 2013, 14). And the gendered pattern continues in the current period; between 1997 and 2011, the male delinquency caseload declined by 38 percent compared to a female caseload that decreased by only 22 percent. As a result, in 2011 females accounted for 28 percent of the delinquency caseload, up from only 19 percent in 1985 (Hockenberry and Puzzanchera 2014). Much of this pattern is explained by soaring increases in arrests of girls for simple assault in over the past few decades. While these have recently leveled off, one study of court referrals found that

"for females, the largest 1985–2002 increase was in person offense cases (202 percent)" (Snyder and Sickmund 2006, 160).

What about other data on girl's violence? The Centers for Disease Control and Prevention in Atlanta has monitored youthful behavior in a national sample of school-age youth in a number of domains (including violence) at regular intervals since 1991 in a biennial survey titled the *Youth Risk Behavior Survey*. As an example, a review of the data collected over the 1990s and into this century reveals that although 34.4 percent of girls surveyed in 1991 said that they had been in a physical fight in the previous year, slightly over half (50.2 percent) of the boys reported fighting. Two decades later, in 2011, 24.4 percent of girls and 40.7 percent of boys said they had been in a physical fight in the last year ("Youth Risk," 1992–2012). In essence, the data shows that girls have always been more violent than their stereotype suggests but also that girls' violence, at least by their own accounts, has been decreasing, not increasing.

To further explore these issues about girl's self-reported violence and likelihood of arrest, Stevens et al. (2011) used several national self-report data sets to compare self-reported behavior with self-reported arrests in two different time periods (1980 and 2000). This research found that girls who admitted to simple assault in 1980 had about a one-in-four chance of being charged with a crime, compared to girls in 2000, who had about a three-in-four chance of arrest. Furthermore, black girls in 2000 were nearly seven times more likely than their 1980 counterparts to be charged with a crime.

In short, while girls had long reported that they were acting out violently, their arrests, particularly in the 1960s and 1970s, did not necessarily reflect that reality. Instead, girls' arrests tended to emphasize petty and status offenses (like running away from home); by the 1990s, that had changed dramatically, as more girls were arrested, particularly for such seemingly "masculine" offenses as simple assault—and this pattern was particularly pronounced among black girls.

Research increasingly suggests that these shifts in girls' arrest patterns are not products of a change in girls' behavior, with girls getting "more" violent. Rather, girls are being more heavily policed, particularly at home and in school (Chesney-Lind and Irwin 2008). Girls are being arrested for assault because of arguments with their parents, often their mothers (Buzawa and Hotaling 2006), or for "other assault" for fighting in school because of new zero-tolerance policies enacted after the Columbine shootings (*Criminalizing the Classroom* 2007). In decades past, this violence would have been ignored or labeled a status offense, like being "incorrigible" or a "person in need of supervision." Now an arrest is made.

Taking a global look at the American obsession with bad, violent, and mean girls is also important. Consider that the work of two recent recipients of the Nobel Peace Prize (Malala Yousafzai and Kailash Satyarthi) reflects a growing global focus on girls' rights, especially their right to education and to be safe from abuse, particularly physical abuse, sexual abuse, and early marriages ("Nobel Peace Prize"). This international concern about girls' victimization and girls' rights stands in stark contrast to the discourse on girls in the past twenty-five years in the United States, where both the media and policymakers have been expressing concern about the growing numbers of "bad" and "violent" girls coming into the juvenile justice system. Clearly, it is time to stop bashing girls in the United States and start entering the global conversation about improving their lives and futures. Our girls are not getting worse—they are getting short-changed.

WORKS CITED

Bennett, Samantha. "Just Between Us Girls: Not Enough Sugar, Too Much Spite." *Pittsburgh-Post Gazette*, June 5, 2002, pp. 3–5.

Bjorkqvist, Kaj, and Pirkko Niemela. *Of Mice and Women: Aspects of Female Aggression*. Academic Press, 1992.

Buzawa, Eve S., and Gerald T. Hotaling. "The Impact of Relationship Status, Gender, and Minor Status in the Police Response to Domestic Assaults." *Victims and Offenders*, vol. 1, 2006, pp. 323–60.

Chesney-Lind, Meda. "Women and Crime: A Review of the Literature on the Female Offender." *Signs: Journal of Women in Culture and Society*, vol. 12, no. 1, 1986, pp. 78–96.

Chesney-Lind, Meda, and Katherine Irwin. *Beyond Bad Girls: Gender, Violence and Hype*. Routledge, 2008.

Chesney-Lind, Meda, Merry Morash, and Katherine Irwin. "Policing Girlhood? Relational Aggression and Violence Prevention." *Youth Violence and Juvenile Justice*, vol. 5, no. 3, 2007, pp. 328–45.

Crick, Nicki R., and Jennifer K. Grotpeter. "Relational Aggression, Gender, and Social-Psychological Adjustment." *Child Development*, vol. 66, 1995, pp. 710–22.

Criminalizing the Classroom: The Over-Policing of New York City Schools. New York Civil Liberties Union/American Civil Liberties Union, 2007.

Elizabeth, Jane. "Girl Bullies Don't Leave Black Eyes, Just Agony." *Pittsburgh Post-Gazette*, April 10, 2002, p. A1.

Federal Bureau of Investigation. *Crime in the United States—2013*. U.S. Government Printing Office, 2014.

Gibbs, B. "Number of Girls in Gangs Increasing." *ABC*, June 19, 2001, abclocal.go.com/wtvd/features/061901_CF_girlsgangs.html.

Hockenberry, S., and C. M. Puzzanchera. *Juvenile Court Statistics 2011*. National Center for Juvenile Justice, 2014.

Leslie, C., N. Biddle, D. Rosenberg, and J. Wayne. "Girls Will Be Girls." *Newsweek*, August 2, 1993, p. 44.

Metcalf, F. "She Devils." *Courier Mail* [Queensland], June 22, 2002, p. L6.

Orpinas, P., et al. "Gender Differences in Trajectories of Relational Aggression Perpetration and Victimization from Middle to High School." *Aggressive Behavior*, vol. 41, 2014, pp. 401–12.

Pollock, Joycelyn. *Women's Crimes, Criminology, and Corrections*. Waveland, 2014.

Puzzanchera, C. M., and S. Hockenberry. *Juvenile Court Statistics 2010*. National Center for Juvenile Justice, 2013.

Read, Phillip. "'Operation Bloodette' Nets 43 Members of Female-Led Drug Ring." *Star-Ledger*, New Jersey On-Line, July 28, 2009, www.nj.com/news/index.ssf/2009/07/operation_bloodette_nets_43_me.html.

Simmons, Rachel. *Odd Girl Out: The Hidden Culture of Aggression in Girls*. Harcourt, 2002.

Snyder, H. N., and M. Sickmund. *Juvenile Offenders and Victims: 2006 National Report (NCJ 178257)*. U.S.

Department of Justice, Office of Justice Programs, Office of Juvenile Justice and Delinquency Prevention, 2006.

Stevens, Tia, et al. "Are Girls Getting Tougher, or Are We Tougher on Girls? Probability of Arrest and Juvenile Court Oversight in 1980 and 2000." *Justice Quarterly*, vol. 28, no. 5, 2011, pp. 719–44.

Talbot, Margaret. "Girls Just Want to Be Mean." *New York Times Magazine*, February 24, 2002, pp. 24–64.

Underwood, Marion K., et al. "Top Ten Challenges for Understanding Gender and Aggression in Children: Why Can't We All Just Get Along?" *Social Development*, vol. 10, 2001, pp. 248–66.

UNICEF. "Nobel Peace Prize Winners Malala Yousafzai and Kailash Satyarthi Make South Asia Proud." www.unicefw.org/pakistan/media_9026.htm.

"Why Girls Are Getting More Violent: Violence is on the Rise Among High School Girls." *Good Morning America*, ABC, March 11, 2006.

Wiseman, Rosalind. *Queen Bees and Wannabees: Helping Your Daughter Survive Cliques, Gossip, Boyfriends and other Realities of Adolescence*. Crown Publishers, 2002.

"Youth Risk Behavior Surveillance—1991–2001." *CDC Surveillance Summaries*, U.S. Department of Health and Human Services, Centers for Disease Control, 1992–2012.

52. • *Elly Belle*

KNEE-JERK BIPHOBIA:
What Responses to Miley Cyrus's Breakup Say About Queer Erasure (2019)

Elly Belle is a writer and digital media strategist based in Brooklyn, NY. Their writings have appeared in *Teen Vogue, Thrillist, InStyle, Playboy, Publisher's Weekly, BUST* Magazine, and *Bitch.* They write mostly on issues of culture, restorative justice, and healing.

Skepticism, erasure, and exclusion is nothing new for bisexual and pansexual people. Some of the most prevalent and harmful stereotypes and accusations about—and even within—the LGBTQ community are about Bi+ people (people who are bisexual, pansexual, or non-monosexual), so it's no surprise that queerphobic hell broke loose when Miley Cyrus, who's been outspoken about being pansexual, announced her split from husband Liam Hemsworth in August 2019, with the separation immediately followed by her dating women. Cyrus and Hemsworth met in 2008 on the set of *The Last Song*, began dating in 2009, and were engaged twice prior to getting married in December 2018, when Cyrus

was 25. Many people were rooting for their marriage to last, creating a fandom that was simultaneously critical of Cyrus's sexuality and the "danger" it posed to their union.

During a break from their relationship in 2015, Cyrus publicly came out as queer and gender nonconforming, an announcement that fans of both stars scrutinized and disbelieved, especially when she released the song "She's Not Him," purportedly about model Stella Maxwell. Cyrus has said that her first romantic relationship was with a girl, and that she's always considered her sexuality to be fluid. In a 2017 *Billboard* interview, Cyrus said, "I always get in trouble for . . . generalizing straight men, 'cause straight men can be my worst nightmare sometimes. And I'm with a straight dude," suggesting that she's well aware that both her relationship and her sexuality are constantly under scrutiny as a result of her fame and a continued cultural misunderstanding of queerness.

Last week's announcement of Cyrus and Hemsworth's split was greeted with both an outpouring of online feelings and a glut of hateful messages that blamed Cyrus's sexuality. One Twitter user wrote that Cyrus is a prime example of why you shouldn't trust bisexual people—although Cyrus has been explicit that she identifies as pansexual, not that that statement would be true, either. The user wrote, "#MileyCyrus splitting and allegedly cheating on Liam with a woman confirms that you shouldn't date bi people. Not offensive, just true. Bi is greedy and never satisfied." Cyrus's fellow musician Halsey—who does identify as bisexual—had a pointed response for such generalizations: "Stop being afraid of women who aren't afraid to do what pleases them and not other people."

As news of the couple's breakup churned through the news cycle, so did photos of Cyrus kissing another woman, Kaitlynn Carter. Straight people on social media were critical of their spending time together, saying that it seems wrong to go on a vacation and flaunt it in an ex's face immediately after breaking up, and that Cyrus was being "slutty" and "inconsiderate." On the other hand, queer women came out in droves to celebrate having Cyrus "back," glad that she had left a man, and suggesting her relationship with Hemsworth had always been temporary—a youthful pit stop on the road to a more valid queerness.

Famous or not, Bi+ people don't become less queer when we start dating someone of one gender versus another, so the idea that Cyrus had been "lost" from her community during her relationship with and marriage to Hemsworth is one I take issue with. Most Bi+ people don't think of their identities as being split in half, so why are we asked to quantify our queerness? Identity policing has always been a cold reminder that even in a space that can be as open and loving as the LGBTQ+ community, there are rules here that can be as rigid as those in hetero spheres. You have to pick a side—and if you don't, well, you're just not like the rest of us.

As a queer person who has experienced my fair share of both internalized homophobia and erasure and biphobia from others, the bitter sting of having your sexuality invalidated and painted over in order to fit a mold that makes sense to others is all too familiar. When I dated cis men and wasn't out, I wasn't being true to myself. But when I came out, it didn't necessarily feel better. Queer people told me I wasn't truly queer if I kept dating cis men, or if I didn't commit to only dating women—a strange thing, considering that bisexuality clearly implies an interest in multiple genders. When I finally did start dating people who weren't cis men, I felt like there was a certain number of people I *had* to date, or kiss, or sleep with to be considered truly queer. None of that was true, of course. But the narrative that to be queer means to eradicate anything that even potentially looks like or mimics heterosexuality from your dating life was deeply rooted in me. It's deeply rooted in many of us.

It doesn't help that representations of queerness are stifled by a popular culture that, despite some promising changes, remains heteronormative. This limited representation is part of why Cyrus's fans—whether they want her to be queer like they are, or they doubt her queerness entirely—are so invested in her sexuality. We don't often see queer characters on TV or moments in pop culture that don't assign a set identity or make a big deal of sexual fluidity. Callie Torres (Sara Ramirez) on *Grey's Anatomy* and Rosa Diaz (Stephanie Beatriz) on *Brooklyn Nine-Nine* are two examples that come to mind: At the start of both shows, the characters were assumed to be straight, Callie and Rosa transitioned to dating people of different genders with a narrative casualness that was meant to normalize their bisexuality.

However, in shows like *Glee*, the queer representation offered by characters like Brittany (Heather Morris) and Santana (Naya Rivera) felt murkier in its intent. Though Brittany identified herself as attracted to both men and women—an ostensibly positive step forward for pop culture given the show's audience and reach—she was also portrayed as comic relief and as an unintelligent, thoughtless character, which only pushed the idea that Bi+ people don't know what they want, and hurt people because of it. Kristen Stewart, a celebrity who, like Cyrus, has been subject to the queer community's ongoing scrutiny, dated fellow actor Michael Angarano until 2009, started seeing her *Twilight* costar Robert Pattinson until 2013, and began publicly dating women in 2015.

Straight people were mad that Stewart was no longer fulfilling their Bella-and-Edward fantasies, while queer women were ecstatic that someone so hot was playing for "our team." Stewart has continued to have relationships with women in the last four years or so (she's currently dating Cyrus's ex, Stella Maxwell), and she's said that she identifies most with bisexuality. "It's cool that you don't have to nail everything down anymore," she told *The Guardian* in a 2017 interview. "That whole certainty about whether you're straight or gay or whatever. You're not confused if you're bisexual. It's not confusing at all. For me, it's quite the opposite." And her openness about her sexuality and being loudly and publicly queer has helped other queer people accept themselves more.

The lack of respect for Bi+ identities has impact. Often, to drive home my own preference for people who are not cis men, I lean on the word "gay" to describe myself, in hopes that no one will invalidate me. In doing so, however, I erase my fuller identity simply to be accepted by others. Comments lobbed at queer women like Cyrus have recently set me back on the path of questioning why queer women in particular are made to feel like our more complex identities are something to be left behind when we're dating someone of one gender, or that we must conform to monosexuality to be true. That, as a community, we often treat queerness or dating as a team sport—saying we have Cyrus's or Stewart's "back"—is not only disingenuous, but deeply harmful.

Invalidation, erasure, and a general disrespect for Bi+ people has real consequences: When tabloids dug into Johnny Depp's abuse of Amber Heard, for instance, they suggested that perhaps he was abusive because she was bisexual and he was afraid she would cheat. The suggestion that Heard's mistreatment could be blamed on an identity that strayed from the "norm" made it clear that mainstream media wasn't sure what to do with someone who resisted easy categorization. Research has repeatedly pointed out that people who identify as bisexual, or as being attracted to many genders, are more likely to struggle with mental health. Approximately 40 percent of bisexual people have considered or attempted suicide, compared to nearly a quarter of gay men and lesbians. Bisexual adults are even more likely to struggle when they are transgender, nonwhite, and/or disabled. Further, bisexuals are much less likely to disclose their sexuality to healthcare professionals, meaning that stigma is preventing us from access to the information, treatment, and care we may need.

As Janelle Monae told *Rolling Stone* in 2018, "Being a queer Black woman in America, someone who has been in relationships with both men and women—I consider myself to be a free-ass motherfucker." Monae's disinterest in one specific label calls out the simple fact that, at times, language simply can't contain human complexity or accurately represent our identities. Labels for sexual and romantic orientation in the queer community should give us freedom from the strict binaries and rules imposed on us by cisheteronormative culture, not used to gatekeep queer people.

I decided to dig into the cultural response to Cyrus's relationships not because I'm interested in defending her (Cyrus has made a number of questionable comments and decisions herself) but because it's crucial to examine how we respond to Bi+ celebrities—and to understand how we harm our community when we shame Bi+ people. If we continue to perpetuate the stereotypes rearing their heads in the wake of Cyrus's split with Hemsworth—to tell queer women that they're only valid when they choose the "right" team, or that those who choose to explore their identities by dating people of any gender are less valid—we'll perpetuate the idea that there is only one way to be queer. Studies continue to find that bisexual people make up more than half of the population of the LGBTQ community but less than half of those people report being out even to the people closest to them. With that in mind, we have to confront our own internalized homophobia and biphobia if we truly want to be free-ass motherfuckers.

SECTION FOUR

Epistemologies of Bodies: Ways of Knowing and Experiencing the World

TABLE OF CONTENTS

53. Janet Mock, from *Redefining Realness* 357
54. *Ari Agha, "Singing in the Cracks" (new) 363
55. *Cheryl Chase, "Hermaphrodites with Attitude: Mapping the Emergence of Intersex Political Activism" 368
56. *C. Winter Han, "Being an Oriental, I Could Never Be Completely a Man: Gay Asian Men and the Intersection of Race, Gender, Sexuality, and Class" 375
57. Dominique C. Hill, "(My) Lesbianism Is Not a Fixed Point" 384
58. *Christina Crosby, "Masculine, Feminine, or Fourth of July" 387
59. Aleichia Williams, "Too Latina to Be Black, Too Black to Be Latina" 392
60. *Kristina Gupta, "Feminist Approaches to Asexuality" (new) 393
61. Gloria Steinem, "If Men Could Menstruate" 398
62. No'u Revilla, "How to Use a Condom" 400
63. *Lailatul Fitriyah, "Can We Stop Talking About the 'Hijab'?: Islamic Feminism, Intersectionality, and the Indonesian Muslim Female Migrant Workers" (new) 401
64. L. Ayu Saraswati, "Cosmopolitan Whiteness: The Effects and Affects of Skin-Whitening Advertisements in Transnational Indonesia" 406
65. Chimamanda Ngozi Adichie, from *Americanah* 416
66. Kimberly Dark, "Big Yoga Student" 421
67. *Jessica Vasquez-Tokos and Kathryn Norton-Smith, "Resisting Racism: Latinos' Changing Responses to Controlling Images over the Life Course" 423
68. *Joanna Gordon, "Sketches" (new) 427
69. *Christina Lux, "10,000 Blows" (new) 428

By the end of this section, you will have a better understanding of:

1. How we know what we know (the epistemology) about the body.

2. How the body becomes an important element in the process of identity formation and the limitations of such a construction.

3. How we inhabit the body influences how others respond to us and how we experience and therefore understand the world we live in.

4. How we need to be more critical of existing discourses (including the "real," medical, and other discourses) about the body in a neoliberal age.

5. How bodies become a medium through and with which we navigate, "talk back to," and challenge the power hierarchy.

Epistemologies: Theories that are concerned with how knowledge is produced and circulated.

Essentialism: A theory that there is an *essence* that defines a particular entity and makes it *innately* different from other groups. Bodies are perceived to be the determining factor for people's identities and behaviors. To argue that women's behavior is inherently different from men's because of their biological differences is to essentialize them.

Does inhabiting a particular body influence how others treat you and how you experience the world? What is the relationship between your body and your identity? And why is it important to ask these questions? This introductory essay and the texts included in this section will help us address these questions and better understand the **epistemologies** of the bodies. Together, the voices collected here point to how labels (such as fit, fat, freaky, feminine, masculine, queer, trans, disabled, racialized, and sexualized) are attached to and provide meanings for the body. Such labels are intersectional categories that both cement and create cultural scripts for how these bodies should be experienced and power hierarchies are maintained. Critically examining the body and its meanings is important because it allows us to peek into the changing constructions of gender, sex, and sexuality as cultural and historical shifts are often represented and "materially inscribed" on the body (Conboy et al. 1997, 8).

BEYOND REALNESS: DECONSTRUCTING ESSENTIALISM

Janet Mock's book *Redefining Realness: My Path to Womanhood, Identity, Love and So Much More* (excerpted here) opens this section with its captivating portrayal of a mixed-race transwoman from Hawai'i whose body does not reflect back the stereotypical postcard image of Hawaiian hula dance girls. Beginning with Mock's essay, this section disrupts the conventions of telling a story about the body, stories that often begin at the center: a young, white, cisgender, heterosexual, middle- and upper-class, abled body. Doing so also allows us to challenge the limited constructions of normative versus deviant bodies, move beyond **essentializing** *any* bodies, and destabilize any categories of identity that may originate in the body, such as gender, race, age, and so on. For example, when we talk about women's bodies, we have to ask *which women* are we talking about? What makes a body a *woman's* body? Who decides?

More important, we begin with an excerpt from Mock's memoir because it serves as a powerful critique that illuminates the disjuncture between the "real" and the represented/idealized bodies as well as the tension between the material and the discursive body. Her story of transitioning illustrates the instability of the body, from hormone therapy and sex-reassignment surgery to the ways in which others respond to her changing body. As the materiality of the body is reconfigured, it shifts not only the semantic and semiotic of the body but also the somatic experience that is felt through and with that body (Prosser 1998, 6). To clarify and complicate this point further, Ari Agha's essay

Janet Mock and Laverne Cox, famous transwomen in American pop culture. Janet Mock became famous after the publication of her *New York Times* bestseller book *Redefining Realness: My Path to Womanhood, Identity, Love & So Much More.* Once the TV host of "So POPular!" on MSNBC, Mock is currently a writer, producer, and director of the television show, "Pose." Laverne Cox is the Emmy-nominated leading actress of the Netflix TV series *Orange Is the New Black.* She has received many awards including the Stephen Kolzak award, the Dorian Rising Star award, and the Courage award from the Anti-Violence Project, among many other things. Here they were seen attending the 26th Annual GLAAD Media Awards in New York in 2015.
Source: lev radin/Shutterstock

"Singing in the Cracks," which details "the impact of testosterone on singing among people assigned female" during their gender transition, is also included in this section.

Mock's insistence that we must move beyond "realness" (or, in her words, "redefine realness") reminds us that, as long as the "success" of a person's transition is measured by their ability to "pass" as a "real" woman or man, we will continue to reinscribe and reinforce the hierarchy of "realness" that leads to discrimination and even violence. Why, one may wonder, is embracing (rather than challenging) "realness" problematic? Susan Pickard, in critically examining the issue of embodiment in "older" people, challenges the notion of the real by arguing that it is not that the real body does not exist. Rather, she invites us to ponder, "why it is that 'real' happens to take the form it does, physiologically as well as phenomenologically and symbolically" (Pickard 2014, 1283–84). Her query pushes us to think more critically about the problematic

INTERSECTIONAL ANALYSIS

A Case Study: Thomas Beatie was the first transman who made his pregnancy public in 2008. An image of him naked at five months into his pregnancy appeared in the magazine *Advocate* alongside an article he wrote about the challenges and discriminations he had faced when trying to conceive a baby as a transman (his wife, Nancy, had a hysterectomy that made it impossible for her to carry a child). When his news became widely known, people posted online comments that highlighted that he was really a "woman having a baby," not a man. His body became the locus of conversations about the anatomy and journey of a transgender body, medical technologies, and transphobia (fear of bodies that are marked deviant and challenge the continuity between bodies and identities).

QUESTIONS

1. What do you think of the online comments that Beatie was a woman, and not a man, having a baby? How do the comments reflect the notion of a "man" as a category of gender that is unstable and intersectional? How does the "real" body discourse affect how people view his body? Why are some people invested in the "real" discourse narrative (real body, real man, real beauty, etc.)?
2. How does his pregnant body shape how he experiences his gender, as an intersectional category, differently? What are the intersecting categories that are at work here? How does his trans identity intersect with and complicate his gender and sexuality?
3. What do the readers' responses to his story reveal about our society's assumption of the relationship between bodies and identities?

production of the real body: why the real body is deemed more desirable and whose body gets to be counted as real, and by whom. For example, as Cheryl Chase's essay "Hermaphrodites with Attitude: Mapping the Emergence of Intersex Political Activism" (in this section) shows, when a baby is born and their genitalia does not fit within the accepted genitalia norms, a medical team "chooses either male or female as a 'sex of assignment,' then informs the parents that this is the child's 'true sex'" (p. 369). In this sense, then, being born intersex does not count as embodying a "real" body. A compulsory surgery often takes place during infancy to reconstruct the gendered materiality of the intersex body, transforming it into what society considers more "real:" a body that fits neatly into either one of the two acceptable gender categories.

KNOWING AND EXPERIENCING BODIES

What do you know about female orgasms, female ejaculation, or women's sexual pleasures in general? According to Nancy Tuana in her 2004 article, "Coming to Understand: Orgasm and the Epistemology of Ignorance," probably not much. Tuana argues that epistemic ignorance about women's sexuality is not simply a "lack" of information but rather a systematic way in which this unknowingness is constructed. Not only by being structurally erased, knowledge about (heterosexual) women's sexual pleasure is also and often attached to "horror" narratives to prevent young women from getting pregnant (hooks 1997, 57). Even body practices such as female genital surgeries and foot binding are/were purposefully done to curb women's sexual pleasures (in the case of female genital surgeries) and to discipline women's bodies for the sake of men's sexual arousal (in the case of foot binding). Indeed, as Rose Weitz argues, repressing women's sexuality has been used as "an effective way to control women's lives" (1998b, 65).

Not surprisingly, then, feminists and **sex-positive** activists have worked toward challenging this ignorance and repression of women's bodies, sexualities, and pleasures. The book *Our Bodies, Ourselves* (Boston Women's Health Book Collective 1973), first published in 1970 as *Women and Their Bodies*, was the first and perhaps best-known book to provide women with a comprehensive knowledge about women's health and bodies, allowing them to take control of their bodies. Activists such as Betty Dodson advocated and taught women to masturbate; her 1974 book *Liberating Masturbation: A Meditation on Self Love* redefines women's sexual pleasure. In the midst of these celebrations of women's sexualities (that is, the "freedom to" do whatever one wants), Breanne Fahs (2014) reminds us that we need to reclaim the "freedom from" discourse (i.e., the freedom from having to be sexual).

A different way of knowing about the body, as phenomenologists would argue, is through experiencing the body itself. Phenomenologists believe that the sensory apparatus of the body or the "lived body" provides us with an insight to knowing about the world (Hammers 2014, 69; McWeeny 2014, 275). In phenomenology, people are viewed "as embodied subjects who think, act, and know through their bodies"; they exercise their "epistemic agency" as they produce knowledge that stems from their everyday experiences (Davis 2007, 57, 59).

The body we inhabit and the identity that we project (whether or not it is in continuity with the body) help shape how we experience and therefore perceive and know ourselves, our bodies, and the world. When certain bodies are attached to specific meanings, however, how we experience these or other bodies will be "mediated" by these meanings (Conboy et al. 1997, 1). In other words, our experiences of, in, and with our bodies are always socially constructed (Bordo 2003, 35). For example, when a person takes on a particular gender identity, there are scripts of how one *should* dress, talk, love, or live. In this case, meanings of gender, as it intersects with other categories of identity, matter because they prescribe how to live in our bodies (Halsema 2006, 159).

It is important to remember, however, that a person's gender does not have to follow their genitalia or the materiality of their body. If someone claims, or is seen to be performing, a particular gender, that person is expected to be familiar with and conform to these roles. What is also interesting, however, is that this gender expectation is intersectional. In his article "Being an Oriental, I Could Never Be Completely a Man: Gay Asian Men and the Intersection of Race, Gender, Sexuality, and Class," C. Winter Han details how gendered expectations for gay Asian men are different from other forms of masculinity—what it means to be a man, such as White, Black, or Latino masculinities.

Also framing intersectionality as a core issue, Dominique C. Hill's creative work "(My) Lesbianism Is Not a Fixed Point" (this section) helps us rethink the fluidity of our own bodies and sexual desires and invites us to dive into this chaotic

Sex-positive: A view that a person can choose whether or not to express their sexuality and in a variety of ways. It highlights the pleasure rather than simply the procreative aspect of sex.

messiness of identity and sexual politics of the body. Indeed, the issue of fluidity is central in understanding the body. Christina Crosby's memoir, "Masculine, Feminine, or Fourth of July" (included in this section), reminds us of the fluidity of one's (dis)abled body. She shares how after an accident her body becomes disabled, and how her disability makes her experience gender and sexuality differently, although she still lives in the one body that has been hers all along.

Although the body we inhabit helps structure how we experience the world, it does not mean that everyone with the same body shape will share the same experience. A light-skinned, thin woman, for example, may not experience the same intensity of **colorism** as another woman with a darker skin tone who is just as thin, because of their intersecting and complex historical, geographical, and other social locations. Thus in this section we include Aleichia Williams's essay, which brings the complexity of intersectionality to the fore even more by reflecting on her experience of being perceived as, to quote from the title of her essay, "Too Latina to Be Black, Too Black to Be Latina." Instead of choosing to be *either* Black *or* Latina, however, she embraces her intersectional identities and even challenges the limited understanding of "Latina" as a homogenous category by sharing her story of being called a "Mexican," when her mother actually came from Honduras. This complexity of intersectionality is also highlighted in Lailatul Fitriyah's essay, "Can We Stop Talking About the 'Hijab'?: Islamic Feminism, Intersectionality, and the Indonesian Muslim Female Migrant Workers," which shows us what it means to really think through the intersectional framework. In her case, she asks that we stop thinking about Islamic feminism through the limiting body-signifier of the hijab and, instead, ruminate on the complexity of experiences that Muslim Indonesian women have to navigate as migrant workers in Singapore, for example.

Bodies matter in how we experience the world and what we know. However, relying simply on the body as a source of knowledge will necessarily limit our claim to the kinds of knowledge we can discern and the identities we can claim. This is why in the Cartesian tradition (the mind/body dualism), the body is considered "a site of epistemological limitation" (Bordo 2003, 227). When a person with a vagina chooses to identify as a man, or **agender**, or advocates for the end of violence against men, for example, society might not readily accept and may even question his identity, credibility, and authority. This certainly speaks to the issue of essentialism and the need to critically rethink such sticky attachments between bodies, identities, and "lived experience"–based knowledge.

Colorism: A form of discrimination based on one's skin color that privileges people with light skin color.

Agender: A person who does not identify to performing a particular gender. This gender-neutral category challenges the gender binary system.

MEDICALIZATION OF BODIES

In the present day, medical discourse is the dominant framework through which we understand our bodies. This, however, has not always been the case. Prior to the late eighteenth century, the scientific community viewed women's and men's bodies as having similar functions and structures, except women's genitalia were inverse while men's appeared outward (Laqueur 1990, 5; Lorber

1998, 12; Martin 1997, 18). By the late nineteenth century, people began to see ciswomen's and cismen's bodies as not only different but also as opposite, and the medical discourse had begun to take hold in society (Laqueur 1990, 5; Martin 1997, 19).

Medical discourse provides a narrative with which we make sense of what happens to our bodies (i.e., a "medical diagnosis") and who we are in relation to the symptom (i.e., a patient with a disease) (Waples 2013, 59). Once we are diagnosed, we *become* a patient in need of a medical intervention, and therein lies the problem.

This process is known as medicalization. However, **medicalization** is not simply identifying symptoms or behaviors through medical discourses. It also involves categorizing certain behaviors or symptoms as "deviant" with the purpose of "eliminating or controlling" them (Riessman 1998, 47–48). As Eunjung Kim (2010) argues, for instance, medical discourse pathologizes, or considers abnormal, asexuality. **Asexual** is defined by the Asexual Visibility and Education Network as "a person who does not experience sexual attraction" (qtd. in Cerankowski and Milks 2010, 651; Van Houdenhove et al. 2014, 179); people who are asexual make up approximately 0.6 to 5.5 percent of the population. Asexuality is not the same as antisexuality, which sees sexuality in a more negative light. According to Kristina Gupta in her essay "Feminist Approaches to Asexuality" (included in this section), the fact that asexuals have been pathologized and minoritized exposes "the operation of *compulsory sexuality* as a system of social control" (p. 394). She argues, therefore, that "feminist visions of gender and sexual justice must reconfigure themselves in order to affirm asexual identities and ways of being in the world" (p. 394).

This pathologization by way of medical discourse certainly has negative effects on the materiality of the body. Transgender people, for example, have been discriminated against by the health care system, from not being able to be reimbursed by insurance companies for certain kinds of care to being retroactively denied insurance when the insurance company finds out the person's transgender status. Insurance companies are also very rigid and limited in understanding the human body: a transgender woman may get health coverage related to female organs (that is, mammograms) but not for prostate problems (Gorton and Grubb 2014, 219). Medicalization thus limits how people understand and experience their own and others' bodies.

Let's use the childbirth process as an example to understand the concept of medicalization. Until the nineteenth century in America, childbirth was experienced at home, attended by friends and family, who would help the midwife (many of whom were immigrant or Black) deliver the baby. At that time, obstetrics was not a common field taught at medical schools (Riessman 1998, 51). By 1910, however, obstetricians (usually men from the "dominant class") became more popular as they claimed that "normal pregnancy" was a medical condition that needed a science-based intervention; this resulted in a significant decrease in childbirth assisted by midwives (Riessman 1998, 51). This shift was partly supported by the women themselves who wanted to

Medicalization: The idea that physicians have the ultimate authority to diagnose a symptom and through this process a person becomes a patient in need of medical intervention.

Asexual: A person who does not experience sexual attraction.

lessen the pain of childbirth by getting the "twilight sleep" ("a combination of morphine and scopolamine") that the physicians used at the time (Riessman 1998, 52). Even Queen Victoria requested such a drug (in her case, "chloroform") to alleviate the pain of childbirth during the delivery of her eighth and ninth children. Indeed, physicians used drugs and childbirth technology to justify their presence and make them seem "indispensable."

This medicalization of ciswomen's bodies in the late nineteenth century also caused some women to undergo unnecessary and dangerous surgeries to have their healthy ovaries or clitorises removed, with up to 30 percent mortality rates (Weitz 1998a, 7). These surgeries were linked to the class ideology at the time that considered middle-class women's bodies frail and thus in need of medical intervention (working-class women, regardless of their race, were seen as "more robust") (Riessman 1998, 53; Weitz 1998a, 6–7). In addition to using medical discourses and class ideologies, these nineteenth-century doctors also used "Christian and Aristotelian" discourses that viewed women with contempt and as emotionally and physically weak, to discourage women, who at the time had begun to work part-time, from working outside the home and furthering their education (Weitz 1998a, 6).

Even menstruation was used to keep middle-class ciswomen from pursuing work outside the home. Around this time, in the nineteenth century, the "process" of menstruation began to be seen as pathological and as having negative effects on women's lives (Martin 1997, 20). After the beginning of World War II, various studies showed that menstruation wasn't responsible for women's "condition" (that made them unable to work) after all (Martin 1998, 224). It is clear that the negative meanings attached to menstruation reflected the dominant gender and political economy ideologies of the time. As Gloria Steinem argues ("If Men Could Menstruate," in this section), the meanings of and practices involved in menstruation would change if, in this man-dominated world, cismen could menstruate. Indeed, reproductive politics is never only about reproduction or women's bodies, but also power, colonialism, and social justice, as No'u Revilla theorizes through her poem, "How to Use a Condom."

Because the medicalization framework mediates women's experiences of their bodies, it becomes problematic if it is the *only* discourse through which women can understand their bodies. Hence, some scholars such as Catherine Kohler Riessman suggest that we demedicalize our relationships with our bodies while being selective about the benefits of medical knowledge (1998, 61). For her, "demedicalization" is about changing "the ownership, production, and use of scientific knowledge;" it is not about being opposed to the biological aspect of it (Riessman 1998, 60). Other strategies that women have used in resisting medicalization, according to Emily Martin's research, is how women, particularly working-class women, pay careful attention to their own body, how it "feels, looks, or smells" rather than referring to the medical model that may alienate women's experience (qtd. in Davis 2007, 58). What do *you* think is the best way to address the medicalization of the body?

CHOICE, CONTROL, AND COMMODITY: UNDERSTANDING BODIES IN A NEOLIBERAL AGE

Body work in today's society is often shaped by neoliberal politics. Michelle Leve offers a definition of neoliberalism that is useful here: "a political-economic ideology and practice that promotes individualism, consumerism, deregulation, and transferring state power and responsibility to the individual" (Leve 2013, 279). A neoliberal economy rests on the assumption that individuals are responsible for improving themselves, preferably through consumption for their own (economic) benefit. The problem with this view is that any inequalities that an individual experiences are merely seen as personal rather than institutional issues (Stuart and Donaghue 2011, 101). To further explore this point and to shed light on how neoliberalism frames our relationship with our bodies as well as others', three popular discourses (choice, control, and commodity) are discussed next.

THE CHOICE DISCOURSE: BEAUTY IDEALS AND IMAGES OF THE BODY

One of the legacies of the second-wave women's movement is a woman's right to choose, especially when it comes to her pregnancy. This feminist discourse, however, has been co-opted by various people and corporations that tell women (or all genders, for that matter) that they are now "free" to choose whatever products they want to buy.

This "free" choice, however, is a mere, if seductive, illusion. Various technologies, ideologies, and political economy conditions, including the neoliberal economy, enable as well as limit these choices. Some choices indeed hold more currency than others. If a woman "chooses" not to practice **body work** that emulates the dominant beauty standard, for example, she may be subjected to the "stigmatization and the loss of social capital" (Dolezal 2010, 357). In this sense, beauty practice is not a mere "choice," albeit framed in such a way. Rather, it functions to normalize and discipline women's bodies. As Naomi Wolf's now-classic 1992 book *The Beauty Myth* has shown, beauty is a systematic structure that keeps women subordinated.

Decades after Wolf's book was published and the women's liberation movement protested against the beauty industry and beauty pageants, many women *still* practice body work. Satu Liimaka, referencing Rubin, Nemeroff, and Russo's research (2004), argues that this persistence in doing body work is related to the fact that although feminism and feminist identity have helped some people to change their "thoughts" about beauty ideals, they have not changed how people "feel" about these beauty standards (Liimaka 2011, 812). Indeed, as L. Ayu Saraswati argues in her 2013 book *Seeing Beauty, Sensing Race in Transnational Indonesia*, beauty practice (in her case, skin whitening), rather than simply reflecting women's desire to look beautiful, is a manifestation of how women *manage* their *feelings* about their body along gender lines, or what she calls as the "gendered management of affect." For example, women

Body work: "[A]n effort to create an alignment . . . between appearance and character, between identity and body" (Shapiro 2010, 144).

are supposed to feel bad when they show signs of aging, and hence in managing this bad feeling, they apply anti-aging cream that makes them feel good about their skin. Men, however, may manage their feelings about their body differently than women (due to the different social constructions between how men and women express and relate to their feelings). This explains why beauty practices are still more common for women. She thus suggests that we pay attention to these feelings (who feels what about which bodies, why, and what we do about these feelings) and even intervene and challenge the very production of these feelings, especially when they are attached to specific bodies and not others. Although these feelings may seem *natural* to us when we feel them, we need to question how these emotions are constructed and how they support the existing power hierarchy of bodies.

Engaged Learning

Choose three parts of your body to focus on (hair, nose, skin color, stomach, thighs, etc.). As you focus on each body part, pay attention to how you feel at this exact moment. Do you feel good, bad, or indifferent about that body part? You may even have mixed, contradicting feelings. Name all of these feelings and write them down in Table 4.1.

Then trace where you might have learned to feel that way about this body part: think of any TV shows, films, or magazines that might have advertised such an idea; then think of any comments or praise your friends and family have uttered about this part of your body. Write as much as you can, and answer the questions in Table 4.1.

Table 4.1: Tracing Feelings About My Body

Body Part	Your Current Feelings	Media's Narrative	Friends' and Family's Comments

QUESTIONS

1. Examine the completed table carefully. Do you notice any patterns and connections between how you feel about your body and the media's narrative? What about your friends' and family's comments? Have you practiced any body work because you feel a certain way about your body? Are any of these practices gendered? Do they reflect your class position? What about your racial background or disabled body status? How do you relate these body works to neoliberalism?

2. If your feelings about these body parts have been mostly unhappy, do you think you might

be able to change these feelings? How? What would this entail? How does shifting our feelings challenge the power hierarchy?

3. If your feelings have been mostly happy, satisfied, or indifferent, where did you learn to feel that way? Might you be able to identify anyone (or anything) that might have helped shape these feelings? How can we reimagine our relationship with our bodies as mindful, critical, and empowering while still being content in our bodies?

What feelings, for example, motivate many women, more than men, to shave their body? Indeed, more than 90 percent of women shave their legs and armpits (only 18 percent of men shave their legs and 30 percent shave their armpits) (Fahs 2013, 562). It is true, however, that a new and growing trend called "manscaping" (men who groom their body hair for aesthetic purposes) has become more popular. Nonetheless, it remains critical to be mindful of how certain beauty practices are manifestations of how people manage their feelings about their bodies based on gender.

In addition to gender, skin color, race, body hair, and body shape, age also plays an important role in defining a beauty ideal. Prior to the 1950s, "older" women were expected to have a "mature" body figure and wear "mature" outfits (Dinnerstein and Weitz 1998, 191). Since then, however, the youthful (and slim) culture has become the beauty standard for all women. By the late 1970s, the "fitness craze" took over American culture and (older) women with "mature" figures were told that they were "a sign of social or even moral failure" (Dinnerstein and Weitz 1998, 191). Aging bodies become the repulsive "abject" bodies that people hope to escape by consuming various beauty products (Carter 2009, 235–36).

New discourses about aging have certainly been articulated. These discourses push for a healthy and "active aging" life, rather than simply aiming for a youthful appearance (Carter 2009, 232). In whatever discourse the process of aging has been articulated thus far (i.e., health, beauty, or both), it nonetheless clings to the neoliberal idea that it is the responsibility of the individual to choose a body project that can keep their body young and vibrant, which is considered the ultimate desirable body. Even contemporary media still continues to circulate advertisements for anti-aging products and to represent older people as sexually inactive (or needing Viagra, for men, and Premarin, for women), "boring," "useless," and "old-fashioned" (Dickerson and Rousseau 2009, 308; Haboush et al. 2012, 669, 673).

The media has been one of the most prevalent means through which beauty ideals are circulated. Unfortunately, as some studies show, it has negatively affected people's body image across the globe (Warren 2014, 551). In the United States, for example, Hollywood films have contributed to people's internalization of the thin ideal, leading to eating disorders (Fox-Kales 2011). Another study shows that when women compare their bodies to models' bodies in the media, it lowers their self-esteem and exacerbates their body image issues (Haboush et al. 2012, 669). In Fiji and Japan, studies show that the exposure to Western media in these countries led to an increase in young women's body dissatisfaction and disordered eating (Jung and Forbes 2007, 382; Warren 2014, 551).

It is important to remember, however, that as we explore how the Western media negatively affects body image in non-Western countries, we do not judge *any* beauty practice as emulating the white beauty standard. In fact, this idea is in and of itself revealing of a racialized and Eurocentric frame of thinking. As L. Ayu Saraswati shows in her essay, "Cosmopolitan Whiteness: The

Skin-whitening cream, a lucrative industry. Skin-whitening cream is one of the top-selling products in the world. In Indonesia, it is dubbed the crisis-proof industry because sales remain steady even in the midst of economic crisis. Desire for whiteness, as L. Ayu Saraswati argues in her article, should not be seen as a mere desire to emulate Caucasian whiteness. Rather, it is an expression of a new kind of whiteness that she calls "Cosmopolitan whiteness."
Source: Barbara Walton/EPA/Shutterstock

Effects and Affects of Skin-Whitening Advertisements in Transnational Indonesia" (included in this section), although skin-whitening practice does suggest a desire for white skin color, this desire is *not* the same as a desire for Caucasian whiteness. Rather, it is a desire for what she calls "Cosmopolitan whiteness," a whiteness that is not attached to any racial background (p. 407). Even the practice of skin tanning that many people assume to show a desire for dark skin, according to Saraswati, actually exposes a desire for Cosmopolitan whiteness.

Chimamanda Ngozi Adichie's fictional story, excerpted from *Americanah* and included in this section, takes us further in examining the complexities of body and beauty norms through the issue of hair from the perspective of a Nigerian woman living in the United States. Her story allows us to peek into the troubling ways in which bodies are marked and read differently as they travel across different communities and how hair becomes a signifier for racialized and gendered beauty ideals and identities.

Beauty ideals may be unattainable. However, some people have used cosmetic surgeries to help them negotiate these standards. Unsurprisingly, then, cosmetic surgery, and the beauty industry as a whole, has become a multi-billion-dollar business (Tables 4.2 and 4.3). (Note that calling it a "surgery" implies the medicalization process of this body work.) Based on 2018 data from

Table 4.2: Cosmetic Plastic Surgery by Race

Race	Number of People Undergoing Cosmetic Surgery
Caucasians	12.4 million
Hispanics	1.9 million
African Americans	1.6 million
Asian Americans	1.1 million

Table 4.3: Top Five Cosmetic Surgeries by Gender

The Top Five Cosmetic Surgeries for Women	The Top Five Cosmetic Surgeries for Men
1. Breast augmentation	1. Nose reshaping
2. Liposuction	2. Eyelid surgery
3. Eyelid surgery	3. Liposuction
4. Nose reshaping	4. Breast reduction
5. Tummy tuck	5. Hair transplantation

the American Society of Plastic Surgeons, Americans spent approximately $16.5 billion on cosmetic surgery alone, and women had 87 percent of these surgeries. In this neoliberal age, however, this act of *choosing* to have surgery (or other body work) remains in the realm of one's personal responsibility, beautifully cloaked under the fraud discourse of "choice."

THE POLITICS OF CONTROL: BODY WEIGHT AND EATING DISORDERS

Eating disorders have become an epidemic in the Western world since the 1980s, although in the nineteenth century the medical world began to take note of how upper-class women were practicing "self-starvation" (Bordo 1997, 93). In contemporary America, eating disorders have been reframed and understood as a form of self-control, a manifestation of being a good neoliberal subject. As M. Cristina Alcalde argues, although the discourse of control over one's body has long been associated with the feminist movement, this is no longer the case. This practice now reflects a way of being in a neoliberal age (Alcalde 2013, 34). Maintaining an ideal body weight involves knowing what to consume (and purge) (Stokes 2013, 59).

However, because not having control over one's body is perceived to be a sign of a failed neoliberal subject, it therefore is used to justify discrimination against "fat" people. (Here, "fat" refers to being 20 percent over the height/weight ratio standard, which is the definition used in many studies [Fikkan and Rothblum 2012, 577]. This, of course, is another example of medicalization of bodies in which certain bodies are deemed "normal," whereas other bodies are "overweight." Fat is indeed a contentious concept, once used to marginalize people considered by societal and medical standards as "over" the "healthy"

ACTIVISM AND CIVIC ENGAGEMENT

You will work in a group to create an online petition as a way to create change and end discrimination based on the body, its meanings, and its social regulation.

1. With your classmates, brainstorm an issue related to the body that has affected many people. For example, you can focus on the discrimination against fat and/or older people in the workplace or request gender-neutral or "gender inclusive" restrooms at your campus. The more specific the issue and the goal, the more effective the petition.
2. Then conduct thorough research to gather as much information as you can about the issue, including statistics and case studies that you can use to support your argument. If possible, find an example from your community.
3. Craft a solid petition that describes the situation, backed up by solid data, and your goals.

Think about the audience for your petition and to whom you will submit your petition.

4. Choose an online petition website that you think will be the best medium to circulate your petition. Some examples include change.org or ipetitions.com. Post and circulate your petition.

QUESTIONS

1. Explain to the class the thought processes of creating your petition. What were the difficulties that your group experienced? What were the most exciting parts of the process? Why?
2. After one week of posting and circulating your petition, assess which group has the most signatures or is closest to reaching their goals. Why? How does this reflect the interest of the audience and the state of our society? What did you learn from working toward an end to body-based discrimination?

weight but that has since been reclaimed by various scholars and activists to challenge this problematic body norm.) Households headed by fat women, for example, have lower income than those headed by non-fat women—an average of 12 percent to 17.51 percent less. This is not the case for fat men, except in the small case of "obese black men," another example of how race, gender, and body weight intersect with each other in creating different experiences of the body (Fikkan and Rothblum 2012, 577, 578). A 2003 study by Hebl and Mannix shows that men who were seen by their employer to have sat next to a fat woman before their job interview were treated more harshly during the interview than men who didn't sit next to a fat woman (qtd. in Fikkan and Rothblum 2012, 577). Regardless of this prevalent discrimination, there is no law that protect people against size discrimination, except in Madison, Wisconsin; Urbana, Illinois; Washington, DC; Binghamton, New York; six cities in California; and the state of Michigan.

Kimberly Dark's "Big Yoga Student" essay in this section creates an intriguing rupture to the dominant narrative about fat people. She makes visible how the normalized body is constructed through narratives of erasures (that is, bodies that don't belong) and disciplinary practices. She playfully animates her everyday experiences of being a fat yoga teacher whose body provokes a certain level of discomfort in her students—some even left the class after seeing her body. However, she insists that fat women keep showing up in yoga classes.

Not participating means being subsumed by the very structure that erases fat women's bodies in these spaces. Nonetheless, showing up in yoga classes also requires that these women *invest* in fees for yoga sessions, mats, and clothes, as a way to invest in themselves, inadvertently turning them into neoliberal subjects.

RELATING TO BODIES THROUGH A COMMODITY DISCOURSE

Bodies are attached to a price tag, as in the adult entertainment industry. Bodies are even fragmented and sold, as in international organ trafficking cases. Bodies, women's bodies in particular, are also used to sell other products or ideas (Conboy et al. 1997, 8, 11). Simply turn to any form of popular culture to see how it relies heavily on the selling (and objectification) of women's bodies to keep the money flowing in.

It is not only the body that is sold as a commodity. Our experiences with and in our bodies have also been commodified. In this neoliberal age, women are expected to do the "third shift of body work"—the second shift revolves around housework (Hallstein 2011, 114). Women are bombarded with advice to "help" them achieve sexy post-pregnancy bikini bodies—for example, by purchasing various weight-loss meal plans and participating in exercise classes, and transforming themselves into a "yummy mummy" (Hallstein 2011, 122, 125).

Moreover, spending time, energy, and money on one's body, as we are told, is a reflection that we love our body. The mainstream "love your body" discourse is indeed a clear example of how all these three discourses merge, overlap, and are articulated through each other. The "love your body" discourse conveniently sits at the intersection of "neoliberal governmentality, emotional capitalism, the growth of social media and commodity feminism" (Gill and Elias 2014, 179). That is, people are taught that to feel good they need to improve and invest in themselves by purchasing various products that are represented to have the ability to empower them. Social media further supports this behavior by functioning as a site where people can post images of the products they purchase or activities that they do (e.g., eating at a fancy restaurant or working out at a gym as a sign of self-love) as well as images of their "improved" bodies. This discourse incorporates "pseudo" feminist messages that tell women and girls that they are "incredible" and have the power to "redefine" beauty (Gill and Elias 2014, 180). Women are told that they are "worth it" and may now *choose* whatever color of lipstick they want. Although telling women and girls to love their body may seem harmless, Rosalind Gill and Ana Sodia Elias argue that this could be dangerous because now not only is the *physical* appearance of the body being disciplined but also women's "psychic life" is being oppressed (2014, 185). This "love your body" discourse is different, of course, from the ways in which women of color, with a long history of gendered, racialized, and sexualized oppression, exploitation, and discrimination, have reclaimed self-care and view it as "self-preservation, . . . an act of political warfare" rather

TRANSNATIONAL CONNECTIONS

Yoga originated in India. When exactly this practice emerged is lost in history, although there are some writings that have provided evidence for its existence such as in the *Vedas* (5000–2000 B.C.), the *Upanishads* (800 and 600 B.C.), and Patanjali's *Yoga Sutras* (200 A.D.) (Simpkins 2012, 12–14). The meaning of the word Yoga is "to join, to unite" (Monroe 2011, 7). In the United States, yoga classes have been popular as a form of exercise that focuses not only on the body, but also on the joining of the body with the mind and the soul. By 2016, the number of yoga practitioners in the United States reached around 36.7 million (Vinoski et al. 2017, 1). Some American yoga teachers have indeed traveled to India to take their yoga teacher's training courses in their desire to attain a more "authentic" experience.

QUESTIONS

1. How does yoga function as a transnational commodity?
2. How does yoga class exemplify how people's experiences with their bodies are mediated by the commodity discourse? How does neoliberalism work in encouraging people to take yoga classes?
3. Who reaps the financial benefits from these yoga classes? Would you consider yoga as a form of cultural appropriation? Why or why not? Are there any other forms of body work that would be considered as a cultural appropriation?
4. Have you ever been to a yoga class? Did you notice how or if the teachers contextualize, historicize, and repackage the teachings of yoga in their classes?
5. Why is the notion of "authenticity" problematic? If you are not familiar with any yoga classes, it may be helpful for you to do some (online) research about these classes.

than a mere "self-indulgence" (Lorde 1988, 131). That is, to care for one's own body when society deems it unworthy and actively marginalizes it is a necessary act, a survival technique, rather than a mere narcissism disguised as liberation (Douglas 2000).

BODY TALK, BODY HACK: AGENCY AND THE BODY AS A SITE OF RESISTANCE

Susan Bordo argues that bodies are a "medium" of or a "metaphor" for culture. That is, what we eat, how we dress, and how we practice body rituals are informed by the culture within which we are a part. However, as she also points out, they are not simply a "tabula rasa, awaiting inscription by culture" (Bordo 2003, 35, 165). We negotiate these (at times conflicting) cultures and in doing so transform our bodies into a dynamic site of contested meanings and practices. In a sense, then, the body becomes a battleground, a site where one can try out different ways of being and identifying with oneself, if not one's body, and talk back to power. Jessica Vasquez-Tokos and Kathryn Norton-Smith highlight this in their essay "Resisting Racism: Latinos' Changing Responses to Controlling Images over the Life Course" (in this section). They show how the Latino men they interviewed exercise their agency in resisting the racist controlling images in their lives.

Catrina Brown, Shelly Weber, and Serena Ali call this mode of communicating with one's body a "body talk" (2008, 93, 94). Body talk, they argue, is different from body project. Whereas in body project women's relationship to their bodies is one of "control" and "repression," in body talk, women exercise their agency to talk back to the dominant body ideal using their bodies. For some "older women," for example, when they do beauty practice as a "coping technique" to help address an early life trauma (i.e., experiencing rape, dysfunctional childhood, or divorce), they are talking back to and taking back their power (Clarke and Griffin 2008, 200, 205). These women no longer let their perpetrators, who once negatively influenced their body image, dictate how they treat their body.

Moreover, in various street protests, bodies have functioned as an instrument of resistance. These bodies stand in solidarity as they march together, or become a "human barricade," in cases such as in Tiananmen Square in 1989, or occupying the building of the People's Consultative Assembly/the People's Representative Council in Jakarta, Indonesia, in 1998 that resulted in a change of government.

Beyond the physical world, activists also use cyberspace as a different way to incorporate the body as a medium of activism. The Egyptian women's rights activist Aliaa Magda Elmahdy, for instance, posts nude photos of herself on her blog to challenge racism, sexism, and violence. Not merely subscribing to existing ideologies of gender and sexuality, she creates a rupture in the convention of female nude protest by embodying an oppositional gaze and a political agency through her nonsubmissive poses (Eileraas 2014, 45–46).

Another form of resistance that uses the body as its medium is the practice of body modification. The body art movement, including tattoos and other forms of "body modification," expands our understanding of body talk by using a more extensive form of technology to create new meanings of the body in order to challenge existing categories of identity such as race, gender, and sexuality (Pitts 2010, 236). The practice of body hacking (biohacking), for example, is a form of non-mainstream body modification that became known in the 1990s through cyberpunk communities (Olivares 2014, 288). An example of a body hack is how Cheto Castellano, a performance artist, had (what look like) horns surgically inserted into his forehead. Because body hacking such as Castellano's aims to contest and decolonize the normative body (Olivares 2014, 292), it is what Victoria Pitts calls "social rebellion through the body" (qtd. in Olivares 2014, 288).

Bodies speak, whether we intend them to or not. As Aimee Rowe points out, "The body is on the table. It becomes the text of pedagogy. All bodies are teaching, whether White and male, queer and Black, South Asian, and foreign. The trick is to become aware of what lessons our bodies are teaching" (Rowe 2012, 1051). It is therefore important to critically and perpetually examine: What stories does our body teach and tell? What knowledge does our body help produce and/or challenge? How can we complicate the stories that our bodies tell? Do these bodies "talk back" to power, or do they become the blank

A woman at a body modification convention in New York City. Body modification is often known as part of the body art movement that aims to challenge the fixity of the body or as a form of what Victoria Pitts calls "social rebellion through the body." In this picture, a woman is seen with tattoos, piercings, and her under-the-skin ring implants.
Source: Photo by Neville Elder/Corbis via Getty Images

screen on which the dominant culture projects and makes visible its power? More important, who's listening? What kinds of bodies get to be heard, and which bodies can only be read in specific ways? What kind of embodiment would allow us to remain faithful to being critical of the dominance of power? How can our body become a site of resistance against systemic and everyday violence? The two poems that end this section, Joanna Gordon's "Sketches" and Christina Lux's "10,000 Blows," allow us to wrestle with these questions, as well as speak to how we can embody resistance in our daily lives.

Critical Thinking Questions

1. How is knowledge about the body produced? Why do some people or agencies have more credibility and authority than others in constructing these knowledges?

2. How do dominant ideas about gendered bodies in your society (in media, religion, etc.) influence how you understand your body and help explain the relationship between your bodily practices and your identity?

3. How does the body influence how we experience the world and our understanding of the world?

4. What are some of the most effective ways to challenge dominant narratives about non-normative bodies?

GLOSSARY

Agender 342

Asexual 343

Colorism 342

Epistemologies 338

Essentialism 338

Medicalization 343

Sex-positive 341

WORKS CITED

Alcalde, M. Cristina. "Feminism and Women's Control over Their Bodies in a Neoliberal Context: A Closer Look at Pregnant Women on Bed Rest." *Feminist Formations*, vol. 25, no. 3, 2013, pp. 33–56.

American Society of Plastic Surgeons. *2018 Cosmetic Plastic Surgery Statistics*, https://www.plasticsurgery.org/news/plastic-surgery-statistics.

Bordo, Susan. "The Body and the Reproduction of Femininity." In *Writing on the Body*, edited by Katie Conboy et al. Columbia UP, 1997, pp. 90–110.

Bordo, Susan. *Unbearable Weight: Feminism, Western Culture, and the Body*. University of California Press, 2003 [originally published 1993]

Boston Women's Health Book Collective. *Our Bodies Ourselves: A Book by and for Women*. Simon and Schuster, 1973.

Brown, Catrina, Shelly Weber, and Serena Ali. "Women's Body Talk: A Feminist Narrative Approach." *Journal of Systemic Therapies*, vol. 27, no. 2, 2008, pp. 92–104.

Carter, Claire. "'Contemporary Ageing: 'Younger, Better, Fresher': How Does This Speak to Feminist Theories of the Body?" In *Feminism and the Body: Interdisciplinary Perspectives*, edited by Catherine Kevin. Cambridge Scholars Publishing, 2009, pp. 228–45.

Cerankowski, Karli, and Megan Milks. "New Orientations: Asexuality and Its Implications for Theory and Practice." *Feminist Studies*, vol. 36 no. 3, 2010, pp. 650–64.

Clarke, Laura, and Meridith Griffin. "Body Image and Aging: Older Women and the Embodiment of Trauma." *Women's Studies International Forum*, vol. 31, 2008, pp. 200–8.

Conboy, Katie, et al., editors. Introduction. In *Writing on the Body: Female Embodiment and Feminist Theory*, Columbia UP, 1997, pp. 1–14.

Davis, Kathy. "Reclaiming Women's Bodies: Colonialist Trope or Critical Epistemology." *Sociological Review*, vol. 55, no. 1, 2007, pp. 50–64.

Dickerson, Bette, and Nicole Rousseau. "Ageism Through Omission: The Obsolescence of Black Women's Sexuality." *Journal of African American Studies*, vol. 13, 2009, pp. 307–24.

Dinnerstein, Myra, and Rose Weitz. "Jane Fonda, Barbara Bush, and Other Aging Bodies: Femininity and the Limits of Resistance." In *The Politics of Women's Bodies: Sexuality, Appearance, and Behavior*, edited by Rose Weitz. Oxford UP, 1998, pp. 189–203.

Dodson, Betty. *Liberating Masturbation: A Meditation on Self Love*. Dodson, 1974.

Dolezal, Luna. "The (In)visible Body: Feminism, Phenomenology, and the Case of Cosmetic Surgery." *Hypatia*, vol. 25, no. 2, 2010, pp. 357–75.

Douglas, Susan. "Narcissism as Liberation." In *The Gender and Consumer Culture Reader*, edited by Jennifer Scanlon. New York UP, 2000, pp. 267–82.

Eileraas, Karina. "Sex(t)ing Revolution, Femen-izing the Public Square: Aliaa Magda Elmahdy, Nude Protest, and Transnational Feminist Body Politics." *Signs: Journal of Women in Culture and Society*, vol. 40, no. 1, 2014, pp. 40–52.

Fahs, Breanne. "'Freedom to' and 'Freedom from': A New Vision for Sex-Positive Politics." *Sexualities*, vol. 17, no. 3, 2014, pp. 267–90.

Fahs, Breanne. "Shaving it All Off: Examining Social Norms of Body Hair Among College Men in a Women's Studies Course." *Women's Studies*, vol. 42, 2013, pp. 559–77.

Fikkan, Janna, and Esther Rothblum. "Is Fat a Feminist Issue? Exploring the Gendered Nature of Weight Bias." *Sex Roles*, vol. 66, 2012, pp. 575–92.

Fox-Kales, Emily. *Body Shots: Hollywood and the Culture of Eating Disorders*. State University of New York Press, 2011.

Gill, Rosalind, and Ana Elias. "'Awaken Your Incredible': Love Your Body Discourses and Postfeminist Contradictions." *International Journal of Media & Cultural Politics*, vol. 10, no. 2, 2014, pp. 179–88.

Gorton, Nick, and Hilary Maia Grubb. "General, Sexual, and Reproductive Health." In *Trans Bodies, Trans Selves: A Resource for the Transgender Community*, edited by Laura Erickson-Schroth, Oxford UP, 2014, pp. 215–40.

Haboush, Amanda, et al. "Beauty, Ethnicity, and Age: Does Internalization of Mainstream Media Ideals Influence Attitudes Towards Older Adults?" *Sex Roles*, vol. 66, 2012, pp. 668–76.

Hallstein, D. Lynn. "She Gives Birth, She's Wearing a Bikini: Mobilizing the Postpregnant Celebrity Mom Body to Manage the Post–Second Wave Crisis in Femininity." *Women's Studies in Communication*, vol. 34, 2011, pp. 111–38.

Halsema, Annemie. "Reconsidering the Notion of the Body in Anti-Essentialism, with the Help of Luce Irigaray and Judith Butler." In *Belief, Bodies, and Being: Feminist Reflections on Embodiment*, edited by Deborah Orr et al. Rowman and Littlefield, 2006, pp. 151–61.

Hammers, Corie. "Corporeality, Sadomasochism and Sexual Trauma." *Body and Society*, vol. 20, no. 2, 2014, pp. 68–90.

hooks, bell. *Wounds of Passion: A Writing Life*. Henry Holt, 1997.

Jung, Jaehee, and Gordon Forbes. "Body Dissatisfaction and Disordered Eating Among College Women in China, South Korea, the United States: Contrasting Predictions from Sociocultural and Feminist Theories." *Psychology of Women Quarterly*, vol. 31, 2007, pp. 381–93.

Kim, Eunjung. "How Much Sex Is Healthy? The Pleasures of Asexuality." In *Against Health: How Health Became New Morality*, edited by Anna Kirkland and Jonathan Metzel. New York UP, 2010, pp. 157–69.

Laqueur, Thomas. *Making Sex: Body and Gender From the Greeks to Freud*. Harvard UP, 1990.

Leve, Michelle. "Reproductive Bodies and Bits: Exploring Dilemmas of Egg Donation Under Neoliberalism." *Studies in Gender and Sexuality*, vol. 14, no. 4, 2013, pp. 277–88.

Liimaka, Satu. "Cartesian and Corporeal Agency: Women's Studies Students' Reflections on Women's Experience." *Gender and Education*, vol. 23, no. 7, 2011, pp. 811–23.

Lorber, Judith. "Believing Is Seeing: Biology as Ideology." In *The Politics of Women's Bodies: Sexuality, Appearance, and Behavior*, edited by Rose Weitz. Oxford UP, 1998, pp. 12–24.

Lorde, Audre. *A Burst of Light: Essays by Audre Lorde*. Firebrand, 1988.

Martin, Emily. "Medical Metaphors of Women's Bodies: Menstruation and Menopause." In *Writing on the Body: Female Embodiment and Feminist Theory*, edited by Katie Conboy et al. Columbia UP, 1997, pp. 15–41.

Martin, Emily. "Premenstrual Syndrome, Work Discipline, and Anger." In *The Politics of Women's Bodies: Sexuality, Appearance, and Behavior*, edited by Rose Weitz. Oxford UP, 1998, pp. 221–41.

McWeeny, Jennifer. "Topographies of Flesh: Women, Nonhuman Animals, and the Embodiment of Connection and Difference." *Hypatia*, vol. 29, no. 2, 2014, pp. 269–86.

Monroe, Marcia. *Yoga and Scoliosis: A Journey to Health and Healing*. Demos Health, 2011.

Olivares, Lissette. "Hacking the Body and Posthumanist Transbecoming: 10,000 Generations Later as the Mestizaje of Speculative Cyborg Feminism and Significant Otherness." *Nanoethics*, vol. 8, 2014, pp. 287–97.

Pickard, Susan. "Biology as Destiny? Rethinking Embodiment in 'Deep' Old Age." *Ageing & Society*, vol. 34, 2014, pp. 1279–91.

Pitts, Victoria. "Feminism, Technology and Body Projects." *Women's Studies*, vol. 34, 2010, pp. 229–47.

Prosser, Jay. *Second Skins: The Body Narratives of Transsexuality*. Columbia UP, 1998.

Riessman, Catherine. "Women and Medicalization: A New Perspective." In *The Politics of Women's Bodies: Sexuality, Appearance, and Behavior*, edited by Rose Weitz. Oxford UP, 1998, pp. 46–63.

Rowe, Aimee. "Erotic Pedagogies." *Journal of Homosexuality*, vol. 59, 2012, pp. 1031–56.

Rubin, Lisa R., Carol J. Nemeroff, and Nancy Felipe Russo. "Exploring Feminist Women's Body Consciousness." *Psychology of Women Quarterly*, vol. 28, 2004, pp. 27–37.

Saraswati, L. Ayu. *Seeing Beauty, Sensing Race in Transnational Indonesia*. University of Hawai'i Press, 2013.

Shapiro, Eve. *Gender Circuits: Bodies and Identities in a Technological Age*. Routledge, 2010.

Simpkins, Alexander. *Yoga Basics: The Basic Poses and Routines You Need to Be Healthy and Relaxed*. Tuttle Publishing, 2012.

Stokes, Jasie. "Fat People of the World Unite!: Subjectivity, Identity, and Representation in Fat Feminist Manifestoes." *Interdisciplinary Humanities*, vol. 30, no. 3, 2013, pp. 50–62.

Stuart, Avelie, and Ngaire Donaghue. "Choosing to Conform: The Discursive Complexities of Choice in Relation to Feminine Beauty Practice." *Feminism and Psychology*, vol. 22, no. 1, 2011, pp. 98–121.

Tuana, Nancy. "Coming to Understand: Orgasm and the Epistemology of Ignorance." *Hypatia*, vol. 19, no. 1, 2004, pp. 194–232.

Van Houdenhove, Ellen, Luk Gijs, Guy T'Sjoen, and Paul Enzlin. "Asexuality: Few Facts, Many Questions."

Journal of Sex & Marital Therapy, vol. 40, no. 3, 2014, pp. 175–92.

Vinoski, Erin, et al. "Got Yoga? A Longitudinal Analysis of Thematic Content and Models' Appearance-Related Attributes in Advertisements Spanning Four Decades of *Yoga Journal*." *Psychology Body Image*, vol. 21, 2017, pp. 1–5.

Waples, Emily. "Emplotted Bodies: Breast Cancer, Feminism, and the Future." *Tulsa Studies in Women's Literature*, vol. 32, no. 2/vol. 33, no. 1, 2013, pp. 47–70.

Warren, Cortney. "Body Area Dissatisfaction in White, Black and Latina Female College Students in the USA: An Examination of Racially Salient Appearance Areas and Ethnic Identity." *Ethnic and Racial Studies*, vol. 37, no. 3, 2014, pp. 537–56.

Weitz, Rose. "A History of Women's Bodies." In *The Politics of Women's Bodies: Sexuality, Appearance, and Behavior*, edited by Rose Weitz. Oxford UP, 1998, pp. 3–11.

Weitz, Rose. "Introduction." In *The Politics of Women's Bodies: Sexuality, Appearance, and Behavior*, edited by Rose Weitz. Oxford UP, 1998, pp. 65–66.

Wolf, Naomi. *The Beauty Myth: How Images of Beauty Are Used Against Women*. Anchor Books, 1992.

53. • *Janet Mock*

FROM *REDEFINING REALNESS* (2014)

Janet Mock is an author, a transgender advocate, and a TV host. Her memoir *Redefining Realness* is a *New York Times* bestseller and winner of the 2015 Women's Way book prize. The excerpt from her memoir below speaks to the complexity and instability of the body and its relationship to one's identity.

[. . .]

What's difficult about being from Hawaii is that everyone has a postcard view of your home. Hawaii lives vividly in people's minds, like the orange and purple hues of the bird-of-paradise flower. It's a fantasy place of sunshine and rainbows, of high surf and golden boys with golden hair, of pigs on a spit and hula dancers' swaying hips, of Braddah Iz's "Somewhere Over the Rainbow" and the North Shore, of hapa goddesses with coconut bras and Don Ho's ukulele.

[. . .]

Ages before Hawaii's sugar boom, voyagers from Tahiti left their home to see what was beyond the horizon. Navigating the seas in handcrafted canoes with the mere guidance of the stars, they arrived in Hawaii and created new lives. Centuries later, I landed in 1995, and it was here, on the island of Oahu, that I would mirror my ancestors on my own voyage, one guided through a system of whispers, to reveal the person I was meant to be. I will forever be indebted to Hawaii for being the home I needed. There is no me without Hawaii.

[. . .]

Though we came from our native Hawaiian mother, Chad and I were perceived and therefore raised as black, which widely cast us as outsiders, nonlocals—and being seen as local in Hawaii was currency.

When we first returned to Oahu, we spoke with a Texas twang that also got us teased. Chad has strong emotions surrounding those first few months: he was traumatized by his apparent blackness, which was a nonevent in Dallas and Oakland, where we were among many black kids. In Hawaii, we were some of the few mixed black kids around. And both our parents taught us that because the world would perceive us as black, we were black.

That didn't erase the unease I felt when the kids in the housing complex took notice of our darkness and kinky hair. Skin color wasn't necessarily the target as much as our blackness was the target for teasing. I say this because the kids who teased us were as brown as us, but we were black. There was a racial order that existed even in this group of tweens. They teased that Chad and I were *popolo*, Hawaiian slang for black people. *Popolo* are shiny berries that grow in clusters in the islands and are so black that they shine purple on branches. Hearing *popolo* on that playground didn't sound as regal as its namesake berries. It sounded dirty, like something that stuck on our bodies, like the red dirt of the playground. I craved belonging, especially to be reflected in my mother and her family, local-bred Hawaiian people, and spent my earlier years trying to separate from my blackness. I've since learned that I can be both black and native Hawaiian despite others' perceptions and their assertion that I must choose one over the other.

Ethnicity is a common part of conversations in Hawaii. Two questions locals ask are: "What high school you went?" and "What you?" Your high school places you on the island, shedding light on your character and where you are from. "What you?" refers to your people, whom you come from, what random mixture has made you. Jeff, whose father was also black, was perceived as Hawaiian, taking after Mom's side, looking like those bronze-skinned local boys who surfed and threw shaka signs at Sandy Beach. Jeff later told me that he didn't even know he was black until he was about eight because he didn't look it and barely knew his father beyond the two-hundred-dollar monthly checks Mom received throughout his childhood.

[. . .]

Wendi's first words to me were "Mary! You *mahu?*"

I was sitting on a park bench as Jeff ran around with his friends on the lawn that separated my school from his. Wendi was passing by with her volleyball in hand, her backpack bouncing on her butt, and her drive-by inquiry in the air. Though there was definitely a question mark floating around, her direct yet playful approach made me internalize her words as a statement. *If she's asking—even kiddingly—then I must be suspect*, I thought.

Everyone took notice of Wendi. She was hard to miss, prancing around Kalakaua Intermediate School in super-short soccer shorts, with her green mop of hair vibrantly declaring her presence. Subtlety was not—and still isn't—her thing. Her irritated red skin, peppered with acne, glistened with sweat as she played volleyball on campus. I'd never been this close to her, and her scrutinizing stare was intimidating.

Jeff, whom I picked up every day after school while Chad was at basketball or baseball practice, wasn't paying attention, but I remember feeling self-conscious. I was afraid that if I got close to Wendi or someone saw me interacting with her, I would be called *mahu*—a word that I equated to *sissy*. In my playground experience with the term, it was an epithet, thrown at any boy who was perceived to be *too* feminine. Until Wendi crossed paths with me, I was under the impression that I was doing a good job at being butch enough that such words wouldn't be thrown my way.

[. . .]

At the time, *mahu* was limited by our Western interpretation, mostly used as a pejorative. What I later learned in my Hawaiian studies classes in college was that *mahu* defined a group of people who embodied the diversity of gender beyond the dictates of our Western binary system. *Mahu* were often assigned male at birth but took on feminine gender roles in Kanaka Maoli (indigenous Hawaiian) culture, which celebrated *mahu* as spiritual healers, cultural bearers and breeders, caretakers, and expert hula dancers and instructors (or *Kumus* in Hawaiian). In the Western understanding and evolution of *mahu*, it translates to being transgender in its loosest understanding: to cross social boundaries of gender and/or sex. Like that of Hawaii's neighboring Polynesian islands, *mahu* is similar to the *mahu vahine* in Tahiti, *fa'afafine* in Samoa, and *fakaleiti* in Tonga, which comes from the Tongan word *faka* (meaning "to have the way of") and *leiti* (meaning "lady"). Historically, Polynesian cultures carved an "other" category in gender, uplifting the diversity, span, and spectrum in human expression.

To be *mahu* was to occupy a space between the poles of male and female in precolonial Hawaii, where it translated to "hermaphrodite," used to refer to feminine boys or masculine girls. But as puritanical missionaries from the West influenced Hawaiian culture in the nineteenth century, their Christian, homophobic, and gender binary systems pushed *mahu* from the center of culture to the margins. *Mahu* became a slur, one used to describe male-to-female transgender people and feminine men who were gay or perceived as gay due to their gender expression. Despite *mahu*'s modern evolution, it was one of the unique benefits of growing up in a diverse place like Hawaii, specifically Oahu (which translates to "the gathering place"), where multiculturalism was the norm. It was empowering to come of age in a place that recognized that diversity existed not only in ethnicities but also in gender. There was a level of tolerance regarding gender non-conformity that made it safer for people like Wendi and me to exist as we explored and expressed our identities.

The first person I met who took pride in being *mahu* was my hula instructor at school. Kumu Kaua'i was one of those *mahu* who reclaimed her place in society—specifically, being celebrated in the world of hula, where the presence and talent of *mahu* was valuable. Some trans women, who actively engaged in restoring native Hawaiian culture, reclaimed *mahu* at that time, choosing to call themselves *mahuwahine* (*wahine* is Hawaiian for "woman"), just as some people in marginalized communities reclaimed formerly derogatory words like *dyke*, *fag*, *nigger*, *queer*, and *tranny*. It was theirs to claim, use, and uplift. Kumu didn't call herself a woman or gay despite her femininity and preference for *she* and *her* as pronouns. She simply identified as *mahu* and had no qualms about the vessel she was given and nor any desire to change it.

[. . .]

Kumu bewildered me initially because I had been raised within the strict confines of male and female. This was a far cry from football Sundays with Dad in the projects. I was shaken by the dissonance of bright floral dresses and long hair on the form of a male-bodied person, someone who expressed her femininity proudly and visibly. Adding to that was the regular presence of Kumu's "husband," a tall, masculine man who appeared Samoan in stature and looks. He would pick up Kumu at the end of our practices, affectionately kissing her and helping her load the truck with the hula instruments—the *ipu* (a drum gourd) and *'ili'ili* (set of smooth black stones)—that she brought for us to dance with. I now realize that my fascination with Kumu wasn't that she puzzled me; I was in awe. She resonated with me at age twelve as I yearned to explore and reveal who I was. With time, I accepted Kumu's own determination of gender and learned to evolve past my ironic need to confine her to the two boxes I had been raised to live within. Kumu Kaua'i, like *mahuwahine* who came before, staked a given righteous place in Hawaii by uplifting, breeding, and spreading many aspects of native Hawaiian culture, specifically through hula. Kumu taught me, this mixed plate of a kid, how to mirror the movements of my ancestors and give thanks for the island culture that respected various other identities.

Wendi similarly captivated me because she refused to be jailed by anyone's categories or expectations. There was no confining this girl. I noticed her everywhere after our brief exchange, during which she recognized something in me that I thought I had expertly hidden behind buzz cuts and polo shirts. I took note of her slamming her volleyball at recess, whipping her flamboyant bob around campus, carrying her black flute case as she sashayed to band practice. What still stuns me about Wendi is that no one tolerated her. She was not something to be tolerated. She was accepted as fact just as one would accept the plumpness of the lunch ladies or the way Auntie Peggy, the counselors' secretary, would grab your palm as you waited for a meeting and read you your future (I recall her telling me, "You're going to get married in white!"). Wendi's changing hues, her originality, her audacity to be fully herself, was embraced and probably even more respected at an age when the rest of us were struggling and striving to fit in.

I refuse to pretend, though, that her uniqueness didn't make her a target. Wendi was called *faggot* at recess and asked when she was going to get her sex change. She used such ignorance as ammunition, threatening to kiss the boys who sought to humiliate her. I wasn't as daring as Wendi, and looking at her I was frightened by what I saw: myself. I told no one about her calling me *mahu* at the swings and avoided her as her long legs in her rolled-up shorts and knee-high socks glided past me in the halls.

Instead, I became all the more unwavering in my commitment to being the good son that year. I didn't put up a fight when it came to haircuts at the beauty school that offered barber discounts. I earned awards for my academic performance in class, was bumped into advanced courses, and even worked as an editor for the yearbook and the quarterly newspaper. My teachers praised and encouraged me, and in the spring of 1996, I was inducted into the National Junior Honor Society. I was the only boy from our class to be inducted. I loved the distinction of *only*, though the boy part I could've done without.

[. . .]

As I look back, what impresses me about my family is their openness. They patiently let me lead the way and kept any confusion or worry to themselves during a fragile period in my self-discovery. I recognize this as one of the biggest gifts they gave me. On some level, I knew they were afraid for me, afraid that I would be teased and taunted. Instead of trying to change me, they gave me love, letting

me know that I was accepted. I could stop pretending and drop the mask. My family fortified my self-esteem, which I counted on as I embarked on openly expressing my rapidly evolving self.

Reflecting on this pivotal time in my life, I think of the hundreds of thousands of LGBTQ (lesbian, gay bisexual, transgender, queer or questioning) youth who are flung from intolerant homes, from families who reject them when they reveal themselves. Of the estimated 1.6 million homeless and runaway American youth, as many as 40 percent are LGBTQ, according to a 2006 report by the Task Force and the National Coalition for the Homeless. A similar study by the Williams Institute cited family rejection as the leading cause of the disproportionate number of homeless LGBT youth. These young people are kicked out of their homes or are left with no choice but to leave because they can't be themselves. That's something both Wendi and I fortunately never faced.

With an air of acceptance at home, it was fairly easy to approach my mother and declare my truth. Sitting at our kitchen table, I told Mom, with no extensive planning or thought, "I'm gay." I was thirteen years old and didn't know how to fully explain who I was, conflating gender identity and sexuality. What I remember about that brief exchange was Mom's warmth. She smiled at me, letting me know that it was okay. I felt loved and heard and, more important, not othered. From her lack of reaction—her brows didn't furrow, her brown irises didn't shift from side to side—I felt as if I had announced that I had on blue today, a simple fact that we were both aware of. Mom later told me that she remembers feeling afraid for me because she sensed that there was more I wanted to say but didn't know how to. "My love for you never diminished, but a part of me was scared that people would hurt you, and that is what I had a hard time with," she told me recently.

A part of me was scared, too. I couldn't acknowledge the gender stuff because I didn't have a full understanding of it. Saying "I think I am a girl" would have been absurd for many reasons, including my fear that it would be a lot for my mother to handle. I didn't know that trans people existed; I had no idea that it was possible for thirteen-year-old me to become my own woman. That was a fantasy.

[. . .]

It was in Wendi's room that I heard about hormones. She mentioned them as if discussing milk, something you had to drink in order to grow. She told me the older girls she knew ("These fierce, un-clockable bitches!") went to a doctor in Waikiki who prescribed hormones for girls as young as sixteen. "I'm going to get my shots down when I turn sixteen," Wendi, who was fourteen at the time, said with excitement. "Trust."

I knew about hormones and puberty and safe sex from the handouts Coach Richardson gave us in health and physical education class. On Tuesdays and Thursdays, he'd lecture us about how we were raging with hormones, changing the shape and feel of our bodies. I felt nothing, barely five-two and a little chunky in the face and thighs: puberty hadn't really touched me. But I noticed the suppleness of the girls in class, the ones who seemed to be towering over many of us in height and shape. They began to separate from the pack swimming way behind in the puberty kiddie pool.

"Your grandparents are going to let you do that?" I asked Wendi, stunned.

"They don't know what *that* is and can barely speak English," she said matter-of-factly. "My aunt's gonna take me."

I trusted that she would do exactly as she said she would, and I admired her unstoppable determination. Wendi's friendship gave me the audacity to be noticed. One morning after one of our beauty experiments, I walked into student council homeroom with arched brows that framed my almond-shaped eyes, which were sparkling with a brush of silver eye shadow that Wendi said no one would really notice because it was "natural-looking." The girls in class, the ones who wore the white SODA platform wedge sneakers I so coveted, said, "I like your makeup." I remember tucking my short curls behind my ears, beaming under the gaze my new look warranted.

One early evening after playing volleyball, Wendi and I visited a group of her friends in a reserved

room at the recreation center. They were rehearsing for a show they did at Fusions, a gay club on Kuhio Avenue in Waikiki. Most of them were drag queens, but a select few were trans women who performed as showgirls. Society often blurs the lines between drag queens and trans women. This is highly problematic, because many people believe that, like drag queens, trans women go home, take off their wigs and chest plates, and walk around as men. Trans womanhood is not a performance or costume. As Wendi likes to joke, "A drag queen is part-time for showtime, and a trans woman is all the time!"

The lines continue to be blurred due to the umbrella term *transgender*, which bundles together diverse people (transsexual, intersex, genderqueer, drag performers, crossdressers, and gender-nonconforming folks) living with gender variance. Unfortunately, the data on the transgender population is scarce. The U.S. Census Bureau doesn't ask about gender identity, how trans people self-identify varies, and many (if asked) may not disclose that they're trans. The National Center for Transgender Equality has estimated that nearly 1 percent of the U.S. population is transgender, while the Williams Institute has stated that 0.3 percent of adults in the United States (nearly seven hundred thousand) identify as transgender, with the majority having taken steps to medically transition. This number does not take into account the number of transgender children or individuals who have expressed an incongruity between their assigned sex and gender identity or gender expression.

Despite the misconceptions, I understood the distinction between a drag queen and a trans woman because I came of age in the mid-nineties, and drag queens were in vogue. There was the 1995 release of *To Wong Foo, Thanks for Everything! Julie Newmar.* I hated that movie because Wendi would tease that Noxeema Jackson—Wesley Snipes's drag character—was my "Queen Mother." Drag queens were on Cori's favorite talk shows, *Sally* and *Jerry Springer*, and then there was RuPaul, "Supermodel of the World." It was a time when a brown, blond, and glamorous drag queen was a household name, beaming on MAC Cosmetics billboards at the mall in shiny red latex.

Like RuPaul, the queens at the rec center staked their claim on a smaller scale in Hawaii, part of the fabric of Oahu's diverse trans community. Toni Braxton's "Unbreak My Heart" was blasting from a boom box, and they were huddled together, about ten of them, discussing their choreography. I watched, seated on the cold tile floor with my backpack and volleyball at my side. They soon reconfigured, gathering in a circle of arms as one woman knelt at the center, hidden by the fort of mostly rotund queens. With the tape rewound, each queen walked clockwise, slowly descending into a kneeling position as the lady in the center rose, lip-synching Toni's lyrics.

[. . .]

Lani, who wore a pair of knee-length denim shorts and a stretched white tank top with black bra straps visible on her shoulders, kissed Wendi on the cheek. I stood behind Wendi, looking at Lani's winged black eyeliner, which she had whipped all the way to a sharp point where it nearly intersected with her penciled-in brows. The other girls gathered around her when Wendi turned around to introduce me. They were the first trans women I had met outside of Wendi.

I extended my hand to Lani, and she pulled me to her fleshy chest and gave me a kiss on the cheek, which left a red lip print on my face. My heart was racing because they were staring at me. Tracy was standing off to the side, uninterested, brushing her hair. I could hear her raking through her mane, strands snapping with each stroke of her brush.

"Mary, she's fish, yeah," Lani said with a chuckle, holding me at arm's length by the biceps. The girls around her nodded. Then, looking directly into my eyes, she added, "You're going to be pretty, girl. Trust!"

I tried my best to smile, aware that she was giving me a compliment—blessing me, even. To Lani, my fishiness was something to boast about. To be called fish by these women meant that I was embodying the kind of femininity that could allow me access, safety, opportunity, and maybe happiness. To be fish meant I could pass as any other girl, specifically

a cis woman, mirroring the concept of "realness," which was a major theme in *Paris Is Burning*, the 1990 documentary about New York City's ballroom community, comprising gay men, drag queens, and trans women of color. Ball legend Dorian Corey, who serves as the sage of the film, offering some of the most astute social commentary on the lived experiences of low-income LGBT people of color, describes "realness" for trans women (known in ball culture as femme queens) as being "undetectable" to the "untrained" or "trained." Simply, "realness" is the ability to be seen as heteronormative, to assimilate, to not be read as other or deviate from the norm. "Realness" means you are extraordinary in your embodiment of what society deems normative.

"When they can walk out of that ballroom into the sunlight and onto the subway and get home and still have all their clothes and no blood running off their bodies," Corey says in the film, "those are the femme *realness* queens."

Corey defines "realness" for trans women not just in the context of the ballroom but outside of the ballroom. Unlike Pepper LaBeija, a drag legend who said undergoing genital reconstruction surgery was "taking it a little too far" in the film, a trans woman or femme queen embodies "realness" and femininity beyond performance by existing in the daylight, where she's juxtaposed with society's norms, expectations, and ideals of cis womanhood.

To embody "realness," rather than performing and competing "realness," enables trans women to enter spaces with a lower risk of being rebutted or questioned, policed or attacked. "Realness" is a pathway to survival, and the heaviness of these truths were a lot for a thirteen-year-old to carry, especially one still trying to figure out who she was. I was also unable to accept that I was perceived as beautiful because, to me, I was not. No matter how many people told me I was fish, I didn't see myself that way. My eyes stung, betraying me, and immediately I felt embarrassed by my visible vulnerability.

[. . .]

With Wendi at my side, I felt I could be bold, unapologetic, free. To be so young and aiming to discover and assert myself alongside a best friend who mirrored me in her own identity instilled possibility in me. I could be me because I was not alone. The friendship I had with Wendi, though, is not the typical experience for most trans youth. Many are often the only trans person in a school or community, and most likely, when seeking support, they are the only trans person in LGBTQ spaces. To make matters worse, these support spaces often only address sexual orientation rather than a young person's gender identity, despite the all-encompassing acronym. Though trans youth seek community with cis gay, lesbian, bisexual, or queer teens, they may have to educate their cis peers about what it means to be trans.

When support and education for trans youth are absent, feelings of isolation and hopelessness can worsen. Coupled with families who might be intolerant and ill equipped to support a child, young trans people must deal with identity and body issues alone and in secret. The rise of social media and online resources has lessened the deafening isolation for trans people. If they have online access, trans people can find support and resources on YouTube, Tumblr, Twitter, and various other platforms where trans folks of all ages are broadcasting their lives, journeys, and even social and medical transitions. Still, the fact remains that local trans-inclusive support and positive media reflections of trans people are rare outside of major cities like Los Angeles, New York, Portland, San Francisco, and Seattle.

Recently, the media (from the *New Yorker* and the *New York Times* to ABC's *20/20* and *Nightline*) has focused its lens on trans youth. The typical portrait involves young people grappling with social transition at relatively young ages, as early as four, declaring that they're transgender and aiming to be welcomed in their communities and schools as their affirmed gender. As they reach puberty, these youth—with the support and resources of their welcoming families—undergo medical intervention under the expertise of an endocrinologist who may prescribe hormone-blocking medications that suppress puberty before graduating to cross-sex hormones and planning to undergo other gender affirmation surgeries.

To be frank, these stories are best-case scenarios, situations I hope become the norm for every young trans person in our society. But race and class are not usually discussed in these positive media portraits, which go as far as erasing the presence of trans youth from low-income communities and/or communities of color. Not all trans people come of age in supportive middle- and upper-middle-class homes, where parents have resources and access to knowledgeable and affordable health care that can cover expensive hormone-blocking medications and necessary surgeries. These best-case scenarios are not the reality for most trans people, regardless of age.

[. . .]

54. • *Ari Agha*

SINGING IN THE CRACKS (new)

Ari Agha is a researcher, writer, musician, and animal lover. They got their Ph.D. in sociology from Pennsylvania State University in 2005. Since then they've worked as a professor as well as a researcher at think tanks and government organizations in the United States and Canada. This essay is part of a larger research-creation project documenting how their singing voice changes with testosterone (www.keyoft.com).

I was assigned-female-at-birth and began hormone replacement therapy with testosterone about 15 months ago, when I was 39 years old. Every other week I draw the viscous liquid into a 3 cc syringe, wipe my thigh with an alcohol swab, insert the needle, and slowly depress the plunger. I started with half of what is considered a "normal" dose and took about ten months to work my way up to my maintenance dose. This gradual approach was intentional, to allow the changes in my body to come about slowly, especially the changes in my vocal folds.

I love singing, and while I don't do it to pay the bills, preserving my ability to sing is very important to me. To help fill the gap in scholarship about the impact of testosterone on singing among people assigned female, Laura Hynes (voice faculty at the University of Calgary) and I have been thoroughly documenting how my singing voice changes with testosterone (www.keyoft.com). Five months after beginning testosterone, we started to notice shifts in my singing voice. Since then my voice has continued to evolve, often in unexpected ways. Before I get into details, please note that the effects of testosterone and the timing of changes can vary a lot from person to person. What follow are my experiences singing through the first 15 months of testosterone therapy. I'm sharing this so readers can better understand both the ways in which my singing voice has changed and also my experience of having a changing voice. I'm presenting a more complex and nuanced description of gender transition than what we often hear in mainstream media.

CHANGES IN VOCAL RANGE

I've been taking voice lessons with Laura for a few years now, beginning well before I started taking testosterone. Before I started T, I could sing from C3 (an octave below middle C) to C6 (two octaves above middle C), the gray-dotted and gray sections on the diagram. Since then I've gained five half-steps at the bottom (white-dotted section) and lost five half-steps at the top (gray section). The transitions between my registers (or breaks) have also shifted down.

It was a regular Thursday afternoon. Laura guided me through some lip trills and humming to begin the warm-up, then asked me to switch to "oo." We were making our way down the scale and I was focusing on maintaining vertical space and relaxing my throat and tongue as we got to the bottom of my range. Laura looked up from the piano.

"P.S., Ari . . . you just sang an A."

I wasn't used to keeping track of my range, so it took me a moment.

"An A?" I asked, not quite comprehending.

She nodded. "An A. Before, the lowest you could sing was a C or maybe a B."

Up until that point I hadn't noticed any differences in how I looked, felt, or sounded, in the five months since beginning testosterone. People close to me hadn't noticed any differences either. I knew starting on a lower dose of testosterone meant that the changes would occur more gradually, but without any outward signs of transition, I could only

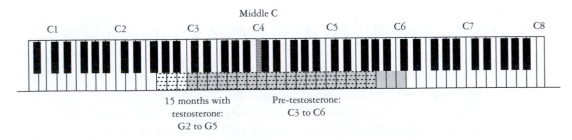

Singing range pre-T and after fifteen months with testosterone

have faith that the hormones were impacting my body. Under my skin, absorbed through my thigh muscle, and transported through my body in my blood, the testosterone I had been injecting had been sending messages to other cells, directing their development and activity. One of the changes was the gradual thickening of my vocal cords. And then that day, in just a split second, I learned my cords had gotten thick enough, that when I brought them together and passed air through them, I could produce vibrations that moved a bit more slowly than they had the week before: I sang an A.

I felt profound, almost miraculous joy at discovering this change in my voice. Realizing that my voice change had begun was about much more than just being able to sing a step lower than I had before: it meant this change I had been anticipating for so long was finally, really happening.

CHANGES IN TIMBRE

While that first shift felt important, I came to realize that the changes at the very top and bottom of my range really didn't make much of a difference in my daily singing life. There's actually a great deal of overlap in the notes I could sing pre-T and what I can sing now (the gray-dotted section on the diagram). While I've always been able to sing in that middle part of my range, the changes in how my voice sounds when I'm singing there have made a far bigger difference than the low notes I've gained or the high ones I've lost.

I absolutely love the power and vibrancy I now have in the lower part of my range. I'm not talking about the "new" low notes at the very bottom of my range, but those middle-low notes I've always been able to sing, which now have greater volume and intensity. While I was happy about the changes in my lower voice, I had a lot of concern about how T would affect the higher part of my range, my head voice. I've always really loved my head voice. Laura describes it as bright and resonant. In cis men, the head voice, sometimes called falsetto, tends to be lighter and more breathy-sounding than that of cis

women. I worried that taking testosterone would cause my head voice to sound more like a falsetto, but so far that hasn't happened. My head voice now sounds darker, richer, more complex than it did before, and to my delight, I haven't lost the clarity I love so much.

NEGOTIATING REGISTER CHANGES

While I've been happy with the way my voice has changed so far, and grateful that my head voice is still available to me, the process has been difficult. My voice has gotten less predictable and much more fragile. I struggle with it breaking and cracking, and while this can happen in any part of my range, it happens more often around the register changes. When my voice is particularly unstable, I can't help but laugh. You just can't take yourself too seriously when your voice bears a striking resemblance to a honking goose.

A few months ago, I worked with Emily, a visiting voice teacher. Emily's laugh is sonorous, and we had been doing a lot of laughing that afternoon, despite (and sometimes because of) my unstable voice. This instability can be incredibly unnerving, though. While we all go through voice changes throughout our lives, the repercussions of experiencing this particular sort of transition as an adult singer in selective choral ensembles are different than they might be for adolescents, even those who are serious singers. We have millennia of human experience and decades of research to help us understand cis boys' adolescent voice changes. We know that while the process may be harrowing, a functional voice is the usual end-product. That is not the case for assigned-female folks who take testosterone. Cis boys going through this change are also usually part of a cohort of peers going through a similar process at around the same time. I'm going through this alone, though. I don't have friends whose voices are changing in similar ways, let alone a parent or older sibling to look to for reassurance that eventually, my voice will settle.

I try to remember that negotiating register changes is a skill that can be learned, and one in which I've already made progress. It's also encouraging to remember that those squeaks and breaks don't necessarily mean I'm doing anything wrong. They are a normal part of the process and are, in fact, signs that my voice is changing. During my lesson with Emily that day I was using my hands to model the movement of my larynx while singing easy glides from five to one, when, as we approached my register change, my voice started cracking.

Feeling self-conscious, I said, "It's landing right in the fuzzy spot for me."

Emily responded, "That's good. Fuzzy stuff is great!" Then, after a long pause, she continued, "If you try and push away the awkwardness, it just gets bigger. So instead, choose to revel . . . You know, you can only be who you are."

I nodded.

Emily continued, "And that means all the cracks and fissures. I, personally, think they're the most fascinating part of any voice."

VOCAL FATIGUE

My voice gets tired much more quickly. I try never to push my voice beyond what is comfortable. This is much easier said than done, though, because I love to sing. I want to sing. In choir rehearsal I'm surrounded by singing voices, and it's frustrating to have to stop for a while or hold back. I've also found that after a long rehearsal, it now takes more rest for my voice to get back to normal.

What makes these changes in my voice much more challenging is that I don't know how long they will last and cannot be totally sure that they will ever resolve. There's growing interest in voice changes among trans singers taking testosterone (Davies 2016; Manternach 2017; Manternach et al. 2017) but there is not yet much research (exceptions are Constansis 2008 and Sims 2017). I try to be optimistic and revel in the present, but it's hard to totally let go of that future uncertainty.

SECTION ASSIGNMENTS

When it comes to ensemble singing, I'm somewhere between alto and tenor. My voice does not fit well into any of the existing categories, and that feels isolating. The in-between position of my voice is often mirrored by my physical location in the choir. When we sit in sections ordered from high to low I am on the low end of the alto section and the high end of the tenors. I'm literally right in the middle, perched on an invisible line, with the altos and sopranos lined up on my right and the tenors and basses on my left. On some songs I sing alto and on others I sing tenor, but I don't really belong in either section. I teeter on the border between the two, not really comfortable or fitting in to either.

SINGING AND LIVING OUTSIDE OF THE BINARY

The parallels between my voice not fitting in the existing structure and my gender not fitting the binary are striking. I use they/them pronouns and am genderqueer. For me, this means that I am neither a man nor a woman. I am not part-man and part-woman. I do not lie somewhere between the man and woman ends of a gender spectrum. I do not move between man and woman. I am not androgynous, and I'm not gender-neutral or gender-free. I exist outside of the binary gender structure, and now, so does my voice.

Singing outside of the existing structure is difficult. Living outside of the gender binary also has painful consequences. I am misgendered and referred to as "she" or "he" or "ma'am" or "sir" every day. I cannot expect that there will be a safe place for me to use the washroom. The washroom issue is magnified by a thousand when it comes to locker rooms at the gym. When filling out forms at doctor's offices, do I check "M" or "F"? When signing up to play softball, will I fill a slot allotted for a "man" or a "woman?" What will happen if I take my shirt off at the beach and reveal the long, pink scars on my chest?

Despite the risks and trials associated with living outside of the gender binary, the identity itself, being genderqueer, feels good and right. It fits. Discovering and embracing this identity has been revolutionary for me. I feel serene and strong and powerful and sexy and beautiful and handsome. I feel safe and vulnerable and open and real. It just feels right.

One of the things I love most about singing in a choir is the intensely personal way it allows me to connect with other singers and listeners. Singing together is so intimate because we use our bodies to produce sound and every voice impacts the ensemble's sound. But not fitting in to any of the sections is painful. What is my place in the choir? What is my role? This kind of not-fitting-in is especially painful because it is connected to my voice, something that has always brought me great joy and pride, and also because I already experience so much alienation and exclusion because I'm genderqueer.

SINGING IN THE CRACKS

When I decided to begin taking T, I knew that there would be a lot of uncertainty, and that I'd have no way of predicting how low my voice would get. I expected the vocal fragility and fatigue. I knew that I could not know for sure what the changes would feel like, how long the transition would last, or what I might sound like afterwards.

Knowing that the future holds uncertainty did not prepare me to live with it, inside of it, slipping and sliding around it and through it. My biggest worry is that I'll forever be stuck in this middle space, between sections, with a fragile voice full of breaks and unable to endure a full rehearsal. But then I pause, breathe, and look around from my spot right in the middle of the choir.

From this vantage point, I can see and hear everyone; to my right are all of the sopranos and altos and to my left are all of the tenors and basses. The conductor is right in front of me. While my voice doesn't fit neatly with the singers on either my right or my left, it allows me to float between them. Maybe I'm both, maybe I'm neither, maybe it depends on the moment. At this point in my transition it feels like I have access to the best of many different worlds. I've maintained a three-octave range. Despite the chaos of different hormones, thickening cords, and unstable breaks, I'm reassured to still feel connected with my voice as I try to embrace the fuzzy stuff and sing through the cracks.

A longer version of this essay is available on my blog: www.genderqueerme.com. This research was supported by the Social Sciences and Humanities Research Council of Canada. Publications with more detailed findings on my voice change are on http://www.keyoft.com.

WORKS CITED

Constansis, Alexandros. "The Changing Female-To-Male (FTM) Voice." *Radical Musicology*, vol. 3, 2008.

Davies, Shelagh. "Training the Transgender Singer: Finding the Voice Inside." *Intermezzo, the e-newsletter of the National Association of Teachers of Singing*, April 14, 2016.

Manternach, Brian. "The Independent Teacher: Teaching Transgender Singers. Part 2: The Singers' Perspectives." *Journal of Singing*, vol. 74, issue 2, November/December 2017, pp. 209–14.

Manternach, Brian, et al. "The Independent Teacher: Teaching Transgender Singers. Part 1: The Voice Teachers' Perspectives." *Journal of Singing*, vol. 74, issue 1, September/October 2017, pp. 83–88.

Sims, Loraine. "Teaching Lucas: A Transgender Student's Vocal Journey from Soprano to Tenor." *Journal of Singing*, vol. 83, issue 4, March 2017, pp. 367–75.

55. • *Cheryl Chase*

HERMAPHRODITES WITH ATTITUDE:
Mapping the Emergence of Intersex Political Activism (1998)

Cheryl Chase is the founder of Intersex Society of North America. She was the recipient of the Felipa de Souza Human Rights Award in 2000. In her efforts to advocate for better social and medical treatment of intersexed people, she has appeared in various media, including *Newsweek*, the *New York Times*, NPR's *Fresh Air*, and NBC's *Dateline*.

The insistence on two clearly distinguished sexes has calamitous personal consequences for the many individuals who arrive in the world with sexual anatomy that fails to be easily distinguished as male or female. Such individuals are labeled "intersexuals" or "hermaphrodites" by modern medical discourse.[1] About one in a hundred births exhibits some anomaly in sex differentiation,[2] and about one in two thousand is different enough to render problematic the question "Is it a boy or a girl?"[3] Since the early 1960s, nearly every major city in the United States has had a hospital with a standing team of medical experts who intervene in these cases to assign—through drastic surgical means—a male or female status to intersex infants. The fact that this system for preserving the boundaries of the categories male and female has existed for so long without drawing criticism or scrutiny from any quarter indicates the extreme discomfort that sexual ambiguity excites in our culture. Pediatric genital surgeries literalize what might otherwise be considered a theoretical operation: the attempted production of normatively sexed bodies and gendered subjects through constitutive acts of violence. Over the last few years, however, intersex people have begun to politicize intersex identities, thus transforming intensely personal experiences of violation into collective opposition to the medical regulation of bodies that queer the foundations of heteronormative identifications and desires.

HERMAPHRODITES: MEDICAL AUTHORITY AND CULTURAL INVISIBILITY

Many people familiar with the ideas that gender is a phenomenon not adequately described by male/female dimorphism and that the interpretation of physical sex differences is culturally constructed remain surprised to learn just how variable sexual anatomy is.[4] Though the male/female binary is constructed as natural and presumed to be immutable, the phenomenon of intersexuality offers clear evidence to the contrary and furnishes an opportunity to deploy "nature" strategically to disrupt heteronormative systems of sex, gender, and sexuality. The concept of bodily sex, in popular usage, refers to multiple components including karyotype (organization of sex chromosomes), gonadal differentiation (e.g., ovarian or testicular), genital morphology, configuration of internal reproductive organs, and pubertal sex characteristics such as breasts and facial hair. Because these characteristics are expected to be concordant in each individual—either all male or all female—an observer, once having attributed male or female sex to a particular individual, assumes the values of other unobserved characteristics.[5]

Because medicine intervenes quickly in intersex births to change the infant's body, the phenomenon of intersexuality is today largely unknown outside specialized medical practices. General public awareness of intersex bodies slowly vanished in modern Western European societies as medicine gradually appropriated to itself the authority to interpret—and eventually manage—the category which had previously been widely known as "hermaphroditism." Victorian medical taxonomy began to efface hermaphroditism as a legitimated status by establishing mixed gonadal histology as a necessary criterion for "true" hermaphroditism. By this criterion, both ovarian and testicular tissue types had to be present. Given the limitations of Victorian surgery and anesthesia, such confirmation was impossible in a living patient. All other anomalies were reclassified as "pseudohermaphroditisms" masking a "true sex" determined by the gonads.[6]

With advances in anesthesia, surgery, embryology, and endocrinology, however, twentieth-century medicine moved from merely labeling intersexed bodies to the far more invasive practice of "fixing" them to conform with a diagnosed true sex. The techniques and protocols for physically transforming intersexed bodies were developed primarily at Johns Hopkins University in Baltimore during the 1920s and 1930s under the guidance of urologist Hugh Hampton Young. "Only during the last few years," Young enthused in the preface to his pioneering textbook, *Genital Abnormalities*, "have we begun to get somewhere near the explanation of the marvels of anatomic abnormality that may be portrayed by these amazing individuals. But the surgery of the hermaphrodite has remained a terra incognita." The "sad state of these unfortunates" prompted Young to devise "a great variety of surgical procedures" by which he attempted to normalize their bodily appearances to the greatest extents possible.[7]

Quite a few of Young's patients resisted his efforts. One, a "'snappy' young negro woman with a good figure" and a large clitoris, had married a man but found her passion only with women. She refused "to be made into a man" because removal of her vagina would mean the loss of her "meal ticket," namely, her husband.[8] By the 1950s, the principle of rapid postnatal detection and intervention for intersex infants had been developed at Johns Hopkins with the stated goal of completing surgery early enough so that the child would have no memory of it.[9] One wonders whether the insistence on early intervention was not at least partly motivated by the resistance offered by adult intersexuals to normalization through surgery. Frightened parents of ambiguously sexed infants were much more open to suggestions of normalizing surgery, while the infants themselves could of course offer no resistance whatever. Most of the theoretical foundations justifying these interventions are attributable to psychologist John Money, a sex researcher invited to Johns Hopkins by Lawson Wilkins, the founder of pediatric endocrinology.[10] Wilkins's numerous students subsequently carried these protocols to hospitals throughout the United States and abroad.[11] Suzanne Kessler notes that today Wilkins and Money's protocols enjoy a "consensus of approval rarely encountered in science."[12]

In keeping with the Johns Hopkins model, the birth of an intersex infant today is deemed a "psychosocial emergency" that propels a multidisciplinary team of intersex specialists into action. Significantly, they are surgeons and endocrinologists rather than psychologists, bioethicists, representatives from intersex peer support organizations, or parents of intersex children. The team examines the infant and chooses either male or female as a "sex of assignment," then informs the parents that this is the child's "true sex." Medical technology, including surgery and hormones, is then used to make the child's body conform as closely as possible to that sex.

The sort of deviation from sex norms exhibited by intersexuals is so highly stigmatized that the likely prospect of emotional harm due to social rejection of the intersexual provides physicians with their most compelling argument to justify medically unnecessary surgical interventions. Intersex status is considered to be so incompatible with emotional health that misrepresentation, concealment of facts, and outright lying (both to parents and later to the intersex person) are unabashedly advocated in professional medical literature.[13] Rather, the systematic hushing up of the fact of intersex births and the use of violent techniques to normalize intersex bodies have caused profound emotional and physical harm to intersexuals and their families. The harm begins when the birth is treated as a medical crisis, and the consequences of that initial treatment ripple out ever afterward. The impact of this treatment is so devastating that until just a few years ago, people whose lives have been touched by intersexuality maintained silence about their ordeal. As recently as 1993, no one publicly disputed surgeon Milton Edgerton when he wrote that in forty years of clitoral surgery on intersexuals, "not one has complained of loss of sensation, *even when the entire clitoris was removed*."[14]

The tragic irony is that, while intersexual anatomy occasionally indicates an underlying medical problem such as adrenal malfunction, ambiguous genitals are in and of themselves neither painful nor harmful to health. Surgery is essentially a destructive process. It can remove and to a limited extent relocate tissue, but it cannot create new structures. This technical limitation, taken together with the framing of the feminine as a condition of lack, leads physicians to assign 90 percent of anatomically ambiguous infants as female by excising genital tissue. Members of the Johns Hopkins intersex team have justified female assignment by saying, "You can make a hole, but you can't build a pole."[15] Positively heroic efforts shore up a tenuous masculine status for the remaining 10 percent assigned male, who are subjected to multiple operations—twenty-two in one case[16]—with the goal of straightening the penis and constructing a urethra to enable standing urinary posture. For some, the surgeries end only when the child grows old enough to resist.[17]

Children assigned to the female sex are subjected to surgery that removes the troubling hypertrophic clitoris (the same tissue that would have been a troubling micropenis if the child had been assigned male). Through the 1960s, feminizing pediatric genital surgery was openly labeled "clitorectomy" and was compared favorably to the African practices that have been the recent focus of such intense scrutiny. As three Harvard surgeons noted, "Evidence that the clitoris is not essential for normal coitus may be gained from certain sociological data. For instance, it is the custom of a number of African tribes to excise the clitoris and other parts of the external genitals. Yet normal sexual function is observed in these females."[18] A modified operation that removes most of the clitoris and relocates a bit of the tip is variously (and euphemistically) called clitoroplasty, clitoral reduction, or clitoral recession and is described as a "simple cosmetic procedure" to differentiate it from the now infamous clitorectomy. However, the operation is far from benign. Here is a slightly simplified summary (in my own words) of the surgical technique—recommended by Johns Hopkins surgeons Oesterling, Gearhart, and Jeffs—that is representative of the operation:

> They make an incision around the phallus, at the corona, then dissect the skin away from its underside. Next they dissect the skin away from the dorsal side and remove as much of the corpora, or erectile bodies, as necessary to create an "appropriate size clitoris." Next, stitches are placed from the pubic area along both sides of the entire length of what remains of the phallus; when these stitches are tightened, it folds up like pleats in a skirt, and recesses into a concealed position behind the mons pubis. If the result is still "too large," the glans is further reduced by cutting away a pie-shaped wedge.[19]

For most intersexuals, this sort of arcane, dehumanized medical description, illustrated with close-ups of genital surgery and naked children with blacked-out eyes, is the only available version of *Our Bodies, Ourselves*. We as a culture have relinquished to medicine the authority to police the boundaries of male and female, leaving intersexuals to recover as best they can, alone and silent, from violent normalization.

MY CAREER AS A HERMAPHRODITE: RENEGOTIATING CULTURAL MEANINGS

I was born with ambiguous genitals. A doctor specializing in intersexuality deliberated for three days—sedating my mother each time she asked what was wrong with her baby—before concluding that I was male, with a micropenis, complete hypospadias, undescended testes, and a strange extra opening behind the urethra. A male birth certificate was completed for me, and my parents began raising me as a boy. When I was a year and a half old my parents consulted a different set of experts, who admitted me to a hospital for "sex determination." "Determine" is a remarkably apt word in this context, meaning both "to ascertain by investigation" and "to cause to come to a resolution." It perfectly describes the two-stage process whereby science produces through a series of masked operations what it claims merely to observe. Doctors told my parents that a thorough medical investigation would be necessary to determine (in the first sense of that word) what my "true sex" was. They judged my genital appendage to be inadequate as a penis, too short to mark masculine status effectively or to penetrate females. As a female, however, I would be penetrable and potentially fertile. My anatomy having been relabeled as vagina, urethra, labia, and outsized clitoris, my sex was determined (in the second sense) by amputating my genital appendage. Following doctors' orders, my parents then changed my name, combed their house to eliminate all traces

of my existence as a boy (photographs, birthday cards, etc.), changed my birth certificate, moved to a different town, instructed extended family members no longer to refer to me as a boy, and never told anyone else—including me—just what had happened. My intersexuality and change of sex were the family's dirty little secrets.

At age eight, I was returned to the hospital for abdominal surgery that trimmed away the testicular portion of my gonads, each of which was partly ovarian and partly testicular in character. No explanation was given to me then for the long hospital stay or the abdominal surgery, nor for the regular hospital visits afterward, in which doctors photographed my genitals and inserted fingers and instruments into my vagina and anus. These visits ceased as soon as I began to menstruate. At the time of the sex change, doctors had assured my parents that their once son/now daughter would grow into a woman who could have a normal sex life and babies. With the confirmation of menstruation, my parents apparently concluded that that prediction had been borne out and their ordeal was behind them. For me, the worst part of the nightmare was just beginning.

As an adolescent, I became aware that I had no clitoris or inner labia and was unable to orgasm. By the end of my teens, I began to do research in medical libraries, trying to discover what might have happened to me. When I finally determined to obtain my medical records, it took me three years to overcome the obstruction of the doctors whom I asked for help. When I did obtain them, a scant three pages, I first learned that I was a "true hermaphrodite" who had been my parents' son for a year and a half and who bore a name unfamiliar to me. The records also documented my clitorectomy. This was the middle 1970s, when I was in my early twenties. I had come to identify myself as lesbian, at a time when lesbianism and a biologically based gender essentialism were virtually synonymous: men were rapists who caused war and environmental destruction; women were good and would heal the earth; lesbians were a superior form of being uncontaminated by "men's energy." In such a world, how could I tell anyone that I had actually possessed the dreaded "phallus"? I was no longer a woman in my own eyes but rather a monstrous and mythical creature. Because my hermaphroditism and long-buried boyhood were the history behind the clitorectomy, I could never speak openly about that or my consequent inability to orgasm. I was so traumatized by discovering the circumstances that produced my embodiment that I could not speak of these matters with anyone.

Nearly fifteen years later, I suffered an emotional meltdown. In the eyes of the world, I was a highly successful businesswoman, a principal in an international high-tech company. To myself, I was a freak, incapable of loving or being loved, filled with shame about my status as a hermaphrodite and about my sexual dysfunction. Unable to make peace with myself, I finally sought help from a psychotherapist, who reacted to each revelation about my history and predicament with some version of "no, it's not" or "so what?" I would say, "I'm not really a woman," and she would say, "Of course you are. You look female." I would say, "My complete withdrawal from sexuality has destroyed every relationship I've ever entered." She would say, "Everybody has their ups and downs." I tried another therapist and met with a similar response. Increasingly desperate, I confided my story to several friends, who shrank away in embarrassed silence. I was in emotional agony, feeling utterly alone, seeing no possible way out. I decided to kill myself.

Confronting suicide as a real possibility proved to be my personal epiphany. I fantasized killing myself quite messily and dramatically in the office of the surgeon who had cut off my clitoris, forcibly confronting him with the horror he had imposed on my life. But in acknowledging the desire to put my pain to some use, not to utterly waste my life, I turned a crucial corner, finding a way to direct my rage productively out into the world rather than destructively at myself. I had no conceptual framework for developing a more positive self-consciousness. I knew only that I felt mutilated, not fully human, but that I was determined to heal. I

struggled for weeks in emotional chaos, unable to eat or sleep or work. I could not accept my image of a hermaphroditic body any more than I could accept the butchered one the surgeons left me with. Thoughts of myself as a Frankenstein's monster patchwork alternated with longings for escape by death, only to be followed by outrage, anger, and a determination to survive. I could not accept that it was just or right or good to treat any person as I had been treated—my sex changed, my genitals cut up, my experience silenced and rendered invisible. I bore a private hell within me, wretchedly alone in my condition without even my tormentors for company. Finally, I began to envision myself standing in a driving storm but with clear skies and a rainbow visible in the distance. I was still in agony, but I was beginning to see the painful process in which I was caught up in terms of revitalization and rebirth, a means of investing my life with a new sense of authenticity that possessed vast potentials for further transformation. Since then, I have seen this experience of movement through pain to personal empowerment described by other intersex and transsexual activists.[20]

I slowly developed a newly politicized and critically aware form of self-understanding. I had been the kind of lesbian who at times had a girlfriend but who had never really participated in the life of a lesbian community. I felt almost completely isolated from gay politics, feminism, and queer and gender theory. I did possess the rudimentary knowledge that the gay rights movement had gathered momentum only when it could effectively deny that homosexuality was sick or inferior and assert to the contrary that "gay is good." As impossible as it then seemed, I pledged similarly to affirm that "intersex is good," that the body I was born with was not diseased, only different. I vowed to embrace the sense of being "not a woman" that I initially had been so terrified to discover.

I began searching for community and consequently moved to San Francisco in the fall of 1992, based entirely on my vague notion that people living in the "queer mecca" would have the most conceptually sophisticated, socially tolerant, and politically astute analysis of sexed and gendered embodiment. I found what I was looking for in part because my arrival in the Bay Area corresponded with the rather sudden emergence of an energetic transgender political movement. Transgender Nation (TN) had developed out of Queer Nation, a post-gay/lesbian group that sought to transcend identity politics. TN's actions garnered media attention—especially when members were arrested during a "zap" of the American Psychiatric Association's annual convention when they protested the psychiatric labeling of transsexuality as mental illness. Transsexual performance artist Kate Bornstein was introducing transgender issues in an entertaining way to the San Francisco gay/lesbian community and beyond. Female-to-male issues had achieved a new level of visibility due in large part to efforts made by Lou Sullivan, a gay FTM activist who had died an untimely death from HIV-related illnesses in 1991. And in the wake of her underground best-selling novel, *Stone Butch Blues*, Leslie Feinberg's manifesto *Transgender Liberation*: *A Movement Whose Time Has Come* was finding a substantial audience, linking transgender social justice to a broader progressive political agenda for the first time.[21] At the same time, a vigorous new wave of gender scholarship had emerged in the academy.[22] In this context, intersex activist and theoretician

Morgan Holmes could analyze her own clitorectomy for her master's thesis and have it taken seriously as academic work.[23] Openly transsexual scholars, including Susan Stryker and Sandy Stone, were visible in responsible academic positions at major universities. Stone's "*Empire* Strikes Back: A Posttranssexual Manifesto" refigured open, visible transsexuals not as gender conformists propping up a system of rigid, binary sex but as "a set of embodied texts whose potential for productive disruption of structured sexualities and spectra of desire has yet to be explored."[24]

Into this heady atmosphere, I brought my own experience. Introduced by Bornstein to other gender activists, I explored with them the cultural politics of intersexuality, which to me represented yet another new configuration of bodies, identities, desires, and sexualities from which to confront the violently normativizing aspects of the dominant sex/gender system. In the fall of 1993, TN pioneer Anne Ogborn invited me to participate in a weekend retreat called the New Woman Conference, where postoperative transsexual women shared their stories, their griefs and joys, and enjoyed the freedom to swim or sunbathe in the nude with others who had surgically changed genitals. I saw that participants returned home in a state of euphoria, and I determined to bring that same sort of healing experience to intersex people. [. . .]

NOTES

My appreciation goes to Susan Stryker for her extensive contributions to the structure and substance of this essay.

1. Claude J. Migeon, Gary D. Berkovitz, and Terry R. Brown, "Sexual Differentiation and Ambiguity," in *Wilkins*: *The Diagnosis and Treatment of Endocrine Disorders in Childhood and Adolescence*, ed. Michael S. Kappy, Robert M. Blizzard, and Claude J. Migeon (Springfield, IL: Charles C. Thomas, 1994), 573–715.

2. Lalitha Raman-Wilms et al., "Fetal Genital Effects of First-Trimester Sex Hormone Exposure: A Meta-Analysis," *Obstetrics and Gynecology* 85 (1995): 141–48.

3. Anne Fausto-Sterling, *Body Building*: *How Biologists Construct Sexuality* (New York: Basic Books, 2000).

4. Judith Butler, *Gender Trouble*: *Feminism and the Subversion of Identity* (New York: Routledge, 1990); Thomas Laqueur, *Making Sex*: *Body and Gender from the Greeks to Freud* (Cambridge, MA: Harvard University Press, 1990).

5. Suzanne Kessler and Wendy McKenna, *Gender*: *An Ethnomethodological Approach* (New York: John Wiley and Sons, 1978).

6. Alice Domurat Dreger, "Doubtful Sex: Cases and Concepts of Hermaphroditism in France and Britain, 1868–1915," (Ph.D. diss., Indiana University, 1995); Alice Domurat Dreger, "Doubtful Sex: The Fate of the

Hermaphrodite in Victorian Medicine," *Victorian Studies* (spring 1995): 336–70; Alice Domurat Dreger, "Hermaphrodites in Love: The Truth of the Gonads," *Science and Homosexualities*, ed. Vernon Rosario (New York: Routledge, 1997), 46–66; Alice Domurat Dreger, "Doctors Containing Hermaphrodites: The Victorian Legacy," *Chrysalis: The Journal of Transgressive Gender Identities* (fall 1997): 15–22.

7. Hugh Hampton Young, *Genital Abnormalities, Hermaphroditism, and Related Adrenal Diseases* (Baltimore: Williams and Wilkins, 1937), xxxix–xl.

8. Ibid., 139–42.

9. Howard W. Jones Jr. and William Wallace Scott, *Hermaphroditism, Genital Anomalies, and Related Endocrine Disorders* (Baltimore: Williams and Wilkins, 1958), 269.

10. John Money, Joan G. Hampson, and John L. Hampson, "An Examination of Some Basic Sexual Concepts: The Evidence of Human Hermaphroditism," *Bulletin of the Johns Hopkins Hospital* 97 (1955): 301–19; John Money, Joan G. Hampson, and John L. Hampson, "Hermaphroditism: Recommendations Concerning Assignment of Sex, Change of Sex, and Psychologic Management," *Bulletin of Johns Hopkins Hospital* 97 (1955): 284–300; John Money, *Venuses Penuses* (Buffalo: Prometheus, 1986).

11. Robert M. Blizzard, "Lawson Wilkins," in Kappy et al., *Wilkins*, xi–xiv.

12. Suzanne Kessler, "The Medical Construction of Gender: Case Management of Inter-sexual Infants," *Signs: Journal of Women in Culture and Society* 16 (1990): 3–26.

13. J. Dewhurst and D. B. Grant, "Intersex Problems," *Archives of Disease in Childhood* 59 (1984): 1191–94; Anita Natarajan, "Medical Ethics and Truth-Telling in the Case of Androgen Insensitivity Syndrome," *Canadian Medical Association Journal* 154 (1996): 568–70; Tom Mazur, "Ambiguous Genitalia: Detection and Counseling," *Pediatric Nursing* (1983): 417–22; F. M. E. Slijper et al., "Neonates with Abnormal Genital Development Assigned the Female Sex: Parent Counseling," *Journal of Sex Education and Therapy* 20 (1994): 9–17.

14. Milton T. Edgerton, "Discussion: Clitoroplasty for Clitoromegaly due to Adrenogenital Syndrome without Loss of Sensitivity (by Nobuyuki Sagehashi)," *Plastic and Reconstructive Surgery* 91 (1993): 956.

15. Melissa Hendricks, "Is It a Boy or a Girl?" *Johns Hopkins Magazine*, November 1993, 10–16.

16. John F. Stecker et al., "Hypospadias Cripples," *Urologic Clinics of North America: Symposium on Hypospadias* 8 (1981): 539–44.

17. Jeff McClintock, "Growing Up in the Surgical Maelstrom," *Chrysalis: The Journal of Transgressive Gender Identities* (fall 1997): 53–54.

18. Robert E. Gross, Judson Randolph, and John F. Crigler, "Clitorectomy for Sexual Abnormalities: Indications and Technique," *Surgery* 59 (1966): 300–308.

19. Joseph E. Oesterling, John P. Gearhart, and Robert D. Jeffs, "A Unified Approach to Early Reconstructive Surgery of the Child with Ambiguous Genitalia," *Journal of Urology* 138 (1987): 1079–84.

20. Kira Triea, "The Awakening," *Hermaphrodites with Attitude* (winter 1994): 1; Susan Stryker, "My Words to Victor Frankenstein above the Village of Chamounix: Performing Transgender Rage," *GLQ* 1 (1994): 237–54.

21. Leslie Feinberg, *Stone Butch Blues* (Ithaca, NY: Firebrand, 1993); Leslie Feinberg, *Transgender Liberation: A Movement Whose Time Has Come* (New York: World View Forum, 1992).

22. See, for example, Judith Butler, *Bodies That Matter: On the Discursive Limits of "Sex"* (New York: Routledge, 1993); Butler, *Gender Trouble*; Laqueur, *Making Sex*; and Julia Epstein and Kristina Straub, eds., *Body Guards: The Cultural Politics of Gender Ambiguity* (New York: Routledge, 1991).

23. Morgan Holmes, "Medical Politics and Cultural Imperatives: Intersexuality Beyond Pathology and Erasure" (master's thesis, York University, Toronto, 1994).

24. Sandy Stone, "The *Empire* Strikes Back: A Posttranssexual Manifesto," in Epstein and Straub, *Body Guards*, 280–304, quotation on 296.

56. • *C. Winter Han*

BEING AN ORIENTAL, I COULD NEVER BE COMPLETELY A MAN:
Gay Asian Men and the Intersection of Race, Gender, Sexuality, and Class (2006)

C. Winter Han is an Associate Professor of Sociology and Contributing Faculty in Gender, Sexuality, and Feminist Studies at Middlebury College. His work focuses on the intersection of race and sexuality, as can be seen from the following essay. Prior to his academic appointment, he was an award-winning journalist.

Even before the last contestant exits the stage, it is bitterly obvious to most in the room who will walk away with the crown. In a flurry of fans and silk, while shaking every muscle in her body, one contestant manages to capture the audience's imagination with a modern rendition of *Madame Butterfly* that is both visually and emotionally inspiring to the largely white audience. As the performance reaches its climax, the audience members, who would later cast their ballots for the winner, are up on their feet, cheering in unison.

"I'm never entering another pageant with Asian girls again," one white drag queen tells me later that evening, "they're just too hard to beat. They're just way too real, it's not even fair."

In the opinion of this white drag queen, and most likely many of the other white drag queens who also competed unsuccessfully for the crown and title, the "realness" of gay Asian drag queens comes from their "more delicate features, smaller statures, and their ability to be more feminine." It is this ability to "pass" as real women, even when the lights go on, that give Asian drag queens a natural advantage in pageants.

While delicate features and smaller size may contribute to the overall illusion of "realness," perhaps it is the audience perception of gay Asian men, and Asian men in general, that ultimately leads to Asian drag queens being perceived as more "authentic." As such, it is not the physical characteristics of gay Asian drag queens, per se, that contributes to the illusion, but rather the inability of white audience members, and judges, to see them as anything other than female that is the real illusion. For example, in what has now become the most famous line from David Henry Hwang's acclaimed play, *M. Butterfly*, the protagonist Song Liling explains his ability to fool Rene Gallimard, a French diplomat, into believing that he was a woman for nearly two decades on Gallimard's inability to see him as anything but a woman rather than on his own abilities of deception.

"The West thinks of itself as masculine—big guns, big industry, big money—so the East is feminine—weak, delicate, poor . . ." Song tells the judge, "I am an Oriental. And being an Oriental, I could never be completely a man" (Hwang, 1986:83). In Song's opinion, it was Gallimard's inability to see him as anything other than a woman, because he was an "Oriental," a result of historical gendering of Asian men necessitated by global domination and conquest, which perpetuated the ruse. Precisely

Reprinted with permission from *Race, Gender & Class*, Vol. 13, No. 3/4 (2006), pp. 82–97.

because Asian men are feminized in Western minds, the Western mind is unable to see anything other than a female when gazing at a male "Oriental" body.

RACE AND MASCULINITY

By now, it is clear that race has always played an integral part of defining masculinity, with racial markers used to define "appropriate" masculine attributes and behaviors. As Michael Kimmel noted:

> The masculinity that defines white, middle class, early middle-aged, heterosexual men is the masculinity that sets the standards for other men, against which other men are measured and, more often than not, found wanting. (1994:124)

In this comparison, white masculinity, practiced in its hegemonic form (Connell, 1995), is largely based on homophobic, racist, and sexist notions regarding those who do not fit the model and maintains itself specifically by defining others as being feminine, constructed to be the opposite of masculine, or having failed at achieving the masculine norm.

Being defined outside of the masculine norm has negative consequences for men of color. In examining masculine identity among black men, Harris (1995:279) noted that black men are not able to achieve the "European American standards of manhood as provider, protector, and disciplinarian" and instead redefine masculinity in a way that emphasizes "sexual promiscuity, toughness, thrill seeking, and the use of violence in interpersonal relations" (280). Denied other cultural markers for being a successful "man," black men become hyper-masculine in the areas of masculinity that are available to them. This hyper-masculinization of black men is further propagated by the media's unrelenting portrayal of black men as being angry, violent, and criminal. As Lemelle and Battle (2004) note, this reliance on hyper-masculinity, in order to counter the stigmatized status of being black, may lead black men to also hold anti-homosexual attitudes and for black men who engage in same-sex

behaviors to remain closeted. As such, the hyper-masculinization of black men has consequences for both gay and straight black men.

Latino men have also been constructed along hyper-masculine lines similar to black men, if slightly less dangerous. Long stereotyped in the popular press, Latino men's machismo has come to be symbolized by sexual aggression, domination, and violence (Mirande, 1997). As such, this misrepresentation of machismo as strictly a hyper-masculine characteristic may lead Latino men to be seen similarly to black men as violent and dangerous (Morris, 2005). Like black men, the focus on machismo has consequences for both straight and gay Latino men. For example, Carballo-Diéguez and colleagues (2004) found that gendered stereotypes often dictate sexual behavior among gay Latino men with more masculine men taking on the dominant role while the more feminine men take on the submissive role during sexual interactions.

While black men and Latino men have been portrayed as hyper-masculine, David Eng (2001:16) points out that Asian American masculinity has always been and continues to be "produced, stabilized, and secured through mechanisms of gendering" that portray Asian men as asexual and/or feminine.

At the root of the process that has constructed Asian men as a gendered body lie various historical processes that have shaped what it means to be an Asian man in the white imagination. Far from a recent phenomenon, the gendering of Asian men has a long history in Western narratives. As Joseph Boone (2001) discusses, early European writings about the "orient" were filled with the sexual politics of colonialization that marked "oriental" men as feminine while at the same time constructing European men as masculine. As Boone puts it:

> For many Western men the act of exploring, writing about, and theorizing an eroticized Near and Middle East is coterminous with unlocking a Pandora's box of phantasmic homoerotic desire, desire whose propensity to spread without check threatens to contaminate, indeed to reorient, the heterosexual "essence" of occidental male subjectivity. (2001:50)

As such, the gendering of "oriental" men was used to disguise western homoerotic desires within the confines of occidental heterosexuality. As the logic goes, if the desired male "oriental" body was not really a male body, then the homoerotic desires of western travelers were not really homosexual. While Boone's analysis is limited to narratives about the Near and Middle East, the same orientalizing narratives were often used to describe Asian men from both East and South East Asia.

For example, early American media products helped to shape a gendered Asian male subject. In examining early American trade cards, Yuko Matsukawa (2002) notes the feminization of Asian men through various tactics such as equating Asian labor with domestic work and infantilizing Asian men during a time when immaturity was equated with femininity. Other writers, too, have rallied against the feminized images of Asian men in American media, most notably the editors of *The Big Aiiieee!* In the introduction, the editors lamented that by the mid-1980s, Asian men in the popular media "[were] at their best, effeminate closet queens like Charlie Chan and, at their worst, [were] homosexual menaces like Fu Manchu" (Chan et al., 1991:xiii). In fact, much of the twentieth-century representations of Asian men are an onslaught of feminine images (Hamamoto, 1994).

For the most part, Asian American men continue to be constructed by the media through this gendered lens. As Nguyen Tan Hoang points out:

> Despite the recent critical attention and popularity of Asian male actors in Asian cinema and its successful crossover into Hollywood (represented by such actors as Jackie Chan, Jet Li, and Chow Yun Fat, and directors such as Ang Lee and John Woo), the representation of Asian men as sexually appealing scarcely figures in mainstream American popular culture. (2004:225)

Thus, while Asian men have managed to stop being domestics or laundry workers in the western imagination, they nonetheless remain sexless.

While popular images are powerful tools in constructing images of the "other," legal policies can also act to construct racial meaning (Omi & Winant, 1986). Particularly, immigrant and racial policies have heavily contributed to the construction of a gendered Asian male. For example, Lisa Lowe (1996) points out that the racialized legal process that constructed Asian people as racial subjects through immigration and naturalization laws also had the effect of making gendered subjects out of Asian men who were denied the more masculine role of citizen and the rights inferred by that designation. Also, Asian exclusion laws, coupled with anti-miscegenation laws, led to the creation of a "bachelor society" among early Chinese male immigrants while labor laws relegated Asian men to feminine occupations such as laundry workers, domestics, and cooks in the largely male dominated west coast of the mid-19th and early 20th century (Chan, 1991; Espíritu, 1997). Thus, not being able to vote, work in masculine occupations, and marry also contributed to the formation of a gendered Asian male in the white imagination. When granted sexuality at all, Asian male sexuality was always depicted as a deviation from the normal white male heterosexuality. (Lee, 1999).

In this paper, I explore the intersection of race, gender, sexuality, and class inhibited by gay Asian men. To do so, I use narratives about Asian men, both gay and straight, from the popular press to examine how Asian men are feminized, and thus gendered, in popular discourse. Then I examine the narratives created by gay Asian men to expose the consequences that gendering can have on gay Asian men's self-esteem and well-being. [. . .]

GENDERING ASIAN MEN

The widespread perception of Asian men, gay, straight, and in-between, as feminine and foreign is blatant in a *Newsweek* article written by Ester Pan called, "Why Asian guys are on a roll." In it, Pan begins by telling us the story of Lisa Rosevear, who, "after getting divorced from an 'All-American guy' . . . was ready for something new." According to Pan, Rosevear "came up with a list of what she wanted in a man: smart, genuine, respectful. Adding it up, it occurred to her that guys who fit the bill were . . . Asian, a group she'd never considered romantically before" (Pan, 2000:50).

In Pan's telling of Rosevear's experience, two things become evident. First, it's apparent from Pan's narrative that "All-American" and "Asian" are mutually exclusive categories. In her portrayal of what Rosevear "wanted" and what she had before, one cannot be both "Asian" and "All-American." Rosevear, after all, goes looking for "something different" after divorcing an "All-American guy." Also, after labeling Rosevear's ex-husband as "All-American," Pan finds no need to elaborate on what it means to be "All-American." Rather, it is assumed that the reader has an intimate understanding of who belongs in that category. In a sense, it is Audre Lorde's "mythical norm" that we are supposed to conjure in our collective consciousness as we envision Rosevear on a quest to find "something different" (Lorde, 1984:116). In this way, the category of "All-American" is the given by which other categories are compared. If Asian men are "different" it is because they are different from the understood category of "All-American." As such, "All-American" is normalized and "Asian" is the problematized category that has to be explained and compared to the All-American norm. In pointing out that Rosevear wanted "something different," Pan places Asian men outside of this norm. What Rosevear finds, using the grocery list of gendered traits that are "different" from the traits possessed by the "All-American" guy, is a man who is "different" because he was envisioned to be so from the beginning. That is, Rosevear sought out difference and found it in a group she already perceived to be different. By extension, "All-American" men are not "smart, genuine, or respectful." In being "different," Asian men are not only non-American, they are also not "male."

In explaining this "phenomenon" of white women dating/marrying Asian men, Pan relies on racial stereotypes. If white women are dating/marrying Asian men at greater rates than before, it's not because stereotypes are proving to be wrong, but

because "in the age of Yahoo's cofounder Jerry Yang, traditionally negative stereotypes of Asian males as smart, studious and hardworking become positive" (Pan, 2000:50). As such, it's not that the stereotypes about Asian men being "smart, studious and hardworking" are proving to be false; rather, these things are becoming positives. By extension, if these things are positives and women are now finding Asian men attractive, then these things must have been true. Furthermore, rather than examining racial notions or racist legal policies that have hindered inter-racial marriages between Asian men and non-Asian women, she argues that the main reason that Asian men have not previously married non-Asian women was because "Asian men born in America face strong family pressure to be dutiful sons by marrying appropriate (read: same race, good family) women" (Pan, 2000:51). According to Pan, it's not white racism that limited the number of Asian men dating/marrying non-Asian women; it was Asian family pressure.

Not surprisingly, then, Pan quotes Rosevear as stating that "Asian boyfriends are the fashion accessory of the moment" (Pan, 2000:51). Much like the Chinese menu method (one from column A, one from column B, and one from column C) of selecting a mate employed by Rosevear, Asian men become nothing more than objectified fashion accessories when one tires of "All-American" husbands and "wants something different." In Pan's narrative, Asian men are an alternative to the "masculine" and patriarchal white male precisely because Asian men are not masculine and patriarchal.

Shortly after Pan's article appeared in *Newsweek*, the *Seattle Times* reprinted a tongue-in-cheek piece from the *Washington Post* on the front-page of the Living section which they marked with the unlikely title, "They're hot, they're sexy . . . they're Asian men" (Nakamura, 2000:E1). The clearly satirical piece, written by David Nakamura, exposed not only exposed the stereotypes that have long characterized Asian American men, but also those rampant in the *Newsweek* article.

What was most striking was not Nakamura's article itself but the flurry of letters to the editor that followed its publication. These letters, as well as letters posted on the website Model Minority, shows that Pan's perception of Asian men as being feminine and foreign is widespread among the general public rather than being a narrowly held interpretation by a single individual.

According to one white woman who posted on the Model Minority website about her Asian boyfriend: "I have found that many Asian men possess the combination of "old-fashioned" values and New Age insights that many women desire . . . Asian men are the best-kept secret around" (Stevenson, 2000).

A white woman wrote in the *Seattle Times*:

I have always preferred Asian males. In high school I was even made an "honorary Asian" and bought a jacket to match my friends . . . My Asian friends say I have "Asian fever." . . . I really like the way most Asian guys treat me—they are polite, highly intelligent, funny, and they have excellent taste in clothing, music, hair styles and cars. Many Asian guys have great respect for their family and native country. I don't like Asian guys who are "too" American—guys who deny their culture . . . (Baldwin, 2000:E1)

When describing the Asian man who was the "most dashing and romantic of [her] loves," one white woman wrote: "With his tight jeans, leather jacket and glorious waist-length black hair pulled into a ponytail, he was, by far, the hottest and sexiest man in the room" (Dell, 2000:E1).

In describing Asian male features, one white woman wrote:

I am a short white woman, and I actually like to be with men who are closer to my height . . . I have dated several men of color, all colors, and have found their semi-outsider status to provide some welcome relief from white male dominance . . . (Phares, 2000:E1)

Another explained her love for her husband of 26 years by stating: "I always loved his slender physique and his beautiful eyes" (Sequeira, 2000:E1). Creating a laundry list of stereotypes, one white woman wrote in:

I found the perfect male: a man my father would like, from a respectable family, with a good work ethic,

who still believed in monogamy . . . Let's just say that Asian men make love even better than they make television sets. (Donohue, 2000:E1)

Even Asian women couldn't help but reduce Asian men to racial stereotypes:

I feel most Asian men lack the "physical" definition of being sexy, but mentally and intellectually they are the top of the crop. If I'm talking to a man and he listens, respects, remembers and understands me, I find it very stimulating. Asian men are that. I have high regard for their tendency to work hard, persevere and be family-oriented. (La, 2000:E1)

Taken together, the narratives provided by white women, and the Asian woman, expose the battery of stereotypes deployed against Asian men to construct them as being more feminine than white men. First, Asian men, when desired at all, are desired for traditionally feminine traits. As much as Rosevear has objectified her attraction toward Asian men, the women represented by these narratives have also come to view Asian men as an "alternative" to the masculine "All-American boy." For one, Asian men are "best-kept secrets" and described in much the same way that white diners often describe "exotic and authentic Oriental" restaurants, even those that are packed nightly with an Asian clientele. Only when whites validate the restaurant's status is the "secret" let out of the bag. One wonders if the hundreds of millions of Asian women who remain in Asia have been let in on the "secret."

The one printed letter from a gay Asian man is indicative of the gendering of Asian men within the gay community. In his letter, he states:

I am a very out Asian gay man . . . I have a master's in architecture from UCLA and a high managerial position in a large firm. My dates, most of them white, admire my dark complexion and smooth skin. Perhaps like Asian women, gay Asian men are seen as exotic and culturally mysterious. It is even better in Europe. (Heng, 2000:El)

Two things are telling about the letter written by a gay Asian man. First is the conflating of both male and female gendered expectations. The writer first begins by describing his "male" accomplishments of a prestigious college degree and his "managerial position in a large firm." At the same time, he emphasizes the "feminine" qualities about himself that he believes are attractive to white men, that of having smooth skin and being seen as exotic and mysterious. So while he claims masculine qualities about himself, he quickly emphasizes his feminine qualities. In the event that anyone would perceive himself being seen this way as a problem, he adds, "It is even better in Europe."

THE GAY ASIAN MALE EXPERIENCE

Portrayals of Asian men in mainstream "gay" magazines haven't deviated from what is found in "straight" media products. In fact, Asian men are even more gendered in gay publications than in mainstream publications (Han, 2008). While several scholars have noted the virtual absence of gay Asian men in "gay" media products, when presented at all, they are often portrayed as the submissive sexual partner only present for white male consumption (Fung, 1996). As Maurice Poon notes, "such images certainly will have a negative impact on gay Asian men's self-esteem and self-worth" (2000:47), particularly in contemporary gay culture where masculinity is valued over femininity, aggressive is favored over submissive, and white is favored over color. Given the invisibility of Asian images in gay publications and the abundance of white male images that are presented as the gay ideal, it isn't surprising that gay Asian men report an overwhelming preference for white sexual partners (Choi et al., 1996; Matteson, 1997; Ridge et al., 1999). In fact:

> The sexually marginalized Asian man who has grown up in the West or is western in his thinking is often invisible in his own fantasies. [Their] sexual daydreams are populated by handsome Caucasian men with lean, hard Caucasian bodies. (Ayers, 1999:91)

So infrequent is the sight of gay Asian men dating other Asian men that Marcus Hu, president of Strand Releasing, was quoted in the *New York Blade*, a local gay newspaper, as stating, "When people saw my Chinese boyfriend and I, other Asian gay guys would stare and ask, 'Oh my god, you two are together?!'" (Noh, 2002).

The problem, of course, is that white men, also subjugated to the same images bombarded on them by the gay press, also favor white men as sexual partners. As such, "Caucasian men interested in Asian men are perceived to be far fewer in number relative to the number of Asian men" (Ridge et al., 1999:57). In such an unbalanced "mate market," social relations between gay Asian men and gay white men illustrate the discrepancy of power we normally see in gendered interactions. In such instances, white men are granted the power to pick their sexual partners while Asian men must be chosen (McCaskell, 1998). In fact, Song Cho writes:

> While white men cruised looking for their prey, most Asians stood back, lined up against the wall like beauty pageant queens waiting to be chosen. With all the attention focused on white guys, I instinctively knew that as a gay Asian, I rarely had the power to choose and would always be the one chosen. (1998:3)

As such, gay Asian men have less power in negotiating with their white partners who are perceived by Asian men as being more desirable than other men. Predictably, gay Asian men come to see each other as competitors rather than potential allies (Chang, 2001; Ridge et al., 1999).

Not surprisingly, gay Asian men report feeling inadequate within the larger gay community that stresses a Eurocentric image of physical beauty (Ayers, 1999; Choi et al., 1998; Chuang, 1999). Given these feelings of inadequacy, gay Asian men may suffer low levels of self-esteem and actively pursue the company of white men in order to feel accepted by the gay mainstream. In addition to seeking the company of white men over that of other Asian men, the obsession with white beauty leads gay Asian men to reject all aspects of themselves as Asian. For example, Chuang (1999:33) writes about how he tried desperately to avoid anything related to his Chinese heritage and his attempts to transform his "shamefully slim Oriental frame . . . into a more desirable western body."

The prevalent belief that Asian men are feminine and thus desirable for only a small subset of gay men looking for "femmes" leads to an unbalanced situation when it comes to interpersonal relationships. As Poon notes: "The beauty standard contributes in part to an observed phenomenon in which many Asian men in their 20s are in relationships with Caucasian men who are often twice their age" (2000:48).

Personal narratives written by gay Asian men also point to this phenomenon. For example, Kent Chuang noted:

> I believed that I was trapped in a circle of old men and leeches in their forties, fifties and sometimes older, unfit or fat, unattractive bordering on repulsive. "The only reason they want us is because they can't get a white boy," one Asian friend told me . . . I concluded that us ugly Asians couldn't get a white boy so we settled for financial and emotional security with old rice queens. Asians sacrificed youth for security, and rice queens sacrificed color for youth . . . I had flashbacks to the gay classifieds: "Mature man has own place and videos, seeks shy Asian for friendship. Students and beginners welcome. I'm patient and discreet." (1999:32)

As for "desirable" white men, Chuang had this to say:

> The reality is that most Asian men wouldn't get a second look from a young, good-looking Caucasian guy. Even if they do look, they still need to be man enough to overcome the stigma of going out with or even picking up an Asian guy in front of their friends. Any Caucasian seen going out with an Asian is in danger of being thought of as desperate unless he is gorgeous, and then everyone is puzzled that he would choose an Asian partner when he could get so many "desirable" white boys. (1999:38)

In fact, in an ad hoc study using gay personal ads, Poon found that white men who were seeking Asian men tended to be between 39 and 58, while Asian men seeking white men tended to be between 18 and 38 (Poon, 2000). Given the difference in age, Poon hypothesizes that gay Asian and white relationships are more likely to be marked by differences in income levels, which "would generally have a negative impact on their self-esteem and self-worth" (2000:51).

Given both the social and economic dominance of white men over their Asian partners, coupled with the age difference of partners, Poon hypothesizes that gay Asian men may also be more vulnerable to domestic violence than white men. While no empirical studies regarding gay Asian men and domestic violence exist, Poon argues that the power imbalance found in gay Asian and white relationships puts gay Asian men at a marked disadvantage while also creating a situation, such as low self-esteem, social isolation, and dependence on the part of the Asian partner and a sense of self-importance and a perception that their behavior will not have negative consequences, where the white partner might be more likely to become a batterer (2000).

As might be expected, gay Asian men are often expected by their white partners to take the "submissive" role of sexual bottoms during anal intercourse (Han, 2006; Kumashiro, 1999). Given the pressure to find a white partner, it is not surprising that many gay Asian men take this role (Murry, 2003). The taking of the "feminine" role within gay relationships by gay Asian men with white male partners also spills over into their public lives (Chuang, 1999; Hwang, 1986). Unfortunately, the expectation by gay white men that gay Asian men will take the "feminine" role, coupled with the scarcity of potential white male partners, leads to the unfortunate situation where gay Asian men have less power within gay relationships and opens them up to potential negative consequences.

While empirical evidence regarding specific sexual behaviors of gay Asian men with white partners is scarce, some anecdotal evidence seems to support the conclusion that the perceived lack of white partners negatively influences gay Asian men's sexual behavior. For example, in an *AsianWeek* article, journalist Alethea Yip quotes Dredge Kang, director of education and prevention services at the

Asian Pacific AIDS Intervention Team in Los Angeles, as stating:

> One of the things that came out [of the focus group] was that Asian men said they don't use condoms with white men . . . They fear rejection and they look up to a white gay-male ideal. They feel intimidation from white partners and they are unable to convince their white partners to use condoms . . . It's power dynamics. (Yip, 1996:12)

Given this "fear" of losing a potential white partner, gay Asian men may also find themselves in unsafe sexual situations, furthering their HIV risk.

DISCUSSION

Rather than simply a matter of academic debate regarding identity construction, failure to see that a person can occupy multiple statuses, that these statuses are not simply additive but are multiplicative, and acknowledging the intersectionality of these "identities" has real-world implications, often of self-esteem and despair, safety and peril, and life and death. I've discussed above how marginalization in the gay and ethnic communities through racializing and gendering may lead gay Asian men to have low self-esteem, possibly be victimized in domestic relationships, and engage in unsafe sex.

Within the dominant gay community, gay Asian men are socially constructed to be feminine, submissive, and undemanding—thus desirable only for a select subgroup of men who favor "femmes" over "real" men. On the flip side of this coin, gay white men are often constructed to be masculine—thus, universally desirable (Levin, 1998). More importantly, gay white men are presented as prizes for gay men of color and rewards for playing by the unspoken rules of the gay community. That is, if gay men of color provide for the sexual fantasies of gay white men, they will be rewarded with the company of those whom the gay community deems acceptable. Swirled in this context, gay Asian men find themselves "performing" the roles of submissive sexual bottoms to white male tops (Carrier, Nguyen, & Su,

1992; Murry, 2003). More importantly, gay Asian men are socially conditioned to not question white male supremacy within the white-centered gay community.

As such, it is likely that stereotypical images of gay Asian men may influence how they come to see themselves and the sexual roles that they take in their relationships with white men and play, at least, a small role in their identity formation and role adoption. Because these "roles" are mediated through race, sexuality, gender, age, and possibly class, it is critical that we examine these intersections for ways to address critical issues among gay Asian men.

According to Walters (1999), the development of healthy group and self identities, including the facilitation of the pressures of the dominant society with the competing demands of their own ethnic, racial, and sexual communities, can lead to psychological well-being for gays and lesbians of color. As such, she recommends not only acculturation into the gay communities, but enculturation into racial and ethnic communities as well. In this paper, I expand the conceptualization of "demands" to include expected behaviors placed on various individuals as a result of their racial, sexual, gendered, and class positions within the communities in which they navigate. I position that it is the unsuccessful negotiation of these demands that can ultimately lead to emotional consequences and unsafe sexual behavior for gay Asian men.

If gay Asian men are heavily acculturated into the dominant gay community, they may be more susceptible to accepting the stereotypes routinely found in the dominant gay community of Asian men being submissive, quiet, non-confrontational, and "feminine." In addition, they are more likely to accept the prevailing belief of "white is best," the mentality found in the dominant gay culture. Once these stereotypes of Asian men and the pedestalization of white men are accepted by gay Asian men, they may be more likely to develop high rates of internalized racism, leading to detrimental consequences for both their emotional and physical health. In order to negotiate within the white-centered community and find acceptance within it, gay Asian men who are so inclined may be more likely to be accepting of their sexual roles within the dominant gay community, leading to a racialized and gendered role performance within interactions with gay white men. However, it is possible that a strong ethnic identity, a stronger sense of ethnic pride, can work to balance the negative racial stereotypes found in the gay community. As such, we need to examine all facets of gay Asian male experiences if we are to arrive at a true understanding of the various social factors that influence their identity formation and their sexual behaviors.

REFERENCES

Ainsworth, S., & Hardy, C. (2004). Critical discourse analysis and identity: Why bother? *Critical Discourse Studies*, 1:225–259.

Ayers, T. (1999). China doll: The experience of being a gay Chinese Australian. *Journal of Homosexuality*, 36:87–97.

Baldwin, S. (2000, June 9). Letter to the editor. *Seattle Times*, p. El.

Boone, J. (2001). Vacation cruises; or, the homoerotics of orientalism. In J. Hawley (Ed.), *Post-colonial Queer*, pp. 43–78. Albany, NY: State University of New York Press.

Carballo-Diéguez, A., Dolezal, Nieves, C. L., Diaz, F., Decena, C., & Balan, I. (2004). Looking for a tall, dark, macho man . . . sexual-role behaviour variations in Latino gay and bisexual men. *Culture, Health and Sexuality*, 6:159–171.

Carrier, J., Nguyen, B., & Su, S. (1992). Vietnamese American sexual behavior and HIV infection. *Journal of Sex Research*, 29:547–560.

Chan, J., Chin, J., Inada, L., & Wong, S. (Eds.) (1991). *The Big Aiiieeeee! An Anthology of Chinese American and Japanese American Literature*. New York: Meridian.

Chan, S. (1991). *Asian Americans: An Interpretive History*. Boston: Twayne Publishers.

Chang, J. (2001, February/March). The truth about GAM. *Magazine*, 58–60.

Cho, S. (1998). *Rice: Explorations into Gay Asian Culture and Politics*. Toronto: Queer Press.

Choi, K. H., Lew, S., Vittinghoff, E., Barret, D., Catania, J. A., & Coates, T. J. (1996). The efficacy of brief group counseling in HIV risk reduction among gay Asian and Pacific Islander men. *AIDS*, 10:81–87.

Choi, K. H., Yep, G., & Kumekawa, E. (1998). HIV prevention among Asian and Pacific Islander American men who have sex with men: A critical review of theoretical models and directions for future research. *AIDS Education and Prevention*, 10:19–30.

Chuang, K. (1999). Using chopsticks to eat steak. *Journal of Homosexuality*, 36:29–41.

Connell, R. W. (1995). *Masculinities*. Berkeley: University of California Press.

Dell, D. (2000, June 9). Letter to the editor. *Seattle Times*, p. E1.

Donohue, P. (2000, June 9). Letter to the editor. *Seattle Times*, p. E1.

Eng, D. (2001). *Racial Castration: Managing Masculinity in Asian America*. Durham: Duke University Press.

Espiritu, Y. (1997). *Asian American Women and Men: Labor, Laws, and Love*. Thousand Oak, CA: Sage Publications.

Fung, R. (1996). Looking for my penis. In R. Leong (Ed.), *Asian American Sexualities: Dimensions of the Gay and Lesbian Experience*, pp. 181–198. New York: Routledge.

Harris, S. M. (1995). Psychosocial development and black male masculinity: Implications for counseling economically disadvantaged African American male adolescents. *Journal of Counseling and Development*, 73:279–287.

Hamamotoa, D. (1994). *Monitored Peril: Asian Americans and the Politics of TV Representation*. Minneapolis: University of Minnesota Press.

Han, C. (2006). Geisha of a different kind: Gay Asian men and the gendering of sexual identity. *Sexuality and Culture*, 10:3–28.

Han, C. (2008). Sexy like a girl and horny like a boy. *Critical Sociology*, 34(6):829–850.

Heng, Y. (2000, June 9). Letter to the editor. *Seattle Times*, p. El.

Huckin, T. (1995). Critical discourse analysis. In T. Miller (Ed.), *Functional Approaches to Written Text* [electronic format]. Paris: USIS.

Hwang, D. (1986). *M. Butterfly*. New York: Plume Books.

Kimmel, M. (1994). Masculinities as homophobia: Fear, shame, and silence in the construction of gender identity. In H. Brod & M. Kaufman (Eds.), *Theorizing Masculinities*, pp. 119–141. Newbury Park, CA: Sage.

Kumashiro, K. (1999). Supplementing normalcy and otherness: Queer Asian American men reflect on stereotypes, identity, and oppression. *Qualitative Studies in Education*, 12:491–508.

La, H. (2000, June 9). Letter to the editor. *Seattle Times*, p. E1.

Lee, R. (1999). *Orientals: Asian Americans in Popular Culture*. Philadelphia: Temple University Press.

Lemelle, A., & Battle, J. (2004). Black masculinity matters in attitudes toward gay males. *Journal of Homosexuality*, 47:39–51.

Levin, M. (1998). *Gay Macho: The Life and Death of the Homosexual Clone*. New York: New York University Press.

Lorde, A. (1984). *Sister Outsider: Essays and Speeches*. Trumansburg, NY: The Crossing Press.

Lowe, L. (1996). *Immigrant Acts*. Durham: Duke University Press.

Matsukawa, Y. (2002). Representing the oriental in nineteenth-century trade cards. In J. Lee, I. Lim, & Y. Matsukawa (Eds.), *Re-collecting Early Asian America: Essays in Cultural History*, pp. 200–217. Philadelphia: Temple University Press.

Matteson, D. R. (1997). Bisexual and homosexual behavior and HIV risk among Chinese, Filipino, and Korean American men. *Journal of Sex Research*, 34:93–104.

McCaskell, T. (1998). Towards a sexual economy of rice queenliness: Lust, power and racism. In S. Cho (Ed.), *Rice: Explorations into Gay Asian Culture and Politics*, pp. 45–48. Toronto: Queer Press.

Mirandé, A. (1997). *Hombres y Machos: Masculinity and Latino Culture*. Boulder: Westview Press.

Morris, E. (2005). "Tuck in that shirt!" Race, class, gender and discipline in an urban school. *Sociological Perspectives*, 48:25–48.

Murry, S. (2003). Representations of desire in some recent gay Asian-American writings. *Journal of Homosexuality*, 45:111–142.

Nakamura, D. (2000, February 27). The Asian advantage; suddenly, it's great to be me. *Washington Post*, p. B05.

Nguyen, T. (2004). The resurrection of Brandon Lee: The making of a gay Asian American porn star. In L. Williams (Ed.), *Porn Studies*, pp. 223–270. Durham: Duke University Press.

Omi, M., & Winant, H. (1994). *Racial Formation in the United States*. New York: Routledge.

Pan, E. (2000, February 21). Why Asian guys are on a roll. *Newsweek*, 50–51.

Phares, M. (2000, June 9). Letter to the editor. *Seattle Times*, p. E1.

Poon, M. K. (2000). Inter-racial same-sex abuse: The vulnerability of Gay men of Asian descent in relationships with Caucasian men. *Journal of Gay and Lesbian Social Services*, 11:39–67.

Ridge, D., Hee, A., & Minichiello, V. (1999). "Asian" men on the scene: Challenges to "gay" communities. *Journal of Homosexuality*, 36:43–68.

Sequeira, L. (2000, June 9). Letter to the editor. *Seattle Times*, p. E1.

Stevenson, M. (2000). Letter to the editor. Model Minority: A Guide to Asian American Empowerment [website]. Retrieved October 18, 2005, from http://modelminority.com/modules.php?name=New&file=article&sid=100

Walters, K. (1999). Negotiating conflicts in allegiances among lesbians and gays of color: Reconciling divided selves and communities. In G. Mallon (Ed.), *Foundations of Social Work Practice*, pp. 45–75. New York: Harrington Park Press.

Yip, A. (1996, December 5). Until there's a cure: APAs step up the fight against HIV and AIDS. *AsianWeek*, 18, p. 11.

57. • *Dominique C. Hill*

(MY) LESBIANISM IS NOT A FIXED POINT (2017)

Dominique C. Hill, Ph.D., is a queer Black feminist creative whose life work is dedicated to highlighting and unearthing overlooked knowledges and experiences emanating from Black life and girlhood. Hill takes seriously making space for Black girls and women to unpack life and imagine anew. Hill is the recent recipient of the Distinguished Dissertation Award in experimental qualitative research by the International Congress of Qualitative Inquiry and co-author of *Who Look at Me?! Shifting the Gaze of Education Through Blackness, Queerness, and The Body.* Dr. Hill is an Assistant Professor of Women's Studies at Colgate University.

I.

I've been scrolling through profiles for hours now. Blackplanet (the black and mostly hetero cyber community for dating) has *way* too many visitors. Why do I have to be in the middle of nowhere? Aside from myself there isn't a lesbian that I would date in sight! It would be a lot easier if I were home in Buffalo or New York City or even Syracuse, I surmise—anywhere but here. In this town of not quite 3,000 people, there are a few girls secretly interested in trying me but that s*** gets old. Don't get me wrong; it's thrilling, momentarily. I respect and understand being confused and/or disinterested in publicly declaring an interest in me, but I don't support performing the character "avid homophobe" in public so your friends who *know* about me (read: know I deal with women) remain unassuming about you. Nor am I moved by the church hugs to keep your distance while whispering in my ear, "You know I want you, right?" No! I want to be with another lesbian. Scratch that, a black lesbian. At the very least, I need someone whose default performance is not "avid homophobe." That means (sigh), that means I'm gonna keep scrolling through these damn profiles. One will jump out at me, I hope.

> She wears dresses
> Pumps and thongs
> I like that.
> She wants me,
> fitted hat and baggy sweats
> Not feeling it!

My lesbian packaging was (and remains) aberrant, to some. Committing to black community solidarity on campus situated me as a rising black nationalist. Working at the Women's Center and leading a women of color awareness and support group made me a strong candidate for the title A-rate black feminist. Somehow my lesbianism could be overlooked, misconstrued as "mannish" femininity. Either way, my sexuality was a craft, something I had to carve up and create for myself. Additionally, being black, female, involved in the black community on campus, interested in black women—with no car—made dating a bit difficult. I took to the Internet and found my first girlfriend—a black woman who, like me, loved wearing thongs and heels. Despite her meeting me through cyberspace as feminine presenting, my degree of femininity slightly bothered her. Maybe it was a predilection for my transgressive behavior or a foreshadowing of her return to men and heterosexuality. Nonetheless, it became abundantly clear that my performance of what it meant to be a lesbian wasn't rebellious enough.

II.

My mom insists on giving me money when going out with my feminine heterosexual friends. Also known as my femme friends. Also known as my ex-girlfriend and her friend who's slightly curious. No curfew. No questions. "Have fun!" she says, waving. Yet, when kickin' it with my masculine girlfriend, a dom, a soft stud as she called herself, there are *always* questions. Like, "Where are you going?" "When are you coming back?" Followed by the demand, "Don't be out all night!" And finally, "Do you have to go out with *those* people?!" I guess it didn't occur to her, I am one of *those* people. I guess I should've kept company with femmes only. Maybe then my lesbianism would remain less of a problem. That's just it—being a lesbian causes disruption.

> Dyke!, she yelled
> I don't want my son 'round
> A bunch of dykes licking and kissing each other!
> Merry Christmas!
> I'm a dyke,
> I guess

Identity involves performance. This epiphany broke me, only to put me back together again in 2003. The fact that my tomboyish ways as a child did not convert into baggy masculine clothing allowed my mother to dismiss my sexuality. Forget that I told her two years before in the local Pizza Hut near my university that I liked women. Forget that I labeled myself a lesbian. Up until this moment, I had not considered that my clothing could mark or in this case allow me to pass as heterosexual. Add my blackness to my style of dress and my sexuality could be disappeared altogether (see Harris-Perry 2011; McCune 2014)! While—prior to this unfortunate encounter with my mother—I deemed the labeling of myself as lesbian enough, I soon realized labels function only as an initial conversation starter. The small talk ends when others begin reading and interpreting my performance.

How do I want to dress up my dykeness?

III.

Labels are flat. This is what I tell myself while sitting on my living room floor thinking about who I am and who I was. How else can I explain that my particular lesbianism includes no disdain for men? How do I call myself a lesbian when I'm attracted and the only things present are a man and his art (DJing/love for music)? I keep asking myself this question. Self? No answer. And how do I make sense of the burst of energy I get after making a man do things (sexual things) he said he would not? Power? A dent in patriarchy? What I know is that I'm ashamed, yet aroused. Overcome by an unsolicited and unjustifiable feeling as well as an intrinsic urge to be me, unapologetically, I—unafraid—go against the grain of what "normal"

lesbians do and enter into a relationship with the opposite sex. Truth is, I feel like someone's gonna come and revoke my "lesbian" card.

"Some Call Me a Misfit"
Some call me a misfit because I say my home is in my mind
Every day I am trying to *trans*cend your limited perception of me
In college, I kissed a woman and smiled afterward
How could home be anywhere but where I am?
Even as we speak I am *trans*itioning into some place, some space
Trying to take responsibility for once deeming myself lesbian and now just ME
Some call me confused because I refuse labels
When I wake up my mind has already been in *trans*it for a
lifetime
Last year I sexed a Black man
Home is nestled in between my soul and spirit *trans*forming in meaning
Some call people like me Black
Some call people like me Feminists
Some call people like me Weird
Some call people like me anything to crush my spirit
Some call people like me Ugly
I call people like me revolutionary
I am a living vessel of Revolution as process
I am a lesbian because I say I am!

IV.

I (silently and reluctantly) turned in my lesbian card for a queer one. Dating a man means you have to, right? Having sex with a man means you have to right? But why?! When I take my clothes off and we have sex, it's just that, sex. I am moved by the possibility of overtaking him, of inciting an earthquake in his body, of controlling him. There is no love in that! No love in control; at least not for me. And yet I stay. Proving (although unintentionally) two points to myself: (1) My sexual identity and its expression is fluid and not fixed; it can, and therefore should be, disruptive; and (2) I am a lesbian. I shoulda kept my lesbian card. Who said I had to turn that s*** in anyway?! And why did I listen to them?!

"Layered Living"
"Which do you put first?" they asked Aunt
  Barbara,
I'm sure she cringed.
Which do I put first?
Depends on the day and what you mean by first.
I suppose Black.
Seems I knew that space first,
Being black in the United States,
raised in highly segregated Buffalo.
Who benefits from me drawing lines around
  myself,
around my lesbianism,
with a separate circle around my blackness,

pretending they don't dance in the dark?
Aunt Cheryl considers my sexuality political.
Resist, she said.
Discourse.
Norms.
Power.
Contest these, she insisted.
Which do you put first,
how you see me or how I see me?
Behavior or labels?
Which do I put first?
Depends on the day and what you mean by first.
I am a blacklesbian,
with a queer aesthetic.
Trying to draw lines around that?
Don't bother.
Resist, I will.

WORKS CITED

Clarke, Cheryl. "Lesbianism: An Act of Resistance." *This Bridge Called My Back: Writings by Radical Women of Color.* Kitchen Table: Women of Color Press, 1981, pp. 128–37.

Harris-Perry, Melissa V. *Sister Citizen: Shame, Stereotypes, and Black Women in America.* Yale UP, 2011.

McCune Jr., Jeffrey Q. *Sexual Discretion: Black Masculinity and the Politics of Passing.* University of Chicago Press, 2014.

Smith, Barbara. *The Truth That Never Hurts: Writings on Race, Gender, and Freedom.* Rutgers UP, 2000.

58. • *Christina Crosby*

MASCULINE, FEMININE, OR FOURTH OF JULY (2016)

Christina Crosby is a Professor of English and Feminist, Gender, and Sexuality Studies at Wesleyan University. She is the author of *The Ends of History: Victorians and the "Woman Question"* (1991) and *A Body Undone: Living on After Great Pain* (2017), from which the following essay was excerpted.

Babe the Dog was a lab and golden retriever mix, born on the Fourth of July, or at least close enough that I could claim the parades and fireworks as a celebration of that auspicious event. At home the dog would get an extra Milk-Bone treat, and the people would get a mint chocolate chip ice cream cake with chocolate fudge icing from Baskin-Robbins. When the local Baskin-Robbins closed, it was replaced by another ice cream franchise. What could we do? Janet called to place the order.

"We don't have fudge icing."

"What do you have?"

"Masculine, feminine, or Fourth of July."

"What? But . . .," Janet stumbled, "but, we want *fudge*. And, and . . . it's for the *dog*—we have a dog, and it's her birthday."

Janet pressed the point but ended up just saying, "Whatever." I don't remember the icing, other than that it was disappointingly *not* fudge. Nor can I recall ordering again from that particular shop. I have, however, many times used the line "masculine, feminine, or Fourth of July" to teach both the absurdity and the normative power of gender. There in a list of choices are its two wholly naturalized categories and a comically out-of-place national holiday, but the seemingly misplaced Fourth of July serves to remind us that a laughably simple and punishingly binary notion of gender is enforced by the powers that be, including the state. Gender, which is a state of mind and embodied attitude, is a site of volatile power, pleasure, and subtle coercion, often used to discipline our thoughts and bodily affects. Normative gender is certainly wielded as a weapon by children anxious to shore up their own selfhood by challenging someone else's. Consult your memory and you'll find that this is true.

Sadly, madly, every birth certificate offers two—and only two—sexes, and only one may be declared. Sex is the first question in every mouth after a birth, and infants are quite ruthlessly assigned to one body or the other, despite the fact that intersex births are far more common than you would think, as the important work of biologist Ann Fausto-Sterling has demonstrated. If innate biology offers no firm foundation for a superstructure of twos, neither does the social world. Parents, teachers, siblings, peers, physicians, pastors, psychologists, and those who enforce the law, all solicit a child to shelter itself under one gender or the other, but many kids refuse, sometimes at considerable cost to themselves.

Gender can also afford embodied pleasures, if one is confident in instantiating it and pleased with the results. It's now possible to modify your body to conform to your felt sense of gender. I've taught students who came to Wesleyan sexed and gendered as (more or less) feminine women, but graduated as trans men (FTM) with deepened voices and beards, their bodies modified by top surgeries—the removal of breasts—and shots of testosterone (T). There's no necessity dictating that a bodymind sexed female at birth will present itself to the world as feminine in adulthood, and no necessary sexuality tied to either sex or gender. "[T]he longer I hang around the various crossroads and deltas of gender, the more I notice that nothing is clear enough to be easy," writes S. Bear Bergman, a trans man who's hung around long enough to be well recognized in the queer-trans community as an author of first-person accounts. Today young people who transform their official gender may be accepted, even celebrated—more than one transgender girl has been elected homecoming queen—but transgender teenagers have been murdered in school, too. Larry (Latisha) King, a slight, effeminate fifteen-year-old boy relentlessly hounded as a "faggot," was killed, shot in the head by a high school classmate offended by Latisha's feminine bearing, flirtatious manner, makeup, and high-heeled boots. Children yoked with a gender they don't recognize as their own or who are confused can be made to suffer cruelly in a world that naturalizes and links together binary sex and gender. If you make it into young adulthood, you may be able to use the force field of gender for your own pleasure and toward your own ends, but straight is the gate and narrow the way.

Once I got to college, I didn't give much thought to my gender and devoted lots to my sexuality. Most of the time I wore flannel shirts and jeans, sneakers and boots. The first lesbian activists in the gay liberation movement whom I met in 1972 declared themselves relieved that they now could go to the bars liberated from the felt necessity to identify as either butch or femme. So those gendered sexualities seemed to me and my friends a thing of the past, something to be playfully gestured toward but not seriously taken up. In the spring of my senior year, for instance, I picked up a black tuxedo jacket at a yard sale and stepped out to a big party wearing it with my freshly washed white painter pants. I stopped on the way to pick a white rose from the president's rose garden for my buttonhole, and joined my friends feeling quite dashing.

This sort of "soft butch" style was not, however, to be taken seriously, because we were lesbian feminists who thought that asserting masculine/feminine anywhere, by anyone, was a patriarchal dead end. Butch/femme was something to sport with rather than a deeply felt commitment to honor. Lesbian sexuality seemed to me to have nothing to do with masculinity—or femininity, for that matter, though lesbianism was integral to a feminism that sought to liberate all women. Sex was just sexy. Commitments to explicitly feminine and masculine styles were to my mind outmoded and irrelevant. I've done a lot of reading and talking since then, and have come to regret this position so insensitive to the complexities of desire and the stylizations specific to race and class, but such was my youthful understanding. When several years ago I read Amber Hollibaugh's book *My Dangerous Desires*, I recognized myself as one who would have discounted her and her sweetheart had we met in the 1970s. She's a big, beautiful, dedicated femme who showed up with her decidedly butch lover at a meeting where they were both written off as relics of a superseded past. She was rejected by a movement for sexual liberation she'd been a part of from the first. Amber, please accept my apologies.

* * *

In the 1950s and 1960s, one place butch/femme genders were elaborated was working-class bar culture—you can get a vivid sense of the stakes by reading *Stone Butch Blues*, an autobiographical

bildungsroman that recounts how a young butch comes of age in the bars and factories of Buffalo, New York. For another approach to the same scene, read *Boots of Leather, Slippers of Gold*, an oral history of working-class lesbian life that famously dedicates itself to "understand[ing] butch-fem culture from an insider's perspective." (Both books have been recently reissued, clear evidence of ongoing interest in how gender is stylized.) My lover in graduate school was older than I, and had grown up in a lower-middle-class neighborhood surrounded by New Jersey affluence. She wanted to have nothing to do with the culture of those bars. When I was in graduate school, Elizabeth and I once went to a bar in Pawtucket, a worn-out working-class town just north of Providence. The place was mostly empty, though several women were playing pool, most of them large, all with short haircuts, wearing shirts and pants. It seemed sad and lifeless to Elizabeth, though I could imagine having fun drinking Miller High Life and hanging out in a place so far distant from my library carrel. I drank a Miller and she had a bad glass of wine. We never returned.

Elizabeth's dislike was, I think, solidly grounded in a refusal to be identified with a lower-class stylization of life. Her mother, a gifted seamstress, conspired with her daughter to transform Elizabeth into a girl who could, without any faltering and with no misstep, date a boy who belonged to the Windy Hollow Hunt Club and rode to hounds. He invited her to the annual Hunt Ball, and had the pleasure of a beautiful, fashionable date on his arm. Elizabeth said he was handsome, but dumb as a brick. Things started looking up her first year in college, when she fell in love with a Jewish girl from New York City—a striver like herself, but from a world entirely different: from suburban New Jersey. I don't know what her girlfriend studied, but Elizabeth was a French major who longed for the elegance and intellectual sophistication of Paris. When they graduated in 1962, they were off to the City of Lights.

Elizabeth was to return to Paris again and again, first as a graduate student studying the most experimental of experimental French novels, and then as a professor of French language and literature. When she spoke to me of those years, she told me that the Katmandou, a nightclub at 21 rue Vieux Colombier, was fabulous, and when we went together to Paris in 1990, we hoped to find it still open, only to be disappointed. I discovered an Internet site memorializing its history when I googled the name. It was "a sophisticated place, patronized by relatively well-heeled women and celebrities, whether lesbian or not: the place was therefore quite exclusive socially," and promised attractive decadence. As the club's publicity pointedly announced, "The girls are young, modern, [and wear] miniskirts, [not the] antique male costume of the other clubs."

* * *

When Janet and I took up gender in the waning years of the 1990s, I once again sported with "masculinity," while Janet elaborated a fabulous "femininity" for her amusement and mine. In those years, lesbian genders often reprised butch and femme styles in a purportedly "postmodern" sort of way—it was the era of the *Rocky Horror Picture Show* revival on Broadway and doing the time warp dance ("Oh, fantasy free me . . ."). We dressed for our own pleasure, certainly, but also as a way of being quickly legible as lesbians. Butches have it easier, in that regard, than femme lesbians, who are almost always read as heterosexual—except when in a butch–femme couple. When we would "go to New York," as we called it when going to some cultural event in the city, we'd dress up, as we did once when heading out for a decidedly feminist/queer musical put on by the rock 'n' roll band Betty. I vividly remember leaving the apartment, because the lobby had a huge mirror that reflected our happiness and high style—I was in a white silk shirt with French cuffs, gold and silver cufflinks (Janet's gift, from Tiffany's no less!), black velvet jacket, red leather boot-cut pants, and black cowboy boots. Janet wore a long-sleeved white shirt that you could see right through, a sleeveless shirt with an icon of the Virgin Mary on its front, a short gray skirt, and gorgeous red pumps with four-inch heels. Off to the first show, we were walking together in the evening light, and on the busy sidewalk passed a homeless man. We dropped our loose change in his cup, and as we walked away he called loudly after us, "You're *both* lesbians!" That short sentence quickly became shorthand for the pleasures of dressing up and stepping out.

In colder weather, instead of the velvet jacket I wore a butter-soft, mid-calf black leather coat with a white silk scarf. The coat had a beautiful satin lining that afforded scant protection in the wintertime, a fact that was borne in on me one January night when we were walking from the subway to a bar called Hell, in the meatpacking district where the wind whips off the Hudson River—but who cares? Janet had a delectable array of bustiers, filmy blouses, leather, velvet, and silk skirts, and many heels, including brown knee-high boots with silver tips from Barney's and those red pumps—so elegant that they were long on display in our bedroom. In 2003 we went to Provincetown over Memorial Day weekend to celebrate Janet's birthday. We were dressed up and on our way to a restaurant for a celebratory meal when a guy sitting on a porch set back from the street hollered out, "You sexy things!" Who's to argue? We both loved making it clear that we were sexual partners, and that we were, as the phrase is, "sex-positive" and queer.

The last time I can remember dressing up this way was to go to a cocktail party Henry was throwing early in the fall semester of 2003, maybe three weeks before I broke my neck. Janet and I were apart, in Middletown and NYC. Because wearing black leather jeans requires a certain frame of mind, in the absence of Janet I was seriously considering how I wanted to dress up for the party. In the end, I decided that such an event hosted by one of the founders of the field of queer studies actually called for those leather jeans, which I chose to complement with a tight, silky, white sleeveless top that did a great job of showing off not only my breasts, but also biceps, triceps, deltoids, and pecs. Silver earrings, silver bracelet, silver rings. Fendi perfume. I got to flirt with the girls *and* the boys—it was a great outfit and just the right gender for the occasion.

* * *

I no longer have a gender. Rather, I have a wheelchair. I'm entirely absorbed into its gestalt. I'm now misrecognized as a man more often than ever before, almost every time I go out. I'm not surprised. I know that 82% of spinal cord injuries are suffered by young men, and middle-aged butchy women must be statistically negligible in that accounting. Besides, when I'm outside wheeling my chair, I'm belted in. For ten years, I used a three-inch belt that went around my chest and fastened with Velcro—I grabbed each end, pushed my torso against the seat back, and brought the belt together as high up on my chest and as tightly as I could, but it still did a pretty good job of flattening my breasts. This I regarded as a great irony and a perverse injury, because I've never wanted to bind my breasts, unlike some butch women. To the contrary, I used to wear my shirts unbuttoned at the top, as Janet likes to remind me, and my zippers pulled down almost to the cleavage. I like my big, gorgeous breasts. I now have a higher back to my wheelchair and a neoprene vest to hold me up, with straps coming down over my shoulders to keep them back, and straps at the bottom, just under my rib cage, that are secured to the side of the chair. There's a zipper up the middle. My breasts are not as smashed by this restraint, which I wear all the time. It's better for my posture, if not for my wardrobe. I joke with Janet that the vest reminds me of the old advertisements for Maidenform bras that lift and separate. There's no "lifting" in this case, only a unisex sort of flattening, and indifferent separating. I love my breasts, and loved to show them off, but there's no way you'd know that seeing me now.

It's actually impossible for me to sit up straight, though it took me two years to understand that simple fact. My body is flat enough when I lie down, but when I sit up, my spine is shaped like a C. Not one of my "core" muscles is functional—those muscles that you work so hard in Pilates—the ones around your abdomen and back that support your torso. "Rake the seat of the chair from front to back," Danielle, my life-affirming physical therapist, said to me. We were talking about the wheelchair I was using in the Hospital for Special Care. "Look, it's built so that you can make the adjustment, using the holes that are drilled right here. You can raise the front so it dumps you on your tailbone. Let gravity work for you." I did as she instructed when I got my own chair, so when I'm seated, I'm always slightly reclined. Check out your own body, and imagine that the muscles below the breastbone have little functional power—you'd flop over without support, like I do. To make things worse, the C-curve of my back is accentuated because the surgery on my neck thrusts my head slightly forward, like a pigeon's when it walks. As I sit slumped in the chair, the chair is what you see. That's my distinctive profile.

I may have no gender, but the chair does. It's masculine. True, most of the time I offer little that would help you see me as a woman. I dress all in black—black pants or dark jeans, black T-shirt, black sweater. The chair is black, the vest is black, and I'm trying to make my body disappear as much as I can. When I am dressing for work, I'll wear a colorful scarf and earrings, but that's it. Maybe I am in permanent mourning. When somebody refers to me as a man, or calls me sir, and then realizes the mistake, profuse apologies follow, as if I had just suffered a grievous insult. The man stocking the grocery store shelves the other day, the shopper in front of me, the boy in the elevator, the barista at the coffee shop, the poll worker where I went to vote—I say to them all, "That's okay. It doesn't matter." The woman standing chatting on the sidewalk tells her friend, "Let that man pass." Then, flustered, "Oh, I'm so sorry. I just didn't realize, I didn't see, I couldn't tell . . ." "Don't worry—it's okay," I say, as I pass by.

And it is. I just don't care that much about my gender, which perhaps tells you all you need to know about how alien I find my body, how alien my life can feel to me.

59. • *Aleichia Williams*

TOO LATINA TO BE BLACK, TOO BLACK TO BE LATINA (2015)

Aleichia Williams is a feminist writer, photographer, and artist. She has been blogging for *Huffington Post* and published her first book, *21 Ways to Live a Fulfilled Life According to a 21-Year-Old*, based on her blog posts. She was born and raised in New York and currently lives in Texas.

I can remember the first time I had a "race crisis."

I was probably twelve or thirteen and I had just moved to the quiet state of North Carolina from my home state and city of New York. North Carolina was a lot different than New York. For one, there wasn't an enormous variety of culture and people. I didn't have class with any Russians. My professors weren't Puerto Rican and there wasn't a whole lot of mixing between kids of one race with kids of another. In fact, at my middle school you had three groups you could classify as: black, "Mexican," or white.

Unaware of this fact I walked into my second class on my first day of school and decided to sit next to a group of friendly looking Hispanic girls. As soon as I sat down the table was quiet. Then one girl snickered to another in Spanish, "Why is she sitting here? I don't want her to sit here." Her friend, who had been in my previous class and had heard my class introduction, blushed and replied to her friend in English, "She speaks Spanish."

That was the first time I could remember being aware of my skin color and the overwhelming implications it held. This was also my first "race crisis."

Now, I know what you're thinking. How could you grow up unaware that you were black? This isn't hard to answer. Growing up in an environment where it was normal to be colored and walk into a store and be spoken to in Spanish did not prepare me for how people in other places perceived my skin. My mom spoke Spanish. My grandmother spoke Spanish. Our family friends spoke Spanish. From the music we listened to, to the church we went to, to the food we ate, everything about me surrounded a Latin-American culture. This was a culture that I knew and belonged to but was excluded from it entirely when I left the melting pot that is New York City.

My crisis continued for years. When the violence broke out in middle school between the African-American gangs and the Hispanic gangs and the students spoke among themselves on who was best I could remember screaming, "I don't know who to side with!" When I got into high school and a classmate told me, "You're the most Mexican black girl I've ever met!" I could remember thinking, "Is that a compliment, because my family is from Honduras?"

Even now as an adult I find people are constantly trying to restrict me into a specific mold and identity. My home language is Spanish so this must mean I eat tacos. I have kinky hair so this must

Aleichia Williams, Too Latina To Be Black, Too Black To Be Latina, *Huffington Post*, December 6, 2017 mean I bang to Meek Mill. For many, I am too black to be Latin and too Latin to be black.

However, that's not how I see things. I currently live in Texas and my identity is unique because you don't have many dark-skinned girls singing along to bachata around here. I've learned, though, that just because I don't fit into one specific mold or the other doesn't mean I'm any less of who I am.

I'm learning to embrace every aspect of my identity and not let small minds put me in a box that just doesn't fit. I'm Latina. I'm black. Also, I'm human. No one can take that from me.

---

60. • *Kristina Gupta*

FEMINIST APPROACHES TO ASEXUALITY (new)

Kristina Gupta is an Assistant Professor in the Department of Women's, Gender, and Sexuality Studies at Wake Forest University. Her work on gender, health, and science can be found in her book *Medical Entanglements: Rethinking Feminist Debates About Healthcare* (Rutgers University Press, 2019). Her work on contemporary asexual identities has been published in a number of journals, including *Signs: The Journal of Women in Culture and Society*. The original chapter below reflects her thinking about the relationship between asexualities, compulsory sexuality, and feminist scholarship and practice.

In the early 2000s, some individuals living in the Global North began to use the term "asexuality" as a sexual identity label and began to form online communities for asexual-identified people. The largest of these communities, the Asexual Education and Visibility Network (AVEN), defines an asexual person as a person who experiences little or no sexual attraction to other people. According to the AVEN website, people who identify as asexual are diverse in many ways—some identify as romantic (interested in romantic relationships) while others identify as aromantic. Of those who identify as romantic, some identify as hetero-romantic, homo-romantic, bi-romantic, or pan-romantic. Some identify as "gray asexual," or located somewhere on an asexual continuum, while some identify as "demisexual," or as experiencing sexual attraction in the context of a long-term relationship. Some individuals who identify as asexual are willing to engage in sexual activity while others who identify as asexual are not (AVEN 2013).

The articulation of asexuality as a sexual identity and the growth of online asexual communities raises a number of interesting questions for feminist scholarship and activism, such as: How do contemporary gender and sexual norms affect the lives of asexual-identified individuals, and how do asexual-identified individuals and communities resist and accommodate themselves to gender and sexual norms? What does the growth of contemporary asexual communities reveal about contemporary systems of inequality? How can feminist activism create space for asexual-identified individuals and nonsexual ways of being in the world? This chapter offers a brief introduction to feminist scholarship on asexuality and then argues that the growth of contemporary asexual communities demonstrates the operation of *compulsory sexuality* as a system of social control. Finally, this chapter argues that feminist visions of gender and sexual justice must reconfigure themselves in order to affirm asexual identities and ways of being in the world.

FEMINIST SCHOLARSHIP ON CONTEMPORARY ASEXUAL IDENTITIES AND COMMUNITIES

As noted above, online asexual communities began to develop in the early 2000s. The largest of these communities, AVEN, was founded in 2001 and, as of 2019, included over 100,000 members. According to AVEN, "an asexual person does not experience sexual attraction—they are not drawn to people sexually and do not desire to act upon attraction to others in a sexual way" (AVEN 2013). However, as AVEN itself notes, while many asexual-identified people agree on this common definition, there is significant diversity in terms of how asexual-identified people experience and even define their asexuality. For example, there are differences in levels of sexual attraction, types of interpersonal relationships sought, and interest in different types of intimacy, physical and otherwise. Some people experience asexuality as a lifelong sexual orientation while others may inhabit their asexuality on a temporary basis, for a variety of reasons. Given this diversity, it is perhaps more appropriate to speak of "asexualities" than "asexuality."

Asexual activists and communities argue that asexuality is stigmatized in contemporary Western society. A number of studies have explored the negative effects of this stigmatization on the lives of asexual-identified individuals. According to this scholarship, asexual-identified individuals can face pathologization (Foster and Scherrer 2014; Robbins et al. 2015), difficulties in relationships and social situations (Carrigan 2011), and disbelief in or denial of their asexual self-identification (MacNeela and Murphy 2015). In my own qualitative research, I found that asexual-identified individuals described experiences of pathologization, social isolation, unwanted sex and relationship conflict, and the denial of their asexual self-identification as a result of the marginalization and stigmatization of asexuality (Gupta 2017).

A number of studies have also explored how asexual-identified individuals work to destigmatize asexuality and challenge contemporary sexual norms. Scholars have argued that asexual-identified individuals disrupt gender and sexual norms by challenging the idea that sexual attraction is a universal, innate drive, particularly for men, and the notion that sexual attraction is part of every healthy, adult form of sexuality (Scherrer 2008; Carrigan 2011; Przybylo 2014). In my research, I found that asexual-identified individuals challenged contemporary sexual and gender norms by (1) describing asexuality as a form of benign sexual variation rather than a deficit; (2) deemphasizing the importance of sexuality to human flourishing; (3) developing new types of nonsexual intimate relationships; (4) describing asexuality as a sexual orientation or identity similar to heterosexuality, homosexuality, and bisexuality; and (5) engaging in asexual community building and visibility work (Gupta 2017).

As the contemporary online asexual movement, particularly AVEN, has patterned itself after other mainstream LGBT movements, some of the same questions arise in regard to mainstream asexual activism as in regard to mainstream gay and lesbian rights activism. In particular, queer activists and scholars have questioned the radical potential of mainstream LGBT activism, given its focus on fixed, essentialized identity categories (e.g., the "born this way" discourse) and assimilation into existing systems of power and privilege (e.g., the campaign for same-sex marriage in the United States). According to critics, a reliance on fixed identity categories precludes a more fluid and contextual understanding of sexuality, and assimilationist politics precludes a more radical attempt to transform systems of inequality (see, for example, Duggan 2002; Conrad 2014). Similarly, feminist asexuality studies scholar Ela Przybylo argues that current asexual activism, which seeks public recognition for asexuality as an innate sexual orientation characterized by a lack of sexual attraction, does not pose a fundamental challenge to contemporary sexual structures. Przybylo writes, "in its current reactive, binarized state, asexuality functions to anchor sexuality, not alter its logic" (2011, 452).

It is also important to ask to what extent asexual communities include people who are disempowered on the basis of their inclusion in more than one marginalized social category. For example, Cuthbert (2015) argues that although asexual-identified individuals may challenge some contemporary Western sexual norms, they may also reinforce ableism through the denial of any links between asexuality and disability. Similarly, Owens (2014) argues that participants in online asexual communities often ignore or deny the importance of racism as a social system of power and privilege. And although AVEN includes members from all over the world, the community draws most of its participants from the United States, Canada, and the United Kingdom (see AVEN 2011; for an analysis of asexual formations in contemporary China, see Wong 2015). Still, in recent years, several asexual communities have made a conscious effort to address these issues; for example, AVEN now includes a forum titled "intersectionality."

COMPULSORY SEXUALITY

The emergence of asexual identities and communities illuminates certain aspects of contemporary Western sexual and gender norms. According to scholars in a number of fields, Western society has become increasingly sexualized (Giddens 1993; McNair 2002; Attwood 2006). This "sexualization of culture" is characterized by the increasing visibility of and importance afforded to sex and sexuality in the public and private spheres (Attwood 2006). Although the sexualization of culture can be liberating in many ways, it also serves a regulatory function. As a result of their engagement with contemporary asexual formations, activists and scholars in the field of asexuality studies have identified *compulsory sexuality* as a system of social control different from *compulsory heterosexuality*. While compulsory heterosexuality privileges heterosexuality over other forms of sexuality, compulsory sexuality privileges sexuality over asexuality and nonsexuality. Thus, for example, an asexual-identified homoromantic person may face marginalization within mainstream society for their homo-romantic and asexual identities and within LGBTQ communities for their asexuality (Chasin 2011, "Notes on Compulsory Sexuality and Asexual Existence"; Emens 2013; Gupta 2015). In my work, I describe *compulsory sexuality* as including:

> the assumption that all people are sexual, the norms and practices that compel people to experience themselves as desiring subjects, take up sexual identities, and engage in sexual activity, and the norms and practices that marginalize various forms of non-sexuality (including a lack of interest in sex, a lack of sexual activity, or a dis-identification with sexuality). (Gupta 2015, 134–35)

Importantly, compulsory sexuality regulates the behavior of all people, not just people who identify as asexual (Gupta 2015). Other names have been used to describe this system, such as "sexual normativity" (Hinderliter 2009; Chasin 2011, "Theoretical Issues in the Study of Asexuality") and "the sexual assumption" (Carrigan 2011), but all of these terms perform similar work.

Of course, how compulsory sexuality affects people depends on the operation of a variety of other systems of oppression, including sexism, racism, classism, colonialism, ageism, and ableism, among others. These other systems of oppression have often relied on specific stereotypes about both hypersexuality and asexuality. For example, sexual norms differ by gender—despite changes, men in the United States are frequently stereotyped as sexually active, while women face pressure from some parts of society to embody sexual passivity and other parts of society to express a "liberated" modern form of female sexuality by actively pursuing sex (Gupta 2019). These gendered sexual stereotypes are further inflected by racism; for example, in the United States, black men are often represented as sexual predators, while black women are represented as both hypersexual (the "Jezebel" stereotype) and asexual (the "Mammy" stereotype) (Collins 2005). Children and older people in the United States are frequently depicted as asexual and/or are denied sexual autonomy, as are people with disabilities (Marshall 2006; Kim 2011). For these reasons, expectations about appropriate levels of sexual activity differ significantly based on gender, age, race, ability, etc., and the potential to assert an asexual identity, and the meaning of such an identity, will vary significantly depending on a person's location within these intersecting systems of oppression.

This reality is made even more complicated by the fact that marginalized groups that are stereotyped as "hypersexual" sometimes respond by asserting their own sexual respectability, while groups that are stereotyped as "asexual" may respond by asserting their own active sexuality. For example, some black communities in the United States responded to myths of hypersexuality by adopting a form of sex-negative respectability politics, or a type of politics centered on assertions that black people are "properly" heterosexual, practice sexual restraint, and conform to mainstream white sexual norms (Collins 2005). On the other hand, some disability rights groups have responded to the desexualization of people with disabilities by asserting that all people with disabilities are inherently sexual (Kim 2011; Gupta 2014). Together, these different sexual stereotypes, as well as counter-norms developed by resistant communities, serve to further limit possibilities for both sexual and nonsexual autonomy.

FEMINIST JUSTICE: AFFIRMING ASEXUALITIES AND NONSEXUALITIES

Moments within the history of feminist thought and activism have offered space for asexualities and nonsexualities. For example, during the 1970s, some radical feminist thinkers and groups in the U.S. women's liberation movement advocated for and/or practiced celibacy as a radical challenge to existing structures of heteropatriarchy (Fahs 2010). However, since the 1990s in the United States, queer feminism and sex-positive feminism have become the dominant feminist discourses in the United States, and, although their virtues are numerous, these discourses have generally either ignored asexualities and nonsexualities or have been outright hostile to them (Barounis 2014; Gupta 2013).

If feminist thought and activism is to be genuinely inclusive, it must be committed to making space for asexual identities and nonsexual ways of being-in-the world. We need to remember that at its core, sexual justice includes a commitment to sexual autonomy, which includes both the right and ability to choose sex and the right and ability to refuse sex. We must also recognize that all expectations about sexuality, whether it is expectations that one is not or should not be sexual or expectations that one is or should be sexual, can be equally limiting and oppressive. These expectations are regulatory for all people, whether they identify as sexual, asexual, or something else. For example, negative attitudes toward asexuality and nonsexuality may place pressure on both sexual and nonsexual people to engage in unwanted sex in order to be perceived as "normal."

Elsewhere I have argued that we should not respond to compulsory sexuality by attempting to "desexualize" society. Rather, we can learn from other progressive movements. For example, trans scholars and activists who have identified our current gender order as a system of oppression have generally not called for a "degendering" of society but have instead called for an end to practices, institutions, and norms that privilege some ways of doing gender and marginalize others. They have also called for a proliferation of representations of gender categories in the expectation that such a proliferation will reduce pressure on all people to conform to specific ways of doing gender. Based on this model, I have argued that we should respond to compulsory sexuality by "challenging the unearned privileges that accrue to sexual people and sexual relationships and by eliminating discrimination against nonsexual people and nonsexual relationships . . . Simultaneously, we can work to proliferate representations of nonsexuality and asexuality" (Gupta 2015, 148). It is my belief that such a vision will create a better world for both asexual and sexual individuals.

WORKS CITED

Attwood, Feona. "Sexed Up: Theorizing the Sexualization of Culture." *Sexualities*, vol. 9, no. 1, February 2006, pp. 77–94.

AVEN. "AVEN Survey 2008: Results." http://www.asexuality.org/home/2008_stats.html. Accessed August 15, 2011.

AVEN. "Overview." http://www.asexuality.org/home/overview.html. Accessed October 18, 2013.

Barounis, Cynthia. "Compulsory Sexuality and Feminist/Crip Resistance in John Cameron Mitchell's Shortbus." *Asexualities: Feminist and Queer Perspectives*, edited by Karli June Cerankowski and Megan Milks. Routledge, 2014.

Carrigan, Mark. "There's More to Life Than Sex? Difference and Commonality within the Asexual Community." *Sexualities*, vol. 14, no. 4, 2011, pp. 462–78.

Chasin, C. J. DeLuzio. "Notes on Compulsory Sexuality and Asexual Existence." *Asexuality and Sexualization: A Panel on Asexuality*, 2011.

Chasin, C. J. DeLuzio. "Theoretical Issues in the Study of Asexuality." *Archives of Sexual Behavior*, vol. 40, no. 4, August 2011, pp. 713–23.

Collins, Patricia Hill. *Black Sexual Politics: African Americans, Gender, and the New Racism*. Routledge, 2005.

Conrad, Ryan, editor. *Against Equality: Queer Revolution, Not Mere Inclusion*. AK Press, 2014.

Cuthbert, Karen. "You Have to Be Normal to Be Abnormal: An Empirically Grounded Exploration of the Intersection of Asexuality and Disability." *Sociology*, vol. 51, no. 2, June 2015, pp. 241–57.

Duggan, Lisa. "The New Homonormativity: The Sexual Politics of Neoliberalism." In *Materializing Democracy: Toward a Revitalized Cultural Politics*, edited by Russ Castronovo and Dana D. Nelson. Duke University Press, 2002, pp. 175–94.

Emens, Elizabeth F. *Compulsory Sexuality*. SSRN Scholarly Paper, ID 2218783, Social Science Research Network, March 7, 2013.

Fahs, Breanne. "Radical Refusals: On the Anarchist Politics of Women Choosing Asexuality." *Sexualities*, vol. 13, no. 4, 2010, pp. 445–61.

Foster, Aasha B., and Kristin S. Scherrer. "Asexual-Identified Clients in Clinical Settings: Implications for Culturally Competent Practice." *Psychology of Sexual Orientation and Gender Diversity*, vol. 1, no. 4, December 2014, pp. 422–30.

Giddens, Anthony. *The Transformation of Intimacy: Sexuality, Love, and Eroticism in Modern Societies*. Stanford University Press, 1993.

Gupta, Kristina. "'And Now I'm Just Different, But There's Nothing Actually Wrong With Me': Asexual Marginalization and Resistance." *Journal of Homosexuality*, vol. 64, no. 8, July 2017, pp. 991–1013.

Gupta, Kristina. "Asexuality and Disability: Mutual Negation in *Adams v. Rice* and New Directions for Coalition Building." *Asexualities: Feminist and Queer Perspectives*, edited by Karli June Cerankowski and Megan Milks. Routledge, 2014.

Gupta, Kristina. "Compulsory Sexuality: Evaluating an Emerging Concept." *Signs: Journal of Women in Culture & Society*, vol. 41, no. 1, 2015, pp. 131–54.

Gupta, Kristina. "Gendering Asexuality and Asexualizing Gender: A Qualitative Study Exploring the Intersections Between Gender and Asexuality." *Sexualities*, vol. 22, no. 7–8, 2019, pp. 1197–1216.

Gupta, Kristina. "Picturing Space for Lesbian Nonsexualities: Rethinking Sex-Normative Commitments through *The Kids Are All Right* (2010)." *Journal of Lesbian Studies*, vol. 17, no. 1, 2013, pp. 103–18.

Hinderliter, Andrew. "Methodological Issues for Studying Asexuality." *Archives of Sexual Behavior*, vol. 38, April 2009, pp. 619–21.

Kim, Eunjung. "Asexuality in Disability Narratives." *Sexualities*, vol. 14, no. 4, 2011, pp. 479–93.

MacNeela, Pádraig, and Aisling Murphy. "Freedom, Invisibility, and Community: A Qualitative Study of Self-Identification with Asexuality." *Archives of Sexual Behavior*, vol. 44, no. 3, April 2015, pp. 799–812.

Marshall, Barbara L. "The New Virility: Viagra, Male Aging and Sexual Function." *Sexualities*, vol. 9, no. 3, July 2006, pp. 345–62.

McNair, Brian. *Striptease Culture: Sex, Media and the Democratization of Desire*. Routledge, 2002.

Owens, Ianna Hawkins. "On the Racialization of Asexuality." In *Asexualities: Feminist and Queer Perspectives*, edited by Karli June Cerankowski and Megan Milks, pp. 119–38. Routledge, 2014.

Przybylo, Ela. "Crisis and Safety: The Asexual in Sexusociety." *Sexualities*, vol. 14, no. 4, 2011, pp. 444–61.

Przybylo, Ela. "Masculine Doubt and Sexual Wonder." In *Asexualities: Feminist and Queer Perspectives*, edited by Karli June Cerankowski and Megan Milks, pp. 225–48. Routledge, 2014.

Robbins, Nicolette K., et al. "A Qualitative Exploration of the 'Coming Out' Process for Asexual Individuals." *Archives of Sexual Behavior*, vol. 45, no. 3, September 2015, pp. 751–60.

Scherrer, Kristin S. "Coming to an Asexual Identity: Negotiating Identity, Negotiating Desire." *Sexualities*, vol. 11, no. 5, October 2008, pp. 621–41.

Wong, Day. "Asexuality in China's Sexual Revolution: Asexual Marriage as Coping Strategy." *Sexualities*, vol. 18, no. 1–2 (2015), pp. 100–16.

61. • *Gloria Steinem*

IF MEN COULD MENSTRUATE (1978)

Gloria Steinem has been a well-known feminist activist and writer since the late 1960s. In 2005, with Jane Fonda and Robin Morgan, she cofounded the Women's Media Center, which aims to make women more visible and powerful in media. She was a cofounder of the feminist *Ms. Magazine*, in which the following essay was first published in 1978. Her works revolve around charting different ways to challenge patriarchy.

A white minority of the world has spent centuries conning us into thinking that a white skin makes people superior—even though the only thing it really does is make them more subject to ultraviolet rays and to wrinkles. Male human beings have built whole cultures around the idea that penis-envy is "natural" to women—though having such an unprotected organ might be said to make men vulnerable, and the power to give birth makes womb-envy at least as logical.

In short, the characteristics of the powerful, whatever they may be, are thought to be better than the characteristics of the powerless—and logic has nothing to do with it.

What would happen, for instance, if suddenly, magically, men could menstruate and women could not?

The answer is clear—menstruation would become an enviable, boast-worthy, masculine event:

Men would brag about how long and how much.

Boys would mark the onset of menses, that longed-for proof of manhood, with religious ritual and stag parties.

Gloria Steinem, "If Men Could Menstruate" *Ms. Magazine*, October 1978. Reprinted with permission.

Congress would fund a National Institute of Dysmenorrhea to help stamp out monthly discomforts.

Sanitary supplies would be federally funded and free. (Of course, some men would still pay for the prestige of commercial brands such as John Wayne Tampons, Muhammad Ali's Rope-a-dope Pads, Joe Namath Jock Shields—"For Those Light Bachelor Days," and Robert "Baretta" Blake Maxi-Pads.)

Military men, right-wing politicians, and religious fundamentalists would cite menstruation ("menstruation") as proof that only men could serve in the Army ("you have to give blood to take blood"), occupy political office ("can women be aggressive without that steadfast cycle governed by the planet Mars?"), be priest and ministers ("how could a woman give her blood for our sins?") or rabbis ("without the monthly loss of impurities, women remain unclean").

Male radicals, left-wing politicians, mystics, however, would insist that women are equal, just different, and that any woman could enter their ranks if she were willing to self-inflict a major wound every month ("you MUST give blood for the revolution"), recognize the preeminence of menstrual issues, or subordinate her selfness to all men in their Cycle of Enlightenment. Street guys would brag ("I'm a three pad man") or answer praise from a buddy ("Man, you lookin' good!") by giving fives and saying, "Yeah, man, I'm on the rag!" TV shows would treat the subject at length. ("Happy Days": Richie and Potsie try to convince Fonzie that he is still "The Fonz," though he has missed two periods in a row.) So would newspapers. (SHARK SCARE THREATENS MENSTRUATING MEN. JUDGE CITES MONTHLY STRESS IN PARDONING RAPIST.) And movies. (Newman and Redford in "Blood Brothers"!)

Men would convince women that intercourse was more pleasurable at "that time of the month." Lesbians would be said to fear blood and therefore life itself—though probably only because they needed a good menstruating man.

Of course, male intellectuals would offer the most moral and logical arguments. How could a woman master any discipline that demanded a sense of time, space, mathematics, or measurement, for instance, without that in-built gift for measuring the cycles of the moon and planets—and thus for measuring anything at all? In the rarefied fields of philosophy and religion, could women compensate for missing the rhythm of the universe? Or for their lack of symbolic death-and-resurrection every month?

Liberal males in every field would try to be kind: the fact that "these people" have no gift for measuring life or connecting to the universe, the liberals would explain, should be punishment enough.

And how would women be trained to react? One can imagine traditional women agreeing to all arguments with a staunch and smiling masochism. ("The ERA would force housewives to wound themselves every month": Phyllis Schlafly. "Your husband's blood is as sacred as that of Jesus—and so sexy, too!": Marabel Morgan.) Reformers and Queen Bees would try to imitate men, and pretend to have a monthly cycle. All feminists would explain endlessly that men, too, needed to be liberated from the false idea of Martian aggressiveness, just as women needed to escape the bonds of menses envy. Radical feminists would add that the oppression of the nonmenstrual was the pattern for all other oppressions ("Vampires were our first freedom fighters!"). Cultural feminists would develop a bloodless imagery in art and literature. Socialist feminists would insist that only under capitalism would men be able to monopolize menstrual blood. . . .

In fact, if men could menstruate, the power justifications could probably go on forever.

If we let them.

HOW TO USE A CONDOM (2011)

No'u Revilla is an 'Ōiwi queer poet, aloha 'āina, and educator. She has performed throughout Hawai'i as well as Toronto, Papua New Guinea, and the headquarters of the United Nations in New York. She has taught poetry workshops at Pu'uhuluhulu University and is an Assistant Professor of creative writing at the University of Hawai'i-Mānoa.

Pleasure Pack variety:
Her Pleasure.
Shared Pleasure.
Deep Impact.

We gotta stop

Ultra ribbed

We gotta stop We gotta stop We gotta stop—
TEAR HERE
and concentrate.
Substance interrupted

if used properly.
will reduce risk of transmission. In-and-out nothings
will eroticize motion and deeper spermicidal tendencies
will lead to murder.

Reproduction is not the problem.
Reproduction is the problem.
making children based on an image.

We gotta stop.

Against highly effective pregnancy.

We are kissing in a picture in a frame on your shelf
(we intercoursed that night while your parents were home) but the fluids stop there.

Our moments like wet hair in the cold: old stories
with low body temperatures, low resistance to virus.

Diminishing diminishing
until lubrication is a product.
For sale.
We gotta stop
I need connection to be source to be predicate to be don't stop don't stop don't stop—
will your lost erections ever find their way home?

TEAR HERE.
Unroll your barrier device.
And leave space at the tip for collection.

No'u Revilla, "How to Use a Condom," in *Say Throne*, Chicago: Tinfish Press, 2011. Reprinted with permission.

63. • *Lailatul Fitriyah*

CAN WE STOP TALKING ABOUT THE "HIJAB"?:
Islamic Feminism, Intersectionality, and the Indonesian Muslim Female Migrant Workers (new)

Lailatul Fitriyah is a Ph.D. candidate at the World Religions and World Church Program, Department of Theology, University of Notre Dame, USA. She is also one of the founders of Feminist Theologies in Global Context Colloquium at Notre Dame. Her current research focuses on the construction of feminist theologies in post-colonial Southeast Asia, feminist theologies of migration, and feminist inter-religious dialogue. She holds an M.A. in International Peace Studies from the Kroc Institute for International Peace Studies-University of Notre Dame, and was also a Nostra Aetate Fellow at the Pontifical Council for Interreligious Dialogue (PCID), Vatican City, Italy.

In mainstream academic discourse, Islamic feminism often focuses on a singular point of contention: the *hijab*, and its relationship with structural and gendered oppression.[1] While the issue is undoubtedly important, it hardly represents the full complexity of the experiences of Muslim women around the world. It is important to note that "Islamic feminism" in this paper is understood as socio-political, religious, and academic movements and discourses that are articulated within an Islamic paradigm and conducted by Muslims. Furthermore, what I call the "dominant discourse" within Islamic feminism in this paper refers to a unitary focus on Muslim women's sexual freedom at the expense of other forms of oppression suffered by Muslim women that are not necessarily linked to an absence of their sexual freedom.

Islamic feminism would thus benefit from a deeper engagement with the intersectional perspective in order to provide a more nuanced analysis of the experiences of Muslim women that goes beyond their religious dress code. I thus propose to expand the focus of Islamic feminism to topics that are outside of its traditional purview, such as the oppressions that Indonesian Muslim female migrant workers face in their work settings in Singapore, Middle East, and Gulf countries. My analysis aims to show: 1) that Islamic feminism needs to embrace an intersectional standpoint in order to provide an inclusive space for the diverse experiences of Muslim women around the world; 2) that despite common homogenizing depictions of the "West" versus "Islam," there are segments of Muslim women who suffer from forms of intra-Muslim violence; and 3) that expressions of agency and aspirations for liberation are as diverse as the contexts that Muslim women find themselves in.

ISLAMIC FEMINISM AND THE INDONESIAN MUSLIM FEMALE MIGRANT WORKERS

In her 1989 article, Kimberlé Crenshaw describes "intersectionality" as the capacity to understand that, for black women, oppression goes beyond simple racism and sexism, but rather includes overlapping multidirectional threats that place black women at the intersection of vulnerabilities (Crenshaw 1989, 149, 152). Over a decade later, in 2013, Cho, Crenshaw, and McCall would define "intersectionality" as

> an analytic sensibility . . . what makes an analysis intersectional is not its use of the term "intersectionality," nor its being situated in a familiar genealogy, nor its drawing on lists of standard citations. Rather, what makes an analysis intersectional . . . is its adoption of an intersectional way of thinking about the problem of sameness and difference and its relation to power. (795)

In this sense, more than any theoretical discourse, "intersectionality" aims to create genuine inclusivity in the process of producing knowledge. In order to be intersectional, Islamic feminism has to broaden its purview to seriously engage with the lives of Muslim women outside of its traditional focus on *hijab*, body-coverings, and the presence or absence of Muslim women's sexual freedom. My study on Indonesian Muslim female migrant workers is one such example of such a broadening perspective that shows us an intersection of oppression that results from the intertwining of the global labor market, socio-political alienation, and racism.

In this essay, I examine the Indonesian female migrant workers who go to Singapore, Saudi Arabia, United Arab Emirates, and Jordan to work as domestic workers. As domestic workers, they face a complex form of oppression due to the gendered view of the nature of their workplace and discriminatory laws that leave them vulnerable to abuses that come from employers, work agencies, and law enforcement officials. In addition, the gendered presumption that caretaking and home-making work

is women's work (especially of women with darker complexions) has also added to the sexualized and racialized dimensions of the oppressions against female migrant workers (hereafter, FMWs).

These trends of sexualization and racialization have in turn resulted in a distinct form of Islamophobia that does not base its claim on ethno-phenotypical distinctions, as it does in the United States and Europe, but rather on perceived socio-economic distinctions. Indonesian Muslim FMWs do not experience Islamophobia because of their darker skin tones, or because of white supremacist narratives that represent them as the hostile "other." Rather, the Islamophobia they suffer is a part and parcel of the commodification process brought about by the context of global labor market (Fitriyah 2019).

Over the course of my field work, I have heard many testimonies from both ex- and active Indonesian Muslim FMWs (especially those who worked/work in Singapore and Hong Kong) who were forced to eat pork and/or prohibited from their five daily prayers because their employers felt uncomfortable with having practicing Muslims as their caretakers and domestic helpers. In this case, the commodification of their labor as domestic workers is compounded by the commodification of their identities that shapes them to be the "perfect laborers" (i.e., laborers whose religious identities are erased to make them more customer-friendly) (Fitriyah 2019).

From this example, it is clear that conventional focus of Islamic feminism cannot understand this phenomenon. These Muslim women experience a different kind of oppression that is not only rooted in racism and ethnocentrism, but also at the intersection of class and gender that is mediated by the global labor market. In order to be able to understand the market-based Islamophobia suffered by non-Middle Eastern Muslim women, Islamic feminism needs to first get out of the conventional orientalist restrictions of Islamic studies that associate "Islam" only with the Middle East (Formichi 2016, 697). Furthermore, the distinctive form of Islamophobia that is suffered by these Muslim women cannot be analyzed simply through a *hijab*-oriented discourse that pigeonholes Muslim women's plight into the issues of sexual oppression and sexual liberation (Abu-Lughod 2013, 88). Only through the inclusion of global context of political economy can we make sense of the intersectional oppression suffered by Indonesian Muslim FMWs.

FORMS OF OPPRESSION IN THE MIDDLE EAST AND GULF COUNTRIES

Market-based Islamophobia is not the only form of intersectional oppression that is suffered by the Indonesian Muslim FMWs. As noted by Tula Connell (2018), the Middle East is notorious for its slavery-like conditions for Indonesian female domestic workers. One major cause of these abuses is a migration policy known as the *kafala* system, which gives employers the legal right to invalidate their employees' work visas (migrant-rights.org). Under the *kafala* system, migrant workers from Qatar to Jordan need to secure their employers' permission in order to quit and change jobs, or else their presence in the country will be rendered illegal. The situation only becomes worst for domestic workers, whose professions are not protected by labor laws in any of the Gulf Countries (migrant-rights.org).

It is within this context that another form of oppression rises up against the Indonesian Muslim FMWs. With the sheer amount of violence that they experience in the Middle East and the Gulf Countries, it is ironic that some of the thirty Indonesian Muslim FMWs that I interviewed in summer 2018 disclosed that the reason they chose these countries was because they thought that Muslim employers would not harm other Muslims. However, in the cases of Turini Fatmah, who was confined to an employer's home for 21 years in Saudi Arabia and was only paid her salary for three times in that period (tribunnews.com, 2019); Eni Suharyati, who was tortured, starved, and confined in a bathroom with her salary partly unpaid for six months in Abu Dhabi (detik.com, 2019); and Diah Anggraini, who was confined to an employer's home for 12 years

by her employer in Amman to the extent that she forgot how to speak in her mother tongue while her salary was also unpaid (antaranews.com, 2019), their Muslim employers in these Muslim majority-countries were torturing them in spite of the fact that they were also practicing Islam.

In this case, the conventional discourse on Islamophobia that places Muslims as a monolithic group facing challenges from an equally monolithic Western society is irrelevant to providing a better understanding of the torture, rape, and abuse that Indonesian Muslim FMWs suffer at the hands of their Muslim employers in the Middle East and Gulf Countries. Practicing the same religion does not protect these Muslim women from their employers' violence. Here, the loci of power in the employer–domestic worker relationships is located at the intersection of race and class that overrides their shared religion. In other words, what is important in these cases is not the fact that both the employers and the domestic workers are Muslims, but rather the fact that the domestic workers are located at a different socio-economic class from their employers. In the eyes of the abusive employers, their violence is justified because the Indonesian Muslim FMWs are seen as the racial other who occupy one of the lowest socio-economic strata in their societies.

Within this atmosphere of socio-economic and political disparity, the traditional focus of Islamic feminism on body-coverings and sexual freedom is irrelevant. The nature of this oppression is an intermingling of politico-economic violence with racial violence, meaning that the FMWs are oppressed because they are seen as labor commodities and racialized others (Southeast Asians, Central Africans, etc.). In the case of those with Muslim employers, their plights come from intra-Muslim violence, rather than from violence done by other religious groups.

Such intra-Muslim violence can also be found within the experiences of Indonesian Muslim FMWs in Southeast Asia (Malaysia and Singapore), where their socio-economic positioning as "maids" is associated with racialized prejudices such as promiscuity, stupidity, and backwardness. In each of these cases, the *hijab* is a non-issue, which means that a shift in focus from *hijab* and sexuality to the socio-political, economic, and racial aspects of Muslim women's lives is necessary. "Muslim women" do not have universal issues. Depending on their sociopolitical, cultural, and economic positionings within the global economy, the oppressions that they suffer go beyond orientalist narratives and mainstream Islamic feminist discourses that stemmed from the presumed absence of Muslim women's sexual freedom.

It is worth noting that some of the Indonesian Muslim FMWs that I spoke with in Singapore considered *hijab* and *abaya* to be critiques against a form of capitalism that commodifies their labor, and erodes their religious identities. Hence, if there is any aspect of the practices of hijab and body-covering among these Indonesian Muslim FMWs that we need to analyze, it is the fact that their preference for wearing the body-coverings is mediated by the political and economic alienations that they suffer from in the global capitalist economy. Thus, when we exclusively analyze the issues that Indonesian Muslim FMWs experience from a unitary framework of Islamophobia that pit "Muslims" as a homogenous group versus the "West" as another, we ignore the complexities of the problems that these women encounter.

INDONESIAN MUSLIM FEMALE MIGRANT WORKERS AND THEIR CONTEXT OF RESISTANCE

Throughout my research, I observed that Indonesian Muslim FMWs in Singapore would construct safe spaces for taking care of themselves and each other within mosques and other religious settings. On Sundays, many of the workers (or at least those whose employers let them leave the house) would gather in religious spaces not only to enrich their religious and spiritual lives, but also meet with their friends and replenish their yearning for individual freedom.

Religious activities such as praying together, learning how to read the Qur'an, and singing religious songs allow these workers to feel empowered and to express their religious subjectivities. Many of the women that I encountered would wear their best clothes, colorful *abayas* and sparkly *hijabs*, to attend their religious activities every Sunday. Rather than representing a system of oppression, religious piety allowed these women to express their individuality amidst the commodification process that attempts to flatten their identities into a homogenous group of laborers. In other words, by deeply engaging in religious life over the weekend, these women build a counter-narrative against the capitalist narrative that is dehumanizing them.

According to Muslim feminist anthropologists Lila Abu-Lughod and Saba Mahmood, one aspect that we need to interrogate in the analysis of "agency" and "liberation" is the many ways that different socio-political and economic contexts influence the localized definitions of both terms (Abu-Lughod 2013, 6; Mahmood 2005, 10, 14–15). There is no definition that can be applied universally when it comes to understanding "agency" and liberation. Within this framework, the conventional narrative of Islamic feminism that focuses on the absence and/or presence of Muslim women's sexual freedom cannot be used to describe the FMWs' experience, for these pietistic practices are liberative expressions amidst the systemic oppression that they suffer as domestic workers.

Since there is no universal definition of what constitutes "liberation" for Muslim women, any discussion on it cannot be separated from the kind of oppression that that specific segment of Muslim women suffers, and the socio-political positions that they occupy. For these FMWs in Singapore, going to the mosque or learning to read the Qur'an is a taste of freedom that they can relish, even as their employers enforce restrictions on their religious identities and practices. For them, religion and religious practices are not parts of their structure of oppression, but are rather their spaces of liberation.

We thus need to reconsider what are the issues that can be validated as a "proper" concern for Islamic feminism. Today, the line is drawn based on the construction of an illusionary "global Muslim imagery" vis-à-vis the Islamophobic West. While Islamophobic discourses have turned representations of Muslim women into a rallying cry to justify Western imperialism against the Muslim world (Abu-Lughod 2013, 6–7), this does not mean that Islamic feminism can only produce reactive discourses that merely seek to prove that Muslim women do have sexual freedom.

Furthermore, the primary focus of Islamic studies that have been disproportionately dedicated to the thoughts and movements of the Arab world (Chaudhry 2015, 5–6) is another factor that allows for the lack of attention on intersectional oppressions suffered by Indonesian Muslim FMWs. It does not matter that the world's largest Muslim population are Southeast Asian people; the fact that Southeast Asian Muslim women are not "Arabs" has already invalidated their experiences. Thus, it is important to ask the question "Who is not included in our conversation?" A commitment to include the diverse experiences of Muslim women has to be an epistemological one that pays attention to their intersectional vulnerabilities. Only then can Islamic feminism serve as a socio-political, academic, and religious movement that aims for the liberation of all Muslim women.

[Acknowledgment: The Summer 2018 field-work on this topic was supported by the Kellogg Institute for International Studies' Graduate Research Grants. An ongoing field-work on the same topic is supported by the Kellogg Institute for International Studies' Graduate Research Grants; the Keough School of Global Affairs' Field Research Award; the Liu Institute for Asia and Asian Studies' Research and Educational Travel Grant; the Department of Theology at Notre Dame's Travel Grant; and, the Ansari Institute for Global Engagement with Religion's Travel Grant.]

NOTE

1. This is mostly due to two factors: 1) The socio-political and regional contexts from which Islamic feminism as a social-political and academic movement come from (Middle East, North Africa, Persia, and South Asia). Early theorists of Islamic feminism such as Margot Badran, Fatima Mernissi, and Leila Ahmed have written that Islamic feminism is part and parcel of the late nineteenth, and early twentieth centuries anti-colonial struggle in those regions in which the practice of Muslim women's body coverings and domestic confinement (including *hijab*) were at the core of colonial and anti-colonial discourses. See: Margot Badran, "Engaging Islamic Feminism," in, Anitta Kynsilehto, ed., *Islamic Feminism: Current Perspectives* (Tampere, Finland: Tampere Peace Research Institute, 2008); Fatima Mernissi, *Le Harem Politique: le Prophète et les femmes* (Bruxelles: Complexe, 1992); Leila Ahmed, *Women and Gender in Islam* (New Haven, CT: Yale University Press, 1992); and 2) The post 9/11 Islamophobic narratives in the US and Western Europe that focus on the presumed absence of Muslim women's sexual freedom on the basis of their body-covering practices, which in turn significantly shaped dominant discourses on Islamic feminism to prove that the presumption is wrong. In this case, Islamophobic focus on 'hijab' resulted in yet another focus on 'hijab'. For further discussion on this topic, see: Lila Abu-Lughod, *Do Muslim Women Need Saving?* (Cambridge, MA: Harvard University Press, 2013); Haideh Moghissi, *Feminism and Islamic Fundamentalism: The Limits of Postmodern Analysis* (London, UK: Zed Books, 1999); Hina Azam, "Islamic Feminism between Islam and Islamophobia," *Journal of Middle East Women's Studies*, 14/1 (2018): 124-128.

BIBLIOGRAPHY

Abu-Lughod, Lila, *Do Muslim Women Need Saving?* (Cambridge, MA: Harvard University Press, 2013), 6–7, 88.

Ahmed, Leila, *Women and Gender in Islam* (New Haven, CT: Yale University Press, 1992).

Azam, Hina, "Islamic Feminism Between Islam and Islamophobia," *Journal of Middle East Women's Studies*, Vol. 14, No. 1 (2018): 124–128.

Badran, Margot, "Engaging Islamic Feminism," in Anitta Kynsilehto, ed., *Islamic Feminism: Current Perspectives*

(Tampere, Finland: Tampere Peace Research Institute, 2008), 25–36.

Chaudhry, Ayesha, "Islamic Legal Studies: A Critical Historiography," in Anver Emon & Rumee Ahmed, eds., *The Oxford Handbook of Islamic Law* (Oxford, UK: Oxford University Press, 2015), 5–44.

Cho, Sumi, Crenshaw, Kimberlé Williams, and McCall, Leslie, "Toward a Field of Intersectionality Studies: Theory, Applications, and Praxis," *Signs: Journal of Women in Culture and Society*, Vol. 38, No. 4 (2013): 785–810.

Connell, Tula, "Migrant Domestic Workers Seek Rights in the Middle East." *Solidarity Center AFL-CIO*, January 31, 2018, last modified December 28, 2018, www.solidaritycenter.org/migrant-domestic-workers-seek-rights-middle-east/.

Crenshaw, Kimberlé, "Demarginalizing the Intersection of Race and Sex: A Black Feminist Critique of Antidiscrimination Doctrine, Feminist Theory and Antiracist Politics," *University of Chicago Legal Forum*, Vol. 1989, Issue 1, Article 8, 1989: 139–167.

Dewi, Anita Permata, "TKI Diah Anggraini Segera Dipulangkan Dari Yordania." *Antara News*, February 12, 2019, last modified September 25, 2019, https://www.antaranews.com/berita/797097/tki-diah-anggraini-segera-dipulangkan-dari-yordania.

Fitriyah, Lailatul, "Islamophobia Beyond Christchurch: Muslims as Tamed Others." *Contending Modernities*, June 18, 2019, last modified September 25, 2019, https://contendingmodernities.nd.edu/global-currents/islamophobia-beyond-christchurch/.

Formichi, Chiara, "Islamic Studies or Asian Studies? Islam in Southeast Asia," *The Muslim World*, Vol. 106, No. 4, 2016: 696–718.

Mahmood, Saba, *Politics of Piety: The Islamic Revival and the Feminist Subject* (Princeton, NJ: Princeton University Press, 2005), 10, 14–15, 17.

Masithoh, Siti, "TKI Asal Cirebon Disekap Majikan di Arab Saudi, Selama 21 Tahun Bekerja Hanya Digaji 3 Kali." *Tribun News*, March 13, 2019, last modified September 25, 2019, https://jabar.tribunnews.com/2019/03/13/tki-asal-cirebon-disekap-majikan-di-arab-saudi-selama-21-tahun-bekerja-hanya-digaji-3-kali.

Mernissi, Fatima, *Le Harem Politique: le Prophète et les femmes* (Bruxelles: Complexe, 1992).

Moghissi, Haideh, *Feminism and Islamic Fundamentalism: The Limits of Postmodern Analysis* (London, UK: Zed Books, 1999).

Motaparthy, Priyanka, "Understanding Kafala: An Archaic Law at Cross Purposes with Modern Development," *Migrant-Rights.org*, March 11, 2015, last modified December 28, 2018, www.migrant-rights.org/2015/03/understanding-kafala-an-archaic-law-at-cross-purposes-with-modern-development/.

Rifa'i, Bahtiar, "Pulang Dari Abu Dhabi, TKI Asal Serang Penuh Lebam Akibat Siksaan." *Detik*, February 6, 2019, last modified September 25, 2019, https://news.detik.com/berita/d-4416751/pulang-dari-abu-dhabi-tki-asal-serang-penuh-lebam-akibat-siksaan.

64. • *L. Ayu Saraswati*

COSMOPOLITAN WHITENESS:
The Effects and Affects of Skin-Whitening Advertisements in Transnational Indonesia (2010)

L. Ayu Saraswati is associate professor in women's studies at the University of Hawai'i. Her book *Seeing Beauty, Sensing Race in Transnational Indonesia* won a National Women's Studies Association Gloria Anzaldúa book award for deftly using the lens of affect theories in exploring issues of race and gender in a transnational context. The following article, published in *Meridians: Feminism, Race, Transnationalism*, exposes the multiplicities of whiteness and introduces a new notion of whiteness as a virtual and affective construction: Cosmopolitan whiteness.

Skin-whitening advertisements dominate the landscape of Indonesian women's magazines. Often, these whitening advertisements appear on the first page of such magazines. In the June 2006 edition of the Indonesian *Cosmopolitan* (hereafter referred to as *Cosmo*), Estée Lauder's "Cyber White" ad appeared on the inside front-cover spread of the magazine. In the following issue of the Indonesian *Cosmo* (July 2006) Kosé's Sekkisei whitening ad with the slogan "Skin of Innocence" appeared as the front-cover gatefold. Neither of these transnational ads employs Indonesian models: a Caucasian woman models the "Cyber White" ad, and a Japanese woman models the Sekkisei ad. These skin-whitening ads, modeled by women of different racial backgrounds and facial features, beg the question: what kind of whiteness is being marketed in transnational women's magazine such as the Indonesian *Cosmo*?

Existing studies on skin-whitening phenomena in a variety of countries fall short of answering this question because these studies operate under the assumption that whiteness is an ethnic or racially based category, however marked it may be by biological, social, and visual signifiers (Burke 1996; Peiss 1998; Kawashima 2002; Hall 2005; Hunter 2005; Rondilla and Spickard 2007; Pierre 2008; Glenn 2009; Parameswaran and Cardoza 2009). For example, when cultural studies scholar Radhika Parameswaran and journalist Kavitha Cardoza point out that whitening advertisements in contemporary Indian media do not necessarily reveal women's desire to be racially white, they are equating "white" with racially Caucasian people (Parameswaran and Cardoza 2009). Similarly, when historian Timothy Burke notes that women's consumption of skin whiteners in modern Zimbabwe was considered as a sign of (re)colonization and "selling-out" to the white regime, he also positioned "white" as a racial category (Burke 1996). Indeed, the term "white-privileging subject position" that Asian studies scholar Terry Kawashima coined in her analysis of contemporary anime, skin-whitening ads, and hair-coloring phenomena in Japan also rests on the same assumed white racial category: Caucasian (Kawashima 2002).

Other important studies on the racial politics of beauty that challenge body-altering practices as merely revealing people's desires for the white beauty norm nonetheless refer to Caucasian whiteness as a frame for referencing "whiteness." Kathleen Zane, although providing us with a different way of reading Asian women's eyelid surgeries that goes beyond Asian women's desire to "imitate a Caucasian appearance" (Zane 1998, 355), still attaches the category of "Caucasian" whiteness to the meaning of a "white" beauty norm. Kobena Mercer has demonstrated the complex "inter-culturation" of so-called "artificial" and "natural" techniques of hairstyling among black people (as well as among people in "white subcultures"), and asked "who, in this postmodern mêlée of semiotic appropriation and counter-creolization, is imitating whom?" (Mercer 1987, 52). Yet he also refers to Caucasian whiteness when he highlights this complexity of whiteness as an embodied racial category. Thus, although critical scholarship on the racial politics of beauty convincingly debunks the myth of racially authentic bodies and points to the unstable quality of "looking white," these studies nonetheless still subscribe to the very notion of Caucasian whiteness as the point of theoretical reference in challenging such whiteness.

This article breaks away from these theoretical trajectories by arguing that desire for "whiteness" is not the same as desire for "Caucasian whiteness." By examining skin-whitening advertisements in the Indonesian *Cosmo*[1] published during the months of June, July, and August, 2006–2008,[2] I argue that in contemporary Indonesia it is what I am calling "cosmopolitan whiteness" that is being marketed through these whitening ads. By cosmopolitan whiteness, I refer to whiteness when represented to embody the "affective" and virtual quality of cosmopolitanism: transnational mobility. In using the term "affect," I am drawing on Teresa Brennan's definition of the term as "physiological shift accompanying a judgment" (Brennan 2004, 5). Here affect is understood as preceding emotions, yet also involving "sociality or social productivity" (Wissinger 2007, 232). In this article I position these ads as a socially productive site where affective qualities about white-skinned women are produced, represented, and circulated.

I propose the notion of cosmopolitan whiteness as a mode for rethinking whiteness beyond racial and ethnic categories and for thinking about race, skin color, and gender as "affectively" constructed. To think about whiteness beyond a racial or ethnic category is not to argue that race and racialization are irrelevant in thinking about whiteness, of course. Rather, I argue that whiteness is also affectively constructed as cosmopolitan and that race and racialization operate in concert with cosmopolitanism in these whitening advertisements.

Redefining whiteness as cosmopolitan whiteness allows me to reveal yet another aspect of cosmopolitanness and whiteness that is not often discussed: its virtuality. Virtuality here is understood as occupying the space between the real and the unreal: the virtual. This notion of virtuality is important in understanding cosmopolitan whiteness because virtuality highlights the lack of "traditional physical substance" (Laurel 1993, 8). I argue that cosmopolitan whiteness is a signifier without a racialized, signified body. Cosmopolitan whiteness can and has been modeled by women from Japan to South Korea to the United States. There is no one race or ethnic group in particular that can occupy an authentic cosmopolitan white location because there has never been a "real" whiteness to begin with: whiteness is a virtual quality, neither real nor unreal.

[. . .]

TRANSNATIONAL CONTACTS AND *COSMO* CONTEXTS

THE RACIALIZED BEAUTY IDEAL IN TRANSNATIONAL INDONESIA

In Indonesia, a country of 300 ethnic groups, the formation of beauty ideals, articulated through racial, skin color, and gender discourses, has historically been transnational. As seen in some of the oldest surviving Indonesian literature, such as

Ramayana, light-skinned women were the dominant beauty norm of the time. The Indonesian (or so-called *Old-Javanese*) version of *Ramayana* was adapted from its Indian origin in the late ninth century. In both the Indian and Indonesian versions of *Ramayana*, beautiful women are described as having white, shining faces, like the full moon. This evidence suggests that: 1) preference for light-skinned women in Indonesia predates European colonialism; and 2) the light-skinned beauty standard in precolonial Indonesia should not be read as merely a "local" or "indigenous" construction. Rather, this idea of light skin color as beautiful is already a "transnational" construction, *avant la lettre*—from India to Indonesia.[3]

This transnational construction of beauty ideals has continued from Dutch and Japanese colonial times into the present day. During the early twentieth century, when Dutch colonialism fully matured in colonial Indonesia (then called the Indies) preference for light (decoded as Caucasian white) skin color was strengthened. Images of Caucasian white beauty represented the epitome of beauty in the beauty ads published in women's magazines during this time. When the Japanese took over as the new colonial power in Indonesia from 1942 to 1945, they propagated a new Asian beauty ideal: white was still the preferred color but not the preferred race. In post-colonial Indonesia, particularly since the late 1960s when the pro-American president Suharto reigned in Indonesia, American popular culture has become one of the strongest influences against which the Indonesian white beauty ideal is articulated and negotiated. . . .

[. . .]

THE COSMO POLITICS OF TRANSNATIONAL CIRCULATION: FROM THE UNITED STATES TO INDONESIA

U.S. popular culture, from its films and magazines to its consumer products, has become one of the most powerful "nodes" (Appadurai 1996) in shaping the terrain of contemporary Indonesian pop culture. Particularly since 1998,[4] there has been a major boom in Indonesian adaptations of American magazines such as *Cosmo*, *Good Housekeeping*, and *Esquire*. Hence, although my focus in this article is on examining skin-whitening ads in the Indonesian *Cosmo*, in this section, I am also looking at U.S. *Cosmo* magazines during the same months (June–August of 2006–2008) to chart the circulation of beauty, racial, and gender discourses through this transnational magazine. Moreover, examining the United States as a site where whiteness is articulated as "desirable," my analysis makes visible how transnational circulations of whiteness from the United States to Indonesia depend on the ways in which whiteness is capable of maintaining its currency globally (hence the notion of cosmopolitan whiteness).

The magazine I examine here, *Cosmopolitan*, is one of the most popular transnational women's magazines in Indonesia. It originated in the United States in 1886 as a literary/fiction magazine. It underwent a significant transformation in 1965 when its new editor, Helen Gurley Brown, then the well-known author of *Sex and the Single Girl*, took a daring step by shifting the magazine's focus to women's sexuality and, as well as in, the workplace (McMachon 1990; Spooner 2001). With the slogan, "fun . . . fearless . . . female," U.S. *Cosmo*'s strategy of marketing to and advocating for sexually independent women saved it from almost certain bankruptcy. Prior to 1965, sexuality was rarely discussed in U.S. women's magazines, which at that time were focused more on women's place in the home (Nelson and Paek 2005). In Indonesia as well, when *Cosmo* (originally called *Kosmopolitan Higina*) first began publication in September 1997, promoting sexually assertive women (albeit in a much subtler way compared to the 2006–2008 editions that I analyzed for this article) meant breaking new ground. Although some Muslim groups in Indonesia sent letters to the editor protesting that the magazine was "helping Indonesian women love sex too much" (Carr 2002), nonetheless, the strategy of putting forth women's independence through sexuality was what made *Cosmo* one of the most successful magazines in the world. . . .

[. . .]

THE CONSTRUCTION OF COSMOPOLITAN WHITENESS IN SKIN-WHITENING ADS

Within its theoretical trajectories, the word "cosmopolitan" is understood to be rooted in the Greek "*kosmos*," which means "world," and "*polites*," meaning "citizen" (Cheah 1998, 22). It conveys the aura of a "citizen of the world." Eighteenth-century French philosophers used the term to highlight "an intellectual ethic, a universal humanism that transcends regional particularism" (Cheah 1998, 22). . . . Moreover, the way the magazine deploys the word "cosmopolitan" also falls within these theoretical trajectories insofar as the magazine seems to make meanings of cosmopolitan, as Bruce Robbins explains it: "the word *cosmopolitan* . . . evokes the image of a privileged person: someone who can claim to be a 'citizen of the world' by virtue of independent means, expensive tastes, and a globe-trotting lifestyle" (Robbins 1998, 248). Here, cosmopolitanism is framed within consumer culture to mean consuming the other's exoticized and commodified culture (Vertovec and Cohen 2002, 7). . . .

[. . .]

. . . The Indonesian *Cosmo*, like the U.S. *Cosmo*, circulates biased, gendered representations of skin color and race that privilege whiteness (oftentimes Caucasian white encoded as cosmopolitan white) in their magazines. Images of African Americans rarely appear in the Indonesian *Cosmo*. Even when African Americans' images appeared in the U.S. and Indonesian *Cosmo*, their numbers were significantly lower than those of Caucasians. For example, out of 308 pages in the August 2006 Indonesian *Cosmo*, only four pages have images of African Americans (1.5%). In comparison, out of 242 pages in the August 2006 U.S. *Cosmo*, only twenty-three pages (10%) contain images of African Americans. The numbers are significantly even lower for images of Asian Americans in the U.S. *Cosmo*. Indonesians or women with stereotypical Southeast Asian features rarely appear in the U.S. *Cosmo*. Indeed, in analyzing thirty-eight issues of U.S. *Cosmo* from 1976–1988, Kathryn McMachon pointed out how models, "if third-world, which is not often the case, are represented in codes which signify difference as the culturally exotic. Paradoxically, actual differences between third-world or minority women and white women in the United States are denied, while racial and ethnic stereotypes are exploited" (McMachon 1990, 383). Conversely, Caucasian women dominate advertisements and images that accompany editorial content in U.S. and Indonesian editions. Having Caucasian white women dominate the Indonesian *Cosmo* highlights the ways in which, within a transnational setting, not only do U.S. citizens travel elsewhere more freely, compared to Indonesian citizens, but their images (mostly of Caucasian Americans) are also circulated more frequently across the globe and therefore are thought to have more value than those of Indonesians.

[. . .]

LOOKING WHITE, FEELING GOOD: RACE, GENDER, AND COLOR AS AFFECTIVELY CONSTRUCTED

My argument that whiteness is cosmopolitan and transnationalized (transcending race and nation) leads us to this article's larger theoretical claim: gender, race, and skin color are "affectively" constructed. Cosmopolitan whiteness is more than just an embodiment of certain phenotypes and vaguely defined skin color, that is, Caucasian whites as having white skin color, big round eyes, and so on. It is also affectively constructed. . . .

At the heart of these ads lie powerful cultural narratives of how happiness is achieved by consuming specific products. As media scholar Sut Jhally argues, "Fundamentally, advertising talks to us as individuals and addresses us about how we can become happy. The answers it provides are all oriented to the marketplace, through the purchase of goods or services" (Jhally 2003, 251). Similarly, Kartajaya emphasizes that the "feel benefit," the benefit of reaching consumers' emotions and promising happiness over rational explanations, rather

than the "think benefit," plays a significant role in helping consumers make their choices. As he succinctly points out, "people's actions are rooted in 'feelings'" (Kartajaya 2004, 34). . . .

In these whitening ads, happiness is offered via the route of whitening practices. Feminist cultural studies scholar Sara Ahmed argues, "some objects more than others embody the promise of happiness. In other words, happiness directs us to certain objects, as if they are the necessary ingredients for a good life" (Ahmed 2007, 127). In these skin-whitening ads, skin-whitening products become the objects necessary for a good life. Happiness is coded as cosmopolitan whiteness.

[. . .]

FACIALIZATION AND THE AFFECTIVE STRUCTURE

One of the most salient features of skin-whitening ads in the Indonesian *Cosmo* is its emphasis on the model's face. All but five whitening ads (Estée Lauder's "Re-Nutriv Ultimate White Lifting Serum," Lux's "White Glamour," Nivea's "Night Whitening Milk," SkinWhite's "Whitening Hand and Body Lotion," and Viva's "White") consist of closeup images of the model's face, which fill almost the entire page. This begs the question: what affective work does this magnification of the face in whitening ads do? I will answer this question by turning once again to the "Cyber White" ad.

In the version of the "Cyber White" ad published in the June 2007 issue of the Indonesian *Cosmo*, as in other whitening ads, the face is the focal point. The face of a blonde-haired, blue-eyed, stereotypical Nordic woman fills the left side of a two-page spread. Her close-up face is magnified. A large, ice-crystal necklace fits perfectly on her smooth, white neck. The neatly arranged light blue ice bricks provide a sense of cool aura to the ad's background. The spectator is invited to feel the "cool"-ness of the ad, of the model, and of the product through the process of a transfer of meanings among these signs (a blue bottle with a white cap, blue ice bricks, a transparent ice-crystal necklace, and the model's blue eyes). She does not smile, which is often requisite in beauty ads. This lack of a smile, however, actually adds to her innocent presence. She peers deep into the spectator's eyes with her sharp and superior look. After all, she is a goddess, or is supposed to make us recall such a mythical figure.

[. . .]

Moreover, in this ad the model's face is represented as surreal in its state of "flawless," poreless, ultra-white brilliance. Here, the "Cyber White" ad positions whiteness as occupying the space in between real and unreal—the virtual. Thus, the invocation of the mythological Greek goddess who looks quite modern in the ad's rendition also makes visible the realness and the unrealness of her whiteness, "Cyber White."

Cyberdiscourse, according to cyber culture scholar Susanna Paasonen, "revolves around notions of mobility and freedom in terms of identity and self-expression" (Paasonen 2005, 2–3). This certainly reminds us of cosmopolitanism: the sense of a globe-trotting lifestyle and the luxury of making claims about multiple (virtual) homes. In this sense, the virtual and the cosmopolitan bleed into each other. However, as some cyberculture scholars have noted, cybercitizens have often been constructed as "white" (here, white usually refers to Caucasian white) (Kolko, Nakamura, and Rodman 2000; Ebo 2001; Nakamura 2002; Paasonen 2005; Nakamura 2008). Hence whiteness becomes one's access to experiencing cosmopolitanness (even if at times only virtually), and cosmopolitanness becomes one's access to experience whiteness.

Virtuality, as it reverberates with cosmopolitan whiteness, also brings to the surface the issue of "real" (authentic) vs. unreal (inauthentic). According to Brenda Laurel, "the adjective virtual describes things—worlds, phenomena, etc.—that look and feel like reality but lack the traditional physical substance" (Laurel 1993, 8). This provides us with yet another understanding of cosmopolitan whiteness: whiteness as lacking the traditional physical substance, traditionally (and discursively) known as Caucasian whiteness. Cosmopolitan whiteness can never be "real" or authentic, nor can any race occupy an authentic white location because there has never been a "real" whiteness to begin with.

Visual studies scholar Nicholas Mirzoeff points out that adding to this lack of authenticity, virtual space is a space that "is not real but *appears to be*" (Mirzoeff 1999, 91; emphasis mine). Thus, cosmopolitan whiteness is not about claiming a form of real whiteness. Rather, it is about appearing white— these creams can only make you *appear* white but cannot make you *become* a "real" white. The body can only be virtually white. The product's label, "Cyber White," therefore captures and exemplifies the cosmopolitanness of the whiteness that is being marketed in this ad. In some sense, this notion of virtuality—real but not real—bears a resemblance to postcolonial theorist Homi Bhabha's notion of colonial mimicry in which whiteness is read as white but not quite (Bhabha 1994).

The question, however, remains: why is the face emphasized in whitening ads? The term "face-to-face conversation" is used to signify the presence of bodies involved in the conversation. This hints at the importance of the face in relation to one's body and its subjectivity. In his analysis of webcam sex Dennis Waskul argues,

> Clearly the face occupies a supreme position in connecting or disconnecting the self with the body. One's face is the most identifiable feature of one's body and self; it is the single human physiological feature that concretely conjoins the corporeal with the self. (Waskul 2002/2004, 51)

Here, the face matters because it links the body and the self. The face becomes, to build on Deleuze and Guattari's argument, a "loc[us] of resonance" (Deleuze and Guattari 1987, 168) that allows us to make meanings out of forms of subjectivity played out in these ads. The face is a source of information through which we approximate the other's subjectivity. The wrinkled old face, the mad person's face, the evil face, the feminine face, the "Asian" face, or the beautiful face could tell us something about the person and how we would feel about them. The meanings of their faces seem so evident that we rarely question where or how these ideas arise, or why certain faces evoke particular feelings in us; that is, a beautiful face may evoke our desire or the mad person's face may incite our fear.

[. . .]

In this era of Photoshop, literally everything is up for alteration. Color is an option. Every pixel's color serves certain (affective, if not aesthetic) purposes. The easiest way to uncover the meanings of these images, according to media scholar Katherine Frith, is to alter the image of the ads and see what different meanings are produced (Frith 1997). For example, would we feel differently about the ad had the model's face been colored red and organized to look angry, that is, instead of having her lips represented as delicate, the model would show her clenched teeth to demonstrate her rage? Of course! These ads hence function as part of the faciality machine because they help the audience "rehearse" (Massumi 2002, 66) their perception of women with white skin color. Moreover, they also help maintain relations of power in which whiteness holds the supreme position. This ad feeds into the reconstruction of her white-skinned face as beautiful, desirable, and positive-affect generating. These are the faces we are "educated" to desire (Stoler 1995). This matters because the micro-management of desire is central to the maintenance of power (Stoler 2002). In other words, whose face we desire is always implicated in the relations of power.

I do not argue, however, that when we look at a white-skinned face, we are *always* positively *affected* by it. This would rob the spectators of their own agency and discount the different degrees of "intensity" (Massumi 2002, 14) that the same face may evoke in different people. This is where I agree with Stoler, who argues that there is "a space for individual affect [to be] structured by power but not wholly subsumed by it" (Stoler 1995, 192). After all, as Terry Kawashima has pointed out, the work of labeling others based on established racial categories involves an active visual reading (Kawashima 2002). That is, readers often dismiss certain parts of the body and simultaneously privilege other parts

to claim that a certain figure looks "white"—in this case the Japanese anime Sailor Moon (a blonde-haired, blue-eyed, small-nosed, petite, young girl). This is what she calls a "white-privileging subject position." (Note that once again, white here is assumed to be Caucasian white.) . . .

COSMOPOLITAN WHITENESS AND HEGEMONIC WHITE SUPREMACY

I wish to end this article with a twist. I would like to preempt a particular question, perhaps unnecessarily. However, it is a question that is almost always raised after I share my reading of these skin-whitening ads in conferences, seminars, or lectures: what about skin-tanning ads? Don't all of these ads simply expose the human desire to want what they don't have? My answer is no: skin-tanning ads actually perpetuate and further strengthen the notion of "cosmopolitan whiteness." Hence in this conclusion, I will provide a succinct reading of these tanning ads to demonstrate how both skin-whitening ads *and* skin-tanning ads function to provide positive affects toward white-skinned women and help construct "cosmopolitan whiteness."

Tanning ads published in the U.S. *Cosmo* during the months of June–August of 2006–2008 provide us with evidence that even in these tanning ads, the color "tan" is advertised *without* undermining the supremacy of the Caucasian white race. Instead, these ads merely affirm positive affects toward women with white skin color and "race," and, of course, their cosmopolitan whiteness. First, unlike whitening ads, none of these tanning ads use the word blackening or browning—words that have racial connotations in the U.S. context. Rather, ads for Banana Boat and L'Oréal, for example, use the word "tan" or "bronze." "Deepest bronze," a surreal color—a color that is not often used to describe skin color—is used to describe the darkest skin tone that these women could achieve by using these tanning products. This suggests that these tanning ads do not even flirt with desires of racial transformation or desires to have black skin, let alone to be black.

Second, whereas none of the whitening ads hint at one's ability to take control of how white one's skin can be, these tanning ads explicitly employ the language of choice and control, an apparatus of white supremacy. Aveeno, for example, sells "moisturizer that lets you customize your color." Olay puts it even more strongly by advertising "the color you control." Hence here, the anxiety of getting too dark is eliminated because Caucasian women can control how "bronze" their skin can be. After all, as Sarita Sahay and Niva Piran found after surveying one hundred South-Asian Canadian undergraduate students and one hundred Euro-Canadian undergraduate students at the University of Toronto, even as Euro-Canadian women desire to have skin that is darker than their current skin color, this "darker skin" still falls within the "white-skin-color-category" (Sahay and Piran 1997, 165). This demonstrates that white skin is indeed the desired norm in North America.

Third, in these ads, tanning is represented within a specific temporal (and therefore contained) context. Most of these ads, such as Aveeno ("you choose the shade for the perfect summer radiance for you"), Dove ("gradually builds a beautiful summer glow in just one week"), and Jergens ("a gradual healthy summer glow, just by moisturizing"), use summer as the time frame for their products. As such, tanning registers within the realm of postmodern playfulness. It invokes temporality, the changing nature of one's skin color, rather than the permanence of desire for darker skin tone. This certainly is not the normative convention of whitening ads that do not highlight any specific time frame in their ads.

Fourth, in these tanning ads, no one is advised to "detox" their white skin color. Whereas in whitening ads we are told that white is "perfect" and that it is a signifier for beauty, in tanning ads, one is advised to simply "enhance" one's skin color. L'Oréal, for example, offers a moisturizer that functions as a "natural skin tone enhancer." This is also the case for Jergens ("natural glow face") and Banana Boat ("natural looking color"). None of these ads insult the white-skinned audience because none of these ads tell them that brown is perfect and their white skin color is toxic.

Last, some of the tanning brands in these ads suggest that tanning is a form of cosmopolitan whiteness insofar as it articulates a sense of "imperialist nostalgia." Renato Rosaldo coined the term "imperialist nostalgia" to mark the colonial's "innocent yearning" for the native's precolonial life imagined as "pure" that had been transformed because of processes of colonialism (Rosaldo 1989). The imperialist nostalgia that haunts these ads can be seen through, for example, the "Hawaiian Tropic" ad, which at a glance resembles a tourism brochure. In this ad an almost fully-naked woman with medium-tanned skin stands seductively displaying her curves. We only see one half of her body, positioned on the right side of the ad, occupying only one third of the page. We see her lips, part of her nose, and one of her eyes, enough to sense that she's smiling coyly. In the background, there is a shadow of a man who is holding a surfboard and is seen walking on the beach. The gender narrative in this ad is too obvious: the man is surfing; the woman is posing for the audience. The colonial narrative, however, lingers subtly in the ad's text: "Hawaiian Tropic sunscreen pampers you with its luxurious tropical moisturizers, exotic botanicals and alluring island scent. . . . With protection up to SPF 70, you can embrace the sun and fully experience the pleasures of the Tropic." Here, tanning practices become a way for white female consumers to inhabit "the exotic other" (Williamson 1986). The Tropic, with a capital T, becomes a colonial site that exists for the purpose of pampering cosmopolitan white consumers. This "going native," the glorification of the exotic other for the consumption of the white self, or "imperialist nostalgia," frames cosmopolitanism as a trope of "colonial modernity"—a mode of engaging the other in the colonizing context (Van der Veer 2002). Hence cosmopolitan whiteness, I argue, is at once a form of longing for the purity of the past and of belonging to the un-rooted and re-routed world culture simultaneously. Hence, I argue that although tanning ads register differently from whitening ads, they both have the same positive affective effects (that is, cosmopolitan, fun, fearless, and beautiful) toward women with white skin color.

In whitening ads the English word "white" and foreign models function to infuse whiteness with a cosmopolitan flair. Skin-tanning ads in the U.S. *Cosmo*, by using the word "tanning" or "bronze" instead of "blackening," urge women to bask in the postmodern desires of playful color transformation while freeing them from the accusation of emulating blackness and hence still privileging (cosmopolitan) whiteness in its ability to travel and consume exoticized others.

In conclusion, in this article I argue that positive affective effects toward women with white skin color are the problematic effects of a transnational women's magazine that circulates within a racially saturated field of visibility. Rather than challenging any racial hierarchies, these skin-whitening (and tanning) ads simply affirm them even if in much more nuanced ways. Moreover, cosmopolitan whiteness illustrates that whiteness works in hegemonic ways. That is, whiteness adapts, mutates, and co-opts new forms of whiteness to maintain its supremacy. As Ahmed points out, "freedom involves proximity to whiteness" (Ahmed 2007, 130). I further argue that the freedom to move transnationally involves proximity to whiteness—and this is the essence of a non-essentialist, "virtual," cosmopolitan whiteness.

NOTES

1. *Cosmopolitan* costs Rp. 35,000 (US$4) and targets upper-middle-class Indonesian women. Class is a significant aspect that begs a more comprehensive analysis, which is beyond the scope of this article.

2. Whitening ads are published throughout the year in the Indonesian *Cosmo*. For this article, I focus on thirty-four whitening ads published in the summer months (June, July, and August) of 2006, 2007, and 2008. This is so because in the larger project from which this article stems, I also provide a comprehensive analysis of a total of nine tanning ads published in the U.S. *Cosmo* (usually published during the summer months).

3. For a thorough racial history of Indonesia from the pre-colonial to the postcolonial period, see Prasetyaningsih 2007.

4. In 1998, Suharto, who had been Indonesia's president for thirty-two years, voluntarily stepped down from his presidency following large-scale protests and the collapse of the economy. His decision was influenced in part because he lost the U.S. government's support. Since 1998 Indonesia has been undergoing a democratization process, one that includes a more open environment for various forms of expressive media that had been repressed under his regime.

WORKS CITED

Ahmed, Sara. 2007. "Multiculturalism and the Promise of Happiness." *New Formations* 63: 121–37.

Appadurai, Arjun. 1996. *Modernity at Large: Cultural Dimensions of Globalization*. Minneapolis: University of Minnesota Press.

Bhabha, Homi. 1994. "Of Mimicry and Man: The Ambivalence of Colonial Discourse." *October* 28: 125–33.

Brennan, Teresa. 2004. *The Transmission of Affect*. Ithaca, NY: Cornell University Press.

Burke, Timothy. 1996. *Lifebuoy Men, Lux Women: Commodification, Consumption, and Cleanliness in Modern Zimbabwe*. Durham, NC: Duke University Press.

Carr, David. 2002. "Romance, in *Cosmo*'s World, is Translated in Many Ways." *New York Times*. May 26. http://tiny.cc/t12ks (accessed August 16, 2010).

Cheah, Peng. 1998. "Introduction Part II: The Cosmopolitical—Today." In *Cosmopolitics: Thinking and Feeling Beyond the Nation*, edited by Peng Cheah and Bruce Robbins. Minneapolis: University of Minnesota Press.

Cosmopolitan (American). 2006–2008. (June, July, August)

Cosmopolitan (Indonesian). 2006–2008. (June, July, August)

Deleuze, Gilles, and Félix Guattari. 1987. *A Thousand Plateaus: Capitalism and Schizophrenia*. Trans. Brian Massumi. Minneapolis: University of Minnesota Press.

Ebo, Bosah. 2001. *Cyberimperialism?: Global Relations in the New Electronic Frontier*. Westport, CT: Praeger.

Frith, Katherine, ed. 1997. *Undressing the Ad: Reading Culture in Advertising*. New York: Peter Lang.

Glenn, Evelynn, ed. 2009. *Shades of Difference: Why Skin Color Matters*. Stanford: Stanford University Press.

Hall, Ronald. 2005. "The Euro-Americanization of Race: Alien Perspective of African Americans vis-à-vis Trivialization of Skin Color." *Journal of Black Studies* 36, no. 1: 116–29.

Hunter, Margaret. 2005. *Race, Gender, and the Politics of Skin Tone*. New York: Routledge.

Jhally, Sut. 2003. "Image-Based Culture: Advertising and Popular Culture." In *Gender, Race, and Class in Media*, edited by Gail Dines and Jean Humez. Thousand Oaks, CA: Sage.

Kartajaya, Hermawan. 2004. *Marketing in Venus*. Jakarta: Gramedia.

Kawashima, Terry. 2002. "Seeing Faces, Making Races: Challenging Visual Tropes of Racial Difference." *Meridians: Feminism, Race, Transnationalism* 3, no. 1: 161–90.

Kolko, Beth, Lisa Nakamura, and Gilbert Rodman, eds. 2000. *Race in Cyberspace*. New York: Routledge.

Laurel, Brenda. 1993. *Computer as Theater*. Reading, MA: Addison-Wesley.

Massumi, Brian. 2002. *Parables for the Virtual: Movement, Affect, Sensation*. Durham, NC: Duke University Press.

McMachon, Kathryn. 1990. "The *Cosmopolitan* Ideology and the Management of Desire." *Journal of Sex Research* 27, no. 3: 381–96.

Mercer, Kobena. 1987. "Black Hair/Style Politics." *New Formations* 3: 33–55.

Mirzoeff, Nicholas. 1999. *An Introduction to Visual Culture*. London: Routledge.

Nakamura, Lisa. 2002. *Cybertypes: Race, Ethnicity, and Identity on the Internet*. New York: Routledge.

Nakamura, Lisa. 2008. *Digitizing Race: Visual Cultures of the Internet*. Minneapolis: University of Minnesota Press.

Nelson, Michelle, and Hye-Jin Paek. 2005. "Cross-Cultural Differences in Sexual Advertising Content in a Transnational Women's Magazine." *Sex Roles* 53, no. 5/6: 371–83.

Paasonen, Susanna. 2005. *Figures of Fantasy: Internet, Women and Cyberdiscourse*. New York: Peter Lang.

Parameswaran, Radhika, and Kavitha Cardoza. 2009. "Melanin on the Margins: Advertising and the Cultural Politics of Fair/Light/White Beauty in India." *Journalism and Communication Monographs* 11, no. 3: 213–74.

Peiss, Kathy. 1998. *Hope in a Jar: The Making of America's Beauty Culture*. New York: Metropolitan Books.

Pierre, Jemima. 2008. "'I Like Your Colour!' Skin Bleaching and Geographies of Race in Urban Ghana." *Feminist Review* 90, no. 1: 9–29.

Robbins, Bruce. 1998. "Comparative Cosmopolitanisms." In *Cosmopolitics: Thinking and Feeling Beyond the Nation*, edited by Peng Cheah and Bruce Robbins. Minneapolis: University of Minnesota Press.

Rondilla, Joanne, and Paul Spickard. 2007. *Is Lighter Better?: Skin-Tone Discrimination Among Asian Americans*. Lanham, MD: Rowman & Littlefield.

Rosaldo, Renato. 1989. *Culture and Truth: The Remaking of Social Analysis*. Boston: Beacon Press.

Sahay, Sarita, and Niva Piran. 1997. "Skin-Color Preferences and Body Satisfaction Among South Asian-Canadian and European-Canadian Female University Students." *Journal of Social Psychology* 137, no. 2: 161–71.

Spooner, Catherine. 2001. "Cosmo-Gothic: The Double and the Single Woman." *Women: A Cultural Review* 12, no. 3: 292–305.

Stoler, Ann. 1995. *Race and the Education of Desire: Foucault's History of Sexuality and the Colonial Order of Things*. Durham, NC: Duke University Press.

Stoler, Ann. 2002. *Carnal Knowledge and Imperial Power: Race and the Intimate in Colonial Rule*. Berkeley: University of California Press.

Van der Veer, Peter. 2002. "Colonial Cosmopolitanism." In *Conceiving Cosmopolitanism: Theory, Context, and Practice*, edited by Steven Vertovec and Robin Cohen. New York: Oxford University Press.

Vertovec, Steven, and Robin Cohen. 2002. "Introduction: Conceiving Cosmopolitanism." In *Conceiving Cosmopolitanism: Theory, Context, and Practice*, edited by Steven Vertovec and Robin Cohen. New York: Oxford University Press.

Waskul, Dennis. 2002/2004. "The Naked Self: Body and Self in Televideo Cybersex." In *Readings on Sex, Pornography, and the Internet*, edited by Dennis Waskul. New York: Peter Lang.

Williamson, Judith. 1986. "Woman Is an Island: Femininity and Colonization." In *Studies in Entertainment: Critical Approaches to Mass Culture*, edited by Tania Modleski. Bloomington: Indiana University Press.

Wissinger, Elizabeth. 2007. "Always on Display: Affective Production in the Modeling Industry." In *The Affective Turn: Theorizing the Social*, edited by Patricia Clough with Jean Halley. Durham, NC: Duke University Press.

Zane, Kathleen. 1998. "Reflections on a Yellow Eye: Asian I(\Eye/)Cons and Cosmetic Surgery." In *Taking Visions: Multicultural Feminism in a Transnational Age*, edited by Ella Shohat. Cambridge, MA: MIT Press.

65. • *Chimamanda Ngozi Adichie*

FROM *AMERICANAH* (2013)

Chimamanda Ngozi Adichie is a novelist who has won many awards, including the Commonwealth Writers' Prize, the Hurston/Wright Legacy Award, and the Orange Prize. Her novel *Americanah*, excerpted here, won the National Book Critics Circle Award for Fiction and the Chicago Tribune Heartland Prize for Fiction. It critically addresses issues of gender, race, and transnationalism in the United States. She was born in Nigeria and divides her time between the United States and Nigeria.

Ifemelu came to love Baltimore—for its scrappy charm, its streets of faded glory, its farmers' market that appeared on weekends under the bridge, bursting with green vegetables and plump fruit and virtuous souls—although never as much as her first love, Philadelphia, that city that held history in its gentle clasp. But when she arrived *in* Baltimore knowing she was going to live there, and not merely visiting Curt, she thought it forlorn and unlovable. The buildings were joined to one another in faded slumping rows, and on shabby corners, people were hunched in puffy jackets, black and bleak people waiting for buses, the air around them hazed in gloom. Many of the drivers outside the train station were Ethiopian or Punjabi.

Her Ethiopian taxi driver said, "I can't place your accent. Where are you from?"

"Nigeria."

"Nigeria? You don't look African at all."

"Why don't I look African?"

"Because your blouse is too tight."

"It is not too tight."

"I thought you were from Trinidad or one of those places." He was looking in the rearview with disapproval and concern, "You have to be very careful or America will corrupt you." When, years later, she wrote the blog post "On the Divisions Within the Membership of Non-American Blacks in America," she wrote about the taxi driver, but she wrote of it as the experience of someone else, careful not to let on whether she was African or Caribbean, because her readers did not know which she was.

She told Curt about the taxi driver, how his sincerity had infuriated her and how she had gone to the station bathroom to see if her pink long-sleeved blouse *was* too tight. Curt laughed and laughed. It became one of the many stories he liked to tell friends. *She actually went to the bathroom to look at her blouse!* His friends were like him, sunny and wealthy people who existed on the glimmering surface of things. She liked them, and sensed that they liked her. To them, she was interesting, unusual in the way she bluntly spoke her mind. They expected certain things of her, and forgave certain things from her, because she was foreign. Once, sitting with them in a bar, she heard Curt talking to Brad, and Curt said "blowhard." She was struck by the word, by the irredeemable Americanness of it. Blowhard. It was a word that would never occur to her. To understand this was to realize that Curt and his friends would, on some level, never be fully knowable to her.

She got an apartment in Charles Village, a one-bedroom with old wood floors, although she might as well have been living with Curt; most of her clothes were in his walk-in closet lined with mirrors. Now that she saw him every day, no longer just on weekends, she saw new layers of him, how difficult it was for him to be still, simply still without thinking of what next to do, how used he was to stepping out of his trousers and leaving them on the floor for days, until the cleaning woman came. Their lives were full of plans he made—Cozumel for one night, London for a long weekend—and she sometimes took a taxi on Friday evenings after work to meet him at the airport.

"Isn't this great?" he would ask her, and she would say yes, it was great. He was always thinking of what else to *do* and she told him that it was rare for her, because she had grown up not doing, but being. She added quickly, though, that she liked it all, because she did like it and she knew, too, how much he needed to hear that. In bed, he was anxious.

"Do you like that? Do you enjoy me?" he asked often. And she said yes, which was true, but she sensed that he did not always believe her, or that his belief lasted only so long before he would need to hear her affirmation again. There was something in him, lighter than ego but darker than insecurity, that needed constant buffing, polishing, waxing. And then her hair began to fall out at the temples. She drenched it in rich, creamy conditioners, and sat under steamers until water droplets ran down her neck. Still, her hairline shifted further backwards each day.

"It's the chemicals," Wambui told her. "Do you know what's in a relaxer? That stuff can kill you. You need to cut your hair and go natural."

Wambui's hair was now in short locs, which Ifemelu did not like; she thought them sparse and dull, unflattering to Wambui's pretty face.

"I don't want dreads," she said.

"It doesn't have to be dreads. You can wear an Afro, or braids like you used to. There's a lot you can do with natural hair."

"I can't just cut my hair," she said.

"Relaxing your hair is like being in prison. You're caged in. Your hair rules you. You didn't go running with Curt today because you don't want to sweat out this straightness. That picture you sent me, you had your hair covered on the boat. You're always battling to make your hair do what it wasn't meant to do. If you go natural and take good care of your hair, it won't fall off like it's doing now. I can help you cut it right now. No need to think about it too much."

Wambui was so sure, so convincing. Ifemelu found a pair of scissors. Wambui cut her hair, leaving only two inches, the new growth since her last relaxer. Ifemelu looked in the mirror. She was all big eyes and big head. At best, she looked like a boy; at worst, like an insect.

"I look so ugly I'm scared of myself."

"You look beautiful. Your bone structure shows so well now. You're just not used to seeing yourself like this. You'll get used to it," Wambui said.

Ifemelu was still staring at her hair. What had she done? She looked unfinished, as though the hair itself, short and stubby, was asking for attention, for something to be done to it, for *more.* After Wambui left, she went to the drugstore, Curt's baseball hat pulled over her head. She bought oils and pomades, applying one and then the other, on wet hair and then on dry hair, willing an unknown miracle to happen. Something, anything, that would make her like her hair. She thought of buying a wig, but wigs brought anxiety, the always-present possibility of flying off your head. She thought of a texturizer to loosen her hair's springy coils, stretch out the kinkiness a little, but a texturizer was really a relaxer, only milder, and she would still have to avoid the rain.

Curt told her, "Stop stressing, babe. It's a really cool and brave look."

"I don't want my hair to be *brave*."

"I mean like stylish, chic." He paused. "You look beautiful."

"I look like a boy."

Curt said nothing. There was, in his expression, a veiled amusement, as though he did not see why she should be so upset but was better off not saying so.

The next day she called in sick, and climbed back into bed.

"You didn't call in sick so we could stay a day longer in Bermuda but you call in sick because of your hair?" Curt asked, propped up by pillows, stifling laughter.

"I can't go out like this." She was burrowing under the covers as though to hide.

"It's not as bad as you think," he said.

"At least you finally accept that it's bad."

Curt laughed. "You know what I mean. Come here."

He hugged her, kissed her, and then slid down and began to massage her feet; she liked the warm pressure, the feel of his fingers. Yet she could not relax. In the bathroom mirror, her hair had startled her, dull and shrunken from sleep, like a mop of wool sitting on her head. She reached for her phone and sent Wambui a text: *I hate my hair. I couldn't go to work today.*

Wambui's reply came minutes later: *Go online. HappilyKinkyNappy.com. It's this natural hair community. You'll find inspiration.*

She showed the text to Curt. "What a silly name for the website."

"I know, but it sounds like a good idea. You should check it out sometime."

"Like now," Ifemelu said, getting up. Curt's laptop was open on the desk. As she went to it, she noticed a change in Curt. A sudden tense quickness. His ashen, panicked move towards the laptop.

"What's wrong?" she asked.

"They mean nothing. The e-mails mean nothing."

She stared at him, forcing her mind to work. He had not expected her to use his computer, because she hardly ever did. He was cheating on her. How odd, that she had never considered that. She picked up the laptop, held it tightly, but he didn't try to reach for it. He just stood and watched. The Yahoo mail page was minimized, next to a page about college basketball. She read some of the e-mails. She looked at attached photographs. The woman's e-mails—her address was SparklingPaola123—were strongly suggestive, while Curt's were just suggestive enough to make sure she continued. *I'm going to*

cook you dinner in a tight red dress and sky-high heels, she wrote, *and you just bring yourself and a bottle of wine.* Curt replied: *Red would look great on you.* The woman was about his age, but there was, in the photos she sent, an air of hard desperation, hair dyed a brassy blond, eyes burdened by too much blue makeup, top too low-cut. It surprised Ifemelu, that Curt found her attractive. His white ex-girlfriend had been fresh-faced and preppy.

"I met her in Delaware," Curt said. "Remember the conference thing I wanted you to come to? She started hitting on me right away. She's been after me since. She won't leave me alone. She knows I have a girlfriend."

Ifemelu stared at one of the photos, a profile shot in black-and-white, the woman's head thrown back, her long hair flowing behind her. A woman who liked her hair and thought Curt would too.

"Nothing happened," Curt said. "At all. Just the e-mails. She's really after me. I told her about you, but she just won't stop."

She looked at him, wearing a T-shirt and shorts, so certain in his self-justifications. He was entitled in the way a child was: blindly.

"You wrote her too," she said.

"But that's because she wouldn't stop."

"No, it's because you wanted to."

"Nothing happened."

"That is not the point."

"I'm sorry. I know you're already upset and I hate to make it worse."

"All your girlfriends had long flowing hair," she said, her tone thick with accusation.

"What?"

She was being absurd, but knowing that did not make her any less so. Pictures she had seen of his ex-girlfriends goaded her, the slender Japanese with straight hair dyed red, the olive-skinned Venezuelan with corkscrew hair that fell to her shoulders, the white girl with waves and waves of russet hair. And now this woman, whose looks she did not care for, but who had long straight hair. She shut the laptop. She felt small and ugly Curt was talking. "I'll ask her never to contact me. This will never happen again, babe, I promise," he said, and she thought he sounded as though it was somehow the woman's responsibility rather than his.

She turned away, pulled Curt's baseball hat over her head, threw things in a bag, and left.

* * *

Curt came by later, holding so many flowers she hardly saw his face when she opened the door. She would forgive him, she knew, because she believed him. Sparkling Paola was one more small adventure of his. He would not have gone further with her, but he would have kept encouraging her attention, until he was bored. Sparkling Paola was like the silver stars that his teachers pasted on the pages of his elementary school homework, sources of a shallow, fleeting pleasure.

She did not want to go out, but she did not want to be with him in the intimacy of her apartment; she still felt too raw. So she covered her hair in a head-wrap and they took a walk, Curt solicitous and full of promises, walking side by side but not touching, all the way to the corner of Charles and University Parkway, and then back to her apartment.

* * *

For three days, she called in sick. Finally, she went to work, her hair a very short, overly combed and overly oiled Afro. "You look different," her co-workers said, all of them a little tentative.

"Does it mean anything? Like, something political?" Amy asked, Amy who had a poster of Che Guevara on her cubicle wall.

"No," Ifemelu said.

At the cafeteria, Miss Margaret, the bosomy African-American woman who presided over the counter—and, apart from two security guards, the only other black person in the company—asked, "Why did you cut your hair, hon? Are you a lesbian?"

"No, Miss Margaret, at least not yet."

Some years later, on the day Ifemelu resigned, she went into the cafeteria for a last lunch. "You leaving?" Miss Margaret asked, downcast. "Sorry, hon. They need to treat folk better around here. You think your hair was part of the problem?"

* * *

HappilyKinkyNappy.com had a bright yellow background, message boards full of posts, thumbnail photos of black women blinking at the top. They had long trailing dreadlocks, small Afros, big Afros, twists, braids, massive raucous curls and coils. They called relaxers "creamy crack." They were done with pretending that their hair was what it was not, done with running from the rain and flinching from sweat. They complimented each other's photos and ended comments with "hugs." They complained about black magazines never having natural-haired women in their pages about drugstore products so poisoned by mineral oil that they could not moisturize natural hair. They traded recipes. They sculpted for themselves a virtual world where their coily, kinky, nappy woolly hair was normal. And Ifemelu fell into this world with a tumbling gratitude. Women with hair as short as hers had a name for it: TWA, Teeny Weeny Afro. She learned, from women who posted long instructions, to avoid shampoos with silicones, to use a leave-in conditioner on wet hair, to sleep in a satin scarf. She ordered products from women who made them in their kitchens and shipped them with clear instructions: BEST TO REFRIGERATE IMMEDIATELY, DOES NOT CONTAIN PRESERVATIVES. Curt would open the fridge, hold up a container labeled "hair butter," and ask, "Okay to spread this on my toast?" Curt thrummed with fascination about it all. He read posts on HappilyKinkyNappy.com. "I think it's great!" he said. "It's like this *movement* of black women."

One day, at the farmers' market, as she stood hand in hand with Curt in front of a tray of apples, a black man walked past and muttered, "You ever wonder why he likes you looking all jungle like that?" She stopped, unsure for a moment whether she had imagined those words, and then she looked back at the man. He walked with too much rhythm in his step, which suggested to her a certain fickleness of character. A man not worth paying any attention to. Yet his words bothered her, pried open the door for new doubts.

"Did you hear what that guy said?" she asked Curt.

"No, what did he say?"

She shook her head. "Nothing."

She felt dispirited and, while Curt watched a game that evening, she drove to the beauty supply store and ran her fingers through small bundles of silky straight weaves. Then she remembered a post by Jamilah1977—*I love the sistas who love their straight weaves, but I'm never putting horse hair on my head again*—and she left the store, eager to get back and log on and post on the boards about it. She wrote: *Jamilah's words made me remember that there is nothing more beautiful than what God gave me.* Others wrote responses, posting thumbs-up signs, telling her how much they liked the photo she had put up. She had never talked about God so much. Posting on the website was like giving testimony in church; the echoing roar of approval revived her.

On an unremarkable day in early spring—the day was not bronzed with special light, nothing of any significance happened, and it was perhaps merely that time, as it often does, had transfigured her doubts—she looked in the mirror, sank her fingers into her hair, dense and spongy and glorious, and could not imagine it any other way. That simply, she fell in love with her hair.

WHY DARK-SKINNED BLACK WOMEN—BOTH AMERICAN AND NON-AMERICAN— LOVE BARACK OBAMA

Many American blacks proudly say they have some "Indian." Which means Thank God We Are Not Full-Blooded Negroes. Which means they are not too dark. (To clarify, when white people say dark they mean Greek or Italian but when black people say dark they mean Grace Jones.) American black men like their black women to have some exotic quota, like half-Chinese or a splash of Cherokee. They like their women light. But beware what American blacks consider "light." Some of these "light" people, in countries of Non-American Blacks, would simply be called white. (Oh, and dark American black men resent light men, for having it too easy with the ladies.)

Now, my fellow Non-American Blacks, don't get smug. Because this bullshit also exists in our Caribbean and African countries. Not as bad as with American blacks, you say? Maybe. But there nonetheless. By the way, what is it with Ethiopians thinking they are not that black? And Small Islanders eager to say their ancestry is "mixed"? But we must not digress. So light skin is valued in the community of American blacks. But everyone pretends this is no longer so. They say the days of the paper-bag test (look this up) are gone and let's move forward. But today most of the American blacks who are successful as entertainers and as public figures are light. Especially women. Many successful American black men have white wives. Those who deign to have black wives have light (otherwise known as high yellow) wives. And this is the reason dark women love Barack Obama. He broke the mold! He married one of their own. He knows what the world doesn't seem to know: that dark black women totally rock. They want Obama to win because maybe finally somebody will cast a beautiful chocolate babe in a big-budget rom-com that opens in theaters all over the country, not just three artsy theaters in New York City. You see, in American pop culture, beautiful dark women are invisible. (The other group just as invisible is Asian men. But at least they get to be super smart.) In movies, dark black women get to be the fat nice mammy or the strong, sassy, sometimes scary sidekick standing by supportively. They get to dish out wisdom and attitude while the white woman finds love. But they never get to be the hot woman, beautiful and desired and all. So dark black women hope Obama will change that. Oh, and dark black women are also for cleaning up Washington and getting out of Iraq and whatnot.

66. • *Kimberly Dark*

BIG YOGA STUDENT (2012, 2019)

Kimberly Dark is a writer, professor, storyteller, and yoga teacher(!) working to reveal the hidden architecture of everyday life so that we can reclaim our power as social creators. She is the author of three books and numerous other publications. This essay appears in her collection *Fat, Pretty and Soon to Be Old* (AK Press, 2019).

She was checking me out. No, really, you can feel that sort of thing, right? Her gaze lingered as I walked into the yoga studio—just that split second longer than a usual acknowledgement. She caught my eye as I rolled out my mat. She looked me up and down—quickly, not in a creepy way—and smiled broadly. Then, as I was picking up a blanket and a block, I could feel her eyes follow me.

So, was there some kind of come-on coming on? A budding yoga studio romance to ensue? I can tell you from experience that this glance likely had a different origin than erotic *tapas.*

We're fat women in a fitness setting.

I know the look—have experienced it for more than twenty years now at yoga studios, gyms, and aerobics classes. I'm accustomed to being looked at because I'm surprising—shocking even. I'm a large woman, and dare I say it—relatively fit, despite being more than one hundred pounds overweight by insurance chart standards. The woman who stared and smiled? She's fit and fat, too. And if she hadn't been so openly interested in looking at my body, I'd have been sneaking peeks at hers, catching glimpses of how her thighs appear in those stretch pants and how her belly or arm fat protrudes from her spandex tank top. The looking is better than the not looking. Sometimes a fat woman will avert her gaze from my flagrant display of largesse. But we were both at peace, happy to see each other. I can't

guess what my admirer was thinking, but based on her smile, I will consider her kindred. Perhaps we were having the same thought: "How wonderful! She's living her life and using her body as she chooses, despite what others might think."

Part of why we find solidarity with one another is because we're scarce—at least at swank studios like that one. When I first started practicing yoga, twenty years ago, there was a range of bodies moving—sometimes struggling—through the postures. Yoga moves seemed a little eccentric and only the bold among us took them into daily life. Back then, I'd catch stares when practicing at the airport in hopes of finding some back-ease mid-flight. You know, those kind of "don't look now, but there's a fat woman doing freaky stuff just over your left shoulder" stares. Sometimes I'm so out-of-the-norm it's hard to tell which aspect of me is being gawked at. However, I receive some glances so frequently, I could make a study.

Nowadays it's easy to recognize the yoga-faithful in public places: the eagle arms in the park at noon on a Tuesday, a deliberate *uttanasana* at Gate 23, the *Virabadrasana I* on the beach. Yoga has expanded its reach, but in the process, it's left some of us behind. The great adjustments, clear instructions, and careful attention to detail of the better yoga studios come with a daunting environment of fitness fanaticism. It's no mystery why these studios market to

"Here's Looking at You," from *Fat, Pretty and Soon to be Old* (AK Press, 2019). Reprinted with permission of Kimberly Dark.

the fitness faithful. They pay. And the rest of us just don't fit in.

Yes, yes, we're practicing *yoga*, so we should all just go within and release our self-judgments. Whoa now. We're working on that, but some have a steeper climb. Or do we? Perhaps it's just easier to look comfortable when one's ego attachment is to the perfect *titibasana* and the $100 recycled yak fur yoga mat. It's inevitable in a consumer culture that the people who can afford to pay a yoga teacher what she's worth will be interested in status. And "hot body" in America definitely equates status. Sometimes the noble fat person can sneak through—the beginner who's assumed to be fighting the good fight against her or his own flab. That person can be jovially accommodated and feel a little bit of love. But what of the average plodder who does a regular practice and never "looks" fit? Well, sometimes it's just not comfortable, so the group support and individual instruction offered by beautiful studios are forfeit.

And that's part of why I became a yoga teacher. Let me not sound too noble here—I love teaching; I've taught a lot of things in a variety of ways for years. And teaching deepens my practice. In addition to these common motivations, I also have a desire to model difference—to encourage others to live fuller lives and to love themselves with greater ease. And sometimes this is personally challenging in ways that it isn't for someone who looks the part, though surely personal doubts about credibility can assail anyone. I've had students at more fitness-oriented establishments see me, look aghast, and walk right out of the class. I've also subbed for classes where students see me and ask if it's going to be a "gentle" class today. To which I jovially respond, "Oh no! We're really gonna kick some ass!"

Ten years ago, I would make the effort to prove my fitness worthiness, but nowadays, I just make my own offering, flawed and brilliant as it can be. (And for pity's sake, if you can't focus on your own breath and asana through a 90-minute class that isn't what you thought you wanted, keep practicing, baby. Just keep practicing.)

We need more fat yoga teachers and old yoga teachers and disabled yoga teachers and anyone with a different body than you think you want. That's what this mess is about, right? Most students want to think of the teacher's body as a goal, an attainable one because she got to look like that by doing this yoga thing. Well, it's not that simple, despite our desire to just pay, participate, and make it so. We want to hop on the yoga conveyor belt and plop off the end looking rested, flexing hot buns, and deserving a martini (or a piece of chocolate cake—choose your poison). The bad news—and the good news—is that living a good life is more about acceptance than it is about attainment. Sure, change is possible, but it's not always the change you were taught to believe you should want.

So, are you thinking about going to a yoga class, but afraid you won't fit in? Chances are you don't. And go anyway. You and everyone else in the room will be better for it. And if you have a body that gets stares—and not always in a good way—and you want to teach, I encourage you. It really will deepen your experience to be the one demonstrating the beauty of a regular practice. Just remember, you may as well get up in front of the class to teach, they're looking at you anyway.

67. • *Jessica Vasquez-Tokos and Kathryn Norton-Smith*

RESISTING RACISM:
Latinos' Changing Responses to Controlling Images over the Life Course (2017)

Jessica Vasquez-Tokos is Professor of Sociology at the University of Oregon. She has published two books: *Mexican Americans Across Generations: Immigrant Families, Racial Realities* (New York University Press, 2011) and *Marriage Vows and Racial Choices* (Russell Sage Foundation, 2017). She specializes in race/ethnicity, Mexican Americans/Latinos, family, intermarriage, and migration. She has been a Visiting Scholar at the Russell Sage Foundation and a Ford Foundation Postdoctoral Fellow. Kathryn Norton-Smith is a doctoral candidate in the Department of Sociology at the University of Oregon. Her research focuses on race and ethnicity, health and illness, intersectionality, and the embodied experience of inequality. This chapter is reprinted, in modified form, with permission. Adapted from: Vasquez-Tokos, Jessica, and Kathryn Norton-Smith. 2017. "Talking back to controlling images: Latinos' changing responses to racism over the life course." *Ethnic and Racial Studies* 40(6):912–30.

In 2015, Donald Trump, a Republican presidential hopeful at the time, disseminated a controlling image (deleterious representation) when he remarked, "When Mexico sends its people, they're not sending the best. They're . . . sending people that have lots of problems and they're bringing those problems. They're bringing drugs, they're bringing crime, [and] they're rapists." "Controlling images," as "major instrument[s] of power," are ideological justifications of oppression that are central to the reproduction of racial, class, and gender inequality (Collins 1991, 68). The function of controlling images is "to dehumanize and control" dominated groups (Collins 1986, S17). The people and institutions that circulate controlling images do so to suppress less privileged groups, restricting minorities' access to upward mobility, self-efficacy, and power of self-definition (Collins 1991).

Controlling images are a hallmark of systemic racism, justifying "the creation, development, and maintenance of white privilege, economic wealth, and sociopolitical power . . . [rooted in] hierarchical interaction and dominance" (Feagin 2000, 14). Controlling images are systemic and cultural and provide a "strategy of action" (Swidler 1986) for prejudice and discrimination. Ann Swidler (1986, 273) conceives of culture (in this case a systemically racist culture) as influencing action "by shaping a repertoire or 'tool kit' of habits, skills, and styles from which people construct 'strategies of action.'" Controlling images are cultural tools that offer "strategies of action," thus bridging systemic racism, prejudice, and discrimination. Patricia Hill Collins (1986, 1991, 2008) theorized controlling images as intersectional depictions of African-descent people that justify racial inequality by masking structural racism. We ask, how well does the controlling images concept extend to Latinos?

Honing in on the two most frequently-reported controlling images of sixty-two mostly middle-class Latino men respondents, we ask: How do controlling images of Latinos as gang members and sports athletes regulate opportunities, impose constraints, and channel emotions? How do Latinos respond to these controlling images? This chapter extends controlling images to Latinos and fills a noted gap concerning subordinated groups' *reactions* to stigma (Lamont and Mizrachi 2012), theorized here as controlling images.

Controlling images (and the institutions and people that communicate them) are a *mechanism* to control underprivileged groups. Controlling images constrain: they divert education, impose suspicion of illegality, block upward mobility, and cause stress. Controlling images are intersectional, specific imagery applying to different groups based on axes of difference such as race, gender, sexuality, and skin color. By focusing on responses, we connect controlling images with their repercussions and we give voice to those whom institutions and people deploying controlling images aim to silence.

This chapter offers three contributions. First, it extends the concept of controlling images to the Latino population. Second, this study focuses on people's agency and theorizes resistance strategies, a move that highlights micro-level power. Third, we demonstrate how stage in life course shapes responses to racist controlling images.

CONTROLLING IMAGES, LIFE COURSE, AND EMOTIONS

Controlling images aim to subdue, dominate, and manipulate oppressed racial groups. These racialized images instruct people on how to perceive and treat racial groups and, in turn, construct a racial order. Alongside the term "controlling images," Collins developed the notion of a "sphere of freedom" (2008, 129), an "'inside' . . . changed consciousness" that is an avenue for empowerment. Life

course literature indicates that this resistance space may be more accessible with age (Eaton et al. 2009), setting the stage to examine how responses to controlling images change over a lifetime. We turn to emotions because people have emotional responses to racism (Lamont and Mizrachi 2012; Fleming, Lamont, and Welburn 2012). Emotions tap into how people respond to what controlling images communicate to them about their position in the racial hierarchy.

Stage in the life course is an under-theorized dimension of power (Utrata 2011). The possession of social power peaks in midlife (Eaton et al. 2009) and self-efficacy and self-assurance also plateau in middle-age (Gecas 2003). This insight into shifting social power as people age stimulates the question of how the age/social power nexus intersects with reactions to racism. Our findings reveal that age affects strategy of resistance, young people utilizing emotional forms and adults employing leadership-oriented tactics.

METHODS

This chapter draws from sixty-two in-depth life history interviews with Latino men. The data come from two research projects conducted by the lead author in 2004–2005 and 2010. Both research projects focused on Latino families and asked questions concerning racial/ethnic identity, family, community, and race and gender issues. The combined data sources include 62 Latino men interviewees that range in age from 15 to 84 years old. All respondents self-identify as Latino, and most as Mexican American (87%). Most respondents are U.S.-born (90%), the remainder foreign-born in Latin American countries. Samples were drawn from two locales: California (San Francisco/Berkeley Bay Area and Los Angeles County) (79%) and northeastern Kansas (Lawrence, Kansas City, Topeka) (21%). The bulk of this sample is middle class. The age breakdown for our respondents follows: 27% were teenagers to twenties, 51% were in their thirties to fifties, and 22% were in their sixties to eighties.

The principal investigator recruited Latinos to interview from Latino-serving institutions (Catholic churches and community organizations), high schools, and Hispanic Chambers of Commerce. The principal investigator then asked respondents for suggestions of family members, friends, and neighbors. The principal investigator conducted in-person interviews (one to three hours) at a location of the respondents' choice, usually their home, workplace, or a coffee shop. All names were replaced with pseudonyms that correspond to interviewees' Hispanic or Anglophone first and last names.

FINDINGS

FORCIBLY CONSTRAINED

Effective controlling images regulate opportunities, impose constraints, and channel emotions. As Latino men interviewees reflected on their youth, they recalled feeling restricted by imagery that depicted them as athletic bodies lacking mental capacity worthy of an education. The controlling image of the athlete curtailed Latino men's aspirations and diverted their educations onto sports fields.

In his youth, the educational system diverted Harry Torres, now sixty-five, out of education and into athletics. Harry uses the phrases "locked me out" and "forced" to explain the institutional racism operating through controlling images that re-routed him toward sports:

> Since I was a straight-A student in grade school, they put me [in] all the AP [Advanced Placement] classes [in high school]. The teacher . . . lock[ed] me out of it. This one teacher knocked me out of the highest English class: . . . she sent me down to a lower English class. . . . They forced me to take . . . shop class . . . I guess they figured this guy is going to pick up one of the manual skills. . . . I didn't fight it. . . . I went out for sports . . . it wasn't as hard.

A strong student in elementary school, high school teachers used race as a proxy for mental ability and "knocked [him] out" of advanced classes. Education is both a racialized and racializing institution

(Vasquez 2011), and here we witness school teachers detouring Harry into menial labor classes. Authority figures racialized him as only fit for "manual skills" that emphasize bodily rather than mental labor. Using "inaction as an emotional strategy for preventing the emotional pain of racism" that struggle would entail (Evans and Moore 2015, 447), Harry "didn't fight it" and instead "went out for sports." As a youth, Harry directed his attention to sports, succumbing to the controlling image and the system's expectations for him. With institutional racism propping up controlling imagery, Harry perceived resisting being typecast as a body without a brain as "hard" whereas not "fight[ing] it" translated to conforming to subpar expectations. The athlete controlling image naturalized sports participation and made bucking a system enforced by authority figures onerous to challenge.

EMOTIONAL RESISTANCE: GAINING ESTEEM IN YOUTH

Emotional resistance involves an internal, psychological, feelings- and attitude-centered struggle to recuperate self- and group-worth. Twenty-eight-year-old Moises Ramos was emotionally committed to proving himself above the low bar of expectations that controlling images establish: "People automatically judge you as being something you're not just because of the way you look." In response, he adopted an "[I] don't give a fuck" attitude as a way to anesthetize the negativity embedded in controlling images. Moises explained his emotional resistance: "just the attitude of 'who cares what others think of me' and 'that's not going to stop me from doing what I need to do to achieve my goals.'"

Given that "stigmatization often triggers indignation" (Fleming, Lamont, and Welburn 2012, 408), this emotional state may guide action. When competing against whites he perceived as racist, Oscar Cota used athleticism to vent his frustration: "We sort of had a chip on our shoulders because we . . . were trying to prove that . . . we weren't going to put up with the B.S. [bullshit] that they were dishing out to us." Rob Esposito was also emotionally dedicated to proving himself equal to others, showing the fine line between emotional and behavioral resistance: "You have to show 'em, show 'em, show 'em that you're just as good as them." Rob tied emotional resistance to specific action: "Just that anger—I was going to have to show them, show them I was better. [That was] a driving force for me, made me competitive." Rob expected that his *objective* achievements in athletics would improve *subjective* opinions of him as a Latino man.

LEADERSHIP AS RESISTANCE: GIVING BACK TO THE COMMUNITY IN ADULTHOOD

Resistance does not stop with emotions but can convert into action as people age and their social power increases. Among adult respondents, most of whom were professionals, resistance materialized as leadership in and "giving back" to their community. Ricardo Torres, a college student, says that people typecast him as a gang member and assume that a facial scar he bears is a gang-related injury. Working against that controlling image, he aims to effect change through "being a teacher" and "really helping people." He elaborates on what "giving back" looks like:

> Just educate. . . . I'd rather work in low-income communities . . . I definitely want to go back to Watsonville [California] to teach . . . I want to see more *raza* [Mexican Americans] come up . . . Not every [teacher] can deal with Spanish-speaking students . . . It's better [for me] to use that skill than to leave it on the floor . . . And I can't lie that I want to see more brown faces here in [University of California campus] or just successful. . . . I'd like to . . . give the biggest voice I possibly can.

While leadership in education was a prevalent theme, some respondents staged resistance through other professions that serve the public, such as sixty-two-year-old architect Gilbert Ornales. As a native of Los Angeles, Gilbert witnessed the relocation of Latino residents of Chavez Ravine to create Dodger Stadium. Wanting to be a "spokesman architect for the people," Gilbert incorporates community representation in his public architectural projects. He sought "input of the gang leaders" when redesigning a park and implemented their suggestions.

By enacting resistance through leadership in professional realms, these Latino men convert frustration with controlling images into constructive action. Emotions remain present in that they undergird and motivate action. By undertaking leadership activities, these men weaken controlling images by promoting life pathways beyond the prescription of controlling images.

ADULT RETROSPECTIVES: LIFE COURSE AND THE TRANSITION OF RESISTANCE STRATEGIES

We now demonstrate how respondents invoke differing forms of resistance throughout their lifetimes. Self-efficacy increases with age, as illustrated by sixty-two-year-old Paul Zagada's reflection on how his reaction to the athlete controlling image changed over time. He describes his high school experience in California and his youthful acquiescence:

> I was really good in . . . track. . . . They called me "the bullet" because I was fast. . . . In order to play, I needed to have a minimum C average. My coach, literally . . . wound up selecting all my classes, dealing with all my teachers. I didn't have to deal with nothin'. I would go to classes: typing classes, business classes, classes that I didn't have to do [anything in] and I thought this was the greatest thing in the world, not realizing what was happening. Because academically . . . they were just passing me . . .

Controlling images of Latinos as sports stars, not smart students, directed Paul into extracurricular activities rather than knowledge-building classes. After achieving his law degree, Paul verbally confronted a college counselor who years earlier had informed him that he would never survive in higher education: "I have survived. . . . I'm probably like many stories where people weren't given the opportunity. Give me the opportunity to survive!" Paul's plea hits at the central nervous system of controlling images: they choke-hold opportunity. Resistance is crafted differently at various life stages. As a youth, Paul passively accepted his place in the racialized school system, unaware of how school practices undermined him. It was not until he reached adulthood that he channeled his emotions into a verbal confrontation meant to resuscitate his agency from years before.

CONCLUSION

Controlling images, as instruments of domination, attempt to contain Latino men as athletes and gang members (among other images), roles that picture them as bodies and offer little chance of upward mobility. While most effective against youth, most Latinos touched by these controlling images resist, their methods of resistance shifting with age. Latino men respond to controlling images principally with emotion in their younger years until they achieve greater social power with age and then resist through leadership in their public-service professions. Latino men recuperate their agency through resistance strategies that are shaped by stage in the life course.

WORKS CITED

Collins, Patricia Hill. 1986. "Learning from the outsider within." *Social Problems* 33(6):14–32.

Collins, Patricia Hill. 1991. *Black Feminist Thought*. New York: Routledge.

Collins, Patricia Hill. 2008. *Black Feminist Thought*. 2nd ed. New York: Routledge.

Eaton, Asia A., Penny S. Visser, Jon A. Krosnick, and Sowmya Anand. 2009. "Social power and attitude strength over the life course." *Personality and Social Psychology Bulletin* 35(12):1646–60.

Evans, Louwanda, and Wendy Leo Moore. 2015. "Impossible burdens: white institutions, emotional labor, and microresistance." *Social Problems* 62(3):439–54.

Feagin, Joe R. 2000. *Racist America: Roots, Current Realities, and Future Reparations*. New York: Routledge.

Fleming, Crystal M., Michèle Lamont, and Jessica S. Welburn. 2012. "African Americans respond to stigmatization: the meanings and salience of confronting, deflecting conflict, educating the ignorant and 'managing the self'." *Ethnic and Racial Studies* 35(3):400–17.

Gecas, Viktor. 2003. "Self-Agency and the Life Course." In *Handbook of the Life Course*, edited by Jeylan T. Mortimer and Michael J. Shanahan, 369–88. New York: Springer.

Lamont, Michèle, and Nissim Mizrachi. 2012. "Ordinary people doing extraordinary things: responses to stigmatization in comparative perspective." *Ethnic and Racial Studies* 35(3):365–81.

Swidler, Ann. 1986. "Culture in action: symbols and strategies." *American Sociological Review* 51(2):273–386.

Utrata, Jennifer. 2011. "Youth privilege: doing age and gender in Russia's single-mother families." *Gender & Society* 25(5):616–41.

Vasquez, Jessica M. 2011. *Mexican Americans Across Generations: Immigrant Families, Racial Realities*. New York: New York University Press.

68. • *Joanna Gordon*

SKETCHES (new)

Joanna Gordon is a writer and educator from the gentrified swamplands of East Honolulu. She graduated from the University of Hawai'i at Mānoa with a degree in English and completed a Master's in Fine Arts at Western Washington University. Her poems and prose have been published with The Shore, Cherry Tree, The Tenderness Project, Blood Tree Literature, and more. She has performed across national stages and participated in length spoken-word productions. She is interested in discussions of white privilege, diaspora, trauma, and tenderness. In her spare time, Joanna enjoys scalding cups of coffee, hiking, bright lipstick, and the company of great friends.

And if you were to draw a body—
draw her in rolls of thick flesh,
in layers of clotted cream and honey,
draw her proper. Sketch the
soft folds of her thighs, her thick
velvet curtains, her hips a country-side
of soft hills, of tiny sloping curves
a landscape not yet seen

And if you were to draw a body,
to really draw a woman, draw her radically
still, draw her radically lonely and
radically whole and radically enough

And perhaps, if you were to actually draw her
body as a revolution—a fist, a foot, a hot sick mouth

what could we be then?

69. • *Christina Lux*

10,000 BLOWS (new)

Christina Lux is a poet and scholar based at the University of California, Merced, where she is Associate Director of the Center for the Humanities. Her poetry has appeared on National Public Radio and in *The Houston Chronicle* as well as in journals such as *Feminist Formations* and *Women's Studies Quarterly*. Her scholarship has appeared most recently in *BioScience*. She previously served as Cultural Envoy to Brazzaville at the invitation of the U.S. State Department, where she worked with youth who had survived the civil war. The two opening lines of this poem were prompted by the story of Freddie Gray, who died in police custody.

when did they teach you
bodies are for breaking?

from our dinner table,
i heard your beating.

we ate in silence,
until the beating stopped.

i stood up once at 12,
to stop that beating.

i stood up just a girl,
pried his hands from your neck
with nothing but eyes, blazing.

who will stand here now,
hand gripping my hand,
to block 10,000 blows?

SECTION FIVE

Science, Technology, and the Digital World

TABLE OF CONTENTS

70. Emily Martin, "The Egg and the Sperm: How Science Has Constructed a Romance Based on Stereotypical Male–Female Roles" 447

71. *Glenda M. Flores, "Latina/x *Doctoras* [Doctors]: Negotiating Knowledge Production in Science" (new) 455

72. *Liam Oliver Lair, "Navigating Transness in the United States: Understanding the Legacies of Eugenics" (new) 459

73. *Clare C. Jen, "Oppositional Scientific Praxis: The 'Do' and 'Doing' of #CRISPRbabies and DIY Hormone Biohacking" (new) 465

74. Wendy Seymour, "Putting Myself in the Picture: Researching Disability and Technology" 470

75. *Vandana Shiva, "The Hijacking of the Global Food Supply" 476

76. *Naciza Masikini and Bipasha Baruah, "Gender Equity in the 'Sharing' Economy: Possibilities and Limitations" (new) 483

77. *Rachel Charlene Lewis, "Technology Isn't Neutral: Ari Fitz on How Instagram Fails Queer Black Creators" 488

78. *Sima Shakhsari "The Parahumanity of the YouTube Shooter: Nasim Aghdam and the Paradox of Freedom" 491

79. Aliette de Bodard, "Immersion" 495

What do inventions in technology, science, and the digital world tell us about the ways in which feminist interventions reconfigure these fields and how these innovations affect our lives? Who gets to create what, for whose benefit, and at whose expense? This introductory essay and the readings that follow help us consider these questions and explore the many faces and facets of science, technology, and the digital world, and their relationships to women, gender, and sexuality issues.

SOCIAL CONSTRUCTION OF SCIENCE

While we often think of science, especially the "hard" sciences, as representing *the* absolute truth, a closer look at how scientists arrive at their findings reveals that dominant ideologies of race, gender, and sexuality shape the kinds of questions they ask, the methods they employ, and the conclusions they draw. Because science creates reality through narratives based on taxonomies and categories (ways of thinking that can be and have been used to justify discrimination), it is problematic to simply accept that whatever science tells us is "true." We need to always be critical of research findings, asking consistently: Who are the researchers? Where are they institutionally located, and who funds their research? What are their methods, and who benefits from these kinds of research?

Many ideas that we now find absurd were once considered "the truth" and circulated in scientific communities as well as the public. For example, in 1760 the Swiss physician Simon Tissot published *Onanism*, a treatise that warned people of the dangerous side effects of masturbation: pain, pimples, memory loss, and even organ failure. To address this issue, a professional society of physicians in Paris published a series of papers in 1864 suggesting chastity belts, cauterizations, infibulations, and amputation of the clitoris as possible methods to treat and deter people from masturbation (Kuefler 2007, 268–73).

Interestingly, around the same time, in late-nineteenth-century Austria, Sigmund Freud was diagnosing women with "hysteria" and enlisting a procedure akin to female masturbation to cure his patients. It was indeed these physicians who developed the electric technology of "anti-hysteria" devices, now known as "vibrators." (This is an example of how science informs technological invention.) Although the myth of masturbation as unhealthy finally came to an end around the mid-1950s when the American sexologist Alfred Kinsey published reports documenting that two-thirds of women and almost all men

Electric hand vibrator, circa 1909. In the late nineteenth century, physicians began to create electric technology of "anti-hysteria" devices, which are now known as "vibrators." The woman shown in this picture is applying the device to her face. Indeed, around that time, the vibrator was advertised to beautify the skin, as well as to relieve pain. Today's vibrators come in different sizes, shapes, colors, and materials and are widely advertised to enhance sexual pleasure.
Source: Library of Congress Prints and Photographs Division Washington, D.C. 20540 USA

in the United States masturbated, all of these examples suggest that science, rather than representing the absolute truth, is socially constructed.

"Science as socially constructed" means that scientific knowledge cannot be regarded as merely an uncontested "fact." The social norms and values that the researchers hold will undoubtedly influence their research. During the 1980s and 1990s, feminist thinkers vigorously criticized the notion of science as "objective" and "value-free." Philosopher Sandra Harding was among the key feminist figures in this struggle. Harding and other feminist **standpoint** theorists call our attention to the importance of questioning science as value-free because the interests and values of the researcher will inevitably shape the research process (Harding and Norberg 2005).

In the first essay that launches this section, "The Egg and the Sperm: How Science Has Constructed a Romance Based on Stereotypical Male–Female Roles," anthropologist Emily Martin examines scientific textbooks used in undergraduate pre-med and medical school classes around the 1980s in the United States and finds that the narratives of the egg and the sperm in these

Standpoint theory: Theories that acknowledge how people's location of and relationship to power, or standpoint, shape their worldview.

textbooks follow existing gender ideologies: the female egg is considered passive and its reproductive process as negative, whereas male sperm is viewed as active, and the sperm production is celebrated. She highlights research in the late 1980s and early 1990s that paints a more nuanced picture of the egg as being active and the reproductive process more complex. Also troubling the medical field, while intersecting issues of gender and race, sociologist and Chicano/Latino studies professor Glenda M. Flores, in her essay included in this section, "Latina/x *Doctoras* [Doctors]: Negotiating Knowledge Production in Science," shows how Latina physicians experience gendered racism in the workplace. She argues, "Latina physicians reflect what Patricia Hill Collins . . . calls the 'outsider within'—in this case, highly educated women of color whose families were at one point marginalized from institutions and who now are in a position to challenge not only how knowledge is produced in the medical profession, but are also repeatedly undermined" (p. 456).

Following Flores's essay, Liam Lair's "Navigating Transness in the United States: Understanding the Legacies of Eugenics" takes on the argument of "born this way" and points out how such an argument "reduces gender to an immutable manifestation of only one of two options: man or woman. This not only limits the possibilities for gender but ignores the multitude of genders already being lived out. These arguments also ignore the historical and cultural specificity of what it means to perform gender. Gender and gendered expectations, even within a limiting binary, change over time and manifest differently depending on cultural and geographical location" (p. 462). His essay allows us to grasp the "enduring legacies of eugenics, particularly in relation to how trans individuals must navigate politics and policies regarding gender in the present day" (p. 460).

SITUATED KNOWLEDGES AND FEMINIST OBJECTIVITY

This evidence showing how science has been socially constructed should not deter us from conducting any scientific research or, worse, cause us to argue that all knowledge is falsely fabricated. An alternative and a feminist mode of addressing this issue, as Donna Haraway (1988) proposes, is to embody feminist objectivity in producing a **situated knowledge** and to avoid occupying the omniscient position of an all-knowing god. Instead, we should always be mindful of our situatedness and be accountable for what we know from that standpoint. This is why it is important to have women with various racial, sexuality, and class backgrounds participate actively as both researchers and research subjects. Including in clinical trials a diverse range of women who bring their different lived experience and biological makeup shapes the research findings.

Situated knowledge: Knowledge is always produced from a specific disciplinary, ideological, and social location.

Unfortunately, based on recent statistics, the percentage of women in different branches of science is still relatively low, although some changes have been

Table 5.1: Women Pursuing Undergraduate Degrees in the Sciences

Field	Percentage of Women Receiving Bachelor's Degrees
Biological sciences	60.5
Computer sciences	18.7
Engineering	20.9
Mathematics and statistics	42.4
Physical sciences	19.3
Social sciences	54.8

Source: https://ncses.nsf.gov/pubs/nsf19304/digest/field-of-degree-women#psychology-biological-sciences-and-social-sciences (2016 data)

Table 5.2: Women in the Science Workforce

Occupation	Percentage of Women
Biological and medical sciences	49.5
Chemical engineers	24.7
Civil engineers	17
Electrical and electronics engineers	12.8
Environmental scientists and geoscientists	25
Industrial engineers	15.9
Mechanical engineers	6.7
Social scientists	58.7

Sources: https://ncses.nsf.gov/pubs/nsb20198/demographic-trends-of-the-s-e-workforce
https://ncses.nsf.gov/pubs/nsb20198/data (2017 Data)

occurring (Table 5.1). In the workforce, women's participation in the sciences is also low (Table 5.2). Thus, although women have made significant changes in the social sciences and medical sciences, the overall number of women participating in the sciences is still low. Inclusion of women in science therefore remains urgent and crucial, as it will change the face of science, from influencing the work culture in the field to producing different kinds of situated knowledges.

TECHNOFEMINIST APPROACHES AND TECHNOLOGY AS GENDERED PRACTICES

What do you think of when you hear the word "technology"? Perhaps you might think of a computer, heavy machinery, or a sophisticated digital gadget. Although all of these certainly count as technology, there are other inventions that we do not often consider as such—for example, vitamins, shoes, and even books. Technology, according to Eve Shapiro, is "the wide variety of objects, knowledge, activities, and processes humans have developed to alter the material (and conceptual) world" (Shapiro 2010, 2). This definition is quite broad and alludes to how science, as a branch of knowledge, and technology may overlap with each other. In this section, when we use the word "science" we emphasize the *process* of knowledge production; the word "technology" is used to highlight the *tools* of production and reproduction.

Science, and the capitalistic market, provides a structure and a realm of possibilities for innovators to imagine new technologies that *can* and *need* to be invented. This means that if science is socially constructed and influenced by the ideologies, interests, and values held by researchers, the technology developed out of this scientific paradigm will inevitably reflect, or in other cases challenge, these dominant values.

As in the sciences, in technology feminists have also made critical interventions that affect our lives in significant ways. Feminist technology and science studies have expanded to move beyond seeing technology as either furthering patriarchal ideologies that are oppressive to women and aim to control women's bodies, such as in the case of reproductive technologies (Faulkner 2001, 80), or improving women's lives, such as better preventive health care technology for women. They have redefined what counts as technology, how to best engage with and influence the field, and how to use technology as a site for activism or resistance. In Clare C. Jen's "Oppositional Scientific Praxis: The 'Do' and 'Doing' of #CRISPRbabies and DIY Hormone Biohacking" (included in this section), she provides us with "key concepts and conversations in oppositional science studies—specifically, intersectional feminist, queer, and trans approaches to science studies critique, as well as their interventions into on-the-ground practices of science, medicine, and technology" (p. 465). Her

TRANSNATIONAL CONNECTIONS

A Case Study: A twenty-one-year-old Thai woman became a surrogate mother for an Australian couple. However, when the twins were born, one of them (a boy), had Down syndrome and a congenital heart condition. The Australian couple took the baby girl but rejected the baby boy. The surrogate mother was supposed to receive 300,000 Thai baht ($9,300) for being a surrogate. She did not, however, get the full amount from the surrogate agency because of the baby's condition. An online campaign in 2014 succeeded in raising $200,000 for the surrogate, who ended up taking the responsibility for raising the baby boy herself.

QUESTIONS

1. How does reproductive technology shape the lives of both the surrogate mother in Thailand and the Australian couple?
2. How does disability matter in this case?
3. How do class, race, gender, and sexuality provide a structure for understanding this transnational dis/connection?
4. Who benefits from this transnational connection?
5. How can we use Wajcman's technofeminist approach to analyze this case?
6. How does technology perpetuate global inequality?

essay serves to challenge the idea that "there is *not* an oppositional way to 'do' science. I argue that there is potential for **femiqueer** STS ways to 'do' science differently" (p. 466).

Similarly, Judy Wajcman considers "technofeminist approaches" crucial in seeing how technology influences the materiality of women's lives in different ways. She argues that advantages for some women happen by exploiting other women (often of color or in other countries). She further reminds us to be critical of why certain technologies receive more funding and attention than others and how these technologies perpetuate global inequalities. In this sense, technology thus becomes "the critical surface for the writing and speaking of power and knowledge" (Masters 2005, 115).

Technological inventions also matter because they have the potential to challenge the fixity of and the fixation with existing gender, sexuality, able-bodied, and racial order. For example, Wendy Seymour, in her article, "Putting Myself in the Picture: Researching Disability and Technology" (included in this section), shares how computer technology has helped her work with her disability. In the case of transgender bodies, hormone injections and surgery have made possible the transition from one gender to another (Alaimo 1994). Other technologies such as birth control pills, available for women since the 1960s, have changed how women experience and express their sexuality. In vitro fertilization has allowed people with the financial resources as well as re-liable access to premium health care to access technology-assisted pregnancies. Dorothy Roberts, in her 1997 book *Killing the Black Bodies: Race, Reproduction, and the Meaning of Liberty*, illustrates the catastrophic ways in which technology has been used to violate Black women's reproductive choices and freedom. These cases show how race, class, sexuality, ability, and gender are "constituted" in the "practices" of technoscience (Gill 2005, 100).

Gendered practices of technology can also be seen in other forms of everyday technology. The telephone as a form of technology, for instance, became a profit-able commodity only after telecommunication companies changed strategy to specifically target women who used the telephone for social purposes, charging them for minutes used rather than for each connection they made. In the late nineteenth and early twentieth centuries, the telephone business failed to thrive because it was primarily marketed to men for business purposes (Lubar 1998, 22). Similarly, it wasn't until Isaac Singer and his Singer sewing machine specifi-cally adapted for home use came on the scene that the sewing machine took off in the United States (Lubar 1998, 22). As Ruth Schwartz Cowan shows in her 1983 book *More Work for Mother*, it was indeed the housewives of America who shaped the kinds of technologies invented and marketed in the United States.

Technology has also been used to manipulate the world's food supply. Van-dana Shiva's essay, "The Hijacking of the Global Food Supply" (included in this section), demonstrates how global corporations, through genetic engineering and patents, as well as monoculture farming, destroy our earth and nature's mechanism to produce diverse food to feed the world's population. She details

Femiqueer: Term used by Rachel Lee to empha-size the intersections of queer theory and feminist studies of science, tech-nology, and medicine.

INTERSECTIONAL ANALYSIS

A Case Study: On Monday, September 29, 2014, Jennifer Cramblett and her partner filed a lawsuit against a fertility clinic in the Chicago area for mistakenly sending them sperm from a Black donor. They claimed that they wanted to hold the clinic accountable for their error so that other people would not have to go through the suffering that they had to endure as a white couple raising a mixed-race child in a 97 percent white neighborhood in Uniontown, Ohio. This hardship includes, they attested, having to travel to an African American community to get a haircut for their daughter and feeling out of place while there. Their therapists advised them to move to a more racially diverse community. The media drew specific attention to Jennifer's sexuality and quoted her saying that as a lesbian she knows what it feels like to be discriminated against and would not want her mixed-race daughter to experience what she had experienced. They sought justice by asking for $50,000 in damages.

QUESTIONS

1. What does it mean to think about "lesbian" as a category of identity that is *not* simply about sexuality but as it intersects with race, class, and parental status?
2. Look online for additional coverage of this case: How do the race, gender, class, and sexual identities of the couple influence the ways in which this story was reported by different news agencies? Why does the news coverage represent Jennifer Cramblett in such a way?
3. In what ways do science and technology affect women's lives (with "woman" as an intersectional category)?
4. In what ways do women engage with science and technology?

the emergence of "food totalitarianism," which she defines as "a handful of corporations control the entire food chain and destroy alternatives so that people do not have access to diverse, safe foods produced ecologically" (p. 482). Technology, in this case, has certainly not been used toward social justice.

Technology as gendered practices can also be seen from the gendered division of labor in this field. Skills associated with high technology are often delegated to men. Men's faces have, quite literally, become the face of innovative technology (think here of the late Steve Jobs of Apple or Mark Zuckerberg of Facebook). Many big tech companies are located in Silicon Valley, a place overpopulated by male tech workers (Hayer 2008, 1361). This, in turn, shapes its masculine work culture and the products and mobile apps they produce (Hayer 2008, 1361; Newton 2001, 73).

This is not to say, however, that women are absent in this field. Some women do work in big tech companies: 36.9 percent of Facebook employees are women (44.2 percent of their total employees are white); 40.2 percent of Twitter (26.3 percent are Asian/Pacific Islander); 33 percent of Apple (14 percent are Latino/as); and 33.2 percent of Google (4.8 percent are Black) (based on 2018 and 2019 data). Women have also created mobile apps to help prevent violence against women, such as "Circle of 6," which won the 2011 White House/HHS Apps Against Abuse Technology Challenge and the 2012 Institute of Medicine/Avon Foundation for Women End Violence @Home Challenge.

Circle of 6 app against sexual violence. Circle of 6 is an award-winning smartphone app—winner of 2011 White House Apps Against Abuse technology challenge. The app works by allowing the person with the app to ask for help by sending a prewritten message to one of the six friends in their "circle" just by clicking the phone twice. It thus aims to prevent rape and sexual violence.
Source: https://www.circleof6app.com/press/

CYBORGS

One of the most important metaphors in feminist technoscience studies is the figure of the "cyborg." In "A Cyborg Manifesto," an influential feminist text in the field first published in 1985, Haraway defines a cyborg as "a cybernetic organism, a hybrid of machine and organism, a creature of social reality as well as a creature of fiction" (Haraway 1991, 149). The concept was first used in the aeronautics field in 1960 to refer to technologies that could improve and repair human bodies and their functions in outer space, although later it came to include everyday lives (Graham 1999, 423). Haraway positions "cyborg" as a figure that embraces the interconnections and relationships among humans, animal, and machines.

Conversations about cyborgs often lead to the binary thinking of technology versus "nature" that, ironically, Haraway attempted to move us away from. Women (more so than men) whose bodies have been touched by technology, specifically for cosmetic surgery, for instance, are perceived by society to have less integrity than those who embrace their natural bodies. However, if we are to pause and ask whose body is *really* natural, we will find that everyone's body, with no exception, has benefited from technologies that protect and prolong our lives: vaccines, shoes, medicines, food, eyeglasses, and cars, among other things. As Eve Shapiro eloquently argues, "technologies shape how we know, understand, and shape the body, and the body is always a product of historically and culturally specific transformative practices" (Shapiro 2010, 143).

Obviously, taking a painkiller is not the same as getting a breast augmentation or a prosthetic leg. The degree to which technology alters our bodies differs based on the form and intensity of that technology, the discourses surrounding the practice, and thence its consequences and meanings. In 2018 in the United States, women made up 87 percent of cosmetic surgery patients. These surgeries and other beauty practices, from eyelid surgeries to applying whitening products, tend to affirm existing notions of racialized white femininity, although not necessarily of "Caucasian" whiteness, as Saraswati suggested in Section Four. These body alterations that conform to current societal beauty standards may create, to an extent, what Brenda Brasher calls the "homogenization of the human by the technological" (1996, 815).

DIGITAL MEDIA

Perhaps we have all indeed turned into cyborgs. In the absence of a smartphone or, for the health-conscious person, a Fitbit wristband literally attached to the body, we can feel as if we're missing a limb. As Sue Thomas proclaims, "the Internet is my body. It's an extra set of senses, an additional brain, a second pair of eyes" (2004, 18). This "extended embodied awareness," or the ways in which the self is now a "networked" self, is what constitutes "posthuman" bodies (Nayar 2010, 8). Not simply an extension of our bodies providing us with a novel way to experience our bodies, virtual space is also a space of dwelling. For some, it is literally the first place they visit, and stay, as soon as they open their eyes in the morning.

But what space is this digital media? Digital media was once referred to as cyberspace, although that term is not commonly used anymore. However, it might be useful here to trace its meanings. Cyberspace is not the same as the internet. Susanna Paasonen (2005) considers cyberspace a narrative about, or a metaphor for, if you will, the internet. For David Bell, cyberspace can be defined in terms of hardware: "as a global network of computers, linked through communications infrastructures, that facilitate forms of interaction between remote actors," or, symbolically, as an "imagined space between computers in which people might build new selves and new worlds" (Bell 2001, 7). Dennis Waskul and Mark Douglass define cyberspace as "a hyperreal technology of social saturation that dislocates space, time, and personal characteristics as variables of human interaction" (1997, 381). Thus, according to these scholars, cyberspace is a way to narrate stories about this imagined space of hyperreality, interactivity, "convergence" (how different forms of media [e.g., radio, books, TV] all come together in this space), and nonlinearity (we don't read websites from beginning to end; we only click on what we would like to see), where time and space are structured and experienced differently than in the offline world.

Seen in its early incarnation as "overly utopian" for having the potential to eliminate limitations set by and in the physical world, cyberspace is now represented by various scholars as a more problematic space that allows for

Engaged Learning

Circle of 6 is a smartphone app that aims to help prevent rape and sexual assaults on campus. It works by allowing the person with the app to ask for help by sending a prewritten message to one of the six friends in their "circle" just by clicking their phone twice. This app won the White House "Apps Against Abuse" technology challenge in 2011. It is still considered as the leading app to prevent sexual assault in 2019. It has 300,000 users in thirty-six countries. If you are comfortable with downloading this app, please feel free to do so. If not, simply learn more about this app or other similar "against abuse" apps from their website. Explore how this app works and answer the following questions.

(Sources: http://www.npr.org/2014/08/13/339888170/smart-phone-apps-help-to-battle-campus-sexual-assaults and https://info.umkc.edu/unews/these-three-apps-can-make-a-difference-for-potential-victims-of-sexual-assault/)

QUESTIONS

1. What technologies are available on your campus to help prevent rape and sexual assaults? Are these innovations efficient? Why or why not?
2. Why aren't more efficient technologies that could address issues of rape and sexual assaults on campus invented? How does this relate to ideas about gender and sexuality?
3. Although Circle of 6 is certainly a great app, it still puts rape and sexual assault prevention in the hands, quite literally, of women, asking *them* to protect themselves. How can we use innovations in science and technology to expand the responsibility of rape prevention to include everyone, not just women, without becoming another means of surveillance?

both change and perpetuation of the power structure. Technology has at times indeed been used against women. Feminist surveillance studies scholars propose the term "white supremacist capitalist heteropatriarchal surveillance" to describe "the use of surveillance practices and technologies to normalize and maintain whiteness, able-bodiedness, capitalism, and heterosexuality, practices integral to the foundation of modern state" (Dubrosfky and Magnet 2015, 7). Moreover, although it may seem that in the virtual world we have the freedom to click whatever we want, the organization of information, links, and advertisements, for instance, reveals the working of capitalism that may shape our choices (Gur-Ze'ev 1999, 447).

Capitalism and globalization played a major role in the development of the internet. First, capitalism fostered the growth of the internet. When the commercial internet was introduced in the late 1980s and early 1990s in the United States, it allowed more people internet access. Prior to that, in the 1970s, only universities/researchers and the military were using the network. This is because it was the US Department of Defense that launched the Advanced Research Projects Agency Network (the precursor of the Internet) in 1969.

Second, access to the internet is made possible by the globalization process that has made the product and the labor that manufactures and transports these technologies less expensive, such as computers, laptops, modems, and so on. This cheap labor is usually people of color who work at factories in other countries. Thus it is important to pay attention to issues of race and postcolonialism as we analyze cyberculture—these are indeed the focus of "digital humanities," a subfield in digital studies.

Interestingly, in the digital world, not only is the labor "cheap," but, in some cases, it is "free" (Terranova 2000, 33). Let's take Facebook as an example. Have you ever imagined discovering that suddenly none of your Facebook friends or the public pages you "like" post anything? How likely would it be for you to keep visiting the site the following day? Perhaps very unlikely. Yet people who attract these visitors on Facebook by posting statuses and images do it for free. Who benefits, then? Certainly many corporations, including Facebook, who turn these postings of information and images into commodities are the ones making the profit.

Why do people willingly become free laborers online? Perhaps it is because most people don't see their online activities in terms of labor and production, unless of course they are part of the new generation of entrepreneurs who use an online platform to sell their products. For example, in the specific case of Black women porn stars that Mireille Miller-Young examines, because these women become their own agents and not only the porn stars on their websites, they are able to enjoy more financial profit for themselves; claiming power over one's own labor is a political act (2005, 214). Most of the time, however, when people go online and become active participants in social media without the intention to sell any product, their activity is driven by the need to manage their identity, seek social approval, or develop relationships (Livingstone 2008, 4). They too have their own self-interest in mind.

It is indeed this belief that people are putting forth their own self-interest and investing in themselves—one of the pillars of neoliberal economy—when they are online that drives the economy in the digital world. In their essay, included here, "Gender Equity in the 'Sharing' Economy: Possibilities and Limitations" Naciza Masikini and Bipasha Baruah analyze the "sharing economy" (the idea that people with access to cars can "share" their cars with peers for a fee or for free) and find that Uber's business models "reinforce rather than challenge social hierarchies based on gender, race and class found in traditional models of entrepreneurship and employment generation" (p. 487). This is because, they argue, Uber has failed to address both safety and equitable access for its female riders and drivers.

SEX, SEXUALITY, AND THE INTERNET

A couple of decades after it became available to the general public, the internet continued to expand and transform itself into the next generation, known as Web 2.0. Now more people than ever, not only those in the internet and computer professions, can participate in this world. For example, in the early days of the internet, one had to learn HTML code to create a website; now users can easily build websites with existing templates, sell their merchandise online, and become authors, singers, and even celebrities using social media platforms and digital self-publishing. Because consumers can also be producers, the line between the two has been transgressed—hence the concept of "prosumers." Customizable information geared toward individual preference is also the feature of Web 2.0 (Nayar 2010, 4).

This advanced development of the internet, as Lewis Perdue argues in his 2002 book *EroticaBiz: How Sex Shaped the Internet*, is heavily influenced by sexual activities (specifically pornography) that happen online. Secure online payment, for example, was born out of the need to conduct safe payment in purchasing access to pornographic materials; the faster download speed was developed to meet the demand of watching porn videos online at the lustful speed of light—imagine pleasuring ourselves to an image that would take five minutes to be completely downloaded, as was the case in the late 1990s.

Online pornography—unlike magazines and television, which are predominantly white and heterosexual—also provides customers with more varied materials; digital technology enables the producers and users with different sexual fetishes, practices, and preferences to post various images and videos on their websites. It does not mean, however, that hetero/sexism and racism no longer exist in the online world. Shoshana Magnet analyzes suicidegirls.com, an unconventional porn website that posts images of women with "alternative beauty" (with body modifications [e.g., tattoos]). Because on this website women stage their own photo shoots and become the "réalisateurs of their fantasies," visitors and feminists alike view this website as liberating and challenging the male gaze (Magnet 2007, 581). However, she argues, the site fails to bring down limiting notions of female sexuality because it prioritizes profit over women's sexuality and includes only a few women of color, and only when it is good for their business (Magnet 2007, 577).

In theory, however, cybersex *can* be liberating. Sadie Plant sees cybersex as the "epitome of disembodied pleasure" because it gives women the autonomy of having sex without physical touch and thus liberates women from getting pregnant or contracting sexually transmitted infections (2000, 460). Cybersex that (hopefully?) leads to "cyberorgasm" also provides a space for talking about "female masturbation," a topic that is still not often discussed openly (Magnet 2007, 584).

The internet can be a liberating space because the anonymity of the virtual world affords some women the possibility to try out a sexual orientation online before coming out in the offline world (Magnet 2007, 583). The internet can also become a relatively safe space (some are safer than others) for LGBTQPAI+ people to meet each other online and learn what it means to be a part of the community (Bryson 2004, 249). For the transgender community, the internet, specifically websites such as gendersanity.com, glamazon.net, and transgendercare.com, has been crucial in providing a space for "bodily transformation," from experimenting with identifying oneself to be of a different gender to learning about the transitioning process (Daniels 2009, 115).

Wikisexuality:
A collaborative- and interactive-based sexuality, not an essence-based sexuality.

The ability for people to express and experience sex online necessarily raises the question of what happens when, for example, women have sex with men offline but have sex only with women when online. Would we call them heterosexual? Bisexual? Hetero-flexible? Saraswati proposes a new category of sexuality that she calls **wikisexuality**. She defines wikisexuality as "a new formation of sexuality that takes into account the fluidity of sexuality as it traverses various layers of reality—the physical and virtual worlds. It is a collaborative- and interactive-based sexuality, rather than an essence-based sexuality . . . . It reflects the non-linear and chaotic formation of sexuality that moves us beyond the mono (i.e., homosexual, heterosexual) versus multiple (i.e., bisexual, pansexual) categories of sexuality and beyond the nature versus nurture debate by evoking the notion of sexuality as constantly shifting with every encounter" (Saraswati 2013, 588). In other words, as the internet provides us with new ways of experiencing our sexuality, it calls for a new category of sexuality, more fluid, playful, interactive, and collaborative, that she calls wikisexuality.

Possible liberatory practices of the internet do not always carry over to material fulfillment, however. Lisa Nakamura (1995) coined the term "identity tourism" to highlight how people can play with their identity online in ways that rely on and perpetuate racial stereotypes. Moreover, the concept of identity tourism allows us to understand how the values and ideas we have about race and gender in the physical world travel with us as we become tourists of identity in the virtual world.

The digital space itself still overrepresents narratives of men and white, able-bodied people. For example, Megan Paceley and Karen Flynn analyzed American online news reports on bullying against queer youth and found that 97 percent of these articles focus on gay male victims and 94.3 percent on white victims (Paceley and Flynn 345). In addition to the race/gender/sexuality/age divide, there still exists the disability divide (Dobransky and Hargittai 2006, 314). This divide is partly due to the expensive "adaptive technology" that is not only hard to learn but also behind in technology compared to those for nondisabled netizens (Dobransky and Hargittai 2006, 329).

On social media, discriminations against queer of color content creators also persist. Rachel Charlene Lewis's "Technology Isn't Neutral: Ari Fitz on How Instagram Fails Queer Black Creators" (included in this section) is an interview with Ari Fitz, a queer Black influencer and YouTuber who left Instagram because the platform never responded to her complaints about the platform's racism and sexism. Instagram removed Fitz's pictures while other queer white people who post semi-nude images did not experience the same level of censorship. Sima Shakhsari's essay "The Parahumanity of the YouTube Shooter: Nasim Aghdam and the Paradox of Freedom" (included in this section) also takes on the issue of social media's "censorship." However, they focus specifically on YouTube's policy on content-moderation and demonetization, and critically analyze what happens when Iranian refugee, activist, and artist Nasim Aghdam responded to YouTube's demonetization of her videos by "injuring three people and killing herself" at the company's headquarters in San Bruno, California. Both essays thus invite us to consider how social media can function as a space of (epistemic) violence and an instrument for the hegemonic maintenance of oppressive, racist, hetero/sexist, and nationalist ideologies.

CYBERFEMINISMS

The digital world has not always been a welcoming place for women. In the online game world, for example, Black and Asian women are often represented as hypersexualized (Nayar 2010, 380). In extreme sports online games, winning means having conquered the racialized others and dangerous/racialized urban spaces and having access to these hypersexualized female bodies (Leonard 2005, 113–16). As such, some online games become a space to imagine white masculinity that structures itself around notions of conquering the bodies and spaces of people of color.

Do women play video games? Of course! Women actually make up half of the PC gamers (Nielsen qtd. in Braithwaite 2014, 707). Some women players, the so-called power gamers, are more active in the gaming world and tend to be more playful in expressing and experimenting with their gendered self. Other women, the "moderate gamers," play games simply to escape everyday life and tend to reinforce gender systems (Royse et al. 2007, 563–67).

Women who are integrated into the mainstream gaming world, however, often receive threats. Websites such as fatuglyorslutty.com collect and post comments sent to female players. Some digital corners of cyberspace, including the online gaming world, have indeed become another site for surveillance of and violence against women.

Against this backlash, feminists have been infiltrating the net in different domains such as in politics, economics, education, care, technology, and romance and transgressing these masculine and masculinized internet spaces. This strand of feminism is called "cyberfeminism"—a term coined by Sadie

ACTIVISM AND CIVIC ENGAGEMENT

In 2017, the hashtag #MeToo went viral. Not only did it catch global attention, but it also strengthened the movement aiming to fight against sexual harassment that had been started in 2006 by Tarana Burke. The hashtag can be considered successful, as it has brought to light, and brought down, some powerful men in the entertainment industry as well as other fields of work, such as in academia: #MeTooPhd.

QUESTIONS

1. How has the internet transformed activism? What are some of the creative ways in which people have used digital media as a site of activism?

2. Can you identify an urgent and important local issue and use a digital platform to raise awareness about it?

Plant in the late 1990s (qtd. in Kuni 2007, 650). Jessie Daniels, referencing Mary Flanagan and Austin Booth, defines it as "a range of theories, debates, and practices about the relationship between gender and digital culture" (2009, 102). An example of cyberfeminism is online activism. Elisabeth Jay Friedman argues that in the specific Latin American lesbian communities that she analyzes, the features of cyberspace such as emails, websites, and chat rooms provide an effective mode of organization and mobilization (791).

EMBODIMENT, DISEMBODIMENT, AND VIRTUAL/POSTHUMAN BODIES

Conversations about science, technology, and the digital world inevitably lead us to the notion of "posthumanism" and the kinds of bodies we can embody in this digital age. But first, let's clarify the meaning of embodiment. Eve Shapiro defines embodiment as "the lived body. A state of being in which the body is the site of meaning, experience, and expression of individuals in the world" (2010, 3). Thus, when people refer to cyberspace as a disembodied space, they think of how in this virtual world people can pretend to have kinds of bodies (gender, race, sexuality, hair color, etc.) that do not correspond to their physical bodies and never have to reveal their offline identities. When some others argue that cyberspace *is* an embodied space, they insist that even when we are online we need our physical bodies to see the computer screen or use the computer keyboard, for example.

Certainly, with new technologies being invented, there are more ways to bring bodies into the digital world. Dianne Currier identifies two forms of virtual bodies. The first is the virtual body as "an informational representation" (2002, 526). In this sense, the virtual body can take the shape of whatever symbol or avatar one wishes and desires. Nonetheless, these virtual bodies become information that other users can decode to gauge the identity of the person behind the virtual body. Second, as a virtual reality body, the physical body is literally brought into a virtual reality environment. For example, when we play bowling with Nintendo's Wii, we use our physical bodies to simulate the movement of "real" bowling in the physical world. This notion of the virtual reality body is also what drives the development of "teledildonic" sex toys and suits that allow people in different locations to have long-distance sex, which is another example of how technology shapes how we experience sex and sexuality.

Posthumanism: A way of being and living where technology, human, and nature seep into each other.

So what does **posthumanism** mean? Posthumanism refers to a "future in which the boundaries between humanity, technology and nature have become ever more malleable" (Graham 1999, 419). It does not mean that we simply leave our human bodies behind, at least not at this time. In this digital world, as Wajcman argues, "wetware —bodies, fluids, human agency" is just as important as "hardware and software" technologies (2004, 77).

Have you ever felt frustrated when clicking on your smartphone keyboard while wishing these buttons could be as convenient as your computer's? This is what Anna Everett is referring to in her "click theory" when she highlights the importance of the body's sense of tactility: the feeling of touching the keyboard that provides us with a certain kind of satisfaction (2003, 14). Her click theory thus reminds us to be aware of the apparatuses of the click, how our bodies emotionally respond, and how we rely on our physical bodies even when we are online. Thus, according to her, cyberspace is an embodied space, even in the age of posthumanism.

What would these posthuman bodies look like in the future? Of course, no one can accurately foretell the shape of these digitally infused cyborg bodies, or if there will be a homogenous version of a posthuman body at all, and how women, gender, and sexuality will be constructed then, when our bodies have been transformed. Aliette De Bodard's "Immersion," a work of science fiction with which we end this section, addresses these issues by provoking questions about culture, technology, and the virtual reality and futurity of identities, allowing us to play with our imaginations of what they may look like. After all, the digital world can be a productive and fun playground of identities.

Critical Thinking Questions

1. How do feminist interventions reconfigure the fields of science, technology, and cyberculture studies? Give specific examples.

2. How do certain technological innovations affect our lives? Provide examples.

3. Who gets to create what technology? Who benefits from this particular technology? At whose expense is this technology invented?

4. How does the internet reconfigure the *materiality* of our bodies?

5. How do we *experience* these new reconstructed bodies in digital media?

GLOSSARY

Femiqueer 435

Posthumanism 444

Situated knowledge 432

Standpoint theory 431

Wikisexuality 442

WORKS CITED

Alaimo, Stacy. "Cyborg and Ecofeminist Interventions: Challenges for an Environmental Feminism." *Feminist Studies*, vol. 20, no. 1, 1994, pp. 133–52.

Bell, David. *An Introduction to Cybercultures.* Routledge, 2001.

Braithwaite, Andrea. "'Seriously, Get Out': Feminists on the Forums and the War(craft) on Women." *New Media & Society*, vol. 16, no. 5, 2014, pp. 703–18.

Brasher, Brenda. "Thoughts on the Status of the Cyborg: on Technological Socialization and Its Link to the

Religious Function of Popular Culture." *Journal of the American Academy of Religion*, vol. 64, no. 4, 1996, pp. 809–30.

Bryson, Mary. "When Jill Jacks In: Queer Women and the Internet." *Feminist Media Studies*, vol. 4, no. 3, 2004, pp. 239–54.

Cowan, Ruth S. *More Work for Mother: The Ironies of Household Technology from the Open Hearth to the Microwave.* Basic Books, 1983.

Currier, Dianne. "Assembling Bodies in Cyberspace: Technologies, Bodies, and Sexual Difference." *Reload: Rethinking Women and Cyberculture*, edited by Mary Flanagan and Austin Booth. Massachusetts Institute of Technology Press, 2002, pp. 519–38.

Daniels, Jessie. "Rethinking Cyberfeminism(s): Race, Gender, and Embodiment." *WSQ: Women's Studies Quarterly*, vol. 37, no. 1/2, 2009, pp. 101–24.

Dobransky, Kerry, and Eszter Hargittai. "The Disability Divide in Internet Access and Use." *Information, Communication & Society*, vol. 9, no. 3, 2006, pp. 313–34.

Dubrofsky, Rachel, and Shoshana Magnet, editors. *Feminist Surveillance Studies*. Duke UP, 2015.

Everett, Anna. "Digitextuality and Click Theory: Theses on Convergence Media in the Digital Age." *New Media: Theories and Practices of Digitextuality*, edited by Anna Everett and John Caldwell. Routledge, 2003, pp. 3–28.

Faulkner, Wendy. "The Technology Question in Feminism: A View from Feminist Technology Studies." *Women's Studies International Forum*, vol. 24, no. 1, 2001, pp. 79–95.

Gill, Rosalind. "Review: Technofeminism." *Science as Culture*, vol. 14, no. 1, 2005, pp. 97–101.

Graham, Elaine. "Cyborgs or Goddesses? Becoming Divine in a Cyberfeminist Age." *Information, Communication & Society*, vol. 2, no. 4, 1999, pp. 419–38.

Gur-Ze'ev, Ilan. "Cyberfeminism and Education in the Era of the Exile of Spirit." *Educational Theory*, vol. 49, no. 4, 1999, pp. 437–55.

Haraway, Donna. "A Cyborg Manifesto: Science, Technology, and Socialist-Feminism in the Late Twentieth Century." In *Simians, Cyborgs and Women: The Reinvention of Nature*. Routledge, 1991, pp. 149–81.

Haraway, Donna. "Situated Knowledges: The Science Question in Feminism and the Privilege of Partial Perspective." *Feminist Studies*, vol. 14, no. 3, 1988, pp. 575–99.

Harding, Sandra and Kathryn Norberg. "New Feminist Approaches to Social Science Methodologies: An Introduction." *Signs*, vol 30, no. 4, 2005, pp. 2009–2015.

Hayer, Heike. "Segmentation and Segregation Patterns in Women-Owned High Tech Firms in Four Metropolitan Regions in the United States." *Regional Studies*, vol. 42, no. 10, 2008, pp. 1357–83.

Kuefler, Matthew, editor. *The History of Sexuality: Sourcebook*. Broadview Press, 2007.

Kuni, Verena. "Cyborg—Communication—Code—Infection: 'How Do Cyborgs Communicate?' Re/Writing Cyberfeminism(s)." *Third Text*, vol. 21, no. 5, 2007, pp. 649–59.

Leonard, David. "To the White Extreme: Conquering Athletic Space, White Manhood, and Racing Virtual reality." In *Digital Gameplay: Essays on the Nexus of Game and Gamer*, edited by Nate Garrelts. McFarland, 2005, pp. 110–29.

Livingstone, Sonia. "Taking Risky Opportunities in Youthful Content Creation: Teenagers' Use of Social Networking Sites for Intimacy, Privacy and Self-Expression." *New Media & Society*, vol. 10, no. 3, 2008, pp. 393–411.

Lubar, Steven. "Men/Women/Production/Consumption." In *His and Hers: Gender, Consumption, and Technology*, edited by Roger Horowitz and Arwen Mohun. UP of Virginia, 1998, pp. 7–37.

Magnet, Shoshana. "Feminist Sexualities, Race and the Internet: An Investigation of suicidegirls.com." *New Media & Society*, vol. 9, no. 4, 2007, pp. 577–602.

Masters, Cristina. "Bodies of Technology: Cyborg Soldiers and Militarized Masculinities." *International Feminist Journal of Politics*, vol. 7, no. 1, 2005, pp. 112–32.

Miller-Young, Mireille. "Sexy and Smart: Black Women and the Politics of Self-Authorship in Netporn." In *C'Lick Me: A Netporn Studies Reader*, edited by Katrien Jacobs et al. Institute of Network Cultures and Paradiso, 2005, pp. 205–16.

Nakamura, Lisa. "Race in/for Cyberspace: Identity Tourism and Racial Passing on the Internet." *Works and Days: Essays in the Socio-Historical Dimensions of Literature & the Arts*, vol. 25/26, 1995, pp. 181–93.

National Science Foundation. *Science and Engineering.* January 2015, www.nsf.gov/statistics/2015/nsf15311/digest/.

National Science Foundation. *Women, Minorities, and Persons with Disabilities in Science & Engineering Indicators*, February 2014, www.nsf.gov/statistics/seind14/.

Nayar, Pramod, editor. *The New Media and Cybercultures Anthology*. Wiley-Blackwell, 2010.

Newton, Stephen. "Breaking the Code: Women Confront the Promises and the Perils of High Technology." *Women's Studies Quarterly*, vol. 29, no. 3/4, 2001, pp. 71–79.

Paasonen, Susanna. *Figures of Fantasy: Internet, Women, and Cyberdiscourse*. Peter Lang, 2005.

Perdue, Lewis. *EroticaBiz: How Sex Shaped the Internet*. Writers Club Press, 2002.

Plant, Sadie. "Coming Across the Future." In *The Cybercultures Reader*, edited by David Bell and Barbara Kennedy. Routledge, 2000, pp. 460–70.

Roberts, Dorothy. *Killing the Black Bodies: Race, Reproduction, and the Meaning of Liberty*. Pantheon Books, 1997.

Royse, Pam, et al. "Women and Games: Technologies of the Gendered Self." *New Media & Society*, vol. 9, no. 4, 2007, pp. 555–75.

Saraswati, L. Ayu. "Wikisexuality: Rethinking Sexuality in Cyberspace." *Sexualities*, vol. 16, no. 5/6, 2013, pp. 587–603.

Shapiro, Eve. *Gender Circuits: Bodies and Identities in a Techno-logical Age*. Routledge, 2010.

Terranova, Tiziana. "Free Labor: Producing Culture for the Digital Economy." *Social Text*, vol. 63, no. 8.2, 2000, pp. 33–58.

Thomas, Sue. *Hello World: Travels in Virtuality*. Raw Nerve Books, 2004.

US Department of Labor, Bureau of Labor Statistics. *Women in the Labor Force: A Databook*. www.bls.gov/opub/reports/womens-databook/archive/women-in-the-labor-force-a-databook-2015.pdf.

Wajcman, Judy. *TechnoFeminism*. Polity Press, 2004.

Waskul, Dennis, and Mark Douglass. "Cyberself: The Emergence of Self in On-Line Chat." *The Information Society*, vol. 13, no. 4, 1997, p. 35.

70. • *Emily Martin*

THE EGG AND THE SPERM:
How Science Has Constructed a Romance Based on Stereotypical Male–Female Roles (1991)

Emily Martin is an award-winning author and scholar. Her book *Bipolar Expeditions* won the 2009 Diana Forsythe prize for the best book of feminist anthropological research on work, science, and technology. She is also the founding editor of *Anthropology Now*. In 2019, she was awarded the Vega Medal in Gold by the Swedish Society for Anthropology and Geography. The following article, first published in *Signs: Journal of Women in Culture and Society*, is one of her best-known and most frequently reprinted works. In it, Martin challenges how science views the female reproductive process.

> The theory of the human body is always a part of a world-picture. . . .
> The theory of the human body is always a part of a *fantasy*.
>
> —James Hillman, *The Myth of Analysis*[1]

As an anthropologist, I am intrigued by the possibility that culture shapes how biological scientists describe what they discover about the natural world. If this were so, we would be learning about more than the natural world in high school biology class; we would be learning about cultural

Reprinted with permission of University of Chicago Press from Emily Martin, "The Egg and the Sperm: How Science Has Constructed a Romance Based on Stereotypical Male-Female Roles." *Signs*, Vol. 16, No. 3 (Spring, 1991), pp. 485–501; permission conveyed through Copyright Clearance Center, Inc.

beliefs and practices as if they were part of nature. In the course of my research I realized that the picture of egg and sperm drawn in popular as well as scientific accounts of reproductive biology relies on stereotypes central to our cultural definitions of male and female. The stereotypes imply not only that female biological processes are less worthy than their male counterparts but also that women are less worthy than men. Part of my goal in writing this article is to shine a bright light on the gender stereotypes hidden within the scientific language of biology. Exposed in such a light, I hope they will lose much of their power to harm us.

EGG AND SPERM: A SCIENTIFIC FAIRY TALE

At a fundamental level, all major scientific textbooks depict male and female reproductive organs as systems for the production of valuable substances, such as eggs and sperm.[2] In the case of women, the monthly cycle is described as being designed to produce eggs and prepare a suitable place for them to be fertilized and grown—all to the end of making babies. But the enthusiasm ends there. By extolling the female cycle as a productive enterprise, menstruation must necessarily be viewed as a failure. Medical texts describe menstruation as the "debris" of the uterine lining, the result of necrosis, or death of tissue. The descriptions imply that a system has gone awry, making products of no use, not to specification, unsalable, wasted, scrap. An illustration in a widely used medical text shows menstruation as a chaotic disintegration of form, complementing the many texts that describe it as "ceasing," "dying," "losing," "denuding," "expelling."[3]

Male reproductive physiology is evaluated quite differently. One of the texts that sees menstruation as failed production employs a sort of breathless prose when it describes the maturation of sperm: "The mechanisms which guide the remarkable cellular transformation from spermatid to mature sperm remain uncertain. . . . Perhaps the most amazing characteristic of spermatogenesis is its sheer magnitude: the normal human male may manufacture several hundred million sperm per day."[4] In the classic text *Medical Physiology*, edited by Vernon Mountcastle, the male/female, productive/destructive comparison is more explicit: "Whereas the female *sheds* only a single gamete each month, the seminiferous tubules *produce* hundreds of millions of sperm each day" (emphasis mine).[5] The female author of another text marvels at the length of the microscopic seminiferous tubules, which, if uncoiled and placed end to end, "would span almost one-third of a mile!" She writes, "In an adult male these structures produce millions of sperm cells each day." Later she asks, "How is this feat accomplished?"[6] None of these texts expresses such intense enthusiasm for any female processes. It is surely no accident that the "remarkable" process of making sperm involves precisely what, in the medical view, menstruation does not: production of something deemed valuable.[7]

One could argue that menstruation and spermatogenesis are not analogous processes and, therefore, should not be expected to elicit the same kind of response. The proper female analogy to spermatogenesis, biologically, is ovulation. Yet ovulation does not merit enthusiasm in these texts either. . . .

[. . .]

But the texts have an almost dogged insistence on casting female processes in a negative light. The texts celebrate sperm production because it is continuous from puberty to senescence, while they portray egg production as inferior because it is finished at birth. This makes the female seem unproductive, but some texts will also insist that it is she who is wasteful.[8] In a section heading for *Molecular Biology of the Cell*, a best-selling text, we are told that "Oogenesis is wasteful." The text goes on to emphasize that of the seven million oogonia, or egg germ cells, in the female embryo, most degenerate in the ovary. Of those that do go on to become oocytes, or eggs, many also degenerate, so that at birth only two million eggs remain in the ovaries. Degeneration continues throughout a woman's life: by puberty 300,000 eggs remain, and only a few are present by menopause. "During the 40 or so years of a woman's reproductive life, only 400 to 500 eggs will have been released," the authors write. "All the rest will have degenerated. It is still a mystery why so many eggs are formed only to die in the ovaries."[9]

The real mystery is why the male's vast production of sperm is not seen as wasteful.[10] Assuming that a man "produces" 100 million (10^8) sperm per day (a conservative estimate) during an average reproductive life of sixty years, he would produce well over two trillion sperm in his lifetime. Assuming that a woman "ripens" one egg per lunar month, or thirteen per year, over the course of her forty-year reproductive life, she would total five hundred eggs in her lifetime. But the word "waste" implies an excess, too much produced. Assuming two or three offspring, for every baby a woman produces, she wastes only around two hundred eggs. For every baby a man produces, he wastes more than one trillion (10^{12}) sperm.

How is it that positive images are denied to the bodies of women? A look at language—in this case, scientific language—provides the first clue. Take the egg and the sperm.[11] It is remarkable how "femininely" the egg behaves and how "masculinely" the sperm.[12] The egg is seen as large and passive.[13] It does not *move* or *journey*, but passively "is transported," "is swept,"[14] or even "drifts"[15] along the fallopian tube. In utter contrast, sperm are small, "streamlined,"[16] and invariably active. They "deliver" their genes to the egg, "activate the developmental program of the egg,"[17] and have a "velocity" that is often remarked upon.[18] Their tails are "strong" and efficiently powered.[19] Together with the forces of ejaculation, they can "propel the semen into the deepest recesses of the vagina."[20] For this they need "energy," "fuel,"[21] so that with a "whiplashlike motion and strong lurches"[22] they can "burrow through the egg coat"[23] and "penetrate" it.[24]

At its extreme, the age-old relationship of the egg and the sperm takes on a royal or religious patina. The egg coat, its protective barrier, is sometimes called its "vestments," a term usually reserved for sacred, religious dress. The egg is said to have a "corona,"[25] a crown, and to be accompanied by "attendant cells."[26] It is holy, set apart and above, the queen to the sperm's king. The egg is also passive, which means it must depend on sperm for rescue. Gerald Schatten and Helen Schatten liken the egg's role to that of Sleeping Beauty: "a dormant bride awaiting her mate's magic kiss, which instills the spirit that brings her to life."[27] Sperm, by contrast, have a "mission,"[28] which is to "move through the female genital tract in quest of the ovum."[29] One popular account has it that the sperm carry out a "perilous journey" into the "warm darkness," where some fall away "exhausted." "Survivors" "assault" the egg, the successful candidates "surrounding the prize."[30] Part of the urgency of this journey, in more scientific terms, is that "once released from the supportive environment of the ovary, an egg will die within hours unless rescued by a sperm."[31] The wording stresses the fragility and dependency of the egg, even though the same text acknowledges elsewhere that sperm also live for only a few hours.[32]

[. . .]

There is another way that sperm, despite their small size, can be made to loom in importance over the egg. In a collection of scientific papers, an electron micrograph of an enormous egg and tiny sperm is titled "A Portrait of the Sperm."[33] This is a little like showing a photo of a dog and calling it a picture of the fleas. Granted, microscopic sperm are harder to photograph than eggs, which are just large enough to see with the naked eye. But surely the use of the term "portrait," a word associated with the powerful and wealthy, is significant. Eggs have only micrographs or pictures, not portraits.

[. . .]

The more common picture—egg as damsel in distress, shielded only by her sacred garments; sperm as heroic warrior to the rescue—cannot be proved to be dictated by the biology of these events.

While the "facts" of biology may not *always* be constructed in cultural terms, I would argue that in this case they are. The degree of metaphorical content in these descriptions, the extent to which differences between egg and sperm are emphasized, and the parallels between cultural stereotypes of male and female behavior and the character of egg and sperm all point to this conclusion.

NEW RESEARCH, OLD IMAGERY

As new understandings of egg and sperm emerge, textbook gender imagery is being revised. But the new research, far from escaping the stereotypical representations of egg and sperm, simply replicates elements of textbook gender imagery in a different form. The persistence of this imagery calls to mind what Ludwik Fleck termed "the self-contained" nature of scientific thought. As he described it, "the interaction between what is already known, what remains to be learned, and those who are to apprehend it, go to ensure harmony within the system. But at the same time they also preserve the harmony of illusions, which is quite secure within the confines of a given thought style."[34] We need to understand the way in which the cultural content in scientific descriptions changes as biological discoveries unfold, and whether that cultural content is solidly entrenched or easily changed.

In all of the texts quoted above, sperm are described as penetrating the egg, and specific substances on a sperm's head are described as binding to the egg. Recently, this description of events was rewritten in a biophysics lab at Johns Hopkins University—transforming the egg from the passive to the active party.[35]

Prior to this research, it was thought that the zona, the inner vestments of the egg, formed an impenetrable barrier. Sperm overcame the barrier by mechanically burrowing through, thrashing their tails and slowly working their way along. Later research showed that the sperm released digestive enzymes that chemically broke down the zona; thus,

scientists presumed that the sperm used mechanical *and* chemical means to get through to the egg.

In this recent investigation, the researchers began to ask questions about the mechanical force of the sperm's tail. (The lab's goal was to develop a contraceptive that worked topically on sperm.) They discovered, to their great surprise, that the forward thrust of sperm is extremely weak, which contradicts the assumption that sperm are forceful penetrators.[36] Rather than thrusting forward, the sperm's head was now seen to move mostly back and forth. The sideways motion of the sperm's tail makes the head move sideways with a force that is ten times stronger than its forward movement. So even if the overall force of the sperm were strong enough to mechanically break the zona, most of its force would be directed sideways rather than forward. In fact, its strongest tendency, by tenfold, is to escape by attempting to pry itself off the egg. Sperm, then, must be exceptionally efficient at *escaping* from any cell surface they contact. And the surface of the egg must be designed to trap the sperm and prevent their escape. Otherwise, few if any sperm would reach the egg.

The researchers at Johns Hopkins concluded that the sperm and egg stick together because of adhesive molecules on the surfaces of each. The egg traps the sperm and adheres to it so tightly that the sperm's head is forced to lie flat against the surface of the zona, a little bit, they told me, "like Br'er Rabbit getting more and more stuck to tar baby the more he wriggles." The trapped sperm continues to wiggle ineffectually side to side. The mechanical force of its tail is so weak that a sperm cannot break even one chemical bond. This is where the digestive enzymes released by the sperm come in. If they start to soften the zona just at the tip of the sperm and the sides remain stuck, then the weak, flailing sperm can get oriented in the right direction and make it through the zona—provided that its bonds to the zona dissolve as it moves in.

Although this new version of the saga of the egg and the sperm broke through cultural expectations, the researchers who made the discovery continued to write papers and abstracts as if the sperm were the active party who attacks, binds, penetrates, and enters the egg. The only difference was that sperm were now seen as performing these actions weakly.[37] Not until August 1987, more than three years after the findings described above, did these researchers reconceptualize the process to give the egg a more active role. They began to describe the zona as an aggressive sperm catcher, covered with adhesive molecules that can capture a sperm with a single bond and clasp it to the zona's surface.[38] In the words of their published account: "The innermost vestment, the *zona pellucida*, is a glycoprotein shell, which captures and tethers the sperm before they penetrate it. . . . The sperm is captured at the initial contact between the sperm tip and the *zona*. . . . Since the thrust [of the sperm] is much smaller than the force needed to break a single affinity bond, the first bond made upon the tip-first meeting of the sperm and *zona* can result in the capture of the sperm."[39]

[. . .]

SOCIAL IMPLICATIONS: THINKING BEYOND

All three of these revisionist accounts of egg and sperm cannot seem to escape the hierarchical imagery of older accounts. Even though each new account gives the egg a larger and more active role, taken together they bring into play another cultural stereotype: woman as a dangerous and aggressive threat. In the Johns Hopkins lab's revised model, the egg ends up as the female aggressor who "captures and tethers" the sperm with her sticky zona, rather like a spider lying in wait in her web.[40] The Schatten lab has the egg's nucleus "interrupt" the sperm's dive with a "sudden and swift" rush by which she "clasps the sperm and guides its nucleus to the center."[41] Wassarman's description of the surface of the egg "covered with thousands of plasma membrane-bound projections, called microvilli" that reach out and clasp the sperm adds to the spiderlike imagery.[42]

These images grant the egg an active role but at the cost of appearing disturbingly aggressive. Images of woman as dangerous and aggressive, the femme fatale who victimizes men, are widespread in Western literature and culture.[43] More specific is the connection of spider imagery with the idea of an engulfing, devouring mother.[44] New data did not lead scientists to eliminate gender stereotypes in their descriptions of egg and sperm. Instead, scientists simply began to describe egg and sperm in different, but no less damaging, terms.

Can we envision a less stereotypical view? Biology itself provides another model that could be applied to the egg and the sperm. The cybernetic model—with its feedback loops, flexible adaptation to change, coordination of the parts within a whole, evolution over time, and changing response to the environment—is common in genetics, endocrinology, and ecology and has a growing influence in medicine in general.[45] This model has the potential to shift our imagery from the negative, in which the female reproductive system is castigated both for not producing eggs after birth and for producing (and thus wasting) too many eggs overall, to something more positive. The female reproductive system could be seen as responding to the environment (pregnancy or menopause), adjusting to monthly changes (menstruation), and flexibly changing from reproductivity after puberty to nonreproductivity later in life. The sperm and egg's interaction could also be described in cybernetic terms. J. F. Hartman's research in reproductive biology demonstrated fifteen years ago that if an egg is killed by being pricked with a needle, live sperm cannot get through the zona.[46] Clearly, this evidence shows that the egg and sperm *do* interact on more mutual terms, making biology's refusal to portray them that way all the more disturbing.

We would do well to be aware, however, that cybernetic imagery is hardly neutral. In the past, cybernetic models have played an important part in the imposition of social control. These models inherently provide a way of thinking about a "field" of interacting components. Once the field can be seen, it can become the object of new forms of knowledge, which in turn can allow new forms of social control to be exerted over the components of the field. During the 1950s, for example, medicine began to recognize the psychosocial *environment* of the patient: the patient's family and its psychodynamics. Professions such as social work began to focus on this new environment, and the resulting knowledge became one way to further control the patient. Patients began to be seen not as isolated, individual bodies, but as psychosocial entities located in an "ecological" system: management of "the patient's psychology was a new entrée to patient control."[47]

The models that biologists use to describe their data can have important social effects. During the nineteenth century, the social and natural sciences strongly influenced each other: the social ideas of Malthus about how to avoid the natural increase of the poor inspired Darwin's *Origin of Species*.[48] Once the *Origin* stood as a description of the natural world, complete with competition and market struggles, it could be reimported into social science as social Darwinism, in order to justify the social order of the time. What we are seeing now is similar: the importation of cultural ideas about passive females and heroic males into the "personalities" of gametes. This amounts to the "implanting of social imagery on representations of nature so as to lay a firm basis for reimporting exactly that same imagery as natural explanations of social phenomena."[49]

Further research would show us exactly what social effects are being wrought from the biological imagery of egg and sperm. At the very least, the imagery keeps alive some of the hoariest old stereotypes about weak damsels in distress and their strong male rescuers. That these stereotypes are now being written in at the level of the *cell* constitutes a powerful move to make them seem so natural as to be beyond alteration.

The stereotypical imagery might also encourage people to imagine that what results from the interaction of egg and sperm—a fertilized egg—is the result of deliberate "human" action at the cellular level. Whatever the intentions of the human couple, in this microscopic "culture" a cellular "bride" (or femme fatale) and a cellular "groom" (her victim) make a cellular baby. Rosalind Petchesky points out that through visual representations such as sonograms, we are given "*images* of younger and younger, and tinier and tinier, fetuses being 'saved.'" This leads to "the point of viability being 'pushed back' *indefinitely*."[50] Endowing egg and sperm with intentional action, a key aspect of personhood in our culture, lays the foundation for the point of viability being pushed back to the moment of fertilization. This will likely lead to greater acceptance of technological developments and new forms of scrutiny and manipulation, for the benefit of these inner "persons": court-ordered restrictions on a pregnant woman's activities in order to protect her fetus, fetal surgery, amniocentesis, and rescinding of abortion rights, to name but a few examples.[51]

Even if we succeed in substituting more egalitarian, interactive metaphors to describe the activities of egg and sperm, and manage to avoid the pitfalls of cybernetic models, we would still be guilty of endowing cellular entities with personhood. More crucial, then, than what *kinds* of personalities we bestow on cells is the very fact that we are doing it at all. This process could ultimately have the most disturbing social consequences.

One clear feminist challenge is to wake up sleeping metaphors in science, particularly those involved in descriptions of the egg and the sperm. Although the literary convention is to call such metaphors "dead," they are not so much dead as sleeping, hidden within the scientific content of texts—and all the more powerful for it.[52] Waking up such metaphors, by becoming aware of when we are projecting cultural imagery onto what we study, will improve our ability to investigate and understand nature. Waking up such metaphors, by becoming aware of their implications, will rob them of their power to naturalize our social conventions about gender.

NOTES

1. James Hillman, *The Myth of Analysis* (Evanston, Ill.: Northwestern University Press, 1972), 220.
2. The textbooks I consulted are the main ones used in classes for undergraduate premedical students or medical students (or those held on reserve in the library for these classes) during the past few years at Johns Hopkins University. These texts are widely used at other universities in the country as well.
3. Arthur C. Guyton, *Physiology of the Human Body*, 6th ed. (Philadelphia: Saunders College Publishing, 1984), 624.
4. Arthur J. Vander, James H. Sherman, and Dorothy S. Luciano, *Human Physiology: The Mechanisms of Body Function*, 3d ed. (New York: McGraw Hill, 1980), 483–84.
5. Vernon B. Mountcastle, *Medical Physiology*, 14th ed. (London: Mosby, 1980), 2:1624.
6. Eldra Pearl Solomon, *Human Anatomy and Physiology* (New York: CBS College Publishing, 1983), 678.
7. For elaboration, see Emily Martin, *The Woman in the Body: A Cultural Analysis of Reproduction* (Boston: Beacon, 1987), 27–53.
8. I have found but one exception to the opinion that the female is wasteful: "Smallpox being the nasty disease it is, one might expect nature to have designed antibody molecules with combining sites that specifically recognize the epitopes on smallpox virus. Nature differs from technology, however: it thinks nothing of wastefulness. (For example, rather than improving the chance that a spermatozoon will meet an egg cell, nature finds it easier to produce millions of spermatozoa.)" (Niels Kaj Jerne, "The Immune System," *Scientific American* 229, no. 1 [July 1973]: 53). Thanks to a *Signs* reviewer for bringing this reference to my attention.
9. Bruce Alberts et al., *Molecular Biology of the Cell* (New York: Garland, 1983), 795.
10. In her essay "Have Only Men Evolved?" (in *Discovering Reality: Feminist Perspectives on Epistemology, Metaphysics, Methodology, and Philosophy of Science*, ed. Sandra Harding and Merrill B. Hintikka [Dordrecht: Reidel, 1983], 45–69, esp. 60–61), Ruth Hubbard points out that sociobiologists have said the female invests more energy than the male in the production of her large gametes, claiming that this explains why the female provides parental care. Hubbard questions whether it "really takes more 'energy' to generate the one or relatively few eggs than the large excess of sperms required to achieve fertilization." For further critique of how the greater size of eggs is interpreted in sociobiology, see Donna Haraway, "Investment Strategies for the Evolving Portfolio of Primate Females," in *Body/Politics*, ed. Mary Jacobus, Evelyn Fox Keller, and Sally Shuttleworth (New York: Routledge, 1990), 155–56.
11. The sources I used for this article provide compelling information on interactions among sperm. Lack of space prevents me from taking up this theme here, but the elements include competition, hierarchy, and sacrifice. For a newspaper report, see Malcolm W. Browne, "Some Thoughts on Self Sacrifice," *New York Times* (July 5, 1988), C6. For a literary rendition, see John Barth, "Night-Sea Journey," in his *Lost in the Funhouse* (Garden City, N.Y.: Doubleday, 1968), 3–13.
12. See Carol Delaney, "The Meaning of Paternity and the Virgin Birth Debate," *Man* 21, no. 3 (September 1986): 494–513. She discusses the difference between this scientific view that women contribute genetic material to the fetus and the claim of long-standing Western folk theories that the origin and identity of the fetus comes from the male, as in the metaphor of planting a seed in soil.
13. For a suggested direct link between human behavior and purportedly passive eggs and active sperm, [see] Erik H. Erikson, "Inner and Outer Space: Reflections on Womanhood," *Daedalus* 93, no. 2 (Spring 1964): 582–606, esp. 591.
14. Guyton (n. 3 above), 619; and Mountcastle (n. 5 above), 1609.
15. Jonathan Miller and David Pelham, *The Facts of Life* (New York: Viking Penguin, 1984), 5.
16. Alberts et al., 796.
17. Ibid., 796.
18. See, e.g., William F. Ganong, *Review of Medical Physiology*, 7th ed. (Los Altos, Calif.: Lange Medical Publications, 1975), 322.
19. Alberts et al. (n. 9 above), 796.
20. Guyton, 615.
21. Solomon (n. 6 above), 683.
22. Vander, Sherman, and Luciano (n. 4 above), 4th ed. (1985), 580.
23. Alberts et al., 796.
24. All biology texts quoted above use the word "penetrate."
25. Solomon, 700.
26. A. Beldecos et al., "The Importance of Feminist Critique for Contemporary Cell Biology," *Hypatia* 3, no. 1 (Spring 1988): 61–76.
27. Gerald Schatten and Helen Schatten, "The Energetic Egg," *Medical World News* 23 (January 23, 1984): 51–53, esp. 51.
28. Alberts et al., 796.

29. Guyton (n. 3 above), 613.

30. Miller and Pelham (n. 15 above), 7.

31. Alberts et al. (n. 9 above), 804.

32. Ibid., 801.

33. Lennart Nilsson, "A Portrait of the Sperm," in *The Functional Anatomy of the Spermatozoon*, ed. Bjorn A. Afzelius (New York: Pergamon, 1975), 79–82.

34. Ludwik Fleck, *Genesis and Development of a Scientific Fact*, ed. Thaddeus J. Trenn and Robert K. Merton (Chicago: University of Chicago Press, 1979), 38.

35. Jay M. Baltz carried out the research I describe when he was a graduate student in the Thomas C. Jenkins Department of Biophysics at Johns Hopkins University.

36. Far less is known about the physiology of sperm than comparable female substances, which some feminists claim is no accident. Greater scientific scrutiny of female reproduction has long enabled the burden of birth control to be placed on women. In this case, the researchers' discovery did not depend on development of any new technology. The experiments made use of glass pipettes, a manometer, and a simple microscope, all of which have been available for more than one hundred years.

37. Jay Baltz and Richard A. Cone, "What Force Is Needed to Tether a Sperm?" (abstract for Society for the Study of Reproduction, 1985), and "Flagellar Torque on the Head Determines the Force Needed to Tether a Sperm" (abstract for Biophysical Society, 1986).

38. Jay M. Baltz, David F. Katz, and Richard A. Cone, "The Mechanics of the Sperm-Egg Interaction at the Zona Pellucida," *Biophysical Journal* 54, no. 4 (October 1988): 643–54. Lab members were somewhat familiar with work on metaphors in the biology of female reproduction. Richard Cone, who runs the lab, is my husband, and he talked with them about my earlier research on the subject from time to time. Even though my current research focuses on biological imagery and I heard about the lab's work from my husband every day, I myself did not recognize the role of imagery in the sperm research until many weeks after the period of research and writing I describe. Therefore, I assume that any awareness the lab members may have had about how underlying metaphor might be guiding this particular research was fairly inchoate.

39. Ibid., 643, 650.

40. Baltz, Katz, and Cone (n. 38 above), 643, 650.

41. Schatten and Schatten, 53.

42. Paul M. Wassarman, "The Biology and Chemistry of Fertilization," *Science* 235, no. 4788 (January 30, 1987), 557.

43. Mary Ellman, *Thinking About Women* (New York: Harcourt Brace Jovanovich, 1968), 140; Nina Auerbach, *Woman and the Demon* (Cambridge, Mass.: Harvard University Press, 1982), esp. 186.

44. Kenneth Alan Adams, "Arachnophobia: Love American Style," *Journal of Psychoanalytic Anthropology* 4, no. 2 (1981): 157–97.

45. William Ray Arney and Bernard Bergen, *Medicine and the Management of Living* (Chicago: University of Chicago Press, 1984).

46. J. F. Hartman, R. B. Gwatkin, and C. F. Hutchison, "Early Contact Interactions Between Mammalian Gametes *In Vitro*," *Proceedings of the National Academy of Sciences (U.S.)* 69, no. 10 (1972): 2767–69.

47. Arney and Bergen, 68.

48. Ruth Hubbard, "Have Only Men Evolved?" (n. 10 above), 51–52.

49. David Harvey, personal communication, November 1989.

50. Rosalind Petchesky, "Fetal Images: The Power of Visual Culture in the Politics of Reproduction," *Feminist Studies* 13, no. 2 (Summer 1987): 263–92, esp. 272.

51. Rita Arditti, Renate Klein, and Shelley Minden, *Test-Tube Women* (London: Pandora, 1984); Ellen Goodman, "Whose Right to Life?" *Baltimore Sun* (November 17, 1987); Tamar Lewin, "Courts Acting to Force Care of the Unborn," *New York Times* (November 23, 1987), A1 and B10; Susan Irwin and Brigitte Jordan, "Knowledge, Practice, and Power: Court Ordered Cesarean Sections," *Medical Anthropology Quarterly* 1, no. 3 (September 1987): 319–34.

52. Thanks to Elizabeth Fee and David Spain, who in February 1989 and April 1989, respectively, made points related to this.

LATINA/X *DOCTORAS* [DOCTORS]:
Negotiating Knowledge Production in Science (new)

Glenda M. Flores is an award-winning author and an associate professor of Chicano/Latino Studies at the University of California, Irvine. Her book, *Latina Teachers: Creating Careers and Guarding Culture*, won the 2018 Outstanding Contribution to Scholarship Book Award from the Race, Gender and Class Section of the American Sociological Association. The following article is a piece from her new book project focused on gendered dynamics in the lives of the Latina/o physicians who are steadily entering prestigious nontraditional careers in medicine. In this project, Flores examines the fluid and often contradicting gendered expectations Latina/o physicians face and how their medical knowledge is received by various actors.

As the US-born daughter of Mexican immigrants, traveling across the US/Mexico border to receive medical care from the city of Santa Ana, California, was not out of the ordinary for my parents. In fact, caravanning almost two hours south of the border was the way they preferred to receive their health screenings with any Latina/o doctor that was available and open for business during their short stay. Part of the reason they did this was because they lacked US health insurance, but another far more important factor was that they were better able to communicate their ailments to Spanish-speaking physicians without needing someone else to translate for them. As I got older, I often accompanied my parents on their medical visits to ensure that the physician understood their symptoms and would provide adequate care. But, while I could translate perfectly what my parents wanted to say to the medical provider, I could not always translate back what the physician was trying to communicate. Kwon (2013, 61) notes that the children of immigrants often serve as language brokers for their parents in various institutions, and in doctor's visits often learn about the seriousness of their ailments.

I had odd interactions with physicians, too. For instance, after looking at my arms during a routine physical examination, a male doctor surmised that I had hirsutism—an excessiveness of hair on the body where hair follicles are normally absent or minimal—and suggested I undergo additional testing. He requested blood tests and other evaluations and they came back normal, yet he also said that this probably ran in my family because we were Mexican, reflective of the medical profession's overreliance on Eurocentric metrics (Saraswati 2013, 108). While my arm hair and full eyebrows were used to denote me as part of the Ramirez (grandfather's surname) brood and indicated beauty and pride, in the United States it meant something completely different. Stories such as these were common among the twenty Latina/x physicians I interviewed in California about their interactions with Latino patients.

At over 17 percent, Latinos are the largest racial/ethnic minority group in the United States, but according to the Association of American Medical Colleges (AAMC 2014), Latinos represent less than 6 percent of all physicians in the nation, and less than 2 percent are Latinas (Dill and Salsbert 2008). Thus, there is a mismatch in the representation of Latinx physicians in the United States in proportion to the overall Latino population. Seeking medical attention in the United States for many Latinx immigrants has not always been met with the warmest interactions, pushing them to seek alternative remedies.

What happens when Latina physicians, who are mostly bilingual and bicultural, enter a white-dominated occupational terrain and provide care to co-ethnic patients? How is their medical knowledge received by various actors? In this essay, I rely on the narratives of twenty Latina/x doctors who are currently practicing physicians in Southern California (Flores 2019) to highlight how science can be biased, especially when providers of color are scarce. I argue that Latina physicians reflect what Patricia Hill Collins (2002, 12) calls the "outsider within"—in this case, highly educated women of color whose families were at one point marginalized from institutions and who now not only are in a position to challenge how knowledge is produced in the medical profession, but are also repeatedly undermined.

SETTING THE CONTEXT

California is an ideal place to study Latina physicians because it has historically been a primary destination for Spanish-speaking Latino immigrants and because there is a high distribution of Latina/o/x physicians—with more than 4,000 (about 4.7 percent) in the state (AAMC 2014). Thus, there were more opportunities to recruit Latina physicians in this region versus new immigrant gateways like the US South, where the Latinx population is barely coming of age.

Of the twenty Latina physicians included in the study, the overwhelming majority (15 of 20) were of Mexican origin, the largest Latinx subgroup in the United States. Two physicians identified as Central American, and three were South American (Colombian or Peruvian). Latina physicians of South American origins had parents who worked in white-collar occupations such as physicians, engineers, and lawyers in the home country. However, ten of the

Mexican-origin physicians had parents who worked in service or factory jobs, and two Central American physicians reported that one or both of their parents experienced downward mobility upon US arrival (Catanzarite and Trimble 2008 159). Only three later-generation Mexican-origin physicians had mothers who worked as teachers in the United States. Sixty-five percent were either 1.5 or second generation, meaning that they migrated to the United States before the age of twelve or were the US-born children of immigrants. Their ages ranged from twenty-nine to sixty-one, and the median age was thirty-seven. Five of the physicians were finalizing their medical residency programs; the rest were working for community clinics or larger medical organizations. Seventy-five percent worked in feminized specialties such as family medicine and pediatrics, mirroring that of women in medicine in general (Murti 2012, 2039; Bhatt 2013, 665; Grijalva and Coombs 1997, 67). With the exception of one physician who self-described as fourth generation and not Spanish proficient, all other doctors were bilingual. The average number of years practicing was eleven and their average salary was over $172,000.

During the interviews the Latina physicians often code-switched between Spanish and English. Therefore, gender and ethnicity facilitated access (Zinn 2001, 159), as all physicians were enthusiastic about participating in a study that examined their experiences in a white-collar field. Below, I rely on the narratives of select physicians to demonstrate what Latinas in science experience in their quotidian interactions with their coworkers and patients.

BROWN WOMEN AND GENDERED RACISM IN THE WORKPLACE

UNDERMINED KNOWLEDGE

Latina physicians explained that their knowledge was repeatedly undermined when pursuing medicine and once in the job. For example, Olivia, a pediatric oncologist of Mexican origins, noted that she constantly bumped into school authority figures who told her she did not "fit" the mold of a physician. She was told, "People like you don't go become doctors." These comments almost prevented her from pursuing medicine altogether. Olivia elaborated, "I kind of wavered for a little period of time because I thought they were authority figures that should be trusted. [I thought] I need to be something else, maybe a teacher? . . . Then I did some volunteer work at some free clinics [and] I met doctors there that really resonated with me." Olivia's father worked as a plumber and her mother was a homemaker, giving others the impression that she did not have the aptitude to become a physician due to her working-class origins.

Not only were Latina physicians questioned about their medical knowledge when pursuing the profession, they also experienced a series of uncomfortable situations rooted in racial conflict once in the occupation. Lisa, a thirty-four-year-old family medicine physician, was born in El Salvador, moved to the United States with her family as an infant, and settled in the Pico Union District in downtown Los Angeles. Lisa explained that while her parents were considered professionals in El Salvador, as undocumented immigrants in the United States they found themselves working in the garment industry. Lisa persevered, but despite securing a prestigious profession, gendered and racial inequities in her interactions with colleagues and patients, both co-ethnics and non-Latinos, were not uncommon. Lisa said:

> I ended up doing way more [work] than that [white] doctor. That doctor slowed me down because his Spanish was broken and he did not know anything about medical Spanish, which I have been studying. So they were using me to interpret [for him] and I was really mad . . . I'm like, "why am I doing that?" . . . I am okay doing it, but it was just funny that [another] Latino [doctor], a Peruvian guy, was putting him [the white doctor] on a pedestal because he is male, white, and older and I am the opposite.

Lisa explained that although patients could communicate better with her, a Latino doctor showed more deference to a white doctor and relegated her to the role of an assistant. Similarly, Rosa, a thirty-six-year-old family medicine physician of Mexican

origins, explained that she was often mistaken for a nurse. She said, "I'm in my scrubs and my patients would immediately assume that I was a nurse. Not that a nurse is anything that I disrespect, but I worked really hard to be a doctor." Here, both Lisa and Rosa elucidate that both Latinx and non-Latinx physicians, and sometimes patients, did not always validate their presence and knowledge.

Elivet, another family medicine physician of Mexican origins, narrated an event where she encountered racialized sexual harassment by an Asian physician. She explained,

> I was at a dinner dance [work event] with my husband and I was very made up . . . I curled my hair and I was wearing a nice dress. [An Asian male doctor] made a comment to me about being Donald Sterling's girlfriend. My husband is Mexican and very fair-skinned . . . [My husband] kind of took it like saying like, "nice job guy" [elbowing] . . . So it looked to me like he was kind of congratulating my husband for getting this hot chick who could be some dumb bimbo, right? I was very offended because I was like, "I'm the doctor here!"

In this case, Elivet narrated that because of her physical appearance she was marked as arm candy and unintelligent.

CULTURAL COMPETENCY AS EXTRA WORK

In an episode of the acclaimed medical drama *ER*, the child of Spanish-speaking immigrants misinterprets the phrase "once a day" written on his mother's prescription bottle as "*once al día*" [eleven a day] and she overdoses. Both of the Spanish-speaking nurses were out for the day and were not there to translate. Latina physicians noted that being Spanish/English bilingual operated in different ways with their coworkers and with their patients: it was an asset but also resulted in extra work. Thalia, an internal medicine doctor, said,

> I sent [a patient] to the GI [gastroenterologist] specialist and they saw her and did all of these tests and she comes and sees me about a month later.

I ask her, "Señora Gutierrez, ¿qué le dijieron, qué entiende usted porque tiene cerosis?" ["Ms. Gutierrez, what did they tell you? What do you understand about having cirrhosis?"]

Y ella me dice, "Pues yo no se." [And she tells me, "I don't know."]

Y le dije, "¿Comó que no sabe, que no fue al specialista, pues que le explicaron?" [And I tell her, "How come you don't know? Didn't you go to the specialist? What did he explain to you?"]

Y ella dice, "No pues nada, que es usted me iba a explicar todo." [And she tells me, "No, nothing. That you were going to explain everything to me."]

So, I took a deep breath and I said, "¿yo?" ["Me?"]

La señora dijo, "Sí porque usted es mi doctora y me va a decir todo lo que esta pasando." [The patient said, "Yes, because you are my doctor and were going to tell me everything that was happening."]

There are very few things that irk me and that is one of them, because if they were Caucasians they wouldn't come back telling me, "You are my doctor and they say you tell me." And it's not that I can't. I am capable of doing that, but I'm not the specialist and you just saw them and I think it's their absolute responsibility to explain to them in a way that they understand or get a translator.

Yvette, who worked in pediatric medicine, explained the different workloads between her male colleagues and herself. She said that in the span of one month she saw over "one hundred patients" while her white male colleague only saw "a little above forty." Yvette explained that "they need [Latino physicians] in clinics" and saw providing treatment as a social responsibility. But Yvette also emphasized the cultural exploitation at the workplace and noticed that because she was bilingual, white doctors relied on her to put the effort to explain to every Spanish-speaking patient what was going on with their health despite the fact that it was not her job to do so. Even specialists from other facilities would fail to provide translations to Spanish-speaking immigrant patients and instead relied on other bilingual doctors.

Lisa, who had a very slight accent indicative of a native Spanish speaker, explained how her pronunciation influenced how patients interacted with her during office visits:

There was an intern who was an Asian [male] and had seen this patient. I am understanding it was [an instance rooted in] race because the [white] patient said . . . "I don't understand you. Bring back the Asian doctor. I don't understand you." [I say] "Sir, I am speaking English!" He says, "No, but I don't understand *your* English." . . . the Caucasian [patients] are the ones that [it has happened with] at least in two situations. It is more race and language because I do have an accent, and I realize that, but I can communicate.

While Lisa felt she was culturally competent to aid patients from various social and economic backgrounds, she was aware that her race/ethnicity and gender meant that both physicians and patients undermined her medical expertise, favoring medical interns who held a lesser rank or less competent white doctors over her. While white women also face gender discrimination in male-dominated jobs, the experience is different for professional Latinas, who encounter gendered racism. Inequality in the professions manifests itself in different ways, and bilingual Latinas working in the "token" context or as the "lonely only" often find themselves doing additional work—like translations—that others performing the same job are not asked to do. The fact that they were bilingual pushed more of the workload in their direction and was met in varying ways.

CONCLUSIONS

I began this piece by demonstrating how the medical profession and science can be biased when treating subaltern and non-English-speaking groups. I posit that as the college-educated daughters of marginalized families, Latina physicians are "outsiders within" who are now in a position to challenge how knowledge is produced in medicine, but they are also repeatedly undermined by various actors in their jobs. While their bilingual abilities are an asset on the job, they often pay a cultural tax where they experience heavier workloads. Yet, Latina physicians recognize that their presence undoubtedly matters for co-ethnic patients.

WORKS CITED

Association of American Medical Colleges. *Diversity in the Physician Workforce*, 2014, http://www.aamcdiversityfactsandfigures.org. Accessed May 10, 2019.

Bhatt, Wasudha. "Little Brown Woman." *Gender and Society*, vol. 27, no. 5, 2013, pp. 659–680.

Cantu, Norma. *Paths to Discovery*. UCLA Chicano Studies Research Center Press, 2008.

Catanzarite, Lisa, and Lindsey Trimble. "Latinos in the United States Labor Market." In *Latinas/os in the United States*, edited by Havidan Rodriguez, Rogelio Saenz, and Cecilia Menjivar. Springer, 2008, pp. 149–67.

Collins, Patricia Hill. *Black Feminist Thought*. Routledge, 2002.

Dill, Michael J., and Edward S. Salsbert. *The Complexities of Physician Supply and Demand. Center for Workforce Studies, Association of American Medical Colleges*, 2008, pp. 1–91.

Flores, Glenda M. "Pursuing *Medicina* [Medicine]." *Sex Roles*, vol. 81, 2019, 59–73.

Grijalva, Cindy A., and Robert Holman Coombs. "Latinas in Medicine." *Aztlán*, vol. 22, no. 2, 1997, pp. 67–88.

Kwon, Hyeyoung. "The Hidden Injury of Class in Korean-American Language Brokers' Lives." *Childhood*, vol. 21, no. 1, 2013, pp. 56–71.

Murti, Lata. "Who Benefits from the White Coat?" *Ethnic and Racial Studies*, vol. 35, no. 12, 2012, pp. 2035–53.

Saraswati, L. Ayu. *Seeing Beauty, Sensing Race in Transnational Indonesia*. University of Hawaii Press, 2013.

Zinn, Maxine B. "Insider Field Research in Minority Communities." In *Contemporary Field Research*, edited by Robert M. Emerson. Waveland Press, 2001, pp. 159–66.

72. • *Liam Oliver Lair*

NAVIGATING TRANSNESS IN THE UNITED STATES:
Understanding the Legacies of Eugenics (new)

Liam Oliver Lair (he/him) is an assistant professor in Women's & Gender Studies at West Chester University. His teaching and research are rooted in feminist studies with a specific focus on sexuality, trans subjectivities, disability, and race. His publications include work examining how constructions of gender "deviance" were shaped by scientific racism and ableism. Dr. Lair has worked with faculty, staff, and students at multiple campuses to create celebratory and affirming spaces for trans, non-binary, and queer folks in institutions of higher education.

INTRODUCTION

Primitive. Abnormal. Pathological. These are terms sexologists used to describe individuals understood to be sexually and gender "deviant" in the early twentieth century; they reveal how eugenics shaped definitions of "deviants." During the first decades of the twentieth century, those adhering to eugenic ideology believed that if they could control who reproduced, they could prevent the (white) race from becoming tainted by "defective" genes. Eugenicists deemed certain people "primitive" or "unfit" to reproduce; the "unfit" included those falling under the new category of "transvestite"—a broad diagnoses of gender deviance describing primarily individuals assigned male at birth who dressed or identified as women.

In what follows, I provide a brief overview of eugenics and highlight connections between eugenics as a social philosophy and sexology as a field of study. Looking at texts written by early sexologists, I demonstrate how eugenic understandings of race and disability shaped the development of diagnoses of gender deviance in the early twentieth-century United States. Furthermore, I provide examples of the enduring legacies of eugenics, particularly in relation to how trans individuals must navigate politics and policies regarding gender in the present day. This will help all of us to consider how we might 1) counter these legacies and 2) move into the future in more transformative and inclusive ways.

A note about language: The language used here reflects language used by sexologists and is not language that I would encourage individuals to use unless they self-identify with one of the terms. For example, most individuals historically identified as "transvestites" now prefer the term "crossdresser." Furthermore, I discuss words like "degenerate," "deviant," "pathological," "primitive," and "savage" and how they were used to denigrate and oppress people. These are terms that should never have been used to describe any person.

NORMAL, VALUABLE

Eugenics was a particular iteration of scientific racism. Francis Galton, a social scientist, coined the term "eugenics" in 1883, distinguishing eugenics from other types of scientific racism through a focus on inheritance. Galton argued that a "wide range of human physical, mental, and moral traits were inherited." As such, he advocated that the only way to achieve a healthy society was by controlling who reproduced.

As eugenics expanded, so did the number of those identified as "unfit" as well as the mechanisms through which to control them. There were consistent categories of individuals deemed unfit to reproduce. Psychiatrist August Forel's 1906 list of the unfit included "criminals, lunatics, and imbeciles, and all individuals who are irresponsible, mischievous, quarrelsome or amoral" (512). In 1909, physician Havelock Ellis—a central figure in sexology and eugenics from the late 1800s until the 1930s—would also identify sexual inverts as unfit. Advocating for state involvement, biostatistician Karl Pearson argued in 1909 that those deemed unfit should be sterilized since only "normal" individuals who were eugenically valuable to the (white, non-disabled, heterosexual) race should produce offspring (1909, 10). With increasing concerns about the unfit and their "deleterious" effect on the nation, eugenics offered ways to curb the spread of these "conditions."

Concurrent to the rise of eugenic philosophy was sexology, a field focused on the study of human sexuality that often relied on eugenic philosophy. Since its emergence, sexology has consistently played a central role in articulating what constitutes "normal" gender and sexuality (Irvine, 1990). Thus, eugenics directly informed sexological proclamations concerning sexual and gender norms (Ordover 2003, Somerville 2014). Because of the influence of eugenics and sexology on one another, ideologies of normality, white racial dominance, ableism, and heterosexuality were foundational to the articulations of sexual and gender deviance.

GENDER DEVIANCE AND TRANSVESTISM

The first iterations of diagnoses of gender deviance—distinct from but related to sexual deviance—emerged from within the field of sexology during the 1910s and 1920s. As with sexual deviance before it, gender deviance was cast as degenerate, pathological, and primitive—all of which were connected to heredity via eugenics. It also reflected a much longer history of connecting disability, racism, and sexual and gender non-normativity. In particular, the use of these terms emerged within medical histories where 1) people of color were considered to be primitive, less mentally developed, and sexually deviant, 2) sexual "deviants" were aligned with psychosis and psychopathology, and 3) deviant gender expression reflected a lack of mental capacity, primitiveness, and pathology.

It was in this context that, in 1910, Magnus Hirschfeld published the first book-length study of "transvestites," individuals (mostly men) who crossdressed. As sexologists were inclined to discuss poor heredity in relation to sexual inversion, Hirschfeld's text did not depart from this trend. Hirschfeld directly engaged heredity in eleven of the seventeen cases he discussed. He argued that transvestism could "be suggestive of a . . . degenerative constitution" (1910, 144). As for the children of transvestites, he worried that they might "be endangered by a heredity burden," or that the deviation of transvestism might "lead to offspring who are . . . unstable, degenerated individuals" (235). In another case, he even referenced notable eugenicist August Forel in asserting that one individual's condition of transvestism was "predetermined by heredity" (321). In this early articulation of gender deviance, Hirschfeld's reliance on eugenics scholars and ideology makes clear the ways in which eugenic philosophy shaped the emergence of transvestism as a diagnosis.

Sexologists would continue to explicitly link gender deviance to poor heredity. In a 1917 article, physicians William Gottheil and Carol Goldenthal cited heredity as the "main etiological factor" for gender ambiguity. They characterized gender deviance as a deformity (a term explicitly rooted in ableist notions of physiological and psychological norms). They went even further to align gender ambiguity with "degeneration, other developmental deformities . . . psychoses . . . and abnormal sexual inclinations" (1917, 933). Undesirable characteristics presented themselves, in one case, in "three successive generations," implying that it would be beneficial if medical professionals could prevent these kinds of "deformities" from passing down through generations of families (933). Eugenic notions of controlling reproduction are explicit in these kinds of statements and helped create the foundation for how gender nonconformity would be characterized for decades to come.

Lastly, in 1928, physician and sexologist Havelock Ellis published the seventh volume in his series on sexuality. In this volume Ellis focused on and defined gender deviance (what he called Eonism) and identified its various manifestations. He asserted that there was a need to recognize "the hereditary and innate factors, the acquired and psycho-genetic factors, in the constitution of this anomaly" (Ellis 1928, 26). He claimed that "among lower races the manifestations of Eonism may occur . . . endemically in groups" and that it was a natural manifestation among those who were more primitive (33). Eonism here is connected to racialized notions of savagery and immorality through the use of the phrase "primitive," and is also reaffirming the connections between Eonism and heredity.

The consistent articulation of gender deviants as neurotic (Hirschfeld), deformed (Gottheil and Goldenthal), or primitive (Ellis) is evidence of how sexologists relied on eugenic ideology to define gendered deviance. In addition, these terms were all assumed to reflect degeneracy and poor inheritance. As such, this language mirrored and incorporated the ableist and racist discourses that were already circulating among the professionals writing and describing gender nonconformity, shaping ideas of who could—and should—reproduce. The grounding of sexology in eugenics shaped the medical profession, and in particular sexology, and its approach to those deemed gender deviant. The work by these sexologists would also lay the foundation for how gender deviance would later be codified in the *Diagnostic and Statistical Manual of Medical Disorders*, solidifying the lasting influence of eugenics on diagnoses of gender variance. Tracing this history allows us to see the connections between eugenics and the historical development of gendered deviance, as well as how both were reliant upon already established systems of racism and ableism.

LASTING LEGACIES

What are the lasting consequences of eugenics on trans folks, particularly those interested in legally and medically transitioning? How do these narratives continue to shape our strategies for trans, racial, and disability justice? This history continues to inform our present moment in numerous ways, but I will discuss three: 1) in debates about what "causes" transness, 2) in determinations of who can and should reproduce, and 3) how transactivists sometimes lack an intersectional approach to justice.

BORN THIS WAY?

Transpeople have historically appropriated explanations for what "caused" transness used by eugenicists and sexologists from the early twentieth century without recognizing the eugenic nature of these arguments. In particular, we too often rely on an argument that insists that "we're born this way." Arguments like this rely on a logic that essentializes what it means to embody or live out a particular gender and minimizes the complexity of gender as something *we do*. If we are "born" as one—and only one—gender, that logic reduces gender to an immutable manifestation of only one of two options: man or woman. This not only limits the possibilities for

gender but ignores the multitude of genders already being lived out. These arguments also ignore the historical and cultural specificity of what it means to perform gender. Gender and gendered expectations, even within a limiting binary, change over time and manifest differently depending on cultural and geographical location.

More importantly, these arguments are ultimately rooted in eugenic thinking, one that grounds the "causation" of our deviation from the norm *in our bodies*. Arguing that our biology "causes" our differences reflects arguments eugenicists provided to justify their racist and ableist approach to medicine and to their supposed "cures" for our "deviance." It offers a narrative whereby gender nonconformity can be understood as an anatomical pathology or a psychiatric disorder (both rooted in biology) and ultimately reinforces who and what subject positions are legitimate and "normal." It is these biological explanations that continue to pathologize not only gender transgressors, but also people of color and people with disabilities, particularly in practices of sterilization. When we rely on biology and genetics to legitimize trans existence—rather than challenging normative and coercive gender expectations more broadly—we fail to distance ourselves from the dangerous rhetoric of degeneracy. Disability scholar Eli Clare advocates for a refusal to even ask if transness is a disorder; instead, we should question the "fundamental relationship between trans people and the very idea of diagnoses" and pathologization (2013, 265). We must disinvest in the ways in which we are medicalized and instead, in tandem with disability rights and anti-racist movements, resist being defined and medicalized by those outside our communities.

REPRODUCTIVE JUSTICE

While many believe eugenics ended after WWII, it in fact continues as an active movement to this day. According to legal scholar Laura Nixon, the continuation is made visible in contemporary assessments of "who is deemed worthy . . . and capable of making [reproductive] decisions for themselves" (2013,

73). Many reproductive justice activists have long been aware of the history and continuing influence of eugenic ideologies. These ideologies have in turn impacted legal policies like immigration restrictions, anti-miscegenation laws, and "laws permitting or requiring sterilization of people convicted of a crime and other people deemed unfit to reproduce . . . based on the supposed genetic inferiority of a targeted group" (Nixon 2013, 92). These laws and policies disproportionly affect people with disabilities, women of color, queer people, and trans people (and of course there are numerous individuals who identify with more than one of these identities). For example, in order to change a gender marker on birth certificates and other government documents, many US states require medical interventions that result in sterilization. While not "forced" sterilization, this is evidence of *de facto* sterilization requirements and is further evidence of the influence of eugenics (Open Society Foundations 2015). This reality reflects, and intersects with, devastating histories in the United States of sterilizing women of color—a practice still offered to women, many of color, in exchange for shorter sentences in prison (Adams 2018). Additionally, Nixon discussed how the lack of fertility-preservation options is evidence of yet another way that eugenics continues to shape transpeople's lives. Often there are no options, and options that might be available are wrapped up in coercive gender expectations. For example, if transpeople want to use their own biological material to reproduce, "gatekeeping healthcare professionals" often interpret this desire as proof that a transperson "had insufficiently embraced his or her 'new' gender identity" (Nixon 2013, 94). Even if the primary intent of these policies is not sterilization, their roots reflect the eugenic philosophies that justified removing people's reproductive choices.

LACKING AN INTERSECTIONAL APPROACH

Without an intersectional approach to achieving justice in the face of oppression, we will continue to undermine our own efforts at creating a more transformative and livable future. Currently, many transpeople are quick to claim their "sanity" in order to distance transness from disability; mainstream LGBTQ movements claim diversity but remain largely white; mainstream disability activists lay claim to normative gender and sexuality in order to distance themselves from queerness. Utilizing these strategies perpetuates the multiple systems that oppress these communities—white supremacy and racism, ableism, and heterosexism—and also evades their complex and overlapping histories. In one example that highlights ableism, Kayley Whalen of the National LGBTQ Task Force asserts that "as long as gender variance is characterized by the medical field as a mental condition, transgender people will find their identities invalidated by claims that they are 'mentally ill,' and therefore not able to speak objectively about their own identities and lived experiences" (2012, n.p.). The underlying assumption of this claim is that those who are "mentally ill" are, in fact, unable to "speak objectively about their own identities and lived experiences" (Whalen 2012). Rather than challenge a) why people are constructed as mentally ill in the first place, or b) how unjust it is that their claims are almost always invalidated, Whalen's first priority is to distance transness from disability. The desire to decouple gender variance from pathology is understandable. However, failing to recognize how this particular move reinforces ableist understandings of psychiatric disability is problematic at best, and at worst reinforces a trans justice approach predicated on the continued pathologization of those with psychiatric disability—a pathologization that is also fully informed by eugenic philosophies and disproportionately applied to people of color (Carter 2007, McWhorter 2009, Samuels 2014, Schwartz and Blankenship 2014).

Working to recognize the lasting influence of eugenics can provide us with tools to create more inclusive movements for change. Knowing our history is important because it provides clearer directions for how we might create more livable futures in the face of oppression. Recognizing the shared histories of various manifestations of oppression is crucial, along with doing the difficult work of building coalitions among communities that we might not immediate understand as our own. Some organizations are already doing this work—Southerners On New Ground (SONG) is one of those organizations. All of their work "strives to bring together marginalized communities to work towards justice and liberation for all people" (SONG 2019). Solidarity among communities working for disability, trans, and racial justice will provide all those involved with more transformative possibilities for all of our futures.

WORKS CITED

Adams, Elise B. "Voluntary Sterilization of Inmates for Reduced Prison Sentences." *Duke Journal of Gender Law & Policy*, vol. 26, no. 23, 2018, pp. 23–44.

Carter, Julian B. *The Heart of Whiteness: Normal Sexuality and Race in America, 1880–1940*. Duke UP, 2007.

Clare, Eli. "Body Shame, Body Pride: Lessons from the Disability Rights Movement." In *The Transgender Studies Reader 2*, edited by Susan Stryker and Aren Z. Aizura. Routledge, 2013.

Ellis, Havelock. "Sexual Inversion: With an Analysis of Thirty-Three New Cases." *Medico-Legal Journal*, vol. 13, no. 3, 1895, pp. 254–67.

Ellis, Havelock. *Studies in the Psychology of Sex: Eonism and Other Supplementary Studies*, Vol. VII. F. A. Davis Company, 1928.

Forel, August. *The Sexual Question: A Scientific, Psychological, Hygienic and Sociological Study*. 1906. Translated by C. F. Marshall. Project Gutenberg eBook; Physicians and Surgeons Book Company, 2009.

Gottheil, William, and Carol Goldenthal. "Pseudohermaphroditism." *New York Medical Journal*, 1917, p. 155.

Hirschfeld, Magnus. *Transvestites: The Erotic Drive to Cross Dress*. 1910. Translated by M. A. Lombardi. Prometheus Books, 1991.

Irvine, Janice M. *Disorders of Desire: Sex and Gender in Modern American Sexology*. Temple UP, 1990.

McWhorter, Ladelle. *Racism and Sexual Oppression in Anglo-America: A Genealogy*. Indiana University Press, 2009.

Nixon, Laura. "The Right to (Trans) Parent: A Reproductive Justice Approach to Reproductive Rights, Fertility, and Family-Building Issues Facing Transgender People," *William & Mary Journal of Women and the Law*, vol. 20, no. 1, 2013, p. 81.

Open Society Foundations. *License to Be Yourself: Forced Sterilization: A Legal Gender Recognition Issue Brief*. 2015.

Ordover, Nancy. *American Eugenics: Race, Queer Anatomy, and the Science of Nationalism*. University of Minnesota Press, 2003.

Pearson, Karl. *The Problem of Practical Eugenics*. Dulau and Co., 1909.

Samuels, Ellen. *Fantasies of Identification: Disability, Gender, Race*. New York University Press, 2014.

Schwartz, Robert C., and David M. Blankenship. "Racial Disparities in Psychotic Disorder Diagnosis: A Review of Empirical Literature." *World Journal of Psychiatry*, vol. 4, no. 4, 2014, pp. 133–40.

Somerville, Siobhan B. "Scientific Racism and the Emergence of the Homosexual Body." *Journal of the History of Sexuality*, vol. 5, no. 2, 1994, pp. 243–66.

Southerners On New Ground. September 8, 2019, http://southernersonnewground.org/.

Whalen, Kayley. "(In)Validating Transgender Identities: Progress and Trouble in the DSM-5." *National LGBTQ Task Force*, 2012. http://www.thetaskforce.org/invalidating-transgender-identities-progress-and-trouble-in-the-dsm-5/

73. • *Clare C. Jen*

OPPOSITIONAL SCIENTIFIC PRAXIS:
The "Do" and "Doing" of #CRISPRbabies
and DIY Hormone Biohacking (new)

Clare C. Jen, Ph.D., is the Director of Women's and Gender Studies Program at Denison University and is jointly appointed as Associate Professor in Women's and Gender Studies and Department of Biology. Her areas of inquiry are in feminist science and technology studies and critical race and gender studies in public health. Her works have been published in *Feminist Formations*, *Ethnic Studies Review*, *Rhizomes*, *Knowing New Biotechnologies: Social Aspects of Technological Convergence* (2015), and the first edition of this reader. In the following article, Jen considers oppositional scientific praxis as feminist, queer, and trans enactments of scientific method and methodology.

This essay introduces *oppositional scientific praxis* as a critical apparatus for joining together the "do" and the "doing" of science. In distinguishing the "do" from the "doing," I refer to feminist approaches to scientific inquiry and practice as theorized by Deboleena Roy (2004), Bonnie Spanier (1995), and Sandra Harding (1987). To "do" science refers to science as method—that is, its techniques, materials, protocols, and procedures. In contrast, the "doing" of science refers to methodology—that is, the ways underlying theories and cultural biases inform method. Feminist science studies continues to ask whether there is a feminist way to "do" science. In other words, do feminists "do" science differently? In congruence with Harding's stance, Roy positions the "do" as distinct from the "doing" of science, and then asserts that feminists do not "do" science any differently than a "conventional, non-feminist, or anti-feminist"[1] scientist (e.g., a feminist scientist does not pipette or centrifuge differently, but the rationale behind the pipetting could be different) (Roy 2004, 261). In contrast, she argues that there is a feminist way of "doing" science, and that

employing a feminist methodological framework could ultimately usher in a practical transformation in how scientific knowledge is produced.

Broadly, this essay aims to provide a window into key concepts and conversations in oppositional science studies—specifically, intersectional feminist, queer, and trans approaches to science studies critique, as well as their interventions into on-the-ground practices of science, medicine, and technology. (I use "femiqueer STS" as shorthand.[2]) Oppositional science and technology studies refers to critiques of "science" as exclusionary and inordinately shaped by neoliberal market forces.[3] Here, critique is not criticism; rather, it is conceptually framed analysis. Critiques in oppositional science studies are inflected by feminist, queer, and critical race perspectives in their interrogations of power and justice. Related to critique, "praxis" refers to theoretically informed and reflexive actions that work towards the liberation of oppressed groups (Freire 2005, 79; hooks 1994, 88). Oppositional scientific praxis is enacted in communities that are typically excluded from Big Bio—that is, the conglomerate of global universities, public–private institutional partnerships, and governmental funding and regulatory agencies that legitimizes what counts as "science" (Kelty 2010; Delfanti 2013). Big Bio excludes those without the "right" pedigrees, credentials, relationships, social capital, and funding sources.

To illustrate methodological concerns regarding the "doing" of science—that is, why particular types of scientific inquiries and methods are prioritized—I turn to disputes concerning CRISPR's human applications at the embryonic scale, which I refer to as #CRISPRbabies, as this essay's first case. As a second case, I position two do-it-yourself (DIY) hormone biohacking projects—Mary Tsang's *Open Source Estrogen* (OSE) and Ryan (Rian) Hammond's *Open Source Gendercodes* (OSG). I tease apart how they put femiqueer STS methodological priorities into action in their "doing" of science, specifically the DIY production and extraction of sex/gender hormones. Finally, I call into question an existing stance that there is *not* an oppositional way to "do" science. I argue that there is potential for femiqueer STS ways to "do" science differently.

#CRISPRbabies AND DIY HORMONE BIOHACKING: CRITIQUING THE "DOING" OF SCIENCE

In early December 2018, #CRISPRbabies tweets steadily populated my Twitter feed. Most were frantic posts from scientists and journalists parsing limited data regarding the "first CRISPR babies." Days before, Dr. He Jiankui shocked the genetic engineering community by announcing births of twin girls, Lulu and Nana. However, this was not an ordinary birth announcement. If true, this was the world's introduction to the first gene-edited human babies using CRISPR, the "hot" gene-targeting and -editing system (Marchione 2018). At present, without a credible publication, He's claims remain unsubstantiated (Cohen 2019). Hence, the global scramble continues—even across my feed—to determine the scientific veracity of his claims and their broader societal implications.

Concurrently, my feed was populating with conversations related to hormone extraction, as offshoots of two high-profile DIY hormone biohacking projects, OSE and OSG. Tsang and Hammond seek to biohack estrogen and testosterone in their efforts to mitigate health care barriers faced by marginalized populations. They "biohack." They work to devise and openly distribute at-home protocols—techniques accessible to non-professional scientists—for extracting hormones from sources they could ultimately distribute like tobacco plants and by using accessible materials like cigarette filters. As separate Twitter conversations, #CRISPRbabies and DIY hormone biohacking converged in my feed due to the company's personalization algorithm. At the same time, I began to discern a different sort of convergence—one not dictated by algorithms but one brought together by oppositional STS, particularly its queries into the "do" and "doing" of science. #CRISPRbabies and DIY hormone biohacking exemplify these separate but connected concerns.

To make sense of #CRISPRbabies and DIY hormone biohacking, I advance feminist methodological concerns into a femiqueer STS approach that more deliberately names the importance of queer and trans ways of knowing and being in the world. I use the term "#CRISPRbabies" as shorthand for the uncertainties and disputes that swell and surge around gene editing and its potential human applications, with He's controversial use of CRISPR as a highly publicized breaking point. "CRISPR" loosely refers to "CRISPR-Cas9," which stands for clustered regularly interspaced short palindromic repeats and CRISPR-associated (Cas) protein 9. He reportedly used the CRISPR-Cas9 system to edit the twins' genes in their early embryonic stages. He's goal was to confer HIV resistance upon Lulu and Nana. Because germline gene editing is sited in the DNA of embryos and gametes, intended (and unintended) genetic changes can be passed on to offspring. Consequences can impact multiple generations (Normile 2018).

As Spanier and Roy apply Harding's four points of feminist methodological inquiry to their own research, we can similarly employ a femiqueer STS approach to query the methodological "doing" of #CRISPRbabies science. First, does embryonic gene editing originate in the "material and political concerns of women- [queer-, trans, and gender non-binary-] centered efforts to improve the quality of life for women, children, [gender and sexual minorities]" (Spanier 1995, 41–42)? Or does #CRISPRbabies science adhere to traditional scientific motivations, such as advancing capitalism and one's career ambition (Spanier 1995, 41–42)? Does the public want scarce resources invested in embryonic genetic engineering, presumably as a strategy for alleviating material and political inequalities borne by vulnerable populations? Second, what is the central purpose of #CRISPRbabies science? Is the central purpose of inquiry to "eliminate constraints based on sex, [gender], race, class, sexual orientation . . . in order to change society for the better" (Spanier 1995, 42)? If structural constraints are the problem, how would engineering social advantages at the genetic level entrench the naturalization of inequalities for successive generations? Third, feminist research pays attention to cultural ideologies and biases that may permeate into how hypotheses are formed and what types of evidence are considered (Spanier 1995, 42–43). Does #CRISPRbabies science take into account how predominant ideologies—like the commodification of technoscientific "solutions" to complex social problems—inform research questions? Finally, feminist researchers interrogate relationships of power between the researcher and those researched (Harding 1987, 8). In #CRISPRbabies science, in what ways do researchers work to mitigate power differentials between themselves and Lulu and Nana, as well as the human participants from whom gametes were retrieved and in whom embryos were implanted? Given that details regarding He's work are still emerging, extensive answers to these concerns are beyond this essay's scope. Nonetheless, it is crucial to raise these questions.

In contrast, OSE and OSG illustrate femiqueer STS approaches to "doing" science differently. Both projects arise from speculative scenarios. Tsang considers whether it would be possible for an at-home biologist to extract estrogen from urine and to detect estrogens concealed in the environment (2017, 37). Likewise, Hammond, described as a "queer artist" and "tactical biologist," wonders whether queer and trans individuals can grow estrogen and testosterone at home using genetically engineered tobacco plants (Paul 2015). They both contextualize their rationale for the "doing" of science in the inequalities of hormonal management, such as institutional barriers to hormonal contraceptives, medical discrimination faced by transgender populations, and the pharmaceutical and health care industries' control of hormone synthesis and distribution (Tsang 2017, 18, 20; Paul 2015). Going even further, Tsang situates her biohacking in a current era of "molecular queering" in which synthetic organic molecules mimic biochemicals and disrupt physiological processes (Tsang 2017, 2).

In applying femiqueer STS methodological concerns to OSE and OSG, it is clear that Tsang and Hammond are "doing" science differently. Their work originates in the "material and political concerns of women- [queer-, trans, and gender non-binary-] centered efforts to improve the quality of life for women, children, [gender and sexual minorities]" (Spanier 1995, 41–42). Their central purpose of inquiry is to "eliminate constraints based on sex, [gender], race, class, sexual orientation . . . in order to change society for the better" (Spanier 1995, 42). They are aware of how systems of power shape cultural ideologies that permeate into how hypotheses are formed and what types of evidence are considered (Spanier 1995, 42–43). For example, Tsang does not position her laboratory hacks as "magic bullet" solutions (Jen 2017). She specifically rejects "scientific solutionism" to environmental toxicities and health care disparities. She also highlights risks faced by feminist, queer, and trans communities when technology hype is upheld as a salve (Tsang 2017, 37). Finally, OSE and OSG mediate relations of power between the researcher and the so-called object of study by designing and employing mechanisms of collaboration.

DIY HORMONE BIOHACKING: HOW-TO-"DO" SCIENCE AS OPPOSITIONAL SCIENTIFIC PRAXIS

I situate OSE and OSG as nodes in the network of DIY, do-it-together (DIT), and do-it-with-others (DIWO) biology. In general, DIY/DIT/DIWO biology are communities, cultures, spaces, and places where individuals and collectives—sometimes known as biohackers, garage biologists, kitchen scientists, science artisans (Kera 2018), feminist biohealth hackers (Jen 2015), and feminist hacktivists (Jen 2017)—work to "hack," or (re)construct scientific instruments often out of everyday materials, and to develop protocols (Delfanti 2013; Meyer 2012). Compared to professional scientists, they practically "do" science differently with respect to their materials and methods. This, in turn, calls into question an existing stance that oppositional science does not "do" science differently.

How Tsang and Hammond "do" science is tied to how they engage with community activism, including their collaborations with so-called research subjects who become (or are envisioned as becoming) partners with whom they "do" science. A self-described "investigative artist," Tsang refines her laboratory hacks through collaborations with Byron Hurt (electronic artist), biohackers, bioartists, and synthetic biologists, at workshops held in Asia, Europe, and North America. Her projects include transforming yeast into a biosensor to detect estrogen and using vodka to hack column chromatography, a technique used to separate mixtures, for estrogen extraction (Tsang 2017, 21, 24–29, 32). She collaborates with queer and transfemme artists to write and produce *Housewives Making Drugs*, a YouTube mini-series in which "transwomen stars host a famous cooking show that teaches the audience at home how to extract estrogens from their urine," and provides a "'natural' open source recipe for upkeeping one's gender transformation" (Tsang 2017, 37–38). In this way, she partners with communities that she cares about and is able to openly distribute knowledges with respect to how to "do" estrogen detection and extraction. In parallel,

Hammond sites much of their work in community biolabs, as they work toward developing a transgenic plant.[4] Their goal is:

> . . . to develop initial prototypes and techniques that I could bring back to community labs . . . to share and develop with others by gaining access to and appropriating these techniques of science, . . . [and] bring a queer agenda into the lab. By teaching others the techniques and by developing open source and collectively owned biological technologies, I'll bring the lab to the queer community. (OSG Crowdfunding 00:01:47–00:02:09)

While Tsang has successfully prototyped, she has yet to establish effective protocol for quality synthesis of "homemade" estrogen for the self-administration of transgender hormone therapy and contraception. OSG, too, remains a work in progress. Yet, it is not just biohacking that resides in the speculative. The effectiveness of He's embryonic genetic engineering also remains unclear. What constitutes evidence determines what remains speculative.

THINKING THROUGH #CRISPRbabies AND DIY HORMONE BIOHACKING

Oppositional scientific praxis yokes the "do" and the "doing" of science. Many oppositional biohackers—including feminist, queer, and trans hacktivists—are driven by the material and political concerns of the marginalized and guided by visions of health equity. They work outside of Big Bio to agitate the status quo. They "hack" the tools and practices of science and work to make hacks accessible to populations most impacted. How do we make sense of #CRISPRbabies, and how does this converge with DIY hormone biohacking? As the concerned public asks "what is CRISPR?" and "what is a CRISPR baby?," scientists ask "how did He do the science?" While these are important questions, there remain other questions that are not being asked. These are the same questions this essay poses to #CRISPRbabies and Tsang's and Hammond's biohacking projects.

Using an oppositional science studies lens, these queries center on the method and methodology of scientific practices and how they are relationally articulated. This lens allows us to illuminate the social, political, cultural, and economic contexts for why particular scientific inquiries are prioritized. By making methodological concerns visible, we are better able to see methods, too, for what they are, which are *not* neutral protocols and procedures. As an example, as CRISPR becomes increasingly accessible as an at-home technology, we must persist in interrogating the "doing" and the "do" of science, particularly as DIY-CRISPR kits scale to more complex organisms. In the future, these at-home technologies could be used to achieve hormone-producing transgenic plants, yet they could also be used in the same #CRISPRbabies vein. We must insist on the significance of transparent femiqueer STS methodological framing.

Femiqueer STS interventions allow us to speculate on the potentialities of oppositional scientific tools. At the same time, OSE and OSG are not merely speculative in their how-to-"do" science, they also enact an oppositional scientific praxis. The "do" and the "doing" of science inform each other. These interventions can be mobilized and coordinated to open science for traditionally excluded communities. Oppositional scientific praxis is the pivot around which method and methodology can relationally bring the lab to the people and the people to the lab, to paraphrase Hammond, and to move toward visions and potential realizations of scientific equity and health justice.

NOTES

1. I refer to Spanier's characterization of traditional science (1995, 41).
2. I borrow "femiqueer" from Rachel Lee's use to denote the intersections of queer theory and feminist studies of science, technology, and medicine (Lee 2014, 33).
3. Donna Haraway contrasts "mainstream science studies" with "oppositional science studies," with the latter focused on formations of gender, race, and sexuality in its analyses of institutionalized scientific knowledge production (Haraway 1997, 35).
4. At times, the pronouns he/him/his and they/their/theirs are used to refer to Hammond. I use they/their/theirs, as later publications seem to have shifted to they/their/theirs.

WORKS CITED

Cohen, Jon. "Did CRISPR Help—or Harm—the First-Ever Gene-Edited Babies?" *Science*, August 1, 2019, https://www.sciencemag.org/news/2019/08/did-crispr-help-or-harm-first-ever-gene-edited-babies.

Delfanti, Alessandro. *Biohackers: The Politics of Open Science.* Pluto Press, 2013.

Freire, Paulo. *Pedagogy For the Oppressed* (30th anniversary edition). Continuum International Publishing Group Inc., 2005.

Hammond, Ryan. *Open Source GenderCodes.* http://opensource-gendercodes.com/projects/osg/. Accessed September 14, 2019.

Haraway, Donna. *Modest_Witness@Second_Millennium.FemaleMan_Meets_OncoMouse* (1st edition). Routledge, 1997.

Harding, Sandra. "Introduction: Is There a Feminist Method?" In *Feminism and Methodology*, Indiana UP, 1987, pp. 1–14.

hooks, bell. *Teaching to Transgress: Education as the Practice of Freedom.* Routledge, 1994.

Jen, Clare. "Do-It-Yourself Biology, Garage Biology, and Kitchen Science: A Feminist Analysis of Bio-Making Narratives." In *Knowing New Biotechnologies: Social Aspects of Technological Convergence*, Routledge, 2015, pp. 125–41.

Jen, Clare. "Feminist Hacktivisms: Countering Technophilia and Fictional Promises." In *Introduction to Women's, Gender, and Sexuality Studies: Interdisciplinary and Intersectional Approaches*, edited by Ayu Saraswati et al. Oxford UP, 2017.

Kelty, Christopher M. "Outlaw, Hackers, Victorian Amateurs: Diagnosing Public Participation in the Life Sciences Today." *Journal of Science Communication*, vol. 9, no. 1, March 2010, http://jcom.sissa.it/archive/09/01/Jcom0901%282010%29C01/Jcom0901%282010%29C03/Jcom0901%282010%29C03.pdf.

Kera, Denisa. "Science Artisans and Open Science Hardware." *Bulletin of Science, Technology & Society*, vol. 37, no. 2, 2018, pp. 97–111.

Lee, Rachel. *The Exquisite Corpse of Asian America: Biopolitics, Biosociality, and Posthuman Ecologies*. NYU Press, 2014.

Marchione, Marilynn. "Chinese Researcher Claims First Gene-Edited Babies." *Associated Press*, November 26, 2018, https://www.apnews.com/4997bb7aa36c45449b488e19ac83e86d.

Meyer, Morgan. "Build Your Own Lab: Do-It-Yourself Biology and the Rise of Citizen Biotech-Economies." *Journal of Peer Production*, no. 2, June 2012, http://peerproduction.net/issues/issue-2/invited-comments/build-your-own-lab/.

Normile, Dennis. "Shock Greets Claim of CRISPR-Edited Babies." *Science*, vol. 362, no. 6418, November 2018, pp. 978–79.

Open Source Gendercodes Crowdfunding Campaign. http://opensourcegendercodes.com/projects/osg/. Accessed September 15, 2019.

Paul, Kari. "Queer Artist Launches DIY Gender Biohacking Project." *Vice*, November 30, 2015, https://www.vice.com/en_us/article/gv5bqw/queer-activist-launches-diy-gender-hormone-biohacking-project.

Roy, Deboleena. "Feminist Theory in Science: Working toward a Practical Transformation." *Hypatia*, vol. 19, no. 1, Winter 2004, pp. 255–79.

Spanier, Bonnie. *Im/Partial Science: Gender Ideology in Molecular Biology*. Indiana UP, 1995.

Tsang, Mary. *Open Source Estrogen: From Biomolecules to Biopolitics . . . Hormones with Institutional Biopower!* MIT, June 2017, https://dspace.mit.edu/bitstream/handle/1721.1/112560/1013184343-MIT.pdf?sequence=1.

74. • *Wendy Seymour*

PUTTING MYSELF IN THE PICTURE:
Researching Disability and Technology (2001)

Wendy Seymour is the author of *Bodily Alterations: An Introduction to the Sociology of the Body for Health Workers*. The following piece was first published in an anthology, *Technologies and Health: Critical Compromises*.

[. . .]

INTRODUCTION

[. . .]

In this chapter I interrogate issues associated with disability and technology, the subject of my research activities over the last two years. While I will draw on the insights given to me by the participants in these investigations, in this chapter I plan to put myself into the picture. While I am involved in collecting data from others, I am concurrently engaging with technology myself—a woman researcher with a disability using technology to engage in research with people with disabilities who use technology.

Seymour, Wendy. "Putting Myself in the Picture: Researching Disability and Technology." In *Technologies and Health: Critical Compromises*. Ed. Jeanne Daly, Marilys Guillemin, and Sophie Hill. Melbourne, Vic, Oxford University Press, 2001. 120–133. OUP Australia

THE ROLE OF THE RESEARCHER

[. . .]

Focusing on the lives of "other people" obscures the researcher's own experiences and concerns. While quantitative methodologies have traditionally been incriminated in this practice, women researchers may also be inclined to approach research in this way, because detachment—the notion of taking oneself out of the picture in order to focus on the concerns of others—conforms to traditional gendered behaviour. The primacy of other people's concerns is established by the diminishment of one's own. Although covert, this practice reflects a view that the researcher is merely a technician who records, documents, and publishes the material of others. However well meaning, this practice is far from neutral.

While the relationship between researcher and the researched is always difficult, disability research has provoked vigorous argument that research which sees the disabled as the objects of research, rather than its authors, exacerbates their sense of exclusion and oppression. These arguments imply that only people with disabilities should research issues related to disability (Bury 1996, pp. 34–5). In examining my own experiences with disability and technology, I am engaging transparent research practices in order to establish a more egalitarian, reciprocal research agenda.

Although some people may dismiss the activity of self-research as mere egocentricity, it is never an easy task to reflect on one's own experience or behaviour. However, neglecting this issue, or failing to engage in the activity, could be seen as both churlish and methodologically reprehensible (Seymour 1998a, p. xi). The researcher is open to criticism for expecting others to participate in an activity in which he or she chooses not to engage, but more importantly, the researcher hides or obscures the role he or she plays in the definition, development, and outcome of the project. What is written is displayed as if it were disconnected from the processes that made it possible (Wynne 1988, p. 103).

A researcher's ability to establish rapport and a trusting relationship with the person who is being interviewed is a critical component of research success.

In collecting data for an earlier, more general study, the informants made it clear to me that my visible disability legitimated my right to conduct the research. In their eyes, the additional fact that I had worked and conducted previous research in the area confirmed that I had paid my dues in terms of commitment (Seymour 1998a, pp. 27–8). All researchers are centrally implicated in the knowledge process, in the writing of culture (Game 1991, p. 7). In terms of this research it is clear that I am far from a neutral component. It is imperative that I "write myself" into the project. In this chapter, I will identify issues related to my own experiences of technological engagement.

RESEARCH AND SELF-RESEARCH

People with disabled bodies are vulnerable to exploitation by others in many aspects of their lives (Albrecht 1992; Deegan & Brooks 1985; Dovey & Gaffram 1987; Lonsdale 1990; Oliver 1990; Smith & Smith 1991) . . . While people with disabilities may engage in a range of strategies to deflect attention from aspects of their bodies, their body is, in effect, "given" to the world for evaluation. Because the body is visible, others feel free to judge and appraise the person without notice or negotiation. When they become the subjects of scholarly inquiry, physical disabilities, with their conspicuous nature, and many specific disabling conditions, because of their rarity, act to heighten the possibility of identification and compromise the possibility of confidentiality. Vulnerability is thus a key issue in disability research.

Only seldom does the researcher experience the process of "being researched." I clearly remember a personal experience of being researched by others. Because of my disability I was asked to participate in a history-taking assessment activity undertaken by health professional students. I had been briefed by the lecturer to answer all questions truthfully, to expand on points if warranted, but not to introduce new topics or lines of inquiry. At the end of the lengthy process of data collection, the students were required to report verbally on what they had found out about me, "the patient," in my presence. Undertaken with serious intention and with much thoughtfulness and good will on the part of both the interviewers and the interviewee, this exercise remains vivid in my memory as an example of the distortions, misinterpretations, and incorrect reportage that may come to constitute a "case history"—the collection of information social scientists call data.

Moreover, as Williams points out (1988, p. 110), the dangers of exploitation may be heightened, not eradicated, by an attempt to create a more equal relationship between the researcher and the researched. Research participants are not dummies; they do not merely comply with our wishes or dutifully respond to our questions. . . . They are capable of subverting and resisting the process by withholding or distorting information, or by using the project to further their own personal or political needs. The dearth of studies that engage social scientists as research subjects may reflect reluctance to engage in work with people who are perceived to have highly developed skills in disruption and subversive activities!

[. . .]

Yet while self-research can be very illuminating, the activity only approximates the experience of being researched by someone else. The researcher remains the information gatekeeper. As with autobiographical writing in general, control remains in the hands of the author, no matter how "revealing" or "insightful" the work purports to be.

[. . .]

DISABILITY AND TECHNOLOGY

Research involving the topic of disability evokes a range of issues other than the issue of vulnerability discussed earlier. People with disabilities make other people feel uncomfortable. Bodily pain and dysfunction are "one's own business" to be managed in silence unless some specific information is required—perhaps by a clinician to confirm a diagnosis or by a social scientist to substantiate a point. People should not speak about their disability unless spoken to: they should remain stoic and silent unless requested to supply specific information about the "problem." Moreover, people with disabilities who are employed full time or who hold responsible positions in the workplace are "not really disabled"—their work status somehow eradicates the disability. Employability still conflicts with the old personal-tragedy model of disability (Oliver 1990, p. 10), and the participation of women with disabilities in public space significantly compounds this stereotype (Seymour 1998b, pp. 164–5).

Living with disability is living a life of constant management, adjustment, and compromise. If the disability is progressive or involves periods of exacerbation and remission, the person must constantly juggle those activities that can be accommodated, and discard or abandon those things that can no longer be accomplished. Making deals with the body—weighing up the losses and gains, trading this for that, pleading a special case, promising to rest up if you can just finish whatever—draws a line between coping and not coping that is fine, and must be continually negotiated; it offers flimsy and precarious support for identity and self-esteem. Living with a disability involves ongoing processes of disembodiment and re-embodiment in response to the challenge of risk, uncertainty, and vulnerability. While not essentially different from the processes by which everyone manages himself or herself in everyday life (Nettleton & Watson 1998), these activities assume heightened importance in the lives of people with physical disabilities.

Augmenting damaged organs with mechanical devices, supplementing strength in muscles and bones, and substituting bodily activities disrupted by blockage, dysfunction, or neural loss have become almost routine techniques of medical practice. Biotechnology now offers a wide range of procedures for bodily restoration and repair. The accelerated development of technology in recent years presents a less comfortable spectre. While promising boundless opportunities for novel bodily experience, sensation, function, and performance, medical technologies expose the body to the risks of surveillance, disembodiment, refabrication, and transcendence (Seymour 1998a, pp. 180–5).

In terms of current practice and use, however, technology offers tantalising opportunities to people with disabilities. Reducing the effect of disease fluctuations, ameliorating pain, and preventing further deformity and destruction must be seen as high priorities in this precarious context. Controlling the physical manifestations of the disease process by invoking the large range of medical, pharmacological, or technical interventions now available will result in a more durable, reliable body. Bodily harmony may be restored by prosthetic substitution and organ bypass. Managing weakness and pain will eliminate the fine line of uncertainty and unpredictability that people with disabilities must constantly negotiate.

Many people feel that technology has taken them by surprise. In fact, technology has been taking us by stealth for a very long time. None of us is immune from technology, though we seldom stop to consider the extent of our immersion and reliance. Workplace restructuring and economic rationalist practices have forced all but the most resistant among us to engage with computer technology. For some, conducting a simple banking transaction through a machine may evoke fear and trepidation. Others may feel that committing personal information to a database for medical, economic, legal, or other "legitimate" purposes effectively strips them of autonomy, knowledge, and control. Anxieties over the "millennium bug" may well be a thinly veiled resentment about our involuntary conscription into the techno-world. Resentment about some technological developments must be tempered by recognition of the enormous potential of others.

PUTTING MYSELF IN THE PICTURE

For me, the computer seemed like my salvation. An inflammatory joint condition since middle adolescence has had a strong impact on my body. While scarcely a joint has escaped the destructive progress of the disease, the major impact has been in my upper limbs, particularly in the joints of my wrists and fingers. The disease has provoked several significant career changes to accommodate deteriorating function and prolong my working life.

The relatively sedentary life of an academic seemed ideal, the advent of the computer heaven sent.

Writing a book in 1988 (Seymour 1989) was a painstaking process of handwriting and laborious rewriting. Construction and placement of elements of the argument involved cutting the written work with scissors and inserting sections into more appropriate locations in the text with clear tape. Once relocated, the selection seldom fitted the developing argument as well as expected, thus requiring another cut, move, fix, and repair of the site, as well as the new location. Paragraphs usually needed reconstruction to accommodate the new material; introductory preamble and concluding comments added to situate the point into the larger argument. Margin notes and other scribbled instructions identified additional tasks to be done and indicated where they should be inserted: direct and instructional, but greatly adding to the visual confusion of the developing manuscript. Correction fluid and an eraser were constantly utilised in an effort to avoid more wholesale change, mostly unsuccessfully. A much-thumbed dictionary averted humiliation, and a thesaurus suggested a range of ways to express the same thing. Photocopying preserved the day's effort and protected the ongoing work. Cluttered, uneven pages cobbled together with sticky tape, additions crabbed between the lines; an expanding pile of paper filled with asterisks, dashes, and other editorial hieroglyphs was the product of my labours. Scissors, sticky tape, correction fluid, erasers, a mountain of pens, and piles of writing pads were the tools of this production. Finding the correct coins for the photocopy machine became a daily obsession. The meaning of "manuscript" is "a handwritten document," and in 1988 this is exactly what I did.

In 1997, a new book (Seymour 1998a). By now there was a computer on every desk. Moving text, trying it out in a new context, inserting a section from another document, locating words or sections easily, committing common phrases or references to memory for future use, spell checks and a thesaurus were basic functions of the new technology. Neat, clean copies could be printed at will, allowing easy identification of issues requiring further work. Automatic back-up ensured document security. For the nervous writer, three floppy discs upgraded daily guaranteed a good night's sleep. The "manuscript" was now a machine-produced document.

Yet despite the indisputable advantages of word-processor computing, the manuscript is still a hand-written document. While the dominant hand no longer guides the pen over the paper, directs the scissor blades, secures the tape, or searches the pages of the dictionary or thesaurus, word processing is an intensely manual activity. Both hands are now required to activate the keyboard. Fingertips, previously little utilised, now interface between body and machine. The smooth, sinuous actions of handwriting learned at school are replaced by the rapid, repetitive, hammer thrusts required to produce typescript. While replacing the pen with the keyboard has dramatically changed the bodily functions and activities required to produce academic work, the hands are no less implicated in this process. Hands remain central to the production of academic capital.

GENDERED WORK

Transforming the work of others to tidy typescript has long been seen as women's work. Girls who were deemed unsuited for serious positions in the workplace, or who, not surprisingly, saw themselves in these terms, were encouraged to "do typing." The "tidying-up" nature of this activity fitted well with the gendered construction of women's work in serving the needs of others (Pringle 1988). Secretarial colleges were filled with girls who "chose" this option because it promised a place in an office, a public space in the world of business, rather than the more deeply gendered work of caring for others involved in nursing, kindergarten, and primary teaching. Men created the ideas, women produced the documents. While presentation greatly enhanced the impact of the ideas, essentially the work could be done by any number of women. Secretarial pools attest to the non-personal nature of the work, with the quality of the typewriter often as important as the skills of the typist. Although the work

was mechanical, poorly paid, and presented few real opportunities for advancement, office work offered women an alternative to even more traditional women's occupations.

The advent of word-processor technology disrupted the gendered relationship between boss and secretary—between the man as creator of office capital and the woman as producer of clean typescript. Seen almost solely as the preserve of women, typing quite suddenly became everybody's business. Secretaries lost their jobs as men's hands hit the keyboards. While computer hardware was expensive, it represented clear opportunities to "downsize" the workforce. Those secretaries who could reinvent themselves in terms of new workplace directions stayed on; the rest left and were not replaced.

While secretarial work remained the domain of low-paid women workers, the conditions under which the work was conducted received relatively little attention. Compared to some other work, the nine-to-five routine, sedentary, and single-task characteristics of office labour were seen as easy work. Like migrant women workers involved in assembly-line production, the bodily damage caused by repetitive work conducted at the behest of others, over many hours each day, often in cramped conditions, was seldom considered (Julian & Easthope 1996, pp. 115–16; Lin & Pearse 1990, pp. 234–7; Petersen 1994, pp. 80–2; White 1994, p. 51). The design of office equipment compounded the deleterious effects of long hours of static back, neck, and upper-limb posture required to facilitate the continual hammering of fingers on a keyboard (Freund & McGuire 1991, pp. 55–8). The long-term effects on muscles, nerves, and joints were obscured by the transitory nature of women's working life.

The pain experienced by relatively powerless migrant women factory workers was only recognised when middle-class, more politically powerful, women began to use the new computer technology and experience for themselves the pain caused by rapid, repetitive movement. Recognition of the condition resulted in the naming of the syndrome repetitive strain injury, though the medical profession remained sceptical of pain that was often unaccompanied by clear clinical evidence. Since a high incidence of the condition was recorded in Australia, the pejorative term "kangaroo paw" became associated with the condition, denoting a political rather than clinical aetiology (Lin & Pearse 1990, pp. 234–7; Willis 1986).

Similarly, the dramatic increase in men's keyboard usage has provoked concern and presaged major changes to computer design. While non-secretarially trained men and women have taken to the keyboard like lemmings in many workplaces, it is the traditional areas of men's work that are receiving particular attention from computer corporations. Law and medicine, for example, have been high employers of female secretarial labour. To reduce the high cost of labour and construct a lean workforce responsive to change, doctors and lawyers have appropriated the keyboard. If professional workers produce their own documents, significant savings can be made in filing, retrieval, and turnaround time, as well as in salaries. While typewriters were strongly associated with women's work, the new technology is not seen to compromise men's integrity.

The keyboard that activated the new technology was the same design as that used by secretaries to operate the old technology, the typewriter of yesteryear. Not surprisingly, new users began to experience pain and subsequent dysfunction. Compelled to address the concerns of their new clientele in order to protect the burgeoning market, computer companies have focused energy on the development of new and less damaging ways to access the computer. Voice-recognition technology has been developed to bypass the keyboard, to replace hand function with the voice. "Hands-free" technology will protect the new user from the consequences of pain and lost productivity that have bedevilled women workers in the past. Targeted at men in particular parts of the workforce, promotional material for early voice-recognition software highlighted the labour-saving advantages of doing the job yourself while, implicitly, protecting the body from damage. A man used to dictating a letter or a report to a secretary could now dictate directly to a computer using the voice-recognition software. A machine replaces a woman; the potential savings are enormous. As long as there is no bodily cost to the user, the technology promises to reconfigure the workplace dramatically.

PROGRESS REPORT

[. . .]

The change from keyboard to voice activation is comparable to the change from pen to computer. Voice activation involves a lengthy process of training the computer to recognise your voice. As with training a dog, "letting the machine get away with it" will result in a lifetime of bad habits. . . .

While I worked hard for many months to fit voice-activation training into my crowded academic workload, I have abandoned the task. Although the deterioration of my hands greatly heightened my motivation to succeed, I gave up. While technological adoption is usually conspicuous, abandonment is often invisible. Why did I do this?

I gave up because the process was difficult and extremely time consuming. I worked long into the night and at weekends to make up the work I had been unable to complete during the training process—invisible, body-tiring labour. I was not resistant to change; indeed I recognised the absolute necessity to adopt new ways of doing work in order to prolong my working life. I gave up as a result of careful analysis and conscious choices—the context of critical compromise within which women manage their lives. In truth, the greatly extended working hours were endangering the very joints I was endeavouring to spare in order to extend my working life. Yet despite the analytical decision-making process, I felt guilty. People with disabilities are judged by how well they can prove to others that they are trying to help themselves. I felt that in failing to master the technology I had failed to help myself. Both gender and age compounded my sense of failure: I felt that I was acting out the stereotypical script associated with older women and, as if this was not enough, I felt guilty about the financial cost to my employer. I now use an old wooden coat-hanger I discovered at the back of a cupboard, a "technology" from a much earlier time. By removing the central hook, I am able to use the curved remaining section to prod the computer keys into life, one by one and slowly. My joints are less painful and I can continue to write. It works for me.

CONCLUSION

[. . .]

In terms of disability, technology can be seen to reproduce some of the characteristics of medicine. While it seems highly desirable to substitute technology for lost function, this seductive solution is underpinned by a mechanistic view of the body, long associated with the "medical model" (Freund & McGuire 1991, pp. 203–29; Petersen 1994, pp. 20–1; Seymour 1989, chapter 4; White 1996, pp. 38–9). In this perspective, the body is viewed in terms of a machine, parts of which may malfunction or wear out. Identification of the problem and isolation of the part prepares the way for remedial intervention. Just as the plumber turns off the water at the meter to work on the kitchen tap, the doctor also assumes that work on a part of the body will have no more than temporary impact on the body as a whole. As the medical model reduced the body to a machine, so too may the technology–machine model compromise and reduce the body.

Technology is not neutral; it is not simply a functional aid. Technology is highly political; it is gendered and intrusive. While seemingly pragmatic and solution driven, technology is capable of reproducing the problems associated with medicine in the past. It may not only be body denying but also threaten the embodied self.

[. . .]

My disability has not only directed my research in particular ways, but the insights of the research participants have helped me to understand my own experiences and frustrations. The participants have enabled me to see that my problems are not located in personal failure or ineptitude, but in the structures of technological production, marketing, and training. Shared experiences, shared fears, reciprocal understandings. Not *my* concerns and *their* concerns, but *our* concerns. We share a range of joys and sorrows. As Wynne suggests, putting oneself in the picture may well raise a Pandora's box of "methodological horrors" (1988, p. 114), but omitting to acknowledge the invisible factors that influence and constitute a research project is to commit a greater sin.

75. • *Vandana Shiva*

THE HIJACKING OF THE GLOBAL FOOD SUPPLY (2016)

Vandana Shiva is a scholar and environmental activist who is based in India. Her interdisciplinary works focus on issues of science, technology, and the environment. She has authored many books, including *The Violence of the Green Revolution*, *Monocultures of the Mind*, *Biopiracy*, and *Water Wars*. She is the founder of Research Foundation for Science,

Technology, and Natural Resource Policy (RFSTN). In 2010, *Forbes* Magazine named her "One of the Seven Most Powerful Women on the Globe." The following essay was originally a chapter in her book *Stolen Harvest: The Hijacking of the Global Food Supply.*

Food is our most basic need, the very stuff of life.

According to an ancient Indian Upanishad, "All that is born is born of *anna* [food]. Whatever exists on earth is born of *anna*, lives on *anna*, and in the end merges into *anna*. *Anna* indeed is the first born amongst all beings."[1]

More than 3.5 million people starved to death in the Bengal famine of 1943. Twenty million were directly affected. Food grains were appropriated forcefully from the peasants under a colonial system of rent collection. Export of food grains continued in spite of the fact that people were going hungry. As the Bengali writer Kali Charan Ghosh reports, 80,000 tons of food grain were exported from Bengal in 1943, just before the famine. At the time, India was being used as a supply base for the British military. "Huge exports were allowed to feed the people of other lands, while the shadow of famine was hourly lengthening on the Indian horizon."[2]

More than one-fifth of India's national output was appropriated for war supplies. The starving Bengal peasants gave up over two-thirds of the food they produced, leading their debt to double. This, coupled with speculation, hoarding, and profiteering by traders, led to skyrocketing prices. The poor of Bengal paid for the empire's war through hunger and starvation—and the "funeral march of the Bengal peasants, fishermen, and Artisans."[3]

Dispossessed peasants moved to Calcutta. Thousands of female destitutes were turned into prostitutes. Parents started to sell their children. "In the villages jackals and dogs engaged in a tug-of-war for the bodies of the half-dead."[4]

As the crisis began, thousands of women organized in Bengal in defense of their food rights. "Open more ration shops" and "Bring down the price of food" were the calls of women's groups throughout Bengal.[5]

After the famine, the peasants also started to organize around the central demand of keeping a two-thirds, or *tebhaga*, share of the crops. At its peak the Tebhaga movement, as it was called, covered 19 districts and involved 6 million people. Peasants refused to let their harvest be stolen by the landlords and the revenue collectors of the British Empire. Everywhere peasants declared, *"Jan debo tabu dhan debone"*—"We will give up our lives, but we will not give up our rice." In the village of Thumniya, the police arrested some peasants who resisted the theft of their harvest. They were charged with "stealing paddy."[6]

A half-century after the Bengal famine, a new and clever system has been put in place, which is once again making the theft of the harvest a right and the keeping of the harvest a crime. Hidden behind complex free-trade treaties are innovative ways to steal nature's harvest, the harvest of the seed, and the harvest of nutrition.

THE CORPORATE HIJACKING OF FOOD AND AGRICULTURE

I focus on India to tell the story of how corporate control of food and globalization of agriculture are robbing millions of their livelihoods and their right to food both because I am an Indian and because Indian agriculture is being especially targeted by global corporations. Since 75 percent of the Indian population derives its livelihood from agriculture, and every fourth farmer in the world is an Indian, the impact of globalization on Indian agriculture is of global significance.

However, this phenomenon of the stolen harvest is not unique to India. It is being experienced in every society, as small farms and small farmers are pushed to extinction, as monocultures replace biodiverse crops, as farming is transformed from the production of nourishing and diverse foods into the creation of markets for genetically engineered seeds, herbicides, and pesticides. As farmers are transformed from producers into consumers of corporate-patented agricultural products, as markets are destroyed locally and nationally but expanded globally, the myth of "free trade" and the global economy becomes a means for the rich to rob the poor of their right to food and even their right to life. For the vast majority of the world's people—70 percent—earn their livelihoods by producing food. The majority of these farmers are women. In contrast, in the industrialized countries, only 2 percent of the population are farmers.

[. . .]

"FREE TRADE" OR "FORCED TRADE"

Today, ten corporations control 32 percent of the commercial-seed market, valued at $23 billion, and 100 percent of the market for genetically engineered, or transgenic, seeds.[7] These corporations also control the global agrochemical and pesticide market. Just five corporations control the global trade in grain. In late 1998, Cargill, the largest of these five companies, bought Continental, the second largest, making it the single biggest factor in the grain trade. Monoliths such as Cargill and Monsanto were both actively involved in shaping international trade agreements, in particular the Uruguay Round of the General Agreement on Trade and Tariffs, which led to the establishment of the WTO.

This monopolistic control over agricultural production, along with structural adjustment policies that brutally favor exports, results in floods of exports of foods from the United States and Europe to the Third World. As a result of the North American Free Trade Agreement (NAFTA), the proportion of Mexico's food supply that is imported has increased from 20 percent in 1992 to 43 percent in 1996. After 18 months of NAFTA, 2.2 million Mexicans have lost their jobs, and 40 million have fallen into extreme poverty. One out of two peasants is not getting enough to eat. As Victor Suares has stated, "Eating more cheaply on imports is not eating at all for the poor in Mexico."[8]

In the Philippines, sugar imports have destroyed the economy. In Kerala, India, the prosperous rubber plantations were rendered unviable due to rubber imports. The local $350 million rubber economy was wiped out, with a multiplier effect of $3.5 billion on the economy of Kerala. In Kenya, maize imports brought prices crashing for local farmers who could not even recover their costs of production.

Trade liberalization of agriculture was introduced in India in 1991 as part of a World Bank/International Monetary Fund (IMF) structural adjustment package. While the hectares of land under cotton cultivation had been decreasing in the 1970s and 1980s, in the first six years of World Bank/IMF-mandated reforms, the land under cotton cultivation increased by 1.7 million hectares. Cotton started to displace food crops. Aggressive corporate advertising campaigns, including promotional films shown in villages on "video vans," were launched to sell new, hybrid seeds to farmers. Even gods, goddesses, and saints were not spared: in Punjab, Monsanto sells its products using the image of Guru Nanak, the founder of the Sikh religion. Corporate, hybrid seeds began to replace local farmers' varieties.

The new hybrid seeds, being vulnerable to pests, required more pesticides. Extremely poor farmers bought both seeds and chemicals on credit from the same company. When the crops failed due to heavy pest incidence or large-scale seed failure, many peasants committed suicide by consuming the same pesticides that had gotten them into debt in the first place. In the district of Warangal, nearly 400 cotton farmers committed suicide due to crop failure in 1997, and dozens more committed suicide in 1998.

Under this pressure to cultivate cash crops, many states in India have allowed private corporations to acquire hundreds of acres of land. The state of Maharashtra has exempted horticulture projects from its land-ceiling legislation. Madhya Pradesh is offering land to private industry on long-term leases, which, according to industry, should last for at least 40 years. In Andhra Pradesh and Tamil Nadu, private corporations are today allowed to acquire over 300 acres of land for raising shrimp for exports. A large percentage of agricultural production on these lands will go toward supplying the burgeoning food-processing industry, in which mainly transnational corporations are involved. Meanwhile, the United States has taken India to the WTO dispute panel to contest its restrictions on food imports.

In certain instances, markets are captured by other means. In August 1998, the mustard-oil supply in Delhi was mysteriously adulterated. The adulteration was restricted to Delhi but not to any specific brand, indicating that it was not the work of a particular trader or business house. More than 50 people died. The government banned all local processing of oil and announced free imports of soybean oil. Millions of people extracting oil on tiny, ecological, cold-press mills lost their livelihoods. Prices of indigenous oilseed collapsed to less than one-third their previous levels. In Sira, in the state of Karnataka, police officers shot farmers protesting the fall in prices of oilseeds.

Imported soybeans' takeover of the Indian market is a clear example of the imperialism on which globalization is built. One crop exported from a single country by one or two corporations replaced hundreds of foods and food producers, destroying biological and cultural diversity, and economic and political democracy. Small mills are now unable to serve small farmers and poor consumers with low-cost, healthy, and culturally appropriate edible oils. Farmers are robbed of their freedom to choose what they grow, and consumers are being robbed of their freedom to choose what they eat.

CREATING HUNGER WITH MONOCULTURES

Global chemical corporations, recently reshaped into "life sciences" corporations, declare that without them and their patented products, the world cannot be fed.

As Monsanto advertised in its $1.6 million European advertising campaign:

> Worrying about starving future generations won't feed them. Food biotechnology will. The world's population is growing rapidly, adding the equivalent

of a China to the globe every ten years. To feed these billion more mouths, we can try extending our farming land or squeezing greater harvests out of existing cultivation. With the planet set to double in numbers around 2030, this heavy dependency on land can only become heavier. Soil erosion and mineral depletion will exhaust the ground. Lands such as rainforests will be forced into cultivation. Fertilizer, insecticide, and herbicide use will increase globally. At Monsanto, we now believe food biotechnology is a better way forward.[9]

But food is necessary for all living species. That is why the *Taittreya Upanishad* calls on humans to feed all beings in their zone of influence.

Industrial agriculture has not produced more food. It has destroyed diverse sources of food, and it has stolen food from other species to bring larger quantities of specific commodities to the market, using huge quantities of fossil fuels and water and toxic chemicals in the process.

It is often said that the so-called miracle varieties of the Green Revolution in modern industrial agriculture prevented famine because they had higher yields. However, these higher yields disappear in the context of total yields of crops on farms. Green Revolution varieties produced more grain by diverting production away from straw. This "partitioning" was achieved through dwarfing the plants, which also enabled them to withstand high doses of chemical fertilizer.

However, less straw means less fodder for cattle and less organic matter for the soil to feed the millions of soil organisms that make and rejuvenate soil. The higher yields of wheat or maize were thus achieved by stealing food from farm animals and soil organisms. Since cattle and earthworms are our partners in food production, stealing food from them makes it impossible to maintain food production over time, and means that the partial yield increases were not sustainable.

The increase in yields of wheat and maize under industrial agriculture were also achieved at the cost of yields of other foods a small farm provides. Beans, legumes, fruits, and vegetables all disappeared both from farms and from the calculus of yields. More grain from two or three commodities arrived on national and international markets, but less food was eaten by farm families in the Third World.

The gain in "yields" of industrially produced crops is thus based on a theft of food from other species and the rural poor in the Third World. That is why, as more grain is produced and traded globally, more people go hungry in the Third World. Global markets have more commodities for trading because food has been robbed from nature and the poor.

Productivity in traditional farming practices has always been high if it is remembered that very few external inputs are required. While the Green Revolution has been promoted as having increased productivity in the absolute sense, when resource use is taken into account, it has been found to be counterproductive and inefficient.

Perhaps one of the most fallacious myths propagated by Green Revolution advocates is the assertion that high-yielding varieties have reduced the acreage under cultivation, therefore preserving millions of hectares of biodiversity. But in India, instead of more land being released for conservation, industrial breeding actually increases pressure on the land, since each acre of a monoculture provides a single output, and the displaced outputs have to be grown on additional acres, or "shadow" acres.[10]

A study comparing traditional polycultures with industrial monocultures shows that a polyculture system can produce 100 units of food from 5 units of inputs, whereas an industrial system requires 300 units of input to produce the same 100 units. The 295 units of wasted inputs could have provided 5,900 units of additional food. Thus the industrial system leads to a decline of 5,900 units of food. This is a recipe for starving people, not for feeding them.[11]

Wasting resources creates hunger. By wasting resources through one-dimensional monocultures maintained with intensive external inputs, the new biotechnologies create food insecurity and starvation.

THE INSECURITY OF IMPORTS

As cash crops such as cotton increase, staple-food production goes down, leading to rising prices of staples and declining consumption by the poor. The hungry starve as scarce land and water are diverted to provide luxuries for rich consumers in Northern countries. Flowers, fruits, shrimp, and meat are among the export commodities being promoted in all Third World countries.

When trade liberalization policies were introduced in 1991 in India, the agriculture secretary stated that "food security is not food in the *go-downs* but dollars in the pocket." It is repeatedly argued that food security does not depend on food "self-sufficiency" (food grown locally for local consumption), but on food "self-reliance" (buying your food from international markets). According to the received ideology of free trade, the earnings from exports of farmed shrimp, flowers, and meat will finance imports of food. Hence any shortfall created by the diversion of productive capacity from growing food for domestic consumption to growing luxury items for consumption by rich Northern consumers would be more than made up.

However, it is neither efficient nor sustainable to grow shrimp, flowers, and meat for export in countries such as India. In the case of flower exports, India spent Rs. 1.4 billion as foreign exchange for promoting floriculture exports and earned a mere Rs. 320 million.[12] In other words, India can buy only one-fourth of the food it could have grown with export earnings from floriculture.[13] Our food security has therefore declined by 75 percent, and our foreign exchange drain increased by more than Rs. 1 billion.

In the case of meat exports, for every dollar earned, India is destroying 15 dollars' worth of ecological functions performed by farm animals for sustainable agriculture. Before the Green Revolution, the byproducts of India's culturally sophisticated and ecologically sound livestock economy, such as the hides of cattle, were exported, rather than the ecological capital, that is, the cattle themselves. Today, the domination of the export logic in agriculture is leading to the export of our eco-logical capital, which we have conserved over cen-turies. Giant slaughterhouses and factory farming are replacing India's traditional livestock economy. When cows are slaughtered and their meat is ex-ported, with it are exported the renewable energy and fertilizer that cattle provide to the small farms of small peasants. These multiple functions of cattle in farming systems have been protected in India through the metaphor of the sacred cow. Govern-ment agencies cleverly disguise the slaughter of cows, which would outrage many Indians, by call-ing it "buffalo meat."

In the case of shrimp exports, for every acre of an industrial shrimp farm, 200 acres of productive ecosystems are destroyed. For every dollar earned as foreign exchange from exports, six to ten dol-lars' worth of destruction takes place in the local economy. The harvest of shrimp from aquaculture farms is a harvest stolen from fishing and farming communities in the coastal regions of the Third World. The profits from exports of shrimp to U.S., Japanese, and European markets show up in na-tional and global economic growth figures. How-ever, the destruction of local food consumption, ground-water resources, fisheries, agriculture, and livelihoods associated with traditional occupations in each of these sectors does not alter the global eco-nomic value of shrimp exports; such destruction is only experienced locally.

In India, intensive shrimp cultivation has turned fertile coastal tracts into graveyards, destroying both fisheries and agriculture. In Tamil Nadu and Andhra Pradesh, women from fishing and farm-ing communities are resisting shrimp cultivation through *satyagraha*. Shrimp cultivation destroys 15 jobs for each job it creates. It destroys $5 of eco-logical and economic capital for every dollar earned through exports. Even these profits flow for only three to five years, after which the industry must move on to new sites. Intensive shrimp farming is a non-sustainable activity, described by United Na-tions agencies as a "rape and run" industry.

Since the World Bank is advising all countries to shift from "food first" to "export first" policies,

these countries all compete with each other, and the prices of these luxury commodities collapse. Trade liberalization and economic reform also include devaluation of currencies. Thus exports earn less, and imports cost more. Since the Third World is being told to stop growing food and instead to buy food in international markets by exporting cash crops, the process of globalization leads to a situ-ation in which agricultural societies of the South become increasingly dependent on food imports, but do not have the foreign exchange to pay for imported food. Indonesia and Russia provide ex-amples of countries that have moved rapidly from food-sufficiency to hunger because of the creation of dependency on imports and the devaluation of their currencies.

STEALING NATURE'S HARVEST

Global corporations are not just stealing the harvest of farmers. They are stealing nature's harvest through genetic engineering and patents on life forms.

Genetically engineered crops manufactured by corporations pose serious ecological risks. Crops such as Monsanto's Roundup Ready soybeans, de-signed to be resistant to herbicides, lead to the destruction of biodiversity and increased use of ag-rochemicals. They can also create highly invasive "superweeds" by transferring the genes for herbicide resistance to weeds. Crops designed to be pesticide factories, genetically engineered to produce toxins and venom with genes from bacteria, scorpions, snakes, and wasps, can threaten non-pest species and can contribute to the emergence of resistance in pests and hence the creation of "superpests." In every application of genetic engineering, food is being stolen from other species for the maximiza-tion of corporate profits.

To secure patents on life forms and living re-sources, corporations must claim seeds and plants to be their "inventions" and hence their property. Thus corporations like Cargill and Monsanto see na-ture's web of life and cycles of renewal as "theft" of their property. During the debate about the entry of Cargill into India in 1992, the Cargill chief executive stated, "We bring Indian farmers smart technologies, which prevent bees from usurping the pollen."[14] During the United Nations Biosafety Negotiations, Monsanto circulated literature that claimed that "weeds steal the sunshine."[15] A worldview that defines pollination as "theft by bees" and claims that diverse plants "steal" sunshine is one aimed at stealing nature's harvest, by replacing open, pollinated varieties with hybrids and sterile seeds, and destroying biodiverse flora with herbicides such as Monsanto's Roundup.

This is a worldview based on scarcity. A worldview of abundance is the worldview of women in India who leave food for ants on their doorstep, even as they create the most beautiful art in *kolams*, *mandalas*, and *rangoli* with rice flour. Abundance is the worldview of peasant women who weave beautiful designs of paddy to hang up for birds when the birds do not find grain in the fields. This view of abundance recognizes that, in giving food to other beings and species, we maintain conditions for our own food security. It is the recognition in the *Isho Upanishad* that the universe is the creation of the Supreme Power meant for the benefits of (all) creation. Each individual life form must learn to enjoy its benefits by farming a part of the system in close relation with other species. Let not any one species encroach upon others' rights.[16] The *Isho Upanishad* also says,

> a selfish man over-utilizing the resources of nature to satisfy his own ever-increasing needs is nothing but a thief, because using resources beyond one's needs would result in the utilization of resources over which others have a right.[17]

In the ecological worldview, when we consume more than we need or exploit nature on principles of greed, we are engaging in theft. In the anti-life view of agribusiness corporations, nature renewing and maintaining herself is a thief. Such a worldview replaces abundance with scarcity, fertility with sterility. It makes theft from nature a market imperative, and hides it in the calculus of efficiency and productivity.

FOOD DEMOCRACY

What we are seeing is the emergence of food totalitarianism, in which a handful of corporations control the entire food chain and destroy alternatives so that people do not have access to diverse, safe foods produced ecologically. Local markets are being deliberately destroyed to establish monopolies over seed and food systems. The destruction of the edible-oil market in India and the many ways through which farmers are prevented from having their own seed supply are small instances of an overall trend in which trade rules, property rights, and new technologies are used to destroy people-friendly and environment-friendly alternatives and to impose anti-people, anti-nature food systems globally.

The notion of rights has been turned on its head under globalization and free trade. The right to produce for oneself or consume according to cultural priorities and safety concerns has been rendered illegal according to the new trade rules. The right of corporations to force-feed citizens of the world with culturally inappropriate and hazardous foods has been made absolute. The right to food, the right to safety, the right to culture are all being treated as trade barriers that need to be dismantled.

This food totalitarianism can only be stopped through major citizen mobilization for democratization of the food system. This mobilization is starting to gain momentum in Europe, Japan, India, Brazil, and other parts of the world.

We have to reclaim our right to save seed and to biodiversity. We have to reclaim our right to nutrition and food safety. We have to reclaim our right to protect the earth and her diverse species. We have to stop this corporate theft from the poor and from nature. Food democracy is the new agenda for democracy and human rights. It is the new agenda for ecological sustainability and social justice.

NOTES

1. *Taittreya Upanishad*, Gorakhpur: Gita Press, p. 124.
2. Kali Charan Ghosh, *Famines in Bengal, 1770–1943*. Calcutta: Indian Associated Publishing Company, 1944.
3. Bondhayan Chattopadhyay, "Notes Towards an Understanding of the Bengal Famine of 1943," *Transaction*, June 1981.
4. MARS (Mahila Atma Raksha Samiti, or Women's Self Defense League), Political Report prepared for Second Annual Conference, New Delhi: Research Foundation for Science, Technology, and Ecology (RFSTE), 1944.
5. Peter Custers, *Women in the Tebhaga Uprising*, Calcutta: Naya prokash, 1987, p. 52.
6. Peter Custers, p. 78.
7. These companies are DuPont/Pioneer (U.S.), Monsanto (U.S.), Novartis (Switzerland), Groupe Limagrain (France), Advanta (U.K. and Netherlands), Guipo Pulsar/Semins/ELM (Mexico), Sakata (Japan), KWS HG (Germany), and Taki (Japan).
8. Victor Suares, Paper presented at International Conference on Globalization, Food Security, and Sustainable Agriculture, July 30–31, 1996.
9. "Monsanto: Peddling 'Life Sciences' or 'Death Sciences'?" New Delhi: RFSTE, 1998.
10. ASSINSEL (International Association of Plant Breeders), "Feeding the 8 Billion and Preserving the Planet," Nyon, Switzerland: ASSINSEL.
11. Francesca Bray, "Agriculture for Developing Nations," *Scientific American*, July 1994, pp. 33–35.
12. *Business India*, March 1998.
13. T.N. Prakash and Tejaswini, "Floriculture and Food Security Issues: The Case of Rose Cultivation in Bangalore," in *Globalization and Food Security: Proceedings of Conference on Globalization and Agriculture*, ed. Vandana Shiva, New Delhi, August 1996.
14. Interview with John Hamilton, *Sunday Observer*, May 9, 1993.
15. Interview Verfaillie, speech delivered at the Forum on Nature and Human Society, National Academy of Sciences, Washington, DC, October 30, 1997.
16. Vandana Shiva, "Globalization, Gandhi, and Swadeshi: What is Economic Freedom? Whose Economic Freedom?" New Delhi: RFSTE, 1998.
17. Vandana Shiva, "Globalization, Gandhi, and Swadeshi."

76. • *Naciza Masikini and Bipasha Baruah*

GENDER EQUITY IN THE "SHARING" ECONOMY:
Possibilities and Limitations (new)

Naciza Masikini holds an M.A. in Gender Studies and Law from the School of Oriental and African Studies (SOAS) in London and a B.A. in Women's Studies and Feminist Research from Western University, Canada. She is a social programming professional who delivers community programs based on anti-oppressive frameworks. Her most notable recent accomplishment is the establishment of the Wellness Centre, a program for racialized minorities and refugees in Croydon, United Kingdom. Naciza currently works for Prince's Trust International as International Programmes Manager for the Eastern Caribbean. Bipasha Baruah is a tenured full professor at Western University, Canada. She holds the Canada Research Chair in Global Women's Issues. She serves frequently as an expert reviewer and consultant to international development and environmental protection organizations.

INTRODUCTION

The "sharing economy" (exemplified by organizations like Uber and Airbnb) prides itself on enabling new forms of employment and entrepreneurship that challenge traditional models of livelihood creation. It distinguishes itself by "opening up" traditional sectors of service and employment in ways that enable everyone who wants to use a service or earn a living to do so on an equal footing. Accessibility, both for riders and drivers, is the unique selling proposition for companies like Uber, and a branding strategy frequently reinforced in its advertising campaigns. It claims to be the easiest way to get around because it offers rides for everyone at any time. Thus, Uber users can get a ride at the "tap of a button." Likewise, drivers just need to "sign up to drive" and to "be their own boss."

In this article, we review existing literature on Uber to analyze the extent to which these claims of equity in use and employment are true. Scholarly literature on Uber is rare and almost exclusively limited to understanding its business model and financial sustainability. By contrast, general media coverage of Uber has grown dramatically over the years so there is no shortage of journalistic coverage to draw upon. We reviewed both scholarly and popular articles about Uber to understand the "accessibility" it claims to offer riders and drivers.

BACKGROUND INFORMATION ON UBER

The two sharing economy giants, Airbnb and Uber, have dramatically altered the lodging and transportation sectors. By connecting drivers to passengers directly, Uber has challenged the traditional car hire model of taxis and limousines. Uber also challenged

the car share model pioneered by ZipCar. Whereas ZipCar allowed car owners to earn additional income by renting out their cars, Uber enabled large numbers of people to give up car ownership altogether and to take up driving as an economic activity. Uber has dramatically changed the way people get around in urban centers around the world. Uber is currently one of the largest and most rapidly growing companies in the world. American entrepreneur Travis Kalanick and Canadian investor Garrett Camp founded Uber in 2009. Uber adopted the "expand first and make money later" business model, which Amazon had relied upon in its early years (Hendriks 2014). Uber reported losses of $31.9 million in 2013 and $237 million in 2014 (Kosoff 2016). By 2018, only 9 years after its founding, Uber operated in 600 cities in 78 countries (International Finance Corporation [IFC] 2018).

Uber considers its drivers "independent contractors" who can "be their own bosses" by setting flexible hours based on individual schedules. By not classifying drivers as "employees," the company is able to prevent drivers from seeking tips, expense reimbursements, overtime, and other benefits. It also prevents drivers from bargaining collectively to improve wages and working conditions.

FINDINGS

Despite Uber's dramatic growth around the world, its services are not accessible for "*everyone* at *any time*" simply because it does not operate in every city in the world. A quick online search of the company's operations in the Americas, Middle East and North Africa, Asia, Australia, and New Zealand reveals numerous cities in which Uber has either decided not to, or otherwise been unable to, establish operations. Uber has also been banned in several cities and countries, on both a temporary and long-term basis, usually for two reasons: (1) conflicts with the taxi industry and (2) reports of sexual assault by Uber drivers and subsequent legal action taken by riders (Ghoussoub 2016).

When Uber establishes operations in a city or town, it often leads to conflict with the taxi industry and increased tension between municipalities and transportation services. Uber's entry into the transportation sector has led to erosion of fares and incomes for taxi drivers and a drop in the cost of taxi medallions (Holodny 2016). City governments' failure or inability to regulate Uber is also a major source of conflict. Uber does not currently have a global standard for its driver screening. The recurring issue for most municipalities is the disagreement over licensing. The laxer requirements for Uber drivers does open up the industry, as it is costly to maintain a commercial driving license. However, it adversely affects taxi drivers, who are, at least in the European and North American context, often highly skilled immigrant workers who are unable to work in the professions they trained for in their countries of origin. Disagreements over regulations led Uber to be banned or to withdraw from various locations in Asia and Europe. Uber's services are thus not accessible for "everyone at any time."

Women have reported being sexually harassed or assaulted by Uber drivers in cities around the world, but Uber has, counter-intuitively, rarely been banned anywhere for this reason. The most widely publicized ban was issued in New Delhi, India. In December 2014, Shiv Kumar Yadav, an Uber driver, kidnapped his fare and raped her. Yadav was subsequently sentenced to life imprisonment (Bhattacharya 2014). Following this incident, Delhi's Transport Department "banned all activities relating to Uber with immediate effect" (BBC News India 2014). Of course, the outcome of this case was strongly influenced by the Indian government's harsher stance on rape and sexual assault following the fatal gang rape of a medical student in New Delhi in December 2012 and the

nationwide protests that ensued (BBC News India 2012). These circumstances may at least partially explain the government's quick decision to ban the service only a few days after the Delhi Uber Rape, as it came to be known (BBC News India 2013). While the government decided to ban Uber almost immediately, enforcing the ban was much harder due to the advantages Uber enjoyed because of its interactive platform, and the fact that its cars are unmarked and therefore not distinguishable from other privately owned vehicles. The ban only affected those who could be easily identified as operating an Uber taxi (BBC News India 2014). Those individuals were indeed fined or had their vehicles impounded. Because the ban did not establish a sustainable enforcement framework, it was short lived. Uber was reinstated in July 2015 after a court ruling clarified that although the government could strictly regulate app-based companies, it could not ban them outright (Reuters 2015). Uber CEO Travis Kalanick responded to the incident by stating that the company would "work with the government to establish clear background checks currently absent in their commercial transportation licensing programs" (BBC News India 2014). In other words, Uber invoked lax licensing regulations in general in India's commercial transportation sector to assert its right to operate. One interesting outcome of the temporary Uber ban in India is that it did lead to the introduction of background check procedures for all operators in the private transportation industry in February 2015 (Isaac 2015).

Beyond such limitations, it is important to remember that Uber's operational platform is inherently restrictive in that it requires both riders and drivers to have a cellphone. To pay, an Uber rider must also have a credit or debit card. These basic requirements make it impossible for large numbers of (typically lower-income) people who have neither to access Uber's transportation services. Owning a cellphone and a credit card requires an individual to have access to both a form of state-approved identification and financial collateral in the form of a job or savings. These requirements are obviously harder to fulfill for women, transgendered people, and racialized and ethnic minorities since they are overrepresented in the ranks of the poor, the undocumented, the unemployed, and the precariously employed. The legal challenges faced by certain groups of people—notably racialized women and transgendered people—in securing photo identification have recently been documented more systematically in the North American context due to the efforts of equity advocacy groups. The story of centenarian Virginia McLaurin, who met and danced with Barack and Michelle Obama but cannot secure photo identification from the Department of Motor Vehicles (because she does not possess a birth certificate), is a much-publicized example (Guild 2016). The efforts made by the US National Center for Transgender Equality (2017) to document the challenges faced by transgendered people in seeking photo identification represent another prominent example.

These basic ridership requirements persisted in all cities in which Uber operated until 2015, when the company began to test cash payment options. Hyderabad, India, was Uber's first test city for cash payments. Uber's motivation for testing cash payments in India grew from the realization that Ola, Uber's major rideshare competitor, in India already allowed cash payments. Over time, Uber realized that its rider requirements were especially restrictive in some non-Western settings. A significant portion of the population that wanted to use Uber's services did not have access to credit cards in cities such as Cairo, Egypt; Colombo, Sri Lanka; Cape Town, South Africa; and Riyadh, Saudi Arabia. Since 2015, Uber has expanded the cash payment option to over 130 cities, mostly in the Global South (Russell 2016).

Of course, Uber has since realized that large numbers of people in North America and Europe also cannot meet its basic ridership requirements. Uber has subsequently expanded the cash payment option to some European and North American cities. In October 2016 Manchester, England,

became the first European city to offer cash payments (Evans 2016) and Colorado Springs, Colorado, became the first city in North America to do so (Heilman 2017). However, payment by credit or debit card remains the norm rather than the exception in most European and North American cities that Uber operates in.

A study conducted by the IFC in 2018 to understand the barriers and opportunities faced by women as Uber drivers and riders reported that women account for just 2.3 percent of drivers in the six countries included in the research, namely Egypt, India, Indonesia, Mexico, South Africa, and the United Kingdom. By contrast, an estimated 41 percent of riders using the Uber app are women across the six countries in the IFC study, ranging from 31 percent in India to 57 percent in Indonesia. Globally, women represent more than 50 percent of Uber riders but only 14 percent of drivers. The vast majority of female drivers (75 percent) are in the United States and Canada (IFC 2018).

People generate income in the sharing economy by monetizing their assets such as cars, houses, or spare rooms. However, to benefit from asset monetization, people must own assets, which is a significant barrier for many women in developing and emerging economies, and for racialized women in industrialized economies. Car ownership rates are significantly lower for women than they are for men in many parts of the world. There are social, financial, and legal barriers that hinder car ownership by women as well as their ability to work as drivers or to travel independently. A Nielsen study (2014) found that of the 65 percent of people in 44 countries planning to purchase a car over the following two years, just 42 percent are women. The gaps were largest in the Middle East and Africa (71 percent, men; 29 percent, women) and Asia Pacific (60 percent, men; 40 percent, women). The IFC study reported that 43 percent of drivers in the six countries studied—rising to 48 percent for female drivers—are leasing or renting or have taken out a personal loan to access the vehicle they use with Uber. Women are also less likely to have a bank account and own assets that enable participation in the sharing economy. Women surveyed across the six countries studied by the IFC are less likely than men to own the car they drive, and identify getting the money to buy or access a vehicle as the biggest sign-up barrier they face, ranging from 17 percent in Egypt to 40 percent in South Africa. Thus, the IFC study concluded that while there are important opportunities for women in the sharing economy, there are also substantial gender-specific barriers to entry, such as digital literacy, financial inclusion, and social stigma.

Women's access to traditionally male-dominated industries, such as transportation, is also often hindered by a lack of access to the social and business networks needed to facilitate initial opportunities and to grow careers or businesses over time. For this and other reasons, 98 percent of traditional taxi drivers in London, for example, are male (Government of UK 2017). For women who want to drive for a living, evidence from focus groups conducted by the IFC suggests that signing up on the Uber app is far easier and less intimidating than applying to work for a traditional taxi operator. Signing up on a sharing economy platform at least partially circumvents some of the institutional enablers of gender bias, such as hiring managers, sponsors, or peer networks (Sundarajan 2016). The fact that the number of women who drive for Uber has remained so low globally despite the lower barriers of entry in the rideshare economy suggests the persistence of other barriers such as digital and financial inclusion, regulatory requirements for commercial licenses, real and perceived concerns about safety, and restrictive social mores.

CONCLUSION

An estimated 18 percent of people globally have used a ride-hailing service in the past 12 months (Holmes 2017), and current estimates anticipate an eightfold increase in ride-hailing by 2030, with total trips approaching 100 million a day (Burgstaller et al. 2017). Supports and detractors of Uber and other ride-hailing companies agree that despite its limitations, the sector will continue to grow in the future. While rideshare companies have indeed changed the transportation industry, our findings suggest that they may reinforce rather than challenge social hierarchies based on gender, race, and class found in traditional models of entrepreneurship and employment generation. This has happened because Uber has not succeeded either in developing an adequately responsive framework to ensure driver and rider safety, or in ensuring equitable access to its platform both for riders and drivers. Women are less likely to participate in the sharing economy because they typically have fewer resources and assets than men do. Since female Uber drivers start out from a weaker financial position than their male counterparts, it is not surprising that they tend to (at least initially) receive a greater boost to their earnings (11 percent in Mexico to 29 percent in Egypt) than men do (IFC 2018). The opportunities and risks of joining the sharing economy may accrue more heavily to women because they have more to gain from participating, but also more to lose if they are excluded from new forms of work, income, or assets.

WORKS CITED

BBC News India. (2012). "Delhi gang-rape victim dies in hospital in Singapore." *BBC News India*, http://www.bbc.com/news/world-asia-india-20860569.

BBC News India. (2013). "Explaining India's new anti-rape laws." *BBC News India*, http://www.bbc.com/news/world-asia-india-21950197.

BBC News India. (2014). "Uber banned in Delhi over taxi driver 'rape'." *BBC News India*, http://www.bbc.com/news/world-asia-india-30374070.

Bhattacharya, Somreet. (2014). "Uber driver Shiv Kumar Yadav tells cops he's raped many women." *Times of India*, https://timesofindia.indiatimes.com/city/delhi/Uber-driver-Shiv-Kumar-Yadav-tells-cops-hes-raped-many-women/articleshow/45483698.cms.

Burgstaller, Stefan, et al. (2017). "Rethinking mobility." *Goldman Sachs*, https://orfe.princeton.edu/~alaink/SmartDrivingCars/PDFs/Rethinking%20Mobility_GoldmanSachsMay2017.pdf.

Evans, Tara. (2016). "Pay as you ride: Now you can pay for your Uber in cash if you live in Manchester." *The Sun*, https://www.thesun.co.uk/living/1998755/now-you-can-pay-for-your-uber-in-cash-if-you-live-in-manchester/.

Ghoussoub, Michelle. (2016). "No Uber for another year, Vancouver City Council decides." *CBC News*, http://www.cbc.ca/news/canada/british-columbia/no-uber-for-another-year-vancouver-city-council-decides-1.3813210.

Government of UK. (2017). "Transport for London—London taxi and private hire." http://content.tfl.gov.uk/taxi-and-phv-demographicsstats.pdf.

Guild, Blair. (2016). "Virginia McLaurin danced with the President but she can't get photo ID." *Huffington Post*, http://www.huffingtonpost.com/entry/virginia-mclaurin-photo-id_us_571e441be4b0d4d3f723efec.

Heilman, Wayne. (2017). "Uber to test cash payments in Colorado Springs." *Denver Post*, http://www.denverpost.com/2017/01/11/uber-cash-payments-colorado-springs/.

Hendriks, Drew. (2014). "5 successful companies that didn't make a dollar for 5 years." *Inc.*, http://www.inc.com/drew-hendricks/5-successful-companies-that-didn-8217-t-make-a-dollar-for-5-years.html.

Holmes, Anisa. (2017). "How big is the transport sharing economy." *Dalia Research*, https://daliaresearch.com/how-big-isthe-transport-sharing-economy.

Holodny, Elena. (2016). "Uber and Lyft are demolishing New York City taxi drivers." *Business Insider*, http://www.businessinsider.com/nyc-yellow-cab-medallion-prices-falling-further-2016-10.

International Finance Corporation. (2018). "Driving toward equality: women, ride-hailing, and the sharing economy." https://www.ifc.org/wps/wcm/connect/topics_ext_content/ifc_external_corporate_site/gender+at+ifc/drivingtowardequality

Isaac, Mike. (2015). "Uber to introduce driver background checks in India," *New York Times*, https://bits.blogs.nytimes.com/2015/01/16/uber-to-introduce-driver-background-checks-in-india/?_r=0.

Kosoff, Maya. (2016). "Uber is hemorrhaging money abroad in quest for world domination." *Vanity Fair*, http://www.vanityfair.com/news/2016/03/uber-loses-money-abroad-in-quest-for-world-domination.

National Center for Transgender Equality. (2017). "Identity documents and privacy." http://www.transequality.org/issues/identity-documents-privacy.

Nielsen. (2014). "Secure tomorrow's car buyers today: four key marketing strategies that will fuel industry growth globally." https://www.nielsen.com/au/en/insights/news/2014/three-key-marketing-strategies-to-secure-tomorrows-car-buyers-toda.html.

Reuters Money News. (2015). "High Court revokes ban on Uber in New Delhi." *Reuters*, http://in.reuters.com/article/india-uber-idINKCN0PI17V20150708.

Russell, Jon. (2016). "Uber begins to see the payout from accepting cash payments." *Tech Crunch*, https://techcrunch.com/2016/02/08/uber-begins-to-see-the-payout-from-accepting-cash-payments/.

Sundararajan, Arun. (2016). *The Sharing Economy: The End of Employment and the Rise of Crowd-Based Capitalism*. MIT Press.

77. • *Rachel Charlene Lewis*

TECHNOLOGY ISN'T NEUTRAL:
Ari Fitz on How Instagram Fails Queer Black Creators (2019)

Rachel Charlene Lewis is a social media strategist and a Senior Editor at *Bitch*. She writes on issues of culture, beauty, sexuality, and relationships. Her works have appeared in *Teen Vogue*, *Refinery29*, *Glamour*, *Allure*, *Catapult*, *The Los Angeles Review of Books*, and *Publisher's Weekly*.

In February 2019, *Out* magazine reported that photographer Tom Bianchi had been locked out of his Instagram account because he'd posted a Polaroid photograph of the back of a nude man sitting on a bed, his butt barely visible. "On Saturday morning I woke up to find that my Instagram account had been removed in its entirety for violating 'Community Guidelines,'" he told *Out*. After artists, fans, and his husband posted their concerns on Instagram, Bianchi's account—and the previously offending post—was reactivated.

Sex-tech startups Dame Products and Unbound protested Facebook, the company that owns Instagram, in July 2019 for continually rejecting their ads and reporting their posts despite their content being much less sexual than those of male-focused brands like Hims. Shadowbanning, a hotly contested term used to describe Instagram's algorithm allegedly deprioritizing certain Instagram posts or accounts, has been rightfully critiqued for harming marginalized people. Women, queer people, and sex workers have begun leaving Instagram entirely, saying it's becoming increasingly difficult to build community on a platform with vague guidelines about what's allowed. (Instagram's policy about nipples has caused a lot of controversy, for instance.) Queer Black influencer and YouTuber Ari Fitz, whose Instagram bio read "HE/HER/DADDY", ditched the platform, leaving behind nearly 140,000 followers. Her final post, captioned, "been fun, @instagram," features a blurred post of Ari posing while topless, her arms covering her chest. A swipe on the post reveals a screenshot of Instagram's notice to Fitz that the original post had been removed for violating the platform's "nudity or sexual activity" policy.

On her final post, Fitz cropped the photo closer to her chest to showcase just how difficult it is to see her nipples, which, she assumes, is why Instagram blocked the image. The top comment on the post reads, "i follow a white [woman] who posts herself completely naked with 2 little scribbles over her nipples. and her posts are still up. bullshit." (White models and influencers like Bella Hadid and Emily Ratajkowski have "poked fun" at Instagram's no-female-nipples policy.)

I interviewed Fitz about her decision to leave Instagram and if Instagram's community guidelines are specifically targeting queer people of color.

Tell me more about your relationship with Instagram. When did you join the platform? How did you originally intend to use it?

I really fell in love with Instagram about three years ago. I had just quit my job and moved to Los Angeles to become a full-time YouTuber, and a major modeling company had seen my older (now defunct) Instagram account and asked me to [sign with] them. The modeling thing didn't work out, but Instagram helped me land major contracts, like UGG and KENZO. I even landed a *NYLON* cover because of Instagram. My first real post was [in] August 2016. At first, Instagram was just a place for me to look cute, show off my fitz (heh), and connect with friends. As I started making more YouTube videos, my audience on Instagram grew in tandem, and IG became more of a place for me to tell stories.

I started producing content specifically for Instagram in 2017, starting with my six-episode "SIXTY SECOND FITZ" series, which [ran for] two seasons. At the time, Instagram felt more raw and real [because there were so] many creatives on the platform. It became addictive to share something raw with artists like me. So many celebrities and people with massive audiences started following me and "liking" my work around then. It was wild to be able to reach people I'd perceived to be unattainable, and to have them see my work. Then I started doing longform photo essay projects with major photographers like Sza's photog Sage who shot my "LEADING MAN" photo essay series or Lula and famous makeup artist Raisa, who shot "ARI-ELLE." I would also do really raw stories in my captions—[and] that's not even touching highlighted stories. Those are dense; [there's] so much of just me in there. My three years on Instagram were raw and real; I bared my whole soul on that app. I have so much of me on it. My goals shifted often, too, but Instagram was always my place to connect with creatives. It was where I fully and freely showed the world people like me existed.

What recent changes have you noticed about how Instagram operates?

I've noticed for about a year (a fucking year!) that people couldn't find me [when] they tried to type my account name in [the search box]. Fan accounts and other accounts would pop up before mine. Most of the time, typing my full name out [was the only way for my page to populate in the search], whereas my friends' usernames would pop up with just a few letters. I always thought it was something I was doing wrong. Isn't that the wild part? Technology has this way of feeling so neutral, like a bug is just a bug, but it's really racism and sexism and bias masquerading as a bug.

As I've gotten more popular on YouTube, I've [received] so many DMs from people saying they thought I blocked them [because they couldn't find my account], or that they had to find me via my friends' accounts. I didn't know what shadowbanning was; I just thought it was somehow my fault. Let's be real: I have [created] a lot of very suggestive posts, but I always censored and tried to be respectful of IG's community guidelines even when I didn't agree with them. I tried to make sure my nipples (even though who is IG to tell me my nipples are female or male?) didn't show. I never showed any sexual or violent activity. My full bare ass has never been shown, even when Justin Bieber made it cool to do that on IG.

I didn't do more than what a white boy or girl influencer has, but IG automatically [deems] my Black queer body [is] wrong.

You recently decided to leave Instagram. What finally pushed you away from the platform? Do you think other Black queer creators or creators of color are doing or will eventually do the same?

I hope so! I hope all the fire, amazing, super-talented creatives leave IG and go to Twitter, YouTube, and my new favorite [platform] TikTok. None of these platforms are perfect, and some seem to have some very shady ties (why exactly was Twitter CEO Jack meeting with Trump?), but most of them seem to at least try to respond to their creators, especially when it comes to racism and bias within their algorithm. I talk to folks at YouTube often; I left Instagram because Instagram never responded. So many of my fellow queer, Black, POC, [and] sex-positive friends were sharing how they were banned too, and IG said nothing. Instagram saw all of our complaints and chose to say nothing or fix anything.

I noticed many of the comments on your final Instagram post point out that many queer white people post semi-nude or fully nude images on Instagram without facing the same level of reporting.

Yup. They're white and I'm not.

What can queer Black creators do to reach their communities in digital spaces, considering increased censorship across the board?

Become software engineers and make a platform (with a diverse group) without racism built into the algorithm! Then send me an invite ;) Until then, creators, run from Instagram as soon as you can. Twitter is great. YouTube is fun (but difficult if you don't do video). TikTok is becoming fun, but the audience is really young—because of this, they're even more sensitive with censorship, so be careful. I think we're all waiting for something new. A new, sexy, racism-free space for creatives sounds so yummy. Build it, and I'm there.

78. • *Sima Shakhsari*

THE PARAHUMANITY OF THE YOUTUBE SHOOTER:
Nasim Aghdam and the Paradox of Freedom (2020)

Sima Shakhsari is an associate professor in the Department of Gender, Women, and Sexuality Studies at the University of Minnesota; the Anthropology, Sociology, and Gender Studies Book Review Editor at the *International Journal of Middle East Studies*; and an editorial team member of *AGITATE!* The following article is an excerpt from their book *Politics of Rightful Killing: Civil Society, Gender, and Sexuality in Weblogistan* (Duke University Press, 2020).

On April 3, 2018, Nasim Najafi Aghdam, an Iranian refugee, vegan activist, artist, and bodybuilder who was upset with YouTube's demonetization of her videos, walked into the company's headquarters in San Bruno, California, injuring three people and killing herself with a gun she had purchased in January.[1] Aghdam had become relatively well-known among Iranian YouTube, Instagram, and Telegram users because of her eccentric videos. Her small number of followers grew after she changed her content about animal rights and veganism and focused on responding to the hostile comments from viewers who ridiculed her. Her campy and slapstick one-woman comedy videos in Persian, Turkish, and English were a combination of exercise routines and social commentaries about animal rights, veganism, consumerism, and objectification of women's bodies, along with a critique of empty claims about freedom of speech in the United States. In the last months of her life, Aghdam produced videos that critiqued YouTube for demonetizing and filtering her four YouTube channels. In one video, Aghdam tells her viewers that while sexually suggestive videos are allowed on YouTube, her exercise video is censored for "inappropriate content."[2] In another (Persian-language) clip, she criticizes the myth of freedom of speech and tells her viewers that the United States has rampant censorship, corruption, suppression of truth, nepotism, animal abuse, and immorality. She explains that because carrying guns in the United States is legal, one is always worried about not coming back home alive. At the end of the video, she is shot at by animated bullets again, giving the message that one gets killed for speaking the truth.[3]

Aghdam's anger at YouTube was a result of the company's change of policy in early 2018. In order to make its service advertiser-friendly, YouTube raised the eligibility requirements for monetization to four thousand watch hours and one thousand subscribers. YouTube announced that it intended to "prevent bad actors from harming the inspiring and original creators around the world who make their living on YouTube."[4] In her videos and on her website (all deactivated now), Aghdam informed her viewers that YouTube's policy is a euphemism for censorship. "People like me are not good for big business," she proclaimed in one of her videos in which she criticizes YouTube's demonetization policy.

Even as YouTube's content-moderation policies at the beginning of 2018 intensified, the company has removed content that it deemed inappropriate and risky since its inception. In 2006 the Google-owned company became one of the first venues where the Digital Millennium Copyright Act and Section 230 of the Communications Decency Act allowed service providers to restrict user-generated content/actions in order to reduce the risk of liability.[5] In addition, after several governments blocked YouTube, the company started to restrict content. For example, in 2007, claiming user complaints as justification, YouTube suspended Wael Abbas, the Egyptian anti-torture activist blogger/YouTube user whose videos revealed police brutality in Egypt. By the end of the first decade of the new millennium, YouTube effectively became the arbitrator of content appropriateness. Ironically, while YouTube removed videos that violated its policy against violence and hate speech, the company allowed graphically violent videos from Iran's Green movement and the Arab Spring. In 2011 the company's manager of news, referring to the violent videos of the Arab Spring, claimed that while normally "this type of violence would violate our community guidelines and terms of service" and result in removal, YouTube makes an exception for videos that have educational and news value.[6] As Jillian York argues, "YouTube, whether its policymakers and executives like it or not, is already an arbiter of speech, not merely a technology company. And so, the decisions it makes reflect its values, and the values of those who make and enforce its policies."[7]

After YouTube demonetized her channels, Aghdam wrote, "Be aware! Dictatorship exists in all countries but with different tactics! They only care for personal and short-term profits and do anything to reach their goals even by fooling simple-minded people, hiding the truth, manipulating science, putting public mental and physical health at risk, abusing non-human animals, polluting the environment, destroying family values, promoting materialism and sexual degeneration in the name of freedom and turning people into programmed robots!"[8] In one of her parody videos titled "Islamic Republic," Aghdam is wearing a dress with décolletage, along with a tightly wrapped hijab on her head. Animated U.S. dollars are raining on her as she dances with a repetitive move and a stern look on her face. In a sing-a-song voice she says, "at least in Iran they kill you with an axe. Here they cut your throat with cotton balls" (phrasing that derives from a Farsi proverb). She tells her viewers about her view of the United States:

> If you are oblivious and superficial, want to walk naked, and have all kinds of sex, like animals, you will think that this is heaven. . . . But if you want to act humane and delve deeply into the system, you will realize, "yuck! yuck! This is hell! This is worse than Iran!" Yes, those who want to raise awareness and go against the system and big businesses will be shut down and repressed. Like Nasim. See how they filtered her on the Internet, on YouTube, on Instagram?[9]

In most of her videos Aghdam appears in exaggerated feminine drag to mock what she considers to be the popular and shallow form of Iranian femininity that attracts viewers. In one of her most famous videos, titled *Dokhtar-e mameh badkonaki* ("Balloon-Boobed Girl"), she dances in a shiny red skirt, a purple top that reveals ample cleavage, a wig, long eyelashes, and makeup. She sings sarcastically:

> Balloon-boobed girl, Balloon-boobed girl. I am very enlightened. Whatever comes to the market, I buy. . . . Breasts like balloons, lips like cheese puffs [alluding to the prevalence of plastic surgery among middle- and upper-class Iranian women]. Yes, this is civilization. It's a form of enlightenment . . . In sexual matters, I have reached the highest level of civilization. No laws, orgy, sex from behind.[10]

At the end of the video, she unbuttons her shirt and takes off the fake large breasts to make a point about the standards of beauty and the objectification of women in the U.S. In fact, in several of her videos Aghdam seems to be condemning what she considers sexual licentiousness in the U.S., while in others she complains about Iranian diaspora's judgements of those who deviate from the mainstream. In one video she sports a see-through scarf, big hair, and a lot of makeup and mimics diaspora Iranians who belittle others (likely herself) by saying, "Wow, look at that girl! Look at her hair and her makeup! She looks like she is stuck in the 60s [1980s according to the Christian calendar]. Thank God we are from the 90s! . . . Yuck! what a bad accent she has! She looks like she's crazy! . . . Look at her long neck! At first, I thought she was a giraffe! God cure these people! It looks like she's trans. She must be trans!"[11]

In fact, before and after Aghdam's death, some speculated that she was trans. In a Twitter post, Laura Loomer, an alt-right journalist, wrote that "#Nasim Aghdam, the #YouTube shooter has very muscular thighs and buff arms. oversized breasts in some of her pics look distorted w/ photoshop. I don't think we are getting the full story. And for the record, Nasim is not traditionally a woman's name. It's a boy's name."[12] Aghdam's immigration status and nationality made her alleged trans-ness even more menacing. Even though Aghdam had moved to the United States as a Baha'i refugee more than two decades before the YouTube incident, she was assumed to have been undocumented and Muslim.[13] While Dana Rohrabacher, a Republican California congressman, speculated that Aghdam was an "illegal alien," Laura Loomer complained that there was no mention of "the fact that the shooter was from a #TravelBan country."[14] The right-wing white supremacists such as Loomer were happy to announce that the YouTube shooting was not a gun problem but the fault of a mentally ill and deceptive "travel-ban," Muslim "tranny." But this transphobia was not just limited to the right-wing conspiracists. U.K. Labour Party member Jennifer James—a TERF feminist—wrote that "the YouTube shooter was a man. This was male violence. Name the problem. Men can shoot, rape, kill, but we have to 'respect pronouns.' No."[15] On the other hand, eager to prove their exceptional citizenship,[16] liberal queer and trans organizations and individuals dispelled the myth of Aghdam's trans-ness and emphasized her Iranian-ness to distance themselves from the figure of the Middle Eastern terrorist.[17] Just as Puar argues, the cultivation of homosexual (and, in this case, transgender) subjects "folded into life, enabled through 'market virility' and 'regenerative reproductivity,' is racially demarcated and paralleled by a rise in the targeting of the queerly raced bodies for dying."[18] Aghdam's video in which she is being shot at becomes an eerie foreshadowing of being destined to die, even as she forecloses that possibility by shooting herself and the others. At the moment of shooting, Aghdam, to borrow from Puar, does not "transcend or claim the rational nor accept the demarcation of the irrational. Rather, [she] foreground[s] the flawed temporal, spatial, and ontological presumptions upon which such distinctions flourish."[19]

While for the likes of Loomer, she embodied the figure of the terrorist, Aghdam's representational body in her daily life did not make her into what Puar calls the "body of excess," read through racial and sexual excesses of the visual.[20] Had Aghdam "looked like" a Muslim man or a hijabi woman (or a black man sleeping in his car in a parking lot), it is unlikely that the Mountainview Police officers—who responded to a missing-person report and questioned Aghdam in a parking lot the night before the shooting, without searching her car—would have treated Aghdam so gently.[21] One wonders if this treatment was not related to the rescue tendencies to liberate Middle Eastern women and girls from their "violent and abusive" families. Undoubtedly, the fact that she was found in Silicon Valley, the hub of model-minority Iranian tech executives, could have also made her Iranian-ness less threatening. Without her animal masks, headscarves, drags, and eccentric, self-made costumes, Aghdam's visual representation offline did not make her body into a "body of excess." It was only after her death, when Aghdam was identified as an Iranian, an angry and eccentric YouTube user, a shooter, and a refugee that her "affective body" and her "informational body" implicated her in danger, irrationality, and terror through contagion and digital cohesion.

Unlike the Boston Marathon bombing or the Orlando Pulse Club shooting where the attackers were Muslim men, and more akin to cases of mass shooting committed by white men, Aghdam was portrayed as a lone wolf with mental health issues, rather than a "terrorist." The gendered framing of her "failure" to kill reiterated the essentialist narratives of women being naturally peaceful and less violent. But this was not the only element that contributed to less demonizing reportage in Aghdam's case compared to other non-white mass shooters. The shooting came at a time when Trump's presidency and his attacks on "fake news" had turned the liberal media into vanguards of resistance against ultraconservatives in the United States. In contrast to previous shootings by Muslim men, the mainstream media (except Fox) were more careful in a hasty characterization of Aghdam as a terrorist. One cannot help but to wonder if the fact that she was a non-threatening Baha'i (and not Muslim) woman in a pink hoodie sweater contributed to the media's less hysterically Islamophobic reactions to this shooting. Yet her Iranian-ness haunted the coverage of Aghdam's shooting after her death. Unlike the male Muslim suicide bomber or shooter, Aghdam was produced as a victim and as an unstable and risky subject whose Iranian-ness, gender, and refugee-ness made her prone to madness, irrationality, and unpredictability. Even as Aghdam condemned sexual promiscuity and anal sex, and even as she was not Muslim, her quirky YouTube personality, her "deviant" behavior (video superimpositions in which she dances with herself dressed as cows, chickens, and horses), and her refusal to act as a model-minority Iranian immigrant made her into a racially queered subject destined to death.

Aghdam committed the act of suicide shooting in defense of the liberal notion of freedom of speech, while revealing the contradictions and the violence of "freedom of speech." The very same technology (YouTube) that machined together Aghdam as a fleeting queer assemblage of human/computer, human/animal, and organic/inorganic constituted her body as an assemblage (metal/flesh) when she walked into the company's property with a gun and at the moment when a metal bullet shattered her heart into pieces. Aghdam was neither a perfect victim nor a perfect villain; neither queer because of her sexuality and identity, nor a hetero-normative subject; neither a perfect embodiment of fear and hate, nor a figure of love. Her parahumanity[22] is not owed to crossing the lines of human/animal, sane/insane, victim/villain, robot/human, but to her failed exceptionalism and affective queerness as an Iranian immigrant—a risky subject who can never be an exceptional citizen despite her desire.[23]

NOTES

1. Aghdam's YouTube channels were removed after her death. Her Instagram account (insta@nasimesabz1) and her website (nasimesabz.com) have also been erased.

2. See "Nasime Sabz/Nasim Aghdam 'YouTube Shooter' Re-Upload." https://www.liveleak.com/view?t=Cm7EX_1522864851, accessed July 6, 2018.

3. YouTube. April 12, 2018. https://www.youtube.com/watch?v=N8BL3kkpx5M, accessed July 6, 2018.

4. See "Additional Changes to the YouTube Partner Program (YPP) to Better Protect Creators." https://youtube-creators.googleblog.com/2018/01/additional-changes-to-youtube-partner.html, accessed July 9, 2018.

5. See Koebler, Jason, and Jillian York. 2018. "A Brief History of YouTube Censorship." *Motherboard* (blog). March 26, 2018. https://motherboard.vice.com/en_us/article/59jgka/a-brief-history-of-youtube-censorship, accessed July 9, 2018.

6. Ibid.

7. Ibid.

8. See "The Many Faces of Nasim Aghdam, Vegan Turned YouTube Shooter." https://www.animals24-7.org/2018/04/05/the-many-faces-of-nasim-aghdam-vegan-turned-youtube-shooter, accessed July 9, 2018.

9. See "Harf-e Raast o Hessab." https://www.youtube.com/watch?v=rGrb9ZbDEk8, YouTube. April 5, 2018, accessed July 6, 2018.

10. See "Meme Balonlu Kizin Sirri." YouTube. December 1, 2016. https://www.youtube.com/watch?v=ZTr_ruw08qo, accessed July 6, 2018.

11. See "Crazy YouTube Shooter videos Nasim Najafi Aghdam." YouTube, April 4, 2018. https://www.youtube.com/watch?v=3kBNAV0Q8yM, accessed April 23, 2019.

12. See Loomer, Laura. Tweet. April 4, 2018. https://web.archive.org/web/20180404225153/https://twitter.com/LauraLoomer/status/981549903016005634, accessed July 6, 2018.

13. See Thomsen, Jacqueline. 2018. "GOP Lawmaker Claims Without Evidence That YouTube Shooter 'Could Be' an Illegal Immigrant." Text. *The Hill*. April 3, 2018. http://thehill.com/homenews/house/381522-gop-lawmaker-baselessly-claims-that-youtube-shooter-could-be-an-illegal, accessed July 6, 2018.

14. See Loomer, Laura. Tweet. April 5, 2018, accessed July 6, 2018. https://web.archive.org/web/20180410063530/https://twitter.com/LauraLoomer/status/982052400168136704

15. See "Anti-Trans Feminists Push 'Conspiracy Theory' That YouTube Shooter Was a Trans Woman." *PinkNews*. April 5, 2018. https://www.pinknews.co.uk/2018/04/05/anti-trans-feminists-push-conspiracy-theory-that-youtube-shooter-was-a-trans-woman, accessed July 6, 2018.

16. Grewal, Inderpal. 2017. *Saving the Security State: Exceptional Citizens in Twenty-First-Century America*. Next Wave. Durham: Duke University Press.

17. Bollinger, Alex. 2018. "Now Conspiracy Theorists Are Claiming the YouTube Shooter Was a Trans Woman." *LGBTQ Nation*. April 5, 2018. https://www.lgbtqnation.com/2018/04/now-conspiracy-theorists-claiming-you-tube-shooter-trans-woman, accessed July 6, 2018.

18. Puar, Jasbir. 2007. *Terrorist Assemblages: Homonationalism in Queer Times*. Durham: Duke University Press, xii.

19. Puar, 218.

20. Puar, 199.

21. See "Police Body Camera Footage Shows YouTube Shooter Nasim Aghdam Sleeping in Her Car in Walmart Parking Lot." YouTube. April 13, 2018. https://www.youtube.com/watch?v=_5aRnIIicYk, accessed July 6, 2018.

22. Amar, Paul. 2013. *The Security Archipelago: Human-Security States, Sexuality Politics, and the End of Neoliberalism*. Social Text Books. Durham: Duke University Press.

23. Some conspiracy theories claimed that she was an artificial intelligence. See https://www.dailydot.com/upstream/nasim-aghdam-conspiracy-theories-youtube, accessed July 8, 2018.

79. • *Aliette de Bodard*

IMMERSION (2012)

Aliette de Bodard is a Franco-Vietnamese writer of fantasy and science fiction. She has written various novels and short stories on artificial intelligence, alternative (Xuva) universe, and Aztec mystery-fantasy. She has won awards for her novel and short fictions, including a British Science Fiction Association Award (2010 and 2015) and a Nebula award (2012 and 2013). The short story included here has won a Nebula and a Locus award (2012).

In the morning, you're no longer quite sure who you are.

You stand in front of the mirror—it shifts and trembles, reflecting only what you want to see—eyes that feel too wide, skin that feels too pale, an odd, distant smell wafting from the compartment's ambient system that is neither incense nor garlic, but something else, something elusive that you once knew.

Originally published in *Clarkesworld Magazine*, June 2012. Reprinted with permission of Aliette de Bodard.

You're dressed, already—not on your skin, but outside, where it matters, your avatar sporting blue and black and gold, the stylish clothes of a well-traveled, well-connected woman. For a moment, as you turn away from the mirror, the glass shimmers out of focus; and another woman in a dull silk gown stares back at you: smaller, squatter and in every way diminished—a stranger, a distant memory that has ceased to have any meaning.

***

Quy was on the docks, watching the spaceships arrive. She could, of course, have been anywhere on Longevity Station, and requested the feed from the network to be patched to her router—and watched, superimposed on her field of vision, the slow dance of ships slipping into their pod cradles like births watched in reverse. But there was something about standing on the spaceport's concourse—a feeling of closeness that she just couldn't replicate by standing in Golden Carp Gardens or Azure Dragon Temple. Because here—here, separated by only a few measures of sheet metal from the cradle pods, she could feel herself teetering on the edge of the vacuum, submerged in cold and breathing in neither air nor oxygen. She could almost imagine herself rootless, finally returned to the source of everything.

Most ships those days were Galactic—you'd have thought Longevity's ex-masters would have been unhappy about the station's independence, but now that the war was over Longevity was a tidy source of profit. The ships came; and disgorged a steady stream of tourists—their eyes too round and straight, their jaws too square; their faces an unhealthy shade of pink, like undercooked meat left too long in the sun. They walked with the easy confidence of people with immersers: pausing to admire the suggested highlights for a second or so before moving on to the transport station, where they haggled in schoolbook Rong for a ride to their recommended hotels— a sickeningly familiar ballet Quy had been seeing most of her life, a unison of foreigners descending on the station like a plague of centipedes or leeches.

Still, Quy watched them. They reminded her of her own time on Prime, her heady schooldays filled with raucous bars and wild weekends, and late minute revisions for exams, a carefree time she'd never have again in her life. She both longed for those days back, and hated herself for her weakness. Her education on Prime, which should have been her path into the higher strata of the station's society, had brought her nothing but a sense of disconnection from her family; a growing solitude, and a dissatisfaction, an aimlessness she couldn't put in words.

She might not have moved all day—had a sign not blinked, superimposed by her router on the edge of her field of vision. A message from Second Uncle.

"Child." His face was pale and worn, his eyes underlined by dark circles, as if he hadn't slept. He probably hadn't—the last Quy had seen of him, he had been closeted with Quy's sister Tam, trying to organize a delivery for a wedding—five hundred winter melons, and six barrels of Prosper's Station best fish sauce. "Come back to the restaurant."

"I'm on my day of rest," Quy said; it came out as more peevish and childish than she'd intended.

Second Uncle's face twisted, in what might have been a smile, though he had very little sense of humor. The scar he'd got in the Independence War shone white against the grainy background—twisting back and forth, as if it still pained him. "I know, but I need you. We have an important customer."

"Galactic," Quy said. That was the only reason he'd be calling her, and not one of her brothers or cousins. Because the family somehow thought that her studies on Prime gave her insight into the Galactics' way of thought—something useful, if not the success they'd hoped for.

"Yes. An important man, head of a local trading company." Second Uncle did not move on her field of vision. Quy could *see* the ships moving through his face, slowly aligning themselves in front of their pods, the hole in front of them opening like an orchid flower. And she knew everything there was to know about Grandmother's restaurant; she was Tam's sister, after all; and she'd seen the accounts, the slow decline of their clientele as their more gen-teel clients moved to better areas of the station; the influx of tourists on a budget, with little time for expensive dishes prepared with the best ingredients.

"Fine," she said. "I'll come."

***

At breakfast, you stare at the food spread out on the table: bread and jam and some colored liquid—you come up blank for a moment, before your immerser kicks in, reminding you that it's coffee, served strong and black, just as you always take it.

Yes. Coffee.

You raise the cup to your lips—your immerser gently prompts you, reminding you of where to grasp, how to lift, how to be in every possible way graceful and elegant, always an effortless model.

"It's a bit strong," your husband says, apologet-ically. He watches you from the other end of the table, an expression you can't interpret on his face—and isn't this odd, because shouldn't you know all there is to know about expressions—shouldn't the immerser have everything about Galactic culture recorded into its database, shouldn't it prompt you? But it's strangely silent, and this scares you, more than anything. Immersers never fail.

"Shall we go?" your husband says—and, for a moment, you come up blank on his name, before you remember—Galen, it's Galen, named after some physician on Old Earth. He's tall, with dark hair and pale skin—his immerser avatar isn't much different from his real self, Galactic avatars seldom are. It's people like you who have to work the hard-est to adjust, because so much about you draws at-tention to itself—the stretched eyes that crinkle in the shape of moths, the darker skin, the smaller, squatter shape more reminiscent of jackfruits than swaying fronds. But no matter: you can be made perfect; you can put on the immerser and become someone else, someone pale-skinned and tall and beautiful.

Though, really, it's been such a long time since you took off the immerser, isn't it? It's just a thought—a suspended moment that is soon erased by the immerser's flow of information, the little arrows drawing your attention to the bread and the kitchen, and the polished metal of the table—giving you context about everything, opening up the universe like a lotus flower.

"Yes," you say. "Let's go." Your tongue trips over the word—there's a structure you should have used, a pronoun you should have said instead of the lapi-dary Galactic sentence. But nothing will come, and you feel like a field of sugar canes after the harvest—burnt out, all cutting edges with no sweetness left inside.

***

Of course, Second Uncle insisted on Quy getting her immerser for the interview—just in case, he said, soothingly and diplomatically as always. Trouble was, it wasn't where Quy had last left it. After put-ting out a message to the rest of the family, the best information Quy got was from Cousin Khanh, who thought he'd seen Tam sweep through the living quarters, gathering every piece of Galactic tech she could get her hands on. Third Aunt, who caught Khanh's message on the family's communication channel, tutted disapprovingly. "Tam. Always with her mind lost in the mountains, that girl. Dreams have never husked rice."

Quy said nothing. Her own dreams had shriv-eled and died after she came back from Prime and failed Longevity's mandarin exams; but it was good to have Tam around—to have someone who saw beyond the restaurant, beyond the narrow circle of family interests. Besides, if she didn't stick with her sister, who would?

Tam wasn't in the communal areas on the upper floors; Quy threw a glance towards the lift to Grandmother's closeted rooms, but she was doubt-ful Tam would have gathered Galactic tech just so she could pay her respects to Grandmother. Instead, she went straight to the lower floor, the one she and Tam shared with the children of their generation.

It was right next to the kitchen, and the smells of garlic and fish sauce seemed to be everywhere—of course, the youngest generation always got the lower floor, the one with all the smells and the noises of a legion of waitresses bringing food over to the dining room.

Tam was there, sitting in the little compartment that served as the floor's communal area. She'd spread out the tech on the floor—two immersers (Tam and Quy were possibly the only family members who cared so little about immersers they left them lying around), a remote entertainment set that was busy broadcasting some stories of children running on terraformed planets, and something Quy couldn't quite identify, because Tam had taken it apart into small components: it lay on the table like a gutted fish, all metals and optical parts.

But, at some point, Tam had obviously got bored with the entire process, because she was currently finishing her breakfast, slurping noodles from her soup bowl. She must have got it from the kitchen's leftovers, because Quy knew the smell, could taste the spiciness of the broth on her tongue—Mother's cooking, enough to make her stomach growl although she'd had rolled rice cakes for breakfast.

"You're at it again," Quy said with a sigh. "Could you not take my immerser for your experiments, please?"

Tam didn't even look surprised. "You don't seem very keen on using it, big sis."

"That I don't use it doesn't mean it's yours," Quy said, though that wasn't a real reason. She didn't mind Tam borrowing her stuff, and actually would have been glad to never put on an immerser again—she hated the feeling they gave her, the vague sensation of the system rooting around in her brain to find the best body cues to give her. But there were times when she was expected to wear an immerser: whenever dealing with customers, whether she was waiting at tables or in preparation meetings for large occasions.

Tam, of course, didn't wait at tables—she'd made herself so good at logistics and anything to do with the station's system that she spent most of her time in front of a screen, or connected to the station's network.

"Lil' sis?" Quy said.

Tam set her chopsticks by the side of the bowl, and made an expansive gesture with her hands. "Fine. Have it back. I can always use mine."

Quy stared at the things spread on the table, and asked the inevitable question. "How's progress?"

Tam's work was network connections and network maintenance within the restaurant; her hobby was tech. Galactic tech. She took things apart to see what made them tick; and rebuilt them. Her foray into entertainment units had helped the restaurant set up ambient sounds—old-fashioned Rong music for Galactic customers, recitation of the newest poems for locals.

But immersers had her stumped: the things had nasty safeguards to them. You could open them in half, to replace the battery; but you went no further. Tam's previous attempt had almost lost her the use of her hands.

By Tam's face, she didn't feel ready to try again. "It's got to be the same logic."

"As what?" Quy couldn't help asking. She picked up her own immerser from the table, briefly checking that it did indeed bear her serial number.

Tam gestured to the splayed components on the table. "Artificial Literature Writer. Little gadget that composes light entertainment novels."

"That's not the same—" Quy checked herself, and waited for Tam to explain.

"Takes existing cultural norms, and puts them into a cohesive, satisfying narrative. Like people forging their own path and fighting aliens for possession of a planet, that sort of stuff that barely speaks to us on Longevity. I mean, we've never even seen a planet." Tam exhaled, sharply—her eyes half on the dismembered Artificial Literature Writer, half on some overlay of her vision. "Just like immersers take a given culture and parcel it out to you in a form you can relate to: language, gestures, customs, the whole package. They've got to have the same architecture."

"I'm still not sure what you want to do with it." Quy put on her immerser, adjusting the thin metal mesh around her head until it fitted. She winced as the interface synced with her brain. She moved her hands, adjusting some settings lower than the factory ones—darn thing always reset itself to factory, which she suspected was no accident. A shimmering lattice surrounded her: her avatar, slowly taking shape around her. She could still see the room—the lattice was only faintly opaque—but ancestors, how she hated the feeling of not quite being there. "How do I look?"

"Horrible. Your avatar looks like it's died or something."

"Ha ha ha," Quy said. Her avatar was paler than her, and taller: it made her look beautiful, most customers agreed. In those moments, Quy was glad she had an avatar, so they wouldn't see the anger on her face. "You haven't answered my question."

Tam's eyes glinted. "Just think of the things we couldn't do. This is the best piece of tech Galactics have ever brought us."

Which wasn't much, but Quy didn't need to say it aloud. Tam knew exactly how Quy felt about Galactics and their hollow promises.

"It's their weapon, too." Tam pushed at the entertainment unit. "Just like their books and their holos and their live games. It's fine for them—they put the immersers on tourist settings, they get just what they need to navigate a foreign environment from whatever idiot's written the Rong script for that thing. But we—we worship them. We wear the immersers on Galactic all the time. We make ourselves like them, because they push, and because we're naive enough to give in."

"And you think you can make this better?" Quy couldn't help it. It wasn't that she needed to be convinced: on Prime, she'd never seen immersers. They were tourist stuff, and even while traveling from one city to another, the citizens just assumed they'd know enough to get by. But the stations, their ex-colonies were flooded with immersers.

Tam's eyes glinted, as savage as those of the rebels in the history holos. "If I can take them apart, I can rebuild them and disconnect the logical circuits. I can give us the language and the tools to deal with them without being swallowed by them."

Mind lost in the mountains, Third Aunt said. No one had ever accused Tam of thinking small. Or

of not achieving what she set her mind on, come to think of it. And every revolution had to start somewhere—hadn't Longevity's War of Independence started over a single poem, and the unfair imprisonment of the poet who'd written it?

Quy nodded. She believed Tam, though she didn't know how far. "Fair point. Have to go now, or Second Uncle will skin me. See you later, lil' sis."

***

As you walk under the wide arch of the restaurant with your husband, you glance upwards, at the calligraphy that forms its sign. The immerser translates it for you into "Sister Hai's Kitchen," and starts giving you a detailed background of the place: the menu and the most recommended dishes—as you walk past the various tables, it highlights items it thinks you would like, from rolled-up rice dumplings to fried shrimps. It warns you about the more exotic dishes, like the pickled pig's ears, the fermented meat (you have to be careful about that one, because its name changes depending on which station dialect you order in), or the reeking durian fruit that the natives so love.

It feels . . . not quite right, you think, as you struggle to follow Galen, who is already far away, striding ahead with the same confidence he always exudes in life. People part before him; a waitress with a young, pretty avatar bows before him, though Galen himself takes no notice. You know that such obsequiousness unnerves him; he always rants about the outdated customs aboard Longevity, the inequalities and the lack of democratic government—he thinks it's only a matter of time before they change, adapt themselves to fit into Galactic society. You—you have a faint memory of arguing with him, a long time ago, but now you can't find the words, anymore, or even the reason why—it makes sense, it all makes sense. The Galactics rose against the tyranny of Old Earth and overthrew their shackles, and won the right to determine their own destiny; and every other station and planet will do the same, eventually, rise against the dictatorships that hold them away from progress. It's right; it's always been right.

Unbidden, you stop at a table, and watch two young women pick at a dish of chicken with chopsticks—the smell of fish sauce and lemongrass rises in the air, as pungent and as unbearable as rotten meat—no, no, that's not it, you have an image of a dark-skinned woman, bringing a dish of steamed rice to the table, her hands filled with that same smell, and your mouth watering in anticipation . . .

The young women are looking at you: they both wear standard-issue avatars, the bottom-of-the-line kind—their clothes are a garish mix of red and yellow, with the odd, uneasy cut of cheap designers; and their faces waver, letting you glimpse a hint of darker skin beneath the red flush of their cheeks. Cheap and tawdry, and altogether inappropriate; and you're glad you're not one of them.

"Can I help you, older sister?" one of them asks.

Older sister. A pronoun you were looking for, earlier; one of the things that seem to have vanished from your mind. You struggle for words; but all the immerser seems to suggest to you is a neutral and impersonal pronoun, one that you instinctively know is wrong—it's one only foreigners and outsiders would use in those circumstances. "Older sister," you repeat, finally, because you can't think of anything else.

"Agnes!"

Galen's voice, calling from far away—for a brief moment the immerser seems to fail you again, because you *know* that you have many names, that Agnes is the one they gave you in Galactic school, the one neither Galen nor his friends can mangle when they pronounce it. You remember the Rong names your mother gave you on Longevity, the childhood endearments and your adult style name.

Be-Nho, Be-Yeu. Thu—Autumn, like a memory of red maple leaves on a planet you never knew.

You pull away from the table, disguising the tremor in your hands.

***

Second Uncle was already waiting when Quy arrived; and so were the customers.

"You're late," Second Uncle sent on the private channel, though he made the comment

half-heartedly, as if he'd expected it all along. As if he'd never really believed he could rely on her—that stung.

"Let me introduce my niece Quy to you," Second Uncle said, in Galactic, to the man beside him.

"Quy," the man said, his immerser perfectly taking up the nuances of her name in Rong. He was everything she'd expected; tall, with only a thin layer of avatar, a little something that narrowed his chin and eyes, and made his chest slightly larger. Cosmetic enhancements: he was good-looking for a Galactic, all things considered. He went on, in Galactic, "My name is Galen Santos. Pleased to meet you. This is my wife, Agnes."

Agnes. Quy turned, and looked at the woman for the first time—and flinched. There was no one here: just a thick layer of avatar, so dense and so complex that she couldn't even guess at the body hidden within.

"Pleased to meet you." On a hunch, Quy bowed, from younger to elder, with both hands brought together—Rong-style, not Galactic—and saw a shudder run through Agnes' body, barely perceptible; but Quy was observant, she'd always been. Her immerser was screaming at her, telling her to hold out both hands, palms up, in the Galactic fashion. She tuned it out: she was still at the stage where she could tell the difference between her thoughts and the immerser's thoughts.

Second Uncle was talking again—his own avatar was light, a paler version of him. "I understand you're looking for a venue for a banquet."

"We are, yes." Galen pulled a chair to him, sank into it. They all followed suit, though not with the same fluid, arrogant ease. When Agnes sat, Quy saw her flinch, as though she'd just remembered something unpleasant. "We'll be celebrating our fifth marriage anniversary, and we both felt we wanted to mark the occasion with something suitable."

Second Uncle nodded. "I see," he said, scratching his chin. "My congratulations to you."

Galen nodded. "We thought—" he paused, threw a glance at his wife that Quy couldn't quite interpret—her immerser came up blank, but there was something oddly familiar about it, something she ought to have been able to name. "Something Rong," he said at last. "A large banquet for a hundred people, with the traditional dishes."

Quy could almost feel Second Uncle's satisfaction. A banquet of that size would be awful logistics, but it would keep the restaurant afloat for a year or more, if they could get the price right. But something was wrong—something—

"What did you have in mind?" Quy asked, not to Galen, but to his wife. The wife—Agnes, which probably wasn't the name she'd been born with—who wore a thick avatar, and didn't seem to be answering or ever speaking up. An awful picture was coming together in Quy's mind.

Agnes didn't answer. Predictable.

Second Uncle took over, smoothing over the moment of awkwardness with expansive hand gestures. "The whole hog, yes?" Second Uncle said. He rubbed his hands, an odd gesture that Quy had never seen from him—a Galactic expression of satisfaction. "Bitter melon soup, Dragon-Phoenix plates, Roast Pig, Jade Under the Mountain . . . " He was citing all the traditional dishes for a wedding banquet—unsure of how far the foreigner wanted to take it. He left out the odder stuff, like Shark Fin or Sweet Red Bean Soup.

"Yes, that's what we would like. Wouldn't we, darling?" Galen's wife neither moved nor spoke. Galen's head turned towards her, and Quy caught his expression at last. She'd thought it would be contempt, or hatred; but no; it was anguish. He genuinely loved her, and he couldn't understand what was going on.

Galactics. Couldn't he recognize an immerser junkie when he saw one? But then Galactics, as Tam said, seldom had the problem—they didn't put on the immersers for more than a few days on low settings, if they ever went that far. Most were flat-out convinced Galactic would get them anywhere.

Second Uncle and Galen were haggling, arguing prices and features; Second Uncle sounding more and more like a Galactic tourist as the conversation went on, more and more aggressive for lower and lower gains. Quy didn't care anymore: she watched Agnes. Watched the impenetrable avatar—a red-headed woman in the latest style from Prime, with freckles on her skin and a hint of a star-tan on her face. But that wasn't what she was, inside; what the immerser had dug deep into.

Wasn't who she was at all. Tam was right; all immersers should be taken apart, and did it matter if they exploded? They'd done enough harm as it was.

Quy wanted to get up, to tear away her own immerser, but she couldn't, not in the middle of the negotiation. Instead, she rose, and walked closer to Agnes; the two men barely glanced at her, too busy agreeing on a price. "You're not alone," she said, in Rong, low enough that it didn't carry.

Again, that odd, disjointed flash. "You have to take it off," Quy said, but got no further response. As an impulse, she grabbed the other woman's arm; felt her hands go right through the immerser's avatar, connect with warm, solid flesh.

***

You hear them negotiating, in the background—it's tough going, because the Rong man sticks to his guns stubbornly, refusing to give ground to Galen's onslaught. It's all very distant, a subject of intellectual study; the immerser reminds you from time to time, interpreting this and this body cue, nudging you this way and that—you must sit straight and silent, and support your husband—and so you smile through a mouth that feels gummed together.

You feel, all the while, the Rong girl's gaze on you, burning like ice water, like the gaze of a dragon. She won't move away from you; and her hand rests on you, gripping your arm with a strength you didn't think she had in her body. Her avatar is but a thin layer, and you can see her beneath it: a round, moon-shaped face with skin the color of cinnamon—no, not spices, not chocolate, but simply a color you've seen all your life.

"You have to take it off," she says. You don't move; but you wonder what she's talking about.

Take it off. Take it off. Take what off?

The immerser.

Abruptly, you remember—a dinner with Galen's friends, when they laughed at jokes that had gone by too fast for you to understand. You came home battling tears; and found yourself reaching for the immerser on your bedside table, feeling its cool weight in your hands. You thought it would please Galen if you spoke his language; that he would be less ashamed of how uncultured you sounded to his friends. And then you found out that everything was fine, as long as you kept the settings on maximum and didn't remove it. And then . . . and then you walked with it and slept with it, and showed the world nothing but the avatar it had designed—saw nothing it hadn't tagged and labeled for you. Then . . .

Then it all slid down, didn't it? You couldn't program the network anymore, couldn't look at the guts of machines; you lost your job with the tech company, and came to Galen's compartment, wandering in the room like a hollow shell, a ghost of yourself—as if you'd already died, far away from home and all that it means to you. Then—then the immerser wouldn't come off, anymore.

***

"What do you think you're doing, young woman?"

Second Uncle had risen, turning towards Quy—his avatar flushed with anger, the pale skin mottled with an unsightly red. "We adults are in the middle of negotiating something very important, if you don't mind." It might have made Quy quail in other circumstances, but his voice and his body language were wholly Galactic; and he sounded like a stranger to her—an angry foreigner whose food order she'd misunderstood—whom she'd mock later, sitting in Tam's room with a cup of tea in her lap, and the familiar patter of her sister's musings.

"I apologize," Quy said, meaning none of it.

"That's all right," Galen said. "I didn't mean to—" he paused, looked at his wife. "I shouldn't have brought her here."

"You should take her to see a physician," Quy said, surprised at her own boldness.

"Do you think I haven't tried?" His voice was bitter. "I've even taken her to the best hospitals on Prime. They look at her, and say they can't take it off. That the shock of it would kill her. And even if it didn't . . ." He spread his hands, letting air fall

between them like specks of dust. "Who knows if she'd come back?"

Quy felt herself blush. "I'm sorry." And she meant it this time.

Galen waved her away, negligently, airily, but she could see the pain he was struggling to hide. Galactics didn't think tears were manly, she remembered. "So we're agreed?" Galen asked Second Uncle. "For a million credits?"

Quy thought of the banquet; of the food on the tables, of Galen thinking it would remind Agnes of home. Of how, in the end, it was doomed to fail, because everything would be filtered through the immerser, leaving Agnes with nothing but an exotic feast of unfamiliar flavors. "I'm sorry," she said, again, but no one was listening; and she turned away from Agnes with rage in her heart—with the growing feeling that it had all been for nothing in the end.

***

"I'm sorry," the girl says—she stands, removing her hand from your arm, and you feel like a tearing inside, as if something within you was struggling to claw free from your body. Don't go, you want to say. Please don't go. Please don't leave me here.

But they're all shaking hands; smiling, pleased at a deal they've struck—like sharks, you think, like tigers. Even the Rong girl has turned away from you; giving you up as hopeless. She and her uncle are walking away, taking separate paths back to the inner areas of the restaurant, back to their home.

Please don't go.

It's as if something else were taking control of your body; a strength that you didn't know you possessed. As Galen walks back into the restaurant's main room, back into the hubbub and the tantalizing smells of food—of lemongrass chicken and steamed rice, just as your mother used to make—you turn away from your husband, and follow the girl. Slowly, and from a distance; and then running, so that no one will stop you. She's walking fast—you see her tear her immerser away from her face, and slam it down onto a side table with disgust. You see her enter a room; and you follow her inside.

They're watching you, both girls, the one you followed in; and another, younger one, rising from the table she was sitting at—both terribly alien and terribly familiar at once. Their mouths are open, but no sound comes out.

In that one moment—staring at each other, suspended in time—you see the guts of Galactic machines spread on the table. You see the mass of tools; the dismantled machines; and the immerser, half spread-out before them, its two halves open like a cracked egg. And you understand that they've been trying to open them and reverse-engineer them; and you know that they'll never, ever succeed. Not because of the safeguards, of the Galactic encryptions to preserve their fabled intellectual property; but rather, because of something far more fundamental.

This is a Galactic toy, conceived by a Galactic mind—every layer of it, every logical connection within it exudes a mindset that might as well be alien to these girls. It takes a Galactic to believe that you can take a whole culture and reduce it to algorithms; that language and customs can be boiled to just a simple set of rules. For these girls, things are so much more complex than this; and they will never understand how an immerser works, because they can't think like a Galactic, they'll never ever think like that. You can't think like a Galactic unless you've been born in the culture.

Or drugged yourself, senseless, into it, year after year.

You raise a hand—it feels like moving through honey. You speak—struggling to shape words through layer after layer of immerser thoughts.

"I know about this," you say, and your voice comes out hoarse, and the words fall into place one by one like a laser stroke, and they feel right, in a way that nothing else has for five years. "Let me help you, younger sisters."

SECTION SIX

Activist Frontiers:
Agency and Resistance

TABLE OF CONTENTS

80. Lila Abu-Lughod, "Do Muslim Women Really Need Saving? Anthropological Reflections on Cultural Relativism and Its Others" 530

81. Beenash Jafri, "Not Your Indian Eco-Princess: Indigenous Women's Resistance to Environmental Degradation" 541

82. Elizabeth R. Cole and Zakiya T. Luna, "Making Coalitions Work: Solidarity Across Difference Within US Feminism" 546

83. *Evette Dionne, "Turning Fury Into Fuel: Three Women Authors on Publishing's New Investment in Anger" 554

84. DaMaris B. Hill, "Concrete" 559

85. *Wangari Maathai, "An Unbreakable Link: Peace, Environment, and Democracy" 563

86. *Christina E. Bejarano, "The Latina Advantage in US Politics: Recent Example with Representative Ocasio-Cortez" (new) 567

87. Michael Winter, "I Was There" 572

88. Sarah E. Fryett, "Laudable Laughter: Feminism and Female Comedians" 574

89. Guerrilla Girls, "When Racism & Sexism Are No Longer Fashionable" 579

90. *Alison Bechdel, "The Bechdel Test" 580

91. Kathleen Hanna/Bikini Kill, "Riot Grrrl Manifesto" 582

92. *Heather Rellihan, "An Interview with Tarana Burke" (new) 583

What is activism, and what forms of activism can we take part in? How can feminist, queer, and other marginalized communities transgress dominant cultural norms in the movement toward social justice? Why is intersectionality important in activist work? In this section, we explore these questions by focusing on different activist strategies. In the interview with her included in this section, long-time community organizer and founder of the MeToo movement Tarana Burke emphasizes that there are many different ways to do activist work. Indeed, as she says, the list of ways that people can get involved in social justice work is "almost endless" (p. 588). What follows is only a partial list, intended to be suggestive rather than definitive. We have selected the following to explore in greater depth: knowledge production, digital activism, community activist organizations, engaging in the political process, nonviolent direct action, humor, creative expression, safer spaces, and speak-outs and testimonials. Within each section there are specific examples of how the strategy has been used by activists. These examples will demonstrate some of the various ways people can get involved around the issues they care about, and that's important because, as Burke notes, "We need different people with varied skills to win the fights of our time" (p. 588).

INTERSECTIONALITY AND COALITIONS

Intersectional approaches are essential to activism in feminist and queer movements because without them there is a danger of reinforcing certain oppressive social hierarchies even as you try to dismantle others. For example, if feminist activism focuses only on straight women, it can reproduce heterosexual privilege while trying to dismantle male privilege. The activists highlighted in this section are not without criticism. Some have been accused of being myopic in their focus on one issue at the expense of others, or of supporting one social hierarchy while they dismantle another. All activist work must be attentive to the ways in which it defines its goals, recognizing, as Lila Abu-Lughod explains in her essay "Do Muslim Women Really Need Saving? Anthropological Reflections on Cultural Relativism and Its Others" (included in this section), that there is a danger of becoming complicit in divisive us/them narratives. In her discussion of transnational activism focused on women in the Muslim world, particularly in conjunction with the post-9/11 rhetoric of salvation and the use of the veil as oppressive symbol, Abu-Lughod reminds us that "[p]rojects of saving other women depend on and reinforce a sense of superiority by Westerners, a form of arrogance that deserves to be challenged" (p. 538).

It is important for feminist and queer activists to reflect on their motivations for their work as well as their complicity in the issues, the ways in which they benefit from the status quo or the ways in which they might benefit from a change. In her article "Not Your Indian Eco-Princess: Indigenous Women's Resistance to Environmental Degradation," Beenash Jafri points to the failure of some transnational environmental activists to acknowledge the **neocolonial** relationships that nation-states like the United States, Canada, Australia, and New Zealand maintain with Indigenous Peoples. She warns that using Indigenous women as symbols of an idealized relationship between women and nature without a critical examination of the history and ongoing effects of colonialism can make invisible the ways in which nonindigenous people have benefited from this oppression.

Abu-Lughod and Jafri point to problems in some activist work and underscore the importance of intersectionality. These critiques are important so that activists can learn from others' missteps. We can't let a fear of making mistakes prevent us from engaging in activism, but at the same time we should see openness and responsiveness to others' critiques as a necessary part of the activist process.

An important component of activist work is **coalition** building. Coalitions are fundamental to social justice, but these collaborations can be difficult because they require working across difference. Feminist activist and musician Bernice Johnson Reagon (1983) argues that acknowledging difference within coalitions is essential. Pretending that everyone is the same, and has come to the table for the same reasons, blocks the transformative potential of coalitions. In their article "Making Coalitions Work: Solidarity Across Difference Within US Feminism" (included in this section), Elizabeth R. Cole and Zakiya T. Luna build on this argument by looking at coalition work in action. They interviewed activists and analyzed their responses to investigate the ways in which coalitions come together and remain strong, as well as the challenges they face around differing interests and agendas.

Neocolonial: The relationship of power developed countries exercise over developing countries using economic relationships and cultural influence instead of military or political control. Neocolonialism is a new form of colonialism, which is a practice whereby European countries conquered, occupied, and exploited countries in Africa, Asia, and the Americas.

Coalition: An association of individuals and/or groups who come together around a shared interest or value.

TRANSNATIONAL CONNECTIONS

Western feminists who are active in campaigns to end female circumcision (also known as female genital cutting or female genital mutilation) in Africa, Asia, and the Middle East frequently argue that the practice stems from efforts to control female sexuality.

1. Research female circumcision. Where is it practiced? What are the arguments given in support of the practice? What are the arguments against it?
2. Research male circumcision. Compare the information you find to what you learned about female circumcision. What are the arguments made for and against male circumcision? How do these arguments compare to those made around female circumcision?
3. Male circumcision is common in the United States. If Western feminists advocate for the abolition of female circumcision, should they also try to end male circumcision?
4. How does this example demonstrate important concerns over transnational activist work?

KNOWLEDGE PRODUCTION: BOOKS, MAGAZINES, AND ZINES

Knowledge production is an integral part of activist work. As Charlotte Bunch explains in her essay "Not by Degrees: Feminist Theory and Education," theory and organizing inform each other: in order to address discrimination, you need a framework for understanding it, and those frameworks need to respond to on-the-ground realities (Bunch 2005, 12). Prior to the online revolution, which democratized publishing by allowing many more people to disseminate their writing at low cost, the production of knowledge was largely limited to those who could get their work published in print. The gatekeepers in the print publishing world represented dominant groups in society, and thus the experience of privileged white men was overrepresented in print media. People from marginalized groups had difficulty getting their work published, which served to maintain their marginalization as their experiences remained outside of mainstream visibility. Furthermore, when marginalized groups don't have access to knowledge production, their stories may be seen only or primarily through the eyes of the dominant group, whose privilege may produce a distorted and self-serving narrative. In "Turning Fury into Fuel: Three Women Authors on Publishing's New Investment in Anger" (included in this section), Evette Dionne interviews three authors—Soraya Chemaly, Gemma Hartley, and Reema Zaman—who talk about the discomfort with women's anger, and how recent books like their own as well as Brittney Cooper's *Eloquent Rage: A Black Feminist Discovers Her Superpower* and Rebecca Traister's *Good and Mad: The Revolutionary Power of Women's Anger* are reclaiming anger as an activist tool. Hartley notes that the publication of these new books contribute to a shift: "[W]e seem to be waking up to the fact that civility is a patriarchal tool that we can't use to our advantage" and "I think the fact that publishers are investing in these narratives helps validate and normalize our anger, which is long overdue" (p. 554, 556).

Providing access to publishing is an essential component of social change because it democratizes knowledge production. Citing an early slogan of the **women in print movement**—"freedom of the press belongs to those who own the press"—Barbara Smith explains that because women, and particularly women of color and lesbians, have had less power in our society, they have had minimal access to publishing, meaning the stories about them were told by others (Smith 1989, 11). Smith and other activists created Kitchen Table: Women of Color Press in 1980 to respond to the dearth of publications by women of color and published influential texts like *This Bridge Called My Back: Writings By Radical Women of Color* and *Home Girls: A Black Feminist Anthology*. While Kitchen Table was an important intervention in the publishing world, limited access for marginalized groups remains a problem. Similarly, while the internet has opened up tremendous opportunities for self-publishing, media companies maintain significant influence over what information we are exposed to online, and so the question of whose opinions are known and whose

Women in print movement: The activist efforts emerging in the late 1960s to increase the amount of published information by and about heterosexual women and lesbians based on the premise that access to information was empowering.

experiences are visible remains central to knowledge production. Writer DaM-aris B. Hill's work is attentive to the power of self-representation and memory. Her memoir, "Concrete" (included in this section), engages with race, gender, and the construction of identity.

The Boston Women's Health Book Collective demonstrates the transformational capacity of publishing as an activist strategy engaged around a particular social justice issue. The members of the group first met in 1969 to talk about their anger with the medical industry and particularly with "doctors who were condescending, paternalistic, judgmental and non-informative" (Boston Women's Health Book Collective 2016). Through those discussions, they decided that in order to improve women's experiences with doctors and the medical community, women needed more information about their bodies and their health, because ignorance detracted from their ability to make informed decisions.

Because increasing women's knowledge about their bodies and their health was the primary goal of the collective, the members initially created a course that they offered locally in schools, churches, and homes. The course was so successful, and the demand for information was so great, that they decided to publish a book based on the course, *Our Bodies, Ourselves*, which was first published in 1971. In addition to providing information about women's bodies, the collective wanted to change the narrative around women's health. For example, cultural norms around menstruation and masturbation were often couched in patriarchal and religious narratives that caused women to

Our Bodies, Ourselves **distributed to every member of Congress.** Judy Norsigian, co-founder of Our Bodies Ourselves (formerly the Boston Women's Health Book Collective), stands behind a copy of *Our Bodies, Ourselves* at the National Press Club in Washington, DC, on October 22, 2012. She announced the new initiative, Educate Congress, which aimed to ensure that representatives and senators are educated about women's bodies and health. The initiative began as a response to Rep. Todd Akin's 2012 statement about "legitimate rape" and pregnancy.
Source: Robert MacPherson/AFP via Getty Images

feel shame about their bodies. *Our Bodies, Ourselves* sought to reframe these topics in positive terms. The book was republished in many new editions and translated into at least twenty-nine languages, selling millions of copies, and was included in the Library of Congress's 2012 exhibit "Books that Shaped America." The story of *Our Bodies, Ourselves* proves that individuals can make a difference: a small group of women created a book that questioned the medical establishment's views on women's bodies and in the process has educated and empowered millions of women globally.

In the preface to her 2014 book *Trans Bodies, Trans Selves: A Resource for the Transgender Community*, Laura Erickson-Schroth says that she was twelve years old when she first looked at her mother's copy of *Our Bodies, Ourselves*. She was inspired by the women who wrote it and hopes that *her* book is just as radical as its predecessor, providing information about trans health and challenging the pathologization of trans identities (Erickson-Schroth 2014, xi).

Trans Bodies, Trans Selves emphasizes the importance of trans visibility by including many first-person narratives like those of prominent trans activists Dallas Denny and Jamison Green. Born in 1949, Denny says, "When I was in my early teens, I could find absolutely nothing about transgender issues. Nada. Zip. There were no zines, blogs, vlogs, Web sites, or radio shows. There was no Internet . . . Libraries and bookstores offered no help. I was alone" (Erickson-Schroth 2014, xix). Born a year earlier, Green agrees, explaining, "I had no idea that others like me existed until the mid-1970s, and I was unable to find reliable information that was reassuring—rather than pathologizing and insulting—until the late 1980s" (Erickson-Schroth 2014, xx). *Trans Bodies, Trans Selves* addresses this deficit by providing information around many aspects of trans lives, with a focus on terminology, identification documents, employment protections, guidelines and inclusion policies for sports, the processes involved in hormone therapy, and immigration policies. It provides strategies for dealing with challenges in employment, a sample doctor's care/carry letter explaining the transitioning process, and tips for how to organize activist groups. The book takes an intersectional approach, with sections like "On Top Surgery, Chests and Race/Class Privilege," "Working for LGBTQ Youth of Color," and "Liberation Doesn't Leave People Behind: Ableism, Transphobia, Classism, and Racism." *Trans Bodies, Trans Selves* provides the type of information that wasn't available to Denny and Green when they were coming of age.

Print and online magazines are also important sources of knowledge production. *BUST* is an example of a magazine (and now a website) that has challenged the status quo within the publishing industry. *BUST* got its start in 1993 when three friends, Marcelle Karp, Laurie Henzel, and Debbie Stoller, saw the need for a women's magazine that appealed to women like them, young feminists "who couldn't relate to the body-sculpting tips of *Cosmo* or the eyebrow tweezing directions of *Glamour*" (Karp and Stoller 1999, xiii). As young twenty-somethings, they had no money and no experience in publishing, but they had a vision for a new type of publication that would empower women to focus less on beauty and more on critically engaging with the world around them. The first issue of *BUST* was a self-published twenty-nine-page zine that they photocopied and stapled themselves (Karp and Stoller 1999, xiii). The print magazine is still being published more than twenty-five years later, now with a companion website, and the content continues to address topics that are too radical for more mainstream publications. Traditional media still encourages women to obsess over their appearance, with damaging effects on female self-esteem, and this obsession with beauty also detracts from the time and energy that women could devote to other interests. Activist publications like *BUST* are important because they send a different message. They encourage a more empowering narrative about femininity and inspire a range of interests that move beyond traditional gender roles for women.

While zines can lead to more formal publications like magazines, as was the case with *BUST*, they don't have to. In fact, the do-it-yourself ethic is an important hallmark of zine culture, which emerged in conjunction with the Riot Grrrl movement (discussed later) with its questioning of power structures and encouragement of personal expression. Zinemakers take the power of publication out of the hands of the traditional publishing industry and put it into the hands of individuals, a democratizing force in the production of knowledge. What generally defines a zine (as opposed to a magazine) is its small circulation (between a hundred and a thousand copies), the fact that it's usually self-published (often via photocopier or online), and its irreverent challenging of traditional genres. Mainstream publications often stay away from controversial issues because they worry about upsetting readers and advertisers, and thereby lowering profits. In contrast, zines often take on these issues directly. Zines might contain personal essays, artwork, graphic novels, or poetry and might address topics like gender bending, body shaming, rape culture, trans history, alternative masculinities, aging, dis/ability rights, parenting, or animal rights. Zine creators see their work as an outlet for creative expression, a channel for voicing anger, and a means of communicating to an audience directly, affectively, and passionately. Therefore, zines are political acts that inform, engage, and persuade.

DIGITAL ACTIVISM

The online revolution is important because it has created greater access to publishing and therefore to knowledge production. It has also created new tools for organizing and an unprecedented level of communication. With over 4.5 million visitors each month, Everydayfeminism.com demonstrates the ways that websites can raise awareness, create community, and inspire action ("About Everyday Feminism"). Started by Sandra Kim in 2012, the mission of Everyday Feminism is "to help people dismantle everyday violence,

INTERSECTIONAL ANALYSIS

Social media hashtag campaigns are an important component of digital activism. Beginning in July 2013, the Black Lives Matter hashtag (#blacklivesmatter) emerged as a grassroots reaction to shooting deaths of young Black men at the hands of police officers or their stand-ins. In 2014, after a man killed six people motivated in part by his hatred of women, activists began using #yesallwomen to raise awareness about gendered violence. The hashtag was also a response to the earlier hashtag #notallmen, which was seen by many feminists as a defensive argument that prevented an honest dialogue around men's role in addressing the issue of violence against women.

QUESTIONS

1. Search on the internet for information on these hashtags. Explain some of the strategies of the Black Lives Matter movement. How are they trying to make change? Explore the relationship between the #yesallwomen and the #notallmen campaigns. What point is each side trying to make?

2. Do you think this form of identity politics is useful in light of what you've learned about intersectional theory? Why or why not? For example, much of the media coverage of the Black Lives Matter campaign has focused on the experience of Black men. Does this marginalize the violence experienced by Black women? Is there enough focus on the violence experienced by queer Black men? Similarly, does #yesallwomen suggest that all women are at equal risk for gendered violence?

3. When asked by protesters how he would address police killings of Black men and women, former Baltimore mayor and 2016 presidential candidate Martin O'Malley said, "Black lives matter. White lives matter. All lives matter." Critics argued that O'Malley's comment is "missing the point." What do you think they mean? What is lost in changing "Black lives matter" to "all lives matter"?

Activists protest the deaths of Michael Brown and Eric Garner. First emerging after George Zimmerman was acquitted of murder charges in the shooting death of black teenager Trayvon Martin, the Black Lives Matter movement has increased public attention to the issues of racial discrimination and police brutality. Slogans "Hands Up! Don't Shoot!" and "I Can't Breathe," used here by activists in New York City in January 2015, have arisen in response to the killing of black men by police officers.
Source: Shutterstock

Hashtags are an important part of social media activism. Here activists highlight the names of individual women at a 2015 event, #SayHerName: A Vigil in Memory of Black Women and Girls Killed by the Police. The hashtag #SayHerName was created by the African American Policy Forum to focus attention on black women's stories in discussions of race and policing.
Source: a katz/Shutterstock

discrimination, and marginalization through applied intersectional feminism and to create a world where self-determination and loving communities are social norms through compassionate activism" ("About Everyday Feminism"). In addition to its online magazine, which features information and discussion through an intersectional lens, Everyday Feminism has also created a School for Social Justice that offers "online learning for healing, justice, and liberation" with courses like "Building a Trans/Non-Binary Inclusive Workplace: A Training for Employers & Employees," "Taking Your Anti-Racism Work to the Next Level: How to Take Risks & Move Out of Your Comfort Zone," and "The Body Love Course: How to Dump Diet Culture & Embrace Radical Self Love" ("School for Social Justice").

Mobile phone technologies like GPS mapping and photo and video recording create unprecedented possibilities for activists. For example, Hollaback! is a crowd-sourced, application-based initiative that documents **street harassment**. Although street harassment is a common form of gender-based violence, it is rarely reported and almost never prosecuted. Hollaback! aims to change this by collecting the stories of women and LGBTQ folks who have been harassed. By downloading an application to their mobile phones, people can document harassment that they see or experience. Documenting the harassment does several things. First, it allows the targets of street harassment to take back the power. Harassers want to make their target scared or uncomfortable, but "[b]y holla'ing back you are transforming an experience that is lonely and isolating into one that is sharable. You change the power dynamic by flipping the lens off of you and onto the harasser. And you enter a worldwide community of people who've got your back" ("About"). Second, sharing individual stories creates awareness and empathy, which can be harnessed into political action. And finally, because all incidents are mapped, data is collected documenting areas with high levels of harassment.

Street harassment: A form of sexual harassment in public places that includes unwanted comments, gestures, whistles, catcalls, or other unwanted attention by strangers.

Online games are another tool that activists have used to raise awareness and create empathy. Urban Ministries of Durham, a North Carolina organization fighting poverty and homelessness, co-created a game called Spent (playspent.org) to dramatize the tough decisions and experiences that many in their community face. Players are given $1,000 and challenged to make it to the end of the month without going broke while negotiating things like changes in employment, unforeseen medical costs, and the lack of affordable housing. As the player progresses through the game and makes difficult choices, the game provides contextual information about the structural causes of poverty and homelessness. Another online game, The Migrant Trail (http://theundocumented.com), educates and engages around the pressing social issue of immigration. Players simulate the experience of either a migrant or a border-control agent on the US–Mexico border, encouraging a greater understanding of the migrants' motivations and the brutal experience of trying to cross the border, as well as the complexities of the job for border agents. It is important that these types of critiques emerge in the gaming world because gaming culture has historically privileged the experiences of those in the dominant group—telling their stories and showing the world through their eyes. It has therefore been less welcoming for women, people of color, and other marginalized groups (see Section Five for more discussion of women and gaming). Games like Spent and The Migrant Trail encourage us to understand multiple perspectives around one issue.

COMMUNITY ACTIVIST ORGANIZATIONS

Community-serving activist organizations are usually designated as nonprofits or nongovernmental organizations (NGOs) because, unlike for-profit businesses, they are not designed to make a profit for owners or shareholders and/or because they operate in civil society outside of governmental structures. HIPS, a support and advocacy organization for male, female, and transgender sex workers in Washington, DC, is an example of community-based activism. HIPS helps with basic needs (such as food and housing) and provides crisis intervention for victims of abuse. The organization also offers physical and mental health services. What defines the organization is its nonjudgmental, respectful, and compassionate outreach to and with sex workers, an approach that makes its mobile van services so successful. On Thursday, Friday, and Saturday nights from 11 p.m. to 5 a.m., HIPS workers drive through the streets of Washington, DC, distributing safer sex materials, candy, and water to sex workers (Montague 2010). They also hand out "Bad Date Sheets," which provide information about individuals who have recently hurt sex workers in the area (Montague 2010). HIPS demonstrates the need for community activist organizations, particularly around issues where government intervention is limited or complicated. Because prostitution is illegal in most places, it is difficult to imagine government services being provided with the same non-punitive approach.

The Green Belt Movement, founded by Nobel Peace Prize winner Wangari Maathai in Kenya in 1977, provides an example of how women have come together in grassroots organizations to address environmental issues and climate change. While the work of the Green Belt Movement began with the simple act of encouraging women to plant trees, it was based on an understanding of the complex ways in which climate change negatively affects women, particularly poor women. As Maathai explains in her essay "An Unbreakable Link: Peace, Environment, and Democracy" (included in this section), "Throughout Africa, women are the primary caretakers, tilling the land and feeding their families. As a result, they are often the first to feel the effects of environmental damage as vital resources become scarce and even unusable" (p. 564). Therefore, an intersectional understanding of the connections between climate change and inequality undergirds the work of the Green Belt Movement: "Professor Maathai saw that behind the everyday hardships of the poor—environmental degradation, deforestation, and food insecurity—were deeper issues of disempowerment, disenfranchisement, and a loss of the traditional values that had previously enabled communities to protect their environment" ("Our History," Green Belt Movement).

While organizations like HIPS and the Green Belt Movement demonstrate the value of community-activist organizations, critics worry that the neoliberal trend toward the increased privatization of social and community services (moving these programs outside of government) may actually have a negative effect on social justice (see Section Three for more discussion of neoliberalism). For example, as Hannah E. Britton and Taylor Price discuss in their article "'If Good Food is Cooked in One Country, We Will All Eat from It': Women and Civil Society in Africa" (included in our supplementary online material at www.oup.com/he/saraswati2e), the **NGOization** of women's activism discourages more radical activism and can contain or even co-opt advocacy through grant-funded financing.

NGOization: The movement of social and community services from government to civil society as a result of neoliberal policies that favor privatization over government intervention.

ENGAGING IN THE POLITICAL PROCESS: VOTING, POLITICAL ACTION COMMITTEES, AND RUNNING FOR OFFICE

Working through the representative government process can be an effective way to make changes in laws and policies, influence how and where governments spend their money, and have your voice heard when it comes to issues that affect your community. For example, in her essay "The Latina Advantage in U.S. Politics: Recent Example with Representative Ocasio-Cortez," Christina E. Bejarano discusses the key role that women of color, and particularly Latinas, have played in recent years—as voters, but also increasingly as elected officials. There are a number of ways to get involved in local, state, and federal politics, including voting; voicing your thoughts and concerns to your government representatives; supporting particular candidates, lobbying groups, or political action committees; and running for office.

Making your voice heard through voting is important, and to support the integrity of the democratic process it's imperative that the right to vote is not unfairly restricted. The League of Women Voters is an activist organization that has been working to promote unfettered access to voting for a hundred years. Starting in 1920, the same year the Nineteenth Amendment was ratified giving women the right to vote, the League was founded to support new women voters, and has continued with the mission "to protect the rights of eligible voters and expand access for those who've been left out of our democratic process" ("Voting Rights"). The League works to increase voter registration and help educate voters through its VOTE411 initiative (vote411.org), where voters can find logistical information like their polling location as well as nonpartisan information on candidates and issues.

Feminist organizations like the National Organization for Women (NOW) argue that we must be vigilant to recognize and oppose voter suppression tactics, which they say have increased in recent years, because they threaten our democratic processes and "disproportionately affect women, especially women of color, low-income women, and immigrant women" ("Voting Rights: A Feminist Issue"). NOW argues that "[w]e must examine voter suppression tactics through a feminist lens," pointing to, for example, the ways in which new voter ID requirements in some states are more onerous for women, because women are more likely to change their name through marriage or divorce, and for trans and gender-nonconforming people whose ID and birth certificate may not match ("Voting Rights: A Feminist Issue"). NOW has also raised concerns about the ways in which cuts to early voting may disproportionately affect women, who may have more childcare responsibilities, and those in low-wage jobs, who may not be able to take off work to vote ("Voting Rights: A Feminist Issue").

Political action committees (PACs) combine donations and resources to encourage specific political goals like the election of candidates or the adoption of policies, initiatives, or legislation. For example, the LGBTQ Victory Fund, a nonpartisan PAC, has been working since 1991 to "change the face and voice of America's politics and achieve equality for LGBTQ Americans by increasing the number of openly LGBTQ officials at all levels of government" ("Our Mission"). Touting the importance of its work, the Victory Fund points to its contribution to the 2018 "Rainbow Wave," which saw a historic number of LGBTQ candidates elected to public office ("Our History," LGBTQ Victory Fund). Similarly, the Feminist Majority PAC, created in 2002, works "to end the under-representation of women and minorities in elected office" and provides support for candidates who they believe will fight for feminist issues, "including women's healthcare and reproductive rights, violence against women prevention, economic equity, civil rights, LGBT rights, collective bargaining, immigration, gun control, CEDAW ratification, Equal Rights Amendment passage, affirmative action and environmental protection" ("Our Work").

Have you ever thought about running for office? There are many organizations that support and mentor aspiring candidates. Groups such as IGNITE, Run for Something, Victory Institute, and EMILY'S List focus particularly on helping folks from under-represented groups get elected. For example, EMILY's List, which supports pro-choice Democratic women, provides in-person and online candidate training as well as networking with its Run to Win online community. Touting thirty-five years of success at getting women elected to local, state, and federal office, EMILY's List helps candidates with various aspects of campaigning, including "fundraising, communications, digital strategy, press and media relations, direct voter contact, and overall campaign management" ("Frequently").

NONVIOLENT DIRECT ACTION

Nonviolent direct action is an essential strategy for activists because it disrupts the lives and thoughts of those it targets, forcing them to take notice. Nonviolent direct action refers to acts of protest or civil disobedience designed to raise awareness, express outrage, and garner attention. It can include a range of activities such as marches, sit-ins, hunger strikes, performances, and acts of civil disobedience. Nonviolent direct action may be used to get people's attention, make people feel uncomfortable, expose people to information, or incite anger, all in the name of making social change. Feminist and queer activists have successfully used nonviolent direct action to disrupt normative narratives and spur critical thinking around social justice issues.

Early AIDS activists often used nonviolent direct action to challenge stereotypes and prejudices about gay men as well as gay sex. In the early 1980s, AIDS was a terrifying epidemic that wasn't well understood by the medical community because of an inadequate amount of funding for research. There weren't enough beds in hospitals, treatments were experimental and ineffective, and ignorance about how the disease spread led to fear and paranoia. Gay activist Larry Kramer insisted that the only reason the public wasn't demanding more action to address the epidemic (and the only reason the public wasn't outraged at the number of deaths) was because of who the disease was primarily affecting: gay men and drug users. In his 1983 essay "1,112 and Counting," Kramer pled for a larger activist response. He said, "If this article doesn't rouse you to anger, fury, rage, and action, gay men may have no future on this earth. Our continued existence depends on just how angry you can get."

Responding to this urgent need and harnessing the anger that Kramer encouraged, the AIDS Coalition to Unleash Power (ACT UP) emerged in 1987. ACT UP's first event was to disrupt traffic on Wall Street: Activists distributed handouts listing a series of demands and highlighting their slogan, "SILENCE = DEATH." Seventeen activists were arrested, and the newspapers featured pictures of the protesters being carried away on stretchers (Hirshman 2012, 197). The following year, ACT UP produced another major protest, this time outside the headquarters of the Food and Drug Administration (FDA): "Wrapped in red tape, bearing fake tombstones, sporting black T-shirts with the signature triangles, for eight hours they surrounded the building. They chanted, stickered the walls of the building, lay down like corpses, and got arrested" (204). The activists achieved their objectives: shortly after the protest, the FDA agreed to expedite the development and approval of new AIDS drugs (204). The success of ACT UP's activists was due in large part to their careful research and preparation. They created a media plan before their protests, they distributed handouts with specific information about how to support their cause, and they made clear demands. Their slogans were memorable: "Know Your Scumbag; The Government Has Blood on Its Hands" and "Kissing

Nonviolent direct action: Acts of protest or civil disobedience intended to raise awareness through disruption or spectacle.

Doesn't Kill: Greed and Indifference Do" (200). Dr. Anthony Fauci, the head of the National Institutes of Health's National Institute of Allergy and Infectious Diseases, described his admiration for ACT UP: "They beautifully combined extraordinarily dramatic, provocative, and theatrical ways to get attention and once they got your attention they were able to talk to you like they were experts in the field" (qtd. in 208).

The frequently theatrical techniques of nonviolent direct action were also important tools in the disability rights movement. In the late 1970s, disability rights activists began a campaign to get wheelchair-accessible lifts on public transportation by blocking the movement of buses with their wheelchairs. They also used nonviolent direct action tactics in a 1990 event called "The Capitol Crawl." At that event, ADAPT activists left their wheelchairs at the foot of the steps of the U.S. Capitol building in Washington, DC, and struggled to move themselves up the stairs, dramatizing how inaccessible public buildings (as the Capitol was at that time) limited their civil rights. In his essay "I Was There" (included in this section), Michael Winter describes his participation in disability rights activism and his motivation for civil disobedience. Thanks in large part to ADAPT activists like Winter, the Americans with Disabilities Act was passed in 1990, requiring public transportation, public buildings, and other sites and goods (such as teaching materials for schools and universities) to be made accessible to people with disabilities.

As with the AIDS crisis and accessibility, nonviolent direct action has also been used to respond to gender-based state violence. As discussed in Section Three, gender-based state violence is often premised on oppressive cultural norms. The transnational activist movement SlutWalk emerged in Toronto in 2011 as a response to comments from a police officer that reflected the unfair treatment that many rape survivors face in the criminal justice system. During a presentation on crime prevention at York University and in reference to the issue of campus rape, one of the invited speakers, Officer Michael Sanguinetti, said, "Women should avoid dressing like sluts in order not to be victimized" (qtd. in Pilkington 2011). His words both revictimized the rape survivor by putting her behavior on trial and shifted the focus off the rapist, the real cause of the crime. SlutWalk emerged as a response to Sanguinetti's words and to **rape culture** in general. The first march in Toronto drew an estimated three thousand people, many of whom carried signs that said things like "Met a slut today? Don't assault her" and "We're here, we're sluts, get used to it" (Pilkington 2011). The event was followed by marches around the world designed to expose and undermine the narrative by which women are blamed for being victims of sexual violence. Some marchers reclaimed the pejorative term "slut" by dressing "slutty," wearing things like fishnet stockings and short skirts. Katt Schott-Mancini, one of the organizers of the Boston SlutWalk, explains the way the narrative of victim blaming causes us to lose our focus on the real culprit: "What you are wearing doesn't cause rape—the rapist causes it" (qtd. in Pilkington 2011). Marches like that used by SlutWalk are a tried-and-true

Rape culture: An environment that normalizes sexual violence against women through a number of cultural practices, including misogynistic social norms, victim blaming, rape myths, and sexual objectification.

ACTIVISM AND CIVIC ENGAGEMENT

Host a viewing party for a documentary that addresses an issue you care about. Invite your friends, family, classmates, and neighbors. Plan for enough time both to watch the film and to discuss it. Create an action sheet to distribute at the end of the party that includes concrete steps people can take to get involved and make change.

1. Choose a documentary. There are a number of curated lists of social justice documentaries available online (see, for example, this one by the *New York Times*: https://www.nytimes.com/watching/lists/social-issue-documentaries), or you could ask your school librarian for help selecting one.

2. Do your research. Read reviews and critiques of the documentary to make an informed judgment about the accuracy of the information presented and to understand how the film presents constrained or situated viewpoints.

3. Create discussion questions meant to stimulate conversation about key points from the film. In writing the questions, use what you've learned in your women's, gender, and sexuality studies course to encourage dialogue about the film from an intersectional perspective. Also use what you learned from your research to provoke discussion about the strengths and/or limitations of the film.

4. Create an action sheet to distribute at the end of the viewing party. List a few specific things that people can do to get involved and make change around the issues presented in the documentary. Searching for related activist organizations and looking at their agendas and initiatives might help you come up with ideas. Encourage action by asking that your guests share any updates about their involvement around the issue with the group.

form of nonviolent direct action. They create a public spectacle that raises awareness and incites dialogue, and they can draw media attention that can pressure those in power to act.

HUMOR

While humor can be used in a disparaging way to legitimate and justify discrimination, humor also has the power to be subversive because it can destabilize what appears self-evidently true. As Sarah E. Fryett notes in her article "Laudable Laughter: Feminism and Female Comedians" (included in this section), laughter can be a useful political tool by "radically [challenging] binaries of natural/unnatural and normal/deviant" (p. 575). Indeed, good comedy encourages us to think critically by uncovering contradiction and exposing absurdity, allowing us to look at something with fresh eyes. This becomes a political act when it is used to reveal the assumptions underlying prejudice and discrimination. For feminist and queer activists, comedy has been a particularly useful strategy for challenging discriminatory beliefs around gender, sexuality, race, religion, and other constructions of difference, thereby providing the space for oppressed groups to create new narratives.

One way in which comedians use their comedy to make social change is by addressing uncomfortable topics in a way that diffuses tension. In 2012 at a stand-up show in Los Angeles, comedian Tig Notaro started her performance by waving to the crowd and saying, "Good evening! Hello. I have cancer! How are you?" (Brownstone 2013). Notaro says that she thought the contrast between the upbeat presentation and the fear inherent in the diagnosis was funny, "trying to make it sound like I'm saying, 'Are there any birthdays tonight, what are you celebrating?' but saying something really horrifying" (qtd. in Brownstone 2013). For Notaro, the relentless positivity that well-intentioned people often impose on cancer patients is problematic, which the contrast in her performance helps expose (Brownstone 2013). Bringing up cancer in a comedy act makes us address an uncomfortable topic by using humor to lower our guard and allow us to listen.

Humor can also create an entry point for the dominant group to engage with the experience of marginalized groups. Amy Schumer, a feminist comedian, has been successful with male audiences. Her TV show, *Inside Amy Schumer*, aired on Comedy Central, which has an audience that is 60 percent male (Dockterman 2014). By making men laugh at "women's issues," she creates a level of consciousness about the role men play in systems of sexism. In one sketch she takes on sexual violence. She's playing a video game (that looks similar to *Call of Duty*) and her female avatar is raped by a superior officer. The game then offers the following prompt: "You were just assaulted by a fellow soldier. Do you wish to report?" "Yes." "Are you sure? Did you know he has a family? Does that change your mind about reporting?" (qtd. in Dockterman 2014). In the context of a game, these questions seem ridiculous—would we ask that question about any other type of crime? With our laughter comes a recognition of the ways in which sexual violence is often trivialized in our culture. Schumer's work demonstrates the way in which comedy can be used to engage with the dominant group.

Negin Farsad and Dean Obeidallah, creators of the 2013 documentary film *The Muslims Are Coming!*, use a similar strategy to address Islamophobia. The film follows Farsad, Obeidallah, and a group of other Muslim comics as they tour the United States offering free stand-up comedy. In addition to their performances, they created conversation and engagement with non-Muslims through witty games like "Name That Religion" and activities like "Hug a Muslim." The documentary includes clips from their performances and activities as well as interviews with comics, celebrities, activists, and religious leaders. Farsad and Obeidallah use humor to address the fear inherent in Islamophobia and to create a less threatening environment for non-Muslims to engage with Muslims. Furthermore, they use satire and irony to expose the irrational assumptions that fuel anti-Muslim discrimination. When we laugh at stereotypes, we acknowledge their constructedness and lessen their power. Farsad and Obeidallah promise that by the end of the movie "you're gonna love the pants out of Muslims" ("A Longer Synopsis").

Comedy can also be a fruitful space for intersectional analysis. The comedian Margaret Cho uses humor to engage with social topics such as beauty image, sexual violence, racism, LGBT rights, and sex work. In the film of her stand-up comedy show, *I'm the One That I Want* (2000), Cho addresses the racism and sexism she experienced during the production of her 1994 TV Show, *All-American Girl*, a sitcom about an Asian American family. She uses her comedy to expose the fetishized constructions of race, explaining how she was coached to act more "Asian." She also talks about the intense pressure to conform to Hollywood beauty standards. After being told to lose thirty pounds, Cho dieted herself into kidney failure. She has since, however, challenged such a beauty standard and now revels in empowering others to embrace their bodies and sexualities. Cho's comedy demonstrates the value of intersectionality as her humor is often produced at the intersection of cultural norms around gender, race, and sexuality.

CREATIVE EXPRESSION: ARTISTS AS ACTIVISTS

The Guerrilla Girls, an activist collective of women artists, reframe the question that has been asked too often and for too long: "Why haven't there been more great women artists?" They ask, instead, "Why haven't more women been *considered* great artists throughout Western history?" (Guerrilla Girls 1998, 7). To answer their question, they highlight how prejudice, restricted access, and biased art critics and historians have both stifled and dismissed the art of women and people of color. Calling themselves the "conscience of the art world," the Guerrilla Girls use posters, billboards, stickers, books, and nonviolent direct action to challenge racism and sexism in the art world (p. 579). They frequently use humor to make their point. For example, in their poster "The Advantages of Being a Woman Artist," they list things like "Working without the pressure of success," "Not having to be in shows with men," and "Having an escape from the art world in your 4 free-lance jobs" (Guerrilla Girls 1998, 9). In their 1989 poster "When Racism & Sexism Are No Longer Fashionable" (included in this section), they turn their gaze on the art collectors, emphasizing the ways in which race and gender affect the art market. The women who make up the Guerrilla Girls want us to question what counts as art, who's included in museums, and which artists are studied in school and to encourage those who feel that women and people of color are inadequately represented in those places to "[w]rite letters, make posters, make trouble" (Guerrilla Girls 1998, 91).

We see similar questions about power and representation in the work of cartoonist Alison Bechdel. "The Bechdel Test" (included in this section), which appeared in 1985 as part of her long-running comic *Dykes to Watch Out For*, features two women talking about going to see a movie. One woman says that she'll only see a film if it meets three basic criteria: "One, it has to have at least two women in it . . . who, two, talk to each other about, three, something besides a man" (p. 581). These simple requirements resonated because most movies at the time, and indeed many movies today, do not meet this low bar. In their analysis of popular films in 2018, the Geena Davis Institute on Gender in Media found that female characters were under-represented as lead characters in popular films, accounted for less overall speaking and screen time than male characters, and were much more likely to be shown in "revealing clothing" (Giaccardi et al. 2019). And the way women are depicted on screen matters. For example, in its global study of how leadership is represented in top films across twenty countries, the Geena Davis Institute found that "[t]hese films show a world which is run by men, for men"; the filmmakers are mostly males employing a male gaze, and what this tells "young people about the world they inhabit keeps girls and young women subservient and anxious" ("Rewrite Her Story"). It also affects how all of us, people of all genders, think about what leadership should look like and who should lead.

Because the gatekeepers of the art and media industries restrict whose eyes we see the world through, subordinate groups have less access to tell their own story. Both despite and because of these limitations, and in conversation with issues of power and representation, women and LGBTQPAI+ folks use creative expression for activist purposes, including (but not limited to) art installations, story quilts, and musical performance (all discussed later), as well as creative writing, dance, and theater. Creativity is an accessible type of activism and can engage people who otherwise don't consider themselves political. Like nonviolent direct action, art can grab our attention; like humor, it can reframe social justice issues in ways that encourage critical thinking. Art can also produce aesthetic pleasure and elicit strong emotional responses, engaging our consciousness in a different way than other forms of activism.

COMMUNITY ART PROJECTS

The AIDS Memorial Quilt demonstrates the power of community art projects to create community, provide healing, raise awareness, and incite action. In 1985, gay rights activist Cleve Jones had an idea for a large quilt including individual squares for people who had died of AIDS; he envisioned the quilt as a way of memorializing the victims and raising awareness around the devastating effects of the disease ("The History of the Quilt"). The NAMES Project emerged in 1987 to organize the production and maintenance of the quilt, which today includes more than 48,000 three-by-six-foot panels, each honoring individuals who succumbed to the disease ("The History of the Quilt"). The fabric panels are decorated with paint, appliques, needlepoint, text, and photos. Two of the squares read: "The Best Daddy in the World Died of AIDS on March 2, 1987. I Love You Forever Daddy" and "I have decorated this banner to honor my brother. Our parents did not want his name used publicly. The omission of his name represents the fear of oppression that AIDS victims and their families feel" (Rutledge 1992, 287). Many of the panels include just a name or imagery.

AIDS Memorial Quilt exhibited in Washington, DC. In 2012 pieces of the quilt were displayed on the National Mall to mark the twenty-fifth anniversary of the beginning of the project. With 48,000 three-by-six foot panels, each commemorating individuals who have died of the disease, the AIDS Memorial Quilt is the largest community art project in the world.
Source: B Christopher/Alamy Stock Photo

The first showing of the quilt was during the National March on Washington for Lesbian and Gay Rights on October 11, 1987, and half a million people came to look at it that weekend ("The History of the Quilt"). In 1988 the quilt was taken to cities across the United States, adding panels and collecting donations at each stop("The History of the Quilt"). The quilt has been displayed numerous times since, and it remains the largest community art project in the world ("The History of the Quilt"). In 2019, the stewardship for the quilt and its accompanying archive of records and memorabilia transitioned to the National AIDS Memorial in San Francisco and to the American Folklife Center at the Library of Congress (Gonzales 2019). What started with Cleve Jones and a small group of friends grew into an international activist project raising money and awareness and forever changing the face of AIDS.

Visual Art

Faith Ringgold is an artist who works in many media, and her work demonstrates the ability of activist art to subvert dominant narratives as well as aesthetic norms within the art industry. Beginning in the 1960s, Ringgold challenged the prevailing norms within the art world. Ringgold was a leader in the **Black arts movement** and the **feminist art movement** and has spent many years advocating for the recognition of Black and female artists. She has organized protests at major museums to draw attention to the exclusion of these artists and created organizations to encourage and foster Black and

Black arts movement: The movement in the 1960s and 1970s to highlight and inspire African American contributions in literature, music, theater, dance, and visual art and to develop a Black aesthetic.

Feminist art movement: Activism beginning in the 1960s and 1970s that promoted female artists, encouraged better representation of women's lives in art, and challenged aesthetic values within the art world, including the privileging of particular media.

female artists. The activism she is best known for comes through her artwork, particularly her story quilts. These quilts use both words and imagery to tell a story, often one of political significance. Ringgold uses materials that challenge the historical subordination of women and people of color in the art world by contesting the traditional distinction between art and craft. While "art" has traditionally involved working with expensive materials (such as oil paints, marble, or bronze) as well as the implied leisure to produce something without secondary use value, the art that marginalized groups have historically created made use of inexpensive, common materials and usually had a secondary use value. Quilts, for example, were long dismissed by the art world as "low art" or craft and were rarely included in museums. By using fabric in her work and making quilts, Ringgold challenges the definition of "art" in a way that highlights how social hierarchies intersect with the construction of aesthetic value.

Ringgold's work also plays with historical narratives in ways that present alternative views of familiar stories. For example, in her story quilt *Who's Afraid of Aunt Jemima?*, Ringgold alternates squares of imagery, patterns, and text to retell the story of Aunt Jemima, a character first emerging in the late nineteenth-century racist minstrel shows that used exaggerated racial stereotypes to legitimate and perpetuate white supremacy. The Aunt Jemima character was later appropriated to sell pancake mix, advertised in ways that perpetuated the mammy archetype. In Ringgold's retelling of the story, Aunt Jemima is a successful businesswoman named Jemima Blakey. While the minstrel imaginings of Aunt Jemima positioned her as a servant understood only in relation to her white employers, Ringgold gives Jemima Blakey her own story. Blakey and her husband open a restaurant and catering business in Harlem, and they have a mixed-race family. The quilt tells Blakey's story through African American vernacular. Using dialect in her art, Ringgold celebrates the value of oral storytelling.

Music

Feminist and queer musicians alike must find their way in a male-dominated industry that both creates and reinforces oppressive narratives around sex and sexuality. However, music, like other creative expression, also creates space for resistance. One strategy has been to create feminist and queer independent record labels like Olivia Records, formed in 1973 to promote women's music. While major music labels still control most of the music that we are exposed to, new forms of self-publishing (including social media) have created new possibilities for music distribution. Musicians can use their work to make social change in a variety of ways. They can use lyrics and imagery to challenge and disrupt dominant narratives, they can challenge norms and tropes within particular musical genres, and they can use their celebrity to create community and raise awareness.

Many feminist musicians have contributed to feminist activism. One of the better-known feminist movements in music is the Riot Grrrl revolution. The feminist punk band Bikini Kill (1990–1997) was credited with starting the Riot Grrrl revolution by centering their music on feminist lyrics and by using their fame to create feminist community in the punk scene and beyond (Marcus 2010). The four-member band included three women—lead singer Kathleen Hanna, bassist Kathi Wilcox, and drummer Tobi Vail— and one man, guitarist Billy Karren. Hanna was drawn to music as a space that embraced contradiction and ambiguity, but even in the punk rock scene she was disappointed to find that most people didn't consider feminism relevant anymore (Marcus 2010 42). The members of Bikini Kill used their lyrics to encourage women to come together and get politically active, to speak up, and to make change.

Other groups that were influential in the early years included Heavens to Betsy and Bratmobile (credited, in part, with coining the term "Riot Grrrl" in its zine) (Marcus 2010). Forming later, bands like Sleater-Kinney and Le Tigre show the enduring influence of early Riot Grrrl bands. The Russian feminist punk group Pussy Riot, which cites Bikini Kill as one of its influences, is known for its guerrilla performances that focus on feminism and LGBT rights (McDonnell 2012). In 2012 Pussy Riot performed at the Christ the Savior Cathedral in Moscow, where they railed against the Russian Orthodox Church and its support of Russian president Vladimir Putin, whom Pussy Riot criticizes for, among other things, his campaign against gay rights. In response to the performance, three members of the group, Nadezhda Tolokonnikova, Maria Alyokhina, and Yekaterina Samutsevich, were arrested and convicted of hooliganism intended to incite religious hatred. They were sentenced to two years in prison, though they were all released before that period. Demonstrations were held around the world in support of Pussy Riot.

Inasmuch as the Riot Grrrl revolution transformed the punk scene, feminist activism is also an important current in other musical genres like rap and hip-hop. Prominent sociologist and scholar Patricia Hill Collins points to the ways in which Black female musicians demonstrate a feminist ethic, noting that "artists such as Salt-n-Pepa, Lauryn Hill, Queen Latifah, India/Arie, and Alicia Keys routinely argue that Black women have the right to be respected, to be loved by their families and partners, to express themselves freely (artistically and sexually), and not to be mistaken for the stereotypes that have been applied to them" (Collins 2006, 192). While images that legitimate female sexual desire can be emancipatory, particularly for women of color, these images are always in tension with what scholar Evelyn Brooks Higginbotham (1993) calls the **politics of respectability**, which accords women value based on perceived notions of sexual restraint.

Hip-hop feminist Joan Morgan argues that although rap is often presented as misogynistic, it's essential for women to engage with it because "it takes us straight to the battlefield" (1999, 72). Morgan maintains that sexism in rap is a mask that African American men wear, one that allows them to deal with the pain that is a product of their oppression (74). Therefore, because hip-hop has

Politics of respectability: A term coined by Evelyn Brooks Higginbotham to describe efforts by those in marginalized groups to police the behavior of their community to encourage conformity with the dominant group's norms as a strategy for gaining greater acceptance.

the capacity to articulate the collective pain of the African American community, it can be an effective tool for analyzing gender, race, and power (80). This tension between the sexist images of mostly Black women and the liberatory potential of hip-hop as a musical genre has prompted the Crunk Feminist Collective (CFC), a group of hip-hop activists, to invoke percussion as a metaphor. Playing on the importance of percussion in Southern rap, the CFC observes "that the tension between competing and often contradictory political and cultural projects like hip-hop and feminism is percussive in that it is both disruptive and generative" (Durham et al. 2013, 724).

Musicians can use their art to teach, engage, and incite action, but consumers also play an important role. Supporting feminist and queer musicians by buying their music and attending their concerts creates a market for their work that finances further projects and encourages others to engage with music in political ways. The reverse is also true: when we buy music that supports ideas we *don't* agree with (e.g., songs with lyrics that trivialize sexual violence or encourage homophobia), we are implicitly encouraging a market that contributes to discrimination.

SAFER SPACES

Safe space/safer space:
A physical or virtual location where marginalized people are sheltered from the prejudice and discrimination that they may face outside the space.

Physical and virtual spaces where people from marginalized groups can expect to be safer from hatred, hostility, and rejection—often called **safe spaces** or **safer spaces**—are important because they create communities that can be healing, energizing, and informative. In her article "On Lesbian-Feminism and Lesbian Separatism: A New Intersectional History" (included in our supplementary online material at www.oup.com/he/saraswati2e), Julie R. Enszer points out that "[s]eparation provides people with time and space to explore the nature of their oppression with others who share similar experiences and without intrusions from individuals who benefit from structural power" (599). This has been an essential tool for creating queer communities as LGBTQPAI+ people have historically been excluded, formally and informally, from communities, organizations, and families. However, separatist strategies raise issues over who is included (e.g., see Tina Vasquez's discussion of the exclusion of trans women from the Michigan Womyn's Music Festival in her essay, "It's Time to End the Long History of Feminism Failing Transgender Women," in Section Two).

Bluestockings, an independent bookstore in New York, is an example of the legacy of separatism that Enszer describes. They carry books, journals, magazines, and zines related to feminist and queer topics, and they use a radical nonprofit business model to run the store (Bluestockings is collectively owned and run by volunteers). It also offers community space for activist events and educational programs that promote "centered, strategic, and visionary thinking, towards the realization of a society that is infinitely creative, truly democratic, equitable, ecological, and free" ("Our History," Bluestockings).

Engaged Learning

Create a social justice playlist.

1. Think about the music you listen to and explore artists who define themselves as activists.
2. Select five songs that you believe have a positive message related to an issue that you care about. The songs can all be from one artist or from a combination of different artists. The songs can be new or old.
3. Look up the lyrics of the songs and do a close reading of the wording. Mark passages that are meaningful to you.
4. Make a one-page handout for your playlist. On the handout, explain how the songs engage in activism around a particular issue. You can talk about the lyrics, the music video for the song, and/or information from the artist(s) themselves. Feel free to add artwork or images of the artist. Be creative!
5. Share your list with your classmates. Read through your classmates' playlists and listen to the songs that interest you.

Women's centers on college campuses are another example of safer space activism. In her article "Campus-Based Women's and Gender Equity Centers: Enacting Feminist Theories, Creating Social Change" (included in our supplementary online material at www.oup.com/he/saraswati2e), Amber L. Vlasnik notes how they emerged on campuses in the 1960s and 1970s in conjunction with the women's movement and to support the increasing number of female students. Vlasnik provides tips on how to get involved with a women's or gender equity center on campus as well as how to start one.

SPEAK-OUTS AND TESTIMONIALS

Testimonials have historically been a powerful tool in social justice activism by giving voice to members of marginalized groups. Feeling silenced is part of the experience of marginalization: a person's story (and experience) isn't valued because it isn't heard. Creating space for people to vocalize their unique experience empowers them because it asserts the legitimacy of their experience and it gives the community a more complex, multifaceted understanding of an issue. Speak-outs are events where people come together to share their stories, usually around a particular social justice issue. Testimonials may also be shared as a part of a larger event. For example, student activists at colleges around the world have organized Take Back the Night events to draw attention to sexual violence by using a variety of strategies, including marches, rallies, and candlelight vigils. These events often feature testimonials where survivors share their stories showing the real people behind the statistics and allowing survivors to see that they are not alone.

The hashtags #ShoutYourAbortion and #MeToo are social media versions of the traditional speak-out. #ShoutYourAbortion was created in 2015 in response to efforts to defund Planned Parenthood, the women's health care provider, and has become a platform for people to share their experience with abortions. After Amelia Bonow posted the story of her abortion on her Facebook page, Seattle writer Lindy West tweeted her story, adding the hashtag #ShoutYourAbortion (Pearson 2015). West explained that she wanted to share Bonow's story, and encourage others to share their stories, saying, "It's about destigmatization, normalization, and putting an end to shame" (qtd. in Pearson 2015). The people who used the hashtag to tell the story of their experience discussed the reasons for their choice, their belief that life doesn't begin at conception, the positive ways that abortion affected their lives, and their reasons for sharing their story, among other topics. Bonow said that she was motivated to talk about her experience because "abortion is still something to be whispered about" (qtd. in Pearson 2015). Testimonials like hers have the potential to challenge misconceptions and offer support to people who may feel alone in their experience.

The hashtag #MeToo, which went viral in 2017, created an international conversation driven by testimonials of sexual violence (see Section Two for more on the history of the MeToo movement). The phrase "me too" emphasizes the solidarity that comes from sharing one's story and feeling recognized and heard. The hashtag #MeToo has provided support and community for survivors of sexual violence and has demonstrated the ways in which sexual violence is both pervasive and insidious in our culture. Therefore, #MeToo shows the power that testimonials can have at the individual level, but also the power that they can have in the aggregate for challenging cultural narratives and making change. As Tarana Burke explains in "An Interview with Tarana Burke" (included in this section), "silence is and has always been a tool of oppression" and the act of breaking the silence has "led to one of the biggest narrative shifts we've seen around sexual violence" (p. 584).

Speak-outs and testimonials have the power to challenge the dominant narrative and create space for feminist, queer, and other marginalized communities to push for social justice. Like the other strategies described here, they can be useful for raising awareness, encouraging critical thinking, and inciting action.

Critical Thinking Questions

1. Think about Abu-Lughod's essay in this section, "Do Muslim Women Really Need Saving? Anthropological Reflections on Cultural Relativism and Its Others." What is the best approach for determining the need for international intervention while respecting cultural difference?

2. What activist strategies would you add to this section?

3. Nonviolent direct action is often successful because it involves acts that are disruptive or make people uncomfortable. Do you think there should be limits on this approach and, if so, what kinds of limits? Is breaking the law appropriate? Is inconveniencing people appropriate?

GLOSSARY

Black arts movement 523

Coalition 507

Feminist art movement 523

Neocolonial 507

NGOization 515

Nonviolent direct action 517

Politics of respectability 525

Rape culture 518

Safe space/safer space 526

Street harassment 513

Women in print movement 508

WORKS CITED

"About." *Hollaback!* 2016, www.ihollaback.org/about/.

"About Everyday Feminism." *Everyday Feminism*, February 29, 2016, everydayfeminism.com/about-ef/.

Boston Women's Health Book Collective. "Preface to the 1973 Edition of 'Our Bodies, Ourselves.'" *Our Bodies, Ourselves*, 2016, www.ourbodiesourselves.org/history/preface-to-the-1973-edition-of-our-bodies-ourselves/.

Brownstone, Sydney. "Tig Notaro: You'll Laugh, You'll Cry." *Mother Jones*, May/June 2013, www.motherjones.com/media/2013/04/interview-tig-notaro-cancer-professor-blastoff-inside-amy-schumer.

Bunch, Charlotte. "Not by Degrees: Feminist Theory and Education." In *Feminist Theory: A Reader*, edited by Wendy K. Kolmar and Frances Bartkowski, 2nd ed., McGraw Hill, 2005, pp. 12–15.

Collins, Patricia Hill. *From Black Power to Hip Hop: Racism, Nationalism, and Feminism*. Temple UP, 2006.

"Compelling Social Issue Documentaries." *New York Times*, www.nytimes.com/watching/lists/social-issue-documentaries.

Dockterman, Eliana. "How Amy Schumer Gets Guys To Think Feminists Are Funny." *Time*, April 1, 2014, time.com/45771/how-amy-schumer-got-guys-to-think-feminists-are-funny/.

Durham, Aisha, et al. "The Stage Hip-Hop Feminism Built: A New Directions Essay." *Signs: Journal of Women in Culture and Society*, vol. 38, no. 3, 2013, pp. 721–37.

Erickson-Schroth, Laura. *Trans Bodies, Trans Selves: A Resource for the Transgender Community*. Oxford UP, 2014.

"Frequently Asked Questions." *Emily's List*. https://trainingcenter.emilyslist.org/faq

Giaccardi, Soraya, et al. "See Jane 2019." Geena Davis Institute for Gender in Media, 2019, seejane.org/research-informs-empowers/see-jane-2019/.

Gonzales, Richard. "AIDS Memorial Quilt Is Returning Home To San Francisco." *NPR*, November 21, 2019, www.npr.org/2019/11/20/781430503/aids-memorial-quilt-is-returning-home-to-san-francisco.

Guerrilla Girls. *The Guerrilla Girls' Bedside Companion to the History of Western Art*. Penguin Books, 1998.

Higginbotham, Evelyn Brooks. *Righteous Discontent: The Women's Movement in the Black Baptist Church, 1880–1920*. Harvard UP, 1993.

Hirshman, Linda. *Victory: The Triumphant Gay Revolution*. HarperCollins Publishers, 2012.

HIPS: Reducing Harm in the Nation's Capital Since 1993. www.hips.org/. Accessed June 3, 2016.

"The History of the Quilt." *National AIDS Memorial*. https://www.aidsmemorial.org/quilt-history.

Karp, Marcelle, and Debbie Stoller. "The Birth of *BUST*." *The BUST Guide to the New Girl Order*, edited by Marcelle Karp and Debbie Stoller. Penguin Books, 1999.

Kramer, Larry. "1,112 and Counting." *New York Native*, no. 59, March 14, 1983. www.indymedia.org.uk/en/2003/05/66488.html.

"A Longer Synopsis." *The Muslims Are Coming!* Written and directed by Negin Farsad and Dean Obeidallah, 2011, themuslimsarecoming.com/about/a-longer-synopsis/.

Marcus, Sara. *Girls to the Front: The True Story of the Riot Grrrl Revolution*. HarperCollins Publishers, 2010.

McDonnell, Evelyn. "Pussy Riot and the Politics of Grrrl Punk." *Los Angeles Times*, September 13, 2012, https://www.latimes.com/entertainment/music/la-xpm-2012-sep-13-la-et-ms-pussy-riot-and-the-politics-of-grrrl-punk-20120912-story.html.

Montague, Candace Y. A. "Helping Individual Prostitutes Survive: On The Van—Part One." In *The Body: The Complete HIV/AIDS Resource*, Remedy Health Media, December 27, 2010, www.thebody.com/content/art59998.html.

Morgan, Joan. *When Chickenheads Come Home to Roost*. Touchstone, 1999.

"Our History." *Bluestockings*. bluestockings.com/about/history/. Accessed October 10, 2016.

"Our History." *Green Belt Movement*, www.greenbeltmovement.org/who-we-are/our-history.

"Our History." *LGBTQ Victory Fund*, victoryfund.org/about/history/.

"Our Mission." *LGBTQ Victory Fund*, https://victoryfund.org/about/mission/.

"Our Work." *Feminist Majority PAC*, feministmajoritypac.org/our-work/.

Pearson, Michael. "Women Embrace, Criticize #ShoutYourAbortion." *CNN*, September 29, 2015, www.cnn.com/2015/09/22/living/shout-your-abortion-feat/.

Pilkington, Ed. "SlutWalking Gets Rolling After Cop's Loose Talk About Provocative Clothing." *The Guardian*, May 6, 2011, www.theguardian.com/world/2011/may/06/slutwalking-policeman-talk-clothing.

Reagon, Bernice Johnson. "Coalition Politics: Turning the Century." In *Home Girls: A Black Feminist Anthology*, edited by Barbara Smith. Kitchen Table: Women of Color Press, 1983, pp. 356–68.

"Rewrite Her Story: How Film and Media Stereotypes Affect the Lives and Leadership Ambitions of Girls and Young Women." Geena Davis Institute on Gender in Media, 2019, seejane.org/research-informs-empowers/rewrite-her-story/.

Rutledge, Leigh W. *The Gay Decades: From Stonewall to the Present; The People and Events That Shaped Gay Lives*. Plume, 1992.

"School for Social Justice." *Everyday Feminism*, February 27, 2020, everydayfeminism.com/school/.

Smith, Barbara. "A Press of Our Own Kitchen Table: Women of Color Press." *Frontiers: A Journal of Women's Studies*, vol. 10, no. 3, 1989, pp. 11–13.

"Voting Rights." *League of Women Voters*, www.lwv.org/voting-rights.

"Voting Rights: A Feminist Issue." *National Organization for Women*, now.org/nap/voting-rights/.

80. • *Lila Abu-Lughod*

DO MUSLIM WOMEN REALLY NEED SAVING? ANTHROPOLOGICAL REFLECTIONS ON CULTURAL RELATIVISM AND ITS OTHERS (2002)

Lila Abu-Lughod is a professor of anthropology and women's and gender studies at Columbia University. Her research focuses on gender in the Middle East, particularly on the ways in which representation and cultural productions affect politics, and the tensions around universalist arguments in human rights discourse. Her books include *Writing Women's Worlds: Bedouin Stories*, *Dramas of Nationhood: The Politics of Television in Egypt*, and *Veiled Sentiments: Honor and Poetry in a Bedouin Society*. In "Do Muslim Women Really Need Saving? Anthropological Reflections on Cultural Relativism and Its Others," Abu-Lughod explores the cultural narratives around Muslim women and the role these narratives play in foreign policy. Specifically, she argues that the image of the oppressed Muslim woman has been used to justify post-9/11 military intervention in Afghanistan.

Reproduced by permission of the American Anthropological Association from *American Anthropologist*, Volume 104, Issue 3, pp. 783–790, 2002. Not for sale or further reproduction.

What are the ethics of the current "War on Terrorism," a war that justifies itself by purporting to liberate, or save, Afghan women? Does anthropology have anything to offer in our search for a viable position to take regarding this rationale for war?

I was led to pose the question of my title in part because of the way I personally experienced the response to the U.S. war in Afghanistan. Like many colleagues whose work has focused on women and gender in the Middle East, I was deluged with invitations to speak—not just on news programs but also to various departments at colleges and universities, especially women's studies programs. Why did this not please me, a scholar who has devoted more than 20 years of her life to this subject and who has some complicated personal connection to this identity? Here was an opportunity to spread the word, disseminate my knowledge, and correct misunderstandings. The urgent search for knowledge about our sister "women of cover" (as President George Bush so marvelously called them) is laudable and when it comes from women's studies programs where "transnational feminism" is now being taken seriously, it has a certain integrity (see Safire 2001).

My discomfort led me to reflect on why, as feminists in or from the West, or simply as people who have concerns about women's lives, we need to be wary of this response to the events and aftermath of September 11, 2001. I want to point out the minefields—a metaphor that is sadly too apt for a country like Afghanistan, with the world's highest number of mines per capita—of this obsession with the plight of Muslim women. I hope to show some way through them using insights from anthropology, the discipline whose charge has been to understand and manage cultural difference. At the same time, I want to remain critical of anthropology's complicity in the reification of cultural difference.

CULTURAL EXPLANATIONS AND THE MOBILIZATION OF WOMEN

It is easier to see why one should be skeptical about the focus on the "Muslim woman" if one begins with the U.S. public response. I will analyze two manifestations of this response: some conversations I had with a reporter from the PBS *NewsHour with Jim Lehrer* and First Lady Laura Bush's radio address to the nation on November 17, 2001. The presenter from the *NewsHour* show first contacted me in October to see if I was willing to give some background for a segment on Women and Islam. I mischievously asked whether she had done segments on the women of Guatemala, Ireland, Palestine, or Bosnia when the show covered wars in those regions; but I finally agreed to look at the questions she was going to pose to panelists. The questions were hopelessly general. Do Muslim women believe "x"? Are Muslim women "y"? Does Islam allow "z" for women? I asked her: If you were to substitute Christian or Jewish wherever you have Muslim, would these questions make sense? I did not imagine she would call me back. But she did, twice, once with an idea for a segment on the meaning of Ramadan and another time on Muslim women in politics. One was in response to the bombing and the other to the speeches by Laura Bush and Cherie Blair, wife of the British Prime Minister.

What is striking about these three ideas for news programs is that there was a consistent resort to the cultural, as if knowing something about women and Islam or the meaning of a religious ritual would help one understand the tragic attack on New York's World Trade Center and the U.S. Pentagon, or how Afghanistan had come to be ruled by the Taliban, or what interests might have fueled U.S. and other interventions in the region over the past 25 years, or what the history of American support for conservative groups funded to undermine the Soviets might have been, or why the caves and bunkers out of which Bin Laden was to be smoked "dead or alive," as President Bush announced on television, were paid for and built by the CIA.

In other words, the question is why knowing about the "culture" of the region, and particularly its religious beliefs and treatment of women, was more urgent than exploring the history of the development of repressive regimes in the region and the U.S. role in this history. Such cultural framing, it seemed to me, prevented the serious exploration of the roots and nature of human suffering in this part of the world. Instead of political and historical explanations, experts were being asked to give religio-cultural ones. Instead of questions that might lead to the exploration of global interconnections, we were offered ones that worked to artificially divide the world into separate spheres—recreating an imaginative geography of West versus East, us versus Muslims, cultures in which First Ladies give speeches versus others where women shuffle around silently in burqas.

Most pressing for me was why the Muslim woman in general, and the Afghan woman in particular, were so crucial to this cultural mode of explanation, which ignored the complex entanglements in which we are all implicated, in sometimes surprising alignments. Why were these female symbols being mobilized in this "War against Terrorism" in a way they were not in other conflicts? Laura Bush's radio address on November 17 reveals the political work such mobilization accomplishes. On the one hand, her address collapsed important distinctions that should have been maintained. There was a constant slippage between the Taliban and the terrorists, so that they became almost one word—a kind of hyphenated monster identity: the Taliban-and-the-terrorists. Then there was the blurring of the very separate causes in Afghanistan of women's continuing malnutrition, poverty, and ill health, and their more recent exclusion under the Taliban from employment, schooling, and the joys of wearing nail polish. On the other hand, her speech reinforced chasmic divides, primarily between the "civilized people throughout the world" whose hearts break for the women and children of Afghanistan and the Taliban-and-the-terrorists, the cultural monsters who want to, as she put it, "impose their world on the rest of us."

Most revealingly, the speech enlisted women to justify American bombing and intervention in Afghanistan and to make a case for the "War on Terrorism" of which it was allegedly a part. As Laura Bush said, "Because of our recent military gains in much of Afghanistan, women are no longer imprisoned in their homes. They can listen to music and teach their daughters without fear of punishment. The fight against terrorism is also a fight for the rights and dignity of women" (U.S. Government 2002).

These words have haunting resonances for anyone who has studied colonial history. Many who have worked on British colonialism in South Asia have noted the use of the woman question in colonial policies where intervention into sati (the practice of widows immolating themselves on their husbands' funeral pyres), child marriage, and other practices was used to justify rule. As Gayatri Chakravorty Spivak (1988) has cynically put it: white men saving brown women from brown men. The historical record is full of similar cases, including in the Middle East. In Turn of the Century Egypt, what Leila Ahmed (1992) has called "colonial feminism" was hard at work. This was a selective concern about the plight of Egyptian women that focused on the veil as a sign of oppression but gave no support to women's education and was professed loudly by the same Englishman, Lord Cromer, who opposed women's suffrage back home.

Sociologist Marnia Lazreg (1994) has offered some vivid examples of how French colonialism enlisted women to its cause in Algeria. She writes:

> Perhaps the most spectacular example of the colonial appropriation of women's voices, and the silencing of those among them who had begun to take women revolutionaries . . . as role models by not donning the veil, was the event of May 16, 1958 [just four years before Algeria finally gained its independence from France after a long bloody struggle and 130 years of French control—L.A.]. On that day a demonstration was organized by rebellious French generals in Algiers to show their determination to keep Algeria French. To give the government of France evidence that Algerians were in agreement with them, the generals had a few thousand native men bused in from nearby villages, along with a few women who were solemnly unveiled by French women . . . Rounding up Algerians and bringing them to demonstrations

of loyalty to France was not in itself an unusual act during the colonial era. But to unveil women at a well-choreographed ceremony added to the event a symbolic dimension that dramatized the one constant feature of the Algerian occupation by France: its obsession with women. [Lazreg 1994:135]

Lazreg (1994) also gives memorable examples of the way in which the French had earlier sought to transform Arab women and girls. She describes skits at awards ceremonies at the Muslim Girls' School in Algiers in 1851 and 1852. In the first skit, written by "a French lady from Algiers," two Algerian Arab girls reminisced about their trip to France with words including the following:

Oh! Protective France: Oh! Hospitable France! . . .

Noble land, where I felt free

Under Christian skies to pray to our God: . . .

God bless you for the happiness you bring us!

And you, adoptive mother, who taught us

That we have a share of this world,

We will cherish you forever! [Lazreg 1994:68–69]

These girls are made to invoke the gift of a share of this world, a world where freedom reigns under Christian skies. This is not the world the Taliban-and-the-terrorists would "like to impose on the rest of us."

Just as I argued above that we need to be suspicious when neat cultural icons are plastered over messier historical and political narratives, so we need to be wary when Lord Cromer in British-ruled Egypt, French ladies in Algeria, and Laura Bush, all with military troops behind them, claim to be saving or liberating Muslim women.

POLITICS OF THE VEIL

I want now to look more closely at those Afghan women Laura Bush claimed were "rejoicing" at their liberation by the Americans. This necessitates

a discussion of the veil, or the burqa, because it is so central to contemporary concerns about Muslim women. This will set the stage for a discussion of how anthropologists, feminist anthropologists in particular, contend with the problem of difference in a global world. In the conclusion, I will return to the rhetoric of saving Muslim women and offer an alternative.

It is common popular knowledge that the ultimate sign of the oppression of Afghan women under the Taliban-and-the-terrorists is that they were forced to wear the burqa. Liberals sometimes confess their surprise that even though Afghanistan has been liberated from the Taliban, women do not seem to be throwing off their burqas. Someone who has worked in Muslim regions must ask why this is so surprising. Did we expect that once "free" from the Taliban they would go "back" to belly shirts and blue jeans, or dust off their Chanel suits? We need to be more sensible about the clothing of "women of cover," and so there is perhaps a need to make some basic points about veiling.

First, it should be recalled that the Taliban did not invent the burqa. It was the local form of covering that Pashtun women in one region wore when they went out. The Pashtun are one of several ethnic groups in Afghanistan and the burqa was one of many forms of covering in the subcontinent and Southwest Asia that has developed as a convention for symbolizing women's modesty or respectability. The burqa, like some other forms of "cover" has, in many settings, marked the symbolic separation of men's and women's spheres, as part of the general association of women with family and home, not with public space where strangers mingled.

Twenty years ago the anthropologist Hanna Papanek (1982), who worked in Pakistan, described the burqa as "portable seclusion." She noted that many saw it as a liberating invention because it enabled women to move out of segregated living spaces while still observing the basic moral requirements of separating and protecting women from unrelated men. Ever since I came across her phrase "portable seclusion," I have thought of these enveloping robes as "mobile homes." Everywhere, such veiling signifies belonging to a particular community and participating in a moral way of life in which families are paramount in the organization of communities and the home is associated with the sanctity of women.

The obvious question that follows is this: If this were the case, why would women suddenly become immodest? Why would they suddenly throw off the markers of their respectability, markers, whether burqas or other forms of cover, which were supposed to assure their protection in the public sphere from the harassment of strange men by symbolically signaling to all that they were still in the inviolable space of their homes, even though moving in the public realm? Especially when these are forms of dress that had become so conventional that most women gave little thought to their meaning.

To draw some analogies, none of them perfect, why are we surprised that Afghan women do not throw off their burqas when we know perfectly well that it would not be appropriate to wear shorts to the opera? At the time these discussions of Afghan women's burqas were raging, a friend of mine was chided by her husband for suggesting she wanted to wear a pantsuit to a fancy wedding: "You know you don't wear pants to a WASP wedding," he reminded her. New Yorkers know that the beautifully coiffed Hasidic women, who look so fashionable next to their dour husbands in black coats and hats, are wearing wigs. This is because religious belief and community standards of propriety require the covering of the hair. They also alter boutique fashions to include high necks and long sleeves. As anthropologists know perfectly well, people wear the appropriate form of dress for their social communities and are guided by socially shared standards, religious beliefs, and moral ideals, unless they deliberately transgress to make a point or are unable to afford proper cover. If we think that U.S. women live in a world of choice regarding clothing, all we need to do is remind ourselves of the expression, "the tyranny of fashion."

What had happened in Afghanistan under the Taliban is that one regional style of covering or veiling, associated with a certain respectable but not elite class, was imposed on everyone as "religiously" appropriate, even though previously there had been many different styles, popular or traditional with different groups and classes—different ways to mark women's propriety, or, in more recent times, religious piety. Although I am not an expert on Afghanistan, I imagine that the majority of women left in Afghanistan by the time the Taliban took control were the rural or less educated, from nonelite families, since they were the only ones who could not emigrate to escape the hardship and violence that has marked Afghanistan's recent history. If liberated from the enforced wearing of burqas, most of these women would choose some other form of modest headcovering, like all those living nearby who were not under the Taliban—their rural Hindu counterparts in the North of India (who cover their heads and veil their faces from affines) or their Muslim sisters in Pakistan.

Even *The New York Times* carried an article about Afghan women refugees in Pakistan that attempted to educate readers about this local variety (Fremson 2001). The article describes and pictures everything from the now-iconic burqa with the embroidered eyeholes, which a Pashtun woman explains is the proper dress for her community, to large scarves they call chadors, to the new Islamic modest dress that wearers refer to as *hijab*. Those in the new Islamic dress are characteristically students heading for professional careers, especially in medicine, just like their counterparts from Egypt to Malaysia. One wearing the large scarf was a school principal; the other was a poor street vendor. The telling quote from the young street vendor is, "If I did [wear the burqa] the refugees would tease me because the burqa is for 'good women' who stay inside the home" (Fremson 2001:14). Here you can see the local status associated with the burqa—it is for good respectable women from strong families who are not forced to make a living selling on the street.

The British newspaper *The Guardian* published an interview in January 2002 with Dr. Suheila Siddiqi, a respected surgeon in Afghanistan who holds the rank of lieutenant general in the Afghan medical corps (Goldenberg 2002). A woman in her sixties, she comes from an elite family and, like her sisters, was educated. Unlike most women of her class, she chose not to go into exile. She is presented in the article as "the woman who stood up to the Taliban" because she refused to wear the burqa. She had made it a condition of returning to her post as head of a major hospital when the Taliban came begging in 1996, just eight months after firing her along with other women. Siddiqi is described as thin, glamorous, and confident. But further into the article it is noted that her graying bouffant hair is covered in a gauzy veil. This is a reminder that though she refused the burqa, she had no question about wearing the chador or scarf.

Finally, I need to make a crucial point about veiling. Not only are there many forms of covering, which themselves have different meanings in the communities in which they are used, but also veiling itself must not be confused with, or made to stand for, lack of agency. As I have argued in my ethnography of a Bedouin community in Egypt in the late 1970s and 1980s (1986), pulling the black head cloth over the face in front of older respected men is considered a voluntary act by women who are deeply committed to being moral and have a sense of honor tied to family. One of the ways they show their standing is by covering their faces in certain contexts. They decide for whom they feel it is appropriate to veil.

To take a very different case, the modern Islamic modest dress that many educated women across the Muslim world have taken on since the mid-1970s now both publicly marks piety and can be read as a sign of educated urban sophistication, a sort of modernity (e.g., Abu-Lughod 1995, 1998; Brenner 1996; El Guindi 1999; MacLeod 1991; Ong 1990). As Saba Mahmood (2001) has so brilliantly shown in her ethnography of women in the mosque movement in Egypt, this new form of dress is also perceived by many of the women who adopt it as part of a bodily means to cultivate virtue, the outcome of their professed desire to be close to God.

Two points emerge from this fairly basic discussion of the meanings of veiling in the contemporary Muslim world. First, we need to work against the reductive interpretation of veiling as the quintessential sign of women's unfreedom, even if we object to state imposition of this form, as in Iran or with the Taliban. (It must be recalled that the modernizing states of Turkey and Iran had earlier in the century banned veiling and required men, except religious clerics, to adopt Western dress.) What does freedom mean if we accept the fundamental premise that humans are social beings, always raised in certain social and historical contexts and belonging to particular communities that shape their desires and understandings of the world? Is it not a gross violation of women's own understandings of what they are doing to simply denounce the burqa as a medieval imposition? Second, we must take care not to reduce the diverse situations and attitudes of millions of Muslim women to a single item of clothing. Perhaps it is time to give up the Western obsession with the veil and focus on some serious issues with which feminists and others should indeed be concerned.

Ultimately, the significant political–ethical problem the burqa raises is how to deal with cultural "others." How are we to deal with difference without accepting the passivity implied by the cultural relativism for which anthropologists are justly famous—a relativism that says it's their culture and it's not my business to judge or interfere, only to try to understand. Cultural relativism is certainly an improvement on ethnocentrism and the racism, cultural imperialism, and imperiousness that underlie it; the problem is that it is too late not to interfere. The forms of lives we find around the world are already products of long histories of interactions.

I want to explore the issues of women, cultural relativism, and the problems of "difference" from three angles. First, I want to consider what feminist anthropologists (those stuck in that awkward relationship, as Strathern [1987] has claimed) are to do with strange political bedfellows. I used to feel torn when I received the e-mail petitions circulating for the last few years in defense of Afghan women under the Taliban. I was not sympathetic to the dogmatism of the Taliban; I do not support the oppression of women. But the provenance of the campaign worried me. I do not usually find myself in political company with the likes of Hollywood celebrities (see Hirschkind and Mahmood 2002). I had never received a petition from such women defending the right of Palestinian women to safety from Israeli bombing or daily harassment at checkpoints, asking the United States to reconsider its support for a government that had dispossessed them, closed them out from work and citizenship rights, refused them the most basic freedoms. Maybe some of these same people might be signing petitions to save African women from genital cutting, or Indian women from dowry deaths. However, I do not think that it would be as easy to mobilize so many of these American and European women if it were not a case of Muslim men oppressing Muslim women—women of cover for whom they can feel sorry and in relation to whom they can feel smugly superior. Would television diva Oprah Winfrey host the Women in Black, the women's peace group from Israel, as she did RAWA, the Revolutionary Association of Women of Afghanistan, who were also granted the *Glamour Magazine* Women of the Year Award? What are we to make of post-Taliban "Reality Tours" such as the one advertised on the internet by Global Exchange for March 2002 under the title "Courage and Tenacity: A Women's Delegation to Afghanistan"? The rationale for the $1,400 tour is that "with the removal of the Taliban government, Afghan women, for the first time in the past decade, have the opportunity to reclaim their basic human rights and establish their role as equal citizens by participating in the rebuilding of their nation." The tour's objective, to celebrate International Women's Week, is "to develop awareness of the concerns and issues the Afghan women are facing as well as to witness the changing political, economic, and social conditions

which have created new opportunities for the women of Afghanistan" (Global Exchange 2002).

To be critical of this celebration of women's rights in Afghanistan is not to pass judgment on any local women's organizations, such as RAWA, whose members have courageously worked since 1977 for a democratic secular Afghanistan in which women's human rights are respected, against Soviet-backed regimes or U.S.- Saudi-, and Pakistani-supported conservatives. Their documentation of abuse and their work through clinics and schools have been enormously important.

It is also not to fault the campaigns that exposed the dreadful conditions under which the Taliban placed women. The Feminist Majority campaign helped put a stop to a secret oil pipeline deal between the Taliban and the U.S. multinational Unocal that was going forward with U.S. administration support. Western feminist campaigns must not be confused with the hypocrisies of the new colonial feminism of a Republican president who was not elected for his progressive stance on feminist issues or of administrations that played down the terrible record of violations of women by the United States' allies in the Northern Alliance, as documented by Human Rights Watch and Amnesty International, among others. Rapes and assaults were widespread in the period of infighting that devastated Afghanistan before the Taliban came in to restore order.

It is, however, to suggest that we need to look closely at what we are supporting (and what we are not) and to think carefully about why. How should we manage the complicated politics and ethics of finding ourselves in agreement with those with whom we normally disagree? I do not know how many feminists who felt good about saving Afghan women from the Taliban are also asking for a global redistribution of wealth or contemplating sacrificing their own consumption radically so that African or Afghan women could have some chance of having what I do believe should be a universal human right—the right to freedom from the structural violence of global inequality and from the ravages of war, the everyday rights of having enough to eat, having homes for their families in which to live and thrive, having ways to make decent livings so their children can grow, and having the strength and security to work out, within their communities and with whatever alliances they want, how to live a good life, which might very well include changing the ways those communities are organized.

Suspicion about bedfellows is only a first step; it will not give us a way to think more positively about what to do or where to stand. For that, we need to confront two more big issues. First is the acceptance of the possibility of difference. Can we only free Afghan women to be like us or might we have to recognize that even after "liberation" from the Taliban, they might want different things than we would want for them? What do we do about that? Second, we need to be vigilant about the rhetoric of saving people because of what it implies about our attitudes.

Again, when I talk about accepting difference, I am not implying that we should resign ourselves to being cultural relativists who respect whatever goes on elsewhere as "just their culture." I have already discussed the dangers of "cultural" explanations; "their" cultures are just as much part of history and an interconnected world as ours are. What I am advocating is the hard work involved in recognizing and respecting differences—precisely as products of different histories, as expressions of different circumstances, and as manifestations of differently structured desires. We may want justice for women, but can we accept that there might be different ideas about justice and that different women might want, or choose, different futures from what we envision as best (see Ong 1988)? We must consider that they might be called to personhood, so to speak, in a different language.

Reports from the Bonn peace conference held in late November to discuss the rebuilding of Afghanistan revealed significant differences among the few Afghan women feminists and activists present. RAWA's position was to reject any conciliatory approach to Islamic governance. According to one report I read, most women activists, especially those based in Afghanistan who are aware of the realities on the ground, agreed that Islam had to be the starting point for reform. Fatima Gailani, a U.S.-based advisor to one of the delegations, is quoted as saying, "If I

go to Afghanistan today and ask women for votes on the promise to bring them secularism, they are going to tell me to go to hell." Instead, according to one report, most of these women looked for inspiration on how to fight for equality to a place that might seem surprising. They looked to Iran as a country in which they saw women making significant gains within an Islamic framework—in part through an Islamically oriented feminist movement that is challenging injustices and reinterpreting the religious tradition.

The situation in Iran is itself the subject of heated debate within feminist circles, especially among Iranian feminists in the West (e.g., Mir-Hosseini 1999; Moghissi 1999; Najmabadi 1998, 2000). It is not clear whether and in what ways women have made gains and whether the great increases in literacy, decreases in birthrates, presence of women in the professions and government, and a feminist flourishing in cultural fields like writing and filmmaking are because of or despite the establishment of a so-called Islamic Republic. The concept of an Islamic feminism itself is also controversial. Is it an oxymoron or does it refer to a viable movement forged by brave women who want a third way?

One of the things we have to be most careful about in thinking about Third World feminisms, and feminism in different parts of the Muslim world, is how not to fall into polarizations that place feminism on the side of the West. I have written about the dilemmas faced by Arab feminists when Western feminists initiate campaigns that make them vulnerable to local denunciations by conservatives of various sorts, whether Islamist or nationalist, of being traitors (Abu-Lughod 2001). As some like Afsaneh Najmabadi are now arguing, not only is it wrong to see history simplistically in terms of a putative opposition between Islam and the West (as is happening in the United States now and has happened in parallel in the Muslim world), but it is also strategically dangerous to accept this cultural opposition between Islam and the West, between fundamentalism and feminism, because those many people within Muslim countries who are trying to find alternatives to present injustices, those who might want to refuse the divide and take from different histories and cultures, who do not accept that being feminist means being Western, will be under pressure to choose, just as we are: Are you with us or against us?

My point is to remind us to be aware of differences, respectful of other paths toward social change that might give women better lives. Can there be a liberation that is Islamic? And, beyond this, is liberation even a goal for which all women or people strive? Are emancipation, equality, and rights part of a universal language we must use? To quote Saba Mahmood, writing about the women in Egypt who are seeking to become pious Muslims, "The desire for freedom and liberation is a historically situated desire whose motivational force cannot be assumed a priori, but needs to be reconsidered in light of other desires, aspirations, and capacities that inhere in a culturally and historically located subject" (2001:223). In other words, might other desires be more meaningful for different groups of people? Living in close families? Living in a godly way? Living without war? I have done fieldwork in Egypt over more than 20 years and I cannot think of a single woman I know, from the poorest rural to the most educated cosmopolitan, who has ever expressed envy of U.S. women, women they tend to perceive as bereft of community, vulnerable to sexual violence and social anomie, driven by individual success rather than morality, or strangely disrespectful of God.

Mahmood (2001) has pointed out a disturbing thing that happens when one argues for a respect for other traditions. She notes that there seems to be a difference in the political demands made on those who work on or are trying to understand Muslims and Islamists and those who work on secular-humanist projects. She, who studies the piety movement in Egypt, is consistently pressed to denounce all the harm done by Islamic movements around the world—otherwise she is accused of being an apologist. But there never seems to be a parallel demand for those who study secular humanism and its projects, despite the terrible violences that have been associated with it over the last couple of centuries, from world wars to colonialism, from genocides to slavery. We need to have as little dogmatic faith in secular humanism as in Islamism, and as

open a mind to the complex possibilities of human projects undertaken in one tradition as the other.

BEYOND THE RHETORIC OF SALVATION

Let us return, finally, to my title, "Do Muslim Women Need Saving?" The discussion of culture, veiling, and how one can navigate the shoals of cultural difference should put Laura Bush's self-congratulation about the rejoicing of Afghan women liberated by American troops in a different light. It is deeply problematic to construct the Afghan woman as someone in need of saving. When you save someone, you imply that you are saving her from something. You are also saving her *to* something. What violences are entailed in this transformation, and what presumptions are being made about the superiority of that to which you are saving her? Projects of saving other women depend on and reinforce a sense of superiority by Westerners, a form of arrogance that deserves to be challenged. All one needs to do to appreciate the patronizing quality of the rhetoric of saving women is to imagine using it today in the United States about disadvantaged groups such as African American women or working-class women. We now understand them as suffering from structural violence. We have become politicized about race and class, but not culture.

As anthropologists, feminists, or concerned citizens, we should be wary of taking on the mantles of those 19th-century Christian missionary women who devoted their lives to saving their Muslim sisters. One of my favorite documents from that period is a collection called *Our Moslem Sisters*, the proceedings of a conference of women missionaries held in Cairo in 1906 (Van Sommer and Zwemer 1907). The subtitle of the book is *A Cry of Need from the Lands of Darkness Interpreted by Those Who Heard It.* Speaking of the ignorance, seclusion, polygamy, and veiling that blighted women's lives across the Muslim world, the missionary women spoke of their responsibility to make these women's voices heard. As the introduction states, "They will never cry for themselves, for they are down under the yoke of centuries of oppression" (Van Sommer and Zwemer 1907:15). "This book," it begins, "with its sad, reiterated story of wrong and oppression is an indictment and an appeal. . . . It is an appeal to Christian womanhood to right these wrongs and enlighten this darkness by sacrifice and service" (Van Sommer and Zwemer 1907:5).

One can hear uncanny echoes of their virtuous goals today, even though the language is secular, the appeals not to Jesus but to human rights or the liberal West. The continuing currency of such imagery and sentiments can be seen in their deployment for perfectly good humanitarian causes. In February 2002, I received an invitation to a reception honoring an international medical humanitarian network called Médecins du Monde/Doctors of the World (MdM). Under the sponsorship of the French Ambassador to the United States, the Head of the delegation of the European Commission to the United Nations, and a member of the European Parliament, the cocktail reception was to feature an exhibition of photographs under the clichéd title "Afghan Women: Behind the Veil."

The invitation was remarkable not just for the colorful photograph of women in flowing burqas walking across the barren mountains of Afghanistan but also for the text, a portion of which I quote:

> For 20 years MdM has been ceaselessly struggling to help those who are most vulnerable. But increasingly, thick veils cover the victims of the war. When the Taliban came to power in 1996, Afghan Women became faceless. To unveil one's face while receiving medical care was to achieve a sort of intimacy, find a brief space for secret freedom and recover a little of one's dignity. In a country where women had no access to basic medical care because they did not have the right to appear in public, where women had no right to practice medicine, MdM's program stood as a stubborn reminder of human rights. . . . Please join us in helping to lift the veil.

Although I cannot take up here the fantasies of intimacy associated with unveiling, fantasies reminiscent of the French colonial obsessions so brilliantly unmasked by Alloula in *The Colonial Harem* (1986), I can ask why humanitarian projects and human rights discourse in the 21st century need rely on such constructions of Muslim women.

Could we not leave veils and vocations of saving others behind and instead train our sights on ways to make the world a more just place? The reason respect for difference should not be confused with cultural relativism is that it does not preclude asking how we, living in this privileged and powerful part of the world, might examine our own responsibilities for the situations in which others in distant places have found themselves. We do not stand outside the world, looking out over this sea of poor benighted people, living under the shadow—or veil—of oppressive cultures; we are part of that world. Islamic movements themselves have arisen in a world shaped by the intense engagements of Western powers in Middle Eastern lives.

A more productive approach, it seems to me, is to ask how we might contribute to making the world a more just place. A world not organized around strategic military and economic demands; a place where certain kinds of forces and values that we may still consider important could have an appeal and where there is the peace necessary for discussions, debates, and transformations to occur within communities. We need to ask ourselves what kinds of world conditions we could contribute to making such that popular desires will not be overdetermined by an overwhelming sense of helplessness in the face of forms of global injustice. Where we seek to be active in the affairs of distant places, can we do so in the spirit of support for those within those communities whose goals are to make women's (and men's) lives better (as Walley has argued in relation to practices of genital cutting in Africa [1997])? Can we use a more egalitarian language of alliances, coalitions, and solidarity, instead of salvation?

Even RAWA, the now celebrated Revolutionary Association of the Women of Afghanistan, which was so instrumental in bringing to U.S. women's attention the excesses of the Taliban, has opposed the U.S. bombing from the beginning. They do not see in it Afghan women's salvation but increased hardship and loss. They have long called for disarmament and for peacekeeping forces. Spokespersons point out the dangers of confusing governments with people, the Taliban with innocent Afghans who will be most harmed. They consistently remind audiences to take a close look at the ways policies are being organized around oil interests, the arms industry, and the international drug trade. They are not obsessed with the veil, even though they are the most radical feminists working for a secular democratic Afghanistan. Unfortunately, only their messages about the excesses of the Taliban have been heard, even though their criticisms

of those in power in Afghanistan have included previous regimes. A first step in hearing their wider message is to break with the language of alien cultures, whether to understand or eliminate them. Missionary work and colonial feminism belong in the past. Our task is to critically explore what we might do to help create a world in which those poor Afghan women, for whom "the hearts of those in the civilized world break," can have safety and decent lives.

NOTES

Acknowledgments: I want to thank Page Jackson, Fran Mascia-Lees, Tim Mitchell, Rosalind Morris, Anupama Rao, and members of the audience at the symposium "Responding to War," sponsored by Columbia University's Institute for Research on Women and Gender (where I presented an earlier version), for helpful comments, references, clippings, and encouragement.

WORKS CITED

Abu-Lughod, Lila.
1986. *Veiled Sentiments: Honor and Poetry in a Bedouin Society*. Berkeley: University of California Press.
Abu-Lughod, Lila.
1995. Movie Stars and Islamic Moralism in Egypt. *Social Text* 42:53–67.
Abu-Lughod, Lila.
1998. *Remaking Women: Feminism and Modernity in the Middle East*. Princeton: Princeton University Press.
Abu-Lughod, Lila.
2001. Orientalism and Middle East Feminist Studies. *Feminist Studies* 27(1):101–113.
Ahmed, Leila.
1992. *Women and Gender in Islam*. New Haven, CT: Yale University Press.
Alloula, Malek.
1986. *The Colonial Harem*. Minneapolis: University of Minnesota Press.
Brenner, Suzanne.
1996. Reconstructing Self and Society: Javanese Muslim Women and "the Veil." *American Ethnologist* 23(4):673–697.
El Guindi, Fadwa.
1999. *Veil: Modesty, Privacy and Resistance*. Oxford: Berg.
Fremson, Ruth.
2001. Allure Must Be Covered. Individuality Peeks Through. *New York Times*, November 4: 14.
Global Exchange.
2002. Courage and Tenacity: A Women's Delegation to Afghanistan. http://www.globalexchange.org/tours/auto/2002-03-05_CourageandTenacityAWomensDele.html.

Goldenberg, Suzanne.
2002. The Woman Who Stood Up to the Taliban. *The Guardian*, January 24. http://222.guardian.co.uk/afghanistan/story/0,1284,63840.
Hirschkind, Charles, and Saba Mahmood.
2002. Feminism, the Taliban, and the Politics of Counter-Insurgency. *Anthropological Quarterly* 75(2):107–122.
Lazreg, Marnia.
1994. *The Eloquence of Silence: Algerian Women in Question*. New York: Routledge.
MacLeod, Arlene.
1991. *Accommodating Protest*. New York: Columbia University Press.
Mahmood, Saba.
2001. Feminist Theory, Embodiment, and the Docile Agent: Some Reflections on the Egyptian Islamic Revival. *Cultural Anthropology* 16(2):202–235.
Mir-Hosseini, Ziba.
1999. *Islam and Gender: The Religious Debate in Contemporary Iran*. Princeton: Princeton University Press.
Moghissi, Haideh.
1999. *Feminism and Islamic Fundamentalism*. London: Zed Books.
Najmabadi, Afsaneh.
1998. Feminism in an Islamic Republic. *In Islam, Gender and Social Change*. Yvonne Haddad and John Esposito, eds. Pp. 59–84. New York: Oxford University Press.
Najmabadi, Afsaneh.
2000. (Un)Veiling Feminism. *Social Text* 64:29–15.

Ong, Aihwa.
  1988. Colonialism and Modernity: Feminist Re-Presentations of Women in Non-Western Societies. *Inscriptions* 3–4:79–93.
Ong, Aihwa.
  1990. State Versus Islam: Malay Families, Women's Bodies, and the Body Politic in Malaysia. *American Ethnologist* 17(2):258–276.
Papanek, Hanna.
  1982. Purdah in Pakistan: Seclusion and Modem Occupations for Women. *In Separate Worlds.* Hanna Papanek and Gail Minault, eds. Pp. 190–216. Columbus, MO: South Asia Books.
Safire, William.
  2001. On Language. *New York Times Magazine*, October 28: 22.
Spivak, Gayatri Chakravorty.
  1988. Can the Subaltern Speak? *In Marxism and the Interpretation of Culture.* Cary Nelson and Lawrence

Grossberg, eds. Pp. 271–313. Urbana: University of Illinois Press.
Strathern, Marilyn.
  1987. An Awkward Relationship: The Case of Feminism and Anthropology. *Signs* 12:276–292.
U.S. Government.
  2002. http://www.whitehouse.gov/news/releases/2001/11/20011117.
Van Sommer, Annie, and Samuel Marinus Zwemer.
  1907. *Our Moslem Sisters: A Cry of Need from Lands of Darkness Interpreted by Those Who Heard It.* New York: Fleming H. Revell Co.
Walley, Christine.
  1997. Searching for "Voices": Feminism, Anthropology, and the Global Debate over Female Genital Operations. *Cultural Anthropology* 12(3):405–438.

81. • *Beenash Jafri*

NOT YOUR INDIAN ECO-PRINCESS:
Indigenous Women's Resistance to Environmental Degradation (2017)

Beenash Jafri is assistant professor of gender, sexuality, and women's studies at the University of California, Davis. Her research centers on issues of race, gender, ethnicity, and culture. Her writing has been published in journals including *American Indian Culture & Research Journal* and *Critical Race and Whiteness Studies* and the anthologies *The Settler Complex: Recuperating Binarism in Colonial Studies*, *Alliances: Re/Envisioning Indigenous-Non-Indigenous Relationships*, and *Speaking for Ourselves: Environmental Justice in Canada.* In "Not Your Indian Eco-Princess: Indigenous Women's Resistance to Environmental Degradation," Jafri analyzes the use of essentialist representations of Indigenous women in feminist discourse.

In November 2012, the Idle No More movement sparked a series of cross-country protests against the Canadian government's plans to pass legislation that would drastically impact First Nations treaty rights, while facilitating resource extraction industries' access to Native land. The movement was led by a group of predominantly Native women: Sylvia McAdam (Cree), Nina Wilson (Nakota and Plains Cree), Jessica Gordon (Cree and Anishnaabe), and Sheelah McLean (non-Native). Also prominent in the movement was Chief Theresa Spence of the Attawapiskat Nation, who went on a hunger fast to demand a meeting about Indigenous rights with the Canadian prime minister. These women are not alone: Indigenous women have been at the forefront of growing transnational movements for climate justice and against exploitative resource extraction industries. Why has this been the case?

It might be tempting to explain the prominence of Indigenous women in climate justice movements as flowing naturally from their identities as Indigenous women. Popular culture certainly suggests as much: from Disney's *Pocahontas* (1995) to Sacagawea in *Night at the Museum* (2006) and Neytiri in *Avatar* (2009), movie audiences are saturated with representations of Indigenous women who have close affinities with the natural world and nonhuman animals. These representations reflect a long-standing assumption that Native women—solely by virtue of being Native—are more in tune with nature than their white, non-Native counterparts. It isn't just popular culture that participates in the production and distribution of these stereotypes, however. Feminist writers, scholars, and activists have participated in this process as well. This was especially true of ecofeminism, a branch of feminist scholarship and activism that emerged in the late 1970s to address the environmental movement's failure to tackle issues of gender. Its proponents examined the connections between women and nature, with some suggesting that women had intrinsic affinities with nature and others focusing on capitalism's exploitation of both women and natural resources. A contemporary example of ecofeminist discourse appears in *Mad Max: Fury Road* (2015), which features the Vuvalini, a tribe of wise older women who have saved seeds from the past in the hopes of reviving green life in the postapocalyptic desert setting of the film. The film's celebration of feminine power—while refreshing—also implies that these

women hold these seeds and knowledge due to their gendered connections to the earth.

Indigenous peoples—and Indigenous women in particular—have featured prominently in the work of many ecofeminists. As Noel Sturgeon argues in *Ecofeminist Natures: Race, Gender, Feminist Theory and Political Action* (1997), many ecofeminists—particularly those writing in the late 1980s—essentialized the relationship between women and nature while holding up Indigenous women as exemplary models of this relationship. For example, Sturgeon cites contributors to the edited collection *Reweaving the Web: The Emergence of Ecofeminism*, who frequently make reference to "the symbols and practices of Native-American cultures" (Diamond and Orenstein 1990, xi) as inspiration for ecofeminist thought. Those endorsing the myth that Indigenous women are intrinsically connected to nature overlook two important points: first, that Indigenous women's social, historical, and political relationships to land are dynamic and shifting, rather than fixed or intrinsic; and second, that colonization has a profound impact on those relationships. I examine each of these points in turn before reflecting on an alternative way to understand Indigenous women's leadership within environmental movements.

I. INDIGENOUS WOMEN'S RELATIONSHIPS TO LAND

Indigenous women are not naturally inclined to be environmental stewards. It is true that Indigenous societies on Turtle Island (North America)—many of which were traditionally matrifocal, centering the leadership of Indigenous women—have historically had far more symbiotic relationships with nature than Western societies. However, these are the result of complex Indigenous philosophies and knowledge systems, cultivated over centuries, that contrast Western ways of knowing and understanding concepts such as "land," "nature," and "culture." These philosophies and traditions did not emerge out of thin air, nor are they static or unchanging. Rather, as described by scholars such as Vine Deloria Jr. (Standing Rock Sioux), they emerge from dynamic *practices* of relating to and interacting with land, water, plants, and nonhuman animals that have been passed down from one generation to the next. Indigenous philosophies and traditions have also shifted and transformed over time, in response to changing political and environmental conditions. For example, in "Land as Pedagogy," Indigenous writer Leanne Simpson, of Michi Saagiig Nishnaabeg ancestry, writes about the grounded, holistic, community-based knowledge system that is tied to making maple syrup in her community in the North shore of Lake Huron near Ontario, Canada (2014, 2 fn2). Simpson anchors her argument through a story about Kwezens (translation: girl), whose participation in maple tapping teaches and reinforces many lessons: for example, how to learn from nonhuman animal teachers such as squirrels, who model ways to collect maple sap; how to creatively adapt squirrel strategies; trusting that her work collecting sap will be recognized by her elders in loving ways; and learning how to prepare the sap for cooking and eating by observing elders (6–7). Simpson describes maple tapping not as a process of resource extraction and production but as part of a process of learning about self, community, and relationships "both *from* the land and *with* the land" (7, original emphasis). She further asserts that:

> It is critical to avoid the assumption that this story takes place in pre-colonial times because Nishnaabeg conceptualizations of time and space present an ongoing intervention to linear thinking—this story happens in various incarnations all over our territory every year in March when the Nishnaabeg return to the sugar bush. Kwezen's presence . . . is complicated by her fraught relationality to the tenacity of settler colonialism, and her very presence simultaneously shatters the disappearance of Indigenous women and girls from settler consciousness. (8)

The active, dynamic Nishnaabeg practice of maple tapping that Simpson describes is a form of resistance

to settler colonialism. Settler colonialism refers to the ongoing colonialism that structures nation-states such as the United States, Canada, Australia, and New Zealand. In these white settler states, Indigenous peoples continue to be subject to colonial laws, policies, and regulations that restrict access to land, modes of governance and social organization, spirituality, language, and medicine. Resistance to ongoing colonialism, including that described by Simpson, also persists: Indigenous peoples across the world engage in acts of what Anishnaabe scholar Gerald Vizenor refers to in his book, *Manifest Manners*, as *survivance*. Beyond mere survival, *survivance* signals Indigenous modes of actively being in the world. It refers to "moving beyond our [Native] basic survival in the face of overwhelming cultural genocide to create spaces of synthesis and renewal" (Vizenor 1994, 53).

II. LAND, ENVIRONMENT, AND COLONIZATION

When popular films, ecofeminist theories/activism, and others uncritically celebrate Indigenous women's relationships to land/nature without paying heed to the context of colonialism, they make invisible an entire system of land dispossession that enabled the establishment of white settler societies. For example, in the classic ecofeminist text, *Woman and Nature*, Susan Griffin frames Sacagawea as a woman highly attuned to her natural surroundings, who is subject to patriarchal oppression by Lewis and Clark, as well as her father, her husband and Shoshone community (1978, 52–53). Yet by failing to examine the constitutive impact of colonialism on Sacagawea's experiences—and by positing patriarchy as the primary source of the marginalization and oppression Sacagawea experienced—Griffin fails to take into account the way in which patriarchy works in conjunction with colonialism, as well as other systems of oppression, including racism, capitalism, and heteronormativity. As Maile Arvin, Eve Tuck, and Angie Morrill write, "Native men are not the root cause of Native women's problems; rather, Native women's critiques implicate the historical and ongoing imposition of colonial, heteropatriarchal structures onto their societies" (Arvin et al. 2013, 18).

The impact of colonialism on Indigenous women's lives cannot be understated. For example, colonialism affected the ways in which Indigenous women experienced relationships to land. As Tonawanda Seneca scholar Mishuana Goeman recounts in *Mark My Words: Native Women Mapping Our Nations*, colonization drastically transformed the landscape of the places we now refer to as the United States, Canada, Australia, and New Zealand. Colonization did not only involve the physical displacement of Indigenous peoples. It also introduced and implemented European modes of imagining, organizing, and relating to space, land, and nature, which relied on scientific knowledge and devalued Indigenous ways of knowing and relating to land. Whereas diverse Native nations had local, often matrifocal, place-based knowledge derived from centuries of caring and cultivating relationships with land, the systematic imposition of European modes of thought through colonial policies and regulations—for instance, through the transformation of matrilineal and/or matrifocal governance into patriarchal governance through the Indian Act in Canada—disrupted these relationships. Colonial constructions of nature and the environment—that is to say, dominant constructions—view these as objects that are fundamentally separate from humans or culture. For instance, the notion that land can be "owned" and made the property of humans relies on the presumption that land is an object or commodity meant to be managed and controlled by humans. This colonial discourse is also gendered: just as patriarchy objectifies women as the property of men, colonial discourse *feminizes* land and nature, framing them as objects belonging to men (e.g., see McClintock, *Imperial Leather*, 1995). The notion that Europeans were better equipped to manage and control land and women has been a salient feature of colonial discourses, one that has been used

to mark Indigenous populations as "savage" in relation to "civilized" Europeans and European men as more properly masculine than Native men. Its effects have been violent, as European colonizers were threatened by the relative egalitarianism and matrifocal organization of the Indigenous societies they encountered. Correspondingly, as Andrea Smith argues in *Conquest: Sexual Violence and American Indian Genocide* (2005), the conquest of Native women specifically, via rape and sexual violence, was central to colonialist ventures. The preponderance of sexual violence combined with the imposition of patriarchal forms of social organization has meant that colonization has been particularly devastating for Native women. Thus the stakes for decolonizing have arguably been higher for Native women than Native men, for whom colonialism has expanded access to patriarchal power.

Resource extraction industries—including mining, oil and gas drilling, and forestry—follow the same logic as their earlier colonial predecessors. These industries, which are fueled by the demands of global capitalist markets, view natural resources as just that: as resources meant to be located, extracted, processed, sold to, and consumed by people. Extractive industries, and their corporate and government supporters, prioritize economic growth above social concerns. The toxic wastes and environmental degradation that extractive processes produce are thus dealt with by these industries as an afterthought. The effects of this toxicity and degradation are experienced unevenly, with distribution largely determined by structural factors shaped by racism, patriarchy, colonialism, and capitalism. As scholars and activists in the environmental justice movement have persuasively demonstrated (e.g., Bullard, *Confronting Environmental Racism*, 1993; LaDuke, *All Our Relations*, 1999), it is poor people of color and Indigenous peoples across the world who are most vulnerable to environmental risk. For example, in North America, extractive industries have targeted First Nations reserves (Canada) and Indian reservations (United States); organizations such as the Indigenous Environmental Network were formed in direct response to that targeting ("About," Indigenous Environmental Network). Colonial policies support these practices: as I mentioned at the start of this essay, in Canada, the federal government passed a series of bills in 2012 that would facilitate resource extraction practices while diminishing First Nations access and authority over their own lands.

III. UNDERSTANDING INDIGENOUS WOMEN'S RESISTANCE TO ENVIRONMENTAL DEGRADATION

I return now to the question I posed earlier in this essay: Why have Indigenous women figured so predominantly in movements for climate justice? To reiterate an earlier point, Indigenous women's leadership on these issues flows from neither their gender nor their ancestry. Rather, this leadership is borne of colonialism's impact on Indigenous communities and nations, which—due to colonialism's disruption of women's leadership within traditional Indigenous societies—has affected Indigenous women in particular. As Freda Huson, spokesperson for the Unist'ot'en Clan, says in relation to addressing the colonial, patriarchal systems supported by Canadian governments and the Indian Chiefs whom they empower through the Indian Act:

> The true traditional decision-making is carried through the clans and through the women who carry the clans. . . . For us, it has been a dual struggle—against government and industry and also against Indian Act chiefs. These male Indian Act chiefs are imposing top-down decisions. That is why we pulled out of the political negotiations and the treaty process. . . . These Chiefs are so worried about funding. The resources being extracted from our territories are worth billions of dollars, and while the government is getting wealthy we are fighting over crumbs. So we are taking action through our hereditary clan system and building awareness and unity through our actions. (qtd. in Walia 2013)

Huson's emphasis on the ways that colonialism and patriarchy mutually reinforce one another is instructive. For non-Native feminists and others wishing to express support and solidarity for Native women, it is crucial that we listen closely to these articulations. Otherwise—if we focus singularly on the impact of patriarchy on Native women's lives—we risk erasing the colonization that is at the root of violence against Native women.

WORKS CITED

"About." *Indigenous Environmental Network*, www.ienearth. org/about/. Accessed October 29, 2015.

Arvin, Maile, Eve Tuck, and Angie Morrill. "Decolonizing Feminism: Challenging Connections Between Settler Colonialism and Heteropatriarchy." *Feminist Formations*, vol. 25, no.1, 2013, pp. 8–34.

Avatar. Directed by James Cameron. 20th Century Fox, 2009.

Bullard, Robert. *Confronting Environmental Racism: Voices From the Grassroots*. South End Press, 1993.

Deloria, Vine Jr. *God Is Red: A Native View of Religion*. Fulcrum Publishing, 2003.

Diamond, Irene, and Gloria Orenstein, editors. *Reweaving the Web: The Emergence of Ecofeminism*. Sierra Club Books, 1990.

Goeman, Mishuana. *Mark My Words: Native Women Mapping Our Nations*. University of Minnesota Press, 2013.

Griffin, Susan. *Woman and Nature: The Roaring Inside Her*. Sierra Club Books, 1978.

LaDuke, Winona. *All Our Relations: Native Struggles for Land and Life*. South End Press, 1999.

Mad Max: Fury Road. Directed by George Miller. Warner Brothers, 2015.

McClintock, Anne. *Imperial Leather: Race, Gender and Sexuality in the Colonial Contest*. Routledge, 1995.

Night at the Museum. Directed by Shawn Levy. 20th Century Fox, 2006.

Pocahontas. Directed by Eric Goldberg and Mike Gabriel. Buena Vista Pictures, 1995.

Simpson, Leanne Betasamosake. "Land as Pedagogy: Nishnaabeg Intelligence and Rebellious Transformation."
Decolonization: Indigeneity, Education and Society, vol. 3, no.
3, 2014, pp. 1–25. decolonization.org/index.php/des/
article/view/22170/17985.

Smith, Andrea. *Conquest: Sexual Violence and American Indian
Genocide*. South End Press, 2005.

Sturgeon, Noel. *Ecofeminist Natures: Race, Gender, Feminist
Theory and Political Action*. Routledge, 1997.

Vizenor, Gerald Robert. *Manifest Manners: Narratives on
Postindian Survivance*. University of Nebraska Press, 1994.

Walia, Harsha. "Indigenous Sovereigntists Speak."
Rabble.ca., February 8, 2013, abble.ca/news/2013/02/
indigenous-sovereigntists-speak.

82. • *Elizabeth R. Cole and Zakiya T. Luna*

MAKING COALITIONS WORK:
Solidarity Across Difference Within US Feminism (2010)

Elizabeth R. Cole is professor of women's studies, psychology, and Afroamerican and African studies at the University of Michigan. Her research focuses on intersectionality and the construction of race, class, and gender. Her work has been published in *Psychology of Women Quarterly*, *Feminism & Psychology*, *Sex Roles*, and *Feminist Studies*, where this article was originally published. Zakiya T. Luna is assistant professor of sociology at University of California, Santa Barbara. Her research interests include reproductive justice, social movements, and inequality. She is co-editor of the University of California Press book series *Reproductive Justice: A New Vision for the 21st Century*, and has had articles published in *Sociological Inquiry*; *Research in Social Movements, Conflicts and Change*; and *Societies Without Borders: Social Science and Human Rights*. In "Making Coalitions Work: Solidarity Across Difference Within US Feminism," Cole and Luna analyze feminist activists who successfully participated in coalition work.

The importance of working in coalition, that is, the process through which groups that define themselves as different work together politically, either long or short term, in the service of some mutually valued end, is a frequent refrain in the writing of feminists of color. In the twenty-five years since Bernice Johnson Reagon addressed the West Coast Women's Music Festival on the importance of coalitions, many feminists—both scholars and activists—have argued for the centrality of coalitional strategies for feminist social change. Feminist coalition work has been variously described as an imperative, an opportunity, and an inevitability, given that difference is culturally constructed and

Cole, Elizabeth and Luna Zakiya, "Making Coalitions Work: Solidarity Across Difference Within US Feminism" *Feminist Studies*. Spring 2010; 36.1: 71-97.

all groups contain heterogeneity.[1] Yet relatively little work has looked at the way these theoretical premises play out in activists' political work. This article aims to bring our models of theorizing coalition into dialogue with practice by listening to activists' own reflections on their work.

[. . .]

. . . What, other than perceptions of basic self-interest, motivates groups that define themselves as different to work together? How do diverse groups conceptualize identity, belonging, and solidarity across difference—what Scott A. Hunt and Robert D. Benford call "external solidarity"[2]—in order to come together in the first place? . . . How do groups work together productively across power asymmetries to achieve common goals, and what practices are necessary to ensure meaningful participation by the most disempowered constituencies?

This article engages these questions based on a reading of the feminist literature on coalitions and activists' narratives recorded as part of a larger project collecting oral history interviews with feminist scholar-activists in four countries. A description of the project, including the US Site Booklet of interview transcripts, from which quotations in this article are taken, is available at "Global Feminisms: Comparative Case Studies of Women's Activism and Scholarship," http://www.umich.edu/~glblfem/. The US-based segment of this project was planned and implemented by an interdisciplinary team of faculty and students. We chose activists whose work addressed sites of intersection between feminist social movements and other axes of oppression such as race/ethnicity, sexual orientation, social class, and ability status. Our selection strategy was intended to generate a sample that could illuminate important fault lines within the women's movement in the United States. Potential participants were told that it was not necessary to identify with the label "feminist" in order to take part and that the interview would include an opportunity to discuss their thoughts about the term. Interviews were conducted at the authors' university, and participants' travel expenses

were funded by the project. Despite the substantial demands of participation, only one invitee declined to participate, due to scheduling constraints.

[. . .]

BUILDING SOLIDARITY ACROSS GROUPS: NARRATIVES OF IDENTITY AND BELONGING

Repeatedly the literature within feminist theory on coalitions suggests that women of color are exceptionally well positioned to apprehend opportunities for, and possibilities presented by, coalitional work because they belong to multiple oppressed communities defined by gender, race, and often class. Of course every individual occupies specific positions with respect to gender, race, class, sexuality, and other socially constructed distinctions associated with political and economic stratification. However, those who claim multiple subordinated identities may be particularly attuned to the ways that organizations, social movements, and public policies based on social identities often frame their analysis to address primarily the concerns of individuals who, but for one marginalized status, are otherwise privileged.[3]

For example, Diane L. Fowlkes observed that when the Combahee River Collective grounded their political analysis in terms of their lived experiences of racism, sexism, and homophobia, they reconstructed their own identities within a social and historical environment in which issues of sexuality were rarely mentioned and issues of gender were often overlooked. In doing so, not only did the collective reveal implicit aspects of the construction of others' identities (e.g., that the concept of "woman" was often assumed to be white and heterosexual), but they also argued that coalitions were necessary because of complex interlocking structures of oppression and privilege. Later work by Chela Sandoval and Gloria Anzaldúa suggested some of the concrete ways that individuals marginalized by multiple statuses might serve as catalysts for such political linkages. Specifically, Anzaldúa argued that her socially marginal position as a lesbian of color rendered her identity inherently hybrid, or *mestiza:* being at once homeless and at home everywhere positioned her to shift between communities and constituencies.[4] Fowlkes observed that in making this argument, Anzaldúa used "complex identity narration" as a tool of struggle. In this reading, women of color scholar/activists have deployed their analysis of the complex layering of their oppression to construct meaningful identities that are themselves tools for social change.[5] Indeed, scholars of the "new social movements," that is, the non-class-based social movements that emerged beginning in the 1960s, emphasized the central importance of identity construction and redefinition to mobilization in these organizations. Importantly then, because identities are constructed categories, so too are solidarity and connection, and therefore alliances are potentially fluid.

However, other theorists, including Chandra Talpade Mohanty and Judith Butler, reject identity as the basis of coalition, worrying that such an approach contributes to the reification and normalization of certain identities. Butler argued that when activists premise a coalition on the assertion of an ideal association between identity and action ("we'll all join hands as women!"), they impose fixed and normative identities on the actors. Kimberlé Crenshaw also argued that identity politics is flawed, however, not because of its emphasis on differences between groups but rather because it is premised on turning a blind eye to differences within groups.[6] For similar reasons, Mohanty urged activists to engage difference, rather than to attempt to transcend it.[7] Although the claim to a common identity may be motivated by the desire for unity within a movement, Butler encouraged those undertaking coalitional politics to embrace fractures and ruptures in identity in order to make the broadest possible movement:

> Without the goal of "unity" . . . provisional unities might emerge in the context of concrete actions that have purposes other than the articulation of identity.

Without the compulsory expectation that feminist actions must be instituted from some stable, unified and agreed upon identity, those actions might well get a quicker start and seem more congenial to a number of "women" for whom the category is permanently moot.[8]

Similarly, Floya Anthias argued that any attempt to describe membership or belonging simultaneously implies a boundary indicating which groups are different or "other."[9] Thus, within the literature on identities and coalition, there is a tension between those who claim that an appreciation for the complexity of identity is a central tool for struggle and those who caution that as a political tool, any identity claim simultaneously engages otherness and exclusion and thus may be an obstacle to successful coalition.

[. . .]

DEFINING SOCIAL IDENTITIES

Several of the activists explicitly discussed their experiences redefining the social identities that had been ascribed to them in ways that were consistent with their own sense of the meaning of their social locations. For example, Grace Lee Boggs, a community organizer in her late eighties, discussed how she became a part of the predominantly Black community in south Chicago where she lived and worked. Her involvement with a tenants' union led to her participation in organizing a delegation for a national march to protest discrimination in defense plants. Even though the march did not materialize, Boggs became more active in the larger struggles of African Americans, which led her to Detroit where she resides today. The daughter of Chinese immigrants, Boggs perceived the definition of community in that time and place not to have been constrained by racial ancestry. She argued that people from generations after hers

> who remember the nationalist phase of the Black movement and the extreme race consciousness that has developed ever since, say, 1960, find it difficult to

recall that in the 1940s and 1950s there was not that sense of color consciousness in the Black community. . . . And I was strange to people. I mean, they . . . considered me a person of color, but I wasn't Black, and kids used to come up and touch my hair and say, you know, "What nice hair you have," because it was so straight, and black. . . . People, I think, accepted me. Particularly, because, you know, I was married to Jimmy [Boggs, who was Black] and we lived in the Black community. And I had a wonderful time. It was the first community I had ever really belonged to.

Later in the interview she elaborated on the extent of her involvement with that community. "I became so active in the Black Movement that the FBI, its records say, 'She's probably Afro-Chinese.' But that's how closely I became identified." However, when the eighty-eight-year-old Boggs reflected on identity explicitly, she commented with humor that "if I were to characterize myself as something particular, I would say I'm old!"

> I don't believe in getting stuck in any one identity. I think that our tendency . . . it's so easy to become fragmented because we live in a fragmented . . . fragmenting society. It's so difficult to be whole, to see yourself as many faceted, to see how many possibilities there are in who we are . . . you know, here I've been Afro-Chinese, I've been Asian American. I've had the opportunity to know so many different people and work with so many different people of all ethnicities and all ages, and of all classes.

Thus, Boggs saw a potential danger in the idea of social identity, in that it can constrain both one's sense of self and the ability to see meaningful connections with others. Her story also pointed to the importance of context as she later reminded the audience that a movement to empower Asian Americans did not exist during her early years of activism. She did not have the option to organize around her racial identity, but, instead of avoiding political action, she became an active ally. Boggs established her commitment to racial justice and local community empowerment over decades. She continued to move beyond activism around obvious identity categories when she founded the Boggs Center, in Detroit, Michigan, which offers community programs, many of which are aimed at youth.

If Boggs's many identifications were grounded locally, Rabab Abdulhadi, an activist who was instrumental in founding the Union of Palestinian Women's Associations, described how, for diasporic Palestinian women, Palestine transcends a specific geographical location to shape their identities and daily lives.

> Thinking about how Palestinian women who are living in the Diaspora, in exile, in the US, people like me and others, have the transnational networks and connections and belongings and identifications with a place called Palestine that is always transnationally imagined. . . . There is a physical place . . . called Palestine . . . geography. At the same time, people are not there, but there is this kind of connection that has . . . that shapes the identity, the thinking, the psyche, everyday life of your existence, and a lot of the women I would call [Palestinian], they have these transnational relations and networks and so on, [but they] are not living actually here and there. They're living here and here. It's always here and here. It's . . . you could be physically here or you could be physically there, but there is this kind of . . . I don't want to call it divided loyalty. I think there is this kind of connection, and I think it is transnational.

In Abdulhadi's reckoning, this transnational experience is so profound that both Palestine and the place of exile may simultaneously be experienced as "here." This view of the world, she argued, allows the transnational feminist living in exile to appreciate the power of borders but also to envision a world in which borders are not fixed in time or space. From this vantage point, Abdulhadi observed that commonalities between women who are widely geographically dispersed may come into view:

> I would say, well, "Global South" is right there in New York City—in the Bronx and in Harlem and in El Barrio, and in Brooklyn, and right there in the streets of NYU, which is supposed to be very

fancy, but . . . You know, so it's . . . everywhere, always when we think . . . if we think about South and North, we don't think about them as like, um, forcefully divided geographically . . . and distinct and discrete units, that there is all . . . a lot of fluidity in them, but we recognize how they are structured . . . in terms of oppression.

In contrast, Cathy J. Cohen, whose political and academic work has mainly addressed queer issues within communities of color, particularly their early disavowal of people with HIV/AIDS, envisaged a shared identity based not on a real or imagined location but on a complete reconceptualization of the ways that the state attempts to control sexuality. Early in her interview, she described her political coming-of-age as a graduate student who became a leader in campus antiracism movements in the 1980s. Many women played leadership roles in her organization; in response, members of older Black organizations sought to discredit them through lesbian-baiting. Cohen recalled that these criticisms led members of her group "to kind of debate and talk about what was the importance of having a broad and inclusive agenda. It meant going back and reading things that we hadn't read." This return to theory led the group to a more nuanced understanding of group identity and its political implications. Cohen recalled, "It wasn't about kind of running away in any way from race, because we are all kind of strong, proud Black women. But it also meant understanding that just because someone shared a racial identity with us didn't mean that they also shared a political identity with us. . . . And it was kind of an important and growing moment in understanding the distinction between the two."

Cohen, who is African American and a lesbian, has worked to explain and challenge how the interests of subordinated constituencies within a minority group may experience a political "secondary marginalization."[10] Her thinking has resulted in a new way to understand the concept of "queer" in structural terms that transcend a straight/gay binary. In her interview she noted that

queer sexuality for me is sexuality that really challenges hetero-normative expectations and assumptions. And what I mean by that [is] it's people who are marginalized on the basis of their sexuality. So you can undoubtedly include lesbian-gay-bisexual-transgender folks in that category. I would also argue that women who are resource-poor and have children are marginalized by their sexual decisions and might be considered queer. Now, I want to be careful because a lot of people will say, "Oh, that's a nice academic argument." And I think at some level it is an academic argument. It's about kind of how do we conceptualize this category "queer." But for me it then becomes, are there political unities between these groups of people that organizers can start to think about how would you build a base for political mobilization?

In Cohen's re-vision of queer identity, mothers who are low-income and people who identify as sexual minorities are not merely potential allies. Because they share political interests by virtue of their common social experience of marginalization in relation to dominant groups, they potentially share an identity as well. Her reconceptualization of "queer" as a very broad politicized identity recalls Anthias's observation that "unities and divisions are constructions rather than representing actual and fixed groupings of people."[11] Cohen's narrative highlights the ways that activists' political work and theory building challenges those who might assume that collective identities are essential, fixed, or ascribed and demonstrates the creative ways identity may be used to generate social change.

These narratives illustrate how feminist activists who occupy multiple subordinated identities have developed from their social locations a complex understanding of the ways that identities are crafted through lived experience, the personal meaning attached to experience, and the power of these identities to generate political alliances. Boggs, Abdulhadi, and Cohen described the development of nuanced understandings of their social locations in ways that suggested their identities were built through reflection (as in Abdulhadi's conceptualization of geography and time), carefully nurtured alliances (as in Boggs's relation to Black communities in Chicago and Detroit), and expansive imagination (as in Cohen's re-envisioning of the category "queer").

EARLY EXPERIENCES AND IMAGINED COMMUNITIES

Many activists recall that early experiences and influences encouraged them to see connections across difference. A common theme in these interviews is the impact of childhood experiences that pushed interviewees to feel empathy toward people whose social identity categories were different from theirs. These examples highlight the flexible and constructed nature of social identity. For example, bioethicist Adrienne Asch recalled how her parents created a social life for their family that included people from diverse backgrounds; moreover, they also refused to define their daughter primarily in terms of the way some others saw her—disabled—thus allowing Asch to recognize that marginalized identities were one part of a person but not a defining feature. Later, Asch would challenge feminists whose work implicitly suggested that women with disabilities were not among the women whose interests the women's movements sought to advance. She took feminists to task both for excluding the experiences of women with disabilities from their theorizing and for their failure to acknowledge the implications of women choosing abortion in cases of fetal genetic anomalies, which Asch argued implicitly devalues the lives of people with disabilities, many of whom are women.

In these interviews, respondents also recalled formative experiences that led them to feel connections with people from outside their own ascribed groups, people whom others might have viewed as stigmatized or marked by difference. Loretta Ross vividly described daily experiences that required her to empathize across difference. One of her sisters was severely disabled, and at times Ross recalled resenting the caretaking role she often had to assume. Looking back, Ross felt the responsibility for her sister that her mother compelled her to take on instilled in her a capacity to empathize with Vietnam veterans with whom she interacted during her work as a hospital volunteer. Later, Ross protested the war, having witnessed firsthand its effects on people she claimed as members of her community.

Verónica Giménez is a member of Sista II Sista, a Brooklyn-based collective of young Latinas and Black women who work to end violence in their community. She recalled that when she first emigrated to the United States she was bused to a school in racially segregated Howard Beach. When white students suggested she could "pass" as Italian American due to her last name, rather than accept the privileges that might come with such an identity, she chose to identify with her less-privileged national identity. Although it had happened years before, a vicious racist attack on a young Black man in that town was foremost in her mind as she actively chose to embrace her racial consciousnesses as a member of an oppressed group.

> So my racial consciousness really became blown when I was not willing to be accepted under the Italian . . . auspice. They were willing to say, well, since my father's last name has an Italian descendency, they were like, "well, you're Italian too." And I was like "No, I'm not, I'm not Italian, I'm not Italian-American," and I related more to being Venezolana and bringing up my identity that way.

Rather than accepting white privilege, which she felt would make her complicit in racial oppression, Giménez worked to challenge oppression on multiple fronts.

Before activists enter into coalition, they have to consider the possibility as not only viable to some degree but also desirable. Many of the activists described how they imagined connections that helped create a worldview in which links across difference were expected and cultivated. Abdulhadi recalled that when she was growing up in Palestine, her mother emphasized the importance of connections with people beyond one's geographic location.

Seeing a newspaper picture of Angela Davis, who was on trial in connection with George Jackson's prison break, her mother insisted Davis was a friend to the Palestinians. Her mother's views led Abdulhadi to develop a sense of solidarity with the African American struggle taking place on a faraway continent, "Because in Palestine you're not interacting with a whole lot of other people from other countries. Little by little you start connecting, and you start seeing the intersections . . . the similarities." In a setting where restrictions on their movement rarely allowed Palestinians to interact with people from other backgrounds, these small moments added up to major changes in her ability to imagine connections. Seeing Davis's picture in newspapers evoked a sense of connection for Abdulhadi's mother who then used the opportunity to teach her daughter about links among oppressed peoples. Although the political contexts were in many ways different for African American and Palestinian women, the understanding of similarities in their experiences of oppression marked an opportunity for feelings of solidarity. Similarly, community organizer and civil rights activist Boggs recalled that upon the start of the Greensboro, North Carolina, lunch counter sit-ins in 1960, Black activists in Detroit held sympathy strikes, even though the right to service in public accommodations had already been secured in the Northern states.

[. . .]

WORKING ACROSS POWER ASYMMETRIES

Activists who described collaborating with groups with greater access to material resources and other kinds of power and privilege recounted the difficulties of what was essentially a translation or cross-cultural understanding. Ross spoke of her years of work as an African American woman in mainstream, predominantly white feminist organizations. In her view, these organizations were fraught with competitiveness and unspoken class conflicts. Ross argued that these group dynamics are very difficult to apprehend, but this understanding was critical to working successfully in such an environment.

> And so for a Black woman, you constantly have to try to figure out what's the normal treatment with which they treat white women versus how they treat me. Is it racism or is this just politics as usual? . . . So I mean, we tend to paint all white women with the same broad brush without understanding the conflicts and tensions within them. We don't understand the role of anti-Semitism in dividing white women, you know, old forms of European nationalism that are still being played out among white people. We don't even understand the construction of whiteness and what goes into that. And so we're not as sharp as I'd like us to be in understanding how to use and manipulate power within the mainstream movement.

But such sensitivity to these dynamics resulted only from years of working within the organization. After she left the organization, Ross continued to act as a bridge even when Black women questioned her engagement with white feminists. Twenty years later Ross was able to use her position to help her organization, SisterSong Women of Color Reproductive Health Collective, gain seats on the steering committing of the 2004 March for Women's Lives. When asked to endorse the march, rather than accept outright, SisterSong set its own terms to reduce the effects of unequal resources between mainstream organizations and smaller women of color organizations. Due to widespread organizing efforts, the march had over one million participants and garnered cosponsors from organizations in multiple movements, not just women's organizations. For example, the National Association for the Advancement of Colored People and the Sierra Club endorsed the march, the first time either group had supported a major pro-choice event. Despite the short-term success of the coalition, Ross expressed her frustration with that kind of work: "It's exhausting to try to study [those dynamics], I mean, getting into that. Not everybody is prepared to be a bridge."

[. . .]

These interviews suggest some of the challenges faced by organizations attempting to work across differences of power. Powerful groups may assume that their practices and internal dynamics are universal and thus should be transparent to all. Such assumptions may pose an additional burden for coalition partners with less power and privilege. Not only must they do the political work, but they must also struggle to decode what is unsaid and then communicate that information back to their coalition partners, who may not be eager to receive feedback reminding them of their blind spots. Activists who recounted such narratives invariably commented on the toll this "double shift" can take. For this reason, some strategically chose only short-term alliances across differences of power.

[. . .]

NOTES

The interviews discussed in this article were funded by a University of Michigan Rackham Interdisciplinary Collaboration Research Grant. Additional support was provided by the College of Literature, Science, and the Arts; the International Institute; Institute for Research on Women and Gender; Women's Studies Program; Humanities Institute; Center for South Asian Studies; the Herman Family Fund; the Center for African and Afroamerican Studies; and the Office of the Provost at the University of Michigan.

1. Bernice Johnson Reagon, "Coalition Politics: Turning the Century" in *Home Girls: A Black Feminist Anthology*, ed. Barbara Smith (New York: Kitchen Table/Women of Color Press, 1983), 3 (imperative); Gloria Anzaldúa, "Bridge, Drawbridge, Sandbar or Island: Lesbians-of-Color Hacienda Alianzas," in *Bridges of Power: Women's Multicultural Alliances*, ed. Lisa Albrecht and Rose M. Brewer (Philadelphia: New Society Publishers, 1990), 220 (opportunity); Kimberlé Crenshaw, "Mapping the Margins: Intersectionality, Identity Politics, and Violence Against Women of Color," in *The Public Nature of Private Violence*, ed. Martha Albertson Fineman and Roxanne Mykitiuk (New York: Routledge, 1994), 114 (inevitability); Cathy J. Cohen, "Punks, Bulldaggers, and Welfare Queens: The Radical Potential of Queer Politics?" in *Feminist Frontiers*, 8th ed., ed. Verta Taylor, Nancy E. Whittier, and Leila Rupp (Boston: McGraw Hill, 2004), 608 (heterogeneity).
2. Scott A. Hunt and Robert D. Benford, "Collective Identity, Solidarity, and Commitment," in *Blackwell Companion to Social Movements*, ed. David A. Snow, Sarah A. Soule, and Hanspeter Kriesi (Malden, MA: Blackwell, 2004), 433–57. The authors make a distinction between internal solidarity, which links the members of a social movement organization to one another, and external solidarity, which is the "identification with groups to which one does not belong" (439).
3. Deborah K. King, "Multiple Jeopardy, Multiple Consciousness: The Context of a Black Feminist Ideology," *Signs* 14 (Autumn 1988): 42.
4. Diane L. Fowlkes, "Moving from Feminist Identity Polities to Coalition Politics Through a Feminist Materialist Standpoint of Intersubjectivity in Gloria Anzaldúa's *Borderlands/La Frontera: The New Mestiza*," *Hypatia* 12 (Spring 1997): 105; Chela Sandoval, *Methodology of the Oppressed* (Minneapolis: University of Minnesota Press, 2000), 57; Anzaldúa, "Bridge, Drawbridge, Sandbar," 222.
5. Gloria Anzaldúa, cited in Fowlkes, "Moving from Feminist Identity Politics," 108.
6. Chandra Talpade Mohanty, *Feminism Without Borders: Decolonizing Theory, Practicing Solidarity* (Durham, NC: Duke University Press, 2003), 300; Judith Butler, *Gender Trouble: Feminism and the Subversion of Identity* (New York: Routledge, 1990), 172; Crenshaw, "Mapping the Margins," 114.
7. Mohanty, *Feminism Without Borders*, 300.
8. Butler, *Gender Trouble*, 21.
9. Floya Anthias, "Beyond Feminism and Multiculturalism: Locating Difference and the Politics of Location," *Women's Studies International Forum* 25 (May–June 2002): 275–86.
10. Cathy J. Cohen, *The Boundaries of Blackness: AIDS and the Breakdown of Black Politics* (Chicago: University of Chicago Press, 1999), 70.
11. Anthias, "Beyond Feminism and Multiculturalism," 277.

83. • *Evette Dionne*

TURNING FURY INTO FUEL:
Three Women Authors on Publishing's New Investment in Anger (2018)

The following interview was a part of a series of articles published by Bitch Media in 2018 called "The Future Is Furious." For this part of the series, Evette Dionne, Bitch Media's editor-in-chief, interviews Soraya Chemaly, Gemma Hartley, and Reema Zaman about their recent books. Chemaly's book, *Rage Becomes Her: The Power of Women's Anger*, encourages women to embrace their anger and use it as a political tool. In *Fed Up: Emotional Labor, Women, and the Way Forward*, Hartley validates women's anger over the gendered burden of emotional labor and "worry work." Reema Zaman shares the story of her fight to free her anger and her voice in *I Am Yours: A Shared Memoir*. In "Turning Fury Into Fuel: Three Women Authors on Publishing's New Investment in Anger," Chemaly, Hartley, and Zaman discuss their own writing, the cultural narratives around women's anger, and role of anger in bringing about social change.

In January, when publishers began sending [Bitch Media] advance copies of their 2018 books, we realized that many authors were exploring a similar theme—women's anger. Receiving those books was the initial catalyst for our weeklong "The Future Is Furious" series. Publishers realizing that multiple books about women's anger are worth putting on shelves; Maxine Waters expressing her anger on national television; and sexual-assault survivors forcing Hollywood and media to reckon with the predators they've long protected gave us the gumption to shine a light on the transformative power of women's anger.

Few people understand the moment we're in better than Soraya Chemaly, Gemma Hartley, and Reema Zaman—three women who've written books about anger and can offer a prescient overview of why publishers are suddenly giving us these books in droves. So, we asked them about it.

People from marginalized communities are driving so many of our cultural conversations about engaging in the political process. Based on the research you've done about anger, would you say we're in a new moment? Or is this a continuation of the anger that has always fueled political shifts?

GEMMA HARTLEY: I think it's both. Our anger is intrinsically linked to the past, but I think we need to claim this moment as our own, to claim our rage as our own. I think (hope) what makes this a new moment is that we seem to be waking up to the fact that civility is a patriarchal tool that we can't use to our advantage. The whole purpose of imposing civility and quelling the expressed anger of marginalized groups is to make sure they can't be heard or effectively harness their power. We're told that engaging "nicely" will lead to change (think white-washed Martin Luther King Jr. memes), but historically, that's not true. There's inherent inequality in demanding civil discourse between two parties when one has significantly more power and privilege than the other. And, of course, this shift in thinking about anger comes from the leadership of Black women, who have always been at the heart of activism and political change. Following their leadership, instead of merely capitalizing on their labor, is necessary if we really want this to be a "new" moment, more than a continuation of the ineffective white feminism of the past.

REEMA ZAMAN: I agree with Gemma. We're in a specific, unique moment, [but it's also] part of a larger story [that's] continually unfolding. The coalescence of all these elements is ideal for enormous change—a perfect storm of sorts. [We've had] enough failures and betrayals on the part of our "leaders," [and it has caused] us to collectively hit our tolerance [limit]. We're simultaneously saying *enough*, and coming forward with our personal stories; our solidarity, our unified commitment to change, is the force that will [make] the defining difference. Our unified commitment gives me such hope amidst all this. Additionally, women in their 30s and 40s were raised on the values of third-wave feminism. We were encouraged to pursue higher education as well as our own income and careers. So, I feel we're equipped, mentally and tactically, to follow through on this fertile rage.

Knowledge is power, and being able to articulate why we're furious is in itself galvanizing, and helps us uncover solutions. Furthermore, in the last 10 or so years, culturally, we've done a lot of work to investigate the ways white hetero activism and white hetero feminism in the past have been nearsighted or downright harmful. Because the thing is, if you're trying to heal a wound using rusted tools, you'll only hurt the body further. Nearsighted activism has done precisely that in the past. Now, we're more intelligent and conscious about leveraging this present moment of fertile rage, with the goal of achieving authentically inclusive, ethical, and sustainable change.

How did you come to the decision to write a book specifically about women's anger (in relation to emotional labor, *the dismissing and denying of women's anger, and an abusive marriage)?*

SORAYA CHEMALY: For many years I'd written about social-justice issues and worked on several book proposals in the process. The 2016 U.S. presidential election was the catalyst for shifting [my] focus to anger. Anger was so palpable in the build up to and the aftermath of [Donald] Trump's election. What was so striking was how powerfully male candidates like Bernie Sanders and Trump could freely, and with added benefit, tap into the rising tide of populist rage. They could pound fists, get red in the face and express righteous political indignation, and [still] be seen as "in touch" with voters. Women, specifically Hillary Clinton, couldn't do this without penalty. We saw the same dynamic in the [Brett] Kavanaugh hearings recently. That double standard and others like it are so defining for women. Anger—its social construction, regulation, expression as an entitlement—seemed like the best filter through which to write about women's experiences, needs, and status.

GH: When I set out to write *Fed Up: Emotional Labor, Women, and the Way Forward*, I didn't intend to write an "angry" book. In fact, you'll probably notice throughout the book the conflation of anger and frustration, because anger is still such a taboo subject. We're not mad at our partners, we're frustrated or disappointed or sad because we can't be angry without also being labeled emotional, crazy, unstable, illogical, etc. But of course, anger is the natural response to injustice and inequality. Anger is the spark that drives change.

RZ: My memoir, *I Am Yours*, is a love letter of healing and a call to action for anyone who has gone through sexual or intimate-partner violence. I was 27 when I left my abusive marriage, and 30 when I decided to write the memoir. During the marriage, I started to connect a few things: I came from a long history of sexual violence, and my entire life, I'd been shamed any time I expressed any morsel of anger or pain. I'm from Bangladesh, the eldest child of an arranged marriage, and I was raised to be the most polite, compassionate, cheerful, understanding, pleasing daughter, woman, and partner, often to my own peril and erasure. [I was] precisely the kind of woman who, upon encountering an abusive man, said, "It's all right. I forgive you. This is just how life and men are. I'll help you."

A lifetime of silenced anger and pain led me straight into an abusive marriage. Inside that marriage, any time I voiced my rage or sorrow toward the things he did, I was further punished. So, I grew to see that the culture of abuse and violence requires our obedience and silence. My personal story spoke to a larger political tale. Once I saw the micro and macro architecture at work, I realized I *had* to write this memoir [because] it's the quintessential narrative of the female condition, the human condition. I felt a deep responsibility to illustrate that by owning our power, validating our rightful rage, and breaking our silence, we heal the past, reclaim authorship in our own lives, and woman by woman, voice by voice, reject the systemic architecture designed to keep us small and caged. To speak is a revolution, and our collective voices are the reckoning the world needs.

I had five years to perfect the book. I began writing in 2013, from my deep need to heal my anorexia and the wounds of sexual trauma, then, with Trump's election in 2016, #MeToo in 2017, and Dr. Christine Blasey Ford in 2018, I've stepped into my voice as a writer and speaker. I've been able to make the memoir an intimate, but shared experience.

Recently, there's been an influx of fiction and nonfiction books that deal specifically with women's anger. Of course, you've all released or will release your books. There's also Brittney Cooper's Eloquent Rage *and Rebecca Traister's* Good and Mad. *Why are publishers so heavily invested in these narratives? What does that convey, if anything, about our cultural moment?*

SC: I think many people were stunned by the course of the presidential election and what Trump means to the state of our culture and democracy. I think this batch of books reflects the surprise that this happened, as well as a greater level of political awareness and editorial activism in the ranks of publishing.

GH: Nothing gives me hope quite like seeing this avalanche of books dealing with women and [other] marginalized experiences with anger. I think the fact that publishers are investing in these narratives helps validate and normalize our anger, which is long overdue. These books convey that we have a lot to be angry about in this cultural moment, and that anger is not only an appropriate response, but one that we can leverage to forge change.

RZ: I'm very close to my publisher, Dayna Anderson, and she's said that publishing my memoir was a personal and social responsibility. Publishing these specific narratives is one way she can use her power and voice in the world to [foster] change, justice, hope, healing, and empowerment. Our marketing tagline for *I Am Yours* is "it is time." Because it is. The silencing of women's stories [has enabled] our globe-spanning oppression in the past, so writing, publishing, and reading our narratives [gives us] the wisdom, fuel, and solidarity we need to heal and evolve.

What obstacles did you encounter as you began the process for publishing your books? How did you push past those obstacles?

SC: First, finding an agent who understood the book and was an excellent advocate. Second, overcoming imposter syndrome! Third, writing at breakneck speed. Fourth, having to do a crash course in the mechanics of publishing. Fifth, really coming to terms with how marginal feminist opinions are in so much of mainstream media. For example, a lot of what I write about isn't family friendly—sexual and domestic violence, racism and racist violence, the difficulties of pregnancy and childbirth, for example. Many editors [are still] profoundly uncomfortable with straightforward descriptions of whiteness or male domination. This has actually improved since Trump's election because of the blunt, self-evident fact of their power and meaning. I tend to weigh risks, benefits, anxieties, and objectives, and the benefits and objectives always seem to win out! That or the fact that I'm angry.

GH: I strongly second what Soraya says about imposter syndrome, and the only cure for that is doing the damn work. Ditto on writing at a fast and furious speed. Another hard thing for me was feeling comfortable "raising my voice" in the writing. My editor often had to coax me out of my conditioned default setting, which is to be safe and palatable for a male audience. That's not who this book is for! It's for women who are fed up with shouldering all the emotional labor without recognition or reprieve. I had to be given permission (and a nudge) to get my full self on the page.

RZ: I've realized that writing this memoir has perfectly equipped me to become the voice and advocate of this memoir, and its larger message. The first three decades of my life held a bizarre volume of adversity, trauma, and violence, so to survive and not die, I've had to redefine my understanding of obstacles, by learning to reframe and compartmentalize my focus and attention. I started writing *I Am Yours* in 2013, long before I'd published a single essay or had any writing credit or accolades to my name. I was on a very strict, high-stakes budget: My parents let me live with them, and I had a year to write a book with the specific goal of publication. [Up until that point], everything else in my life had failed. I was a "failed" wife and actress, and producing a publishable book was my plan B. I wrote with intense pressure, concentration, and discipline—a process that works very well for my personality.

The writing flowed without pause or obstacle. *I Am Yours* was on submission from June 2016 to November 2017. Others may have found this crushing, but this length of time played to my advantage. My agent, Lisa DiMona, and I realized *I Am Yours* needed that time in submission [because] it's a book that required an ideal fit, a [book editor] who understands it and loves it as her own. I spent that year-and-a-half training and launching myself as a speaker and essayist. By the time we found [my book editor] Dayna [Anderson], I'd stepped into my voice as an author, speaker, and thought-leader.

Moreover, over that time, society's consciousness and palate matured on the themes in my memoir, so the timing of my book is uncannily ideal.

Writing this book and becoming its voice has made me unshakable. I've released toxic people, and learned how to value, protect, and advocate for myself in ways I never did before. Harsh criticism, rejection, backlash, and trolls haven't mattered thus far, and they won't. Whenever I encounter misogyny, I laugh, knowing it's the last, vain, dying gasps of a system that knows its days are numbered. By rejecting the confines and privileges reaped from the hetero male gaze, I threaten the very people who profited off the pleasing behavior, silence, and docility of my past.

You've all written about the various ways that women are penalized for being vocal—in the workplace, in public spaces, and in personal relationships. Have you personally encountered those consequences? If so, how have you found the strength to continue speaking truth to power and people? What are steps other women can take to tap into that anger and wield it effectively?

SC: Yes, I think like most women, I have. Some of the limits and regulation are so built into our social mores, traditions, and habits that they're hard for some people to see [and] difficult to call out. For example, women are often ritually silenced in patriarchal religions—not allowed to serve in ministerial positions in churches, mosques, and synagogues. That teaches children powerful lessons about who has the right to public speech and authority. I think the denial of women's ability to represent divinity is a direct assault on girls and women. Online, women are also subjected to more direct policing in the form of sustained, sexualized, and often double- or triple-threat abuse. In my case, online harassment has involved everything from stereotypical name calling to violent and graphic rape threats.

GH: Every bit of writing I've published has received vitriol from men who are outraged that I've had the gall to write about my life on my terms. I'm really strict with my "don't read the comments" rule, but I've been assured by curious friends and family that there's some truly horrifying stuff down there about me. I delete a lot of emails without opening them. The bulk of the response to my writing, however, comes from women thanking me for using my voice in a way that resonates with them—that makes them feel less alone. That's what gives me the strength to keep doing this work. Of course, I want my work to impress visible change on our culture, but even if it did nothing more than make a few people feel less alone in their struggles, that would be wholly worth it.

RZ: Yes. For the first three decades of my life, I was penalized for being vocal. Now, I've found the strength to speak and continue speaking truth to power and people because of the revelation I had during my abusive marriage. Abusers require our silence [for them] to thrive. So, we *must* break silence. For me, the high stakes of that are the fuel I need to keep speaking. I encourage women to take [the following] steps: Do something that gives your voice a place to be heard. Keep a journal for yourself, even if you're lucky enough to have a supportive network of friends and family. Having a journal and writing essays in my laptop was quintessential [to] breaking free from my abusive husband. Gaslighting is a highly effective tool used by abusive partners, relatives, coworkers, politicians, and society to invalidate our feelings, particularly our anger; keep us second-guessing our intelligence, clarity, power, and self-sustenance; and disregard our right to respect, kindness, and justice.

Shaming and silencing our rightful rage is another part of an abuser's arsenal. They shame and gaslight us into silence and submission, manipulate us into thinking we deserve their cruelty, thereby normalizing their behavior. Consequently, by writing down your thoughts and giving voice to your anger on the page, especially if you're surrounded by people who continually invalidate and disregard your voice, you'll begin seeing that you're indeed intelligent and correct to feel and think the things you do. By bearing witness to your truth on the page, you'll begin filling with the courage and validation you need to start speaking up for yourself, start owning your power, and taking steps toward

leaving that harmful relationship, job, lifestyle, or environment. [Since] women have been conditioned to be highly empathic, nurturing creatures that are forever attuned to the wellbeing of others, women's rage is always felt in the presence of injustice. It's not something we that should be ashamed of.

Soraya, in Rage Becomes Her, *you write that there's a difference between anger, assertiveness, and aggression. Can you expand on this? How do we begin separating these out?*

SC: Anger is an emotion, whereas assertiveness and aggression are better described as behaviors. A confident girl can be assertive, which does not mean she's automatically aggressive or angry. Similarly, a person can be aggressive—stridently confronting someone, for example, without being angry at all. As we know, it's also possible to feel profoundly angry but not be assertive or aggressive. These are so often unhelpfully conflated, largely in an effort to tone police or silence girls and women.

We often associate anger with courage. In order to be vocal, we have to be brave. Is that something you believe in? If so, why?

SC: Yes, I really do believe this. It's so often the case that speaking, saying difficult truths out loud means challenging our families, teachers, coworkers, [and] employers. There are real risks and often threats. For me, speaking is still very challenging. However, I have found a good path in writing. While [speaking] can often be difficult, virtually anything I believe is worth saying comes flying out of my fingertips with little inhibition.

GH: In a culture where anger is essentially "forbidden" for women, I think it takes a lot of bravery to speak up about our anger and its sources without hedging to make everyone comfortable. Honestly, it's something I still struggle with.

RZ: I absolutely believe voice and courage go hand in hand, but thinking you have to be brave before you can speak can often work against you. [It can] keep you quiet until you have the courage to speak. I became brave because I began speaking; using my voice led to courage. The voice is a muscle. The more we use it, the stronger it grows. By practicing the muscle, you engage and develop audacity, until courage becomes synonymous with who you are, as easy as breathing, as seamless as speaking. In addition to writing, I've been performing spoken-memoir for a long time, and I love every minute of speaking truth to power. I love the feeling of connecting emotion with the visible or invisible audience. It's invigorating and liberating for both artist and audience to feel validated and unified in our humanity, be it our rage, our past wounds, our hope, our healing, our strength. By voicing our truth, we alleviate the ache of being human.

Who are the cultural figures you look to as you attempt to navigate and define anger? For instance, Serena Williams is it for me. When I look at how she's policed and how she responds, it offers me a chance to really examine the relationship between anger and race. Who is that person(s) for you?

SC: I thought a lot about this when I was researching the book. I found that I kept, over and over again, coming back to feminist philosophers whose work I admired or whose work I was only just finding through research. I was struck by how remarkable their descriptions and analyses and very deep thinking on the topic were. In particular, I found Miranda Flicker's work on epistemic justice clarifying. It resonated very deeply.

RZ: Lidia Yuknavitch's work has been monumental in shedding my shame about women's rage. Reading her memoir *The Chronology of Water* was enormously empowering, and [gave me] permission to accept and own the power of my rage. Gloria Steinem has always been an inspiring role model as well. To me, she emulates a different route to fighting and breaking patriarchy, of battling the system from the inside out. Steinem's Playboy exposé will always [be] one of the most inspiring and brilliant pieces of work and activism. [It was] brilliant in conception and execution. Infiltrating the toxic architecture, learning and exposing its mechanics, cutting the wires, and burning it all down is my type of Trojan Horse chess play—being strategic and precise, turning fury into fortitude.

84. • *DaMaris B. Hill*

CONCRETE (2017)

DaMaris B. Hill is an associate professor of creative writing and African American and Africana studies at the University of Kentucky. Her work examines the individual and collective realities of the human experience and includes fiction, poetry, and criticism. The anxieties of the contemporary world and representation in popular narratives are themes in her work; She explains, "I belong to a generation of people who do not fear death but are afraid that we may be forgotten." Hill won the Zora Neale Hurston/Richard Wright Creative Writing Award for Short Fiction in 2003 for her story "On the Other Side of Heaven—1957," and she was the 2016 Scholar in Residence for Critical Conversations Concerning Race and Teaching for the Center for the Enhancement of Learning and Teaching at the University of Kentucky. "Concrete" is a memoir that explores ideas of spirituality and citizenship within the context of black girlhood.

My Granddad was Captain America, but my father was just a man. He was not the defender of democracy that his father was, nor was he a flower. He wasn't the feminine lilac luster of bee balm like his mother, but weedy, maybe like the lush leaf of wild cane. Granddad raised him tough like a tin can of seasoned tobacco, taught him to lock away savory scents of life. He was something like his beard, soft and prickly. There was nothing left for him to be but a preacher. My daddy taught me to breathe, the power of the voice, and commanded me to have my say. So when I threatened Robert with death, I most likely meant it. I was nine.

Riley Curry is my favorite person on TV. She is much lighter than a paper bag and only little girls the color of Oreo cookies qualify as "cute" to me, but Riley's smile is well worth me ignoring my prejudice; she is stunning. She is loud in her laughter and loved, black girl magic. Her skin must be a soufflé mixture of honey and stardust. I know that her Afro puff acts as her human helmet. It allows her to breathe on this planet. She is something like an angel. I bet, she only looks like flesh and dense matter. I bet her daddy can't hold her still without her permission. Like if he reached for her, she would become ethereal and float away.

I may look like a sweet confection, some blend of *Werther's* hard caramel candy, the kind with a special space in the center to rest your tongue, but I am a concrete woman, something like a fountain among the cityscape. I am all phosphates and resin, the kind that gives the wet look to lush rough of rock. I lived a long time in Charm City, where divas chime in the voices of church bells. You know us when you see us; we carry our beauty like an heirloom. In Baltimore, we fancy and prettier than the women who powder their faces like porcelain.

All daddy's girls get an extra portion of "don't-do-right" when they leave Heaven for the birth canal. And this "don't-do-right" is nurtured from forgiving hugs, a daddy's arms can cover us from any evil like the wings of Michael the Archangel. So by the time we are in the world, we have forgotten all the instructions, the dos, the don'ts and the

never forgets. We don't know the boundaries, can't recall the expectations. How was I ignorant to the fact that I could frighten a bully, a boney white boy named Robert, into working with his worst enemy? I heard that the vice principal's office was a palace of punishments. She was a tall white woman with short hair, and she was rumored to have rulers ready for wristing in her right hand drawer.

Riley Curry is my role model. She is like the love child of Ma Rainey and The Beastie Boys, but her and her grandmother look like Anna Julia Cooper, the black woman that couldn't get a PhD at Columbia University so she sailed to France to study at the Sorbonne. She stunned them. Curtains and table clothes must hide the pixie dust trailing behind Riley; those reporters treat her ratchet. Are they mad that she is blessed? She is a Gabriel kind of girl. She already has enough money to buy them and the networks.

Baltimore is a land where the river and seas meet. It can't keep quiet or still. So when people tried to bind it in legal contracts, they had no right. They couldn't keep it there. Next, they steamed rolled it, prisoned it in tar and rocked it over. They were bent on paving it into submission. They tried to fix it by plaquering it with people names. Jailed it in fencing and blasted it with basketballs, like loose confetti. These balls keep the Baltimore seagulls at bay. No nesting or chicks near the courts, places where basketballs ricochet from backboard to black man to white guy to lesser known women to ghostly reporters to microphones across fiber optics and cameras that crowd around Steph Curry and the fluid swish of his satin shorts—and capture the glimmer image of an American hero, the man—until she stops it, this renegade role model Riley.

I had no choice and righteous words. Anna Julia Cooper said "Bullies are always cowards at heart and may be credited with a pretty safe instinct in scenting their prey." I didn't know her, but she was AME like me and my daddy was a local celebrity, a preacher, so church was all I knew. I wish my daddy would have known that my mighty words were perfumed in the moral right, not anger. They be from a fire shut up in my bones. The Old Testament is full of legacy and justice. Then, they were the only stories I knew. And, like my daddy, I was good with words. I could wield them like the sleeves of a wide satin robe and gold lined sash or like my daddy did silly church ladies that were easily moved by piano chords.

Robert had no business reaching for Lisa's hind parts, making her out to be the wrong kind of girl for me to play with. She was the only girl on the block, besides my sister. Her mamma looked like a Greek Janet Jackson, the kind of white woman that could be called pretty in public, and her step-daddy hung nude pictures on the wall, you know art, where a woman's lady parts would be apples or something. The kind that gave you an idea about what you will look like when you became a woman, somewhere around sixteen and Lisa had a big brother named Niko, who looked like Tarzan and taught us how to swing trees and one day when I became a woman I was going to kiss him and that bully Robert had no business touching "some body" that wasn't his.

I was just warning him, giving him a chance to choose righteousness. Anna Julia Cooper calls for us to be women who are so sure of our own social footing that we need not fear leaning to lend a hand to a falling sister. This, I remembered. So right there in the middle of recess, between Four Square and the basketball games, I stopped discussing all the mysteries of the sun with a boy named Daniel who had a special talent for setting ants on fire with a magnifying glass, to write Robert, the bully, a warning letter. I wasted no righteousness. I decorated it with expletives and illustrations. I stabbed it up, the note, to encourage him not to lay a finger on my friend. The bastard, bastard being the word that I am sure I misspelled in the letter, he ratted me out and ran to the vice-principal, a woman who promptly conspired with her enemy, the bully Robert, and called my daddy with their stories.

Daddy Curry is a believer; some think he is saintly. But everybody knows that calling out for Jesus doesn't make a black man bullet proof, so it's best to be a celebrity. The fans, some of them preachers and policemen, will recognize this kind of man as a citizen. They praise him because they believe he loves the game of basketball. False. Daddy Curry loves his daughter Riley and basketball protects them both, pads Daddy Curry and Riley from basic bias like the gear of an ice hockey goalie. Basketball celebrity is mighty, but it barely protects her from angry reporters, who tell us all about how disruptive she is. They want to shame her for having her say just like they did Jarena Lee, Sojourner Truth, Frances Harper, Anna Julia Cooper, Billie Holiday, Shirley Chisholm, Vashti McKenzie, Sandra Bland. . . .

In the city, concrete springs up like trees. From New York to DC, we have five story brownstones that are made of marble, some are rust colored or have gray faces. They line the streets in groves, up and down town. We have penthouses; they are the tree houses of the heavens. Sometimes they are so near to the sun that the rays threaten to bleach and scorch every fabric in the place. We use thick drapes and layer in curtains to protect all that is inside from damage.

I bet Daddy Curry likes high rises and thinks a penthouse is the closest thing on earth to living in Heaven. I bet Riley has heard about angels and their wings. I bet they are the inspiration for the way she wears them. You know, dressing the curtains over her like a cape. I bet when she is home, she flies around freely. I bet her smile is a blinding sunbeam in her daddy's face. Or maybe he forgets to look for her in the curtains, because he is busy with a reporter's request? Maybe Riley is a little too comfortable and close to getting burnt by her environment. They are both full of promise like a new beam of dawn, living miracles, but her daddy's skin is deep yellow and tough like a brass tobacco can and he doesn't know that Riley is lilac soft in her skin and sensitive to all types of things. He is a daddy and maybe he forgets that even girls that are the magic you made them will need protection from the elements that are harmless in isolation, but sting when collected against her.

Robert, the white boy, the bully, the boney one with the coffee cup haircut, did not die. He was rescued. I was beaten for not behaving. My daddy became something that resembled a man. He stormed in the house like he was pure lightning wearing a weather coat and wool hat. Not much for zoot suits, I'm sure all was nicely tailored underneath. I wouldn't know. Never taking off his coat or hat, he darted toward me with his belt in hand and cut me. I screamed. And in the chaos and commotion of him defending the common good, my protests were fleeting. I wanted to remind him that I only had confections for skin, wanted to remind him how sweet I was, not the soft chew of a tootsie roll, but I was dazzled like rock candy on a stick. I wanted him to remember that I was one of those good gifts.

Riley Curry retired from news reporting at age two. The night her father won it all in basketball. So when I hear that nine AME church members have been murdered while studying the Old Testament, I wish for Riley's smile. I wish she was in the way of the day-to-day of our lives, singing how blessed she is over top the funeral bells and sirens. Without her, there is nothing left to smile about on TV. Anna Julia Cooper said, "Let woman's claim be as broad in the concrete as the abstract." Susie Jackson was probably praying for the killer when she was shot. I know this and wonder; what is to be gained by staring into the sun? "Life must be something more than dilettante speculation."

Icarus flies too high. Some think the same of black women, particularly of those from Baltimore, who wear their grandmother's prayers and collected histories like bustles. They boast about a league of black women geniuses, brag on how blessed they are, saying things like "we raise our women from stars, not soil." Baltimore ain't got an earthy clutch of women. We are gilded, all waxed and wonderful, glossy. Even old women sparkle like glass in the streets. We take care, scrub our steps clean without dirtying our knees. We avoid the company of water rats. A kitchen table community, we feed folks with our politics, steam crabs and corn. Then we weight them with cake. We sweet and sweat. Even when we spit in your face, it tastes like salt water taffy.

I am hard-headed and mouthy. My Granddad was Captain America—he knew how this country worked. He knew my opinion was only worth cents on the dollar. He knew that I was made of light, but

my life would be murky. My daddy knew I needed a bit of faith to see my way through. Who knew that "don't-do-right" was some sort of a nickname for "don't-do-righteous"? A black woman being able to have her say was a calculated concern, a risk. Captain America kept warning my daddy about me, this grown mouth girl, lush with guts and giggles. He was the first to tell my daddy that nothing good could come from it and how he should reel me in on the edge of a whip. Zora Neale Hurston, another black woman they denied a PhD from both Columbia or Northwestern Universities, she too was determined to have her say. She traveled the world and wrote it all down. She say women be the mules of the world. I believe her.

Riley Curry put on your curtains and come to the rescue, fly by to see about me. The impossible is beginning to happen, the world is dressing me in a saddle and calling it a bodice. They keep telling me that it is all right and that it pinches because it is cased in coins. I say, I can't breathe. They tell me not to worry, stay pretty as a gypsy, but the harness at my mouth is a fancy cut of lace, the cheap kind made of recycled credit cards and plastic promises. It bites me in the corners of my mouth leaving blood in my words.

Be more careful. In Baltimore two young men got it wrong. They wrestled a black girl to the ground. They whipped her. Reports say rape. And while we celebrate Riley for being our heartbeat and number one, black women are keeping count of democracy's debt, staking our claims early, tacking the sidewalk with big chalk. When it looks like hopscotch, we are dancing and calling out for the drums. This is one of the ways black women pray, boldly in broad daylight, giggly and all up in your face, but some ain't no wiser. They smug and just one way, like them streets designed to slow you down at the Inner Harbor. It is like the whole world has abandoned their feet and has taken to those rental boats. They lack faith. They are paddling backwards and crashing into one another. They never notice the schools of mermaids below the tides or the light riding the water. Maybe all of this is hard to see, because the trash floats and white foams in caps of waves.

85. • *Wangari Maathai*

AN UNBREAKABLE LINK:
Peace, Environment, and Democracy (2008)

Wangari Maathai was a Kenyan activist who won the Nobel Peace Prize in 2004 for her work addressing deforestation and environmental conservation in conjunction with efforts to promote democracy, peace, and women's rights. Among her many achievements, she is perhaps best known for the Green Belt Movement, an environmental NGO she founded in 1977 to address the ways environmental degradation was affecting rural Kenyan women's access to food, water, and firewood. In "An Unbreakable Link: Peace, Environment, and Democracy," Maathai articulates the necessary interconnectedness of peace and sustainable development, and explains how the Green Belt Movement empowered women to improve their lives and their communities through grassroots activism. This piece was first published in the *Harvard International Review*.

The reality that sustainable development, democracy, and peace are indivisible concepts should not be denied. Peace cannot exist without equitable development, just as development requires sustainable management of the environment in a democratic and peaceful space. In order to advance peace, we must promote its underlying democratic institutions and ideals. In large part, this is only possible if management of the environment is pursued as a universal priority. Only a holistic approach that takes these interlinked factors into account can ensure effective, ecologically sustainable development.

The Norwegian Nobel Committee challenged the world to appreciate this link and, in doing so, broadened our understanding of peace and security. The task at hand is to act on this challenge. This entails motivating leaders to build fair and just societies in which resources are shared equitably; to protect the environment to ensure that the needs of future generations are not compromised; and to expand democratic space, particularly for women and minorities, so that minority representation can exist alongside majority rule. Setting a foundation for peace and development requires that citizens feel vested in a common future and empowered to realize their own potential in addressing the problems they face.

SUSTAINABLE DEVELOPMENT AND THE ENVIRONMENT

In many developing countries, particularly in Africa, environmental problems are relegated to the periphery because they do not appear to be as urgent as other issues. Protecting the environment is often seen as a convenient luxury when, in reality, it is a question of life and death. People cannot survive

Wangari Maathai, "An Unbreakable Link: Peace, Environment, and Democracy," *Harvard International Review*, vol. 29, no. 4, 2008, pp. 24–27. Reprinted with permission of *Harvard International Review*.

without clean drinking water, which comes from the forested mountains, or live without the food that is grown in fertile fields watered by the rains. Even the air we breathe needs trees to provide oxygen and recycle carbon dioxide. Our very survival depends on the survival of our fragile ecosystems.

The Green Belt Movement (GBM) was initiated in 1977 with the planting of seven trees on World Environment Day. It was conceived as a practical way to address the needs that rural women were facing, specifically for clean drinking water, nutritious food, firewood, and fodder. These are all benefits that come from the land. Simple methods of caring for the environment have a huge impact on the health of communities as well as on economic empowerment and growth. Because the land had been so degraded, an obvious solution was to rehabilitate it by planting trees. Trees stop soil erosion, thus conserving water. In addition, tree planting is a simple and realistic goal which guarantees successful results within a reasonable amount of time. In the Green Belt Movement model, trees provide women with the basic needs they require to sustain their families—food, fuel, shelter, and income— since women receive monetary compensation for every tree that survives up to three months.

Working with women to teach them how to plant and care for trees was a natural choice. Throughout Africa, women are the primary caretakers, tilling the land and feeding their families. As a result, they are often the first to feel the effects of environmental damage as vital resources become scarce and even unusable. Environmental degradation forces them to walk farther to attain wood for cooking and heating, to search for clean water, and to find new sources of food as old ones disappear. When the environment is destroyed, plundered, or mismanaged, it is their quality of life, and that of their children and families, that is ultimately undermined.

In addition to planting and nurturing new trees, it is imperative to protect and conserve the trees that still stand in forests around the world. Forests are catchment areas for water; without them, flash floods would carry away the soil and nutrients needed for agriculture. Forests also serve as major carbon sinks, trapping carbon dioxide and thus helping to maintain the climate. Finally, forests filter and purify water supplies, while providing a habitat for wildlife.

The United Nations recommends that each country have at least 10 percent of its land covered with forests. Very few countries are able to claim that they have achieved this goal. In Kenya, for example, forest cover is less than 2 percent; from 1950 to 2000, Kenya lost 90 percent of its forests. To compound this problem, for the last 80 years, the Kenyan government has been planting exotic species of trees for the timber industry, often in indigenous forests. As the trees are planted, people are invited to go into the forests and grow crops along with the exotic trees in a system known as *shamba*. Under *shamba*, subsistence farmers are supposed to plant trees before moving on to a fresh plot of land after three years of farming. Unfortunately, much of the clear-felled plantations have not been replanted with tree seedlings, and some farmers refuse to vacate land earmarked for tree planting, resulting in a serious lag in reforestation. Currently, the Kenyan government is trying to reintroduce this destructive practice, partly to appease demand for agricultural land and partly to win favor with voters. Eventually, *shamba* will undermine the livelihood of millions of Kenyans unless the process is quickly reversed. Commercial plantations are not forests; on the contrary, they are biological deserts. The Green Belt Movement and similar organizations are trying to fill this gap by prioritizing tree planting with communities in degraded forest areas. So far, these efforts have proven highly successful, and there is great hope for further forest restoration.

PEACE AND EQUITABLE RESOURCE MANAGEMENT

A degraded environment leads to a scramble for scarce resources and may culminate in poverty and conflict. As resources become scarcer or are squandered—whether they be land, water, hydrocarbons, timber, or minerals—some will seek to control them by excluding others. Consequently, the excluded seek justice and dignity through whatever means they can, often resulting in conflict. In fact, most conflicts in the world today relate in some way to competition over the access, control, and distribution of resources. Sometimes these conflicts take form within a state's own borders as local disputes over water, grazing ground, and agricultural land. Others are international conflicts, such as those in the Middle East. Almost without exception, these conflicts are over the distribution of these limited resources: who will own them, who will control them, and who will be excluded.

Inequality often results from such situations, contributing to desperation and further conflict. To ensure the equitable provision of resources, a country must guarantee the rule of law and basic human rights—including the right to be heard, to eat, to have water, to receive quality education, and to live in a clean and healthy environment. Good governance is necessary to give a voice to societies' weak and vulnerable populations, even while it accepts the decision of the majority. Most importantly, it seeks justice and equity for all, irrespective of race, religion, gender, and any other parameters, which can be used to discriminate and exclude.

Many African leaders have recognized the need for good governance in their respective countries and in the greater region, realizing that despite the continent's wealth in resources, development has sorely lagged. Through multinational deliberation and cooperative organs like the African Union, there is movement toward greater engagement by leaders in order to consult with one other and decide amongst themselves how to end conflicts, rather than wait for assistance from external resources. To further promote these initiatives, African governments need to be supported—both by their own people and by one other. While challenges such as corruption and resource mismanagement do remain in many countries, it is encouraging to see leaders committing to resolve conflicts peacefully and give development a chance.

DEVELOPMENT AND PEACE THROUGH PARTICIPATION

The strengthening of civil society and grassroots movements to catalyze change is essential for development and peace. Doing so enhances the democratization process and respect for human rights. Weak civil societies cannot hold their leaders accountable to the people. As a result, it becomes much easier for citizens to ignore the rule of law. In contrast, a strong civil society can also be an important vehicle for the delivery of services like health, education, and protection of the environment.

As a civil society institution, the Green Belt Movement initially started off as a way to address the immediate needs of rural women. It quickly grew into a movement that educated citizens about the links between the problems they were facing, the degradation of the environment, and governmental policy. Initially, empowering citizens was difficult because they had been persuaded to believe that they were poor not only in capital, but also in the knowledge and skills they needed in order to address their challenges. They were conditioned to believe that solutions to their problems had to come from the "outside." This way of thinking led to a dependency syndrome that was disempowering.

In order to help communities to understand these linkages, the Green Belt Movement developed a citizen's education program. In this program, women identify their problems, the causes of these problems, and then possible solutions. They make connections between their own personal actions and the problems they witness in the environment and in society. Women then come to understand that meeting their needs depends on their environment being healthy and well-managed, and that they must be part of the solution.

This is one of the most significant messages of the Green Belt Movement's holistic approach toward development: the need to expand "democratic space" by educating, mobilizing, and empowering local communities to take action and create change. People must come to realize that they should not wait for local authorities, government, or development agencies to bring about change. Rather, all individuals themselves can and should take action, no matter how small that action may seem. These individual, small acts have resulted in the planting of over 30 million trees in the past 30 years. Furthermore, the courage and commitment of ordinary citizens can push for political change and demand reform from the government. In 2002, ordinary people and civil society organizations realized Kenya's peaceful transition from a one-party state to a democratic government.

TURNING THEORY INTO ACTION

The experience of the Green Belt Movement underscores the link between the environment, development, democracy, and peace. A country cannot develop where there is no peace; peace, in turn, will not prevail if resources are mismanaged or put in the hands of a few at the expense of many. Finally, sustainable development and peace can only be ensured if citizens participate in protecting and restoring their environment and demanding a place at the decision-making table. Understanding these indivisible links is critical to promoting sustainable development.

A number of excellent initiatives indicate that leaders, international organizations, and civil society are already acting to promote these fundamental pillars of development. One example at the regional level is the Congo Basin Forest Partnership. The forests of the Congo Basin are among some of the last remaining large areas of primeval forested lands in the world, second only to the Amazon Basin. Together with the forest ecosystem in Southeast Asia, they are considered the "three lungs" of the planet. The Congo Basin ecosystem includes almost one-quarter of the world's tropical forests and is home to 400 mammal species and more than 10,000 plant species.

It provides food, materials, and shelter for over 20 million people and plays an important role as a global sink for carbon dioxide. However, logging, hunting, agriculture, and the oil and mining industries are degrading these forests at a rate of two million acres every year.

The Congo Basin Forest Partnership brings together about 30 governmental and non-governmental organizations to manage the Congo Basin in a sustainable manner. The Congo Basin Forest is located within the boundaries of Cameroon, Central Africa Republic, Democratic Republic of Congo, Equatorial Guinea, Gabon, and Republic of Congo. The goal of the partnership is to promote economic development and alleviate poverty through conservation programs in the region, improve local governance through natural resource conservation, and enhance resource management through control of illegal logging and wildlife poaching. This partnership is the result of a growing understanding that managing forest ecosystems' resources sustainably and equitably can help stabilize the planet's atmosphere and ecology. Additionally, doing so can also help foster peace in an area that has been historically torn by conflict over resources. Under the leadership of Former Canadian Prime Minister Paul Martin and myself, the government of Britain has been the first to make a substantial contribution to support the implementation of the Congo Basin Forest Partnership agreement. We are currently working hard to develop a governance structure that will allow other donor agencies to provide similar financial support.

Another important example of an effort to expand democratic space and bring the voices of African people into decision-making processes is the formation of the African Union's Economic, Social, and Cultural Council (ECOSOCC). According to its Statutes adopted in 2004, ECOSOCC's objective is to establish an assembly of civil society organizations from all African countries to facilitate dialogue between governments and civil society and to promote African civil society's participation in implementing policies and programs of the African Union. It provides African civil society with an opportunity to have a voice during the AU Heads of State summit.

In 2005, I was asked to preside over the formation of this assembly and was proud to do so. I strongly believe that until a critical mass of Africans are sufficiently empowered to hold their leaders responsible and accountable, Africa's resources will continue to be plundered for the benefit of others.

The Green Belt Movement is not alone in recognizing the importance of empowerment through environmental action. Indeed, thousands of other organizations around the world are educating and mobilizing citizens and instilling in them a sense of responsibility that deliberate, doable steps can and do make a difference. One such effort is The Billion Tree Campaign, which is an initiative that encourages people, communities, business and industries, civil society organizations, and governments to plant trees. Participants record their pledges on the campaign's website. The campaign strongly encourages the planting of indigenous trees and trees that are appropriate to the local environment, demonstrating the power of organized efforts.

A CALL TO ACTION

It is imperative that humanity stops threatening its life-support system and starts treating the earth and its resources with respect. This is wonderfully articulated in the word *mottainai*, which is a Japanese concept that means "do not waste resources," "have respect for the resources around us," and "use them with a sense of gratitude." It personifies the need to respect our environment and encapsulates the concept that the Green Belt Movement has been actively promoting for decades: reduce, reuse, and recycle. To this, we should add one more word: "repair."

The concept of *mottainai* captures how each one of us can protect the environment through simple, deliberate, conscious efforts every day. We can use both sides of a piece of paper before discarding it; we can conserve water every time we turn on the tap; we can use public transportation; and we can always plant more trees. Finally, we must remember that while the rest of the species on the planet can survive without us, we cannot survive without them. In protecting the survival of other species and respecting their right to be, we can, in turn, ensure our own.

86. • *Christina E. Bejarano*

THE LATINA ADVANTAGE IN US POLITICS:
Recent Example with Representative Ocasio-Cortez (new)

Christina Bejarano is professor of multicultural women's and gender studies at Texas Woman's University. Her research examines the increased political success and power of racial/ethnic minority women in US electoral politics. Her two books, *The Latina Advantage: Gender, Race, and Political Success* and *The Latino Gender Gap in US Politics*, focus on Latinx political participation and political candidates. In "The Latina Advantage in US Politics: Recent Examples with Representative Ocasio-Cortez,"

Bejarano looks at the rising political influence of Latinas and how this trend challenges traditional assumptions about viable political candidates and the impact of Latinas on the electoral environment in the United States.

Women of color are proving vital to our changing political climate, both as key voters and political candidates. Their recent campaigns are also broadening our traditional political models for candidates and their particular style of campaigns. Their rising political influence has become even more evident with the results of the 2016 US presidential election and the 2018 midterm election. We now more regularly discuss politically influential women of color, like "The Squad" of four women elected to Congress in 2018 who are now household names and celebrities: Representatives Ilhan Omar, Alexandria Ocasio-Cortez, Rashida Tlaib, and Ayanna Pressley. These electoral wins are significant not just because women advanced to win their contests, but also because they are breaking the mold for who is considered an ideal, traditional, or viable candidate.

This growing attention toward women of color in US politics has also sparked renewed discussions about the potential for diverse and intersecting identities to shape and influence our electoral environment. In my larger work such as *The Latina Advantage: Gender, Race, and Political Success* and *The Latino Gender Gap in U.S. Politics*, from which this essay is drawn, I question how diverse identities can intersect to create a unique set of not only opportunities but challenges as well. In addition, I analyze the growing political influence of women of color, as well as their potential impact on the political environment and prospective staying force. These questions become even more pressing given the results of the 2016 and 2018 elections, as they continue to challenge our traditional notions of what motivates people to get involved in political activism and what helps a political candidate be successful. This essay delves into these important questions while focusing on the recent success of women of color in elective office, most notably the success of Representative Ocasio-Cortez. This research contributes to the larger political debate

over identity and the rising influence of women of color in US politics.

FOCUS ON WOMEN OF COLOR IN POLITICS

We should take an intersectional approach to study women of color's experiences in politics. This includes highlighting how women of color are gaining more political authority and voting power in US politics. This growing phenomenon is significant in that it challenges researchers' focus on the white majority in studies of political impact. Our traditional assumptions about politics need to be broadened to more fully understand the growing political impact of women of color.

Political participation rates for US racial and ethnic minority females have increased dramatically, exceeding increases for their male counterparts (Bejarano 2014). Compared to their male counterparts, women of color not only participate more; they also express distinctive policy views that have helped them lead the way in boosting and attracting increased minority political participation in US politics. This phenomenon within communities of color is consistent with the modern gender gap in political participation rates, vote choice, and policy attitudes that we see across all racial and ethnic groups (Bejarano 2014). For example, women of color have gained increased political attention in recent elections given their high voter turnout rates that exceeded those of their male counterparts. In particular, women of color had increased support for Democratic presidential candidates in the recent elections, compared to their male counterparts, and this support often proved pivotal by helping the winning candidate gain needed votes.

Racial and ethnic minority women have also made significant strides in attaining political office in the

United States. Female representatives of color, both in the US Congress and state legislatures, make up a greater proportion of all representatives of color, as compared to the proportion of white female representatives among white elected officials. In 2019, there were 2,131 women serving in state legislatures, which is about 29 percent of the total available seats (CAWP 2019). This includes 543 racial/ethnic minority women, who represent about 26 percent of the total number of female state legislators: 312 African Americans, 46 Asian American/Pacific Islander, 127 Latinas, and 22 Native American females (CAWP 2019). For context, the women of color elected to state legislatures was 250 in 1999 and 350 in 2009 (CAWP 1999, 2009). However, despite the fact that women of color candidates are gaining success, it is important to keep in mind that they are still underrepresented in comparison to their numbers in the overall population.

Women of color have also made steady progress getting elected to Congress with their number of seats in Congress increasing from 18 in 1999 to 21 in 2009 (CAWP 1999, 2009). In 2019, there were 47 members of Congress identifying as women of color, out of a total of 127 women serving in the 116th Congress. The 2019 delegation of women of color constitutes 37 percent of all women members or about 9 percent of the total members of Congress (CAWP 2019). This diverse delegation included the first two Native American women to join the House of Representatives with the election of Representatives Deb Haaland and Sharice Davids. In addition, the first two Muslim women were elected to the House with Representatives Omar and Tlaib. The 2018 election also marked some distinctive records for Latinas in Congress, with the first two Latinas elected to Congress from Texas with Representatives Escobar and Garcia, as well as the election of the youngest women to Congress with Representative Ocasio-Cortez (who was 29 at the time of her election). The election of these women of color drew increased national attention especially since they did not fit the mold of traditional candidates: the women challenged conventional wisdom on when and how to run for elective office. They also continue to challenge the expectations for how elected officials should behave once in office. A recent example is Ocasio-Cortez, who, even though she is a newcomer to congressional office, has consistently challenged not only the Trump administration and the Republican Party, but also the leadership of the Democratic Party.

LATINA DISTINCTIVENESS IN POLITICS

In particular, Latinas are increasingly attracting political attention as voters, political candidates, and elected officials (Navarro et al. 2016). Latinos are 16.3 percent of the total US population according to the 2010 Census—up by 43 percent over the previous decade. As their numbers grow, Latinos are becoming more active and influential in politics. Latinas, in particular, are often catalysts of political change, the ones who take the lead in mobilizing families and communities. There is also a growing distinctiveness of Latinas in their support for political parties and their political participation rates, which are setting them apart from their male counterparts (Bejarano 2014). As a result, Latinas are gaining ever more political authority and voting power—and using them to dramatically influence American politics.

The growing political presence of Latinas can significantly influence the nature of Latino political representation in the United States. Latinas first attained national electoral office in Congress in 1989 with Representative Ros-Lehtinen and have gained increased representation since the 1990s. In 2019, there were 127 Latina state legislators, which represents 6 percent of all female state legislators (CAWP 2019). In 2019, there were also 13 Latinas in Congress, which is about 10 percent of all females in Congress and 35 percent of all Latinos in Congress. Latinas have increased their presence in Congress and 2016 marked the first Latina elected to the Senate with Senator Cortez Masto.

Even though Latinas are making gains in US politics, they—like women in general—are still underrepresented overall, which means their number in the general population is not comparable to their number in elective office. For example, Latinas are about 17 percent of the US population but only represent less than 2 percent of the total elected officials across Congress, statewide elected executive offices, and state legislatures (Bejarano 2018). Therefore, even though Latinas and other women of color have made steady strides in political office and represent a substantial proportion of all minorities elected to office, there remains progress left to be made to attain a more equitable share of political offices.

With recent examples of historic electoral wins for Latinas, such as the win for Representative Ocasio-Cortez, we also need to keep in mind that these non-traditional candidates will have to navigate the unique challenges that can come from their distinction of being the possible "first" in their campaigns and elective positions. There are challenges and advantages that can come from the "first" distinction for many of the women of color running for office in recent elections. In addition to being the "first" Latina or woman of color to be elected from key states, there are additional challenges they will face as first-time candidates running for politics. For example, Representative Ocasio-Cortez did not have prior political experience before she decided to run for political office for the first time. While all first-time candidates face challenges by virtue of being new to the effort of running for office, female candidates may face particular and gendered challenges. For example, women are more likely to question whether they are prepared and qualified to run for office (Lawless and Fox 2016). Representative Ocasio-Cortez highlights this challenge for first-time candidates, especially those who are women of color, in her 2018 powerful campaign ad which starts with her saying, "women like me aren't supposed to run for office" (Bejarano 2018).

LATINA POLITICAL ADVANTAGES

Minority female political candidates are often represented as facing compound electoral disadvantages. In my 2013 book *The Latina Advantage*, however, I challenge this assumption and show that multiple subordinated identities can bring political advantages too—in this instance, helping Latina candidates overcome burdens from either their gender or ethnic identities.

Certainly, my argument does not assume that minority women completely escape the double disadvantages that come from being female and racial and ethnic minorities—both historically underrepresented and marginalized identity groups within US politics—but rather that these disadvantages may also come with certain advantages.

As a result of their diverse identities, Latinas and other women of color have the potential to attract more diverse voter coalitions than their male counterparts. Instead of being a hindrance, a candidate's gender can help her deemphasize disadvantages that come from ethnic differences from many voters. In addition, a female minority candidate may get a boost in electoral support from both fellow minorities and women of all backgrounds. Due to their dual identities, Latinas are actually able to attract more diverse voter coalitions than their male counterparts. Generally, in fact, Latinas are more likely than their male Latino counterparts to win elections to represent districts with a majority of non-Latino residents.

In addition, Latinas benefit from their diverse set of political skills or candidate qualities. Latinas have a long history of community activism and civic participation (Hardy-Fanta 1993; Gutierrez et al. 2007), which is a key source of their electoral support or their "Latina advantage." Latinas often serve as key actors in Latino community involvement, providing both the essential leadership and organizational tools to effect change (Garcia et al. 2007; Hardy-Fanta 1993). For example, Representative Ocasio-Cortez had not held political office before she decided to run for office; in fact, she had a job as a bartender a year before she ran for Congress. However, she did have extensive experience working in community organizing and was politically active.

Previous research has also found that Latinas have a different view of political involvement than

Latino men (Hardy-Fanta 1993). Latinas generally have a more participatory vision of politics, where they focus on grassroots organizations and community work, while Latino males tend to focus more on electoral politics (Hardy-Fanta 1993; Jones-Correa 1998; Pardo 1998). In addition, Latinas are socialized to have a different set of civic skills than Latino males, which include more community involvement and increased responsibility within the family (Lopez 2003). Moreover, Latinas often view their political participation "as an extension of their daily lives, which informs their mobilization strategies and effectiveness with the Latino community" (Hardy-Fanta 1993, 2; Bejarano, 2013, 60). For example, Representative Ocasio-Cortez was able to relate and connect on a deeper level with a younger generation of supporters by strategically and expertly using social media.

Latinas and other women of color are increasingly motivated to get involved in their communities as political activists, especially when there is an issue of importance at stake. Latinas are also likely to take the initiative and personally organize their communities to attempt to bring about change. Latinas often motivate other Latinos to participate in US politics, by organizing naturalization and voter registration drives and volunteering for local political campaigns (Jones-Correa 1998). They apply their leadership and organizational skills to their political work on political campaigns, social movements, and community organizations (Garcia and Sanchez 2008; Pardo 1998). As a result, Latinas are perceived to be the key to mobilizing Latino families and communities. Overall, Latinas' increased community participation may very well provide them with stronger civic skills and stronger ties to their community and political institutions. In addition, Latinas' community involvement can also be linked to their higher political participation levels and high success rates as political candidates (Bejarano 2014).

Latinas like Representative Ocasio-Cortez were able to draw on her unique experiences, background, and perspectives to bring together a winning coalition of supporters. In particular, Representative Ocasio-Cortez's win, especially during the Democratic primary, was shocking for several reasons, including the fact that she was able to unseat a ten-term incumbent, Representative Joe Crowley, and was able to do so by implementing a grassroots campaign. She sent a tweet after the 2018 primary election and clarified that she did not win for solely "demographic" reasons; rather, she was able to gather the support of voters of all kinds (Bensman 2018). She also remarked that the incumbent candidate may have had money and experience going for him, but she was able to pull together a cadre of dedicated volunteers and supporters (Bensman 2018). She also clarified that she won because she outworked the competition and went door-to-door to contact as many Democrats as possible, especially those who were unregistered and unlikely voters (often the more diverse and younger communities) (Bensman 2018). In addition, "Ocasio-Cortez's campaign highlighted the value and significance of Latina/o political engagement, the long trajectory of immigration that bolstered (not threatened) the entire country and the district specifically, and how a mobilized electorate could not just change the fate of the primary but also the composition of Congress" (Sampaio 2018).

Therefore this set of multiple political and civic strengths exhibited by Latinas and other women of color in the United States gives them potential advantages when they choose to get involved in politics. However, they often have to be encouraged to channel their strengths and unique experiences toward a political career, since they may not think they are prepared or the stereotypical candidate or activist. As women of color continue to think and act differently from their male counterparts in politics, they are likely to accumulate more political authority and voting power, putting them in a position to dramatically influence the course of American politics for everyone in their community and beyond.

WORKS CITED

Bejarano, Christina. *The Latina Advantage: Gender, Race, and Political Success*. University of Texas Press, 2013.

Bejarano, Christina. *The Latino Gender Gap in U.S. Politics*. Routledge Press, 2014.

Bejarano, Christina. 2018. "Measuring Success for Latina Politics in 2018." GenderWatch2018.org. http://www.genderwatch2018.org/measuring-success-latina-politics-2018/.

Bensman, Miriam. "They Had Money, We Had People." *Dissent Magazine*. July 9, 2018. https://www.dissentmagazine.org/blog/they-had-money-we-had-people-alexandria-ocasio-cortez.

Center for American Women and Politics (CAWP). "Fact Sheet: Women of Color in Elective Office 1999." https://cawp.rutgers.edu/women-color-elective-office-1999. Accessed November 2019.

Center for American Women and Politics (CAWP). "Fact Sheet: Women of Color in Elective Office 2009." https://cawp.rutgers.edu/women-color-elective-office-2009. Accessed November 2019.

Center for American Women and Politics (CAWP). "Fact Sheet: Women of Color in Elective Office 2019." https://cawp.rutgers.edu/women-color-elective-office-2019. Accessed August 2019.

Garcia, F. Chris, and Gabriel R. Sanchez. *Hispanics and the U.S. Political System*. Pearson/Prentice Hall, 2008.

Garcia, Sonia R., Valerie Martinez-Ebers, Irasema Coronado, Sharon A. Navarro, and Patricia A Jaramillo. *Politicas: Latina Public Officials in Texas*. University of Texas Press, 2007.

Gutierrez, Jose Angel, Michelle Melendez, and Sonia Adriana Noyola. *Chicanas in Charge: Texas Women in the Public Arena*. AltaMira Press, 2007.

Hardy-Fanta, Carol. *Latina Politics, Latino Politics: Gender, Culture, and Political Participation in Boston*. Temple University Press, 1993.

Jones-Correa, Michael. 1998. "Different Paths: Gender, Immigration and Political Participation." *International Migration Review* vol. 32, pp. 326–49.

Lawless, Jennifer L., and Richard L. Fox. *It Takes a Candidate: Why Women Don't Run for Office*. Cambridge UP, 2016.

Lopez, Nancy. *Hopeful Girls, Troubled Boys: Race and Gender Disparity in Urban Education*. Routledge Press, 2003.

Navarro, Sharon A., Samantha L. Hernandez, and Leslie A. Navarro, eds. *Latinas in American Politics: Changing and Embracing Political Tradition*. Lexington Books, 2016.

Pardo, Mary. *Mexican American Women Activists, Identity and Resistance in Two Los Angeles Communities*. Temple UP, 1998.

Sampaio, Anna. 2018. "Alexandria Ocasio-Cortez and the Myth of the Morena Tide." GenderWatch 2018.org. http://www.genderwatch2018.org/myth-morena-tide/.

87. • *Michael Winter*

I WAS THERE (2008)

Michael Winter was a disability rights activist who served as president of the National Council on Independent Living. In "I Was There" he describes his participation in nonviolent direct action in support of the Americans with Disabilities Act (ADA), the landmark civil rights law passed in 1990 that provides protections against discrimination for people with disabilities. His first-person account of civil disobedience demonstrates how the work of activists in the disability rights movement raised awareness about the barriers faced by those with disabilities.

On the afternoon of March 11th, I was very excited as I thought about the next day's activities. I had been elected President of the National Council on Independent Living and had dedicated myself and the organization to working with ADAPT to ensure that we do anything and everything necessary to get the Americans with Disabilities Act signed. At the same time, I was on a Transit Board and the Executive Director of the Berkley Center for Independent Living. I felt very fortunate that I was able to participate in this historical event.

The next morning, I thought about the many times that I had been discriminated against: being forced to go to a "special" segregated school instead of integrated ones, not being allowed on a Continental Trailways bus because of my disability, and being told in a restaurant that "We don't serve disabled people." But I also had very positive thoughts about what a great life and great opportunities I had to that point. I was determined to work to overcome the injustices of discrimination and create more positive opportunities for myself and for others with disabilities.

As I listened to the speakers on that day, I considered how life had prepared me for this moment of civil disobedience. Although I had taken part in such "street theatre" before, this seemed like the crowning glory of them all.

After the speeches, we started chanting "What do we want?" "ADA!" "When do we want it?" "NOW!" The chants became louder and louder, and ultimately my good friend Monica Hall told me that it was time to get out of my wheelchair and crawl up the steps to the Capitol Building. Monica took my wheelchair, smiled and said, "I'll meet you at the top!" I started to climb step by step towards the top. At the very beginning, I looked up and thought that I would never make it. But right below me was a seven-year-old girl who was making the same climb, step by step, her wheelchair left somewhere below or whisked somewhere above. This was Tom Olin's young niece. I felt an obligation to be a role model for this girl and we ultimately made it to the top together.

Some people may have thought that it was undignified for people in wheelchairs to crawl in that manner, but I felt that it was necessary to show the country what kinds of things people with disabilities have to face on a day-to-day basis. We had to be willing to fight for what we believed in.

The next day, we visited the Capitol under the pretense of wanting to go on a tour. I was one of the only demonstrators wearing a tie; my Board of Directors insisted that as the CEO of a nonprofit organization, I might as well look professional if I was going to get arrested. There was a lovely young woman who was volunteering at the Capitol to give tours over the summer, and as more and more people arrived she approached me and shared her excitement at giving a tour to so many people with disabilities.

A few minutes later we all began chanting, and Congressmen came to assure us that the ADA would be passed. These individuals included House Speaker Foley, Republican leader Michel, and Congressman Hoyer. We got louder and louder and all of a sudden, chains came out and people began to chain themselves in a circle. The young volunteer came up to me and asked, "Do you think they're ready for their tour now?" I was sorry and somewhat amused to be the one to tell her that no one would be touring on that day and that many individuals would probably be arrested.

Soon after this, the Capitol police began arresting people and cutting chains. The whole process took 2 to 3 hours and resulted in my own arrest. We were all sent to the Capitol jail and were scheduled to appear before a judge late that evening. In jail, I had the honor of being with Wade Blank, Michael Auberger, and many other disabled activists. It is ironic and perhaps fitting that I now oversee the implementation and compliance to the transportation provisions of the ADA, the law that we all fought so hard for.

I remember Evan Kemp watching the proceedings very closely from the back of the courtroom, and I remember our attorney, Tim Cook, informing the judge that we all pled guilty, that all of the defendants were part of the "Wheels of Justice" campaign to end the segregation of and the discrimination towards people who use wheelchairs. All of the defendants were released on our own recognizance and were given one year of probation.

I was the only one who was fined, because I held a job with significant income, and I was proud to "donate" $100.00 to the cause of justice and equality. Those few days and the passing of the ADA were monumental for me as an individual and an activist, but also for people across the United States of America. We now have taken steps to move towards inclusion and away from segregation and discrimination of people with disabilities.

I often think of these days and the lessons and power that they brought me in my current job as Director of the Office of Civil Rights at the Federal Transit Administration. It is important to keep these memories fresh in our minds and to avoid complacency in the face of injustice.

88. • *Sarah E. Fryett*

LAUDABLE LAUGHTER:
Feminism and Female Comedians (2017)

Sarah E. Fryett is an assistant professor in the department of English and writing at the University of Tampa. Her work revolves around feminist and queer theory, as well as humor/comedy studies, pedagogy, and media studies. Her recent publications include a piece on late-night television show host Samantha Bee, an essay on hegemonic masculinity in bromance films, and a forthcoming article on the television show *Orphan Black* and the image of the female hero. In "Laudable Laughter: Feminism and Female Comedians," Fryett argues that female comedians challenge reigning normative discourses surrounding sexuality and gender through humorous reversals, incongruity, and frankness.

Comedian Elvira Kurt—imagining an audience member's thoughts in one of her skits—inquires: "If you're a lesbian, and we are laughing at you, does this mean we're gay?" She responds, after a pause and a widening of the eyes: "Yes, yes, it does. Let the parade begin!" ("Elvira"). Titters, guffaws, and clapping follow this bit. Why is the audience laughing? Why do I laugh each and every time I hear this piece (which is a lot, after all, as I am writing an essay on it)? The answer is simple: Kurt's comedy challenges a number of stereotypes—being gay is contagious/gays and lesbians love parades—that pervade our heteronormative culture. This observation led me to contemplate comedic performance as critical of cultural norms, and if, as Kathleen Rowe notes, our culture prefers "women's tears over their laughter," we must ask what might laughter enable (Rowe 1995, 214)?

In thinking about female comedians, the following question comes to mind: Is comedy a viable arena for a feminist critique of patriarchy and heteronormativity? Yes. Laughter is political in its capacity to be critical and creative through a challenge to the institutions of patriarchy and heteronormativity. Though there are many forms of laughter, such as nervous laughter and laughter at awkward moments, here I am referring to the physical and mental laughing moment elicited from a comedic performance. Using the nineteenth-century German philosopher Friedrich Nietzsche in conjunction with an interspersing of feminist theorists, I construct a framework for theorizing the transformative power of comedy and its potential ramifications. Focusing on Elvira Kurt, Wanda Sykes, and Amy Schumer, I offer an interdisciplinary textual analysis that demonstrates how female comedians challenge reigning normative discourses surrounding sexuality and gender through humorous reversals, incongruity, and frankness.

I first look to Nietzsche because, though not explicit, a close reading of his works advances a conceptualization of laughter as a transformative practice or, as he would phrase it, a practice of transvaluation. Transvaluation is a process whereby concepts are forced into a rigorous examination—challenged and destroyed. Through that challenge and destruction, an opening is created to allow for new possibilities/new ways of thinking. Though Nietzsche was responding, in his conceptualization of transvaluation, to what he saw as societal problems of the nineteenth century, the process can be applied to any structure of values that portends to construct the *truth*. I borrow his term to articulate a twenty-first-century feminist practice of laughter that radically challenges binaries of natural/unnatural and normal/deviant.

Often overlooked is *how* transvaluation occurs, and I argue that one possibility is laughter. In Nietzsche's *Thus Spoke Zarathustra*, he makes apparent this idea. *Thus Spoke Zarathustra* offers a variety of critiques concerning religious values such as morality, good and bad, and notions of the body, using an odd amalgamation of philosophy and narrative. The text chronicles the character Zarathustra as he travels through the countryside. Zarathustra, remembering his own council, notes, "I told them to overthrow their old professorial chairs wherever that old conceit [good and evil] had sat; I told them to laugh at their great masters of virtue and their saints and poets and world redeemers" (Nietzsche 2006, 157). Laughter, a physical and mental phenomenon, functions as a method and a tool to overcome the old conceits of the great masters. That is,

laughter—allowing a lightness of mood to infiltrate the serious—forces a questioning of what is conceived to be truth, the supposed natural and innate. Toward the end of this section, Nietzsche writes: "let each truth be false to us which was not greeted by one laugh" (Nietzsche 2006, 169). Each "truth" must be greeted with a laugh because the laugh challenges foundations and refuses closure and sedimentation; it is the catalyst for change and revision. This Nietzschean laugh of transvaluation is essential to a feminist practice that is rooted in destabilizing the institutions of patriarchy and heteronormativity and the narratives that maintain those systems.

Feminist theorists less than a hundred years later interested in challenging the institutions of patriarchy and heteronormativity are many, but only a small sampling engage with the notion of laughter. Hélène Cixous is one of them, and she tackles the discourse of psychoanalysis—a direct corollary of the institution of patriarchy—within her essay "The Laugh of the Medusa." She interrogates structures of language, specifically phallocentric (privileging of the masculine) language, among other discursive practices, which erase and silence women and women's sexuality. Though not employing the Nietzschean term "transvaluation," Cixous transvalues the narrative of psychoanalysis, through a laughing, parodic revisioning of the Medusa myth. Medusa, a Greek mythological figure beheaded for supposedly desecrating a temple, is conceptualized as a female monster. Cixous questions and answers:

> Wouldn't the worst be, isn't the worst, in truth, that women aren't castrated, that they have only to stop listening to the Sirens (for the Sirens were men) for history to change its meaning? You only have to look at the Medusa straight on to see her. And she's not deadly. She's beautiful and *she's laughing*. (my emphasis, Cixous 1976, 885)

By transforming the raging snake-haired woman into a laughing beauty, Cixous accomplishes two actions. On one level, this reimagining destabilizes the mythological Medusa (of Ovid, of Freud), thereby focusing a critique on how narratives manipulate images and characters for specific purposes.

On another level, her laughter challenges a tradition that erases and silences, physically and mentally, women and their bodies. Medusa's laugh conceptualizes an alternative possibility, a bodily practice of disruptive laughter that momentarily "speaks." This "speaking" laughter transvalues the logic of phallocentrism. The laugh as critical engagement, a method for a feminism of the twenty-first century, at once demonstrates the pitfalls of a language entrenched in patriarchal and heteronormative narratives while simultaneously and creatively offering a new space to think that is inextricably linked to the body's sensations.

Informed by these theories, I turn to Kurt's performances because they play with and reverse heteronormative narratives. In the following example, homosexuality replaces heterosexuality as the natural/normal sexuality—calling into question this very divide. She says, somewhat playfully: "The more I hang around straight people the more I find them like me. As long as they keep it to themselves. As long as they don't flaunt it. [Pause] Stay away from my kids!" ("Elvira Kurt—Giggles Comedy Agency"). In this controversial time period with the repeal of Don't Ask, Don't Tell, the recent Supreme Court ruling on same-sex marriage, among other controversial issues, the traditional narrative goes: "If gays and lesbians keep their sexuality to themselves, I'm okay with them." Kurt's humorous statement reverses that narrative to demonstrate the absurdity of that common sentiment. She also implicitly interrogates heterosexuality as the norm, what Adrienne Rich refers to as "compulsory heterosexuality." Rich defines compulsory heterosexuality as "a political institution which disempowers women" because it supports the male/female binary, keeping intact hierarchical understandings of gender relations (Rich 1993, 203). Compulsory heterosexuality is reinforced on every level from Disney narratives to advertisements to history books. Rich observes:

> The lie of compulsory female heterosexuality today afflicts not just feminist scholarship, but every profession, every reference work, every curriculum, every organizing attempt, every relationship or conversation over which it hovers. It creates [. . .] a profound falseness, hypocrisy, and hysteria in the heterosexual dialogue. (Rich 1993, 221)

Kurt's reversal in this example encourages a critical examination of that "falseness, hypocrisy, and hysteria"—a transvaluation of heteronormativity. Kurt, by substituting "straight people" into a derogatory statement usually reserved for gays and lesbians, creates a reflective moment where we recognize the institution of normative sexuality.

In another moment of transvaluation through sarcastic humor, Kurt tackles her mother's disappointment upon learning that she is a lesbian. In Kurt's skit from "Giggles Comedy Agency," she flips the pages of an invisible album, imitates her mother's voice, and points to pictures saying: "This was the university she was supposed to go to. This was the guy she was supposed to marry. This was her first girlfriend, Brenda. They said they were roommates." Applause and laughter follow this bit. A similar routine that Kurt often concludes with centers on her mother meeting a friend in the supermarket and, as they compare their children, Kurt, impersonating her mother's Hungarian accent, says, "My daughter, she's a comedian and a lesbian. Both at the same time. Oh yeah, like a dream come true." Kurt brings these erased encounters into the open, creating awareness and recognition. In relating her experiences with parental disappointment, she turns these shameful, rarely discussed encounters into an occasion for comedy; in doing so, Kurt advocates for lesbian voices and visibility. This cultural commentary steeped in humor transvalues the institution of heteronormativity.

The next skit I turn to that offers a similar critical commentary is from Wanda Sykes's HBO performance *I'ma Be Me*. Sykes poses a poignant reimagining of the "coming out" narrative—coming out black instead of coming out gay. This reimagining functions on a number of levels as it: (a) offers a humorous yet critical space from which to view the "coming out" narrative and the concept of the closet, (b) showcases the absurdity of heterosexist responses to "coming out," and (c) challenges the institution of heteronormativity. As Eve Kosofsky Sedgwick notes in *Epistemology of the Closet*, "The closet is the defining structure for gay oppression in this century," and though Sedgwick is referring to the twentieth century, the closet still functions as a limiting structure today, in the twenty-first century (Sedgwick 1990, 71). Sykes—acknowledging these structures—begins the routine with: "It's harder to be gay than black [. . .] *I didn't have to come out black*." Without delving into whether this is an accurate statement regarding oppression, Sykes does offer a poignant observation concerning the coming out process. She continues—pausing after each word—with: "I didn't have to sit my parents down and tell them about my blackness." In this juxtaposition, Sykes challenges the audience to examine the relationship between discriminatory practices and (in)visibility, thereby casting light on the proverbial skeletons in the closet.

In the remainder of this short piece, Sykes relates a conversation with her mother that humorously brings the coming out story to the stage, prompting transvaluation. Sykes—taking a deep breath—says: "I hope you still love me. Mom, Dad, I'm black." What follows is Sykes intoning her mother in a heartbroken, slightly hysterical voice: "Oh, lawd. [. . .] Anything but black, Jesus. Give her cancer. Anything but black. [. . .]." Saying something of this ilk is unimaginable; no one would dream of articulating this thought as it relates to race. Why, then, is it okay to mutter it in relation to being gay or lesbian? It is in the incongruity of Sykes's statement that a critique emerges. Continuing in her mother's voice, she blurts: "You've been hanging around black people, and there you go thinking you're black. What did I do? I knew I shouldn't have let you watch *Soul Train*." Here the notion that hanging out with black folks will somehow make one black pokes fun at the idea that being gay is somehow contagious—similar to the Kurt quote that opened the essay. There is also the infamous self-blaming that Sykes's mother does, which again emphasizes the ridiculousness of these comments.

Her mother's final comment is: "Oh, you weren't born black. The Bible says Adam and Eve not Adam and Mary J. Blige." The decry of "not being born" and the resemblance to an anti-LGBT slogan that emerged in the late 1970s (Adam and Eve not Adam and Steve) create a further contrast between the narrative of coming out black and coming out gay. Through this reversal, Sykes critically tackles the space of the closet and the coming out narrative, cementing a practice of transvaluation.

In a slightly different—but no less powerful—humorous moment, Amy Schumer substantiates a transvaluation of patriarchy in her sketch "Last F**kable Day." The blunt and ironic comedy skit, which opened the third season of her show *Inside Amy Schumer* on Comedy Central, confronts unrealistic female beauty ideals that pervade Hollywood. The skit begins with Schumer jogging through the woods when she happens upon a picnic attended by Julia Louis-Dreyfus, Tina Fey, and Patricia Arquette. Schumer is invited to join the party and asks: "Is it someone's birthday here?" Arquette answers: "The opposite. We are celebrating Julia's last f**kable day." Schumer's confused look prompts Louis-Dreyfus to add: "In every actress' life, the media decides when you're not believably f**kable anymore." The irony of celebrating, as one would a birthday, Louis-Dreyfus's last f**kable day generates the humor in this sketch, and that humor elucidates Hollywood's fetishistic standards for female actresses. When you reach a certain age, your appeal dramatically plummets. Anti-aging advertisements from antiwrinkle creams to surgical procedures saturate our world, and the imperative is: *you must stay young*. Hollywood maintains this discriminatory practice, which silences and erases older female voices and bodies. Schumer's sketch, however, names this practice of erasure, and by naming, initiates transvaluation and a Cixousean "speaking" moment.

The next part of the conversation encourages transvaluation by unearthing the contradictory nature of these female beauty standards. Schumer inquires: "Well, how do you know [that you are not f**kable]? Who tells you?" Fey replies: "No one really tells you. There are signs, though. Like, when Sally Fields was Tom Hanks's love interest in *Punchline* and twenty minutes later she was his mom in *Forrest Gump*." Arquette also observes: "Another common sign is when they start remaking your best movies with younger and more f**kable actresses." These responses show how Hollywood determines a woman's worth based on age. The clearest critique, though, occurs when Schumer asks: "Wait, what about men? Who tells men when it's their last f**kable day?" Raucous laughter ensues, and Arquette plainly states: "Honey, men don't have that day." This comment calls attention to the double standard that exists in Hollywood and patriarchy's control of female beauty standards. Passivity, weakness, and submissiveness are the female beauty ideals; activity, strength, and power are the male beauty ideals. These sexist standards of beauty pervade Hollywood and firmly sustain a gendered binary: male = active/female = passive. The sketch

however, through frank humor, destabilizes these ideals of female attractiveness—cementing a transvaluation of patriarchy.

Kurt, Sykes, and Schumer challenge the institutions of patriarchy and heteronormativity through humorous reversals, incongruity, and candor. They advance a critique by contesting traditional norms of sexuality and gender. Kurt and Sykes tackle heteronormativity by insisting on visibility and creating stark, laughable contrasts; Schumer confronts patriarchy through an embrace of strong language and candid observations. All three comedians destabilize the all-encompassing narratives that disallow difference and create false hierarchical dichotomies. These comedic moments break through the silenced and erased bodies—undermining the institutions' truth. By laughing at these false truths, as Nietzsche and Cixous enjoin us to do, we substantiate transvaluation. A feminist practice for the twenty-first century must embrace this *laudable laughter*.

WORKS CITED

Cixous, Hélène. "The Laugh of the Medusa." Edited by Keith and Paula Cohen. *Signs: Journal of Women in Culture and Society*, vol. 1, no. 4, 1976, pp. 875–93.

"Elvira Kurt—Giggles Comedy Agency." Uploaded by WE Talent Group, April 17, 2009, www.youtube.com/watch?v=DCI5maHosiU.

"Elvira Kurt—Stand Up." Uploaded by frmtransguy, May 11, 2015, www.youtube.com/watch?v=H6qVzyr4yhY.

Nietzsche, Friedrich. *Thus Spoke Zarathustra*. Edited by Adrian Del Caro and Robert Pippen. Cambridge UP, 2006.

Rich, Adrienne. "Compulsory Heterosexuality and the Lesbian Existence." In *Adrienne Rich's Poetry and Prose*, edited by Barbara Charlesworth Gelpi and Albert Gelpi. W. W. Norton, 1993.

Rowe, Kathleen. *The Unruly Woman: Gender and the Genres of Laughter*. University of Texas Press, 1995.

Schumer, Amy. "Last F**kable Day." *Inside Amy Schumer*, season 3, episode 1, Comedy Central, April 21, 2015, www.youtube.com/watch?v=XPpsI8mWKmg.

Sedgwick, Eve Kosofsky. *Epistemology of the Closet*. University of California Press, 1990.

"Wanda Sykes: I'ma Be Me—Gay vs. Black." Uploaded by HBO, February 1, 2010, www.youtube.com/watch?v=1_wWJ-_4uSY.

89. • *Guerrilla Girls*

WHEN RACISM & SEXISM ARE NO LONGER FASHIONABLE (1989)

The Guerrilla Girls are a group of anonymous feminist artists who use humor to fight discrimination in the art world. They wear gorilla masks in public to keep their identities secret. Their name references the unconventional tactics of guerrilla warfare that influence their protest art, which includes provocative posters and billboards designed to raise awareness and incite conversation. The group had its start in 1985 as a reaction to the Museum of Modern Art's 1984 exhibition of contemporary art where only 13 of the 169 artists included were female. When they realized that just protesting in front of the museum wasn't effective, they started their first poster campaign. Since then they've used other strategies to get their message out, including publishing books like *The Guerrilla Girls' Bedside Companion to the History of Western Art* and *The Guerrilla Girls' Art Museum Activity Book*. "When Racism & Sexism Are No Longer Fashionable" is one of their best-known posters.

90.   •   *Alison Bechdel*

THE BECHDEL TEST (1985)

Alison Bechdel is a cartoonist and graphic memoirist and was awarded the MacArthur Foundation "Genius" Grant in 2014. She has published two graphic memoirs. *Fun Home: A Family Tragicomic* was published in 2006 and later adapted into a Tony Award–winning musical. Her second graphic memoir, *Are You My Mother?: A Comic Drama*, was published in 2012. Bechdel is also well known for her comic *Dykes to Watch Out For*, which in 1985 featured a strip that articulates a metric for gender inequality that has come to be known as "The Bechdel Test," "The Rule," or "The Bechdel-Wallace Test" (Liz Wallace is the friend who inspired Bechdel in the creation of the conversation between the two characters).

Alison Bechdel, Dykes to Watch out For

91. • *Kathleen Hanna/Bikini Kill*

RIOT GRRRL MANIFESTO (1992)

Bikini Kill is a punk band that was a major contributor to the Riot Grrrl movement, a feminist subculture emerging out of the punk music scene and focusing on political activism around issues like rape, domestic violence, and gender inequality. The Riot Grrrl movement also espoused a DIY ethic that gave rise to a vibrant zine culture. Bikini Kill began in Olympia, Washington, in 1990 and became known for its feminist lyrics and for encouraging a more welcoming environment for women in the sometimes hostile punk scene. Kathleen Hanna was the lead singer for Bikini Kill, and her "Riot Grrrl Manifesto" evokes the energy and ethos of the movement, particularly its focus on female empowerment.

BECAUSE us girls crave records and books and fanzines that speak to US that WE feel included in and can understand in our own ways.

BECAUSE we wanna make it easier for girls to see/hear each other's work so that we can share strategies and criticize-applaud each other.

BECAUSE we must take over the means of production in order to create our own meanings.

BECAUSE viewing our work as being connected to our girlfriends-politics-real-lives is essential if we are gonna figure out how what we are doing impacts, reflects, perpetuates, or DISRUPTS the status quo.

BECAUSE we recognize fantasies of Instant Macho Gun Revolution as impractical lies meant to keep us simply dreaming instead of becoming our dreams AND THUS seek to create revolution in our own lives every single day by envisioning and creating alternatives to the bullshit christian capitalist way of doing things.

BECAUSE we want and need to encourage and be encouraged in the face of all our own insecurities, in the face of beergutboyrock that tells us we can't play our instruments, in the face of "authorities" who say our bands/zines/etc are the worst in the US and

BECAUSE we don't wanna assimilate to someone else's (boy) standards of what is or isn't cool.

BECAUSE we are unwilling to falter under claims that we are reactionary "reverse sexists" AND NOT THE TRUEPUNKROCKSOULCRUSADERS THAT WE KNOW we really are.

BECAUSE we know that life is much more than physical survival and are patently aware that the punk rock "you can do anything" idea is crucial to the coming angry grrrl rock revolution which seeks to save the psychic and cultural lives of girls and women everywhere, according to their own terms, not ours.

BECAUSE we are interested in creating non-hierarchical ways of being AND making music, friends, and scenes based on communication + understanding, instead of competition + good/bad categorizations.

BECAUSE doing/reading/seeing/hearing cool things that validate and challenge us can help us gain the strength and sense of community that we need in order to figure out how bullshit like racism,

Hanna, Kathleen /Bikini Kill, "Riot Grrrl Manifesto" *The Essential Feminist Reader*. Ed. Estelle B. Freedman. New York: The Modern Library, 2006. 394-396.

able-bodieism, ageism, speciesism, classism, thinism, sexism, anti-semitism and heterosexism figures in our own lives.

BECAUSE we see fostering and supporting girl scenes and girl artists of all kinds as integral to this process.

BECAUSE we hate capitalism in all its forms and see our main goal as sharing information and staying alive, instead of making profits or being cool according to traditional standards.

BECAUSE we are angry at a society that tells us Girl = Dumb, Girl = Bad, Girl = Weak.

BECAUSE we are unwilling to let our real and valid anger be diffused and/or turned against us via the internalization of sexism as witnessed in girl/girl jealousy and self defeating girltype behaviors.

BECAUSE I believe with my wholeheartmind-body that girls constitute a revolutionary soul force that can, and will change the world for real.

---

92. • *Heather Rellihan*

AN INTERVIEW WITH TARANA BURKE (new)

Tarana Burke is a social justice activist and the founder of the "Me Too" movement. Burke has worked with several activist organizations, including the 21st Century Youth Leadership Movement and Girls for Gender Equity. In 2006 she founded Just Be Inc., an organization designed to promote the health, self-esteem, and empowerment of girls and women, particularly girls and women of color. In 2017 Burke and other activists who were dubbed "the silence breakers" were named Person of the Year by *TIME* magazine for their role in creating an international conversation around sexual violence. In the following interview Burke discusses her long history in activism, the origins of the phrase "me too," and the role of hashtag activism in conjunction with other types of social justice work.

HEATHER RELLIHAN: You have a long history of activist work. Can you share some of that history? What initially motivated you to get involved in your communities to make change? What are some of the programs or initiatives that you have worked on that have been the most meaningful to you? How has your previous activist work and your lived experiences informed your vision for the MeToo movement?

TARANA BURKE: There's not a time I can recall, outside of my early childhood, where activism wasn't a part of my life. Growing up in the Bronx, New York, I saw and experienced the painful impact systemic oppression has on Black, brown, and poor people every day. My family, particularly my grandfather, was committed to ensuring that I understood what it meant to be Black in America. Early on he started teaching me about the rich history that we descended from, as well as the injustices that Black people had faced in this country. At the same time, my mother was grounding me in Black feminist literature that helped shape my young identity. These foundational experiences helped me understand how to identify and speak up about injustice.

As a pre-teen, I joined a youth organization called the 21st Century Youth Leadership Movement. There I deepened my understanding of systemic oppression and learned about community organizing and activism from elders who had championed racial and social justice issues decades prior during the Civil Rights Movement and other movements of the '60s and '70s. I launched initiatives around issues like racial discrimination, housing inequality, and economic justice while still a teenager and young adult. I also went to work for 21st Century after college and continued the work of developing young leaders. It was during that experience that I began to encounter other young people who had also survived sexual violence. The vision of The 'me too.' Movement grew out of a desire to impact the lives of the young survivors who I was working with and to put into action the mantra that the elders who trained me had imparted: Community problems need community solutions. I had seen and experienced how collective action could change the course of history regarding things like discrimination, economic injustice, and equal rights, and I believed it was possible for sexual violence.

HR: What was the context in which you first came to use the hashtag #MeToo? What did the phrase "me too" mean to you when you first used it?

TB: The name 'me too.' —which didn't start as a hashtag—derives from a conversation I had with a student I was working with in Selma, Alabama. After participating in an exercise where other girls shared their experiences, she eventually shared her story with me. At that point in my career and in my advocacy, I wasn't equipped to navigate that conversation with the necessary empathy. While I felt an overwhelming sense of compassion for her and deeply identified with what she was sharing, I

regretfully wasn't able to tell her what I was thinking as she shared her experience . . . which was simply "*this* happened *to me too*." So in remembrance of that moment I created 'me too.' and decided that from then on, all the work that we did around, for, and in support of survivors, would be rooted in the principle of "empowerment through empathy."

HR: In 2017 you were among a group of activists named "the silence breakers" who were honored as *TIME* magazine's Person of the Year. What does it mean to you to be one of "the silence breakers"? How does silence function in a culture of violence against women? How can the MeToo movement break silences at the individual and structural levels?

TB: For me, 2017 was a whirlwind that completely changed my life. When Alyssa Milano Tweeted #metoo in response to the Harvey Weinstein scandal unfolding on October 17th, I had no idea what was on the horizon. Within hours of the viral moment, I saw my life's work being shared by millions. All over the country and around the world, people were saying #metoo and sharing stories of sexual violence with bravery, transparency, and a level of vulnerability that touched me deeply. I couldn't believe what I was seeing. People who knew me started reaching out and were feverishly sharing online that 'me too.' wasn't just a hashtag that was created that day, but a decades-old body of work that was created to support all survivors of sexual violence, but especially Black women and girls.

Being named one of *TIME*'s people of the year was one of the honors of my life. That moment allowed us and others to have intentional conversations about why so many survivors never disclose their assaults and why millions of people are forced to remain silent. Being able to publicly name that silence is and has always been a tool of oppression led to one of the biggest narrative shifts we've seen around sexual violence. Silence functions as the lynchpin that perpetrators of sexual violence depend on . . . which is why they often target the most vulnerable people they have access to. If there are no words, it's almost as if there was no harm or at least that is what they would like to believe. One of the things our work does is make clear that silence doesn't erase the harm so that people can understand that just because you can't hear the people screaming about their pain doesn't mean that they aren't holding any. We also help survivors understand that they don't owe their stories to anyone, but if and when they are ready to share they deserve the safest spaces possible to break their silence.

HR: Hashtag activism can help break the silence around sexual violence and can amplify the voices of survivors, raising awareness and creating community. How has the hashtag #MeToo worked to make change around the issue of sexual violence?

TB: "Hashtag activism" is quite the complicated cultural phenomena. The use of the words 'me too.' was part of the grassroots work we did and has been a tool we've used in storytelling and digital organizing since the beginning. All of that changed the day the hashtag went viral, reaching millions of survivors who, before that moment, had probably held the weight of their experience alone. Personally, I felt a mix of emotions that day seeing thousands upon thousands saying #metoo. In one vein, it was what I had worked most of my life for; we were finally seeing a narrative shift around survivorhood. People were sharing their experiences and finding support and community with other survivors around the world. These acts of vulnerability and bravery forced the prevalence of sexual violence into the mainstream in a way that many of us hadn't seen before. It was amazing to witness and deeply gratifying.

However, at the same time, I saw that people were speaking about the hashtag separate from the movement and body of work that was rooted in years of grassroots organizing. I began to worry that people would assume that #metoo was just another viral hashtag that would fizzle out after people grew tired of hearing about the scandals involving rich, powerful people in Hollywood. I feared that, yet again, everyday survivors would be left without a voice in this long-overdue conversation.

Upon recognizing that #metoo was indeed connected to a body of work (due largely in part to Black women and other survivors who jumped into action, correcting the record), Alyssa Milano reached out to me personally and said that she wanted to support the movement and my leadership. That act of support and allyship meant a great deal to me and it helped us retain control of the developing narrative around #metoo.

Many might not understand why I would include that information here, but as students of gender studies and social movements, it is paramount that you understand that for generations, Black people and other people of color have contended with movements that we both created and labored in being co-opted and commodified by white people. Look no further than the modern feminism movement for an example of this phenomena. Even though there wouldn't be a feminist movement without the labor and leadership of Black women like Sojourner Truth, Mary Church Terrell, bell hooks, and Audre Lorde, the mainstream understanding of feminism still centers white women and largely ignores the experiences of women of color, which works to reinforce deep-seated racial hierarchies.

Good allies and accomplices are needed in The 'me too.' Movement and all fights for justice and equality. We need those who understand how to leverage their privilege to mitigate harm for those experiencing the oppression at hand. So Alyssa's willingness to elevate my leadership over hers and her desire to leverage her celebrity and resources to support the work of the movement were indicators that she was indeed an ally in the work to end sexual violence.

Since that time, we've worked hard to maintain that #metoo is an element of the broader 'me too.' movement. The hashtag is incredibly valuable because it reached millions who otherwise may have never felt safe or seen enough to say that they, too, are a survivor. It created an opportunity for us to have nuanced conversations about sexual violence and survivorhood that people from all walks of life could participate in. #metoo changed the world. To date, more than 40 million people have shared the hashtag across various online platforms, making it one of the most shared hashtags in recent history. But people wouldn't still be sharing it two years later if it wasn't grounded in transformational work.

HR: Some people use the pejorative term "slacktivism" to question the value of hashtag activism and other low-commitment, easy-to-do, digital activist engagements like signing an online petition or reposting something on Facebook. What do you see as the value of things like hashtags in making change, and what do you see as the limitations?

TB: When it comes to "hashtag activism" people often conflate very different actions and designations, resulting in points of frustration for those who are working in communities in real time. Just because something gains traction on social media doesn't automatically make it a "movement." To some, sending a tweet or sharing a post about a particular issue is activism, but others might say that's advocacy or the act of amplifying someone else's advocacy. All of those things are valuable and necessary to our movements, but it is important that people understand what movements are, how they work, and what they require in order to grow and sustain.

We need people sharing information about social movements because it's a strategic way to expand reach and galvanize the energy needed to affect change. Social media is a powerful tool that when used effectively can amplify messages, unite and mobilize people en mass. But that level of virality can be detrimental when comments and opinions are applied haphazardly and/or without knowledge of the associated movement. For example, people putting #metoo on posts that share messages that are not in alignment with the movement's core values and beliefs isn't actually serving the movement, no matter how many people it reaches.

Regardless of the channels you use to organize or share information, I encourage young people and students to remember that social change movements like 'me too.' are about changing the material conditions of people experiencing a particular kind of oppression, and that is a serious endeavor.

HR: Since #MeToo has gone viral, you have been involved in several efforts to educate the public about sexual violence, share the stories of survivors, and connect survivors to resources. Can you talk about the work you've done creating a public service announcement (PSA) campaign and the development of the metoomvmt.org website? What was the motivation for these projects, and what do you hope to achieve with them? What has been the response to these projects?

TB: The Survivor Story Series was a PSA campaign produced and launched in partnership with Deutsch, a creative agency that shared the same desire to rally survivors and supporters together in the movement to end sexual violence through personal testimonies. It's important for us to consistently refocus the movement on the dignity, humanity, and healing of survivors, and connect with other survivors to these stories. The PSAs debuted in partnership with HBO at the 2019 Sundance Film Festival.

The development of the website is an ongoing project, with the goal of providing a wealth of resources for everyone and anyone to heal and take action. I've been doing this work for over two decades and hadn't come across a digital space that directed survivors to safe spaces in their communities and neighborhoods. The metoomvmt.org aims to be a clearinghouse for survivors and supporters to find the help they need and get involved in the movement.

Survivors have expressed gratitude in being able to see themselves in these stories and witness courage in narrative form. The website continues to highlight the disparity of access to healing resources in marginalized communities, which only fuels our work. Both of these projects were truly enlightening. I think it also underscores the responsibility we all have—as individuals, organizations, and corporations—to address sexual violence in our own lives, in our communities, and the cultures we are part of.

HR: What do you see as the conditions that made #MeToo go viral at this historical moment? Do you see this as a watershed moment for changing the culture regarding sexual violence, and if so, why? What do you see as the next steps for the MeToo movement?

TB: Several factors created the necessary conditions for The 'me too.' Movement. First and foremost, we acknowledge that we stand on the shoulders of generations of women and allies who fought for the rights of survivors of sexual violence long before 'me too.' became a global rallying cry. Their labor, brilliance, sacrifices, and successes are the foundation of the movement we see today. And for that we're truly grateful. The work we're doing now is a continuation of their legacy.

Secondly, several years before the viral moment, the nation experienced a series of cultural awakenings that prepared the ground for a movement like 'me too.' Mainstream conversations about abuse of power, privilege, and sexual assault dominated news and popular culture. Shortly after the election and re-election of President Barack Obama in 2008 and 2012, many in this nation believed we had arrived at a post-racial society, one in which race no longer played a role in people's conditions or their ability to access their full civil and human rights. But the unrelenting shooting deaths of Black people at the hands of police and vigilantes quickly upended that argument. The 2012 shooting of Trayvon Martin ignited a new iteration of a decades-long fight for Black liberation and civil rights, and the death of Mike Brown, Jr., in 2014, sent the city of Ferguson and several others around the nation into months of unrest. These deaths, and countless others that preceded and followed, forced the country to face the hard reality that Black lives are not valued equally in this country.

Publicly dissecting antiBlackness led to deeper conversations about issues that intersect with it like homophobia, transphobia, xenophobia, sexism, misogyny, and toxic masculinity, all of which play into the pervasiveness of sexual violence. We saw these issues addressed in the mainstream with more nuance and intentionality than ever before. The days of being able to claim willful ignorance were over, and we were moving into a time where being "woke" and having a cultural and socio-political consciousness was not only popular, but celebrated . . . something deemed unusual outside of progressive spaces.

That moment in time, along with others like Occupy Wall Street, reminded Americans that protest and other forms of united resistance are deeply rooted parts of our democracy. It showed a generation of people too young to have experienced the civil rights, women's liberation, and anti-war movements of the '40s, '50s, '60s, and '70s, that change is possible when people of goodwill rally around a shared goal. That shift in cultural consciousness, coupled with the righteous indignation of millions of fed-up people, was paramount, but the election of Donald Trump in 2016 was the boiling-over point for many.

Millions believed that 2016 would render yet another historic election, with Hillary Clinton posed to be the nation's first woman president. But a different kind of history was made when we ended up with a president who had zero political track record, but a list of sexual assault accusations miles long. The fact that the stories shared by dozens of women he allegedly assaulted didn't end his campaign sent a very loud message to survivors and allies that something had to be done.

HR: Do you think it's important for students to see themselves as activists? What suggestions do you have for students who would like to participate more actively around issues that are important to them? Given your long history of working with advocacy organizations, what advice would you give to students who want to pursue a career in community activism work?

TB: When I meet students, it's rare that I'm not asked "How can I become an activist?" The energy and innocent desire to fight for change always moves me. But the first thing I tell young people is that activism doesn't work if you don't truly believe change is possible. You'd be surprised how many people are committed to struggles they don't believe can be won. So before you start working on an issue, be certain that you believe change will come and that you're not just being active for the sake of being woke and involved.

Secondly, I recommend spending some time figuring out how you want to be of service and then analyze if that's actually the most effective use of your time and skill set. For me, my expertise is informed by my experience as a community organizer. I am passionate about fashion and art; both have been a part of my life for many years. But I know that I am most effective in this work when I tap into my training and long history as an organizer.

There's various ways people support social justice work: Activism, advocacy, organizing and base building, education and research, journalism, art and culture work, technology, business . . . the list is almost endless. Activism and organizing are central to most movements for change, yes, but that's not everyone's skill set and that's okay. We need different people with varied skills to win the fights of our time. So figure out what you're good at and ask people working within movements you care about what the needs are and use your skills to help fill critical gaps.

For those who are considering making their activism or advocacy a career, know that you're needed. If you are committing even a part of your professional life to fighting for a more just world, you are contributing to a long legacy of freedom fighters who made it possible for us to keep moving toward the future we all deserve. But know that this work isn't easy. It often comes with challenges, dangers, and obstacles that at times may feel insurmountable, especially when everything around you, from the current state of our nation's politics to the rapidly changing climate, feel like they're out of our control. But I can say from personal experience that there's nothing more beautiful or fulfilling than offering your time to the cause of justice. And because of that, I truly believe being in service to your people, to humanity, is the best career choice there is.

Index

Photos and illustrations are indicated by italicized page numbers. Notes and tables are indicated by n and t following the page number.

ableism, 58–59
abolitionist movement, 90–94
    "An Appeal to the Christian Women of the South,"
      112–113
    suffrage movement and, 91–92
    Truth and, 117
    women in, 90–91
abortion, 25, 100, 146, 200–201. *See also*
    reproductive choice
    birth control and, 277–278
    June Medical Services v. Russo (2020), 200
    pro-choice/pro-life advocates, 201
    Roe v. Wade (1973), 201
    #ShoutYourAbortion, 527
Abu-Ghraib, 317–321
Abu-Lughod, Lila, 404
    "Do Muslim Women Really Need Saving?
      Anthropological Reflections on Cultural Relativism
      and Its Others," 506, 530–541
activism, 7, 17. *See also* feminist activism
    art and, 521–526
    body and, 353–354
    community activist organizations, 514–515
    CRC, 145–146
    digital, 511–514
    history and, 88
    HIV/AIDS, 517–518
    housewife, 98–100
    intersectionality and, 506–507

lesbian, 123
LGBTQPAI+, 102–103, 124
mobile phone technologies and, 513
online, 443–444
print media and, 508
queer, 88–89, 104, 139, 253n4
reproductive justice, 203
sex and sexuality, 101–104
technology and, 433–436, 511–514
transgender, 8–9, 253n4
voting rights, 94
ACT UP (AIDS Coalition to Unleash Power), 517–518
ADA. *See* Americans with Disabilities Act
Adichie, Chimamanda Ngozi, 79, 348
    Americanah, 416–420
ADL. *See* Anti-Defamation League
adolescence, 46–48
adoption
    Adoptive Family v. Baby Girl (2013), 188
    of Native American children, 187
advertising
    "Cosmopolitan Whiteness: The Effects and Affects of
      Skin Whitening Advertisements in Transnational
      Indonesia," 347–348, 406–415
    Photoshop for, 412
    skin-tanning, 412–414
    skin-whitening, 347–348, 410
    for vibrators, 430, *431*
affirmative action, 241

affirmed gender, 9t
Afghan women, 506, 530–541
    RAWA, 536–538
    under Taliban, 535–537
Africa
    activism in, 78–79, 514–515, 563–567
    colonialism in, 79
    gender roles in, 40–43
    homosexuality in, 76
    "Queer/African Identities: Questions, Limits,
        Challenges" (Currier & Migraine-George), 17, 76–79
    sexuality and, 77
agency
    activism and, 78–79
    body and, 353–354
    of Muslim women, 404
agender, defined, 9t, 342
Agha, Ari, "Singing in the Cracks," 363–367
aging, beauty ideals and, 347
agriculture, corporate hijacking of, 477–478
Ahmed, Leila, 405n1, 532
Ahmed, Sara, 85, 266, 414
AIDS Coalition to Unleash Power (ACT UP), 517–518
AIDS Memorial Quilt, 522–523, 523
Ain't I a Woman? (hooks), 15
Airbnb, 484
Alcalde, M. Cristina, 349
Ali, Serena, 353
Allen, Emma, 171
Allen, Paula Gunn, "Where I Come from Is Like This,"
    186
Alloula, Malek, The Colonial Harem, 539
ally, defined, 9t
America and the Pill: A History of Promise, Peril, and
        Liberation (May), 200
Americanah (Adichie), 416–420
Americans with Disabilities Act (ADA), 518
    "I Was There," 572–574
American Woman Suffrage Association (AWSA), 92
"An Appeal to the Christian Women of the South"
        (Grimké, A.), 112–113
Anderson, Eric, 327
androgyny, 9t
"And When You Leave, Take Your Pictures With You"
        (Carrillo), 106, 147
Anthias, Floya, 548, 550
Anti-Defamation League (ADL), 310, 316n16

antidiscrimination laws, 253n5
    ENDA, 252
    SONDA, 252
anti-LGBT violence, 17, 76, 312–313
anti-lynching campaigns, 3, 92–93
    "A Red Record," 92–93, 117–120
antiviolence movement
    "A Black Feminist Reflection on the Antiviolence
        Movement," 206–207, 299–302
    class and, 300–301
    LGBT, 309
    NCAVP, 308–309
    racism and, 300–301
Anzaldúa, Gloria, 547–548
    "La Conciencia de la Mestiza/Towards a New
        Consciousness," 106, 156–161
    This Bridge Called My Back, 15
Applebaum, Anne, 261
aromantic, 9t
art
    activism and, 521–526
    community art projects, 522–523
    visual, 523–524
Arvin, Maile, 543–544
Asch, Adrienne, 551
Asexual Education and Visibility Network (AVEN),
        393, 394
asexuality
    affirming, 396–397
    defined, 9t, 343
    "Feminist Approaches to Asexuality" (Gupta), 343,
        393–398
    feminist scholarship on, 394–395
Asian Americans
    "Being an Oriental, I Could Never Be Completely a
        Man: Gay Asian Men and the Intersection of
        Race, Gender, Sexuality, and Class" (Han), 341,
        375–384
    gay male experience of, 380–382
    gendering Asian men, 377–380
    masculinity and, 376–377
Aslan, Ozlem, 259
As Nature Made Him (Colapinto), 37
assigned sex, 9t
assigning gender, 37–38
Atkinson, Ti-Grace, 133, 150
avatars, "Immersion," 445, 495–503

AVEN (Asexual Education and Visibility Network), 393, 394

AWSA (American Woman Suffrage Association), 92

Babcock, Linda, *Women Don't Ask: Negotiation and the Gender Divide*, 194–195

Badran, Margot, 405n1

Bailey, Courtney, "A Queer #MeToo Story," 207, 302–306

Baltz, Jay M., 454n35

Barkley Brown, Elsa, 88

Barrett-Fox, Rebecca, "Constraints and Freedom in Conservative Christian Women's Lives," 185–186, 200, 216–220

Baruah, Bipasha, "Gender Equity in the 'Sharing' Economy: Possibilities and Limitations," 440, 483–488

Battle, J., 376

beauty ideals and images, 577–578
    "Big Yoga Student," 350, 421–422
    choice discourse and, 345–349
    colonialism and, 409
    cosmetic surgery, by gender and race, 349t
    "Cosmopolitan Whiteness: The Effects and Affects of Skin Whitening Advertisements in Transnational Indonesia," 347–348, 406–415
    facialization, 410–412
    feminine, 345–347
    hair and, 417–420
    media and circulation of, 347–348
    racialized, 407–409
    skin-whitening, 347–348
    transnational construction of, 409
    Western culture and, 347–348

The Beauty Myth (Wolf), 345

"Because You're a Girl" (Ijeoma A.), 6, 40–46

Bechdel, Alison, "The Bechdel Test," 521–522, 580–581

"Before Intersectionality" (Caballero), 18, 80–81

"Being an Oriental, I Could Never Be Completely a Man: Gay Asian Men and the Intersection of Race, Gender, Sexuality, and Class" (Han), 341, 375–384

Bejarano, Christina E., "The Latina Advantage in US Politics: Recent Example with Representative Ocasio-Cortez," 515, 567–572

Bell, David, 438

Belle, Elly, "Knee-Jerk Biphobia: What Responses to Miley Cyrus's Breakup Say About Queer Erasure," 212, 333–336

benefit programs. *See* social service and benefit programs

"Big Yoga Student" (Dark), 350, 421–422

Bikini Kill, 525
    "Riot Grrrl Manifesto," 582–583

binary gender, 245, 250, 254n9
    beyond, 8–13

binary system, defined, 9t

biohacking. *See* body hacking

biology
    birth sex/biological sex, 10t
    "The Egg and the Sperm: How Science Has Constructed a Romance Based on Stereotypical Male–Female Roles," 431–432, 447–454

Birch, Jessica E., "Love, Labor, and Lorde," 220–224

birth control, 200–201
    abortion and, 277–278
    access to, 278
    Christianity and, 217
    Little Sisters of the Poor v. Pennsylvania (2020), 200
    medicalization of, 278
    movement, 275–277

"Birth Control" (Ferguson), 202, 275–279

birth sex/biological sex, 10t

bisexuality
    defined, 10t
    HIV/AIDS and, 78
    "Knee-Jerk Biphobia: What Responses to Miley Cyrus's Breakup Say About Queer Erasure" (Belle), 212
    queer African communities and, 77–78

black arts movement, defined, 523

black communities
    "Reflections on the Black Woman's Role in the Community of Slaves," 141
    sexism in, 152

black feminism, 105, 141–146, 149. *See also* Combahee River Collective
    "A Black Feminist Reflection on the Antiviolence Movement," 206–207, 299–302
    contemporary, genesis of, 141–142
    organizing, 144–146
    issues and projects, 146
    "Multiple Jeopardy and Multiple Consciousness: The Context of a Black Feminist Ideology," 13
    politics of, 142

Black Feminist Criticism (Christian), 15

"A Black Feminist Reflection on the Antiviolence Movement" (Richie), 206–207, 299–302
"A Black Feminist's Search for Sisterhood" (Wallace), 144
"A Black Feminist Statement" (Combahee River Collective), 105, 141–146
Black Feminist Thought (Collins), 210
Black Lives Matter movement, 2, 512
black women. *See also* women of color
    "Concrete," 559–562
    gender roles and, 144–145
    in labor market, 143
    "Love, Labor, and Lorde," 220–224
    in music, 525–526
    "Reflections on the Black Woman's Role in the Community of Slaves," 141
    reproductive justice and, 202
    stereotypes of, 142
    sterilization of, 100–101
    "Too Latina to Be Black, Too Black to Be Latina," 342, 392–393
Bluestockings (bookstore), 526
body
    activism and, 353–354
    agency and, 353–354
    aging, 347
    beauty ideals and images of, 345–349
    "Being an Oriental, I Could Never Be Completely a Man: Gay Asian Men and the Intersection of Race, Gender, Sexuality, and Class" (Han), 341, 375–384
    "Big Yoga Student" (Dark), 350, 421–422
    birth sex/biological sex, 10t
    commodity discourse on, 351–352
    "Cosmopolitan Whiteness: The Effects and Affects of Skin Whitening Advertisements in Transnational Indonesia" (Saraswati), 347–348, 406–415
    disembodiment, 444–445
    embodiment, 444–445
    epistemologies of, 338–354
    female, 130
    "Feminist Approaches to Asexuality" (Gupta), 343, 393–398
    gender and, 8–9
    "Hermaphrodites with Attitude: Mapping the Emergence of Intersex Political Activism" (Chase), 339–340, 368–374
    "How To Use a Condom" (Revilla), 344, 400
    identity and, 341, 357–363
    "If Men Could Menstruate" (Steinem), 344, 398–399
    knowing and experiencing, 340–342
    "(My) Lesbianism Is Not a Fixed Point" (Hill), 341–342, 384–387
    "Masculine, Feminine, or Fourth of July" (Crosby), 342, 387–391
    masculinity and male, 51
    medicalization of, 342–344
    modesty and, 218–219
    modification, 353, *354*
    neoliberalism and, 345–352
    Our Bodies, Ourselves (Boston Women's Health Collective), 341, 509, 509–510
    Redefining Realness: My Path to Womanhood, Identity, Love and So Much More (Mock), 338–339, 357–363
    "Singing in the Cracks" (Agha), 363–367
    "Sketches" (Gordon), *354*, 427–428
    "10,000 Blows" (Lux), *354*, 428
    "Too Latina to Be Black, Too Black to Be Latina" (Williams), 342, 392–393
    Trans Bodies, Trans Selves: A Resource for the Transgender Community, 510
    transgender, 340
    virtual/posthuman, 444–445
body hacking (biohacking), 353
    "Oppositional Scientific Praxis: The 'Do' and 'Doing' of #CRISPRbabies and DIY Hormone Biohacking" (Jen), 434–435, 465–470
"Body of Knowledge: Black Queer Feminist Pedagogy, Praxis, and Embodied Text" (Lewis), 82
body talk, 352–353
body size
    "Big Yoga Student," 350, 421–422
    expression of, 349–352
body work, defined, 345
Bonaparte, Marie, *Female Sexuality*, 131
Booksmart (film), 326
Boone, Joseph, 376–377
Booth, Austin, 444
Bordo, Susan, 352
Boston Women's Health Collective, 509
    Our Bodies, Ourselves, 509, 509–510
Boston Working Women's League, 96
Boxer, Marilyn, *When Women Ask the Questions*, 3
Brasher, Brenda, 438

Bridesmaids (film), 325

Britton, Hannah E., "'If Good Food is Cooked in One Country, We Will All Eat from It': Women and Civil Society in Africa," 515

Brod, Henry, 33–34

"'Broken Hearts, Broken Families': The Political Use of Families in the Fight Against Deportation" (Das Gupta), 188–189, 224–229

Brown, Catrina, 353

Brown, Kimberly Williams, "Trans-forming Bodies and Bodies of Knowledge," 19, 81–86

Brown, Wendy, 258

Budig, Michelle, "The Fatherhood Bonus and the Motherhood Penalty," 194

bullying, 329–330, 442

Bunch, Charlotte, "Not by Degrees: Feminist Theory and Education," 508

Burke, Tarana, 109, 175
  "An Interview with Tarana Burke," 528, 583–588

burqa, 533–538

Burwell v. Hobby Lobby (2014), 275–276

BUST (magazine), 510–511

Butler, Judith, 52–53
  Gender Trouble, 8

bystander intervention, defined, 206

Caballero, M. Soledad, "Before Intersectionality," 18, 80–81

CAH (congenital adrenal hyperplasia), 37

"Campus-Based Women's and Gender Equity Centers: Enacting Feminist Theories, Creating Social Change" (Vlasnik), 527

"Can We Stop Talking About the 'Hijab'?: Islamic Feminism, Intersectionality, and the Indonesian Muslim Female Migrant Workers" (Fitriyah), 342, 401–406

Carballo-Diéguez, A., 376

Carby, Hazel, "White Woman Listen!," 15

care work
  child care policies, 241
  devaluing of, 186
  "Love, Labor, and Lorde," 220–224
  neoliberalism and, 221

Carrillo, Jo, "And When You Leave, Take Your Pictures With You," 106, 147

CFC (Crunk Feminist Collective), 526

Chase, Cheryl, 35–36
  "Hermaphrodites with Attitude: Mapping the Emergence of Intersex Political Activism," 339–340, 368–374

Chemaly, Soraya, 508, 554–559

Chesney-Lind, Meda, "Mean Girls, Bad Girls, or Just Girls: Corporate Media Hype and the Policing of Girlhood," 211, 329–332

Chicanas, "La Conciencia de la Mestiza/Towards a New Consciousness," 106, 156–161. *See also* Latina/o/x

childbirth, medicalization of, 343

child care policies, 241

Chinese Exclusion Act of 1882, 94, 187

Cho, Song, 380

Cho, Sumi, 402

Chodorow, Nancy, 48, 325, 326

Christian, Barbara, *Black Feminist Criticism*, 15

Christianity, 185
  "An Appeal to the Christian Women of the South," 112–113
  birth control and, 217
  "Constraints and Freedom in Conservative Christian Women's Lives," 216–220
  gender roles and, 23–24
  marriage and, 26
  reproductive choice and, 26
  sexuality and, 217–218
  slavery and, 112–113
  women's role and, 216–217

Chuang, Kent, 380–381

Circle of 6 (app), 436, 439

cisgender, defined, 9, 10*t*

cisgender privilege, defined, 11*t*

cissexism, defined, 10*t*

Cixous, Hélène, 575, 578

Clare, Eli, 462
  "The Mountain," 7–8, 55–62

class
  antiviolence movement and, 300–301
  "Compliance Is Gendered: Struggling for a Gendered Self-Determination in a Hostile Economy" (Spade), 196, 245–256
  feminism and, 24–25
  imprisonment and, 164
  "Policies to End the Gender Wage Gap in the United States," 195–196, 239–243

class (*continued*)
    "The Politics of Survival" (Tormos-Aponte), 197,
        270–274
    "The Rise of Neoliberal Feminism" (Rottenberg),
        196–197, 257–268
Class and Feminism (Diana Press), 24
class inequalities, 24–25, 96–97
    education and, 256n35
    in labor market, 239–274
    legal services and, 250–252
    reproductive choice and, 100
click theory, 445
climate justice, 291–292, 542, 545
clitoridectomy, 134–135
clitoris, 101–102, 130
    anatomy, 132–133
    female circumcision, 134–135, 507
closeted (or in the closet), 10*t*
coalition
    defined, 507
    early experiences and, 551–552
    identity and, 547–548
    imagined communities and, 551–552
    importance of, 546–547
    "Making Coalitions Work: Solidarity Across Difference
        within US Feminism," 507, 546–553
    power asymmetries and, 552–553
    solidarity and, 547–548
    women of color and, 547
coercion, 176–177
Cohen, Cathy J., 550
Colapinto, John, *As Nature Made Him*, 37
Cole, Elizabeth R., "Making Coalitions Work: Solidarity
    Across Difference within US Feminism," 507,
    546–553
collaborative pedagogy, 19, 81–86
Collins, Jennie, *Nature's Aristocracy: A Plea for the
    Oppressed*, 96
Collins, Patricia Hill, 423–424, 456, 525
    Black Feminist Thought, 210
    "It's All in the Family," 186
The Colonial Harem (Alloula), 539
colonialism
    in Africa, 79
    beauty ideals and, 409
    environment and, 544–545

feminism and, 537
    indigenous women and, 543–545
    Muslim women and, 532–533
    neocolonialism, 507
    patriarchy and, 544
    settler-colonials, 185
    whiteness and, 412
colorism, defined, 342
"The Color of Choice" (Ross), 202, 279–291,
    551–552
The Color of Fear (film), 63
Combahee River Collective (CRC), 141–146, 547–548
    "A Black Feminist Statement," 105, 141–146
coming out, 10*t*, 360, 576
"Coming to Understand: Orgasm and the Epistemology
    of Ignorance" (Tuana), 340
community
    imagined, 106, 551–552
    queer community, 4, 60, 79, 104, 335
    "Reflections on the Black Woman's Role in the
        Community of Slaves," 141
    *Trans Bodies, Trans Selves: A Resource for the Transgender
        Community*, 510
community activist organizations, 514–515
community art projects, 522–523
comparable worth, 241–242
"Compliance Is Gendered: Struggling for a Gendered
    Self-Determination in a Hostile Economy"
    (Spade), 196, 245–256
compulsory heterosexuality, 110–111, 395, 576, 578
    defined, 102
"Compulsory Heterosexuality and Lesbian Existence"
    (Rich), 102
compulsory sexuality, 394, 395–396
Comstock Laws, 276
    defined, 199
"La Conciencia de la Mestiza/Towards a New
    Consciousness" (Anzaldúa), 106, 156–161
"Concrete" (Hill), 509, 559–562
Cone, Richard, 454n38
congenital adrenal hyperplasia (CAH), 37
Connell, R. W., 49, 107–108, 325
Connell, Tula, 403
Conquest: Sexual Violence and American Indian Genocide
    (Smith), 544
consciousness-raising groups, for men, 155

consent
  gendered violence and, 304, 306
  to sexual activity, 78
"Constraints and Freedom in Conservative Christian
    Women's Lives" (Barrett-Fox), 200, 216–220
controlling images, 423–427
Coontz, Stephanie, 100, 186
Cooper, Brittney, *Eloquent Rage: A Black Feminist Discovers
    Her Superpower*, 508
cosmetic surgery, by gender and race, 349*t*
Cosmopolitan (magazine), 409–414
cosmopolitan whiteness, 347–348, 407–408
  hegemonic white supremacy and, 413–414
  realness and, 411–412
  skin-tanning and perpetuation of, 412–414
  skin-whitening advertising and, 410
"Cosmopolitan Whiteness: The Effects and Affects of
    Skin Whitening Advertisements in Transnational
    Indonesia" (Saraswati), 347–348, 406–415
covert aggression, 329–330
COVID-19 pandemic, 197
Crazy Rich Asians (film), 325
CRC. *See* Combahee River Collective
creative expression, 521–526
  community art projects, 522–523
  music, 524–526
  visual art, 523–524
Crenshaw, Kimberlé, 15, 85, 176, 402
criminality, 166–167
  gender and, 330–331
criminal justice system, 301. *See also* law enforcement
  LGBT violence and, 308–309
#CRISPRbabies, 434–435, 465–470
Crosby, Christina, "Masculine, Feminine, or Fourth of
    July," 342, 387–391
Crunk Feminist Collective (CFC), 526
cultural competency, 457–458
cultural differences, awareness of, 538
cultural relativism
  "Do Muslim Women Really Need Saving?
    Anthropological Reflections on Cultural Relativism
    and Its Others," 506, 530–541
  issues of, 536
Currier, Ashley, "Queer/African Identities: Questions,
    Limits, Challenges," 17, 76–79
Currier, Dianne, 444

Cuthbert, Karen, 395
cyberculture, 410–411
cyberfeminisms, 443–444
cybernetic model, 452
cybersex, 441
cyberspace, 438–440
"A Cyborg Manifesto" (Haraway), 437
cyborgs, 437–438

Daniels, Jessie, 444
Dark, Kimberly, "Big Yoga Student," 350,
    421–422
Darwin, Charles, 452
Das Gupta, Monisha, "'Broken Hearts, Broken Families':
    The Political Use of Families in the Fight Against
    Deportation," 188–189, 224–229
Daughters of Bilitis (DOB), 102, 123–124
Davies, Sharyn Graham, 5
Davis, Angela, 552
  "Masked Racism: Reflections on the Prison Industrial
    Complex," 105, 163–167
  "Rape, Racism and Myth of the Black Rapist," 206
  "Reflections on the Black Woman's Role in the
    Community of Slaves," 141
  Women, Race & Class, 15, 201
de Bodard, Aliette, "Immersion," 445, 495–503
"The Declaration of Sentiments" (Stanton), 114–116
Defense of Marriage Act, 189
Delaney, Carol, 453n12
Deleuze, Gilles, 411
demisexual, 10*t*
deportation, "'Broken Hearts, Broken Families': The
    Political Use of Families in the Fight Against
    Deportation," 187–189, 224–229
Diagnostic and Statistical Manual of Mental Disorders
    (DSM), 104, 432, 462
DiAngelo, Robin, "Nothing to Add: A Challenge to
    White Silence in Racial Discussions," 13–15,
    62–73
digital activism, 511–514
  hashtag campaigns, 512
  online games and, 513–514
digital media, 438–440
Dionne, Evette, "Turning Fury into Fuel: Three Women
    Authors on Publishing's New Investment in
    Anger," 508, 554–559

disability
    ADA, 518
    employment and, 472
    living with, 472
    "Masculine, Feminine, or Fourth of July" (Crosby), 342, 387–391
    "The Mountain" (Clare), 7–8, 55–62
    "Putting Myself in the Picture: Researching Disability and Technology," 470–476
    research, 470–471
    social construction of, 7–8
    supercrips, 55–62
    technology and, 472
disability rights movement, 518
    "I Was There," 572–574
disaster capitalism, 197
discrimination. *See also specific types of discrimination*
    antidiscrimination laws, 252, 253n5
    employment, 192
    gender identity, 253
    of LGBTQPAI+ people, 102
    racial, 92–93
    transgender, 173
    in workplace, 240–241
disembodiment, 444–445
divorce, 115, 194, 326
DOB. *See* Daughters of Bilitis
doctors, "Latina/x *Doctoras* [Doctors]: Negotiating Knowledge Production in Science" (Flores), 432, 455–459
domestic violence, 205
    in queer relationships, 313–315
    survivors of, 315
domestic workers, 96
dominance
    controlling images and, 423
    male, 24, 177, 261, 263
    masculinity and, 48, 51, 52, 108, 159
    #MeToo movement and, 303
    patriarchy and, 30, 32
    racial, 63, 64–65, 66, 460
    violence against LGBTQ community and, 309
    women's friendships and, 326
"Do Muslim Women Really Need Saving? Anthropological Reflections on Cultural Relativism and Its Others" (Abu-Lughod), 506, 530–541

double bind, 219
    defined, 13
Douglass, Frederick, 90, 91, 114
Douglass, Mark, 438
drag queens, 361–362
Driver, Susan, *Queer Girls and Popular Culture: Reading, Resisting, and Creating Media*, 211
DSM. *See* Diagnostic and Statistical Manual of Mental Disorders
Dyer, R., 64, 68

eating disorders, 349–352
ecofeminism, 542
education
    class inequalities and, 256n35
    gender and, 42
    "Not by Degrees: Feminist Theory and Education," 508
    sex, 199
"The Egg and the Sperm: How Science Has Constructed a Romance Based on Stereotypical Male–Female Roles" (Martin), 431–432, 447–454
Eisenstein, Zillah, 283
Ejlersen, Mette, 133
Elias, Ana Sodia, 351
Ellis, Albert, 134
Ellis, Havelock, 460, 461
Ellman, Mary, *Thinking About Women*, 131
Eloquent Rage: A Black Feminist Discovers Her Superpower (Cooper), 508
emasculation, 47
embodiment, 444–445
EMILY's List, 516
employee benefits, 241
employment discrimination, 192
Employment Non-Discrimination Act (ENDA), 252
Eng, David, 264, 376
Enszer, Julie R., "On Lesbian-Feminism and Lesbian Separatism: A New Intersectional History," 526
environment
    colonization and, 544–545
    degradation of, 541–546
    indigenous women and, 543–545
    "Not Your Indian Eco-Princess: Indigenous Women's Resistance to Environmental Degradation," 507, 541–546
    "An Unbreakable Link: Peace, Environment, and Democracy" (Maathai), 514–515, 563–567

epistemologies
"Coming to Understand: Orgasm and the Epistemology of Ignorance," 340
defined, 338
equal opportunity statutes, 240–241
Equal Rights Amendment (ERA), 95–97
class inequalities and, 96–97
Erickson-Schroth, Laura, *Trans Bodies, Trans Selves: A Resource for the Transgender Community*, 510
EroticaBiz: How Sex Shaped the Internet (Perdue), 441
essentialism
deconstructing, 338–340
defined, 338
eugenics, 201
defined, 199
movement, 199
"Navigating Transness in the United States: Understanding the Legacies of Eugenics" (Lair), 432, 459–464
reparations for, 201
white supremacy and, 280–289
Everett, Anna, 445
Everydayfeminism.com, 511
expectations, gendered, 31–32

Facebook
activism on, 586
gender options on, 174
#MeToo movement and, 175
profit model of, 440
shadowbanning on, 489
#ShoutYourAbortion on, 528
women employed at, 436
women's friendships and, 327
facialization, 410–412
factory workers, 95–96
Fahs, Breanne, *Liberating Masturbation: A Meditation on Self Love*, 341
"False Promises: Criminal Legal Responses to Violence against LGBT People" (Mogul, Richie & Whitlock), 207, 307–317
Families for Freedom (FFF), 225–227
family
"'Broken Hearts, Broken Families': The Political Use of Families in the Fight Against Deportation," 187–189, 224–229
"Constraints and Freedom in Conservative Christian Women's Lives" (Barrett-Fox), 200, 216–220

gender pay gap and, 241
immigrants and, 187–189
"Love, Labor, and Lorde" (Birch), 220–224
Native Americans and, 186
nuclear, 185–186
"Popaganda: Queering Family Values" (Mirk), 229–239
power and, 185
rejection by, 360
responsibility to, 43
rethinking, 184–190
slavery and, 187
structure, 186
Women, Work & Family, 184
Family Medical Leave Act (FMLA), 196
Farris, Sara, 260
"The Fatherhood Bonus and the Motherhood Penalty" (Budig), 194
Fausto-Sterling, Anne, "The Five Sexes Revisited," 5, 35–40, 388
Feinberg, Leslie
"I'm Glad I Was in the Stonewall Riot," 103, 124–126
Transgender Liberation: A Movement Whose Time Has Come, 373
female circumcision, 134–135, 507
Female Sexuality (Bonaparte), 131
The Feminine Mystique (Friedan), 99–100, 223
femininity, 8, 31, 138, 385
beauty ideals and images, 345–347
"Masculine, Feminine, or Fourth of July" (Crosby), 342, 387–391
women's roles and, 99
feminism, 2–5
American, 44–45
black men and, 144–145
cisgender, 174
class differences and, 24–25
colonial, 537
history of, 89
hooks on, 23
humor and, 574–578
"It's Time to End the Long History of Feminism Failing Transgender Women," 171–174
lifestyle, 25
"Making Coalitions Work: Solidarity Across Difference within US Feminism," 546–553
men and, 148, 154–155, 161–163
misunderstanding of, 23

feminism (*continued*)
    neoliberal, 196–197, 257–268
    in pop culture, 209
    queer and, 4–5
    radical, 171
    reformist, 24–25
    "The Rise of Neoliberal Feminism" (Rottenberg),
        196–197, 257–268
    stereotypes, 2
    technofeminist approaches, 433–436
    third world, 106
    transgender, 171–174
    violence against women and, 299–300
Feminism Is for Everybody (hooks), 212
feminist activism, 88–89
    art and, 521–522, 523–524
    black, 105
    community activist organizations, 514–515
    CRC, 145–146
    defining women's issues and, 107
    digital, 511–514
    humor, 519–521, 574–578
    lesbians and, 135
    men in, 106–108, 161–163
    music and, 524–526
    print media and, 508–511
    third world feminism and white, 147
"Feminist Approaches to Asexuality" (Gupta), 343,
    393–398
feminist arts movement, defined, 523
Feminist Majority PAC, 516
feminist movement
    hierarchy in, 100, 104–105
    masculinity and, 48–49
    privilege in, 104–105
    roots of, 2–3
    separatism in, 150, 153–154, 526
feminist objectivity, 432–433
"Feminist Politics: Where We Stand" (hooks), 2,
    23–25
feminist theory
    on coalitions, 547
    Feminist Theory: From Margin to Center (hooks), 23, 25
    "It's Time to End the Long History of Feminism Failing
        Transgender Women" (Vasquez), 171–174
    "Not by Degrees: Feminist Theory and Education," 508

"Trans-forming Bodies and Bodies of Knowledge"
    (Brown & Washburn), 83, 84
    women's friendships and, 327
feminization, 48
femiqueer, defined, 435
Ferguson, Kathy, "Birth Control," 202, 275–279
fertility, 219–220
FFF (Families for Freedom), 225–227
Fifteenth Amendment, 92
    suffrage and, 93–94
Fitriyah, Lailatul, "Can We Stop Talking About the
    'Hijab'?: Islamic Feminism, Intersectionality, and
    the Indonesian Muslim Female Migrant Workers,"
    342, 401–406
"The Five Sexes Revisited" (Fausto-Sterling), 5,
    35–40
Flanagan, Mary, 444
Fleck, Ludwik, 450
Flores, Glenda M., "Latina/x *Doctoras* [Doctors]:
    Negotiating Knowledge Production in Science,"
    432, 455–459
Flynn, Karen, 442
FMLA (Family Medical Leave Act), 196
food supply
    corporate hijacking of food and agriculture, 477–478
    free trade and, 478–479
    genetic engineering and, 481–482
    "The Hijacking of the Global Food Supply" (Shiva),
        435–436, 476–483
    import insecurity and, 480–481
    monocultures and, 479–480
Forel, August, 460, 461
For Men Against Sexism: A Book of Readings
    (Snodgrass), 155
Fourteenth Amendment, 92
    suffrage and, 93–94
Fowlkes, Diane L., 547–548
Frankenberg, R., 63
Fraser, Nancy, 259, 268n7
Freud, Sigmund, 101, 430
    on vaginal orgasm, 131–132
Friedan, Betty, 4, 135, 261
    The Feminine Mystique, 99–100, 223
Friedman, Elisabeth Jay, 444
frigidity, 130, 131
Frye, Marilyn, "Oppression," 13

Fryett, Sarah E., "Laudable Laughter: Feminism and Female Comedians," 519, 574–578
Fugitive Slave Act, 91
Fundamentalist Church of Jesus Christ of Latter-Day Saints (FLDS), 186

GAA. *See* Gay Activists Alliance
Gambetti, Zeynep, 259
Gardiner, Judith Kegan, 51
    "Women's Friendships, Popular Culture, and Gender Theories," 210, 324–328
Gay Activists Alliance (GAA), 104, 124
gay, defined, 10*t*
Gay Liberation Front (GLF), 104, 124
    "A Leaflet for the American Medical Association," 139–140
gay rights movement, 124
Geena Davis Institute on Gender in Media, 522
gender
    affective construction of, 410–412
    ambiguity, 39
    in American society, 43–44
    assigning, 37–38
    body and, 8–9
    categories, 52
    cosmetic surgery by, 349*t*
    criminality and, 330–331
    defined, 10*t*
    education and, 42
    expectations and, 31–32
    history and, 115
    juvenile delinquency and, 331
    in labor market, 191–197
    learning and unlearning, 5–8
    masculinization process, 6–7
    regulation of, 247–248
    as social process, 5–6
    social services access and, 250–251
    spectrum, Southern Poverty Law Center, 9–12*t*
    status, defined, 5
    stereotypes, 8
    in youth culture, 46
gender-based state violence, 226, 315, 518
gender dysphoria, 10*t*
gendered division of labor, 185–186, 473–474

gendered violence, 204–209, 299–300
    "A Black Feminist Reflection on the Antiviolence Movement" (Richie), 206–207, 299–302
    consent and, 304, 306
    "False Promises: Criminal Legal Responses to Violence against LGBT People" (Mogul, Richie & Whitlock), 207, 307–317
    "June" (Prince), 293–298
    "Making Feminist Sense of Torture at Abu-Ghraib" (Nusair), 208, 317–321
    "A Queer #MeToo Story" (Bailey), 207, 302–306
"Gender Equity in the 'Sharing' Economy: Possibilities and Limitations" (Masikini & Baruah), 440, 483–488
gender expression, 10*t*
gender-fluid, defined, 10*t*
gender identity, 139
    defined, 5, 10*t*
    discrimination, 253
    intersexuality and, 38–39
    sexuality and, 52
gender ideologies in science, 431–432
gender inequalities
    globally, 40–46
    housework and, 100
    masculinity and, 48
gender-neutral, defined, 10*t*
gender-neutral bathrooms, 172–173
gender nonconforming, defined, 10*t*
gender pay gap, 192–197, 239–243
    comparable worth, 241–242
    defined, 192
    ending, 243
    equal opportunity statutes and, 240–241
    families and, 241
    pay secrecy and, 242–243
    "Policies to End the Gender Wage Gap in the United States," 195–196, 239–243
    unionization and, 242
genderqueer, defined, 4, 10*t*
gender rights
    International Bill of Gender Rights, 39–40
    litigation, 252
gender roles
    in Africa, 40–43
    black women and, 144–145

gender roles (*continued*)
Christianity and, 23–24
defined, 10*t*
"The Egg and the Sperm: How Science Has Constructed a Romance Based on Stereotypical Male–Female Roles," 431–432
family and, 185–187
housework and, 127–128
immigrants and, 228
male, 160
masculinity and, 48
patriarchy and, 31–32
gender-transgressive people, 251
Gender Trouble (Butler), 8
genetic editing and engineering
agricultural, 481–482
human, 434–435, 465–470
genital surgery, female, 134–135, 507
Ghosh, Kali Charan, 477
Gill, Rosalind, 352
girls
"Mean Girls, Bad Girls, or Just Girls: Corporate Media Hype and the Policing of Girlhood," 329–332
rights of, 331–332
violence and, 329–331
Girschick, Lori B., 305
Glamour (magazine), 510
glass ceiling, defined, 195
GLF. *See* Gay Liberation Front
Goeman, Mishuana, 544
Goldenthal, Carol, 461
Good and Mad: The Revolutionary Power of Women's Anger (Traister), 508
Gordon, Joanna, "Sketches," 354, 427–428
Gordon, Linda, *Woman's Body, Woman's Right*, 276
Gottheil, William, 461
government policies
crime control, 166–167
gender-neutral bathrooms, 172–173
immigrants, 187–189
welfare policy, 248
Green Belt Movement, 514–515, 563–567
Greif, Geoffrey, 324
Griffin, Susan, *Woman and Nature*, 543
Grimké, Angelina, 90, 91
"An Appeal to the Christian Women of the South," 91, 112–113

Grimké, Sarah, 90, 112
#growinguptrans, 7
Guattari, Félix, 411
The Guerrilla Girls, 521
"When Sexism and Racism Are No Longer Fashionable," 579
Gupta, Kristina, "Feminist Approaches to Asexuality," 343, 393–398

Hall, Stuart, 209, 266, 267
Hammond, Ryan (Rian), *Open Source Gendercodes*, 466–469
Hamtramck Women's Committee, 98–99
Han, C. Winter, "Being an Oriental, I Could Never Be Completely a Man: Gay Asian Men and the Intersection of Race, Gender, Sexuality, and Class," 341, 375–384
Hanna, Kathleen, 525
"Riot Grrrl Manifesto," 582–583
Haraway, Donna, 432, 469n3
"A Cyborg Manifesto," 437
Harding, Sandra, 465, 467
Hardisty, Jean, 285
Harris, S. M., 376
Hartley, Gemma, 508, 554–559
Hartman, J. F., 451
Harvey, David, 269n13
hashtag activism, 512, 584–586
#BlackLivesMatter, 2, 512
#CRISPRbabies, 434–435, 465–470
#growinguptrans, 7
#MeToo, 108, 109, 174–177, 207, 302–306, 527–528, 583–588
#ShoutYourAbortion, 527
hate crimes
defined, 207
legislation, 310–313
LGBT violence and, 309–310
race and, 310
Hate Crimes Statistics Act, 311
Hawaiian culture, in *Redefining Realness: My Path to Womanhood, Identity, Love and So Much More*, 357–363
healthcare
SRS and, 256n32
transgender access to, 172, 343
hegemonic masculinity, 49, 108

Heritage Foundation, 283
"Hermaphrodites with Attitude: Mapping the
　　Emergence of Intersex Political Activism" (Chase),
　　339–340, 368–374
hermaphroditism, 35–36. *See also* intersexuality
Hersh, Seymour, 319
heteronormative, 4, 51
　　defined, 5, 11*t*
heterosexism, 11*t*
heterosexuality, 50
　　ally, 9*t*
　　compulsory, 102, 110–111, 576, 578
　　defined, 11*t*
　　masculinity and, 47
　　patriarchy and, 102
　　privilege, 11*t*, 105
heterosexual privilege, defined, 11*t*
hierarchy
　　in feminist movement, 100, 104–105
　　in labor market, 96
　　Nature's Aristocracy: A Plea for the Oppressed, 96
　　"There Is No Hierarchy of Oppressions" (Lorde), 15–16,
　　　75
　　third world women and, 106
high school, 46–47
"The Hijacking of the Global Food Supply" (Shiva),
　　435–436, 476–483
Hill, DaMaris B., "Concrete," 509, 559–562
Hill, Dominique C., "(My) Lesbianism Is Not a Fixed
　　Point," 341–342, 384–387
hip-hop, 525–526
HIPS, 514
Hirschfeld, Magnus, 461
HIV/AIDS
　　activism, 517–518
　　AIDS Memorial Quilt, 522–523, 523
Hoang, Nguyen Tan, 377
Hochschild, Arlie, 192
Hollaback!, 513
Hollibaugh, Amber, *My Dangerous Desires*, 389
Holmes, Morgan, 373
Home Girls (Smith), 15
homeless
　　LGBT youth, 360
　　transgender, 253n7
homophile movement, 102–103
　　"Statement of Purpose," 123–124

homophobia, 11*t*
　　violence, 207
homosexuality. *See also headings starting with "LGBTIQPA+"*
　　in Africa, 76
　　"A Leaflet for the American Medical Association,"
　　　139–140
　　medicalization of, 102, 104, 139
hooks, bell (Gloria Jean Watkins)
　　Ain't I a Woman?, 15
　　on feminism, 23
　　Feminism Is for Everybody, 212
　　"Feminist Politics: Where We Stand," 2, 23–25
　　Feminist Theory: From Margin to Center, 23, 25
　　"Men: Comrades in Struggle," 106–107, 148–155
hormones, 36, 250
Hornacek, Paul, 151
housewives and housework, 100–101, 126
　　activism, 98–100
　　devaluing of, 186
　　gender roles and, 127–128
　　"The Politics of Housework," 100, 126–129
　　technological innovation and, 435
"How To Use a Condom" (Revilla), 344, 400
Hubbard, Ruth, 453n10
Human Rights Watch, 281
human trafficking, 197–198
humor, 519–521
　　feminism and, 574–578
　　Islamophobia addressed through, 520
　　"Laudable Laughter: Feminism and Female Comedians,"
　　　574–578
　　transvaluation and, 576–577
hyper-masculinity, 376

ICWA (Indian Child Welfare Act), 188
identity. *See also* gender identity; queer identity
　　bodies and, 357–363
　　coalition and, 547–548
　　female, 138
　　high school and, 46–53
　　politics, 104–109
　　privilege, 104–109
　　social, defining, 548–551
　　tourism, 442
"'If Good Food is Cooked in One Country, We Will All
　　Eat from It': Women and Civil Society in Africa"
　　(Britton & Price), 515

"If Men Could Menstruate" (Steinem), 344, 398–399

Ijeoma A., "Because You're a Girl," 6, 40–46

Illegal Immigration Reform and Immigrant Responsibility Act (IIRIRA), 226

imagined community, 106, 551–552

IMF (International Monetary Fund), 478

"I'm Glad I Was in the Stonewall Riot" (Feinberg), 103, 124–126

"Immersion" (de Bodard), 445, 495–503

immigrant labor, 188–189

immigrant rights movement, 225

immigrants, 18, 81

    "'Broken Hearts, Broken Families': The Political Use of Families in the Fight Against Deportation," 188–189, 224–229

    factory workers, 95, 121–123

    family and, 187–189

    gender roles and, 228

    government policies, 187–189

    IIRIRA, 226

    The Migrant Trail (online game), 513–514

imprisoned population, 164

    in labor market, 165–166

India

    food supply in, 435–436, 476–483

    sharing economy in, 485–486

Indian Child Welfare Act (ICWA), 188

indigenous women, 507

    in climate justice movement, 542

    colonization and, 543–545

    environmental degradation and resistance of, 545

    environment and, 543–545

    land and, 542–545

    "Not Your Indian Eco-Princess: Indigenous Women's Resistance to Environmental Degradation," 507, 541–546

    pop culture representations of, 542

    sexual violence against, 544

Indonesia

    "Can We Stop Talking About the 'Hijab'?: Islamic Feminism, Intersectionality, and the Indonesian Muslim Female Migrant Workers" (Fitriyah), 342, 401–406

    "Cosmopolitan Whiteness: The Effects and Affects of Skin Whitening Advertisements in Transnational Indonesia," 347–348, 406–415

    Seeing Beauty, Sensing Race in Transnational Indonesia, 345–346

In Search of Our Mother's Gardens (Walker), 15

Instagram

    censorship by, 489, 492

    hashtag activism on, 7

    queer black creators failed by, 442, 488–490

    shadowbanning on, 489

    YouTube shooter's account on, 491, 492

interdisciplinarity, 19–20, 184

interlocking oppression, 15

International Bill of Gender Rights, 39–40

International Monetary Fund (IMF), 478

Internet

    EroticaBiz: How Sex Shaped the Internet, 441

    pornography, 440–443

    sexuality and, 440–443

interpersonal sexual violence, 204–207

    defined, 204

intersectionality, 13–19, 148

    activism and, 506–507

    analysis, 14

    "Before Intersectionality" (Caballero), 18, 80–81

    "Can We Stop Talking About the 'Hijab'?: Islamic Feminism, Intersectionality, and the Indonesian Muslim Female Migrant Workers" (Fitriyah), 342, 401–406

    defined, 15

    "Trans-forming Bodies and Bodies of Knowledge" (Brown & Washburn), 19, 81–86

    whiteness and, 19

intersex, 249, 255n22

    defined, 11t

    "Hermaphrodites with Attitude: Mapping the Emergence of Intersex Political Activism" (Chase), 339–340, 368–374

intersexuality

    in babies, 37

    classifying, 39

    defined, 37

    gender identity and, 38–39

    rates of, 36

"An Interview with Tarana Burke" (Rellihan), 528, 583–588

intimate partner violence, 77. *See also* domestic violence

Iranian women, 537–538

Islam, 319. *See also* Muslim women
"Can We Stop Talking About the 'Hijab'?: Islamic Feminism, Intersectionality, and the Indonesian Muslim Female Migrant Workers" (Fitriyah), 342, 401–406
Western culture and, 538
Islamophobia, 208
defined, 208
humor for addressing, 520
"It's All in the Family" (Collins), 186
"It's Time to End the Long History of Feminism Failing Transgender Women" (Vasquez), 171–174
"I Was There" (Winter), 518, 572–574

Jacobsen, Margaret, 189, 229–239
Jafri, Beenash, "Not Your Indian Eco-Princess: Indigenous Women's Resistance to Environmental Degradation," 507, 541–546
Jen, Clare, "Oppositional Scientific Praxis: The 'Do' and 'Doing' of #CRISPRbabies and DIY Hormone Biohacking," 434–435, 465–470
Jhally, Sut, 170, 209
Johnson, Allan, "Patriarchy, the System: An It, Not a He, a Them, or an Us," 3–4, 26–34
Johnson, Virginia, 101
"June" (Prince), 293–298
June Medical Services v. Russo (2020), 200
juvenile delinquency, gender and, 331

Kaba, Mariame, "Solidarity Not Charity: Mutual Aid and How to Organize in the Age of Corona Virus," 197
Kalish, Rachel, "Suicide by Mass Murder: Masculinity, Aggrieved Entitlement and Rampage School Shootings," 170
Katz, Jackson, "Memo to Media: Manhood, Not Guns or Mental Illness, Should Be Central in Newtown Shooting," 108, 167–170
Kawashima, Terry, 412
Kellner, Douglas, "Rage and Rampage: School Shootings and Crises of Masculinity," 170
Kelly, G. Lombard, *Sexual Feeling in Married Men and Women*, 132
Kessler, Suzanne J., *Lessons from the Intersexed*, 39
Killing the Black Body: Race, Reproduction, and the Meaning of Liberty (Roberts), 201, 286, 435

Kim, Marlene, "Policies to End the Gender Wage Gap in the United States," 195–196, 239–243
Kimmel, Michael, 326, 376
"Suicide by Mass Murder: Masculinity, Aggrieved Entitlement and Rampage School Shootings," 170
King, Deborah, "Multiple Jeopardy and Multiple Consciousness: The Context of a Black Feminist Ideology," 13
Kinsey, Alfred, 101, 139, 430–431
Kipnis, Laura, 305
Kitchen Table: Women of Color Press, 508
Klein, Naomi, 197
"Knee-Jerk Biphobia: What Responses to Miley Cyrus's Breakup Say About Queer Erasure" (Belle), 212, 333–336
knowledge
production of, 508–511
situated, 432–433
Koedt, Anne, "The Myth of the Vaginal Orgasm," 101–102, 130–135
Kramer, Larry, "1,112 and Counting," 517
Ku Klux Klan, 119
Kwon, Hyeyoung, 455

labor market
black women in, 143
"Compliance Is Gendered: Struggling for a Gendered Self-Determination in a Hostile Economy" (Spade), 196, 245–256
disability in, 472
gendered division of, 185–186
"Gender Equity in the 'Sharing' Economy: Possibilities and Limitations" (Masikini & Baruah), 440, 483–488
gender in, 191–197
hierarchy in, 96
immigrants in, 188–189
imprisoned population in, 165–166
LGBTQPAI+ in, 192, 195–196
men in, 185–186
"The Politics of Survival" (Tormos-Aponte), 197, 270–274
race in, 96
"The Rise of Neoliberal Feminism" (Rottenberg), 196–197, 257–268
science, 432–433, 433*t*

labor market (*continued*)
    second shift, 192
    sexuality in, 191–197
    women in, 99–100, 185–186, 191–192
labor organizing, 95–97
    "141 Men and Girls Die in Waist Factory Fire,"
        121–123
    Mine-Mill Ladies Auxiliary and, 98
    unionized workers, 193–194, 242
Lair, Liam, "Navigating Transness in the United States:
        Understanding the Legacies of Eugenics," 432,
        459–464
land
    colonialism and, 543–545
    indigenous women and, 542–545
language
    patriarchy and, 31
    reproductive anatomy, 448–450
Larner, Wendy, 258, 267
Laschever, Sara, *Women Don't Ask: Negotiation and the
        Gender Divide,* 194–195
Latina/o/x. *See also* women of color
    defined, 11*t*
    "The Latina Advantage in US Politics: Recent Example
        with Representative Ocasio-Cortez" (Bejarano), 515,
        567–572
    "Latina/x *Doctoras* [Doctors]: Negotiating Knowledge
        Production in Science" (Flores), 432, 455–459
    masculinity and, 376
    political advantage of, 570–571
    "Resisting Racism: Latinos' Changing Responses to
        Controlling Images over the Life Course" (Vasquez-
        Tokos & Norton-Smith), 352, 423–427
    "Too Latina to Be Black, Too Black to Be Latina," 342,
        392–393
"Laudable Laughter: Feminism and Female Comedians"
    (Fryett), 519, 574–578
Laurel, Brenda, 411
"lavender menace," 135
law enforcement
    anti-LGBT violence and response of, 308, 312–313
    "False Promises: Criminal Legal Responses to Violence
        against LGBT People," 207, 307–317
    LLEEA, 311
    Violent Crime Control and Law Enforcement Act, 311
Lazreg, Marnia, 532–533

"A Leaflet for the American Medical Association" (GLF),
    139–140
League of Women Voters, 515
Lean In: Women, Work, and the Will to Lead (Sandberg),
    97, 196, 257–267
Lemelle, A., 376
"(My) Lesbianism Is Not a Fixed Point" (Hill), 341–342,
    384–387
lesbians
    activism, 123, 135
    defined, 11*t*
    experience, 136
    humor and, 575–577
    label, 136–137, 385
    "lavender menace," 135
    "(My) Lesbianism Is Not a Fixed Point," 342, 384–387
    "A Quick History of TV's Elusive Quest for Complex
        Black Lesbians" (Turner-Williams), 321–323
    separatism, 143–144
    violence against, 310
Lessons from the Intersexed (Kessler), 39
Levitt, Steven D., 284
Lewis, Mel Michelle, "Body of Knowledge: Black Queer
        Feminist Pedagogy, Praxis, and Embodied Text," 82
Lewis, Rachel Charlene, "Technology Isn't Neutral: Ari
        Fitz on How Instagram Fails Queer Black
        Creators," 442, 488–490
LGBT movement
    in Africa, 78–79
    mainstream, 251–252
LGBTQPAI+
    activism, 102–104, 123, 124, 139
    antiviolence movement, 309
    defined, 4
    domestic violence survivors, 315
    "False Promises: Criminal Legal Responses to Violence
        against LGBT People," 207, 307–317
    gendered violence and, 205
    history of, 88
    homeless youth, 360
    identities, in media, 211–212
    in labor market, 192, 195–196
    marriage equality and, 189–190
    sexual violence, 207
    in sex work industries, 198
    violence against, 309–310

LGBTQ Victory Fund, 516
Liberating Masturbation: A Meditation on Self Love (Fahs), 341
Little Sisters of the Poor v. Pennsylvania (2020), 200
Local Law Enforcement Enhancement Act (LLEEA), 311
Lorde, Audre
    "Love, Labor, and Lorde," 220–224
    Sister Outsider, 15, 19, 184
    "There Is No Hierarchy of Oppressions," 15–16, 75
"Love, Labor, and Lorde" (Birch), 220–224
Lowe, Lisa, 377
Luna, Zakiya T., "Making Coalitions Work: Solidarity Across Difference within US Feminism," 507, 546–553
Lux, Christina, "10,000 Blows," 354, 428
lynching, 93, 117–120. *See also* anti-lynching campaigns

Maathai, Wangari, "An Unbreakable Link: Peace, Environment, and Democracy," 514–515, 563–567
machismo, 160
Magnet, Shoshana, 441
Mahmood, Saba, 404, 538
mahu, 358–359
Mainardi, Pat, "The Politics of Housework," 100, 126–129
"Making Coalitions Work: Solidarity Across Difference within US Feminism" (Cole & Luna), 507, 546–553
"Making Feminist Sense of Torture at Abu-Ghraib" (Nusair), 208, 317–321
"Making Masculinity" (Pascoe), 6–7, 46–53
male gaze
    defined, 209
    in media and pop culture, 212
    suicidegirls.com and, 441
male privilege, 33–34, 151
March for Women's Lives, 552
marginalized women, privilege and, 104–105
marriage. *See also* same-sex marriage
    Christianity and, 26
    Defense of Marriage Act, 189
    divorce, 115
    power and, 185
    slavery and, 187
marriage equality, 189–190

Martin, Emily, 344
    "The Egg and the Sperm: How Science Has Constructed a Romance Based on Stereotypical Male–Female Roles," 431–432, 447–454
"Masculine, Feminine, or Fourth of July" (Crosby), 342, 387–391
masculinity, 8, 31
    adolescent, 48
    complicit, 49
    defined, 48–50
    dominance and, 48, 51, 52, 108, 159
    gender inequalities and, 48
    gender roles and, 48
    hegemonic, 49, 108
    heterosexuality and, 47
    in high school, 47
    "Making Masculinity," 6–7, 46–53
    male body and, 51
    "Masculine, Feminine, or Fourth of July" (Crosby), 342, 387–391
    "Memo to Media: Manhood, Not Guns or Mental Illness, Should Be Central in Newtown Shooting" (Katz), 108, 167–170
    multiple masculinities, 49
    power and, 49
    queer theory approach to studying, 51
    race and, 48, 376–377
    rethinking, 52–53
    sexuality and, 48, 50–51
    sociology of, 49
    violence and, 167–170
masculinization process, 6–7
Masikini, Naciza, "Gender Equity in the 'Sharing' Economy: Possibilities and Limitations," 440, 483–488
"Masked Racism: Reflections on the Prison Industrial Complex" (Davis), 105, 163–167
mass incarceration, 166, 205
Masters, William, 101
masturbation, 430–431
    cybersex and, 441
    vibrators, 430, 431
Matsukawa, Yuko, 377
May, Elaine Tyler, *America and the Pill: A History of Promise, Peril, and Liberation*, 200
McCall, Leslie, 402

McCandless, Cathy, "Some Thoughts about Racism, Classism, and Separatism," 153–154
McCullough, Laurence B., 38
McIntosh, Peggy, "White Privilege: Unpacking the Invisible Knapsack," 13, 16
McMachon, Kathryn, 409–410
McRobbie, Angela, 263, 268n8
"Mean Girls, Bad Girls, or Just Girls: Corporate Media Hype and the Policing of Girlhood" (Chesney-Lind), 329–332
meanness, 329–330
media and popular culture, 209–212
    anti-feminism in, 211
    beauty ideals circulated through, 347–348
    feminism in, 209
    indigenous women represented in, 542
    "Knee-Jerk Biphobia: What Responses to Miley Cyrus's Breakup Say About Queer Erasure" (Belle), 212, 333–336
    knowledge production in print, 508–511
    LGBTQPAI+ identities in, 211–212
    male gaze and, 209
    "Mean Girls, Bad Girls, or Just Girls: Corporate Media Hype and the Policing of Girlhood" (Chesney-Lind), 329–332
    postfeminism in, 210–211
    print media, 508–511
    queer identities in, 209
    "A Quick History of TV's Elusive Quest for Complex Black Lesbians" (Turner-Williams), 321–323
    transnational circulation of, 409
    "Women's Friendships, Popular Culture, and Gender Theories," 210, 324–328
Medicaid, SRS and, 256n32
medicalization
    of birth control, 278
    of bodies, 342–344
    of childbirth, 343
    defined, 343
    hermaphrodites, 368–371
    of homosexuality, 102, 104, 139
"Memo to Media: Manhood, Not Guns or Mental Illness, Should Be Central in Newtown Shooting" (Katz), 108, 167–170
men
    anti-sexist, 107, 151, 161–163
    consciousness-raising groups for, 155
    feminism and, 148, 154–155, 161–163
    in feminist activism, 106–108, 161–163
    friendships of, 324–325
    gender role, 160
    "If Men Could Menstruate" (Steinem), 398–399
    in labor market, 185–186
    sexual violence against, 207
    women defined by, 138
"Men: Comrades in Struggle" (hooks), 106–107, 148–155
Mennel, Eric, "Payments Start for N.C. Eugenics Victims," 201
menstruation
    "If Men Could Menstruate," 344, 398–399
    scientific representation of, 448
Mernissi, Fatima, 405n1
Messner, Michael, 49
mestiza consciousness
    defined, 106
    "La Conciencia de la Mestiza/Towards a New Consciousness," 106, 156–161
#MeToo movement, 108, 109, 174–177
    "An Interview with Tarana Burke" (Rellihan), 527–528, 583–588
    "A Queer #MeToo Story" (Bailey), 207, 302–306
Mexican American women, 98.
Mexican-Indian culture, 160
microaggressions, 66, 74n4
Middle East, oppression in, 403–404
Migraine-George, Thérèse, "Queer/African Identities: Questions, Limits, Challenges," 17, 76–79
The Migrant Trail (online game), 513–514
Miller-Young, Mireille, 440
Mine-Mill Ladies Auxiliary, 98
Mirk, Sarah, "Popaganda: Queering Family Values," 229–239
Mirzoeff, Nicholas, 411
misgendering, defined, 11t
misogyny, 32
mobile phone technologies
    activism and, 511–514
    Circle of 6, 436, 439
Mock, Janet, Redefining Realness: My Path to Womanhood, Identity, Love and So Much More, 338–339, 357–363
Mogul, Joey L., "False Promises: Criminal Legal Responses to Violence against LGBT People," 207, 307–317

Mohanty, Chandra Talpade, 85, 88, 106
monocultures, 479–480
More Work for Mother (Schwartz Cowan), 435
Morgan, Robin, *Sisterhood is Powerful*, 146
Morrill, Angie, 543–544
mothers
    paid leave for, 195–196
    pay penalty, 194
"The Mountain" (Clare), 7–8, 55–62
Mountcastle, Vernon, 448
"Multiple Jeopardy and Multiple Consciousness: The
    Context of a Black Feminist Ideology" (King), 13
multiple masculinities, 49
Mulvey, Laura, 209, 212
Muñoz, Jose, 85
music, 524–526
    black women in, 525–526
    feminist activism and, 524–526
    "Riot Grrrl Manifesto," 582–583
The Muslims Are Coming! (film), 520
Muslim women, 208
    in Afghanistan, 531–532, 533, 536–538
    burqas, 533–538
    "Can We Stop Talking About the 'Hijab'?: Islamic
        Feminism, Intersectionality, and the Indonesian
        Muslim Female Migrant Workers" (Fitriyah), 342,
        401–406
    colonialism and, 532–533
    cultural explanations of, 531–533
    "Do Muslim Women Really Need Saving?
        Anthropological Reflections on Cultural Relativism
        and Its Others," 506, 530–541
    salvation rhetoric applied to, 538–540
    veiling and, 533–538
My Dangerous Desires (Hollibaugh), 389
Myers, Kristen, 211
"The Myth of the Vaginal Orgasm" (Koedt), 101–102,
    130–135

NAFTA (North American Free Trade Agreement), 478
Nair, Yasmin, 189, 229–239
Najmabadi, Afsaneh, 537–538
Nakamura, David, 378
Nakamura, Lisa, 442
NAMES project, 522–523
Nardi, Peter, 325–326
NATFI (North American Task Force on Intersexuality), 39

National Black Feminist Organization (NBFO),
    141, 142
National Coalition of Anti-Violence Programs (NCAVP),
    207, 308–309
National Indian Health Services, 201
National Organization for Women (NOW), 4, 135, 516
National Organization for Men Against Sexism
    (NOMAS), 107
    "Tenets," 161–163
National Woman Suffrage Association (NWSA), 92
Native Americans, 542. *See also* indigenous women
    adoption of, 187
    Adoptive Family v. Baby Girl (2013), 188
    family structure, 186
    ICWA, 188
    Sacagawea, 543–544
    sterilization of, 101, 201
    voting rights, 94
nature. *See* environment
Nature's Aristocracy: A Plea for the Oppressed (Collins), 96
"Navigating Transness in the United States:
    Understanding the Legacies of Eugenics" (Lair),
    432, 459–464
NBFO. *See* National Black Feminist Organization
NCAVP. *See* National Coalition of Anti-Violence
    Programs
neocolonial, defined, 507
neoliberalism
    bodies and, 345–352
    care work and, 221
    defined, 187
    "The Politics of Survival" (Tormos-Aponte), 197,
        270–274
    in Puerto Rico, 270–274
    rationality in, 258–259
    "The Rise of Neoliberal Feminism" (Rottenberg),
        196–197, 257–268
    xenophobia and, 187–188
Newtown school shooting (2012), 108, 167–170
New York City Shirtwaist Strike, 121
New York Radical Feminists, 130
New York States Sexual Orientation Non-Discrimination
    Act (SONDA), 252
New York Times, "141 Men and Girls Die in Waist
    Factory Fire," 121–123
NGOization, defined, 515
NGOs (nongovernmental organizations), 514

Nietzsche, Friedrich, 575
   Thus Spoke Zarathustra, 575
Nineteenth Amendment, 94, 515
Nixon, Laura, 462–463
NOMAS. *See* National Organization for Men Against Sexism
nonbinary, defined, 11t
nongovernmental organizations (NGOs), 514
nonprofit organizations, 514
nonviolent direct action, 517–519
   defined, 517
   disability rights movement, 518
   HIV/AIDS activism, 517–518
   "I Was There," 572–574
North American Free Trade Agreement (NAFTA), 478
North American Task Force on Intersexuality (NATFI), 39
Norton, Ann, 260
Norton-Smith, Kathryn, "Resisting Racism: Latinos' Changing Responses to Controlling Images over the Life Course," 352, 423–427
"Not by Degrees: Feminist Theory and Education" (Bunch), 508
"Notes for Yet Another Paper on Black Feminism, or, Will the Real Enemy Please Stand Up?" (Smith), 152–153
"Nothing to Add: A Challenge to White Silence in Racial Discussions" (DiAngelo), 13–15, 62–73
"Not Your Indian Eco-Princess: Indigenous Women's Resistance to Environmental Degradation" (Jafri), 507, 541–546
NOW. *See* National Organization for Women
Nusair, Isis, "Making Feminist Sense of Torture at Abu-Ghraib," 208, 317–321
NWSA (National Woman Suffrage Association), 92

Obergefell v. Hodges (2015), 189
occupational segregation, 193–194, 241
   defined, 193
Oliver, Michael, 58
"141 Men and Girls Die in Waist Factory Fire" *(New York Times)*, 121–123
"1,112 and Counting" (Kramer), 517
"On Lesbian-Feminism and Lesbian Separatism: A New Intersectional History" (Enszer), 526
online activism, 443–444

online games, 443–444, 513–514
Open Source Estrogen (Tsang), 466–469
Open Source Gendercodes (Hammond), 466–469
"Oppositional Scientific Praxis: The 'Do' and 'Doing' of #CRISPRbabies and DIY Hormone Biohacking" (Jen), 434–435, 465–470
oppression, 13–19
   of black women, 142–143
   defined, 13
   hierarchy of, 15–16, 75
   in Middle East, 403–404
   Nature's Aristocracy: A Plea for the Oppressed, 96
   patriarchy and, 32
   privilege and, 13–14
   psychology of, 128–129
   racial, 13–15, 142–143
   racial-sexual, 143–144
   solidarity and, 551–552
   "There Is No Hierarchy of Oppressions" (Lorde), 15–16, 75
   of women, 128
   of women of color, 13–15
"Oppression" (Frye), 13
orgasm
   "Coming to Understand: Orgasm and the Epistemology of Ignorance," 340
   female, 130, 132–133
   Freud on, 131–132
   "The Myth of the Vaginal Orgasm," 101–102, 130–135
   psychologically stimulated, 133
Orientalism, 318–319
   defined, 208
Origin of Species (Darwin), 452
othering
   cultural, 536
   "Do Muslim Women Really Need Saving? Anthropological Reflections on Cultural Relativism and Its Others," 506, 530–541
otherness, 548
Our Bodies, Ourselves (Boston Women's Health Collective), 341, 509, 509–510
out (or out of the closet), outing, 11t
Owens, Ianna Hawkins, 395

Paasonen, Susanna, 411, 438
Paceley, Megan, 442

PACs (political action committees), 516
Page Act of 1875, 187
Palestinian women, 549–550, 551–552
pansexual, defined, 11t
Pantsuit Nation, 175
Papanek, Hanna, 533
"The Parahumanity of the YouTube Shooter: Nasim
    Aghdam and the Paradox of Freedom" (Shakhsari),
    442–443, 491–495
parents. *See also* family
    deportation of, 227–228
    "The Fatherhood Bonus and the Motherhood
        Penalty," 194
    paid leave for, 241
Pascoe, C. J., "Making Masculinity," 6–7, 46–53
patriarchy
    colonialism and, 544
    contexts of, 27
    culture of, 31
    defined, 3–4
    dominance and, 30, 32
    elements of, 30–31
    experience of, 33
    gender roles and, 31–32
    heterosexuality and, 102
    language and, 31
    male defensiveness and, 26
    oppression and, 32
    participation in, 27, 32–34
    power and, 31
    privilege and, 32–34
    process of, 33
    reproductive choice and, 100
    as social system, 29–30
    structure of, 32
    system of, 26
"Patriarchy, the System: An It, Not a He, a Them, or an
    Us" (Johnson), 3–4, 26–34
Paycheck Fairness Act, 243
Pearson, Karl, 460
pedagogy
    "Body of Knowledge: Black Queer Feminist Pedagogy,
        Praxis, and Embodied Text" (Lewis), 82
    of possibility and social difference, 84–86
    "Trans-forming Bodies and Bodies of Knowledge"
        (Brown & Washburn), 19, 81–86

Perdue, Lewis, *EroticaBiz: How Sex Shaped the Internet*, 441
"the personal is political," 100–101, 126, 143
Personal Responsibility and Work Opportunity
        Reconciliation Act of 1996 (PRWORA), 248
Photoshop, 412
Pickard, Susan, 339
the pill, 200–201
Pitts, Victoria, 353
Planned Parenthood, 101, 200, 527
Plant, Sadie, 441, 443–444
police brutality, 16, 124, 205. *See also* law enforcement
"Policies to End the Gender Wage Gap in the United
        States" (Kim), 195–196, 239–243
political action committees (PACs), 516
political engagement, 515–516
    "The Latina Advantage in US Politics: Recent Example
        with Representative Ocasio-Cortez" (Bejarano), 515,
        567–572
"The Politics of Housework" (Mainardi), 100, 126–129
politics of respectability, defined, 525
"The Politics of Survival" (Tormos-Aponte), 197, 270–274
Poon, Maurice K., 381
"Popaganda: Queering Family Values" (Mirk), 229–239
pop culture. *See* media and popular culture
population control
    climate crisis and, 291–292
    "The Color of Choice" (Ross), 279–291
    white supremacy and, 279–291
"Population Control Is Not the Answer to Our Climate
        Crisis" (Susskind), 202–203, 291–292
pornography, 440–443
postfeminism, 210–211
posthumanism, defined, 444
poverty
    compliance and, 248–249
    legal services and, 250–252
    reproductive justice and, 283
    social services and, 245
power
    coalition and asymmetries in, 552–553
    family and, 185
    feminism and, 144
    marriage and, 185
    masculinity and, 49
    patriarchy and, 31
    white silence and, 68

praxis, defined, 19
preferred pronouns, defined, 11t
Prince, V. Efua, "June," 293–298
print media, 508–511
prison industrial complex
    defined, 105
    economics of, 165–166
    "Masked Racism: Reflections on the Prison Industrial
        Complex," 105, 163–167
prisons
    mass incarceration, 166, 205
    sex segregation in, 255n25
privilege, 13–19. *See also* white privilege
    cisgender, 11t
    defined, 13
    in feminist movement, 104–105
    heterosexual, 11t, 105
    identity, 104–109
    male, 33–34, 151
    marginalized women and, 104–105
    "Nothing to Add: A Challenge to White Silence in
        Racial Discussions" (DiAngelo), 13–15, 62–73
    oppression and, 13–14
    patriarchy and, 32–34
property ownership, 254n10
prostitution, 197–198, 514
PRWORA (Personal Responsibility and Work
    Opportunity Reconciliation Act of 1996), 248
Przybylo, Ela, 395
Puar, Jasbir, 493
Puerto Rico
    COVID-19 pandemic in, 197
    "The Politics of Survival" (Tormos-Aponte), 197,
        270–274
Purvis, Jennifer, "Queer," 4
Pussy Riot, 525
Putnam, Robert, 327
"Putting Myself in the Picture: Researching Disability
    and Technology" (Seymour), 435, 470–476

queer, 2–5, 386
    activism, 88–89, 104, 139, 253n4
    defined, 4, 12t
    "La Conciencia de la Mestiza/Towards a New
        Consciousness," 106, 156–161
    social identity and, 550
    stereotypes, 77

"Queer" (Purvis), 4
"Queer/African Identities: Questions, Limits,
    Challenges" (Currier & Migraine-George), 17,
        76–79
queer Africans, 76–77
    bisexuals and, 77–78
    identities, 78–79
    literary and cultural representations of, 79
*Queer Girls and Popular Culture: Reading, Resisting, and
    Creating Media* (Driver), 211
queer identity, 106, 550
    African, 78–79
    in pop culture, 209
"Queering Family Values" (Jacobsen & Nair), 189,
        229–239
"A Queer #MeToo Story" (Bailey), 207, 302–306
queer relationships, domestic violence in, 313–315
queer theory, 50–51
queer youth, bullying of, 442
questioning, defined, 12t
"A Quick History of TV's Elusive Quest for Complex
        Black Lesbians" (Turner-Williams), 210, 321–323
Quiverfull Movement, 186, 217, 219

race and racism
    affective construction of, 410–412
    antiviolence movement and, 300–301
    in beauty ideals and images, 407–409
    cosmetic surgery by, 349t
    cyberculture and, 410–411
    discrimination, 92–93
    dominance and, 63, 64–65, 66, 460
    The Feminine Mystique and, 100
    feminist movement and, 24–25, 146, 149–150
    hate crimes and, 310
    imprisonment and, 164
    in labor market, 96
    masculinity and, 48, 376–377
    "Masked Racism: Reflections on the Prison Industrial
        Complex," 105, 163–167
    profiling, 205
    stereotypes, 93
    voting rights and, 94
    "When Sexism and Racism Are No Longer
        Fashionable," 579
    white silence and, 62–73
    in workplace, 456–457

racial-sexual oppression, 143–144
radical activism, 125–126, 277–278
Radicalesbians (group), 3
  "The Woman-Identified Woman," 135–139
radical feminism, 171
rape. *See also* sexual violence
  in Abu-Ghraib, 320
  interpersonal, 205
  lynching for, 120
  "Rape, Racism and Myth of the Black Rapist" (Davis),
    206
Rape, Abuse and Incest Network (RAINN), 205
rape culture, 205–206, 304, 518
rap music, 525–526
RAWA. *See* Revolutionary Association of Women of
  Afghanistan
Reagon, Bernice Johnson, 507, 546
"Reckoning with the Silences of #MeToo" (Tambe), 109,
  174–177
*Redefining Realness: My Path to Womanhood, Identity, Love
  and So Much More* (Mock), 338–339, 357–363
"A Red Record" (Wells), 92–93, 117–120
Redstockings, 3, 126
"Redstockings Manifesto," 149
"Reflections on the Black Woman's Role in the
  Community of Slaves" (Davis), 141
relational aggression, 329–330
Rellihan, Heather, "An Interview with Tarana Burke,"
  528, 583–588
reproductive choice, 100–101
  "Birth Control" (Ferguson), 202, 275–279
  Burwell v. Hobby Lobby (2014), 275–276
  Christianity and, 26
  mobilizing for, 287–289
  Roe v. Wade (1973), 201
reproductive justice, 201–203
  activism, 203
  "The Color of Choice" (Ross), 279–291
  "Population Control Is Not the Answer to Our Climate
    Crisis" (Susskind), 202–203, 291–292
  poverty and, 283
  white supremacy and, 279–291
  women of color and, 202–203
reproductive politics, 199–203. *See also* reproductive
  choice; reproductive justice
  "Birth Control" (Ferguson), 202, 275–279
  "The Color of Choice" (Ross), 202, 279–291, 551–552

"Population Control Is Not the Answer to Our Climate
  Crisis" (Susskind), 202–203, 291–292
reproductive technologies, 200
"Resisting Racism: Latinos' Changing Responses to
  Controlling Images over the Life Course"
  (Vasquez-Tokos & Norton-Smith), 352, 423–427
respectability, politics of, 525
responsibility
  to family, 43
  of women, 41
Revilla, No'u, "How To Use a Condom," 344, 400
Revolutionary Association of Women of Afghanistan
  (RAWA), 536–538, 540
Rich, Adrienne, 325, 326, 576
  "Compulsory Heterosexuality and Lesbian Existence,"
    102
Richie, Andrea J., "False Promises: Criminal Legal
  Responses to Violence against LGBT People,"
  207, 307–317
Richie, Beth, "A Black Feminist Reflection on the
  Antiviolence Movement," 206–207, 299–302
Riessman, Catherine Kohler, 344
right-wing politics, 311
Riot Grrrl movement, 511, 525
  "Riot Grrrl Manifesto" (Bikini Kill), 582–583
"The Rise of Neoliberal Feminism" (Rottenberg), 196–
  197, 257–268
Ristock, Janice, 305
Rivera, Sylvia, 9
  "I'm Glad I Was in the Stonewall Riot," 103, 124–126
Robbins, Bruce, 409
Roberts, Dorothy, *Killing the Black Body: Race,
  Reproduction, and the Meaning of Liberty*, 201, 286,
  435
Roe v. Wade (1973), 201
Rose, Nikolas, 258
Rosheuvel, Janis, 227
Ross, Loretta, "The Color of Choice," 202, 279–291,
  551–552
Roth, Benita, 105
Rottenberg, Catherine, "The Rise of Neoliberal
  Feminism," 196–197, 257–268
Rowe, Aimee, 353
Roy, Deboleena, 465, 467

safe space/safer space, 526–527
same-gender loving, defined, 12*t*

same-sex marriage
  in Africa, 77
  Defense of Marriage Act, 189
Sandoval, Chela, 547–548
Sandy Hook Elementary School shooting (2012), 108,
    167–170
Saraswati, L. Ayu, 438, 442
  "Cosmopolitan Whiteness: The Effects and Affects of
    Skin Whitening Advertisements in Transnational
    Indonesia," 347–348, 406–415
  Seeing Beauty, Sensing Race in Transnational Indonesia,
    345–346
Schatten, Gerald, 449
Schatten, Helen, 449
Schwartz Cowan, Ruth, *More Work for Mother,* 435
science. *See also* technology
  "The Egg and the Sperm: How Science Has Constructed
    a Romance Based on Stereotypical Male–Female
    Roles," 431–432
  "Latina/x *Doctoras* [Doctors]: Negotiating Knowledge
    Production in Science" (Flores), 432, 455–459
  "Navigating Transness in the United States: Understanding
    the Legacies of Eugenics" (Lair), 432, 459–464
  "Oppositional Scientific Praxis: The 'Do' and 'Doing' of
    #CRISPRbabies and DIY Hormone Biohacking"
    (Jen), 434–435, 465–470
  social construction of, 430–432
  social effects of, 452
  technology, 433–436
  women in, 432–433, 433*t*
Scott, Joan, *Women, Work & Family,* 184
secondary marginalization, 77–78, 550
second shift, defined, 192
secretarial work, 473–475
Sedgwick, Eve, 51
Seeing Beauty, Sensing Race in Transnational Indonesia
    (Saraswati), 345–346
self-control, eating disorders and, 349
self-reflexivity, defined, 19
Seneca Falls Convention of 1848, 91–92
  "The Declaration of Sentiments," 91, 114–116
separatism, 526–527
  in feminist movement, 150, 153–154
  lesbian, 143–144
September 11, 2001 terrorist attacks, 531
settler-colonials, defined, 185

sex
  activism, 101–104
  assigned, 9*t*
  assignment surgery, 37–38
  birth sex/biological sex, 10*t*
  categories, 137
  Internet and, 440–443
sex education, 199
sexism
  in black communities, 152
  machismo, 160
  unlearning, 153
  "When Sexism and Racism Are No Longer
    Fashionable," 579
sex object, 137
sex-positive, defined, 341
sex reassignment surgery (SRS), 37, 172, 253n3,
    255n26, 256n32
sex roles, 136
sex segregation, in prisons, 255n25
sex trafficking, 197–198
sexual activity, consent to, 78
sexual assault, 205. *See also* sexual violence
sexual behavior, "appropriate," 139
Sexual Feeling in Married Men and Women (Kelly), 132
sexuality
  activism, 101–104
  Christianity and, 217–218
  female, 101–102, 130–131
  five-sex system of, 36
  gender identity and, 52
  Internet and, 440–443
  labels and, 385
  in labor market, 191–197
  learning and unlearning, 5–8
  masculinity and, 48, 50–51
  regulation of, 247–248
  rethinking, 52–53
  two-sex system of, 36
  in youth culture, 46
sexually transmitted infections (STIs), 78
sexual orientation, 12*t*
sexual response, 130
sexual violence, 27
  against indigenous women, 544
  interpersonal, 205–207

LGBTQPAI+, 207
men, 207
sexual orientation and, 207
in sharing economy, 485
women of color, 207
sex work, 197–198
Seymour, Wendy, "Putting Myself in the Picture: Researching Disability and Technology," 435, 470–476
Shakhsari, Sima, "The Parahumanity of the YouTube Shooter: Nasim Aghdam and the Paradox of Freedom," 442–443, 491–495
Shapiro, Eve, 433–434, 437, 444
sharing economy, gender equity in, 440, 483–488
She Hate Me (film), 322
Shiva, Vandana, "The Hijacking of the Global Food Supply," 435–436, 476–483
#ShoutYourAbortion, 527
Simpson, Leanne, 543
"Singing in the Cracks" (Agha), 363–367
Sista II Sista, 551
sisterhood, 24
"A Black Feminist's Search for Sisterhood," 144
Sisterhood is Powerful (Morgan), 146
Sister Outsider (Lorde), 15, 19, 184
SisterSong Women of Color Reproductive Health Collective, 202, 288, 289n4, 552
situated knowledge, defined, 432
"Sketches" (Gordon), 354, 427–428
skin-whitening
advertising, 347–348, 409
"Cosmopolitan Whiteness: The Effects and Affects of Skin Whitening Advertisements in Transnational Indonesia," 347–348, 406–415
facialization and, 410–412
Slaughter, Anne-Marie, "Why Women Still Can't Have It All," 257, 265–266, 268
slavery
"An Appeal to the Christian Women of the South," 112–113
Christianity and, 112–113
family and, 187
Fugitive Slave Act, 91
marriage and, 187
SlutWalk, 518–519
smallpox, 453n8

Smith, Barbara, 508
Home Girls, 15
"Notes for Yet Another Paper on Black Feminism, or, Will the Real Enemy Please Stand Up?," 152–153
Snodgrass, Jon, *For Men Against Sexism: A Book of Readings*, 155
social constructionism
defined, 5
of disability, 7–8
of gender, 5–6
of science, 430–432
social institutions, defined, 3–4
socialization, 28, 30
social media, 211, 512. *See also* Facebook; Instagram; Twitter
social service and benefit programs, 247–248
gender and access to, 250–251
for LGBTQPAI+ communities, 246
for low-income people, 245
for transgender, 246
for violence against women, 299
social systems, 27–28, 28f
participation in, 28–29
patriarchy as, 29–30
solidarity
coalition and, 547–548
"Making Coalitions Work: Solidarity Across Difference within US Feminism," 507, 546–553
of oppressed people, 551–552
"Solidarity Not Charity: Mutual Aid and How to Organize in the Age of Corona Virus" (Kaba & Spade), 197
Solinger, Rickie, 202
"Some Thoughts about Racism, Classism, and Separatism" (McCandless), 153–154
Southerners On New Ground (SONG), 464
Southern Poverty Law Center, gender spectrum overview, 9–12t
Spade, Dean
"Compliance Is Gendered: Struggling for a Gendered Self-Determination in a Hostile Economy," 196, 245–256
"Solidarity Not Charity: Mutual Aid and How to Organize in the Age of Corona Virus," 197
Spanier, Bonnie, 465, 467
speak-outs, 527–528

Spent (online game), 513–514

Spivak, Gayatri Chakravorty, 532

SRS. *See* sex reassignment surgery

standpoint theory, defined, 431

Stansell, Christine, 261

Stanton, Elizabeth Cady, "The Declaration of Sentiments," 114–116

STAR. *See* Street Transvestite Action Revolutionaries

"Statement of Purpose" (Daughters of Bilitis), 102, 123–124

state violence, 208

    defined, 205

    gender-based, 226, 315, 518

Steinem, Gloria, "If Men Could Menstruate," 344, 398–399

stereotypes

    of black women, 142

    "The Egg and the Sperm: How Science Has Constructed a Romance Based on Stereotypical Male–Female Roles," 431–432, 447–454

    feminist, 2

    gender, 8

    queer, 77

    in reproductive biology, 448

sterilization. *See also* eugenics

    forced, 201

    of women of color, 100–101, 146

STIs (sexually transmitted infections), 78

Stone, Sandy, 373

Stonewall riots, 103, *103*, 124–126

street harassment, defined, 513

Street Transvestite Action Revolutionaries (STAR), 124, 125

Stryker, Susan, 106, 373

    Transgender History, 8–9

Suares, Victor, 478

submission of women, 41–42. *See also* dominance; patriarchy

suffrage movement, 90–94

    abolitionist movement and, 92

    arguments against, 92

    "The Declaration of Sentiments," 114–116

    Truth and, 117

suicidegirls.com, 441

Supreme Court

    Adoptive Family v. Baby Girl (2013), 188

    Burwell v. Hobby Lobby (2014), 275–276

    June Medical Services v. Russo (2020), 200

    Little Sisters of the Poor v. Pennsylvania (2020), 200

    Obergefell v. Hodges (2015), 189

    Roe v. Wade (1973), 201

Susskind, Yifat, "Population Control Is Not the Answer to Our Climate Crisis," 202–203, 291–292

sustainable development, 514–515, 563–567

Swidler, Ann, 423

Sylvia Rivera Law Project, 245

Take Back the Night events, 527

Taliban, 531–532, 535–537

Tambe, Ashwini, "Reckoning with the Silences of #MeToo," 109, 174–177

technofeminist approaches, 433–436

technology. *See also* science

    activism and, 433–436, 511–514

    click theory, 445

    cyberspaces, 438–440

    cyborgs, 437–438

    digital media, 438–440

    disability and, 472

    gendered practices of, 433–436

    "Immersion" (de Bodard), 445, 495–503

    mobile phone, 511–514

    neutrality and, 475–476

    "The Parahumanity of the YouTube Shooter: Nasim Aghdam and the Paradox of Freedom" (Shakhsari), 442–443, 491–495

    "Putting Myself in the Picture: Researching Disability and Technology," 470–476

    secretarial work and, 473–475

    voice activation, 475

"Technology Isn't Neutral: Ari Fitz on How Instagram Fails Queer Black Creators" (Lewis), 442, 488–490

"10,000 Blows" (Lux), 354, 428

TERFs (trans-exclusionary radical feminists), 171–173

terrorism, 531–532

testimonials, 527–528

"There Is No Hierarchy of Oppressions" (Lorde), 15–16, 75

Thinking About Women (Ellman), 131

third gender, defined, 12*t*

third world feminism
    black feminism and, 146
    defined, 106
    white feminists and, 147
third world women
    defined, 15
    hierarchy and, 106
This Bridge Called My Back (Moraga and Anzaldúa, eds.), 15
Thomas, Sue, 438
Thus Spoke Zarathustra (Nietzsche), 575
Tilly, Louise, *Women, Work & Family*, 184
Tissot, Simon, 430
"Too Latina to Be Black, Too Black to Be Latina"
    (Williams), 342, 392–393
Tormos-Aponte, Fernando, "The Politics of Survival,"
    197, 270–274
torture, 317–321
Traister, Rebecca, *Good and Mad: The Revolutionary Power
    of Women's Anger*, 508
*Trans Bodies, Trans Selves: A Resource for the Transgender
    Community* (Erickson-Schroth), 510
trans, defined, 4
trans-exclusionary radical feminists (TERFs), 171–173
"Trans-forming Bodies and Bodies of Knowledge"
    (Brown & Washburn), 19, 81–86
transgender
    activism, 253n4
    body, 340
    defined, 8–9, 12t, 38
    discrimination against, 173
    feminism, 171–174
    gender-neutral bathrooms, 172–173
    healthcare access of, 172, 343
    in homeless shelters, 253n7
    "It's Time to End the Long History of Feminism Failing
        Transgender Women," 171–174
    mahu, 358–359
    narratives, 510
    "Navigating Transness in the United States:
        Understanding the Legacies of Eugenics" (Lair), 432,
        459–464
    social services for, 246
    statistics on, 361–362
    studies, 8–9
    violence against, 173, 310
    youth, 363

Transgender History (Stryker), 8–9
Transgender Liberation: A Movement Whose Time Has Come
    (Feinberg), 373
Transgender Nation (TN), 373
transitioning
    defined, 12t
    voice changes associated with, 363–367
transnationalism
    in *Americanah*, 416–420
    in beauty ideals and images, 409
    social identity of, 549–550
transphobia, 12t, 174, 207
transsexualism, defined, 12t, 38
transvaluation, 575, 576–577
Triangle Shirtwaist Factory fire, 95, 95–96
    "141 Men and Girls Die in Waist Factory Fire,"
        129–131
Tsang, Mary, *Open Source Estrogen*, 466–469
Tuana, Nancy, "Coming to Understand: Orgasm and the
    Epistemology of Ignorance," 340
Tuck, Eve, 543–544
Turner-Williams, Jaelani, "A Quick History of TV's
    Elusive Quest for Complex Black Lesbians," 210
"Turning Fury into Fuel: Three Women Authors on
    Publishing's New Investment in Anger" (Dionne),
    508, 554–559
Twitter
    #CRISPRbabies on, 466
    hashtag activism on, 7, 175, 466, 512, 527–528
    marginalized voices on, 211, 490
    #MeToo movement on, 108, 109, 174–177, 207, 302–
        306, 527–528, 583–588
    as transgender support resource, 363
    women employees at, 436
Two Spirit, defined, 12t

Uber, 484–487
"An Unbreakable Link: Peace, Environment, and
    Democracy" (Maathai), 514–515, 563–567
unionized workers, 193–194, 242
utopias, 81–86

vagina
    anatomy, 132–133
    "The Myth of the Vaginal Orgasm," 101–102, 130–135
Vasconcelos, José, 156

Vasquez, Tina, "It's Time to End the Long History of Feminism Failing Transgender Women," 171–174

Vasquez-Tokos, Jessica, "Resisting Racism: Latinos' Changing Responses to Controlling Images over the Life Course," 352, 423–427

vibrators, advertising for, 430, *431*

victim blaming, 518–519

violence. *See also* domestic violence; gendered violence; sexual violence

    antiviolence movement, 206–207, 299–302, 308–309

    bullying, 329–331, 442

    covert aggression, 329–330

    criminal justice system and, 301

    "False Promises: Criminal Legal Responses to Violence against LGBT People," 207, 307–317

    feminism and, 299–300

    hate crimes, 309–310

    homophobic, 207

    against indigenous women, 544

    against LGBT people, 17, 309–310

    masculinity and, 167–170

    "Memo to Media: Manhood, Not Guns or Mental Illness, Should Be Central in Newtown Shooting" (Katz), 108, 167–170

    police brutality, 16

    public awareness of violence against women, 300

    relational aggression, 329–330

    social services for victims of, 299

    state, 205, 208, 518

    against transgender people, 173, 207, 310

    voting rights-related, 119

Violent Crime Control and Law Enforcement Act, 311

virtuality, realness and, 411–412

virtual/posthuman bodies, 444–445

visual art, 523–524

Vlasnik, Amber L., "Campus-Based Women's and Gender Equity Centers: Enacting Feminist Theories, Creating Social Change," 527

voice activation technology, 475

voice changes

    register changes, 365–366

    timbre, 365

    vocal fatigue, 366

    vocal range, 364–365

VOTE411 initiative, 515

voting. *See also* suffrage movement

    political engagement and, 515–516

    violence related to, 119

Voting Rights Act of 1965, 94

wages. *See also* gender pay gap

    equity, 241

    fatherhood bonus, 194

    livable, 185–186

    motherhood pay penalty, 194

    negotiating, 194–195

    "Policies to End the Gender Wage Gap in the United States," 195–196, 239–243

    secrecy, 242–243

Wajcman, Judy, 435, 444

Walker, Alice, *In Search of Our Mother's Gardens*, 15

Wallace, Michele, "A Black Feminist's Search for Sisterhood," 144

Walters, K., 382

War on Terrorism, 531–532

Washburn, Red, "Trans-forming Bodies and Bodies of Knowledge," 19, 81–86

Waskul, Dennis, 411, 438

Watkins, Gloria Jean. *See* hooks, bell

wave model of feminist history, 89

Weber, Shelly, 353

Weitz, Rose, 341

welfare reform, 247–248, 255n16

Wells, Ida B., 3, *93*

    "A Red Record," 92–93, 117–120

"Wheels of Justice" campaign, 573

"When Sexism and Racism Are No Longer Fashionable" (The Guerrilla Girls), 579

When Women Ask the Questions (Boxer), 3

"Where I Come from Is Like This" (Allen), 186

whiteness, 13–15. *See also* cosmopolitan whiteness

    colonialism and, 412

    defined, 63–64

    intersectionality and, 19

    as multidimensional, 63

white privilege, 407

    "Nothing to Add: A Challenge to White Silence in Racial Discussions" (DiAngelo), 13–15, 62–73

    "White Privilege: Unpacking the Invisible Knapsack" (McIntosh), 13, 16

white silence, 62–73
  antiracist education and, 64–65
  effects of, 65
  rationales for, 66–72
  theoretical framework, 63–64
white supremacy
  cosmopolitan whiteness and hegemonic, 413–414
  eugenics and, 280–289
  feminism and, 25
  promotion of, 247–248
  reproductive justice and, 279–291
"White Woman Listen!" (Carby), 15
Whitlock, Kay, "False Promises: Criminal Legal
    Responses to Violence against LGBT People,"
    207, 307–317
wikisexuality, defined, 442
Williams, Aleichia, "Too Latina to Be Black, Too Black
    to Be Latina," 342, 392–393
Winch, Alison, 327
Winter, Michael, "I Was There," 518, 572–574
WITCH (Women's International Conspiracy from Hell),
    3
Wolf, Naomi, *The Beauty Myth*, 261, 268n9, 345
Woman and Nature (Griffin), 543
"The Woman-Identified Woman" (Radicalesbians),
    135–139
Woman's Body, Woman's Right (Gordon), 276
Women, Race & Class (Davis), 15
Women, Work & Family (Scott & Tilly), 184
Women Don't Ask: Negotiation and the Gender Divide
    (Babcock & Laschever), 194–195
women in print movement, 508
Women of African Descent for Reproductive Justice, 288
women of color
  coalitional work of, 547
  criminal justice system and, 301
  defined, 13
  "The Latina Advantage in US Politics: Recent Example
      with Representative Ocasio-Cortez" (Bejarano), 515,
      567–572
  oppression of, 13–15
  police brutality of, 16
  in print media, 508

reproductive justice and, 202–203
  sexual violence against, 207
  sterilization of, 100–101
  victimization of, 301
women's and gender equity centers, 527
women's and gender studies
  historical perspectives in, 88–109
  interdisciplinarity of, 19–20, 184
  queer in, 4–5
  roots of, 3
  "Trans-forming Bodies and Bodies of Knowledge"
      (Brown & Washburn), 19, 81–86
"Women's Friendships, Popular Culture, and Gender
    Theories" (Gardiner), 210, 324–328
Women's International Conspiracy from Hell (WITCH),
    3
Women's Liberation Movement, 137
Women's March, 108, 175
  "Guiding Vision and Definition of Principles," 178–182
Women's Trade Union League (WTUL), 95
workplace, discrimination in, 240–241, 456–457
World Bank, 478
World Trade Organization (WTO), 478

xenophobia
  defined, 187
  neoliberalism and, 188–189

Young Lords, 125–126
youth, 46–48
  gender and sexuality in, 46
  high school, 46–47
  homeless LGBT, 360
  juvenile delinquency, gender and, 331
  queer, bullying of, 442
  transgender, 363
YouTube, "The Parahumanity of the YouTube Shooter:
    Nasim Aghdam and the Paradox of Freedom"
    (Shakhsari), 442–443, 491–495

Zaman, Reema, 508, 554–559
zines, 510–511
ZipCar, 484